CONWAY COUNTY HERITAGE:
THEN AND NOW

CONWAY COUNTY
ARKANSAS

Turner®
PUBLISHING COMPANY

Nashville, Tennessee

TURNER PUBLISHING COMPANY

Publishers of America's History

200 4th Avenue North • Suite 950
Nashville, Tennessee 37219
615-255-2665

www.turnerpublishing.com

Copyright © 2006 Conway County
Genealogical Association
Publishing Rights: Turner Publishing
Company.
All rights reserved.

Library of Congress Control Number:
2006920386
ISBN 978-1-68162-160-9
Limited Edition

TABLE OF CONTENTS

FOREWORD

The Train Depot

The people of Conway County can be proud of the important and significant roles they have played in the history of Arkansas. This is the second attempt to preserve the records of families of Conway County, the first being produced in the 1980s. The records of over 600 families are preserved in this new volume of local history, and will serve as an historical source of genealogical and historical information for generations to come.

We believe the names, dates and places included in this book to be correct, according to our sources of information. In some cases the family names were modified over the years, and every attempt was made to leave these as spelled in the original documentation.

We would like to thank the hundreds of Conway County families, both near and far, for sharing the rich legacy of your ancestors. May you all enjoy this permanent record of our community history.

Conway County Genealogical Association

CONWAY COUNTY GENEALOGICAL ASSOCIATION

The Conway County Genealogical Association was formed in February 1997. A group of people consisting of Burnie Beavers, Euna Beavers and Amanda Sefton, who were interested in genealogy, called a meeting January 13, 1997 at the Farm Bureau meeting room in Morrilton in hopes of forming a genealogy group. The possibility of forming a genealogy group was discussed. A second meeting was held February 6th to complete the process. A name was selected for the group and a regular meeting day was set.

The first officers of the group were Euna Beavers, President; Mary Brents, Vice President; Rosemary Norwood, Secretary; Bonnie Chism, Treasurer; Mickey Zachary, Historian; Barbara Marler, Reporter; and Gerri Willcutt, Telephone Chairman. It was decided that the group would meet on the third Monday night of each month. At the third and regular monthly meeting of the group, Rhonda Norris, a licensed genealogist from Russellville, was the speaker. The group was made up of all levels of genealogists from beginners to professionals. The membership consisted and still does consist of people who come to each and every meeting, those who come occasionally as time permits and many who for one reason or another are not able to attend meetings at all. We have many long distance members. Members are scattered from California to Delaware to Florida. A monthly newsletter is published by the group. This newsletter tells of local events, reunions, homecomings, cemetery decorations, ancestor fairs and other things that would be of interest to genealogists. One of the goals of the group has always been for the more experienced to help those who are new to genealogy. The first Conway County Ancestor and Heritage Fair was held August 23, 1997 at the AP&L Ready Room in Morrilton. The fair featured gatherers of information, providers of information and vendors offering books and materials that were genealogy related. The heritage portion of the fair featured people of the area who were demonstrating quilting, cotton carding and many other old arts. There was also a display of quilts, handmade chairs, churns, etc.

Charter members were Burnie and Euna Beavers, Mary Ellen Brents, Bill and Bonnie Chism, Ted Hutchcroft, Leona Carter, Gerry Willcutt, Tarci Davidson, Cathy Barnes, Jeannie Price, Helen Dickens, Dorothy Youngblood, Kip and Rosemary Norwood, Mickey Zachary, Ken Charton, Tambra Lewis, Dale James, Dorothy Beal and Barbara Marler. Many members were added in the coming months.

Soon after being formed the group began the project of taking a census of all the cemeteries of Conway County. This was a long and sometimes difficult project and took a couple of years to complete. A four volume set of books was published from this information. CDs were made available later. The year 2005 finds us doing updates for the cemetery books. The new books will be available in late 2005 or early 2006. The group is now working on other books about Conway County as well.

Meetings are now held the first Monday night of each month at the Morrilton Depot Museum. The CCGA has also set up a Conway County Research Library in one of the museums. Many books, CDs, microfilm, etc. are available for researchers to use when visiting. A computer is set up to utilize the CDs. It also stores a family history database. Individuals can contribute their family histories to it. These records are privatized so as to protect those still living. Anyone can contribute to this project. The library houses many family history books also. CCGA has compiled a new history book of Conway County. It is entitled *Conway County Heritage: Then and Now*. This book should be available in the fall of 2005. The group is compiling other books also.

The goal of the CCGA has always been to promote interest in genealogy and to aid in research. Many of the group volunteer to help researchers from other areas by doing lookups. This is a group of dedicated genealogists and volunteers. Another goal is to add to the Conway County Research Library so that researchers can have many sources to work with when they visit the library. *Submitted by Euna Beavers.*

Lienhart Creamery in Morrilton.

CONWAY COUNTY HISTORY

Old Store Porch, 1971. The post office and grocery store was a community gathering place in Cleveland, AR. In good weather men gathered on the porch of the Halbrook Grocery and Post Office. Lyonell Halbrook is sitting in a rocker with his step granddaughter, Becky Skipper, in his lap. John Skipper is standing in front of them. Thomas Williams is sitting at Lyonell's right and Hi Bowling is on his left. Byron Shewmake is sitting on the edge of the porch.

A Brief History of Conway County, Arkansas

Conway County formed in 1825 out of Pulaski County and is named for Henry Wharton Conway, who was territorial delegate to the U.S. Congress. At one time, Conway County covered an area of about 2,500 square miles and included most of Faulkner, Van Buren, Pope, Perry and part of Yell County. This large territory—as large nearly as some of the smaller United States—has been divided and carved from time to time, until the present area of Conway County is but 567 square miles. The county seat was moved numerous times as the county kept reforming and it was the intention to keep the county seat housed in a central location in the county.

The first county seat was at Cadron. The house of Stephen Harris was the second location of the county seat in Harrisburg (now Portland). In 1831 the seat was moved to Lewisburg. The courthouse was moved to Springfield in 1850. The Springfield courthouse was demolished by a tornado in 1858 and a new courthouse built in its place. There was a fire in 1863, which destroyed the courthouse in Springfield a second time. Another courthouse was built in 1869 in Springfield. The courthouse was returned to Lewisburg in 1873. The county seat was permanently moved to Morrilton in 1883-1884.

The Cherokee Indians owned land temporarily in north central Arkansas between 1817 and 1828, which included most of Conway County. The Southeast corner of the Western Cherokee Nation was located on Point Remove Creek, not far from Morrilton. Sequoyah, father of the Cherokee Alphabet, came to Arkansas in 1818 to bring his alphabet. The Cherokee were eventually pressured into signing a treaty to give up their Arkansas lands.

There is a marker on the corner of Jackson and S. Cherokee in Morrilton that reads as follows: Conway County Cherokee Indian Boundary. On the north bank of the Arkansas River at the mouth of Point Remove Creek a line was run in a Northwesterly direction to Batesville. On White river this line crosses the highway here and was designated as the Eastern Boundary of the lands ceded by treaty in 1817 to the Western Cherokee Indians in exchange for lands given up by them in the states of Georgia and Tennessee. The Cherokee Nation followed the Trail of Tears through Conway County. It is estimated that the forced emigration claimed over 4,000 lives by the time the last Cherokee reached Oklahoma in 1839. At times, the line formed by the Indians on their trek was about 85 miles long.

During the Civil War, companies for both the Confederate and Union Armies were recruited from Conway County. Five regularly-organized Confederate companies, which were largely recruited by volunteers strictly from the county, and the fragment of a company raised by Dr. Davis, represented at least 700 men from Conway County. Two hundred more recruits from Conway County to companies recruited in other Arkansas counties, made a total of 900 in all that entered the Confederate Army from Conway County. No more than 200 ever returned, the others dying on the battlefield, of camp sickness or in Northern prisons.

Two companies, raised by Capt. Anthony Hinkle and Capt. L. S. Dunscomb, and recruited mainly in Conway County, joined the Third Arkansas United States Cavalry (Federal Army). They were mostly stationed in Central Arkansas, at Lewisburg and other points and saw but little fighting during the war.

The following official list includes the names of all those who occupied positions of responsibility within the county from its organization until 1890 (from Goodspeed History of Conway County - 1890)

County Judges. —H. G. Saffold, 1830 to 1832; B. B. Ball, 1834 to 1835; Robert McCall, 1835 to 1836; W. T. Gamble, 1836 to 1838; J. W. Comstock, 1838 to 1842; W. G. Gamble, 1842 to 1844; John Quindley, 1844 to 1846; R. R. Gordon, 1846 to 1848; H. H. Higgins, 1848 to 1850; James Campbell, 1850 to 1854; Robert Stell, 1854 to 1856; J. T. Hamilton, 1856 to 1858; J. M. Venable, 1858 to 1860; U. A. Nixon, 1860 to 1862; Henry McFearson, 1862 to 1864; W. J. Vance, 1866 to 1868; A. B. Gaylor, 1868 to 1872; A. F. Woodward, 1874 to 1876; Joshua Moses, 1876 to 1878; M. W. Steele, 1878 to 1882; John W. Todd, 1882 to 1884; William Blankenship, 1884 to 1886; G. H. Taylor, 1886 to 1888; J. R. Hamm, 1888 to 1890.

Clerks. —David Barber, 1826 to 1829; James Ward, 1830 to 1832; Thomas Mathers, 1832 to 1834; J. I. Simmons, 1834 to 1842; H. H. Higgins, 1842 to 1846; E. Morrill, 1846 to 1852; Joshua Moses, 1852 to 1856; J. R. Bill, 1856 to 1858; Joshua Moses, 1858 to 1864, and 1866 to 1868; W. R. Hinkle, 1864 to 1866, and 1868 to —; D. H. Thomas, to 1872; William Kearney, 1872 to 1874; H. A. Nations, 1876 to 1880; W. F. Conlee, 1880, died in February, and F. J. Willis elected to fill vacancy; also, re-elected 1880 to 1882; M. L. Ashbury, 1882 to 1884; C. E. Hawkins, 1886 to 1888; Jeff. Wright, present incumbent, elected in 1888.

Sheriffs. —Kinkead, resigned, July, 1827, was succeeded by James Kellam, who served out the term; was re-elected in 1830 to 1833; James Barber, 1827 to 1829; B. F. Howard, 1833 to 1835; T. S. Haynes, 1835 to 1842; John Murray, 1842 to 1846; John Quindley, 1846 to 1852; W. G. Harrison, 1852 to 1854; R. S. Cargill, 1854 to 1860; A. A. Livingston, 1860 to 1864; R. T Markham, 1866 to 1868; N. W. Moore, 1868 to 1872; T. B. Stout, 1872 to 1874; W. E. Dickinson, 1874 to 1876; W. M. Clifton, 1876 to 1878; D. B. Russell, 1878 to 1880; G. W. Griffin, 1880 to 1882; L. Sleeper, 1882 to 1884; R. H. Speer, 1884 to 1886; J. H. Coblentz, 1886 to 1888; M. D. Shelby, present incumbent, elected in 1888.

Treasurers. —D. D. Mason, 1836 to 1840; B. H. Thompson, 1840 to 1842; H. H. Berry, 1842 to 1844; J. G. Musser, 1844 to 1846; L. Stockston, 1846 to 1848; Peter Clingman, 1848 to 1850; H. C. Watson, 1850 to 1860; J. W. Willbanks, 1860 to 1864; J. W. Scroggins. 1866 to 1868, and 1872 to 1878; Jesse Schumake, 1868 to 1872; John Wells, 1878 to 1882; W. T. Gordon, 1882 to 1884; Z. T. Kindred, 1886 to 1888; R. N. Vail, present incumbent, elected in 1888.

Coroners. —Reuben Blunt, 1826 to 1827; John Houston, 1830 to 1832; William Ellis, 1832 to 1833; William Ellis, Jr., 1834 to 1835; W. H. Robertson, 1835 to 1836; George Fletcher, 1836 to 1838; James Darling, 1838 to 1840; W. H. Robertson, 1840 to 1846; Thomas Weston, 1846 to 1848; J. C. Webster, 1848 to 1850; H. Gregory, 1850 to 1852; John Buwie, 1852 to 1854; John Wells, 1854 to 1858; William Hibbin, 1858 to 1860; J. A. Westerfield, 1860 to 1862; M. Porter, 1862 to 1864; Uriah Dickens, 1866 to 1868; J. Lyon, 1868 to 1872; R. T. Harrison, 1872 to 1874; John Houston, 1874 to 1876; Lafayette Moize, 1876 to 1878; C. E. Francis, 1878 to 1880; F. W. Morrow, 1880 to 1882; J. A. D. Hale, 1882 to 1884; E. K. Turner, 1886 to 1888; Alvis Hugg, present incumbent, elected in 1888.

Surveyors. — E. W. Owen, 1830 to 1832; James Ward, 1833 to 1834; L. C. Griffin, 1835 to 1836; D Harrison, 1836 to 1838; C. M. Robert, 1840 to 1842; Harrison, 1842 to 1854; L. Rankin, 1854 to 58; William Dungan, 1858 to 1862; W. L. Harwood, 1862 to 1864; A. B. Henry, 1866 to 1872; W. C. Watkins, 1872 to 1874; J. Maratta, 1874 to 1876; G. W. Howard, 1876 to 1878; J. G. Bennett, 1878 to 1880; N. Dixon, 1880 to 1884; M. Brown, 1884 to 1886; T. J. Holbrook, 1886 to 1888; John Beck, present incumbent, elected in 1888.

Assessors. - P. B. Norwood, 1868 to 1872; W. G. Gray, 1872 to 1874; J. R. K. Hobbs, 1874 to 1876; J. W. Harrison, 1876 to 1878; G. W. Griffin, 1878 to 1880; A. B. Simmons, 1880 to 1884; William Taylor, 1884 to 1886; H. L. Kennamere, 1886 to 1888; J. H. Littlejohn, present incumbent, elected in 1888.

Delegates in Constitutional Conventions. — From January 4th to 13, 1836, Nimrod Menifee; from March 4 to 21st, and May 6 to June 3, 1861, S. J. Stallings; from January 7 to February 18, 1868, Anthony Hinkle; from July 14 to October 31, 1874, William S. Hanna.

Members of Council and House of Representatives in Territorial Legislatures. —A. Kuykendall and R. J. Blount were the only members of the Council from the formation of the county in 1825 until the admission of the State in 1836. The members of the House were Conway and Pulaski Counties, A. H. Sevier in 1827 and 1828; N. Menifee in 1831, and J. C. Roberts in 1833.

Senators in the State Legislature. — Conway and VanBuren Counties: A. Kuykendall, 1836 to 1840. Conway and Pope Counties, J. Williamson, 1840 to 1844. Conway and Perry Counties, D. Q. Steel, 1844 to 1846 Conway, Johnson and White Counties, D. Maxwell, 1848 to 1849.

Conway, Jackson and White Counties, F. DeShough, 1850 to 1853; W. L. Keith, 1854 to 1855. Conway, Perry and Yell Counties, J. J. Sterman, 1856 to 1859; G. W. Lemoyne, 1860 to 1862; F. M. Stratton, 1864 to 1865; same counties, S. Forrest, 1866 to 1867. Conway, Searcy and Pope Counties, A. D. Thomas, 1871 to 1873; same counties, J. R. H. Scott, 1874. Conway, VanBuren and Searcy Counties, John Campbell, 1874 to 1877; same counties, W. S. Hanna, 1878 to 1882; same counties, Z. B. Jennings, 1882 to 1886; same counties, W. S. Hanna, 1886 to 1890, during which time Mr. Hanna was President of the Senate.

Representatives. — John Linton, 1836 to 1838; N. Menifee, 1838 to 1840; J. Stephenson and D. Q. Stell, 1840 to 1842. Conway and Perry Counties, T. S. Haynes and G. W Lemoyne, 1842 to 1843; J. J. Simmons and John Hardin, 1844 to 1845; Richard Griffin and A. Kuykendall, 1846; J. Gordon and H. H Higgins, 1848 to 1849; E. W. Adams and J. Gordon, 1850 to 1851; A. Hayes and J. Quindley, 1852 to 1853; A. Gordon and J. J. Jones, 1854 to 1855; James P. Venable, 1856 to 1857; W. W. Edwards, 1858 to 1859; Robert. N. Harper, 1860 to 1862; Russell Welborn, 1862 to 1863; G. W. Galloway, 1864 to 1865. Conway, Searoy and Pope Counties, W. W. Bradshear, J. R. Hall and H. W. Hodges, 1868 to 1870; same counties, T. D. Hawkins, B. F. Taylor and N. C. Cleland, 1871 to 1872; same counties, Benton Turner, Y. B. Shephard and J. F. Stephenson, January 6th, to April 25, 1873; same counties, L. W. Davis and J. P. Venable, 1874 to 1875. Conway alone, F. P. Hervey, 1877; Lewis Miller, 1879; E. B. Henry, 1880 to 1881; W. S. Hanna, 1883; Hiram Dacus, 1885; G. E. Trower, 1887; Z. A. P. Venable.

2005 ELECTED CONWAY COUNTY OFFICIALS

Jimmy Hart - County Judge; Terry Alvey - Justice Of The Peace; Kathy Cooper - Justice of the Peace; Billy Deaver - Justice of the Peace; Michael Hammons - Justice Of The Peace; Phillip Hoyt - Justice Of The Peace; Wayde Prince - Justice Of The Peace; Gary Sams - Justice Of The Peace; Robert Stobaugh - Justice Of The Peace; John Trafford - Justice of the Peace; Lawrance Williams - Justice Of The Peace; Lyle Wilson - Justice of the Peace; Richard Neal County - Coroner; Mark Flowers - County Sheriff; Wayne DeSalvo - County Treasurer; Helen Noll - County Assessor; Catherine Bradshaw -County Collector; Debbie Hartman County Clerk; Carolyn Gadberry - County Circuit Clerk.

As of the 2000 federal census, there are 20,336 people, 7,967 households, and 5,736 families residing in Conway County.

BLACKWELL COMMUNITY
By Everlean "Bea" Garrett Webb

Blackwell was a 1arge community where most of the landowners and residents were black.

The first post office was owned by a black man named William Black and the town was named for him. The second postmaster was Archie Hill.

There was a railroad station across from the post office operated by Bill Tate. A cotton gin was owned and operated by two black men, Edd and Sam Sanders. Later, owners of the gin were Earl Howard, Jim Cheek, Guy Smirl and Carl Peters. Fee Anderson worked at the gin. There was a saw mill owned and operated by Buster Collins, which furnished jobs for a lot of people in Blackwell.

At one time, there were four stores in the community, and the merchants were Henry Alford, Gus Peters, Sam Swain and Allen Bryles. In addition to owning a grocery store, Bryles was an undertaker and sold coffins. He also had a barber shop in his building and Walter Ackerson was the barber.

Blackwell once had four cafes, two of the owners were Cletis Thurman and Forest Bryles.

Mrs. Lucinder Franklin operated a taxi cab service and rented rooms to people passing through. She also ran a ballpark and a dance hall. Another ballpark and dance hall was run by Allen Bryles. Blackwell had a real nice band which played there. Forest Bryles, Rosevelt, Wilmer Bland, and other men were in the band. They were all black. Also, there was a skating rink that was owned by Sam Swain and people came from all over the county to dance and skate there.

There was also a theater in Blackwell where W.B. Kelley showed motion pictures which everyone really enjoyed.

Our people were active and industrious. The first black train foreman in Blackwell was Allen Bryles and Mamon Woody was the first black porter. W.M. Jessie was a deputy sheriff, as was John Neely. Philip Bailey raised tobacco and Josh Robinson made molasses for the whole county.

Most of the early settlers and the first families in the Blackwell area came from South Carolina and Atlanta, Georgia, while the white families came from Alabama and Atlanta, Georgia.

I remember we had a high school and the kids from Morrilton came up to Blackwell to school. We had a home demonstration agent who would come to the school and teach us how to can with steam pressure canners and how to make mattresses. Her name was Josephine Hudlow.

There were several large farms growing cotton owned by Emit Carter, Lonnie Carter, Jack Fields, and Bill Embry. My father, Josh Robinson, had a blacksmith shop. He shoed lots of horses and made wagon Wheels.

The community has not grown in size, but we are proud to say that there is now a body shop (automobile) owned by Harold Black, a fire station, two liquor stores, and a trailer place.

I am having a time trying to get a store. We have to go to Morrilton or Atkins to get milk and bread.

CAMPGROUND CEMETERY THE STORY BEHIND THE PICTURE
By Jarrell Rainwater

They say that every picture is worth a thousand words. There is not that many words behind this picture, but there is a powerful, sad and tender story behind this one.

Let's begin with the tallest monument. It is in the second row from the front, then there are a number of tiny stones, barely above ground level-just beyond, leading

Campground Cemetery with Lake Overcup beyond the tree showing a twister that recently went through in spring 2004.

toward the lake. This is a story of love, compassion and sacrifice.

The tall monument is for Burr, a young man who never married and never really had a girlfriend. A teen-age girl, Janey, lived across from the girl who dated Burr's younger cousin. Burr was a shy boy, the youngest child in his family. Jeff, his cousin, finally persuaded Burr to have a few tentative dates - more like walk along the road or attend church. They would accompany Jeff and his future bride, Maggie Parker.

Soon, Fred appeared on the scene and swept Janey off her feet. They and Jeff and Maggie were soon tied in matrimony. This left Burr alone, again. His brothers and sisters were all married. His mom had been dead almost 10 years. He and his dad who was in his mid-70s lived alone together in the old two-room cabin that his father and mother had built after homesteading in 1870. Burr was not born until almost 1900.

Burr had a sister, Arkie, who was married to Henry. Henry had fought in World War I and had been poisoned-gassed. Henry and Arkie had two little boys. Both Henry and the baby died in 1923. Arkie and little Henry then moved in with her father and Burr. She cooked and cleaned for them to earn her "keep."

At this time, Burr was in his mid-20s, but he began running around with boys in their teens. In the spring of 1927, Arkansas and the mid-south experienced the worst floods of the century.

The boys talked Burr into going onto the sunken lands where overflow and backwater had covered area. They were wading in the shallows and Burr stepped off a hidden bluff and plunged 10-20 feet at once under water. He couldn't swim.

The boys ran to find someone to help. They found Fred and Janey's cousin. Fred was a great swimmer and after an hour or two, he found Burr by sinking himself and using his feet to search for the body.

The water was so high that they were unable to get the body to town. They had to use wagon and mules to go into town to purchase a coffin and bring it to the body. We lived near the flooded area and the cemetery. They brought his body to our front porch and laid it out; using our porch as a temporary slab. They were unable to get to the cemetery, as all roads were covered by high water.

Finally, after a couple of days had passed, they put the coffin in the mule-drawn wagon and went through the cornfield and pasture. They cut a gap through the fence right across from the cemetery.

All of this was just too much for Burr's dad. About four weeks later he and Arkie sat down to Sunday dinner after church, he collapsed and died at the table.

Now, Arkie is left alone with little Henry, age 4. They moved in with Fred and Janey and Janey's mom, who owned the house they all lived in. Little Henry, always in poor health, died three months later in August 1927.

Arkie was now truly alone, but she was a survivor. She lived longer than any of her siblings or their spouses. She never remarried. She devoted the rest of her life to her nieces and nephews and to God.

In World War II, she read how a Bible with a steel cover saved lives when a soldier carried it in his left shirt pocket. She mailed one to me and one to my cousin, Jack. Jack became a Baptist minister. His grandson is a Catholic priest in the Diocese of Little Rock. Arkie died a week before Christmas in 1976. Jack died in the spring of 1978.

Fred and Janey had several children die at young ages. They are buried next to Burr. When Fred died, Janey had him placed near Burr, with space for herself. She, too, along with her entire family is gone now.

So, now, you have the story of row two. Arkie, Henry, Little Henry and the baby. There are Burr's parents, Burr, Fred, Janey and all of their children lying peacefully beside the still waters. I can't say for anyone else, but, their little story of love, caring and sacrifice restores my soul. Surely, goodness and mercy shall follow them all of their days and ours. We shall dwell in the house of the Lord forever. Amen.

P.S. It is now May 2004. This story began in World War I. I am the only survivor. Burr's body was brought to the house where I lived in April 1927. I was born in that house in September 1926. Burr was my uncle, Arkie was my aunt, brother and sister of my father. Henry was my mother's first cousin.

I still have Arkie's steel-plated Bible. In engraved letters on the front, it says, "May God Bless You." On the inside first page, it says "from Aunt Arkie." God has blessed me by giving me caring, loving people throughout my life.

In front row of the picture are my mom and dad and Sharon, our only little girl, our daughter. She died with cancer at age 41.

CENTER RIDGE

Center Ridge at the turn of the century circa 1905. This was, what is now, Arkansas State Highway 9. A busy shopping day, probably Saturday. At that time, Morrilton was a hard day's journey (one-way) and not much larger than Center Ridge. The boy, leaving the road and walking toward the photographer with a lettered sign above his head, in the background was George Richardson, father of Millard Richardson, former longtime circuit clerk of Conway County. George's older brother Jake was a former Center Ridge post office rural carrier during this period. According to legend, one of the two rural carriers was murdered on his route (not Jake). The man who did the killing was apprehended, and according to the story I was told, he was the last person that was hanged at the Conway County Courthouse. After this executions were carried out at the state penitentiary. Submitted by Jarrell Rainwater, nephew of George Richardson.

CLEVELAND

Old Store Buildings, 1956, "Downtown" Cleveland, Arkansas, on SH 95 in north Conway County. The building on the left was a general store, post office and residence with a Masonic Hall on the second floor. Next is an automobile repair garage. On the right is Frazier's general store and just beyond it is Bost's general store.

Cleveland Grocery, 1978. The old store building in Cleveland, AR, a few years before it was torn down to be replaced by a more modern structure.

Men in Post Office, 1965, Doyle O'Neal, rural route carrier, is on the left, and Lyonell Halbrook, postmaster, is on the right in this photo of the interior of the Cleveland Post Office in the Halbrook Grocery store.

Group in Early Automobile about 1916. Luther Maxwell and friends were out for a Sunday afternoon walk and came upon this automobile stopped in the road for a flat repair. Note that the rear tire is flat. They decided to have their photograph taken in the car. Luther is in the driver's seat and the photographer's shadow is included. The car may be a 1916 Dodge.

Three Men about 1946. From left to right, brothers Lyonell, Clyde and Opie Halbrook on the front porch of their parents' home in Cleveland, Arkansas.

HATTIEVILLE

"Jump Ball" community basketball ca. 1920. I remember that my grandfather, Luther A. Maxwell, told me that this photo was taken in Hattieville.

LEWISBURG

Home built by W.P. and Kate Egan at Lewisburg.

MORRILTON

The "Depot" in Morrilton - 1930s.

Main Street Morrilton.

Morrilton Cotton Warehouse Co. - Jan. 21, 1914. Percival Norman Totten was manager (front row, 5th from right).

Morrilton Cotton Warehouse Co. - Jan. 21, 1914.

Morrilton Cotton Warehouse Co. - Jan. 21, 1914.

Morrilton, AR - 1915, "This car won 1st prize. Mother, Gladys Totten, decorated our T-model with cotton. Daddy, Percy Totten, was manager of the cotton compress and had small bales of cotton compressed for the event. Daddy, with derby hat, was driving the car.

DOWN MEMORY LAND...
by Jarrell Rainwater

If you don't think Mother and Grandmother are not masters of efficiency experts - attempt to be on time with a couple of teens in the house and only one bathroom.

Back in 1930s many homes in Overcup had only one or two bedrooms with the living room doing double duty as a sleeping room. Large families were the rule. It was not unusual for five girls and five boys plus mother and father in two bedrooms and no bathroom. So came the old maxim - a room and a path.

The few automobiles and pickups were used almost exclusively for work, seldom used for ordinary errands. Children always walked to school and walked home in the afternoon. No rushing little Susie to school because she overslept. A child was entirely responsible for his ownself. If he was late or tardy, he suffered the consequences. Seldom if ever, do I remember a child not being on time.

Almost every child had chores - both before and after school and during the summer vacation. A child beginning at age 10-12, sometimes earlier, spent 10-hour days working hand labor in the fields.

There would be cows to milk, hogs to slop, cotton to chop and pick, strawberries, potatoes to set out, cultivate and pick or dig. Almost every farm grew most of their own food and if the kids didn't help there would be a serious food shortage.

To us, school and church were our recreation as well as our education and religious faith. Compared to our demanding labor, they were anxiously awaited by us. At school, as at home, there were no electric lights, no bathrooms, no running water. At school we had the familiar outdoor facilities.

There was no janitor - children were delegated for school jobs. Someone had to draw water from the well across the playground and tote and fill up the water container in the school daily. Someone had to get to school early in cold weather to start up a fire in the big wood heater. Someone had to sweep and empty the waste basket daily. Children did all of these tasks along with walking to school and chores at home '

We had one teacher, Mrs. Alice Carroll, for grades 1-6. The first three grades were on one side of the room; the other three on the other side of the room. The center of the room was open and contained the stove.

This was where Mrs. Alice sat in a wooden folding chair. She called classes for recitation. We would get up from our desks and stand in a row by the teacher. After our class, we would sit down and she would call another.

We were motivated by the fact that adults and family needed us, depended on us, and trusted us. We wouldn't have let them down for the world. We learned early that education was the key to try to better our life and our country.

We had lots of good times with playing in the swimming holes, Friday night play parties, playing checkers at the store, hanging out at the cotton gin seed house.

Every Christmas, Overcup Methodist Church had a play: readings, Christmas carols and an old-fashioned cedar Christmas tree that went all the way to the ceiling. Santa Claus came at the end of the program with a gift for every child.

On Christmas Day there was an old-fashioned turkey shooting contest. Our frontier skills were tested against one another.

During the '30s, a CCC camp was built out the WPA road east of Highway 9 between Overcup and Solgohachia. Young men were taught forestry conservation and construction skills. They were given barracks-style living, a uniform, all they could eat, and $21 per month. Another CCC camp

OVERCUP

Overcup children circa 1936, Easter Sunday, third and fourth grades to seventh and eighth grades, ages 9-13 approximately. From left, front row, lying on ground: Orville Denham, Bud Charton, Audrey Bostian (partially hidden) and Clayton Charton; sitting (partially hidden) Irple Bostian, Howard Charton, Doris Woodard, Lavene Poteete, Lorraine Bostian, Aileen Wilkinson, and Dorothy Holder; kneeling, Jarrell Rainwater, Afton Underwood, Quincy Stockindale, Arlona Underwood, Geraldine Bostian, Bernice Laster, Loretta Yocum, Athalene Bostian, and Muriel Holder, standing in rear, Elsie Williams, J.R. Crowder, Ione Yocum, Helen Yocum, Lorene Underwood, Edith Mae Adams, Ruthie Muriel Faulkner, Katherine Bostian, daughter of Gene Bostian.

Overcup group of young people, 1916-17, almost all of the boys went into the Army in 1917 for WWI. Back row, standing: Velma Underwood Yocum and Arkie Rainwater Tiner at end of row. The two boys and the 2nd and 3rd girl are unknown. Bottom row, sitting: 3rd boy is Monroe Rainwater (brother of Arkie) and last boy is David Henry Bostian. Emil Mourot and Andy Underwood are also in picture.

was located atop Petit Jean Mountain. They built much of our state park system.

For a real treat we got to go to Morrilton about once a month on Saturday for a 5-cent hamburger, Pepsi Cola or RC Cola, and a double feature cowboy western serial and cartoon at the Rialto or Petit Jean Theatre for 10 cents.

As you might imagine with hand milking, drinking raw milk and using untested well water and no refrigeration, the third world diseases such as malaria, tuberculosis, and stomach and bowel diseases were commonplace. Typhoid fever had just been conquered a few years previously, so with the health department shots that was no longer a problem. I lived near Campground Cemetery and I went to many funerals; many of them just babies and children.

Our teacher, Mrs. Alice Carroll, had one son, James Berry. He and two other teen-age boys were killed in an auto accident one Friday night. On Saturday my Dad took me to the funeral home to see them. They had been cleaned up and placed on stretchers but had not been placed in coffins.

On Sunday, Dec. 7, 1941, when we heard the Pearl Harbor attack news, many of us young people gathered at the little Methodist church. We talked in hushed tones, we sang and prayed. I don't think there was a preacher there that night. Our '30s Overcup experiences had taught us life's lessons well.

A preacher and a teacher could inspire and enlighten us, but ultimately only our faith in God and in ourselves could carry us through to victory over the enemies of our country and the enemies of our spirit. We would build a great America.

PLUMERVILLE

About 1833, Samuel Plummer, a young orphan from Boston, migrated to present day Conway County where he purchased 160 acres of land with a one-room log cabin. He added another room to his cabin and began a saddlery business. The Fort Smith and Little Rock Stage Coach route passed in front of Plummer's residence and the cabin soon became known as Plummer's Station and became a regular stage stop. Other settlers moved to the area and Plummer's Station continued to grow. The railroad obtained right-of-way through that area in 1870. The first business in Plumerville was a saloon, opened in 1872, by L.M. McClure. The Simms Hotel, the most known of all hotels, was built in 1880. The Peel Hotel was built a short time later. On October 4, 1880, Plummerville was incorporated as a town. Dr. G.W. Smith was the first mayor of Plummerville. He opened a drug store in the town in 1883.

At its peak, from 1910 to 1930, Plummerville boasted about 50 businesses, a telephone exchange, wagon yard, livery stables, at least five hotels, several rooming houses, three theaters, two drug stores and a goodly number of warehouses and at least three cotton gins. A number of years ago the post office dropped the second "m" from Plummerville and today it is spelled both ways.

At present the town has 12 businesses, a day care center, Arch Ford Educational Co-Op, a police department and court, and a volunteer fire department. Plumerville is the only town in Conway County that experienced growth between the census years of 1990 and 2000. Interstate 40, located on the north side of the city, was opened to traffic in 1970.

In 2004, Plumerville has Plummerville United Methodist Church, organized in 1884; the First Baptist Church, organized in 1891; the Portland Baptist Church, originally located in the Portland area; the Church of Christ; Mount Carmel Baptist Church, and Shady Grove Baptist Church.

In 1999, William C. "Bill" Plummer, great-great grandson of Samuel Plummer, took office as Mayor. During his first term as mayor he was instrumental in obtaining funding to renovate the old agricultural school building into a modern, up-to day facility for a Senior Citizen Center and Community Building. A new post office facility was opened to the public in 2000.

CCC CAMP

Letter to David Tilley from his cousin Ginny

Dear David,

Back in 1937 during the great depression, most of the families in Lost Corner and Cleveland were having a hard time keeping a roof over their heads and food for their children.

Marlin Hawkins, who later became the high sheriff of Conway County and for years ran a political operation that practically ran the state of Arkansas, was working for the Welfare Office, now called Human Services. Marlin was from a poor family himself and he knew the hardships the families in Conway County were suffering. So, when President Roosevelt set up the Civilian Conservation Corps to help poor families during the depression, Marlin took advantage of it. He went over the county notifying families that had young men aged 18-22 years to sign up for the program. It paid $30.00 per month, which, at the time was nothing to sneeze at. Marlin signed up your daddy, Paul Tilley, your uncle Arlie Watkins and their friend, Leon Brents. The three of them were sent to Pierce, Idaho to work in the Clear Water National Forest. They stayed there for six months, cutting trees, fighting forest fires and blasting stumps for roadways. The camps, were set up like army camps and they wore uniforms and followed certain rules and regulations. The boys spent from April to September of 1937 in Idaho. (Leon Brents gave me a lot of this information. Daddy couldn't remember all the details when I talked to him.) The program was a really good idea and it meant that grandpa Sam and grandma Maga got $180.00 that year to live on from Daddy. That was about the profit of a cotton crop off that sorry farm grandpa was renting. I'm sure that your daddy's family also appreciated the money from his work.

Grandpa Sam worked for the Works Progress Administration (WPA). He walked 5 miles each day from his farm to Wonderview, Arkansas where they were building a new school house. They paid him

CCC Camp in Pierce, Idaho "Clear Water National Forest." Arlie Watkins in front row on left side. Paul Tilley far right side in back. April thru September 1937. They made $30 per month.

50 cents a day for his work. Daddy said Grandpa carried his lunch in a tin pail and most of the time his lunch was cornbread and molasses or cornbread and turnip greens.

Grandpa Sam helped build the Wonderview School and also the school here in Plumerville where I live. Times were really hard around here and didn't get better until after World War II.

Daddy married Momma in December of 1937 right after he got back from the CCC Camp. Your daddy didn't marry Aunt Ola until 1939 after her first husband died of Typhoid Fever. I suppose he met her because he and daddy were friends.

Daddy said his time in the CCC Camp was OK. He said he only got into one fight. It was at night and daddy had worked hard all day and wanted to go to sleep. Some other boy wanted the lights on and refused to turn them off when everyone got ready to go to bed. Daddy beat the tar out of him. His only injury was when a bed spring broke and pierced his thumb and made it bleed. Anyway the result was everyone slept in the dark that night. (Ha) I don't remember him saying if your daddy had any adventures. Being a young frisky boy, I'm sure he did.

I've got a picture of the boys taken in front of their barracks. Daddy is on the front row on the left side. Your daddy (I think) is on the other end on the right of the picture. He has a cigarette in his mouth. Some of the boys were "acting tough" and put cigarettes in their mouth for the picture. I gave Pat a good copy. I don't know what she did with it. She said I would have to tell you all about everything because she couldn't remember it. (reckon she is getting old?)

This brings back memories. I sure wish I could talk with daddy and momma again. I miss them so.

I hope you and your family are well and happy. Pat tells me about you sometimes, when she can remember to do so. (Ha)

I am doing pretty good. I have reached my five year mark on my breast cancer and have not had any sign of its return. I'm so grateful.

My husband, Jimmy, is still farming in the Plumerville bottoms.' I don't work. (just stay home and watch grandkids. I have four, three girls and one boy.

Lynn, my youngest brother, is the only immediate family I have left. Buddy and Narvin have both gone on to be with Momma and Daddy. Lynn lost his only son,

Gary, this year. It sure has been hard for him and his wife.

I guess you know that Aunt Clara died a couple of months ago. She had a grand funeral and so many beautiful flowers. They buried her at the lower end of the cemetery in the newer part of the cemetery. She is across from Daddy. Uncle Willie who is almost 90 years old seems to be doing OK. Burl has remarried (his first wife, Lois, died of breast cancer); his second wife has done him a world of good. He goes clean and well kept now and seems to be happier than he has been in years. They still live at Lost Corner on Uncle Willie's land. Most of the, other children live at Lost Corner or near Cleveland. Buck, Louise, Betty and Sonny all still live in Little Rock. We seldom see them. Pat is the only one of the cousins that I have contact with, I sure do love her. She seems more a sister than a cousin.

Well, I guess I will stop. I hope this helps you. I know the older we get, the more we appreciate our family. I can think of so many things I wish I had talked with Daddy about.

Pat said you were going to Japan? If so, Please take care of yourself

Love, your Arkie cousin, Ginny.

Holiness Church - Morrilton, Arkansas

Conway County Fire Department

In September 1969, the Conway County Communications Club, a group of citizen band radio buffs, also known as 4-C'ers, started one of the first countywide fire departments in the nation. The department answered calls from all parts of the county excluding the cities of Morrilton and Plummerville.

The Conway County Fire Department's first truck was a 1941 model pumper that had been replaced by the Morrilton Fire Department and donated to the county at the request of then County Judge Tom Scott. It was housed in a rented metal building adjacent to Morrilton Motors on Railroad Avenue. The station also housed a mobile communications van, equipped and operated by the 4-C'ers, to be used at night and in remote parts of the county.

Serving as officers were Chief David Brewer, Assistant Chiefs Johnny Williams and R.E. Grooms, and Captain/Station Master Robert Swope. Other members included B.L. Hurley, George Reidmueller, Keith Dotson, Roy Coffman, Raymond Hardin, A.W. Wyllia, Clarence Bridgman, Lindell Roberts, W.B. Stracner, L.W. Ruff, Oran Oates, J.D. Huddleston, V.O. Conley, Ira Sanders, Jerry Eubanks and Harvey Roberts.

After a few years the department started to grow as many communities expressed interest in forming their own local stations. The first station outside Morrilton was formed at Hattieville. Jerusalem and Birdtown soon followed. Over time some stations were closed and others formed. There are now 13 stations in the county with Sardis, formed in 1989, being the most recent.

In 1973, Petit Jean resident Win Paul Rockefeller gave the fire department a much-needed boost when he donated three emergency vehicles and a modern radio system.

On September 6, 1977, County Ordinance 77-15 was passed by the Quorum Court to formally establish the Conway County Fire Department as an agency of the county and establish a five-member board. The five member is appointed by the county judge to formulate policies and procedures for the fire department as required by state law. On September 18, 1991, County Ordinance 91-29 was passed by the Quorum Court to establish an Advisory Board to furnish advise, gather information and make recommendations to the Administrative Board. County Ordinance 97-26, passed October 20, 1997, adopted the by-laws which define the organization of and set requirements for membership into the Conway County Fire Department.

In 2000 voters of Conway County passed 1/4 cent sale tax, which has been used to greatly increase the level of service provided to the public. These monies have also made possible the computerization of

Conway County Fire Department

records, upgrading of the radio system, building of new stations, and provided additional funds to purchase much needed training materials to be made available to members.

Today there are 260 volunteer members staffing 13 stations in communities around the county. The districts are Springfield, Jerusalem, Birdtown, St. Vincent, Petit Jean, Cleveland, Center Ridge, Hillcreek, Menifee, Blackwell/Kenwood, Overcup, Sardis and Ada Valley. Each district consists of a chief, assistant chief, captains, and between 10 and 25 members. *Submitted by Steve Beavers.*

Sardis Volunteer Fire Department (Conway County Fire Dept. District 12)

On April 3, 1989 the newly formed Sardis Volunteer Fire Department held its first meeting. This department was formed to serve the area of Conway County between Morrilton and Plumerville and from Interstate 40 to Oppelo. Charter members of this department were Dennis McCoy-Chief, Carroll Atkinson, Jr.-Secretary/Treasurer, David Speights, John Trafford, Greg Mourot, Doug Hunter, Randy Gilley, Gary Gilley, Ronnie Mourot, Donnie Hervey, Steve Atkinson, Phil Thomas, Harold McCoy, Gene Young, George Wade, Bill Craig, Chester Speights and Mark Atkinson-reserve.

Since its inception the Sardis Volunteer Fire Department has served the community by responding to fires, auto accidents, train accidents, and medical emergencies. They have also responded to areas outside of their district and even outside of the county to help other fire departments when they were needed.

Current members are: Tim Bengston-Chief, Steve Beavers-Assistant Chief, Bobby Beavers-Captain, Steve Trafford-Captain, Marcus Canady-Captain, Jimmy Brown-Captain, John Trafford, Johnathan Trafford,

Mark Trafford, David Speights, Rachel Beavers, Luke Berry, Matthew Speights, Sam McCallie, Shawn Lentz, Brandon Hunter and Jason McCoy.

In the 16 years since the department was formed they have strived to serve the community to the best of their ability and the members of the department look forward to serving the community for many more years to come. *Submitted by Steve and Rachel Beavers.*

Center Ridge Volunteer Fire Department

The history of Center Ridge Volunteer Fire Department began in the late 1970s when several area residents got together to form the original group of firefighters. This group included Drew Kissire, Sue West, Bernard Dusher, Rick and Norma Bryant (who were the first EMTS), James and Andrea Polk, Robert Birch, Bud Flowers, Randall Dixon, Bobby Bryant, Rick West, Allen Powell and several others.

Money was raised through many fund raising events - turkey shoots, a spook house, drawings for donated prized and some very successful fish fries. Sue West, the first secretary/treasurer went door-to-door soliciting donations to help buy protective gear and build the firehouse. She also convinced merchants in Morrilton and other communities to donate prizes for raffles, food items for fish fries, turkeys for the turkey shoot and other items used to raise money. Because of the combined efforts of Sue, Drew, Bernard and the others, and the generosity of the community at large, over $20,000 was raised initially. The land where the fire department sits was donated and the Wootens performed much of the labor to build the building. The members of the fire department performed most of the labor, donating their time and effort.

During this time Drew was elected the

first chief. Bernard Dusher was captain and Sue was elected as secretary/treasurer.

The members underwent training on safety procedures, firefighting techniques, equipment operation and even arson investigation. One memorable and frightening training session took place in Russellville, where they learned how to fight a propane tank fire. It was hot and dangerous.

The first piece of equipment was a donated brush truck from the forestry department, who by the way was indispensable in the early days. They donated equipment protective gear and assistance. Their expertise in fighting brush fires was invaluable as the fire department was getting on its feet.

One important goal was realized when the firefighters ' were certified. This led to the reclassification of the fire rating for insurance purposes. Most area residents received a reduction in their insurance premiums.

Being a volunteer fireman had to be a labor of love. They are unpaid; give up their time for training and equipment maintenance. They are called out in the middle of the night, the heat of the day, and in the dead of winter when it is so cold the pumps have to be started in the firehouse and the hoses routed through the water tanks. If the water wasn't kept circulating it would freeze on the way to the fire. They would be cold, wet, and tired. After the fire was out they had to clean, maintain and prepare the equipment for use before going home. But they continue to do it day after day, year after year.

As well as being exhausting, dirty work, firefighting is also dangerous. Injury was always a possibility when caught up in the excitement and confusion of a fire scene.

Bernard Dusher injured his hand while on a brush fire and had to go the hospital to have it repaired. Many firefighters suffered burns, cuts, bruises and sprains while on duty. Randall Dixon continued to serve while battling with terminal cancer.

One of the more serious injuries was suffered by Sue West, the treasurer, when she fell off of the back of the brush truck in 1980 while fighting a grass fire. She was busted up pretty badly and had to spend five days in the hospital.

Another time the fire dept was mobilized when the missile exploded in Damascus. Thankfully all that was required was to alert residents and point out escape routes. Most people gained a few extra gray hairs over that incident. Especially when we were alerted that the cloud of fuel vapors was heading our way. Mercifully the wind dissipated it.

After Drew resigned as chief, Bobby Bryant replaced him. Bobby served as chief until his untimely death in 2004. His casket was carried to the cemetery on the back of a fire truck, and there were fire trucks from several local departments in the procession. He was a credit to the department and will be sorely missed.

A few of the first volunteers are still active in the department. Norma Bryant re-

Captain Bob Ike Rieske, Cleveland Fire Dept., in front of the first fire station built in 1976. He stands beside the first pumper, a 1941 Ford Hale 500 GPM pumper.

ceived her 25 year service pin as a testament to her service. Norma not only continues as an EMT, but teaches classes on the subject.

This group of dedicated volunteers is responsible for saving many homes, barns and other buildings, as well as fighting brush fires, many of which threaten property, houses and even lives. Because of this brave group, the area residents and their property are much safer.

Current members are Rick Beck, Chris Bryant, Lynn Bryant, Norma Bryant (treasurer), Peggy Bryant (secretary), Joseph Conner, Curtis Conner (asst. chief), Terry Davidson (1st captain), Ed Hart, John Hart, Sherry Hart, Michelle Keith, Dennis Maxwell, Kenneth Meyer, Eddie Phillips, Becky Shipp, Tommy Stanley (chief), Charles Wilson (2nd captain), Darlena Wilson. *Submitted by Rick West.*

CLEVELAND FIRE DEPARTMENT DISTRICT #6

On September 3, 1976 the people of the Cleveland community met at the Methodist Church to discuss forming a fire department for the community. All were in agreement that this would be an added benefit for Cleveland. At this meeting the decision was made to organize the Cleveland Volunteer Fire Department. At this time donations

Cleveland's latest addition, a 1995 Freightliner, 1250 GPM pumper, bought in November 2004.

Cleveland Dist. #6, new station that houses all the trucks.

were taken to start the building of a station to house two fire trucks. Bob Ike and Betty Rieske leased enough land between their home place and the Cleveland Community building to erect the first fire department building.

The two bay 30'x35' wooden station was built on a concrete slab. This station housed a 1941 Ford 500 gpm pumper and a 1967 Jeep brush truck. In 1981 the community, through donations and fund raisers, bought a 1956 International 750 gpm pumper for $8,000 from Long Green, Maryland. A third bay door was added to the station.

The following is a list of firemen that originally started when the department was organized: Chief Louis McNew, Captain

Charlie Parham and Firemen: Tony Hofherr, A.O. Thompson, L.L. Halbrook, Ronnie Hendrick, Clell Stobaugh and Bob Ike Rieske.

At this time if someone had a fire and it was between 7 A.M. to 5 P.M., they would call the Cleveland Grocery to report it. A few years later some of the men in the department installed a siren that could be sounded from the store and this helped with the response time. After 5 P.M. one of the firemen was notified of a fire and his wife was responsible to call the other firemen.

After the 911 system was put into service all firemen received a pager or radio and got the call at the same time, making response time much quicker.

Back in the first days of the department when you had a bad battery or the truck was broken down someone had to go see the county judge to see if they had any spare batteries or parts at the county barn. Each department in the county was faced with this problem while trying to operate with old equipment.

Several years later the county had a survey taken and all fire districts were told they would have to have three water tankers and two pumpers per district. Cleveland started buying or getting tankers from the Arkansas Forestry Department. This caused a need for more housing for the added trucks. The department leased land from the Cleveland Baptist Church south of the old station to build an additional station. In 1992 and 1993 a 2 bay 40'x40' metal station was built to house the three additional trucks.

In December of 1996 the department received a $15,000 state matching grant and was able to purchase a 1974 International pumper. The 1941 Ford pumper was taken out of service at this time.

On August 22, 2000 the people of Conway passed a 1/4 cent sales tax for the rural fire departments. With this much needed money we have been able to make many improvements in our station and fire fighting equipment.

Knowing our old station was to small and beginning to deteriorate the department agreed to ask Betty Rieske if the old station was tom down if she would lease extra footage to build a larger building. She graciously did that for the department. In 2003 the old original station was torn down and a 4 bay 70'x40' metal building was erected. This building was tied to the 40'x40' giving us a total building of 110'x40'. Thanks to the Conway County voters.

One of the greatest benefits from the 1/4 cent sales tax, was that it enabled the department to buy a 1995 Freightliner 1250 gpm pumper.

As the new year of 2005 begins the department is working on lowering ISO ratings so that the community can reap the benefits of lower insurance premiums. The department now has 18 active firefighters with nine being first responders. The following is a list of the volunteer fire fighters and first responders for the Cleveland

Community: Chief Ronny Campbell, Asst. Chief Harles Hoyle and Firefighters: Debbie Hoyle, Bob Beavers, Jimmy O'Neal, Rick Emerson, Tommy Nelson, Angela Bennett, Jimmy Jones, Lynn Bennett, William Bennet, David Hull, Vicki Hull, Alex Campbell, Bob Carr, Rusty Deckard, Wesley O'Neal, Karman O'Neal and Cindy O'Neal.

The Cleveland Volunteer Fire Department now proudly houses seven trucks in our six bay station. They are as follows: 1990 Chevrolet Kopiak tanker, 1989 GMC tanker, 1979 GMC Sierra 7000 tanker, 1986 Chevrolet 1 1/4 service truck, 1974 International 1000 gpm pumper, 1967 jeep brush truck, 1995 Freightliner 1250 gpm pumper.

SAINT VINCENT FIRE DEPARTMENT CCFD DISTRICT 4

The Saint Vincent District of the Conway County Fire Department was organized at a community meeting on July 8, 1976. Fifteen men signed the first roster and began training to become volunteer firefighters. Otto Zimmerman was elected as the first fire chief and served until December of 1977.

Conway County supplied the first firefighting vehicles to the department in September of 1976. The 1952 international pumper truck and 1967 military jeep were repaired, equipped and put into service by the volunteers. Louis Pfeifer agreed to house the trucks in an unheated building at Pfeifer's Feed Mill until a fire station could be constructed. To protect the trucks from freezing, they were covered with a plastic tarp and an electrical heater was placed underneath.

During the summer of 1977, fire department members and other community volunteers constructed a pre-fabricated 40x80 foot metal building on church property in St. Vincent. The building was originally designed as a farm building and had one exit with sliding doors and no insulation. After numerous modifications, this building has served the fire department well. It is now, after 28 years, being replaced with a modern fire station.

Gerald Gangluff was elected fire chief in January of 1978 and served until his death in August 1998. During this time, the fire department received its first insurance services office rating. The department improved from a Class 10 to a Class 9 rating which saved the citizens approximately 20% on their insurance premiums. In 1982, a pumper truck was purchased from the Tulsa Fire Department using community funds

and donations. This truck greatly improved the fire department's firefighting capabilities with its large pump and water tank.

A "First Responder" Medical Program was started by the fire department in the mid-90s. The fire department responds to all emergency medical calls and accidents to immediately begin medical treatment and to assist the ambulance service with patient care. This program has been very well received by the citizens of the district.

Chief Gangluff started a program of upgrading equipment and vehicles as he prepared the fire department for a new insurance services office rating. A newer pumper was purchased to replace the 1952 International. Two tanker trucks were constructed for use in a "Tanker Shuttle System" which replaces the need for fire hydrants in areas of the district without water mains.

Charles Gangluff, the current fire chief was elected following his father's death in 1998. Charles is the only remaining charter member of the fire department. Work on a new insurance services office rating was continued and a Class 6 rating was received September 1, 2001. This rating was important for the fire department since it is similar to the rating received by most small cities. The citizens of this rural fire district now pay an insurance premium equal to many small municipalities.

The fire department continues to expand and improve. A sub-station has been constructed in the Lanty Community with the hopes of extending the insurance savings into this area. Additional trucks and equipment were purchased to make this station operational. Two Automatic External Defibrillators (AEDs) were purchased for the First Responders to use during cardiac emergencies.

The members of the Saint Vincent Fire Department wish to thank the citizens of the county, the local community and especially St. Mary's Church for their support and financial contributions over the last 28 years. Special thanks to the many men and women that have donated their time and efforts to volunteer for this fire department in the past. Each firefighter has helped develop this department into the success that it is today.

Saint Vincent Fire Department pumper.

KILLED IN THE LINE OF DUTY

John L. Emerson
Second District Engineer
Box #158 Nov. 17, 1914

Captain Thomas J. Strahler
Truck Co. No. 11
Box #3423 May 27, 1916

Ladderman William R. Halloran
Truck Co. No. 5
Box #246 Apr. 17, 1915

Frederick Branon
Third District Engineer
Dec. 31, 1918

Lieut. John A. Watson
Engine Co. No. 27
Box #72 Apr. 24, 1919

Lieut. Howard A. Davis
Engine Co. No. 47
Box #72 Apr. 24, 1919

Fireman Walter Musgrove
Engine Co. No. 30
June 18, 1919

Engineman Daniel Rogers
Engine Co. No. 9
Box #235 Sept. 18, 1919

Fireman Charles Parks
Engine Co. No. 32
Box #4 May 8, 1920

Captain George A. Lenz
Engine Co. No. 7
Box #446 Sept. 12, 1922

Captain Harry Jones
Water Tower Co. No. 2
Box #516 Dec. 26, 1925

Fireman William Hesse
Engine Co. No. 40
Box #8945 Dec. 14, 1924

Fireman Claude McGee
Truck Co. No. 18
Box #47 Jan. 14, 1929

Fireman William H. Hundertmark
Engine Co. No. 44
Box #8349 Jan. 5, 1931

Fireman John King
Truck Co. No. 4
Box #35 May 9, 1931

Firefighter William H. Grief
Engine Co. No. 35
Box #6546 Mar. 3, 1954

Francis P. O'Brien
Fourth Battalion Chief
Box #12 Feb. 16, 1955

Captain William J. Lamb
Engine Co. No. 25
Box #389 Nov. 13, 1933

Fireman Edward L. Rithmiller
Engine Co. No. 12
Box #149 Dec. 10, 1934

Fireman Pemberton Warmsley
Truck Co. No. 15
Box #294 Sept. 9, 1935

Fireman George J. Reif
Truck Co. No. 3
Box #1841 Feb. 21, 1936

Fireman Lawrence F. Wheatley
Truck Co. No. 25
Box #8646 Nov. 20, 1936

Captain Murray L. Byrne
Truck Co. No. 10
Box #457 Jan. 7, 1937

Lieut. James K. Harrison
Engine Co. No. 5
Box #528 Oct. 13, 1937

Fireman John H. Sommers
Engine Co. No. 15
Box #528 Oct. 13, 1937

John F. Steadman
Deputy Chief No. 2
March 7, 1940

Fireman Herman W. Jackson
Truck Co. No. 6
Box #514 Apr. 23, 1940

Captain James T. Wheatley
Engine Co. No. 44
Silent Alarm Nov. 29, 1941

Fireman Eugene F. Kernan
Engine Co. No. 43
Box #8248 July 28, 1942

Fireman John H. Naumann
Engine Co. No. 10
Box #463 Jan. 1, 1943

Harry B. Scheve
Acting Deputy Chief
August 27, 1943

Fireman John Pfadenhauer
Engine Co. No. 30
Box #7126 Apr. 10, 1944

Firefighter Joseph F. Taylor
Engine Co. No. 24
Box #288 Jan. 11, 1956

Firefighter Charles M. Jerschied
Engine Co. No. 24
Box #288 Jan. 11, 1956

Lieut. Frederick Klaburner
Engine Co. No. 42
Box #8231 Feb. 1, 1946

Fireman Carl E. Humphreys
Truck Co. No. 1
Box #2127 Jan. 11, 1948

Lorenz A. Dolle
Second Battalion Chief
May 9, 1948

Fireman Joseph A. Remeikis
Truck Co. No. 22
Box #8664 Nov. 9, 1949

Fireman Joseph B. Magaha
Truck Co. No. 22
Box #8664 Nov. 9, 1949

Fireman Charles A. Paff
Engine Co. No. 46
Box #8664 Nov. 9, 1949

Fireman James W. Haynie
Engine Co. No. 46
Box #8664 Nov. 9, 1949

Captain Daniel Riordan
Engine Co. No. 15
Box #4121 Feb. 4, 1950

Fireman Andrew Duffy
Engine Co. No. 15
Box #4121 Feb. 4, 1950

Captain Harry E. Tuckey
Engine Co. No. 21
Box #8559 Apr. 10, 1952

Firefighter George J. Hand
Hose Co. No. 3
Box #1039 June 3, 1952

Firefighter William R. Smith
Truck Co. No. 9
Box #1039 June 3, 1952

Lieut. Oscar W. Slitzer
Engine Co. No. 6
Box #23 Apr. 18, 1953

Firefighter Albert E. Reiley
Truck Co. No. 19
May 2, 1953

Asst. Engineman Herman Leyh
Engine Co. No. 22
Box #1932 Sept. 5, 1953

Firefighter Morris G. Hunt
Truck Co. No. 6
Box #563 July 9, 1965

Firefighter Jennings G. Moser
Chemical Co. No. 1
Box #1937 Mar. 29, 1966

Firefighter William W. Barnes
Engine Co. No. 17
Box #12 Feb. 16, 1955

Firefighter Joseph P. Hanley
Engine Co. No. 13
Box #12 Feb. 16, 1955

Firefighter Anthony Reinsfelder
Truck Co. No. 16
Box #12 Feb. 16, 1955

Firefighter Rudolph a. Machovec
Engine Co. No. 15
Box #12 Feb. 16, 1955

Firefighter Richard F. Melzer
Engine Co. No. 15
Box #12 Feb. 16, 1955

Firefighter Thomas J. Eagen
Truck Co. No. 19
Box #549 Nov. 21, 1955

Firefighter Stephen Chearney
Truck Co. No. 6
Box #576 Feb. 25, 1963

Lt. Joseph H. Zajac
Truck Co. No. 24
Box #1944 May 6, 1968

P. O. James E. Carter
March 24, 1970

Lt. Joseph B. Goonan
April 4, 1971

Capt. Frank J. Sappe, Jr.
March 4, 1977

FF Donald G. Knopp
March 25, 1979

Capt. Martin Kleinsmith
April 19, 1980

FF Melvin S. Rosewag, Jr.
July 29, 1984

Lt. John T. Killian, Jr.
March 10, 1985

Lt. Nelson Taylor
Nov. 22, 1985

Lt. John N. Plummer
Jan. 27, 1991

E.V.D. Eddie Arthur
June 1, 1991

Firefighter Joseph J. Gray
Chemical Co. No. 3
Box #6321 Jan. 4, 1958

Lieut. Charles A. Leutner
Engine Co. No. 24
Box #1934 Oct. 31, 1958

Firefighter Thomas E. Reynolds
Truck Co. No. 13
Silent Alarm Mar. 13, 1960

Christian F. J. Reynolds
Sixth Battalion Chief
December 17, 1960

Firefighter James M. Gallagher
Truck Co. No. 14
Box #8474 July 15, 1961

Pump Operator Francis Marney
Engine Co. No. 2
Box #5624 Jan. 10, 1962

FF Joseph P. Hanley
Engine Co.No. 13
Box #12 Feb. 16, 1955

FF Anthony Reinsfelder
Truck Co. No. 16
Box #12 Feb. 16, 1955

FF Rudolph A. Machovec
Engine Co. No. 15
Box #12 Feb. 16, 1955

FF Richard F. Melzer
Engine Co. No. 15
Box #12 Feb. 16, 1955

FF Thomas J. Eagen
Truck Co. No. 19
Box #549 Nov. 21, 1955

FF Joseph Taylor
Engine Co. No. 24
Box #288 Jan. 11, 1956

FF Charles M. Jerschied
Engine Co. No. 24
Box #288 Jan. 11, 1956

FF Joseph J. Gray
Chemical Co. No. 3
Box #6321 Jan. 4, 1958

Lt. Charles A. Leutner
Engine Co. No. 24
Box #1934 Oct. 31, 1958

FF Thomas E. Reynolds
Truck Co. No. 13
Silent Alarm Mar. 13, 1960

Batt. Chief Christian F. J. Reynolds
Sixth Battalion Chief
Dec. 17, 1960

Firefighter Paul J. Herauf
Engine Co. No. 17
November 29, 1966

Lieut. John E. Hoschstedt
Engine Co. No. 44
Box #8144 Dec. 18, 1966

Firefighter Thomas Brand
Engine Co. No. 25
Box #324 Jan. 2, 1967

Firefighter James L. Grahe
Truck Co. No. 5
Box #8268 Dec. 2, 1967

Firefighter William A. Bernhard
Engine Co. No. 51
Box #1835 Mar. 28, 1968

Lieut. Joseph H. Zajac
Truck Co. No. 24
Box #1944 May 6, 1968

FF James M. Gallagher
Truck co. No. 14
Box #8474 July 15, 1961

Pump Operator Francis
Marney Engine Co. No. 2
Box #5624 Jan. 10, 1962

FF Stephen Chearney
Truck Co. No. 6
Box #576 Feb. 25, 1963

FF Morris G. Hunt
Truck Co. No. 6
Box #563 July 9, 1965

FF Jennings G. Moser
Chemical Co. No. 1
Box #1937 Mar. 29, 1966

FF Paul J. Herauf
Engine Co. No. 17
Nov. 29, 1966

Lt. John E. Hochstedt
Engine Co. No. 44
Box #8144 Dec. 18, 1966

FF Thomas Brand
Engine Co. No. 25
Box #324 Jan. 2, 1967

FF James L. Grahe
Truck Co. No. 5
Box #8268 Dec. 2, 1967

FF William A. Bernhard
Engine Co. No. 51
Box #1835 Mar. 28, 1968

Firefighter Eric Schaffer
Rescue #1
Sept. 16, 1995

CEDAR CREEK SCHOOL

Cedar Creek School Group

CENTRAL WARD SCHOOL

Located at N. Division Street where the U.S. Bank is now. This 4th grade class graduated in 1944 - MHS, Springfield, Oppolo, where bused in to high school. Some in 9th grade were not at Central Ward. Miss Ruth Moore was the principal.

Arkansas Centennial 100 years - l-r: James Fleming, Lois M. Loyd, Laurance Brookings, Carolyn Farish, Charles Bridewell, Virginia Martin, H.T. Avants, Doris Danials, Royce Tester, Pearl Newkirk, _, Kelley Pryor, Roger Brooks(?), Norma James, O.H. Wood, Ermalene Gray, Edward L. Marshaw, Edith Bizell, Ben White Walters, Jimmie F. Carey, Wendel West. Seated: Dorothy McCarrol, Imogene Stroud, Billie Jean Cole, Peggy Jackson, Laverne Sledge.

L.W. SULLIVAN HIGH SCHOOL

Hymon King Sr. was the last principal of Sullivan High School. He was principal from about 1948 until May 1965 when the schools in Morrilton were desegregated. He came to Morrilton from the Rosenwald School at Bigelow in Perry County.

Mr. King was a graduate of Western University in Kansas with further study done at Wayne State University in Detroit, Michigan. His wife, Zeophus Nelson King was a teacher and librarian at Sullivan High School.

Mr. King was responsible for many improvements during the time he was principal. Sullivan received its first A-rating by the

L.W. Sullivan High School

State Department of Education and he worked until the school was accredited by the North Central Association. All teachers who taught during his tenure had accredited degrees from accredited colleges. A National Honor Society Chapter, Mathematics Club, and Future Teachers of America Club were organized at the school while he was administrator.

Mr. King was a Steward and Trustee at St. Paul A.M.E. Church where he, his wife and son, Hymon Jr. were members. *(Information from personal knowledge and from a news clipping in Mattie Brown's Journal that was clipped from the Morrilton Headlight about 1963.)*

LOST CORNER SCHOOL

Lost Corner School Group, May 1, 1925.

Class of 1934, taken day of Jr.-Sr. Banquet. Front row: Jimmie Cunningham, Robert Whitley, Carl Davis, Ralph Helloms, Maxine Bissett, Harold Farish, Allan Merritt, Jimmy Austin. Row 2: Helen Fiser, Sophie Miller, Maxine Stover, Gladys Totten, Naomia King, David Leach, Jim Egan, Irene Brown, Ruby Farish. Row 3: Mary Ellen Webb, Dorothy Todd, Maudine Clerget, Lillian Green, Sybil Bradshaw, Irene Griffith, Clin Lee, Johnnie Scroggin, Sam Patterson. Row 4: Christine Jones, Marie Wear, Wilma Jones, Ruby Cooke. Row 5: Floy Groom, Dora Harrington, Helen Isley, Elon Groom, Opal Gordon, E.W. Littleton, J.A. Crain, Allen Riggs, D.L. McArthur. Row 6: Robert Bradley, Alva Gordon, Waymon Freyaldenhoven, Hildegard Croon, W.M. Stell.

Taken by Edmond Flowers, a former student, in June 1971.

POTEETE SCHOOL

According to those asked, it was located across the road from Lone Oak Baptist Church. Both are now gone. Lone Oak Baptist Church was located on Lonoke Road. It was moved to near Overcup on Hwy. #9 and is now called Lonoke Baptist Church. It

Poteete School - Picture taken about 1894-96.
Back Row: Arthur Poteete, Mayne Rainwater, Luther Poteete, S.J. Rainwater, "Poley" Poteete, John Denton, Elmer Ross, Elbert Dugger, May Poteete, Arkie D. Rainwater, Ida Poteete. 3rd Row: Charles Rainwater, Rufus Poteete, Dora Poteete, Vernonia Poteete, Mary Poteete, Maudie Dugger, Emma Poteete, Ella Denton, Bob Poteete, Joe Denton. 2nd Row: Edmund Rainwater, Arch Dugger, Miles Poteete, _ Poteete, "Fate" Poteete, Benny Denton, Lee Denton, Albert Poteete. Front: Tollie Poteete (blurred), _ Dugger, Ellis Rainwater, Annie Thomas, Annie Denton.

was established by the Poteete/Rainwater families. Was not able to read the first name of one Poteete and one Dugger; the rest were all identified by Warren's father, Luther Eugene. He was born in Conway County in 1882 and lived among these people most of his life until age 18 when the family moved to Oklahoma (then Indian territory).

Families represented: Joseph Daniel and Rhoda Jane (Rainwater) Poteete, Warren's grandparents. Luther Eugene (1882-1958); Mary (1883, died before 1900); Bob (Robert Lafayette, 1879-1916).

Simeon Vinson and Nancy Christina (Rainwater) Poteete: Joanne Gatliff's great-grandparents. Ida (b. 1883), Vernonia (b. 1878), Emma (b. 1880), Albert (b. 1877), Annie Thomas (granddaughter).

William Humphrey and (1st) Martha (Ross) Poteete and (2nd) Jacqueline (Autry) (Ross) Poteete: Arthur D. (b. 1883), "Poley" Napoleon (b. 1880), Elmer Ross (Jacqueline's 1st husband) (b. 1884), May (b. 1885), Rufus (b. 1875), Dora (b. 1870), John Miles (b. 1871), "Fate" Lafayette (b. 1873), Tollie or Tolley (1892).

Edmund E. "Hoda" and Sarah Virginia "Jennie" (Poteete) Rainwater: "Mayne" William M. (b. 1881), "S.J." Simeon J. (b. 1884), Arkie D. (b. 1893), Charles (b. 1879), Edmund E. (father), "Ellis" Edmund E. (b. 1890).

Joseph E. and Mary Elizabeth (Poteete) Denton: John F. (b. 1880), Ella (b. 1879), Joe (father), Benny (b. 1875), "Lee" Robert L. (b. 1877).

J.C. and Julia A. (Autry) Dugger: Julia was sister to Jacqueline (Autry) (Ross) Poteete. Elbert, Maudie (b. 1879), Archy (b. 1875), ??, Annie (b. 1889).

SARAH CLARK ELEMENTARY SCHOOL

Sarah Clark Elementary School

SUCKER CREEK BASEBALL TEAM - 1914

Top Row, l-r: Cary Scroggins, Ollie Pimpleton, William Rhodes, Orville Kissire, Samuel Garfield Watkins. Bottom Row, l-r: Dennis Scroggins, Levi Rhodes, Wash Keith, Frank Rhodes.

WONDERVIEW SCHOOL

School at Jerusalem in 1933. Ruth Maxine Thompson, Dorothy Lee Reynolds and Delilah Dale Reynolds.

CONWAY COUNTY ARKANSAS

CHURCHES, SCHOOLS, BUSINESSES, CLUBS & ORGANIZATIONS

George Washington Hawkins holding gear.

"No farewell words were spoken, no time to say good-by, you were gone before we knew it, and only God knows why."

Don Louis McMillan was the son of USAF Capt. George Louis McMillan Jr. and Bonnie LaVelle Littig of Ft. Worth, Texas, and born in Panama City, Florida.

When Don was three months old, his father, a highly decorated Air Force fighter pilot, died when his plane crashed in Bangor, Maine. Later, Don and his older brother, Ricky, were adopted by Air Force pilot, Major Marvin Paty. With Paty's death, Don lost another father, and was 9 years old when his mother married Air Force pilot, Lt. Col. John Ross Rhoads, who also adopted the boys.

Don grew-up living in Japan, Montana, Arizona, Texas, and Arkansas. He enjoyed sports, pitched baseball, and was basketball team captain. Riding motorcycles, hunting, fishing, reading, and rodeo riding were his favorite hobbies. Don was tops academically and a notorious practical joker. At 10, he landed his first job and braved the harsh Montana winters delivering newspapers on his bicycle. At 14, he bagged his first trophy, an Elk. By 16, he bought his first motorcycle, owned a string of rodeo steers traveling on weekends throughout the country leasing them to rodeo producers, and pro-riding. Don learned the art of horse training, was a bronc rider, bull rider, roper, and bulldogger bringing home many trophies for his successes. Bull-doggin' was his specialty and, Don, and his horse, Crash, made quite a team continuing to rodeo in college and later, while working for Arkansas Power & Light Company. Fun-loving and daring, he also helped as a rodeo clown luring the bulls and bucking broncs from the cowboys in the arena.

A licensed journeyman lineman, he retired in 1988, after a 20 year career in electrical distribution and construction with Arkansas Power & Light Company in Little Rock and Russellville. Thriving on challenges, he trained and worked on electrical transmissions lines, towers, and sub-stations as well.

On December 1, 1973, Don married, Marsha Jewell Elkins, daughter of USMC CWO-3 (Ret.) James Lewis and Ruby Mae Thompson Elkins, in Little Rock where they were living because their respective parents retired from the military and settled near the Little Rock Air Force Base.

In 1975, Don and Marsha established their home in Granny's Hollow near Jerusalem, and Don's dream of owning a farm became reality. He worked long hours pioneering a farm from a brush and tree covered wilderness. He had a passion for hard work tackling every situation with determination and valor. In 1976 they started a cattle operation, and in 1980, added poultry houses. A swine farrow-to-finish facility was constructed in 1988 when Don retired from AP&L to farm full-time. In 1994, a farrow-to-finish farm at Center Ridge was added to the operation.

The loves of his life were Marsha, and their only child, a son, Blake Halston, born October 20, 1983. For 30 years, Don and Marsha were partners and soul mates. They were members of the Church of Christ, active in community service, and politics. They devel-

Don Louis "Cowboy" (Rhoads) McMillan
November 21, 1948 - September 13, 2003
Photo taken ca. 1967.

oped several businesses, Rocky Roads Farms, which later became DonMar Farms LLC, Rhoads Construction, D & R Forestry Services LLC, Beach Haven Senior Care LLC, and DonMar Properties LLC.

Don was in *Who's Who in Executives and Professional* in 1998-99, served as County Election Commissioner and Republican Party Chairman from 1994-97, 1st vice chairman, and treasurer. In 2003, after working with the Republicans for many

Don & Marsha McMillan, 1988.

Don L. and Blake H. McMillan, father and son. Harding Academy Choir concert, Searcy, AR. Spring 2001.

USAF Capt. and Mrs. George Louis McMillan, Jr., Ft. Worth, TX, 1946.

years, he joined the county Democrats. Other activities included the AR Pork Producer's Association, Cattleman's Association, Brotherhood of Electrical Workers, the AR Home School Association, and the Cub Scouts.

After the death of his parents, Don petitioned the court to reinstate his birth name. On August 26, 2002, the Rhoads family became the McMillan's.

September 13, 2003, at the age of 54, Don, was tragically killed near Hot Springs and is at rest in the McMillan family mausoleum at the Robertstown Cemetery near Jerusalem. Genesis 9: 6-16.

Blake, 19, at the time of his father's death, was a college student majoring

A1c Blake H. McMillan, Lakeland Air Force Base, San antonio, TX. Basic Training, June 2004.

in engineering, science, and computer systems. In March 2004 because of his concern for his mother's future, and putting hers before his own as he knew his father would have done, he accepted deferred military enlistment. On June 8, 2004, he began his Air Force life leaving behind all he knew and loved, his family, his home, and his dreams.

As a friend, Don was always there; for a chat, a smile, hug, or helping hand. He cared deeply and his love was true and strong. He loved life and lived each day giving us his all. Being selfless, Don was a devoted husband, father, and son, and a gentle, loving, motivator. Each word from his lips was a blessing and his laugh, like music. Our greatest joy was being with Don. He was "Our Sunshine" and our love for him, infinite. His memory glows in our hearts as he continues to light our path with his love.

Written in loving memory by James and Ruby Elkins and Blake and Marsha McMillan.

Donnie, Bonnie and Rickey McMillan, Summer 1950.

25

FIRST BAPTIST CHURCH OF PLUMERVILLE

The First Baptist Church of Plumerville began August 25, 1891. On that date a council composed of Elder G.W. Ford, Elder M.S. Kirkland, and Elder H.W. Melton was called for the purpose of organizing a church. Since it was the earliest of its kind in this area, the church was given the name of First Baptist Church of Plumerville, the name it holds to this day.

First Baptist Church of Plumerville

Elder M.S. Kirkland was the first pastor and W.E. Overstreet, the first church clerk. The church voted that regular services be held on the fourth Saturday and Sunday of each month. On September 26, 1891, two months after the organization of the church, a presbytery was called and organized to ordain deacons who had been previously elected by the church. Tins presbytery was composed of Elder G.W. Ford, Elder M.S. Kirkland, and Bro. Sim Poteete, a deacon from the Lonoke Church. Bro. Riley Parker and Bro. J. H. Overstreet were ordained as deacons. A short time later, W.F. Kirkland, and J.W. Overstreet were ordained as deacons.

During those two months, 40 persons were baptized into the fellowship of the church and a number were received by letter.

The first building was a one room frame structure erected in 1892. This building stood for 33 years, until on February 4, 1925 it was destroyed by fire. A building committee was soon appointed and they began immediate, active efforts to plan and erect a new building. Under the capable leadership of Rev. C.P. McCraw, a new building was erected within six months and twenty six days from the date that the old building was destroyed.

On March 3, 1929, the church voted to dedicate their new house of worship on the fourth Sunday in May of the same year. On that day, a special program was rendered, and addresses were made by Dr. J.S. Compere, Editor of *The Baptist Advance*, Dr. J.S. Rogers, General Secretary of the Arkansas Baptist State Convention; and Dr. E.P.J. Garrott, pastor of the First Baptist Church of Conway.

As the church prospered, the congregation decided to purchase a pastor's home and in 1960 build a new Educational Building. In 1965, new carpets were added and a new Baldwin organ was given to the church in memory of Mr. and Mrs. W.F. Kirkland and Deacon F.M. Ramer by their children. In June of 1966, the church purchased a new central heating and cooling system.

Several improvements have been made to the church plant: a colonial-type porch was added to the front, a steeple was placed on top of the sanctuary, baptistery curtains, and pew cushions were purchased and a lighted cross was hung in front of the sanctuary. An addition of 50 feet was added to the south end of the church and provided a new baptistery as well as five additional Sunday School rooms. In 1983, a sound system was donated to the church and later was upgraded.

The church receives a percentage of the W.D. Kirkland and Miss Glenn Kirkland estate each year. The church has used this money for various expenditures such as a scholarship fund and as an addition to the building fund to enrich church grounds and building. This financial bequest has been evidenced in aluminum siding, storm windows, mini-blinds, remodeling of the parsonage and Educational Building. The parsonage basement was remodeled into a Fellowship Hall with a full kitchen. In 1989 central heat and air was added to the parsonage, a second bathroom was added in 1990. A newer, smaller organ was donated to the organ also in 1990. In 1991 the pastor's office was improved with new carpet and bookcases and cabinets.

In 2000 a new church sign was purchased band a new Fellowship Hall was built behind the existing buildings. The new Fellowship Hall has served the church well with a capacity of over 150.

The first weekend in December, it is used for the annual Senior Citizen's Christmas Banquet.

In 2004 a church bus was purchased and a food ministry was also begun to help provide for the needs of our community.

This short history does not give the complete story of the First Baptist Church of Plumerville. The full history is written in the hearts of the great number of souls ministered to by Southern Baptists throughout our world, the ones reached here in our community, and those yet to be ministered to. As Plumerville First Baptist Church continues to march forward under the banner of Jesus Christ our Lord, history will continue to be made.

FORMER PASTORS

M.S. Kirkland	1891-1893	J.B. Graves	1942-1943
T. Moody	1893-1894	L.L. Jordan	1943-1949
Giles C. Taylor	1895-1896	M.E. Wilfong	1949-1951
A.H. Wilson	1897-1900	C.H. Holland	1951-1952
G.A. Miller	1901	Merle Johnson	1952-1956
S.B. Barnett	1903-1905	Don Gravenmier	1956-1958
W.P. Kirne	1905	William Brown	1958-1960
E.J.A. McKinney	1907-1909	John Graves	1967-1970
W.V. Walls	1910	Herald Quisenberry	1970-1971
T.J.D. King	1911	Jerry Cothern	1972-1973
E.J.A. McKinney	1912-1914	Marvin Ferguson	1974-1976
O.M. Stallings	1915-1916	Jimmy Milloway	1976-1981
J.K. Smith	1916-1917	Don Hook (interim)	May-Oct 1982
W.C. Hamil	1919	Tommy Monk	1982-1985
L.P. Guthrie	1920	Matt Harness	1985-1990
A.A. Dulaney	1921-1922	William West (interim)	Oct-Dec 1990
G.E. Jones	1923-1924	Fred Holst	1990-1992
C.P. McGraw	1925-1928	Jerry Threet	1993-1996
W.O. Taylor	1929	Kenny Dunham	1997-1999
J.S. Rogers	1930-1938	Jack Bean (interim)	May-Oct 1999
J.T. Elliff	1939	Fred Fretz	1999-2004
C.H. Cutrell	1940-1941	Steven McCann	2005-

SUNDAY SCHOOL SUPERINTENDENTS

Riley Parker	Bill Gwin	Gene Burgess
Collie Bean	Larry Hogan	Hunter Crawford
Everette Parker	Woodrow Parker	Bob Bean
F.M. Ramer	C.A. Ramer	Roy B. Bane
Mrs. Dan Patterson	Lowell Winningham	Larry Hogan
Arel Fox	Junior Garrett	

CHURCH CLERKS

W.E. Overstreet	Mae Ruth Moore Reed	Billy Jean Bean
J.B. Loggins	Wanda Brown	Mrs. Bradley Thomas
J.R.G.W.N. Adams	Colleen Fields	Mrs. Emmette O'Boyle
W. A. Moody	F.M. Ramer	Charlene Mulvaney
G.H. Taylor	Mrs. I.A. Deaver	Karen Price
A.L. Goatcher	Mrs. Ed Reed	Jo Garrett
Robert Parker	Mrs. Sam Gilmore	Linda Mason

CHURCH TREASURERS

A.L. Goatcher	Bobbye and Bradley Thomas
John Reed	Janet Bean
Mrs. I.A. Deaver	Bobbye and Bradley Thomas
C.A. Ramer	Bob and Janet Bean

DEACONS

Riley Parker	C.A. Ramer	Robert Parker
J.H. Overstreet	Sam Gilmore	Ray Atkinson
W.F. Kirkland	Ira Dixon	Art Wiman
J.W. Overstreet	Dave Bean	Roy B. Bane
John Reed	Bill Gwin	Bob Bean
W.A. Moody	Ray Trafford	Bradley Thomas
Hunter Crawford	Collie Bean	Junior Garrett
W.R. Beckham	Emmett O'Boyle	Bill Garrett
F.M. Ramer	Lloyd Greene	Larry Hogan
W.D. Kirkland	Earl Smith	
A.L. Goatcher		

FIRST PRESBYTERIAN CHURCH

The First Presbyterian Church of Morrilton was established in 1883 and is approaching its 125th anniversary. There are currently 180 members of the church which is affiliated with the Presbyterian Church U.S.A.). Presbyterians believe that the Bible is the inspired word of God, and that is the foundation of our faith. Presbyterians also believe that salvation is a gift of grace, that no human being is good enough to warrant the gift of Heaven in his/her own right, and that no one is so bad that he/she can not be saved by God's redeeming grace.

Ministers serving our congregation through the years and the year each was installed include Samuel J. Martin (1906), T.R. Best (1912), John P. Kidd (1913), J.P. Robertson (1915), R. Guy Davis (1918), Samuel Stanworth (1920), Samuel J. Patterson (1924), Andrew E. Newcomer (1941), S.N. Harris (1945), George T. McKee (1947), Lyndon M. Jackson (1950), Edwin Walthall (1954), Robert J. Stewart (1959), Daniel W. Adams (1963), T. Stratton Daniel Jr. (1966), Edsel Granger (interim 1987), Karl F. Young (1988), David Davies (interim 1998, Mark Richie (1998), Jimmie Thames (interim 2001), Kris Crawford (2002), and Gail Perkins (interim 2004).

Current First Presbyterian Church in Morrilton, AR.

The present church building located at 105 W. Church Street was dedicated in 1952 and through the years has been refurbished and remodeled to maintain its stately architecture. In 1980 the church obtained the properties at the corner of Morrill and Valley Streets and the property of Miss Louise Ashley which adjoined the church on the west side of the church. The structures on these lots were torn down to make more parking spaces available. The old manse, located to the east of the church next to the county library, was demolished in 1987. The manse at 605 W. Church, which had been purchased in 1966, was sold in the 1990s and a housing allowance became a part of the pastor's benefits.

Current programs at the church, in addition to Sunday church school and worship, include fellowship meals, women's circle groups, weekly breakfasts for men, a large multicultural youth group, and Thrive which is an after school program for children. The church also sponsors a twice weekly exercise program called Temple Toning. In 1993 the church began holding biennial fund raisers named Talents for the Lord. The activities feature games, crafts, silent auctions, and a barbecue dinner.

Ministers of First Presbyterian have been active in the Morrilton Ministerial Alliance since its inception. Both the ministers and the members have participated in establishing and maintaining the Conway County Care Center and the Conway County Christian Clinic. The chapel at the Christian Clinic was a gift from the church to the community.

In our community the Presbyterian Church has been a leader in placing women in leadership positions. Athalene McConnell was installed as the first female deacon in 1965, and in 1976 Mary Virginia Cheek and Vida Cravens were installed as elders. In 2001 the church called Rev. Kris Crawford to fill the pulpit as pastor. While serving the church as interim pastor in 2005, Rev. Gail Perkins was installed as moderator of the Presbytery of Arkansas.

With the grace of God First Presbyterian Church will strive to continue God's work and worship. Buildings, ministers, members, and programs may change with time, but the work of the Lord is eternal. *Submitted by Mary Clyde Rasmussen.*

Old Manse First Presbyterian Church - 1921 (Courtesy Mickey Poindexter).

Some members of FPC shown at the dedication of the Morrilton Christian Clinic Chapel in 2005 are Anne Johnston, Brink Butler, Rev. Kris Crawford, Judy Calhoun, Anne Neeley, Beverly Parks, Mollie Williams, Rev. Gail Perkins, Edie Harris, Charles Jackson, Gary Harris, Jim Johnston, Baxter Sudduth, Rev. Stan Larson, Valery Jackson, Valerie Peck, Sue Spivey, Charles Spivey, Nikki Sudduth, Rev. Jimmie and Alene Thames. (Courtesy Sue Spivey.)

GRANDVIEW CHURCH OF CHRIST

A two-story building was constructed and finished in 1906. This building was to serve as a school, church, and community building. The Masonic Lodge members, the Odd Fellows and the Eastern Star groups used the upper level. The lower level was used for school and church services of many different denominations.

Among the first preachers to speak in this building were Frank Stobaugh and Joseph T. Paxson. Mr. Paxson was a member of the Church of Christ. He traveled on a mule to speak at Grandview and surrounding churches in the early 1900s. Some of the other preachers to hold services in this building were R.H. Johnson, George Reece, Mr. Hart, Mr. Bradley, Henry Cates, J.L. Gordon and Henry Prather. Mr. Cates lived in Van Buren County. Having no transportation, he walked the 12 miles to teach the people of the community about God. J.L. Gordon not only was a preacher at Grandview, but also along with his wife, taught school on the lower floor of the building. Henry Prather was a schoolteacher at the Middleton School during the time that he preached for the Grandview Community.

Around 1945, two groups shared the building. On Sunday morning Ollie Crawford held services for the undenominational church and in the afternoon, Arnold Polk held services for the Church of Christ with Gutherie Dean preaching part time. One of the first full time preachers was Gerald Weeks, during the early 1950s. Later in the 50s, Richard Hale took the congregation over. In the 1960s Richard Batten worked very hard to keep the church going. Although he had a full time preaching position at the New Liberty Church of Christ, he used his Sundays off to preach for Grandview, along with five young men he was training to speak. They took turns speaking to the congregation. The boys were not old enough to drive, so Clell Stobaugh, from the New Liberty Church of Christ provided their transportation to Grandview each week. The young men were David Stobaugh, Jackie Smart, Billie Moore, Tommy Acton and Steve Crow. Some of these young men continued to help the congregation out for several years. Burlin Gray and his family worked very hard with the church for about one and a half years. In 1970 Burlin preached and his wife, Nelta and their daughters started classes for all the children. Because of responsibility in another congregation, mid-week classes were held on Tuesday night. Around 1971, David Stobaugh came and preached for almost six months. After David left Ray Moore, from Culpepper Mountain, was the preacher until late 1972. Ray's wife, Nadene, and their daughter, Doris Honeycutt, along with Betty Dixon and Donna Hardin kept the children's classes going.

Time finally

Grandview Church of Christ, 2005.

took its toll on the structure, services had to be curtailed in 1972. Thus, the Grandview faithful were forced to attend other congregations in the surrounding communities until funds could be raised to renovate the structure. In February 1975, the community started renovation of its building. Mr. and Mrs. Jack Ethridge of Flint, Michigan provided much needed funding, on an annual basis, until the materials were completely paid for. 1975 saw the downstairs renovated; carpeting was added in 1976. The upstairs was restored, with new classrooms, which were carpeted. The following October, the modern convenience of gas heat was installed. Air conditioning was the next major acquisition in August 1982. A fellowship room was added in the mid-80s. The frame and the large church bell were also repaired and put back into working order during this time. Once again it became time for another renovation. This meant fund raising of a large scale. Many people of the community, as well as those who once lived here but were in other towns and states, gave graciously and from their hearts to help finance the next renovation. The downstairs was in need of an over-haul of a massive scale. Through faith, prayer and an abundance of hard work the renovation took place and was completed in May 1999.

The spirit of the Lord is certainly manifest in the many hours expounded by the many workers who have turned this run-down structure into the Lord's House. During the first renovation period, Brother Rick West led our community spiritually by preaching twice monthly from 1982 to 1984. At that time, he became our full-time preacher. January 1986 saw Brother West move to Wichita, Kansas. Brother Bobby Parks from Harding School of Biblical Studies in Searcy graciously filled our need for a preacher until Brother Bruce Bradford decided to start preaching in July 1986. He diligently worked for God and our community until October 1987. Since then Brother Rocky Fulkerson, Brother Gary James, and Brother Julian Reynolds worked with us for many years helping united to stand in God's Word. Brother Brian Bryant has been with us since September 9, 2004. He is currently continuing the work of the Lord, started so many years previously.

Deep gratitude and debt is owed to many who have formed our community, both spiritually and with physical labor. To the memory of all of these, past and present, this historical summation is dedicated. We also acknowledge that without the presence of God, manifest through His people, none of the foregoing events would have been possible.

JERUSALEM CHURCH OF CHRIST

January 2005

In 1881, Jasper W. Wilson donated land on Cedar Creek to the elders of the Church of Christ. The elders were: J.C. Winn, A.J. Wiley and G.R. Reynolds. This land was to be used for Church of Christ worship and a subscription school. Some of the early preachers were T.P. Saylors and J.C. Winn. Some of the early members of the church were the Staffords, Winns, Saylors, Stobaugh, Nowlins, Griffins, Wilsons, Joneses, Underhills, and possibly others.

In 1913, Lawson Wilson donated the land where the church is now located and a frame building was erected. The congregation then moved from the Cedar Creek site to the present location of the Church of Christ at Jerusalem. In 1917, George Wooldridge held a protracted meeting and baptized about 107 people. A protracted meeting was a gospel meeting held in the summer for a duration of 10-14 days.

A tabernacle was built between 1925 and 1930 on the west side of the church building; also, called an arbor. This was used in the summer months for comfort due to no fans or air conditioning in the building. The tabernacle had wooden shingles with cedar post support. There were no enclosures on the sides or ends and the pews were brought from the church building in the spring and carried back in the fall.

Some of the preachers that held protracted meetings in the 1930-1950s included: W.F. Lemmons, R.H. Johnston, John Reece, Tillman Pope, E.L. Whitaker, George Housley, Bro. Curtis, Barber, Earnest Finley, John Teel, Steve Williams, Charles Stovall and Billy Moore. Beginning in 1960 to present day 3-5 day meetings have been held and some of the preachers were Will Slater, Bro. Evans, Bill Baker, B.G. Hogan, Paul Hanna, Johnny French, Billy Hale, Olen Fullerton, Bro. Connors, Al Jolly, Ronnie Hale, LeRoy Wood, Eddie Clower, Wesley Hylton, Leon Barnes, Jack Smith, Eddie Bowman, Loyd Brents, Jim Love, Ted Knight, Bill Graddy, Carroll Sites, Charles Bane, Jim Woodall, Ben Putterbaugh, Don Adkins, Dan Lightfoot, Bill Roderick, Burt Wilkerson, Bruce Bradford, Mickey Burleson, Carl Clem and David Riley.

In 1964, the tabernacle and the frame building were torn down and a new brick building was erected on the same site. The new building included auditorium, class rooms, bathrooms and foyer. The first sermon was preached in the new building May 10, 1964, by Bro. Carthel Healy. That day, the Jerusalem Church and the Pleasant View (known as Granny Holler Church) were united to form a larger congregation.

In 1981, the first full-time minister was hired and this was 100 years after the church was formed. Wesley Hylton was the first full-time minister, moving here with his wife, Deana. Wesley served as the minister from 1981 to 1986. He was followed by Ray Earnhart 1987-1989, Maurice Crowley 1989-1992, Burt Wilkerson 1993-1997 and Randy Gray 1997-1998. In 1998, the Church of Christ at Appleton approached the members of the Jerusalem Church of Christ about consolidation. On July 5th, the Appleton Church of Christ merged with the Jerusalem Church of Christ. Scott Roderick became the minister in November 1998 and has remained until the present time (1-2005).

The Jerusalem Church of Christ building ca. 1913.

In 1983, a brick house was built west of the church building for the minister's home. In 1992, a multi-purpose building was built and is attached by a breeze way to the church building. This serves as a classroom and a dining room with a complete kitchen. The building is also used for showers, pot-luck meals and other special events.

Many improvements have been made to the church building since it was built. These include: new larger bathrooms, new tile in the foyer and bathrooms, carpet and drapes in the auditorium and classrooms, central heat and air, ceiling fans and new light fixtures, safety lights and paved parking lot. The minister's home and multi-purpose building have central heat and air, also. In 1995, a pre-used 15 passenger van was purchased for church use. It was used to pick up young people for Vacation Bible School, take the young people from here to Vacation Bible Schools at various locations, transport them to and from Camp Caudle for a week's camp, to Youth Devotions held monthly at different locations and any other function that was church related. In 1999, a new 15 passenger van was purchased to replace the old one.

The Jerusalem Church of Christ still meet in this location at 9:30 a.m. Sunday mornings for Bible Study, 10:30 a.m. for worship service, 6:00 p.m. Sunday evening and 7:00 p.m. Wednesday evening.

New Liberty Church of Christ

New Liberty Church of Christ

Churches of Christ were thriving in rural southern Van Buren County immediately after the Civil War, a time when the Restoration Movement, with its plea for a return to simple New Testament Christianity with the Bible as the sole rule of faith and practice, was sweeping the country. In 1870 there were two congregations, one at Liberty and one at Liberty Springs. No records were kept in those early years, but it is known that D.F. Draper, a Texas preacher, held several meetings at Liberty Springs, and that in 1917 he held a two or three weeks meeting in the schoolhouse at Gravel Hill and baptized 75. In a second meeting there in 1918, 50 or 60 more were baptized. It was at this time that Draper suggested a new meeting house, and several sites were considered, Mr. and Mrs. Henry Scroggins and Mr. and Mrs. John Halbrook each donated an acre of ground for a building site at what would later be 4813 Highway 95, the location of the present church building. It was called "New Liberty" to distinguish it from the former location, which naturally became "Old Liberty." Trees around the property served as hitching posts for those who came in wagons and buggies. The building was built in 1919 with private donations and the help of churches at Center Ridge and Liberty Springs. Simon and Charlie Brents built the building, for which each received one dollar per day in wages.

The first meeting in the new building was in late December 1919, a singing held at the conclusion of a singing school that had been taught by Will Slater at Liberty Springs. People came from far and wide, in wagons, hacks and buggies, and on horseback, and the new building was filled. D.F. Draper held several meetings in the '20s. Many other capable preachers have held meetings here, including such giants of the faith as Joe H. Blue and Joe S. Warlick, and other notables such as Henry Cates, a Bee Branch farmer, Jeff Reece, a blacksmith from southwest Arkansas, J. Will Henley, a prosecuting attorney from southwest Arkansas, Lowell Davis, long-time missionary to China, and S.A. Bell, professor of Bible at Harding College. Since there was no baptistery in the old building, all baptizing was done in Point Remove Creek and later in stock ponds.

Some of those attending here at the beginning were the families of Henry Scroggins, John Halbrook, John Koone, Hicks Stroud, Joe Swain, Robert Russell, William Guinn, Owen Lentz, Matt Williams, Wayne Tilley, Jackson Meeler, and others.

More than 60 preachers have preached here on a monthly or weekly appointment basis, but of that number only four: Richard Batten, Charles Pierce, Burlin Gray, and Loyd Brents, have lived here and served as full time preachers. Currently Loyd Brents and Neil Chism, a teacher in South Conway County Schools, share pulpit duties. Others have come from Arkansas Christian College (now

Harding University), Harding College, both students and faculty members, students from Harrison School of Preaching, from surrounding communities. In many instances, "home grown" preachers have done a re-

New Liberty Church of Christ

markably fine job of filling in. Among the latter were Wylie Scroggins, Ray Moore, Joe Scroggins, Carl "Boad" Brents, Joe Reeves, Bobby Smart, Steve and Randall Crow, and David Stobaugh. The church has produced five full time preachers: Tommy Acton, Loyd Brents, Bobby Carey, Billy Moore, and Jacky Smart. Billy Moore is currently serving as a missionary in Mexico City. Numerous others who have supported themselves in secular work have nevertheless given much of their time to preaching the gospel.

The first elders were Green Scroggins, Wylie Scroggins, and Hicks Stroud, and those currently serving in that position are Gerald Freeman, Clell Stobaugh and Ned Smart. The latter is a son-in-law of the late Wylie and Blanche (Stubblefield) Scroggins, and grandson-in-law of the late Henry and Martha Jane (Reid) Scroggins, one of the original land donors. His wife, Janita, is the only direct descendent of any of the original families still in attendance at New Liberty. Others who have served as elders include Oscar Koone, Joe Swain, Orville Stroud, and Dewey Crow.

In 1971 a new brick veneer, centrally heated and air conditioned auditorium, complete with baptistery, nursery, and restrooms was completed as an addition to the 1919 building, and the old building is still in use as classrooms and fellowship hall.

The church is mission minded, and currently contributes to the support of the Southern Christian Home in Morrilton and Children's Homes of Paragould, as well as to the support of the Billy Moore family in Mexico City, the Paul Kee family in Cameroon, Africa, the *"Search for the Lord's Way"* TV program, Truth for Today, and the Eastern European Missions Bibles for Russia program, and has contributed to mission trips for individuals or groups to Alaska, Russia, Romania, Honduras, Guyana, Haiti, and other places.

The above was compiled by Alma (Scroggins) Reeves, a daughter of the late Henry and Martha Jane (Reid) Scroggins, with additions by Nellie (Mrs. Clell) Stobaugh and Jean (Mrs. Dewey) Crow.

SAINT ELIZABETH CATHOLIC CHURCH

St. Elizabeth Catholic Church is located at Oppelo, 12 miles southwest of Morrilton in the foothills of Petit Jean Mountain. A settlement of German families settled in the area on land purchased from the Iron Mountain Railroad Company. The head of these families were Valentine Bahr, Englebert Dold, Gebhard Hock, Bernard Drilling, Joseph Hoyt, Clem Fisher and Henry Rehm. In 1882 Mass was held in the homes of these settlers and presided over by their first pastor Reverend Felix Rumph O.S.B. who came from his home in Dixie by horse and buggy. The first small church was built in 1885 on five acres of land given to the community by the Iron Mountain Railroad. St. Elizabeth Church was named after the 13th patron saint of Hungary who though she was of royal birth, was noted for her dedication of helping the sick and the poor. The pastor of the church at this time was Rev. Matthew Saettele O.S.B. Soon after the church was built an additional 35 acres of land was purchased from the railroad. During this period other early settlers joined the community: Bruck, Flucks, Grabherr, Isenman, Nagel, Nord, Thien and Welter. This original church served the Parish for 32 years.

In 1917 a second, larger church was built. Rev. Othmar Wehrl O.S.B. was pastor. In 1923 the original church was transformed into a school and a seven room home was built for the Sisters of Mercy from Mount St. Mary's Academy in Little Rock. Sister Mary Augustine Fargo and Sister Mary Dalorosa Madden were the first teachers at the new school. Frank Miller, S.W. Rehm and Nick Nagel were directors of the school which had an enrollment of 40 students. The school grew so rapidly that a lay teacher Elizabeth Drilling of Morrilton was hired. The school soon became part of the Perry County school district in order to survive financially. In the summer of 1929 a two room school building was constructed on the site of the first church. A.O. Hoyt was the principal carpenter. Wardens of the Parish were John Grabher and Emil Rehm. School Directors were Nicholas Nagel, Albert Hoyt and Emil Rehm. Sisters M. DeChantal Devine, Angela Corcoran, Jerome Nash and Angela Janesko each spent several years teaching in the 1930s and 1940s . During and after WWII such a few young people remained in the area that the Sisters of Mercy withdrew from the school in 1948. Lay teachers kept the school open two more years. This school served the families of the area for 27 years, closing in 1950. The two room school building built in 1929 is a now a Knife Museum in Ada Valley.

The third and present church was built in 1964 during the Pastorate of Rev. Lawrence Maus. A

The third and present church, built in 1964.

Parish Hall was built 10 years later. St. Elizabeth is presently a mission church with about 100 families. Our founders are gone, but descendants of these early settlers still attend church at St. Elizabeth - the Dolds, Grabhers, Hoyts, Rehms and Zimmermans. The current pastor is Rev. Richard P. Davis, who resides at Saint Boniface Parish in New Dixie. *(Above information is from the archives of the Catholic Diocese of Little Rock and April 25, 1930 Morrilton Democrat.)*

Pastors of Saint Elizabeth Church
1883-2005

Rev. Felix Rumpf, O.S.B	1883-1885
Rev. Matthew Saettele, O.S.B.	1885-1888
Rev. Charles Zang	1888-1889
Rev. Udalricus, O.S.B.	1889-1890
Rev. Matthew Saettele, O.S.B.	1890-1893
Rev. Benedict, O.S.B.	1893-1894
Rev. Matthew Saettele, O.S.B.	1894-1898
Rev. Aloysius Baumgaertner, O.S.B	1898-1900
Rev. Boniface Spanke, O.S.B.	1900
Rev. Othmar Wehrl, O.S.B.	1900-1919
Rev. Francis, O.S.B.	1919
Rev. William Kordsmeier	1919-1925
Rev. A.H. Metz	1925
Rev Joseph Feldkamp	1925-1926
Rev. John Duffy	1926-1927
Rev. Henry W. Nix	1927-1931
Rev. Joseph Burns	1931-1932
Rev. Francis X. Dollarton	1932-1935
Rev. Charles F. Stanowski	1935-1936
Rev. John Flaherty	1936-1938
Rev. George Carns	1938-1939
Rev. Lawrence P. Maus	1939-1942
Rev. John Mulligan	1942-1945
Rev. Paul McLaughlin	1945-1947
Rev. Francis X. Prendergest	1947-1951
Rev. Joseph J. Enderlin	1951-1956
Rev. Lawrence P. Maus	1956-1972
Rev. John Hlavacek	1972-1974
Rev. H. Paul Strassle	1974-1976
Rev. Al Baltz	Feb 1976-Aug 1976
Rev. James Savery	Aug. 1976-1982
Rev. Joseph Correnti	1982-1983
Rev. Amos Enderlin	1983-1996
Rev. Edward G. Marley, C.S. Sp.	1986-1990
Rev. James P. West	1990-1996
Rev. Richard P. Davis	1996- present pastor

Approximate dates: Copied from Church records and archives diocese of Little Rock, Arkansas. *Submitted by Frances Grabher Donaldson.*

The original church built in 1883.

The second building, built in 1917.

Petit Jean Vo-Tech, 1963. This building served as both the Administration Building and the classroom and lab areas for vocational and training areas.

In 1959, Arkansas' first post-secondary vocational-technical school had opened in Pine Bluff, Arkansas, and it was originally intended to serve the needs of the entire state. However, the Arkansas General Assembly, recognizing the need for expanded vocational education opportunities, provided state funds for the construction and operation of a second post-secondary vocational-technical school in 1961.

Cities throughout the state competed strongly for consideration as the location for the new school. While the decision was up to the State Board of Education, Governor Orval Faubus encouraged the board to select a site north and west of Little Rock, since the first school was established south and east of Little Rock.

In 1962 the State Board of Education voted unanimously to consider sites at Morrilton and Fort Smith, and after the two sites were visited, the board voted for locating the new school in Morrilton. On June 10, 1962, the board officially named the school Petit Jean Vocational-Technical School, after a local landmark—Petit Jean Mountain. The first classes began in September 1963.

Petit Jean VoTech served Arkansas well for 30 years as an adult vocational school. In 1991, the "Two-Year Post-secondary Education Reorganization Act of 1991" (Act 1244) became law, converting 14 of the state's post-secondary vo-tech schools to two-year colleges. As a result of this legislation, Petit Jean Vo-Tech became Petit Jean Technical College (PJTC), and the college expanded its curriculum to include general education courses that were transferable to other state colleges and universities. In 1997, Petit Jean Technical College changed its name to Petit Jean College in order to better reflect its more comprehensive mission.

During its first nine years of operation as a college, Petit Jean College's enrollment increased 289 percent from 318 students in fall 1990 to 1,238 students in fall 1999. During that same period, the college achieved accreditation with the North Central Association, Higher Learning Commission (1996); gained approval to award the associate of applied science degree, the associate of general studies degree, the associate of arts degree, and a variety of technical certificates; completed several renovation projects and two additions to existing buildings; and constructed a dining hall and Phase I of a Fine Arts Complex.

On August 22, 2000, the citizens of Conway County approved a permanent 1/4 cent sales and use tax in support of the college. By means of a bond issue, Phase II of the Fine Arts Complex and a new Business Technology Center were constructed in 2001.

In 2001, the Petit Jean College Board of Trustees voted unanimously to affiliate with the University of Arkansas System and be known as the University of Arkansas Community College at Morrilton. Record enrollments continued, increasing from 1,290 students in 2001 to 1,511 students in fall 2004.

The college's growth created a need for more classroom space, as well as expanded student service facilities. In May 2004, construction was completed on the University Center a two-story building approximately 33,000 square feet in size. This building was funded through a $3,000,000 bond issue.

Today, the University of Arkansas Community College at Morrilton is a dynamic two-year, public college that is dedicated to meeting the multi-dimensional needs of the communities it serves

through open access and affordability. UACCM offers a comprehensive curriculum of university-transfer and career-specific technical programs, as well as adult education, community education, and workforce training.

University Center, 2004. This building, officially opened in May 2004, houses the administrative offices of UACCM as well as 10 classrooms, a math tutoring lab and student study lounge.

Technology has changed the world of work as well as how students are trained. Here, a surveying student uses computer-aided software to map a location.

Students in UACCM's business program receive in-depth training in a number of computer software programs.

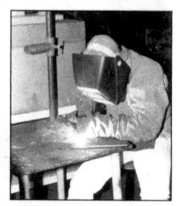

Welding is one of the applied technology programs offered by the college for the past four decades.

MORRILTON SECURITY BANK

M orrilton Security Bank was founded in 1955 by Mr. Claude M. Farish. He opened the bank at 201 North Moose Street on March 11, 1955.

In 1962 the bank opened the very first drive-up window in the Morrilton area. The bank changed locations on April 9, 1965, to its present location on the corner of Moose and Elm Street. A branch was opened in Plumerville in 1974, followed by another branch office in 1975 at Highway 9 Business North. It is still currently running and a remodel of the current building is scheduled for early 2005.

The second president of Morrilton Security Bank was Howard E. Jones, husband of Claude Farish's daughter, Marilyn. During his tenure in May 1984 Morrilton Security Bank merged with First Commercial Corporation. Mr. Jones retired from banking in 1986. Mr. Sam W. Callihan became the new president until his retirement in 1987.

Mr. Callihan was succeeded by Mr. Billy Gene Staton in 1987. In 1998 Morrilton Security Bank (owned by First Commercial Corporation) merged with Regions Bank. Mr. Staton retired in 1999. Succeeding Mr. Staton as president was Mr. Fred C. Tanner. He served as president until April 2004.

In June 2004, Michael L. Dunaway became president. Currently Regions Bank of Morrilton has 21 employees and operates as a community focused bank with local leadership. The board of directors are Mr. Edward Lee Eddy (Chairman), Mr. Allen Gordon, Mr. Ronald Mobley, Mr. Kenny Shipp, Mrs. Alice Fleeman, Mr. David Ruff and Mr. Benny Koontz.

ROBERSON TIRE SERVICE

The newest Roberson Tire facility in 2005.

J.T. and Faye Roberson with their two children, Virginia and Jim, began selling Kelly – Springfield tires when they purchased the Lion Oil bulk plant in 1951 in Morrilton. These tires were sold on a carry – out basis.

Later, they added Goodyear, Mohawk, Bridgestone, Firestone and farm implement tires when they purchased a building at 204 East Railroad in 1970; with the added space they began mounting and balancing tires, fixing flats and were able to do front-end alignments.

When they retired in 1973 they sold the business to their son Jim and his wife Judy Roberson. They began teaching their sons: Ted, Landy and Mark, the business from the bottom up, fixing flats. Ted and Mark stayed with the tire business, while Landy chose a profession in petroleum engineering.

In 1978, the Roberson's bought the City Garage, which was located across the alley from the store. Again, they were able to offer new services that included oil changes, brake work, shocks, struts and other minor car repairs.

In 1990 they opened a store at 1330 East Oak Street in Conway with Ted as manager. Mark stayed with the Morrilton store. Mark and Ted bought the two stores in 1994 when Jim and Judy retired.

A new building was constructed in 1998 at #4 Bruce Street in Morrilton with the old location being sold to Conway County. At this new location they are able to provide even better service to their customers and better working conditions for their employees.

Customers can enjoy television while waiting for their vehicles or admire the mounts of deer, bobcat, ducks or marlin. There is also a snack room for coffee and refreshments. Also a line of Mossy Oak apparel and accessories has been added with deer stands and feeders.

In 2005 another change has been made with the sale of the Conway store bringing Ted back to Morrilton to help Mark with the everyday operations.

Other employees are Larry McCoy at the front desk, and

Jim, Virginia & Mark assisting customers, 1994.

Roberson Tire Service in 1989.

Virginia Roberson Wright and Melissa Payne in the office. Mechanics and tire techs include: Freedie Guinn, Royce Parker, Carl Shipp, Leslie McCoy, Travis Russell, William Turner, David Nellis, Jerry McCoy.

STROUD'S HOME FURNISHINGS

Stroud's has been in business on Moose Street in Morrilton for well over 55 years. It began as Stroud's Grocery and Feed around 1945. Over the years, the name has changed along with the products sold to the current name of Stroud's Home Furnishings.

Stroud's Home Furnishings' original owner, Amos Price Stroud, was born on January 11, 1928, in Cleveland, Arkansas. His parents were Roy Louis Stroud and Sally Halbrook Stroud. He had an older brother, Lee Stroud, and an older sister, Vernona Stroud. His father owned a sawmill and grocery store in the Gravel Hill area. During his elementary and junior high school years, Price attended school at Cleveland, Scotland, then Wonderview. He was remembered during this time often riding his little spotted pony. Sadly, his mother fell sick with cancer when he was only 10, and passed away. He spent a lot of time at his father's grocery store in Cleveland and often told how he could add up the groceries in his head as he bagged them. He also did the ordering for his father at a very young age and basically ran the family store. Sometimes, a salesman would stop and tell his father that Price gave him an order, figuring it definitely needed to be approved by Roy Louis Stroud himself. Price's daddy told the salesman to order whatever Price told him to and there was no need to check with him again. Also, customers sometimes would say that Price did not charge them enough, thinking he surely could not add the groceries in his head. Price's father would only say, "You just keep it and don't worry about it."

Price and his father moved to Morrilton around 1943. Price did not think there was any need to go out for the basketball team in such a bigger school. However, a friend told him he was sure that they could make the team and they did. His fondest memories were of playing basketball at Morrilton. He practiced all the time. He loved the story of how the white boys would practice, then they turned the gym over to the black team. He took great pride in the fact that the black boys would invite him to stay around and practice with them also. Those were some of his most enjoyable times and he loved to sit and reminisce about them. He never cared much for bookwork, but continued to enjoy playing ball.

He graduated from Morrilton around 1946. His father, Roy Louis, had a grocery & feed store on Moose street, with Rupert Lynch, at that time. He asked Price if he wanted to go to college or into business. Price didn't really have to think about this choice. He often told that his dad made a merchant out of him the last year he raised a crop, when he was 13. He said he knew then that he never wanted to do any agriculture work again. So, Price told his father he didn't think there was a chance he could make the basketball team in college, and he believed he would just go into business. Price's father helped put him into business with Rupert Lynch, and he moved off to California. Price bought out his father's half of the business. Not long after this, he went into the United States Air Force, during the Korean conflict. He sold his half out to Rupert Lynch, and reported for duty at Kelly Air Force Base in September of 1950. He spent three years in the Air Force, stationed at Edwards Air Force Base during the time that Chuck Yeager broke the sound barrier. While in the Air Force, he saved as much as he could out of his pay, and spent most of his free time trying to win at poker. He saved quite a sum of money while in the service.

He was discharged from the Air Force on September 10, 1953 and returned to Morrilton, where he promptly bought his half of the grocery store back from Rupert Lynch. After a short time, he bought out Rupert's part of the store and began to run the business by himself. At this time, he was living over the former Wood's Variety Store, on Moose Street. (This is where a pawn shop is now located, across from the city police station.) His business was located at 215 Moose Street. He dated June Boyle some during this time. However, she moved to Washington D.C. and then to California to work for the FBI. Around 1957, he decided he wanted to marry June, and he and a friend drove out to California and brought her back to Morrilton. They married on June 20, 1957. They had a son on April 12, 1958 named Roy Lewis Stroud. Then, they had two daughters, Cynthia Renee Stroud, on June 20, 1959, and Cheri Lynn Stroud on October 29, 1961. He often talked about having three babies at one time. He loved to tell of paying Dr. Thomas Hickey for the delivery of his youngest daughter, with a portable black and white television.

Stroud's Home Furnishings, east side of Moose Street, in Morrilton - 2005.

During the time around 1957, black and white televisions sets were just becoming popular. He decided he would try to sell them. On Saturdays, or in the evenings, he and an employee would load two or three TVs in the truck and drive until they could find homes where the people would let them set the TVs up for a trial. They asked the people if they could just leave it in

Price Stroud and wife June Boyle Stroud at the store in 1990.

their home for about a week and come back and see what they thought of it. Some people did not like them, but some were taken by the new invention and decided to buy them. He continued to sell televisions, and kept the TVs up in his apartment above Wood's Variety Store. He took people up there to see them when they were interested.

Gradually, he started keeping TVs and other household items in his grocery store. Over time, he went from groceries to home furnishings. He stayed in business at 215 N. Moose for several years. Then, in 1964, he moved from there down the street to the present location at 308 N. Moose. They moved the store safe, which had originally been used in the Bank of Scotland, to the new location by rolling it down the street. The safe is still used in the store today. Around 1993, he bought the buildings directly across from 308 N. Moose. These buildings now house a Living Room Showroom, metal beds, sleepers, and some used furniture. Stroud's Home Furnishings is also about to expand to a 2nd location, selling flooring once again, at 16 10 Hwy 9B N., soon.

For many years, Stroud's has had in-store financing. In the last few years, Price Stroud has begun trading with the children and grandchildren of his customers he originally started trading with in the 1950s and 1960s. They have many customers that are loyal to Stroud's and tell of the fact that their parents or grandparents said Price Stroud gave them credit when no one else would. He has always valued the loyalty of his customers. He gave them credit and service when he traded with them. He would often tell customers not to worry about the brand name of a product, just be sure they get it at Stroud's. He would then say, "If you have a problem, I will make you proud you traded at Stroud's."

Price Stroud is definitely one of a kind. There's no doubt, as many people will tell, that he has always been outspoken. He has often been heard to say, "I'm just as sure when I am wrong as I am when I'm right." One thing you never had to worry about with Price Stroud, he was never undecided. He now lives on Hwy 95, with his 2nd wife, Louise. His daughter, Cheri Pruitt, recently bought Stroud's Home Furnishings from her father. She and her son, Kyle Pruitt, now run the business. Kyle began working for his grandfather at Stroud's at the age of 13. They are now in the process of opening a 2nd location soon, at 1610 Hwy 9B North, where they will offer many types of floor covering as well as other home furnishing items. They hope to continue the same family traditions of dealing honestly with their customers and providing good service for whatever they may sell.

HAWKINS INSURANCE AGENCY

Bruce and Phyllis Hawkins

Ask Bruce Hawkins for the secret to success in the insurance business, and he'll give you an answer as basic and steadfast as the man himself. "Pay attention to the customer, not just the employer in a group case, but their employees as well. Drop by, go through the business and shake hands. People like to put a name with a face. Don't just go by at renewal time."

Hawkins and his wife, Phyllis, began their Morrilton life and health agency in August 1979 and their property and casualty agency in March 1985. He decided to enter the insurance field after purchasing a life insurance policy before getting married. "I liked the agent's lifestyle," said Hawkins. "The freedom to choose whom you work with, when you work, and play golf when you want, was very appealing to a 22-year-old about to get married. But the people contact was the main focus."

With a background in banking, marketing, and education, Phyllis didn't so much choose to join the family business as much as it chose her. "I had no plans to be an insurance agent," she said. "It sort of happened by default. We had lost a secretary, who was our only employee at that time. I came in after my school job and worked during the summer. Once I was here, I never left!" Today, she oversees the property and casualty side of the agency.

In 1984, the Hawkins Insurance Agency was one of the first independent agencies appointed by Arkansas Blue Cross and Blue Shield. Affiliation with a nationally respected company opened a broader market for the local agency. "Arkansas Blue Cross has always been the Rock of Gibraltar for our business," said Hawkins.

"We sometimes say our blood is almost blue," he joked. "We have a tremendous amount of respect for Arkansas Blue Cross," he added. "It is a company that makes us feel comfortable, whether we're visiting with those in customer service or with Ms. Sharon Allen. We know [Sharon] will listen because she cares."

Now in his 25th year of business, Hawkins said their staff has been the true key to their success. "Each employee has customer service as their highest priority. Not one of our employees will back up from a challenge." Their team includes Cindy Sutton, Lorie Clary, Shirley Koontz, Donna Zimmerman, Paula Hearne, Tom Hale and Jim Sutton.

Bruce and Phyllis see their biggest business challenge as expanding beyond their demographic borders. "To grow in a small town is difficult due to limited businesses and resources," said Hawkins. To meet that challenge, they associated their business with another insurance agent, Ross Honea, who was in life insurance estate planning and worksite marketing, and established H & H Employee Benefits Specialists. "This gave us added expertise to offer our clients," explained Phyllis, "and a Little Rock metropolitan identity for our hometown agency."

Hawkins cited rising costs of health care as one of the greatest changes in the industry during the last decade. "As all of us are aware, the cost of health care is a tremendous burden on employers, employees and individuals. The challenge we face is to make sure that we, as agents, give our clients every possible service, every option available, with every quality company doing business in Arkansas."

He said that, along with cost considerations, keeping up with rules, regulations and law changes also is a tremendous challenge to doing business. A former state representative, Hawkins has been a lobbyist since 1995. You may contact Hawkins regarding lobbyist matters at *dbhawkins@cox-internet.com*.

They said they enjoy working side by side. "It's funny sometimes, because we are a true 'mom and pop' organization. We have been fortunate to have a business that we love where we can truly help others," said Phyllis. "It's what insurance is all about."

Lifelong residents of Morrilton, they have one son, Clayton, 18, who Phyllis calls "the joy of our lives."

WINROCK INTERNATIONAL

Making a Difference for People in Arkansas And Around the World

In 1953, Winthrop Rockefeller came to Arkansas to visit an Army buddy and decided to make it his home. He purchased nearly 1,000 acres on the top of Petit Jean Mountain about 70 miles northwest of Little Rock in central Arkansas, and began Winrock Farms. Winthrop Rockefeller wanted to create a model farm to test ideas and showcase practical farming systems, but farming that could benefit any farmer. Farming was just one of Rockefeller's interests.

In 1955, he became the first chairman of the Arkansas Department of Economic Development, an organization he helped establish to attract industry to the state. In its first year, the ADEC created 10,000 new jobs. Under his leadership, Arkansas led all states in attracting new industry and the jobs they created.

Rockefeller died of cancer in 1973, but the commitment he made to Arkansas and the world continues through trusts, organizations, and the peoples' lives he touched.

Winrock International Institute for Agricultural Development was created in 1985 with the merger of three organizations: the Winrock International Livestock Research & Training Center founded by Winthrop Rockefeller and located at Winrock Farms; the Agricultural Development Council founded by John D. Rockefeller III; and the International Agricultural Development Service inspired by John D. Rockefeller III and funded by Rockefeller Foundation. Barns and other buildings at Winrock Farms were converted into office space for Winrock International.

Once called Winrock International Institute for Agricultural Development, the name has been shortened to Winrock International to better reflect the broad nature of its programs. During its

early years, Winrock International continued to build on the agricultural work of its predecessor organizations - helping people help themselves by producing more food. Winrock's focus has expanded since then, addressing to address the interrelated problems of food production, economic and social development, equity, and natural resource management. Its mission is to work with people in the United States and around the world to increase economic opportunities, sustain natural resources and protect the environment.

Currently Winrock International works in some 65 countries around the world. Its work is funded through grants and contracts from national and international agencies, foundations and corporations, and contributions from public and private sources.

For 20 years Winrock International called Petit Jean Mountain and Conway County home. In mid-December 2004, Winrock International completed a new headquarters facility in Little Rock and relocated there. The new 'green' building illustrates Winrock's commitment to its mission - it is good for people and the environment.

KIWANIS CLUB OF MORRILTON
Compliments of Cat Claws

The Kiwanis Club was organized on February 12, 1925, and was sponsored by the Kiwanis Clubs of Conway and Little Rock. This was some 10 years after the very first Kiwanis Club began, which was in January 1915. Our charter was presented on April 9, 1925. The first president was Edward Gordon and the first secretary was Joe Nemec. There were a total of 34 charter members, including J.N. Armstrong, Ben Kordsmeier, S.J. Laux and Billie Earl. C.A. Imboden, Mayo Gordon, J.M. Matthews, Bryce Mobley, H.E. Mobley and J.B. Pinkham were other charter members. Herbert Fiser, James L. Lucas, J.W. Johnston, J.L. Williams and Carroll W. Johnston were among the first few presidents.

Other early leaders were Cleo Cheek, S.E. McReynolds, George Kordsmeier, Earl Haynes, Claude Matthews and William Gibson. During the 40s the presidents were J.E. Brazil, Horace Crofoot, Jack Jumper, Olen Fullerton, Dr. Hugh M. Biggs, A.A. Hudspeth, Victor Kordsmeier, Ernest Coleman, Charles V. Webb, O.G. Abanathy, Royce Loveless and Theo. Roberts. Other presidents included Arthur Ormond, Lyndon Jackson, S.E. Sewell, Charles Bettis, Robert Mitchell, Raymond Evans, Dr. Virgil Engelhoven, Robert Mobley and Grady Hayes.

Through the years the club has been known for their annual pancake day. During the 90s, the club also sold hamburgers at the Great Arkansas Pigout, as well as sponsor a coed softball tournament. Little League baseball tournaments, peanut sales, Arkansas Traveler tickets and other projects have helped fund scholarships for many area seniors. We currently fund five $500 scholarships for seniors and one for a single parent. Other projects include giving pumpkins to needy children, annual prayer breakfast, books to area day care centers, sponsoring a Morrilton Youth Association team and the annual angel tree project. We also sponsor sacred Heart High School's Key Club.

In 1989, the formerly all-male club became coed. Shawn

Kiwanis club members - ca. 1950

Mittledorf was the first female member. Now the club is about 50/50 male and female. Delores Hartman was the first female president.

Each year since 1965 the club honors a member as Kiwanian of the Year for their dedicated service. Previous winners of the Kiwanian of the Year are O.O. Smith, Bud Lienhart, Joe Gunderman, Joe Massey, and Garland Eddy during the 60s. The winners in the 70s were S.E. McReynolds, Leland Brents, Jewell McKinney, Herman Kordsmeier, A.V. Ormond, Vesper Akin, John Webb, Bud Lienhart, Billy Roper and Carroll Trent. The recipients during the 80s were Charles Hamling, Cleon Lyles, S.E. McReynolds, Horace Crofoot, Ray Hall, Ted Gipson, Lefty McReynolds, Tim Hill, Max Sellers and Malcom McLain. The winners during the 90s were Carroll Trent, Charles Lovelace, John Winningham, Bill Wofford, Greg Flowers, Delores Hartman, Ray Konklin, Laverne Massingill, Becki Griffey, and Carroll Trent. Since 2000, Charles Lovelace, Karen Hofford, Laverne Massingill and Delores Hartman have won the award.

Tablets of Honor (the highest in Kiwanis) have been given to Carroll Trent, Delores Hartman, Larry Williams, Ray King, Bill Deaton, Lefty McReynolds and Joe Gunderman.

Compliments of Cat Claws

CONWAY COUNTY EXTENSION HOMEMAKERS

The first Home Demonstration Clubs were organized in 1917 by Mrs. Byrd Tatum, Home Agent. Mrs. L.E. McClaren and Mrs. Alma Chism were charter members of the first organized Home Demonstration Club at Lanty. In the early days, women met in each other's homes and were taught to preserve food.

The clubs in Conway County have quite a history which was shown in 2002 when the Petit Jean Extension Homemakers Club celebrated its Diamond Jubilee with friends from the county and the mountain.

Since 1926, the needs and interests of the club have changed.

Educational classes were based on immediate family needs such as canning kitchens in the 1930s and making mattresses in the 1940s. Also in the 1940s some clubs raised money to obtain war bonds.

Over the years the programs changed with the times, focusing on their mission statement: The mission of this organization shall be to empower individual families to improve their quality of living through continuing educational, leadership development, and community service.

Today, the clubs educational programs teach and inform members about the concerns of modern life, nutrition, health and safety, family resources, and relationships.

Community service has always been an important part of Extension Homemaker Club programs with each club being involved in many worthwhile projects. Some of these include youth projects such as 4-H programs, Body Walk, choir robes for the high school, scholarships, angel tree, Kids First, and the Child Development Center. Other projects include: cemeteries, fire departments, Care Center, Safe Place, Petit Jean State Park, Relay for Life, Senior Adult Center, Christian Clinic, county fair and many more.

Currently, the six clubs in Conway County are Birdtown, Hilltoppers, Lewisberg, New Horizons, Oppelo Twilight, and Petit Jean. The EHC County Extension Council is made up of all club members and is guided by the EHC Board. These officers are: Linda Chapman-President, Bea Thompson-Vice President, Christine Williams-Secretary, Gaynelle McNew-Treasurer, and Emma Carothers-Reporter.

The Arkansas Extension Homemakers Council is a partner with the Cooperative Extension Service, University of Arkansas' adult education program in agriculture and family and consumer sciences. Adult education is made available under the leadership of County Extension Agents - Family and Consumer Sciences. These agents have previously been known as Home Demonstration Agents and Extension Home Economists.

PETIT JEAN GARDEN CLUB HISTORY

1933-2005

The Petit Jean Garden Club was organized September 3, 1933 and became a Federated Club in October 1934. The first president was Elizabeth McLean. As part of the National Council of State Garden Clubs, Inc., it is also part of the South Central Region of the National Council of Arkansas Federation of Garden Clubs, Inc.

Monthly meetings are held the second Friday of each month, September through May at 1:00 p.m. at member's homes unless otherwise noted. At meetings club members recite the Gardener's Prayer and the Gardener's Creed. Hostesses provide refreshments and a speaker related to a gardening topic. Reports are given from committee chairpersons on civic, environment/conservation, horticulture, ways and means, and the annual garden show.

Past and present club projects include; The Nature Trail gardens, flowerbeds at the Morrilton Museum, Arbor Day plantings, Conway County Library flower arrangements, Morrilton City Park landscaping and planting of bushes, flowers and trees, Adopt a Highway #113 (two miles), Main Street Morrilton plantings, Reynolds and Northside Elementary School gardens, Greater Arkansas Clean-Up, T.C. Vaughn Senior Center plantings, Annual Rialto Garden Show, Garden tours, Highway beautification (wild flowers), judges at Perryville County Fair, clerks at Conway County Fairs, attendance at Arkansas State Flower and Garden Show.

The club's flower is the Crape Myrtle with the club colors of pink and green. The club motto is "To make the beautiful more beautiful." The object of the club is "to stimulate a knowledge of

and interest in gardening and flower arranging; to aid in the preservation of native trees, plants, birds and animals; and to encourage cooperation with officials and groups for civic improvements."

Petit Jean Garden Club. Front row: Emily Bost, Anita Walker, Dee Curry, Bev Hutchcroft, Gladys Mock. 2nd row: Mollie Williams, Ann Franklin, Mary Hope Moose, Pearl Jones. 3rd row: Mary Dale Laux, Annie Rae Gray, Mary Lore, Cetherine Pinter, Charolette Goins. 4th row: Vicki Ennis, Merlene Tucker, Ella Mae Willis. Absent: Liz Goats, Johnna Howell, Jane Virden, Margarette Oliver, Mary Ellen Gray and Fannie Linn.

38

ADELAIDE CLUB OF MORRILTON

The Adelaide Club of Morrilton became an organized club on December 2, 1948 as a branch of the Pathfinder Club and named for Mrs. Adelaide Witt, a leading citizen of Morrilton at that time. Mrs. W.A. Riddick was the sponsor. The new club received a certificate for membership in the General Federation of Women's Clubs on March 14, 1949 and so became a part of the Little Rock District of the General Federation of Women's Clubs of Arkansas.

The first officers of the Adelaide Club were president, Mrs. Herbert Laux; vice president, Mrs. Jess Scroggins Jr.; recording secretary, Mrs. John A. Sadler; treasurer, Mrs. S.C. Mitchell; historian, Mrs. Frank France and parliamentarian, Mrs. Joe B. Montgomery. Other charter members were Mrs. V.H. Merrick, Mrs. Bonor Moore, Mrs. Allen Stallings, Mrs. William Hobert Jones Jr., Mrs. Gerald Laux, Mrs. Rudolph Montgomery, Mrs. Edward Gordon, Mrs. Charles Owens, Mrs. D.T. Black and Mrs. Guy Thompson.

In early 1958 club members campaigned house-to-house, gathering funds, clothing, and supplies to help the underprivileged families, especially children, of Conway County, becoming known as the Adelaide Club's Children Fund. This endeavor enabled Judge Aubrey Strait to continue in efforts to establish a community help system which was the beginning of the Conway County Community Service, whose purpose is the coordinating of all services offered by the state, civic and county agencies for the benefit of the people of Conway County. Other counties have adopted the service and it is now one of the strongest agencies in Arkansas.

In 1960 fluoridation of the Morrilton Water System was installed due to a movement started by the Adelaide Club.

Over the years the, club has donated TV sets and pianos to public and private schools; provided air conditioning for the high school; furnished wall clocks for each hospital room; donated the first Isolette for the old hospital nursery in 1960 and a bilirubin lamp in 1961 for newborns with RH negative blood; sponsored Boy and Girl State Delegates; parties for special education classes; supplied the Morrilton Fire Department with street markers that point out hydrants at night; participated in Project Smile; helped with the Community Service Cajun Night fundraisers and Meals on Wheels for the elderly.

In 1979 the Adelaide Club initiated the first test for Scoliosis disease working with the Public Health Services.

In 1983 the Adelaide Club sponsored a young women's club, the Century League, into the General Federated Women's Clubs.

In March 1989, the Conway County Care Center opened its doors through the club's efforts in organizing and volunteer work. The center's purpose is to provide food, clothing and emergency care for families or individuals in a crisis situation. Members still volunteer to work in the thrift store and pantry.

The club met with county officials in March 1991, to initiate the 911 emergency system for Conway County. In October of that year Adelaide members manned the polls for a special election and in the spring of 1996 the 911 system went into effect.

Each year the club sponsors on-going projects such as presenting two scholarships to deserving graduates - one for Morrilton High School and one to Sacred Heart High School; work with the City Beautiful program; volunteer in the art department (almost 2000 pieces of children's art were hung) and horticultural department of the county fair; works at the Great Arkansas Pig Out festival sponsored by the Chamber of Commerce; donates to Safe Place, a shelter for battered women; donates to the Conway

County Community Center; volunteers for Monsters on Main Street (an afternoon of Halloween treats for children) and furnish two Thanksgiving baskets each year.

Since 1986 one of the Adelaide Club's largest programs has been the Angel Tree working through the Department of Human Services. 300 to 500 children are provided a Christmas each year. Those whose names are not "adopted," the club donates $500 for Christmas gifts.

Club members participate in the Walk-A-Thon and Walk America for the March of Dimes, Relay For Life for the cancer drive and the Conway County Road Show For Life. Members also participated in the Body Walk, a health program for young children.

An Adelaide member has served as president of the library board of directors; several members serve on the board of Friends of the Library and a member is chairman of the library's Poetry Night. Members also help with the library's book sales.

A successful fundraiser the last 10 years has been the winter dances held on the eve of the Super Bowl and a Trinkets & Treats rummage sale held every other year with proceeds going to the Conway County Library, Conway County Care Center, Safe Place, Conway County Christian Clinic, Angel Tree, Conway County Single Parent Scholarship Fund, and other programs.

In 1996 the club decorated and partly furnished a children's holding room in the new Department of Human Services building.

Members worked on committees for Fire Safety House which is sponsored by the Arkansas Children's Hospital as a special project for children.

In 2004, Adelaide members participated in the 50 year celebration of the late Governor Winthrop Rockefeller that was held on Petit Jean Mountain.

Members served refreshments at the ribbon cutting for the beginning of the Downtown Morrilton Renovation Project.

Morrilton celebrated their 125th year birthday with Adelaide members helping with the food table.

One of the Adelaide members has served as president for the state General Federation of Women's Clubs of Arkansas after serving in state and district offices. Several members have served as chairmen for the state and district GFWCA.

A special year for the club was 1999, celebrating their 50th anniversary with an afternoon tea.

The club's current civic program is the Conway County Christian Clinic that provides health care free to those who are in need. Doctors, dentists, pharmacists and health personnel donate their time to this program.

Current officers and members are president, Leah Dell Ward; vice president, Marie Kordsmeier; second vice president, Sue Noble; recording secretary, Elinor Rohlman; corresponding secretary, Bonnie Coffman; treasurer, Katherine Foust; historian, Darlene Cree; parliamentarian, Martha Bostic, and Jeannie Andrews, Vickie Buchanan, Vickie Ennis, Wanda Delacerda, Ene Guinn, Beebe Huett, Pearl Jones, Barbara Loh, Martha Nelson, Jeannie Price, Barbara Wade, Sharon Knighten, Leona Koch, Jean Owens and Jan Ruff.

There are very few community projects or programs in which a member of the Adelaide Club does not have an active part. These are on a part of the club's volunteer activities.

The Adelaide Club's theme is "To Thine Own Self Be True." The club flower is the red rose and the colors are green and white.

1st row: Billie Jeanne Scroggin, Jean Stallings, Marie Mitchell, Ruth Laux. 2nd row: Juanita Semmes, Farris Mitchell, Margaret Montgomery, Jean Owens, Catherine Black. 3rd row: Kitty Sadler, Nell Thompson, Laurie VanMeter, Dorothy Butler, Margery Moore, Marvelle Jones, _ Newkirk.

lst row: Marie Kordsmeier, Bonnie Coffman, Leah Dell Ward, Elinor Rohlman, Katherine Foust, Jean Owens. 2nd row: Martha Bostic, Darlene Cree, Pearl Jones, Vickie Buchanan, Barbara Wade, Ene Guinn. 3rd row: Jeannie Hutchison, Jeannie Andrews, Wanda Delacerda, Sue Noble, Beebe Huett. Not shown: Jeannie Price, Martha Nelson, Barbara Loh, Vickie Ennis, Leona Koch, Jan Ruff, Sharon Knighten.

CONWAY COUNTY LIBRARY

In 1897, a ladies club was formed in Morrilton known as the Path finder Club. From its conception the club's primary goal was to establish a library for the community. The first library began in a small way as club members collected books and appointed a "librarian" from their membership. The library was originally housed in various members' homes and circulation was limited to the club membership.

The result of a 1914 town meeting was a community commitment to help the Pathfinder Club obtain and maintain a library for the community. Funds were solicited to purchase the Old School Presbyterian Church. The building was remodeled by residents who contributed their time and talent to the project. After the club moved their books into the newly purchased building, the library was opened to anyone who had a club member's sponsorship and they were charged a small fee. Mrs. J.I. Ellis was hired as the first librarian with a salary of $25 a month.

During this time, a Morrilton resident, Mr. W.S. Cazort had purchased a collection of 1,800 rare books from a reclusive Chicago engraver and book lover, Mr. William H. Porter. Soon after the library opened, Mr. Cazort asked the library to take care of his Porter Collection.

Until 1916, funding for the library was made possible through public subscription, dues, and gifts. The Pathfinder Club petitioned the Andrew Carnegie Foundation for a grant with which to build a new library. The Club used the Porter Collection, along with a downtown Morrilton lot that they had purchased with the proceeds from the sale of the Old School Church building as a testament of their commitment to a community library.

Andrew Carnegie, was often referred to as the "Patron Saint of Libraries," because during his lifetime he made new library buildings available to hundreds of communities all over the world. Very few communities were denied funds after they agreed to his terms, which included the community's legal ability to levy a tax for the annual support of the library. Morrilton agreed to the Foundation's terms and on September 29, 1915, the Andrew Carnegie Foundation granted the city of Morrilton $10,000 for the purpose of building a free public library, making Morrilton the smallest town in the south to have a Carnegie Library.

In October 1916, the books were moved into the building. The construction cost was $7,500 leaving $2,500 to purchase coal and furniture. The 3,628 square foot facility consisted of a top floor for books and a lower floor with a meeting room, small kitchen, furnace, and coal bin. There were originally four public libraries built in Arkansas through the philanthropic work of Andrew Carnegie; however, today the Conway County Library is one of only two public libraries in the state of Arkansas that still operates from its original Carnegie building.

In 1938, the Library became a part of the state-wide library system. In November of 1948 a one-mill library tax was passed by over 90% of eligible county voters which replaced the voluntary one-mill tax that was granted twenty-five years earlier.

In March 1971, Victor Boren headed a committee made up of members of the Pathfinder Club, Literary Coterie, and Adelaide Club for the purpose of remodeling the library. The Quorum Court levied a voluntary one-mill property tax to help finance the renovation. On December 3, 1972 an open house was held in the newly remodeled Library.

In 1991 on the 75th Anniversary of the Library, the Library Building fund was established for the purpose of providing funds to renovate and expand the Conway County Library. On June 25, 1999 a Ground Breaking Ceremony was held for the 1,300 square-foot addition and renovation of the Conway County Library, which was made possible through donations, grants, and the Library Building Fund. The extensive remodeling of the 83-year-old basement provided an entrance from the new addition and reconfigured the existing space for improved public services by incorporating

Above & below: The front and back of the Conway County Library.

new technology and an area for children's activities. The new addition and renovated basement were opened on June 4, 2000. The new addition is an example of blending the old with the new. The building is a focal point in the community and is treasured by the citizens of Conway County.

Today the Conway County Library is supported by funds from the city, county, state, and a vibrant Friends of Conway County Library group. The present challenge that the library faces is finding funds for automation. Automation would make our collection more accessible for the patrons, which would be reflected in our circulation and collection development. Automation will insure the survival and growth of our library, community, and children. It is about providing our children with the tools they need to succeed in the workplace and giving our patrons information on healthcare, retirement, and entertainment.

The Conway County Library will continue its tradition of building on the past, while working toward the future. *Submitted by Peggy Havener, Library Director, Conway County Library*

The Pathfinder Club Of Morrilton

Inset: Mrs. W. G. Stout. Above: Conway County Library.

The Pathfinder Club of Morrilton had its beginning in 1897 when a group of women met to discuss the need for improving the educational and cultural environment of their hometown, Morrilton, Arkansas. These early meetings led to the formation of a literary club. Mrs. W.G. Stout was the first president. She served from 1897-1899. Mrs. Stout's husband, Rev. Stout had bought 5,000 acres on the south side of the Arkansas River, at the foot of Petit Jean Mountain. The home they established there was a magnificent plantation named, Hawkstone, which was the second place opened on the south side of the river.

The Stouts introduced the first piano and the first pleasure carriage in Conway County. There was a steamboat landing, Stout's Ferry, and a large store on the plantation. Later, Rev. and Mrs. Stout moved to Morrilton where he built another handsome home. Mrs. Stout, a brilliant, educated woman, was a charter member of the Episcopal Church in Morrilton. That church was organized at the Conway County Courthouse on July 19, 1885.

Early meetings of the Pathfinder Club were conducted in the homes of members. Each member purchased a set of Shakespeare's plays which became their programs for several years.

At this time, Andrew Carnegie began offering grants to public libraries. The club applied for and received one of these grants in 1916. This money was used to build the present Conway County Library which is one of only two Carnegie libraries in the state which is still open.

In addition to literary programs, the club was active in community and school affairs. They helped to beautify the town, purchased street markers and playground equipment for schools, helped to obtain lights for railroad crossings, assisted in the installing of traffic lights and sponsored clean-up campaigns. The club sponsored the first kindergarten and later a program for illiterate adults.

Pathfinder Club members organized another General Federated Women's Club in 1931. This was the Junior Pathfinder Club, which later became the Literary Coterie and then helped to organize a second GFWC, the Adelaide Club, in 1948.

Pathfinder Club members consider sponsorship of the public library to be their most significant accomplishment to community education and culture. Support of the library has continued through the years. In 1982, the club organized the Friends of the Library to increase support of the library through gifts of time, talent and financing. Several *Roast and Toasts* to recognize local citizens have been held. The first Roast honored a local physician, Dr. Gastor Owens, who had served the citizens of the community and as Devil Dog physician so faithfully for many years; the second honoree was Marlin Hawkins, well-known local servant, sheriff and politician; the third, respected local Mayor Stewart Nelson, better known as Santa Claus; the fourth, former Lieutenant Governor Nathan Gordon who was a Congressional Medal of Honor winner and generous financial supporter of the Library; fifth, Diana Denton, a very talented local drama teacher; and the sixth, Katherine Foust, a GFWC member who served at president of Arkansas GFWC and an outstanding community leader. All proceeds of the *Roasts and Toasts* events, a total of $35,356, were donated to the library. Annual Used Book Sales by Friends of the Library provide further financial assistance.

These contributions have helped with the building of a 500 square foot addition to the library. It is now a beautiful building which has an elevator and handicapped accessible entrances and exits. The Pathfinder Club continues to work toward improvement of the educational and cultural environment of the community.

Daughters of the American Revolution
General William Lewis Chapter

Daughters of the American Revolution (DAR) is a patriotic lineage organization whose members descend directly from a person who aided the American Revolution. Its 3-fold purpose is historical preservation, education and patriotism. The national DAR motto is "God, Home and Country." In 1969 women of Morrilton organized the General William Lewis Chapter.

Organizing Regent Jean Walt Stallings beside monument to General William Lewis at Mount Holly Cemetery in Little Rock. (Photo by Pearl Jones)

Names of charter members are in *Conway County - Our Land, Our Home, Our People*, 1989, p. 60.

The chapter was named for William Lewis, who served in the Virginia Militia at age 12. After a military career in Virginia and Kentucky, he resigned in 1815 and migrated west. He settled in Arkansas Territory at Pecannerie on the Arkansas River near present day Morrilton in 1918. His great-granddaughter, Mary House, was a charter member of the chapter.

Regents have been Mrs. Alan Stallings, Mrs. James Upton, Mrs. A.V. Ormond, Mrs. W.C. Cheek, Mrs. Bernard Brazil, Mrs. Jord Sadler, Mrs. Euna Mae Wortham, Mrs. W.R. Vandivere, Miss Sharon Bell, Mrs. Robert C. Wallman, Mrs. Roger V. Hamilton Jr., Mrs. Ansel Swain, Mrs. Horace M. Crofoot III, Mrs. Rayford Windle, Mrs. Travis Bonds Mrs. Bob J. Mobley and Mrs. Travis Bonds.

Activities of the chapter have included placing Korean War 50th Anniversary monument to its veterans at courthouse in Morrilton, Louisiana Purchase Bicentennial, Bicentennial of death of George Washington, soldiers of Iraq honored before and after their service, support of six schools for needy children, annual American heritage essay contests, annual observance of Constitution Week, promotion of U.S. Flag display and etiquette, cemetery clean-up, annual recognition of veterans' service, and scholarships.

Citizens' accomplishments recognized by the chapter include Kevin Shipp, winner of state 8th grade history essay; Rachael Hays and Laura Conley, winners of state Christopher Columbus essay; Jared Jones national DAR scholarship; Stephanie Taylor, Joshua Langston, Traci Hopkins, and Stephanie Hamling, DAR state scholarships; and DAR Medal of Honor to Nathan Green Gordon, recipient of U.S. Congressional Medal of Honor for valor in World War II.

General William Lewis Chapter members have organized DAR chapters in Conway, Clinton and Russellville. *Submitted by Pearl Newkirk Jones (Mrs. Meredith G.), Chapter Historian.*

Gunderman Scrap Metals
65 Years of Recycling

Buying scrap metals started in the later 1930s by T.P. Austin. During this time, scrap iron, copper, brass, eggs, cream, cow hides and animal furs were bought. Sometime about 1950, the business was taken over by Osco and Carthal Coleman. They also bought batteries and chickens, and ran the business until early 1972 when Osco began to have bad health.

In June of 1972, John and Chris Gunderman bought the business and operated at the same location, also buying pecans and other metals. During those days, everything was loaded and unloaded by hand. Later, a magnet and a front-end loader was bought to help with the loading and unloading.

In 1979, the business was moved to 100 South Cedar Street on a much larger lot. After moving to this location, a forklift and track loader with grapple were purchased for loading and lifting the heavy loads. Now the company was purchasing all scrap metals, batteries and pecans.

This has been a family business operated by John, Chris, Butch and Eddie Gunderman, with some part-time labor to help out.

First Church of the Nazarene

Morrilton's First Church of the Nazarene was organized in 1913. In October of that year there were two meetings held to organize the Pentecostal Church of the Nazarene. One meeting was held by Rev. and Mrs. Allie and Emma Irick and the other was held by the District Superintendent Rev. B.H. Haynie at the home of Mrs. A.V. Hombree.

Rev. L.L. Hamric of Vilonia was called to serve as the first pastor. He came two Sundays a month to pastor the new church. After a year, he entered the evangelistic field and Rev. C.P. Roberts was called to be the new full time pastor. At this time the church had approximately 20 members and met in the "Old Tabernacle" on North Morrill St.

In 1921, under the leadership Rev. S.N. Erwin, the church purchased some property at 106 N. Morrill St. for $3,000 and a new church was constructed. There was a house on the south side of the lots which served as the parsonage. In 1947, under the leadership of Rev. Boyd C. Hancock, an educational building was added to the church. In 1960, under Rev. Mike Courtney, the parsonage was sold and moved to make way for a new parsonage.

In 1985, under the leadership of Rev. Jewell McKinney, a new parsonage was purchased across the street from the church. The old parsonage was used for classrooms until it was torn down to make room for the new sanctuary.

On April 12, 1992, still under the leadership of Rev. McKinney, ground was broken for a new sanctuary. The new sanctuary was built and the old sanctuary was used for a reception area and classrooms.

In 2004, under the leadership of Rev. Ellis Clark, it was decided that the old sanctuary, being in very poor condition, needed to be torn. down to make room for a new reception and educational building. At this time, plans are being made for the construction of this building.

The First Church of the Nazarene has been a part of Morrilton for 92 years and we look forward to many more years of service in this community.

Pastors

1913-1914	Rev. L.L. Hamric	1939-1943	Rev. A.L. Chaffin
1914-1916	Rev. C.P. Roberts	1943-1944	Rev. Noble J. Hamilton
1916-1916	Rev. E.H. Kunkre	1944-1948	Rev. Boyd Hancock
1917-1918	Rev. G.O. Crow	1948-1950	Rev. Oscar Stallings
1918-1919	Rev. R.M. Parks	1950-1952	Rev. Nolan Culbertson
1919-1920	Rev. C.H. Lancaster	1952-1954	Rev. W.E. Latham
1920-1921	Rev. F.H. Bugh	1954-1955	Rev. J.G. Rushing
1921-1922	Rev. S.H. Erwin	1955-1958	Rev. Harvey Rathbun
1922-1924	Rev. R.E. Dunham	1958-1961	Rev. M.O. Courtney
1925-1926	Rev. J.W. Henry	1961-1966	Rev. Cordell Hudson
1926-	Rev. Josiah Tucker	1966-1995	Rev. Jewell McKinney
1930-	Rev. Russell	1995-1996	Rev. John Martin
1934-1936	Rev. V.F. Paul	1997-2001	Rev. David Black
1936-1936	Rev. R.T. Morris	2001-Present	Rev. Ellis Clark
1936-1939	Rev. L.A. Richardson		

Submitted by Rachel D. (Langle) Beavers.

CONWAY COUNTY
ARKANSAS

FAMILY HISTORIES

The following family histories were researched and compiled by children in the Conway County school system.

BEALLS - In the beginning Jill and Gordon Beall came to Arkansas. They decided to stay close to their relatives Dorothy Beall, and Jan and Jerry Perkins. With there four children: Sarah, Shannon, Alex and Brayden, they moved from Little Rock to north hills. Jill, a lawyer fresh from school, went to work in Little Rock while Gordon, an electrician, went to work in Russellville. Despite the long drive to work they still had time for their kids.

Through the years Jill and Gordon Beall have been getting job promotions and Jill has even moved to a new job though she stayed in Little Rock. The Beall's now live in a new, much better, house. Also, the children have grown to high levels. Sarah, the oldest daughter, is almost done with college. Shannon, the older middle child, has made it to the middle of college. Both girls went to USA.

Alex, the youngest middle child, is in 8th grade while Brayden, the youngest child, sits in 3rd grade. The family has been through ups and downs, but all live and prosper.

BEIJEN - As a part of her advanced English class, Breanna Raye Beijen had to write an essay on her family history. Breanna Raye Beijen is the daughter of Brian and Patti Beijen. She has one sister named Hart LaShaye Beijen, who attends school at North Side Elementary, which is located in Morrilton. Breanna is 13 years old and attends Morrilton Middle School, where she is a member of the Morrilton Junior High Cheerleading Squad, where she is a flyer. She is also a part of the Career Orientation Club, and is active in many sports during the summer.

Breanna's grandparents' are Tuffy and Patricia Hart. They are the current owners of Surplus City. They both attend Bethel Missionary Baptist Church in Morrilton. Breanna's mother, Patti Beijen, has three siblings: Paula Dahlke, Steve Hart, and Janel Hart. Patti Beijen is an account manager at AMCS. Breanna's other grandparents are Jim and Ilse Beijen. Jim Beijen is an engineer. Ilse Beijen is a operating room technician. They both attend Lutheran and Redeemer. Breanna's family attend Mt. Pleasant Baptist Church.

BENGSTON - Katelyn Bengston is in the 8th grade at Morrilton Middle School. She was born in November 1990. Katelyn is the daughter of Timothy Gordon Bengston and Cheryl Lynn (Henderson) Bengston. Katelyn has one older brother, Timothy Ryan Bengston, who was born in January in 1988.

Katelyn's Dad was born in 1963. His parents are Robert and Lorraine Bengston. Tim was born in Watertown, New York. In 1966, Tim, his sister Lora and brother Brian, moved to Morrilton, where Robert got a job at the paper mill in Oppelo. Tim's dad, Robert, was born in 1932 to Harold and Agnes Bengston. Tim's mom, Lorraine, was born in 1930 to Edward and Mabel Teufert.

Katelyn's mom was born in 1964. Her parents are Benny and Joyce Henderson. Ever since Benny and Joyce married, they have lived in Birdtown. Cheryl has one brother, Benny Jr. Cheryl's mom, Joyce, was born in 1946 to Leon and Alma Dean Kellar. Cheryl's dad, Benny, was born in 1944 to Earl and Louise Henderson.

BRADFORD - On March 16, 2005 Miranda Bradford was given the challenge in her eighth grade English class to write about her family history. Miranda Bradford is an eighth grade student at Morrilton Middle School. She is the daughter of Bruce and Cindy Bradford of Plumerville. Miranda has two brothers, John Price, a senior at Morrilton High School, and Cody, a sophomore at Morrilton High School. Bruce is the son of John A. and Eulene Bradford of Damascus. He has two brothers, Gary and Johnny Bradford, both of Damascus.

Cindy is the daughter of Amos Price and the late June Boyle Stroud of Morrilton. She has one brother, the late Roy Stroud, and one sister Cheri Stroud Pruitt of Solgohachia. Price Stroud was the owner of Stroud Home Furnishings located on Moose Street, which is currently owned by his daughter Cheri Pruitt. John Price is an 18-year-old graduate with the class of 2005 in May. He is a member of the Morrilton High School basketball, and baseball teams, and Future Farmers of America. John Price plans to attend Harding University, located in Searcy, on a baseball scholarship in the fall. Cody is a member of the Morrilton High School football team and Future Farmers of America. Miranda is a member of the Morrilton Middle School basketball and volleyball teams, and Beta Club. He plays on the summer team '14 and under Hi Voltage'.

The Bradford family attends Downtown Church of Christ in Morrilton where Bruce is a deacon of the church. Also, where John Price, Cody, and Miranda are members of the youth group. That is the history of the Bradford family.

BRIDGES - In May 1953 Mary Bridges gave birth to a boy and she named him Ronald Bridges. When 10 years passed Mary Bridges gave birth to Stephanie Bridges (Walkins). Ronald Bridges grew up in College Station with his mother, sister, and his grandparents next door, Louise "Bamp" and Jimmy "Pap." After finishing high school he went to college at University of North Little Rock (UNLR), where he majored in English and minored in math.

After finishing college, he worked at Baptist Health for about two years as a RN. Then went on to work in Sears where he meet Barbara Cross of Plumerville, AR, daughter of Harrison and Vivian, and youngest of three children: Duel (Vera) of Plumerville and Cubia (Tommy) Fair of Shreveport, LA. They were married in October 1989 and about a year later Ronald got a job at US Corps of Engineers in North Little Rock and has worked his way to assistant manager. They moved to Plumerville and had two daughters, Alexandria Delores Bridges, the eldest, is an 8th grade student. She is class secretary, a member in Beta, math, and C.O. Club. She also is in the band as a flute player. Allyson Denise Bridges, the youngest, is a 5th grader and a straight "A" student with a math level of 12.3 and 2nd top reader in her class.

BRIDGES - Linda and Robert Bridges are the parents of Tarra Bridges. Linda Bridges currently works at the Lodge on Petit Jean Mountain. As a cook she makes steak, chicken, French fries, onion rings, eggs, bacon and other foods. Robert Bridges currently works at Sticks Deli and Diner in Morrilton. As a cook he also makes steak, chicken, French fries, onion rings, eggs, bacon and other foods.

Buddy Pruitt is the step-brother of Tarra Bridges. He is in the fifth grade. He also suffers from bipolar disorder, which causes much havoc within the household. Tarra Bridges is in the eighth grade. She does not participate in any sports. She is a library aide during her first period class. She also writes poetry. Some of the titles of her poetry are: *Alone*, *Giving Up* and *Mom*. Tarra Bridges has many friends and just moved to Morrilton, Arkansas.

This is an assignment given to her by her eighth grade advanced English teacher. Tarra Bridges also has a dog named T.C.

BROCKMAN - This is the history of Cassie La'Shae Brockman of Morrilton. She has a lot of history but her present history, being her parents, seems a good place to start.

Cassie's parents, Kevin Brockman and Youlonda Reed, grew up down the street from each other when they came from Centeridge and Menifee, their home towns. You could say their relationship grew. They decided to get married in 1989 after their first child, Brittany Renae Reed, was born. She was spoiled rotten by both parents, but it was Cassie's grandparents who spent the most time with her. Then a year, one month and a week later, Cassie was born. She was named after her great-grandmother Cassie Reed, who died days before she was born. Cassie and her sister had their times. One day her mom had just got done with her and Brittany's hair and they messed it all up by pouring powder on it.

In December 1992 her little brother Kevin was born. Kevin had no problems at

...ll. When he was one year old, Kevin played his first game. Well actually, he wasn't really playing, Cassie's daddy gave him a controller which he soon got to plug in. In 1993, Cassie suffered an accident where she fell off the slide at the Manier II Apartments. She was picked up in a helicopter where she died twice before reaching the Little Rock Children's Hospital, where she was revived.

In April 1994, a year later, Khadejah was born. This was Cassie's second sister. She has a story too. When she was old enough to crawl she went under her parents kitchen sink. Cassie's dad was washing dishes and she poked her head out of the cabinet and her dad screamed because he thought she was a spider.

Cassie and her siblings grew older and matured more. She was 12 years old and her parents divorced. This was a sad day for the children, but a regretful decision for their parents. The kids separated with two going to each parent.

CAHILL - Drew Cahill is a 14-year-old student that currently attends Morrilton Middle School, in Morrilton, AR. He is a member of the Beta Club, Math Club and the Library Club. His birthday is February 1991 and he is the first child in his family. His parents are David and Martha Cahill. David Cahill is from Pine Bluff, AR and Martha is from Danville, AR. They both attended college at Arkansas Tech University. They later married and moved to Illinois with Drew and had a second child named Tyler Cahill.

They currently live in Morrilton, AR. David and Martha later divorced. David later married Leslie Qualls, and she had a son named Will Qualls. Martha is now dating Steve Deason who currently works at Cogswell Motors and is general manager. Martha is currently a teacher at West Side Kindergarten. David is a salesman in a business called AMS (Advanced Marketing Specialists). He sells Mossy Oak band camo, bog boots, Imperial Whitetail Clover and many other things.

CANADY - Tai'hsia Canaday was born in Little Rock, Arkansas in 1991. She currently attends Morrilton Middle School in Conway County. In 1992 her parents, Bridgette Mann and Terry Canady, had a divorce and she continued her life living with her mother.

She was an excellent student from preschool at Tots and Landing in Plumerville in 1994 to her current grade, eighth, now at Morrilton Middle School. She was and A and B student up until the third grade. Then she was a straight A student. She is and active child as well. She plays basketball, volleyball, runs track, and plays summer basketball, which is called AAU. She is part of the Beta, math and future business leaders of America clubs and is in the Duke Talent program.

Bridgette remarried in 1998 to Lynn William. They divorced in the year of 2002. Tai'hsia's two sisters are twins, Tina and Trina. They were born in 1986. Tina was a cheerleader from her fifth grade year in 1996 to her senior year in 2004. Trina was on the basketball team from her seventh grade year until her senior year in 2004. She also played soccer her sophomore year until her senior year. They both played tennis and softball for some time as well.

Trina received MVP of the soccer team her sophomore year and her basketball team won the state championship her junior year in 2003. She had defensive player of the year her junior and senior year in soccer as well. Tina was captain of the cheerleading squad her senior year. Tina was in the Beta Club, Fellowship of Christian Athletes, Science Club, future business leader of America, Math Club, Library Club, and French Club. She was also on the student council. She was an "outstanding" senior and graduated with honors and was all conference as a tennis player in 2004.

Trina was in fellowship of Christian athletes, student council, MAST, science, math, and thespian clubs. Tina now attends the University of Arkansas in Fayetteville and Trina attends the University of Arkansas at Pine Bluff. There she is playing soccer as the goalie. She is ranked third in the nation and she is on the basketball team. She is majoring in industrial technology and Tina is majoring in psychology.

Bridgette is the supervisor over materials at IC Corporation in Conway. She has been working at IC Corporation for about 11 years and she played basketball and softball in high school.

COOK - Kaitlyn Cook attends Morrilton Middle School where she is a member of the Junior High Cheerleading Squad, Math Club, Beta Club, Historian of the C.O. Club and the Morrilton Band. Peter Paul and Jeanette Leigh (Hayes) Rossi are Kaitlyn's grandparents. Pete is former owner of Rossi Electric and Veteran of the Korean War.

Pete's parents traveled over to the United States by ship from Italy. They both attend St. Joseph's Catholic Church in Center Ridge. They have three children: Michael Rossi born in May 1956, Andrea Kay (Rossi) Dobbins was born on May 20, 1958 and died on February 21, 1997 and Marilyn Joyce (Rossi) Swope.

Marilyn was married to David Gary Cook and they had two children, Angela Marie, born in 1985, and Kaitlyn Leigh, born in 1991. Angela is now 19 and attends Arkansas Tech University. Kaitlyn attends Morrilton Middle School where she is a member of the Junior High Cheerleading Squad, Math Club, Beta Club, Historian of the C.O. Club and the Morrilton Band.

Kaitlyn's parents divorced in 1994. Kaitlyn's mother remarried in 1998 to Louis Edward Swope, who has one child named Taylor Reed Swope who is 13 and lives in Ohio. Currently in 2005, Marilyn Swope is the office manager at Arkansas Specialty Hand and Upper Extremity Center.

Andrea (Rossi) Dobbins has two children, Jamianne (Polk) Honeycutt and Taylor Polk. Jamianne has two sons, Preston Tyler and Wesley Barker. Jamianne is currently a senior at Arkansas Baptist Radiography School.

EDMUNDS - Tim Edmunds was born in 1961. He met Melissa Mooney and her one-year-old daughter, Chelsea LaNae. Soon after, Tim and Melissa got married in 1993. One year later they had their first child Taylor Breanne. At this point Tim works as an electrician at CEICO. Melissa is employed at Olympia in Conway.

Chelsea is in the eighth grade at Morrilton Middle school and she participates in many school clubs such as Beta Club, Science Club, Career Orientation Club, Quiz Bowl Club, and Math Club. Chelsea played the flute in the Morrilton Middle School Band for two years.

Taylor is now in the fourth grade at Northside Elementary. So far in her life she has played soccer. In the year of 2001 Tim and Melissa got a divorce. Melissa is currently married to Allen Johnson. Allen already had two boys, David and Dustin, and one girl, Britney.

ELLIOTT - Sonny Beth Elliott is the daughter of Jenny (Baker) Roller and John David Elliott Jr. Jenny was born in 1964 and John was born in 1959. Sonny's parents divorced in 1993, two years after her birth. Jenny moved to Morrilton and soon married a man named Charles Roller, born in 1962. His birth name was Charles Edward Luebker, but he was adopted by Ed Roller at a younger age. He has two daughters, Meghan Roller, age 11, and Elizabeth Roller, age 13. They live in Fayetteville with their mom, Christie. They are both very smart and every other weekend and on all the holidays, they come down to visit everyone here in Conway County. Jenny has two brothers and two sisters, Charles, on the other hand, has six sisters and two brothers.

Sonny has two brothers, Alex and Cliffton Elliott. Alex is now in heaven and at a better place. Cliff attends Morrilton High School and will graduate in 2006. Sonny and her family attend the First Presbyterian Church on Sundays, and Sonny is a member of their Wednesday youth group. Sonny, class of 2009, is in the Math, Beta, Science, Career Orientation, FCCLA and FBLA clubs.

The Roller and Elliott families are very academic and enjoy spending time with the rest of the family.

ETHERIDGE - The Etheridge-Greer family has been living in this area for over 100 years. Both of the families are of Native American descent. Both Georgia May Greer and Walter Etheridge Jr. were born in 1956. In 1974, they married at the Pentecostal Church of God in Morrilton. In 1991, they had a daughter that they named Amber Caroline Etheridge.

Amber is now 14 and attends Morrilton Middle School and is in choir, Beta Club, Math Club, a Science Club officer, and the eighth grade reporter. Walter is now a contractor in Ralls and Etheridge Construction. Georgia works as a cook at Northside Elementary School.

The Etheridge family are currently members of a southern gospel group called Heaven's Highway. They also currently attend Lewisburg Miracle Lighthouse Church along with Walter's mother, Eunice Etheridge. The Etheridge family now lives in Plumerville, Arkansas.

FORNASH - In 1987 Bobby Fornash and Kelly Halbrook Fornash got married. Bobby and Kelly had two daughters, Meagan and Lindsay. Meagan Elizabeth Fornash was born in 1988, and she was the oldest of the two daughters. Lindsay Nicole Fornash was born in 1990, and she was the youngest of the two daughters.

Meagan and Lindsay were part of the Beta Club at their school. Meagan and Lindsay also played softball, basketball, volleyball, and ran at least one year of track. Meagan was on a state championship softball team (The Gary's Angels) in 1998. Lindsay was part of a softball team (Strike Force) that won district and got first runner up in ASA, and USSSA state tournament in 2003. Bobby, Kelly, Meagan, and Lindsay lived in Morrilton all their lives. Bobby and Kelly got a divorce in 2004.

Kelly is the daughter of Arlene Windsor Halbrook and the late Gary Halbrook. Arlene and Gary had Kelly in 1968 and had Shawn in 1972. Gary died in 1996 after being married to Arlene for 28-1/2 years.

Bobby is the son of Doris Reiter Fornash and Robert Fornash. Bobby was born in 1968 and had one younger sister, Melanie Tipton Fornash, and one younger brother, Bradley Fornash. *Submitted by Lindsay Fornash.*

FRANKLIN - As a student at Morrilton Middle School, Araya Franklin was challenged to write a report on her family history. Araya Franklin is the daughter of Rayford Franklin Jr. and Tameria Wert in Little Rock, Arkansas on July 19, 1991. She has two sisters, Jessica, who is 10, and Andrea, who is 22. She also has a stepbrother named Adrien, who is 24. Adrien is serving in the military and is now stationed in West Virginia. Araya's father is employed at Amtran Incorporative. Araya serves in many clubs, such as Beta Club, Math Club, Duke Talent, FCCLA, CO Club, and more. Araya is the historian of the FCCLA club. Araya's family attends the Philadelphia Missionary Baptist Church in Menifee, Arkansas. Araya's parents have attended this church for over 13 years.

Tameria Wert was born to Opha Jackson and Leroy Wert in 1956. Tameria has two sisters named Regina Hogan and Marcia Johnson. Regina doesn't have any children, and Marcia has 2 children, Elizabeth Nicole and Natalie. She also has a brother named Roy Wert, and he has three children named Sherita, Joanna and Roy Jr. Regina, Marcia and Roy are all married. She graduated from

Menifee High School and afterwards attended a business college.

Tameria now works at Arkansas Educational Television Network in Conway, Arkansas. There, she programs and broadcasts the television shows. She is happily married to Rayford Franklin Jr. Tameria's mother was born to Elmo Jackson and Colodius Seaton. Colodius and Elmo had five children together. For Araya's grandfather, Leroy Wert, we could not trace back because of his death.

Rayford Franklin Jr. was born to Rayford Franklin Sr. and Betty Bland. Rayford has two sisters named Shawna and Deirdre. Shawna has no kids and she is not married. Deirdre has four kids and her husband's name is Fredrick. Her children's names are Brianna, Ki, Sean and Asha. Deirdre is currently going to school to become a hair stylist, and Fredrick recently returned from Iraq. Rayford graduated from Morrilton High School and afterwards attended a college in Pine Bluff. He graduated from that college with a degree in biology. Rayford's mother was born to Lloyd Franklin and Lucille Webb. The information on Rayford Franklin Sr. cannot be traced because of his death.

Araya Franklin's family now lives in Blackwell, and their history will be remembered.

GUNDERMAN - Charles Anthony Gunderman, son of the late John and Ottila (Beck), and Ruth Ann Swope, daughter of the late John and Hattie (Edwards), were married in 1961. They had two children, Kimberly Renee and Robert Allen. Charles owns Central Locksmith at 209 N. Moose St. Ruth is a LPN; she worked at Conway Human Development Center for 19 years until she retired in 2002. She then went to work for Perryville Center for Exceptional Children until she became ill in January 2005. Ruth died of colon cancer on March 26, 2005 at the age of 60. Kimberly married Billy Joe Thompson, son of Othell and Revadell Thompson, in 1980 and had two children, Joshua Ryan and Heather Nicole.

Robert married Esta Mae Prince, daughter of Roy Gene and Patricia Ann (Kuettle), in 1986. They had one child Stacie Marie. Kimberly and Billy moved to Orlando, Florida in 2001. Joshua graduated from Conway High School in 2001. In 2005, he is currently attending the University of Arkansas. Heather graduated from West Orange High School in Orlando in 2004. In 2005, she is currently attending the University of Central Florida. Robert works at Conway County Regional Water as the chief plant operator and has been a member of the Morrilton Fire Department for 18 years. Esta Mae works at Fred's Pharmacy as a pharmacy technician and volunteers at the Conway County Christen Clinic.

Stacie attends Morrilton Middle School. She is in the Beta Club, Math Club, Science Club, and the treasurer of the CO Club. Stacie also plays the clarinet in the Morrilton Band.

HARVEY - Shula Leavell was born in April 1906 in Cleveland, Arkansas and grew up in the Morrilton area He spent his young adult years traveling to California to pan for gold. Then on to Oklahoma to live with his brother, Wilbur Leavell, raise quarter horses and play minor league baseball. He found his way back to Morrilton and served as a police officer for several years. During this time he meet Ms. Emma Stallings who was born in June 1914 in Morrilton, Arkansas, Shula and Emma married in March 1936. Shula Leavell served as temporary police chief and mayor when his town needed him. He served as a Morrilton City Alderman for 36 years. After retirement Mr. Leavell was called back into service to stand in as mayor and chief of police again because he knew and understood the people of Morrilton so well.

Emma Leavell graduated with Mr. Sam Walton, from the University of Arkansas and began her career as an accountant for 1st State Bank and eventually 1st Security Bank. She also served as the bookkeeper for her brothers at the Stallings Brothers Feed Mill for many years. The mill was a fixture of Morrilton for many more years. The Leavell's were also long time members of the First Presbyterian Church.

Shula and Emma Leavell had two children, the first a daughter named Prudence in December 1944, the second a son named Calvin in June 1946. Calvin went on to live in Texas, where Prudence married Bill Seidenschwarz in February 1965 and had three children. One of whom is Stacia Seidenschwarz born in April 1967, who married Ken Harvey in August 1985 and bore to sons, Joshua Harvey, born in September 1987, and Jacob Harvey, born in June 1991. Stacia worked as an employee of Levis Straus for many years until the long time business of Morrilton closed it doors, Stacia is now married to John Finkbeiner. They married in May 1998, the family resides in Plumerville, Arkansas to this day.

HILL - As a student at Morrilton Middle School, Destanie Hill was challenged to write a report on her family history. Destanie was born in Russellville, Arkansas on July 30, 1991 to Stacy and Lisa (Wade) Hill. Stacy and Lisa married in Hot Springs two years before Destanie was born, and they are still married to this day.

Destanie and her family attend Lonoke Missionary Baptist Church in OverCup, Arkansas. Destanie has been attending Lonoke since she was a baby. Her father, Stacy, owns a shop in Overcup, Arkansas. In his shop, he fixes mobile homes and his father, Jerry Hill, sells the mobile homes at the shop. He owns "Cabin Creek RV Sales and Services." Her mother, Lisa, is a preschool teacher at West Side Kindergarten in Morrilton. Lisa is attending night classes at a college in Morrilton to become a permanent teacher. Lisa has two brothers, Kevin and Steven Wade, who are both older than her.

Kevin has two kids, Kevin Jr. and Jessica, and two step-kids, Kayla and Dustin. Kevin's wife is Michelle whom he married as a 2nd wife when Destanie was 7. Steven also has two kids, Steven "Stevie" and Jacky, and two step-kids, Nikki and Brandon. Steven got a divorce and is not married now. Stacy has one sister, Melissa Shipp, who has three kids: Andrew, Kaden and Libby, and is married to Steven "Stevie" Shipp.

Destanie has one sibling, Joshua "Josh" who is 11 years old, in 5th grade. Destanie is in many clubs at Morrilton Middle School such as FCCLA Club, C.O. Club, Math Club, FBLA Club and Beta Club. Destanie is the secretary of FCCLA Club and the reporter of FBLA Club. Josh is involved in Little Pups Football at North Side Elementary, where he attends school.

Destanie's grandparents include Jerry and Rachel Hill, Stacy's parents, and Bobby and Carolyn Wade, Lisa's parents. Jerry helps Destanie's dad and Rachel works in a tax store. Bobby cuts wood and sells it. He also builds things and sells them to people. Carolyn owns many, many dogs. She breeds them and sells the puppies. All of her grandparents have awesome jobs! Rachel's father was full Indian so Destanie has some Indian in her. His name was Hueaska Wanataw.

Destanie's family still lives in OverCup, Arkansas to this very day and they hope to be remembered long from now.

HOLLABAUGH - Christina Y. Hollabaugh was born in 1965 in Detroit, Michigan. Throughout most of her life she moved through the east part of the United States, but finally went back and stayed, for a while in Michigan. Christina, nicknamed Tina, went to Michigan State University where she received a four year degree in accounting after which she married.

In 1989, Tina had a daughter, Taira, who was loved and protected by Deserae, the dog Tina had gotten as a present. Another daughter, Taylor, was born in 1991, who ended up as the middle child in 1993 when Shelby, Tina's youngest was born.

When her middle daughter was about 4 or 5, Tina moved to Russelville, Arkansas, then when her eldest daughter was 9, divorced. A couple years after that Deserae died when hit by a car. She was deeply missed.

By then, Tina and her daughters had moved to Morrilton, where Tina already had a job as manager of Conway County Center for exceptional children. They bought another dog, Sierra, who didn't take Des's place, but had an exceptional amount of room in their hearts. Taylor was also given a dog, Brittany, who receives lots of love too.

Christina, even though she lived in Michigan a majority of her life, proved to be a very important person in the community.

HUGGINS - Grandpa Robert M. Huggins was born Jan. 18, 1862 at Atkins, AR. He died Apr. 11, 1939 at Tulsa, OK. He was married May 9, 1890 in Conway Co. to Mattie Cumi Gasaway. Mattie was born Aug. 15, 1871 in Dardnelle, Yell Co., AR to Mary Bird and Thomas Marion Gasaway. She died Oct. 10, 1949 in Fresno, CA and is buried beside Robert in Fairview Cemetery in Shawnee, OK.

Robert Mathew Huggins and Martha Cumi Gasaway

On Sept. 2, 1892, Robert and Mattie established their actual residence on Section 31, Conway Co., AR, by homestead, he being 37 years of age. He states that in Sept. 1892 he built a house and out buildings and cleared 16 acres of ground. He had farmed 15 acres for six years at that time.

Robert and Mattie are in the 1900 census of Cedar Falls District, Conway Co., AR, with five children, probably all born in Conway Co. The family continued to live on this property until 1921, when part of the family migrated to Seminole Co., OK. Robert told his grandchildren stories about building the cabin on Pettit Jean Mountain, and that the family moved into the unfinished cabin. There was no fireplace, only a huge hole in the wall over which they hung a quilt. Robert had gone back down the mountain to Casa to bring another load of household goods to the new cabin. Wolves, bears and panthers roamed the mountain, and while he was gone, Mattie would sit in a rocking chair all night with a gun across her lap to protect her children, all probably under five years of age.

Their children include: Rue (b. Sept. 18, 1891, d. Jan. 14, 1972, m. Clarence [Lump] Montgomery); Viola (b. Dec. 5, 1892, d. Nov. 19, 1977, m. Zack Upchurch); Bertha (b. Mar. 18, 1894, d. Feb. 2, 1977, m. Evander West); Burton (b. Jan. 20, 1898, d. 1956, m. Clara Yates); Ethel (b. Jan. 4, 1896, d. June 3, 1979, m. Albert M. Deeter); Elmer (b. Aug. 1, 1900, m. Lilly Shirley); Clifford (b. Nov. 5, 1902, d. Feb. 6, 1950, m. Edith Bowerman); Mary (b. May 17, 1906, m. James Davis); Harley (b. Sept. 14, 1908, d. Apr. 9, 1984, m. Mavis Jones); and Syble (b. Jan 3, 1911, m. Garland Owen).

Clifford told never-ending stories of the beauty of Arkansas and especially of Pettit Jean Mountain and Conway Co. Mattie's uncle, John Bird, raised fruit and he and Robert would go to Morrilton with loads of apples and other fruit to peddle from house to house. He told about their Easter sunrise celebrations and favorite picnic areas. During this time, Mattie worked as a midwife and delivered many babies.

About 1921, Robert and Mattie with their younger children moved to Seminole Co., OK, where Robert's half-brother, Samuel Jacob Gasaway, lived. Clifford, along with Elmer, Harley and Syble all migrated to OK. Rue Montgomery and her husband, Clarence, and Bertha West and her husband, Evander, all lived and raised families in the area of Conway Co. Ethel m. Albert Deeter, Viola m. Zack Upchurch, Burton m. Clara Yates, and Mary m. James Davis, spouses all from the area, but all later spent time in Oklahoma near the family. Elmer, Clifford, Harley, and Syble all married in OK. No matter how far these children roamed, they stayed close and never forgot their wonderful childhood on Pettit Jean Mountain.

Submitted by: Gerthel Jean, daughter of Clifford Huggins.

JOHANNES - Thomas Dee Johannes was born 1972 in Iowa City, Iowa. In 1973, he moved to Dickinson, TX. He attended Primary School for kindergarten, 1st, and 2nd grades. He continued Dickinson public schools until 6th grade when he moved to Judsonia, AR. From 6th grade until 10th grade, he attended Central School. In 9th grade, Thomas was in FFA, FHA, and he ran track. In 10th grade, he was in FFA and the student council. Thomas transferred to Kensett High School in 1988. In 11th grade, he was in FFA and many other school clubs. His senior year, he was in FFA, cutest couple, and he won Mr. Kensett High School both with his future wife, Scarlet.

Scarlet Michelle Walker was born 1972 in Brinkley, Arkansas. She attended school in Brinkley until 7th grade. In 5th grade, she took dance. Scarlet moved to Searcy, Arkansas and went to school until she was in 10th grade. She was in many school clubs and the student council. In 11th grade, Scarlet took tae-kwon-do and participated in school clubs. In 12th grade, she won cutest couple and Miss KHS with Thomas.

In 1991, Thomas and Scarlet had Emily Breanne Johannes in Galveston, Texas, and in 1992 they had Thomas Dee Johannes II. On August 28, 1993, Thomas and Scarlet were joined in holy matrimony. Shortly after, the family moved to Stamps, Arkansas, where Emily attended kindergarten in 1995. That summer, the family moved to Tyler, Texas. In Tyler, Thomas II started kindergarten and went on to the 1st grade and Emily went in to 1st and 2nd grade. Thomas's job transferred him back to Arkansas in 1999. Thomas and Scarlet found a house in Conway County, Arkansas. Emily and Thomas II started attending school in Morrilton.

When Emily was in 4th grade, she was in dance and the next year she continued dance, was inducted into the National Junior Beta Club, and was who's who-most friendliest. When Thomas II was in 5th grade, he was also inducted in the Beta Club and he played soccer. In 6th grade, Emily was in the Beta Club, Science Club, Math Club, was a cheerleader and did dance. When Thomas II was in 6th grade, he was in the Beta Club and played basketball. When Emily was in 7th grade, she was in the Beta Club, Science Club, Math Club, was the reporter for the Beta Club, and the secretary for the Science Club. She also participated in her last year of dance. Thomas is currently in the 7th grade where he is in the Beta Club and the Science Club. He also plays the guitar and is in lessons. Emily is currently in the 8th grade and is active in the Beta Club, Math Club, Science Club, Career Orientation Club, Quiz Bowl Club, and takes piano lessons. Both children are in advanced classes.

JONES - Bruce Jones and Sarah Underwood married in 1985. They have four children: Aaron, Lyndsey, Brett and Blake. Sarah is the daughter of James Jr. Underwood and Cheryll Ann Underwood. She has three sisters and one brother. Their names are Angel, Lori, Michelle and Toni.

Bruce is the son of Virgel Jones and Martha Jones. He played football at Morrilton High School. He now works at Green Bay Packaging. Aaron is a student at Morrilton Middle School. He plays football and basketball at Morrilton Middle School. He also plays baseball at Plumerville Youth Association.

MANNING - Emma Eileen Wilson Manning was the only person in her family to be born in Conway County. Her family history in Conway County began when her grandfather Woody (Colonel Waring Woodrow Wilson) retired from the Air Force and moved to Morrilton. His family at the time consisted of his wife, Beulah Eileen Miller Wilson, and youngest daughter, Barbara Jean Wilson. Woody's other children: Donald Allen Wilson, Mary Jane Wilson (Kennedy), Carol Anne Wilson) had already married and moved out. In January 1974, the family (Woody, Beulah and Barb) moved to a farm in Sheepskin Valley, Center Ridge, Arkansas.

In 1990, Barbara gave birth to Emma. In 1997, Eldridge Snow (a family friend and retired pastor) married Barb to Marshall Stuart Manning (Stu).

In 2001, Barb became a high school physical science, chemistry, and physics teacher for the South Conway County School District. Emma attended school with Barb. Stu became a self-employed welder on the farm.

By the end of her eighth grade year, Emma had been receiving dance lessons from Judi King, in Clinton, AR for 10 years. She had been a member of the Red River Cloggers for three years, and had performed with them several times. She had performed at Solgohachia Days, the Great Arkansas Pig-out, the Conway County Fair Talent Show, the AR State Fair Talent Show, the National Chuckwagon Races in Clinton, AR, a Carnival Cruise ship and Silver Dollar City.

Emma Manning wrote this on March 29, 2005 for a school report. Therefore, this was all she could record since she could not predict the future.

NEVAREZ - Ernesto Nevarez was born in Chihuahua, Mexico in 1965. He married Sandra R. Arias, who was born in 1970, in December 30, 1988. They immigrated to Forth Worth, Texas in 1990, where they had their first child, David E. Nevarez. They stayed there for about a year. Then decided to have their second child in Mexico, their only girl, Sandra I. Nevarez in 1991. They

decided to stay in Mexico, and had their third child, Jonathan Nevarez in 1993.

Later in 2001, the whole family came to Morrilton, AR to visit Sandra's sister, Maria Rosas. The kids liked the town so they all decided to stay here in Morrilton.

Ernesto works as a painter, painting houses in Little Rock, Conway, and other towns near or far away from home. Sandra doesn't work, but she stays home and takes care of her three kids.

With Ernesto's hard work, they saved some of the money and bought a house in December of 2004. They fixed the house inside and outside and they are very happy to live in it.

NORBERG - In the summer of 1998, the Norberg family moved to Morrilton, Arkansas. The family includes Michael Norberg, Charlotte (Gibby) Norberg and Stephanie Norberg.

Michael Norberg is currently working at Woodruff Elementary in Little Rock as a third grade school teacher. He is also an adjunct psychology professor at UACCM. He is the son of the late Larry Norberg, and Herman and Norma Vandiver. The Vandiver's are currently living in Andrews, Texas. Michael also has three siblings: Cindy Richardson, Teresa Young and the late Tommy Norberg.

Charlotte Norberg currently works at Reynolds Elementary in Morrilton as a second grade school teacher. She is the daughter of Don and Euna (Turner) Gibby. The Gibby's and Turner's have lived in Conway County all of their lives. Charlotte has one brother and one sister. Their names are Deborah Gibby and Randy Gibby.

In 1980, Michael and Charlotte met at the Southwestern College in Waxahachie, Texas. In 1981, they started dating and by 1982 Michael and Charlotte were married.

In 1990 a wonderful thing happened! They had their first child. A beautiful baby girl named Stephanie. She is now 14 years old and is an 8th grader at Morrilton Middle School. She is 8th grade class president, Junior Beta President, an 8th grade cheerleader, a member of CO Club, a member of FBLA, a member of band, and is in track.

Michael, Charlotte and Stephanie are all very active members of Morrilton First Assembly of God. They are all in the adult choir. Michael and Charlotte both teach a Sunday School class. Stephanie is in her youth group's Praise and Worship Team, is very active in special events, and enjoys going on many youth trips.

NORWOOD - In September of 1991 Paula and Daniel Norwood gave birth to a baby girl which they named Loren Ranell Norwood. Then in 1993 Daniel passed away. Loren was only 1-1/2 years old; she hardly knew him. Then in 1996 Paula remarried to Douglas Smith. In April 1997 they gave birth to a baby girl which they named Morgan Leighann. Then in November 1998 they gave birth to a baby boy which they named Hayden Douglas.

In November 2000 Loren was saved and baptized, Brother Joel Summers was the pastor then, but for the remaining year of 2005, Loren and her church are without a pastor. Loren enjoys going to church every Sunday with her granddaddy Paul Mourot, who takes her and her sister Morgan to and from church every Sunday morning. Loren attends Solgohachia Baptist Church, which she has attended for several years. Loren sometimes leads the singing and teaches the younger children for Sunday school.

Loren was 14 in September 2005, while her little sister Morgan was 8 in April 2005 and her little brother turned 7 in November 2005.

Loren says she would like to be a wildlife officer or a model, she also says that is her goal in life to become one or the other or maybe even both of them - she thinks that would be really cool!

ORTIZ - In the summer of 1999, the Ortiz family came to Morrilton, Arkansas. The Ortiz family consisted of five siblings, and two parents, Samuel and Juana Ortiz. The children's names are Samuel Ortiz Jr., Jose Raul Ortiz, Luis Carlos Ortiz, Jose Guadalupe Ortiz and Neli Guadalupe Ortiz. Samuel and Juana's families both live in the same town in Mexico.

Part of the Ortiz family was born in Mexico, and part in the U.S. Samuel Ortiz was born in Las Liebres, GuanaJuato, Juana Ortiz was born in Mexico City. She went to Las Liebras and met Samuel, then they married and had Samuel Jr. He was born in Mexico D.F. Later, they had Jose Raul. He was also born in Mexico D.F. Samuel and Juana came to Bakersfield, California with Samuel Jr. and Jose Raul. That is when they had Luis Ortiz. Then they moved back to Mexico D.F. and had Jose Guadalupe. Later they came back to California and moved to Arkansas. Neli Guadalupe was born in Conway.

Samuel Ortiz works very hard in Plumerville at Hixon Lumber Sales. Juana only works part-time so she can care for her young daughter, Neli.

Samuel Ortiz Jr. attends Morrilton High School where he plays on the football team. Jose Raul Ortiz attends Morrilton Middle School and Luis Carlos Ortiz attends Northside. Jose Guadalupe Ortiz is in the second grade at Reynolds elementary. Neli doesn't attend school.

Samuel and Juana love their children very much and work very hard to make good lives for them.

RHODA - Darryl W. Rhoda was born in 1961 in Memphis, Tennessee. He married Wendy R. Morin in October 1988. Wendy was born in 1965 in Connecticut. The first two years of their marriage, Darryl and Wendy lived in Crossett, Arkansas, then moved to Harrison, Arkansas.

In 1990, they moved to McGhee, Arkansas where they had their first of two children, Emily S. Rhoda. Then in 1992, they had Tara L.C. Rhoda in McGhee. The Rhoda family lived in McGhee until 1994 when they moved to Rogers, Arkansas. They lived in Rogers for about one year, then moved to Russellville, Arkansas where they lived for eight months. Just in time for Emily's kindergarten year, they found a house on five acres in Morrilton, Arkansas.

In December 2001, Darryl and Wendy divorced. Wendy now lives in North Little Rock, Arkansas while Emily and Tara live in Morrilton with their father, Darryl.

ROBIN - Aimee Denise Robin was born February 17, 1991 in Conway, Arkansas. Her parents are Nelson Robin and Linda Robin. Her dad (Nelson) was born October 23, 1964 in Morrilton, Arkansas and her mom (Linda) was born January 31, 1970 in Dos Palos, California.

She has three sisters Heather Nicole Beck born October 15, 1988 in Conway; Ashley Nichole Robin born June 21, 1986 in Morrilton; and Christiane Danielle Robin born May 20, 1984 in Morrilton. Aimee's grandparents' on her mother's side are Joycelyn Ellise Moore born September 23, 1931 in San Francisco, California and Edward Dale Ingram born in Monroe, Louisiana, died in May 1983.

Her great-grandparents' on her mother's side are Lyle Stanley born in Eureka, California and died in Fort Bragg, California in 1980. Clara Smith Stanley, born in Santa Clara, California, died in 1997 in Fort Bragg, California. Her great-great grandmother was Felicia Smith, died in California in 1950. Robert Ingram was born in Louisiana and died in Lake Providence, Louisiana in 1983. Mary Ingram was also born in Louisiana and died in Lake Providence, Louisiana in 1993.

Nelson Robin Sr., born in Arnaudville, Louisiana March 15, 1934, died in Morrilton, Arkansas in 2000. Linda Eaton Pavatt, born March 5, 1942 in Center Ridge, Arkansas and now resides in Morrilton, Arkansas.

ROBERSON - On March 16, 2005, Kimberly Roberson was given the challenge to write an article about her family. Kimberly is an eighth grade student at Morrilton Middle School. Her family includes her dad, Greg Roberson, her mom, Debbie Roberson, her sister, Brittany Roberson, and her adopted brother, Nick Williams. Greg Roberson was born into the Roberson family in 1965 to Jerry and Erma Dean Roberson (Cossey), retired dairy farmers of Bee Branch, Arkansas.

Greg was born in Conway, Arkansas on December 20, 1986 and married Debbie Stein. Debbie Stein was born to the late Richard and the late Daisy Stein (Carter). Debbie was born in Judsonia, Arkansas. In December 1987, Greg and Debbie received a gift from God, a baby girl. Brittany Roberson was born at Harrison, Arkansas. Brittany is now 17 years old and a junior at Morrilton High School. She is a member of Beta Club, Spanish Club and was selected for the Who's Who Among American High School Students and All-American Scholar.

In May 1991, Greg and Debbie received

another gift from God, another baby girl. Kimberly was born in Blytheville, Arkansas and is now 13 years old. She is a member of Beta Club, Duke Talent, Junior High manager for the Morrilton volleyball team, plays softball for Koontz High Voltage, was selected for All-Region Band, and a member of the Morrilton Christian Center Praise Team. Kimberly and Brittany are both members of the Morrilton Christian Center youth group. Nick was born in February of 1981. The Roberson family adopted him in July 1996. In July 2000, he went into the army. Since then he has been back and forth from Iraq and the United States. In December 2004, he was sent back to Kuwait. He was not with the family when they moved to Morrilton. Greg, Debbie, Brittany, and Kim moved to Morrilton in November 2000 on the account of Greg getting another job as the pastor at Deerwood Assembly of God.

In October 2004, Greg was offered a job as the Christian Education Director at Morrilton Christian Center. He accepted the job and changed churches. Now not only is he the Christian Education Director, he is also the chairman of the Conway County Care Center, vice president of the Ministerial Alliance, sports director for Morrilton Community Channel 6, and a member of the Pastoral Associates. Debbie is a patient accounts representative at St. Anthony's Healthcare Center, a member of the Morrilton Christian Center Praise Team, and helps with the sports on Morrilton Community Channel 6. The Roberson family is very active in Morrilton and hopefully will be remembered in the future.

SCROGGIN - The Scroggin's history extends beyond the sixteen hundreds when our ancestors immigrated to the United States from the countries of England and Scotland. Some of the research goes back to George Scroggin who was born in 1660. He died between 1696 and 1700 in the state of Maryland. His wife Susanna was also born in England about the same time.

Skipping several generations to Dennis Quilla (sometimes spelled Quiller) Scroggin, the first child of Roberta Humphrey Scroggin and Sarah Barnes, was born September 9, 1883 at Springfield, AR. He died April 21, 1958, at Morrilton, AR. He married Matilda Jane Starkey, daughter of Richard Isiah Starkey and Margaret Spence, October 30, 1899. Matilda was born October 9, 1879, in Springfield, AR. She died November 24, 1962, at Springfield, AR. They had 12 children, one of which was Junia Jewell Scroggin, Kacie's great-grandmother. She is 91 years old and the only child living as of March 2005. She was born 1914 near Center Ridge, AR and married Willie Everett "Shine" Stover on September 28, 1935. He was born Dec. 3, 1912, at Center Ridge and died August 2, 1987, at Conway, AR. They have one daughter, Willie Gay, born 1939, at Center Ridge.

Willie Gay married Lewis Earl Miller at Morrilton in 1959. He was born in 1937,

in the Hill Creek Community, near Plumerville, AR. They have two daughters, Tawnia Gay born 1965 and Crystal Ann born 1968 at Morrilton. Tawnia married Kenneth Michael Hoelzeman, October 3, 1986, at Mt. Pleasant Baptist Church near Plumerville. He was born 1958 at Morrilton. They have three children: Kacie Lynn, born 1990; Haley Renee, born 1994; and Bret Andrew, born 1997. All were born in Little Rock, AR. They attend schools in Morrilton and church at Mt. Pleasant. Tawnia teaches second grade at Reynolds Elementary School in Morrilton. Kenny is a self-employed chicken grower for Pilgrim's Pride and raises cattle north of Plumberville.

Crystal married Kevin Emil Rehm, December 17, 1988 at the First Baptist Church in Morrilton. He was born 1966, at Morrilton. They have two daughters, Stephanie Leigh, born 1991, and Hannah Maria, born 1994, at Little Rock. Both attend St. Joseph School in Conway, Arkansas. Crystal is a librarian at Theodore Jones Elementary School and Kevin owns Central Arkansas Electronics in Conway.

Other children born to D.Q. and Matilda were James Madison "Matt," born March 23, 1901, died, February 23, 1982, married Irene Hawkins; Jesse Baxter "Jess," born December 18, 1903, died July 8, 1982, married first Vivian Lacefield, second Hazel Williams; Christopher Columbus "Lum," born October 2, 1905, died September 3, 1998, married Beatrice Blanch Mallett; Chloia Easter, born April 19, 1908, died April 26, 1997, married William Edgar Dowdy; Genevia Icillene "Icie," born March 3, 1916, died October 29, 1981, married Marie Mallett; Leoda, born February 1, 1920, died March 23, 1929. Four other children died in infancy. *Written by great-great-granddaughter, Kacie Lynn Hoelzeman.*

SHARP - Kristen Sharp's family actually started way back in 1987. In 1987 Ronnie Wayne Sharp married Kathy Lynnette Yarbrough in Bismarck, Arkansas at Pleasant Hill Church of Christ. A year after they married they had Tiffany Lynn Sharp. Also four years after marriage they had Kristen Lee Sharp in Hot Springs, Arkansas.

Martins - Generations ago W.O. Martin and Anna (Bartlett) Martin married and were proceeded in death by an infant child named Loretta Lynn Martin. W.O. Martin was the son of W.S. and Gladys Martin of Nadda Valley. Anna (Bartlett) Martin was the daughter of L.D. and Epsie Bartlett of Cleveland, Arkansas. Anna had two daughters, Carol Ann and Maryland Rose.

Carol Ann married in 1965 at the age of 16 to Kenneth David Sharp. Two years after marriage they had their first son, Ronnie Wayne.

Yarbrough - Debra Lewis married Gene Yarbrough in 1964. In 1965 they had their first child named Gene J.R. Their second child born in 1966 they named him Nelson Lee. Three years later they had their first daughter and third child named Kathy Lynnette in 1969. Their very last child was born four years after their daughter in 1973 they named him Nathan Shane. Ronnie Wayne met Kathy Lynnette in January 1987 and they married in June. The Sharp family started generations ago.

SHIRLEY - As an 8th grade student at Morrilton Middle School, Ryan Shirley was challenged to write a report on her family history. Ryan will be in the graduating class of 2009. Her parents are John and Deborrah Shirley. John and Debbie moved to Conway County from Cleveland, Ohio in 1999. Her siblings are Tracie, 26, Amon, 22, Michael, 21, Kerry, 20, and Travis, 19. Tracie married George Perkins in 2001. Together they had two children, Grace, born in 2003, and Benjamin, born in 2005.

John Shirley's parents are Von and Tressie Michell Shirley, who in 2001 celebrated their 50th anniversary. His siblings are Tom, Janis, Lavon, Samuel and Joe. Von's parents are Rufus and Vivin Shirley. Tressie's parents are Hubert and Nora Michell Jones.

Deborrah Shirley's parents are Bruce Dopp and Doris Bernstine. Her brother is Bruce and her twin sister is Dawn. Bruce's parents are Fancheon and Cleo Shinn Dopp. Doris's parents are Opal and William Justice.

SMITH - Joseph Wesley Smith is the son of Charles and Tina Smith. Charles works for ADT and Tina works for Morrilton Housing Authority. Grandparents, Charles and Judy Smith, own their own business, JW's Fireworks and Arkansas Valley Scrap Metal. His great-grandparents, Dolly and Joe Smith, are both retired. His oldest relative is Granny Mac.

On his mother's side, his grandmother works for ICT. His great-grandparents, Hurly and Maxine Sigler are both retired. In 1991, Tina and Charles had a baby boy, Joseph Smith. Charles was not there; he in Saudi Arabia in the war. He was in the Marine Corps - so was Joe and Charles Smith. All of his grandparents and great-grandparents have been in a major war.

SMITH - Oral Smith was born July 30, 1934 in Formosa, Arkansas, Van Buren County, to Elmer and Susie Smith. Oral had one sister, Penny Conley of Morrilton, and the late Sherman Smith of Memphis, Tennessee. Oral served four years, stationed in Germany, in the United States Army. Oral returned to Formosa after his tour of duty with the Army, shortly after returning, Oral's father died, and Oral and his mother moved to Morrilton. Oral worked for a short time at Soundcraft on Petit Jean Mountain, after being laid off at Soundcraft he began work at Oberman Manufacturing, which later became Levi Strauss & Co., and remained working there until his retirement when the plant closed.

On Friday, January 13, 1961, he met Joy Garrett of Plumerville at a ballgame between Plumerville and Nemo Vista. Joy was the daughter of C.D. and Irene Garrett of the Lone Star Community. Joy had six broth-

ers: the late Leo Garrett of Paragould, Arkansas; the late James Garrett of Ola, Arkansas; the late Eugene Garrett of Rover, Arkansas; Martineau "Bud" Charles; and Harold Garrett, all of Lone Star; also, two sisters, Nelle Trafford of Hill Creek and the late Betty Brice of Lanty. They had a whirlwind romance and married July 1, 1961 at Caney Valley Baptist Church in Plumerville. Joy was employed by Dr. H.C. Carruthers until the birth of their first child, Angela Renee, on July 4, 1962. Shortly after the birth of Angela they bought a home in the Lone Star Community close to Joy's childhood home. Sharon Kay was born March 30, 1965 and completed the family. Oral worked as a mechanic at Levi Strauss and Joy was a homemaker.

Sharon married Hal Walker, son of Aubrey and Golda (Pet) Walker of Plumerville, July 27, 1984; they live in Plumerville. Sharon and Hal blessed Oral and Joy with four grandchildren: Rebekah Ann (born November 18, 1987), Seth Thomas and Shannon Kay (born October 30, 1989) and Elysha Rene (born February 19, 1994). Angela married Rick Summers, son of David Summers of North Little Rock and Betty Smith of Little Rock; grandson of Merdie and Wilma Martin of Solgohachia, December 31, 1985, they live in the Caney Valley Community. They gave Oral and Joy two more grandchildren, Martin "Marty" Lynn (born January 28, 1988) and Erika Renee (born August 31, 1991).

Oral and Joy built a home in the Hill Creek Community in 1989 and remain there today. Oral serves as a deacon and Sunday School teacher at Bald Knob Baptist Church in Plumerville. After retirement Oral and Joy spend their time attending various functions that their grandchildren are participating in, and visiting hospitals, nursing homes, retirement homes, and churches, singing Southern gospel with a group of friends.

SUMMERS - Ricky Lynn Summers was born in 1955 in St. Anthony's hospital in Morrilton, Arkansas. Rick is the son of John David Summers and Betty "Martin" Summers. When Ricky was born he lived in Solgohachia, Arkansas and moved to Little Rock, Arkansas at age 8 and lived there until age 19 when he joined the Marines for two years and moved back to Little Rock.

Angela Renee Smith was born in Morrilton, Arkansas in 1962. Angela is the daughter of Oral Smith and Joy "Garrett" Smith. Angela lived in Morrilton, Arkansas for one year, moved to Plumerville, Arkansas and has lived there from then on. Angela attended Plumerville High School until it was moved to Morrilton and she graduated from Morrilton High School.

In 1983 Rick and Angela met in Caney Valley at the house they live in now. In 1985 Rick and Angela were married at Caney Valley Church. They lived in Plumerville for 10 months and moved to Caney Valley where they still live today. In 1988 Martin "Marty" Lynn was born at the Conway hospital. In 1991 Erika Renee was born at the

Little Rock Baptist hospital. Rick currently works at Hendrix College in the grounds department and Angela is employed at the Plumerville Post Office. The family attends Bald Knob Missionary Baptist Church in Plumerville. Rick is the song leader and Angela is the piano player and a Sunday school teacher.

TYNER - Chuck Tyner and Cheryl Fitzgerald both originally of Dallas, Texas were married in 1989. In December 1990 they had their first son, Dalton C. Tyner, two years later they had their second son, Dakota S. Tyner. Chuck first worked for Mark Cambino after first moving to the Morrilton area. After working for Mr. Cambino for about three years, Chuck opened his own carpentry business which is still operating today. It is known as Tyner's Carpentry.

While all this is happening Cheryl has been working at a Shell gas station then at Phillip's 66. After working these two jobs, she got a job at the Morrilton Police Department. As a dispatcher in 2000, then as police officer, still at Morrilton Police Department. Recently she has been promoted to corporal. Not only is she on the Police Department she is also on the Police Department's Entry Team which is sort of like Morrilton's version of a SWAT TEAM.

Dalton is a member of eighth grade football team. He is also a member of a local band known as Chris And The Martions in which he plays lead guitar. When not at band practice or football practice, he can be seen around town with his buddies, Shane Wilson and Chris Jones, skateboarding.

Dakota is a member of the MYA baseball program in which he plays on the LA Dodgers that are sponsored by Roberson Tire and U.S. Bank. Dakota is also a member of the Morrilton Youth Bowling Association.

VIRDEN - In 1971, four people moved to Morrilton, Arkansas. They were Jerry Virden, Martha Virden, and their two children Bart, age 11, and Lynlee, age 7. The Virden family came here from Clarksville because of Jerry's new job at the lumber mill. He was the head honcho over there. They were a lovely family and were respected throughout the community. They were a family that wanted one to think for himself. Little Bart and Lynlee's parents were very different from one another. Jerry was a Republican, and Martha was a Democrat, so you see their views differed on lots of things. But, Martha and Jerry never let their differences get in the way of raising their family or their love for one another.

Time went on, and the children grew up as children tend to do. Bart went off to college to become a lawyer, and Lynlee set off to become a teacher. Bart also married his off-again-on-again girlfriend, Janna Jennings, as he was starting law school. Lynlee married a man by the name John Maus.

Bart and Janna had three lovely children of their own, the youngest one in curls.

These children are named Jessica, Bryant and Eli Virden. Jessica is currently 18 years old and is attending college with a full-paid scholarship. Bryant is 17, a member of the popular band "Diddly and the Squats," and a future college student. The youngest child is Eli. He is a fiery 14-year-old redhead that attends Morrilton Middle School. These children of Bart and Janna are all gifted in many areas and are very interesting characters.

Lynlee beat her brother in the baby contest by having four children with John. The oldest, J.B. Maus, goes to Sacred Heart along with his brothers. He is 12, plays the piano, and is the absolute biggest fan of the Arkansas Razorbacks. Hamilton Maus is 10 years old, plays the piano like his brother, and is near the top of his class. Next is 7-year-old Stephen Maus. He is in first grade and is doing well. He has yet to start playing, but he says he wants to learn the violin instead of the piano. Last, but certainly not least, is little Annalee. She is 2 years old and is as cute as a bug in a rug! For a child her age, she is very smart; she can walk, talk, solve problems like how to get over the fence or get the candy off the counter, and can speak a little Spanish thanks to Dora the Explorer.

All of Jerry and Martha's grandchildren play soccer and other sports. The Virden and Maus tribes are very close and will put their family first. They may have their differences, but they are a family drawn together by love.

WILLIAMS - Kendreylla Williams was born in Conway in 1990. In 2000 her family moved to Conway County. So now she participates at Morrilton Middle School. She also participates in the following clubs: Math Club, Science Club, Beta Club, and President of FBLA Club. Divine Williams was born in 1998. This little girl is very smart. They are the children of Lamont and Nicole Williams. They married in 1996.

Kendreylla's mother had her at the age of 17, and had Divine at the age of 23 years old. Nicole is employed at International Corporation (make parts for buses). She's been working there for 10 years. Her husband Lamont is now 34. He has a lawn service and really works hard to earn what he deserves. This lawn service is called "The Williams Lawn Service".

Now you know a little about the Williams family that now live in Plumerville, Arkansas and is now part of Conway County.

WILSON - Lillie Karen "Kay" Kimbrough was born in Newport, Arkansas in 1945. Her parents were Joseph C. and Joanne Dunn Wilson who moved from Newport, Arkansas to Menifee, Arkansas around 1966. Lillie married Herbert Kimbrough in 1965 and they lived in Little Rock, Arkansas. They moved to Menifree, Arkansas in 1971.

They had children: Herbert Jr., Leslie, Lisa, Demetria and Christian. Lillie's parents were Joseph C. and Joanne Dunn Wilson. Joseph's father and mother were

Marion and Ruth Wilson. He had two brothers. All are now deceased.

Joseph's grandfather was a relative of McWilson who was Irish. He fought in the Civil War and lived in Menifree, Arkansas after the war. His granddaughter was born (name unknown) are both deceased. Joanne's father and mother were Lillie and Jeri Dunn, both are deceased. Her grandmother was a Cherokee Indian (name is unknown). The family name was dropped over time and they became Wilsons.

WOFFORD - In 1952 Bobby O. Wofford and LaVerne Sledge were married in Morrilton. Bobby O. Wofford is the son of Charles Wofford and Bernice Poteete. LaVerne Sledge is the daughter of Columbus Sledge and Sarah Jordan. A few years after Bobby and LaVerne were married they had a son, Bobby C. Wofford, on January 31.

On August 21, 1987, Bobby C. Wofford married Glenna Dickson. Glenna is the daughter of Glen Wade Dickson and Bernadine Wilhelm. A couple of years later they had a son, Clayton Wofford, on October 31.

The Woffords are members of Morrilton Country Club. Clayton is a current member at Morrilton Middle School in Morrilton, Arkansas. Clayton is in all advanced classes and is in many clubs. Some clubs are Beta, Science, Quiz Bowl and FBLA (Future Business Leaders of America).

Bobby O. Wofford passed away on March 4, 2004; the rest of the family still lives in Morrilton.

WOFFORD - Joseph Gotsponer and Clemmie Weisen met on a boat from Switzerland in 1882. They settled in St. Vincent in 1883 and were married. They had five children. Their daughter Josephine married John Zimmerman in 1915. They had eight children and moved to St. Elizabeth. Daughter, Helen Zimmerman, born in 1923, married Carl Hoyt, born in 1915. They had 11 children. Their daughter Stephanie married Steve Wofford in 1978 and had four daughters. The oldest of the four is Kim Wofford who was born in 1979 and lives in Morrilton. She works at Conway County Center for Exceptional Children and has two sons, Colton and Lamar, ages 5 and 3.

Their second oldest daughter Melissa was born in 1982 and recently graduated in the Spring of 2004 from the University of Central Arkansas. She graduated with a degree in accounting. She moved to Los Angeles, California and works at Wells Fargo Financial Bank.

Their next and third daughter, Sarah, was born in 1986 and lives in Oppelo with her parents and younger sister. Sarah graduated from Morrilton High School in the Spring of 2004. She is now a freshman at the University of Arkansas Community College of Morrilton. She wants to pursue a career in nursing.

The last of the four daughters is Hannah Wofford born in 1990. She attends Morrilton Middle School and is a member

of the Math Club, Science Club, Career Orientation Club and the National Junior Beta Club. Hannah enjoys playing golf and soccer. Every year Hannah attends Junior Golf Summer Program at Morrilton Country Club and has won Junior Club Champion in the girls division two times. I hope you enjoyed my family history.

YORK - Allison York is the daughter of Angie and her second husband Dr. Craig York. Allison was born in Little Rock, Arkansas on April 1, 1991. Allison's mother remarried to Dr. York when Allison was two years old. Allison and her family lived in Little Rock for four years, then they moved to Morrilton, Arkansas, where they live presently. She now attends Morrilton Middle School and is in the eighth grade. When Allison was eight years old, her half-brother Sam was born. Sam was born at the York's home in Morrilton, and is now 5 years old.

Angie York's maiden name is Clausen, like the pickles, Clausen Pickles. The Clausen's have six children including my mom. Most of the Clausen family lives in other places like, South Dakota and Arizona.

Craig York's family lives mostly in West Virginia and South Carolina. The York family only consists of four children. When Angie and Craig started dating, Craig's career was launching in Chiropractic care. Dr. York now has a business of his own in Morrilton and is becoming very successful. The York family also attends First United Methodist Church, where Allison will be going on a mission trip to Mexico with them this summer. The York family still lives happily in this small town of Morrilton and hopes to be in a generation sometime long from now!

ABEL – Konrad Ludwig Abel (b. 1729 in Wurtemburg, Germany) married Eva Regina Boson in 1749. Eva Boson (b. March 5, 1730 in Wurtemburg, Germany) was a daughter of Jacob and Eva Boson. Konrad and Eva immigrated to America and settled in Philadelphia, PA prior to December 1758. Eva died at Philadelphia on Dec. 19, 1758, three days after the birth of their last child, who died the day before his mother died. Konrad was a "dryer" by trade. He became a naturalized citizen in 1764. Konrad and Eva had eight children.

Ludwig Heinrich Abel (b. Sept. 9, 1752 in Wurtemburg, Germany) was the son of Konrad and Eva. He moved to Montgomery County, VA about 1773 and later moved to Wythe County, VA, where he acquired land. Ludwig married Elizabeth Wampler in 1774. Elizabeth (b. Aug. 12, 1752 in Lancaster County, PA) was daughter of Hans (John) Michael and Anna Elizabeth Wampler. Ludwig was a private in Capt. Bosseroa's Volunteers under General George Rogers Clark, 1778-79. Ludwig died March 10, 1801 in Wythe County. Elizabeth then married George Davis. She later moved to Roane County, TN. Ludwig and Elizabeth had at least 11 children.

Jonathan Abel (b. Feb. 2, 1783 in Wythe County, VA), son of Ludwig and Elizabeth, married Catherine Cleaver Jan. 12, 1809. Catherine, born between 1783-89, was a daughter of Frederick Cleaver. Jonathan, a farmer, moved his family to Greene County, TN prior to 1830. Catherine died between 1835-40 in Greene County. Jonathan died there between 1852-60. Jonathan and Catherine had at least nine children.

Joseph Abel (b. April 13, 1831 in Greene County, TN) was the son of Jonathan and Catherine. Joseph married Christina Kiesel Nov. 12, 1850 in Greene County. Christina (b. June 11, 1830 in Greene County) was the daughter of John Kiesel and Anna Headrick. Joseph moved his family to Keokuk County, IA prior to 1855. Joseph was a farmer. He died Aug. 11, 1894 at Ollie in Keokuk County. Christina died Jan. 25, 1918, in Prince Edward County, VA. They had at least 12 children.

Christopher Columbus Abel (b. Feb. 28, 1855, Keokuk County, IA), son of Joseph and Christina, married in 1878 to Elizabeth Emiline Kirby (b. Feb. 18, 1860 in Iowa, d. Nov. 7, 1934). Columbus was a farmer and killed when hit by a train while walking across the railroad track in Ollie on Christmas Day 1936. Their children (all born in Keokuk County) were:

1) Zina Abel (b. 1879, d. young).

2) Earl Abel (b. June 25, 1880, d. 1958).

3) James Marion Abel (b. Aug. 10, 1885, d. Jan. 1, 1970) md. Blanche Amelia Bush (dau. of Louis Edwin Bush and Anne Adamson). Children: Lewis, John, Hazel and Margaret Abel.

4) Merle H. Abel (b. Aug. 6, 1888, d. 1963).

5) Mary Myrtle Abel (b. June 28, 1893, d. Aug. 19, 1981) md. Earl Louis Bush (son of Louis Edwin Bush and Anne Adamson). Children: Leona, Edgar, Vera, Walter, Henry and Elizabeth "Betty" Bush (married Robert Wren and Willie Felkins).

6) Infant Abel (b&d. before 1899).

7) Elmer Baker Abel (b. Aug. 15, 1899, d. August 1965) md. Freda Locke, then Fern Locke.

ADAMSON – William Sheppard Adamson was born Feb. 16, 1838 in Ohio. Census records indicate his parents were born in Ohio. William married Rebecca A. Maiden prior to 1865. Rebecca Maiden (b. May 29, 1836 in Ohio) was one of at least 10 children born to William and Margaret Maiden.

The family appears on the 1870 Henry County, IA census. William was a farmer with real property valued at $1950. Living nearby was Rebecca's brother, Henry Maiden and his wife Margaret. Rebecca's parents lived a short distance away. William moved his family to Winfield, Henry County, IA prior to 1874. William and Rebecca had a child born in April 1874 in Winfield, Henry County. The infant died the same day and is buried in Winfield, Henry County, prob-

ably in the Winfield-Scott Cemetery. William moved his family to Louisa County, IA prior to 1880. William and his two sons farmed in Elm Grove Township. In 1900, William and Rebecca's daughter Ann (Adamson) Bush, with her husband and children, lived with William and Rebecca for a short time. William and Rebecca's son, John Adamson, and his family lived on the farm beside William's. William, his son and son-in-law all worked the land together. William died Feb. 19, 1908 at Winfield in Henry County. Rebecca died there on June 16, 1922. They are buried in Winfield-Scott Cemetery.

Children of William Adamson and Rebecca Maiden were:

1) Anne "Annie" H. Margaret Adamson (b. May 20, 1865, d. Jan. 2, 1927) md. Louis Edwin Bush. Children: Esther (md. Clyde Jones); Blanche (md. first, James Marion Abel and second, E.F. Rohren); Earl Louis Bush (md. Mary Myrtle Abel).

2) Grant Harrison Adamson (b. Sept. 8, 1867, d. Oct. 20, 1937) md. Amelia Ellen Webster. Children: Lloyd Earl, Lee Roy, William, Dewey, Iona, Cecil and John Adamson.

3) John William Adamson (b. May 12, 1870, d. Aug. 15, 1935) md. Rosa Anna Rahiller. Children: Edith, Vern, Walter, Flossie, Pearl, Lela and Viola Adamson.

4) Infant Adamson (b&d. April 1874).

A number of Adamson descendants settled in Conway County in the early to mid-1900s. Several descendants remain in the area today.

ALLEN – Drury McNairy "Mack" Allen came to Arkansas in 1867 after having served four years in Co. E., 35th Regiment of the Alabama Infantry. He was born May 27, 1840 in Madison County, AL, the son of Drury M. Allen and Martha "Patsy" Cabaness Allen. In 1872, he married Martha C. Huggins, the widow of Amos M. Johnson. She was born 1850 in Alabama, the daughter of Robert and Nancy Huggins. Martha had two daughters with Amos, Lilly and Allice. Drury and Martha had two daughters: 1) McWillie "Mackie" (b. Dec. 30, 1873, d. May 1, 1937 in Eugene, Lane County, OR) md. James Eli Thomas Lovett March 13, 1892 in Conway County. They had five sons: Charlie Allen, Walter Murphy, Dallas Wesley, William Bryan and Ernest Elmer. They also had two daughters who died as infants in Oklahoma. 2) Francis Catherine "Kate" (b. December 1876, d. bef. 1914). Martha died in 1876.

Drury M. Allen and unknown grandchildren. Circa 1910.

Drury married Sarah F. Carroll, widow of Thomas Yarborough, on Dec. 27, 1877 in Conway County. Sarah already had four sons: William Franklin, James Sidney, John B. and Thomas Lee. Sarah was born about 1840 in Georgia. Her parents are unknown. Drury and Sarah had three children:

1) Martha Ada (b. April 1879, d. bef. 1914).

2) Charles Carroll (b. Aug. 6, 1880, d. Aug. 28, 1949) is buried Walnut Lake Cemetery, Dumas, AR. On July 20, 1913 he married Betsy Dortch, daughter of William F. Dortch and Ara Savannah Carroll Dortch. She was born March 17, 1891, died Jan. 17, 1964 and is buried at Ada Valley Cemetery beside her second husband, Oscar Camp. Charlie and Betsy had nine children: Charles Vernon, Ada, Oletha, Nina Estelle, O.C., Emma Lee, Lucille, Billy Earl and Betty Jewel.

3) Walter Cabaness (b. June 9, 1883, d. March 26, 1952) is buried at Ada Valley Cemetery along with his wife Mattie Porter whom he married Dec. 3, 1905 at Morrilton. Mattie (b. Jan. 20, 1887, d. April 29, 1973) was a daughter of John Jacob Porter and Anna Josephine King Porter. They had 10 children: Ruby

Berniece, Charles Edgar, Walter Basil, John Carroll, Luther McNarry, Opal Irene, James Hamilton, Anni Monteen, James Ervin and Minnie Viola. Sarah died in 1886 and was buried at Barnes Cemetery.

On July 11, 1889, Drury married his third wi Mrs. Mary H. Morris, in Perry County. He continue to live in Higgins Township in Conway County. He was a farmer and justice of the peace. Mary died sometime before the 1900 census and Drury died Jan. 24, 1918 from influenza and was buried at Ada Valley Cemetery. Charlie and Walter moved their families to Desha County in 1930, where they continued to farm for the remainder of their lives. *Submitted by Mary Allen Brown.*

ALLEN - Pinkney Allen and Susannah Bryant filed for their marriage license Dec. 18, 1873 and were married the next day Dec. 19, 1873. They were married in Winchester, TN. Susannah was born in Tennessee May 28, 1856 to Alexander John Bryant of Virginia, and Susannah Phillips Bryant of North Carolina. There is no information on Pinkney Allen. Pinkney and Susannah Allen had two children while living in Tennessee, Hattie Allen (b. June 1876) and Sam Houston Allen (b. Oct. 15, 1878).

Sam and Georgia Allen with eight of their children. Standing in back row: Jewell, Hiram, Ruby, Fay; front row: Romie, Georgia holding Mary, Sam holding son Sam, Ila and Allen.

Pinkney and Susannah with their two children soon moved to Conway County. By the year 1882, Pinkney said he had a toothache and was going to Little Rock to see a dentist. He was never seen again. It has been said he had taken all their gold with him, and it is unknown if he met up with foul play or left on his own accord. Susannah, now left alone at the age of 26 with two small children, married Thomas Dunlap on April 18, 1882.

Susannah and Thomas Dunlap had five children: Agnes, Thomas, Susanna, John and Emma Faye. When Thomas Dunlap died, Susannah married J.W. "Dutch" Spires. They made Cedar Creek their home in Conway County.

Pinkney and Susannah Allen's son, Sam Houston Allen, married Georgia Ann Brinkley May 25, 1896. She was born March 4, 1877, daughter of Alexander Brinkley and Nancy Jones Brinkley, who also had a son John Harrien Brinkley. Sam and Georgia Allen made Lick Mountain their home along with 10 children. Georgia died Aug. 26, 1916 at the age of 39. Sam and Georgia Allen's children are:

1) Eugene (b. May 27, 1897, d. Jan. 13, 1987) md. Mae Green. Their children are Vivian, Sally, Betty and Jack.

2) Robert (b. April 18, 1899, d. Jan. 1, 1929) md. Victoria Abbott who died of swamp fever in April 1928, leaving five young children: Monteen, Arthareen, Aubrey, Calvin and Royce. Royce married Marion Smith Oct. 15, 1948. Royce and Marion's children are Vicky, Kathleen, James, Kenneth, Rebecca, William and Paula. Robert could have been a great baseball player, but Victoria wouldn't hear of it.

3) Hiram (b. April 8, 1901, d. June 27, 1956) was the father of Mary, Johnny, Flora and Teddy.

4) Jewell (b. May 15, 1904, d. April 12, 1980) md. Erma Gwin of Morrilton. Their children are Ermaon Allen, Dorothy Marleen, James Loloan and

Howard Reed. Dorothy Gwin married Donald Benafield and their children are Donald Gwin, John Dwight, Michael Duane and Susan Lavonne.

5) Ruby (b. June 6, 1906, d. March 9, 1997) md. Alvin McCowan and had nine children: Robert, James, Paul, Jerry, Danny, Bill, Cloteen, Sylvia and Larry.

6) Fay (b. March 5, 1908, d. March 9, 1997) md. Donia Schuler. Their two children are Fay Jr., who had twin daughters, Karen and Beth, and Betty, who married Al Brandt and had one son Michael.

7) Ila (b. May 6, 1910, d. 1974) md. Floyd Carrol. They had three children: Georgia (died at birth), Bobby Gene and John Gary.

8) Romie (b. Jan. 6, 1912, d. May 11, 1985) md. Carrie Green and had two children, Georgia Ann and Romie Darrell.

9) Sam (b. Oct. 28, 1914, d. Sept. 20, 1985) md. Mary Thompson Aug. 4, 1951. They had six children: (a) Samuel Wade married Donna Efird and had two children: Matthew and Mary Jeannine (died as a baby). Matthew Allen married Becky King and their children are Emilea and Zackary Samuel Allen. They all live in Rapid City, SD. (b) John Jacob Allen of Texarkana, TX, whose stepsons are Jeremy, Josh and Jordan Sutton. (c) Thomas Richard Allen married Katrina Clark of Morrilton. Their children are Hannah and Abbey Allen. All live in North Little Rock, AR. (d) Rebecca Amanda "Mandy" Allen Hall married Carl Hall and their children are Beth Suzanna (md. Eric McKinnon) and Christopher Allen Hall. All are from Benton, AR. (e) Bonnie Laurie Allen Patterson married B.J. Patterson of Little Rock. His children are Debbie Munn, Kim Weidower, Bobby Patterson Jr., Amanda and Amy Patterson. (f) David Joseph, who died at birth.

10) Mary Volage (b. Nov. 25, 1915, d. 1999) md. Remmel Cody and had two children, Marilyn and Gayle. She then married Andy Fowler and had one daughter, Andrea.

When Georgia Allen died, Sam Houston Allen married Nethie Harris of Solgohacvhia on Feb. 25, 1917. Nethie was a widow with two children, Jessie and Lorene. Nethie and Sam had three children together: Opal Lee, Edna and Sam Houston, who died of water on the brain. It was said he was so smart, his head was too big! Sam Houston Allen was a farmer all his life. He grew the tobacco he smoked and drank his own brew. He never owned a fell team. He had only one horse and one mule. Sam didn't have much to say, but when he did, it was funny. In his later years he lived in Oppelo and died Oct. 30, 1948. Sam Houston Allen left behind a large and loving family. *Submitted by Bonnie Laurie Allen Patterson.*

ALLEN - Roy Edward Allen (b. Dec. 29, 1918 in Statesboro, GA) was a son of Rufus Green Allen and

Roy Edward Allen, taken ca. 1940/1941.

Sallie Mae Cason. Rufus Green Allen, after the death of his first wife, married Vera Surrency. Roy Allen enlisted in 1939 in the US Army, serving during WWII in Hawaii, Philippines, Okinawa and Guam before the war ended. Mr. Allen reached the rank of tech sergeant E-6 and was a tank commander. After the war he worked for awhile at Fort Jackson, SC as a light weapons repairman.

In 1947 he married Barbara June Wilkinson (b. July 14, 1925 in Lawety, FL), daughter of Forrest Delmar Wilkinson and Lille Griffis. To Roy and Barbara were born three sons: Lester Earl "Smokey," Robert "Bobby" Edward and Richard Green Allen. Roy and Barbara came to Arkansas seeking property and landed in Morrilton. They bought property in Ada Valley where Roy farmed and had a milking operation until Barbara came down with tick fever, then moved to Doctor Hardison's old home place on Petit Jean Mountain. Roy decided to return to his trade of construction and masonry work for many years. In the 70s Roy Allen was called to the ministry and preached for many years. In 1992 Roy Allen developed lymphoma and passed away on Oct. 27, 1997, at McClelland Veteran's Hospital in Little Rock. He was buried near his son, Robert Edward Allen, on Petit Jean Mountain Cemetery.

Lester Allen, ca. 1966.

Lester Allen joined the US Army, April 23, 1965 and remained in the military service until retiring Nov. 30, 1985. He married Anna Elizabeth Ruf, born April 15, 1926, who was widowed and had three sons: Reinhardt, Dietman Podolski and Jurgen Ruf. Jurgen passed away in 1991 at Norfolk, VA. He was cremated and his ashes were interred in Petit Jean Cemetery. Anna Elizabeth Allen was the daughter of Anton Ruf and Centha Renzhofer, of Wettenhausen, Germany. Mr. Ruf had a total of six daughters and no sons.

Lester, while in the service, received his bachelor's degree in history from the University of Maryland. After retirement Lester attended Petit Jean Vocational Technical School two certificate one in horticulture and landscaping and the other in marketing and management. In 1993 he returned to Arkansas Technological University and received a second bachelor's degree in German language. Lester spent four tours in Germany and one in Vietnam. Lester is currently serving as Commander of American Legion Post 39 and also serves as quartermaster/adjutant of VFW Post 4453. Lester is a life member of the Disabled American Veterans.

Robert Edward "Bobby" was injured in a car accident in May 1966, just before graduation from Morrilton High School, and passed away at Old Saint Anthony's Hospital in September 1966. Richard Green Allen graduated from Morrilton High School in 1967, and went to Arkansas Tech. University and graduated with a bachelor's degree in English. Richard went on to Tulsa and received his master's degree. Richard, while in Tulsa, operated his own business in the construction industry for several years. Richard decided to go back to school and received his doctor's degree in Osteopathic Medicine. Richard presently lives and works in Wagoner, OK. *Submitted by Lester E. Allen.*

ANDERSON – In the 1880 census of Bentley Township in Conway County, my great-grandfather Harry Anderson was listed as 31 years of age. He was born in 1849 and was from Denmark. His mother and father were also from Denmark.

Harry married Miss Phebe E. Louisa Sims on June 6, 1881. She was born March 11, 1864 and was orphaned. Harry and Phebe had two children. John Anderson was born

William Henry Anderson

February 1883 and died of a bleeding ulcer. William Henry Anderson, my grandfather, was born March 8, 1885 and died July 16, 1967. After Henry died, Phebe met and married Ulysses Hack and they had three children: Rosa, Katie. and Leslie.

William Henry Anderson, my grandfather, married Syble Rorie on Dec. 8, 1917. Syble died March 9, 1928. They had five children:
1) William Henry Anderson Jr. (b. July 31, 1921,

d. March 17, 1986) md. Miss Imo Ethel Payne on March 29, 1941. They had four children: (1) William David Earl (b. Jan. 14, 1942) md. Roberta Bingham (b. July 4, 1939) on Dec. 24, 1961. They have three children: Lex, Sonya and Jon Paul. (2) Henry Gene (b. July 17, 1943, d. April 16, 1992) md. Barbara Ann Mosely. They had two children, Victor and Victoria. Henry Gene then married Carol Cody Jan. 31, 1975 and they had two children, Jamie Carol and Shannon Dale. (3) Patricia Jeanette (b. Aug. 8, 1945, d. Dec. 1, 2003) was married three times: (1st) Jackie Boyd, no children; (2nd) Gene Potts, two children, Kim and Michael Potts; (3rd) Johnny Strassle, one child, Melissa Strassle. (4) Barbara June (b. July 9, 1951) md. Delbert Vales (b. Sept. 17, 1967) and they have two children, Candy and Mark.

2) Vernon Leon Anderson (b. Oct. 23, 1923, d. May 27, 2002) md. Ila Mae Yarbrough Feb. 1, 1949 and they had three children: Terry, Danny and Donald. Ila died July 28, 2002.

3) Geneva Anderson (b. July 12, 1925).

4-5) Twins, Millard and Mildred (b. July 12, 1925).

When Syble died, William Henry Anderson married again April 19, 1929 to Miss Estella Lusas. Estella (b. Aug. 12, 1911, d. Sept. 13, 1993) and William lived at Ada Valley and had seven children: Monteen (b. April 29, 1929, d. Feb. 8, 1995); Ulion (b. Jan. 12, 1933); Charles (b. Sept. 3, 1935, d. Sept. 9, 1996); Shirl (b. Oct. 24, 1938); James Edward (b. Oct. 10, 1941); Floyd Allen (b. Aug. 29, 1943, d. March 20, 2004); William Earl (b. Dec. 6, 1950). *Submitted by David Anderson.*

ANDERSON – My great-grandfather, Commodore Perry, was born around 1854 in Ohio or Pennsylvania, (parents currently unknown) and married Elizabeth "Susie" (Stone) ca. 1876. Susie (b. ca. 1855) was a daughter of Tolliver Stone (b. ca. 1829 in Wayne County, IL) and Elizabeth Horn.

Susie birthed 10 children in 19 years, dying of a lung condition in 1895, the year their last child, Franklin, was born. There is a beautiful stone on her grave that Perry made for her. Perry died in 1912 in Arkansas and is beside Susie in the Dewey Cemetery in Elizabeth, Fulton County, AR.

Back row (l-r): Columbus H. Flowers, Clara (Anderson) Flowers, Oda Flowers, Bytha Flowers. Front row (l-r): Joseph and Edmond Flowers. Picture taken in mid to late 1920s.

Their children are:
Eddie Tolliver (b. ca. 1877) md. Minnie Wheat. Family legend indicates he died after they moved to Oregon.

Sarah Rosetta (b. ca. 1880, d. 1965, Beedeville, Jackson County, AR) md. Cyrus Columbus Reynolds in 1901.

Perry Walter (b. ca. 1882 maybe in Missouri, d. 1956 in Conway County, bur. in Grandview Cemetery). His first wife is unknown at present. Second wife was Ider Maybelle Wagley (b. Nov. 10, 1884, d. Nov. 23, 1958, bur. in Sunnyside Cemetery), daughter of James Wagley and Josephine White.

My grandmother, Drucilla Claretta, was named Drucila for her maternal aunt and called Clara, was born around 1895. She married Columbus "Hoop"

Henderson Flowers in Conway County around 1905. His parents were Henry Edmond and Elizabeth Janie (Sweeden) Flowers of Conway County. They are the parents of my father, Edmond Columbus Flowers (b. 1914 in Conway County). Clara was in Conway County living and working for a Hill family when he met Grandpa Hoop. All of her young siblings followed her there. Clara died in 1939 at Olyphant, Jackson County and is buried at Coffeyville Cemetery, Jackson County.

Joseph (b. ca. 1890 in Baxter County, AR) md. Tennie B. Grayson (b. June 1, 1895 in Arkansas, d. Feb. 1, 1975 in Morrilton, Conway County), daughter of Robert Grayson and Bettie Wilson. They had a daughter named Bertha (b. ca. 1926) who married Arlie Williams Sr. She lives in Bird Township. Joseph was a farmer, died in 1938 and is buried in Sunnyside Cemetery. Tennie is buried at Grandview Cemetery.

Nancy Ann, twin of Joseph and called "Annie," was born about 1890. She married a Mr. Clowers and had two children, Delmas and Elsie.

Ada Mae (b. ca. 1891) had a daughter named Alpha. Ada married a Mr. Womack and had Bill, Rena and Robert.

Fannie Bell (b. ca. 1895) md. Oscar Ferrel in 1912. They had a son Clifton and a set of twins. Fannie died in 1914, the same year the twins were born.

Franklin was born in 1895, the same year his mom died, and disappeared ca. 1911 at age 16.

After Susie's death, Perry remarried in 1896 to Zula Womack in Fulton County and had three or four more children. *Submitted by their great-granddaughter, Carolyn Flowers Tucker.*

ANDERSON - Zula (Womack) Anderson married Commodore Perry Anderson in 1896. Zula may be the daughter of Tennessee born parents, Isom and Elizabeth Womack. Isom was born ca. 1853 and Elizabeth was born ca. 1862. In the 1920 Conway County Census, the children of Perry and Zula were with Isom and Elizabeth in Bird Township.

There is some confusion about their children - I have them as Alta (b. ca. 1899); Odie (b. ca. 1905); and William Otto (b. ca. 1907). Odie used to visit my parents, Edmond and Mildred Flowers, often in the 1970s in Newport, Jackson County, AR. If memory serves, he was a minister and lived with his wife in Missouri. William Otto married Avis Katherine Hawkins and they have a daughter Mary Pearl. *Submitted by their great-granddaughter, Carolyn Flowers Tucker.*

ANDREWS – Newton Floyd Andrews (b. January 1858 in Fayette County, AL) was the son of William and Elizabeth Jane Simmons Andrews. Newton lived in Fayette County until 1867 when he and his family moved to Conway County, AR. He was married twice. His first marriage was to Margaret Ellen Williams on Oct. 21, 1875. Ellen was the daughter of George W. and Alosia E. Prince Williams. Their marriage produced three children. (1) William Jasper Andrews (b. Dec. 10, 1877) md. Ida Belle Barnes. He died June 4, 1869 and was buried in the Old Salem Cemetery. (2) Lavinia Andrews (b. 1879, d. after 1963, bur. Atkins

Elva E. Andrews and Family–Anadarko, Oklahoma. First row: Elva (sitting), Maxine, Rhoda (sitting), Melvin Andrews. Back row: Calvin, William, Roy, Barney, Nute, Ruby, Rosie, Thomas Andrews.

Cemetery) md. Robert S. Reid. (3) James Andrews (b. Aug. 9, 1883, d. Jan. 27, 1964, bur. Old Liberty Cemetery) md. Mintie Scroggins.

Margaret Ellen Williams Andrews died in 1883 and Newton married Letha Frances Wallace Sept. 27, 1884. Letha was the daughter of Levi W. and Sena Anne Wells Wallace. Newton and Letha lived on their farm at Hattieville, ARK until their deaths. Newton died in 1916 and Letha died in 1940. They are buried in the Wallace Wells Cemetery, located on Levi Wallace's old homestead at Hattieville. Their union produced the following children:

First row: Newton Andrews, Letha Wallace Andrews. Back row: Hava Andrews, Novel Andrews, Dora Andrews - 1910.

Elva Eli Andrews (b. Nov. 15, 1886, d. Nov. 4, 1973 at Anadarko, OK) md. Rhoda Harris; Levi Andrews (b. 1886) md. Rosa Pierson; Martha Ellen Andrews (b. Dec. 8, 1892, d. Jan. 27, 1970, bur. Lost Corner Cemetery) first married Henry Harris Chambers, then N.A. Nicholson.; Elza Andrews (b. 1898, d. Dec. 17, 1973, bur. Rosemont Cemetery, Benton, AR) first married Zula Dunn, then married Effie Dutton; Novel O. Andrews (b. Nov. 23, 1901, d. Jan. 28, 1979, bur. Elm Wood Cemetery) md. Minnie Pierce; Dora Andrews (b. Jan. 30, 1903, d. March 15, 2002, bur. Vincent Chapel Cemetery) md. Edward O'Brien; Hava R. Andrews (b. Oct. 8, 1905, d. Nov. 11, 1986, bur. Vincent Chapel Cemetery) first married Rena Nicholson, then Elzada Pierson; Frances Andrews (b. 1895, d. March 15, 1918) md. Matthew Franklin; Taffy Andrews (b. March 1909, d. March 2, 1915, bur. Wallace Wells Cemetery). *Submitted by Maxine Redin.*

ANDREWS – Oscar "Floyd" Andrews and Lucy Maunita Ridling were married Oct. 10, 1939 in Conway County at the home of E.M. Harrington, JP. They lived for a while on Hwy. 95 about halfway between Morrilton and St. Vincent. Four children were born between 1940-46. They left Conway County in late 1948 and eventually settled in North Little Rock, Pulaski County. Three more children were born between 1949-55. Lucy died in 1982 and Floyd in 1997. They are buried at Arkansas Memorial Garden in North Little Rock.

Lucy (b. 1921 at Solgohachia) was a daughter of Henry "Lee" Ridling and Pitha "Jane" Lilly. Lucy's great-grandparents, Moses Franklin Ridling and Sarah Rogers, were married Nov. 21, 1822 in Jackson County, GA. They began their journey westward shortly after 1846. In 1850, they were living in Cherokee County, AL. They moved on to Mississippi for a short time and arrived in Arkansas in 1854. In 1860, they were living in Ouachita County. Shortly after the Civil War, they settled in Conway County and were among the first settlers at Lone Grove. Their son, Rev. Henry C. Ridling, gave Lone Grove its name.

The first burial at Lone Grove Cemetery in about 1876 was one of their great-grandchildren. Several generations of the Ridling family are buried there. Moses and Sarah's youngest son, Moses Jr., known as Frank Ridling and born 1837, enlisted in the Civil War on Sept. 14, 1861 at Camden and fought at Murfreesboro, TN. Between 1860 and 1863, he married Melissa Brazzell (b. 1873 in Sumner County, TN). Six children were born between 1864 and 1877. The three oldest children were born in Kentucky. In 1870, they were residing in Christian County, KY. They settled in Conway County before April 1873. Their oldest son, Lee Ridling, and Jane Lilly were married between 1915 and 1919. Jane (b. 1885 at Springfield) was the daughter of Henry "Sampson" Lilly and Mary Ann Ward. Her paternal grandparents were Robert

Sampson Lilly and Martha Patricia Summers. Maternal grandparents were Claiborn Ward and Martha Cargile. Sampson Lilly enlisted in the Civil War at Springfield. He fought at Port Hudson, LA. Sampson and Mary Lilly are buried near Springfield on property that once belonged to the family.

Floyd (b. 1922 at Hattieville) was a son of Elza Floyd Andrews and "Effie" Eva Evalee Dutton. Elza (b. 1898) and Effie (b. 1901) were married Aug. 17, 1918 at Center Ridge. They are buried at Rosemont Cemetery at Benton. Floyd's paternal grandparents were Newton Floyd Andrews and Letha Frances Wallace. They are buried at Wallace Wells Cemetery. His maternal grandparents were Wiley M. Dutton and Florence Catlin. Wiley was the youngest son of Wiley J. Dutton and Evaline Rose. Wiley and Evaline came from Franklin County, TN in late 1849 or early 1850 and settled on Dutton Mountain. Wiley M. Dutton and his parents are buried at Middleton County. Florence is buried in Oklahoma. *Submitted by Kathy Andrews.*

ANDREWS – Roland Andrews (b. 1802 in Laurens County, SC) was the son of Howell and Mary Andrews of Virginia. Howell Andrews' great-grandfather, Thomas Andrews (b. 1663 in England), arrived in the Colony of Virginia on the ship *Richard and Elizabeth* in 1685. Roland was a farmer and migrated to Monroe County, MS with his family in the 1820s. He married Matilda Maddox in Monroe County, MS on Dec. 15, 1823. Roland, his family and his parents were living in Tuscaloosa County, AL in 1830.

Matilda (b. 1810 in Tennessee) is thought to be the daughter of William Maddox and had at least six children, but only three are known. Ezekiel (b. 1824 in Monroe County, MS), her first son; Mary Jane Adeline Andrews (b. 1825, in Mississippi); William Roland Andrews (b. 1835 in Alabama). According to census records three other children were born to the couple, two females and one male, but their names are unknown.

Roland was living in Fayette County, AL on a 120-acre homestead in 1867 when he decided to move to Conway County, AR. Roland, his sons, Ezekiel and William, and his daughter, Mary, who had married Amos Roberts, moved to Conway County with several other Fayette County, AL families who were trying to make a new start after the Civil War.

Matilda Maddox Andrews died in 1869 from an asthma attack, shortly after her arrival in Conway County. Roland took a second wife, Julia B. Prince, in 1872. It is unknown when Roland died or where he and Matilda Maddox Andrews are buried. *Submitted by Dee Andrews.*

ANDREWS – Thomas Andrews (b. 1663 in England) emigrated to Virginia from England Jan. 25, 1685 aboard the ship, *Richard and Elizabeth*. He settled in the Curles Neck area, 15 miles southeast of Richmond. He was issued a land grant for 396 acres on Oct. 20, 1704 for paying for the passage of eight immigrants to the colonies. The name of Thomas' wife was unknown. Children known to have been born to this union were: Thomas Jr. (b. 1686); William (b. 1688) md. Avis; John (b. 1698) md. Elizabeth; Benjamin (b. 1690); Richard (b. 1700) md. Mary; Donna-Donivant (b. 1692); and Anne, who married Benjamin Granger. Thomas' children are registered in the Bristol Parish Register of Henrico County, VA. Henrico County Colonial records contain deed and will records of Thomas. He died April 21, 1731.

William Andrews (b. 1693 in Henrico County, VA) md. a woman named Avis, probably in Dinwiddie County, VA. He died there May 22, 1770. Children born to this union were: Ephraim (b. March 2, 1721) md. Ann; George (b. Jan. 14, 1723) md. Mary Walker; Winnifred (b. June 1, 1724) md. John Granger; William (b. ca. 1725) md. Anne Vodin; Avis (b. July 7, 1727); John (b. July 7, 1729); Lucianna (b. Sept. 7, 1731); Mark (b. 1733) md. Winnifred Lyell; Abraham (b. ca. 1735) md. Anne; Thomas (b. ca. 1740) md.

Francis; and Roland or Richard who was born between 1735-45.

Thomas Andrews (b. ca. 1740 in Mecklenburg County, VA) md. a woman named Frances (maiden name unknown). Thomas sold the land he inherited from his father, William, in 1779 and moved to Lancaster County, SC where he died in 1783. The names of Thomas' children are unknown. It is thought these are their five sons: Rowland, Howell, Exechial S., Terrell and John. Roland died in South Carolina. In 1819 Howell, Exechial, Terrell and John Andrews moved to Tuscaloosa County, AL and died there.

Howell Andrews (b. ca. 1771 in Mecklenburg County, VA) md. a woman named Mary (b. 1777 in Virginia). Her maiden name is unknown. Howell died in Tuscaloosa County, AL in 1839 and Mary died in Fayette County, AL after the 1860 census was taken. Children born to Howell and Mary Andrews were: Sara Anne (b. July 9, 1794) md. Abraham Howell; Elizabeth (b. 1796-1798) md. William J. Bryant; unknown female; Roland (b. 1802 in South Carolina) md. Matilda Maddox Dec. 15, 1823 in Monroe County, MS; Nancy; unknown female; Frances; Daniel (b. 1809); John William (b. 1816); Franklin (b. December 1811) md. 1st, Mittie Winters and 2nd, Sarah Winters.

Known children born to Roland and Matilda were: Ezechial (b. 1824 in Monroe County, MS) md. Sarah J. in Alabama and died after 1870 in Arkansas or Oklahoma; Mary Jane Adeline (b. 1825 in Monroe County, MS, d. 1907 in Pontotoc, OK) md. Amos Pleasant Roberts in Alabama; William Roland (b. 1835 in Tuscaloosa County, AL) md. Elizabeth "Louisa" Jane Simmons. Roland and Matilda migrated to Conway County, AR from Fayette County, AL in 1867 after the Civil War.

ANDREWS – William Roland Andrews (b. 1835 in Fayette County, AL) was the son of Roland and Matilda Maddox Andrews. William married Elizabeth "Louisa" Jane Simmons on Nov. 8, 1851 in Tuscaloosa County, AL. William and his family moved to Conway County, AR in 1867. He settled at Lick Mountain and was listed on the 1870 census of Conway County as living in Lick Mountain Township. It is unknown when William and Louisa died or their place of burial. They are not listed on the 1880 census of Conway County.

Letha F. Wallace Andrews and daughter, Martha Andrews Chambers–1930.

William and Louisa had the following children:
John Roland Andrews (b. 1854 in Alabama) first married Mary Williams and later married Mary Conley.

James H. Andrews (b. 1856 in Alabama) md. Jane Elizabeth Holbrook. He died in 1914 and is buried in the Roberts Cemetery near Jerusalem, AR.

Newton Floyd Andrews (b. 1857 in Alabama) first married Margaret E. Williams, then married Letha Frances Wallace. He died 1916 and is buried in Wallace Wells Cemetery.

Sarah Jane Andrews (b. 1858) md. Mitchell Macy.

Matilda Adeline Andrews (b. 1859 in Alabama) md. William Watkins. She died in 1899 and is buried in Bolton Cemetery near Hattieville, AR.

Sarah Andrews (b. 1860 in Alabama) may have married G.M. Hinkle.

William Roland Andrews (b. 1862 in Alabama)

md. Joanna Wade. He died 1917 in Franklin County, AR.

Charles M. Andrews (b. 1864 in Alabama) first married Rutha Jones, then married Sena Idora Wallace.

Daniel Andrews (b. 1867) first married Manda Ragsdale Harris, then Rosa Harris. He died 1917 in Coweta, OK.

Miranda Andrews (b. 1874 in Conway County) md. William Jackson Kyle. She died 1905 at Citra, OK.

Melinda Andrews (b. 1869 in Conway County, d. May 1870, in Conway County, AR). *Submitted by Delena Bradford Watkins.*

ARNN – Abihu Arnn (b. Sept. 23, 1807 in Pittsylvania County, VA) was one of 11 children of George Washington Aaron (b. ca. 1772 in Virginia, d. July 11, 1855 in Henry County, TN) and Sarah Walker (b. ca. 1784, d. June 21, 1849), who were married Dec. 10, 1797.

Abihu's grandfather was Abraham Aaron (b. ca. 1734 in Lancaster County, PA) who moved to Virginia about 1771. Abraham provided aid during the Revolutionary

Abihu Arnn

War by providing beef for the Virginia militia in 1777. Various spellings of this family name are Aaron, Aron and Arnn. On Oct. 26, 1829 in Pittsylvania County, VA, Abihu married Margaret R. Blair (b. April 24, 1811), a daughter of Samuel Blair and Mary "Polly" Reynolds, all of Pittsylvania County VA. Shortly after their marriage they moved to Henry County, TN where their seven children were born. The 1850 census lists him as a tinner.

In 1853 they all moved to Conway County, AR. The 1860 census lists them as living in Griffin Township where he is a painter and tinner. The 1880 census lists him as a tinner living in Gregory Township. Abihu died Feb. 24, 1893 and his wife Margaret died Nov. 9, 1875. She is buried at Mt. Vernon Cemetery and it is thought he is also buried there.

Their children are Mary Ann (b. Nov. 11, 1831, d. Jan. 30, 1884) md. John Houston March 6, 1856; George Samuel (b. July 25, 1834, d. July 4, 1863) md. Synthy Ann Jones Sept. 27, 1858; Francis Alabama (b. Oct. 23, 1836, d. Jan. 11, 1906) md. (1) Richard C. Griffin Sept. 3, 1854 (2) Gregory Hawkins (3) W.R. Welch and (4) D.M. Morning; James Wilson (b. Dec. 20, 1838, d. Nov. 22, 1886) md. Sarah Wyatt Aug. 16, 1860; Sarah Elizabeth (b. May 30, 1841, d. Sept. 9, 1867) md. William S. Jones March 8, 1866; Edward McBride "Mack" (b. Jan. 21, 1849, d. Oct. 5, 1884) md. Martha "Mattie" Washington Stepp Dec. 20, 1874; John Henry (b. June 12, 1852, d. Dec. 7, 1930) md. Anna J. Arnn June 30, 1889.

George Samuel and James Wilson served in the Confederacy as privates with the 36th Arkansas Infantry, Company C, Arkansas Cavalry.

Martha Stepp, wife of "Mack" Arnn was born Oct. 19, 1856 to William W. Stepp and Clarissa Pew. William W. Stepp died of measles at Corinth, MS while serving in the Confederate Army (Company C, Arkansas Cavalry). "Mack" and Martha had five children before he died in 1884 at age 35. The 1880 census lists his occupation as undertaker.

Their children are Roxanna (b. Nov. 2, 1875, d. Nov. 21, 1934) md. Joe Williams in 1902; Henrietta "Etta" (b. Sept. 12 1877, d. May 5, 1967) md. Edward Payson Cunningham Feb. 5, 1905; Thomas (b. Dec. 3, 1879, d. Aug. 13, 1880); Wilma Myrtle (b. Oct. 27, 1881, d. Nov. 10, 1965) md. first, William H. Stout in 1909 and second, Edward L. Schrimscher; Alabama (b. Nov. 4, 1883, d. Dec. 16, 1884). All of this family except Roxanna and Henrietta are buried in Atkins City Cemetery. Roxanna and Joe are buried in Old Hickory Cemetery, as is James Williams, and Henrietta is bur-

ied in National Memorial Cemetery, Falls Church, VA.

On Oct. 3, 1886 Martha Stepp Arnn married her second husband, James Madison Williams. Their five children are Dinkie Lou (b. Dec. 25, 1887, d. Jan. 9, 1974) md. Alvie Barton Tate; Dorothy "Dottie" (b. March 11, 1891, d. Aug. 26, 1958) md. Elijah C. Palmer; James Forrest (b. Aug. 26, 1893, d. Nov. 8, 1968) md. Lela Tucker; Clara Louise (b. Sept. 21, 1895, d. Aug. 9, 1989) md. Edward Teeter; baby brother (b. April 4, 1898). Martha died Jan. 26, 1948.

Henrietta Arnn and Edward Cunningham were both living in Hattieville, Conway County, at the time of their marriage in Pope County. As soon as their first child was born, they took the train to northeast Oklahoma, which at that time was Indian Territory of the Cherokee Nation, where they raised four children: Edward Perry (b. Dec. 24, 1905, d. Oct. 25, 1989) married Elma Lou Kitchen, Sept. 1, 1934; Forrest Truesdell (b. June 8, 1908, d. Sept. 5, 1964) md. Ruby Fay Fain May 18, 1934; Harry Howard (b. April 10, 1911, d. March 18, 1996) md. Thelma Rountree April 1935; and Warden Young (b. Nov. 1, 1912, d. June 8, 1971). Henrietta and Edward have eight grandchildren, 13 great-grandchildren and 14 great-great-grandchildren. *Submitted by Maridell Cunningham Loomis.*

ASHCRAFT - Byron Ashcraft was born Sept. 3, 1880, son of William Columbus Ashcraft and his wife and cousin, Nancy Jane Ashcraft, born 1848. Byron married Cornelia Huggins (b. June 6, 1889 in Carden Bottoms), daughter of Abraham Lincoln Huggins and Frances Olivia Rook.

Byron descends from a long line of Ashcraft back to John Ashcraft (b. ca. 1737 in Orange County, NC). He married first Mary Brown, daughter of John Brown, and second Rebecca __. Byron and Cordelia Huggins Ashcraft's children are Ernest (b. Dec. 3, 1906, Rose Creek, Perry County, d. June 9, 1908); Thelma Leon "Tom" (b. Nov. 11, 1909, Perry County) md. Elizabeth Sikes; Thurman Frank (b. Oct. 16, 1912) md. Louise Williams; Anna Drucilla (b. Feb. 20, 1914, Rose Creek, Perry County) md. Wm. Edward Haynes; Alpha Lorene (b. Nov. 11, 1918, Rose Creek, Perry County) md. Don Barclay; Alma Joe (b. Aug. 10, 1922, Casa, AR).

Cousin Michele Barclay Coffman wrote and I quote: "Cornelia Huggins and Byron Ashcraft were married in 1904, she was 15 and he was 24. Byron farmed in Rose Creek, Perry County on 88 acres of land planted in vegetables. Byron was later a justice of peace in Conway County, and it is said married couples from atop a horse."

"Ann was six when the family moved to Bigelow (1920) and was 12 years old when the family moved to Little Rock (1926)."

On April 23, 1940 Cordelia Huggins Ashcraft suffered a stroke. She is buried In Martin Cemetery in Mablevale, AR beside Byron who died Feb. 13, 1972. *Submitted by F.H. Huggins.*

ASHCRAFT - Leonard Ashcraft (b. ca. 1872, d. 1960) was a son of William Columbus Ashcraft and his wife, Nancy Jane Ashcraft. Leonard married Mahala Josephine Story (b. ca. 1871, d. 1923), daughter of James Story and Mahala E. Jones. Leonard married second, Minnie Van Diver.

Ashcraft homestead in Ada Valley, Conway County, AR. All of John Leonard's children were born here.

Children born to John Leonard Ashcraft and Mahala Josephine Story are (1) Willie (md. Pinnie Lewis); Cappie (md. Jody Jones); (2) Johnnie (b. 1898, d. February 1988); (3) Mary (d. February 1988) md. Mr. Fuqua; (4) Ethel (md. Homer Freeman); (5) Elbert Martin (md. Lilly Montgomery); (6) Minnie (b. April 1894) md. Will Holderfield; (7) Irene (b. April 13, 1911) md. Mr. Newkirk; (8) Annie Lucille (b. 1913, d. 1990) married first, Leo Huett and second, J. Richie. Children: Mary Louise (b. 1936) md. Billy Jack Kelly, Betty Joe (b. 1938) md. Fred Meeks, Jimmie Lee (b. 1940) md. Mitzie Kay Mosely; (9) Lottie Estell (b. 1915) married first, Carl Franklin Ashcraft and second, Mr. Patterson. Children: Lee and Jessee.

According to the obituary of John Leonard Ashcraft, he was a farmer and carpenter. He was survived by his wife, Minnie, and his children as named. He was also survived by two brothers, Byron Ashcraft and Eugene Ashcraft, both of Little Rock. John had 33 grandchildren, 61 great grandchildren and three great great grandchildren.

John Leonard Ashcraft died Feb. 16, 1960 and was buried in the Pettit Jean Mountain Cemetery. He was a member of the First Nazarene Church in North Little Rock. *Submitted by Jim Huett.*

ASHCRAFT - William Columbus Ashcraft (b. ca. 1847, York County, SC) was the son of James Leonard Ashcraft (b. ca. 1827 in York County, SC) and Catharine Crook (b. ca. 1823 in York County, SC). William Columbus married Nancy Jane Ashcraft (a cousin), daughter of John Morton Ashcraft and S. Sides.

Their children were:
1) Cora, (b. ca. 1871 in Cleveland County, AR) never married.

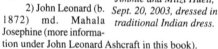
Jimmie and Mitzi Huett, Sept. 20, 2003, dressed in traditional Indian dress.

2) John Leonard (b. 1872) md. Mahala Josephine (more information under John Leonard Ashcraft in this book).

3) Byron, (b. ca. 1880) md. Cordelia Huggins, daughter of A.L. Huggins (see more under Byron Ashcraft in this book).

4) Mary (b. Feb. 25, 1885, d. Dec. 4, 1952) md. Robert Theophilus "Op" Robertson. "Op" farmed in Carden's Bottom and ran a sawmill on Pettit Jean Mountain. Their children: Ethel (b. Dec. 28, 1903) md. Bob Counts; Earl (b. Sept. 30, 1905) md. Edna Sever; Evie (b. Dec. 11, 1906) md. Earl Gilley; Ettie (b. July 30, 1908) md. Doyle Gilley; Elvis (b. April 28, 1910) md. Iva Lee Webb; Elmer (b. July 11, 1913, d. at 9 months); Erma (b. Oct. 5, 1915, d. at age 17 in 1932); Edith (b. Feb. 18, 1918) md. Talmage Deeter; Eula (b. Nov. 22, 1920) md. Otis Osborn; Eunice (b. Aug. 23, 1922) md. James Stewart; Robert Everett (b. Aug. 4, 1925) md. Winnie Rhodes.

5) Eugene Arthur Ashcraft (b. ca. 1890, d. 1968) md. ca. 1910 to Maude W. Walker, they had two children, Theo T. (b. ca. 1912) and Valerie A. (b. ca. 1916) md. a Locke. *Submitted by Jimmie Huett.*

ATKINS - Benjamin D. Atkins (b. 1822 in South Carolina), son of Benjamin and Margaret (Howell) Atkins, moved to Georgia in his youth. He was among the first landholders in the newly formed Cherokee County, AL, after Cherokee Indian lands were opened. Benjamin's first wife Elizabeth died ca. 1849, leaving him with two young sons. In 1850 he married Nancy D. Strickland in Cass County, GA.

In 1859, Benjamin D. Atkins and his family moved to Conway County, AR, where they settled in Cadron Cove. An owner of over 400 acres of land, he also operated a sawmill in the pine forest about 12 miles northeast of Springfield. In August 1871, Benjamin and Nancy deeded a parcel of land, lying north of the Batesville Road, to the Cadron Cove congregation of the Cumberland Presbyterian Church for as long as the congregation remained in Cadron Cove.

Conway County court records show that Benjamin served as a petit juror, an election judge, a commissioner, and a grand jury witness. On Feb. 28, 1872, Benjamin died at the age of 49. In 1876 his widow moved with family members to Ellis County, TX, where she died on Jan. 31, 1877. Benjamin's children were: Fletcher Leonidas Atkins (d. March 1864 during the Civil War); James A. Atkins (md. Lettie L. Connally); and Mary Ann Stacia Atkins (md. F.M. Mallett). *Submitted by D. Baker.*

ATKINSON - The name Atkinson means "son of Atkins" … that is the way all surnames ending in "son" had their origin. Atkinson is either a Scottish or English surname. We have hit an impasse, as frequently happens in genealogy, and have not been able to learn the parents of, or county of birth, or residence of our Burrell and Mary Atkinson while they were still in North Carolina. These are our oldest (known) ancestors. From federal census records we know that they were both born in North Carolina in the late 1700s, and from Orange County, NC marriage records, we learned that a Burrell Atkinson and "Polly" Price were married Sept. 21, 1820.

Standing: T.C. (Texas), Cora, Jess. Seated: Sophronia, Margaret, Mary Jane (Sis) Atkinson, ca. 1910.

A Burrell Atkinson is shown on Camden County, GA census and a Burrell and James Atkinson were in Hall County, GA in 1830. We have evidence to show the one in Hall County to be our ancestor. It is believed that he may have gone to Georgia from North Carolina because of the land lotteries taking place in the northern Georgia counties in 1820-30, but we have not found his name on these lottery lists.

Burrell and Mary's first daughter Emily H. was born in North Carolina, ca. 1827, with the remainder of the children being born in Georgia. James W., a blacksmith, born in Georgia, ca. 1829, is believed to have been their oldest son.

Kavanaugh Tucker of Morrilton (now deceased), stated in August 1977, "My father, Sam Tucker, told me that my grandfather, Wilson Tucker (b. ca. 1830, North Carolina) married my grandmother, Emily Atkinson, in Rome, GA and they came to Arkansas in ox-wagons in 1859." Wilson volunteered and served in the Confederate Army from Arkansas.

Mrs. Cora Atkinson Gordon of Plumerville, (also now deceased) had an extremely good memory, but like many of us, did not keep a lot of written information about her ancestors. Mrs. Gordon's children are "Peck" Gordon and Mrs. Hobbs (Lena) Horton. Her brothers were Dolph and Cliff Atkinson, both deceased. Cliff was head of the Arkansas State Police at one time. Mrs. Gordon stated that her grandfather was James Atkinson and she was always told that he was killed in the Civil War in Missouri. Her father James Monroe Atkinson (b. June 16, 1864, d. 1940) was nicknamed Jimmy Day. He is buried in Friendship Cemetery, a few miles south of Solgohachia.

Burrell and Mary "Polly" and their children still living at home, had moved to Union Township, Conway County by 1860. Burrell's occupation is listed on census as "wagonmaker." Children still at home

were Gideon, Amdrian (a female listed as Tumely A. on 1850 census), William Fletcher, and Joseph Banks. Burrell and Mary's known children were:

1) Emily H. (b. ca. 1827, North Carolina) md. Wilson Tucker. Their children were Benjamin A. (b. ca. 1852, Georgia); Mary (b. ca. 1855, Georgia); Samuel (b. ca. 1856, Georgia); and James (b. ca. 1863, Arkansas).

2) James W. (b. ca. 1828, Georgia) was a blacksmith by profession … mentioned earlier.

3) Thomas Capers (b. 1833) was a field doctor in the Confederate Army and stayed on in Alabama after the war.

4) Gideon (b. ca. 1837, Georgia) md. Sarah Hill. Their known children are Jim and William W.

5) Tumely Amdrian (b. ca 1841, Georgia) is believed to have died very young.

6) William Fletcher (b. ca. 1843, Georgia) served in the Confederate Army in Arkansas. He married Sarah J. Shewmake on June 12, 1866. His mother "Polly" Atkinson is shown living with this son and family on both 1870 and 1880 censuses. Fletcher and Sarah's children were Margaret "Martha" Julia, Charity, Mary and Wilson A.

7) Joseph Banks (b. Jan. 15, 1845, Hall County, GA) served in the Confederate Army from Conway County. He married Nancy Mahan July 25, 1868. Nancy was the daughter of James M. and Emily White Mahan. Joseph B. died Aug. 10, 1901 and Nancy died June 11, 1906, both are buried in Center Ridge Cemetery. Their children were:

a) Margaret L. (b. Aug. 11, 1869) md. James Fulkerson and had children: Mandy (md. Perry Graham), Nora (md. Homer Harris), Allen (md. Lizzie Marlow) and Beulah (md. Albert Rainey). After James' death, Margaret married Mr. Williams.

b) Mary Centelia Jane (b. Nov. 24, 1870), called "Sis" all her life, married James Harrison Mason on Jan. 8, 1893 at Center Ridge. They were members of the Church of Christ. He was a Justice of the Peace and a Mason. James' first wife, Rebecca Hill, had died, leaving five children: John C., James Blaine, Frances, Roxie A. and Chester A. The children of James Harrison and Mary Centelia Jane were Emma Viola (b. Jan. 23, 1894, d. July 6, 1975) md. John Calloway Bradley; Fred Orville (b. June 7, 1895) md. Isabelle Miller; Samuel L. (b. Dec. 27, 1896, d. Oct. 5, 1897); Isaac Dewey (b. Sept. 9, 1898, d. July 1976) md. Minnie E. Fullerton; Joseph Theodore (b. Sept. 9, 1900, d. Sept. 9, 1901); Mary Damaras (b. Oct. 10, 1902, d. Feb. 19, 1911); Ada Lee (b. Jan. 1, 1905) md. Hulan Epperson; Laurice Harrison (b. July 22, 1909, d. Feb. 18, 1911).

c) Sophronia E. (b. Oct. 11, 1873) md. John C. Mason (b. Nov. 25, 1873). Their children: Elmer (md. Lora Prince), Aaron (md. Ida McMahan), Lonnie (md. Celia Davis), Lee (wives names unavailable) and Wilburn (md. Edna Masterson). John C. and Sophronia were buried in Center Ridge Cemetery.

d) William Jesse (b. Nov. 11, 1875) md. Tennessee Newberry. Children: Audry (md. 1st, Lena Thomason and 2nd, Cassie Prince), Jean (md. Calvin Hollowell), Lois (md. Willie Hall) and Ivan (md. 1st, Mildred Parker and 2nd Lenora Hogue).

e). Samuel Melton (b. Dec. 31, 1877, d. Feb. 6, 1907) was unmarried.

f) Cora Lee (b. Oct. 14, 1882) md. Charles Cullum and they lived most of their lives in Mariana, AR. Their children are Charles Jr., Cecil, Tula and Freeda.

ATKINSON - Burwell Boneville Atkinson was born in 1793 in Nash County, NC to James Atkinson (his spouse is possibly Martha). The family moved to Chattooga County, GA in the early 1800s, more than likely due to a land grant. They settled in what is known as Broom Town Valley and that is where James died sometime in 1850.

James' father was Ephraim Atkinson who had a brother Burwell who was also found in Georgia. They are named as beneficiaries in their father's will - James Atkinson (Adkinson) who died in 1799 in Nash County, NC. However, Ephraim and Burwell are not the only children of this James Atkinson. He and his wife Margaret had John, Thomas, Burwell, Ephraim, Henry, Elijah and unnamed daughters. All of these records can be found in the history of Nash County and census records. They owned quite a bit of land and the buying and selling of lots are recorded in the land exchanges of Nash County, NC.

The history of the name Burwell, which is found in every generation of the Atkinsons to date, is an interesting one which helps in tying our past together. A gentleman by the name of Shadrack Atkinson was born in 1708 in England to a Thomas Atkinson. He came to Virginia with his parents as a child and grew up to marry a Jane Burwell. They had seven sons, but only the two youngest, John and Nathan, are named in any records I have found. I do know that the Conway and Faulkner County Atkinsons did NOT descend from either of these two sons, but given the Burwell name, it is quite possible that the first James Atkinson was a grandson or great-grandson of Shadrack. Hence, the English connection is complete.

Burwell Boneville Atkinson, being the oldest child, was the first in the family to come to Arkansas. It is probably because of his settling here that the others followed suit, but not for another generation. His brother, Irvin, owned a plantation in Broom Town Valley, GA, and was a Methodist minister. The plantation house stood until 1994 when it was finally demolished. There are documented war transcripts about Irvin's plantation from his wife after the Civil War where she attempted to receive war reparations after Sherman's army marched through and destroyed much of the plantation. Another brother of Burwell, Sion, apparently died at a young age but his sons W.S. (Whitmell Samuel), Sion Jr., John, and William all fought in the Confederate Army of the Civil War. W.S. and William were the only two to return home, and it was W.S. who moved his family to Greenbrier, AR in the late 1870s. He and his wife are buried in Greenbrier. After Burwell, Irvin, and Sion, there followed three sisters: Susan, Elizabeth, and Martha "Patsy." Since it is more difficult to trace females, there is no other information available at this time. *Submitted by Jamie Atkinson Bryant.*

ATKINSON

ATKINSON - The first recorded James Atkinson in this family was born in 1766 in North Carolina. His children were Burwell (pronounced Burrell) (b. 1793); Irvin (b. 1798); Sion (b. 1800); Susan (b. 1802) and Elizabeth (b. 1805). He moved his family to Chattooga County, GA in 1826.

James Monroe

Burwell Atkinson was a wagon maker. He brought his family to Conway County, AR in 1856, traveling by oxen and wagon, and settled on Tucker Mountain. (Tucker Mountain is located between Solgohachia and Birdtown.) He brought his wife (Mary Price) and six of his seven children with him. Traveling in the same group were members of the Tucker and Garrison families. The Atkinson children were James W. (b. 1828), Gideon (b. 1837), Tumley A. (b. 1841), Emily H. (b. 1825), William Fletcher (b. 1843) and Joseph Banks (b. 1845). The seventh Atkinson child was Thomas Capers. He was a Confederate Army doctor in the Civil War and who later migrated to Texas. Emily Atkinson was married to Wilson Tucker and Tucker Mountain was named after them. William Fletcher and Joseph Banks both served in the Confederate Army. Joseph B. was severely wounded and was captured. James W. was killed in Missouri during Price's raid.

James W. married Martha E. Durham while in Georgia and they brought their two children, Joseph (b. 1853) and Mary (b. 1855), with them. After their arrival in Arkansas they had Gideon (b. 1857), Thomas Jefferson (b. 1860) and James Monroe (b. 1864). Martha, the mother, died in 1866 and their aunt, Emily (Atkinson) Tucker, raised the Atkinson children along with her own. Joseph lost a leg while living on Tucker Mountain and moved to Massachusetts to work in the mills. Mary married William P. Bradshaw. Gideon was blind from an early age and never married. He was noted for making cane bottom chairs and other handicrafts. Thomas Jefferson married Pollie Lacefield and had two sons, Elbert, born 1884 and Clarence, born 1886. He later married Sarah Jane Edlin Rice and moved to Stony Point, AR, where they had six children: Willie, Duffie, Walter, Cora (b. 1886), Thomas (b. 1888) and Clifford (b. 1893). Willie, Thomas and Clifford all served in the US Army during WWI.

In 1901 James Monroe and his family moved to Solgohachia and he later owned and operated the cotton gin there. He was elected to the Arkansas Legislature in 1917. Cora married Paul Gordon and had Othello and Lena. Willie married Gladys Kidd and had no offspring. Duffie married Pearl Ramer and had Howard Neil (b. 1923) and Maxine (b. 1928). Walter died as a teenager. Thomas married Alice Koonce and had Jerrold (b. 1907). He later married Myrtle Ramer and had Elwanda and Kenneth (b. 1929). Clifford married Stella Lasater at Solgohachia and had Millicent (b. 1920), Randal (b. 1922), Drexel (b. 1926), Robert (b. 1930) and James (b. 1929).

Clifford was elected sheriff of Conway County in 1933 and moved his family to Morrilton. In 1935 he was appointed one of the original Arkansas Rangers and moved to Little Rock. The Rangers later became the Arkansas State Police and Clifford was promoted to Chief of the Arkansas State Police in 1944. None of Clifford's family returned to Conway County to live. *Submitted by James D. Atkinson.*

BAILEY

BAILEY - Sarah Ann Bailey (b. Sept. 11, 1851 in Tennessee) was the daughter of Benjamin C. and Nancy Wade (Sullivan) Bailey. She married James W. Chism July 19, 1870 in Pope County, AR. James, son of Obadiah Parker and Elizabeth (Gaylon) Chism, was born about 1848 in Arkansas. He died Dec. 31, 1881 with burial place unknown. Sarah and James had three children: Mary Elizabeth, John Pleasant and Kizzie. James had a daughter, Selena Jane "Janie" by Mary "Polly" Ann Hudson.

Thomas S. Wells and Sarah Ann Bailey Chism Wells.

Janie (b. March 14, 1868 in Newton County, AR) md. Charles Frank Ridling Feb. 2, 1885 in Conway County, AR. Charles (b. Nov. 18, 1866, d. Jan. 15, 1924) and Janie had 12 children: Nora R. Ridling Greer, Lillie Ridling Spence, James F. Ridling, Maggie Ridling Lilly, Annie Ridling, Tennie Vana Ridling Bailey, Dolly M. Ridling Hawkins, Caudine Ridling Mantus, Mae Ridling, Corene Ridling, Cleo Ridling and Theo Ridling. Janie died Feb. 1, 1958 in England, Lonoke County, AR. She and Charles are buried in the Robertstown Cemetery, Conway County, AR.

Mary Elizabeth "Betty" Chism (b. Sept. 9, 1872 in Newton County, AR) md. John Albert Welch Feb. 25, 1894 in Conway County, AR. John (b. April 3, 1871, d. Dec. 18, 1929) and Mary were the parents of

11 children: Lillie B. Welch, Thomas M. Welch, Herbert Lee Welch, Susil A. Welch, Bert Doyle Welch, Arazona Welch, Tilda Emogene Welch Tilley, Marvin H. Welch, Sidney Fred Welch and Hobert Sicil Welch. Mary Elizabeth died Oct. 4, 1955. Mary and John are buried in the Lone Grove Cemetery, Lanty, Conway County, AR.

John Pleasant "Doc" Chism (b. Oct. 4, 1874 in Newton County, AR) md. Maggie Lou Conley March 10, 1901 in Conway County, AR. Maggie (b. Jan. 30, 1878 in Conway County, AR, d. Feb. 15, 1923 in Carrizo Springs, Dimmitt County, TX), daughter of William Lewis and Sarah Caroline (Beeson) Conley, is buried in the Mt. Hope Cemetery in Carrizo Springs. Doc and Maggie had one child, William Archie Chism. Doc is buried in the Adams Cemetery, Lanty, Conway County, AR.

Kizzie Chism (b. Dec. 4, 1875 in Newton County, AR) md. Joe Cephas Blankenship on Jan. 28, 1894 in Conway County, AR. Joseph (b. March 10, 1876 in Greenup County, KY, d. Aug. 5, 1948 in Conway County, AR) was the son of William and Elizabeth (Keeton) Blankenship. Kizzie and Joseph were the parents of four children: Annie Blankenship Baker, Jimmy Blankenship, Artency Blankenship and Flarra Bell Blankenship Elam. Kizzie died Oct. 21, 1903 and is buried in Old Hickory Cemetery, Conway County, AR. Joe is buried in Robertstown Cemetery, Conway County, AR beside his second wife, Ruby Zachary Hanna Blankenship.

After the death of James W. Chism, Sarah married Thomas S. Wells on April 6, 1896 in Conway County, AR. He was born July 25, 1834 in Morgan County, AL and died on Sept. 7, 1917 in Cleveland, Conway County, AR. Sarah died June 16, 1925 in Conway County, AR. They are buried in the Cleveland Cemetery, Conway County, AR. *Submitted by William Alan Chism.*

BALCH

BALCH - Ralph E. Balch moved to Morrilton in January 1987 after living in Texas for 25 years. He was born in Nashville, AR on July 27, 1934 to Walter A. and Della Myrick Balch, the third of their three children.

After graduating from Nashville High School in 1952 he served in the US Navy as a Hospital Corpsman. In 1955 he was attached to the US Marine Corps and spent his fourth year of active duty in Japan with the Third Marine Division.

W.L. Wood residence, photo made around 1910.

After completing his military service he enrolled in the University of Arkansas where he completed his BS and MA degrees in political science. While attending college he married Virginia Lea MacDonald of Springdale in 1960. They had one daughter Virginia Suzanne (b. 1962). She is now a college professor in New Mexico, having graduated from Texas Tech University with a PhD in history.

Balch worked in the insurance profession for over 43 years, starting with Crawford and Company Adjusters in Atlanta, GA in 1961. From there he was transferred to Austin, TX where he worked for eight months before being transferred to Dallas. After six years there he was promoted to manager of their Lubbock office where he served until 1972 when he was promoted again to manager of the Odessa/Midland office.

In 1974 a career change moved them back to

Lubbock where he worked as manager for a large independent insurance agency, Jim Finley and Associates. An important part of that decision was so his wife, Virginia Lea, could complete her MA and PhD in history at Texas Tech University. Part of that plan was not completed as Virginia Lea died of breast cancer at age 44 in 1984 just before completing all the requirements for the PhD. Their daughter Suzanne was diagnosed with the same disease at the same age as her mother, 39, in 2001. She is now a three-year survivor.

In 1982 the Finley Agency was sold to a national independent agency chain and Balch left to form his own insurance and real estate agency. He continued that until after the death of his wife and eventually sold his agency in 1985. Then he sold his home and for the next two years traveled all over the United States in his van and trailer with his basset hound, Rex V. From 1962 until 2003 he owned six bassets. He refers to this being his "first retirement."

In January 1987 Balch took a job as claims manager with American Underwriters Insurance Company in Morrilton. In October 1987 he was promoted to vice president of the company and was responsible for overseeing the company's Arkansas operations. AUIC is a division of American Management Corporation that moved from Morrilton to Conway in 1992.

Balch served as an officer and president of the South Plains Claims Association twice, on the Texas Claims Association charter Board of Directors, as president of the Arkansas Field Club, manager of the Arkansas Rural Risk Underwriters Association, member of the Arkansas Auto Plan and vice chairman of the Arkansas Earthquake Board. He also received the CIC designation in 1996.

After living here almost a year he bought the W.L. Wood house at 709 N. Morrill St., Morrilton, AR. The house had been owned and occupied by W.L. and Alice Sleeper Wood since construction in 1906. They were parents of two children, Lee C. and Bertha. After the untimely death of Bertha's husband, Edgar Earle Love, in 1919, she and her two sons, William Earl and Charles Allen, moved into the house with her parents. She and her brother Lee took equal ownership in 1928 although their parents continued to live there until their deaths in 1935 and 1936. In 1937 Lee sold his half to Bertha. After Bertha Love's death in 1965, Charles Allen and William Earle inherited equal ownership. Later Charles sold his half to William Earle and Marion Ryland Love. They continued to hold ownership and occupy the house until 1985. The Woods and the Loves were prominent farmers, merchants and civic leaders in Conway County. Bertha Love was instrumental in getting a grant for the library from the Carnegie Foundation. In 2002 the Queen Ann style Victorian house was placed on the National Register of Historic Places with an emphasis on its architectural importance in the community. The photograph of the W.L. Wood House was made around 1910. The land where the house stands was originally a cotton field.

Balch entered semi-retirement in 2000 after undergoing treatment for prostate cancer in 1996. He is an eight-year cancer survivor and is active in the Arkansas Prostate Cancer Foundation, which is involved in encouraging early detection awareness.

Suzanne has two children, Virginia Leigh and Kenneth Franklin Slater. Virginia is attending college at Eastern New Mexico University where her mother teaches, and Frank attends high school in Lubbock where he lives with his dad, Jerry Slater.

In his "second and final retirement" Balch travels a lot, mostly in Arkansas, but he has made trips to California, Alaska, Florida, New Mexico and many points in between. He also spends a lot of time in Cabot visiting his best good friend, Gail Ahart. *Submitted by Ralph E. Balch.*

BARKER - In 1900, Julie Etta Stripling and Robert Don Barker were united in marriage. Julie and Robert were both born and raised in Van Buren County. They moved to Conway County in 1927 from Bee Branch

in Van Buren County. Robert ran a small grocery store and farmed at the James farm river bottoms.

Julie and Robert had 11 children (three died in infancy). Julie died in her early 40s in 1928 leaving six sons: Jessie, Elmer, Harvey, Arvil, Roy and Hulon, and two daughters, Ova and Ona.

Robert and Minnie Barker

In 1932 Robert married Minnie Mae Mathes. Minnie was born and raised in Conway County area. Her parents both died when she was just 12 years old so this was to be her first real home in a long time. Being a young woman and marrying a man with eight children was quite a challenge, but she was up to the task. They had three sons: Junior, Robert and Jacob, and three daughters: Helen, Evelyn and Betty. They lost Robert in infancy.

Their children grew up and went their separate ways. Jessie Lee married Flossie Presley and they made their home in Little Rock. Ova Jane married Alton Sanders and they made their home in Los Angles, CA. Ona Mae married Loyce Freeman and they made their home in Los Angeles, CA. Elmer Thurman married Hazel Rogers and they made their home in Little Rock. Harvey Afton married Lucille Sanders and they made their home in Little Rock. Arvil Syrus married Edith Autry and they made their home in Little Rock. Roy Edward married Dolly Marie Caple and they made their home in Little Rock. Hulon Harold married Faye Duggins Davis and they made their home in Little Rock. Arvil Junior married Kathleen Davis and they made their home in Dallas, TX. Helen Mae married William Charles Hubbard and they made their home in Overcup. Evelyn Sue married Ray Jones and they made their home in Overcup. Betty Lou married Clarence Bridgman and they made their home in Solgohachia. Jacob Edward married Judy Petty and they made their home in Overcup.

In 1937 they bought a farm on Hwy. 64 where they raised their family. In the summer of 1954 they lost their home to a fire, but Robert rebuilt his home and stayed there until about 1956. Then be bought land on Hwy. 9 in the Overcup area. There was an old store on the land and he renovated it to use as the family home. There was plenty of space to raise a few horses, cows and chickens and a nice place for a large garden. They remained in their home in Overcup until their death. Robert died in 1966. Minnie died 30 years later in 1996.

Five of the children are still living in Arkansas. Helen, Evelyn, Betty and Jacob are in Conway County. Roy, one of Julie's children, lives in Little Rock. There is still a very large family of grandchildren, great-grandchildren and great-great-grandchildren. *Submitted by Linda Kay Hubbard (granddaughter).*

BARRIMORE - Ellen Barrimore, age 28, was born W, Canada (I was told this denotes Welch Dist. of Canada, which would be near Nova Scotia). Ellen is listed as head of household in the 1850 census of Yell County, AR with her daughters, Victoria (b. 1841, Arkansas), Mary (b. 1844, Arkansas) and Angelina (b. 1847, Arkansas). A boarder, Richard Brison, age 21, born Tennessee, is also in the home.

By the 1860 census of Galley Rock, Victoria, age 20, has married John C. Isom, age 31, born Tennessee. Victoria's sisters are living with them: Mary (age 18, Arkansas) and Angelina (age 12 Arkansas) and a male child, Francis A. Isom (age 8, born Arkansas).

In 1989 Vol. 14, No. 2 *Yell County Quarterly* printed an account by Wayne Banks of a wagon train leaving Yell County for the Gold Fields of California

and I quote: "Joseph C. Johnson commanded a wagon train which left 1 April 1849 from Yell County. This train was of considerable size. Organization was as follows: R. Rogers, Captain, John May, 1st Lieutenant, other divisions was commanded by John Barrimore and John B. Johnson."

I believe this John Barrimore is the same John Sidney Barrimore who had land grants in Pope County, and who lived there in the 1840 census where daughter was born in 1841. It appears that John Barrimore may have stayed in California. Perhaps Ellen hopped the next stagecoach going West as she disappears from the census after 1860. Perhaps Angelina also went along, as I find no other mention of her. *Submitted by Agnes Walrod.*

BASKIN(S) - Thomas Twine Baskin was born in 1856 in Abbeville, SC. His wife, Emma Swain, was probably from a neighboring farm. "Emma was white and content to become colored" as the legend goes. They were married in Abbeville, SC. Although Twine was born a free man, the name Baskin was taken from the original slave owner, a John Baskin. Twine and Emma, with their nine children, migrated to Morrilton, AR probably during the spring and summer after the birth of their daughter Ida in October 1884 in Abbeville, SC and before the birth of their son Eurskin in August 1895 in Solgohachia, AR. The Baskins settled in Morrilton and later settled in Solgohachia to farm and raise cotton.

Emma bore a total of 11 children for Twine. They were Mary Janie Baskin-Parker (b. 1874, d. 1934); Lizzie Baskin-Black (b. 1880-); Ida Emma Asula Baskin-Jenkins (b. 1884, d. 1948); Eurskin Thomas Baskin (b. 1895, d. 1975); Iola Baskin-Edwards (b. 1890, d. 1978); Brennie Baskin (b. 1900-); Johnnie William Baskin; Eugene Harrison; and Clarkie Baskin.

Thomas Twine Baskin (1856-1928) and Emma Elizabeth Swain (1864-1905).

Mr. Baskin was rumored to be a wanderer and a musician. This wandering may account for limited information on the family intact in Arkansas.

We have been unable to locate information on Emma Swain neither in South Carolina nor in Arkansas. It is believed that Emma died in 1905 after the birth of the last child named Brennie. Brennie was born in 1900. After Emma's death, 10-year-old Eurskin went to live with his older sister Mary Janie Baskin-Parker, in Hopewell Ridge, AR. They attended the Hopewell Ridge Presbyterian church. Five-year-old Brennie went to live with another older sister Lizzie Baskin-Black.

After the death of Emma, Twine moved to Russellville, AR and worked in the coal mine, digging Anthracite coal. Eurskin later joined him.

The 1910 census shows Thomas Twine Baskin living in Russellville City, Illinois Township, Pope County, AR. He is listed as 56 years old. He is also listed as a "mulatto," widowed, renting land and a general laborer. Eurskin is listed as 14 years old and working odd jobs.

The 1920 census shows Twine living in Russellville, widowed, and living alone. He is listed as living on West David Street. His age is listed as 64 years old. Eurskin married and moved to Kansas City. Thomas Twine Baskin died 1928 in Russellville, AR.

BATSON - Joseph D. Batson (b. ca. 1818 in Greenville County, SC) md. Mary Elizabeth Carolina Bishop in 1838 and resided in South Carolina until the fall of 1846, when he moved his family to Gilmer County, GA and operated a stock farm. About 1849 he was a captain in the 195th Battalion, Gilmer County. He served as Justice of the Inferior Court in Gilmer County from Jan. 10, 1861 to Jan. 23, 1865. After the Civil War, Joseph moved his family west to Conway County, AR, where he was a farmer and carpenter. He died Jan. 21, 1871, but his wife Mary lived until after 1880.

Joseph Batson and Mary Bishop had the following known children: Elizabeth Batson (b. 1839, d. bef. May 1888) md. Harrison Moose in Conway County, AR in 1870; Malissa A. Batson (b. 1840, d. 1925 in Georgia) md. Joseph N. Hancock in 1866; William Asbury Batson (b. 1841, d. 1910) md. Margaret Heatherly in 1861; Nancy Adeline Batson (b. 1845, d. 1912 in Georgia) md. Charles Tolbert Carnes in 1869; Sterling Turner Batson (b. 1848, d. after 1871); Terrell Wilkie Batson (b. 1848, d. 1903 in Ft. Smith, AR) md. Mattie J. Myers ca. 1880; Joseph B. Batson (b. 1850, d. aft. 1860); Jasper Philip Batson (b. 1852, d. aft. 1870); Henry C. Batson (b. 1855, d. 1891 in Conway County) md. Sarah J. Hollyfield in Conway County in 1880; Larkin Columbus Batson (b. 1858, d. 1926 in Conway County) md. Effie Carpenter in Conway County in 1879; Hawkins Batson (b. 1860, d. Dec. 5, 1890 in Palarm, AR). *Submitted by Dorothy Baker.*

BATSON - William Asbury Batson (b. Nov. 21, 1841 in Greenville County, SC) was the third child of Joseph D. and Mary C. (Bishop) Batson. He moved with his family in 1846 to Gilmer County, GA and reached adulthood there. While working for his uncle, he met and married Margaret S. Heatherly in Henderson County, NC. Shortly thereafter, in July 1862, he joined the 64th North Carolina Regiment, where he was voted a lieutenant. On Aug. 3, 1863, the regiment was surrendered at Cumberland Gap and William spent the remainder of the war as a prisoner, primarily at Ft. Delaware. He was released on June 12, 1865 and returned to Georgia to join his wife and parents. He went into business as a retail grocer and remained in Georgia until 1873, when he moved to Conway County, AR to join his parents and younger siblings.

Like other family members, William was a carpenter. He also was a merchant and justice of the peace in Conway County. In 1879 he signed a petition to incorporate the town of Morrilton, and served as the town's first Marshal. Some time after Margaret's death in 1899, he remarried and moved to Coleman County, TX, where he died in 1910.

William Asbury Batson and Margaret S. (Heatherly) Batson had the following known children: Viola V. Batson (b. 1866 in Georgia, d. bet. 1870 and 1880); Annie Batson (b. 1869 in Georgia, d. Jan. 20, 1901) md. John T. Crutchfield in 1888. She is buried in Plumerville; Harley Lafoon Batson (b. 1871 in Georgia, d. Aug. 22, 1927 in Muskogee, OK) md. Celia Hutson; Valentine Wilkie Batson (b. 1873 in North Carolina, d. Sept. 12, 1892 in Plumerville); Dora Lillian Batson (b. 1875 in Conway County, AR, d. Oct. 6, 1964) md. 1st, Neil Donaghey and 2nd, Hugh Roberts; Leslie Victoria Batson (b. 1878 in Conway County, AR, d. Dec. 21, 1961 in Muskogee, OK) md. John Henry Baker in Conway County. *Submitted by Ms. Dorothy Baker.*

BEAN - Charles David Bean (b. 1935 in Plumerville, Conway County, AR) is the son of Collie Raymond Bean and Mattie Yancey Bean. He attended Plumerville Public Schools, graduating in 1953. In 1955 he married Shirley Anne Jackson, who was born in 1938 in Morrilton, Conway County, AR where she attended Morrilton Public Schools, graduating in 1955. She is the daughter of Cecil Everette Jackson and Minnie Kimberlin Jackson. She was the first woman to be elected to the Plumerville School Board of Education

and was vice president of that board for five years. She retired from South Conway County School District in 2002.

Plumerville American Revolution Bicentennial 1776-1976 (L-R) State Representative Bunk Allison, City Council Member Ronnie Deavor, City Recorder DeLoyte Bean, City Council Member Jim Campbell, Mayor Charles Bean.

Charles served in the Arkansas National Guard and as an alderman for the city of Plumerville for several years. He was elected mayor of Plumerville in 1974 and served until 1979. He was a meat market manager for Safeway, retiring after 40 years with Safeway/Harvest Foods in 1997. He retired from the Plumerville Fire Department with 24 years of service in 1997. He served on the Conway County Equalization Board and the Plumerville Fire Department Pension Board. He is an avid hunter and a lifetime member of the M-P Hunting Club.

During his service as Plumerville Mayor, the city celebrated the American Revolution Bicentennial 1776-1976. At this time a capsule was filled with mementos by many of the citizens living in Plumerville. On July 4, 1976 this capsule was buried on the town square, corner of Church and Springfield Streets. It is to be opened on July 4, 2076.

They are Christians and of Baptist faith, raising their three children and attending the First Baptist Church of Plumerville.

Charles "David" Bean Jr. was born at St. Anthony's Hospital in Morrilton, AR in 1956 and resides in Charleston, SC. He was a 1975 graduate of Plumerville Public Schools and a 1980 University of Central Arkansas graduate. He has one son, Forrest Tyler Bean, born in Charleston, SC.

Deborah Anne "Debbie" Bean was born at St. Anthony's Hospital in Morrilton, AR in 1958. She was a 1976 graduate and salutatorian of Plumerville Public Schools. She attended University of Central Arkansas and was a graduate of Capital Business College. She resides in Russellville, AR and is married to Dr. Wm. Bruce Brown an orthopaedic surgeon. Dr. Brown opened the Arkansas Orthopedic Center in Russellville in 1994. They have two children, Austin Jacob Brown, born in Newport News, VA and Taylor Ashley Brown, born at Ft. Lewis, WA.

Derrick Jackson Bean was born at St. Anthony's Hospital in Morrilton, AR in 1964. He attended Plumerville Public Schools until the consolidation of the Plumerville, Menifee, and Morrilton Schools in 1980. He was a 1982 graduate of the South Conway County School District. He is a master electrician and resides in Plumerville, AR. He is married to Andrea Reece Bean, formerly of Englewood, CO. They have two daughters, Whitney Reece Bean and Lindsey Marie Bean, both living in Plumerville, AR since birth.

Mr. and Mrs. Bean built their home in Plumerville in 1964 and reside there today. *Submitted by Shirley Bean.*

BEARDEN - Berryman Hicks Bearden (b. March 10, 1824 in South Carolina), son of John and Rhoda Bearden, married Harriet N. Smith Aug. 3, 1843 in Spartanburg, SC. Harriet was born Feb. 23, 1823 in South Carolina. Berryman and his family were in Conway County by the 1860 census. He had children born in South Carolina from 1844-53 and then in

Conway County from 1859-68. Berryman was a Missionary Baptist minister and a farmer.

Berryman Hicks and Harriet Bearden.

Children of this couple include Robert (b. 1844 in South Carolina); Elizabeth J. (b. 1846 in South Carolina); Nancy Polina (b. Oct. 17, 1847 in South Carolina); Cormelia (b. 1849 in South Carolina); Gustovus F.D. (b. 1851 in South Carolina); Mary Catherine (b. Jan. 7, 1853 in South Carolina); John Will (b. July 1859 in Arkansas); Emily Francis (b. Dec. 1, 1861 in Arkansas); George B. (b. 1864 in Arkansas); and Victoria (b. 1868 in Arkansas). According to Berryman's obituary he had 12 children, seven of whom were living when he died. According to his obit, he fell at the pulpit while preaching and died shortly afterward on Dec. 18, 1893 in Conway County, AR. Harriet died Feb. 7, 1897 in Conway County. Both are buried in Friendship Cemetery at Solgohachia in Conway County.

Nancy Polina Bearden married George Washington Baker May 2, 1867 in Conway County. George (b. March 23, 1842 in Conway County) was a son of Moses and Rebecca Callahan Baker. George was an undertaker in Morrilton for many years before moving to Oppelo. Children born to this couple include Alis Victoria (b. March 8, 1870, d. July 27, 1873); Rosa Lee (b. Oct. 30, 1872); Viola May (b. Sept. 11, 1874); Mary Florence (b. Feb. 9, 1878); Georgia Anna (b. Oct. 20, 1880); Perry Verner (b. Oct. 7, 1883); Ulah Bell (b. June 4, 1886); and Arley Less (b. Feb. 18, 1889). Nancy died July 18, 1905 and George died June 6, 1908. They are both buried in Wolf Cemetery in Oppelo, AR.

Ulah Bell Baker married Bennett Floyd Wood in Conway County July 15, 1914. Bennett Floyd was born Dec. 13, 1881 to Wilburn and Mary Ann Moore Wood in Oppelo. Ulah and Floyd had three children: Lilburn Lester "Bill," Don and Bess Marie. Floyd was a farmer in Oppelo until about 1951 or 1952. He was a member of Woodmen of the World. Ulah died Nov. 6, 1965 and Floyd died Aug. 1, 1967. Both are buried in Wolf Cemetery in Oppelo. *Submitted by Fay Wood Beavers.*

BEAVERS - Burnice Lee "Burnie" Beavers (b. July 13, 1946 in Jerusalem, AR), son of Elmer Lee and Epsie Edith Cato Beavers. When he was about 3 years old, the family moved just north of Morrilton on what was known as Monastery Ridge No. 2. He married Euna Fay Wood March 8, 1973 in Morrilton, AR. They have three children: Steven Lee, Bobby Allen and Timothy David. Steve is married to Rachel Deanne Langle and has two children, Alanna Jordan and Evan Lee.

Burnice Lee Beavers

Burnie was a carpenter. He worked at the Crompton Arkansas Mills in his early years, then went into carpentry. Some years later he returned to the Crompton Mills and was employed as their carpenter. When the mill shut down in 1984, he began his own carpentry business. He remained in this business until his death. Burnie was one of the early Conway County Volunteer Firemen. The county volunteer fire department then consisted of one department for the entire county.

Burnie was an avid genealogist and was a charter member of the Conway County Genealogical Association. He attended many ancestor fairs and helped his wife organize reunions for the four lines of their families. He loved family and friends and was always delighted to find a new "cousin." Burnie loved to garden and work in the yard. He loved to fish and did deer hunt a little each year. Burnie fell while working on the family's home on Aug. 28, 2000 and died in Little Rock, AR on Aug. 29, 2000. He is buried in Cedar Creek Cemetery at Jerusalem, AR. *Submitted by Euna Wood Beavers.*

BEAVERS - Elmer Lee Beavers (b. Aug. 20, 1908 at Brock Creek in Van Buren County, AR), son of Reuben Wakefield Beavers and Fredona Bell "Donie Bell" Bates Beavers. He married Epsie Edith Cato Feb. 10, 1934 in Conway County. Epsie was born June 16, 1910 at Doyle Flat in Conway County to Willis Franklin and Elsie Emmaline Harris Cato. Elmer died in Morrilton, March 2, 1972 after a long illness with cancer. Epsie died March 30, 1974 in Morrilton after a long battle with cancer.

Elmer and Epsie Beavers

They are buried in Cedar Creek Cemetery in Jerusalem.

Elmer and Epsie were the parents of the following children: Frances Alene (b. April 16, 1935, d. June 10, 1937); Juanita Faye; Burman Eudell; Burnice Lee (b. July 13, 1946, d. Aug. 29, 2000); and Bobby Dale. Frances Alene "Dinky" is buried in Cato Cemetery at Jerusalem.

Juanita Faye Beavers married Robert Thelton Bird. They have five children: Kevin Robert, Anita Robin, Jerry Wayne, Terry Alan and Melissa Renee.

Burman Eudell married Virginia Lynn Jones. They have two children, Michael Keith and Michelle Lynn.

Burnice Lee married Euna Fay Wood. They have three children, Steven Lee, Bobby Allen and Timothy David.

Bobby Dale married Carlys Israel. They have three children: Richard Keith, Lindsay Ann and Kasey Lauren. *Submitted by Tim Beavers.*

BEAVERS - John Willis Beavers Sr. (b. 1825 in Tennessee) md. Elizabeth Owens (b. July 1823 in Tennessee or Kentucky). John Willis was in Welborn Township in Conway County by the 1840 census. John Willis Sr. had died by the 1880 census. John Willis and Elizabeth had nine sons. Three of these were John Willis Jr., Charles W. and Lou. I have not been able to find any of the others for certain. John Willis Sr. is said to be buried in the mountains out from Jerusalem near where the old Sain Post Office was at one

John Willis and Mary Jane Beavers

time. Elizabeth is buried in Rocky Valley Cemetery just over in Van Buren County.

John Willis Jr. (b. Dec. 25, 1847 in Arkansas, d. Jan. 25, 1933) md. Mary Jane Reid, daughter of Rhesa and Martha Reid, on Aug. 30, 1868 in Conway County, AR. Mary Jane was born March 28, 1851 and died Aug. 18, 1929. They lived in Liberty Township and White Oak Township in Van Buren County, AR. John Willis and Mary Jane had the following children:

Cary, Martha E., William Luke, Luther, George W., Ella A., Larkin Lee, Cora A., Ruben Wakefield, John Elbert, Ida and Ollie. John Willis Jr. and Mary Jane are buried in Rocky Valley Cemetery. *Submitted by S.L. Beavers.*

BEAVERT - John Beavert was born in South Carolina on Feb. 2, 1804. His parents are unknown. John can first be found in the 1830 federal census living in Hickman County, TN. He must have had itchy feet because by 1840 he and his family were living in Welborn township in Conway County, AR. He kept moving and in 1850 was living in Pope County, AR. Then "Oregon Fever" hit and in 1853 traveled the Oregon Trail to the Oregon Territory.

Very little is known about John Beavert. His first wife was Mima Flowers, probably the daughter of Henry and Elizabeth Marshall Flowers. Elizabeth Flowers was living in Conway County, Point Remove Township in 1840 without her husband. John and Mima were the parents of Cynthia Arilla, William, Henry, Nancy, Mahala and John. In 1847 John married Jane Montgomery Weston, a widow with three children. The children born from this union were Sarah, Mary, Naomi and James. Jane's brother-in-law from her first marriage had been Thomas Weston, Conway County's Coroner from 1846-48.

John did not read or write so his name has been spelled with several variations: Bevert, Bevart, Beavers, Bevers. John Beavert returned to Arkansas in 1890. He died June 20, 1890 in Pope County and is buried in the Center Valley (or old Baptist) Cemetery. *Submitted by Vicki Bonagofski.*

BEDINGER - After the deaths of Solomon Singleton Bedinger and his wife Mildred Berry Bedinger, the oldest daughter Henrietta "Netta" Gray Bedinger, at age 18, was left to hold the family together. She and her younger sister Lavinia, now 15, cared for the infant, Singleton Berry, and the young son, Henry Clay, age 13. The children kept the homestead near Lewisburg. In 1875, the homestead was proved and title of the homestead was vested with Henrietta, her sister and two brothers. The children stayed together and lived as a family in Conway County, AR.

Silhouette cutout art of Netta Gray Bedinger.

Henry Clay Bedinger grew up in Conway County and in 1888 married Nancy Sultena Meeks. They lived in Polk County, AR before relocating to Texas where they raised three boys: Henry Clay Jr., Charles Arthur and William Elbert Singleton.

Lavinia Bedinger married Edward Henry Morrill in 1882. He was the son of E.J. Morrill, prominent merchant of Conway County. Edward Morrill's untimely death in 1888 left Lavinia with four young children: Edward Henry, Netta Washington, Edna Lavinia, and Mildred Antoinette. Lavinia and her children lived in Morrilton until the early 1900s when they moved to Terrell, Kaufman County, TX.

Singleton Berry Bedinger was raised by Netta and Lavinia in Conway County. He later settled in Terrell, TX after attending Tulane University, New Orleans and working at various jobs in south Texas. In 1904 Singleton Berry Bedinger married Nina John Terrell, daughter of John Love Terrell and granddaughter of Robert Adams Terrell after whom the town of Terrell, TX is named. Singleton and Nina Bedinger

had five children: John Terrell, Singleton Berry Jr., Nina Celeste, Edward Rentfro and George Terrell. Nina (Terrell) Bedinger died soon after the birth of her son George Terrell in January 1917. From 1907-14 Singleton was superintendent of the Masonic Home in Fort Worth, TX. Singleton traveled over much of the state of Texas as sales representative for various companies.

To keep the family together, Henrietta "Netta" Gray Bedinger may have taught school in the early years after her father's death. In 1858, when Netta was not yet 4 years of age, her aunt died, leaving her property. As provided in the will of her aunt, Sarah "Salley" Eleanor Washington, the proceeds from the property were to be accrued until Netta reached the age of 18, when it was to "...be used to send her to school and give her both useful and ornamental education." Her ownership of the property willed her did not survive the ravages of the Civil War. However, by her strength of character and fortitude, Netta did attain the education her aunt wished for her. Netta's education included the study of art in St. Louis. She became a teacher of art and attained wide recognition as a gifted artist.

An early position she held was principal of the art department at Hiram and Lydia College in Altus, AR. Her long career in teaching art took her to Pass Christian Institute, Mississippi and schools in Kansas, Alabama, and Tennessee. She was the first teacher of art at the University of Arkansas. Her artwork includes oil paintings on canvas, paintings fired on china and sculpture. She was especially well known for her outstanding talent at freehand silhouette cut art, two pieces of which reside in the Sue H. Walker collection at the University of Arkansas.

In her later years she moved to Terrell, TX where her sister, Lavinia Morrill, had made her home. Netta taught art at Toon College in Terrell. Netta G. Bedinger died at the home of her brother Singleton Berry Bedinger in Terrell on Aug. 31, 1923. *Contributed by Marion Singleton (Doug) Bedinger.*

BEDINGER - Solomon Singleton Bedinger, son of Henry Clay Bedinger and Judith Rust Singleton, was born in Lewis County, KY in 1828. Henry Clay Bedinger was the son of Major George Michael Bedinger and Henrietta Clay. Henrietta was the daughter of Dr. Henry Clay and Rachel Povall and second cousin of the American statesman Henry Clay. On Feb. 9, 1854 at the Washington home, Cedar Lawn in Jefferson County, VA (now West Virginia), Solomon Singleton Bedinger was married to his second cousin Mildred Berry Washington, daughter of John Thornton Augustine Washington and Elizabeth Conrad Bedinger.

Solomon Singleton Bedinger

John T.A. Washington was the grandson of Col. Samuel Washington, younger brother of George Washington the President. In 1856, Solomon Singleton and Mildred Bedinger, with Solomon's brother and several brothers and sisters of Mildred, moved to Johnson County in western Missouri, where Solomon acquired government land and built a home, "Sunnyside." There on May 22, 1857, Henry Clay Bedinger, younger brother of Solomon, married Susan Ellsworth Washington, sister of Mildred Berry Washington.

By 1862 four children were born to Solomon and Mildred. They were Henrietta Gray, Lavinia, Henry Clay and Arthur Singleton. The fertile lands of Johnson County brought prosperity to Solomon and Mildred and a bright future seemed to lie ahead. This encouraging picture was to be blotted out not only by the disastrous Civil War, but also raids on farms in western Missouri by gangs of lawless renegades.

Solomon and his brother gave their services to the southern cause, serving in Company E of the 10th Missouri Cavalry and taking an active part in the struggle until its close. Mildred and her four children went to live with her sister, also living in Johnson County during the war. A modicum of safety from pro-union raiders was afforded because her sister, George Anna, was the wife of Union Army officer Major John Wheeler Smith. Following the close of the war, Solomon and Mildred Bedinger, having lost most of their personal estate, sold or bundled the remains and moved to Conway County, AR.

Solomon Bedinger filed to homestead 80 acres southwest of present-day Morrilton, overlooking the Arkansas River floodplain. Solomon owned and operated the ferry on the Arkansas River below Petit Jean Mountain and entered into partnership with his brother-in-law, John Wheeler Smith. The partnership acquired 300 acres of Arkansas River bottomland where Solomon managed the cotton farming enterprise. In 1871, bright days appeared to be ahead in Conway County for Solomon and Mildred Bedinger and their children, Henrietta Gray, Lavinia and Henry Clay.

Their few years in Arkansas had been saddened by the death of their youngest child, Arthur Singleton at age 7 years, 8 months in 1869, but Mildred was expecting her fifth child in November. The joy of the birth of Singleton Berry Bedinger on Nov. 7, 1871 was soon followed by tragedy of Mildred's death. Bad climate and crop failures in the following years. On Feb. 8, 1873 Solomon died leaving four children, aged 14 months to 18 years. Solomon Singleton Bedinger and Mildred Berry (Washington) Bedinger are buried in Oakland Cemetery, Little Rock, AR in the same plot with their son Arthur Singleton Bedinger. *Contributed by Marion Singleton (Doug) Bedinger.*

BELL - The Bell family origins are in Great Britain, and the Conway County branch came to the area by way of Murfreesboro, TN, in the 19th century.

Joseph Thompson Bell (b. March 1, 1850) was killed by lightening while taking shelter under a tree on his farm near Plumerville on June 9, 1899. On May 29, 1872 he married Edna Virginia "Jane" Ledbetter (b. 1853, d. December 1899). They had nine children (listed below), all of whom lived in the Plumerville area most of their lives and worked as merchants, farmers and wives in their community into the 1950s and 1960s.

1) Francis Jane "Jennie" Bell, (b. 1873) md. D.Q. Stell and had six children: Myrtle Elinor, Edna Ethelma, Christopher Columbus, Clyde, Hugh, and Margaret Mae.

2) Hugh Machelhannon Bell (b. 1874) md. Byrd Stell and had two children, James Batey and Alice, who both died in infancy.

3) Sallie Mae Bell (b. 1878) md. George McAlister and had four children before his death: Ira, Orville, Willie Bell and Leila Mae. Sallie married a second time to Ed L. Tiner, a widower with seven children: Dovie, Laney, Arkie, Orpha, Susie, Herman and Emily. Together they had Carl Audry, Earl Marie and Calista Agnes.

4) Margaret Ann Bell (b. 1881) md. J. Sam Moses; they had no children.

5) Joseph Thompson Bell Jr. (b. 1884) md. Grace Miller and had three boys: Buford Winston, Burwell Thompson and E.J.

· 6) Samuel Peyton Bell III (b. 1887) had no children.

7) Bennie Barrett Bell (b. 1888) died as a child.

8) Lue Zella Bell (b. 1892) had no children.

9) Edd McKinley Bell (b. 1895) md. Maude Teresa Crawford (b. 1898); they had four children: Edna Elizabeth, Jack Lee, C.J. and William Robert

Of all the descendants, only Edna "Betty" Bell Harris lived in Conway County as recently as 2003. She and her husband (Clarence L. Harris, who grew

up in Morrilton) lived on Petit Jean Mountain during their retirement years.

BENNETT - Thomas Ransom Bennett (b. ca. 1834 in Wayne County, MO, d. between 1888 and 1900 in Conway County, AR) was a son of Coleman (b. ca. 1803 in Kentucky, d. ca. 1875 in Stoddard County, MO) and Elizabeth Smith Bennett (b. ca. 1802 in North Carolina, and d. ca. 1875 in Stoddard County, MO). Coleman is thought to be a son of Larkin Cyrus (b. ca. 1775 in Virginia, d. ca. 1859) and Dorothy Jones Bennett (b. ??, d. ca. 1812). Larkin C. Bennett is reported to be a descendant of Thomas F. (b. ca. 1742 Pittsylvania County, VA, d. 1809 Livingston County, KY) and Margaret "Peggy" Roysden Bennett.

Thomas and Nancy Douglass Bennett

Thomas F. Bennett's parents were William (b. June 2, 1703, d. 1778, Pittsylvania County, VA) and Hannah Goode Bennett. William Bennett's parents were William (b. ca. 1684, King and Queen County, VA, died ??) and Sarah Brumwell Bennett. William's grandfather was also William Bennett (b. ca. 1659 King and Queen County, VA, d. Feb 18, 1683/84) md. Mary Smith. The latter William Bennett was a son of John Bennett (b. ca. 1624 in Wiveliscombe, Somerset, England, died ??) md. Mary Sawyer Berry. This family has been traced back four more generations in Wiveliscombe, Somerset, England. Parents of John were Thomas Bennett Jr. and Agnes Beard. Thomas' parents were Thomas Bennett Sr. (b. April 2, 1750) and Anstie Tomson Als Spicer Bennett. Robert Bennett (b. 1537) and Elizabeth Edyne Bennett were Thomas Bennett Sr.'s parents. John Bennett (b. ca. 1500) and Margery were the parents of Robert.

Children of Coleman Bennett and Elizabeth Smith are:

1) John (L. or S.) Bennett (b. ca. 1822, d. April 5, 1888) md. Elizabeth Graham (b. Oct. 28, 1829, d. Dec. 11, 1892).

2) Larkin Bennett (b. ca. 1825, Missouri) md. Eliza Jane Marr?? (b. ca. 1825, Tennessee).

3) James Bennett (b. Dec. 9, 1828, Missouri) md. Margaret (b. ca. 1831, Illinois) in Wayne County, MO.

4) William Bennett (b. Dec. 9, 1828, Wayne County, MO, d. Nov. 21, 1901, Missouri) md. Mary Jane Ward (b. Dec. 15, 1830, Clay County, TN, d. Oct. 17, 1912) on Aug. 11, 1847, Missouri.

5) Ransom "Ranse" Bennett (b. Oct. 18, 1830, Missouri, d. Feb. 16, 1917, Wayne County, MO) md. Mary E. Pike (b. June 19, 1836, Tennessee, d. March 31, 1904) on June 24, 1859, Conway County, AR.

6) Thomas Ransom Bennett (b. ca. 1834, Wayne County, MO, d. bet. 1888-1900, Conway County, AR) md. Nancy Ann Douglass (b. 1837, Kentucky, d. Sept. 17, 1916, Van Buren County, AR) on Jan. 12, 1860, Conway County, AR.

7) Mary Smith Bennett (b. ca. 1838, died at a young age).

8) Perry Coleman Bennett (b. November 1838, Wayne County, MO, d. aft. 1900) md. Susan F. Fulkerson (b. 1848, Tennessee, died aft. 1900) on Aug. 30, 1866, Conway County, AR,

9) Noah Bennett (b. 1841, d. aft. 1888).

10) Francis Marion Bennett (b. 1843, d. in childhood).

Children of Thomas Bennett and Nancy Douglass are:

1) Sarah Francis Bennett (b. 1860, d. ??) md. John H. Lockhart (b. ca. 1854, Arkansas, d.??) on Aug. 9, 1877, Conway County, AR.

2) John Oliver Hazard Bennett (b. May 17, 1862, Arkansas, d. June 13, 1933, Faulkner County, AR) md. Rebecca Melinda Talley (b. Sept. 10, 1861, Arkansas, d. Dec. 21, 1901, Faulkner County, AR) in 1877, Van Buren County, AR.

3) Mary Ellen Bennett (b. April 30, 1864, Arkansas, d. March 28, 1937, Conway County, AR) md. Thomas J. Lockhart (b. March 5, 1859, d. March 21, 1930, Conway County, AR) in 1880, Van Buren County, AR.

4) Oragon Elizabeth "Betty" Bennett (b. December 1865, Van Buren County, AR, d. 1916, Van Buren County, AR) md. Melvin Green Brewer (b. May 1856, Orange County, NC, d. 1924, Formosa, Van Buren County, AR) on Jan. 9, 1887, Van Buren County, AR.

5) Coleman Rufus Bennett (b. June 2, 1867, Arkansas, d. Nov. 10, 1914, Van Buren County, AR) md. Mary A. Lackey (b. June 2, 1866, North Carolina, d. Jan. 11, 1945, Arkansas) in 1891, Van Buren County, AR.

6) Daisy Rancen Bennett (b. November 1878).

7) Nancy Myrtle Bennett (b. Feb. 12, 1879, d. 1978) md. Adolphus Taylor (b. 1874, d. 1943).

8) Cora Adeline Bennett (b. ??, d. 1965) md. Cole.

9) Roxie Emeline Bennett (dates unk.) md. Weber.

Children of John Bennett and Rebecca Talley are William T. Bennett (b. June 1885, died young age); Roxy E. Bennett (b. March 1886, d. ??) md. Henry Stephens (b. 1882, d. ??) on Dec. 27, 1903, Faulkner County, AR; Lou Bennett (b. October 1889) md. Hartsfield; Maggie Bennett (b. October 1890) md. Carmichael; Jela Lee Bennett (b. February 1892, died young age); Claude Bennett (b. December 1896, Arkansas, d. 1978) md. James May Vaughn (b. 1901, died ??) on Feb. 13, 1916, Faulkner County, AR; Walter Garland Bennett (b. ca. 1904, d. 1991, Arkansas) md. Flora Davis.

Children of Thomas Lockhart and Mary Ellen Bennett are Ben Lockhart (md. Lucille); Andrew Lockhart (md. Irene); Coleman Lockhart (md. Lizzie Mallett); Beryl Lockhart; Nora Lockhart (b. March 20, 1886, d. Sept. 19, 1977) md. Joe Benjamin Williams (b. March 8, 1883, d. Feb. 17, 1948, Conway County, AR).

Children of Melvin Green Brewer and Oragon Elizabeth "Betty" Bennett are:

1) Stella Brewer (b. Feb. 27, 1888, Arkansas, d. Jan. 16, 1989, North Little Rock, Arkansas) md. Charles H. Bailey (b. Dec. 10, 1886, died Jan. 20, 1970, Atkins, Arkansas).

2) Arrie Anna Brewer (b. Aug. 12, 1889, Formosa, Van Buren, AR, d. Oct. 24, 1969, Morrilton, AR) md. Samuel Lewis Henley (b. March 26, 1873, Arkansas, d. Jan. 8, 1961, Morrilton, AR).

3) Bertie Brewer (b. June 1, 1894, Okemah, OK, d. Feb. 24, 1975, Little Rock, Pulaski County, AR) md. Melvin Franklin Crownover (b. Jan. 4, 1890, Bee Branch, Van Buren County, AR, d. Feb. 22, 1970, Clinton, Van Buren County, AR) on Dec. 1, 1912, Van Buren County, AR.

4) Mary Esther Brewer (b. Jan. 25, 1897, Formosa, Van Buren, AR, d. Dec. 22, 1995, Clinton, Van Buren AR) md. Amos Oliger (b. April 7, 1894, d. May 16, 1945, Van Buren County, AR).

5) Buleah Brewer (b. Dec. 2, 1900, Formosa, Van Buren, AR, d. Jan. 14, 1994, Conway, Faulkner County, AR) md. A.C. "Aud" Shofner (b. Oct. 19, 1900, d. Nov. 22, 1987, Conway, Faulkner County, AR) in November 1918, Conway County, AR.

6) Hazel Lavern Brewer (b. Nov. 1, 1906, d. June 27, 1998, North Little Rock, Pulaski County, AR) md. 1st, Forest Myron Sickler (b. ??, d. December 1977) and 2nd Cheek.

Children of Coleman Rufus Bennett and Mary Lackey are:

1) Charles O. Bennett (b. Oct. 5, 1892, Springfield, MO, d. July 17, 1952, Conway County, AR) md. Rebecca J. Banning (b. March 1, 1905, d. July 17, 1952, Conway County, AR) on May 23, 1921, Van Buren County, AR.

2) Arthur L. Bennett (b. February 1894, Bee Branch, AR, d. April 24, 1960, Morrilton, Conway County, AR) md. Carlie L. Winningham (b. Feb. 24, 1900, d. May 12, 1980) on Dec. 24, 1917.

3) Minnie Bennett (b. Dec. 18, 1895, d. Aug. 18, 1991, Conway County, AR) md. 1st, James Smith and 2nd, Vasco Johnson (b. April 18, 1888, d. Sept. 13, 1977, Conway County, AR.

4) Dora M. Bennett (b. March 10, 1897, AR, d. Nov. 9, 1914.

5) Roy A. Bennett (b. Jan. 1, 1899, Arkansas, died Dec. 21, 1957, Arkansas.

6) Nancy Myrtle Bennett (b. Oct. 13, 1900, d. June 29, 1971, Conway County, AR) md. Walter McKinley "Kin" Shipp (b. Nov. 16, 1896, Conway County, AR, d. July 31, 1962, Conway County, AR).

7) Frank Rufus Bennett (b. Sept. 15, 1904, d. May 14, 1947, Merced, CA) md. Mary Ann Cargile (dates unk.).

8) William G. "Jesse" Bennett (b. 1909) md. Hazel Cargile.

Children of Adolphus Taylor and Nancy Myrtle Bennett are: Dolphia Ann Taylor (b. 1898) md. John Allen Marlar (b. 1890, d. 1976); Jerry Alvin Taylor (b. 1899, d. 1900); Harold Dan Taylor (b. 1901, d. 1985) md. Lillian Dale Ledbetter (b. 1908); Richard Lyle Taylor (b. 1910, d. 1965) md. Maude Isabelle Smith (b. 1913); Nelly Marie Taylor (b. 1910) md. 1st, Earl Jennings and 2nd, John Kelly. *Submitted by Charlotte Crownover West.*

BENTLEY – Eli Bentley came to Pecanerie (Peconery, Pecanary), Conway County's first white settlement, in 1820. Well known for its abundance of pecan trees and rich bottomland, Pecanerie was situated about a mile-and-a-half south of Sardis, a small community halfway between Morrilton and Plumerville. Eli and his family entered the territory of Arkansas from the state of Virginia.

In 1838 Eli Bentley moved to nearby Lewisburg, a small settlement on the north bank of the Arkansas River, where he established the mercantile firm of Eli Bentley and Co. Among the early Lewisburg planters and merchants were the Breedens, a family who emigrated from Tennessee and settled on the bank of the Arkansas River at Howard's Landing. In 1871 the mercantile firm of L.O. Breeden and Son was established in Lewisburg. A union of these two families occurred when P.O. Breeden, son of L.O. Breeden, was married to Miss Mary Jane Bentley, a daughter of Eli Bentley.

In time the railroad came through the region and was routed through Morrilton. This profoundly changed the fortunes of Lewisburg and eventually stole away much of the Arkansas River commerce from Lewisburg, causing the latter to steadily lose population to Morrilton and to its railroad. Eli Bentley's family was among those in Lewisburg who resettled in the newly created town of Morrilton. Among them was Oliver Tolls "O.T." Bentley (b. Dec. 31, 1854, d. March

12, 1918), a son of Eli Bentley, who practiced law in Morrilton and was a member of the Conway County Bar Association. O.T. Bentley was a graduate of the University of Arkansas, and of the Law Department of Vanderbilt University. He served as a Conway County judge for two terms: 1896-98 and 1898-1900. One of O.T. Bentley's daughters, Mae/May Bentley, married Robin Cruce, a son of Columbus Erasmus "C.E." Cruce, founder of the *Morrilton Democrat.*

C.E. Cruce was born in Paris, TX in 1862. He moved with his family to Warrensburg, MO in 1866. As a youth, he worked on his father's farm in Warrensburg for several years. In 1880 he joined the *Warrensburg Journal-Democrat.* He came to Arkansas in 1885 and was employed as make-up and ad man on the *Ft. Smith Times.* In 1890 C.E. Cruce purchased the interest of Jesse A. Bell of the firm of Hampton and Bell, publishers of the *Greenwood Democrat.* Four years later he bought out Mr. Hampton. He sold the *Greenwood Democrat* in 1896 and moved to Morrilton where he established the *Morrilton Democrat.* After an illness of several years, he died on Dec. 28, 1920 at age 58. On March 26, 1929 the *Morrilton Democrat* was purchased by Curtis B. Hurley, then president of the Arkansas Press Association, and former publisher of the *Camden News. Submitted by Robert (Robin) Cruce Jr.*

BERRY - Johnnie Keith Berry (b. Dec. 2, 1945, in Hot Springs), son of Orville Benjamin Berry and Susie Mae Chote Berry, served in the US Army as an airborne ranger during the Vietnam War. His military career was ended prematurely when his plane was shot down by enemy fire, resulting in physical injuries requiring his discharge.

He owned a trucking company and spent many years working in the transportation industry. Johnnie moved from Hot

Johnnie K. Berry 2004

Springs to Conway County in October 2004, making his home in Granny Hollow near Jerusalem, and he is an owner in JonMar Trucking. *Submitted by J. Berry.*

BERRY - William Berry's father emigrated from England, sailing from Belfast, Ireland about 1740 and settling in Virginia. William Berry was born prior to 1755 in Virginia. He served as a private under General George Washington in the Revolutionary War. William married Susannah Taylor, daughter of Grant Taylor, prior to 1776. About 1795, William and Susannah moved from Virginia to Oglethorpe County, GA, where William purchased over 400 acres of land. In 1804 William received a land grant in Franklin County, GA and in 1807 he sold 601 acres in Franklin County to his brother, Taliaferro Berry. William died prior to July 1809.

On the first Monday in July 1809, Susannah Berry, widow, and Taliaferro Berry were made administrators of the Estate of William Berry. William and Susannah had at least eight children (order of birth unknown): William Berry; "Polly" Berry (md. Thomas B. Landers); Frances Berry (md. Samuel Brightwell); Taliaferro L. Berry; Edmund G. Berry; John D. Berry; Susannah Berry (md. Beverly Daniels); Patsy "Martha" Berry (md. Jesse Wyatt Hewell).

William Berry (b. ca. 1776 in Virginia), son of William and Susannah, married Cally (last name unknown) ca. 1795. William's family moved to Georgia about 1795. In 1808 William appeared on the Tax Digest of Morgan County, GA. He was a landowner and farmer and fought with Andrew Jackson in the War of 1812. On Jan. 1, 1818 William sold land in Morgan County to his brother Edmund Berry. On Sept. 1, 1818, William and his mother, Susannah Berry (widow), released their rights to one tenth part of 100 acres, part

of the estate of William Berry, his father, deceased. William died soon after September 1818. Soon after William's death Cally moved the family to Hardin County, TN. She appears on the 1820 Hardin County census with her son and seven daughters. Cally died about 1830.

William Berry (b. 1807 in Georgia), son of William and Cally Berry, married Sarah Weatherford about 1827 in Hardin County, TN. Sarah (b. 1806 in Tennessee) was the daughter of William Weatherford and Margaret Ann Polk. Prior to 1830, William and Sarah moved their family to Wayne County, TN. Sarah died in Wayne County between 1851-57. William married Lucinda King on Dec. 10, 1858 in Wayne County. Lucinda (b. Jan. 27, 1821 in Tennessee) was the daughter of Samuel King. William signed his will on Sept. 18, 1866, in which he listed his children. The will was probated in the Wayne County court on Feb. 3, 1869. Lucinda died July 1, 1883. William and Lucinda had no children.

William and Sarah (Weatherford) Berry's children were: (1) Mary Margaret "Peggy" Berry (b. 1828, d. Nov. 21, 1897) md. Nathaniel H. Horton; (2) William Alderson Berry (b. 1829, d. Jan. 5, 1910) md. Mrs. Mary Martin; (3) Rebecca Berry (b. 1830, d. Dec. 18, 1864) md. Thomas Madison Alexander; (4) John Wyatt Berry (b. 1832, d. December 1872) md. Nancy Margaret Newman; (5) Joseph George Berry (b. Jan. 22, 1834, d. Dec. 8, 1889) md. Elmira Jane Cypert; (6) Sarah Ann Elizabeth Berry (b. July 19, 1836, d. Jan. 4, 1916) md. David Cook Greeson; (7) James Ellison Berry (b. May 19, 1838, d. Jan. 30, 1907) md. Mrs. Frances Wayne Hensley (or Hamm); (8) Nancy Emaline Berry (b. 1842, d. 1920) md. Franklin Cole.

BESCHORNER - August Beschorner (b. Sept. 12, 1836 in Germany) came to Morrilton, AR with his wife Agnes and their children in 1880. August was a day laborer. They had three sons: Paul, William and Andrew. The only thing known of Andrew is that he settled in St. Louis, MO and was still living at the time his brother William died.

August and Agnes Beschorner.

Paul Beschorner (b. April 1876 in Germany) md. Mary Thome on Oct. 9, 1900 in Morrilton. They had one son Paul who died at the age of 6 years. Paul and Mary moved to North Little Rock, AR where he became the proprietor of Argenta Bottling Works. He remained in this business until he died of a heart attack in his back yard on April 26, 1921.

William Beschorner (b. Feb. 1, 1879 in Germany) md. Magdalena Comes, the daughter of a prominent Morrilton businessman, John Richard Comes and his wife Marguerite, on May 9, 1905. She was born in LaRochette, Luxembourg Nov. 11, 1878. They moved to North Little Rock, AR where William joined his brother Paul as co-owner of Argenta Bottling Works. They had two daughters, Eleanor and Margaret. Later they adopted a daughter Elizabeth. William passed away April 23, 1929 in El Paso, TX where he had gone for his health. Magdalena died May 20, 1937 in North Little Rock. William and Magdalena are buried in Calvary Cemetery in Little Rock.

Eleanor passed away at the age of 6 years. She is buried in Sacred Heart Cemetery in Morrilton, next to her paternal grandparents, August and Agnes.

Margaret (b. Jan. 9, 1906) md. Thomas Buton

Jones of Lonoke, AR on Nov. 7, 1928. Thomas was born Aug. 9, 1904. Upon the death of her father, they took over as proprietors of Argenta Bottling Works, which they ran until 1961 when it was sold. They had five children: Rosalyn (b. Sept. 11, 1930), Thomas B. Jr. (b. Sept. 21, 1932), Margaret Ann (b. Nov. 5, 1935), Mary Comes (b. Jan. 23, 1938) and Elizabeth "Betty" Sue (b. Dec. 5, 1940). Margaret and Tommy and their deceased descendants are buried in Calvary Cemetery in Little Rock.

Rosalyn married Harry Lee Hastings Jr. and lives in Little Rock, AR. They have three children: Harry Lee III, Catherine Marre and Stanley Thomas.

Thomas married Jean Ann Pratt and resided in North Little Rock. They had one son, Thomas B. Jones III. Thomas Jr. passed away May 23, 1991 and his wife Jean Ann died July 4, 1998.

Margaret Ann married James Lawrence Phillips and lives in Little Rock. They have six surviving children: Deborah Kay, Cynthia Ann, Michael Thomas, Ronald Clark, Mary Denise and Matthew James. The oldest, David Ray, passed away Sept. 12, 1980. Another child John Barron passed away shortly after his birth.

Mary married Don Engle Crain and resides in Little Rock. They have three children: Donald Clay, Dore Lynn and Tracy Marie.

Betty married Ross Richard Mayfield of El Dorado, AR and lives in Dickinson, TX. They have three daughters: Kimberly Ann, Terry Lynn and Lisa Marie.

Elizabeth Beschorner married Thomas Davis and resided first in North Little Rock and later in Little Rock. He worked at the bottling works for Margaret and Tom Jones. They had three children: Isabelle, James Thomas and Robert Marion. *Submitted by Mary Jones Crain.*

BINGHAM

BINGHAM - Robert Lee Bingham and Margie Luellen Lawson married on July 30, 1938 in Oppelo, AR. Robert Lee (b. April 6, 1920, d. Jan. 14, 2001) was the son of Alexander Bingham and Edith Hopkins. Margie (b. Oct. 4, 1917, d. Aug. 27, 1996) was the daughter of Otto Allison Lawson and Lillie Bell Jones. Both are buried at Ada Valley, AR.

Robert and Margie Bingham

Their children are:

1) Roberta Luellen Bingham (b. July 4, 1939, Ada Valley, AR) md. William David Earl Anderson Dec. 24, 1961. Their children are: (a) Lex Allen Anderson (b. Feb. 27, 1963) md. May 4, 1999 to Cathy Arleen Zimmerman (b. Aug. 10, 1965). Their child is Margie Mae Anderson (b. Feb. 10, 1992). (b) Sonya Letitia Anderson (b. July 28, 1964) md. first, Russell Robert Walker Pelc (b. Aug. 20, 1960) on Dec. 31, 1987. Their children are Shawna Latricia Anderson (b. May 17, 1984), Roberta Alish Anderson (b. July 21, 1991) and Chance David Anderson (b. Aug. 16, 1992). They divorced in May 1988 and Sonya married again to James Meyer on June 18, 2004. (c) David Jon Paul Anderson (b. Oct. 29, 1965) md. Rebecca Kay Caldwell (b. Feb. 24, 1969) on May 30, 1987. Their children are Dylan Wayne Anderson (b. May 9, 1991) and Summer Kay Anderson (b. July 12, 1995).

2) Bonnie Lee Bingham (b. July 26, 1941) md. Aug. 17, 1957 to Coy Lee Jones (b. May 22, 1937). Their children are Steven Coyle Jones (b. Feb. 24, 1959), Vernon Keith Jones (b. March 4, 1961) and Gregory Lynn Jones (b. Feb. 17, 1963). They have seven grandchildren and three great-grandchildren.

3) Edith Loretta Bingham (b. Sept. 16, 1943) md. Feb. 20, 1961 to Charles Raymond Jones (b. July 6, 1938). Their children are Carlotta Marietta Jones (b.

Sept. 27, 1961); Ronda Raylene Jones (b. Nov. 25, 1962, d. Jan. 20, 1996); Susan Kathlene Jones (b. Dec. 17, 1963) and Charles Wade Jones (b. May 15, 1965). They have four grandchildren and two great-grand-children

4) Edwin Leon Bingham (b. Jan. 6, 1947 at Oppelo) md. April 7, 1969 to Patty Relli (b. June 22, 1949). Their children are Robert Dominic Bingham (b. March 17, 1971) and Laura Ann Bingham (b. Jan. 23, 1973). Laura married Alex Whitley on Nov. 11, 1996. After getting a divorce Edwin Leon Bingham married July 24, 1993 to Tami Ferguson Miller (b. March 15, 1962). Edwin's stepchild is Abby Miller (b. Dec. 3, 1986). Edwin has two grandchildren

5) Guy Lawson Bingham (b. June 23, 1956 in Morrilton) md. March 13, 1978 to Linda Marie Armor Stone (b. Nov. 16, 1955). Their children are Margie Lynn Stone Bingham (b. Dec. 23, 1973 and adopted by Guy); Megan Renee Bingham (b. Aug. 29, 1977) and Brittiany Marie Bingham (b. July 15, 1983). Guy divorced Linda and has not remarried. He has three grandchildren.

BIRD

BIRD - James W. Bird was born in January 1836 in Union County, MS, and his wife Susan F. was born March 1840, also in Mississippi. Both of their parents were from Tennessee. James was a Civil War veteran, having served in both the 17th Mississippi Infantry, and the 18th Mississippi Cavalry. About 1873, the family moved to Arkansas. Perhaps first to Sharp County, then Conway County. They lived first in Union Twp., then Washington Twp. at Solgohachia. James was a farmer, both in Mississippi and Arkansas. At one time or another, he had three parcels of land in and around Solgohachia.

Left to right: Adolf "Dolf" Gordon, son, born Oct. 6, 1887 (approx. 8 years old). Jerome E. Gordon, father, born Sept. 24, 1865 (approx. 30 years old). Laura Lola Gordon (Loly), daughter, born Aug. 4, 1892 (approx. 3 years old). Susan Alice "Sally" (Bird) Gordon, mother, born March 10, 1868 (approx. 27 years old). Luther Gordon, son, born Nov. 21, 1894 (approx. 1 year old, on mother's lap). James "Jim" Campbell Gordon, son, born April 26, 1889 (approx. 6-1/2 years old). Young man standing is unknown (family friend).

James and Susan had a total of seven children, the first three born in Mississippi and the last four born in Arkansas: Luretta (b. 1864), Elizabeth (b. 1866), Susan Alice (b. March 10, 1868), Emma (b. 1873), William (b. 1876), Mattie (b. 1878) and Luther H. (b. November 1880).

The third daughter, Susan Alice, married Jerome E. Gordon of Solgohachia on Oct. 15, 1886. Jerome was the fourth of 15 children of Hiram Campbell Gordon and Sarah Angeline Bearden of Solgohachia. They were married by the Rev. Berryman H. Bearden of Solgohachia, Jerome's great-uncle (Jerome's mother being Sarah Angeline [Bearden] Gordon). Jerome and Susan lived in the Solgohachia area after they were married. Approximately three months after the birth of their fifth child, Sally died on Oct. 28, 1897, of Diabetes or Bright's disease. She is buried on private property north of Solgohachia on Highway 9, South of Cypress Creek.

James applied for a Confederate pension while living in Solgohachia, and was granted the sum of $25.

His pension papers state that he died on June 21, 1905, and his wife applied for his pension after his death. James' and Susan's gravesite are not listed in Conway County's cemetery listings. Although a Confederate veteran and pensioner, James is not listed in the Arkansas Confederate veterans gravesite listings.

BIRD

BIRD - John Bird's early life is written in the *Biography of Arkansas* as a fruit grower in Conway County. It named his parents as Jacob Bird Jr. and Nancy Brickey Bird. My great-grandmother, Mary C. Bird Gasaway, was one of his sisters. John (b. Oct. 7, 1852 in Walker County, GA, d. June 22, 1914) is buried on Pettit Jean Mountain.

John Bird's father, Jacob Bird II, was a child of Jacob Bird Sr. and Amelia Dunn. Jacob Sr. was the son of the Revo-

John Bird, fruit grower in Conway County.

lutionary Soldier John Bird who is buried in Greenville, TN. Amelia was the daughter of Daniel Dunn, another Revolutionary Soldier. John Bird was born in Henrico County, VA in 1749.

Nancy Brickey Bird was born in Blount County, TN, child of another Revolutionary soldier, William Brickey. The Brickey family bought up about 8,000 acres of land near Maryville, TN and an old cabin built by Brickey still stands on land still in the family.

Our migrating ancestor on the Brickey line is John who first appeared in Westmoreland County, VA, Court records in 1690. This John Brickey was appointed Constable of the Precinct 5, June 1710, and served three years. John's wife is unknown. We descend from John through his son Peter, who married Winifred Lucas. Their son John who married Mary Garner, to William Brickey who married Eleanor Dobkins and were the parents of Nancy Brickey who married Jacob Bird II and were parents of John, Mary and others. The Lucas Courtneys, Garners and Keenes lead us into the earliest settlement of this country.

The Garners patented land on Cherry Point, MD which is located across the Potomac River from the area near where John Washington, George's Washington's father lived, and the Garners seem to have come to this area about the same time as George Washington's family from England. Nancy Brickey's father, William Brickey, was the son of John Brickey and Mary Elizabeth Garner (b. 1740 Westmoreland County, VA) and her parents were Thomas Garner and Rosemond Courtney. John Garner, the progenitor of this line of Garners, came to the County of Northhumberland in the Colony of Virginia about 1650 at the age of 17, probably of English origin. John married Susanna Keene, daughter of Thomas and Mary Keene. Susanna was probably born on Kent Island in the Potomac River during the period of 1634-1649.

Thomas Keene, father of Susanna Keene, was born presumably in England in 1593. He is first found on Kent Island, which lays just off the coast of Maryland in Chesapeake Bay. Thomas is thought to be the son of Thomas and Elizabeth (Gosnold) Keene.

Elizabeth Gosnold was the daughter of Robert Gosnold of Earleshall County, Suffolk, England. Gosnold was a Justice of the Peace for Suffolk. His wife was Ursula, third daughter of William Naunton of Leatheringham Abbey. He is said to have descended from John Gosnold of Otley, Suffolk, England, who lived during the reign of Henry VII. A prominent member of this family was Bartholomew Gosnold, nephew of Robert, who commanded the *Goodspeed* and was vice admiral of the fleet of three vessels, including *The Sarah Constant* and the *Discovery*. The *Goodspeed* and the *Discovery* landed at Jamestown, VA in 1607. In 1602 he discovered the

Island of Martha's Vineyard and named it for one of his daughters. A chart of this Gosnold family may be found in the Library of the Virginia Historical Society of Richmond, VA. *Submitted by Mrs. C.B. Wingert.*

BIRD - John Bird's early life is written in the *Biography of Arkansas* as a fruit grower in Conway County. It named his parents as Jacob Bird Jr. and Nancy Brickey Bird. My great-grandmother, Mary C. Bird Gasaway, was one of his sisters. John (b. Oct. 7, 1852 in Walker County, GA, d. June 22, 1914) is buried on Pettit Jean Mountain. His siblings were Wm. Buford, Amelia, Jacob H., Jane, Elizabeth E., Mary, Susan, Talitha, Daniel G., John A., Richard Othnice and James Martin Bird.

Mary Bird Gasaway and her husband, Thomas Marion Gasaway, started West after the 1870 census of Walker County, GA.

My grandmother Mattie Cumi Gasaway Huggins (b. Aug. 15, 1872, Dardnelle, Yell County, AR) had two other brothers born in this area. About 1880 the Thomas Marion Gasaway family moved from central Arkansas into Scott County where we have many relatives in that area and on into Eastern Oklahoma, probably to the coal mines near McAlester and Sallisaw, OK. James Madison Bird was a miner and died near Sallisaw, OK of Black Lung, a disease of coal miners. When James died, his brother John came from Arkansas and took his children back to Arkansas and raised them as his own. James Martin Bird's children were Arthur Othonel, James Jacob, Josie, Nettie and Matin Bird who all died young.

John Bird's father, Jacob Bird II, was a child of Jacob Bird Sr. and Amelia Dunn. Jacob Sr. was the son of the Revolutionary soldier, John Bird, who is buried in Greenville, TN. Amelia was the daughter of Daniel Dunn, another Revolutionary soldier. John Bird was born in Henrico County, VA in 1749 and this is the area where the Birds of Virginia first settled, but at this time no connection with that family has been made.

Nancy Brickey Bird was born in Blount County, TN, another child of a Revolutionary soldier, William Brickey. The Brickey family bought up about 8,000 acres of land near Maryville, TN and an old cabin built by Brickey still stands on land still in the family; also, an old cemetery is on the property that has graves since the Revolutionary War. Nancy Brickey Bird was born in this cabin and lived there probably until she married Jacob Bird II.

Our migrating ancestor on the Brickey side is John who first appeared in Westmoreland County, VA Court records in 1690. This John Brickey was appointed Constable of the Precinct 5, June 1710; he served three years. John's wife is unknown. We descend from John through his son Peter who married Winifred Lucas, their son John who married Mary Garner, to William Brickey who married Eleanor Dobkins and were the parents of Nancy Brickey who married Jacob Bird II and were parents of John, Mary and others. The Lucas Courtneys, Garners and Keenes lead us into the earliest settlement of this country. The Garners patented land on Cherry Point, Maryland which is located across the Potomac River from the area near where John Washington, George's Washington's father lived, and the Garners seem to have come to this area about the same time as George Washington's family from England.

Nancy Brickey's father, William Brickey, was the son of John Brickey and Mary Elizabeth Garner, born 1740 Westmoreland County, VA and her parents were Thomas Garner and Rosemond Courtney. John Garner the progenitor of this line of Garners, came to the County of Northhumberland in the Colony of Virginia about 1650 at the age of 17, probably of English origin. John married Susanna Keene daughter of Thomas and Mary Keene. Susanna was probably born on Kent Island in the Potomac River during the period of 1634-1649.

Thomas Keene, father of Susanna Keene, was

born presumably in England in 1593. He is first found on Kent Island. This island lays just off the coast of Maryland in Chesapeake Bay. Thomas is thought to be the son of Thomas and Elizabeth (Gosnold) Keene.

Elizabeth Gosnold was the daughter of Robert Gosnold of Earleshall County, Suffolk, England. Gosnold was a Justice of the Peace for Suffolk. His wife was Ursula, third daughter of William Naunton of Leatheringham Abbey. He is said to have descended from John Gosnold of Otley, Suffolk, England who lived during the reign of Henry VII. A prominent member of this family was Bartholomew Gosnold, nephew of Robert, who commanded the *Goodspeed* and was vice admiral of the fleet of three vessels, *The Sarah Constant* and the *Discovery*. The *Goodspeed* and the *Discovery* landed at Jamestown, VA in 1607. In 1602 he discovered the Island of Martha's Vineyard and named it for one of his daughters. A chart of this Gosnold family may be found in the Library of the Virginia Historical Society of Richmond, VA. *Submitted by Jean Huggins Wingert.*

BISHOP - William Daniel Bishop (b. March 18, 1844 in Pulaski County, KY), son of Johnathan and Sarah Price Bishop, married Artymace Helena Vanhook on Aug. 29, 1867, in Pulaski County, KY. Artymace's parents were Benjamin Vanhook and Miss Kirtley. William Daniel and Artymace Bishop brought their family to Arkansas from Kentucky around the late 1880s. They settled first in Van Buren County, AR, then moved to Conway County in the Birdtown area.

Tolbert Francis Bishop with what was known as the "Rauleigh Hack."

William and Artymace Helena had seven children: Tolbert Francis (md. 1st, Lillian Stobaugh and 2nd, Mary Susan Carolina Allen); Kittie Bell (md. Dr. I. Harman Pavatte); John (md. Sarah Quinn); Thomas (md. 1st, Mary Iola Harmon and 2nd, Bertha P. Huie); Catherine Mae (md. 1st, David Benjamin Waters and 2nd, Jim Herrin) and two children who died young.

Tolbert Francis, known as Tollie or T.F. Bishop, was born Aug. 31, 1872 in Louisville, KY, son of William Daniel and Artymace Bishop. Tollie traveled around Conway and Van Buren counties in his horse and buggy selling "Rauleigh" products (spices, extracts, toilet articles and etc.) Tollie married Lillian Stobaugh on Dec. 3, 1894 and they had four children: Violet (md. 1. James Jamerson, 2. James Fred Gongeau, 3. James Furlong Sr., 4. Truman Hill); Winnie (md. Roy Barton); Norene (md. 1st, Willie Jones and 2nd, Mitt Scroggins); and a baby who died along with Lillian during childbirth.

Tollie married Mary Susan Carolina Allen on Feb. 20, 1906 in Van Buren County, AR and they had 12 children: Sybil (died young); Iris married David Wesley Huett and together they owned and operated Huett's Grocery Store at Birdtown; William Perry (md. Leta Faye Fitzgerald); Cyril Clyde Bishop (md. Hazel Goldie Flora New); Wilma Inez (md. John Tom Chambers); Gladys (md. Tony Bernard DeSalvo); Baby Girl (died at birth); Lawrence Wilburn (md. Florabel Douglas); Allen Dalton (md. Betty Eoff), Frank (died young); Lena (md. Robert Earl Groom); and Tolbert Francis Jr. (died at 2 months).

Cyril Clyde Bishop, son of Tolbert, was a preacher, editor, writer and missionary. Bro. Bishop, as he preferred to be called, was converted and bap-

tized by the Pleasant Springs Baptist Church, Springfield, AR (Conway County), in the summer of 1925. He was licensed to preach by Pleasant Springs Church on March 17, 1929 and ordained to the ministry by this church on Sept. 14, 1930.

Thomas L. Bishop (b. June 6, 1880 in Jefferson County, KY), son of William and Artymace Bishop, married Bertha Huie and they had Opal (md. Claud Martin), Carmie (md. Loulee Martin), Addie, Lola (md. Taft Berry), and Emmer Eveline (md. Carroll Sigler).

Thomas had four children with his second wife, Mary Iola Harmon: James Elmer (md. Rubye Ernest McCasland), Lois (md. Dan Pearson), Nobie Lee (md. Horace Weaver Waddell) and Robert Earl Bishop (md. Lela May Andrus).

Catherine Mae Bishop, daughter to William and Artymace Bishop, married Jim Herron and they had Elsie and Jessie. Catherine then married David Benjamin Waters and they had Sadie and Harvey.

John Bishop, son of William and Artymace, married Sarah Quinn and had Farrie.

BLACKMON - Daniel Blackmon was born a slave about 1846. Family oral history recalls that he told them that when he was being sold, he was put on the auction block and given a piece of gingerbread so he would stand still for the buyers to inspect him. Daniel became a farmer. He married Amelia in the 1800s. The family moved to Conway County, AR.

Daniel Blackmon appears in the 1910 census of Washington Township, Conway County, AR, as a 63-year-old widower born in South Carolina. There were four children in the household with him. The children of Daniel and Amelia Blackmon were Hattie, Mattie, Edward Stokes, John, George, Liza, Jane, Ben, Minnie and Ella.

Hattie Blackmon married Spain Mitchem (Meacham) Dec. 23, 1897. They were parents of Fred, Morgan, James, Wendell, Elbert, Jewel, Scipio, Josie and Goldie.

Mattie - no information available.

John Blackmon married and was the father of two children, Beulah and Dessie Blackmon.

Daniel's son, my Uncle Ed, lived next door. Ed was born in South Carolina and married Emma Brown. They were the parents of 12 children: Huey, Edgar, Robert, Elliott, David, Ethel, Girtha, Willie, Jeremiah, Obadiah, Edward Stokes Blackmon (d. June 1957) and one who died in infancy.

Rev. George Washington Blackmon (b. 1895 in Solgohachia, AR, d. 1945 in Little Rock, AR) married three times. He and first wife, Rena were the parents of George Jr. He and Virgie were the parents of Booker C. Blackmon. When he was 38 years old, he married 15-year-old Mildred Vera Catherine Webb on May 1, 1934. They became parents of Melie Pauline, Daniel, Paul Lawrence, Maxine Elizabeth, Wayne Apollis and Georgia Ann.

Jane Blackmon was the mother of Arthur Bryant.

Liza Blackmon Scott married and was the mother of James and Nathaniel.

Benjamin Blackmon II married Bertha Jefferson. To this union six children were born: Lula Mae Blackmon Robinson, Annie Blackmon Erby, Jessie Lee, Ruby Blackmon Ausler, Arbie Blackmon Blackwell Templeton and Lamond Blackmon.

Ella Blackmon, the youngest of Daniel's Blackmon's children, married Willie Carolina.

Minnie Blackmon Gunnels (b. 1899 in Arkansas) md. Matthew Gunnels and they became parents of following children: Marzetta Gunnels Shephard, Mattie Lee, Sherman, Leroy, Lillie Mae Gunnels Dorris, Leola Gunnels Dorris, Maella Gunnels Scott, Onella Gunnels Kindle, and Loreatha Gunnels Mayberry.

Daniel Blackmon had a brother named Benjamin and also a son named Benjamin. Daniel's brother Ben married Matilda Mitchem (also spelled Meacham). Ben and his wife were traveling to Arkansas and became separated. Two of the children were with Ben (names unknown) and two were with Matilda. Those two were Hattie and John. Hattie married a Rose and they were parents of three children: Annie, Dewey and Earl Blackmon. John Henry married Alice Jackson and they were the parents of three children. *Submitted by Rev. Loreatha Gunnels Mayberry.*

BOOZER - Richard was born September 1861 in South Carolina and died in Morrilton, Conway County, AR in 1901. Richard's siblings included John Hampton Boozer, Hattie Boozer Thornton, and Lemuel Boozer Thornton. John Hampton Boozer married Caroline Brockington. Their children were Moses, Addie, Hattie Boozer McGill, Bernice, Hazel Boozer, Evalina Boozer Flournoy, and Bernice Boozer Foster. Richard married Alice Ponds in 1883.

Alice Ponds (b. May 1861 in South Carolina, d. 1918 in Morrilton, Conway County, AR) is buried in Oddfellows Cemetery in Morrilton under the double headstone of Richard B. and Alice Boozer.

Annie Boozer, Alice's oldest daughter, married F.M. Mason, a brick mason and business owner, on Dec. 27, 1893. They resided in Little Rock, AR and were the parents of three children.

The oldest son Moses Davis (b. July 1, 1877 in South Carolina, d. Feb. 8, 1954 in Morrilton, AR) md. Elizabeth Washington. They were parents of seven children: Oliver Davis; Salena Davis (b. ca. 1908, d. May 30, 1923 in Morrilton, Conway County, AR); Aretha Davis (b. ca. 1910); Lovell Davis (b. ca. 1914) md. Lovie Tresvant about 1933 in Morrilton, AR. Lovie (b. Dec. 14, 1917 in Morrilton, d. July 16, 1992 in Kansas City, MO) was the daughter of Rev. George W. and Katherine Tresvant.

Pauline Boozer Oliver (b. Sept. 18, 1886, Morrilton, AR) md. Grant "Bo" Oliver, son of Rena Oliver. They resided in Morrilton, AR. When her sister Naomi died, Pauline raised her two daughters. Pauline died Oct. 12, 1963, in Chicago, IL, and is buried in Morrilton's Oddfellows Cemetery.

Otto Boozer (b. Nov. 20, 1892 in Morrilton, AR, d. May 10, 1955, Morrilton).

Naomi Boozer (b. March 9, 1896 in Morrilton, d. May 23, 1923 in Morrilton) md. Will Hensley (b. Jan. 18, 1894, d. Jan. 7, 1950 in Chicago, IL). Their children were Claudia Louise Hensley Lambert Ray and Jerlean Hensley

Richard Boozer Jr. (b. ca. 1902, d. ca. 1925) and his wife Mary, who was from Hempstead County, AR, were the parents of four children: Richard III, James C., Annie Jerlean, and Tollie H. When Richard died, Mary and the children moved to Hempstead County. Richard III and James are deceased; Tollie died in Ozan, AR in September 2001; and Annie Jerlean lives in Nashville, AR

A daughter, Rachel Boozer, was born in 1898 but I have no further information about her. *Submitted by James Oliver.*

BRADLEY - Isaac Taylor Bradley (b. 1844) md. Elisabeth "Lizzie" Prince (b. September 1840, d. July 25, 1905). Records say that their families came to Arkansas from Tennessee. They settled first in the Mt. View, Leslie, Marshall areas of Searcy and Van Buren counties. Isaac Taylor Bradley is buried in the Grandview Cemetery near Center Ridge, AR. Elisabeth was buried in Halbrook Cemetery between Center Ridge and Formosa. Her first husband was a Mr. Gordon and her mother was Charity Halbrook and her father was Miles Prince. Charity Halbrook's father was Wm. Erwin Halbrook (1782).

Isaac Taylor was killed by a team of run-away mules. Elisabeth's children by Mr. Gordon were Joe P. (b. July 11, 1860); Roxie (b. March 15, 1863, d. Jan. 10, 1944) md. Jim Bryant; Wm. M. (or F) (b. May 19, 1864). All three are buried at Halbrook Cemetery, as are most of Lizzie's brothers and sisters. John Thomas (b. July 1, 1867, d. July 12, 1947); Charity Bradley (Smith) (b. 1869); Bluford (b. 1872); Mariah Jane (Stobaugh) (b. 1874); Isaac Newton (b. 1876); and

Jasper (died at 3 months of age). *Submitted by Eva L. Bradley Cralle.*

BRADLEY - In 1717, James and Elizabeth Scroggins sailed to America from England and settled in Baltimore, MD. Their great-grandson Larkin Scroggins (b. 1775 in Virginia) md. Sarah and had four children: Henson, John, Sarah and Floyd. Of these four children, Henson Scroggins (b. 1800 in Georgia) and his wife Melinda had nine children including Green Scroggins (b. March 17, 1841, Conway County, d. Aug. 5, 1899). Green married Elizabeth "Granny" Franklin (b. April 12, 1847, d. Oct. 11, 1935). Green and Elizabeth had several children including Jessee James Scroggins (b. Nov. 22, 1874, d. June 24, 1927) md. Mary Elizabeth "Lizzie" Reid (b. Aug. 11, 1880, d. June 16, 1959).

Bottom row: Lee Roy Ridling Sr. and Loretta Gail Scroggins Ridling. Top row: Malinda Jean Ridling Rhea, Lee Roy Ridling Jr. and Margaret Ann Ridling Bradley. Photo taken 2001.

Annie Scroggins with family, 1977. Bottom row: Loretta, Annie, Linda. Standing l-r: Johnny, Mary, Betty, James, Jean, George, Ruby and Marie.

The Jessee James Scroggins' Family. Standing l-r: Jessee Scroggins, George Monroe Scroggins, Annie Scroggins. Seated: Jessee James Scroggins and Mary Elizabeth Scroggins with baby, Ira Pete Scroggins. Taken approximately 1914.

Jessee and Lizzie Scroggins were the parents of six children: Annie, George Monroe, Ira Pete, Jessee, Lloyd and an unnamed daughter who died in infancy. George Monroe (b. May 7, 1898, d. April 21, 1964), commonly known as Monroe, was born in Cleveland, AR. On Aug. 24, 1919, George Monroe married Annie Lee Huffman (b. March 12, 1906, d. Nov. 27, 1983). Annie was born near Marshall, AR to William Henry (b. 1864, d. 1957) and Nancy Adline House Huffman (b. 1868, d. 1938). George and Annie Scroggins lived in Jerusalem, and they had 11 children: Virgil Marie (b. April 28, 1922, d. July 2, 2001); Ruby May (b. May 1, 1924); Jessie Monroe (b. Nov. 15, 1927, d. Dec. 15, 1927); George William (b. June 14, 1930, d.

George Monroe and Annie Scroggins, background Linda Scroggins with baby Charley Burnett, 1959.

Aug. 16, 1985); Jean (b. Oct. 3, 1933); James Marion (b. Sept. 3, 1935, d. Aug. 2, 1979); Betty Sue (b. May 4, 1938); Mary Lou (b. April 22, 1941); John Everett (b. Sept. 8, 1944); Linda Dale (b. Dec. 11, 1946, d. May 3, 1989) and Loretta Gail (b. Nov. 14, 1948).

On Aug. 6, 1966, George and Annie's youngest child, Loretta Gail, married Lee Roy Ridling (b. Aug. 16, 1947) from Lanty. Lee is the son of Oscar Earl (b. Feb. 14, 1915, d. Oct. 5, 1979) and Sarah Margaret (b. June 18, 1925). Lee served in the army during the Vietnam War. After Lee's military service, they moved to Rockford, IL. They have three children: Lee Roy Jr. (b. July 7, 1970), Margaret Ann (b. Dec. 26, 1971), and Malinda Jean (b. April 28, 1976). After living in Rockford, IL for many years, Lee and Loretta moved back to Morrilton in 1976. They presently live in Lanty, AR.

Lee Roy Jr. married Betty Kimberly Phelps (b. Oct. 12, 1971) on May 18, 1996. They reside in Seattle, WA and have two daughters, Calissa (b. Aug. 14, 2001) and Regan (b. Oct. 3, 2003).

Margaret married Jerry Norman Bradley (b. Oct. 13, 1966), known as Norman, on June 23, 1990. They live in Morrilton and have two boys, Jerry Norman Jr. (b. Oct. 1, 1990), who is known as Judd, and Spencer Lee (b. Aug. 28, 1995). Margaret also has a stepdaughter, Alicia Nicole Bradley (b. Oct. 18, 1983) and a grandson, Kalyb Xay Phomsithi (b. Oct. 19, 2000).

Malinda married Christopher Rhea (b. June 30, 1974) on July 6, 1996. They currently reside in Battle Creek, OK. *Submitted by Margaret Bradley.*

BRADLEY - John Thomas Bradley (b. July 1, 1867, d. July 12, 1947) md. Nancy Emaline Pierce (b. Jan. 6, 1870, d. Sept. 23, 1933) from Murrill, AR in Searcy County. Both are buried at the Grandview Cemetery, west of Center Ridge. Nancy's mother was Stacy Maybelle Sikes, whose first husband was a Mr. Cotton and her second husband was Thomas J. Pierce, born in 1826. She had three children by Mr. Cotton: Bea, Patrick and another daughter. Bea and Patrick were in the Searcy County area and listed in the *History of Van Buren County* as early settlers at Archey, AR. Mr. Pierce died young, but Grandmother Pierce lived to be 97 years old. We think Stacy Maybelle's mother was Ellen Cothern. "Little Sarah Pierce" lived with Ma Bradley for a while after her mother died.

Children of John Thomas and Nancy Emaline Bradley are Wm. "Willie" (d. ca. 1886 at 1 year of age); John Calloway (b. Sept. 28, 1888, d. Oct. 26, 1967); Riley J. (b. Aug. 4, 1890); Eddie (died at age 9); Patrick C. (b. May 7, _); Alex Joseph (b. Jan. 2, 1899); Alta May (b. May 7, 1901); Judy Catherine (b. April 18, 1903); Samuel (b. Nov. 25, 1905); Delmas Vincent (b. March 14, 1907, d. July 12, 1945); Ardith Lynn (b. Feb. 9, 1909, d. Nov. 25, 1951); Charity Jane (b&d. Feb. 14, 1911); Nella Lou (b. June 8, 1912, d. March 24, 1967).

John Calloway married Emma V. Mason and had two daughters, Eva Lee (Cralle) and Thelma (Bradley). Eva Lee and Ralph Cralle had one daughter, Emma Karen Weatherford and two grandchildren, Kara Kimberly and David Noble "Stormy" Weatherford. Thelma and Borden Bradley had two daughters, Borda Jean Guinn Sessions, who had three children: Ben,

Todd and Marcie Guinn. Kathryn Lee Bradley Blackstock had one daughter, Christy.

Riley J. Bradley md. Sarah Bryant and had Eulene and Joy Faye; Patrick C. md. Cyretha Parker and had Edna Mae, Erma and Benny Leon; Alex. J. md. Esther Edwards and had a son Wilbern; Alta Mae md. Tom W. Leonard and had four children: Geneva, Alfred, Glenna Mae and Vincent; Judy md. Orville Bryant and had four sons: Herschel, Harriet (Jim) Theo and Landon; Samuel married Gertrude Baker and had a son Leathal (Jim); Delmas V. md. Opal Mahan and they had one daughter, Loretta; Ardith Lynn md. Mary Kissire and had two daughters, Elene and Joyce Lynn. He later married Marvelle Bryant. Nellie married Mr. Stover, then a Mr. Conley. *Submitted by Eva L. Bradley Cralle.*

BRADSHAW - William Jasper D. Bradshaw (b. Nov. 22, 1851, d. April 30, 1928) was the seventh child and only son of Mary Ann Sutterfield and Henry Bradshaw Jr. On July 12, 1874, in Stone County, AR, William Jasper married Mary Elizabeth Bradshaw, his first cousin. They had four children: Henry (b. ca. 1875, d. Sept. 26, 1930); William Jasper Jr. (b. ca. 1876); Cynthia (b. ca. 1877); and Nathaniel (b. ca. 1879).

Henry married Mary Bell Freeman about 1901. They had seven children. Cynthia married John B. Bergis on Nov. 8, 1896 in Stone County, AR and they had at least one child.

In the middle of the year 1890, Mary Elizabeth Bradshaw died.

About 1877, Malinda Caroline Wilks (b. Aug. 20, 1862) md. Col. Jonas M. Wallace. Her first two children were twin boys born in September 1879. Two months later both would be dead. She told her granddaughter Shirley Watts in 1937 that she had been so proud of those twins that she never wanted another child unless it would be twin boys. She would have Shirley's mother, Florence Louemmer in 1884 and in 1885 she had a son, Anderson Wilson Wallace. Also in the middle of 1890, Jonas Wallace died.

On Nov. 30, 1890, William Jasper Bradshaw and Malinda Caroline Wallace (a first cousin, one generation removed) were married in Morrilton, AR. They had four children: two died in infancy; Ed (b. 1893, d. April 30 1934 in Fort Smith, AR, bur. in the Bolton Cemetery just out from Alma, AR); and Martha (b. Aug. 23, 1894, d. June 21, 1967 in Little Rock).

William and Malinda were divorced in Stone County, AR, on Dec. 17, 1908. Malinda died in Little Rock on Feb. 13, 1945.

Malinda's daughter from her first marriage, Florence Louemmer, married Lafayette Jefferson Richardson on Jan. 6, 1901. Malinda's son from the first marriage, Anderson Wilson, married Myrtle Elizabeth Tilley.

William and Malinda's daughter, Martha, married first, a Mr. Bice and second, John Q. Skipper. William and Malinda's son, Ed, married Julia Gabrielle Mourot on July 13, 1913. Julia (b. Oct. 12, 1890, d. Jan. 23, 1987 in Little Rock, AR) and Ed had six children: Sybil (b. June 12, 1915, d. June 28, 1980); a son who died at birth March 21, 1917; Mable (b. March 29, 1918, d. Feb. 12, 2001); Ruby (b. Nov. 30, 1919, d. Jan. 12, 2004); Ellen Ruth (b. April 20, 1922) and Iris (b. Dec. 11 1995). Mable married first, Rosston Harris and second, Bill Murray. Ruby married Jay Beal Thomas. Ellen Ruth married Wilson Redditt. Iris married first, James Halbrook and second, Carl Anderson.

Mable had two step-children, Jan and Bill Murray Jr. Ruby and Jay Thomas had five children: Robert, Larry, Donald, Sherry and Charles. Ellen Ruth and Wilson Redditt had three children: Linda, Victor and Melba. Iris had three children: Frances, Carl Jr. and Dudley. *Submitted by Linda Redditt Francis.*

BRANHAM - Sources indicate the Branham family emigrated to America prior to 1740, settling in Georgia by the mid-1700s. There are many variations of the spelling.

William Branham was born 1812 in Georgia. His mother was probably Frances "Fanny" Branham and his siblings probably included Hannah Jane (md. Blake Tidwell), Lewis L., James W. and John. William married Arenna R. (last name unknown) about 1830. Arenna was born 1812 in North Carolina. William and Arenna's first child was born in Tennessee. The family moved to Blount County, AL in 1834. In 1855, William, Francis, J.W. and L.L. Branham all paid taxes in Blount County. A short time later, L.L. Branham moved to Searcy County, AR. In 1857 and 1858 William received land patents in Blount County. William was a farmer and in his later years a preacher. William left Alabama in 1861 and moved his family to Searcy County, AR. His son, James, enlisted in the Searcy County militia on Nov. 1, 1861. William is listed on the 1862 Searcy County tax list. He moved his family to Macon County, IL, 1862-65. One of his daughters married in Macon County in 1865. William and Arenna moved back to Blount County prior to 1870, then moved to Colbert County, AL between 1870 and 1880. Arenna died between June 1880 and July 1884 in Colbert County. She is probably buried in the Mitchell Cemetery near Tuscumbia in Colbert County.

William married Theodoshia "Doshie" Davis on July 17, 1884 at Tuscumbia, in Colbert County. Doshie (b. April 30, 1856 in Alabama) was the daughter of Dennis Denmark Davis and Euphemy Gowers. William was 72 when he married the 28 year old Doshie, who had two small children. Five children were born after their marriage. All seven children used the Branham surname, but spelled it Branom. William died Feb. 19, 1898 in Colbert County and is buried in Mitchell Cemetery near Tuscumbia in Colbert County. There is a marker at his grave and an unmarked grave beside him that is probably Arenna's grave. Doshie died Dec. 16, 1914 at Tuscumbia in Colbert County and is buried beside William in Mitchell Cemetery.

William and Arenna's children (all born in Blount County, AL, except the oldest child who was born in Tennessee) were Susanna E. Branham (b. 1834) md. Oliver T. Hill; Frances Branham (b. 1836); Jane H. Branham (b. 1838, d. 1915) md. first, William H. Farley and second, Franklin D. Gloden; Uriah Branham (b. 1839); James Lacey Branham (b. 1841, d. 1914) md. Eliza Jane Osborn (Ausburn); Lucinda Adaline Branham (b. 1844, d. 1878) md. Michael M. Gloden; Jeremiah Branham (b. 1847); Rolen E. Branham (b. 1853) md. first, Mrs. Lucretia King and second, Margaret McCochran; Arenna May Branham (a twin) (b. 1858, d. bet. 1860-70) and Samantha Elizabeth Branham (a twin) (b. 1858) md. Spencer Tyler.

William and Doshie's children: Maggie "Alice" Branom (b. 1881, d. 1904) md. Logan Mitchell; Maudenia Branom (b. 1884, d. 1959) md. Elmer Cole; John S. Branom (b. 1886) md. Belle Wright and Essie Greenhill; Marshall S. Branom (b. 1890, d. 1962) md. Annie Moland; Harvey Terrell Branom (b. 1891, d. 1952) md. Pearl White; William Wesley Branom (b. 1896, d. 1969) md. America Isabel Garrett; and Lucy R. Branom (b. 1897, d. 1976) md. Elizah Masterson.

BRANHAM - James Lacey Branham (b. Sept. 21 1841, in Blount County, AL), son of William Branham and Arenna R. (last name unknown). In 1861, James Lacey moved with his family to Searcy County, AR. They settled at Leslie near Lewis L. Branham, who was probably a brother to William. James Lacey and Lewis L. Branham both joined the 45th Arkansas Confederate Militia, Co. C, in November 1861 at Leslie. After the outbreak of hostilities in 1862 the militia was reorganized into an infantry unit. James Lacey enlisted with the 32nd Arkansas Infantry, Co. F, on June 16, 1862 at Burrowville (now Marshall), in Searcy County. Lewis Branham enlisted at the same time as James Lacey and in the same unit. James Lacey enlisted in the Union Army on July 13, 1864 at Lewisburg, in Conway County, AR. He enlisted in Co. I of the 3rd Arkansas Cavalry. James Lacey was mustered out at

Lewisburg on June 30, 1865. He returned to Alabama in 1867.

On July 30, 1871, James Lacey married Eliza Jane "Liza" Osborn (Ausburn), probably in Cherokee County, AL. Liza Jane Osborn was born January 1855 in Illinois. James Lacey returned to Arkansas in 1871 with his new bride. They settled in Searcy County near Leslie where they lived until 1910 when they moved to Culpepper in Van Buren County, AR. James Lacey was a farmer. On Oct. 11, 1911, he applied for his Civil War pension and drew $15 per month. He filed another pension application on May 31, 1912. It was approved and his pension increased to $19 per month.

James Lacey died Sept. 27, 1914 at Culpepper, in Van Buren County. He is buried in the Culpepper Cemetery. A Civil War monument marks his grave.

Liza Jane applied for a widow's Civil War pension on Oct. 29, 1914. About 1930, Liza Jane moved to Hominy, OK to live with her daughter Tennie. Liza Jane died Nov. 16, 1940 at Hominy and is buried in Blackburn Cemetery near Hominy.

James Lacey and Liza Jane had at least 11 children, but only six lived beyond infancy. Their children (all born in Arkansas) were:

1) Mandy Jane Branham (b. Aug. 27, 1876, d. April 15, 1967) md. Andrew Daley. Children, Mary Jane and John Robert Daley. She then married William Franklin Gloden. Children: Harry Alonzo, Lillian Grace and Frank Gloden.

2) Sarah Ann Arenna "Renie" Branham (b. June 2, 1879, d. Aug. 19, 1967) md. Joshua Howell. One child, Flora Howell.

3) James William Branham (b. Aug. 8, 1885, d. March 7, 1958) md. Gertie May Adaline Gloden. Children: Leroy, Velma, Della, Clyde, Odious, Effie, Pearlie and Jewel Branham.

4) Tennessee Paralee "Tennie" Branham (b. Feb. 25, 1888, d. May 16, 1984) md. Mansfield F. Sheridan. Children: Homer, Verlie and Dovie Sheridan. She then married Harlen Edgar Van Dusen. Children: Albert, Marie and Edgar Van Dusen.

5) Frances W. Branham (b. August 1890) md. Duncan "Dee" Snook. Children: James, Frank, Edith, Irene, June, Ruby and Carl Snook.

6) Viona "Onie" Branham (b. January 1897, d. 1964) md. John Watson. Children: Charlie, Oscar and Dave Watson.

BRANHAM - James William "Will" Branham (b. Aug. 8, 1885 at Leslie, Searcy County, AR) was the son of James Lacey Branham and Eliza Jane Osborn (Ausburn). Will Branham married Gertie Mae Adaline Gloden on Oct. 16, 1911 in Conway County, AR. Gertie Mae Gloden (b. April 13, 1894 at Covington, Tipton County, TN) was the daughter of William Franklin Gloden and Etta "Ettie" Melvina Taylor. Will and Gertie were cousins. Will Branham and Gertie's father, William Franklin Gloden, were first cousins. (Will's father, James Lacey Branham, and William's mother, Lucinda Adaline Branham Gloden, were brother and sister.)

Will and Gertie settled in Van Buren County, AR where they farmed. Shortly before 1920 they moved to Leslie in Searcy County. The 1920 Searcy County census shows Will, Gertie and their children living in the house with her father and step-mother, William and Mandy Gloden. Will was working as a tie loader with the railroad at that time. They soon moved into their own house next to the Gloden house. Will soon returned to farming. In the early 1930s Will moved his family to Humphrey, in Arkansas County, AR where they farmed. About 1940, Will and Gertie moved their family to Missouri where Will farmed as long as his health would allow. Will died March 7, 1958 at Kennett, in Dunklin County, MO. Gertie died Feb. 12, 1959 at Campbell, in Dunklin County. They are buried in the Tucker Cemetery at Campbell. Will Branham and Gertie Gloden had eight children. Several of their children and their descendants settled in Conway County. Their children were:

1) Leroy Branham (b. Sept. 4, 1912, d. Jan. 24, 1981) md. Mae Speaks. Children: Mary Frances, Gail, Barbara Jo, Joyce and Gary Branham.

2) Velma Mae Branham (b. March 20, 1914, d. March 12, 1987) md. Charles William McClure. Children: Gracie, Virgil, Dorothy, Charlene, Darrell, Bobbie, Jo Ann, DJ and Roy McClure. This family settled in Conway County.

3) Della Branham (b. 1917) md. Benjamin Franklin Ramsey on Oct. 15, 1934 in Conway County. Della and Ben lived in Conway County several years and operated a grocery store located on Highway 64 on the west end of Morrilton. They had no children. They later moved to Missouri. Della moved back to Conway County after Ben died in 1976. Della married Onva Williams on Jan. 1, 1984, in Conway County.

4) Clyde William Branham (b. 1920) md. Mary Lucille Anderson, Lorene Griggs, Inez Griggs and Susie Belle Whitehead. Children: Loretta, Larry, John and Debra Branham.

5) Odious Lee Branham (b. 1923).

6) Effie Mae Branham (b. Aug. 13, 1927, d. July 14, 1995) md. Earl Hefner, Ray Christopher and Walley Shawn. One child: Rick Hefner.

6) Pearlie Ann Branham (b. April 4, 1933, d. March 11, 1991) md. Tommy Bates, then Oral Dunlap. No children.

7) Jewel Dean Branham (b. 1937) md. D.W. Carpenter, James Harman Meese Jr. and Coyus Moore. Children: John Meese and Pat, Coyus and Ralph Moore.

BRAUD – Gilbert Gay Braud, aka "GG Braud," was born in Destrehan, LA in 1928 to Yve Pierre and Pamela Marie Braud. He graduated from Destrehan High in 1945. He joined the Army and served in Japan in the Army of Occupation after the dropping of the atomic bombs during WWII. He visited the bomb sites many times.

After leaving the Army in 1949, he attended Louisiana State University, where he majored in accounting, economics and business administration. He was also captain of the swim team and was on the rodeo team. In June 1951 he married Phyllis Ann Nauman. Their first two children, Karen Gay and Alton Lewis, were born in Baton Rouge. In 1953 he graduated from LSU with a BS in accounting and went to work for Gulf State Utilities. They moved to Beaumont, TX and Terri Lynn was born in 1957.

In 1958 he married Betty Aldredge. They had a son, Gilbert Gay Jr. (b. 1959). In 1960 they moved to Colorado and Gilbert adopted Betty's son, Steven David. Gilbert worked for the Colorado State Tax Commission as an appraiser until 1970, when they moved to Arkansas.

Gilbert bought land in Conway County in the Cypress Valley Community and finally realized his dream of raising cattle. He joined St. Joseph Church at Catholic Point and went to work for the state of Arkansas. At one time, he was Conway County Director of Social Services, later he became financial manager for DHS.

In 1982 he retired from the Marines Reserves as a master gunnery sergeant.

In 1985 he married Rachael Anne McKinney Wills, who was born in Little Rock. Rachael had a daughter, Roseanne Wills, who was born in Little Rock in 1982. Roseanne attended school in Morrilton and graduated in 2000. She attended UCA and married Ryan Austin Henson in October 2000. Ryan, son of Linda and Grady Henson, was born in 1981. Roseanne had a son, Keegan Ryan Henson, on Christmas Eve 2001.

In 1990 Gilbert retired from DHS to become a full time rancher.

Steven married Shirley Bowdle in 1980. They had a daughter, Serena Joyce. She married David Schneblen and they had a daughter, Ivy Mercedes, in 1998. Steven later married Susan Sutherland. Steve plays the drums and has played with several different groups. He is a supervisor with a manufacturing company in Conway, AR, where they live.

Gilbert Jr. married Colette Marie Lovelady in 1984. They had three boys: Jacob Pierre (b. 1986) and twins, Joshua Ryan and Jeremy Kyle (b. 1991). Collette is a registered nurse and also teaches nursing. Gilbert Jr. works in maintenance at the Nuclear Plant. They live in the Cypress Valley Community also. The twins attended Morrilton Schools and Jacob graduated from the Arkansas Math and Sciences Academy in 2005. *Submitted by Rachael Braud.*

BRENTS - Alvin Garfield Brents was born March 10, 1894 outside the small community of Cleveland in Conway County, AR. He was the oldest child of Noah Sherman and Margaret "Belle" Isabelle Williams. Alvin had six sisters: Mary Ann, Mae, Lucy, Rose, Ruth and Rea. He attended school through the eighth grade in Cleveland and temporarily moved to Formosa, AR, to complete his formal education.

He worked on the family farm until he was drafted in September 1917. Alvin went with his uncle, Thomas McKinley Brents (b. Aug. 30, 1894), son of Wesley Columbus, to join the Army. They trained at Camp Pike in North Little Rock, AR. From Camp Pike, Alvin traveled to Camp Beauregard, Pineville, Rapides Parish, LA, to await transport to France where he was a replacement soldier with the American Expeditionary Forces.

Noah Sherman family.

Noah Sherman and Belle Williams

Alvin and Thomas Brents

In March 1919, Alvin was discharged from the Army and returned to the family farm. He married Rose Couch Nov. 16, 1919. While living in England, AR, Alvin contracted typhoid fever. When Alvin's sister, Mae, learned Alvin was sick, she drove her wagon to England, loaded Alvin up, and took him to Cleveland. The doctor said Alvin might not live, but Mae insisted she would pull him through, and she did.

After Alvin's recovery, he was recruited by Henry Brisbane to help rebuild Key West, FL, after the hurricane in 1919. Henry asked Alvin what he could do, and Alvin replied, "I can drive nails." To which Henry replied, "Well, I can tell you where to drive those nails." Alvin worked in Key West, learning carpentry, until Henry's death.

At his sister Lucy Phillips' home, Alvin met Thomas "Belle" Bellflower Phillips, Lucy's sister-in-law. Alvin and Belle married Oct. 12, 1921 and settled on a farm outside Cleveland. Alvin and Belle raised three sons: Rafel, Louis and Charles "Lynn" Linberg.

Alvin became well known as a carpenter. He built a house in Morrilton for Dr. Coley in 1936/7 that was patterned after Nathaniel Hawthorne's *The House of the Seven Gables*. He built a house for Marshall Robinson in 1937/8 located near Morrilton's Cotton Gin. Alvin built houses for B.R. Little in the early 1930s, for Sherman Scroggins in mid-1930s, for Lyonell Halbrook in the late 1930s and for Marvin Scroggins in 1950/1, all in Cleveland. He built a house in North Little Rock for his son Louis in 1955, and built two houses in Little Rock, one for his son Rafel, in 1956 and one for Hubert Harness, in 1959. Some of these houses are still standing. In addition to houses, barns, and furniture, Alvin built coffins complete with padding, lining, and silver decorations.

Alvin was considered a competent "doctor" for setting broken bones. When Rafel broke his arm by holding on to the rope around the neck of a run away calf, Alvin set the arm. Rafel also had a dislocated shoulder that Alvin reset. When John McCoy fell off the roof of his house and broke his leg, he insisted that Alvin be called to set his leg. Alvin came and tried to convince John to see the doctor, but set John's leg and cared for him until his leg healed.

In July 1967, Alvin and Belle moved to a house on Church Street in Morrilton to live with Rafel and his two children. Alvin died in December 1968 and Belle in December 1979. Both are buried in the Brents' Cemetery. Rafel still lives in the house on Church Street.

BRENTS - The name Brent originated from the Anglo-Saxon word meaning "to burn." Family records have been traced back to the Norman Conquest of 1066 A.D. when Odo de Brent was Lord of the Manor of Cossington in the county of Somerset, England. The Brents family immigrated to North Carolina in the 1600s when the family set out from England in search of new lands. They remained in North Carolina until the early 1800s when the family moved into Kentucky and then into Tennessee. Finally, in the mid-1800s, Arkansas was chosen as a permanent homestead.

Berma Brents, late 1950s.

Berma Brents was born in Morrilton, AR on July 26, 1924 to parents Landy McKinley Brents (aka Mac) and Una Scoggins. Son of Thomas Landy Brents and Mary Elizabeth Lynch, Mac was born in Scotland, AR on Jan. 15, 1897. Una was the daughter of Erastus Scoggins (aka Raz) and Dora Elizabeth Roberts. The Lynch family had migrated from Georgia around 1877 and homesteaded in the Overcup Community.

Growing up in a community in southwest Morrilton, then referred to as Hannaford, Berma often reminisced of horseback rides and swims in a nearby creek. The family had a farm and received supplemental income from the bottling company, which Mac worked at bottling Grapette soda. First married in 1940, Berma had four children during this union. On Nov. 8, 1958, she married Afton Walter Lewis, son of Walter Lewis and Cornelia Wagley. They had one child, Linda Lee Lewis (b. Sept. 18, 1959). Linda married James Alvin Newsom and three children were born: Crystal

Dawn Newsom, Ashley Michelle Newsom and James Lewis Michael Newsom.

In the early 1970s, Berma attended beauty school and opened Berma's Beauty Place from her home. She kept her business going for over 15 years before retiring in the mid-1980s. Berma remained in Morrilton throughout her lifetime and was buried in Elmwood Cemetery after her death on April 27, 1999. *Submitted by Christie Newsom Brown*

BRENTS - Wesley Columbus "Babe" Brents was born Oct. 23, 1847 in Perry County, TN. In early 1850, the family moved to Arkansas.

Wesley Brents

He was still a young boy when the Civil War began, however, on March 22, 1864, at age 16, he enlisted in Company B 3rd Arkansas Cavalry, USA under Capt. Gibbons at Lewisburg, AR. Wesley's enlistment states he was 18 years old, but he falsified his age in order to enlist. His description is listed as: 5'9", gray eyes, dark hair, and dark complexion. He supplied his own horse and received compensation from the government for the use of his horse. He was in several skirmishes and minor engagements. At the battle of Point Remove and Glass Village, on Sept. 10, 1864, he received a serious wound. His horse jumped a ditch and threw himself on the breech of his gun injuring his left chest. He was taken to Little Rock that night by ambulance wagon and treated for the wound, but it caused him suffering for the rest of his life. He was discharged June 13, 1865, and thereafter pursued the occupation of farming.

Wesley met Millie Ann Frazier, whose family had come to Arkansas by riverboat from Mississippi. She was born Nov. 22, 1850 in Mississippi. They married Jan. 23, 1868 and raised eight children on their farm near Cleveland. James "Jemes" Wesley (b. Nov. 20, 1868); Robert Washington (b. June 9, 1871); John Mansfield (b. March 9, 1874); Noah Sherman (b. Jan. 19, 1877); Minnie Mae (b. April 30, 1879); Logan Blain (b. Nov. 11, 1883); Benjamin "Ben" Harrison (b. Jan. 21, 1886); Marvin Luther (b. Aug. 14, 1889); and Thomas McKinley (b. Aug. 30, 1894).

Wesley's older brother, Pleasant Mitchell, and his wife, Priscilla D. Upchurch, had a farm at Springfield, where they lived with their eight children: Suraney (died as a child); Vesta (b. Oct. 17, 1866); Simon Alexander (b. April 20, 1868); Alverda (b. May 28, 1872); Minor Hamilton (died as a child); Eunice (b. 1873/4); Charles Wesley (b. Dec. 5, 1875); and Priscilla Jane (b. 1876/7). In March 1878, Priscilla died, leaving Pleasant with small children and a farm to manage by himself. Then in October 1881, Pleasant died of pneumonia and Wesley and Millie Ann took the eight children to raise as their own.

They built a home about two miles from Cleveland near the home place of his father, Joshua. The home, built with large logs, was in the style of its day. It had two sections with two rooms each, and these were joined together with a wide hallway called a "dogtrot" which served as a breezeway. There was a fireplace in each section, at opposite ends of the house, and one large upstairs room over both sections and the "dog-trot." This house stood for about 100 years.

Wesley was a charter member of the Cleveland Masonic Lodge and a member of the M.E. (Methodist Episcopal) Church South. He was civic minded and concerned with the growth of the community. He deeded land for a school, a Methodist Church, and a cemetery. The school never materialized, but the Methodist Church was built and used until it was destroyed by fire. It was located across the road from the cemetery.

Wesley and Millie's son, John "Big John" Mansfield, moved on to the old home place when age forced Wesley and Millie to move to a home in Cleveland. About 1912, a party system telephone exchange was installed in Cleveland and "Central" was in Wesley's home with Millie Ann as operator.

Wesley died July 29, 1920 and Millie lived on in the home of her youngest son, Thomas and wife Wilma, until her death March 28, 1933. Both are buried in the Brents Cemetery, Conway County, AR.

BRICE-MOORE – The Brice-Moore family of Solgohachia, Morrilton, Cleveland: Gertrude Brice (b. 1890, d. 1979) md. George W. Moore (b. 1887, d. 1965) in Cleveland, AR on Aug. 20, 1911. Children: Lillian Cleo Moore-Williams (b. 1912, d. 2000); Cloa Agnes Moore-Hallsell (b. 1914, d. 1997); Wilburn Washington Moore (b. 1917, d. 1993); Wilma Grace Moore-Spradley (b. 1920-); Alma Hazel Moore-Bridgman (b. 1924, d. 2003); George

Gertrude Brice-Moore, George W. Moore

Winfred Moore (b. 1927, d. 1988); Guy'lene Brice Moore-Dwyer (b. 1931-); and Gwyn Dolyn Moore-Mitchell (b. 1934-).

Gertrude Brice Moore's ancestry: Anglo-Irish and Welsh Irish. Parents, Sarah Alverda Brents-Brice and William Thomas Brice II, married Cleveland, AR (Dec. 22, 1887). Maternal grandparents, Priscilla Upchurch-Brents and Pleasant Mitchell Brents. Paternal grandparents, Emily "Emma" Butler-Brice and William Thomas Brice.

Brief history: Gertrude Brice's heritage included the Butlers, one of the 10 most historic and powerful families in Irish history. They came into Ireland with the Normans – conquered and ruled from the 11th through the 16th century. They were Marquises, Dukes and Earls of Ormonde. One castle still stands in Ireland. It is Kilkenny Castle, and it still dominates Kilkenny and the southeast of Ireland. Standing over 800 years, it houses Butler history. The Brices from Ireland were Welch-Irish. The Upchurchs and Brents were Anglo-Irish (also coming in with the Normans). They were Lords and Ladies of England.

All intermarried with the native Irish, and as history tells it: "became more Irish then the Celtics." When all of these families came to the New World in the 1600s, they were influential in the New Colonies. One was Deputy Governor of Maryland. His sister married the first Governor of Maryland. One Brents' judge in Kentucky started a law school, they served in the legislative branches from Maryland, the Carolinas, Kentucky, Virginia, Tennessee and Georgia. After the "Old South" was brought to her knees, our people came into Arkansas as pioneers, lawyers, teachers, farmers, etc. after the Civil War. They located in Cleveland, AR and the surrounding areas in the 1860s.

George Washington Moore ancestry: Ancient Irish and Cherokee Indian. Parents, Sarah Hannah Estes-Moore (Cherokee) and William Howard Moore (Ancient Irish). Maternal grandparents, Josie Morningstar - Estes and Joseph Nathaniel Estes. Paternal grandparents, Mariah Palmer-Moore and John Howard Moore.

Brief History: Looking back at our history and ancestry it is amazing how our parents came together in Cleveland, AR. Our mother's people came into Arkansas after the Civil War. Her grandmother (Emily) and her father (a little boy) came from Georgia after the loss of her grandfather in the Civil War. Our father's people also came from Georgia. They came into Arkansas years earlier, when the "Great Cherokee Nation" consisting of Georgia, North and South Carolina, Alabama, Tennessee and the western part of West Virginia, was forced off their well-developed lands and farms. From their homes, they were made to travel to the reservations in Oklahoma. One of their stops on this tragic "Trail of Tears" (in the winter of 1838-39) was Arkansas. Solgohachia was the Indian Center of this forced migration and a third of Arkansas was "Indian Territory" at the time.

Much more could be written on our history, but suffice to say: wars, economic changes, laws enforced, political powers, etc. have a great affect on countries, communities and families - many times life-changing. From Ireland, through the colonies to Georgia, through two great tragic events, "The Trail of Tears" and the Civil War, our families were brought together, finally, in Cleveland and Solgohachia, AR to establish the Brice-Moore connection. Our parents were a blessing to our lives, and all the history they brought to us, make up who we are and who will be a part of generations to come. *Submitted by Guy'lene Brice Moore-Dwyer.*

BRIDGES - Sarah Jane "Sallie" Autry, daughter of John and Mary Mahalia (Roberts) Autry, was born around 1872. She is first listed on the 1880 Welborne Township, Conway County, AR Census in the household of her father, John Autry. It stated that she was 8 years old and born in Missouri.

Stella Bridges Pope family.

Sarah Autry married James L. Bridges on May 17, 1885 in Conway County, AR, Book "E" Page 151. Her mother, Mary M. Autry, gave consent for her daughter to marry, her father being dead. It stated that James was 23 years of age and Sallie was 17. This would put her birth year as 1868. Other records suggest she was born around 1872. Census records state that James was born in December of 1864 in Louisiana. James and Sallie were the parents of two children, Matthew Hawkins Bridges and Stella Adeline Bridges.

Sarah Bridges died of cancer between 1890 and 1900. She is buried beside her father in the Johnston Cemetery, Sardis Community, Conway County, AR. After Sarah's death, Matthew and Stella lived with their grandmother, Mary Mahalia, on Wills Mountain in Van Buren County, AR. Matthew and Stella stayed there until their father sent for them around 1908.

Matthew was born on Dec. 28, 1888 near Petit Jean Mountain, Conway County, AR. According to his tombstone, Matthew was a private in Company "F," 157th Arkansas Infantry during WWI. Further research is needed on this, due to the fact that there was no 157th Arkansas Infantry.

Matthew married a Josephine and they were the parents of Wilma, J.W. and Floyd. On the 1920 Webster County, MS, Census, Matthew is listed with wife Josephine and daughter, Wilma. He later moved to Louisiana and married Lela Mae Lowry in 1933. They are the parents of eight children: Joyce Fay Bridges Cason and Billy Ray Bridges (twins), Judy Bridges, Richard Bridges and Robert Bridges (twins), Marilyn Bridges and Carolyn Bridges (twins), and Charles Bridges. Matthew left the family and the children were raised in foster homes except the oldest two. An aunt raised Joyce and Billy Ray was adopted. Lela Mae later married a Tom Conley, and they were able to get all the children back together, except for Billy Ray, who chose to stay with his adopted family.

In frail health, Matthew moved back to Arkansas and lived with his aunt, Annie Wills Freeman, and a cousin, Artie Freeman Creach. He died Jan. 5, 1965 in Morrilton, Conway County, AR. He is buried in the Liberty Springs Cemetery, Van Buren County, AR.

Stella (b. March 6, 1890 near Petit Jean Mountain, Conway County, AR) md. Esrom Isom Pope on July 26, 1908 in Perry County, AR. Esrom, son of Frank and Elizabeth (Sharp) Pope, was born Dec. 24, 1885 in Conway County, AR. Esrom died Sept. 19, 1970 and Stella died Oct. 5, 1970. They are buried in the Lanagan Cemetery, Lanagan, McDonald County, MO. Stella and Esrom were the parents of four children: William Izak Pope, Ruby Neal Pope Murphy, Ida Belle Pope Thompson and Fredrick Pope.

After Sarah's death, James Bridges married Mrs. Malinda Lawson on Feb. 6, 1900 Perry County, AR and they are the parents of four children: John Robert Bridges, Carrie Bridges Chadwick, Ollie Bridges Eagle and Mary Jane Bridges Spradlin.

Malinda Bridges died of pneumonia when Mary Jane was an infant. James died on Jan. 10, 1917 in Pulaski County, AR. The children were placed in the Methodist Orphanage in Little Rock. The older children left the orphanage and Mary Jane was adopted out to a family by the name of Gardener. Later, Carrie, Ollie and John Robert searched for Mary Jane until they found her, and Carrie raised her as her own daughter. *Submitted by Eathel Campbell Freeman.*

BRIDGMAN - The Bridgman family immigrated to America prior to 1640. Franklin Bridgman, born prior to 1765, settled in Wythe County, VA prior to 1800. Franklin appears on the 1810 Wythe County census with his wife and 11 children.

William Bridgman (b. 1782 in Henrico County, VA) may have been the son of Franklin Bridgman. William had several siblings, including John W. Bridgman, and a sister Martha "Patty" Bridgman who married Sampson David. William married Mariam Brown in 1805 in Wythe County, VA. Mariam (b. 1782 in Tennessee) was the daughter of Isaac Brown. About 1815 William moved his family to Campbell County, TN. He is listed in a Campbell County property inventory in 1816 when his brother-in-law, Sampson David, died. William served several terms as juror in the Campbell County Circuit Court and was appointed inspector of elections. He was also a farmer. William died August 1840 in Campbell County. An inventory was made after his death and an estate sale was held in October 1840. Mariam died about 1860 in Campbell County. Records indicate as many as 18 children may have been born to William and Mariam. Their children included:

1) Charlotte S. Bridgman (b. Sept. 23, 1807, d. after 1887) md. Richard Drummond Wheeler, son of Benjamin C. Wheeler. Children included: Penelope, John, James, Benjamin, Marguis, Hugh, Ephraim, Elizabeth, Eliza, Richard Drummond Jr. and Joseph Wheeler.

2) Mary Brown Bridgman (b. Nov. 3, 1808, d. Oct. 3, 1868) md. Sampson David, son of James David. Children included: William, James, Eliza, Thomas, Emily and Charlotte David.

3) Martha D. Bridgman (b. April 14, 1810, d. Nov. 2, 1880) md. John Archer, son of Richard Archer. Children: Mary, Sarah, William, Eliza, Emily, Martha, Richard, John, Isabella and David Samuel Archer.

4) Isaac Bridgman (b. 1811, d. August 1859) md. Jane Butler, dau. of Taliafarro Butler and Mary "Polly" Miller. Children: William T., Mary, Franklin David, John, Howard, James, Eliza, Thomas, Miller Creed, Lucinda and Emily Bridgman and her twin sister (unnamed) who died at birth.

5) John Washington Bridgman (b. Aug. 1, 1812, d. Jan. 7, 1898) md. Lucinda Gibson, dau. of George Gibson. Children: William, James Franklin, Eliza, John Washington Jr., Mariam, Martha, Zacharia, Missouri Belle, Dora and Robert E. Lee Bridgman.

6) Benjamin Franklin Bridgman (b. 1813, d. bef. 1880) md. Martha. Children: Mary, Josephine, Eliza, Elizabeth, John and Benjamin Bridgman.

7) William Calvin Bridgman (b. 1815, d. Jan. 23, 1897) md. Matilda J. Prock. Children: Calvin, Thursa Jane, Ann, James, William, John, Mary, Sampson D., Lucinda and Marion Bridgman.

8) James Bridgman (b. 1817) md. Adelia Proctor. Children included: Marion Franklin, William and John Bridgman.

9) Sampson David Bridgman (b. February 1819, d. Feb. 18, 1873) md. Mary Queener. Son: Benjamin Elliott Bridgman. He then married Sarah Jane Hinkle. Children: William, David, Thomas, Mary, Charles, Robert E. Lee and Martha Bridgman.

10) Emily J. Bridgman (b. 1825) md. James Vowell.

11) Andrew Jackson Bridgman (b. Jan. 19, 1828) md. Rebecca Kidwell. Children: Lucinda, James, Margaret and Eliza Bridgman.

12) Ann E. Bridgman (b. 1829) md. William Bruce, son of Daniel Bruce.

13) Oliver P. Bridgman (b. 1829/30) md. Sarah Jane Owens. Children: William, Eliza, Mary, Alfred and Oliver P. Bridgman Jr.

14) Nancy Bridgman (b. 1832) md. Willis Bruce, son of Daniel Bruce. Children included Mariam Bruce.

BRIDGMAN - Herbert Howard Bridgman (b. Sept. 26, 1916 at Timbo in Stone County, AR), son of Thomas Jefferson H. Bridgman and Frances Adaline Catherine Holden, moved with his family to Conway County in 1917 where they farmed in the Morrilton bottoms. Herbert began his formal education at the Monastery Ridge School. In 1924 the family moved to Solgohachia in Conway County.

Solgohachia was a thriving community in the 1920s and 30s. Some of the businesses at that time were Ruff's Grocery, Serove Zimmerman's Blacksmith, a drug store, Tice Grist Mill, Oscar Miller's store, and a shoe and barber shop located under the Woodman's Hall and run by Herbert's brother, Bill Bridgman. Cora Gordon ran the Post Office, which was located inside Ruff's Grocery. During the depression of the 1930s, the Civilian Conservation Corps (CCC) was established and a camp operated at Solgohachia from 1935-37. Herbert worked for the CCC in 1938-39. He was headquartered at Lost Corner, AR, working with the forestry division, planting trees and building roads.

On May 4, 1940 Herbert married Maggie May Horton (b. May 25, 1915 at Una in Searcy County, AR), daughter of James William Monroe Horton and Effie Ann Harmon. Herbert and Maggie settled at Solgohachia where they farmed. They also raised and sold hogs, sold eggs to Montgomery Hatchery, sold milk to the Morrilton Cheese Factory and cream to Linhart's Creamery. In 1944 they moved to Portland Bottoms and farmed until the big flood in the spring of 1945 forced them to leave. They returned to Solgohachia and from 1950 until 1958 Herbert was farm manager for Henry Thines who owned property at Solgohachia. In 1958 Herbert moved his family to Morrilton where he worked for over 31 years as farm manager for Col. Roy R. Chaney. In 1989 failing health forced Herbert to retire. He and Maggie moved to Plumerville to be near their daughter Katherine and her family. Herbert died April 26, 1994 and is buried in Friendship Cemetery near Solgohachia. After Herbert's death, Maggie moved into the house with Katherine and her husband. Herbert and Maggie's children are:

1) Katherine Ann Bridgman (b. 1949 at Solgohachia) md. Roy McClure (b. 1948 at Morrilton), son of Charles William McClure and Velma Mae Branham. Roy retired from the military in 2004 after almost 34 years of combined active duty, National Guard and Army Reserve enlistment. He saw action in Vietnam and in Enduring Freedom in Iraq (2003).

In civilian life he worked over 21 years as a sheetmetal mechanic and has been a civil service employee for the Army since 1994. Katherine has served as City Recorder for Plumerville since 1988. They have two sons: (1) Scott McClure (b. 1972) md. Tammie Lovelady and has a son, Jonathan; (2) Clint McClure (b. 1975) md. Shannon Hancock.

2) Carol Susan Bridgman (b. 1951 at Solgohachia) md. Albert Wren. Albert (b. 1950 in Iowa) is the son of Robert Wren and Elizabeth "Betty" Bush (Felkins). Albert retired from the Army in 1991 after 20 years active service. He is currently a long distance trucker. They have two children: (1) Anthony Wayne Wren (b. 1972) md. Leigh Huie and has a son Devon, he then married Tammi Gay and has step-children: Kenneth, Kevin and Kindall Gay. (2) Tonya Wren (b. 1984).

BRIDGMAN - Isaac Bridgman (b. 1811 in Wythe County, VA) was the eldest son of William Bridgman and Mariam Brown. Isaac married Jane Butler about 1834 in Campbell County, TN. Jane (b. 1814 in Virginia) was the daughter of Taliaferro Butler and Mary "Polly" Miller. Isaac served often on the Campbell County Circuit Court jury and worked from 1838 to 1841 as road overseer. Isaac was also a farmer. Isaac and Jane left Campbell County in 1849 and after visiting with Isaac's brother, Benjamin Franklin Bridgman, who operated a dry goods store in Marion County, TN, the family settled in Walker County, GA. Isaac farmed in Walker County until his death from a heat stroke in August 1859. Jane and nine of her children appear on the 1860 Walker County, GA, census. Living near Jane was her oldest child, William T. Bridgman, and his family. Also living nearby was her father, Taliaferro, and her brother Miller Creed Butler.

The Civil War divided Jane's family in their loyalties. Two of her sons fought with the Confederate Army, one son fought with the Union Army and one son was a member of first the Confederate Army, then the Union Army. The story is told that in 1862 Jane went after her son who was ill in the Confederate Army. She brought him home and nursed him, then became ill herself and died on Oct. 27, 1862 at her home at Pond Spring near Chickamauga.

Isaac and Jane's children (the eight older children born in Campbell County, TN and the four younger in Walker County, GA) were:

1) William T. Bridgman (b. Jan. 25, 1835, d. Dec. 27, 1887) (served in both the Confederate and Union Army).

2) Mary Catherine Bridgman (b. 1837, d. 1861) md. Joseph Lafayette Stanfield. One child: Hannah Catherine Stanfield.

3) Franklin David Bridgman (b. Nov. 18, 1838, d. Feb. 1, 1889) served in the Union Army and was taken captive by the Confederate Army and held as a POW at Chattanooga, TN. He married Susan Barron. Children: William, James, Isaac, Creed and Franklin Bridgman. He then married Margaret Ann Hall. Children: Susan, Annie, Thomas and Mary Bridgman.

4) John F. Bridgman (b. 1841) enlisted March 4, 1862 in 39th Confederate Regt. Georgia Infantry.

5) Howard Bridgman (b. 1843) (enlisted Feb. 23, 1863 in 1st Confederate Regt. Georgia Infantry).

6) James Everett Bridgman (b. March 25, 1844, d. May 1, 1911) md. Cynthia Barron. Children: Mary, Cora, John, Eva and Charles Bridgman.

7) Ann Eliza L. Bridgman (b. June 3, 1845, d. June 17, 1903) md. Joseph C. Carson. Children: Mary, James, Hannah, Creed, Horace and Georgia Carson.

8) Thomas W. Bridgman (b. 1848, d. 1918) md. Ruth E. Lamb. Children: William, Claudius and Vandver Bridgman. He then married Ruth Davis. Children: Orville, Frank, Maude, Grady, Emmett and Jewell Bridgman.

9) Miller Creed Bridgman (b. 1851, d. 1867 from sleeping sickness).

10) Lucinda Jane Bridgman (b. 1853) never married.

11) Emily Susan H. Bridgman (a twin) (born November 1857, d. Dec. 9, 1915) md. George Crum. Children: Minnie, Riley and Arno Crum.

12) Infant daughter Bridgman (a twin) (died at birth November 1857).

BRIDGMAN - Thomas Jefferson H. Bridgman (b. Oct. 3, 1872 near Timbo in Stone County, AR), son of William T. Bridgman and Dicey Jane Maxey, married Frances Adaline Catherine Holden Oct. 25, 1894 at Timbo. Adaline (b Oct. 14, 1872 near Timbo) was the daughter of Richard James D. Holden and Martha Caroline George. Thomas farmed for several years in Stone County. In 1917 he moved his family to Conway County. They settled in the Morrilton bottoms and the children attended the Monastery Ridge School for a time.

In 1924, Thomas moved his family to Solgohachia in Conway County. There he and his sons farmed. The younger children attended school in the two-story wood frame school building, which burned in the 1920s. A new two-room brick building was built, where grades 1 through 8 were taught. (Some of the teachers during the 20s and early 30s were Gladys Nation, Lee Ruff, Gladys Yates, Bessie Brawdway, Marion Williams, Reba Henley and Will Hutchison.) Thomas and his sons raised cotton on farm land along Point Remove Creek. The family lived on Tucker Mountain in 1941, but moved to a farm on Solgohachia Road in 1942. Thomas died there on July 2, 1947 and is buried in Friendship Cemetery at Solgohachia. In 1950, Adaline moved into the house with her youngest son Herbert and his family. Adaline died Oct. 17, 1964 at Morrilton and is buried beside her husband. All eight of Thomas and Adaline's children settled in Conway County.

1) William Berry "Bill" Bridgman (b. Dec. 19, 1895, d. Jan. 12, 1970) md. Dessie Fryer, daughter of Fate Fryer and Annie Taylor. Eight children: Mildred, Lonnie, Harmon, Hellen, Clarance, Ellen and (twins) Leo and Cleo Bridgman. Bill was a WWI veteran and a farmer.

2) Willis Andrew Bridgman (b. June 2, 1898, d. Feb. 10, 1981) md. Ina Fryer, daughter of Fate Fryer and Annie Taylor. Ten children: Infant, Nora (died at 3 mos.), Sherman, Thurman, Herman, Willis "Junior," Betty, Sandra, Verna and Linda Bridgman. Willis was a farmer and produce dealer.

3) Aggie Josephine Bridgman (b. Sept. 2, 1901, d. July 22, 1935) md. Robert Honeycutt. Nine children: Gertrude, Hubert, Ruby, Houston, Tom, J.W., Arthur, Audistie and Lorine Honeycutt.

4) Leonard Archie Bridgeman (b. Feb. 10, 1904, d. March 11, 1975) md. Lillie May Cargile, daughter of George W. Cargile and Rosa Frances Barnes. Six children: John B., Harold, Rosa (died in infancy), Sturl, Christine and Jimmy Bridgeman. Leonard was a farmer. Leonard added an e to the surname.

5) Gertha Mayona Bridgman (b. Jan. 19, 1905, d. May 21, 1991) md. Roy Jefferson Martin, son of Rob Martin and Hannah Sutterfield. Four children: Jemolee, Billy, James and Frances Martin. Roy was a farmer and a carpenter.

6) James Franklin Bridgman (b. April 7, 1907, d. Jan. 14, 1967) md. Dorothy (York) Moss. Frank was a farmer. He and Dorothy had no children. Dorothy had a daughter, Audie.

7) Lillian Myrtle Bridgman (b. Dec. 21, 1910, d. Dec. 31, 1910).

8) Herbert Howard Bridgman (b. Sept. 26, 1916, d. April 26, 1994) md. Maggie May Horton, daughter of James William Horton and Effie Harmon. Two children, Katherine and Carol Bridgman. Herbert was a farmer and farm manager.

BRIDGMAN - William T. Bridgman (b. Jan. 25, 1835, in Campbell County, TN) was the son of Isaac Bridgman and Jane Butler. His middle name was probably Taliaferro and he was named for his grandfathers, William Bridgman and Taliaferro Butler. In 1849 William T.'s family migrated from Campbell County, TN to Walker County, GA. In 1858 William T. married Elizabeth Stanfield (b. 1842 in Tennessee), the daughter of James Stanfield. William T. was a farmer. In 1861, with war nearing, William T. moved his family to Searcy County, AR. He enlisted in Co. E, 45th Regiment Arkansas Confederate Militia of Searcy County where he served from Dec. 22, 1862 until Dec. 20, 1863. On Feb. 13, 1864, he enlisted in the Union Army in Co. H, 3rd Arkansas Cavalry. He mustered out June 30, 1865 at Lewisburg, in Conway County and was discharged July 18, 1865. After the war William T. settled in Izard (now Stone) County, AR, where he homesteaded 80 acres of land. In 1866 he purchased an adjoining 80 acres. Elizabeth died there between 1866-1868, probably in childbirth. They had one son.

William T. married Martha Ann Maxey about 1869 in Izard (now Stone) County. Martha (b. 1846 in Oglethorpe County, GA) was the daughter of Bennett Hail Maxey and Frances Eason. William T. and Martha had a son born March 1870. Martha died between August 1870 and early 1871.

About 1871, William T. married Martha's sister, Dicey Jane Maxey (b. 1843 in Oglethorpe County, GA) and they had five children. Dicey died July 5, 1885, in Stone County, possibly in childbirth

On Sept. 20, 1885, two months after Dicey died, William T. married Eliza Bradshaw. They had no children. William T. died Dec. 27, 1887 in Stone County. William raised cotton as a money crop and owned 345 acres of land at the time of his death.

William T. Bridgman and Elizabeth Stanfield had one son: James Isaac Bridgman (b. February 1860, Walker County, GA, d. between 1905-1910) md. Nancy Teague. Children: Ettie Jane, Anna, Mary, Aggie and Ada Bridgman.

William T. Bridgman and Martha Ann Maxey had one son: John Butler Bridgman (b. March 1870) md. Sarah Bunker. They moved to Conway County and settled near Grandview soon after their marriage. Sarah was born Dec. 18, 1881 and died Sept. 1, 1907 in Conway County Children: Perry, Frank and Edgar Bridgman. The family is buried in Grandview Cemetery, Conway County

William T. Bridgman and Dicey Jane Maxey had five children born in Stone County:

1) Thomas Jefferson H. Bridgman (b. Oct. 3, 1872, d. July 2, 1947) md. Frances Adaline Catherine Holden. This family settled in Conway County.

2) William Henry Bridgman (b. April 7, 1874, d. March 3, 1943) never married. He lived in Conway County for a time.

3) Rufus Calvin Bridgman (b. Nov. 8, 1878, d. April 24, 1914), never married.

4) Mary Jane "Sis" Bridgman (b. Oct. 3, 1880, d. Sept. 4, 1962) md. James S. Gray. Children: Williem Troy, Bitha, Dennie, Willis, Ellis and Arlie Ann Gray.

7) Hazine J. Bridgman (b. Sept. 3, 1882, d. Dec. 19, 1912) md. Robert Daniel Sutterfield. Children: Ulysses, Dessie, William, Baby (died in infancy) and Howard Sutterfield.

BRIMMAGE – George Allen Brimmage, second son of Luther Marvin and Alta Mae Yarbrough Brimmage, was born Dec. 4, 1911 in Yell County, AR. He moved with his parents and a brother to Ada Valley as a young boy. His father was a storekeeper and a farmer. On Dec. 24, 1931, Allen married Hazel Odelia Hale (b. May 2, 1916, in Drake, Carter County, OK), daughter of Luther Jackson and Mary Luella Conn Hale, then living in Ada Valley.

Allen and Hazel bought property just across the creek from his parents home. Allen hired out as farm hand and Hazel stayed home and tended the children, farm, livestock, garden, and orchard and worked with Allen's parents when needed.

In 1954 they divorced and Hazel married Ruel Ware and moved to Houston in Perry County. She died in 1996 and is buried in Ada Valley Cemetery. Allen worked on the Winrock Ranch on Petit Jean Mountain and by 1958 moved to Hot Springs, in Garland County.

Allen died in 1973 and is buried in Pleasant Valley Cemetery near Mountain Valley Water Plant, just off US Highway No. 7. Allen and Hazel had eight children, seven born in Ada Valley and one born in Morrilton.

The Brimmage family: left to right, back row, Katheryn, Henry, Allen, Hazel and Eugene. Front row: Elizabeth, Dorothy, Fay and Marie. Thomas not in picture.

1) George Eugene (b. 1934, Ada Valley) was killed in 1955 by accidental death while working on a ranch at Herford, TX, and is buried in Ada Valley Cemetery.

2) Henry Evrett Allen (b. 1936, Ada Valley) served in USAF. He married Roxie Arant of Florida and had one daughter Betty. They divorced and he married Sandy Jane Whitney of California. They have two daughters, Beverly Ann and Mary Luella, and reside at Raytown, MO.

3) Katherine Louise (b. 1938, Ada Valley) md. Cephus Warren of Ada Valley and had six children: Mary Frances, Emma Jean, Shirley Jean, Nila Sue, Angela Louise and George Franklin. Katherine resided in Ada Valley until the 1980s. She currently resides at Morrilton.

4) M.E. married Robert Collier of Hot Springs and had one daughter Cheryl Lynn who lives at Hot Springs.

5) Dorothy Mae (b. 1943, Morrilton) md. True Fitch of Rose Creek and had six children: Paul Marion, Wanda Sue, Terry Dale, Tressa Gail, Dain S. "John," and Grover Allen. They resided at Bryant's Cove. Dorothy died of cancer in 1994 and is buried in Fitch Cemetery at Rose Creek.

6) Ruby Marie (b. 1944, Ada Valley) md. Eliga Wilson of Houston and had five children: Andrea Jane, Maryrose Marie, George Allen, Lora Ann and Eliga Allen. They resided Little Rock, AR. Ruby died of leukemia in December 2000 and buried at Lonoke, AR

7) Georgie Fay (b. 1947, Ada Valley) md. Jimmie Johnson of Houston and had two sons, Jimmie Carroll Jr. and Carroll Gene; divorced and married Curtis Miller of Kansas City, MO, and had a daughter Michelle Fay. They reside at Independence, MO.

8) Luther Thomas (b. 1951, Ada Valley) md. Jeannie Turner of Perryville and had two daughters, Heidi Murriell and Autum Hazel; divorced and married Opal Turner of Perryville and had two sons, Stephen Shane Turner and Thomas Prescott. They reside at Wye Mountain. *Contributed by Fay Brimmage.*

BRIMMAGE - The first Brimmage in Conway County was Luther Marvin Brimmage and his wife Alta Mae Yarbrough. Marvin (b. Aug. 8, 1888 in Danville, Yell County, AR) was the only child of William Henry and Lizzy Piney Brimmage. Marvin married Alta Mae Yarbrough (b. Aug. 15, 1889), daughter of Thomas L. and Frances M. Yarbrough. (The Yarbroughs are buried in Ada Valley Cemetery.

Marvin and Alta had two sons both born in Yell County. Marvin bought farmland and moved his family to Ada Valley, and set up a small store in an old wagon shop on his property just north of the Valley's original crossroads. He sold groceries and pumped

Luther Marvin and Alta Yarbrough Brimmage

gasoline. He also did mail orders for customers who couldn't instantly pay. He always said he did well on selling bologna sandwiches and cold soda pops. That was when a soda pop and a candy bar were five cents each.

He and Alta grew a large truck patch and sold fresh vegetables when in season. Alta died June 15, 1948 and Marvin continued his business and farmed until about 1958 when his health failed, then he moved from the Valley. Marvin sold his holdings to Roy and Alfred Kendrick and moved into a cabin that he kept reserved and it sat where the fire station is today. He then moved to Hot Springs, Garland County, to live with Allen. Marvin was diagnosed with diabetes and on May 5, 1962, it took his life. Marvin and Alta are both buried in Ada Valley Cemetery.

Their first son Henry Holland Brimmage (b. June 30, 1909 in Yell County) md. Marnie Ellison (b. April 21, 1910 at Ada Valley), daughter of Happ and Mary Jane Ellison. They moved to National City, CA and had two children, Alton (b. 1933 in Ada Valley) and Sharon (b. 1943 at National City). Holland died and is buried in National City. Alton died and is buried in Ravensdale, WA. Marnie and Sharon still reside in California.

Their second son George Allen Brimmage (b. Dec. 4, 1911 in Yell County) md. in 1931 to Hazel Odelia Hale (b. May 2, 1916), a daughter of Luther Jackson and Mary Luella Conn Hale, then living in Ada Valley. They bought property near Allen's parents and had eight children born in Conway County, seven of them in Ada Valley. Children: George Eugene, Henry Evrett Allen, Katherine Louise, Mary Elizabeth, Dorothy Mae, Ruby Marie, Georgie Fay, and Luther Thomas. The Brimmages all left the Valley by 1959 except for Katherine, who married Jess Cephus Warren and lived in the valley for over 50 years. She now resides at Morrilton. Her daughter Shirley still lives in Ada Valley. *Contributed in memory of Brimmage families.*

BRINKLEY - Alexander "Alex" Brinkley (b. 1860, d. July 1898), son of Bumpass Brinkley and Martha Ann Hill, was the first white man to be hanged in Conway County. He was accused of shooting Dr. Gilbert Chamness, a crime Alex denied on the gallows. His handmade headstone in Grandview Cemetery says "Innocently Hanged."

Alexander Brinkley

Alexander Brinkley married Nov. 25, 1858 in Conway County to Julia Scroggins, daughter of Lee Roy Scroggins and Julia Ann Williams. Their children were William, Martha J. (md. John Henry Williams), Bumpass B. (md. Laura Lee Wagley), Marietta (md. Ance Flowers), John, Joseph (md. Hattie Bruce), Peggy Dove (md. William Louis Kirtley), Alexander (md. Margaret Maxwell) and Kerry (md. Alma Smith). *Submitted by Phyllis Maulding Campbell.*

BRINKLEY - Bumpass B. Brinkley (b. in 1842) was a native of Henderson County, TN. His parents were Bumpass Brinkley and Elizabeth Jinkins Brinkley. As far as anyone knows, he had three brothers: Simeon Brinkley (b. 1825, d. 1858); John Brinkley (b. 1836); William B. Brinkley (b. 1843, d. 1880). Bumpass enlisted in the 3rd Arkansas Cav., Co. I, in 1863 and was discharged in 1865. He was granted a bounty land grant for his service during this terrible War.

Bumpass B. Brinkley and two unidentified

In 1859, Bumpass B. Brinkley had married Mrs. Martha Ann Hill Williams, widow of Leroy P. Williams and daughter of Jonas Hill and Mary Barnes. Her first husband, Leroy Williams, was the son of Nathan and Rebecca (Jackson) Williams. Leroy had died between 1857 and 1859, leaving Martha with five children of the marriage. The union of Bumpass and Martha Ann produced nine children: William U. "Bill" (b. 1859); Alexander (b. 1863, d. 1898) md. Julia A. Scroggins in 1879; Bunk (b. 1861); Margaret Ann (b. 1861, d. 1936) md. George Washington Stobaugh in 1878; Martha Ann (b. 1865, d. 1949) md. George C. Honeycutt in 1880; Betty (b. 1867, d. 1930); William H. (b. 1867, d. 1926) md. Martha J. Jones in 1883; Bumpass B. (b. 1872, d. 1948) md. Mary L. Winters; and Ethel (b. 1858).

The name Bumpass is so unusual, yet there are so many by that name in the Brinkley family, one has to wonder about the origins of it. During some research, it was uncovered quite by chance. There was a woman whose name was Winifred Bumpass (b. 1745 in Orange County, NC) who married Anthony Cozart III in 1761. One of their daughters was named Agnes Bumpass Cazort and she married William Brinkley in 1784. Their child, in turn, Bumpass Brinkley, is the father of the subject of this sketch. So, this name was once a surname and the tradition of naming the children after this old name continued for many generations.

BRINKLEY - Bumpass B. Brinkley, son of Alexander Brinkley and Julia Scroggins was born August 1881 in Center Ridge, Conway county. He died in 1945 in Dumas, AR and is buried there in Walnut Creek Cemetery.

Bumpass first married Laura Lee Wagley, daughter of James Wellington Wagley and Josephine White Wagley. Their children were Thelma and Bunk, who died in infancy, and are buried in Sunnyside Cemetery. Their only surviving son was Berlin Brinkley.

Bumpus Brinkley

After Laura Lee died Berlin married Ida Ann Stobaugh Robbins, daughter of Franklin Owen Stobaugh and Martha Jane Maddox. Their children were Lola May, Joel Alexander and Jessie Lee. *Submitted by Phyllis Campbell.*

BRINKLEY - John Alexander Brinkley was born in 1859 to Bumpass B. Brinkley and Martha Ann Hill Williams Brinkley. His story is one of both tragedy and injustice, On July 31, 1879, in Conway County, he married Julia Ann Scroggins (b. June 1863), a daughter of Leroy Scroggins and Julia Ann Williams. The couple had nine children: Bumpas (b. 1881, d. 1945); Maryetta D. (b. 1884); John S. (b. 1899); Peggy Dove (b. 1891, Alexandria, d. 1894); Kerry (b. 1896, d. 1945);

William; Martha Jane (b. 1884, d. 1973); Joseph B. (b. 1889, d. 1938). Not much is known about their early life, but events in life often will overshadow our ordinary lives. One such event was reportedly the entry of Marshall Black, a black man who had moved from Chicago to Center Ridge, buying land, building a home and opening a saloon. It is said that Alex and Dr. Gilbert Chamness shot Mr. Black to death and stole money from him.

Then, on a June evening in 1897, the 16th, Dr. Gilbert C. Chamness was shot to death on his front porch. The next day, an article appeared in the *Arkansas Gazette* relating the case. "The doctor was sleeping on the porch when the cowardly villain slipped up within gunshot distance and sent a Winchester ball crashing through his head." They arrested Alex Brinkley, and upon a search of his person, found a pocketwatch with the initials "M.B." and on the inside, a photo of Marshall Black and his wife. The authorities assumed that Brinkley and Chamness had argued over the splitting of the money, and Brinkley killed him for it. Now, the grand jury which indicted him had among its members, Mrs. Gilbert Chamness and a Dr. Virgil Cross, a fact which is very suspect, at best. At any rate, they held him for trial, he was found guilty and sentenced to death by hanging.

Brinkley's statement at the time of sentencing was this: "I did enough to be hung for, but I didn't kill Dr. Chamness." No matter, he was indeed hung on Oct. 14, 1898 at Morrilton. Speculation has it that Mrs. Chamness, who was afraid of her husband, and Dr. Cross, who needed money, conspired together by first putting ether to Dr. Chamness's nose, then propping him in a rocking chair, then fatally shooting him. Now none of this was ever proved in a court of law, but in an article by Sandy Jones (a great-great-granddaughter of Alex's) she reported that her mother knew a woman who may know something about it. Mrs. Minnie Harwood's father was the deputy sheriff during that time and she was 13 years old when it happened and remembered it (and, probably, all the rumors that ensued). Also, Mrs. Fannie Lockhart, a friend of Mrs. Harwood's also recalled some of the facts for Sandy Jones. They both concurred that the whole town was surprised when Alex was convicted.

Alex and Julia Ann Brinkley are both buried at Grandview Cemetery. His tombstone reads, "Alex Brinkley, Innocently Hanged."

BROWN - Arlene Marie Brown, daughter of Robert Warren Brown and Shirley Marie Edwards, was born July 18, 1954 in Biloxi, MS at Kessler Air Force Base. Arlene married Bobby Wayne Price (b. Dec. 28, 1950) on Aug. 17, 1970. Their children are Jeffrey Lynn Price (b. Aug. 18, 1972) and Jennifer Marie Price (b. June 20, 1975).

Bobby and Arlene Brown Price family.

Arlene was a resident of Springfield, AR until after her marriage. She was only 16 at the time of their marriage and went on to finish school and worked to make a good wife and mother.

Bobby served in the US Army, worked in the oil fields, delivered mail and retired from the US Postal Service. Bobby sang with the Promise Land Gospel Group, which we all enjoyed. Arlene and Bobby are both dedicated to their church and are active members at Friendship Baptist. Arlene loves her work at Kimberly Clark where she is employed but still has time to check on her parents and we thank her for her love and care.

Jeffrey Lynn Price, son of Bobby Wayne and Arlene Marie Price, graduated from Vilonia High School in May 1991 and graduated from Pulaski Technical College in May 1992. He then served in the US Air Force. Jeffrey married Michelle Lynette Jarett (b. April 21, 1972) on Dec. 3, 1994. Their child is Jeffrey Austin Price (b. Aug. 13, 1996). Jeffrey Lynn enjoys his job at Axiom.

Jennifer Marie graduated from Vilonia High School May 28, 1993, then graduated from the University of Central Arkansas with a degree of bachelor of business administration in accounting May of 1997 and her master's degree in accounting in May 2001. Jennifer is now employed at St. Anthony's Hospital in accounting. Jennifer married Charles Harrell (b. Aug. 30, 1968) on Dec. 20, 1997. Charles Harrell has a master's degree in industrial education and is an automotive collision repair instructor at UACCM in Morrilton, AR. Their child is Madison Marie (b. Dec. 16, 2004).

BROWN - Mattie Perry Brown (b. Aug. 9, 1877 in Memphis, TN), daughter of George and Martha Ann Perry, was born the same year the family moved to Arkansas. Mattie's name was actually Martha also, but she was called Mattie all her life so as not to confuse her with her mother.

William Henry and Mattie Brown.

Mattie was baptized Oct. 4, 1889 at Pleasant Hill Church in Oppelo by Brother Harry Miller. She attended school at Oppelo. Mattie married Logan Cyrus Dec. 25, 1894. Logan was the son of Pilot and Isabella Cyrus from Giles County, TN. His brother, named Isham Cyrus, lived in Howard Township. Mattie and Logan were parents of four children: Lola Cyrus Lafayette Wood, James Roy Cyrus and Walter and Charlie who both died in infancy. Lola married and divorced Will Lafayette. She later moved to Omaha, NE where she married Chester Wood. James Roy Cyrus married Katie Broadnex. He lived and died in California.

Mattie and Logan divorced. Mattie married William Henry Brown in 1901 and they were the parents of William Perry, Ulysses, Celestine Brown Roberts, Mae Esther Ponds and Audrey Brown.

She was a charter member and deaconess of Trinity Baptist Church. She made the bread, bought the "wine" and kept the communion table linens bleached. She was at times president, secretary, or treasurer of the Missionary Society, taught Sunday School and Baptist Training Union, prayed, led praise services, sponsored special events, fed the preachers and their wives, represented the church at conferences and conventions, provided flowers, cleaned the church, planned programs, and everything else except preach, which wasn't allowed. She had to settle for becoming a missionary and teacher. Mattie completed classes offered by Silent Unity at 917 Tracy Avenue, in Kansas City, MO. She bought their books and subscribed to their magazines, including the *Wee Wisdom* for children. She has quotes from *Daily Words* throughout her Journal. She also took every training class she could that was offered by the district and state church bodies. She studied the Bible constantly and it was her custom to begin to read it from beginning to end on an

annual basis. She could recite lengthy Bible passages and remember where to find scriptures without a concordance. She distributed Bibles to community youth, and was well known in the community as a good Christian woman. She also was known as an "herb doctor" who practiced African and Native American remedies to heal infants and adults.

Mattie worked as a cook for the Oscar Hargis family in Morrilton, owners of O'Neal's Dry Goods store. Mattie raised her daughter Mae Esther's only child from the time she was four years old until she was an adult. She also kept her two great-grandchildren briefly while their mother attended school and worked out of town. Mattie departed this life Feb. 4, 1971 at the age of 94 and is buried in Odd Fellows Cemetery in Morrilton, AR. *Submitted by Keith and John Lewis.*

BROWN - Terry Lee Brown (b. May 4, 1953 in Biloxi, MS at Kessler AFB), son of Shirley Marie Edwards and Robert Warren Brown, was a long-time resident of Springfield, AR. While growing up he had a natural talent for art and could draw just about anything. His work was very impressive for someone with a natural ability. He loved the rodeo and rode the bulls and saddle and bareback horses; as a teen he rode in the high school rodeo and received the award and trophy. He also had a great passion for his motorcycle.

Carri, Elizabeth Carol, Terry and Amanda Brown.

Terry married Elizabeth Carol Boyer (b. Sept. 13, 1956, d. Sept. 28, 2000) on Oct. 26, 1973. She is buried in the Springfield Cemetery. Their children are:
1) Carri Lee Brown (b. May 25, 1977) md. Chris Whitbey. They have two children, Alexa Page Whitbey and Broady Hayes Whitbey.
2) Amy Lanay Brown (b. Jan. 11, 1980) was the product of a 29 week gestation and unable to survive. She is buried in the Springfield Cemetery.
3) Amanda Ann Brown (b. May 20, 1982) has a child, Kay Lee.

Terry loved his family, especially his children. His time spent with them was very special.

BROWN - William Perry Brown (b. March 23, 1902 in Morrilton, AR), son of William Henry and Martha Perry Cyrus Brown. He attended Morrilton Schools and completed eighth grade under the principalship of Professor B.T. Braggs. He graduated from the Oregon School of Welding in 1943 and from Universal Trade School Body and Fender Repair and Gas Welding in Omaha, NE. He was a barber, carpenter, plumber, bricklayer, electrician, and welder. The majority of his work was done away from Morrilton, although he worked many years for the Morrilton Oil Mill.

W.P. Brown

W.P. worked at Thomas Barber Shop, 1927-30. He worked for the Missouri Pacific Railroad in Kansas and Colorado in 1930 and 1940. He worked for

the Behr Company in Joliet, IL and in Rockford, IL. He returned to Morrilton Oil Mill for a while. He retired from Behr and once again moved to Morrilton where he continued to work independently as a carpenter and handyman and of course in the church and community.

W.P. joined Trinity Baptist Church in 1916 where he remained a member throughout his life, although he united with churches wherever his employment took him. These churches included Paradise Baptist and Zion Baptist churches in Omaha, NE. He was a member of Zion's Choir and Men's chorus.

He was a deacon and devoted member of Trinity Baptist Church in Morrilton. He built the last addition to the church building. He served as president of the Baptist Training Union at Trinity 1926-30. He was a member and soloist in the church choir and served as superintendent of the Sunday School.

W.P. was a 33rd Degree Mason (Prince Hall Affiliation), and a Shriner. His membership in Silver Trowel Lodge No. 9 in Morrilton where he was Past Most Worshipful Master, extended over a period of 50 years. He served as High Priest for Triple Tau Chapter No. 11 of Royal Arch Masons from its inception until his death. He was also Past Grand Joshua of the Heroines of Jericho.

W.P. was a member of the Conway County NAACP, and served as a Reserve Deputy Sheriff for Conway County. He was a board member of the Arkansas River Valley Community Action Council (ARVAC) where he was named to their Hall of Fame for more than 30 years of service. As late as 1983, at age 81, W.P. was a volunteer for the Meals on Wheels food program for the elderly, drove his neighbors to and from medical care, and took care of his brother, Ulysses, for as long as he was physically able.

William Perry married Emily Virginia Thomas on Aug. 12, 1927. (Her biography appears in the Education section.) William Perry Brown departed this life Jan. 13, 1992 at Baptist Medical Center in Little Rock, AR, and is buried in Oddfellows Cemetery in Morrilton, AR. He left a legacy of which we can all be proud. *Submitted by Kimberly Brown.*

BRYANT - Frank Bryant married Ina May Jones (b. May 25, 1894 in Webb City, MO), daughter of George William Jones and Susan Matilda Fivecoat (the name was originally Funfrock, a German name, changed by her grandfather). George was from Howard County, IN. He met and married Susan Fivecoat in Iowa. The family moved in the fall of 1878 to Ness County, KS where most of the children were born. The western Kansas economy collapsed in 1888 and

Eurie Frank and Ina May Jones Bryant

Webb City, MO was booming because of the lead and zinc mines. The Jones family moved there in 1888, where son Lester was born and lastly my grandmother, Ina May Jones who was born in 1894.

Frank Bryant and Ina May Jones had the following children: 1) Mattie Mae (this writer's mother) was born Aug. 14, 1912 in Webb City, MO. She didn't like the name Mattie and in adult life went by the name Delores; 2) Evelyn Pearl (b. 1914, Webb City) md. Alfred Morrison; 3) Nadine Lucille (b. December 1915 in Orango, Jasper County, MO) md. Loren Page; 4) Hazel Leota (b. September 1917 in Commerce, OK) md. Thomas Lang; 5) twin-Frances Beatrice (b. September 1919 in Scottsville, Allen County, KY) md. 1st, Sig Lett Sr. and 2nd, Johnny Bennett; 6) twin-Franklin (b. September 1919 in Scottsville, KY, d. December 1919); 7) Billy Gene Bryant (b. December 1926 in Santa Anna, TX) md. Maxine (last name unknown).

Frank Bryant worked in the mines and later did drilling for a lady. His family moved a great deal after 1916. They lived in Missouri, Oklahoma, Kansas, Kentucky and Texas. During WWII, the family moved to Long Beach, CA in 1943 and Frank Bryant worked in the shipyards. By the end of 1943, the family moved to Richmond, CA, that is near Oakland and across the bay from San Francisco. Frank Bryant and this writer's mother, Mae Bryant, worked at the Kaiser Ship Yards in Richmond.

It was in Richmond after the war that my mother met Ova Levon Cline, who was in the Navy. Mom had one daughter, Beverly Jean, born in 1937 when the Bryants lived in Coffeyville, KS. Mae and Lee married in Richmond and several months later Lee Cline (find more on him under Cline) was discharged after six years of service. *Submitted by David Cline, second great-grandson of Louis and Adalaide Richardet Charton.*

BRYANT

BRYANT – T. Wesley Bryant was the firstborn child of Drayton Bryant (b. July 25, 1817 in Spartanburg District, SC) and Minerva Ann Ragsdale Bryant (b. April 4, 1821 in Tennessee). I don't know anything of their lives before they met.

Drayton and Minerva were married Dec. 22, 1841 by Peter Clingman, Esq., in Conway County, AR. Wesley was born 11 months later on Nov. 18, 1842. Wesley married Sarah George on Oct. 7, 1866 in Conway County. If Wesley and Sarah had children, I am not aware of them. In a later census, Wesley is married to a woman named Lenora and they have three children: Lenora, Thomas W. and Frances E.

T. Wesley Bryant

Drayton and Minerva had several more children. They were Sarah J. (b. May 7, 1844);

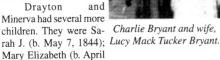
Charlie Bryant and wife, Lucy Mack Tucker Bryant.

Mary Elizabeth (b. April 10, 1846); Martha (b. April 11, 1848); John (b. ca. 1849); Nancy A. (b. ca. 1852); Levi (b. ca. 1855); Amanda (b. ca. 1857); Howell (b. April 9, 1860); Caroline M. (b. June 15, 1862); Charles Decatur (b. June 1, 1864); and Minerva (b. ca. 1867).

My great-aunt, Mildred Ballew, told me that Charlie Bryant (my great-great-grandfather) had itchy feet. I believe it. His daughter, Elizabeth Bryant Culpepper, wrote an informal autobiography in 1988. In it she recounts stories of the family moving between Arkansas, Texas and Oklahoma – year in and year out.

The opening paragraphs of Lizzie's manuscript gives a glimpse of the family's life in Conway County: "On March the 28th, 1902 a little girl was born ... to Charlie and Lucy Bryant, who already had eight children. They lived in the Arkansas River Valley, or river bottom as it was called at the time. They were very poor. My father did farm labor and raised a garden. Mother and the older children canned or dried what was raised. We lived on the north side of the Petit Jean Mountain. Morrilton was the nearest town. A ferry boat crossed the river going to town each morning and back home in the evening.

There was no town on the top of the Petit Jean Mountain. I was 3 months old when Ma and Pa lost their first child, who was just older than I. There was a bend in the river named the Paw Paw Bend. That is where the baby was buried, in the Paw Paw Cemetery." *Submitted by Regina Gualco.*

BURKE

BURKE - The original name was spelled (Bourq) "French." It was changed when they moved from Louisiana to Arkansas. Probably because it sounded more like the spelling of Burke. Pauline Hebert was born April 4, 1839 in Louisiana. Her parents came from France. Her father was Abian Hebert, born in France. She married Francois (Frank) Burke March 9, 1866 in Louisiana.

They moved to Conway County, AR, date unknown. Their children were all born in Louisiana: Lillie; Ollie; Lou Noline,; Leo; Albert; Louis Arthur; Paul Maxilian (Mack Burke);

Mack and Ellen Burke and daughter Pauline

Louis Arthur (b. Jan. 7, 1868, d. Oct. 23, 1896, bur. Oak Grove Cemetery at Morrilton, AR); Pauline Hebert (b. April 7, 1839, d. Feb. 11, 1915, bur. Oak Grove Cemetery at Morrilton, AR).

All of their children married and moved away from Conway County, except for Mack Burke, their youngest. He stayed on the farm with his mother, which was located about 2-1/2 miles north of Plumerville, AR. Mack Burke married Sarah Ellen Haworth Dec. 25, 1898. He died April 22, 1934 and is buried at Plumerville Cemetery. Their children are:

1) Ozzie Frank (b. Oct. 26, 1899, d. Feb. 4, 1964, bur. at Combs Cemetery, TX) served in WWI. He married Lee Bradford and moved to Harlingen where he became a self-employed paint contractor.

2) Lela Frances (b. Oct. 10, 1900, d. March 30, 1943) md. Erwin Bradford and moved to Harlingen, TX.

3) Fronia (Josephine) (b. Aug. 24, 1906, d. Dec. 9, 1975) married Rocky DeSalvo. She became a teacher and taught in Needles, CA and Amarillo, TX. She also served in WWII.

4) Mack Neal (b. Jan. 4, 1910, d. March 30, 1973) md. Lucille Stobaugh. After serving in WWII he went to work for the Federal Government in the Labor Department. Mack and Lucille lived in Ft. Smith and later moved to Ft. Worth, TX.

5) Afton Allen (b. Oct. 8, 1912, d. June 1, 1994) served in WWII. He married Edith Robinson and they moved to Corpus Christi, TX. He became a self-employed builder.

6) Ollie Pauline (b. Aug. 15, 1918, d. Jan. 16, 1988) md. Alvie Williams and they lived in Morrilton, AR.

7) Irene Muriel (b. June 30, 1920) md. Burton Williams (d. June 1959). She served in the Korean War as a Crypto Operator. After she got out of the USAF, she went to work for the Federal Government in the General Services Administration and retired after 20 years of government service. She married James M. Harvey and now lives in Burleson, TX.

Mack and Ellen raised all their children on the original farm the Bourqs bought when they came to Arkansas. We raised cotton, corn and all the vegetables we ate. We had milk cows for the family milk and butter, lots of chickens and eggs, raised pigs which we butchered for meat. The farming was done with hand held plo'ws and mules - no tractors - everything was done the hard way. Dad sold cotton to support the family. During the depression, times were very hard. Dad learned to make whiskey and sold it to help support the family. This was not legal, but he did what he could to take care of his family. My Dad was well known in Conway County and had lots of friends. Ozzie, Lela and Fronia went to school at Sardis Crossing School. Mack Neal, Afton, Pauline and Irene went to school in Plumerville School.

This information was complied by Irene Burke Harvey, from family records. Irene is the youngest of Mack and Ellen's children and the only one still living at age 84 years old.

BURROW

BURROW - The first Phillip Burrow immigrated to America between 1654 and 1663. The second Phillip was born about 1670 in Surry County, VA; but moved to Prince George County, VA where his son John was born. John moved to Orange County, VA. The third, fourth and fifth Phillips were all born in Virginia. The fifth Phillip, with his brothers, moved his family to Bedford County, TN in 1805. One of the first, if not the first, still was owned by Phillip and was situated near the town of Flat Creek. His son, Hiram, held office in the Methodist Episcopal Church. He raised 13 children in Tennessee; several of whom moved to Arkansas. His son, Handsel Wesley "Hance" graduated from Bethel College and taught four years. He married and brought his wife, Fannie, to Fourche La Fevre Creek in Perry County. They had three sons, but only Charles Christmas and Thomas Ewell survived. When war came, Hance moved his wife back to Tennessee and received a commission in the Confederate Army.

After the war, Fannie died and Colonel "Hance" Burrow brought his sons back to Conway County, settling in Lewisburg near Morrilton. He built a beautiful home within 25 acres surrounded by orchards and gardens. It may be seen at the east end of Burrow Street on Bridge Street. He married Sallie E. Howard with whom he had three children: Oscar Sayle, Lydia Ann and Mabel S.

Charles Christmas Burrow married Eugenia Moose in the Methodist Church in Morrilton. "Gene" was active for many years in the Morrilton Women's Missionary Society, and was a president of the Robert Dowdle Chapter of the United Daughters of the Confederacy. She was also a member of the Arkansas Pioneer Society in Little Rock. "C.C." established a mercantile business in 1886. He was very successful both in business and in farming cotton, a life-long interest. They had eight children: Hance Wesley, Allie Hannagan, Linnie Moose (Mrs. Thad Wells), Frances Elizabeth (Mrs. Tom McClean), Emma Gene (Mrs. Joe Byrd), Mary Fletcher (Mrs. Audrey Strait), Lula Doyle "Dump" (Mrs. Cloud Knight Rainwater), and Mabel Louise. In 1898, the Burrows moved to Little Rock where "C.C." devoted his energies to the cotton trade and farming. In addition to a large plantation in Lincoln County, he owned farming land from just west of Morrilton to past Blackwell. His land surrounded the communities of Kenwood and Blackwell. In about 1905, Charles and "Gene" moved back to Morrilton and built the Burrow Mansion on Green Street that later became Morrilton's first hospital. It probably became a hospital about 1918 when they again moved to Little Rock. Charles was regarded as one of the most able men in the state in the cotton industry and for a time was president of the Little Rock Cotton Exchange.

Some descendants still living in Arkansas are Max J. Mobley III, H. Blaise Mobley, Jeremiah B. Mobley, Benjamin M. Mobley, Max J. "Mickey" Mobley, Evan J. Mobley, William T. Mobley, Mary Lou Strait (Mrs. Ron Comstock), and William "Bill" Strait.

Many of the people mentioned in this article were buried in the Elmwood Cemetery in Morrilton.

Information for this article came from articles from the *Morrilton Headlight* and the *Arkansas Gazette,* an article by Hance W. Burrow Jr., research in the Arkansas Historical Commission, Tennessee State Archives, Morrilton Public Library and from interviews of Mrs. Mary E. Cholvan Mobley Strait. *Submitted by Max and Sally Mobley.*

BUSH

BUSH – Elbridge G. Bush (b. Dec. 8, 1829, Ohio) settled in Fulton County, IL prior to 1850. Elbridge married Anna E. Nichols on Oct. 16, 1856, in Fulton County. Anna (b. Aug. 20, 1836 in Illinois) was the daughter of Edwin F. and Hester Nichols. Elbridge was a prosperous farmer in Fulton County. In 1871, he moved his family to Winfield, Henry County, IA. Elbridge died there on Feb. 7, 1872, and was buried in the Winfield-Scott Cemetery.

Anna moved to Louisa County, IA prior to 1880.

There she bought land that she and her sons farmed. Anna died Feb. 14, 1916 and was buried beside her husband. Elbridge and Anna had seven sons but only five grew to manhood and only one married. Children of Elbridge and Anna were Carl W. Bush (b. 1857, d. 1861); Louis Edwin Bush (b. 1859); Walles Edward Bush (b. March 21, 1862, d. Jan. 17, 1863); Frank Leflie Bush (b. Feb. 3, 1864, d. July 30, 1942); Artimus Beil Bush (b. Sept. 7, 1866, d. July 11, 1952); Edward A. Bril Bush (b. Nov. 17, 1869, d. July 11, 1942) and Eugene Lawrence Bush (b. June 3, 1871, d. Sept. 16, 1930).

Louis Edwin Bush (b. Aug. 29, 1859, in Fulton County, IL) was the son of Elbridge and Anna. Louis married Anne "Annie" H. Margaret Adamson on Sept. 1, 1887 in Louisa County, IA. Annie (b. May 20, 1865, in Iowa) was the daughter of William Sheppard Adamson and Rebeca A. Maiden. Louis and his father-in-law farmed together in Louisa County for a time. Prior to 1920, Louis and Anna moved to Henry County, IA, where Louis and his brother Eugene farmed together for a time. Annie died Jan. 2, 1927 and Louis died Sept. 29, 1950. They are buried in Winfield-Scott Cemetery at Winfield in Henry County. Louis and Annie had three children: Esther Ethel Bush (b. June 15, 1888, d. 1970) md. Clyde Jones; Blanche Amelia Bush (b. March 10, 1892, d. Feb. 6, 1941) md. first, James Marion Abel and second, E.F. Rohren; Earl Louis Bush.

Earl Louis Bush (b. June 2, 1893 at Marshalltown, in Marshall County, IA), the son of Louis and Annie Bush. He married Mary Myrtle Abel on Oct. 11, 1911. Mary (b. June 28, 1893 at Ollie, in Keokuk County, IA), the daughter of Christopher Columbus Abel and Elizabeth Emiline Kirby. Earl and Mary farmed and raised their family in Iowa. They later sold the farm and moved to Missouri. In the 1950s, Earl and Mary moved to Conway County. During their years in Conway County they lived at Opello, Overcup and Morrilton. After a few years, the couple moved back to Missouri. Two of their children settled in Conway County. Earl died June 3, 1971, at Rolla, MO and Mary died Aug. 19, 1981, at St. James, MO. They are buried in Winfield-Scott Cemetery at Winfield in Henry County, IA.

Children of Earl and Mary Bush: Leona LaToska Bush (md. Gordon V. Bennett); Edgar Edwin Earl Bush (md. Louisa Brent); Vera Bush (md. Virgil David Reid, then Mark Woodrow Wilson; Walter Christopher Bush; Henry Earl Bush (md. Edith Ledger); Elizabeth Annie "Betty" Bush (md. Robert Laverne Wren, then Willie Felkins).

BUTLER - The Butler family immigrated to America in the 1600s. By 1799, hundreds of Butler families were living in the fertile farmlands of Virginia. William Butler (b. bet. 1724-1734 in Prince William County, VA) md. Mary (last name unknown), about 1754 in Prince William County. Mary was born about 1736. William served in the Revolutionary War. He was a farmer and died between 1805-07 in Culpeper County, VA. Mary died there about 1810. They had at least seven children: Joseph Butler (b. 1755, d. 1818); Spencer Butler (b. 1757, d. 1818); Armstead Butler (b. 1760, d. 1837); William Butler (b. 1762, d. 1843); Charles Butler (b. 1764); Nancy Butler (b. 1766); and Benjamin Butler (b. 1768).

Joseph Butler (b. 1755 in Culpeper County, VA) was the eldest son of William and Mary. He married Nancy Embry (Emery) on April 15, 1769, in Culpeper County. Nancy Embry was the daughter of Robert and Anne Embry and granddaughter of William and Ann Embrey from Gravesend, England. Joseph is listed in the Fauquier County, VA tithables list in 1782, 1783, and 1784 and in the Culpeper County tithables list in 1787, next to his brother Spencer. Joseph was the operator of a saw and grist mill.

Upon his death, his son Taliaferro Butler inherited the mill lot. Joseph died 1818 in Culpeper County. His son, Taliaferro, was administrator of the estate.

Estate records name Joseph's children (birth order unknown): Taliaferro Butler; Joshua Butler; Robert Butler (md. Delilah Yeates/Yates); Susan Butler (md. John Estes); James Butler (md. Mary C. Purks); Charles Butler (md. Susanna Neale); William Butler (md. Tabithy Settle); John Butler (md. Nancy Butler); Sarah Butler (md. John Peyton); Joseph W. Butler (md. Mary Ann "Polly" James, then married Sarah Witt); Nancy Butler (md. John Wharton); and Elizabeth Butler (md. William Priest).

Taliaferro Butler (b. April 20, 1781, in Virginia) was the son of Joseph Butler and Nancy Embry/Emery. Taliaferro was married twice. He first married Janny Grimsley on Dec. 28, 1804 in Culpeper County, VA and they had three children: Henry R. Butler (b. 1805); Hillary Butler (a twin) (b. 1808, d. 1838) and Catharine Butler (a twin) (b. 1808, d. 1809). Janny died between 1810 and late 1813, probably in Culpeper County.

Taliaferro married second, Mary "Polly" Miller on Nov. 30, 1813, in Culpeper County. Polly Miller (b. 1786 in Virginia) was probably the daughter of William Miller. Upon the death of his father in 1818, Taliaferro inherited the mill lot where his father operated a saw and grist mill in Culpeper County. Prior to 1825, Taliaferro and Polly moved their family to Campbell County, TN. Prior to 1850, the family moved to Walker County, GA. Polly Butler died Aug. 1, 1858 near Chickamauga, GA. Taliaferro died Nov. 4, 1865 near Chickamauga. Taliaferro and Polly had four children: Jane Butler (b. 1814, d. 1862) md. Isaac Bridgman; William E. Butler (b. 1821, d. 1842); John H. Butler (b. 1822, d. 1842); and Miller Creed Butler (b. 1825, d. 1900) md. Mary Carlock.

CAMPBELL - Benjamin Campbell (b. April 14, 1894 in Van Buren County, AR), the son of William Frasier and Mazie Elizabeth (Coats) Campbell. Benjamin married Bessie Belle Ingram on Oct. 26, 1915 in Conway County, AR. Bessie (b. March 4, 1895 in McLeansboro, Hamilton County, IL) was the daughter of James Robert and Mary Eldora (Burton) Ingram. Besse's parents moved to Clay County, AR when she was just a small girl and settled in the Rector area. Her mother died Dec. 4, 1904 in Clay County. James married Ada Hedgecock in 1907 and moved the family to Conway County in about 1914 and settled in an area north of Cleveland.

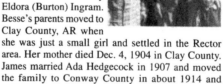

After Benjamin and Belle married, they stayed with his parents on top of White Oak Mountain in Van Buren County, AR for a few months, then moved to the Illinois Bayou in Rhett, Pope County, AR. Their first son, Raymond Claud, was born there on Dec. 17, 1916. The next year, they returned to White Oak Mountain to help care for Ben's father who was ill.

On Aug. 8, 1918, Benjamin and Belle had a son, William Francis "Frank" Campbell. After the birth of Frank, they homesteaded an 80-acre farm on White Oak Mountain. Two daughters were born there, Mary Eathel Campbell (b. Dec. 13, 1920) and Lela Marie Campbell (b. Feb. 26, 1924).

Later in 1924, the family moved to Smyrna, a small community north of Cleveland on Point Remove Creek. Their children attended the one-room country school and later Wonderview High School. After the kids were grown, Benjamin and Bessie finally settled in Hattieville, Conway County, AR and lived there the remainder of their lives. Bessie Belle died July 7, 1975 in Morrilton. Benjamin died at the home of his daughter Eathel on July 12, 1977 in Cleveland. They are buried in the Elmwood Cemetery in Morrilton.

Raymond married Wilda Branscum Sowells on Aug. 21, 1937 in Conway County, AR. She was born

March 29, 1906 and died Sept. 20, 1987. Raymond died Dec. 9, 1992 in Perry County, AR. They are buried in the Elmwood Cemetery in Morrilton.

Frank Campbell married Nellie Bridges on Oct. 10, 1936 at Scott's Chapel, Van Buren County, AR. Nellie (b. Jan. 11, 1918 in Dabney, Van Buren County, AR, d. Jan. 27, 1997 in Sioux Falls, SD) and Frank (d. April 6, 1988 in Morrilton). Frank and Nellie are buried in the New Hope Cemetery in Van Buren County, AR.

Mary Eathel married Arden William Freeman on Dec. 23, 1939 in Conway, Faulkner County, AR. Arden (b. Jan. 17, 1915, in Gridley, Van Buren County, AR, d. Sept. 17, 1992 in Morrilton) is buried in the Liberty Springs Cemetery in Van Buren County, AR.

Lela Marie married Laudis Ray Huffman on May 3, 1941 in Cleveland. Laudis died Dec. 29, 1991 in Jerusalem, Conway County, AR and is buried in the Reid Cemetery north of Cleveland. *Submitted by Mary Freeman Chism.*

CAMPBELL - Cindella Weaver (b. March 1863 in Van Buren County, AR) was the daughter of Joshua Weaver and Martha Sowell Weaver. Joshua Weaver (b. 1822 in Lawrence County, TN), son of Mark Weaver Jr. and Christina Lucretia Null Weaver, was a farmer and a blacksmith. His wife Martha Sowell Weaver (b. 1834 in Tennessee) was the daughter of Martin D. and Elizabeth Sowell. Mark Weaver Jr. (b. 1795 in

Cindella Weaver Campbell

Wilkes County, NC) md. Christina Null in Lawrence County, TN on March 5, 1818. They both died between 1850-1860 in Van Buren County, AR.

Mark Weaver Jr.'s father, Mark Weaver Sr., was born 1770 in North Carolina and served in the War of 1812. Mark Sr.'s father, Isaac Weaver, fought in the Revolutionary War. He was born in 1747 in Virginia and died in 1814.

Cindella Weaver's family descended from a William Weaver who was born about 1540 in Shropshire, England. Samuel Weaver, a grandson of William Weaver, came to the colonies as an indentured servant on the ship *Bonnybess* in 1622.

Cindella's parents had the following children: (1) James M. Weaver (b. 1852) md. first, Nancy Christopher in 1872 and second, Mary B. Christopher in 1878; (2) Lucretia Elizabeth Weaver (b. 1855) md. Richard E. Caldwell in 1869, died about 1885 in Van Buren County; (3) Joshua Weaver Jr. (b. 1856); (4) Alsey Jane Weaver (b. 1856) md. James Hooten in 1872; (5) Mary Anne Weaver (b. 1859) md. Andrew Caldwell in 1877; (6) Cindella Weaver (b. 1863) md. Elijah C. Campbell on Dec. 24, 1882 in Van Buren County, AR. She and her husband were living in Conway County, AR when she died in 1919. She was buried in the Bradford Cemetery located near Shirley, AR. *Submitted by Della Campbell Matlock.*

CAMPBELL - Elijah C. Campbell (b. Aug. 12, 1860) was known as "Lidge" by the family. Elijah was the first born child of Richard Campbell and his second wife, Elizabeth Anne Bean. Elijah's parents were living on a farm in Union Township in Van Buren County, AR when he was born.

Elijah had two half brothers and four half sisters. Alexander and Will-

Elijah C. Campbell

iam H., Lucretia, Miranda, Elizabeth and Louisa, were children of Elijah's father, Richard, and his first wife Mary Anne.

Elijah had two younger sisters, Lorilda Anne Campbell (b. December 1866) md. Annual Davis in 1888. They had five children: E.C. Davis, James A. Davis, Hattie E. Davis, William Davis and Floyd B. Davis. Lorilda died in 1903.

Artie Elizabeth Campbell (b. March 19, 1875) md. Irving J. Eoff in 1894. They had two children, Ora Eoff and Daniel Grady Eoff. She married second, William J. Davis in 1902. They had four children: Ernest V. Davis, Annual Garland Davis, Leonard O. Davis and Gyva Davis.

The Civil War raged during the first five years of Elijah's life in Van Buren County. When he was older, he helped his brothers, Alexander and William, work on his father's farm. Family legend tells that Elijah's brother, Alexander, or "Coleman" as he was called, left their home one day and never returned. William Campbell married Nancy Bailey in 1879.

Elijah met and fell in love with a neighboring farmer's daughter named Cindella Weaver. She was the daughter of Joshua Weaver and Martha Sowell Weaver. Her grandfather, Mark Weaver Jr., was born in North Carolina, migrated to Lawrence County, TN and had settled in Independence County, AR by 1830.

Elijah Campbell and Cindella Weaver were married on Christmas Eve in 1882 at the Presbyterian Church by Rev. J.B. Fortner. Both were members of the church. Elijah was later ordained an elder of the church on Sept. 4, 1886.

Elijah was a farmer and an owner of a shingle mill. He made an application for a homestead grant of 160 acres in 1896. He received title to this land and in 1897 donated one-half acre of his land to be used as school property. A school named "The Blue Star" school was built on this property and Elijah's children attended school there.

Elijah and Cindella Weaver Campbell had the following children: Ollie Gertrude (b. February 1884, d. Jan. 18, 1940 in Missouri) md. Charles Dowdy; William Daniel Campbell (b. November 1888, d. Nov. 18, 1945 in Missouri) md. Florence Shipp; Augie Dee Campbell (b. February 1890, d. July 26, 1961 in Missouri) md. Belle Harness; Pata Elizabeth Campbell (b. July 1893, d. Feb. 8, 1981 in Kennett, MO) md. Louis D. Ward; Martha Elizabeth Campbell (b. October 1897, d. Feb. 18, 1975 in Plumerville, AR) md. Rudolph Lute; Grace Bretta Campbell (b. September 1899) md. Clarence Adams; Ira Dickson Campbell (b. March 28, 1902, d. May 1, 1986, Plumerville, AR) md. Cora Anne Gordon; Troy Pace Campbell (b. July 1907, d. Dec. 14, 1976, Kennett, MO) md. Irene Flemming.

Elijah and Cindella moved to Conway County, AR in 1919 and settled in the Paw Paw Bend Community for a while, later they moved to Plumerville. Cindella Weaver Campbell died in 1919 and is buried in the Bradford Cemetery near Shirley, AR. Elijah C. Campbell died Nov. 2, 1932 and is buried in the Plumerville Cemetery. The inscription on his head stone reads as follows: "His spirit smiles from that bright shore and softly whispers, weep no more." *Submitted by Jimmy Campbell.*

CAMPBELL - Grover Cleveland Campbell was the third generation of his Campbell line to live in Arkansas. His grandparents, Henderson McNeal Campbell (b. ca. 1829 in Kentucky) and Lou Ellen Fraser (b. ca. 1833 in Maryland), settled in Conway County, AR around 1870.

Grover (b. Nov. 3, 1887 at Oak Grove, Conway County, AR), son of William Fraser Campbell (b. Feb. 28, 1859, d. Nov. 29, 1917) and Mazy Elizabeth Wright (b. Oct. 20, 1861, d. June 24, 1926), was one of six children: Mary Elizabeth, Laurie, Grover Cleveland, Henry Sterling, Benjamin, and Clarence E. His family homesteaded a place on White Oak Mountain in Pope County, AR. Oral history indicates that he was of Scotch-Irish descent. A hunting license for 1928-29,

states that Grover, age 41, was 6 feet 5-3/4 inches tall, weighed 185 pounds, had black hair, and blue eyes.

A receipt, from the store of S.W. Simpson & Son dated 1908, gives a snapshot of the time when Grover was a young man. His father purchased the following: Eagle Thistle Soda $0.25, 3 pkgs. pepper $0.30, 50 lbs. salt $0.35, 4 spools of thread $0.20, 6 yds. denim $1.00, 3 doz. rubbers $0.25, 2 pr. shoes $4.40, and 2 pr. overalls $1.70 for a total of $8.45.

Grover married Permela Elizabeth "Lizzie" Roberson, daughter of William Marshall Roberson and Mary Francis Lowder, on Oct. 13, 1912 in Conway County. Lizzie (b. Jan. 10, 1892 near Gridley, Van Buren County, AR. They had four children: infant son (b. Sept. 7, 1913, d. Sept. 13, 1913); William Arlie (b. Sept. 28, 1914, d. Aug. 15, 1995); Grover Marshall (b. April 4, 1918); and Alvin Clemo (b. Aug. 2, 1922, d. Dec. 1, 1939).

William Arlie was born at New Hope and in 1935 he married Lois Reid. They had one child, Betty Joann (b. Oct. 27, 1936 at Cleveland), who married Robert Ike Reiske in 1953. They have two daughters: (1) Deborah Gayle (b. Aug. 5, 1954) md. Harles Hoyle and (2) Beverly Ann (b. Jan. 31, 1956) md. Jerry Golden. Arlie's second marriage was to Imagene Lefler. Arlie passed on Aug. 21, 1995.

Grover Marshall, the third son of Grover and Lizzie, married Joyce Mills. They have three children: Norma Loeta, Leta Virginia and Sherrill Marshall. (See subsequent article on Grover Marshall Campbell.)

After the birth of their first child, Grover and Lizzie homesteaded 80 acres at New Hope. Around 1925, they bought a farm near Cleveland in Conway County for $1,100. The land in Pope County was sold back to the United States for $240 for the 80 acres. The deed was executed March 4, 1929.

School records show that Grover was a director of Smyrna School. On Oct. 23, 1929, Thomas Mills, Grover Campbell and Homer Reid, as Directors of School District No. 82 in Conway County, AR, hired Theodore Kincanon to teach school for three months. School started Oct. 28, 1929. The salary was $60 each month, with room and board provided by Grover and Lizzie.

Lizzie's philosophy is illustrated by her two favorite sayings: "Don't cry over spilled milk," and "Don't say anything if you can't say something good about somebody." After Grover died on May 1, 1961, Lizzie lived alone for many years and died Nov. 17, 1989. *Submitted by N. Loeta Campbell Sweetwood.*

CAMPBELL - Grover Marshall Campbell was born April 4, 1918 at New Hope, Pope County, AR. His parents were Grover Cleveland Campbell and Permela Elizabeth Roberson. He was one of four children: an infant boy, William Arlie, Grover Marshall and Alvin Clemo. Around 1925, the family purchased a farm near Cleveland, in Conway County and left New Hope.

Marshall married Joyce Mills (b. Sept. 22, 1917 on Brock Creek near Cleveland), daughter of Thomas Roland Mills and Lela Virginia Brown, on Dec. 19, 1936. She was one of 12 children: Lillian Vina, Cleora Ava, Thomas Roosevelt, Oma, Weldon Taft, Ulysses Grant, Eunice Wilma, Zela, Joyce, Shelton, Lavola and Luman. Marshall and Joyce have three children: Norma Loeta (b. Nov. 9, 1938); Leta Virginia (b. Oct. 30, 1941, d. Feb. 25, 1994); and Sherrill Marshall (b. Feb. 4, 1948).

Loeta married Virgil L. Sweetwood. Their children are Kimberly Ann (b. March 12, 1963); Kevin Levern (b. Sept. 4, 1965); Bonnie Michelle (b. Jan. 12, 1967); and Steven Shawn (b. Dec. 6, 1975). Kimberly married Denny Calvin McVey. They have three children: Ashley Elizabeth, Brooke Nicole and Courtney Michelle. Kevin is an alternative education teacher at South Lindhurst High School. Michelle married Thomas Donald Spindler. They have two children, Thomas Donald Jr. and Tyler Daniel. Steven is a senior release planner with Bayer Healthcare.

Leta married Christopher Paul deBuzna. Their

children are Andrea Joyce (b. Dec. 3, 1966) and Krista Paulette (b. Jan. 8, 1976).

Sherrill married Patricia Irene McQuown. Their children are Cambria Christina (b. Nov. 7, 1972), Catrina Cathlene (b. Oct. 14, 1974), and Casey Christopher (b. Feb. 28, 1977). Catrina married Thomas Yost. They are the parents of Noah, Samuel and Kiersten. Cambria has a son, Zachary Monk. Casey is a sales representative for HCL Machine Works, Inc.

During the Depression, Marshall quit school at the age of 12 to earn a living. His first job was removing the bark from logs. Later he plowed for Taylor Miller and then set a crop for his Uncle Will Roberson. Subsequently, he toiled in a CC Camp working on soil conservation.

Upon being drafted into the US Army in WWII, Marshall was assigned to the 203rd Anti-Aircraft Artillery Air Warning Battalion. His campaign was in the Rhineland of Central Europe where he operated a heavy truck and half-track vehicle on which machine guns were mounted. He served his country from May 8, 1944 to June 25, 1946.

After the war, Marshall bought land at Cleveland and tried farming, but eventually, the family migrated to California. He learned to operate heavy equipment and worked in central and northern California as a land leveler. In 1957, after several back and forth stays in California and Arkansas, the family settled in Yuba City, CA.

Marshall and Joyce wanted their children to have opportunities for an easier life. The importance of a good education and hard work were stressed. When Marshall's work required moving, Joyce tried to stay behind until the children finished the school year. Due to their encouragement and help, all of their children graduated from a four-year college.

Upon retirement from land leveling in 1981, Marshall and Joyce returned to Cleveland, AR where they started a new career in farming. *Submitted by Steven S. Sweetwood.*

CAMPBELL - Henderson McNeal Campbell (b. ca. 1829 in Kentucky) md. Lou Ellen Frasier about 1852 in Alabama. She was born about 1831 in Maryland, the daughter of Daniel R. and Elizabeth Frasier. Henderson and Lou Ellen's known children are Mary Frances, Nancy, Susan, William Frasier and Sterling Price.

Seated: William F. Campbell, Benjamin Campbell, Marjie Elizabeth Wright Campbell. Standing: Grover Cleveland Campbell, Henry Campbell, Mary Elizabeth Campbell, Laura Campbell.

Mary Frances (b. July 27, 1853 in Alabama) md. 1st, Jesse Arnold on Jan. 11, 1872 in Conway County, AR. Shortly after Jesse and Mary were married, they moved to Lawrence County, AR. Mary and Jesse's children are: Susan Lidda Arnold Covington Harris Grigsby (b. July 26, 1874, d. Jan. 23, 1948); Clara A. Arnold Tunstall (b. Feb. 7, 1876, d. Jan. 26, 1900); Osellia "Zella" Arnold Mosely Felts (b. Feb. 18, 1878, d. Oct. 19, 1968); John W. Arnold (b. 1880, d. 1900); Jesse E. Arnold Vandiver (b. Nov. 16, 1881, d. August 1969); and James Carroll "Jack" Arnold (b. May 26, 1886, d. June 11, 1949).

Jesse Arnold died Oct. 11, 1886 and buried in the Arnold Cemetery, Swifton, Jackson County, AR. Mary's second marriage was to Dr. Thomas J.

Moneyhon on April 15, 1890 in Lawrence County. They had one daughter, Mary Bessie Moneyhon Smith Belk Westmoreland (b. January 1892). Mary and Thomas Moneyhon divorced before 1900 and she never remarried. Mary died on Feb. 22, 1914 in Alicia, Lawrence County, AR and is buried beside her first husband, Jesse.

Nancy Campbell was born about 1855 in Franklin County, AL. Susan Campbell was born about 1857 in Franklin County, AL. Nothing else is known about these two girls.

William Frasier Campbell (b. Jan. 28, 1859 in Franklin County, AL) md. Mazie Elizabeth Wright on Feb. 22, 1885 in Conway County. Mazie (b. Oct. 29, 1861 in Hawkins County, TN) was the daughter of Elijah and Catherine Elizabeth (Coats) Wright. William and Mazie's children are Mary Ellen Campbell Coffman (b. Feb. 19, 1886, d. Jan. 8, 1981); Grover Cleveland Campbell (b. Nov. 3, 1887, d. May 1, 1961); Henry Sterling Campbell (b. July 7, 1890, d. June 22, 1959); Laura Gertrude Campbell Furr (b. Sept. 13, 1892, d. Aug. 15, 1974); Benjamin Campbell (b. April 14, 1894, d. July 7, 1975); and Clarence Elijah Campbell (b. Sept. 11, 1899, d. July 27, 1900).

William and Mazie moved their family from the Oak Grove Community in Conway County to Van Buren County sometime in 1891. Family history states that he moved his family from the river to the mountains to get away from the "fever" epidemic that had killed his parents and siblings. Family history also states that the cemetery that William's parents were buried in was washed away by a flood in the late 1800s.

William Frasier died Nov. 29, 1917 on White Oak Mountain, Van Buren County, AR. Marie Elizabeth died on June 24, 1926 in Cleveland, Conway County, AR. They are buried in New Hope Cemetery, White Oak Mountain, Van Buren County, AR.

Sterling Price Campbell (b. Aug. 7, 1862 in Booneville, Tishomingo County, MS) never married and lived in the Cleveland area with the family most of his life. He was a furniture maker by trade and made a good living from it. He died May 23, 1943 and is buried in Ried Cemetery, Cleveland, Conway County, AR. *Submitted by Darrell Dean Freeman.*

CAMPBELL - Ira Dickson Campbell, known by the family as "Dick" was born on March 28, 1903. He was the son of Elijah C. and Cindella Weaver Campbell. Dick lived the first 18 years of his life in Van Buren County, AR, working on his father's farm and in his shingle mill, which was located near Shirley, AR. Dick and his family left Van Buren County around 1920 and moved to Conway. After living a short while at Paw Paw Bend at the foot of Petit Jean Mountain, they eventually settled in the Portland Bottoms near Plumerville, AR.

Dick married Cora Anne Gordon, the daughter of William and Laura Hill Gordon, in Conway County on Dec. 23, 1923. They farmed in the bottoms until the flood of 1927, which destroyed their home and made it necessary for them to look elsewhere for land to farm.

Dick followed his older brother, William Daniel, and several other family members to the boot heel area of Missouri where he remained until 1959. Dick and Cora returned to Plumerville, AR in 1959 and Dick farmed the Mary House Farm in Menifee, AR until his retirement in 1971. Cora Anne Gordon Campbell (d. June 1, 1979) and Dick (d. May 1, 1986) are buried in the Plumerville Cemetery in Conway County, AR. Their 56-year-marriage produced the following children:

William I.D. Campbell (b. Jan. 22, 1925 in Plumerville, d. April 5, 2000 in Kennett, MO) md. Betty Ruth Harrison. Children: Jennie Ruth and Cynthia Anne.

Ancel Byron "Buddy" Campbell (b. Dec. 31, 1927 in Plumerville) md. first, Irene Scallins. Children, Robin Elizabeth and Allen Byron. Married second, Jane.

Dick Campbell family, 1947. First row, r-l: Jimmy Campbell (little boy), Dick Campbell, Della Campbell, Buddy Campbell, Glen Campbell Jr. Back row, l-r: Ruby Campbell, Cora Gordon Campbell, I.D. Campbell, Ira Campbell. Not pictured - Jerry Campbell.

Ira M.D. Campbell (b. Sept. 24, 1930 in Senath, MO, d. Sept. 4, 1987) md. Johnette Parks. Children: Sharon Lee, Gary Lynn, Karen Sue, Ira Michael, John Paul and Lisa Elaine.

Glen Dickson Campbell (b. Oct. 1, 1932 in Senath, MO, d. Nov. 13, 2001) md. Marjorie Hart and Billie Pettingill. Children: Glen Dickson Jr. and Sherry Anne.

Ruby Anne Campbell (b. March 6, 1934 in Senath, MO, d. April 21, 2002) md. Charles F. Mauk. Children: Cheryle Lee, Dennis Charles, David Fredrick, Richard Dale and Lisa Gail.

Della Jean Campbell (b. Sept. 28, 1938 in Senath, MO) md. J.V. Matlock. Children: Maracella Anne and Danny Jay.

Jimmy Dale Campbell (b. Jan. 11, 1942 in Senath, MO) md. Virginia Lee Watkins. Children: Kelli Beth and Christopher Dale.

Jerry Wayne Campbell (b. Aug. 11, 1949 in Gideon, MO) md. Jemica Deaver and Jeanette McNeal. Children: Kathy, Candy and Joshua. *Submitted by Kelli Campbell.*

CAMPBELL – Jimmy Dale Campbell (b. Jan. 11, 1942 in Senath, MO) is the son of Ira Dickson and Cora Anne Gordon Campbell. After graduating from Parma High School in 1959, Jimmy left Missouri and moved to Menifee, AR with his family.

Jimmy married Virginia "Ginny" Lee Watkins on March 23, 1963. She is the daughter of Arlie Lee Watkins and Eva Frances Chambers Watkins. Jimmy farmed with his father until 1971 when his father retired and Jimmy bought the farming operation. Ginny worked for the law offices of J.G. Moore and the insurance company of James L. Martin.

Jimmy Dale Campbell, Summer 1987.

Jimmy and Ginny are members of the Portland Baptist Church in Plumerville, AR. Jimmy is active in community affairs, serving on the Plumerville Volunteer Fire Department for a period of 23 years and as an alderman for the city of Plumerville. Their marriage produced two children:

Kelli Beth Campbell (b. July 22, 1967) md. Howard Smith. Children: Miranda Laine and Kaci LeAnne Smith.

Christopher Dale Campbell (b. July 16, 1971) md. Jennifer E. Humphries. Children: Samantha Elise and Aaron Christopher Campbell. *Submitted by Christopher Dale Campbell.*

CAMPBELL - Richard Campbell, the father of Elijah C. "Lidge" Campbell, was born in middle Tennessee between 1822-24. His parents are unknown.

Richard married Mary Anne (maiden name unknown) in Tennessee about 1842. Richard moved to Kentucky in 1848 and was living in Ripley County, MO when the 1850 census was taken. He and Mary Anne had moved to Van Buren County, AR by 1852. They had the following children: Lucretia Campbell (b. 1844); Miranda B. Campbell (b. 1846) md. Martin Anderson in 1868; Elizabeth M. Campbell (b. 1848); Louisa J. Campbell (b. 1850) md. Lewis Pate in 1869; Alexander Campbell (b. 1852); and William H. Campbell (b. 1855) md. Nancy Bailey in 1879.

Census records show that Mary Anne Campbell died prior to 1860, and that Richard had married Elizabeth Anne Bean. Richard and Elizabeth Bean Campbell had the following children: Elijah C. Campbell "Lidge" (b. Aug. 12, 1860, d. Nov. 2, 1932 in Conway County, AR) md. Cindella Weaver in 1882; Lorilda Anne "Rilda" Campbell (b. December 1866, d. bet. 1900-03 in Van Buren County, AR) md. Annual Davis in 1888; Artie Elizabeth Campbell (b. March 19, 1875, d. Jan. 17, 1941 in Conway County, AR) md. first, Irving J. Eoff and second William J. Davis.

Richard Campbell died about 1890 in Van Buren County. Elizabeth Bean Campbell was living with her daughter, Artie F. Davis, when she died sometime after the taking of the 1910 census. Richard Campbell was a farmer. He and Elizabeth were members of the Cumberland Presbyterian Church of Van Buren County, AR. *Submitted by Jerry Wayne Campbell.*

CANADY - Theoda "Pete" Canady was born south of Cleveland in a small region called the Center Community on Jan. 9, 1919. He married Sarah E. Moore Dec. 7, 1940. Pete grew up trying to farm on very poor soil, but managed to survive. He was unable to attend school often, but his sense of wit helped him master several jobs at a sawmill, including learning to drive a truck, count money and sign his name legibly. When sawmill work declined, he worked in the pulpwood business with his brother, Roy, and his grandsons, when they were old enough to help out.

Front (L-R): Kelsey, Mae, Theoda, Sarah and Charles. Back (L-R): Runall, Theauther and Curtiss.

Sarah (b. Dec. 7, 1922) attended several years of school occasionally, then she became a housewife that helped with gardening and other outdoors jobs, like chopping and picking cotton, until 1962. She fortunately got a job at Oberman's, a pants making facility, later purchased by Levi's in Morrilton. She worked there until retirement, then returned to doing things she enjoyed, like making quilts, traveling, church work, and community activities. She traveled to at least 10 states outside of Arkansas. In November 2004, at age 81, she suffered a light stroke. Until then, she was able to do most anything she wanted, like drive herself to town, sing in the choir, etc. Theoda and Sarah Canady had six children.

1) Mae Ester, who married Willie James Wright of Morrilton, had eight children: Anita and husband Donnie have two daughters, Chandra and Candace, and one son Marcus with two children; James has three daughters: Alicia, Erica and Kierra, and one son Cameron Blake; Barbara has a daughter Andrea and a son Darius; Martin is deceased and had two sons, Brandon and Trey, and one grandchild; David and wife Christy have two daughters, Shyra and Danielle, and one son Christopher; Joseph has a daughter Chelsey

and a son Jalen; Willene and husband Cortez Sr. have three daughters: Brittany, Toni and Briaunna, two sons, Damein and Cortez Jr., and one grandchild Shawna Rae who has two sons, Dorian and Geron.

2) Runall and wife Sharon have three sons: Derrick, Texford and Galen, and three grandchildren.

3) Curtiss and wife Carlene have one son Greg, one daughter Kesha and two grandchildren.

4) Kelsey and wife Mary have three daughters: Christina, Tanisha and Tia; one son Bryan and three grandchildren.

5) Theauther and wife Gwen have four daughters: Joyel, Tynisha, Trista and Victoria; one son Thedore "Teddy" and three grandchildren.

6) Charles has one daughter Tiffany, one son Derek and three grandchildren.

The old home place is still the setting for most family get together's, nestled in the country air with cool breezes under the walnut trees. *Submitted by daughter Mae Ester Wright.*

CARGILE
The Cargile family originated in Scotland. The surname is a place name derived from the ancient lands of Cargill, lying in the present Parish of Cargill in Perthshire, Scotland. Cornelius Cargill was born about 1680. It is unknown when he immigrated to America, but he appeared in Virginia records in 1712. Cornelius married Mary Anderson, widow of Thomas Anderson, before July 8, 1712 in Virginia. Mary died about 1718. Cornelius and Mary had two children, John (b. 1714) and Mary (b. 1718). Cornelius married several times after Mary's death. He died after June 10, 1763 in Halifax County, VA.

John Cargill (b. 1714 in Surry County, VA) was the son of Cornelius and Mary. John married Rachel Tinsley, daughter of John Tinsley and Susannah Chiles. John and Rachel had at least 11 children: John, Clary, Sarah, Cornelius, Elizabeth, Thomas, Mary, Daniel, Clement, Keziah and Lucy. John moved to South Carolina after 1763. He received 1100 acres in land grants in South Carolina. He died 1777 in Craven County, SC.

John Cargill, eldest child of John and Rachel, was born 1740 in Virginia. He married Keziah (last name unknown). John appears on the 1790 and 1800 Laurens District, SC, census. John and Keziah had several children.

John Cargill Jr. (b. bet. 1775-77) was the son of John and Keziah. John married first about 1796-1800. The name of his first wife is unknown. They had three children. John's wife died prior to November 1803. John married Nancy Elizabeth Lewis on Nov. 27, 1803 in Christian County, KY. Elizabeth (b. 1785) was the daughter of Alexander and Elizabeth Lewis.

John and Elizabeth appear on the 1810 Christian County census. The family moved to Graves County, KY prior to 1830 and to Arkansas about 1837. John appears on the 1838 tax records of Johnson County, AR, and the 1839 tax records of Searcy County, AR. He appears on the 1840 Searcy County census. John and Elizabeth probably died before 1850.

Children of John Cargill Jr. and his first wife:
(1) Unknown Son Cargill (b. 1794-1800); (2) Unknown Daughter Cargill (b. 1794-1800) and (3) Unknown Son Cargill (b. 1800-1803).

Children of John and Elizabeth (some of the children spelled their name Cargile):
4) Unknown Daughter Cargill (b. 1804, d. young)
5) Keziah Cargill (b. 1806, d. 1879) md. Benjamin Palmer Jr. Children: Mariah, William, Nancy, Sarah, Martha, Margaret, Mary, Benjamin, Minerva, Susan and Robert Palmer.
6) Edward P. Cargile (b. 1808) md. Mary. Children: James, John, Nancy, Jessie, Pelina, Daniel and Louisa Cargile.
7) Nenion Elijah Cargile (b. 1810) md. Sarah, then married Elizabeth Plant.
8) Delemore Burvel Cargile (b. 1812, d. 1876) md. Mary Plant. Children: Charles Thomas, William, Sabre, Dennis Stell, Marvin, Mary, Nancy, Laura and

John Cargile. He then married Elizabeth (last name unknown).
9) Robert Lewis Cargile (b. 1814, d. 1880) md. Margaret Plant. Children: Sabre Elizabeth, Charles, M.A., Sarah and Lucinda Cargile. He then married Hannah (probably Livingston). Children: Hannah, Lydia, Mary Elizabeth, Martha Kellie and Katie Cargile.
10) Thomas H. Cargill (b. 1816) md. Mary Palmer. Children: Benjamin, Elizabeth, John, Martha, Edward, William, Robert and Keziah Cargill.
11) Martha P. Cargile (b. 1820) md. Clarborn Ward. Children: Nenion, Nancy, Mary, Margaret, Ezekiel, John, W.C. and Benjamin Ward.
12) William W. Cargile (b. 1825, d. 1864 in the Civil War) md. Cynthia Martin.
13) Nancy Jane Cargile (b. 1829).

CARGILE
Nenion Elijah Cargile (b. 1810 in Kentucky) was the son of John Cargill Jr. and Nancy Elizabeth Lewis. Nenion married Sarah Johnson Aug. 14, 1835 in Hickman County, KY. Sarah Johnson (b. 1820 in Tennessee) was under age when she married and her mother, Elizabeth, gave written permission for her to marry. Nenion moved his family to Arkansas about 1837. Several families made the trek together. Nenion appears on the 1839 Searcy County tax list, along with his father John Cargill and his brother Thomas Cargile. On the 1840 Searcy County census an older woman, who may have been Sarah's mother, was living with the family.

Living nearby were Nenion's parents, his brother Robert Lewis Cargile and his sister Keziah Palmer. Prior to 1850, Nenion moved his family to Benton Township of Conway County, near his brother William Cargile. Sarah died between 1855 and 1859. On July 1, 1859, Nenion patented 160 acres of land in Walker Township of Conway County. (In 1873 both Benton and Walker Townships of Conway County became part of the newly formed Faulkner County.) Nenion's family appears on the 1860 Conway County census in Walker Township near his brother Thomas Cargill.

Nenion married Elizabeth Plant on April 27, 1862 in Conway County. On Feb. 8, 1867, Nenion appeared before the Conway County Chancery Court to seek a divorce from Elizabeth. Elizabeth did not appear in court and the judge continued the final action until the "next term." Chancery Court records for the August Term 1867 show the divorce decree was made "final and absolute." In 1867, Nenion bought property in Benton Township of Conway County. He paid taxes on the property for several years. The 1870 Conway County, Benton Township, census shows Nenion living near his brother Delemore Cargile. Nenion probably died prior to 1880. Besides being a farmer, Nenion was a Justice of the Peace for over 30 years. County records contain countless marriages he performed.

Nenion and Sarah had eight children:
1) Nancy Elizabeth Cargile (b. May 29, 1836) md. William Holliway S. McClure on Jan. 14, 1855 in Conway County. Children: Nenion, Robert Conway, Sarah Ann Priscilla (md. John Alvy Laycook), Dora Bannon, Harriet (md. John Wesley Maupin, then Curtis Powell), and Millard McClure.
2) Keziah Cargile (b. 1837) md. Lewis Hanley on Feb. 7, 1856 in Conway County.
3) Mary J. Cargile (b. 1840) md. William A. Elliott Jr. on Dec. 30, 1858, in Conway County. William (b. 1836, d. 1864 in the Civil War) was the son of William A. Elliott Sr. and Mary Graves. One child: Ara Adna Elliott (md. George Riley Smith). Mary then married Alex K. Livingston on Aug. 7, 1865 in Conway County.
4) Cyntha Margaret Cargile (b. 1843).
5) Martha Eliza Cargile (b. 1846).
6) Mahala A. "Milla" Cargile (b. 1848) md. Alonza W. Bennett on Nov. 6, 1870, in Conway County. Alonza was the son of George W. Bennett and Nancy Williams.

7) John W. Cargile (b. 1851).
8) Delemore Burvel Cargile (b. 1855) md. Amy E. Butler on July 22, 1881, in Stephens County, TX.

CASHARAGO
Gilbert Casharago was born in Italy June 2, 1806. Mara Tacchin (b. ca. 1816) md. Gilbert by 1835 or 1836. Gilbert and Mara arrived in New York aboard the ship, *La Rosa*, on Sept. 11, 1849. With them were their daughters: Josephine, Heneritta, Louisa and Delilah. They had a son Louis that was brought over with Mara's sister and husband, Josephine and Henry Nicolaides, and another daughter, Mary Jane, was born in Arkansas. They then traveled to Arkansas where they first lived in Prairie County, and later moved to Conway County, which is now Faulkner County. They settled on the south bank of Pea Vine Creek on a small flat with a good spring. The community became known as Cash Springs, because of the Casharagos. Later the name was changed to Republic, as it is still today.

Louis Casharago enlisted in the Civil War and fought for both the North and the South, which was not unusual. He returned from the service, married Jane Havens and had a son, James Calvin. Louis fell off a barn roof and died from a broken neck when James was quite small. Jane married A.B. Jones after the death of Louis. James Calvin married Mary Salter, and to this union Minnie Casharago was born. Minnie married twice, (1st) Lewis Wharton and (2nd) William Louis Mallett. No children were born to either marriage.

Josephine Casharago married twice, (1st) Reuben Haywood Hawkins and had children: Reuben, Mary Fannie, Thomas D., Martha and (2nd) Walter Ford DeJarnett. To this union was born Alice, md. Dr. J.S. Kessinger; James Walter md. Ada M. Donell; Lavina; Tennie; Stephen md. Laura Kessinger; and Soudie Louisa md. Peter Mathew Douglas.

Heneritta Annett "Hetty" Casharago md. George Washington Mallett and to this union was born: Amanda md. Jessie Price Jordan; Anderson Gordon; Kelly md. William Earnheart; William Lewis md. (1st) Nancy Ollie Kennamer and (2nd) Minnie Casharago; Daniel Harrison md. Molly Perry; Edwin Monroe; Joseph Columbus md. (1st) Lula Abbie Duncan and (2nd) Lena Elizabeth; Lydia Bell md. Jack Miller; Alma Heneritta md. John Cunningham; Virgil; and Sarah Catherine md. Lafayette Lee.

Louisa "Lou" Casharago md. Marshall LaFayett Cate and to this union was born Jannette who md. James M. Adams.

Delila "Lila" Casharago md. Green McMillen and to this union was born Mary; Thomas md. (1st) Lancy Lance and (2nd) Mattie Parson; Samuel; and Jefferson.

Mary Jane Casharago md. (1st) James Bradshaw and to this union was born James and Sarah. Mary Jane md. (2nd) Samuel P.C. Smith and to this union was born John Lewis who md. Salley Mallet; Mary Elizabeth md. Joe Mallett; William Gilbert md. Mary Lena Kendall; Susan Jane md. Timothy Owen Rowlett; George Lincoln md. Ara Margaret Moore; and Sam Houston md. Del Crump. *Submitted by Jane Bliss, Marry Lemire and Betty Ruble.*

CATO
Willis Cato (b. 1827 in Arkansas) is thought to be the son of James Cato, but no proof of that has been found. He married Epsie ? who was born in 1834 in Missouri. Willis was in Pulaski County in the Bayou Meta Township by the 1850 census, and in Polk County in the Big Fork Township by the 1860 census. Children of Willis and Epsie include William Jackson (b. March 20, 1850 in Arkansas); Edna Caroline (b. 1853); George Washington (b. Jan. 15, 1856 in Bayou Meta, Faulkner County, AR); Sarah A. (b. 1857); and Rebecca Jane (b. 1860).

William Jackson married Edith Catherine Sparrow in 1877. Edith Catherine (b. March 28, 1860 in Arkansas) was the daughter of John and ? Sparrow. William Jackson was in Pulaski County in 1860, Searcy

County in 1880 and then in Conway County by 1900. William Jackson and Edith Catherine had the following children: Margaret (b. Jan. 10, 1878); Willis Franklin (b. July 31, 1879); Nora B. (b. Nov. 21, 1881); George T. (b. March 16, 1887); May Survilla (b. March 17, 1889); Selah L. (b. Feb. 17, 1891); Nevada Kansas (b. May 8, 1893); Millie Florence (b. Sept. 18, 1899); and Edith or Epsie Cato (b. May 18, 1902). William Jackson died Aug. 18, 1910 and Edith Catherine died Jan. 19, 1911. Both are buried in Cato Cemetery in Jerusalem, AR.

Willis and Elsie Cato

Willis Franklin Cato married Elsie Emmaline Harris March 21, 1904. Elsie (b. Oct. 31, 1885 in Appleton, AR), daughter of Jim Owens and Elizabeth Harris. Willis was a farmer. He and Elsie had two children, Walsie A. (b. May 3, 1908 in Jerusalem) and Epsie Edith (b. June 16, 1910 in Jerusalem). Willis died Nov. 20, 1957 and Elsie died Sept. 27, 1974. They are buried in Cedar Creek Cemetery in Jerusalem, AR. *Submitted by Bobby A. Beavers.*

CHAMBERS - Bennett Chambers was born in 1805 in Davidson County, TN. His parents are unknown, however, census records from Perry County, TN indicate that his father was named Thomas C. Chambers.

Bennett married a woman named Rebecca. Her maiden name is unknown. Sometime after the 1840 census of Weakley County, TN, Bennett and his brother, Greenbarry, moved to Pope County, AR. Greenbarry had married Jane Buford in Lawrence County, TN in 1830.

Eva Frances Chambers, 1934, great-great-granddaughter of Bennett Chambers.

Bennett settled in the Dover area. He and Rebecca had the following children: (1) Greenbarry Chambers (b. 1827 in Tennessee, d. bet. 1860-70 in Pope County, AR) md. Janie Burris; (2) Thomas J. Chambers (b. 1831 in Tennessee, d. bet. 1862-70 in Pope County, AR) md. Phoebe Catherine Burris; (3) Elizabeth Jane Chambers (b. 1832 in Tennessee) md. John Brady, then Green Owens; (4) William C. Chambers (b. 1840 in Tennessee, d. 1879) md. Matilda Catherine Reynolds. He is buried St. Paul Cemetery in Pope County, AR. (5) Mary Eliza Chambers (b. 1845 in Arkansas) md. James W. Booker. Also according to census records, an unknown male Chambers was born in 1839 in Tennessee.

Bennett was a farmer. He served as a private in Company A of the Arkansas Mounted Regiment under Captain J.R.H. Scott during the Mexican War in 1846. Bennett was 58 years old when he joined the Union Army in 1863. Bennett's two sons, Greenbarry and Thomas, joined the Confederate States Army in 1862. Later, Greenbarry deserted and joined the Union Army in 1863. William C. Chambers, another son of Bennett, also joined the Union Army in 1863. Bennett was discharged on March 2, 1865 and returned home.

Rebecca died after the 1870 census of Pope

County was taken. Bennett married a second time to Denisha Garner Poindexter Baker in 1871. He sold his farm in Pope County and moved to Logan County. He died there in 1876 and was buried in the Red Bench Cemetery in Logan County, AR. Several of Bennett's grandsons moved to Conway County and made their lives there after the Civil War. *Submitted by Beth Campbell.*

CHAMBERS – Henry Harris "Horace" Chambers (b. 1879 in Conway County, AR) was the son of Willis C. Chambers and Nancy Emoline Johnson. Horace, as he was known in the family, was raised in the household of Jackson McCoole after the death of his parents. He was a farmer and married three times. His first marriage produced one child, William Chambers (b. 1902). William married Ada Price and lived the latter part of his life in Rogers, AR. He died March 23, 1987 and was buried in the Price Cemetery near Russellville, AR.

Henry Harris Chambers (Horace) and wife Martha E. Andrews.

Henry married a second time to Martha Ellen Andrews, the daughter of Newton and Letha Wallace Andrews, on Jan. 31, 1907. Their daughter Eva Frances Chambers (b. March 20, 1920) md. Arlie L. Watkins. Eva died May 12, 1996 and was buried in the Lost Corner Cemetery near Cleveland, AR.

Henry's third marriage was to Ethel Camp and produced three children: (1) Lorene Chambers (b. 1929, d. 1940). (2) Wilburn Chambers (b. 1931) md. 1st, Minnie Lamkins. Children: Peggy and Pamela Chambers. Wilburn married 2nd, Lessie Jones. Children: Penny and Eugene Chambers. (3) Milburn Elmer Chambers (b. 1933) md. Rosetta Moses. Their children were Hazel, Milton and Jerry Chambers.

Henry Harris "Horace" Chambers died Oct. 12, 1933 in England, AR and buried in the Wallace Wells Cemetery near Hattieville, AR. *Submitted by Virginia Campbell.*

CHAMBERS - Willis C. Chambers (b. 1854 in Pope County, AR) was the son of Thomas Chambers, a farmer and Confederate veteran of the Civil War, and Phoebe Catherine Burris, a daughter of John and Cynthia Anne Ashmore Burris. Upon the deaths of his parents, Willis followed his brothers, James Albert and William Bennett Chambers, to Conway County.

Willis married Nancy Emoline Johnson on June 4, 1875. Nancy was the daughter of Martin Van Buren and Emoline McGehee Johnson. Willis was a farmer and settled on a 160 acre homestead in Union Township to begin his marriage.

Willis C. Chambers and wife, Nancy Emoline Johnson Chambers.

Willis and Nancy had the following children:
1) Henry Harris Chambers (b. Jan. 1, 1878).

2) Ruth Chambers (b. 1878, d. 1950) md. James Isaac Barnes in 1895. children: Bertha, David, Reese, Tom and Jeff Barnes.

3) Samuel Ernest Chambers (b. 1881, d. 1952) md. May Dry. Child: Idella Chambers.

4) Mary Claudia Chambers (b. 1886) md. Edward Price. Children: Darwin, Bud, Edna, Roy, and Ina Grace Price.

5) James B. Chambers (b. 1888, d. 1914) md. Maude Skipper. Child: James Eugene Chambers.

6) McDaniel "Mack" Chambers (b. 1890, d. Dec. 9, 1975) md. Beulah Williams. Children: Hetty, Delton, Claudia, James, Syretha and Carolyn Chambers.

7) Annie L. Chambers (b. March 14, 1892) md. Charles King. Children: Cuba, Bill, Virgil, Carl, Calvin, Evelyn, Wanda and Rheba King.

Willis C. Chambers died about 1895 and Nancy Johnson Chambers died about 1897. They are buried in the McClaren Cemetery near Lanty, AR. *Submitted by Ralph Redin.*

CHARTON – Alphonse Auguste Charton (b. Oct. 5, 1848 in France) was the son of Nicholas Charton, as our family knows him. There were several old letters saved by Alphonse and Rosalie that were mailed from La Grange Rouge, France starting on April 18, 1903 from Orcole Charton. The first of these letters came addressed to Monsieur Alphonse Charton, "Solgohachia Conway County, AR Etats. Unis., Amerique." Some of these letters were postmarked Monthureux S Saone Vosges, and some were postmarked Gruey Les Surance Vosges. After 1906 they were addressed to RFD No. 2, Morrilton. There are several of these letters from Orcole, so he must have been a close relative, that was near and dear, for these letters to have been saved for such a long time. They were written in French and there is no one in our family at this time that can read them.

A passport was issued to Alphonse Auguste Charton in Mirecourt, Department of Vosges on Aug. 31, 1873 to go to New York, United States of America. The passport was good for one month for departure from France. Alphonse would have been about 25 years of age when he immigrated to America.

Little is known about the time between 1873-81. John Rochelle, a tailor residing in East Saint Louis, IL and having a tailor shop in Saint Louis, MO, purchased Lot 1 Block 2, Morrilton from George H. Morrill on the first of November 1878. On March 19, 1881 Alphonse purchased land from M. Brown. On April 23, 1881 Alphonse got a marriage license from the Conway County Courthouse to marry Rosalie Rochelle, but they were not married until May 5, 1881. On the 21st of December that same year, he purchased a place from W.L. Hannah. Alphonse lived in Plumerville for a short time before he purchased the old Box place from Mr. Hannah. The original log house is still part of the old Harry Charton home.

On Aug. 12, 1882 Nicholas and Adrien Charton, two adults purchased a steamship ticket to sail on the steamer *Sabradod* to depart from Havre, France to go to New York. Nicholas signed a Contract De Transport Par Mer in Paris for their passage. Adrien (Andre or just Andrew) stayed with his brother Alphonse for the rest of his life. Clarence and all of the other children of Harry and Lena Hainley Charton just knew him as Uncle Drew.

The following is quoted from the local and state newspapers. From the *Morrilton Democrat:* "A very sad occurrence was the death of our friend, Alphonse Charton, by drowning of which will always be shrouded in mystery as to whether he fell in the river accidentally or for purpose. He was an old resident of this community and made his home with his son. The old man had become practically blind and was very feeble in both body and mind and had become somewhat despondent over his condition because he could not work, so about two weeks ago on the 26th of September he left his home. Going a little ways, he fell in company with a colored man going to Morrilton so he went with him. The man ask him if he wanted to go back with him and where he would find him. The old man said he would be at Mr. Austin's Store.

"The colored man looked the town over and made inquiry and could find no trace of him. The colored man notified his son of the matter that evening. But he thought his father was visiting some of his old French friends around Morrilton as he had done before and that he would be home in a day or so, but as he did not return in a few days, he became uneasy and started to search for his father. He could find no trace of him.

"They searched three of four days but all in vain, not a word could they hear but on the third day of this month they saw an account of a man being found on Sunday floating down the Arkansas River below Little Rock fitting the description, so one of them in the company of another man went down to make investigation, and found it to be the body of his father buried in a shallow grave near the edge of the water just as he was found. He had the body cared for and sent home and buried Saturday with the help of his friend.

"The funeral service was conducted by Bro. Chaney of Solgohachia. Our friend was a native of France, has two boys who are very highly respected in this community, and we extend our sympathy to them in their great trouble, for if their father committed the last act of taking his own life by drowning, it was not their fault, for he was well cared for himself. So the mystery will never be solved. He was a man of 76 years and had worked very hard."

From the *Arkansas Gazette:* "The body of a white man found floating down the Arkansas River below Little Rock last Sunday morning was identified Thursday by Harry and Gus Charton of Morrilton as that of their father, Alphonse Charton, 76, who disappeared last week. Mr. Charton disappeared from his home south of Morrilton, on the river, on September 26th. The brothers could advance no theory except that their father fell into the river by accident. The body was brought to Morrilton Friday for burial." *Submitted by Ken Charton.*

CHARTON - Clarence Elmer Charton (b. June 21, 1916 in Overcup, Conway County, AR) was the first of 12 children born to Harry and Lena Hainley Charton. Clarence made several trips to Texas and run the wheat harvest. They would start in Texas and run through Oklahoma and Kansas into Nebraska. In the 1930s, Clarence, after age 19, made several annual trips to California to work on a farm around the Cutler-Orosi-Dinuba area, and he delivered produce to the Los Angeles area at times. Several men would go together each spring to make the trip. Some of the men going were Louie Charton, Emmett Charton, Clifton Charton, and Trot Yates.

When Clarence came home in 1939 on Christmas Eve, he and Ruby Bostian went to Hot Springs to get Bro. A.H. Burroughs, Arthur's father, to marry them. Ruby's parents would not let her go without a married chaperone. Arthur and Wilma went and got married on December 23 and came home and chaperoned them.

In 1940 Clarence and Ruby lived in a small log house on the south side of the dirt road, where in 1942 they built a new three room house across the road, where the present home is located. In 1949 Clarence added two bedrooms, living room and a bathroom. Clarence and Ruby had three children: Kenneth Winston (b. Sept. 2, 1941), Betty Carolyn (b. Jan. 18, 1946) and Danny Charles (b. Jan. 25, 1954).

In the 1940s he ran a dairy operation until he came down with rheumatism. Ruby and Ken milked the cows by hand, until he was able to resume the job. The milk was put in large cans and left at the highway and a man from Center Ridge picked it up and carried it to the Morrilton Cheese factory. He was a farmer and rancher, and in about 1959-60 he built a chicken house and went into the chicken business. Later he bought the Sam Underwood place and acquired another chicken house.

In the 1950s Clarence contracted with the Atkins Pickle Co. to sign up growers to raise cucumbers. We ran a grading station in Morrilton and had one at Center Ridge for a couple of years. In 1958-59 he got 30 farmers to plant 80 acres of Allgold sweet potatoes to supply to Kroger, Safeway and other outlets in Little Rock. He built a storage facility in Plumerville and about 4,000 bushels of potatoes were stored. Clarence also bought peas and other vegetables for a processing plant in Fort Smith. In the late 1950s we built a cattle auction barn and pens for beef cattle on the Carruthers place on Branch Street.

In 1964 Clarence was elected to the Farm Bureau Board of Directors and in 1991 he was elected to the Board of the Cattlemen's Association. He served both until his death. He was also on the Board of Directors of the Farmers Co-op. He had also served on the board of the Farmers Home Administration. He was a member of the Overcup Methodist Church and had been on the board of the Overcup Community Building several years after helping build it.

Clarence died of pancreatic cancer on May 3, 1993. *Submitted by Danny Charton.*

CHARTON - Louis Charton was born in Nancy, France on Jan. 18, 1831. A researcher in France, who is a Charton, was unable to locate any information. So far, no information on his entry into the United States has been found. The family tradition is that he came to this country through New Orleans, LA at the age of 12. Who he stayed with or what connection there is to the other Chartons which were in St. Louis, MO and later moved to Morrilton, AR is not known. There is probably some link, but further research is needed.

His wife was Adalaide Richardet, also from France. She was born about 1838. It is said she was from Sabandia, France. However, the only Sabandia I have found is in Peru. So, she was probably from a place that sounds similar. She was Jewish by birth and is said to be a Palestinian Jewess. I have also heard it said that her parents were from Egypt. Palestinian or Egyptian, Adalaide would be a Shephardic Jewess as opposed to the Ashkenazi Jews of eastern Europe.

It is also said that her parents died in a house fire in France when she was an infant. So, their surnames are not known. Richardet was given to her. She was raised in a Catholic convent. When or how she came to this country is not known. How she met Louis Charton or where they married is not known. There are Richardets, which settled in Perryville, MO. Whether there is any connection to that family through adoption or some other way is not known at this time.

With all the family tradition and speculation, it is certain that Louis and Adalaide were both from France. The first documented record is the 1860 census from Ohio. They were living there near Canton. This is also where my first great-grandmother, Zora "Zoy" Charton, was born about 1856. There was a French settlement near Canton, OH.

By 1870, the Louis Charton family is found on the census in Tennessee living in Franklin County. It is not certain when they moved from Ohio to Tennessee, but it was most probably after the Civil War. It was here that Zoy Charton met and married Robert Henry Bryant on Aug. 27, 1874.

Another problem for research is that Zoy Charton made a point, which is on record, that the family name was originally Chastain and not Charton. So, that may be the name Louis had when he entered the United States.

CHARTON - Ruby Katherine Bostian was born in Arkansas, Aug. 9, 1920, the sixth child of seven born to Charles W. and Willie Mae Watkins Bostian. Ruby graduated in May 1939 as salutatorian of her class. Dec. 24, 1939 after Clarence Charton came home from working on farms in California, they went to Hot Springs to get A.H. Burroughs to marry them. Ruby's parents would not give their consent to travel to Hot Springs without having a married chaperone, so Arthur Burroughs and Wilma Charton were going to get mar-

ried, so they went to Hot Springs and married on December 23 and came back to Overcup and took Clarence and Ruby to Hot Springs. A.H Burroughs was Arthur's dad and was a former pastor of the Overcup Methodist Church.

After marriage her father, C.W. Bostian, let them have 80 acres that had an old log house on it. The old log house is where they lived until 1942 when they built a three room house across the road on the north side. While living in this three room house, Kenneth was born on Sept. 2, 1941 and Betty Carolyn was born Jan. 18, 1946. In 1949 they added a living room, two bedrooms and a bathroom on to the house. Danny Charles was born on Jan. 25, 1954.

Clarence worked for C.W. Bostian on his farm to get the use of his tractor. Even though the tractor had lights on it, C.W. believed that it had to be in the barn by dark, just like the mules and horses. When Clarence came down with rheumatism, Ruby and Ken kept the cows milked and sent to market. The milk had to be put in large cans and put by the mailbox at the highway so a fellow from Center Ridge could pick it up and deliver it to the Cheese factory in Morrilton.

In the 1950s when we had the cucumber shed, Ruby would take care of it while Clarence was baling hay. Ken and Phillip James would haul the cucumbers to the Atkins Pickle Co. in 1958. I don't remember who drove the truck before we started.

Ruby was active in the Overcup Rural Community Improvement Club, Overcup Home Demonstration Club, 4-H Club Leaders, Morrilton High School Band Parents, Overcup Community Building, Parents Teachers Association, and Methodist Church activities.

Ruby died on Nov. 18, 1997 of leukemia at the age of 77 years. *Submitted by Kenneth Charton.*

CHARTON - Zoy Charton/Chastain's husband, Robert H. Bryant, was born Oct. 22, 1856 in Franklin County, TN. He was the son of Alexander Bryant and Susan "Susa" Phillips. Alexander may have been born in Virginia, but by 1840, he was settled in Cannon County, TN. Susan Phillips was originally from Guilford County, NC. Her father settled with his large family in Cannon County. Benjamin H.F. Phillips was married five times with 18 children. Susan's mother was the third wife.

Robert Bryant had brothers on both sides in the Civil War. Franklin County, TN was a very secessionist region and even threatened to leave Tennessee and join Alabama, if it didn't secede from the union. One brother who fought for the union was killed. Another brother, William, fought in the First Tennessee Regiment at First Manassas. He was discharged for medical reasons not long after and later settled in Benton, AR.

The Charton family left Franklin County, TN for Nashville, and by 1880 had settled in Morrilton, AR. Robert Henry Bryant and Zoy Charton moved at the same time (or about the same time). They had two sons while in Nashville, John Barry Bryant and William. By 1881, the Bryants were in Morrilton and lived there until probably 1888. Two children were born in Morrilton. One was a daughter who died soon after birth and the second was Walter Bryant.

The Bryants left Morrilton before Zoy Charton Bryant's mother died. Adalaide (Richardet) Charton died on Sept. 13, 1888. She was buried at the Catholic cemetery. Louis Charton married a second wife, Martha Ann Edmundson, in July 1889. Louis Charton died on Jan. 28, 1891. Adalaide originally buried him at the Catholic cemetery. His second wife later had him moved to Elmwood Cemetery in Morrilton.

By July 1888, the Bryant family was living in Ft. Smith, AR where a fourth son was born, Benjamin "Bennie" Bryant. The next place the family moved was Webb City, MO. It was here on Oct. 1, 1891 that my maternal grandfather, Eurie Frank Bryant, was born. (See more on him under Bryant.)

The family also lived for a time around Peoria,

Indian Territory. It was in Peoria in 1894 that Zoy Charton passed away. She was buried at Benson Cemetery just a mile across the Oklahoma-Missouri border from Peoria in Newton County, MO. After his death on Dec. 30, 1928 in Baxter Springs, KS, Robert H. Bryant was buried next to Zoy.

CHISM - Alta (b. Oct. 14, 1881), daughter of John W. and Margaret S. (Beeson) Adams, married Eugene E. Tilley on Feb. 3, 1899 in Conway County, AR. Eugene (b. April 1, 1876, d. Feb. 24, 1909) is buried in the McClaren Cemetery, Lanty, Conway County, AR. Alta and Eugene were the parents of William Roosevelt "Ted" Tilley, Metty Tilley Koonce, John Tilley and Mabel Tilley Hazelwood.

After Eugene's death, Alta Maud Adams Tilley married David Obadiah Chism on July 18, 1918 in Conway County, AR. David, son of William Henry and Nancy E. (Wells) Chism, was born Dec. 5, 1872 in Conway County, AR. David and Alta are the parents of two children: Carroll Cecil Chism and William Parker "Bill" Chism.

Carroll (b. Sept. 13, 1919, d. July 22, 1979) never married. He is buried in the Adams Cemetery. William Parker Chism married Bonnie R. Harrell on Dec. 26, 1952. After retirement, William and Bonnie built their home on his father's old home place in Lanty, AR where they currently reside.

Alta Adams Tilley Chism died Oct. 4, 1970 and is buried in the Adams Cemetery. David Obadiah Chism died Oct. 1, 1944 and is buried beside his first wife, Nellie, in the Lanty Cemetery. *Submitted By Cynthia Ann Chism Efird.*

CHISM - Carolyn "Callie" Chism (b. March 1877 in Conway County, AR, d. May 13, 1914) was the daughter of William Henry and Nancy Wells Chism. Callie married Henry N. Ferguson on Dec. 30, 1893 in Conway County, AR. Callie and Henry were the parents of two children: Birtha Ferguson (b. January 1895) and Henryetta Ferguson (b. March 1897). After the death of Henry Ferguson, Callie married Joseph T. "Joe" Moore on Sept. 30, 1897 in Conway County, AR. Joe was born in April 1855 and died April 24, 1929 in Conway County, AR. Callie and Joe are the parents of three girls: Ora Moore, Rhea Moore and Katie Moore. Callie and Joe T. Moore are buried in the Skinner Cemetery, Conway County, AR. Rhea Moore (b. 1904) md. William E. "Buddy" Fellers. Rhea died Jan. 5, 1925 in childbirth and is buried in the Skinner Cemetery, Conway County, AR.

Katie Moore (b. 1905, d. 1994) md. Wes Bridges and they had one son, Carl Deon Bridges. Katie and Wes divorced and she married William "Bill" Garrett (b. 1904). Bill Garrett adopted Carl Deon.

Joe T. Moore was married the first time to Elizabeth Ida Beeson and they were the parents of six children: Sarah Elizabeth Moore, Emma Lou Moore, Lydia Otis Moore, Ambrie Moore, Walter L. Moore and Bennie Lou Moore. *Submitted by Carl Garrett.*

CHISM - David Obadiah Chism, son of William Henry and Nancy E. (Wells) Chism, was born Dec. 5, 1872 in Conway County, AR. He married Nellie E. Harrington on Nov. 2, 1892 in Conway County, AR. Nellie, daughter of Hezekiah Dempsey and Bellefane (Johnson) Harrington, was born Oct. 20, 1875 in Conway County, AR and died Oct. 30, 1917. David Obadiah Chism died on Oct. 1, 1944 and he is buried beside Nellie in the Lanty Cemetery. David and Nellie were the parents of seven children.

1) William Harmon Chism (b. Oct. 29, 1894 in Lanty, Conway County, AR, d. July 15, 1971) md.

Johnnie Victoria Sutton on July 22, 1916 in Conway County, AR. Johnnie (b. Aug. 6, 1893, d. March 8, 1961) was the daughter of James Everett and Mary Alice (Bizzell) Sutton. William Harmon and Johnnie are buried in Lanty Cemetery.

2) Eva Ethel Chism (b. Sept. 29, 1898, d. Sept. 19, 1983) md. James V. Maxwell on May 12, 1918 in Conway County, AR. James (b. July 28, 1895, d. April 23, 1975) and Eva are buried in Kilgore Cemetery, Birdtown, Conway County, AR.

3) Famie Jewell Chism (b. 1901, d. 1950) md. Tollie L. Brown on Dec. 23, 1919 in Conway County. Tollie (b. 1897, d. 1979) and Famie are buried in the Lanty Cemetery.

4) Mary Elmus Chism (b. May 12, 1903, d. March 13, 1975) md. 1st, Stanley Cole. They divorced and she married Max W. Morphis Sr. on Nov. 23, 1920. Max (b. Jan. 12, 1899, d. Sept. 29, 1981) and Mary are buried in Lanty Cemetery.

5) Zora Bell Chism (b. June 6, 1905 in Conway County, AR, d. Oct. 13, 1992) md. Jasper Joe Marion Haney. Jasper (b. Aug. 4, 1896, d. Jan. 10, 1967) and Zora are buried in the New Hope Garden of Memories, Spiro, OK.

6) James Roscoe Chism (b. April 16, 1908, d. May 1, 1990) md. Ruby Lee Orr on Aug. 21, 1929. Ruby (b. Feb. 17, 1911, d. April 13, 1992) and James are buried in Grandview Cemetery, Conway County, AR.

7) Thomas Reno Chism (b. Feb. 2, 1911, d. Dec. 6, 1966) md. first, Vernie Mae Wells (b. Aug. 21, 1916) on Oct. 15, 1932. Thomas and Vernie divorced and he married Esta R. Telay Scroggins (b. Jan. 6, 1910, d. Sept. 6, 1995) on Oct. 2, 1941. Thomas and Esta are buried in Lanty Cemetery.

After Nellie's death, David Obadiah Chism married Alta Maud Adams Tilley on July 18, 1918 in Conway County, AR. Alta, daughter of John W. and Margaret S. (Beeson) Adams, was born Oct. 14, 1881 and died on Oct. 4, 1970. She is buried in the Adams Cemetery. David and Alta are the parents of two children: Carroll Cecil Chism and William Parker "Bill" Chism. *Submitted by Krista Chism Gray.*

CHISM - Eva Ethel Chism (b. July 29, 1898, d. Sept. 19, 1983) was the daughter of David Obadiah and Nellie (Harrington) Chism. Eva married May 12, 1918 to James Victor Maxwell, the son of John Westerfield and Josephine (Robinson) Maxwell. James (b. July 28, 1895, d. April 23, 1975) and Eva are buried in Kilgore Cemetery, Birdtown, Conway County, AR.

Eva Ethel and James Victor are the parents of 10 children:

1) Vivian Jewell Maxwell (b. April 19, 1919, d. May 2000) md. Aldon McCoy on Oct. 5, 1940. They were parents of four children: Larry Winston McCoy, Elmore Art McCoy, William Victor McCoy and Betty Jewell McCoy.

2) Wesley Obadiah "Bud" Maxwell married Billye Ruth Bull and they are parents of three chil-

dren: Marilyn Lance Maxwell, Gary David Maxwell and Vicki Annette Maxwell.

3) Pauline Euna Maxwell (b. April 16, 1923, d. April 14, 1963, buried in California) md. Edgar Jackson Buie and they are the parents of three children: Una Faye Buie, Jarvis Lee Buie and Jean Buie.

4) Edith Melvinia Maxwell (b. June 22, 1925, d. Nov. 18, 1955) never married and lived with her parents until they passed away.

5) James Milburn "Gib" Maxwell married Bernice Bull and they are the parents of four children: Kenny Allen Maxwell, Randy Howard Maxwell, Barry Wade Maxwell and Janet Denise Maxwell.

6) Melvin Hayes Maxwell married Frances Foshee and they have one daughter, Linda Diana Maxwell. Melvin and Frances divorced and he married Virginia Cain. They are the parents of three children: Dana Lynn Maxwell, Gordon Lee Maxwell and Gregory Lance Maxwell.

7) Ida Mae Maxwell married Irvin Foshee and they are the parents of eight children: Rentha Mae, Sharon Jacqueline, Stanley Irvin, James Andy, Allen Lynn, Pamela Jean, Angela Gail and Lisa Ann.

8) Elna Louise Maxwell married Floyd Erman Stell and they are the parents of three children: Floyd Wayne Maxwell, Mary Evelyn Maxwell and Steven Erman Maxwell.

9) Barbara Ellen Maxwell married Leo Brasier and they are the parents of three children: Deborah Kay Brasier, Ernest Ray Brasier and Melvin Keith Brasier.

10) Mary Lena Maxwell (b. Oct. 18, 1939., d. Jan. 9, 1987, buried in Kilgore Cemetery, Birdtown, Conway County, AR) md. Thomas Dean Boyd II and they had two sons, Thomas Dean Boyd III and Morris Scott Boyd. Lena and Thomas divorced and she married Clarence Hearn. Lena and Clarence have one son, Nathan Kelly Hearn. Lena and Clarence divorced and she married Charles Bruce. They had one son, Danny Bruce. *Submitted by Louise Maxwell Stell and Ida Mae Maxwell Foshee.*

CHISM – Famie Jewell Chism (b. 1901, d. 1950) was the daughter of David Obadiah and Nellie (Harrington) Chism. Famie married Tollie Lucien Brown (b. 1897, d. 1979) on Dec. 23, 1919. Tollie was the son of Wallace and Ellen (McClaren) Brown. Famie and Tollie are buried in the Lanty Cemetery, Lanty, Conway County, AR. Famie and Tollie were the parents of five children: James Doyne

Brown, Ellen Faye Brown, twins-Thelma Brown and Velma Brown, and Mary Jane Brown.

1) James Doyne Brown (b. Sept. 25, 1920) md. Marie Sledge on Sept. 12, 1936. Doyne and Marie are the parents of three children: Shirley Ann Brown (b. Jan. 14, 1937, d. Jan. 16, 1937); Henry Wallace Brown (b. Sept. 28, 1945, d. Sept. 2, 1964) and Margaret Ann Brown. Margaret married Eugene Waight. They divorced and had no children. James Doyne died on May 21, 2001 and is buried in the Lanty Cemetery, Conway County, AR.

2) Ellen Faye Brown (b. March 21, 1925) md. Jimmy Mitchell (b. Jan. 18, 1918, d. April 9, 1944, buried in Grandview Cemetery, Conway County, AR). Ellen and Jimmy had no children. Ellen Faye married second to Alvis Leroy Delong (b. Jan. 1, 1920, d. Feb. 27, 1970, buried in the Lanty Cemetery) and they were the parents of three children: Joyce Faye Delong, Donnie Alvis Delong and Teresa Ellen Delong.

(a) Joyce Faye Delong married Arnold Dee Moody and they have one daughter, Elizabeth Ellen

Moody. Elizabeth Moody married Clinton Wayne Gilbert on Oct. 7, 1989 and they have two daughters, Ashley Elizabeth Gilbert and Allison Cheyenne Gilbert. Joyce and Arnold Moody divorced and she married a Sensabaugh. They divorced and she married Earl Brockway on March 21, 1999. Joyce and Earl have no children.

(b) Donnie Alvis Delong (b. July 19, 1949, d. Aug. 18, 2000, buried in Lanty Cemetery) married first to Terry Lou Zachary on Aug. 30, 1969. They were the parents of one daughter, Donna Annette Delong. Donna married Fred Peters Jr. and they have two children, Corey Wayne Peters and Wyatt Andrew Peters. Donnie and Terry Lou divorced and he married Betty White. Donnie and Betty were the parents of three children: David Anthony Delong, twins-Carroll and Cheryl Delong. Donnie and Betty divorced and he married Rose Settlemire.

(c) Teresa Ellen Delong married David Anderson on March 10, 1979 and they are the parents of two children, Famie Marie Anderson and Katie Renee Anderson.

After Alvis' death, Ellen Faye married Robert Lewis; they had no children. Ellen Faye Brown Mitchell Delong Lewis died July 20, 1989 and is buried beside Alvis Delong in the Lanty, Cemetery, Lanty, Conway County, AR.

3) Twin-Thelma Brown (b&d. Oct. 11, 1931) is buried in the Lanty Cemetery.

4) Twin-Velma "Snooks" Brown (b. Oct. 11, 1931, d. July 15, 1998) md. Herbert Hoover McCoy in 1949. Snooks and Hoover are the parents of two children: Rickey Lynn McCoy and Shirley Louise McCoy. Snooks and Hoover divorced and she married Earl Brockway on Nov. 11, 1974.

5) Mary Jane Brown (b. Nov. 14, 1937, d. Dec. 4, 1937). *Submitted by Joyce Brockway.*

CHISM – James Billy Chism (b. March 1, 1933 in Jerusalem, AR), son of Willie Ellen Massey (b. Feb. 22, 1910) and John Leonard Chism (b. Dec. 22, 1910).

John and Willie were married Sept. 16, 1928. James' older sister was Wanda Faye Chism (b&d. June 6, 1930). There is no marker for her in the Jerusalem Cemetery. His younger sister is Johnnie Sue Chism (b. Feb. 10, 1939 in Jerusalem, AR).

James Billy Chism married Vereta Jean Castleberry in Piggott, AR, March 14, 1953. She was born in Sikeston, MO on March 1, 1933. They have two daughters:

James Billy Chism (son of John L. Chism and Willie Ellen Massey) and Vereta Jean Castleberry Chism.

Shirley Jean Chism Dold (b. Jan. 6, 1956 in Morrilton, AR at old Saint Anthony Hospital) md. Gerald Wayne Dold (b. Aug. 17, 1954) on June 1, 1972. They have five children: Theresa Jean Dold Payment (b. Nov. 20, 1972); Elizabeth Ellen Dold Norwood (b. Nov. 21, 1974); Catherine Marie Dold (b. July 2, 1977) is not married; Phillip John Dold (b. Nov. 2, 1982) is not married yet; and Angela Joan Dold Denova (b. April 10, 1979).

James and Vereta's second daughter, Janet Sue Chism Speights, was born Aug. 4, 1960 at old Saint Anthony's Hospital in Morrilton, AR. Janet married David Marion Speights on June 16, 1978. Their children: Aaron Joseph Speights (b. Oct. 6, 1980) md. Kathryn Leigh Jacobi (b. July 31, 1982) on June 19, 2004; Matthew James Speights (b. Jan. 16, 1985); and Elizabeth Anne Speights (b. Dec. 4, 1994). All children were born at Russellville, AR. *Submitted by Jean Chism.*

CHISM - James Monroe Chism (b. Jan. 30, 1885, d. Jan. 7, 1978) was the son of William Henry and Nancy

(Wells) Chism. James Monroe Chism married Cynthia Allie Byers (b. Feb. 15, 1884, d. July 25, 1950) on Jan. 14, 1903 in Conway County, AR. They are buried in the Cedar Grove Cemetery, Francis, Pontotoc County, OK. After Cynthia's death, he married Nora Nance Rinehart Stobaugh

(b. Jan. 8, 1886, d. 1968) on Oct. 6, 1951. Nora is buried beside her second husband, Inglish Stobaugh in Matthews, MO.

James Monroe and Cynthia Allie moved to Oklahoma after her sister sent them a message to come out west. They settled in the Weleeka area where there was a farm to work on. It took a week to go from Jerusalem, AR to Oklahoma. They traveled by horse and wagon, camped out at night and traveled during the day.

James Monroe and Cynthia Allie are the parents of eight children:

1) William Duel (b. Feb. 24, 1904 in Cleveland, Conway County, AR, d. April 29, 1995) md. Earnie Lee Ramsey (b. Jan. 10, 1904, d. April 1984). Their children are Dean Chism, Juanita Chism Bishop, Norma Jean Chism Smith and Wanda Corine Chism Geiger.

2) Alvin Henry (b. Jan. 9, 1906 in Cleveland, AR, d. Feb. 26, 1995) md. Norma Griffin in 1925. They were the parents of one son, Kenneth Alvin Chism.

3) Tollie David (b. Nov. 29, 1908 in Cleveland, AR, d. _) md. Lovie Griffin (b. May 10, 1908) in 1926. Tollie and Lovie had one daughter, Barbara Chism Price. Tollie married his second wife, Cleo (b. Aug. 28, 1912, d. May 1984), in 1962.

4) John Leonard (b. Dec. 22, 1910 in Cleveland, AR, d. Sept. 9, 2003) md. Willie Ellen Massey (b. Feb. 22, 1910 in Jerusalem, AR, d. May 17, 2001). They were the parents of three children: Wanda Faye Chism, James Billy Chism and Johnnie Sue Chism.

5) Leo Thomas (b. Feb. 27, 1916 in Jerusalem, AR, d. April 12, 2003) md. Evelyn West on Aug. 11, 1934. They were the parents of three children: Donna Chism Shaw, June Chism Boggs and Tommie Dale Chism.

6) Robert Cleo (b. March 4, 1919, d. April 22, 1997) md. Quida (b. Sept. 13, 1917, d. Sept. 20, 1995) in 1938. They were the parents of two children, Brenda Chism and Robert Chism.

7) Mary Lucille married Mirl Melvin Moon in September 1941. Mirl died Nov. 6, 2001. They were the parents of one son, Joe Edd Moon.

8) Hazel was born in Jerusalem, AR. She married Lester Kymes and they are the parents of three children: Charles Kymes, Barbara Ann Kymes Frantz and Dennis D. Kymes. *Submitted by James Billy Chism.*

CHISM - James Roscoe Chism (b. April 16, 1908 in Macedonia, Conway County AR), son of David Obadiah Chism and Nellie E. (Harrington) Chism, was 8 years old when his mother died. At the age of about 12 he went to live with his older sister, Fammie and her husband Tollie Brown. Roscoe was married to Ruby Lee (Orr) Chism Aug. 23, 1929 in Conway County, AR. He died May 1, 1990 in Cleveland, Conway County, AR. Ruby (b. Feb. 17, 1911, Grandview, Conway County, AR, d. April 13, 1982 in Grandview, Conway County, AR) and

Front: Ruby and Roscoe Chism. Back, l-r: Betty, Jimmy and Nellie.

Roscoe are buried in Grandview Cemetery, Conway County, AR.

Roscoe and Ruby were the parents of three children:

1) Nellie Louise Chism (b. April 23, 1935 in Lanty, Conway County, AR) md. Clell Laudis Stobaugh on May 6, 1954 in Atkins, Pope County, AR. Clell is the son of Arlie Laudis Stobaugh and Virginia Jean (Cupp) Stobaugh. Nellie and Clell are the parents of two children, (a) David Glenn Stobaugh (b. April 30, 1955) md. Ann Addison on April 21, 1971 in Lipan, TX. They have one son Justin David (b. March 9, 1987). (b) Cynthia Louise "Cindy" Stobaugh (b. Oct. 17, 1959) md. Donald Karman O'Neal on May 25, 1978 in Cleveland, Conway County, AR. Cindy and Karman have two children, Felicia Dawn and Wesley Shawn. Felicia Dawn O'Neal (b. Jan. 2, 1979) md. Steven Davenport on July 17, 1999. Their child is Brook Nichole Davenport (b. Dec. 18, 2001). Wesley Shawn O'Neal was born Nov. 19, 1980.

2) Betty Marie Chism (b. Jan. 17, 1943 in Lanty, Conway County, AR) md. Jimmy Harold "Jim" Dixon on April 28, 1961 in Morrilton, Conway County, AR. Jim is the son of Olen Dixon and Marie (Polk) Dixon. Betty and Jim are the parents of three children.

(a) Betty Gail Dixon (b. Oct. 9, 1962) md. Leslie Dixon (divorced), they were the parents of one son, Mitchell Keith Dixon (b. Sept. 9, 1985). Betty Gail then married Donald Eller on Oct. 17, 1987. They are the parents of Luke Ashdon Eller (b. Feb. 10, 1989) and Andrew Randall Eller (b. June 25, 1993). Betty Gail died Sept. 13, 1997 and is buried at Grandview Cemetery, Conway County, AR.

(b) Deronda Lee Dixon (b. April 23, 1966) md. Tony Freeman (divorced), they are the parents of one child, Ashley Nichole Freeman (b&d. Aug. 2, 1985, buried in Grandview Cemetery, Conway County, AR). Deronda married Fred Givens Jr. Oct. 17, 1987. They are the parents of two children, Heather Lee Givens (b. March 3, 1989) and Jenna Marie Givens (b. Aug. 19, 1994).

(c) Randall Harold Dixon (b. March 7, 1970) md. Lynice Leann Sharp (b. May 5, 1989). They are the parents of two children: Krysten Lynice Dixon (b. Nov. 15, 1989) and Stephanie Janell Dixon (b. July 1, 1991). Randall Harold died Jan. 10, 1994 and buried at Grandview Cemetery, Conway County, AR.

3) James Riley "Jim" Chism (b. Oct. 5, 1949 in Grandview, Conway County, AR) md. Mary Evelyn Guinn on Oct. 4, 1968 in Center Ridge, Conway County, AR. She is the daughter of Otho Guinn and Jewell Freeman Guinn. Jimmy and Evelyn are the parents of two children. (a) Dena Lynn (b. June 23, 1972) md. Boyce Smith on Sept. 4, 1999. They are the parents of one child Morgan Nicole Smith (b. July 4, 2001). b) James Gregory Chism (b. July 26, 1978).

During their life together Roscoe and Ruby lived at Lanty, until 1943 when they moved to the Grandview Community where they lived on Ruby's family farm. This is where they raised their family and lived the rest of their lives.

They both worked very hard, milking cows, plowing and picking the fields of cotton, corn, peas, and cucumbers. Roscoe also worked as a barber and a blacksmith. He would spend all day shoeing horses.

Although they worked extremely hard they always seemed to manage to have time to socialize, sometimes all night. Their home was always open to anyone who came by.

Roscoe and Ruby were blessed with 53 years of marriage together. *Submitted by Nellie Chism Stobaugh.*

CHISM - John Pleasant "Doc" Chism (b. Oct. 4, 1874 in Newton County, AR) was the son of James W. and Sarah Ann (Bailey) Chism. Doc married Maggie Lou Conley on March 10, 1901 in Conway County, AR. Maggie (b. Jan. 30, 1878 in Conway County, AR) was the daughter of William Lewis and Sarah Caroline (Beeson) Conley. Doc and Maggie had one child, William Archie Chism (b. Dec. 31, 1910 in Lanty, Conway County, AR).

John Pleasant Chism, wife Maggie Conley Chism and son William A Chism.

When Maggie was diagnosed with tuberculosis, she was told to move to a dry climate and it would ease her symptoms. William was just a small boy when his father moved the family to Carrizo Springs, Dimmitt County, TX. They lived there until her death on Feb. 15, 1923. She is buried in the Mount Hope Cemetery, Carrizo Springs, Dimmitt County, TX. Doc and little William returned to Conway County where Doc settled in the Lanty Community and never remarried. He died on Feb. 27, 1947 in Vinson Chapel and is buried in the Adams Cemetery, Lanty, Conway County, AR.

William married Evelyn Faye Adams on April 16, 1933 in Conway County, AR. Evelyn Faye (b. March 23, 1917 in Little Rock, Pulaski County, AR) was the adopted daughter of Ben Q. and Mabel (Smith) Adams. William and Evelyn had one child, Norma Jean Chism (b&d. April 5, 1934 in Lanty, Conway County, AR), who is buried in the Adams Cemetery, Lanty, Conway County, AR. Evelyn died June 4, 1934 from complications during childbirth and is buried with her baby in Adams Cemetery.

After Evelyn's death, William married Rose Mildred Zachary on Feb. 2, 1937 in Conway County, AR. Rose, daughter of George Washington Zachary Jr. and Mary Jane (Hasler) Zachary, was born in Vinson Chapel, Conway County, AR. William and Rose are the parents of five children: Betty Ruth Chism, Howard Lee Chism, Kenneth Edward Chism Sr., Billy George Chism and Carl Eugene Chism.

Howard married Cheryl Ann Helton, daughter of Joe and Gertie (Underhill) Helton, and they have two daughters, Valerie Diane Chism and Michelle Lee Chism. Kenneth married Mary Joyce Freeman, daughter of Arden and Eathel (Campbell) Freeman, and they have four children: Tammie Joyce Chism Shipp, Rosemary Chism Norwood, Kenneth Edward Chism Jr. and William Alan Chism. Billy married Margaret Ann Norwood, daughter of Virgil and Opal (Mansfield) Norwood, and they have three children: Michael Clint Chism, Crystal Jane Chism Gullett and Billy Lance Chism. Carl married Deborah Eugenia Caudell, daughter of Elmer and Sherry (Rainbolt) Caudell, and they have three children: Robert William Caudell, Deborah Chism and Zachary Todd Chism.

William Archie Chism died Oct. 5, 1974 in Morrilton and is buried in the Vinson Chapel Cemetery, Conway County, AR. *Submitted by Kenny Chism.*

CHISM - Kenneth Edward Chism Sr. (b. April 5, 1942 in Vinson Chapel, Conway County, AR) is the son of William Archie and Rose Mildred (Zachary) Chism. He married Mary Joyce Freeman of Cleveland, Conway County, AR on May 27, 1961 in Morrilton, Conway County, AR. Mary is the daughter of Arden William and Mary Eathel (Campbell) Freeman.

On March 31, 1985, Kenneth was tragically killed in a one-vehicle accident in St. Vincent on his way home from work. He is buried in the Liberty Springs Cemetery, Van Buren County, AR. Mary currently resides in Cleveland and works for Wal-Mart.

Kenneth and Mary had four children: Tammie Joyce Chism Shipp, Rosemary Chism Norwood, Kenneth "Kenny" Edward Chism Jr. and William Alan Chism.

Kenneth and Mary (Freeman) Chism Family. Children: Tammie, Rosemary, Kenny and Alan.

Tammie married Dewey "Lynn" Shipp on Dec. 17, 1988 at Center Ridge, Conway County, AR. Lynn is the son of Dewey Lee and Mary (Ward) Shipp of Cleveland. Lynn and Tammie have two children, Sarah Lynne Shipp and Jonathan Thomas Shipp. Both children were born in Conway, Faulkner County, AR. The Shipps currently make their home in Cleveland where Lynn is self-employed and in the chicken litter business. Tammie works as an administrative assistant for the Wonderview School District at Hattieville, Conway County, AR where Sarah and Jonathan both attend school.

Rosemary married Kippy Dale Norwood on March 4, 1983 at Morrilton, Conway County, AR. Kippy is the son of Wayne Norwood and Mabel (Roberts) Norwood. Kippy and Rosemary have three children: Nicholas O'Neal Norwood, Mary Whitney Norwood and Nathan Edward Norwood. They all currently reside in Morrilton. Kippy is employed at Green Bay Packaging, Arkansas Kraft Division of Morrilton, where he has worked for 25 years. Rosemary is a stay-at-home mom and in her spare time, quilts, researches the family history and gardens. The two oldest children, Nicholas and Whitney, both graduated from Morrilton High School. Nicholas currently attends the University of Arkansas Community College at Morrilton and Whitney attends the University of Central Arkansas at Conway, AR. Nathan was born with Down Syndrome and is currently a student at Morrilton High School.

Kenny married Tern Tilley in 1994 at Clinton, Van Buren County, AR. They have one daughter, Maegan Hope Chism. The couple later divorced. Kenny resides in Cleveland, AR and has been employed by Green Bay Packaging, Arkansas Kraft Division of Morrilton for 16 years. Maegan attends school at the Clinton School District.

Alan is unmarried and resides in Conway, Faulkner County, AR. He is currently employed by Detco Industries of Conway. *Submitted by Tammie Chism Shipp.*

CHISM - Mary Angeline "Molly" Chism, daughter of Obadiah Parker and Elizabeth Rebecca (Gaylon) Chism, was born December 1855 in Arkansas and died sometime between 1927-30 in Conway County, AR. She is buried in Skinner Cemetery, Conway County, AR. She married Newton J. Anderson on Sept. 5, 1882 in Conway County, AR. The marriage record is in Book "D" Page 291 Conway County, AR. Newton, son of Nathaniel and Elizabeth (Hale) Anderson, was born March 1851 in Scott County, MO. He died Nov. 14, 1914 in Conway County, AR but it is unknown were he is buried.

Mary Angeline (Chism) Anderson

Mary Angeline's brothers and sisters are Samuel B. Chism, Pleasant Obadiah Chism, William Henry Chism, John Jasper Chism, James W. Chism, Elizabeth Jane Chism, Rebecca Sophronia Chism and George Washington Chism.

Newton Anderson's known brothers and sisters are George W. Anderson, Mary Anderson, James Anderson, Jane Anderson, Louisey Anderson, John Anderson, Charles Anderson and Ida Anderson.

Mary Angeline and Newton were the parents of two children, Marintha A. Anderson and Emma E. Anderson. Marintha (b. ca. 1879, died sometime after 1880) was listed on the 1880 Van Buren County, AR Census in the household of her grandparents, Obadiah and Rebecca Chism.

Emma E. Anderson (b. January 1880 in Arkansas, died sometime before 1910 in Arkansas) md. Richard McDonald on Feb. 21, 1897 in Yell County, Conway County, AR. Richard, son of John S. and Caroline McDonald, was born in December 1869 in Arkansas and died before 1910 in Arkansas. Emma and Richard were the parents of one son, Newton A. "Newt" McDonald (b. Dec. 25, 1903 in Arkansas, d. Sept. 25, 1981 in Conway County, AR).

Newt served in the US Army during WWII. Newton married Madlin M. Wells on June 28, 1945 in Conway County, AR. Madlin is the daughter of Franklin and Mary (Prince) Wells. Newton and Madlin are the parents of one son, Doyle Newton McDonald.

Doyle McDonald married Tammy Medlock, daughter of Louie and Gloria Jean (Mayall) Langley. Doyle and Tammy are the parents of three daughters: Lindsey Gail McDonald, Kristy Kay McDonald and Jennafer Janell "Jenna" McDonald. *Submitted by Doyle and Tammy McDonald.*

CHISM - Mollie Chism (b. Dec. 23, 1878 in Conway County, AR) was the daughter of William Henry and Nancy Wells Chism. Mollie's first marriage was to W.J. Treadaway on Jan. 23, 1896 in Conway County, AR. It is unknown what happened to this union.

Mollie married second to James Irvin Gaylor on Oct. 14, 1897 in Conway County, AR. James was born in September 1875 in Conway County, AR. Mollie and James had five children: Lloyd Brown Gaylor, J.I. Gaylor, Mabel Clara Gaylor, Sidney "Buster" Gaylor and Edith Lee Gaylor.

James Irvin Gaylor and Mollie Elizabeth Chism Treadaway Gaylor

James Irvin Gaylor died Aug. 5, 1924 in Oklahoma and is buried in Spiro or Round Mountain Cemetery in Oklahoma. Mollie Gaylor died on April 26, 1975 and is buried in Cedar Grove Cemetery, Frances, OK.

1) Lloyd Gaylor and his wife, Bernice, have two children, James Irvin Gaylor and Lenora Gaylor. Lloyd died young and is buried in Fairlawn Cemetery, Stillwater, Payne County, OK.

2) J.I. Gaylor died at the age of 12 years old. He is buried in the Fairlawn Cemetery, Stillwater, Payne County, OK.

3) Mabel Clara Gaylor (b. March 27, 1913 in Jerusalem, Conway County, AR, d. Oct. 16, 1960 in Oklahoma is buried in the Cedar Grove Cemetery, Frances, OK. Mabel married Herley Lee Kelley on Oct. 9, 1927. Herley (b. Aug. 8, 1908 in Jerusalem, Conway County, AR, d. Dec. 15, 1984) is buried in Cedar Grove Cemetery, Frances, OK. Mabel and Herley were the parents of five children: Ollie Elizabeth Kelley, Rob-

ert Leroy Kelley, Hershel Herley Kelley, Charles David Kelley and Donny Eugene Kelley.

4) Sidney "Buster" Gaylor married Mattie "Kate" Long and they have three children: Irvin Sidney Gaylor, Mary Alice Gaylor and Yvonne Marie Gaylor.

5) Edith Lee Gaylor (b. March 22, 1918, d. June 4, 1993) md. Leon Scroggins and they have three children: James Willie Scroggins, Donna Kathryn Scroggins and Betty Virginia Scroggins.

CHISM - Mary Elmus Chism (b. May 12, 1903 in Lanty) md. Max W. Morphis Sr. on Nov. 23, 1920. Max (b. Jan. 17, 1899 in Atkins, Pope County, AR) and Mary had seven children.

1) Charles McKinley Morphis (b. Sept. 5, 1921, d. June 10, 1976, buried at Lanty Cemetery) md. Goldie Ridling and they had two children, Billy Charles and Jo Ann. Billy had three children: Scott, Cynthia and Benjamin. Jo Ann Morphis married Hamid Malik and they have one son, Shawn.

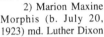

2) Marion Maxine Morphis (b. July 20, 1923) md. Luther Dixon on July 14, 1938. They have five children: Dewey Landon, James Luther, Willie Earl, John Maxey and Mary Betty. Dewey Landon married Sue and they had two children, Dewey Landon II (who is now deceased) and Tammy. He and Sue divorced. He is now married to Dorothy and they have no children. Maxine passed away two years ago and is buried in St. Louis. James Luther married Esther, they have no children. John Maxey married Ski and they have four children: Chris, Dallas, Danny and Maria. Willie Earl died at age 3. Mary Betty married Dave Muich. They have two children, Kenny and Jamie. Luther passed away and Maxine married Carl Wolf.

3) Don Paul Morphis (b. Aug. 18, 1926) md. Johnnie Griffin from Sikeston, MO. They had two sons, Phillip Don and Stephan Paul. Stephan died of cystic fibrosis at a young age and is buried in California. Phillip has a son Kevin and daughter Gail. Don and Johnnie divorced and he married Dorothy. They had a son Scott, who died of a brain tumor at age 3. Don passed away and is buried in California.

4) Ruby Jewell Morphis (b. Sept. 22, 1929) md. Dick Weems and they have three children: Mary Odell, Loetta Ann and Debbie. Mary married David White and they have three children: Angie, Kim and David Jr. Loetta has 10 children - three by her first husband, Darrell Baker, and seven by her second husband. She is now divorced and lives with her children. Debbie married Eddy Watson and they have one daughter, Christa. She is now married to Phil May and they have no children. Ruby passed away and is buried at Arnold, MO.

5) Anne Morphis (b. Jan. 22, 1932) md. Farrell Stacks. They have three children: Stephen Farrell, Charlotte Ann and Danny Carl. Stephen married Deana Sell and they have one child, Trisha Nichole. Charlotte married Kenneth Higgins, they have no children. She has a stepson, Skye Higgins. Danny is not married.

6) Ruth Elaine Morphis (b. March 26, 1934) md. Bill Martin and they have two children, Ricky Lynn and Rita Gail. Ruth and Bill divorced and she married Kenneth Beezley. They had one son, Michael. Kenneth passed away. Ruth and Michael live with Rita and her husband, Max Garrison.

7) Max Morphis Jr. (b. July 17, 1941) md. Patsy Durham and they have one son, Leslie Earl. Max and Patsy divorced and he married Neoma Chandler in Checotah, OK. They had two children, Shannon and Gary Lance Taf.

Max and Elmus Morphis are buried in the Lanty Cemetery, Conway County, AR. *Submitted by Anne Stacks.*

CHISM - Obadiah Parker Chism, son of John W. and Sarah (Parker) Chism, was born March 23, 1814 in Kentucky and died July 9, 1889 in Conway County, AR. He married Elizabeth Rebecca Gaylon about 1838. She was born Feb. 15, 1817 in Tennessee and died April 6, 1898 in Conway County AR. They are both buried in the Skinner Cemetery, Conway County, AR.

Descendents of Obadiah Parker Chism.

Obediah and Elizabeth were the parents of nine children:

1) Samuel B. Chisum (b. ca. 1839 in Tuscumbia, Franklin County, AL).

2) Pleasant Obediah Chisum (b. Sept. 1, 1841 in Jackson Park, Jackson County, AR, d. Dec. 21, 1932, Tulsa, Tulsa County, OK) md. Louisa D. Conley on Feb. 14, 1867 in Conway County, AR. Louisa (b. May 22, 1847 Walker County, GA, d. Sept. 22, 1919 in Ada, OK) was the daughter of James T. Conley and Rachel Evatt Conley.

3) William Henry Chisum (b. October 1843 in Newton County, AR, d. April 15, 1909 in Conway County AR) md. Nancy Elizabeth Wells on Sept. 28, 1872 Conway County, AR. Nancy (b. October 1855 in Arkansas, died in Jerusalem, Conway County AR) and William Henry are buried in the Skinner Cemetery, Conway County, AR.

4) John Jasper Chisum (b. March 4, 1846 Newton County, AR, d. Dec. 28, 1928 in Tulsa, Tulsa County, OK, buried in Blanco Cemetery, Pittsburg County, OK) md. Kisiah Emeline Standridge in about 1870. Emeline (b. Nov. 16, 1847, d. July 29, 1918) was the daughter of Lemuel and Margaret Standridge. She is buried in Hewitt Cemetery, Daisy, OK.

5) James W. Chisum (b. ca. 1848 in Arkansas, d. Dec. 31, 1881) md. Sarah Ann Bailey on July 19, 1870, Pope County, AR. After James' death, Sarah (b. Sept. 11, 1851, Tennessee, d. June 16, 1925, Conway County, AR) md. Thomas W. Wells of Cleveland. Sarah and Thomas are buried in the Cleveland Cemetery. It is unknown where James is buried.

6) Elizabeth Jane Chisum (b. ca. 1849) md. Samuel Doss on Aug. 5, 1867 in Pope County, AR. Nothing else is known of her. We assume she died young. Samuel Doss married second to Cynthia Finnery on Aug. 25, 1870, Conway County, AR.

7) Mary Angeline "Molly" Chisum (b. December 1855 in Arkansas, died between 1927-30 in Conway County, AR) is buried in Skinner Cemetery, Center Mountain, Conway County, AR. She married Newton J. Anderson on Sept. 5, 1882 in Conway County, AR. Newton (b. March 1851 in Scott County, MO, d. Nov. 14, 1914 in Conway County, AR) was the son of Nathaniel and Elizabeth (Hale) Anderson.

8) Rebecca Sophronia Chisum (b. December 1855 in Conway County, AR, d. Aug. 6, 1907 in Conway County, AR) md. Lorenzo Boyd Merrick on Feb. 16, 1879 in Conway County, AR. Lorenzo (b. Aug. 6, 1857 in Conway County, AR, d. Oct. 19, 1915 in Conway County, AR) was the son of Griffith and Martha (Wells) Merrick. Rebecca and Lorenzo are buried in Skinner Cemetery, Center Mountain, Conway County, AR.

9) George Washington Chisum (b. ca. 1862 in Arkansas) md. first to Susan Milligan (b. March 14, 1861, d. April 27, 1927). They divorced and George married Mary Jane Upchurch (b. ca. 1862) on March 15, 1887. *Submitted by Stanley Dean Chism.*

CHISM - Thomas Reno Chism (b. Feb. 2, 1911 in Lanty, Conway County, AR) was the son of David Obediah Chism and Nellie Harrington Chism. After the death of Reno's mother, his father married Alta Maud Adams Tilley.

Reno married Vernie Maie Wells on Oct. 15, 1932. Reno and Vernie Maie had two children, Sherman Doyle (b. Sept. 15, 1933) and Renia Mae (b. Dec. 3, 1934).

Sherman Doyle married Genevieve Louise Green on July 4, 1952, and they had one son, Steven Dwayne Rogers (b. Sept. 9, 1953). Steven married Rebecca Lopes and they had two children, Jayson Michael (b. Oct. 30, 1977) and Angelina Nacole Rogers (b. Aug. 3, 1979). Sherman Doyle was killed in a house fire on Sept. 4, 1965. Steven Dwayne died April 1996.

Renia Mae married George Franklin Lenzi on Feb. 21, 1953. Renia and George had two children, George Arthur and Thomas Gordon. George married Cynthia Ann Motto on July 12, 1975, and they had two children, Shera Kristine (b. Oct. 31, 1979) and George Ryan (b. June 11, 1982). Thomas Gordon Lenzi never married.

After Reno and Vernie Maie divorced, Reno met and married Esta Artelia Scroggins. Reno and Esta married Oct. 2, 1941 and had three children: Etta Ruth, David Humphrey and Thomas Earl.

Etta Ruth (b. Jan. 21, 1944) md. Sturl D. Bridgeman on Feb. 21, 1961 and they had four children: Terry Gene Bridgeman (b. Sept. 21, 1962), Timothy Wayne Bridgeman (b. Oct. 28, 1968) and Travis D. Bridgeman (b. Nov. 16, 1980). Terry married Vickie Gayle Price on June 4, 1988. Terry and Vickie have two children, Marcus Allan (b. Oct. 9, 1988) and Katie Elizabeth (b. June 31, 1991). Terry and Vickie are now divorced. Tim married Sandee Dae Trafford on June 17, 1989. Tim and Sandee have two children, Stephanie Nichole (b. Feb. 11, 1998) and Jacob Aaron (b. May 16, 2001). Tonya married Allison Dale Thomas on May 15, 1999. Dale and Tonya have two children, Nathaniel Lane (b. Dec. 8, 1998) and Savannah Grace (b. Oct. 25, 2001). Travis died Nov. 17, 1980. Etta Ruth died of cancer Dec. 16, 2001. Both Etta Ruth and Travis are buried at Friendship Cemetery in Solgohachia, AR.

David Humphrey (b. Nov. 11, 1946) md. Glenda Grace Bridges on June 29, 1968. David and Glenda have one child, David Todd Chism (b. Nov. 16, 1971). Todd is not married.

Thomas Earl (b. Nov. 7, 1948) md. Rita Ann Brown on May 30, 1969. Tommy and Rita have two children, Danny Earl (b. Oct. 14, 1969) and William Reno (b. Aug. 10, 1974). Danny is not married. William married Carla Jean Zimmerman on Oct. 9, 1996. William and Carla had one child, Cole Gary Thomas Chism (b. Nov. 21, 1997). William was killed in a truck accident Feb. 10, 1998. Tommy died May 19, 1989. Tommy and William are both buried at Ada Valley Cemetery.

Reno died Dec. 6, 1966 and Esta died Sept. 6, 1995. They are both buried in the Lanty Cemetery, Lanty, Conway County, AR. *Submitted by Tonya Thomas.*

CHISM - William Harmon Chism (b. Oct. 29, 1894 at Lanty, AR) was the eldest son of six children born to David Obie Chism and Nellie Bell Harrington. On July 22, 1916 Harmon married Johnnie Victoria Sutton (b. Aug. 6, 1893), daughter of James Everett Sutton and Mary Alice Bizzell of Lanty. Harmon and Johnnie had nine children:

Earle Chism (b. Nov. 5, 1917, d. Nov. 6, 1917) is buried in Bizzell Cemetery.

James Harold Chism (b. Sept. 9, 1918) md. Betty Bostian on March 11, 1939. They had four children:

LaVonda Ruth (Chism) Heffington (b. May 1, 1940), retired teacher; Eva LaNelle (Chism) Millsap (b. Nov. 13, 1942), retired teacher; James Harold Chism Jr. "Jim" (b. Aug. 5, 1946), Arkansas State Department of Education; and Judy LaDene (Chism) Carte (b. Feb. 22, 1959), social work and management.

The W.H. Chism family.

Eulysis Athel Chism (b. May 3, 1920, d. 1996) md. Abbie Bostian Parker (d. 1976) on May 28, 1939. Abbie had Kenneth Parker (d. 1950) and Janice Parker (d. 2002). Together they had one son, Eulysis Weldon Chism "Eulas" (b. July 20, 1940), a retired manufacturer. Athel and Abbie are buried in Lanty Cemetery and Kenneth and Janice are buried in Mt. Pleasant Cemetery.

William Ralph Chism (b. March 8, 1923, d. 2003) md. Sylvon Boone (d. 2002) on Feb. 7, 1941. They had six children: Johnnie Marilyn (Chism) Robertson (b. Aug. 18, 1942), retired teacher; twin girls (b. Nov. 26, 1947) - Dr. Diana (Chism) Julian, Superintendent of Benton Schools and Dana (Chism) McMahon, College Professor; Dr. William Ralph Chism Jr. "Bill" (b. May 14, 1950), Ophthalmologist; Phyllis Ann (Chism) Howard (b. Jan. 17, 1953), teacher; and Pamela Renee (Chism) Goodman (b. Dec. 10, 1957), teacher and counselor. Ralph and Sylvon are buried in Springfield, MO.

Marion G. "M.G. or Doc" (Chism) (b. Oct. 22, 1924, d. 2003) md. Odelphia Williams "Dee" on Nov. 1, 1947. Doc served in Special Forces in the US Army during WWII. They had three children: Mary Dalene (Chism) Stover (b. Aug. 10, 1948), teacher and librarian; Sherry Ann (Chism) Rogers (b. Oct. 17, 1950), teacher; and Marion Steven Chism (b. Feb. 27, 1954), production. Doc is buried in Plumerville Cemetery.

Wendell Cecil Chism (b. Sept. 7, 1926, d. 1990) md. Dorothy Stroud on March 24, 1954, a teacher. Cecil served in the US Army during WWII. They had two sons: Michael David Chism (b. July 7, 1955), teacher, and Wendell Neal Chism (b. Sept. 2, 1957), teacher. Cecil is buried in Lanty Cemetery.

Twins (b. April 6, 1929), Rayburn Chism and Reba Chism Miller. Rayburn married Fern Sparks on Nov. 28, 1956. They have two daughters, Cheryl Lynn (Chism) Linsenby (b. Oct. 1, 1958), secretary, and Lisa Dawn (Chism) Jackson (b. Jan. 30, 1966), domestication. Reba, a teacher, married Hershell D. Miller on Aug. 16, 1947. They have one daughter, Carolyn J. (Miller) East (b. Oct. 27, 1949).

The last child born to Harmon and Johnnie was Ruby (Chism) Truelove (b. Sept. 28, 1931, d. 1992), a teacher. She married Fred Truelove (d. 2000) on Dec. 3, 1955. They had two daughters, Victoria Cecilia Truelove (b. Aug. 6, 1956) and Cathy Rebecca Truelove (b. Feb. 1, 1962). Both girls drowned in 1968. Ruby and her girls are buried in Plumerville Cemetery.

Harmon and Johnnie's family were primarily farmers and educators. Between 1926-67, they settled in Lanty, Cypress Valley, Portland Bottoms, into Missouri, returning to Caney Valley in '67.

Harmon died July 15, 1971 and Johnnie died March 8, 1961. Both are buried in Lanty Cemetery. To date, Harmon and Johnnie have nine children, 23 grandchildren, 33 great-grandchildren, and 23 great-great-grandchildren. *Submitted by Betty Chism.*

CHISM - William Henry Chism, son of Obadiah Parker and Elizabeth Rebecca (Gaylon) Chism, was born October 1843 in Newton County, AR and died on April 15, 1909 in Cleveland, Conway County, AR. He married Nancy Elizabeth Wells on Sept. 28, 1872 in Conway County, AR. Nancy, daughter of David A. and Jane Wells, was born March 1855 in Conway

County, AR and died Sept. 18, 1916 in Conway County, AR. They are buried in the Skinner Cemetery, Conway County, AR. William Henry Chism served in the Civil War in the Union Army, Second Arkansas Cavalry, Company D.

William Henry and Nancy Wells Chism

William Henry and Nancy Elizabeth are the parents of five children: David Obadiah Chism, Carolyn "Callie" Chism, Mollie Elizabeth Chism, William Robert Chism and James Monroe Chism.

David Obadiah Chism (b. Dec. 5, 1872 in Conway County, AR, d. Oct. 1, 1944 in Conway County, AR) md. Nellie E. Harrington on Nov. 2, 1892 in Conway County, AR. Nellie (b. Oct. 20, 1875 in Arkansas, d. Oct. 30, 1917 in Conway County, AR) was the daughter of Hezekiah Dempsey and Bellefame (Johnson) Harrington. David's second marriage was to Alta Maud (Adams) Tilley on July 18, 1918 in Conway County, AR. Alta (b. Oct. 14, 1881 in Conway County, AR) was the daughter of John W. and Margaret (Beeson) Adams. Alta's first marriage was to Eugene E. Dotson Tilley on Feb. 3, 1899 in Conway County, AR. Alta died Oct. 4, 1970 in Conway County, AR and is buried in the Adams Cemetery, Conway County, AR. David and Nellie are buried in the Lanty Cemetery, Conway County, AR.

Carolyn "Callie" Chism (b. March 1877 in Conway County, AR) md. first to Henry N. Ferguson on Dec. 30, 1893 in Conway County, AR. After his death, she married Joseph T. Moore on Sept. 30, 1897 in Conway County, AR. He was born April 1855 and died between 1920-30. Callie and Joe are buried in the Skinner Cemetery, Conway County, AR.

Mollie Elizabeth Chism (b. Dec. 23, 1876 in Cleveland, Conway County, AR) md. first, W.J. Treadaway on Jan. 23, 1896 and second, James Irvin Gaylor on Oct. 14, 1897 in Conway County, AR. James, son of A.B. and Elizabeth (Dempsey) Gaylor, was born Sept. 2, 1875 in Conway County, AR. James died Aug. 5, 1924 in Spiro, LeFlore County, OK and is buried in the Short Mountain Cemetery, LeFlore County, OK. Mollie died April 30, 1975 in Ada, Pontotoc County, OK and is buried in the Cedar Grove Cemetery, Francis, Pontotoc County, OK.

William Robert "Bob" Chism (b. Sept. 14, 1878 in Conway County, AR, d. Oct. 20, 1923 in Conway County, AR) md. first to Linda Newton. After her death, he married Josie E. Shoemake (b. Oct. 30, 1885, d. Feb. 16, 1920). William Robert and Josie are buried in the Cleveland Cemetery, Conway County, AR.

James Monroe Chism (b. Jan. 30, 1885, d. Jan. 7, 1978) md. Cynthia Allie Byers on Jan. 14, 1903 in Conway County, AR. She was born Feb. 15, 1884 and died July 25, 1950. They are buried in the Cedar Grove Cemetery, Francis, Pontotoc County, OK. After Cynthia's death, he married Nora Nance Rinehart Stobaugh (b. Jan. 8, 1886, d. 1968) on Oct. 6, 1951. Her first husband, Inglish Stobaugh, is buried in Matthews, MO and Nora is buried by him. *Submitted by William Parker "Bill" Chism.*

CHISM - William Parker "Bill" Chism, son of David Obadiah and Alta Maud (Adams Tilley) Chism, married Bonnie R. Harrell on Dec. 26, 1952 in Peoria, Peoria County, IL. Bonnie is the daughter of William V. and Tennie Edith (Bullington) Harrell.

Bill worked in Peoria, IL for Armour Meat Com-

pany for 28 years. Bonnie was in nursing school, graduated in 1953, then worked as a registered nurse in the Methodist Hospital in Peoria. Later, she worked as an occupational health nurse for Cameron Iron Works in Houston, TX for 20 years.

Bill and Bonnie are the parents of three children: Stanley Dean Chism, Cynthia Ann Chism and Krista Marie Chism.

Stanley Dean Chism married Emily Ruth Whisenot on Dec. 17, 1977 in Cullman, Cullman County, AL. Stanley and Emily both graduated from Harding University in Searcy, AR. Stan is a minister and Emily is a registered nurse. They are the parents of three daughters: Jennifer Ruth Chism, graduate of Harding University in Searcy, AR; Heather Nicole Chism, currently attending the University of Alabama; and Amber Jeanette Chism, currently a senior in high school.

Cynthia Ann Chism is a graduate of Abilene Christian University and is currently a teacher. She married Phil Autry on June 30, 1980 in Houston, TX. They had one son, Phillip Aaron Autry. Cynthia and Phil divorced and she married Robert Adolph Efird on June 29, 1985 in Houston, Harris County, TX. Robert graduated from the University of Houston and works for Union Pacific Railroad. Robert Efird adopted Phillip as his legal son. Phillip Adolph Efird married Sandy Laree Green on June 14, 2003 in Glorietta, NM. Sandy and Phillip graduated from Lubbock Christian University in May 2004. Cynthia and Robert have one daughter, Haley Marie Efird, who is a freshman in high school.

Krista Marie Chism is a nursing graduate of Harding University. She married William "Buddy" Lonnie Gray on Feb. 14, 1988 in Houston, Harris County, TX. Buddy is a graduate of Abilene Christian University. Currently, Krista is a nurse and Buddy is a Church of Christ minister in Modesto, CA. Krista and Buddy adopted a son, Matthew Dee Gray in 2000. *Submitted by Bonnie Harrell Chism.*

CHISM - William Robert "Bob" Chism (b. Sept. 14, 1878 in Conway County, AR, d. Oct. 20, 1923 in Conway County, AR) md. Linda Newton and they had two daughters, Lillis Pearl Chism Adams Passmore and Wilma Liddie Chism Reid.

William Robert Chism, Lillis Pearl Chism, Grandpa Newton, Wilma Liddie Chism, Linda Newton Chism.

Lillis Pearl (b. Nov. 28, 1907, d. Oct. 17, 2001) md. Sylvester Adams and they have one daughter, Leverda Faye Adams. Lillis Pearl and Sylvester divorced and she married Jodie H. Passmore (b. Dec. 26, 1888, d. June 17, 1963). Lillis and Jodie are buried in the Springfield Cemetery, Conway County, AR.

illis and Jodie's children are Jodie H. Passmore, twins-Wendell Earl Passmore and Ella Pearl Passmore Moses, Clarence Passmore, Duel Passmore and Joseph Chism Passmore.

Wilma Liddie Chism (b. March 29, 1912) md. Lester J. Reid (b. Aug. 23, 1910, d. June 7, 1972). He is buried in Stockton, CA. Lester and Liddie had four children: Darrel Eugene Reid, Emma Jean Reid Kinney and Helen Ruth Reid Pierce David. Liddie and an infant son died in childbirth on March 8, 1942. They are buried in the Reid Cemetery at Cleveland on Point Remove Creek. The community used to be known as Smyrna.

After Linda's death, William Robert "Bob" Chism married Josie E. Shoemake (b. Oct. 30, 1885, d. Feb. 16, 1920). Bob and Josie both died of tuberculosis and they are buried in the Cleveland Cemetery, Conway County, AR. Bob and Josie are the parents of one son, Raymond Chism.

Raymond married Jonnie Raye Reid on June 20, 1948. Raymond and Jonnie Faye are the parents of two children, Darrell Chism and Karen Joann Chism. *Submitted by Darrell Reid.*

CHISM - Wilma Liddie Chism (b. March 29, 1912) md. Lester Jay Reid (b. Aug. 23, 1910, d. June 7, 1972). He is buried in Stockton, San Joaquin County, CA. Lester was the son of James Henry and Emma Senora (Byers) Reid.

Lester and Liddie's children are Darrell Eugene Reid, Emma Jean Reid Kinney, Helen Ruth Reid Pierce David Robert. Liddie and an infant son died in childbirth on March 8, 1942 in Cleveland, Conway County, AR. They are buried in the Reid Cemetery at Cleveland on Point Remove Creek.

Wilma Liddie (Chism) Reid and Lester Jay Reid

1) Darrell Eugene Reid married Betty Louise Church on Dec. 23, 1955. They are the parents of four children: Donald Eugene "Don" Reid, Terry Ellen Reid, James Bruce Reid and Cynthia Ann "Cindy" Reid.

Donald Eugene "Don" married Angie Smith on June 23, 2001. Angie is the daughter of Richard and Shirley Smith. Don has one son, Brian James Reid. Angie has three children: Derrick Joseph Smith, Leann Lucas Mulligan and Brodie Calhoun Mulligan.

Terry Reid married Allen Hays on April 1, 1982. They are the parents of three children: Matthew Hays, Lacie Delane Hays and Tyler Reid Hays. Terry and Allen are now divorced.

Bruce Reid married Tarita Signs on June 6, 1990 and divorced on Feb. 4, 1995. They have one son, James. Bruce later married Beverly Spears Wilson; they have no children. She has five children from a previous marriage: Christopher Wilson, Chad Wilson, Clint Wilson and twins, Courtney and Casey Wilson.

Cynthia Ann "Cindy" Reid married Mike McCoy and they are the parents of three children: Jeremy McCoy, Jonathan McCoy and Aimee McCoy. Cindy and Mike are now divorced.

2) Emma Jean Reid married William D. Kinney on May 31, 1959. Emma Jean and William are the parents of three children: Lester Glenn Kinney, William Hollen Kinney and Jeffrey Curtis Kinney.

Lester Glenn Kinney married Mary Ann Ott and they are the parents of two children, Sarah Ann Kinney and Clinton Lester Kinney. Lester and Mary Ann divorced and he is married to Alesia. William Hollen Kinney married Theresa Fullmer on June 6, 1998 and they have one daughter, Dana Jean Kinney. Jeffrey Curtis Kinney married Karen Graham in September 1990.

3) Helen Ruth Reid married Leon Pierce. They

divorced and she married Dale David. Helen and Dale have two children, Gary David and Doug David. Dale David died of cancer and Helen married Jim Robert. Helen and Jim have two children, Robin Robert and Tara Robert. *Submitted by Jean Reid Kinney.*

CHISM - Zora Bell Chism (b. June 6, 1905 in Conway County, AR, d. Oct. 13, 1992, buried in New Hope Garden of Memories, Spiro, OK) md. Jasper Joe Marion Haney (b. Aug. 4, 1896, d. Jan. 10, 1967). Zora and Joe were the parents of one daughter, Molly Ruth Haney (b. Nov. 2, 1924, d. April 22, 1988), who married Elmer Carter (b. Oct. 22, 1922, d. April 8, 1994). They are both buried in New Hope Garden of Memories in Spiro, OK. They were the parents of two children.

Zora Honey and Eva Maxwell, Roscoe's sisters.

1) Vicki Lynn Carter (b. May 5, 1950) md. Kenneth Rayself (divorced). They have one child Kendra Lynn Rayself (b. Oct. 4, 1977). Vicki Lynn married Michael Glen Redden on May 9, 1968; they have one child, Angel Renee Redden (b. July 30, 1986).

2) Darrell Carter (died in military service) md. Wilda Rivera Garcia. They had two children: Nicholas Alexander Carter (b. 1977) and Nancy Marie Carter (b. 1978). *Submitted by Betty Chism Dixon.*

CHOLVAN - Jean Baptiste Cholvan, born in Alsace-Lorraine, fought in the Franco Prussian War. When it ended in 1871, Jean and his wife, Elizabeth, emigrated to the United States with their children: Amelie, Alphonse, Mary, Celestine, and John Louis. They moved across the northern part of the United States, staying for a while in Indiana, where Elizabeth fell ill and died. Jean, Mary, Celestine, and John moved to a farm near Morrilton, across the road from the Parette family, another family that emigrated from France.

John Louis did not like farming, so he moved to Little Rock where he met and married Ellen O'Brien in St. Vincent's Infirmary Chapel. Their children were Louis, John, Mary Ellen and Frances. Jean Baptiste and Louis moved their families to Monrovia, CA, where the young Mary Ellen recalls hearing the church bells ring in the new century. Jean, Louis and Ellen died and were buried in Monrovia, CA. Mary Ellen's Aunt Celestine took in Louis and Frances; but sent Mary Ellen to Ramona Convent to be educated. She graduated from Ramona and returned to Little Rock to live with her godparents. There she met and married Max James Mobley, who moved her back to live in Morrilton. See the Mobley Family article.

Information for this article came from Mary Ellen Cholvin Mobley Strait and was submitted by Sally Mobley.

CLARK - Sarah Elizabeth Perry Clark (Aunt Sally) (b. Oct. 1, 1869 in Shelby County, TN), daughter of George W. Rabun-Perry and Martha Ann Ferguson White Gates-Perry. She was brought to Arkansas on a steamboat by her parents in 1877. The family lived in Perry County, then moved to Conway County.

Sarah Elizabeth was baptized in Perry County by Elder Bert Haynes and became a member of the St. Matthew No. 1 Baptist Church in Oppelo. When she moved to Morrilton, Sarah became a member of the Trinity Baptist Church

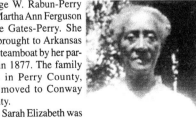

Sarah E. Clark

where she taught Sunday School and was active in the Missionary Society. She was married to John W. Clark in 1888. John Clark taught school in Perry County. She and John were parents of three children: Pearl Elizabeth Clark Ware, John Henry Clark and Mary Ellen Clark. Sarah and John divorced and he remarried. Sarah remained single.

Sarah Elizabeth's college education was received in the Perry County Church School, at Arkansas Baptist and Philander Smith Colleges in Little Rock and at Arkansas AM & N College in Pine Bluff.

She was the matron at Arkansas Baptist College while attending school there. Her three children lived with her there while she was in school. John and Pearl were also Arkansas Baptist graduates. She taught school at Marche, AR before returning to Conway County to teach.

In Conway County she taught school in the communities of Spring Valley (about five miles north of Morrilton), James Farm, Kenwood (about 5 miles west on Highway 64), Blackwell (about 10 miles west on Highway 64) and Oliver School (located at the foot of St. Matthew Hill). She taught also at Bend of the Lake, Union Church, Burville, Mount Pisgah, and Ash Slough. Her last assignment was at Morrilton Colored School that later became Sullivan High School, where she taught for 21 years before retiring in 1945 at the age of 76. Sarah F. Clark taught school for a total of 58 years.

In 1949, two rooms of Morrilton's new elementary building were completed and the rest of that school was added in 1951. When the building was finished, it was named the "Sarah F. Clark Elementary School" at ceremonies held in her honor. The school later was renamed Westside.

When Sarah's health began to fail, she moved to Little Rock to live with her daughter, Pearl. She died Oct. 30, 1958 and is buried at Oddfellows Cemetery in Morrilton. *Submitted by Dr. Perry W. Brown.*

CLEMMONS - William J. Clemmons (b. January 1855 in Darlington County, SC, d. Dec. 24, 1912 in Little Rock, Pulaski County, AR) md. Hellin Brockington in Darlington, Darlington County, SC. She was born May 1865 in Darlington County, SC and died Oct. 29, 1960 in Morrilton, Conway County, AR. She was the daughter of Phillip and Peggy (Margaret) Brockington. They also had son, Sam C. Brockington (b. 1860 in Darlington, SC); he married first to Martha in Morrilton, AR. She was born 1862 in Darlington, SC and died in Morrilton, AR. She was the daughter of Jerry Russell and Margaret Lee. They had two children: 1) Charlie Brockington (b. March 6, 1894 in Morrilton, AR, d. August 1979 in Little Rock, AR) md. Gertrude; 2) Addie Brockington. Sam married a second time to Julia McDaniel. Martha married a second time to William McKeever (McIver).

William and Hellin's children were:

1) Frazella Clemmons (b. November 1878 in Darlington, SC, d. Oct. 29, 1970 in Morrilton, Conway County, AR) md. Jason Stewart in Morrilton.

2) Phillip Clemmons (b. April 1881 in Darlington, SC, d. April 1975 Tulsa, OK) md. Sally Donley in Morrilton, AR.

3) Willie Clemmons (b. June 1883 in Darlington, SC, d. 1927 in Morrilton, Conway County, AR) md. Matilda Wright in Little Rock, Pulaski County, AR. She was born 1895 in Lewisville, Lafayette County, AR, died in Little Rock, AR and is buried in Fraternal Cemetery of Little Rock, AR. She was the daughter of Doss (D.E.) Wright and Lettie Walker. Their children were: (a) Willie Mae Clemons born in Little Rock, AR, died in St. Louis, MO. She married Toussaint Crump in Fordyce, Dallas County, AR. (b) Helen Clemmons born in Little Rock, AR, died in San Bernardino, CA. She married Cornelius Henry Smith in Little Rock, AR.

4) Oliver (Dime) Clemmons (b. May 1884 in Darlington, SC) md. LuLu.

5) Mary Clemmons (b. September 1886 in

Morrilton, Conway County, AR, d. 1907 in Morrilton, Conway County, AR).

6) Sarah Clemmons (b. February 1888 in Morrilton, Conway County, AR, d. May 1973 in Morrilton, Conway County, AR) md. Leon Love.

All are buried in Odd Fellows Cemetery.

Some people are of the belief that Martha Brockington and William Clemons are brother and sister. It is also, believed that William Clemons changed his name from Dolphus Clements.

Dolphus Clements was born 1857 in Darlington SC. His mother's name was Margaret Lee born 1828 in Darlington, SC. He was married to Helen ? (b. 1858 in Darlington, SC). Their children were Frizella (b. 1879 in Darlington, SC); Phillip (b. 1880 in Darlington, SC); Willis Clements (brother) (b. 1863 in Darlington, SC).

CLINE - John Cline emigrated to America in 1770 with his sons, Jacob, John Jr. and George. George Cline (b. 1740 in Germany) md. Susanah Buck in 1770, Ulster County, NY. Susanah (b. 1750 in Germany) may have been the daughter of Joseph Buck. George and Susanah settled in Northumberland County, PA. George served as a sergeant in the Pennsylvania 3rd and 12th Regiments in the Revolutionary War. About 1782, he moved his family to Ohio County, VA (now WV). About 1795 he moved to Washington (now Monroe) County, OH. George died there on April 14, 1801. Susanah married Anthony Evans on Oct. 13, 1808. She died in 1840 in Washington County.

The Cline families were among the first settlers of Washington Township in Monroe County, OH. Joseph and William, sons of George Cline, built the first cabins and settled in Washington Township in 1804. John, another son of George Cline, was living in Virginia in 1804, but purchased land in Washington Township in 1805, and moved his family to the area. The first child born in the settlement was born to Joseph Cline. The first grist mill was built by John Cline in 1810. The first church (Methodist-Episcopal) was organized at the house of Joseph Cline in 1817. George and Susanah Cline had at least nine children.

John C. Cline, son of George and Susanah, was born Oct. 27, 1772 in Northumberland County, PA. He married Mary Brown in 1791 in Ohio County, VA (now WV). Mary was born 1773 in Virginia. John and Mary settled in Virginia. In 1805, John purchased land in Washington Township of Monroe County, OH and moved his family to the area. John built the first grist mill in Washington Township in 1810. The mill was destroyed by fire in 1816 and rebuilt in 1817, along with a saw mill. John was also a prosperous farmer. Mary died 1825 in Monroe County. In 1830, John married Sarah Williamson (b. 1797 in Virginia). John died May 25, 1859 in Monroe County. John and Mary had at least 10 children.

George L. Cline, son of John and Mary, was born June 26, 1795 in Virginia He married Nancy C. Cline on Feb. 16, 1816 in Monroe County, OH. Nancy (b. Nov. 5, 1798 in Ohio) was the daughter of John Clines' brother, Joseph G. Cline and Sarah Linn. George and Nancy were first cousins. George was a farmer and owned many acres of rich farmland in Monroe County. George died there on Sept. 25, 1875. George and Nancy had at least nine children, including Peter Cline (b. Oct. 25, 1824 in Monroe County).

Peter married Dorcas Brown (b. 1830, in Ohio) in 1847 in Ohio. Peter farmed in Monroe County for many years. Between 1865-68 Peter moved his family to Spencer County, IN. Peter died after 1880. Dorcas died about 1896. They had eight children: (Etholinda Cline (b. 1848); Josiah Cline (b. 1850); Vincent Cline (b. 1851); Amelia Cline (b. July 7, 1853, d. Sept. 17, 1932) md. William Paceley, then George Harris; Nancy Cline (b. 1856); Sally Cline (b. 1859, d. before 1870); Elizabeth Jane Cline (b. 1864) md. Horace Edward Paceley; Warren D. Cline (b. 1869).

CLINE - Lee Cline was from Taylorsville (actually near Hiddennite), Alexander County, NC. He was the son of Nathan Scippio Cline and Crettie May Bowers. The Cline/Klein family had lived in western North Carolina since the immigrant ancestor Johannes Sebastian Bostian Klein moved from Postroff, Alsace, France (formerly Germany before 1648) to Pennsylvania. He arrived on the ship *Robert & Alice* on Sept. 3, 1739. He moved to Reading, PA and after 1750 when land opened in western North Carolina, he moved his family there. Lee Cline was a fourth great-grandson of the immigrant.

He worked for a few months with his father-in-law, Frank Bryant, wildcatting as Frank had gotten into drilling for oil. Frank Bryant continued with this occupation until his death in 1963 in Oklahoma. As for the Bryants, they soon moved to Wann, OK and in 1955 settled in South Coffeyville, OK, which is just across the border from Coffeyville, KS. Frank Bryant had a small independent drilling operation.

As for Lee Cline, he went to work at Certain-Teed Roofing in Richmond, CA in June 1947 and worked there for 40 years until he retired in June 1987. He was the president of Paper Workers Union Local No. 334 for over 25 years.

He had many hobbies, which included building and flying model airplanes with a club, the Richmond Sky Knights. He rebuilt a 1930 Ford Model A, which won first place in a contest and later became a model railroad enthusiast. He was also a music lover, especially bluegrass music. He played guitar, banjo, harmonica, piano, etc. He also loved books, history, and travel.

After Mae (Bryant) Cline married, she became a full time housewife. She and Lee had two children: David (b. September 1947) never married; (2) Karen Darlene (b. August 1950) md. Thomas Arnn of Johnson City, TN. They have two children. Mae's first daughter, Beverly (d. 1988 of cancer), married Hoover Crittenden of Hulbert, OK and had two sons. One works for Boeing in Wichita, KS and the other is a lawyer in the Tulsa, OK area. Both have five children each.

Mae was involved in the local PTA and other activities. She was an excellent cook, loved making candy like her grandmother Zoy, and was a prolific letter writer. I never knew until later years how much writing she did.

Mae (Bryant) Cline died in March 1987 in San Pablo, CA. Lee Cline died nine years to the day Mae was buried in March 1996. They are both buried at Rose Hill Cemetery in Richmond, CA. *Submitted by David Cline, second great-grandson of Louis and Adalaide Richardet Charton.*

CODY - Will and Sarah Jane Robinson Cody built and moved into their house in 1921. They had a merchant store, a gas station and a hardware store, and joining the store was a kerosene (coal oil) pump where customers got fuel for their lamps. Will had a black smith shop, a car house, three cow barns, a mule barn, and a potato house where everyone stored their potatoes. He also had a large smoke house for storing meat.

Will and Sarah Jane Robinson Cody left a legacy that remains through their descendants and a place on the map.

Will and Sarah raised six sons, four daughters and had 68 grandchildren. As their children married, they all settled near their parent's farm.

The area soon came to be called Cody Town and was listed on the Arkansas map. It lies in the Rose Creek Community, south of Petit Jean Mountain and very near to the Perry/Conway County line. On the 4th of July, a big celebration with ice cream, lemonade, games and story telling was held in Cody Town.

Cody Town can be accessed off Highway 155 in the western part of Perry County, very near the Conway County line. Before county lines were redrawn, Perry County extended north to the Arkansas River and west to the Petit Jean River. *Submitted by Ruby Cody Hubbard.*

COMES - John Richard Comes was a prominent business man in Morrilton, AR at the end of the 19th and early 20th centuries. John R. was born in Reuland. Luxembourg on April 16, 1844 to John and Margaret (Feyen) Comes. He married Marguerite Rodange, a milliner, on Feb. 12, 1872 and moved to LaRochette, Luxembourg. Five children were born to them there, but only two survived. On Oct. 10, 1881 John and Marguerite left LaRochette and came to America with their children, John Theodore and Madeleine (Magdalena) and settled in St. Paul, MN close to a brother of Marguerite's. Twins were born to them there in 1883, but both soon passed away.

Marguerite and John Richard Comes

John R. attended college in Cologne, Germany where he studied architecture. He worked as a carpenter and cabinet maker for 17 years in Cologne and LaRochette. In St. Paul he engaged in contracting and architectural work. In 1897 he moved to Morrilton to join his twin brother, John Adam, and younger brother, John. There he established a contracting business and also won prominence as a fruit grower, specializing in peaches and grapes. Marguerite died Jan. 14, 1899 and on Feb. 16, 1904 John R. married Bertha Theis of Little Rock. John Richard Comes passed away in Morrilton on July 27, 1928.

His son John Theodore became a prominent ecclesiastical architect in Pittsburgh, PA. He married Nora Webber and had three daughters: Eleanor, Marcella and Alice. He died there April 13, 1922.

John R.'s daughter, Magdalena, married William Beschorner of Morrilton. William emigrated from Germany in 1880. They moved to North Little Rock, AR where he joined his brother Paul as co-owner of Argenta Bottling Works.

They had two daughters, Eleanor and Margaret. Eventually they adopted a daughter, Elizabeth. Eleanor passed away at the age of 6 years and is buried next to her paternal grandparents in Sacred Heart Cemetery in Morrilton. William died April 23, 1929 and Magdalena passed away May 20, 1937.

Margaret married Thomas Buton Jones of Lonoke, AR. Upon the death of her father, Margaret and Thomas took over the management of Argenta Bottling Works which they operated until 1961 when it was sold. They had five children: Rosalyn, Thomas B. Jr., Margaret Ann, Mary Comes and Elizabeth "Betty" Sue.

Elizabeth Beschorner married Thomas Davis and had three children: Isabelle, James Thomas and Robert Marion.

John A. married Magdalena Meyers in 1875 in

Germany. They came to America in 1880 with his widowed father, John, and immediately settled in Morrilton. The father John, a carpenter, died in 1881. In 1882 John A. and his wife moved to St. Paul, MN where they lived until 1884. They returned to Morrilton where he made contracting and building his sole occupation until 1890, when he formed a partnership with Mr. Reuter. They operated a planning mill in Morrilton where they dressed 6,000 to 7,000 feet of lumber per day. John A. died Dec. 6, 1915 and his wife, Magdalena, died Jan. 2, 1938.

In 1897 Sacred Heart Catholic Church was built in Morrilton. John Adam was a member of the building committee as well as general contractor for the church. John Richard was the carpenter that did the woodwork inside the church. The vestment cabinet from this church is housed in the museum in Morrilton.

Their younger brother, John, also settled in Morrilton. He was a farmer and married to Maria. They had four children: Maggie, Edward, Annie and John Jr. John died June 26, 1918 and Maria died Jan. 3, 1919. The three brothers and their wives are all buried in Sacred Heart Cemetery in Morrilton. *Submitted by Betty Jones Mayfield.*

CONLEY - John Burge (b. March 27, 1900 in Conway County) was the son of William Lewis and Millie Ann (Carr) Conley. Burge married Delena "Lena" Jane Wells on May 16, 1922. Lena was the daughter of William David and Minnie (Jones) Wells of Hattieville, AR. Burge and Lena were married for 49 years and bore 13 children.

John Burge and Lena Conley, 1944.

1) William Hobert (b. June 16, 1923) md. Virginia Sims in 1944. Virginia died in 1981 of breast cancer. Hobert then married Martha McDonald. They live at Hill Creek AR.

2) Lucille (b. Nov. 7, 1924) md. Perry Anderson of Solgohachia, AR. They had two girls, Nita Ann and Shirley Ann.

3) John Burge Jr. "JB" (b. April 25, 1927) md. Wanda Dean Long in 1945. They had three children: Georgia Ann (b. May 12, 1947), Ted (b. July 4, 1948) and Wanda Jean (b. Sept. 30, 1954). In 1971 JB was married to Lois Nell Solcom until her death in June 12, 2003. JB and children live in Texas.

4) Herbert Inell (b. 1928, d. Aug. 13, 1949 while serving in the United States Air Force).

5) Loeta (b. 1932, d. 1935).

6) Millie Ann (b. 1934, d. 1938).

7) Cecil Elmo (b. 1936, d. Dec. 14, 1938 during a diphtheria epidemic).

8) Deanna (b. Sept. 10, 1937) md. Charles Berry of Huntsville, AR on Dec. 16, 1960. They had one girl, Elizabeth Janice (b. Dec. 4, 1964).

9) James Weldon (b. June 3, 1939, d. March 19, 2004) md. Evelyn Caudell of Morrilton, AR on May 31, 1959. They had one son Steven Wayne (b. Aug. 5, 1964, d. July 14, 1989). Both are buried at Lanty Cemetery in Conway County.

10) Rita Sue (b. July 31, 1942) md. James Black Lewey of Little Rock, AR on Nov. 3, 1961. They had one son John Edward Lewey (b. Oct. 7, 1962).

11) Lyndell (b. Sept. 2, 1946) md. Janice Singleton of Dover, AR on Jan. 28, 1967. They had two children, David Lynn (b. Dec. 27, 1970) and Wendy (b. Nov. 10, 1977).

12) Delena Ann (b. Jan. 19, 1948) md. Joe Bush in 1964. They had one son Johnny Keith (b. March 30, 1970). She later married Larry Crafton on April 13, 1973, who adopted Johnny.

13) Millie Jane (b. April 12, 1951) md. Michael Loyd on Dec. 23, 1969. They have two children, Lena Ann (b. June 12, 1971) and Michael Jason (b. March

11, 1973). She later married Glenn Max Mayhew on Jan. 13, 1978 and they have one son Douglas Bradley Mayhew (b. March 3, 1979).

Burge and Lena spent their life in Conway County. Burge started off as a farmer and carpenter in Lanty, AR. They moved to Morrilton in 1944 and ran a neighborhood grocery store. Lena was a devoted mother and housewife. Both were members of the Trinity Cumberland Presbyterian Church, where Burge was an elder. Lena died May 7, 1970 and Burge died March 6, 1971. Both are buried at Lanty Cemetery in Conway County. *Submitted by Rita Sue (Conley) Lewey.*

CONLEY- William Lewis Conley (b. Oct. 7, 1841 in Walker County, GA) was the eldest son and one of five children born to James T. Conley (b. 1808, d. 1863) and Rachel P. Evatt (b. 1806, d. 1863). James and Rachel moved their family from Iuka, MS (1860 census records) and eventually settled in Conway County, AR.

2nd Lieutenant William Lewis Conley, Company I, 3rd Arkansas Cavalry, 1863-65.

During the Civil War, William and his only brother Virgil were involuntarily recruited into the Confederate Army. The following is a quote by William about his military service, for a Pension Deposition: "I enlisted in Company C, 1st Arkansas Infantry in March, 1863. Wounded June 1, 1863 (at Big Creek, Newton County, AR) and after my recovery I recruited for, enlisted a (unreadable) Company D, 2nd Arkansas Cavalry, and afterward served in Company I, 3rd Arkansas Cavalry as 2nd lieutenant. Previous to my enlistment, I enlisted or was enrolled in the 16th Arkansas Confederate Infantry, Captain Lawrence's Company and deserted in March 1862, in Benton County, AR. I was not conscripted into this service but circumstances connected with our Union utterances before the battle of Oak Hill made it necessary for me to enlist in the Confederate service, after the defeat of Lyons and the overrunning of this country by the Confederate forces. My father was afterward hanged for the same cause by the Confederates."

William Lewis Conley, est. 1870-1880.

(L-R) Charles Irving Conley, William Ervin Conley and William Hobert Conley, sons of William Lewis Conley (est. 1906).

The family story was that William and his brother Virgil, after hearing about their father's hanging, deserted the Confederate Army and hunted down the men who did the hanging, shot them dead, then went to join the Union Army. Virgil joined the 1st Arkansas Infantry on Feb. 12, 1863 at Fayetteville, AR. He was

killed May 28, 1863 in Pope County, AR. Burial location is unknown.

William spent part of his time in the Army as an ambulance driver with the 3rd Arkansas Cavalry out of Lewisburg. During that time, he met George W. Tinney (b. 1842, d. 1925). George was the eldest son of Harvey Allen Tinney (b. 1820, d. 1877) and Missouri Ann Williams (b. 1825, d. ?). While serving with the 2nd Arkansas Cavalry, George Tinney suffered a heart attack. William took him to the hospital in Little Rock, then stayed on to help care for him. They became close friends and remained friends after the war ended. They apparently lived near each other.

On Oct. 4, 1868 William Lewis Conley married Sarah Caroline Beeson (b. 1850), daughter of and one of 10 children born to Ambrose Haywood Beeson and Nancy Jane Blount. William and Sarah had seven children together: Virgil Obediah (b. 1869, d. ?); Ambros Cicero (b. 1871, d. 1874); James Thomas Monroe (b. 1873, d. 1901); Ida Lewis (b. 1875, d. 1923); Maggie Lou (b. 1878, d. 1923); Gracie Lee (b. 1879, d. 1888) and Mareyetta Linnie (b&d. 1881).

Sarah died in 1883, leaving William with several small children. His friend, George W. Tinney, sent his eldest daughter, MayVan Tinney (b. 1868, d. 1953), to the Conley house to help care for the children. Although they did not marry, MayVan became pregnant and gave birth to a son, William Ervin Conley (b. March 18, 1888, d. 1968). MayVan and William Ervin lived with his Grandfather, George Tinney, until he was a young man. He then went to live with his father's family.

On May 24, 1894, William married his second wife, Milley Ann Carr (b. 1866, d. 1948). William and Milley had eight children together: Charles Irving (b. 1891, d. 1936); Walter Dewitt (b. 1894, d. 1895); William Hobert (b. 1896, d. 1917) was killed during WWI in France; George Dewey (b. 1898, d. 1978); John Burge (b. 1900, d. 1971); Vera Lavern (b. 1902, d. 1991); Wiley Parker (b. 1904, d. 1987); and Joseph Lewis (b&d. 1906).

William was an influential and important member of the community. He assisted his friends and neighbors with many legal and financial matters. He served as Postmaster in Nichols, AR and was a well respected Justice of the Peace in Conway County, AR. He and his sons also farmed a large area of land in the county. The family still has many original legal documents that he hand-drafted, as well as the sword that he carried during the Civil War and the rifle carried by George W. Tinney. Having out-lived many of his 16 children, he passed away on July 27, 1923 at the age of 82. He is buried, along with many family members, in the Lanty Cemetery, Lanty, Conway County, AR. *Submitted by Karen Moon-Tinker, granddaughter of William Ervin Conley and great-granddaughter of William Lewis Conley.*

CRABTREE - James C. "Jim" Crabtree (b. Dec. 25, 1882, Arkansas, d. Feb. 27, 1980 Plumerville, Conway County, AR) was the son of George Crabtree and Lucy Mahan-Yow. He is buried at Kilgore Cemetery. He was a Baptist minister and member of the Pleasant Springs Missionary Baptist Church. He married Lilly May Tucker, a daughter of Benjamin A. Tucker and Mary "Molly" Woodard. Lilly (b. July 16, 1882, Arkansas, d. Oct. 12, 1957, Conway County, AR) is buried at Kilgore Cemetery. James and Lilly Crabtree did not have any children.

George Crabtree (b. 1839, Tennessee, died before 1920 in Conway County, AR) worked as a laborer and farmer. He had five known children: William W. "Bill" (b. 1880), James C. "Jim" (b. 1882), Louise C. "Lue" (b. 1888), Berlie (b. 1890) and Charles "Charlie."

James C. Crabtree had very close ties with the Gordon family of Conway County, AR and was always referred to as a "cousin" although no actual relationship has been found.

Information is based on data received prior to March 2001. *Submitted by Sharon Smith.*

CREACH - John Calvin Creach (b. Jan. 22, 1903 in Apple Springs, MO) was the fifth child of Benjamin and Elizabeth Agnes (Roney) Creach. The Creach family moved to Marion County, AR around 1905. On Nov. 19, 1927 John Creach married Artie Mahalia Freeman, daughter of Homer and Annie M. Wills Freeman and granddaughter of Lewis J. Wills and Willis Freeman.

John Creach Family 1956.

John and Artie Creach had four children: 1) Zelma Dewel Creach (b. Sept. 17, 1928, died of pneumonia Jan. 23, 1934, buried at Kessee Cemetery, Marion County, AR); 2) John Dempsey (b. Jan. 16, 1930, d. Jan. 9, 2002, buried in Elmwood Cemetery, Morrilton, AR); 3) Cletus Carroll "C.C.;" 4) Mary Elizabeth.

John Dempsey married Lois Lynn Koone, daughter of Gus and Etta Koone from Alread, northwest of Clinton, AR. They had three children: John, Gale and Dianna.

CC married Shirley Ann Sharp of Longview, TX, the only child of Rufus and Bonnie Pepper Sharp. They had three sons: David, John Dennis and Terry. He then married Barbara Barrett Lyons, daughter of Charles and Lucille Barrett of Dallas, TX. She had one son, Gary Lyons, from previous marriage.

The John Creach family moved to Morrilton, Conway County, AR in 1936. Mary Elizabeth was born in the Lewisburg Community. In 1957 Mary married Kenneth Pettingill, the sixth child of W.L. and Mary Lola Pettingill of Plumerville. They have two sons, Kenneth Jr. and Timothy Scott.

John Creach's skills included musician, lumberman, saw miller, mechanic, carpenter, woodworker, and he retired as a steam engineer. He worked for Pierce and Young Lumber Co., Chevrolet dealership, Case Implement Co., and Crompton Mills. His fascination with automobiles started at a young age when he saw his first Model T. He ran after it, barefoot, until he was exhausted.

The Creach family helped in the war effort by gathering scrap metal, a Victory garden, and rationing of critical commodities. After WWII, the family moved north of Morrilton on Monastery Ridge. They started farming with truck patches, cows, chickens, ducks, geese, hogs, etc. Hunting, fishing, and trapping helped sustain the household. They preserved food by canning, drying, butchering, and curing meat. When school closed for harvest, Artie Creach would take the children to pick cotton. The money earned bought school clothes, shoes, supplies, etc.

Creach family recreation included music, fishing, hunting, campouts, and family gatherings. These gatherings around July 4th in conjunction with Arden Freeman's family and relatives was the beginning of the annual Freeman Family Reunion which continues today by third generation Freemans.

John Creach moved to 1601 Poor Farm Road, Morrilton AR, in 1953 and retired in 1965. Artie Creach started day care for small children which was expanded with John's help. She cared for the second generation of several of these children.

John Creach (d. April 23, 1985) and Artie Creach (b. Oct. 31, 1909, d. Dec. 30, 1999) are buried at Liberty Springs Cemetery, Van Buren County, AR.

CREE - William "Bill" Jr. (b. Jan. 9, 1926 in Kansas City, MO) was the adopted son of William John Cree

William "Bill" Cree

Sr. and Mary Rose (Matson) Cree of Kansas City, KS. Bill attended Rockhurst College in Kansas City and joined the US Navy in 1944, where he served on submarine duty in WWII until his discharge in 1946. In April 1953, he married Mary Darlene Hinds (b. Feb. 27, 1929), daughter of Ray and Grace (Powers) Hinds. They had three sons: Paul Alan (b. Oct. 11, 1954), David Ray (b. Feb. 25, 1956) and Michael Linn (b. Jan. 4, 1959). Darlene has one sister, Donna Thompson, in Coronado, CA.

The family moved to North Little Rock in 1954 where Bill was claims manager for Employers Mutual Casualty, and where he passed the Arkansas Bar in 1965. They lived two years in Minnesota before coming to Morrilton in June 1969. Bill practiced law with Joe Cambiano and in 1977 was elected Municipal Judge where he served until his death on Dec. 21, 1984.

Paul graduated from Morrilton High School in 1972 and Arkansas Tech in 1985. He is an environmental health specialist for Arkansas. Paul married Karen Elaine Deeter in May 1977. Dr. Karen is the daughter of Dewitt and Emma (Whittington) Deeter. Karen earned her doctorate in pharmacology and is Director of Pharmacy at St. Anthony's Healthcare Center in Morrilton. Her father served in the US Air Force and died at the young age of 23 in 1960. Her mother, Emma, was a teacher at Morrilton High School and died in April 1997. Karen has a half-brother, Steve Robertson.

David graduated from Sacred Heart High School in 1974 and attended United Electronics Institute in Little Rock. He is field service technician for Hugg and Hall Equip. Co. In March 1977, he married Judy Ann Huffman, daughter of Doyle and Bobbie (McCoy) Huffman. Judy is office manager for Child Support Enforcement for Arkansas. They have two daughters, Danielle Ray and Jessica Ann. Danielle "Dani" married Nathan Matthew Reel in July 1997 and they have a son, Kase Ethan, and a daughter, Kennedy Elaine. Jessica married Scott David Keeton in May 2001 and they have a daughter, Wyleigh Danielle. Judy's father is retired from Mobil Oil Co. and her mother works for the Area Agency on Aging. Judy has a brother, Rev. Jim Huffman.

Michael graduated from Sacred Heart High School in 1977 and attended North Pulaski VoTech in Little Rock. He is a radio personality for Station KVOM in Morrilton. He married Shannon Lea (Sisson) Stone in April 2003, daughter of Willie and Robbie Sisson of Conway. She has a son, Christopher Stone.

CROUTHERS - Andrew N. Crouthers (b. 1809, probably in North Carolina) md. Frances (last name unknown) about 1833, probably in Tennessee. Frances was born 1815 in Tennessee. About 1836 Andrew moved his family to Pope County, AR, where he later bought land that he farmed. Andrew died prior to 1880. Children included: James Crouthers (b. 1834), Andrew N. Crouthers Jr. (b. 1836), David Crouthers (b. 1838), Adaline Crouthers (b. 1841), Frances Crouthers (b. 1842), Henry Crouthers (b. 1844), Sarah Crouthers (b. 1847), Eliza Crouthers (b. 1849), George W. Crouthers (b. July 17, 1851, d. May 22, 1925) md. 1st, Maggie __ and 2nd, Nannie Norman on Feb. 23, 1888, Conway County, AR, and Robert C. Crouthers.

Robert C. Crouthers (b. Oct. 1, 1858, in Pope County, AR) the youngest son of Andrew and Frances, married Emma H. Maddox (b. March 25, 1865, in Alabama) on Sept. 10, 1883 in Conway County, AR. Robert and Emma lived near Hattieville in Conway County for many years. About 1914, the family moved to Morrilton. Robert died Aug. 7, 1926 and Emma died Feb. 15, 1940. They are buried in

Elmwood Cemetery at Morrilton. Children included: Minnie M. Carruthers, Robert Q. Carruthers, Paul B. Carruthers, Roy Maddox Carruthers, Harl C. "Doc" Carruthers, Rebecca E. Carruthers and Emma Carruthers.

Roy Maddox Carruthers (b. Dec. 26, 1898, at Hattieville, Conway County, AR) was the son of Robert and Emma Maddox Crouthers. Roy and his brother Harl changed the spelling of their name to Carruthers. Roy married Susie Holt on April 16, 1922, in Conway County. Susie Holt was the daughter of Miles Holt and Sarah Stoakes. Roy and Susie had two children, Jack and Betty. The marriage ended in divorce prior to 193[0?]. For a number of years during the mid-30s to mid-40s, Roy was owner and operator of Blue Mountain Dairy at Morrilton.

Roy married Bertha Martha Belle Horton on Nov. 24, 1948, in Conway County. Belle (b. March 28, 1908, in Pope County, AR) was the daughter of Will Horton and Effie Harmon. Belle worked at the dairy for a few years before she and Roy married. After their marriage, they lived for several years in the old Crouthers house located on Will Street in Morrilton. The dairy had been at that same location, and the barn and milk house stood until the early 1960s.

About 1955, Roy bought land at Kenwood in Conway County. He also bought an old church building and remodeled it into a nice house, where he and Belle lived until their deaths. Roy bought farm land and became a prosperous farmer in the Kenwood and Atkins bottoms. After being injured in a farm accident, Roy had to retire from farming. He and Belle then spent much of their time traveling. Roy and Belle had no children. Roy (d. Jan. 27, 1973) and Belle (d. May 13, 1983) are buried in Elmwood Cemetery.

CROW - The Crow family originated in England and began immigrating to America as early as 1620. John Crow was born 1683 in St. George's Parish, Baltimore County, MD. Records indicate he married three times. He married his first wife Mary (last name unknown) in 1713, in St. George's Parish. Mary was born 1687 and died Nov. 16, 1713 in St. George's Parish, just five days after giving birth to her only child, James Crow. John married second, Margaret Compton on April 6, 1719 in St. George's Parish. John married his third wife, Judith Magee, before 1732. John died Feb. 16, 1744 in St. George's Parish. John and Judith had at least five children: Margaret (b. 1734), John (b. 1736), James (a twin, b. 1740), Thomas (a twin, b. 1740) and Mansfield (b. 1742).

John Crow (b. Feb. 23, 1736 in Baltimore County, MD) was the eldest son of John and Judith. He married Sarah (last name unknown). John probably served with the Chatham County, NC Militia in 1772, in Captain Isaiah Hogan's Company. In 1790 John bought 320 acres of land in Rutherford County, NC, which he later willed to his son James. John's family appears on the 1790 Hillsborough District, Chatham County, NC census. John was a wealthy planter, with a great deal of property and several slaves. He acquired a land grant in 1797. John signed his will on May 25, 1815 in Chatham County. In it he named his wife Sarah, and children Ruben, James, John, Jesse, Gabriel, Johnson, Rachel, Elizabeth and Sarah. Census records indicate John and Sarah had at least 11 children. John died between 1815-20 in Chatham County. Sarah died between 1830-40 in Chatham or Guilford County, NC.

James Crow (b. bet. 1780-86 in Chatham County), son of John and Sarah, served in the War of 1812 in the Chatham County Militia. He was named in his father's will in 1815 to receive slaves and 320 acres of land. James and his brother Ruben were named executors of their father's will. James was appointed trustee of his sister Elizabeth, who apparently was disabled. James married Diana McClanahan on May 1, 1821. About 1830-34, James moved his family to Guilford County, NC. Diana died there between 1840 and 1850. James married Sarah (last name unknown) between 1850 and early 1857. He signed his will on March 3, 1857, in which he names his wife Sarah, children: John, James W., Eliza, and Sina, and grandchildren by his daughter Sarah, who was deceased. James died about July 1859 in Guilford County. His will was executed in the August 1859 term of the Guilford County Court.

Children of James Crow and Diana McClanahan are 1) Sarah Crow (b. 1824, d. 1854) md. John Worth Gray. Children: James, Stephen and Mary Gray. 2) John Henry Crow (b. 1826, d. 1874) md. Sarah Jane Rollins. 3) Eliza Crow (b. 1828) md. Green Parsons. Child: Mary Parsons. 4) Unknown Son Crow (b. 1830, d. bef. 1840). 5) Sina Crow (b. 1837). 6) James William Crow (b. 1839) md. Elizabeth C. Armfield.

CROW - John Henry Crow (b. 1826 in Chatham County, NC) was the son of James Crow and Diana McClanahan. John married Sarah Jane Rollins about 1845 in North Carolina. Sarah Rollins was born 1830 in Randolph County, NC. The Rollins family moved to North Carolina from Virginia prior to 1790.

John and Sarah settled in Guilford County on land given to them by John's father when they married. John was a farmer. On March 2, 1850, John's sister, Sarah Crow Gray, her husband and children left North Carolina headed for Missouri. They settled instead in Independence County, AR. In July 1853 the Gray family returned to North Carolina for a visit. When they returned to Arkansas in November 1853, John and Sarah Crow and their four children returned to Arkansas with them. John and Sarah settled near the Gray family at Cave City, in Independence County. John bought land, which the family farmed. Eight more children were born to John and Sarah in Independence County.

John was named in his father's will in 1859, to receive a share of the money derived from the sale of any items not disposed of in the will. The will stated that no land was left to Sarah, John Henry and Eliza by their father because those children had already had been give their share of the land.

John Henry died August 1874 in Independence County and Sarah Jane died November 1886. They are buried in the Cave City Cemetery.

Children of John Henry Crow and Sarah Jane Rollins:
1) James William Henry Crow (b. 1846, d. 1912) md. Mrs. Elizabeth Lawrence Mobley Ball. Children: William Jefferson, Andrew and Andy Crow. He then married Nancy "Nannie" Patterson. Children: Henry, Louis, Sarah (md. James West), James, Albert, Nora (md. Louis Andrews), Ruben and Martha Jane (md. Thruman Drewery).
2) Mary Eliza Crow (b. 1848, d. 1917) md. John Kibby. Children: William, Florence (md. Jasper Allen), Robert, Margaret (md. Jim McLeod) and Alice (md. John Hallmark).
3) Sina Elizabeth Crow (b. 1850, d. 1921) md. James Dockins. Children: Travis, Sarah (md. Frank Helms), Manuel and Margin Magnolia (md. George Rawlings).
4) Oliver Lamen Crow (b. 1853, d. 1906) md. Eliza Wilson. Children: John Thomas, Sarah Elizabeth, Annie, Margaret, Willie May and Virgie Lee Crow.
5) William Ruben "Rube" Crow (b. 1855, d. 1929) md. Melissa Copeland. Children: James Virgin, Rachel, Rosalee Belle (md. James Duncan), Nora Ann (md. Lauther Chadwick), Martha (md. Monroe Brown) and Mary Almeda (md. Annias Watkins).
6) Christina Malissa "Sis" Crow (b. 1857) md. James Holly.
7) Martha Jane Crow (b. 1858, d. 1915) md. James Louis Harmon. Children: Almeda (md. Richard Walker), Sherman, Schuyler, Effie (md. Will Horton) and Willie Harmon.
8) Thomas Jefferson "Jeff" Crow (b. 1863, d. 1948) md. Arena M. Green. Children: Fletcher, Paralee, John, Sarah Jane (md. John Dolphus Lentz), Effie, Jim and Jeff Crow.

9) Christopher Columbus "Lum" Crow (b. 1864, d. 1946) md. Victoria Copeland. Children: Verdo, Dottie, Azlee (md. Thomas Wilson), Alvice, Viola (md. Pleasant Mobley), Nettie (md. Jettre James) and Esther Crow.
10) Sarah Ann Crow (b. 1867, d. 1881).
11) Rachel Margaret Lucretia Crow (b. 1869, d. 1931), md. Amos James. Children: Talmage, Leroy, Sarah, Petris, Adaline, Margie, Retha, Archibald, Maude and Paralee James.
12) Nancy Paralee Crow (b. 1872, d. 1936) md. Robert King. Children: Ida May and Edna Matilda King.

CRUCE - Columbus Erastus Cruce (b. May 6, 1862 in Paris, TX), son of Lafayette and Mary Cock Cruce, moved to Warrensburg, MO, as a child then moved to Fort Smith, AR, when he was just over 20 years old. He worked with his brother, Richard Allen Cruce, for *The Daily Times* newspaper in Fort Smith for a while before moving to Greenwood where he owned an interest in *The Greenwood Democrat* and served as editor for a short time. In 1896 he moved to Morrilton and was the founder and publisher of *The Morrilton Democrat*, first issue on Feb. 21, 1896.

While in Fort Smith he married Cora Lee Reed, a native of Fort Smith and the daughter of Jesse C. and Francis Burt Reed, Jan. 12, 1887. Their first three children were born in Sebastian County, AR: Myrtle, Clarence (died in infancy), and Robin. Their fourth child, Pryor Reed Cruce Sr., was born in Morrilton, Sept. 15, 1897.

Myrtle Cruce married Raymond Lewis of Danville where she lived until her death in 1945.

Robin Cruce married Mae Bentley in 1920 They lived in Morrilton where he edited *The Morrilton Democrat* for a few years, following the death of C.E. Cruce, she worked at the Public Library. They had two children, Bobby and Mary Bentley.

Pryor Reed Cruce Sr. married Alma Ross Nov. 7, 1920. He operated the Crow Burlingame auto parts store until his death in 1957. They had three children who were born, raised and graduated from High School in Morrilton:

Sallie Lee Cruce married Tom Caviness Jr. and they lived in Carlsbad, NM and Texarkana, AR, where they both died. They had three children: Douglas, Mary and Martha.

Jimmy Cruce married Sammye Lee McKinley of Morrilton, and lived in Little Rock a few years and now lives in Lonoke, AR. They had three children: Phyllis, Greg and Jan.

Pryor Reed Cruce Jr. married Doris Hodges in North Little Rock. He is a United Methodist Minister serving as pastor throughout Arkansas, now retired and living in Fort Smith. They have five children: Martin, Daniel, Steven, Pamela and Kenneth.

Alma Ross Cruce was born in Missouri and lived in Clarksville, AR before moving to Morrilton around 1915 when her parents, George N. Ross and Sally Davis Ross, came to Morrilton to start the first steam laundry.

The George Ross family had four children: Carl Ross who married a Missouri girl, Florence Barlin, in 1907 and lived most of his life in Kansas City, MO. Rex Davis Ross spent much of his life in Morrilton. He was married and his wife died young. They are both buried in Elmwood Cemetery, Morrilton. Audra Ross married Albert Basham at Morrilton on Dec. 9, 1917. He was killed in a truck accident leaving her with three children to raise: George Albertine, Carl and Jack. They had a grocery store on Main Street, which she ran a short time after his death and then started teaching school, working summers on her college degree. She spent most of her teaching career in the Morrilton School System. She died Feb. 23, 1988. Alma Ross married Pryor Reed Cruce Sr. (see above about the Cruce Family).

The following members of these families are buried at Elmwood Cemetery: Albert and Audra

Basham, C.E. and Cora Reed Cruce, Pryor R. and Alma Ross Cruce, George Albertine Basham Riggs, George and Sally Davis Ross, Rex Ross and his wife. *Prepared by Pryor R. Cruce Jr.*

CRYE - Willie Belle Crye (b. May 12, 1912) md. Arlon Dewey Edwards on Dec. 14, 1929. They were the most beloved people you could ever meet. To this marriage were born two children: A.D. Edwards Jr. (b. Feb. 8, 1934, d. March 10, 1934) and Shirley Marie Edwards (b. Feb. 14, 1935) who married Robert Warren Brown.

Willie Belle Crye and Arlon Dewey Edwards

Arlon Edwards (b. Jan. 16, 1908) met Willie at the Baptist Church at Hill Creek, AR. She was 17 years old and he was 21 years old when they married. They both worked hard at farming and I was told the first year of their marriage they started out with only 50 dollars to live on and that was to last them the whole year. They could not make it farming for themselves, so they tried share cropping and from that to many other jobs. In WWII Dad and Mom moved to Covina, CA, where Dad worked at Douglas Aircraft and mother packed oranges and did house work for other people.

When I was 12 years old Mom moved back to Springfield and I came with her and Dad transferred his work to Tulsa, OK. After he retired from Douglas Aircraft he worked for Mr. Vic Kordsmier, then some for Mr. Hightower, and was still doing part-time work at North Side Service Station when he passed away from a massive heart attack on Oct. 10, 1980. Willie Belle died Nov. 15, 1989. I, Shirley Brown, their only living child miss them very much. I was born weighing only 2 pounds and they struggled hard to keep me alive. Mother said it was cold and they kept fruit jars filled with hot water around me in an apple box, and I lay on a small pillow in the box. She said I was too weak to nurse so she took milk from her breast and with a medicine dropper would feed me. They sure fought hard for me and continued to show me the way of life with love and understanding.

My mother was known as "Bill" and my father was called "Doc." *Submitted by Shirley Brown.*

CRYE - Elder Joseph Alexander Crye (b. Jan. 25, 1859, d. Oct. 8, 1922) md. Nancy Della Satterfield (b. March 23, 1859, d. Nov. 29, 1940). Elder Crye was a minister at Cadron Ridge Baptist Church in 1907 and was known as a strong missionary preacher and full of fire. Some of the traditions and customs of the church are interesting to note. The women and girls always sat on the left side of the church and the men and boys sat on the right. The Crye's are buried on the hill behind the church as it is now. Joseph and Della Crye had a family of seven children.

Dave and Fannie (Hairston) Crye.

1) Fannie Crye White buried in Beaumont, TX.
2) Dave Thomas Crye (b. Aug. 30, 1882 in Macon, GA, d. Oct. 28, 1964, buried in Springfield Cemetery) was my grandfather. He married Fannie Lamar

Hairston (b. Oct. 31, 1885, d. Jan. 29, 1966) and they were life-long residents of the Springfield Community. Papa Dear (Dave Crye) was a foreman on the WPA and other construction jobs. Their children were:

a) Lois Mae Crye (b. May 28, 1907) md. James A. Mallett and they had three children: Mae, James O. and Fannie.

b) George Thomas Crye (b. Aug. 6, 1909, d. Nov. 10, 1950) md. Nona and they had three children: George, Betty Crye Brashier and Gene.

c) Willie Belle Crye (b. May 12, 1912, d. Nov. 15, 1989) md. Arlon Dewey Edwards (b. Jan. 16, 1908, d. Oct. 11, 1980) on Dec. 14, 1929. Arlon and Willie were the most beloved people you could ever meet. To this marriage were born two children: A.D. Edwards Jr. (b. Feb. 8, 1934, d. March 10, 1934) and Shirley Marie Edwards (b. Feb. 14, 1935).

d) Jack Joseph Ray Crye (b. Oct. 15, 1915) md. Ima Hartwick. Their children are Billy and James Crye.

e) James David Crye (b. April 17, 1921) md. Leone Thomas and their children are Sharon, Barbara and Jimmy.

f) Della Irene Crye (b. Feb. 3, 1924) md. Lloyd Brents and their child is Patsy.

3) Charlie Alexander Crye - Irene's family.

4) Nola Crye Turner.

5) John Crye (b. Nov. 3, 1888, d. November 1947).

6) Jo Crye Stringer.

7) George Crye.

Mr. and Mrs. Dave T. Crye were loving parents and grandparents and beloved by all in the community. They took care of family members throughout the years as they were needed. They married Aug. 3, 1906 and while Dave T. Crye worked mostly away from home, Fannie Lamar stayed home, farmed and took care of her family. They raised cows and had horses, pigs and chickens. They butchered and smoked their own meats, raised vegetables and fruits and canned to provide for their family. Fannie Lamar cooked on a wood cook stove and heat was provided by a fire place. I remember we would all get close to it to get warm and our legs would burn, but when you moved back away you would get cold real quick.

My mother was Willie Belle Crye Edwards and known to most as Bill or Mamabill. She was the third child of Dave and Fannie Crye. She married may father Arlon Dewey Edwards and was so loving and protective. They had a good 50 years of marriage but Dad died before the 51st year with a massive heart attack it seemed like mother never was the same. It seemed her life wasn't worth living after Dad died and also, she just was not well. They had a farm in the early years of marriage but could not make a good living at it, so during WWII they moved to Covina, CA, where Dad worked at Douglas Aircraft and Mom packed oranges. I had a good life. *Submitted by Shirley Marie Edwards.*

CUNNINGHAM - Aaron Fred Cunningham, a native of Greenville, SC came to Arkansas with his parents when he was 6 years old. He began teaching at the age of 20 in 1907, and taught in Johnson, Van Buren, Conway and Pope counties. Aug. 16, 1912 is a day the writer never forgot because of a self-inflicted accident. He shot himself in the foot, which had to be amputated. He had an artificial leg, used a walking stick and walked with a limp. This

A.F. Cunningham

happened while teaching in Pope County in a school in an abandoned farmhouse used for a schoolroom. Quite a change has occurred since that time. This article came from his write up Aug. 26, 1954, *Morrilton Democrat*. We now have more modern buildings with comfortable seating and other articles that make teaching more satisfactory.

A.F. Cunningham, one of the most widely read news correspondents for the *Democrat* with his "Meditations" from Blackwell-Kenwood, died at the home of a niece, Corrie M. Wilson, March 11, 1962.

His column appeared weekly in the Democrat and was an outstanding feature. His variety of subjects added to the interest of his writings and it was generally expected that he would have words of wisdom on any topical subject. He was survived by a son, Aaron F. Cunningham III of Tulsa, OK; a daughter, Edna M. Johnson of Oakland, CA; a stepson, James J. Davis of Los Angeles, CA; a stepdaughter, Leta Braxton of Tulsa; two grandchildren; four great-grandchildren; and many nieces and nephews. Funeral services were held at St. Matt. No. 3 Baptist Church Blackwell March 15, 1962.

Pallbearers were Active: W.A. Templeton, N.A. Ausler, Forrest Bryles, Leonitte Leapheart, Cullin FLetcher, and Felmo Washington; Honorary: P.P. Evans, E.H. Bagby, J.W. Ackerson, A. Moore, Brooks Wilson and Charlie Bowden. *Submitted by Voicy M. Cunningham Steward, my great-uncle.*

CUPP - In 1924, Lester Cupp and his wife, Gertrude Cupp, with his father, W.F. Cupp, opened a grocery in Morrilton on North Division Street. The location is now the Conway County industrial Development Commission.

People from all over the county would shop at the store. I remember my dad had a large floor truck. He would stack cases of salt and other things on it and roll it outside by the street. He also had a Philco radio that he put on the boxes of salt. Customers and local people would sit or stand and listen to the New York Yankees play the Brooklyn Dodgers, the two main ball teams at the time. My father played and pitched a little baseball in his younger years.

This picture is from the grocery store on North Division Street, around 1924. From left to right: Lester Cupp, Ezra Edwards, Gertrude Cupp, Rebecca "Granny" Cupp, Jack Cupp and W.E. "Grandpa" Cupp.

In 1937, Lester and Gertrude leased where the Morrilton Feed Mill is located, adjacent to the railroad, and moved their business from Division Street to Railroad Avenue. The building was of wooden construction and used as a strawberry shed. They added later to the building. A spur track fed off the main railroad tract and went by the building. Boxcars of feed and flour and even cars of salt would be spotted at three doors of the building brought up by the Missouri Pacific local from Little Rock.

About 1941, my brother Jack went to World War II. He landed on Iwo Jima against the Japanese as a corpsman in the 5th Marine Division. He had his pack shot off his back but kept going. The war was over and the government quit drafting young men. Lloyd and Floyd, twins, were at the right age but they were not drafted because of the end of the war.

Lester then got enthused in raising goldfish for fish bait. They were used for catching bass and catfish on troutline. The stores in town would close on Thursday. On Thursday afternoon when the stores closed, we would rent them the containers for 25 cents. Most everyone would bring them back to us and we would rent them again the next Thursday.

When Winthrop Rockefeller built the airport on Petit Jean Mountain, we had people fly in from Kentucky and Tennessee to buy oxygen bags of Israeli Carp to put in stock ponds to eat the algae and vegetation. *Submitted by Floyd Cupp.*

CYPERT - The Cypert family originated in Germany. They probably came from the area called Alsace-Lorraine. Alsace-Lorraine is now located on the eastern border of France, along the Germany border. At one time it was part of Germany. The Cypert surname has many varied spellings. Larrance Scypeart was born about 1680-1690, in Germany. He married Margaret (last name unknown) about 1715 in Germany. They immigrated to America between 1725 and 1735. Records indicate they settled in Pennsylvania and probably died in Pennsylvania. They were Quakers. Larrance and Margaret had at least two children:

1) Margaret Scypeart (b. 1716, in Germany, d. 1799, Pennsylvania) md. Peter Stout.

2) Francis Scypeart (b. between 1718-24 in Germany). He married Charity Townsend about 1743 in Lancaster County, PA. Francis and Charity settled in Lancaster County. About 1750 Francis moved his family to Orange (now Chatham) County, NC. Francis owned at least 640 acres of land in Chatham County. The Cypert name appears often in Quaker records. The family attended meetings at Cane Creek Meeting House in Orange (now Chatham) County. Many family members were married at the meeting house and several family members are buried in the meeting house cemetery. Charity died prior to 1788 in Chatham County. Francis died there about 1788. Francis and Charity Scypeart's children included: Margaret Scypert (md. Jacob Marshall); Thomas Sypert; Francis Cypert II and Robert Scypert. (Each of the three sons spelled his surname differently.)

Francis Cypert II, referred to as Francis Cypert Jr., was born about 1750 in Orange (now Chatham) County, NC. He served in the North Carolina Militia in 1774-75. Francis Jr. married Abigail Johnson in 1783, probably in Chatham County. Abigail (b. ca. 1760 in Virginia) was the daughter of Jesse Johnson. In 1789, Francis bought his brother Robert's portion of their father's 640 acres of land in Chatham County. About 1795, Francis sold his land to his brother Thomas.

Francis then moved his family to Tennessee. Francis was living in Overton County, TN in 1805 and in Jackson County, TN in 1807. He was an early settler in Maury County, TN before moving with his family to Wayne County, TN about 1815-18. His brother Robert settled his family in Wayne County at the same time. Francis settled in the Indian Creek Valley, then known as Rain's Creek, on land he received as a land grant for his military service in the war. Francis was a founding member of the Providence Baptist Church in 1831 in Wayne County. He continued as a member there until his death. Abigail died September 1828 in Wayne County and was buried in the Providence Church Cemetery. Francis died there Nov. 12, 1839 and was buried beside his wife.

Children of Francis Cypert II and Abigail Johnson included: Jesse Newton Cypert (md. Jemima Worthen); Baker Cypert (md. Malinda Neal); Charity Cypert (md. Zachariah Thompson); John William Cypert (md. Nancy Anderson); Thomas Cypert (a twin); Francis Cypert III (a twin) md. Nancy Whidbee; Comfort Annis Cypert (md. John Loyd); Abigail Cypert (md. James Arnett Jr.); Mary "Polly" Cypert (md. Joseph Woody); and William T. Cypert.

DEATON - Bill Deaton, farmer and civic leader, was born Billie Eugene Deaton, Sept. 6, 1927 to James Alex and Etta Irene Williams Deaton of Morrilton. A brother Jimmy Dean Deaton, 65, died of cancer April 7, 2001; a sister Marietta, 62, married and divorced LeRoy Driggers, married Ray Russell, who died in 2004, lives in Winkleman, AZ. Four daughters: Deana, Donna, Debbie and Dodie. Jim Deaton married and divorced Delores Rainwater. Three children: Mark Deaton, unmarried; Phyllis Deaton Reidmueller and Lisa Deaton Trafford. Jim married Ruth Coffman Trafford, aunt of Lisa's husband, Steve Trafford.

Bill Deaton, 2004.

Bill's grandparents were Riley and Nanny Gordon Deaton and Ferd and Martha Johnston Williams.

Drafted in the fall of 1945 following the end of WWII, Bill served with the US Air Force 8th Photo Tech Unit with occupation forces in Japan. He returned home in June 1946 and married Helen Louise Long Deaton (b. Sept. 1, 1930) on Oct. 9, 1947. Her parents were Elmo (b. July 6, 1908, d. July 2, 1988) and Marmary Dicus Long (b. July 20, 1910, d. Feb. 2, 1995). Employed at J.T. Roberson Wholesale Grocery, he and several local veterans took on-the-job training classes offered by the government. They earned $90 a month from the government and $20 a week from employers. At the end of the war, times were hard for young married couples. Refrigerators were scarce, and couples were on lists at appliance dealers; it took months for the Deatons to get one—a Frigidaire; family help was a blessing.

In 1951, Bill joined his father-in-law in farming the J.E. Ketchum farm in the Sandtown bottoms south of Morrilton. It was later bought by V.R. (Judge) Edwards, Rufus Morgan Jr. and Cleo Priba, brothers-in-law, who owned it until their deaths and their spouses. In 2002, it was willed to Harding University, Freed-Hardeman University and the TV religious program, *Search*. Bill was joined in the family farming operation in 1972 by his son, William Randyl "Randy" Deaton (b. May 31, 1954) who now farms it alone since Bill retired in 2002. Through the years, they accumulated several hundred more acres. As farming is a gamble, there have been lean years: the devastating drought of 1980 and a flood in 1986 when the family lost almost a thousand acres of a bumper soybean crop and the Arkansas River floods at least once most years - often on growing crops.

Bill and Helen also have a daughter, Cheryl Ann Blansett (b. July 16, 1956) who married Ralph Andrew "Andy" Blansett of Searcy (b. Dec. 3, 1955) on Oct. 6, 1978, a pharmacist and drug store owner in North Little Rock. They live in Cabot with three sons: twins-Joshua Deaton Blansett and Jonathan Andrew Blansett (b. Nov. 10, 1984), students at the University of Arkansas, Fayetteville and Harding University, Searcy; and Luke Allan Blansett (b. Jan. 9, 1990). Cheryl graduated from Harding with a BS degree in mathematics, with graduate work in the actuarial field, and taught four years part-time at Harding. Randy married Cheryl Ann Riggs (b. Sept. 9, 1955) on Aug. 14, 1975. Two daughters, Jennifer Lynn (b. April 28, 1980) married Dewey Wesley Mahan (b. Feb. 18, 1974) on June 26, 1999, and Whitney Ann (b. Nov. 26, 1989). Jennifer has a bachelor of business administration degree (2002) and a master's in accountancy from University of Central Arkansas (2003).

The Deaton family was twice Conway County Farm Family of the Year: 1967 and 1984. Bill has received many awards for community service, recognition for serving on all boards connected to farming, including 11 years serving 41 counties as a Western Arkansas Production Credit Association director and chairman; president, Agri Co-op; president, Conway County Fair Association for which he received in 1992 the Award of Individual Accomplishment through the Arkansas Community Development Awards Program for improvements to the fairgrounds, including a new livestock building and multi-purpose building. This brought a state award to the city of Morrilton and for

him the Citizen of the Year from the Morrilton Chamber of Commerce; Conservation Service board since 1987; and the Farm Bureau board. He has served many years on the Extension Service Advisory Committee; 4-H Foundation board; 17 years in Kiwanis Club, receiving in 2001 Kiwanis highest honor, the Tablet of Honor from Kiwanis International Foundation, presented by agricultural friends of Conway County.

Bill has been a deacon at Downtown Church of Christ since 1967; Helen, a Bible teacher 48 years, has been a feature writer with the *Morrilton Headlight, Petit Jean Country Headlight* and the *Arkansas Democrat Sunday Magazine*. Witty and a perpetual kidder, Bill began his political service as committeeman of Morrilton Ward 4; then in 1962 as Morrilton city alderman serving 37 years, the longest of any Conway County elected official; except for four years under Mayor Gerald Laux, he served continuously under the administrations of Mayors Dr. T.H. Hickey, John Davidson, Jim Sutton and Stewart Nelson and often as vice mayor. He retired Dec. 31, 2002, then accepted a part-time position with the city's wastewater commission as manager and marketer of crops grown on city-owned land, a position he continues to fill in 2004. *Submitted by Helen Deaton.*

DEAVER - Joshua and Rebecca Hauser Deaver lived in Rowan County, NC in the early 1800s. They had at least six children, one of whom came to Conway County, AR around 1840, namely Samuel Deaver.

Rebecca Hauser was descended from Casper Hartman and Martin Hauser. Joshua Deaver was the son of Samuel Deaver and Elizabeth Farmer, who married in 1787 in Rowan County, NC. His brother, Samuel, married Susannah Hauser (Rebecca's sister). He was in manufacturers and trades and his son Alexander is listed as a tobacco planter after his death.

Of Joshua and Rebecca's children, only three are known at this time: Nathan, Samuel and Alexander. Joshua died in 1842 in Davie County, NC and is buried at Joppa Cemetery in Mocksville. Rebecca moved to Arkansas sometime after 1860, along with her son Nathan. She, Nathan, his wife Ada and their son Thomas, are all buried at Springfield Cemetery, in Springfield. AR. Rebecca died on Aug. 21, 1882.

Samuel Deaver married Fannie Burgess. Samuel died between 1864 and 1870. Fannie died sometime after 1880. Children were:

Emily (b. 1848).

James (b. 1849).

Adolphus (b. ca. 1849-51) md. Emaline Brinkley in 1872, and had one child, Minnie. He married Francis Self in 1881.

Samuel Jr. (b. 1854, d. 1912) md. Susan F.E. Cullom in 1891 in Conway County. Children were David "Davie," Nettie, Annie, Allie and Nora.

Franklin (b. 1857).

Nathan (b. 1861, d. 1920) md. Fannie Lee in 1888 Conway County. He was a farmer and a "tinker."

Colonel Marion (b. 1864) md. Lenora Magdaline Salter in 1887 Conway County. They had three surviving children: (1) Irvin (md. Ruth German), no children; (2) Boyd; (3) Doyle married first, Lela Douglas, two children, Martha Anne and Helen Louis. He married second, Lottie Milam, no children. Boyd (d. 1910) is buried at Mt. Pleasant Cemetery at Hill Creek Community. Maggie died in 1944 and is buried at Plumerville Cemetery.

Boyd Taylor Deaver (b. 1892) md. Alma Flara Rice in 1912 in Conway County. Children:

1) Maxine (b. 1913, d. 1972) md. first, Harold Masters and second, Bud Clayton.

2) Burl (b. 1915, d. 1972) md. Mildred Lacefield.

3) Charles K. (b. 1916, d. 1978) md. Faye Cates.

4) Margie Marie (b. 1919) was killed by a drunk driver on Christmas night, 1936.

5) Mildred LaVelle Deaver (b. 1921) md. Jack Arlie "Red" Walker in 1937. They had eight children together, namely: Naomi, Harold, C.B., Lucretia, An-

thony, Gwyned, Arlianne and Kevin. LaVelle died in 2003 and is buried at Plumerville Cemetery.

6) Frank (b. 1924, d. 1995) md. Oleta Carter.

7) Naomi Mozelle (b. 1926) md. Junior Carr. She died in 1950 from complications from heart and liver failure.

8) Alton Norris "Sonny" (b. 1930, d. 1999) was a hairdresser in Morrilton. *Submitted by Jennifer Hill Russell.*

DENNISTON - Michael Edward Denniston (b. Sept. 25, 1949 in Fort Smith, AR) was trained as a helicopter pilot for the Vietnam War and continued to fly helicopters after his honorable discharge from the Army - first in the Gulf of Mexico to the oil rigs and then for medical emergency transport. On Dec. 12, 1987, he married Jeannie L. Culbertson (b. May 3, 1951 in Jackson, MS). Their daughter Sara Elizabeth Denniston was born Nov. 30, 1988 in Little Rock.

The family moved from Little Rock to Morrilton in 1994, following Jeannie's graduation from the UALR School of Law. Mike continued to fly helicopters until his death from a heart attack on Oct. 28, 2002. He is buried in Hagarville, AR.

Jeannie was the first female attorney to practice in Conway County. She opened her office in private practice and also served for two years as the county's deputy prosecuting attorney. She joined the law firm of Gordon, Caruth and Virden in 1998 as an associate attorney and remained there until 2004. At that time, she went to work for the state of Arkansas full time as a dependency-neglect ad litem, representing children found to be neglected and/or abused.

Sara was active in school activities of the South Conway County School district, maintaining her position on the honor roll, as a starter for the junior high school volleyball team, a starter for the high school bowling team, theatrical productions, Beta Club and the school newspaper.

Both Jeannie and Sara are members of the Baha'i Faith and are certified scuba divers.

DeSALVO - Amelia Beatrice (b. Nov. 2, 1911), daughter of Joseph Luke and Mary Louise Rossi DeSalvo, married Angelo Anthony "Doc" Paladino on Nov. 20, 1929 at St. Joseph Catholic Church. Doc (b. Feb. 27, 1905, d. Nov. 15, 1962) was the son of Barbato and Donato Chavlerila Paladino. Their children were:

1) Leo Bernard (b. Feb. 17, 1931, d. April 14, 2000) md. Florence Dornak on March 2, 1957. Their children are Leo Bernard Jr. "Dino" and Mark Anthony.

2) Carl Richard (b. Dec. 15, 1932, d. June 1, 1979) md. Malthilda Josephine Miller on Feb. 25, 1959. Their children are: Marilyn Rose, Patricia Marie, Carl Richard Jr. "Ricky," Angelo Anthony.

3) Edward Joe (b. Oct. 16, 1935) md. Joann Scroggins on Nov. 29, 1966. Their children are Pamela and Sherry.

4) Kenneth Charles (b. Aug. 1, 1937, d. Jan. 21, 1939).

5) Rose Ella (b. June 2, 1942) md. John Martin Beck on Aug. 19, 1961. Their children are Janice Lynn and Kimberly Ann.

After Amelia and Doc married, they lived with his parents for two years. In 1932 they built and moved into the house where she resides now. Each year they would kill hogs and make sausage, growing the animals themselves. The vegetables out of the garden were canned for the winter's use. Doc went to work in about 1948 for the State Highway Department as a road worker. He was employed with them at the time of his death. Amelia, what a wonderful cook, only serving homemade bread, pasta, sauces, jams, and jellies, always the homemaker. There was nothing better.

Doc was continually bringing a group home for a meal. Armed with her pots, pans and skillets, Amelia would whip up a delicious meal in no time (fried pies a special treat, and a favorite). Amelia gardened all through the spring and summer months. She was quite the seamstress as well, and made all their clothes - shirts for the men and boys and dresses, skirts and blouses for herself and daughter. Over the years she has sewn for her grandchildren and great-grandchildren as well, making them all quilts, knitting, and crocheting all kinds of beautiful and useful things. She taught herself to do all of these wonderful crafts and even to tat, which is an art that is slowly fading.

Amelia has worked very hard all of her life, teaching herself so much. Now she is passing all that love and inspiration, as well as the wealth of information she holds, on in a legacy of four generations that follow her. Amelia has five children, 10 grandchildren, 18 great-grandchildren and 13 great-great-grandchildren. Now at the age of 93, her mind is sound as ever, she is still eager to learn and to share her knowledge. *Submitted by John C. Hawkins.*

DeSALVO - Anthony Luke (b. April 10, 1899 in Catholic Point, Conway County, AR, d. July 23, 1991) was the son of Luca and Beatrice DeSalvo. He married first, Josephine "Giuseppa" Marie Rossi on Nov. 9, 1916 at St. Joseph Catholic Church. Marie (b. April 4, 1896, d. April 18, 1934) was the daughter of Joseph and Maria "Mary" Pedrazolli Rossi. Their children are Augustine Luke "Gus" (md. Anne Marie Lanni); Louis James "Father Raphael;" Michael Edward (md. Genevieve Harriette Tankersley); Marie Rose "Sister Marie Rose;" Henry Joseph (md. Gloria Maria Rossi; Clara Beatrice (md. Arvel Andy Granger); Emma Ligouri (md. Harley Frank Petty); Virginia Arlene (md. Weymon Douglas Lambert); Abraham Charles married first, Rosalie Antoinette Keenan and second, Vera Lou Kendrick.

Tony and Josephine (Rossi) DeSalvo and Gus about 1918.

About some five months after having her last child, Josephine became ill. One day a cow stepped on her foot and caused an infection turning into blood poisoning, which led to her death. After the death of Josephine, Tony having nine very small children, one an infant, to care for and feed, needless to say *Tony and Frances DeSalvo* he was somewhat over-whelmed and in great need of help. His sister-in-law, Minnie Paladino, feeling sorry for him, asked that her daughter, Frances, go down to help him out a few days a week with the children and the household chores. This of course meant cooking for the family as well. Frances was taught to cook at a very young age and took to the task quite nicely.

In the few short months that Frances was helping at Tony's home he came to depend on her greatly and decided, hey she's a really good cook too. So Tony took the next step and on Sept. 12, 1934 Tony and Frances were married at St. Joseph Catholic Church. Frances was the daughter of Tony and Minnie Paladino (see "Our Land Our Home Our People") she was born Sept. 4, 1903 and died April 20, 2001. When she was born weighing in at about 2 pounds, she was placed in a shoebox on the windowsill in the sunshine to help

keep her warm, and in hopes that the sunrays would make her healthier. It must have done the trick!

Tony and Frances had 10 children together, their children are Helen Patricia (md. Russell Andrew Hart); Margaret Frances (md. Clarence Milton Hart); Christina Beatrice (md. John Peter Koch); Angela Ann (md. James Joseph Malik); Delores Mary (md. Clemens Theodore Hartman); Thomas Patrick (md. Ida Ann Wenger); Mary Antonette (md. Thomas Weldon Hall); Beatrice Frances md. Carl Matthew Miller; Raphael Anthony "Brother Tobias; "Anthony James (md. Pamela Watts - marriage legally dissolved).

Tony and Frances were strong in their faith and supporters of their community. Tony was the kind of neighbor that would do anything he could do to help a fellow out, always willing to go that extra mile. Not only were their doors open to friends and neighbors, but also usually the table was fully spread with a variety of homemade delights from the kitchen of Frances (always the hostess). The family as a whole worked very hard to maintain the farm and vineyards. This was, as everyone knows, Tony's first great love, instilled in him by his father, who taught him everything he knew about the vineyard. They raised animals, which provided all the meat for the family and vegetables in the gardens that were used for canning and preserving for the winter months.

Tony was a member of the Catholic Knights of America, Past Agricultural Stabilization Conservation Service Board, and past director of the Conway County School Board. Tony was very instrumental in keeping the Catholic Point School open until the late 60s. He was an avid fisherman; always out by the pond bank with not one but two or three poles in the water at one time. He really knew how to pull them in! Tony and Frances both lived to be in their 90s, both very well loved and respected pillars of their community. Leaving behind the kind of legacy that most only dream of. Nineteen children, 78 great-grandchildren, and at the time of her death, eight great-great-grandchildren. *Submitted by Beatrice DeSalvo Miller and Anthony James DeSalvo.*

DeSALVO - Camillo came to the United States from Italy about 1880. He settled in St. Louis, MO, where he married Leonesia. They had four sons: Heliodora "Ollie," Luca, Dominico and Joseph. In the early 1880s they all moved to Center Ridge, Conway County, AR, settling in a small community known as Catholic Point. Camillo was born July 25, 1824 in Italy and died July 26, 1884 in Center Ridge, Conway County, AR. His wife Leonesia was born June 15, 1824 in Italy and died Dec. 17, 1886 in Center Ridge, Conway County, AR. Both are buried in St. Joseph Cemetery.

1) Heliodora "Ollie" was born in 1857 in Italy and died while living in Missouri. Ollie married Roccena, who was called either "Lena" or "Katie," Farino. She was born 1869 in Italy and died in Missouri. Their children were Paschal, Luke, Joe, Tony, Mary, Louise, Marie, Isabella, Paul, Virginia and Josie. Ollie moved his family from St. Louis, MO to Center Ridge, AR several times before settling in St. Louis.

2) Luca Antonio (b. Sept. 20, 1859 in Italy, d. Feb. 3, 1936 in Center Ridge, AR) was also known as Luke. He married Beatrice DeSalvo in St. Louis on Oct. 4, 1881. She was born Sept. 7, 1860 in Italy and died March 11, 1940. Both are buried at St. Joseph Cemetery. Their children were Nicholas "Will," Camillo "Kell" Annie Marie, John, Joseph Luke, Louis, Julia, Amelia, Anthony Luke, Pete and Rocco J.

3) Dominico (b. Nov. 19, 1861 in Italy, d. Aug. 27, 1934) md. Jarginta on Oct. 26, 1884 at St. Joseph Catholic Church. She was born July 4, 1869 in Italy and died March 21, 1933. Both are buried at St. Joseph Cemetery. Their children were Micheal, Conchetta, Angelo, Mary, Josephine, Tony and Jane.

4) Joseph "Joe" (b. May 1870 in Italy) md. Johannia Lombardo. Their children were Frank, Carmie, Martin, Thomas, Vincent, Maria, Elizabeth, Virginia, Frances, Jim and Lena.

These pioneers were of the strongest and bravest of individuals. They came here to Conway County not knowing anyone. Not knowing how or where they would live, upon coming here they had to clear the land and build houses and barns. In the beginning they almost starved, because they didn't know how to farm. So some chose to go back to St. Louis but then would return in a few years to Conway County. Those who did return with help from friends and neighbors were able to build new lives for themselves. They built a community embracing their culture with a mixture of the new world they had found. Those who stayed found it was very difficult but rewarding, giving them a better way of life for themselves and their families. Many sent for other family members to come and live in their new-found community. They built a church and a school, thus completing the community. Not all returned, some stayed in St. Louis, or moved on to New York, never returning to Conway County.

DeSALVO - Luca "Luke" Antonio (b. Sept. 20, 1859 in Campabosso, Italy, d. Feb. 3, 1936 in Center Ridge, AR) md. Theresa Beatrice DeSalvo (b. Sept. 7, 1860 in Italy, d. March 11, 1940 in Center Ridge, AR) on Oct. 4, 1881 in St. Louis MO. Both are buried in St. Joseph Cemetery. Luke and Beatrice stayed in St. Louis until about the mid-1880s. Having trouble with her breathing while living in St. Louis, due to all the smoke from the factories, they decided to move to Arkansas. They settled in the community of Catholic Point near Center Ridge. Before leaving St. Louis they had two sons, Nicholas and Camillo.

Luca and Beatrice DeSalvo

1) Nicholas "Will" (b. June 20, 1883 in St. Louis, MO, d. Aug. 27, 1963 in Center Ridge) md. first, Virginia Moser (b. Jan. 2, 1882, d. Oct. 12, 1922) on Nov. 12, 1901. She was the daughter of Thomas and Maria Rossi Moser. Will and Virginia's children were Frank, Katherine, Thomas, Phillip, Amelia, Andrew, Marie and Josephine. After Virginia's death, Will married second, Jessie Jones (b. May 30, 1902, d. Nov. 30, 1946). Their children were Dorothy, William and Georgia Fay.

2) Camillo "Kill" (b. April 10, 1855 in St. Louis, MO, d. Jan. 1, 1968) md. Carmalla Paladino (b. Feb. 25, 1889, d. Feb. 3, 1925), daughter of Barbato and Donato Chavlerila Paladino. Their children: Angelo, Johnny, Luke A., Dan, Tony B., Angeline M. and Annie Marie.

3) Annie Marie (b. Dec. 10, 1886 in Catholic Point, Conway County, AR, d. Aug. 24, 1978) md. Rockie Paladino (b. Oct. 26, 1883, d. Nov. 21, 1928), son of Frank and Lena Annuizo Paladino. Their children: Frank, Anthony, Maria Rose, Mary, Elizabeth, Luke, Louis, Theresa, Katherine, Regina, Pete and Rosie.

4) John (b. Sept. 3, 1888 in Catholic Point, Conway County, AR, d. July 10, 1909 of typhoid fever).

5) Joseph Luke (b. Jan. 10, 1889 in Catholic Point, Conway County, AR, d. March 30, 1963) md. Mary Louise Rossi (b. June 19, 1889, d. Jan. 4, 1985) on Nov. 20, 1910. Mary was the daughter of Joseph and Maria Pedrazolli Rossi. Their children were Amelia Beatrice, Paul Anthony, Edward Luke, Julia Marie, Robert Anthony, Vencent Anthony, Joseph Luke Jr.,

Richard Valetine, Irene Marie, Lorene Marie, Eugene Carl and Minnie Katherine.

6) Louis (b. Jan. 4, 1894 in Catholic Point, Conway County, AR, d. Nov. 5, 1976) md. Linzy Marie Zarlingo on Nov. 29, 1919. Their children were Josephine, Rose Marie and Lucille.

7) Julia (b. Jan. 28, 1895 in Catholic Point, Conway County, AR, d. Nov. 25, 1938) md. Robby Paladino, son of Frank and Lena Annuizo Paladino, on Oct. 28, 1912. He was born Dec. 10, 1890 and died May 27, 1961. Their children were Frank, Pauline, Tony, Josephine, Louise, John, Lawrence, Adolph, Carmella, Victor, Phillip, Margaret and Beatrice.

8) Amelia (b. June 26, 1898 in Catholic Point, Conway County, AR, d. Aug. 7, 1909).

9) Anthony Luke (b. April 10, 1899 in Catholic Point, Conway County, AR, d. July 23, 1991) md. first, Josephine "Giuseppa" Marie Rossi (b. April 4, 1896, d. April 18, 1934), daughter of Joseph and Maria Pedrazolli Rossi. Their children were Augustine Luke, Louis James "Father Raphael," Michael Edward, Marie Rose "Sister Mary Angela," Henry Joseph, Clara Beatrice, Emma Ligouri, Virginia Arlene and Abraham Charles. After Josephine's death, Anthony Luke married a second time to Frances Paladino (b. Sept. 4, 1903, d. April 20, 2001) on Sept. 12, 1934. She was the daughter of Tony and Minnie Rossi Paladino. Their children were Helen Patricia, Margaret Frances, Christina Beatrice, Angela Ann, Delores Mary, Thomas Patrick, Mary Antonette, Beatrice Frances, Raphael Anthony "Brother Tobias," and Anthony James.

10) Pete (b. Oct. 2, 1901 in Catholic Point, Conway County, AR, d. Jan. 16, 1996) md. Rose Miller and their child was Linda.

11) Rocco J. (b. Nov. 11, 1903 in Catholic Point, Conway County, AR, d. Oct. 9, 2000) md. Josephine Burk (b. 1906, d. 1975). Their children were Bea and Rocco Jr.

Luke "Luka" and Beatrice were among the first settlers in the Catholic Point Community. His parents and brothers all settled here as well. They were dedicated to building their homes and lives, along with helping to build their community and church better than they had known in their former lives in Italy. Working side by side there was an abundance of blood, sweat and tears that were shed in order to have this new life, as time passed they grew to be a happy, tight knit community. The clothing they wore was obtained by making it themselves or by way of trade. Everything was grown or made by hand, they planted vineyards, from the vines brought here from the old country, Italy. In the gardens they had corn, beans, herbs and tomatoes. The corn was ground by the gristmill and made into meal, out of the ground meal they made a dish called polenta. This was made by boiling water and adding the ground meal until it was thickened then poured out on a dish, topped with tomato sauce and cheese. They raised a few cattle, which they milked. Hogs were raised and used to make sausage and cured meats. Beatrice loved to sing. She would sing a solo every Sunday at church. She had a very beautiful voice. When I was a child, I can remember spending time with my grandmother. Almost each time I would visit, it seems like she would have a nickel for me. Back then that was big money!

DICUS - Loonie Albert Dicus' ancestors came to Kent County, MD via the British Isles—Scotland or North Ireland, in 1705. He was born Dec. 10, 1882 at Hazen, AR, to George R. Dicus and Mandy Wilson Dicus. He had two brothers, Edward and William Isaac Dicus, who died without descendants. Loonie married Georgia Lee Martin June June 30, 1907, and they lived in Hattieville. They had six children, all now deceased: Walter Lee (b. Feb. 27, 1908); William Earl (b. Oct. 12, 1912); Roy Edward (b. Jan. 14, 1915); James Albert (b. Aug. 13, 1921); Levi Alvin "Dub" (b. July 3, 1924) and one daughter, Marmary Truman Dicus (b. July 20, 1910). Two or three died in infancy.

Walter married Anna Dortha Long and had six

children: Charles Edward (b. Jan. 8, 1929, deceased) md. Lois Mae Siemens; Dorthy Lee (b. Feb. 28, 1931) md. Billy Hallett, deceased; William Harold (b. Dec. 31, 1933) md. Lela June Brown; Betty Irene (b. Dec. 28, 1935) md. Robert Lee Hester, divorced and married Sherrill Mayall; Georgia Faye (b. May 21, 1937) md. Doyle "Zeke" Davidson, deceased; Lois Katherine (b. March 31, 1939) md. Reuben Eugene Parish Jr., deceased, married Mike Arndt.

L.A. Dicus Family, Golden Anniversary, June 30, 1957: (l-r) Earl, Marmary, James, Walter and Alvin "Dub."

Will Martin, his brother-in-law Loonie Dicus "Jot'em Down Store," 1950's.

Earl Dicus married Lela Reddig, one son, William Earl Jr. (b. June 10, 1944, deceased). Marmary T. married Elmo Floyd Long on Sept. 24, 1929; one daughter, Helen Louise (b. Sept. 1, 1930), md. Bill E. Deaton Oct. 9, 1947. Roy married Edith Engle, twins Raymond Leslie and Rayburn Wesley (b. Aug. 24, 1933, both deceased); a daughter, Hazel Ruth (b. Sept. 27, 1939, deceased) md. David Parette, one son, Gary, deceased. James married Syble Scroggins on May 14, 1924, two children: a son, Jimmie Earl (b. April 3, 1944) md. Sammie, divorced, married Georgia; and a daughter, Martha Sue (b. Nov. 1, 1945) md. Jerry Syck. Alvin "Dub," unmarried but fathered a daughter, Margaret Robinson Tutor, and possibly a son.

"Loon," as he was known, was a farmer in the Sandtown bottoms along the Arkansas River south of Morrilton, on the farms of Dr. Bradley and Dr. B.C. Logan. Retiring from farming, Loon and Georgia moved to the Lewisburg Community on Bridge Street south of Morrilton. He later worked down the street as a part-time employee for the late Joe Kissire's Grocery. He liked it so much, he opened his own (known to the family as his "Jot 'em Down Store") in front of the family home.

A favorite story about him is his extending credit to customers. One was way behind in paying, and Loon shook his unpaid tickets in the man's face and said, "You see these? If you don't pay them, I'm going to tear them up!" Another family favorite is about carrying dentures in his pocket. He would feed cattle and get hay in the pockets, but when he wanted to eat, he'd shake off the hay and put them in his mouth! When the family lived on the Logan farm, they raised, butchered, and smoked many hogs, and the Dicus "ham" was well-known. Both Loon and Georgia were in old St. Anthony's Hospital at the same time when she died Jan. 2, 1959. He then lived with his son-in-law and daughter, and because of a stroke spent time in a nursing home before dying Sept. 16, 1965. *Submitted by Katherine Dicus Parish Arndt.*

DIXON - Allen A. Dixon, son of Logustine and Mary Dixon, had siblings John C., David R. and Elizabeth F. Logustine Dixon - also known as Augustine (b. North Carolina about 1801-05, died after 1860), and Mary (b. about 1805, d. after 1860) were in Sumner County, TN in 1830, and were in Pope County, AR by 1840.

John C. Dixon (b. Dec. 1, 1828, Sumner County, TN, d. Aug. 17, 1887, buried at Center Valley Cemetery, Pope County, AR) md. Sarah P. Stout on Nov. 25, 1847 in Pope County and they had 11 children: Mary Ann (b. 1848, d. _), David Clinton (b. 1850, d. 1903), James Warren (b. 1852, d. 1924), Alfred B. (b. 1854, d. 1882), Nancy Isabell (b. 1856, d. _), William M. (b. 1858, d. _), Elizabeth Ann (b. 1860, d. 1955), Margaret (b. 1862, d. _), Houston (b. 1865, d. 1920), Eliza Catherine (b. 1870, d. 1931) and Henry Lee (b. ca. 1874).

David R. Dixon (b. 1830 Sumner County, TN, d. March 30, 1875, Pope County, AR) md. first, Mary Crouch on March 29, 1854 and they had three children: Tennessee Ann (b. 1856, d. 1936), John A. (b. 1859) and Eliza E. (b. 1861). He then married Harriet Coffman June 4, 1866 and they had six children: William (b. 1866), Hugh (b. 1869), James (b. 1870), Wallace (b. 1873), Noah (b. 1874) and Mary Alice (b. 1875).

Elizabeth F. Dixon (b. 1833, died apparently between 1860 and 1870). Elizabeth was not on the 1870 census and the 1880 showed William as a widower. Elizabeth married William Garner April 7, 1851 in Pope County and they had five children: Harriet (b. 1852), Sabrina (by 1854), Lavina (1855), Barney (b. 1857) and Elizabeth (b. 1859).

Allen A. (b. 1825 in Tennessee, d. Dec. 7, 1880) md. Columbia Garner (b. 1832, d. Aug. 31, 1899) on Aug. 8, 1849 in Pope County. she was the daughter of Barney B. and Elizabeth Purvis Garner. Their children were Martha (b. 1850/51), John G. (b. February 1852), William (b. 1854), Julia (b. 1856), Barney D. (b. 1857), Mary (b. 1858), Martin (b. 1859), Robert (b. 1867), Margarette (b. 1870) and Chester (b. 1872). There may have been another daughter, Almira (b. 1859) and possibly other children between 1860 and 1867. A.A. served as a corporal in the Mexican War from June 1846 to April 1847 in Company B of the Arkansas Battalion Infantry and Mounted Rifles.

John G. (George?) Dixon was born February 1852, died between 1880 and 1885. We have been unable to find the date or cause of death of this young man. He was married July 29, 1875 in Conway County to Mary Spence, daughter of Rick D. and Elizabeth Spence. They only had two children: John Quincy "Buster" and Alice.

Alice (b. Sept. 18, 1880, d. Jan. 19, 1967) md. William Vardman Bennett and their children were: Vonnie, Pearl, Stella, Oscar, Charles and Oval. Both Alice and William are buried at Middleton Cemetery, Conway County.

John Q. Dixon (b. Dec. 15, 1977, d. Feb. 11, 1959) md. July 9, 1899 to Eva Darcus Stracener, daughter of Henry Jordan Stracener and Mary (Sarah) Elizabeth Kirtley Stracener. They had 10 children: Arlie E., James Orville, Jewel E., Edgar, Olen Quitman, L.M., Luther Otis, William Curtis, Elbert Doyle and Euna Faye Dixon. See the additional write up on the John Quincy Dixon family. *Submitted by John C. Dixon*

DIXON - Billy Joe Dixon (b. Sept. 17, 1954, in Morrilton, Conway County, AR) was the fifth child of William Curtis "Curt" Dixon Sr. and Ruby Marvell (Little) Dixon. He was self-employed at Dixon Water Conditioning Company for 20 years, then went to work for Conway County Regional Water Distribution District (CCRWDD) in 1993. He married Mary Elizabeth Pettingill (b. Nov. 29, 1955, in Morrilton, Conway County, AR) on July 5, 1974 in Plumerville, Conway County, AR.

Their oldest son David Lynn Bolin (b. Feb. 11, 1973, in Morrilton, Conway County, AR) md. Deborah Gail Russell (b. Aug. 28, 1973, in Morrilton, Conway

County, AR) on June 28, 1997, in Morrilton, Conway County, AR. They have one child, Hunter Lynn (b. Dec. 13, 2002, in Russellville, Pope County, AR).

l-r: Wayne, Michelle, Alyssia. Billy Joe, Mary, Hunter, Debbie and David.

Their youngest son, Billy Wayne (b. Oct. 29, 1974, in Morrilton, Conway County, AR) md. Susan Michelle Mourot (b. Feb. 9, 1978, in Little Rock, Pulaski County, AR) on June 17, 2000, in Morrilton, Conway County, AR. They have one child, Alyssia Ruell (b. April 15, 2003, in Conway, Faulkner County, AR).

DIXON - Jimmy Harold Dixon (b. Aug. 26, 1942 in Center Ridge, AR) was one of seven children born to Olen Quitman Dixon and Martha Marie Polk Dixon. Jimmy "Jim" met and married Betty Marie Chism (b. Jan. 17, 1943 in Lanty of Conway County), daughter of Roscoe and Ruby Chism. They made their home in the old Grandpa Buster Dixon's house for several years. They both worked at the Cotton Mill at Morrilton. In 1966 they moved to Kansas City, MO, where Jim worked for General Motors for about a year.

Jim and Betty Dixon family.

They decided that Arkansas was home, so they moved back to the Grandview area. Jim was self-employed timber pulpwood cutter and hauler who sold to the Paper Mill for 13 years. After Jim got out of the timber business, they were dairy farmers for 27 years on Randall Dixon Rd. Jim and Betty Dixon had three children. Betty Gail Dixon (b. Oct. 9, 1962), Deronda Lee Dixon (b. April 23, 1966) and Randall Harold Dixon (b. March 7, 1970).

Gail married Leslie Alan Dixon of Plumerville Dec. 22, 1979. They had Mitchell Keith Dixon on Sept. 9, 1985. Gail later married Donald Eller on Oct. 17, 1987 and they had two children, Luke Ashton Eller (b. Feb. 10, 1989) and Andrew Randall Eller (b. June 25, 1993). Don already had four children when they married - they were Cindy, Adam, Paul and Sarah Eller. Jim and Betty have six step great-grandchildren from them. They are Brianna, Ashley, Alex, Gail, Tyler and Camry Eller.

Deronda Givens married Tony Freeman (son of Wayne and Jane Freeman) on Jan. 17, 1985 and later had one daughter Ashley Nicole Freeman Aug. 3, 1985. Unfortunately Ashley died at birth. This devastated their new family. Deronda later married Fred Thomas Givens Jr. (son of Fred and Judy Givens) on Oct. 17, 1987. They had two children, Heather Lee Givens (b. March 3, 1989) and Jenna Marie Givens (b. Aug. 19, 1994). Fred, Deronda and the girls lived at Center Ridge and operated the dairy farm for sev-

eral years, then moved to Morrilton and now reside at Plumerville.

Randall Harold Dixon married Lynice Sharp (daughter of Gordan and Lori Sharp) on May 5, 1989. They had two daughters, Krysten Lynice Dixon (b. Nov. 15, 1989) and Stefanie Janelle Dixon (b. July 1, 1991). Lynice later married Dale Martin and had three boys named Dustin, Dillon and Jordan Martin.

The children were a big part of the family farm. We all worked hard together at all aspects of the dairy business, milking, hay making, and lots of gardening. We enjoyed many years of work and play together until 1992 when Randall was diagnosed with cancer. He went through 18 months of treatments and a lot of sick days before the cancer took him on Jan. 10, 1994. We miss him so much. We seemed to be just getting ourselves pulled back together when Gail died in a fatal automobile accident on Sept. 12, 1997. This left us all in total shock. We still miss them both very much but are so thankful for all the closeness we were blessed with when we were all together. We are very thankful for all the children they both left to carry on their legacy. We have, through God's love and our faith and great friends and family, went on with our everyday lives.

The summer of 1999 Mitch (Gail's oldest son) came to help on the family farm and did not return home in the fall. He decided that he was needed by his grandparents on the farm due to their health. Jim and Betty finally decided to sell the dairy business in 2003 and are now raising beef cows still in the Grandview area. *Submitted by Mitch Dixon.*

DIXON - John Quincy Dixon (b. Dec. 15, 1877 at Center Ridge, Conway County, AR), son of John G. Dixon and Mary Spence Dixon. He was a farmer and a lifelong resident of Conway County with the exception of a few years they lived in England, AR in the late 1920s. He died Feb. 11, 1959 and is buried at Grandview Cemetery, Conway County.

On July 9, 1899, in Conway County he married Eva Darcus Stracener, daughter of Henry Jordan Stracener and Mary (Sarah) Elizabeth Kirtley. Eva's mother gave permission for her daughter to marry. Eva (b. March 25, 1885 in either Faulkner or Conway County, d. Aug. 19, 1948 in Morrilton) is buried at Grandview Cemetery. After Eva died, Buster married Beulah Virginia Greer.

John Quincy "Buster" Dixon and wife Eva Darcus Stracener.

Buster and Eva had 10 children, four of whom died young.

1) Arlie Edwin (b. Dec. 8, 1902, d. Nov. 27, 1963) md. Lavada Hill in 1920. Their children were Leonard Edward (b. Feb. 18, 1921, d. Dec. 9, 2002); Vondon Walter (b, Aug. 13, 1923); Lymon Jardine (b. Feb. 29, 1925, d. Nov. 7, 1991); and a baby boy (b&d. April 4, 1934).

2) James Orville Dixon (b. Oct. 17, 1906, d. Jan. 10, 1922, buried at Grandview Cemetery). The family says he had a pain in his head for about a week before he died. He would probably have survived with today's medical knowledge.

3) Jewel E. Dixon (b. May 17, 1909, d. May 2, 1990). She died while living with a son in South Carolina and is buried at New Hamburg, MO. She married in 1927 to Connie Bennett and their children were

William E. "Bill" (b. Dec. 22, 1928, d. July 20, 1999), Charles Bennett, Harold Mendel and Richard Wayne "Curly" (b. Jan 20, 1943, d. Dec. 19, 1967).

4) Edgar Dixon (b. June 17, 1912, d. July 1, 1931 at England, AR) drowned not long before he was to be married.

5) Olen Quitman Dixon (b. Sept. 22, 1914, d. Sept. 28, 1961 of a gunshot wound) md. Martha Marie Polk on Nov. 3, 1934 in Matthews, MO. They had seven children: Betty Sue Dixon (b&d. July 22, 1935), Vivian Lue, Eula Jean, Edward Earl, Jimmy Harold, Olen Ray and Roddy Lynn.

6) L.M. Dixon (b. June 25, 1917, d. Sept. 24, 1917). No one can tell me what his "name" was or if he had any other than initials.

7) Luther Otis "Luke" Dixon (b. March 10, 1919, d. Sept. 15, 1984 in Rolla, MO) md. first, Maxine Morphis and their children were Dewey L., John M., Mary Betty, James Luther and Willie Earl (b. Feb. 20, 1944, d. Feb. 16, 1947). He married second, Dorothy Wilson.

8) William Curtis Dixon (b. July 19, 1922, d. Dec. 30, 1999 at Conway, AR) md. Ruby Marvell Little on Aug. 1, 1942. They had six sons: John C., James Donald, William Curtis Jr., Steven Owen, Billy Joe and Lloyd Clay.

9) Elbert Doyle Dixon (b. May 24, 1925, d. Jan. 22, 1926).

10) Euna Faye Dixon md. Garland Jackson on Dec. 24, 1946. Their two sons are Gary and Larry. *Submitted by Curtis Dixon Jr.*

DIXON - Olen Quitman Dixon (b. Sept. 22, 1914 near Center Ridge in Conway County, AR) was one of 10 children of John Quincy "Buster" Dixon and Eva Stracener. He had blond hair and blue eyes, and was medium height and build. He was very outgoing and never met a stranger. He played on a baseball team in the Grandview Community. He was married in Matthews, MO on Nov. 3, 1934 to Martha Marie Polk (b. Sept. 27, 1917). They had seven children.

Olen and Marie Dixon

When they first married they lived in the "weaning house." This was a very small house near his parents, that was built with the sole purpose being for newlywed children. Several of Buster and Eva's children used the "weaning house." It was across the field from the family, near enough to be helped out by the parents yet far enough to have privacy. Olen lived and raised his family near the Middleton Community in Conway County. He was a farmer and construction worker in road building. The family milked 30 plus cows by hand and sold milk daily. They had fields of corn, cotton, peas and cucumbers, which were picked by the family and sold for a living. They worked very hard but enjoyed good times together fishing. They were one of the first families around to have a TV and also a truck. Olen was a Good Samaritan of the community. He drove everyone to the doctor when needed. They seem to always have visitors at their home.

His life was tragically taken on Sept. 28, 1961 while working at Danville, AR for Freshour Construction. He was shot and killed by a fellow worker. He is buried at Grandview Cemetery near Center Ridge. Shortly afterward the farm was sold. Marie moved to Morrilton and stayed until she moved back to Center Ridge.

Their children are as follows:
Vivian (b. July 22, 1935) md. William "Mickey" Williams on Sept. 9, 1953. They were married 35 years until Mickey's death. They had four children: Helen (md. Gary Sams), James (md. Gwen Wooten), Thomas "T" (b. Sept. 22, 1958, d. Nov. 6, 2001) md. Karen

Rankin; and Rowdy (married Jamie Cidlik). Vivian lives in Morrilton. Vivian's twin, Betty Sue (b&d. July 22, 1935) is buried at Grandview Cemetery.

E. Jean (b. Nov. 17, 1937) has lived and worked in Washington DC and Ashland OH. She married first, Jimmy Reef and they had four children: Kimberly (md. Kurt Krueger), Mike (md. Carol Burke), Jamie (md. Amy Rohr), and Joe. She married second, Phil Miller and they live in Ohio.

Edward E. (b. April 22, 1940) md. Delores Kirtley on May 21, 1960. They had four children: Brenda (md. Franklin Benson); Regina "Gena" (md. Lynn Mallett); Bill (md. Samantha Russell); and Donna Kay (md. Tommy Hill). Ed lives in the Center Ridge area.

Jimmy H. "Jim" (b. Aug. 26, 1942) md. Betty Marie Chism on April 28, 1961. They had three children: Betty "Gail" (b. Oct. 9, 1962, d. Sept. 13, 1997) md. first Leslie Dixon, then Don Eller); Deronda Lee (md. Fred Givens Jr.); Randall (b. March 7, 1970, d. Jan. 10, 1994) md. Lynice Sharp). Jim and Betty live near Center Ridge.

Olen "Ray" (b. Dec. 19, 1944) md. Helen Bryant on Dec. 21, 1963. They have three children: Tammy (md. Steve Lucas), Tim (md. Dona Pickard), and Amy (md. Eddie Terhune). Ray and Helen live in Cabot, AR.

Rod (b. Jan. 14, 1952) md. Patsy Stacks June 6, 1970. They had three children: Bobby (md. Nancy Payne), Shelly (md. Greg Andrews), and Kelly. Rod and Patsy live at Center Ridge. *Submitted by Jim Dixon.*

DIXON - William Curtis "Curt" Dixon Sr. (b. July 19, 1922) was the eighth child born to John Q. "Buster" Dixon and Eva Stracener. He worked for a construction company, then went into business for himself. He was self-employed at Dixon Water Conditioning Company until his retirement in 1973. He married Ruby Marvell Little (b. Dec. 16, 1926) on Aug. 1, 1942 and they had six sons.

William and Ruby Dixon family.

They both enjoyed raising a garden and going fishing for Crappie. "Nanny" was a very special grandmother and "Papa Curt" enjoyed spending time with the grandchildren. They were lifelong residents of Conway County. Curt (d. Dec. 30, 1999) and Ruby (d. Sept. 23, 1994) are buried at Grandview Cemetery. Their children are:

1) John Claud Dixon (b. Oct. 12, 1944) md. Brenda J. White (b. Oct. 19, 1950) on Aug. 25, 1973. There are three children: Rebecca "Becky" (Dixon) Bullard (b. Dec. 30, 1962), John David Dixon (b. Aug. 30, 1965), and Tanya Marie (Dixon) Teague (b. Aug. 30, 1965). John and Brenda have seven grandchildren: Travis Wesley Bullard (b. Aug. 12, 1985), Arthur William Bullard (b. Oct. 15, 1990), John Aaron Bullard (b. July 10, 1992), Raymond Lee Bullard (b. July 18, 1995), Laina L. Teague (b. Dec. 9, 1986), Kevin W. Teague (b. April 2, 1990) and Kyle Everett Dixon (b. Feb. 28, 1995).

2) James Donald Dixon (b. Aug. 10, 1946) md. Karen June Dixon (b. June 18, 1950) on Aug. 15, 1969. There are two children, Donna Kay (Dixon) West (b. Aug. 19, 1971) and Jennifer Gail Dixon (b. June 16, 1976). Don and Karen have two grandchildren, Kaylynn Michelle Wood (b. Sept. 7, 1992) and Calihan C. West (b. June 24, 1997).

3) William Curtis "Bug" Dixon Jr. (b. June 15, 1949) md. Brenda Henderson Ayers (b. Nov. 2, 1960) on April 12, 2002. There are three children: Brian Curtis Dixon (b. April 7, 1969), Kimberly Dawn Dixon (b. Dec. 18, 1973, d. Sept. 10, 1983) and Shawna Lachelle Dixon (b. Feb. 3, 1987). Bug and Brenda have two grandchildren, Shelby Faith (b. April 16, 1999) and Gracie Dawn (b. Oct. 10, 2003).

4) Steven Owen Dixon (b. July 29, 1953) md. Donna Townsend on Sept. 19, 2004. There are two children, Tina Marie (Dixon) Beard (b. Dec. 27, 1980) and Rusty Owen Dixon (b. Aug. 5, 1983). Steve and Donna have one grandchild, Bailey Nicole Beard (b. May 21, 2001).

5) Billy Joe Dixon (b. Sept. 17, 1954) md. Mary E. Pettingill (b. Nov. 29, 1955) on July 5, 1974. There are two children, David Lynn Bolin (b. Feb. 11, 1973) and Billy Wayne Dixon (b. Oct. 29, 1974). Billy Joe and Mary have two grandchildren, Hunter Lynn Bolin (b. Dec. 13, 2003) and Alyssia Ruell Dixon (b. April 15, 2003).

6) Lloyd Clay Dixon (b. Feb. 28, 1965) md. Seavia Ellen Bohannon (b. Sept. 8, 1966) on Dec. 3, 2002. There is one child, Jade R. Dixon (b. Jan. 23, 1990). *Submitted by Mary E. Pettingill Dixon.*

DOCKINS - James Richard and Sarah Elizabeth Rucker married April 20, 1857 in White County, AR. James Richard (b. March 1827 in Tennessee, d. April 17, 1914) served in the Civil War, Co. A, 36th Arkansas Infantry, 1862-63, White County, AR. Sarah (b. May 22, 1833 in Tennessee, d. 1921) was the daughter of Taylor Rucker, mother is unknown. They are buried in Woolverton Mountain Cemetery.

James Richard and Sarah Elizabeth Rucker Dockins.

Making their home between Van Buren and Conway Counties they eventually settled in Conway County. Their children were:

1) L.E. "Beth" (b. 1850, d. 1939) md. John H. Rainey (b. 1846, d. 1930) on May 27, 1877. They had no children. They are buried in Woolverton Mt. Cemetery.

2) Margaret J. "Meg" (b. March 11, 1866, d. Feb. 29, 1956) md. Thomas Mayall (b. March 7, 1864, d. Jan. 2, 1934) on July 12, 1855. They are buried in Woolverton Mt. Cemetery. Their children are Elmer and Leona.

3) James Robert (b. Jan. 16, 1869, d. July 27, 1952) md. Sarah Elizabeth Prince Polk (b. Jan. 23, 1870, d. Dec. 30, 1960) on Jan. 20, 1889. They are buried in Center Ridge Cemetery. Their children are Loretta "Rettie," Nettie Mae, Cyretha Ann, Lillard Catherine and Vernon Dow.

4) Susan Mattie (b. June 20, 1875, d. Nov. 30, 1940) md. Samuel Alexander Smith (b. Oct. 17, 1865, d. Dec. 24, 1938) on Nov. 29, 1894. They are buried in Center Ridge Cemetery. Their children are Laudis, Lora and Orvell. *Submitted by Kevin L. Ruff.*

DOCKINS - James Robert (b. Jan. 16, 1869 in Center Ridge, AR, d. July 27, 1952) was the son of James Richard and Sarah Elizabeth Rucker Dockins. On Jan. 20, 1889 he married Sarah Elizabeth Prince Polk, daughter of William Jasper and Martha Elizabeth Owens Prince. She was born Jan. 30, 1870 in Center Ridge, AR and died Dec. 30, 1960. Her first husband was William Thomas Polk (b. 1866, d. Dec. 26, 1888).

This was about one month after their son, Jasper Allen, was born.

James Robert "J.R." and Sarah Elizabeth Prince Polk Dockins

Jasper Allen Polk (b. Nov. 29, 1888, d, April 5, 1928) md. Linner Ethel Mahan (b. April 13, 1893, d. Sept. 26, 1928) on Oct. 6, 1908. Their children are Laudis Thelbert, William Jesse, Glyn Wood, Ardith Taylor and Doris Bratton. Sarah then married J.R. and had five children of their own, raising all six of the children in Center Ridge. Their children were:

1) Loretta "Rettie" (b. Dec. 24, 1889, d. July 20, 1914) md. Lowell Mahan on Nov. 18, 1910. They had one child Opal (b. Sept. 30, 1911, d. Aug. 29, 1996) md. Delmas V. Bradley (b. March 14, 1907, d. July 8, 1966) on Sept. 28, 1928. They had one child, Loretta (b. Oct. 15, 1936, d. Oct. 17, 1983).

2) Nettie Mae (b. Dec. 24, 1894, d. Aug. 27, 1982) md. John Carl Hawkins (b. Jan. 29, 1891, d. July 9, 1931) on Jan. 20, 1910. Their children were Leona Inez (b. Aug. 27, 1910, d. Dec. 8, 1910); Clemmie Helen (b. Sept. 18, 1911, d. Sept. 22, 1991); Marlin Conover (b. April 22, 1913, d. Sept. 16, 1996); James Hugh "Jimmy" (b. Jan. 28, 1915, d. Aug. 13, 1993); Estes Ray (b. Jan. 29, 1921, d. April 25, 1959); Glenna Cathelene (b. Sept. 19, 1926); and J.C. (b. Jan. 8, 1929, d. Sept. 23, 1982).

3) Cyretha Ann (b. September 1897, died in California) md. Fred Prince (b. July 12, 1899, d. March 17, 1937), son of William and Rosie Hammonds Prince. They had one child, Robert Hervey.

4) Lillard Catherine (b. Nov. 28, 1904, d. June 24, 1991) md. Olen F. Maxey (b. April 4, 1904, d. Aug. 12, 1977) on Aug. 29, 1919. Their children are Lorene, Marie, Jerald, Bobby John.

5) Vernon Dow (b. July 31, 1907, d. Aug. 22, 1977, in California) md. Reba Hazel Brinkley on Oct. 30, 1925. Their children are Reba Dow, Bob George, Mary Helen, Carby Richard, Sara Ann, Ray and Larry Wayne.

To all of us James Robert and Sarah Elizabeth were always known as PaBob and MaSarah Dockins. He was a blacksmith in Center Ridge. My grandmother told me stories of how when she was a child, she would sit and watch him as he was working in his shop. She talked about all the things he worked with and worked on. The one thing that will always stand out in my mind is the way she described his very large calloused hands, and how they seemed to masterfully move somehow gently about his work, making sure the smallest of details were done in such precise and proper order.

PaBob's blacksmith shop was located where Meador's Paint and Body Shop is now in Center Ridge. MaSarah had hens that she kept for laying the eggs she and PaBob used. She had names for each one of them (they were her pets). She was well known for the aroma of her oversized yet delectable biscuits. MaSarah kept her yard full of hollyhocks and larkspurs and numerous other flowers and bushes. She loved to garden. She and PaBob both were full of humor and laughter.

They lived to have a long and happy life of 63 years together. *Submitted by Gary L. Hawkins.*

DOLD - Louise is the granddaughter of Frank and Albertine Gottsponer Zimmerman, who came to America from Switzerland, as children with their parents in 1883. They were married at St. Vincent in 1892 and were the parents of 14 children: Emil, Ida, Albert, Otto, Hattie, Clara, Ben, Herman, Cecilia, Paul, Joseph, Ernest, Marie and Louis.

Herman married Ann Hamling of St. Vincent and they were the parents of Herman, Frances, Louise,

Frank, Mary Ann (who died at age 9), Loretta and Wilma.

Hubert Dold is the grandson of Engelbert Dold, who came from Germany when he was 18 years old. Engelbert married Anna Florian of Conway and they were the parents of Joseph, George, Walter, Elizabeth, Bertha, Marie, Theresa, Margaret and Albert. Joseph married Theresa Miller of Bigelow and they had one son, Hubert.

Hubert and Louise Dold Family – 1968. Front row: Annise, William, Anthony. Second row: Raymond, Louise, Janet, Hubert. Third row: Richard, Mary, Julie, Susie, Gerald.

Hubert Dold married Louise Zimmerman on Oct. 19, 1949 at Sacred Heart Catholic Church in Morrilton. Hubert and Louise lived in Little Rock when they were first married. In December 1949 they returned to Oppelo and lived with Anna Dold on the old Dold Homestead, which they purchased in 1953. Their children are Julie Dold Palmer, Susie Dold Mooney, Gerald Dold, Mary Dold Wofford, Richard Dold, Janet Dold Huett Ogle, Denise Clara Dold (died at birth), Raymond Dold, William Dold (died at age 21), Annise Dold Ryan and Anthony Dold.

Seven of their children have stayed in Conway County. Raymond moved to North Carolina and Gerald lived in Conway County and worked at Arkansas Kraft paper mill for several years. He now lives in Zachary, LA.

Their children and grandchildren have built homes near the homestead where Hubert and Louise still live, located on what is now known as Dold Road.

DONALDSON – Frances Grabher Donaldson was born at St. Anthony's Hospital, Morrilton, Conway County, AR on Dec. 3, 1933, the second daughter of John Fred Grabber (b. 1901, d. 1987) and Anna Marie Nutt (b. 1904, d. 1933).

Her early education was at St. Elizabeth School, a two-room structure where Mercy Nuns taught first through eighth grades. The school was located at Oppelo, AR. Frances graduated from Sacred Heart High School, Morrilton, AR in 1952 These school years

Donaldson Family– Stephanie, Frances, Ben and Greg (standing), 1985.

were a time of many fond memories and friendships that have lasted a life time. Growing up on a farm Frances recalls a time when she, her sister Rita and friends Berniece and Regina Zimmerman dug sweet potatoes for an entire week. As a reward her dad treated the four girls to their first movie in Morrilton, a film starring Bob Hope and Dorothy Lamour.

She attended Saint Vincent School of Nursing in Little Rock, AR receiving a R.N. Diploma in 1955 then worked in surgery at U.A.M.S, for seven years. Frances joined the Air Force Nurse Corps in 1962, receiving her commission as first lieutenant. While stationed at Greenville AFB, MS, she married Benjamin Marion Donaldson, a career officer, on June 29, 1963 in the base chapel.

Ben (b. Oct. 4, 1937 in Pine Bluff, Jefferson County, AR) is the son of Olen Walton Donaldson (b. 1914, d. 1967) and Helen Dixon Donaldson Kraft (b. 1917-). Ben graduated from Pine Bluff High School then attended Henderson State Teachers College in Arkadelphia, AR, graduating in 1958 with a BS in education. Frances and Ben are parents of two children:

1) Gregory Keith Donaldson (b. March 15, 1966 at Sheppard AFB Hospital, Wichita Falls, TX) md. Christine Alison Boone on Aug. 3, 1990 at Christ the King Catholic Church, Little Rock, Pulaski County, AR. Their sons are Warren Chandler Donaldson (b. March 3, 1996 in Chesterfield, MO) and Adam Garrett Donaldson (b. Feb. 11, 2004 in Little Rock, AR).

2) Stephanie Lynne Donaldson (b. Dec. 28, 1968 in Enid, OK) md. Jeffrey Lee Fox on May 28, 1994 in Trinity Episcopal Cathedral, Little Rock, AR. Their sons are Johnathon Jerry Fox (b. March 4, 1998 in Clarksdale, MS) and Andrew Freeman Fox (b. Dec. 1, 2000 in Decatur, IL).

Ben's military tours were in Mississippi, Texas, Oklahoma, Florida, Hawaii and overseas assignment to Philippines, Okinawa, Korea and Vietnam. Following Ben's retirement from the Air Force, the Donaldson's moved to Little Rock, where Ben served as senior counselor for St. Francis House. Frances continued her nursing career in surgery at Doctor's Hospital. Following their second retirement, Ben and Frances moved to the John Grabher homestead in Oppelo in 1997, later building their present home nearby on Arena Road. *Submitted by Stephanie Donaldson.*

DOOLEY - Will Jones was married to Martha Luella Dooley in 1924. He was born on March 21, 1908 to Daniel and Ella Smith Jones in Damascus; AR. Martha Luella Dooley was born to Will and Elizabeth Dooley on July 24, 1903 in Center Ridge, AR. He died Jan. 4, 1991 and she died Dec. 24, 1964.

He was the third generation of Reddick Jones Sr. and Mary Jones who came from Nashville, TN and settled in Damascus, AR in 1874. He was the fourth of 11 children: Augusta, Jessie, Annie, Cozetta, Tommy, John, Pearl, Vearlie Mary, Genettie.

Martha was the third generation of Elbert Dooley and Ella Morris Dooley, who came from Georgia in 1899. Her maternal grandparents were Louis Kemp and Martha Knox Kemp, who also came from Georgia and settled in the Morris Mountain Community near Center Ridge, AR. Morris Mountain was later named the Friendship Community. Martha was the oldest of seven

Rev. W.C. Jones, Martha Jones, Willy Jones, daughter.

children: Holcy, Georgia, Mary, Velva, Orlean and Effie Mae.

Will and Martha were the parents of 10 children: Gequitter, Alicesten, Willie Jean, Daniel, Melanese, Johnny, Isaac, Miley, two died at a very young age. Will was a farmer, carpenter, and a Minister of the Gospel. He was a very industrious man; he built homes all around Conway County and the surrounding counties. He pastored Mt. Olive MBC at Mt. Vernon, Sweet Home MBC at Center Ridge, Pilgrim MBC, Solgohachia; Mt. View MBC at Clinton. He served as District Missionary, Dean of the Congress, and President of Institute, Vice-Moderator and Moderator of the Cypress Creek District. He was active in State and National Conventions. His life was dedicated to his family, helping others and magnifying Christ.

Martha Dooley Jones was a homemaker and mother. She was dedicated to her family and her church. She served as secretary to Cypress Creek District Women's Association, president of the Women's

Missionary Society of the Friendship Baptist Church, where she held membership all her life and was a diligent worker in the church and community. *Submitted by Willie J. Heaggans.*

EDDY - Garland and Clara Marie Eddy were citizens of Morrilton throughout their 65 plus years of marriage. He was born May 4, 1912 in Blackwell to Dr. John D. and Annie Louise Shoptaw Eddy. Dr. Eddy arrived in Conway County in 1898 and lived at Blackwell, Jerusalem and Morrilton. Living in Morrilton her entire life, Clara Marie was born Dec. 23, 1914 to Wiley and Ollie Charton Brown. Her great-great-grandparents, Thomas and Viola Aldridge, were landowners in the county in 1847, having moved from Indiana the prior year. Their daughter, Susan Helen, married a prominent Virginia farmer, John Miller, in 1858. Their eldest child, Eliza Louella, was the mother of four children (and twice a widow) when she married Henry Charton. Ollie was their first child.

Garland and Clara Marie were the parents of Edward Lee, Mary Ann and Louise. They worked hard in church, business and community. He served as an elder at the Downtown Church of Christ; owned Arkansas Valley Wholesale Grocery Co.; was Fire Chief (assistant chief and fireman) on the Morrilton Fire Dept.; served in many capacities on the County Fair Board and Kiwanis Club and the Morrilton Summer Baseball Program; and was City Water and Sewer Commissioner.

Perhaps this quote from the *Morrilton Headlight*, January 1946, paints the best picture of the team of Garland and Clara Marie Eddy:

"Becoming partners in a business where 14 years before he began work as a general utility man at one dollar a day, is the record of Garland "Buster" Eddy, who effective January 1st, purchased a half interest in the Arkansas Valley Grocery Company, North Moose Street, from W.W. Ketcheside of Conway.

Following his entrance into the grocery business, Mr. Eddy advanced from truck driver where he resigned to accept the agency for Colonial Bread Products in the Morrilton territory. By close application to details Mr. Eddy developed the wholesale bread business in this area. He continued a program of saving a portion of his income each month, started when he went to work for Arkansas Valley in 1932, so when the opportunity came for him to purchase an interest in the wholesale grocer, he had sufficient cash to handle the transaction."

He enjoyed hunting and fishing, was a member of The Fish Lake Club, and loved Arkansas' beautiful lands, rivers, and lakes.

She was always involved in her children's activities, judged county fair clothing entries, enjoyed family history, worked intricate jigsaw puzzles, and was widely known as a good cook.

They loved their children and set examples of honesty and hard work before them. They built and left a good name for their descendants. Edward Lee, his wife DeLois and grandsons, Kent and Phil Eddy, still live in the area. Mary Ann Brown lives in Searcy and has two sons and three grandchildren. Louise lives in Houston, TX.

Mr. Eddy died Sept. 30, 1997 and Mrs. Eddy died April 20, 2000. They are buried in Elmwood Cemetery.

EDWARDS - Shirley Marie Edwards, daughter of Willie Belle Crye and Arlon Dewey Edwards, was born prematurely at home Feb. 14, 1935. Her parents had a son a year before she was born, but he only lived eight weeks and they wanted a child so much. At the time of her birth she was weighed on cotton scales and with her clothes on and wrapped in a blanket they showed only two pounds. Her parents took wonderful care of her.

Shirley Marie Edwards and Robert Warren Brown

At the age of 17 Shirley met Robert Warren Brown (b. Aug. 13, 1928 in Argon, GA), son of Doyle and Ethel Brown. Always calling Robert "Bob," they were married Aug. 1, 1952. From the first time she met Bob she felt like he was the most handsome man and loved him from then on. He was a US Air Force career man and retired after 20 years with the Air Force. To them were born two children:

1) Terry Lee Brown (b. May 4, 1953, d. Aug. 8, 2002) md. Elizabeth Carol Boyer.

2) Arlene Marie Brown (b. July 18, 1954) md. Bobby Wayne Price.

Both children were born in Biloxi, MS and what was good - the same doctor delivered both of them - which is luck because, as most know, on base you hardly ever saw the same doctor twice.

Shirley worked at several jobs before deciding on what she wanted to do. First she worked in Tulsa, OK as a nurse's aide for six years at St. John's Hospital. Then they moved back to Springfield, AR, and she started work at the old St. Anthony's Hospital on the hill as a nurse's aide. That was in November 1963. She loved it and at that time decided to go to school at Petit Jean Votech. In 1965 she became a LPN. She had a wonderful teacher, Mrs. Elizabeth Talley, RN. Nursing has changed much throughout the years, but it is a wonderful profession and she truly cared for all she encountered. Shirley retired in December 2000.

All her family were very supportive throughout the years, and she loves them all so much.

EDWARDS - William "Bill" Edwards married Norma Lizzie Williams. Their children were:

1) Andrew Jackson Edwards (b. July 4, 1884, d. May 9, 1952) md. Emily Isabelle "Belle" Gilbert Powell (b. Dec. 25, 1881, d. April 28, 1958), daughter of Sir Thomas Gilbert and Martha Gilbert. They came to the US from Salisbury, England. Andrew and Belle were married Sept. 30, 1902 and were long-term residents of Center Ridge, AR.

Andrew and Belle Crye Edwards

Ma Belle Edwards was first married to a man with the last name of Powell. They had a son named Arlie Powell (b. March 28, 1900) who married Sally. They had one son Ray who married Meriden and they had four children.

Arlie's father died, then Belle married Andrew Edwards. Their children were:

(A) Esther Lavester Edwards (b. June 21, 1903, d. Dec. 29, 1973) md. Alex Brandley. Their son Wilburn married Elenore and had three children.

(B) Effie Edwards (b. Sept. 30, 1904) md. Robert Russell. Their son Orvid Farrell Edwards (b. June 28, 1931, d. Sept. 13, 2000) md. Doris Marie Harrell (b. Aug. 15, 1935) on May 16, 1953. Their children were:

(i) Karen Sue Edwards (b. April 28, 1955) md. July 3, 1975 to Tommy Allan Kiser (b. June 24, 1950).

Their children are Terisa Jo (b. Jan. 20, 1977) and Crystal Rae (b. Nov. 11, 1980).

(ii) Virgina "Jenny" Ann Edwards (b. Nov. 13, 1957) md. Brady Claude Goen (b. Dec. 4, 1955). Their children are Brandon Claude Goen (b. Sept. 5, 1976) md. June 28, 1996 to Amy Cody (b. Aug. 15, 1976) and their children are Brittney Glenn Goen (b. Feb. 20, 1997) and Byron Claude Goen (b. June 22, 2001). Jashua Neal Goen (b. May 11, 1979) md. Bethany Odam (b. May 22, 1978) and their child is Travis Jessie Goen (b. July 20, 1984).

(iii) Janet Marie Edwards (b. Jan. 23, 1961) md. Dec. 26, 1977 to Festus Asbury Watson III (b. Oct. 21, 1952). Their children are (1) Heather Dawn Watson (b. May 11, 1978) md. Dec. 23, 1994 to Shanan Dale Lytle and their children are McKinzy Michelle Lytle (b. June 15, 1995) and Sky Ashley Lytle (b. July 19, 1997). (2) Festus "Bear" Asbury Watson IV (b. Feb. 15, 1981).

(iv) Brenda Gail Edwards (b. April 19, 1965) md. Jan. 16, 1988 to Alvin Garner Stamps (b. July 10, 1960). Their children are Hannah Marie Stamps (b. March 4, 1996) and Aaron Garner Stamps (b. March 4, 1996).

(v) Darrell Lynn Edwards (b. Dec. 16, 1971) md. June 3, 1990 to Robin Antionette Denny (b. Dec. 30, 1971). Their child is Chelsea Renee Edwards (b. March 18, 1997).

(C) Arlon Dewey Edwards (b. Jan. 16, 1908, d. Oct. 11, 1980) md. Willie Belle Crye on Dec. 14, 1929. Their children were A.D. Edwards Jr. (b. Feb. 8, 1934, lived only eight weeks) and Shirley Marie Edwards (b. Feb. 14, 1935) who married Robert E. Brown (see her history).

(D) Vida Edwards (b. Nov. 25, 1913) md. Lawrance Jackson. Their children: Billy Dean Jackson (b. Dec. 30, 1932) md. Sept. 3, 1955 to Judy (b. Dec. 29, 1935) and their child is Beverly Gail Jackson Golden (b. Aug. 14, 1956); Susan Diane Jackson (b. May 23, 1958); Steven Andrew Jackson (b. March 9, 1962); Betty Sue Jackson (b. April 8, 1940) md. March 28, 1964 to Richard Van Valkenburg (b. May 17, 1935).

(E) Opal Edwards (b. Dec. 18, 1918) died at 2 years of age.

(F) James Admiral Edwards (b. Oct. 10, 1924).

2) Ruthie Edwards had three children.

3) Charles Edwards (b. March 6, 1878) md. first, Sara Lockhart, a teacher who taught in Oklahoma. They had three children: twin boys (b. Sept. 7, 1900), Otis and Owen who died in 1910; and Ezra Edwards (b. April 27, 1903). Charles married a second time to Mary (b. March 2, 1888) and they had the following children: Homer Edwards (b. Sept. 8, 1909); Pearline Edwards (b. May 19, 1912); Luther Edwards (b. March 6, 1914); Ruby Edwards (b. Nov. 4, 1916); Florene Edwards (b. Aug. 28, 1918); Evelean Edwards (b. Oct. 19, 1920); Columbus Edwards (b. Dec. 25, 192_) who is now a Baptist minister; Calvin Edwards (b. March 26, 1925); Suliver Edwards (b. Aug. 20, 1928); twins-Bennie and Glenn Edwards (b. June 27, 1931).

EGAN - Phillip Kearney Egan (b. July 2, 1875 at Lewisburg, AR), son of William Pitt and Kate Kearney Egan. He was a farmer of medium build, 5'7-1/2" tall, weighing 150-155 pounds with blue eyes and black hair. While attending the annual Conway County dance he met a beautiful dark-haired and brown-eyed girl named Camilla Roach. He courted her for a couple of years before they married on April 30, 1906.

They moved to a small house about 20 miles west of Little Rock along the Maumelle River. About a year later they moved to Ola, AR where they lived for a time before finally moving back to Morrilton. Phillip

K. Egan (d. Feb. 2, 1968 in Contra Costa County, CA) is buried in Elmwood Cemetery, Morrilton. The children born to Phillip and Camilla Egan were:

1) Kate Kearney Egan (b. March 1907 at Morrilton) was training to become a nurse but died July 6, 1929 of a ruptured appendix and is buried in Elmwood Cemetery.

2) Grace Egan (b. Feb. 9, 1919 at Morrilton) md. Thomas Wilkinson on June 26, 1933. She finished nursing school in Pittsburgh, PA. For many years she lived in Gibsonia, PA in an early 19th century farmhouse she and her husband restored and furnished with antiques. He died Oct. 9, 1968 and she died June 14, 1990 in Gibsonia, PA. They had two sons, Thomas Charles Wilkinson II and Phillip Robert Wilkinson.

3) James William Egan (b. Oct. 1, 1911 at Ola, Yell County, AR, d. Aug. 16, 1926). He died of an abrasion or insect bite on his face that developed into septicemia and was buried in Elmwood Cemetery at Morrilton.

4) Phillip Egan (b. Jan. 18, 1914 at Lewisburg, Conway County) md. Maxine Brant of North Little Rock and was a building superintendent and manager with the Arkansas Louisiana Gas Company. He served in the Army during WWII. He belonged to Gardner Memorial United Methodist Church in North Little Rock. Phillip and Maxine had one daughter, Jennie Linda Egan. He died Feb. 27, 1988 and was buried in Edgewood Cemetery in North Little Rock.

5) Mary Gladys Egan (b. Dec. 26, 1916 at Morrilton) was a registered nurse and served in the Army Nurses Corps during WWII. She belonged to the Methodist Church. She married first, Frank P. Hanna and they had one son, Frank P. Hanna IV. She married second, Mr. Johns. Mary Gladys died March 22, 1989 at Stone Mountain, Dekalb County, GA and is buried in Elmwood Cemetery at Morrilton.

6) Frank Walter Egan (b. 1918, d. 1924 of typhoid fever).

7) Dr. Robert Lee Egan (b. May 9, 1920 in Morrilton, d. Feb. 4, 2001). (See article Robert Lee Egan).

8) Marian Julia Egan (b. August 1922 in Morrilton) md. Robert Warren Meggelin on July 15, 1945 at Chicago, Cook County, IL. Robert served in the US Marine Corps in WWII. They had four daughters: Sandra Lee, Patricia Ann, Pamela Jean and Barbara Jo Meggelin. Robert Meggelin died July 3, 1988 of Alzheimer's disease and Marian Julia Egan died August 1992 at Pleasant Hill, Contra Costa County, CA. *Submitted by Lynda Suffridge.*

EGAN - Robert Lee Egan (b. May 9, 1920 at Morrilton, Conway County, AR), son of Phillip Kearney Egan and Camilla "Miller" Roach, and grandson of William Pitt Egan who first moved to Conway County in 1867. He was seventh of eight children in an Irish-American family ravaged by the Great Depression. A graduate of Morrilton High School, he was one of the few Eagle Scouts, Boy Scouts of America, in his home area and served in the armed forces during WWII and the Korean Conflict. Furthering his education, he became Robert L. Egan, M.D., a pioneer in the development of mammography.

He married Mary Alice Vetterly and they had five daughters: Kathleen Louise (b. 1954), Deborah Ann (b. 1956), Cheryl Lynn (b. 1959), Melissa Jean (b. 1961) and Patricia Lee Egan (b. 1963).

Over a career of 30 years, Dr. Egan wrote 14 books and more than 200 articles for medical journals. He developed the team approach in the diagnosis and treatment of breast cancer. He traveled world-wide to share this vital information with other physicians and to train them in the use of mammography in the early detection of breast cancer. He received the American Cancer Society Distinguished Service Award for the Physician of the Year presented in New York City on Nov. 5, 1975.

During the 14th annual Conference on Detection and Treatment of Early Breast Cancer, the American College of Radiology selected him as the third annual Wendell G. Scott Lecturer in San Juan, March 12, 1975, "In recognition of your pioneering and continuing scientific contribution to the detection of early breast cancer." The Lucy James Wortham Clinical Research Award given by the Society of Surgical Oncology was presented on May 6, 1977. In 1986, Dr. Egan was recognized as "The pioneer whose unique and monumental work has appropriately earned him the title of "The Father of Mammography" at the first Robert L. Egan Lecture Series of the annual Breast Imaging Conference. In 1992, the American College of Radiology presented him their highest honor, the Gold Medal, "for the greatest contribution to radiology ever made by an individual."

He enjoyed outside activities, woodworking and growing orchids. He lost his personal battle with cancer Feb. 4, 2001, at his home in Cumming, GA. He was preceded in death by his wife, Mary Alice. His five daughters: Kathy Egan, Debbie Egan, Cheryl Lane, Lisa Fyfe and Patty Harper and six grandchildren survive him. He is buried in Sewanee View Memorial Gardens in Cummings, GA. *Submitted by Lynda Suffridge.*

EGAN - The 1870 Conway County, AR Census indicates William Pitt Egan (b. 1833 in County Roscommon, Ireland) immigrated to America before 1851, as indicated by his signature in a book purchased in Covington, KY. According to family legend, he arrived in New Orleans where his parents and all but one brother died from yellow fever. He traveled north on the Mississippi River settling in Cincinnati, OH. He was employed from 1856-61 as a store clerk for G.W. Ball and Company, manufacturers of Stoves and Hollow Ware.

William Pitt Egan and Kate Kearney, wife of W.P. Egan.

With the outbreak of the Civil War, he enlisted as a private in Company "D," 2nd Regiment, Ohio Volunteer Infantry, mustering in at Camp Dennison, OH, April 17, 1861. Appointed Pioneer on June 20, 1861, and participated in the First Battle of Bull Run on July 21, 1861. Mustering out of the Army Aug. 9, 1861, he returned to Covington, KY, to organize Egan's Company which mustered in as Company "E," 23rd Regiment, Kentucky Volunteer Infantry, USA, Dec. 9, 1861, with Egan holding the rank of captain. He participated in the Battle of Stones River, Murfreesboro, TN, on Dec. 31, 1861, and Jan. 2, 1862.

In a strange turn of events, he was promoted to lieutenant colonel, then a few days later arrested and court-martialed for leaving his command during the battle. He was found guilty, but due to irregularities in the proceedings, was only cashiered from the army. He moved to Memphis, then in Federal hands, where he was a grocer and commissary merchant with John G. Wallace at 316 Front Street and a member of the Federal Militia, Department of Memphis. He was subsequently drafted for Federal Service, but the war ended prior to re-enlistment.

By November 1866, he had opened a mercantile store at Lewisburg, Conway County, AR. He returned to Warren County, OH, and on June 20, 1867, married another Irish immigrant, Kate Kearney (b. February 1842 in County Tipperary, Ireland), the daughter of Patrick Kearney and Sophia Apjohn, formerly of Pallas Green, County Limerick, Ireland. By the time of their

marriage, the Kearney family had moved from Cincinnati to Waynesville, Warren County, OH. The Kearney family immigrated to the United States, arriving Oct. 11, 1849, at New York City from Liverpool, aboard the *S.S. Cornelia*.

W.P. and Kate returned to Lewisburg where he was a planter and merchant until businesses moved to Morrilton when the railroad came through there instead of Lewisburg. He then served as Conway County Deputy Clerk for several years. The last years of his life he was a bookkeeper for the Stout Plantation. Nov. 26, 1890, he drowned at Stout's Landing above Lewisburg at the base of Petit Jean Mountain. His wife Kate died Feb. 12, 1907. Both are buried in Elmwood Cemetery at Morrilton. *Submitted by Lynda and Buford Joseph Suffridge Jr.*

ENDICOTT - John Endecott (b. 1588 in Dorchester, England) was first Governor of Massachusetts Bay Colony. He was a physician and surgeon in England. In 1628, John and five others were granted a patent for the "Governor and Company of Massachusetts Bay in New England." Before sailing to America, John married Anna Gouer. In June 1628, John and Anna set sail for America. They arrived at Naumkeag, MA, on Sept. 6, 1628. Anna died in 1629 in Salem leaving no children. John governed the Massachusetts Bay Colony until John Winthrop arrived in 1630.

John married Elizabeth (Cogan) Gibson in 1630. Elizabeth (b. 1607) was the daughter of Philobert Cogan and Ann Marshall. Elizabeth was a widow.

John served several terms as Governor of Massachusetts Bay Colony. He died March 15, 1665 and was buried in Granary Burying Ground at Boston. Elizabeth died Sept. 18, 1676 and was buried at Granary. John and Elizabeth had two children.

Zerubbabel Endecott (b. Feb. 14, 1635) was the younger of two sons born to John and Elizabeth. He married Mary Smith, daughter of Samuel Smith of Norfolk County, England. Zerubbabel was a physician and an ensign in the Salem Militia. Mary died in 1677 and Zerubbabel married Elizabeth (Winthrop) Newman, widow of Rev. Antipas Newman and daughter of Governor John Winthrop of Connecticut. Zerubbabel died March 27, 1684. Zerubbabel and Mary had 13 children.

Joseph Endecott (b. July 14, 1671 at Salem, MA), son of Zerubbabel and Mary. He moved to Northampton, NJ in 1698 and married Hannah Gosling. His will was probated May 1747 in Burlington County, NJ. Joseph and Hannah had at least five children.

Joseph Endecott Jr. (b. 1711 in Burlington County) was the son of Joseph and Hannah. He married Anne Gillam on May 12, 1736. Joseph was a farmer and died in 1748. Joseph and Anne had at least six children.

Joseph Endicott III (b. June 8, 1738) was the son of Joseph and Anne. He married prior to 1774 and moved to North Carolina. At least three children, a son and two daughters, were born to Joseph. The family migrated to Kentucky prior to 1797.

Joseph Endicott IV (b. 1775 in North Carolina) was the son of Joseph Endicott III. Joseph IV married Welmet Nation on Jan. 28, 1792 in Stokes County, NC. He moved his family to Kentucky prior to 1797. In 1807, he bought land in Nicholas County, KY and died there in 1833. Welmet moved to Indiana and died after 1855. Joseph and Welmet had 11 children.

Joseph Nation Endicott (b. Feb. 18, 1795 in North Carolina) was the son of Joseph and Welmet. He served in the War of 1812. He married Elizabeth Varner in 1815 in Kentucky. Elizabeth (b. 1797 in Kentucky) was the daughter of Jacob Varner and Sarah Ficklin. Joseph moved his family to Posey County, IN in 1820. He was a carpenter by trade and owned a sawmill. He later moved to Franklin County, IL. Elizabeth died 1870, in Franklin County and Joseph died there June 24, 1874. They had 14 children: John, James, George, William, Joseph, Arvis, Sarah, Emily, Charles, Samuel,

Elizabeth (b. 1834) md. Wilson Harmon, Welmet, America and Martin Endicott.

EOFF - On June 21, 1963, Mary Rebecca Harwood of Center Ridge became the bride of Freddie Earl Eoff of Plummerville. Becky was the daughter of G.L. and Edith Harwood, and Fred was the son of Grady and Hettie Eoff.

They met in Morrilton as the two were running around with their friends. A popular hangout, Hoover's Drive-In was the place to go and Becky worked there. They were introduced by Fred's cousin Jim *Fred and Becky Eoff* Campbell and girlfriend Virginia "Ginny" Watkins. The two couples married in 1963 within months of each other at Portland Missionary Baptist Church, and they served as witnesses for each other.

Fred and Becky lived in Little Rock in their early years of marriage, but they came home every weekend to spend time with friends and family. Becky worked for the University of Little Rock and Fred worked for Rockefeller as a surveyor. Later they moved home to Plumerville and both got jobs with Brooks and Curry Surveying in North Little Rock. Becky switched jobs and moved to the Coca-Cola Bottling Company in Morrilton. Their first child, Sharon Leigh (b. August 1967) md. James Wilson of Center Ridge on June 21, 1986. They have three children: Geoffrey, Juleighanna and Jacquelynn.

After working for years for others, Fred and Becky decided to change their lifestyles and go into the dairy business with Becky's brother and sister-in-law, Jeff and Brenda (McCoy) Harwood. In 1977, E & H Dairy was formed and work was started on a new milk barn on Jeff and Becky's family farm. Later Fred and Becky took over the operation when Jeff and Brenda built chicken houses. In 1978, Fred and Becky had a second child, a son Garrett Daniel. Garrett was born prematurely and weighed only 3 lb. and 4 oz. He overcame the size issue and followed the steps of the Eoff men, eventually becoming over 6 feet tall. Garrett plans to wed Katie Burns of Bono, AR in the summer of 2005.

The daily work of the dairy farm was a hard one. Days usually began around 4 am and sometimes ended at midnight. The Eoffs worked tirelessly at all aspects of farm life, from haying season to breeding and raising calves. Fred and Becky ran Eoff Dairy for 23 years before selling the land and retiring to Plumerville. Becky works part time for her brother, Jeff Harwood, at Center Ridge Grocery. They spend other free time chasing grandkids: Geoffrey, Juleigh and Jacque Wilson, and going to son Garrett's baseball games to watch him coach.

EOFF - Grady Daniel Eoff married Hettie Melvina Gordon on Dec. 18, 1926 in Morrilton, AR. They lived most of their lives in the Portland Bottoms in Plumerville. Hettie was the daughter of Laura Elizabeth Hill Gordon and William Robert Gordon. Grady was the son of Artie Elizabeth Campbell Eoff Davis and Irvin Eoff.

Hettie's siblings were Robert Edgar (b. April 18, 1900, d. May 8, 1978); Ora Jane "Sis" (b. Oct. 18, 1902, d. Oct. 7, 1977); Cora Ann Gordon Campbell (b. June 1, 1906, d. June 1, 1979); Ollie Elizabeth Gordon Brown (b. April 24, 1913, d. Feb. 6, 1992); and Alex Jefferson "Jack" Gordon (b. 1922). When Irvin died, Artie married William Jefferson Davis. Their children were Ora Eoff (b. 1898), Grady (b. 1926), Soloman, Ernest, Garland, Gyva and Leonard whose birthdates are unknown.

Hettie and Grady were the proud parents of William Hoover (b. Dec. 1, 1927, d. June 20, 1956); Erma

Lorene "Lee" (b. 1930); Betty Jo Bishop (b. 1932); twins-Freddie Earl and Edna Pearl (b. 1937, Pearl d. Aug. 8, 1986); Patton Arnold (b. May 21, 1942, d. Feb. 17, 2004); James Gordon (b. Sept. 17, 1943, d. Sept. 2, 1993); Grady Lynn (b. 1947); Carolyn Elizabeth (b. Sept. 12, 1949, d. Sept. 17, 1949); and Michael Wayne (b. 1953).

Hettie and Grady were farmers and enjoyed having friends and family over to visit. Their home was filled with laughter. Hettie loved to feed people especially her grandchildren. She is remembered for her chocolate gravy. She loved gardening, going to town, quilting and cooking. Helen Gordon, Jack's wife, spoke of Grady, "When we first married, we practically lived at Hettie and Grady's house. We played Rook and laughed all night. Your daddy always had a funny story ready. He was fun to be around and very good natured." They were charter members of Portland Missionary Baptist Church - the church "on the hill."

Grady (d. 1965) and Hettie (d. Aug. 17, 1985) are both missed greatly by their children and grandchildren.

EVANS - Augustus "Gus" and Minus. Gus and Minus are the two brothers that are responsible for the Evans families that settled in the Solgohachia area, Conway County, in the late 1800s. The area that they settled and farmed is located astride present day state highway 278, just south of Point Remove Creek and north of Solgohachia. These farms are further described as being in the Evans and Tucker Mountain area. In addition to Gus and Minus, there was a half brother, Charley, that settled in the same area but Charley had no children.

Gus and Minus are descendants of Reddick and Almyra Jane Evans and their grandparents were Thomas and Louisa Evans. There is a detailed record of this family in their movement from North Carolina to Tennessee and into Arkansas in a loose leaf book entitled *"The Descendants of Thomas and Louisa Evans"* by the descendants of Thomas and Louisa Evans, December 1992, reprinted in 1996 with minor revisions/additions. This book is no longer in print, but a donated copy is on file at the Conway County Library. Also, on file is an addendum to this book, giving a detailed record of Reddick's descendants and movement of his family from Tennessee to Arkansas.

Augustus "Gus" Evans (late 1920s).

Minus Evans (about 1900).

After Gus and Minus's father died in the 1889-90 timeframe and buried in Line Cemetery, Faulkner County, Gus, being the oldest of the siblings, becomes the family leader along with Almyra Jane, his mother. Also, at this time Gus takes on an additional responsibility by marrying Mary Savannah Fielder, Aug. 31, 1889. Mary is the daughter of Nick and Ann Fielder, the next door neighbors of the Evans family. Gus and Mary move their newly acquired family to the Solgohachia area in Conway County in the mid-1890s. Shortly after the move to Solgohachia, Minus marries Genara Jobe, Dec. 10, 1896. The two brothers are now family men. Except for Gus moving his family to Independence County in the late 1890s, where they lived for about four years before returning to the Solgohachia area, the two brothers farmed in close proximity to each other for about the next 25 years.

The following Arkansas census' for 1900, 1910 and 1920, show Minus's family for each of those years. The 1900 census shows that Minus inherited Genara Jobe's brother; Ona (8), and six sisters: Grettie (17), Gerlina? (16), Cynthia (12), Lona (10), and twins-Lovie and Dovie (2) along with a step sister's son, Guss Dodd (16). Also, the 1900 census shows that Minus and Genara had one son, Alvis (2).

The 1910 census shows the family of Minus and Genara being: Alvis (10), William Clarence (9) and Floyd A. (6).

The 1920 census has the following children for Minus and Genara: Alvis (22), William Clarence (19), Floyd A. (16), twins-Orvel and Arbie (7). It must be pointed out that Genara died in 1913, probably in child birth with the twins. Minus remarries Oct. 1, 1916 to widow Georgia Mayhue, which brings four Mayhue sons: Frank (16), Jasper (12), Aubrey (10), Reba (5) and one daughter Nona? (8) to the marriage. Georgia and Minus had one son, Elmo (2), which is shown in the 1920 census. Elmo is the last child for Minus and Georgia. Minus continues to farm in the Solgohachia area until his accidental death in 1933.

Minus's children marry the following spouses: Alvis to Etta Guess, Oct. 16, 1920; William Clarence to Carlena Bostian, April 25, 1920; Floyd A. to Julie Deaton, Feb. 21, 1925; Orvel Lee to Viny Rhodes, Oct. 12, 1931; Arbie to Arthur Hillis, Nov. 14, 1940; and Elmo to Eva Nell Minton, April 11, 1942.

We shift now to Gus's family development in the Arkansas 1900, 1910 and 1920 censuses. The 1900 census finds Gus with his family located in Liberty Township, Independence County with the following family members: Martha A. (9), Jennie N. (7), Claud (2), Gus's mother, Almyra J. (60) and three Dodd children: Alice (12), Charley (10) and Bryant (9). The three Dodd children belonged to Sarah, a daughter of Almyra's from a previous marriage.

In the 1910 census, Gus is back in the Solgohachia area with the following family members listed: Martha (19), Jennie (17), Claude (12), Elisha (8), Maye (6), William W. (3), Jane, mother (74) and a sister Harriet (28) a widow with one child, Cory (1).

The 1920 census lists Gus's family as Lish (18), May (16), Willie (13) and Clara (9). Almyra Jane, Gus and Minus's mother, dies between 1911-14 and is buried in the Friendship Cemetery near Solgohachia. Harriet, their sister, marries an Ellis Dorrell in 1911 and they have three children: Loey, Odis Reddick and Lester, plus Harriet's daughter Cory by a previous marriage. Gus continues to farm in the Solgohachia area until the depression of 1930s forces him to give up his farm. After giving up his farm, he moves to Lonoke County to be near his children that moved there in the 1920s and 30s. Gus's children married the following individuals: Martha to William "Bud" Loyd, Dec. 13, 1913; Jennie to Earnest Krissell, Dec. 3, 1911; Claude to Anna Skipper, April 20, 1917; Elisha to Anna Bostian, Dec. 10, 1921; Maye to Arthur Skipper, July 28, 1923; William "Bill" to Wilma Sanders, Aug. 8, 1929; Clara to Avery Davis, July 13, 1931.

During the 1920s and 1930s most of Gus and Minus's children moved from the Solgohachia area to the four winds. Most moved to the Arkansas delta area

Minus Evans sons about 1941: back row l-r: Alvis, Clarence, Floyd. Bottom (kneeling): Orvel, Elmo.

near the town of England, where they continued to farm. Prior to leaving Solgohachia, most met their spouses at the "all" night dances, the swimming hole on Point Remove Creek and the baseball games. These, along with other activities, allowed the Evans-Bostian-Skipper-Krissell siblings to meet, court and marry. If your last name is one of the mentioned and your folks came from the Solgohachia-Lanty-Overcup area you're probably kinfolk. *Submitted by Eulus E. "Rusty" Evans.*

EVANS - Thomas Pope Evans (b. ca. 1792 in Kentucky, d. Nov. 11, 1832 in Conway County) md. Elizabeth Campbell Sept. 26, 1811 in Madison County, AL. She died about October 1858 in Conway County. They had one son, Leroy Pope Evans (b. Nov. 23, 1812) near Huntsville, AL. They came to Arkansas in 1822 and settled four miles southeast of Morrilton.

Leroy married Margaret Henry on July 16, 1835 in Conway County. She was the daughter of James Henry and Catharine. James was born in Tennessee and came to Arkansas in 1826 and was an own cousin to Patrick Henry.

Leroy Evans and Margaret Henry had 13 children (four girls and nine boys), most of them died before 1900. The Evans are buried in the Evans Cemetery on the old home place, just south of the sewer treatment ponds southeast of Morrilton.

One of Leroy's sons was Peter H. Evans. He was a lawyer in Morrilton and had three children: Eva, Edith and Carl Edward. Carl Edward was a druggist in Morrilton. He had the nickname of "Whitey."

Another son of Leroy's was Lee Gettus Evans. He had eight children, one of them was Dotch Leroy Evans. He ran the Evans Dairy North of Morrilton on Highway 9 and a little grocery store just west of the Morrilton City Park.

One other son of Leroy's was my great-great-grandfather William A. Evans. He was born Sept. 15, 1845 in Conway County and died ca. 1903 in Conway County. He married Susan C. McCaige March 24, 1870 in Conway County. She was the daughter of John McCaige and Sarah Sutter, born in Tennessee, Jan. 8, 1848 and died about 1898 in Conway. They had three children: Lonnie Lee, Azora George and Benjamin.

Lonnie Lee (b. Jan. 13, 1874, d. Feb. 12, 1941) was my great-grandfather. He married Tennessee Lee McCullough (b. Nov. 1, 1870 in Tennessee, d. Feb. 13, 1941) on Sept. 24, 1895 in Conway County. Lonnie was a farmer and also owned the ice plant, cotton gin, light plant, bottle works (soda pop) plant, Atkins Phone Co., and Atkins Roller Mill in Atkins, AR. He was also mayor of Atkins in 1923.

Lonnie and "Tennie" had eight children (six girls and two boys). Their daughter Susan Lorean (b. Oct. 29, 1898 in Plumerville, d. Aug. 14, 1987 in Russellville, AR) was my grandmother. She married Pleasant Earl Horton on June 23, 1920 in Atkins, AR. She was a teacher and housewife. P. Earl Horton (b. Jan. 21, 1897 in Atkins, d. Feb. 16, 1972) was a Navy Veteran of WWI. He worked for Arkansas Power and Light for 21 years, then worked for General Water Works of Russellville as manager for 21 more years, retiring in 1963. They had three boys. The youngest is my father, Haskell Horton (b. Aug. 4, 1924 in Russellville, AR).

Haskell "Hack" Horton is a veteran of WWII serving in the Merchant Marines. He married Mary Ellen Haney, Jan. 28, 1945 in Russellville. He owned and operated "Hacks Cleaners" in Russellville from 1953-89. Hack and Mary Ellen have one son James Lee "Jimmy" Horton (b. Sept. 30, 1946). *Submitted by James L. "Jimmy" Horton.*

FAULKNER - Loma Ishmel Faulkner (b. Jan. 19, 1886 in Sugar Tree, TN, d. July 22, 1976) was the son of John Faulkner and Leanna Garner. He married Millie Ann Vaughn on Dec. 20, 1908. Millie (b. June 28, 1890 in Morrilton, AR, d. Feb. 8, 1986) and Loma had the following children: Roy Franklin, Herman Floyd and William Elmo.

Roy Franklin Faulkner (b. Nov. 12, 1909 in Plumerville, AR) md. Ethel Lee Groom on Oct. 15, 1927 and they had daughter, Ruth Muriel. Roy married Bonnie Ledbetter on March 9, 1937 and they had daughter, Barbara Ann.

Standing: Roy Faulkner, Ruth Faulkner (daughter of Roy). Seated: Loma and Millie Vaughn Faulkner -

Herman Floyd Faulkner (b. March 26, 1911 in Plumerville, AR) md. Jessie Fay Davison and their son is William Floyd.

William "Whitey" Elmo Faulkner (b. Nov. 12, 1913 in Plumerville, AR) md. Anna Corene McInturff Sept. 27, 1945. Corene (b. May 1, 1926 in Plumerville, AR) and Elmo had two children, William Larry and Mary Ann. In 1942 at the age of 28, Elmo was drafted into the Army and sent, along with 13,000 other troops, to North Africa aboard the *Queen Mary.* Very soon after landing in North Africa, Elmo was taken prisoner by the German Army and remained a prisoner for 26 months in a POW camp in Poland. Elmo was freed in 1945 when the Russian Red Army captured the POW camp. Upon discharge from the Army, Elmo and Corene moved to California and

Loma Ishmel Faulkner and Millie Ann Vaughn, 1970.

William Elmo Faulkner and Anna Corene McInturff, 1945.

settled in Orosi. He became a master mechanic and received several awards of excellence from Chrysler Corporation. Along with two other veterans, Elmo founded the Cutler-Orosi VFW. Elmo died Nov. 22, 1984.

Ruth Muriel Faulkner (b. Aug. 24, 1928 in Morrilton, AR) md. Norman Holland on July 3, 1947. Ruth and Norman had children: David Lynn, Geary Lee, Linda Carol and Donna Sue. Ruth was married to Jerome Warner in 1972.

Barbara Ann Faulkner (b. Nov. 30, 1937 in Bakersfield, CA) md. Bobby Robertson in 1956. She was married to Louis Corazza in 1973. Barbara and Louis had one child, Donald Faulkner.

William Floyd Faulkner (b. July 17, 1942 in Oakland, CA) md. Helen Ayers in 1964. Floyd and Helen had two children, Michael and Karen. Floyd was married to Ann Fairbanks in 1982. Floyd and Ann had the following children, Jessica Ruth and Megan Ann.

William Larry Faulkner (b. Aug. 16, 1947 in Richmond, CA) md. Barbara Smoljan and they had three children: Larry Lee, Jeanne Corene and William Nathan. Larry married Linda Nichols March 25, 1972 and had two children, Kimberly Diane and Jennifer Megan.

Mary Ann Faulkner (b. July 30, 1948 in Richmond, CA) md. Gary Evans Jan. 3, 1981. *Submitted by MaryAnn Evans, granddaughter to Loma Ishmel and daughter to William Elmo Faulkner.*

FELKINS - James Ervin Felkins (b. February 1852) was the son of Henry Felkins and Keziah Prewitt (Pruitt). James married Mary Young on March 19, 1876

in Pope County. James was a farmer. Mary died about 1886. James married Josephine Dillon on March 28, 1887, in Pope County. Josephine (b. 1876) was the daughter of Joshua H. and Susan Dillon. Josephine died about 1889. James moved his family to Johnson County, AR prior to 1891. He married Missouri Tennessee Dillon on March 8, 1891, in Johnson County. Missouri (b. May 1870) was Josephine's older sister. James died prior to 1920. Missouri died February 1963 in Johnson County.

Children of James Felkins and Mary Young:

1) William Martin Felkins (b. March 30, 1878, d. Dec. 18, 1961) md. Mary Nordin on Dec. 6, 1903, Johnson County. Children: John, Mary Frances, Jack, Bessie, Aaron, Beatrice and Lee Felkins.

2) Harrison Felkins (b. 1880).

3) Margaret "Maggie" Felkins (b. Aug. 28, 1881, d. November 1976) md. Aaron C. Wheeler. Aaron (b. December 1877, d. Sept. 10, 1954) was the son of Wylie Wheeler and Emmaline Owen. Children included: James, Mary, Emma, Marie, Edia and Stella Wheeler.

Children of James Felkins and Missouri Dillon: Henley J. Felkins (b. 1897); Emma Felkins; Eva Felkins married Riley Bennett on Oct. 27, 1919, Johnson County, AR; George Felkins; Keziah Felkins; and Rachel Felkins.

Henley J. Felkins (b. March 28, 1897, in Johnson County, AR) was the son of James Ervin Felkins and Missouri Tennessee Dillon. Henley served as a private in the 7th Co., 13th Bn., MPC, in WWI. Henley appears on the 1920 Johnson County census at home with his widowed mother. Henley married Mrs. Nancy Eastep on Jan. 20, 1920, in Johnson County, AR. Nancy (b. ca. 1900) had a daughter, Delie Eastep, by her first marriage. Henley was a farmer and died Dec. 15, 1966 at Clarksville in Johnson County, AR. Children included: Willie Ervin Felkins, James W. Felkins, Juanita Felkins (md. _ Holt), and Flora Felkins.

Willie Ervin Felkins (b. Oct. 18, 1931, in Johnson County, AR) was the son of Henley J. Felkins. Willie joined the Arkansas State Police and served as a state trooper for a number of years. Willie married prior to 1954 and had two sons, Billie Felkins and Willie Felkins. On June 2, 1956, Willie married Elizabeth Annie "Betty" (Bush) Wren in Mississippi. Betty (b. Jan. 5, 1927, at Wayland, Henry County, IA), daughter of Earl Louis Bush and Mary Myrtle Abel. Betty was first married to Robert Laverne Wren, by whom she had six children: Carol, Richard, Diana, Albert, Nancy and Donald. Willie was injured in a traffic accident in Missouri on Oct. 11, 1957. The accident left him paralyzed from the waist down. Willie and Betty moved to Morrilton, Conway County, AR soon after his accident. Betty was a licensed nurse and cared for him at home as long as she was able. Willie died at Morrilton on Sept. 19, 1963, at the age of 31 years. Willie and Betty had no children.

FELKINS - John Felkins (b. 1759 in Virginia) was the son of William and Sarah Felkins. John served in the North Carolina Continental Line in the Revolutionary War. He married Anna (last name unknown) prior to 1780. John was a farmer. His family was in Pulaski County, KY in 1810. Prior to 1820, the family moved to Cumberland County, KY. John was in Tennessee when he began receiving his military pension on June 7, 1831. He died Jan. 21, 1839 in Overton County, TN. Children included:

1) Sally Felkins (b. 1780) md. Shadrack Cundiff on Jan. 16, 1799, Bedford County, VA.

2) Martin Felkins (b. 1784, d. 1857) md. Esther Doss on April 28, 1808, Pulaski County, KY. (Children: William, Joel, Edna, Elizabeth, Nancy, Annie, Jimmy, John, Allen, Lucinda, James and Aaron).

3) John Felkins Jr. (b. 1787, d. aft. 1860) md. Bersheba Cundiff on May 26, 1808, Pulaski County, KY. Children included: James, Marinda and William.

4) William Felkins (b. 1792).

5) Elizabeth Felkins (b. 1795) md. Thomas Hill

on Oct. 19, 1815, Pulaski County, KY. Children included: Nancy, Moses, Jamima, Mary, Elizabeth, Lucinda and Thomas Jr.

6) Lucinda Felkins (b. 1803) md. Isaac Wells on July 15, 1819, Cumberland County, KY.

7) Reuben Felkins (b. 1805).

8) Wilson Clemence Felkins (b. 1806, d. 1881) married prior to 1828, one son, William Felkins. He then married Malinda Shepard in 1833. Children: Hetta, James, John, Thomas, Sarah, Eliza, Willy, Bathsheba, Nancy, Tennessee and Richard.

William Felkins (b. 1792, in Virginia) was the son of John and Anna Felkins. He married Jane (June) Williams (b. 1792, d. 1833 in Garrards County, KY) on May 1, 1813, Pulaski County, KY. William was a farmer. Prior to 1850, he moved to Madison County, AR, where he died in 1869. Children included: Anne Felkins (b. May 1814, d. January 1877) md. Rev. Parris Teeter; Henry Felkins (b. 1817); Elizabeth Felkins; Sarah Felkins; Thomas Felkins (b. November 1825); Harriet Jane Felkins (b. 1832) md. East Monroe; Artemesia Felkins; and William Felkins Jr.

Henry Felkins (b. 1817 in Kentucky) was the eldest son of William Felkins and Jane Williams. Henry married Keziah Bell Prewitt (Pruitt) on June 2, 1837, in Madison County, KY. Keziah Prewitt (b. 1818 in Kentucky) was the daughter of John Prewitt and Mary Ford. Henry moved his family to Indiana in 1839 and to Madison County, AR in 1846. They moved to Searcy County, AR prior to 1860 and to Pope County, AR prior to 1867. Henry was a farmer. Children included:

1) William Thomas Felkins (b. 1838, d. Oct. 17, 1864, from typhoid fever in the Civil War) md. Elizabeth Standridge. Children: Margaret and John.

2) Nancy Felkins (b. 1840, d. Nov. 26, 1901) md. Richard Standridge. Children: Samuel, Tennessee, Louisiana, Alabama, George, Arkansas, Missouri, James and Virginia.

3) Elizabeth Felkins (b. 1842, d. Jan. 24, 1930) md. Carter Guthrie. Children: James, Susan, Mary, Roxey, Lucy, Sally and Thomas.

4) Thomas Felkins (b. 1845, died in the Civil War).

5) Mary Susan Felkins (b. 1847, d. October 1888) md. Martin Tarlton Ross. Children: Henry, Nelly, John, Betsey, Grant, Louisey and Susan.

6) John Felkins (b. 1850) md. Angeline Standridge, then married Elizabeth Ross. Children by Elizabeth included: Andrew, Mary and Sally.

7) James Ervin Felkins (b. February 1852).

8) Keziah Felkins (b. 1855) md. Richard Burns.

9) Lucinda Ann Felkins (b. 1858).

FLOWERS - My Grandfather, Columbus Henderson "Hoop" Flowers was born around 1884 in Lick Mountain Township, to Henry Edmond and Elizabeth Jane (Sweeden) Flowers of Conway County. He was a farmer and a blacksmith. He got the name "Hoop" by hollering ahead while walking, alerting all of his coming and "calling" square dances. He loved to dance.

Columbus married Drucilla Claretta Anderson in Conway County around 1905. Her parents were Commodore Perry Anderson and Elizabeth "Susie" Stone of Fulton County, AR. Clara was in Conway County working for a Hill family, babysitting their children, when she met Grandpa.

In the 1910 Lick Mountain Township Census, they own an unmortgaged farm on the Center Ridge and Cleveland Roads. Grandma Clara is also working on the farm. They moved to Old Glaze Township in Olyphant, Jackson County, AR in 1930.

Grandma Clara was born around 1890, died at age 49 in 1939 while asleep of a heart attack. My parents were there. My mother became suspicious when she woke and my Grandma was still "asleep," she was always the first one awake. Grandma and my 2-year-old sister Martha had been playing with the baby chicks the day before. Grandpa Hoop did not live long after she died. He died on Christmas Eve 1941 in his 50s.

Their children, all born in Lick Mountain Township, were: Bytha Tennessee (b. April 11, 1906) md. John Earnest Williams, of Lick Mountain Township in 1925. His parents were Henry Clay and Laura (Keith) Williams of Lick Mountain Township. They had no children. She died at age 52 on May 14, 1958 of diabetic complications. I was just shy of my first birthday and was just learning to walk. I had been walking to her the day she died. Uncle Earnest lived many years after her death but he never remarried. They both are buried near their parents in Coffeyville Cemetery, at Possum Grape, Jackson County.

Oda McArthur Flowers (b. Nov. 11, 1908) md. Bessie Polk in 1929 in Lick Mountain Township, daughter of May Olliger and Alvin Polk. They are buried near Possum Grape at Oakland Hill Cemetery, Jackson County.

Edmond Columbus Flowers (b. Nov. 14, 1914), my dad, married my mom, Mildred Pauline Ray, daughter of Esther Elizabeth Kirkpatrick and Toney Nathan Ray, on Nov. 4, 1933 in Jackson County, AR. Their children are Martha, Raymond, Donald, Ronald and Carolyn. Dad died in 1996 in Newport, Jackson County. They are buried in the family plot at Gracelawn Cemetery, Tuckerman, Jackson County.

Joseph Alonzo Flowers (b. Oct. 1, 1919) md. Eunice Epperson, daughter of Earnie and Frankie Epperson. He died Feb. 10, 1992 in Newport and is buried at Coffeyville Cemetery, Jackson County near his parents. *Submitted by their granddaughter, Carolyn Flowers Tucker.*

FLOWERS - My brother Donald Ray "Don" Flowers, was born the son of Edmond and Mildred (Ray) Flowers on Oct. 14, 1946, after Dad returned home from the war. Don attended the Newport Class of 1964, served in the Vietnam War in the USN. Our parents cried in each other's arms when Don was drafted. They drove in a horrible snowstorm to Houston, TX after getting a hospital call that Don was near death. Renting a room nearby, Mom fed him liquid meals thru a straw; he was over 6 foot tall and weighed less than 90 pounds.

One of the most beautiful moments captured in my mind is of an earlier homecoming, around 1965 or so, maybe from boot camp, I'm not sure. Our home at 1404 Dewey in Newport was lovely with a lush green lawn, roses galore and a white picket fence. I was standing in the doorway watching as my mom ran down the porch to the sidewalk, throwing open the gate. My tall handsome big brother, dressed in his Navy whites, was walking up the sidewalk. He dropped his duffel bag reaching out his arms to Mom as she was running to him. Bending over he scooped her effortlessly up into the air into his arms and twirled her around in a long happy tearful embrace.

Don was Commander of the Jackson County, AR, VFW, Justice of the Peace and a Jackson County Quorum Court member.

He married Jeanette Stewart. They had Linda Lynette and Donald "Donnie" Flowers Jr. Linda graduated from Arkansas State University-Jonesboro and is a registered nurse. Donnie graduated from ASU-Newport and is an auto mechanic. Don has four beautiful grandchildren: Dustin, Zack, Ashlyn and Drew.

Then Don married Debra Hanley. They had James Raymond and Edmond Columbus. James served in the US Marine Corps, is engaged and attending college in New York. Edmond is in high school in Independence, MO.

Don's last wife was Christine Ward. Don was very proud of his Conway County heritage. He died there unexpectedly in the home of our cousin Elsie (Holmes) Bryant on Sept. 30, 2000. I know his heavenly homecoming was even grander than the lovely one I was blessed to witness as a small child.

The following was written by our mama on his 19th birthday, Oct. 14, 1965:

My Little Boy
Of all the boys in the world, there is none quite like my little boy.
God gave him to me just at the close of the war,
I thought he was beautiful at first sight.
He has brought us much happiness.
His Dad and I saw him grow year-by-year, step-by-step from baby boy to wonderful manhood.
Today he is 19.
He has gone to serve his country, got his call to join the fighting forces.
He is much too young to go, he is but a boy at heart.
I pray he will return to me— Just as his daddy did 20 years ago.
Submitted with love by his "Little Sis," Carolyn Tucker.

FLOWERS - Edmond Columbus Flowers was born Nov. 14, 1914 in Lick Mountain Township. His Arkansas Flowers line begins at Point Remove Township, in 1840, then Arkansas Cherokee Indian Lands. His parents were Columbus "Hoop" and Clara (Anderson) Flowers. He attended Sunnyside School and loved playing ball and running fast. He worked hard very young.

Edmund and Mildred (Ray) Flowers, 1983, 50th year of marriage.

His family moved to Old Glaze Twp., Olyphant, Jackson County, AR around 1930. Jokingly he'd say, "I had to leave Conway County to avoid marrying a cousin." He married Mom, Mildred Pauline Ray, on Nov. 4, 1933 in Newport, Jackson County. He told me "She was the prettiest thing I ever saw." Mom (b. June 14, 1918 at Village Creek, Jackson County) was the daughter of Toney Nathan and Esther Elizabeth (Kirkpatrick) Ray. Mom loved her in-laws, especially Clara, very much. Daddy was a proud patriotic WWII Navy Veteran. Married 11 years, their war letters were filled with love and longing. Their marriage would last 62 years.

He worked for the Post Office in Newport from 1947-75, carrying our neighborhood mail for 15 years. They bought old houses, fixing them up as rental property. He was always smiling and whistling a happy tune. They traveled to research their family history. Proudly, Daddy traced his Flowers line to 1500s England, via the book, *The Flowers Chronicles*, by P.B. Flowers. Henry and Jane (Underwood) Flowers are on the records of "America's First Families."

Daddy was a Deacon. He worked the Election Day polls. He restored antique furniture. He was in the Veterans of Foreign Wars, providing military burials to local veterans. They helped raise their grandchildren.

Pleasant Hill Cemetery Decoration Days and trips to Center Ridge to see Aunt Nancy (Flowers) and Uncle Bud Holmes are precious memories. I loved to wade in the cool beautiful running streams at Sunnyside. Dad proudly showed me his Sunnyside School.

Their five children, born and raised in Jackson County, are Martha, Raymond, Donald, Ronald and Carolyn. They have nine grandchildren, 10 great-grandchildren and two great-great-grandchildren.

Daddy died peacefully at home with dignity on Sunday, Jan. 14, 1996, near the end of church services.

Church members, old friends and family lovingly encircled his bed in prayer just moments after his passing. He had fought the good fight just as his Conway County Pioneer ancestors had before him. He had lived an exemplary life. Mom passed peacefully Aug. 8, 2001 at home with her daughters. They are buried at Gracelawn Cemetery, Tuckerman, Jackson County - him to her left as he requested, so she wouldn't be next to the street.

Dad was very proud of his Conway County heritage, as all his children are. He was a hard-working easy-going family man. The world sorely needs more just like him. Words cannot express how proud we were he was our Dad. He lives forever in our hearts. *Submitted in his memory by their daughter, Carolyn F. Tucker.*

FLOWERS – Edwin Flowers was the last born child, born in the 1820s to my ancestors Henry and Elizabeth (Marshall) Flowers in Tennessee. His mom, Elizabeth, was in the 1840 Point Remove Census. Edwin's first born and only son, Elmer Sevier, was probably the youngest child listed by age. Point Remove was then a part of the Arkansas Cherokee Indian Reservation. Edwin may be one of the two males younger than 30. They are farming and mining, unable to read or write. Edwin is on the Pope County Tax Lists for 1843, 1844 and 1847.

By 1850, Edwin marries Lavicia Elizabeth Gilliam. She was my ancestor Eliza Jane (Gilliam-Duron) Flowers' sister. On their way to be married, Eliza and Jacob Flowers stopped to visit his brother Edwin. The girls realized they were sisters! The Gilliams had been killed in a buggy accident and the Durons had adopted Eliza, then left the area for a while. So the sisters married brothers! All their direct descendants are double cousins!

Edwin raised his family near Jerusalem, Conway County. In 1850 Griffin Twp., December 3, Edwin is age 30, a blacksmith, born in Tennessee; Lavicia is 24, born in Tennessee and son Elmer Sevier is 12.

Elmer Sevier marries Areminta Sides July 12, 1855, Pope County, daughter of Joseph Sides and Elizabeth Wyatt. Elmer dies by 1860.

In the 1860 Conway County Census Griffin Twp., Old Hickory Post Office, July 24, Edwin is age 44, born in Tennessee, a blacksmith, $464 in property; Lavicia is 34, born in Arkansas, with two daughters.

Edwin buys his Conway County 120 acre homestead in August 1861, Doc. No. 18940, Part 1=N NE, Sec 17, Twp 9N, R17W. Part 2=SE NE, Sec 17, Twp 9N, R17W.

In the 1870 Conway County Census, Griffin Twp., Springfield Post Office, September 2, Edwin is 54, born in Tennessee, farming with $1,000 in property, Elizabeth is 46, born in Arkansas, with three daughters.

In the 1880 Census of Liberty, Van Buren County, Edwin, 64, born in Tennessee, parents born in North Carolina, is farming with wife Luvicy, 54, born in Arkansas, parents born in Georgia, with three daughters and three grandchildren.

These Sweeden grandchildren are William S., age 6, born Arkansas; Anetta, age 5, born Arkansas; Robert E., age 2, born Arkansas.

Edwin died after 1880 and before 1900; his wife is a widow in 1900 Van Buren County, White Oak Twp. She is then 73.

Son Elmer addressed above, so their daughters were:

Mary Ann Josephine Elizabeth Flowers (b. November 1855, Arkansas) md. Henry Sweeden, September 1872, Conway County, son of Thomas Sweeden and Emmaline Spray.

Louisiana J. Flowers (b. March 1, 1861 in Arkansas) md. John "Cal" Jax Linker, July 9, 1882 in Pope County, son of Ransome Linker and Priscilla Furr.

Nancy Arilla Flowers (b. May 23, 1864 in Arkansas) md. J.E. Fuller Sept. 10, 1883 in Pope County. *Submitted by Carolyn Flowers Tucker.*

FLOWERS - Elizabeth Jane (Sweeden) Carr Flowers, my great-grandmother, was born in Arkansas, probably Clark County, around 1850, to Thomas Levi and Emmaline Sweeden. I think Emmaline's maiden name could be Spray or Sprague. Janie's parents and siblings are in Clark County, AR in 1850 Census. By 1860 Thomas Levi has left the family, remarried to Rachel Clark and is in Panola County, TX with another set of children.

She is with her brother Henry Sweeden, his wife Nancy Caroline Sides and their mom Emmaline in Griffin Township, Conway County in 1860. She is listed as a male, Jne. E., age 9. Based on my extensive research I feel sure it is she and the male entry is an error. Her brother Parrium is also with them.

Her first marriage takes place March 2, 1868 in Griffin Township, Conway County at the home of her brother Henry to J.M.D. Carr, by Shadrack Jones. Shadrack Jones was the father of her brother Patrick's first wife, Eleanor. The ages of the couple are difficult to read, they are age 20 or 28. They both live in Conway County at the time, filed at Conway County Courthouse April 7, 1868. I do not know who J.M.D. Carr's parents are yet, although there are lots of Carrs in the county.

In 1870 I think I have found the couple in Galla Rock Township, Dover Post Office in Pope County on July 20, 1970. They are living with Thomas and Martha Kendrick, both born in Arkansas, ages 21 and 19. Jim Carr is 21, born Arkansas, Jane E. Carr is age 20, born Arkansas. They have an unnamed Carr female baby, age 1 month. They are surrounded by African-American families listed as black. It is possible these were Indian families, as then they often gave a different race for their heritage to avoid harassment.

I don't know what happened to J.M.D. Carr. She marries Henry Edmond Flowers before 1880. I suspect they married in Van Buren County, those records for those times are destroyed. Henry was born in 1849 in Pope County, AR, to Jacob and Elizabeth Jane (Gilliam-Duron) Flowers. His Arkansas Flowers line begins at Point Remove on the Arkansas Cherokee Indian Reservation in 1840.

The unnamed female baby is not with Janie and my Great Grampa Henry Flowers in the 1880 Census. All of the older children are in school. Then Janie is a widow living with their children in 1900 in Lick Mountain Township. She is living with her daughter Elzonia (Flowers) Keith in 1910 in Lick Mountain Township in Conway County. That census has her the mother of seven children, all-living. She dies in 1919 in Conway County. She and Henry are buried in Pleasant Hill Cemetery, Center Ridge, Conway County.

Their children are Jacob Marion, Louis Jefferson, John Henry, Robert Ance, Columbus "Hoop" Henderson (my Grampa), Ellen Arizona "Elzonia" Keith, and Nancy Miranda Holmes. *Submitted by her great-granddaughter, Carolyn Flowers Tucker.*

FLOWERS - Elmer Sevier Flowers was born around 1838, probably in Tennessee. He was the son of Edwin and Lavicia Elizabeth (Gilliam) Flowers. His grandmother, my ggg-grandmother, Elizabeth (Marshall) Flowers was in Point Remove Twp. in 1840. Based on their ages, I think Elmer and his dad were with her. I think his mom died before he was 2 years old. Point Remove Twp. was then Arkansas Cherokee Indian Land.

Elmer married Areminta Sides on July 12, 1855 in Pope County, AR, daughter of Joseph Sides and Elizabeth Wyatt. She was born Sept. 29, 1835 in Alabama. Elmer doesn't live long after their wedding; he dies before 1860. Areminta and the children are then living with her sister, Cynthia (Sides) Kelly and her family in Pope County, Moreland Twp.

Children of Elmer and Areminta were: 1) Elizabeth A. (b. 1858 in Arkansas) md. Samuel S. Clark on June 22, 1879, in Conway County, AR. He was born May 11, 1858. 2) Joseph E. (b. September 1856 in Arkansas) md. Sarah Fannie Griffin on Nov. 5, 1882

in Pope County, AR. She was born Nov. 11, 1864 in Georgia or Alabama. Joseph has a Land Patent, Sept. 20, 1889, in Van Buren County, AR. They were living in Conway County in 1900 in Griffin Twp. In 1910 they are in Van Buren County, AR on the Ozark National Forest Preserve, married for 27 years. Sarah is the mother of 10 children, seven living. All eligible children are in school. They are farming their own unmortgaged farm. Their children were: Susan A. "Annie" Flowers (b. 1883), John T. Flowers (b. 1885), James P. Flowers (b. 1889), Walter Flowers (b. 1896), Lisa Flowers (b. 1899), Addie Flowers (b. 1903) and Alma Flowers (b. 1908).

Sarah died Aug. 4, 1914 with burial at Mt. Zion Cemetery, Conway County, AR. *Submitted by C. Flowers Tucker.*

FLOWERS - Henry Edmond Flowers was born around 1849 in Pope County, AR to Jacob and Elizabeth Jane (Gilliam-Duron) Flowers. A Duron couple adopted his mom after the Gilliams were killed in a buggy accident. Henry was a saddle maker and might have been part Indian. He married Elizabeth Jane Sweeden before the 1880 Census. His grandmother Elizabeth (Marshall) Flowers was in Point Remove Township in 1840, then Indian Land.

(l-r) Clara Mae Flowers, Martha Ann Flowers, Grandpa Hoop Flowers is holding my brother Ray and James Edmond Flowers, Columbus Flowers.

Janie was born in Arkansas, probably Clark County, around 1850 to Thomas and Emmaline Sweeden. Janie is widowed living with their children in 1900 in Lick Mountain Township. She is living with her daughter Elzonia Keith in 1910 in Lick Mountain Township. She dies there in 1919. They are buried in Pleasant Hill Cemetery at Center Ridge.

Their children and grandchildren are: 1) Jacob "Marion" (b. June 11, 1867) md. Sarah Velia Polk, Jan. 31, 1889 in Conway County. She is the daughter of William Thomas Polk. Uncle Marion died Feb. 4, 1940. They are buried at Pleasant Hill. Their children were Allen, James Monroe and Sula Nova.

2) Louis Jefferson (b. July 3, 1868) md. Nancy Polk, daughter of William Polk, on Oct. 16, 1890 in Conway County. Uncle Jeff died March 21, 1952 in Conway County. They are buried at Pleasant Hill Cemetery.

3) John Henry (b. ca. 1874) md. Ida Polk (b. 1877, d. 1959), daughter of William Polk, on April 15, 1894 in Van Buren County. Uncle John died Oct. 17, 1934, in Conway County. They are buried at Pleasant Hill. They had Mary and adopted son, Jewel McNabb.

4) Robert Ance "Uncle Ance" (b. Feb. 14, 1876) md. Ella Mae Wagley on Feb. 4, 1906. She was the daughter of James and Josephine (White) Wagley and died April 11, 1960. They are buried at Pleasant Hill. Children were Alice, Alta, Henry "Peck" and Millard.

5) My Grampa, Columbus "Hoop" Henderson (b. February 1882 in Lick Mountain Township, Center Ridge, Conway County) md. Clara Anderson around 1905. She was the daughter of Commodore Perry and Elizabeth "Suzie" (Stone) Anderson. Grampa Hoop died Christmas Eve 1941 in Olyphant, Jackson Count, AR. Grandma Clara died just two years before him. They are buried in Coffeyville Cemetery, Jackson County. Children: Bytha, Oda, Edmond (my dad) and Joseph.

6) Ellen Arizona, "Elzonia/Aunt Ell" (b. ca. 1883) md. John "Lee" Keith, son of John Keith and Sarah Harwood, on Nov. 7, 1902 in Conway County. She died in 1953, just two years after him. They are buried at Pleasant Hill. Grandma Janie (Sweeden) Flowers is living with them in 1910. They had Seretha, Willie and Marion Houston.

7) Nancy Miranda, "Aunt Nancy," (b. ca. 1889, in Lick Mountain Township) md. William "Uncle Bud" Holmes, son of Jim and Surilda (Hill) Holmes, Nov. 10, 1905, died March 17, 1980. They are buried at Pleasant Hill Cemetery. Their daughter is Elsie Bryant. *Submitted by their great-granddaughter, C. Tucker.*

FLOWERS – Jacob "Marion" Flowers. Uncle Marion, as my dad called him, was born around June 11, 1867, the son of my great-grandparents, Henry and Elizabeth Jane "Janie" (Sweeden) Flowers in Conway County. He was attending school in Lick Mountain Township in the 1880 census. At age 20, per the Conway County Marriage Record, he married Sarah Vella Polk, on Jan. 31, 1889. Two of his brothers, Louis Jefferson and John Henry Flowers, married her sisters, Nancy and Ida Polk.

Jacob "Marion" Flowers, 1867-1940; picture may have been taken in 1920s.

J. Marion Flowers is listed on the 1890 tax records of Conway County. He was a farmer. He and "Vellie," as she was called, are living in Lick Mountain Township in the 1900 and 1910 census. They owned their mortgaged farm and he can read and write. Their oldest two children, Allen and James, are in school, their youngest, Sula, is only 6.

They, Sula and her husband, Bailey Cole, moved to Texas in the 1920s. That may not have been a permanent move. Uncle Marion died at Center Ridge, Lick Mountain Township in 1940, his wife in 1948. They are both buried in Pleasant Hill Cemetery at Center Ridge.

Their children were all born at Center Ridge, Lick Mountain Township. Allen (b. ca. 1890) md. Genia Hillis; James Monroe (b. ca. 1893) md. Claudia Josephine Wagley; Sula Nova (b. ca. 1905) md. Bailey Cole. *Submitted by Carolyn Flowers Tucker.*

FORT - Wallace R. Fort was born in Waukegan, IL. In 1987 he married Dannie S. McCoy. Dannie was born in Morrilton, AR, at the church in Middleton.

Dannie is the daughter of Dan McCoy and Virginia Bennett. She has a sister, Brenda Harwood, and a brother, Jack McCoy (deceased). Dannie served in the US Navy and was discharged in June 1966 at the North Island Naval Air Station in San Diego, CA.

Dannie S. and Wallace R. Fort.

Wallace is the son of Edward Fort and Ann Cherry McGill. He has a brother Edward Fort, who lives in Chicago, and a sister, Geraldine Springston (deceased). Wallace served in the US Marine Corps and was discharged in March 1952 at Camp Pendleton, Oceanside, CA.

Wallace and Dannie worked for the same aircraft manufacturer in Chula Vista, CA, for over 30 years each in various management positions prior to retirement. They currently live in the Center Ridge area in the home they had built in 2000. *Submitted by Wallace R. Fort and Dannie S. Fort.*

FOWLER - Billy Dale Fowler (b. Aug. 18, 1925 in Casa, Arkansas, in Perry County) was the second child of Armour and Addie Billings-Sosbee-Fowler. Armour and Addie had four children: Marquis Lyndon, Billy Dale, Mildred Louise, and Wilma Jean. Addie was a widow when she and Armour were married and had a daughter, Marjorie, who died in her teenage years and is buried at Casa Cemetery. Armour was an iron worker and Addie a school teacher. They are buried in Galt, CA.

Bill and Mary Ann Fowler, November 1991.

Bill attended Casa and Adona schools and lived part time with his grandparents, James "Jim" Robert Lee and Mary Bell "Molly" Ghrell Fowler. Bill left Perry County in 1943 and went into the Marine Corps, serving in the South Pacific during WWII. After his discharge, he settled in California. He married Leta Loftus and they had seven children: Mark Billings, Stephen Lee, Glen Marion, William James, Joan Camille and two were still born and buried in Pasco and Seattle, WA.

Bill later moved to Washington where he worked and retired as an ironworker. He worked for several companies and was an independent contractor for several years. The Space Needle was one of his contracts. He had nine contracts at the World's Fair Center. He worked in Alaska seven years, and his work took him to Hawaii for a time. Bill and Leta were divorced in 1968.

In 1988 he returned to Perry County to visit relatives. He went to Hattieville Church of Christ with Ghrell and Anna Mae Fowler, his uncle and aunt. There he met Mary Ann Allen-Heistand-Gullett on June 4. Not a 24-hour period has separated them since. Ivy Davenport, preacher at the church where they met, married them on October 15 of the same year. Brother Davenport also baptized Bill on June 24, 1988.

Bill moved to Hattieville, AR where Mary Ann had lived since 1973. They still reside there today. Mary Ann was owner and operator of Mary Ann's Beauty Shop in Hattieville since March of 1988. She retired in 2002. She has three sons: Glen Heistand (b. June 24, 1956), Grady Randall Gullett (b. Feb. 15, 1967) and Mark Allen Gullett (b. Feb. 2, 1976). Bill and Mary Ann make frequent trips to the northwest to visit Bill's children: three live in Seattle, WA, one in Turlock, CA, and one in Portland, OR.

Mary Ann is a native of Conway County. She was born on Jan. 15, 1939 to James Andrew and Mary Louvenia Blankenship Allen. Mary Ann was the third child of eight. Her siblings are Lola Ruth Ulry, James Benton Allen, Evelyn Faye Baxley, Judy Lane Allen Freeman, Rita Jo Gipson, Paul David Allen and Gloria June Woods. They lived at Pleasant View, on Granny Hollow Road, south of Jerusalem, AR.

FREEMAN - Alta Freeman, daughter of Homer and Annie Mary (Wills) Freeman, was born Oct. 29, 1912 at Gridley, Van Buren County, AR. Alta's brothers and sisters are Artie Mahalia Freeman Creach, Arden William Freeman, Alene Bretty Freeman Campbell and Lewis Ardee Freeman.

Alta married Weldon Taft Mills on Sept. 26, 1938 in Cleveland, Conway County, AR. Weldon, son of Thomas Roland and Lela Virginia (Brown) Mills, was born Oct. 4, 1908 in Gridley, Van Buren County, AR.

Weldon died Dec. 26, 1972 and is buried in the Cedar Creek Cemetery, Jerusalem, Conway County, AR..

Weldon's brothers and sisters are Lillian Vina Mills Morgan Elliot, Cleora Ava Mills Holcomb, Thomas Roosevelt Mills, Oma Mills Hawkins, Ulysses Grant Mills, Eunice

Alta Freeman Mills

Wilma Mills Blake Stroud Acton, Zela Mills Blake, Joyce Mills Campbell, Shelton Mills, Lavola Mills Reid Harrison and Luman Moses Mills.

Alta and Weldon are the parents of six children: Evern Edwin Lawless, Mack Sheldon Mills, Virginia Aleda Mills, Lena Joy Mills, Barney Aldon Mills and Alta Cordell Mills.

Evern Edwin Lawless married Glynna Sue Roper on Sept. 2, 1957 in Hernando, DeSoto County, MS. Glynna Sue is the daughter of Reedy Eugene and Bertie Lee (Stroud) Roper. Evern and Sue are the parents of one son, Bobby Evern Lawless.

Mack Sheldon Mills married Martha Faye Hall on Dec. 7, 1961 in Pinnacle, Pulaski County, AR. Martha is the daughter of Mark Alan and Jessie (France) Hall. Mack and Martha are the parents of two children, Michael Aldon Mills and Mary Annette Mills Brown.

Virginia Aleda Mills married Lonnie Gene Bateman on Sept. 30, 1967 in North Little Rock, Pulaski County, AR. Lonnie is the son of Jesse and Bessie (Dickey) Bateman. Aleda and Lonnie are the parents of two children, Barry Alan Bateman and Corinne Deanna Bateman Keeton.

Lena Joy Mills married Eddie Poe on Feb. 15, 1964 in Arkansas. Eddie is the son of Tazel and Merle (Ball) Poe. Lena and Eddie are the parents of one daughter, Carla Michelle Poe. Lena and Eddie divorced and she married Charles Wayne Cossey on June 3, 1977 in Arkansas. Charles is the son of Radis and Stella (Duncan) Cossey. Lena and Charles are the parents of one daughter, Charlie Nicole Cossey Osborne.

Barney Aldon Mills married Penny Hawkins Nov. 15, 1970 in West Plains, Howell County, MO. Penny is the daughter of Ralph and Elizabeth (Penn) Hawkins. Barney and Penny are the parents of one daughter, Natalie Yvonne Mills Wright Miller.

Alta Cordell Mills married Jimmy Dale "Jim" New on July 27, 1965 in Little Rock, Pulaski County, AR. Jim is the son of Carlos and Wanda Lee (Riggan) New. Cordell and Jim are the parents of two daughters, Marquita Renae New Sanchez Johnson and Melissa Rachelle New Doyle Barry.

When Alta's children were older, she moved to Little Rock and worked at Levinson Cleaners for a while. She later worked at the Baptist Medical Center in Little Rock until her retirement. She moved back to Jerusalem, Conway County, AR where she currently resides. Her hobbies include growing flowers and crocheting. She lives beside her daughter, Aleda and likes to spend a lot of time with her family. *Submitted by Cordell Mills New.*

FREEMAN - Arden William Freeman was born on Jan. 17, 1915 in Gridley, Van Buren County, AR to Homer and Annie Mary (Wills) Freeman. He lived the early part of his childhood in southwest Van Buren County. His father left the family when he was just a young man, so he quit school and took on the responsibility of supporting his mother and four siblings. They all lived on Wills Mountain in Van Buren County with his grandparents, Lewis Joseph and Mary Mahalia (Roberts) Wills. He joined the Civil Conservation Corp in 1935 and was able to send money home for the family. He was stationed in Solgohachia, Berryville and Jasper. He learned a lot from the CCC and put that knowledge to use all of his life. Later, he was employed

by the Corp of Engineers and worked at the Lock and Dam No. 9 in Morrilton for 15 years until his retirement in 1980. It was while he worked at the Lock and Dam that he studied and received his high school diploma. He was so proud of his accomplishment.

Arden and Eathel Freeman

Arden married Mary Eathel Campbell on Dec. 23, 1939 in Conway, Faulkner County, AR. Mary Eathel is the daughter of Benjamin and Bessie Belle (Ingram) Campbell. She was born in Okay, AR which is just about on the Pope, Conway, Van Buren County lines. She taught school for over 40 years in Van Buren and Conway Counties. In 2002, Eathel had her memoirs published entitled, *Journey of a Depression Kid.*

Arden and Eathel are the parents of four children: Mary Joyce Freeman Chism, Janice Arden Freeman Roberts, Gerald Don Freeman and Darrell Dean Freeman.

Mary Joyce married Kenneth Edward Chism, son of William Archie and Rose Mildred (Zachary) Chism, on May 27, 1961 in Morrilton. Their children are Tammie Joyce Chism Shipp, Rosemary Chism Norwood, Kenneth Edward Chism Jr. and William Alan Chism.

Janice Arden married James Roy "Jim" Roberts, son of James Roy and Sarah Bernice (Holt) Roberts, on Nov. 26, 1970 in Huntsville, Madison County, AL. Janice and Jim have one son, John Arden Roberts.

Gerald Don married Judy Lane Allen, daughter of James Andrew and Mary Louvenia (Blankenship) Allen, on Aug. 24, 1967 in Jerusalem, Conway County, AR. Gerald and Judy have two children, Karen Elizabeth Freeman Shaw and Gregory Don Freeman. Judy died on May 2, 1985 and Gerald married Sharon Beth Crawford Wells, daughter of Thomas Tabor and Ina Geneva (Jones) Crawford, on July 22, 1989 in Jerusalem, Conway County, AR.

Darrell Dean married Laura Jean Eiseman, daughter of George Edward and Betty Jane (Richardson) Eiseman, on April 1, 1991 in Old Alexandria, VA. Darrell and Laura have no children. *Submitted by Mary Whitney Norwood.*

FREEMAN - Loyd Freeman (b. July 27, 1910 in Conway County, AR) was the son of Dyke Freeman and Melinda "Lindie" Victory. Dyke was married to Martha Maxwell and had 10 children. After her death he married Lindie and had three more children: Arlie, Abe and Loyd. Loyd was the youngest of 13 children. Dyke's father was Jessee Freeman from Pope County. He fought in the Civil War for the Union Army. Jessee married Elizabeth Flowers from

Loyd Freeman and Walsie Cato

Van Buren County. Jessie's father was William Freeman, who migrated from Illinois to Arkansas. His wife's name was Mary Ward. They owned a large cotton farm in Pope County.

Lindie Victory's parents both came to Arkansas from Tennessee. Her father was William Victory and her mother was Mirah Wayne Tackett.

Loyd married Walsie Cato in 1931 at Jerusalem. She was the daughter of Ailsey Harris and Willis Cato. Willis was born in Searcy County, AR and Ailsey was born in Pope County. Ailsey is the daughter of Elizabeth Harris and Jim Owens. Her grandparents were Charles Harris and Ailsey Tompkins.

Willis' father was William Cato and he lived in the Doyle Flat Community until his death. His wife's name was Edith Sparrow. They are both buried in the County Line Cemetery, or Cato Cemetery as it is sometimes called. The Catos came to Arkansas from South Carolina. They lived in Searcy County before moving to Conway County. Walsie's paternal great-grandfather, Willis Cato, died fighting for the Confederacy.

Loyd and Walsie lived part of their married life in the Doyle Flat Community on 40 acres she inherited from her parents. They moved to the Mt. Zion Community in 1942 where they had a cotton farm. Loyd started to do construction work so they sold the cotton farm and moved back to Doyle Flat and later to Morrilton, where they lived until their death. After moving to Morrilton they started a chicken raising business. She died in 1989 and he in 2001.

They had five children (two girls and three boys): Odell, Clovie, Ovie, Vernon and Willard. Clovie died as an infant, Willard died when he was 18 in an automobile accident. Odell has five children: Michael, Edward, Deborah, Marcus, Margo and Leonard. He resides in Ocala, FL with his wife, Beverly, and sells real estate. Ovie married Don Reynolds and had four girls: Donna, Anita Christian, Katrina and Rita. She lived many years in Alaska and is now retired and lives in Logan, UT. Vernon has four children and two step children: Ronda, Steve, Susan, Jonathan, and step daughters, Kendra and Karissa Brown. He and his wife Anita have tax offices in Morrilton and Conway. They live part of the time in Ocala, FL and the rest in Morrilton, AR.

FULLER - Nancy A. Flowers Fuller, widow of Johnathan Fuller, of the Cherokee Nation returned to Hattieville in 1900 from the Indian Territory of Oklahoma. She was one of the original members of the Hattieville Church of Christ that had their building built in 1925, and which still stands. Nancy's father, Edward Flowers, was an Indian Scout during the Civil War. She was born in 1865. Edward Flowers homesteaded land in Van Buren County, which is now owned by a Summers family.

James and Arkie Russell Fuller

Nancy married Johnathan Fuller of Georgia in Russellville. They homesteaded in Waldron, AR. Together they had five children. When the oldest child was 13, Johnathan died of complications of the measles after chasing cows that had gotten into the corn. He was 65 years old. After Johnathan died, Nancy packed her family into a wagon and traveled with her sister's family from Waldron to the Indian Territory of Oklahoma, and remained there two years. She qualified for the Land Grant to the Indians of 160 acres but did not accept it as she had a mistrust of the offer.

The Fuller children were James, Edna, Cephous, Melvin and Bostian. Bostian died in his teens of a possible aneurysm. James Fuller married Gladys Arkie Russell, daughter of Sid Russell, a deputy sheriff in Hattieville. Their children were David Fuller, who gave his life for his country in New Guinea in WWII, Clarence, Basil and Elizabeth Kent.

Clarence married Edith L. Coffman, a daughter of Charlie Coffman and Ada Beverage, and their children are Doris Wells, James who died in the year 2000, Annette White and Linda Briggler. Doris is the proprietor of Wells Grocery on Highway 95 at the Lord's School Community. Annette has a small farm in Hattieville. Linda is the Administrator of the Conway County Health Department and is married to Raymond Briggler formerly of the St. Vincent Community.

Clarence and Edith farmed for a living early in

their marriage. Clarence worked for Arkansas Power and Light Company. Edith began working in Morrilton for the Oberman Company, maker of men's pants, about 1951. She then worked for the Coca Cola Bottling Company and from there retired. She currently writes local news for Hattieville for the Petit Jean Country Headlight. Clarence worked for AP and L until 1970. He continues to raise a garden and cattle.

GARRETT - On Oct. 9, 1934 in Ramer, TN, Johnny Vinson Garrett was born Joseph Archie and Neelia (Leatherwood) Garrett, the second of five children. Upon graduation from high school in Kossuth, MS, Johnny moved to Memphis, TN, where he met and married JoAnn Green. JoAnn was born in Ripley, MS in 1940 to Freddie (Aldridge) Green and Joe Tom Green. In September 1957, Johnny received an honorable medical discharge from the US Army in Fort Chaffee, AR.

Johnny Garrett (left) presenting Kiwanis Club attendance award to S.E. McReynolds.

Johnny and JoAnn have two daughters, Trisa Kaye (b. June 4, 1959) and Angela Dawn (b. March 14, 1962), both were born in Memphis, TN. In September 1964 the family moved to Little Rock, AR, where Johnny was employed in sales and service for Remington Rand Office Machines, a division of Sperry Rand, Inc.

While attending Twelfth Street Baptist Church in Little Rock (now Heritage Baptist Temple) they developed a close friendship with Larry and Winona Adams. Mr. Adams worked at Little Rock Air Force Base for his employer, the University of Dayton Ohio Research Institute. He and his wife Winona, had two children, a daughter Jennifer (age 2), and a son Jason (age 8 months).

While helping with machine repair for Mr. John D. Webb, who owned Morrilton Typewriter Company, Mr. Garrett learned that the business was for sale, and he and Mr. Adams decided to move their families to Morrilton and establish a new business partnership. On Dec. 8, 1969, Mr. Adams and Mr. Garrett purchased Morrilton Typewriter Co., located at 104 West Broadway and re-named the business Morrilton Office Machines. They later purchased a larger building, expanded the business, and relocated to 608 West Broadway.

In 1983 the partnership also purchased Poindexter Office Supply at 118 North Division Street. They later opened Johnny's Office Products in Clinton and Cleburne County Office Products in Heber Springs. Both families were active in their communities and churches throughout the years. Mr. Adams was a member and past president of the Morrilton Lions Club. Johnny was a member and past president of Morrilton Kiwanis Club.

Winona and JoAnn worked in their businesses as well as the newly established Riverview Christian School, from which all four children graduated before going on to their colleges of choice. Trisa Kaye Garrett being the first graduate. In addition to enjoying the role of wife and mother, JoAnn enjoyed working with other children, teaching kindergarten for six years She was a member of Child Evangelism Fellowship International, teaching Neighborhood Bible Clubs and presenting Christmas and Easter lessons in various public schools.

In 1988. Mr. Garrett and Mr. Adams divided the partnership, with Mr. Adams retaining the office machines portion and Mr. Garrett retaining the office supply portion. In 1998 Mr. Adams sold his business to Robert Adamson of Quality Office Inc. of Searcy. Larry and Winona are both now retired and enjoy travel in their motor home. They have two grandsons, Tyler and Trey Smith of Batesville, AR.

While making time for his hobbies of hunting and fishing, Johnny, at age 70, continues to operate his office supply stores. This includes Poindexter Office Supply, which has continued to be a downtown merchant since its establishment in 1953 by Mr. Paul Poindexter Senior. Johnny and JoAnn have three grandsons: David Scott Steele, Trisa's son; Jon Deven Russell and Shawn Eric Russell, Angie's sons.

Johnny and JoAnn, as well as Larry and Winona, are charter members of the church Morrilton Baptist Temple since its establishment in 1979. *Submitted by JoAnn Garrett.*

GARRISON - After the death of his first wife in Georgia, Capel Garrison, the son of a Methodist Episcopal minister and the grandson of a Revolutionary War veteran, brought his family to Conway County and settled at Springfield about 1858. Capel was a farmer and wagon maker. His wife, Elizabeth Baker Garrison, had died in the summer of 1854 during an episode in which a man came to their Chattooga County, GA home, intent on hurting her son. After Capel asked him to leave, the man tried to attack Capel, whereupon Elizabeth fainted. According to her 1854 obituary, Elizabeth probably expected to see her husband stabbed or shot, and "…fainted away, sank down, and died instantly."

During their 23-year-marriage, Capel and Elizabeth had eight children. Two of their sons were Allen W. Garrison (b. ca. 1836) and Andrew Jackson Garrison (b. 1840). Both settled in Conway County. In 1854, Capel married his second wife, Jane Tucker, in Georgia, and they had at least one son, William D. Garrison, who lived to marry in Conway County and raise a family.

Allen W. Garrison married Elizabeth Jane Durham, daughter of Joseph and Leona Huff Durham, in 1859. The Garrisons made their home in Springfield, where Allen farmed until the outbreak of the Civil War. He and Elizabeth had several children. Leona California (b. 1860) md. C.C. Moore on Sept. 1, 1878; James H. (b. 1864) md. Melissa Josie Garrett in 1883; Geneva (b. 1866) md. Charles M. Wilson in 1885; Bedford F. (b. 1870) md. Effie Fields in 1891; Ella M. Garrison (b. 1875) md. Ben W. Duncan in 1893.

During the Civil War, both Allen and his brother Andrew served in Company I, Third Regiment, Arkansas Cavalry, CSA. The regiment joined the Army of the West at DeValls Bluff and by order of General Earl Van Dorn the Third Cavalry served dismounted at the Siege of Corinth, suffering horrible casualties. Allen became ill and, under surgeon general's orders, was discharged at Camp Tupelo. In 1863 at Lewisburg, he enlisted in Company B, Third Regiment, Arkansas Cavalry, Volunteer Regiment of the Union Army. He was a 26-year-old farmer of medium height with blue eyes, light hair and a fair complexion. Allen's cousin, James F. Garrison, served in the same company.

Allen's brother, Andrew, continued to serve in the Third for the rest of the war. Paroled in 1865, he came home to marry Elizabeth's sister, Sarah Ann "Sally" Durham, later that year. Andrew and Sally had children: Thomas (b. 1866); Albinus (b. 1868) and James M. (b. 1871). Sally apparently died in the 1870s and Andrew married Martha Cagle in Conway County. They had a son John R. (b. 1880).

After Allen's 1873 death at the age of 38, his widow, Elizabeth, married James F. Garrison. She became his third wife when they married in 1886. James (d. 1901) and Elizabeth (d. 1908) are buried at Mount Pleasant Cemetery. *Submitted by Diane H. Norton.*

GARRISON - James Franklin Garrison (b. Sept. 13, 1827 in Hall County, GA) was the eighth child of Caleb Garrison and Rachel Box. He was married to Susan M. Webb Jett, a widow, in 1845. They came to Conway County in 1854. Susan died in 1858, leaving James to raise her son, John Wyatt Jett, as well as their sons, James C. (b. 1849) and Franklin M. (b. March 14, 1851).

James was conscripted several times into the Confederate Army, but each time obtained a release. He enlisted in the Union Army in September 1863 and served in Company B, Third Arkansas Cavalry until discharged May 22, 1865. As a result of a wound received June 1, 1864, he was blind by October 1870.

James married Julia McCravin on March 31, 1860. Julia (b. 1829 in South Carolina) was the widow of William McCravin. They were the parents of Martha Melinda and Thomas Monroe. James and Julia had twin daughters, Louisa Missouri and Louisa Tennessee (b. Jan. 5, 1869). James and Julia divorced Oct. 20, 1870.

On Dec. 17, 1886, James married Elizabeth Durham Garrison, the widow of Allen Garrison. James was a member of the Springfield Lodge of Masonry and the Napier Post of the Grand Army of the Republic in Center Ridge. He died March 1, 1901 and is buried in Mt. Pleasant Cemetery. Also buried at Mt. Pleasant are Julia McCravin Garrison; her daughter Martha McCravin Durham, wife of Samuel Durham; Louisa Missouri Garrison Garrette, wife of William T. Garrette; Louisa Tennessee Garrison Trout, wife of Henderson Trout; Franklin M. Garrison; James' father Caleb Garrison; and James nephew, Francis Marion Thomas.

Son Thomas C. died before maturity. Son Franklin married Ursula Jane "Sula" Stacks on May 16, 1872. Ursula was the daughter of Benjamin and Ursula West Stacks from Georgia. Franklin and Sula had the following children: James Benjamin, Martha Ellen, Thomas Monroe, Benjamin Franklin, Susann, Alvalee, Annabelle, Oma Dell, Berlie and Dorothy. Franklin was a Mason, a farmer and half owner of the first Conway County steam cotton gin. He donated the land for the Caney Valley Baptist Church. Franklin (d. Dec. 17, 1917) and Sula (d. April 17, 1940) are buried in Wetumka, OK beside daughter Martha Ellen.

Thomas Monroe Garrison (b. Dec. 9, 1877) md. Vida Hawkins on Aug. 20, 1898. She was the daughter of Henry E. Hawkins and Susanna Whitson and called Sudy and Charlie. They had the following children: Bessie Irene (md. Carl Dyton Garrett); Eugene Melton (md. Maude Mildred Patterson); Bernice Ann (md. Clyde Carl Garrett); Benjamin Homer (md. Josephine Bowling); Maudie Lee (died in infancy); Thomas Gloid (md. Bessie Biggers); Everett Elliot (md. Vernell Hipkins); Charles Aubrey (md. Ruby LaFever); and Sudy Jane (md. Carl Livesey). Vida (d. Nov. 3, 1918) is buried at Mt. Pleasant and Thomas (d. March 14, 1940) is buried in Hobart, OK, as are all his sons. *Submitted by Mildred Garrison Cox.*

GASAWAY - Thomas Marion Gasaway, the father of these children, was born in Ringgold, Catoosa County, GA in 1840. He served in the Civil War with the Walker County Invencibles and later with a unit that his father joined. His father, Samuel F. Gasaway, was killed at the battle for Warwick Dam in Tennessee during the Civil War.

Thomas first married Amelia "Millie" Bird, a sister of Mary Bird, and they had four children: Nancy Ellen, Samuel J., Jennie Louise and Amelia/Millie Gasaway. Samuel J, "Uncle Sam," and Jennie Louise married and raised their families in Indian Territory, OK. Nancy Ellen and Amelia have not been so easy to trace. These children lost their mother, Amelia Bird, ca. 1867, and Thomas then married my great-grandmother, Mary Bird. Ida Gasaway Gottberg (b. 1869 in Georgia) was their first child.

Mattie Cumi Gasaway Huggins was the daughter of Mary Bird and Thomas Marion Gasaway. Mattie was born 1871 in Dardnelle, Yell County, AR, shortly after the family arrived from Walker County, GA. Mattie's sister Ida (Gottberg) was born in Walker County in 1869; brothers, David Crockett and Levi Gasaway, were born in Yell County; and another brother, Walter Gasaway, was born in Indian Territory near present day McAlester, OK.

About 1888 when Walter was about 7 years of age. Thomas Marion died near McAlester and is buried somewhere in that area; we have not been able to find the exact location. At that time, Mary Bird Gasaway's brother, John Bird, of Pettit Jean Mountain came and moved Mary and her children back to Cedar Falls District, Pettit Jean Mountain, Conway County, AR.

Mary then applied for a land grant on 11th of April 1891. This document has her signature on it (land is near the Tennis Courts on Pettit Jean Mtn.). Mary's land was located in Section 33 and her witnesses are J.W. Carlock, J.H. Barton, Robert Huggins and John Bird. She raised her children in that area. Later that land was sold and the place nearby that Walter had was bought. Great Grandma Mary lived out her life with Walter's family and is buried on Pettit Jean Mountain beside her son Levi who died a young man. Mary planted a Catalpa tree near his grave to mark this site.

Our Gasaways descend from Col. Nicholas Gassaway, who was baptized March 11, 1634, St. Margaret's Church, Westminster, London, England, who died 1692 in Anne Arundel County, MD. He was the son of Thomas and Anne Collingwood Gasaway of London, England. Col. Nicholas married Ann Beeson and our line is John married Elizabeth Lawrence; their son Nicholas married Elizabeth Hawkins; their son James Gasaway Sr. married Elizabeth Scruggs; their son Thomas and Dorcas Smith Gasaway were the parents of Samuel F. Gasaway; Samuel F. and his wife Elizabeth were the parents of my great-grandfather Thomas Marion Gasaway (b. 1840 in Ringgold, GA, d. ca. 1888 in Eastern, OK. *Submitted by Mrs. Bland Wingert.*

GEORGE - James Sevier George (b. 1804 in Tennessee) may have been the son of Benjamin George (b. 1780) and Rachel (last name unknown). James married Nancy (last name unknown) about 1828 in Tennessee. James was a farmer. He appears on the 1830 Lincoln County, TN census and is listed on the 1832 Lincoln County tax list. He moved his family to Searcy County, AR about 1840. They appear on the 1840 Searcy County census with five children. Nancy died 1840-41 in Searcy or Izard County, AR from complications from childbirth.

After Nancy's death, James returned to Tennessee where he married Margaret J. Stewart, on Nov. 2, 1841 in Lincoln County. Margaret was probably a relative or an old acquaintance. Margaret Stewart was born 1808 in South Carolina. James and Margaret returned to Arkansas immediately after their marriage and settled in Izard County.

James paid personal property taxes in Izard County in 1843. The 1850 Izard County census shows the family living in Richwood Township. The 1860 and 1870 Izard County census shows them in Sylamore Township (now located in Stone County). The 1880 census shows them in Stone County, still living in Sylamore Township. Margaret died 1881-87 in Stone County. James died November 1887. An Application for Letters of Administration was issued Dec. 6, 1887 in Stone County, in the matter of the estate of James S. George, deceased. It listed his children and heirs.

James George and Nancy had five children, all born in Tennessee:

1) Mary Jane George (b. 1830, d. 1856) md. Peter Avey, son of John Avey. Children: James Epson, Nancy Jane (md. Henry Harris) and Delila Avey.

2) Benjamin George (b. 1832, d. before 1887-not mentioned in the letter of administration).

3) Permelia Catharine George (b. 1835) md. John Cole. Children: Josephine Victoria (md. Archibald Roberts) and Sarah Delila "Dilly" (md. James Ingram).

4) Martha Caroline George (b. 1838, d. 1874) md. Richard James D. Holden. Children: Presley Sanford Holden (died young); Margaret Elizabeth Holden (md. Jess H. Holt); James W. "Jim" Holden (md. Sarah Pierce); and Frances Adaline Catherine Holden (md. Thomas Jefferson H. Bridgman).

5) Sarah A. George (b. 1840) md. _ Cooper.

James George and Margaret Stewart had five children, all born in Izard County:

6) Rachel Adaline "Addie" George (b. 1843, d. 1928) md. the outlaw John William "Bill" Dark. One child, William J.B. Dark. Adaline then married D. Hugh "Dock" Martin. Children: Robert, Molly and James Martin.

7) Richard George (b. 1846, d. before 1887-not mentioned in the letter of administration).

8) Robert H. George (b. 1848, d. before 1887) md. and produced children. His heirs are mentioned in the letter of administration.

9) Andrew Jackson George (b. 1851). Andrew married Mary Ellen Rebecca Taylor. Children: Littleberry, Lilborn William, James Albert, Clinton Hall, Lovie Beatrice, Eula Agnes and Ella Leona George.

10) William Francis George (b. 1854, d. 1916) md. Mary Ann Shipman. Children: Francis Marion George and Anderson Nathaniel George.

GEYER - John Christopher Geyer (b. ca. 1819 in Asch, Austria) was the eldest child of John Michael Geyer and Maria Sophie (Ludwig) Geyer. John sailed alone to America around 1849 and settled in Conway County. His parents and siblings, brother John Erhardt and sister Sophie, sailed together on the ship *Rebecca* a few years later, and chose Little Rock as their new home.

Over the course of several years, John bought *John Christopher Geyer* land in both Perry and Conway counties on the Arkansas River. But Conway County, near Lewisburg, was where he made his home and earned a living as a farmer.

He married Nancy Adeline around 1856 and this union produced his only children, Charles Michael and George Anderson Geyer. Nancy died before 1870, and John married Lucinda Stover.

Besides farming, John was also active in his community. He was appointed Justice of the Peace in 1868, and court examiner in 1869 for Howard Township.

John died in 1878, at 59 years of age. His widow Lucinda and his two sons moved to Perry County. George Anderson Geyer died young and never married, but his brother, Charles Michael, married May Hamilton around 1881.

One child, Charlie Anderson Geyer, was born to Charles and May in 1882, and Charles Michael died soon after. When he was a young man, Charlie Anderson moved to Conway in Faulkner County, where he attended Hendrix College.

He married Maggie Lee Middleton there in 1903, and moved his young bride to Perry County, where he built a home and worked as a farmer and a carpenter.

Charlie and Maggie had one son, Charlie Adolph Geyer (b. 1904 in Perry County, in the old Dixie Community near Stoney Point). From Charlie Adolph Geyer there are only four Geyer males left, two sons and two grandsons. *Submitted by Linda Mills, great-great-great-granddaughter of John Christopher Geyer.*

GIVENS - Fred Thomas Givens Sr. (b. April 11, 1943), the son of Jack Newton Givens and Mabel "Patsy" Clay King, in Abilene, TX. Fred joined the Army National Guard and left Texas. He was stationed at Fort Chaffee, at Fort Smith and loved Arkansas. Fred came to visit our area with one of his buddies, Tim Givens, and met Judy Caroline Scroggins (b. July 5, 1941), daughter of Sherman and Stincy Dee Roberson Scroggins. They met and fell in love. They were married on April 19, 1964.

Fred and Judy Givens

Fred loved the Conway County area and made it his home. Fred had a partnership with Volkswagen dealership in Russellville for several years and sold automobiles. In 1974 Fred Givens was one of the first 13 people hired for Arrow Automotive in Morrilton. He took great pride in Arrow and the products it produced. He worked there until it shut it doors. He was instrumental in its success for many years.

Fred and Judy had three children:

1) Fred Thomas Givens Jr. (b. Dec., 13, 1964) md. Deronda Lee Dixon, daughter of Jimmy and Betty Dixon, on Oct. 17, 1987. They have two children, Heather Lee Givens (b. March 3, 1989) and Jenna Marie Givens (b. Aug. 19, 1994). They live in Plumerville, AR.

2) Tara Lea Givens (b. Nov. 30, 1965) md. Benny Lloyd McClure, son of Darrell Benjamin and Peggy Janell Brown McClure, on Oct. 6, 1984. They have three children: Derrick Shane Jack McClure (b. July 5, 1987); Charles Blaine Thomas McClure (b. Oct. 22, 1989) and Lauren Lea Brooke McClure (b. July 24, 1991). They live in Springdale, AR.

Gaysha Lynn Givens (b. Nov. 12, 1968) md. Robert Bartlett Aug. 25, 1989. They have one child, Joshua Newton Bartlett (b. Nov. 4, 1993) and live in Morrilton, AR.

GLODEN - Michael M. Gloden was born 1830-36 in Luxembourg, one of the smallest and oldest countries in Europe. He was the son of John Gloden and M. Stomuel. He immigrated to America in 1857 and became a naturalized citizen.

Michael enlisted on Aug. 14, 1862 at Decatur, IL in Co. I, 116th Illinois Volunteer Infantry. He was discharged on June 7, 1865. He married Lucinda Adaline Branham on Sept. 6, 1865 at Decatur, IL. Lucinda (b. May 3, 1844 in Blount County, AL) was the daughter of William and Arenna Branham. Lucinda died Aug. 18, 1878 at Decatur and is buried in Wheeler Cemetery. Michael married Margaret Herman on Feb. 2, 1880 in Macon County. Margaret Herman (b. 1854 in Aultbiren) was the daughter of Andrew Herman.

On June 3, 1895, Michael filed for an invalid pension on his Civil War service. His application indicated he was unable to earn a support by manual labor because of a gunshot wound in the left arm and rheumatism, impaired vision, disease of the heart and general disability. Michael filed again for his Civil War pension on Feb. 27, 1907. He died Aug. 28, 1911, at Decatur. Margaret died there on Aug. 18, 1914. They are buried in Wheeler Cemetery.

Children of Michael and Lucinda: (1) John Michael Gloden (b. 1867, d. 1948) md. Lillie Coulter; (2) William Franklin Gloden (b. 1869, d. 1939); (3) Margaret Irene Gloden (b. 1871, d. 1902) md. Ernest Harkness; (4) Mary J. Gloden (b. 1872) md. Clarence Molter, then William Gaines; (5) James Moses Gloden (b. 1874) md. Elizabeth Babcock.

William Franklin Gloden (b. May 7, 1869 at Decatur, IL) was the son of Michael and Lucinda. He married Etta Melvina "Ettie" Taylor in 1891. Ettie Taylor (b. Aug. 10, 1875 in Illinois) was the daughter of Oral Taylor who was said to be 3/4 Cherokee Indian. Frank and Ettie moved to Tennessee soon after November 1892. They moved to Arkansas and divorced about 1903-05.

Frank married his cousin Mandy Jane (Branham)

Daley on July 31, 1906 at Memphis, TN. Mandy (b. Aug. 27, 1876 at Leslie, AR) was the daughter of James Lacey Branham and Eliza Jane Osborn. Mandy was the widow of Andrew Daley. Mandy and Frank were first cousins and had to go to Tennessee to marry because the state of Arkansas would not allow first cousins to marry. Frank's mother, Lucinda, and Mandy's father, James Lacey, were brother and sister. The family settled at Leslie where Frank farmed and for a time worked in a barrel factory.

Ettie (Taylor) Gloden married David White on March 25, 1921 in Searcy County. David White was first married to Mary Jane Daley, daughter of Mandy Jane Branham who Frank married after he and Ettie divorced. Frank died April 25, 1934 at Leslie. Mandy died April 15, 1967 at Marshall, AR. Ettie died in the 1930s.

Children of Frank Gloden and Ettie Taylor: William Penn Gloden (b. 1892, d. 1894); Gertie Mae Adaline Gloden (b. 1894, d. 1959) md. James William Branham; Jesse Michael Gloden (b. 1898); Josey Gloden (b. 1901, d. 1902).

Children of Frank Gloden and Mandy (Branham) Daley: Harry Alonzo Gloden (b. 1907, d. 1908); Lillian Grace Gloden (b. 1909, d. 1986) md. Thomas Eli Campbell; Frank Gloden (b. 1914, d. 1996) md. Mamie Elen Garner.

GOODALL - About 1880 four Goodall Brothers left Marion County, AR, after their father, James Matthew Goodall, mysteriously vanished from the face of the earth. He was a soldier in the Confederate Army during the Civil War.

Uncle Tom and Uncle Bill Goodall settled in Yell County, while Uncle George Goodall and my father, James Madison, settled in Conway County. For a brief time my father moved to Yell County. After his wife died and was buried in a Bluffton, AR cemetery, he remained single until he met and married my mother, Minnie Bell Wells, in 1900.

This picture has all 13 of the children together as adults, along with both parents. Seated l-r: James Madison Goodall, Minnie Bell Wells Goodall, Lillie Goodall Simons, only daughter of James Madison and Annie Reynolds Goodall. Standing l-r are Mattie Goodall Tanner, Elba Goodall Clemons, Lottie Goodall Meeks, Opal Goodall Yielding, Maggie Goodall Peters, Thomas W. Goodall, Henry James Goodall, Esther Goodall Rea, Hester Goodall Torbert, Floy Goodall McGee, William "Bill" Goodall and George Goodall. Margie Goodall, the second child born to my parents died at about 3 months old.

My mother, Minnie Bell Wells, was born and partially raised at Cleveland, AR. Both sides of her family came from Alabama. Her mother's name was Fannie Kelly. The story goes that Fannie rode a grey mare side-saddle all the way from Alabama to Arkansas. Her husband, Henry Wells, died at the age of 28, leaving her with six children to bring up alone.

When all of Grandma's children were grown, the entire family, except for Grandma and my mother, moved to Texas and stayed, except to visit Arkansas occasionally. Grandma had 80 acres of land she and her husband had purchased. When she died, she willed it to mother and until this day that land is still in the family. I almost forgot to tell you that when my dad

came to Conway County he drove a team of oxen named Buck and Charlie for Uncle George Tilmon Goodall. Both my dad and Uncle George are buried at the Old Hickory Cemetery. Uncle Tom is buried in Atkins, AR, Cemetery. Uncle Bill Goodall wanted to be buried in the Cowan Cemetery in Marion County, AR.

Three of the Goodall brothers who left Marion County about 1880 became farmers. The other one, Uncle Bill, was a blacksmith by trade. He not only did blacksmithing work, but he also had a gristmill that ground corn into cornmeal. The most prominent of the Goodall brothers, at least financially, was Uncle George Tilmon. He raised cattle, horses, mules and hogs. I have been told that in the late 1800s and early 1900s people had free range, which meant they had unlimited pastures. Uncle George also hauled freight by wagon and team from Toad Suck Ferry to Galla Rock. That was especially true when the Arkansas River was low. Uncle George was also a guard for the state of Arkansas, guarding prisoners on a farm near Morrilton. It has been said he was one of the wealthiest men in Conway County for a number of years. When the banks went bankrupt in 1929, he lost all his money but $3,500 to $4000; this lasted him until his death in 1952.

To James Madison, Annie Reynolds and my mother (after the death of Annie), 14 children were born. Thirteen of them lived to be adults, however, all of them were high school drop-outs. One of them did get a high school diploma by means of the GED test. That one also went on to three colleges and universities for about eight years, earning both a bachelor's and master's degree. Thomas W. has been advised to admit that he was the one who got the high school diploma and the two college degrees.

Uncle Bill Goodall, the blacksmith, was the only brother who had no children of his own. He was also a Baptist preacher. *Submitted by Thomas W. Goodall.*

GORDON - Alexander Gordon (b. ca. 1822 in Robertson County, TN, d. March 1, 1864 in Conway County, AR) is buried at Grandview Cemetery. His parents were Robert Boaz and Millie Pitts Gordon. He married Nancy Ragsdale about 1846. She was the daughter of William and Sarah Ragsdale. Nancy died prior to 1859 in Conway County. Alexander's second wife was Elizabeth Prince, daughter of Miles and Charity Halbrook Prince. They married July 26, 1859 Conway County.

Alexander Gordon, 1822-1864, Co. C, 5th AR Inf., CSA.

Alexander worked as a miller, farmer and justice of the peace. He purchased 80 acres of land under the Homestead Act with the final certificate being issued May 1, 1860. He enlisted June 10, 1861 in Co. C, 5th AR Infantry, CSA and was wounded Oct. 8, 1862 during the Battle of Perryville in Kentucky and sent to the hospital in Harrodsburg, KY. His grandfather was Alexander Gordon (b. 1755, d. 1831), who fought in the Revolutionary War, enlisting Aug. 11, 1782 in the first South Carolina Regiment under the command of Colonel C. Pinckney. His grandmother was Sarah Lee, daughter of John and Mary Cassels Lee.

About 1800, his grandparents migrated from Chester County, SC to Robertson County, TN to Carroll, TN, then to Graves County, KY and then to the Center Ridge area of Conway County, AR in the mid-1840s. Robert Boaz Gordon served as County Judge in Conway County between 1846-48 and in 1850 served on the committee of three to locate the county seat and arrange for the building of a new courthouse in Conway County.

Children of Alexander and Nancy:

1) Johnathan "John" (b. ca. 1847 in Arkansas,

d. before 1900 Conway County, AR) md. Mary "Polly" Starkey on Dec. 10, 1871 in Conway County. She was the daughter of Caleb and Sarah Huie Starkey. They did not have children.

2) Robert Bolen (b. Dec. 31, 1849 Conway County, AR, d. April 5, 1920, Conway County, AR, buried at Kilgore Cemetery) md. Nancy Elizabeth Reed Sept. 5, 1872 in Conway County. She was the daughter of James and Sarah Elizabeth Smith Reed. Their children were James A. "Jim," Mary Ann "Molly," William Robert "Will," John W. "Red," Joseph Lucian, Elizabeth Ann "Lizzie," Ira Austin, Lonnie Houston and two infants that died at birth.

3) Alexander Bruce (b. July 4, 1855 in Conway County, AR, d. Feb. 1, 1910 Conway County, AR, buried at Kilgore Cemetery) md. Melvina Reed on July 5, 1874 in Conway County. She was the daughter of James and Sarah Elizabeth Smith Reed. Their children were Nancy Ann "Nannie," Lucian R. "Luce," Jane, Lewis, Lucinda "Cindy," Sarah, John Bruce, Emma Jeanette, Elmer Alexander, Rosa Narsis "Sissy," Sreathie Ethel and Allie Melvina.

4) Lucian (b. ca. 1858, Conway County, AR, d. unk.) md. Ophelia A. Doty Feb. 8, 1885 in Conway County.

Children of Alexander and Elizabeth:

1) Joseph P. (b. July 11, 1860, Center Ridge, Conway County, AR, d. Oct. 28, 1928, Center Ridge, Conway County, AR, buried at Halbrook Cemetery) md. Amelia Hogue. Their children were William, John Alexander, Roxie L., Martha Elizabeth, Charity Palmer, Lucy Jane and Isabell.

2) Roxie Ann (b. March 15, 1863, Center Ridge, Conway County, AR, d. Jan. 10, 1944, Center Ridge, AR, buried at Halbrook Cemetery) md. J. Newton Halbrook Aug. 16, 1878 in Conway County. Their children were Sarah Ann, Charity Elizabeth, Joseph T. and Mary Nora. Roxie married second, James Monroe Bryant in 1889 Conway County, AR. Their children were Myrtle J. "Myrtie," Nancy Zellar "Zella," John Thomas "Johnnie." Lou Ella "Ellie" and Cerrena "Renie."

3) William Miles (b. May 9, 1864, Center Ridge, Conway County, AR, d. Nov. 17, 1958, Perryville, Perry County, AR, buried at Halbrook Cemetery) md. Martha Barnes "Marthie" about 1890 in Conway County. She was the daughter of Andrew and Rebecca Williams Barnes. They had one daughter Lillie (b. December 1909 in Conway County). William's second wife was Annie Bell Oliger-Clowers, daughter of Charles F. and Sallie Eoff Oliger. They married June 15, 1910 in Conway County. Their children were Archie, Olen, William Elba, Ruby, Willie Mae and Charlie Raymond.

Alexander and Nancy Gordon are my great-great-grandparents. All information on this family is based on data obtained prior to January 2001. Additional information on the Gordon Family can be found at http://www.angelfire.com/tn/gordongenealogy. *Submitted by Sharon Smith.*

GORDON - Alexander Gordon (b. 1822 in Robertson County, TN) was the son of Robert Boaz Gordon and Milly Pitts Gordon. Robert married Nancy Ragsdale in Tennessee and moved to Conway County, AR between 1844-50. He is shown living in the Point Remove Township on the 1850 census of Conway County. Alexander was a Justice of the Peace of Conway County and a farmer. Nancy died between 1856-59. Alexander took a second wife on July 26, 1859 when he married Elizabeth Prince. Alexander is shown on the 1860 census living in Lick Mountain

Alexander Gordon

Township. Alexander died March 1, 1864. Conway County Administrations and Bonds Records 1859-85, page 89-90, March 17, 1864 mention Alexander's death.

Judith Elizabeth Prince Gordon was administrator of Alexander's estate and later, Loyal C. O'Barr received letters of administration. William Ragsdale, a relative of Nancy Ragsdale Gordon, was at one time also an administrator of Alexander's estate.

Alexander had four children by his first wife and three children by his second wife. Children of Alexander and Nancy Ragsdale Gordon: John E. Gordon (b. 1847 Conway County) md. Holly Starkey; Robert Bolen/Bolin Gordon (b. Dec. 31, 1849) md. Nancy Elizabeth Reed, died April 6, 1920 Conway County, AR; Alexander Gordon III (b. July 1855) md. Melvina Reed; Lucian M. Gordon (b. 1857) md. Ophelia A. Doty.

Children of Alexander and Elizabeth Prince Gordon: Joseph P. Gordon (b. July 1860, d. October 1928) md. Permelia P. Hogue; Roxie L. Gordon (b. March 1863, d. January 1944) md. Isaac Halbrook; William M. Gordon (b. May 1864, d. November 1958) md. Martha. *Submitted by Kaci Smith.*

GORDON - Alexander Bruce Gordon was born July 4, 1855 in Conway County, AR to Alexander and Nancy Ragsdale Gordon. He died Feb. 1, 1910 in Conway County and is buried at Kilgore Cemetery. He married Melvina Reed July 5, 1874 in Conway County. Melvina was born Dec. 11, 1855 in Tennessee to James and Sarah Elizabeth Smith Reed. Melvina died Dec. 9, 1925 in Conway County and is buried at Kilgore Cemetery.

Alexander Bruce Gordon, Melvina Reed-Gordon and Allie Gordon about 1906.

Alexander's mother died before 1859 and his father died in 1864, a few months before his son's ninth birthday. He and his brothers then went to live with their grandparents, William and Sarah Ragsdale, until they were adults. Alexander farmed for a time on rented land and one winter worked at a gin for his brother-in-law, William W. Reed. In December 1881, he moved onto 80 acres of land which he purchased under the Homestead Act with the final certificate being issued May 31, 1890. He was a member of the Pleasant Springs Missionary Baptist Church, where he also served as church clerk.

Alexander and Melvina had 12 children:

1) Nancy Ann "Nannie" (b. May 2, 1875, Center Ridge, Conway County, AR, d. May 24, 1951 Morrilton Conway County, AR, buried Kilgore Cemetery) md. William Ryly Deaton Feb. 10, 1898 in Conway County. Children: Margaret, Alex and Julia.

2) Lucian R. "Luce" (b. March 3, 1877, Center Ridge, Conway County, AR, d. Sept. 2, 1880 Ridge, Conway County, AR, buried Pleasant Hill Cemetery).

3) Jane (b. Nov. 3, 1878, Center Ridge, Conway County, AR, d. March 3, 1911, Center Ridge, Conway County, AR, buried Kilgore Cemetery) md. H. Dempsey Harrington Dec. 28, 1897 in Conway County. Children: Alexander, Fronia, Arkey, Anna, Lola, Sam, Selma and Myrtle.

4) Lewis (b. Dec. 9, 1879, Center Ridge, Conway County, AR, d. Aug. 25, 1881, Conway County, AR, buried Pleasant Hill Cemetery).

5) Lucinda "Cindy" (b. July 13, 1881, Center

Ridge, Conway County, AR, d. Nov. 17, 1960 in Oklahoma) md. James P. Scroggin "Pleas" on March 20, 1901 in Conway County. Children: Nettie and Jennie.

6) Sarah (b. Jan. 13, 1882, Ridge, Conway County, AR, d. July 15, 1882, Conway County, buried at Pleasant Hill Cemetery).

7) John Bruce (b. Dec. 26, 1886, Center Ridge, Conway County, AR, d. Feb. 12, 1969, England, Lonoke County, AR, buried Union Valley Cemetery) md. Carrie Etta Tucker Dec. 3, 1905 in Conway County. She is the daughter of Benjamin A. and Mary Woodard Tucker. Children: William Stanley, Edward Earl, Edna Pearl, Muriel May, Velma Virginia, Iris Noreen, Lindel and Fred.

8) Emma Jeanette (b. July 20, 1888, Center Ridge, Conway County, AR, d. May 14, 1967, Morrilton, Conway County, AR, buried Kilgore Cemetery) md. John Amos Huett about 1909 in Conway County. He is the son of David "Uncle Doc" and Carlotta "Lottie" Williams Huett. Emma and John did not have any children.

9) Elmer Alexander (b. April 18, 1892, Center Ridge, Conway County, AR, d. Aug. 13, 1975, Springfield, Conway County, AR, buried Kilgore Cemetery) md. first, Eugene Tucker "Jeannie" on Nov. 24, 1917 in Conway County. Their son was premature and died at birth Dec. 23, 1918. Jeannie died Dec. 25, 1918. Elmer married second, Ollie Ann Meeler on Feb. 10, 1920 in Conway County. Ollie is the daughter of Stephen Lard "Lardie" and Safronia Adeline Brents Meeler. Children of Elmer and Ollie: Pauline and Carl D.

10) Rosa Narsis "Sissy" (b. Nov. 17, 1893, Center Ridge, Conway County, AR, d. Aug. 21, 1967, Morrilton, Conway County, AR, buried Kilgore Cemetery) md. Samuel Porter Bird "Port Bird." Children: Edther, Elbert Samuel, Ruth, Fay M., Ralph Dale, Imogene Gladys, Robert L., Dewey Gordon, Roy Lane and Huett Franklin.

11) Sreathie Ethel (b. July 4, 1896, Center Ridge, Conway County, AR, d. Jan. 31, 1985, England, Lonoke County, AR, buried at Kilgore Cemetery) md. Jacob Calvin Huett "Cabin Huett," a son of David "Doc Huett" and Lue Ella Allgood Huett. Children: Freddie and Mable.

12) Allie Melvina (b. July 21, 1901, Springfield, Conway County, AR, d. Jan. 27, 1975, in San Antonio, Bexar County, TX, buried at Fort Sam Houston Cemetery) md. Jessie Lee Wilson Oct. 22, 1916 in Conway County. Children: Edith Melvina, Emma Lee, Wilma Allie, Mary Francis and Gordon Neil.

Alexander and Melvina Gordon are my grandparents. All information on this family is based on data available prior to January 2001. Additional information on the Gordon Family can be found at http://www.angelfire.com/tn/gordongenealogy. *Submitted by Sharon Smith.*

GORDON - Jerome E. Gordon (b. Sept. 24, 1865, at Lewisburg, Conway County, AR, at the end of the Civil War) was the fourth of 15 children, all born in Arkansas. His father was Hiram Campbell Gordon, and his mother was Sarah Angelene Bearden. His father, at various times, ran a grist mill on Point Remove Creek, farmed, ran a store in Solgohachia, and was the Solgohachia Postmaster for about a year and a half before his death. The land that the mill was located on is still in the hands of Gordon descendants.

Jerome was married to Susan "Sally" Alice Bird on Oct. 17, 1886, in Conway County. Susan was the daughter of James W. and Susan F. Bird, of Solgohachia. Susan Alice was born in Desoto County, MS, the third of seven children. The Bird family came to Conway County about 1873.

Jerome and Sally had five children, all born in Solgohachia: Laura Iola (b. Aug. 4, 1892) md. Tallie Williams; Adolf "Dolf" (b. Oct. 6, 1887) md. Addie Williams; James Campbell (b. April 26, 1889) md. Emma Taylor; Luther (b. Nov. 21, 1894) md. Katie Reed; Susan "Sadie" (b. Nov. 9, 1896) md. Horace Blackshear.

Mother Susan Alice died on Feb. 8, 1897 at age 29, three months after the birth of their fifth child, Susan "Sadie" and was buried the next day on private property north of Solgohachia on Hwy. 9, south of Cypress Creek. She died from complications of either Diabetes or Bright's Disease.

Grandparents, Hiram and Sally Gordon, as well as Jerome's sister, Elisia Jane Gordon Nation, helped raise the motherless children until Jerome remarried about three years later on Feb. 24, 1900 to Dora Ella Williams, at Solgohachia. Dora was originally from the Conway County area. Jerome and Dora had 12 children together (thus Jerome had fathered 17 children altogether).

Their children together were Pompei Eugene "Gene" (b. Nov. 15, 1900); Ben White "Doc" (b. June 9, 1902); Laurence Crawford (b. Aug. 6, 1904); Freda Helen (b. March 28, 1906); Arka "Arkie" (b. June 30, 1908); Inez Orlinda (b. Aug. 22, 1910); Hiram Harvey (b. March 14, 1914); twins-Marion Wilson and Maude Dickson (b. Dec. 22, 1916); Christina "Tina" Elizabeth (b. Dec. 3, 1920); William Alfred (b. Jan. 24, 1923); Unknown Infant.

Jerome (known as "Uncle Bud" to his many nephews and nieces) and Dora lived in Solgohachia until sometime between 1910-20, when the family moved to Kansas. Jerome and Dora resided there until their deaths. Dora (d. 1951) and Jerome (d. Oct. 28, 1957) are buried in Wilson, KS.

GORDON - Joseph Lucian Gordon (b. Aug. 30, 1884, in Center Ridge, Conway County, AR, d. March 1, 1960, in Lonoke, AR) was the son of Robert Bolin Gordon and Nancy Elizabeth Reed, and the grandson of Alexander Gordon and Nancy Ragsdale, daughter of William and Sarah Ragsdale. Lucian's great-grandparents were Robert Boaz Gordon and Milly Pitts. All four generations of this family owned land in Grandview or Center Ridge. Lucian's maternal grandparents were Rev. James Reed and Sarah Elizabeth Smith. Sarah died in Tennessee before James moved his family to Arkansas. James Reed first settled in Peter's Creek, Van Buren County in 1856 and by 1871 he was in Conway County.

Reginald, Gerald, Robert, Lucian Gordon and Paxson.

On Feb. 13, 1910, Lucian Gordon married Chloe Bell Paxson (b. March 8, 1898 in Grandview, AR, d. Sept. 4, 1967 in Little Rock, AR), daughter of Joseph Taylor Paxson and Mathilda Agnes Kelley of Grandview. Joseph Lucian Gordon was a schoolteacher at Grandview and Center Ridge Schools. For a short time, the family lived in Cleburne County and he taught at Davis Special and Greer's Ferry. Lucian's son, Robert, remembers his father going by horseback on Sun-

day, staying Monday through Friday and coming home for the weekend. They farmed but always had a hired man, and of course the manual labor of the children.

Lucian helped to build the Grandview Church and School, as did his father-in-law, Joseph Taylor Paxson. Lucian was very active in the Church of Christ - teaching and leading singing

Leona Stripling Bradley, in *The Valentine of 1899,* her book of memories of her life in Conway County, wrote on page 6, "Chloe Paxson and Lucian Gordon went to church at Center Ridge. Some of us can remember when husbands and wives didn't sit together at church. The mothers sat on one side and took care of the little ones and Daddies sat on the other side. It was different with Chloe and Lucian and it made a very deep impression on me as a young lady. I remember saying, "If I ever get married, how I hoped I'd get a man like that…"

In the summer of 1931, the Gordon family moved to Lonoke County near other relatives. They loaded their belongings into a truck, in which the parents and three youngest children rode. The other children and belongings were placed in their wagon, which was pulled by mules. The cows were tied to the wagon and they made the long, 3-day journey down to Oldham, Lonoke County, camping out along the way. Arlie Clowers, Lucian's farm hand, moved with the family to assist in planting crops. The family later moved to Bain's Chapel. Lucian farmed full time at these locations. When they moved to the town of England, Lucian went into contract construction work. In 1939 they moved to Lonoke, AR where Lucian worked as a case worker for a government social service agency. During WWII, he did carpentry work on a large defense plant in Pine Bluff. Lucian continued to work in his carpentry and cabinet shop in Lonoke until his death.

Lucian and Chloe felt blessed that all five of their sons served their country in the Pacific, and all returned alive and healthy. Chloe and Lucian enjoyed singing. It was always church songs and we would often have a singing whenever there was a family gathering. Lucian and Chloe had seven children: Helen, Leonard, Lorene, Robert, Paxson, Gerald and Harold Reginald.

1) Helen Nema Gordon (b. March 18, 1912, at Davis Special, Van Buren County, AR, d. Oct. 13, 1985 in Morrilton, AR) md. Jeff Thomason ca. 1935, divorced, one son Jeff (b. Jan. 1, 1938). She married second, Vernon Anderson, in 1950 in Lonoke, AR. Helen was a LVN.

2) Joseph Leonard Gordon (b. Jan. 11, 1916 at Center Ridge, AR, d. July 14, 1961) md. Jan. 10, 1937 in Coy, Lonoke County, AR to Cuba V. King (b. Oct. 1, 1911, in Lanty, Conway County, AR, d. Oct. 11, 2000 in Lonoke, AR). Leonard served in the Army in the Pacific Theater during WWII. He took up flying and owned a Piper Cub airplane.

3) Agnes Lorene Gordon (b. Sept. 18, 1918, Center Ridge, AR, d. May 2, 1989, in N. Little Rock, AR) md. Alvin McClain, divorced. On June 16, 1966, she married Dennis Dallas in N. Little Rock, AR. Dennis was born 1903 in Valonia, Faulkner County, AR and died Aug. 28, 1985, in N. Little Rock, AR. Lorene had no children, but was like a special mother to her niece, Aleta Ann Gordon.

4) Robert Paxson Gordon (b. Nov. 16, 1922 at Edgemont, Cleburne County, AR) md. Peggy Evelyn Pike on Sept. 3, 1946 in Houston, Harris County, TX. Robert served in the Navy on the repair ship, USS *Ajax*, which was in the Pacific Theater during WWII. After the war, he went back to Harding College to finish his degree in accounting. While there, he was the first of his brothers to take flying lessons from his cousin, Lowell Beavers. For nearly 30 years, Robert was in hospital administration at Hermann Hospital, Houston, TX and at Angelo Community Hospital, San Angelo, TX. In 1978 he opened his own CPA practice and as of 2005, is still working full time. Robert and Peg have five children: Drexel Reed, Kearby Lynn, Sharla Jan, Blair Kevin and Kyle Duncan.

5) Lucian Paxson Gordon (b. April 28, 1925 in

Grandview, Conway County, AR) md. Opal Fae Shaffer on July 14, 1946, in Briscoe, Wheeler County, TX. Paxson served in the Air Corps in the Pacific Theater during WWII. They both graduated from Harding College and received higher degrees in education. Paxson and Opal were both schoolteachers in Beaver, OK and Liberal, KS. Paxson also preaches for the Church of Christ. He and Opal spend several months each year in Sibiu, Romania, helping with church work. Paxson and Opal have five children: Norma Lee, Larry, Linda Fae, Sylvan and Alma Ruth.

6) Gerald Leland Gordon (b. May 18, 1927 in Grandview, AR, d. Oct. 27, 1951 in Griffithsville, AR) md. Jorene Bogan (b. Jan. 14, 1931, d. Oct. 31, 1951 in Griffithsville, AR) on Aug. 28, 1949. Gerald was in the Navy and served in the Pacific Theater during WWII. After the war, he attended Harding College. He also became a pilot and owned a Piper Cub airplane. He gave up school for flying and marriage, and became a crop dusting pilot. Gerald and Jorene had one daughter, Aleta Ann Gordon.

7) Harold Reginald Gordon (b. Aug. 16, 1930 in Grandview, AR) md. Claudia Emmaline Middleton June 9, 1950, divorced. He has three daughters: Mary Deborah, Trina and Kathy. Reginald attended Harding College for a very short time before he joined the Navy. He also learned to fly and, as most Piper Cub pilots, had many "adventures" landing in the wrong place! When he retired from the Navy, after 20 years, he went to work for Hewlett-Packard in Georgia. He married Cynthia Elizabeth (Sinclair) Partridge (b. June 17, 1972, d. April 17, 2001 in Roswell, GA). On May 4, 2002, Harold married Guerry (Graham) Myers in Atlanta, GA. They now live in Virginia. *Submitted by Peggy Pike Gordon.*

GORDON - Our earliest ancestor to arrive in Conway County was the Robert Boaz Gordon family. Robert Boaz (b. 1800 in Chester County, SC, d. Aug. 3, 1853 in Conway County, AR, buried at Grandview Cemetery), was the son of Alexander Gordon (born in Virginia) and Sarah Lee, daughter of John and Mary (Cassels) Lee of Fairfield County, SC. In 1802, the family moved to Robertson County, TN. About 1819, Robert Boaz Gordon married Milly Pitts (b. 1787, Chatham County, NC, died before 1870 in Conway County), daughter of Joseph Pitts and Martha "Patsy" Barbee.

Robert Boaz and Milly (Pitts) Gordon began their migration west with a move to Carroll County, TN, then to Mayfield, Graves County, KY. Their last move west was to Lick Mountain Township in Conway County. Robert Boaz Gordon is first recorded in Conway County as County Judge in the November Term 1845. On Nov. 6, 1850, Commissioners Robert Boaz Gordon, John W. Gilbert and John H. Fryer were elected to choose a site for the County Seat and to build a Courthouse for Conway County. They chose Springfield, AR. Robert Boaz Gordon also farmed and served as Justice of Peace. Robert Boaz and Milly (Pitts) Gordon had eight children:

1) Angeline Gordon (b. July 1821 in Robertson County, TN, died after 1900 in Oklahoma) md. James Armstrong in 1840 in Graves County, KY. Their children were Mary Ann, William A., James, Missouri, Freeman Patrick and Melissa.

2) Alexander Gordon (b. 1822 Robertson County, TN, d. March 1, 1864, Conway County) md. first to Nancy Ragsdale (b. 1825 Tennessee, d. ca. 1857, Conway County). There is a biography of Alexander Gordon and Nancy Ragsdale in this book.

3) Elzanna Gordon (b. Nov. 29, 1824 in Robertson County, TN, d. bef. 1861 in Pope County, AR) md. Samuel N. Wilson (b. Feb. 2, 1822 in Tennessee, d. Oct. 1, 1866 in Pope County, AR) on Dec. 4, 1845. Their children were Margaret Lane, Alexander D., Mary, Missouri Tennessee, Gullet "Gully" Sylvester and Finis Ello.

4) Elvira Gordon (b. Dec. 22, 1827 in Robertson County, TN, d. bef. Sept. 19, 1860 in Pope County,

AR) in about 1846 married Robert S. Wilson, brother of Samuel Wilson. He was born 1822 and died April 21, 1859. Children: Mary Angeline and Joseph.

5) Eisora Gordon (b. 1832 Robertson County, TN) married three times: (1st) William Erastus Prince on Oct. 9, 1851 in Conway County. He was born 1830 in South Carolina, son of Cary Prince and Beulah Smith. (2nd) William Carter Shearon about 1860 in Conway County. (3rd) William Thomas Parsley before August 1870.

6) Joseph Pitts Gordon (b. July 20, 1833 in Carroll County, TN, d. July 31, 1891 in Collin County, TX) md. Unie Pate Aug. 4, 1859 Conway County, AR, sister to Judge James Pate of Van Buren County, AR. Joseph and Unie had eight children: Robert Bolden, Joseph, David Alexander, Mary Molly, James W., Sarah, infant son born and died Collin County, TX, and Dixie Cleveland

7) John James Gordon (b. 1837 Carroll County, TN, d. Sept. 24, 1861, Conway County) md. America Griggs, daughter of Samuel Griggs and Fanny Maddox. She later married James Wilson Pate, brother of Unie Pate, who married Joseph Pitts Gordon. John and America had no children.

8) Missouri Gordon (b. Feb. 11, 1839 Graves County, KY, d. Sept. 13, 1894 Pope County, AR) md. Phillip Manly Austin in Conway County, AR on Sept. 28, 1859. Children: Sarah M. and Parallie. Missouri and Phillip also raised the children of her sisters, Elzana and Elvira. *Submitted by Peggy Pike Gordon.*

GORDON - Robert Bolin Gordon (b. Dec. 31, 1849 in Center Ridge, AR) the son of Alexander Gordon and Nancy Ragsdale. Alexander migrated to Arkansas from Tennessee prior to 1850 and was living in Point Remove Township at the time of the 1850 census.

The Gordon family. Seated: William Robert Gordon and Laura Elizabeth Hill Gordon. Standing, l-r: Ollie Gordon Brown, Hettie Gordon Eoff, Edgar Gordon, Cora Anne Gordon Campbell, Jack Gordon.

Robert, according to family history, entered the Confederate States Army when he was 14 years old. He was a member of Col. McCroy's Regiment of Cavalry from Arkansas. He served in the 10th Regiment from 1863-65. He was discharged Feb. 15, 1865 in Cape Girardeau, MO. Mrs. Cora Gordon Campbell said it took Robert two years to return home to Center Ridge, AR after his discharge.

She also said Robert Bolin Gordon enlisted in the Confederate Army at Lewisburg, AR in 1863. Robert lived at Center Ridge, AR with his family. One day a neighbor rode up and told Robert's father that Northern Sympathizers were riding through the county killing all boys old enough to fight. That night Robert and one of his friends rode to Lewisburg and enlisted the next day."

Robert Bolin Gordon married Nancy Elizabeth Reed on Sept. 5, 1872 in Conway County. Nancy was the daughter of James and Sarah Elizabeth Smith Reed. Robert was a farmer. He and Nancy lived all their lives in Conway County.

The couple had 10 children: James A. Gordon (b. 1873, d. about 1891 in Oklahoma); Mary Ann Gordon (b. September 1874) md. Will Scroggins; William Robert Gordon (b. Dec. 25, 1875, d. Feb. 25, 1963) md. Laura Elizabeth Hill; John W. Gordon (b. December 1877) md. Dollie Bell Gordon; Joseph Lucian

Gordon (b. Aug. 30, 1884, d. March 1, 1960) md. Chloe Belle Paxon; Elizabeth Gordon (b. March 1886) md. Allen Powell; Ira A. Gordon (b. February 1892) md. Josie A.; Lonnie Houston Gordon (b. July 1, 1893, d. Aug. 24, 1953) md. Geneva Mae Maxwell.

Robert died April 6, 1920 in Conway County. Nancy died Oct. 22, 1939 in Lonoke County. They are buried in the Kilgore Cemetery in Conway County, AR. *Submitted by Miranda Smith*

GORDON - Robert Bolen Gordon (b. Dec. 31, 1849 at Center Ridge, Conway County, AR, d. April 6, 1920 in Conway County, AR) was the son of Alexander Gordon and Nancy Ragsdale. On Sept. 5, 1872 he married Nancy Elizabeth Reed (b. May 5, 1853 in Bradley County, TN, d. Oct. 22, 1939 in England, Lonoke County, AR), the daughter of James Reed and Sarah Elizabeth Smith of Tennessee and Georgia. Nancy and Robert Bolin are buried at Kilgore Cemetery. Census records show Robert Bolin as a farmer and he also served as a Justice of Peace.

Robert Bolin Gordon served three years in the Confederate States Army in the 10th Arkansas Cavalry under Col. McCroy. According to dates listed in his Pension Application, he was only 14 years old when he enlisted.

For a short time in the 1890s, the family lived in Indian Territory, around McAlister, OK. We have not found any records of the time period they were there.

After Nancy was widowed, she rotated staying with her children and their families. Robert Paxson Gordon has memories of his Grandmother during the times she stayed with his family. "Grandma Gordon was very jolly and quite a talker. She sat in front of the fire in her rocker and talked. She knew everybody in the country, it seemed; also, who was kin to whom. She was the story teller type, the words just flowed. I remember she made a lot of quilt tops." After I married into the family, my mother-in-law gave me two quilts, the tops of which had been made by Grandma Nancy Gordon, who had made quilt tops for all of her grandchildren. She had 46 grandchildren.

Nancy and Robert Bolin had 10 children:

1) James A. Gordon was born 1873 in Conway County and died about 1891 in Oklahoma or Texas, when he fell from a train and was killed.

2) Mary Ann Gordon, "Molly" (b. Sept. 24, 1874 at Center Ridge, d. March 14, 1950 at Springfield, AR) md. George Robert Scoggins on Nov. 17, 1901.

3) William Robert Gordon (b. Dec. 25, 1875 in Conway County, d. Feb. 25, 1963 in Plumerville, AR) md. Laura Elizabeth Hill on Oct. 23, 1897 in Conway County. She was born Jan. 9, 1882 in Conway County, AR and died Sept. 1, 1966 in Plumerville, AR.

4) John Wesley Gordon (b. Dec. 27, 1878 in Conway County, d. April 10, 1953 in Lonoke County, AR) md. Dollie Bell Flowers (b. Aug. 30, 1877, d. Dec. 24, 1954 in Lonoke County, AR) in 1898.

5) Infant Gordon born Conway County, AR, buried at Kilgore Cemetery.

6) Joseph Lucian Gordon (b. Aug. 30, 1884 in Center Ridge, AR, d. March 1, 1960 in Lonoke, AR) md. Chloe Bell Paxson on Feb. 13, 1910 in Conway County. This family is featured in another biography in this book.

7) Rosa Elizabeth Gordon "Lizzie" (b. March 1886 in Conway County, AR, d. April 14, 1942) md. Moses Allen Powell (b. ca. 1884, d. Dec. 14, 1952) on Feb. 13, 1906.

8) Infant born Conway County, AR, buried at Kilgore Cemetery.

9) Ira Austin Gordon (b. Feb. 4, 1892 in Center Ridge, Conway County, AR, d. Aug. 28, 1976 in Patterson, Stanislaus County, CA) md. Josephine A Meeler (b. Jan. 17, 1886 in Arkansas, and died about 1929).

10) Lonnie Houston Gordon (b. July 1, 1893 in Center Ridge, AR, d. Aug. 24, 1953 in Conway County, AR) md. Geneva Mae Maxwell (b. Oct. 14, 1894, d. Feb. 7, 1955 in Conway County, AR) on Feb. 14, 1914. *Submitted by Mrs. P.P. Gordon.*

GORDON - William Robert Gordon (b. Dec. 25, 1875, Conway County, AR) was the son of Robert Bolin Gordon and Nancy Elizabeth Reed Gordon. William married Laura Elizabeth Hill, daughter of Thomas Jefferson Hill and Hannah Jane Polk, on Oct. 23, 1897 in Conway County.

William was a farmer. He and Laura lived and worked in Conway County, AR, most of their lives. William Robert Gordon died Feb. 25, 1963 and Laura Elizabeth Hill Gordon died Sept. 1, 1966. Both are buried in the Plumerville Cemetery in Plumerville, Conway County, AR.

William Robert and Laura (Hill) Gordon with their son, James Henry "Shafter."

Their union produced the following children: James Henry "Shafter" Gordon (b. July 28, 1898 in Conway County, AR, d. Dec. 14, 1930, buried in the Plumerville Cemetery) md. Ollie McCarver; Robert Edgar Gordon (b. April 18, 1900, d. May 8, 1978, buried Plumerville Cemetery) md. Etta Adams; Ora Jane Gordon (b. Oct. 18, 1904, d. Oct. 7, 1977) md. Joseph M. "Bud" Huie; Cora Anne Gordon (b. June 1, 1906, d. June 1, 1979, buried Plumerville Cemetery) md. Ira Dickson Campbell; Hettie Melvina Gordon (b. July 23, 1908, d. Aug. 17, 1985, buried in Plumerville Cemetery) md. Grady Eoff; Ollie Elizabeth Gordon (b. April 24, 1913, d. Feb. 6, 1992, buried Plumerville Cemetery) md. Therlo Brown; Alex Jefferson Gordon (b. Dec. 22, 1923) md. first, Helen Rice and second, Lena Bird. *Submitted by Samantha Campbell.*

GRABHER – John Albert Grabher (b. Nov. 8, 1868 in Baden, Germany) was the son of Joseph Grabher (b. 1833, d. 1899) and Theresia Kreidness (b. 1840, d. 1918). He arrived with his parents in the United States in 1876, first living in Peoria, IL and arriving in Oppelo, AR in late 1880. John Albert married Emerelia "Emma" Isenman Jan. 10, 1899 in the original St. Elizabeth Catholic Church near Oppelo, AR. Emerelia (b. Sept. 22, 1877 in Decorah, IA) was the daughter of Johan "John" Isenman (b. 1842, d. 1906) and Anna Marie Willman (b. 1845, d. 1893).

John Albert Grabher family about 1931. Front row: John Albert, Albert, Emma. Back row: Joseph, Marie, Sister Albertine, John Fred and wife Anna Marie, Carl and Johanna.

John Albert and Emma lived in a log cabin on land that was purchased for 50 cents an acre. This land had belonged to the Isenman. They subsisted on food from their vegetable garden, fruit from the orchard and meat from cows, pigs and sheep. Later a smokehouse was built as well as a fruit cellar, which acted as a winter store for their provisions. They shared the responsibility of managing the farm, John Albert working the land while Emma maintained the ledgers since she could write in English. Emma enjoyed receiving letters from the Old country while John eagerly awaited German language newspapers published in the East and reading from a family Bible written in his native language. On social occasions, wine produced from cuttings brought from the vineyard section of Austria was shared with guests and family. One room of the log cabin was relocated around 1909 and became the kitchen area of the present Grabher home on Arena Road. Residents referred to the area as Grabher's Corner and in later years became known as Rehm's Corner. Electricity was installed in the home in the late 1920s with funds from the sale of all the family sheep.

The parents of 11 children, seven who lived to adulthood were John Fred Grabher (b. 1901, d. 1987) md. Anna Marie Nutt (b. 1904, d. 1933) and second marriage to Josephine Louise Barborek b. (1899, d. 1987); Elizabeth Mary Grabher became Sister Mary Albertine R.S.M. (b. 1906, d. 1997); Joseph Albert Grabher (b. 1908, d. 1982) md. Irene Marie Meyer (b. 1913, d. 1972) and second marriage to Velma Wetzer Dare (b. 1908-); Johanna Freda Grabher (b. 1910-); Marie Elizabeth Grabher (b. 1912, d. 1997) md. John Andrew Gunther (b. 1910, d. 1984); Carl Henry Grabher (b. 1915, d. 2002) md. Eleanor Eddy Meyer (b. 1920, d. 2004); Albert William Grabher (b. 1920-) md. Theresa Louise Breyel (b. 1928-). The four children who died in infancy were Anna Marie Grabher (b. January 1900, d. March 1900); Mary Theresa Grabher (b. December 1902, d. September 1905); Rose Marie Grabher (b. November 1904, d. September 1905); Anna Marie Grabher (b. 1917, d. 1920).

John Albert and Emma Grabher were active members of St. Elizabeth Catholic Church and participated in many community activities which included dances held in various homes with music provided by fiddlers from the area. The Grabher family always went to the Fourth of July Picnic in Perry, and each child was given a quarter to spend and cokes were a nickel. Their first car was a Bush made in St. Louis, MO. John and Emma never learned to drive so their sons did the driving. John Albert died July 25, 1933 at home. His obituary stated he came from Germany as a baby. He was an honest upright citizen and was held in high esteem by his neighbors and friends, his death being learned with much sadness by all. Emma Grabber died as a result of gallbladder cancer on May 24, 1951 at St. Anthony Hospital, Morrilton, AR. Note: John Albert was listed as stepson and last name of Steel in 1880 Illinois Census. *Submitted by Johanna Grabher.*

GRABHER – John Fred Grabher (b. Jan. 22, 1901 in Oppelo, Conway County, AR) was the son of John Albert Grabher (b. 1868, d. 1933) and Emerelia "Emma" Isenman (b. 1877, d. 1951). John attended the lower Oppelo School, and as a young boy in 1909, he helped his dad build the present Grabher home located now on what is known as Arena Road. He attended Subiaco Academy, Polk County, AR for two years before returning home to help his family with the farm.

John Fred married Anna Marie Nutt on Feb. 12, 1931 in St. Boniface Church in the New Dixie Community. Anna Marie (b. Dec. 17, 1904 in New Dixie, Perry County, AR) was the daughter of Joseph Andreas Nutt (b. 1873, d. 1955) and Caroline Strott (b. 1872, d. 1911). John and Anna Marie were members of St. Elizabeth Catholic Church at Oppelo. They built their home on what is now known as Timberlake Road. Two children were born of this marriage, Rita Emma Grabher (b. May 16, 1932) and Frances Johanna

Grabher (b. Dec. 3, 1933 in Morrilton, Conway County, AR). Eight days after the birth of Frances, Anna Marie died at St. Anthony's Hospital in Morrilton on Dec. 11, 1933 and is buried in St. Elizabeth Cemetery, Oppelo, AR. John and his two daughters moved back to the Grabher home where he continued farming with his mother and younger brothers and sisters. They made their livelihood from the sale of dairy products and sweet potatoes. They also had a fruit orchard and vegetable garden. A large sweet potato house was heated by a wood stove to cure the potatoes in the winter months. In the spring, the milk and butter was lowered in a bucket into a well to keep it cool. In the hottest months, a block of ice was delivered for their ice box. On the Fourth of July homemade ice cream was a memorable treat for the family. John was very proud to be one of the first in the community to raise whiteface cows and purchased a John Deere tractor for the farm.

John Fred Grabher and Anna Marie Nutt married Feb. 12, 1931.

Rita Emma Grabher married Charles Benson Gray on Oct. 6, 1951 in Sacred Heart Church, Morrilton, AR. Their son, Michael John Gray (adopted) (b. Jan. 8, 1959 in Baden, Germany) md. Cynthia Dianne Halter on Nov. 10, 1979 in St. Joseph Church, Conway, Faulkner County, AR. Michael and Cynthia's three sons are Jeremy John Gray (b. Jan. 13, 1981 in Oppelo, AR); Sean Michael Gray (b. July 16, 1982 in Abilene, TX) and Ryan Christopher Gray (b. May 14, 1993 in Mountain Park, NM). Rita Emma Gray died Aug. 7, 1977 in Oppelo and is buried in St. Elizabeth Cemetery, Oppelo, AR. Charles Gray's second marriage was to Nancy Bearden Koontz on Dec. 8, 1979. Frances Johanna Grabher married Ben Marion Donaldson on June 29, 1963 (See Grabber-Donaldson history).

John Fred's second marriage was to Josephine Louise Barborek on April 4, 1958 in Church of the Assumption at Atkins, Polk County, AR. Josephine (b. Feb. 11, 1899 in Sealy, TX) was the daughter of Frank Barborek (b. 1863, d. 1944) and Rosalie Kasalek (b. _, d. 1950). Josephine died March 13, 1987. John Fred died May 11, 1987. Both died at Doctors Hospital, Little Rock, AR and are buried at St. Elizabeth Cemetery, Conway County, AR. *Submitted by Stephanie Fox.*

GRABHERR – Joseph Grabherr (b. Sept. 14, 1833 in Austria) and Theresia Kreidness (b. Sept. 22, 1840 in Baden, Germany) emigrated to the United States in 1876, first settling in Peoria, IL. They traveled from Peoria, IL in a wagon train, walking most of the way, a journey which took three months. They arrived in Perry County in the late 1880s and settled in an area east of the present Highway 9, near the Perry-Conway County line. Joseph was a farmer and Theresia was a housewife. They were members of St. Elizabeth Catholic Church near Oppelo. Joseph and Theresia were the parents of six children:

1) Caroline "Lena" Grabherr (b. May 16, 1862 in Baden, Germany) md. Fred Isenman about 1885. She died Sept. 11, 1898 in Morrilton, AR and is buried at Sacred Heart Cemetery.

2) John Albert Grabherr (b. Nov. 8, 1868 in Baden, Germany) md. Emerelia "Emma" Isenman on Jan. 10, 1899 at St. Elizabeth Catholic Church at

Oppelo, AR. He died July 25, 1933 in Oppelo, AR and is buried at St. Elizabeth Cemetery.

Joseph Grabherr and Theresia Kreidness Grabherr.

3) Otto Robert Grabherr (b. July 26, 1872 in Peoria, IL) md. Sarah E. Berger on May 17, 1897 in St. Elizabeth Church. Otto died Oct. 27, 1940 in Oppelo, AR and is buried at St. Elizabeth Cemetery.

4) Mary Grabherr (b. March 20, 1874 in Peoria, IL) md. Joseph Miller on Feb. 20, 1895 at St. Boniface Catholic Church in New Dixie, AR. She died April 7, 1944 in Bigelow, AR and is buried at St. Boniface Cemetery, New Dixie, AR.

5) Fredrick Grabherr (b. March 22, 1877 in Peoria, IL, d. April 21, 1904 in Oppelo, AR) is buried at St. Elizabeth Cemetery in same plot as his parents.

6) Fredricka "Freda" W. Grabherr (b. March 9, 1880 in Peoria, IL) md. William W. Nord on Nov. 12, 1903 in St. Elizabeth Church at Oppelo. She died Nov. 11, 1959 in Little Rock, AR and is buried at St. Elizabeth Cemetery in Oppelo, AR.

Joseph Grabherr died Nov. 4, 1899 in Oppelo. After Joseph died, Theresa lived with her children and at the time of her death she was living with her daughter, Mary Miller, in Bigelow, Perry County, AR. Theresia Grabherr died March 20, 1918. Both are buried at St. Elizabeth Cemetery near Oppelo, AR. Note: Carolina Grabherr and John Albert Grabherr were listed as stepchildren with the last name of Steer in the 1880 Illinois census. *Submitted by Frances Grabherr.*

GRABHER - Otto Grabher (b. July 26, 1872 in Peoria, IL) md. Sarah Berger May 17, 1897 in St. Elizabeth Catholic Church at Oppelo, AR. Sarah was born Aug. 6, 1876.

Otto and Sarah Grabher with children Charlie and Theresa, about 1907.

Otto and Sarah bought land in southwest Oppelo where they farmed and raised their family. They were members of St. Elizabeth Church and were known in the community as Uncle Ott and Aunt Sis. They were parents to five children:

1) Sarah Theresa Grabher (b. April 23, 1889, d. April 28, 1898).

2) Charles Joseph Grabher (b. Feb. 26, 1904, d. Dec. 31, 1967) md. Gertrue Bingham on Oct. 5, 1928. They had one daughter, Jeweldean "Judy" Martin.

3) Theresa E. Grabher (b. March 20, 1906, d. Sept. 9, 1982) md. Cecil Horton and their children were Sarah Lee Lavern Franklin and Robert Henry Horton.

4) Albert John Grabher (b. Feb. 11, 1914, d. Dec. 14, 1979) md. Laura Lee on Oct. 28, 1939. Albert and Laura are parents of four children: Carl Edmond Grabher (b. July 26, 1940); Sarah Frances Grabher Martin (b. Jan. 24, 1942); Otto Robert "Bud" Grabher

(b. Oct. 3, 1944) and James Arthur "Pete" Grabher (b. Aug. 9, 1947).

5) James Otto Fredrick Grabher, (b. Nov. 19, 1916, d. March 21, 1977) md. Sybelene Cassity in 1940. James and Sybelene had three children: Betty Ellen Grabher Kirby, James Odell Grabher and David G. Grabher.

In the summer of 1940, Otto Grabher became ill from heat exhaustion and was incapacitated, dying suddenly in his home on Oct. 27, 1940. His obituary states he was a farmer by trade and a man highly respected. He is buried at St. Elizabeth Cemetery. Sarah Berger Grabher died Oct. 11, 1952 from a stroke and is buried at Wolf Cemetery in Oppelo, AR. *Submitted by Sarah Martin.*

GRAY - Jesse Gray (b. Nov. 25, 1832, in Maury County, TN) was the oldest child of Zachariah and Jemima Gray. In 1842 Zachariah purchased land in Conway County from Samuel Arendall. Jesse was among the early settlers of Lewisburg, AR in Conway County. He married Minerva Jane Northern on March 9, 1852, in Franklin County, AR, and they had three children: Tennessee Elizabeth Jane, John Z. and Sarah.

Standing: Cassandra Smith Gray and her daughter (seated) Fannie Gray.

Jesse was a Confederate soldier in Company B, Gordon's Regiment, Arkansas Cavalry, having enlisted at the beginning of the conflict and serving for four years. A Morrilton newspaper printed an article about the time after the war that Jesse and his two oldest daughters were forced to give food and a night's shelter at their home to Jesse James and one of the younger brothers. Before they left after breakfast the outlaws gave Jesse money to cover the cost of his hospitality. They also commended him for serving as a Confederate soldier.

Following the death of Minerva, Jesse married Cassandra Haziltine Smith on June 2, 1864, in Perry County, AR. They had seven children: Fannie, John Laney, Minnie, Nellie, Annie Jessamine, James and Willie. The Gray family was residing in Lewisburg during the 1880 census.

Jesse and Cassie's bed has survived the years and is currently placed in a great-grandson's home. According to the printing on the bed, it was shipped around the Horn and delivered to Gray's Landing in Lewisburg, which was owned and operated by Jesse. The bed, together with a trunk of Gray/Humphrey memorabilia survived a fire in Morrilton at the 204 South Ola home of Gene and Annie Waller (Jesse's granddaughter). Jesse and Cassie moved to Morrilton when the city was established, erecting a multi-floor building across from the depot on Broadway which still bears his name (owned by M.A. Metzger in 1936 and occupied at that time by the Rexall Drug).

Jesse enjoyed financial success, though he could not read or write. His many papers, which survived the fire, indicate he signed with an X as "his mark" which was always witnessed.

Jesse's obituary noted that he was the father of 10 children. Cassie's obituary says the same for her. Actually, as noted above, seven were from Cassie and the first three were from Jesse's previous marriage to Jane Northern.

About 1900 Jesse and Cassie divorced. Jesse bought land and built a house at 201 North Morrill Street in Morrilton. As of December 2004, Jesse's granddaughter, Annie Mae Hawkins, age 92, still resides in this house. Cassie remained on the family farm in Lewisburg until she died on May 13, 1913, at which time her daughter Annie inherited the property.

About 1904 Jesse married for the third time to a Mrs. Parker (first name unknown) in Morrilton. They lived in the North Morrill house for a short time, then they divorced. Jesse spent the last two years of his life with cancer-caused blinded eyes and was cared for in his North Morrill home by his daughter, Minnie, and her husband, Will Hawkins. He died Jan. 20, 1916. Jesse, Cassie, three daughters, and one son are buried in the Elmwood Cemetery along with family members of his daughter, Fannie Gray Humphrey. *Submitted by Frances Jensen.*

GRAY - Dr. Norman E. Gray (b. 1932 in Linn County, KS) graduated from Kansas State College in 1956, with a doctor of veterinary medicine degree.

In 1954 he married Mary Ellen Wolfinger, who was born in 1934 in Linn County, KS. He served in the Army from 1956-58, at Fort Stewart, GA. A son, Franklin John, was born there in 1957.

Dr. Norman Gray, Mary Ellen and Franklin moved to Morrilton on Aug. 15, 1958, when he established a general practice in veterinary medicine. He opened a clinic at 1104 North St. Joseph Street in 1959. He stayed there until August 1971 when he built a new clinic at 404 East Harding Street. That clinic still exists and is now owned by Dr. Chris Ward.

Franklin graduated from Morrilton High School in 1975 and from Arkansas Tech University in 1981. He played tight end and punter on the 1973 football state championship team (for the Morrilton Devil Dogs). He now lives in Conway with his wife, Cindy (French), and their three children: John, Joseph and Jessica.

Mary Ellen opened the Fabric and Drapery Shop in 1976 and sold it to Laura Lock in 1998. In 1982, Mary Ellen was elected the first woman president of the Morrilton Chamber of Commerce.

Dr. and Mrs. Gray are both retired and live in Morrilton. *Submitted by Dr. Norman E. Gray.*

GRIFFIN - James Bennett "J.B." Griffin (b. Jan. 13, 1881 at Jerusalem, AR) was the son of Robert Henry and Lucinda C. Griffin. J.B. married Rosie Stroud Sept. 8, 1902 at Jerusalem and they had two children, James Irving "Barney" Griffin (b. Aug. 30, 1911) and a daughter Lovie. Rosie died March 13, 1914. J.B. married Rosie Jolly on June 27, 1914; she had two children, Albert and Lorene.

Barney and Luva Griffin, about 1950.

Barney married Luva Ferguson (b. 1914) on Dec. 25, 1932 in Booneville, AR, and moved to Morrilton. Their only daughter LaVada Marie Griffin was born in 1935. Barney worked as a millwright for M.H. Pierce Lumber Co. for many years and for J.B. Porter. Luva worked first at The Cotton Mill and at Oberman Mfg. Co.

Their daughter LaVada married her high school sweetheart, Romie Willis Price, in 1951. She graduated from Morrilton High School in 1952 and worked at Price Motor Co., the Willys Dealership, till Willis joined the US Air Force and they lived in San Antonio, TX. While there LaVada went to Draughon's Business School and worked at Lackland AFB at the 3700th USAF Hospital Personnel Office and later at the Air Force Personnel Training and Research Branch. Upon returning to Morrilton in 1957, Willis opened Price Motor Co. on Broadway until 1966, when he joined Allison Ford Co. as sales manager. LaVada began working at the US Forest Service in Perryville, AR in 1961 where she served until 1994.

Their only son, Romie Griffin Price (b. 1967) attended school in Morrilton. During the 1970s Willis remained as sales manager at the Ford Dealership until purchasing the Chevrolet Dealership in Morrilton in 1979.

In the early 1960s, Barney and Luva Griffin opened Griffin Floral Co. and later bought the Hillcrest Floral Co. at 810 N. Morrill St., Morrilton. They operated the florist until 1978. Barney died in 1977. Luva traveled and spent some time in Oklahoma and Phoenix, AZ, and returned to Morrilton in the 1980s and remained here. She enjoyed working in the greenhouse and her garden; she also traveled with Willis and LaVada.

Willis and LaVada purchased the Chevrolet Dealership in Morrilton in 1979, and in 1989 Willis sold Price Chevrolet, Inc. During the early 1990s he operated Price Motor Co. in Russellville and eventually moved the company back to Morrilton. Their son, Griff, married Donna Windsor, daughter of Mike and Phyllis Windsor of Morrilton, in 1991 and later attended Petit Jean Vocational School. In 1989 he graduated from the University of Arkansas in Fayetteville with a bachelor degree in architecture. His wife, Donna, graduated from the University of Central Arkansas in 1991 and later became a teacher in the Perryville School District.

Griff and Donna's only child, Romie Ethan Price (b. 1999), attended school at Perryville, AR. In 2004, Griff and Donna returned to Morrilton, where Griff established himself as an architect and started his own business, taking on many architecture projects. Willis and LaVada spent their retirement years operating their car lot and traveling around the country. *Submitted by Mrs. R.W. Price.*

GRIFFIN - John W. and Eliza Griffin were the only Griffin family living in Union Township in 1850. Other Griffins were in Conway County then, but were evidently not related to John W. He was the only Griffin born in New York. Why or how he came to be in Arkansas is unknown. He was a cooper and a farmer and was well-respected in Conway County. The citizens petitioned to have him appointed county commissioner in August 1853, to fill the vacancy created by R.B. Gordon's death. The petition was approved and John was appointed the same month.

By 1860 John and Eliza were parents of four children: William Thomas, 9; John King, 7; Fletcher Alexander, 4; and Martha Emily Griffin, 1. About 1868 another son, James, was born. John and Eliza both died before 1870, and their children resided with Venable relatives. The two youngest children, Martha Emily and James, lived with James Venable; King lived with Zeb Venable; Alexander lived with the John R. Morgan family, who were unrelated, it seems.

Thomas (b. 1851) had married Sarah (b. _) and established his own household by 1870. A daughter was born to them in 1871. Sarah died and Thomas married Susan Humphrey in Conway County in 1875, then to Mary Spears in Faulkner County in 1881.

King (b. 1853) md. Margaret Ann Allen, daughter of Asa and Dinah Allen, in 1875. Their family moved to Faulkner County after 1900.

Fletcher Alexander (b. 1857) lived with Capt. Zeb Venable's family in 1880. In 1886, he married Mrs. Lula (Shaddox) Ward. Alex died of lung disease in 1894.

Martha Emily (b. 1858/59) possibly was the Mattie Griffin that married Robert B. Stell in 1878. If so, she had a daughter born about 1881 in Conway County.

James (b. ca. 1868) probably died while a young child. There is no further record for James Griffin, his age, in Conway or surrounding counties.

Some descendants of John W. Griffin's children were:

Sarah Ellen "Sallie" Griffin born in November 1871 to Thomas and Sarah Griffin. Sallie married Loke Harley Sinyard in Faulkner County in 1887. Their daughter Ollie Sinyard married Albert Pallmer in Faulkner County in 1914. Their children were Lena, Verlon and Cordia Pallmer.

King and Margaret Griffin raised six children. Their eldest child, John, married Ollie Jordan in 1899. Their children were Willie and John Carl Griffin.

Thana Parilee (b. 1880, d. 1950) md. first, John Wiley Jr. Their children were Otis, Roy, John and Bill Wiley. Thana married John Sibley in 1917. Their offspring were Herman and Mary Ellen Sibley.

Martha Elizabeth "Lizzie" (b. 1886, d. 1920s) md. Abner Daniel Hogan. in 1909. The Hogan children were Emmett, Alleen, A.D. III, Marie and Norman.

James Edgar "Bud" (b. 1888, d. 1961) md. Alice Mobbs about 1912. Their children were Bonnie, Chester, James Jr., William, Doyle, Juanita, Joyce and Maxine Griffin.

Emma Lorene (b. 1894, d. 1981) md. John Bose Milam in 1913. Their children were Chester, Dorothy, J.B., Gene and Emma Lee Milam. Chester Paul (b. 1897, d. 1916) died of pneumonia. He was single.

Alex and Lula Griffin had four children: Ella (b. 1887, d. 1926) md. Arthur Norwood; Myrtle (b. l888, d. 1981) md. Samuel B. Sledge; John (b. 1891, d. 1893 at 18 months); Ada (b. 1894, d. 1973) md. Chester Owens.

Martha Emily "Emmy" may have been the mother of Bennie (or Bernie?) Viola Stell (b. 1881, d. 1970) who married George Washington Faulk in Conway County in 1897. Mattie died before 1895 (when R.B. Stell married again) or else she and Robert separated or divorced during the 1880s. Emmy (Mattie?) lived in Portland, OR in the 1890s and had a half-grown son, George (birth date and surname remain unknown). *Submitted by Carlene Guthier.*

GRIFFIN - The only Griffin family in Union Township in 1850 was John W. Griffin, 30, and his wife, Eliza, 21. There were other Griffins in Conway County, but only John claimed New York as his place of birth. Why, how, or when he came to Arkansas is unknown. He was a cooper, a farmer, and well-respected in Conway County. The citizens petitioned to have him appointed County Commissioner in August 1853 to fill the vacancy created by R.B. Gordon's death. The petition was approved and John was appointed that month.

John's wife, Margaret Eliza, was from Georgia and a daughter of Thomas William and Martha (Stell) Venable.

By 1860, John and Eliza had four children: William Thomas, John King, Fletcher Alexander, and Martha E. Griffin. Emily was born about 1862 and James in 1868.

John and Eliza were deceased by 1870, and most of their children resided with Venable relatives. Emily and James (and possibly Martha) lived with James Venable. King lived with Zeb Venable and Alexander lived with the John Morgan family.

Thomas (b. 1851) had married Sarah __ by 1870. Their daughter Sarah Ellen "Sallie" was born about 1871. After Sarah's death, Thomas married Susan Humphrey in Conway County (1875), then Mary Spears in Faulkner County (1881). Thomas' daughter, Sallie Griffin, married Loke Harley Sinyard in 1887. Their daughter, Ollie Sinyard, married Albert Pallmer in Faulkner County in 1914.

King (b. 1853) md. Margaret Ann Allen, daughter of Asa and Dinah Allen, in 1875. They moved to Faulkner County after 1900, where they raised five of their nine children. Three children were deceased and the eldest son John had married Ollie Jordan in 1899.

Thana Parilee (b. 1880, d. 1950) md. John Wiley Jr. in 1905. He died of typhoid fever in 1915. Thana married John Sibley in 1917.

Martha Elizabeth "Lizzie" (b. 1886, d. 1920s) md. Abner Daniel Hogan in 1909.

James Edgar "Bud" (b. 1888, d. 1961) md. Alice Mobbs about 1912.

Emma Lorene (b. 1894, d. 1981) md. John Bose Milam in 1913.

Chester Paul (b. 1897, d. 1916) died of pneumonia, unmarried.

Alexander "Elic" (b. 1857) lived with Capt. Zeb Venable's family in 1880. In 1886, he married Lula Ward, daughter of Nancy Lucinda (Carson) and Ezekiel Shaddox Jr. Elic and Lula Griffin had four children: Mary Ella/Ellen (b. 1887, d. 1926) md. Arthur Norwood; Myrtle Mae (b. 1888, d. 1981) md. Samuel B. Sledge; John Franklin (b. 1891, d. 1893 at 18 months); Ada Fletcher (b. 1894, d. 1973) md. Chester Owens. Elic died of lung disease on April 13, 1894, just 12 days after Ada was born.

Martha E. may have been the M.E. Griffin, 18, who married S.D. Ferrin, 24, in Faulkner County in February 1876. (Stephen Decatur Ferrin was a ward of Martha's uncle, James Venable in 1860, and he farmed for James Venable's sister-in-law, Rebecca Pearl, in 1870.) Their marriage was probably annulled, because it appears Mr. Ferrin was already married.

At any rate, Martha E. probably was the "Mattie" Griffin, 19, who married Robert Bayliss Stell, 19, on Oct. 13, 1878 in Conway County. The marriage record states both parties were from Springfield (Union Township). Their daughter, Bernie Viola Stell (b. 1881, d. 1970) md. George Washington Faulk in Conway County in 1897.

Mattie evidently died before 1895, because Robert Stell remarried that year.

Emily (b. 1862) lived in Portland, OR in the 1890s. She mentioned her son George in a letter she wrote her brother Elic, but we have yet to learn the name of her husband, since she signed her letter only as "Emmy."

James (b. 1868, died before October 1871) was not listed as one of the "only heirs" of Thomas W. Venable in a Chancery Court record of 1871.

GROOM - James Thomas (b. July 22, 1853 in Weakley County, TN) was the only child of James Marshall Groom (b. June 1829, d. May 10, 1897) and Nancy Ellen Carlton (b. 1831, d. 1853/55), daughter of Wade H. Carlton (b. Aug. 10, 1809, d. June 5, 1888) and Sarah Putnam (b. March 1813, d. March 23, 1873). It is believed Nancy died in childbirth or shortly after the birth of James Thomas. James Marshall remarried in 1855.

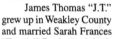
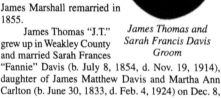

James Thomas and Sarah Francis Davis Groom

James Thomas "J.T." grew up in Weakley County and married Sarah Frances "Fannie" Davis (b. July 8, 1854, d. Nov. 19, 1914), daughter of James Matthew Davis and Martha Ann Carlton (b. June 30, 1833, d. Feb. 4, 1924) on Dec. 8, 1871. J.T. and Fannie had the following children: Hewaska Wanata "H.W." (b. Nov. 3, 1872, d. Aug. 23, 1951); Mollie F. (b. Nov. 11, 1874, d. ___); Katherine Crawford "Kate" (b. Jan. 12, 1877, d. May 29, 1929); Charles Thomas (b. Dec. 16, 1879, d. June 27, 1967); Robert Fulton "R.F." (b. Nov. 13, 1881, d. June 17, 1966); Lela Blanche (b. Aug. 5, 1888, d. June 26, 1966); and Velma L. (b. March 17, 1895, d. March 18, 1950). All the children were born in Tennessee.

In December 1899, the family moved to Conway County, AR. Fannie's mother, Martha Ann Davis (b. June 30, 1833, d. Feb. 4, 1924), came with the family. In letters written back to Tennessee, they described the area as having good-looking land, nicely dressed and healthy looking people. The land the family settled was near Overcup and known as Center Valley.

Hewaska Wanata married in Tennessee to Rachel Etta Reddick (b. Feb. 24, 1876, d. June 18, 1942), daughter of John Lewis Martin Reddick (b. Jan. 26, 1852, d. June 19, 1929) and Mary Evaline Black (b. May 21, 1856, d. March 29, 1900). They had two children who were born in Weakly County: Clyde (b. Sept. 6, 1896, d. Aug. 3, 1988) and Bryan (b. May 24, 1899, d. Aug. 10, 1893). After moving to Arkansas, their family increased with the following births: Clarence Hewaska (b. Aug. 19, 1901, d. Nov. 2, 1983); Nell (b. July 18, 1905, d. Dec. 17, 1982); Myrtle (b. July 23, 1908, d. April 15, 1995); Mary Frances (b. July 13, 1914, d. Oct. 20, 1996), plus four children who died as infants.

Katherine Crawford "Kate" married Stanford Marion "S.M." Lasater D.V. (b. Feb. 14, 1868, d. Sept. 2, 1945) on Feb. 25, 1903. He was a widower with six children. His first wife, Malvina S. Reddick (b. Oct. 12. 1872, d. abt. Aug. 24, 1901), died in childbirth. Kate and S.M. lived in the Overcup Community where they raised S.M.'s children and nine of their own. Their children were: Lillie Mae (b. Nov. 10, 1903, d. Feb. 22, 1988); Joe Todd (b. May 18, 1905, d. Nov. 13, 1975); Lela Blanche (b. Dec. 9 1906, d. Aug. 8, 1996); Jimmy Lee (b. March 30, 1908, d. Nov. 16, 1908); Lessie Ada (b. April 21, 1910, d. Dec. 3, 1993); Brooxie Ann (b. April 5, 1912, d. June 26, 1981); Lillian Margie (b. July 5, 1914, d. Sept. 12, 1944); and twins, Fanny and Margaret Lucille (b. Aug. 13, 1919). Fannie died Aug. 13, 1919.

Charles Thomas married Lona Taylor (b. Feb. 25, 1884, d. July 15, 1925) and they had one son. His second wife was Hazel Lucas (b. about 1904-).

Robert Fulton married Susan Metta Reddick. (See Robert Fulton Groom).

Blanche married George P. Mourot (b. about 1886, d. about 1939) and they had no issue.

Velma L. married Thomas Houston Bostian (b. Sept. 13, 1893, d. Sept. 12, 1968). They had the following children: James E. (b. ca. 1913, d. June 5, 1983); George T. (b. ca. 1914, d. before 1994); Emmet E. (b. Jan. 16, 1917, d. Jan. 22, 1917); Virgil David (b. March 22, 1918, d. March 16, 1999); Edith Mae (b. March 1, 1921, d. March 5, 1921); Orville Wayne (b. ca. 1924, d. Oct. 24, 1994); Bonnie Lee (b. June 3, 1926-); and Charles Waymon (b. ca. 1939-).

After the death of Fannie, James Thomas married Josephine Burks (b. Jan. 28, 1876, d. Aug. 23, 1966) on June 17, 1915. They adopted a daughter, Eva Mae (b. Jan. 26, 1913, d. Oct. 4, 1988) who married Muriel Crowder (b. Nov. 10, 1914, d. Aug. 31, 1997) on Nov. 5, 1932. Eva Mae and Muriel had six children: Dorothy (b. May 27, 1935, d. Nov. 28, 1938); Murielene; Linda; Charles; Frank and James.

The Groom families lived in and around Morrilton until their deaths. Most of them are buried in Campground, Kilgore, Elmwood and Solgohachia Community (Friendship) cemeteries. *Submitted by Ruth M. Faulkner Warner and Jenny Hoang.*

GROOM - Robert Fulton "Bob" Groom (b. Nov. 13, 1881 in Gibson County, TN), the son of James Thomas and Sarah Frances Davis Groom. In December 1899 he moved with his family to the Center Valley Community in Conway County, AR. After his arrival in Center Valley he worked on the Scroggin Brothers farm as an overseer. While working there he was able to come home to see his family only one weekend per month.

Robert Fulton and Susan Reddick Groom

In 1902 he returned to Weakley County, TN to marry Susan Metta Reddick (b. March 8, 1882, d. Feb. 2, 1962), daughter of John Lewis Martin Reddick (b. Jan. 26, 1852, d. June 19, 1929) and Mary Evaline Black (b. May 21, 1856, d. March 29, 1900). Susan was a sister of Rachel Etta Reddick (b. Feb. 24, 1876, d. June 18, 1942), wife of Hewaska Wanata "H.W." "Buck" Groom, Bob's older brother.

After returning to Arkansas, Bob and Susie settled into farming near their families in the Center Valley Community. Here, they purchased 80 acres of land from N.T. Hawkins. This section of land was part of the land granted to the state of Arkansas by the US

Government in 1853 for the use of the Little Rock and Fort Smith Railroad. Over the next few years, Bob bought additional land. Along with his brother, H.W. and their father, the Groom family owned several hundred acres in Center Valley.

Center Valley had its own schoolhouse and Bob and Susie boarded some of the teachers before it was consolidated with the Morrilton School System. The school building was left vacant after consolidation. In 1932 after Bob and Susie's house burned down, they bought the school building and converted it into a six-room home for their family.

Bob and Susie were the parents of nine children, three of whom died as infants. Their children were: Bessie Evaline (b. Oct. 28, 1903, d. Dec. 3, 1987); Ethel Lee (b. Dec. 13, 1905, d. June 19, 1954); Emmet Edward (b. May 30, 1908, d. Aug. 14, 1908); Carl (b. Aug. 26, 1909, d. April 3, 1993); Ernest Walter (b. Dec. 29, 1911, d. March 22, 1913); Elon Irene (b. May 24, 1914, d. Feb. 28, 1999); Floy May (b. July 4, 1917); Robert Earl (b. Sept. 1, 1920, d. Aug. 1, 2000); and infant (b&d. July 6, 1925).

Bessie Evaline married Eugene Orville Bostian (b. Oct. 23, 1901, d. July 29, 1992). Their children were:

1) Wilma Dale (b. Oct. 31, 1922) md. first, Herman Haston (b. Oct. 23, 1916, d. Dec. 24, 1944) and whose sons were Billy Ray (b. Oct. 7, 1939) and James Allen (b. Oct. 12, 1944, d. Dec. 7, 1945). Wilma married second, Wilbur Warren (b. Feb. 1, 1919). They had a son Garry (b. June 21, 1947).

2) Ellie Kathryn (b. Aug. 19, 1928) md. William James (b. March 6, 1923). They had two daughters, Janet Lynn (b. March 10, 1955) and Susan Ann (b. May 17, 1960).

3) Robert Wesley (b. Feb. 26, 1933) md. Beverly West (b. April 5, 1934) and their children were Mark (b. June 21, 1955, d. May 29, 2000) and Philip (b. Dec. 1, 1960).

Ethel Lee married Roy Franklin Faulkner (b. Nov. 12, 1909, d. Jan. 22, 1998), son of Loma Ishmel (b. Jan. 19, 1886, d. July 22, 1976) and Millie Ann Vaughn Faulkner (b. June 28, 1890, d. Feb. 8, 1986). They had one daughter, Ruth Muriel (b. Aug. 24, 1928). She first married Norman Nathan Holland (b. June 20, 1923, d. Aug. 7, 1986). Their children were David Lynn (b. June 16, 1948); Geary Lee (b. March 17, 1951, d. April 6, 1974); Linda Carol (b. April 6, 1952); and Donna Sue (b. Feb. 9, 1954). Her second husband was Jerome Warner (b. July 7, 1946).

Carl married Mildred Lucille Johnson (b. Sept. 25, 1914). They had two children, James Carl (b. Feb. 9, 1936, d. March 19, 1937) and Betty Carolyn (b. March 14, 1938).

Elon Irene married first, Orville Tolbert Horton (b. Aug. 24, 1912, d. Sept. 16, 1968). Their children were (1) Orla Irene (b. March 16, 1936) who married Robert Roberts (b. Aug. 16, 1931) and they have four children: Gloria (b. June 9, 1953), Terry (b. May 28, 1970), Kimberly (b. Dec. 14, 1975), and Justin (b. Dec. 20, 1979); (2) Jenwyl Dean (b. Oct. 13, 1937) md. Mike Miller (b. Aug. 5, 1930). Their children are Sylvia (b. Nov. 28, 1957) and Ricky (b. March 4, 1960); (3) Betty Joyce (b. Feb. 9, 1939) md. Roger Winter (b. April 27, 1945) and they have a son Matthew (b. Aug. 9, 1983); (4) David Tolbert (b. Dec. 30, 1942, d. Dec. 11, 1994); and (5) Darrell Lendon (b. Oct. 13, 1948) md. Karen Kuespert (b. Sept. 13, 1949). They have a son Adam (b. Jan. 4, 1979). Elon later married William Shaw (b. Nov. 18, 1898, d. Feb. 25, 1977).

Floy May taught school in Arkansas, Missouri and Louisiana where she taught for 32 years before retiring in 1981. After the death of her mother in 1962, she took her father to Louisiana to live with her during the school year. When school was out for summer they would return to their home in Center Valley for the summer months. Bob died in Morrilton June 17, 1966.

Robert Earl married Lena P. Bishop (b. Oct. 12, 1927) and their children were Merideth Susan (b. June 23, 1947); Roger Earl (b. Sept. 22, 1948, d. July 3, 1976); and Lela Rebecca (b. Sept. 10, 1951). Rebecca married Steven R. Shepherd and they have three sons: Russell W. (b. July 24, 1972); Steven R. (b. Sept. 26, 1974); and Terrence Clay (b. March 8, 1976). In addition to farming the usual crops of cotton, corn and hay, Bob grew strawberries and boysenberries, which he shipped to markets outside of the state. At one point in time they raised turkeys that they sold to the Arlington Hotel in Hot Springs. Bob also did blacksmith work for people in the community and was known county wide for his sorghum molasses. He also contracted with neighbors and friends to make their molasses.

Bob and Susie sold their home and the acreage it was located on in 1952, and built a new home on another section of their land. This home had all the modern conveniences and they lived there until their deaths. Part of the land they owned is still owned by their children and grandchildren. *Submitted by Ruth M. Faulkner Warner and Jenny Hoang.*

GULLETT - Sarah is the daughter of the late Henry Clay Hallett Jr. and Annie Jewel (Jones) Hallett of Oppelo. Sarah is a lifelong resident of Oppelo, having been born here, and went to school at Oppelo and graduated from Junior High School in 1950. Later attending Morrilton High School and graduating in 1953. After graduation Sarah begin work at Oberman Mfg. Co. She later met her husband Bill Gullett of Hector. After marriage

Bill and Sarah Gullett

they went to live in Flint, MI, where Bill was employed at the Buick Motor Division.

Bill has been employed in Morrilton since they returned from Michigan. He worked hauling rock off Petit Jean Mountain to build the dikes on the Arkansas River. Later he worked for Otis Cook, doing TV repair work and then he went to work for Price Stroud, doing TV work and helping out in the grocery store. At one time he worked for Kenneth Morgan doing auto repair work, but later went back to work for Price Stroud, helping in the furniture business. Later he decided to enter business for himself and he opened Bill Gullett Auto Sales and Service at 706 West Broadway.

Bill served in the Korean War, where he was a mechanic working on heavy equipment and driving a wrecker. After he had been in the auto business for a while he decided to go into the wrecker business because that was a love he carried from service. He now operates a car business part time and has Gullett Wrecker Service, which keeps him busy most of the time, still located at the same place.

Sarah has worked most of her life. After she returned from Michigan she went back to work at Oberman Mfg. Co. She has worked at Soundcraft on Petit Jean Mountain and Morrilton Plastic Co. In 1970 she entered beauty school and opened the first beauty shop in Oppelo as Sarah's Hair Fashions. After 14 years she returned to work at Levi Strauss and Co. where she retired in 1999 when Levi closed their plant here in Morrilton. Sarah stayed home for a while, but having a need to be around people she went to work for ICT Group where she was employed part-time for a little over three years.

They have three daughters: Deborah K. Keener of Harris Brake, Marilyn F. Winberry of Fayetteville, and Donna R. Hawthorne of Cabot. Ten grandchildren, one step grandchild 10 great-grandchildren round out the family.

They are active members of the Bethel Missionary Baptist Church in Morrilton. Bill loves to hunt and fish when time permits and Sarah enjoys working in her yard and tending to her flowers.

When asked, if you could live any where in the world, where would you want to live? Bill replied, right where I am living now. It is quite and peaceful, not too far from town and we have some of the best neighbors in the world right around here. I'm satisfied. *Submitted by Sarah Gullett.*

GULLETT - Grady Cecil Gullett was born May 23, 1925 in Hattieville, AR to J.W. (also called Jim) and Chloe Craig Gullett. His siblings were Lois Jewel, Willa Dean, Billy Donald, Bobbye Jean, Sarah Catherine, and Jimmy Doyle. Grady's dad was married the first time to Sally Johnson of Pope County. They had six children: Clarence, Evie, Vida Ann, Homer, Nita, and Emmelton. J.W. died April 1, 1937 of pneumonia and is buried at Childer's Cemetery in Pope County.

Grady was only 12 at the time. Chloe died Aug. 31, 1938 and is buried at Crossroads Cemetery in Pope County, AR. Jimmy was only 16 months old. The children were handed out at the funeral to relatives that would take them. Grady, being the oldest, was passed around to labor with local families. He was staying with Emmelton and family when he became sick with what they suspected to be tuberculosis. Emmelton's wife burned his things and put him out. Mr. Bluchard Jordon picked him up and took him to Booneville, AR to a TB sanitarium. He didn't have TB, but an abscess on his lung. Dr. C. Ray Williams did his first surgery on Grady. After being released, he hitchhiked to Peach Orchard, MO to pick cotton and was taken in by a Johnson family there.

Grady went into the Army and received a medical discharge. His brothers and sisters had not been reunited until Grady came back from the service.

Grady was married to Ellen Reid, of Pope County. Grady was a jack-of-all-trades and went to Arizona to pick cotton. He picked 744 pounds of cotton in one day, the most he had ever picked. They lived in Oklahoma and had two daughters, Kathy (b. July 12, 1951) and Sue (b. March 18, 1954). While working for Meadow Gold Ice Cream Company, driving a truck, he fell from a loading dock and hurt his back. Grady had an unsuccessful surgery and was confined to wear a brace the last 14 years of his life. Grady and Ellen were divorced in 1965.

Grady attended Morrilton Beauty School where he met Mary Ann Allen Heistand, a former graduate. Mary Ann was a widow with an 8-year-old son, Glen, who lived in Jerusalem, AR. Grady and Mary Ann were married March 5, 1966 and together built Jerusalem's first beauty shop. They had two boys, Grady Randall (b. Feb. 15, 1967) and Mark Allen (b. Feb. 2, 1976). They moved to Hattieville in 1973. Grady died Aug. 10, 1980 at age 55 of congestive heart failure and is buried at Robertstown Cemetery. He was a member of the Church of Christ. Mary Ann reopened the beauty shop in Hattieville in 1988. Mary Ann married Bill Fowler on Oct. 15, 1988. Both Randall and Mark graduated from Wonderview High School. Randall graduated from Arkansas Tech University in Russellville with a BS in business and marketing. He married Hope Warren of Dardanelle on Oct. 20, 1990 and had a daughter, Gillian Grace (b. Dec. 20, 1997). They were divorced in 2001. Mark traveled the US playing music with a band. He is currently attending UACCM in Morrilton but stills plays music locally.

GUNDERMAN - John F. Gunderman (b. March 21, 1936 in Conway County) went to grade school and high school in Conway County. He worked on the family farm until he got work around Central Arkansas on different jobs.

1985–John, Chris, Butch and Eddie Gunderman.

In 1958 he married Sarah Christine Swope (b. March 2, 1938 in Conway County). He served in the Army Reserves for six years, with 10 months active duty during the Berlin and Cuban Crises.

A son, David Bernard, was born in 1959 at St. Anthony's Hospital in Morrilton. A second son, John Ed, was born in 1968, also at St. Anthony's Hospital in Morrilton.

In June 1972 they bought Osco Coleman Scrap Metal. They ran the business at St. Joseph and Elm Street until 1979 when they bought property on South Cedar Street. They still run the business as a family group, Gunderman Scrap Metal, Inc.

David "Butch" lives in the St. Vincent Community. He has two children, Brooke and Emily. John Ed lives on the farm that they bought from the Gunderman family at Wonderview. They raise Black Angus cattle and hay for the cattle.

Christine worked for the Morrilton public schools for 25 years as a lunchroom cook until she retired. Mr. and Mrs. Gunderman are both retired, but still work part-time at the scrap metal business and on the farm. *Submitted by John Edward Gunderman.*

HAIRSTON - Thomas B. Hairston, the eldest son of Benjamin R. and Fata T. Hairston, was 15 years of age at the time of the family's arrival in Springfield. For the next five years, until his marriage to Jennie I. Smith, Thomas was the "chief bread winner" of the family. Jennie I. Smith (b. Aug. 2, 1860 in Arkansas) was 18 years of age at the time of their marriage in Plumerville. She was the daughter of John Smith. Thomas B. Hairston

Thomas and Jennie Hairston

died July 13, 1922 at the age of 63. Jennie S. Hairston lived with her daughter and son-in-law, Fannie and David T. Crye, until her death on May 11, 1928, at the age of 67. Their children and grandchildren were as follows:

1) Benjamin R. (b. 1879, d. 1959) md. Effie Tindall. Their children: Thomas B., Myrtle, Freda, Edna Marie, Oleta and Norman.

2) James H. (b. 1883, d. 1968) md. Vinnie Thomas. Their children: Carl, Edith, Lester, Leslie, Irene and Robert.

3) Fannie L. (b. 1885, d. 1966) md. David T. Crye. Their children: Lois, Tom, Willie Belle, Jack, James D. and Irene.

4) Thomas C. (b. 1889, d. 1959) md. Minnie Brannon. One child, Nan.

5) Fred E. (b. 1890) md. Myrtle McClaren. Their children: Amos, Everett, Irene, Freeda, T.B., Iva Lee and Fred Jr.

6) Jennie May died in infancy in 1900.

HALBROOK - Andrew Jackson Halbrook and Hester "Hettie" Ann Cordelia Rhoads were life-long sweethearts and residents of the upper reaches of Point Remove Creek along the border between Conway and Van Buren counties. They eventually moved southwest into Cleveland.

Andrew's father was John Reynolds Halbrook. John was only 5 when his grandfather, William Erwin Halbrook; his father, Joseph Erwin Halbrook; and some uncles made a scouting

1954-Andrew Jackson Halbrook and Hester Cordelia Rhoads

trip into Arkansas. John must have stayed in Memphis with his mother and the other women and children. The Halbrook family eventually settled in the area near Woolverton Mountain at the headwaters of East Point Remove Creek.

John Reynolds Halbrook married a Huie woman and they had William Thomas Halbrook. She died during a subsequent childbirth and John then married Frances Driver. John and Francis had nine children: Allen, Paralee, Matthew, Judie, Prudie, Andrew, Minnie, Sallie and James.

Sometime around 1880, John Halbrook and his family moved to Texas. The move was about the time Andrew was born in 1882. Andrew was just a little boy when they moved back to Arkansas. The group had a goal of traveling 10 miles per day. At a speed of two miles per hour, that would have meant five hours of travel each day. The rest of the day would have been spent preparing meals and making and breaking camp. At 10 miles per day, it would have taken them nearly a month to make the trip. Not long after little Andrew and his family got back to Conway County, Hettie Rhoads was born. The family told Andrew that he now had a little girlfriend and he always claimed that she was his girlfriend. I guess they were boyfriend and girlfriend all her life.

In the late 1800s, the Rhoads family moved to Oklahoma to farm new land. They crossed the Arkansas River on the old Lewisburg Ferry and a colt fell into the river. The colt was able to swim beside the ferry near its mother and made it out on the south bank. Andrew would have gone to Oklahoma to marry Hettie and bring her back, but the family moved back to Conway County before he could make his move.

Andrew and Hettie were married in 1902 and lived with relatives for awhile. They got a job picking cotton with a family that farmed along West Point Remove Creek where Highway 124 crosses it and turns north toward Jerusalem. One of Andrew's older brothers and his wife were also picking cotton. They got room and board with the farm family and wages for the cotton by weight. It was only natural that a rivalry would develop between the couples about who could pick the most cotton. It may not have been a spoken challenge, but each kept an eye on how the others were doing. Hettie and the other wife stayed just about even, but Andrew was a little faster than his brother, and he and Hettie had picked the most by the time the crop was finished. It seems that it actually hurt the feelings of the older couple to be beaten by the newlyweds.

Andrew and Hettie took the money they had earned picking cotton and went to town to buy what they would need for their new home together. They bought a small cast iron cook stove, a can of kerosene, a box of matches, and some staples and had enough money left over to last the winter.

Andrew and Hettie had a piece of land to settle on and their relatives and friends came to help them build a cabin. Someone had a mule and used it to pull logs to the site. Two men would work a log to notch it for the walls. Part of the procedure was to cut the ends of the logs off even at the corners of the walls after the

walls were up. Andrew was anxious to get it all roofed and ready to move into and told the helpers not to worry about the logs ends, he would cut them off later. Someone said, "I'll bet you a goose you'll never cut them off!" But he still wouldn't let them and he never did cut them off.

Clyde was Andrew and Hettie's first child. He was born in 1904 and in those days the babies and little children went to the fields with their parents. Clyde was left on a pallet in the shade at one end of the rows and the family's little dog stayed with him. One day a young colt was allowed to follow its mother during the plowing, but it got bored walking up and down the rows and started exploring. When Hettie went to check on Clyde, she found the colt nosing around the pallet with the little dog standing between it and Clyde to make it keep its distance.

Daughter Rose was born in 1909. Clyde now stayed at the pallet to watch Rose while his parents worked in the fields. One time they came to check on the children and found a large snake near the pallet. They asked Clyde, "What would you have done if the snake had crawled onto the pallet with Rose?" and he replied, "I would have dwagged her off!"

Opie, their second son, was born in 1915.

When Lyonell, the fourth child, was born, Clyde was about 15. He was too old to be hanging around the house during the birth, so, since he had not been allowed to go out hunting alone with the rifle before, he was given the rifle and told that he could go hunting. That kept him away until the baby came. Rose was about 12 years old and she probably took care of Opie who was 5. At the time, they lived north of Cleveland on the west side of SH95.

Andrew and Hettie moved on the north edge of Cleveland in a house just north of the gin and west of the school. Hettie's brother Elbert died there and her daughter Reva Dale was born there in 1924. The land in front of the gin was swampy and SH95 was not an improved road. Andrew kept a team ready to pull folks out when they got stuck in the road.

After a few years they moved a couple of miles west of Cleveland, to a place on the south side of what is now called Copeland Cave Road. They then moved back to the west edge of town and lived in a house on the little hill on the south side of Copeland Cave Road not far from where the Methodist Church building is now located. They were building a nice new house on the north side of the road and it was completed in time for Hettie Mae to be born there in 1929. When the time for Hettie Mae's birth had come, they sent Clyde to take 5-year-old Reva Dale to stay at Rose's. After the baby was born, Clyde brought Reva Dale home. He told her that the doctor had brought them a new baby sister She had a hissy fit and insisted that they tell the doctor to take the baby back. Hettie had the "milk leg" after Hettie Mae was born, and was confined to the bed for several weeks. Doc Coley came to check on her every day and Reva Dale had such a fit whenever he was there that they had to have Rose come to keep her under control.

In their later years, Andrew farmed with his sons and sons-in-law, and Hettie supported him from home and helped her daughters and daughters-in-law with their families. Hettie died April 29, 1959 and Andrew died Nov. 15, 1965. *Submitted by Hettie Mae Halbrook Hofherr.*

HALBROOK - Lyonell Halbrook, postmaster at Cleveland, AR from 1957-83, was a life-long resident of Cleveland. Born to Andrew Jackson Halbrook and Hester "Hettie" Ann Cordelia Rhoads Halbrook on July 7, 1920 at their home just north of downtown Cleveland, he was the fourth of six surviving children: Clyde, Rose, Opie, Lyonell, Reva Dale and Hettie Mae.

He attended elementary school in Cleveland and helped with his father's farm, later attending high school at the Wonderview Consolidated School. When the building burned, the school was temporarily moved back to Cleveland, but the new Wonderview School building was completed in time for Lyonell and his class to hold their graduation there in 1938.

During high school, he had driven the school bus, a converted truck, but following graduation he worked in the Civilian Conservation Corp. As part of the CCC experience, he was able to take some college courses at ASU in Jonesboro and gained practical construction experience.

Lyonell Halbrook and Louise Maxwell Halbrook in front of their new home in Cleveland, AR (1948).

WWII resulted in the only length of time spent away from Cleveland. Following basic training, he was assigned to the Signal Corps. He shipped out from Yakima, WA and spent most of the next four years in the Philippines, and then Japan, following their surrender. After discharge, he returned to Cleveland, vowing never to leave.

He became reacquainted with Louise Maxwell Skipper, who had lost her husband, James Skipper, during the war. She and her two children, Jimmy and Jeanne, were living in Lanty with her parents, Luther and Eugenia Maxwell. They were married Aug. 22, 1947 and soon built a rock home in Cleveland. Their children were Brenda, Marinelle, Sherry and John.

Lyonell worked with his brothers and brother-in-law at construction, traveling to work-sites in Arkansas and, occasionally out of state, but he always farmed. In 1957 he was appointed postmaster of the Cleveland Post Office and combined that with a retail business when he bought the contents of the Kordesmeier's variety store in Morrilton. He soon added groceries to the inventory and lots of wood, ensuring plenty of warmth for the wintry days of socializing around the old iron stove. He retired in 1983 with an encyclopedic memory of people and events with ties to Conway County.

He bought land as he could, raised cattle and range turkeys and, while the children were at home, raised a large garden (later cutting it down to a mere half-acre). He was an active leader of the Cleveland Methodist Church, served as a board member on the Conway County Farm Bureau for over 30 years, worked with the Cleveland Volunteer Fire Department and served as a trustee for the Old Liberty Cemetery.

Willie "Marie" married F.E. Scroggins (both deceased). They have three children: Kay Marie, Marilyn Jo, and Bruce Eugene.

J.C. married Alice Elma White. They live in Oklahoma City. Their daughters are Barbara Lynn Mallett and Janet "Jan" Gayle (Mallett) Lake.

Milton Leon (deceased) has a daughter, Lona Ruth "Sue."

Gwynnith Louise married Lester Ledbetter (deceased). They share three children, Lynnette, Sanford Leslie "Les" and Kevin Gwynne.

Grace LaVerne married Robert Bane (both deceased). Their children: Robert Keith (deceased), John Warren, Nancy LaVerne (deceased), and Karen Elizabeth (Bane) King.

Papa's homeplace is currently being restored by Karen (Bane) King and her husband David. It has been kept in the family where loved ones often return "home to remember." The house holds many memories of "Papa" and family. *Submitted by Jan Lake.*

HALBROOK - Lyonell Halbrook liked to tell the family stories that he remembered from early childhood. His father, Andrew Halbrook, owned several hundred acres in the bottom lands where Brock Creek joins West Point Remove in north Conway County. One time Brock Creek flooded and washed a narrow ditch across the field to Point Remove. Weeds had grown up head-high so the ditch was not visible. Andrew was standing in the front of the wagon bed to get a better view over the weeds, but didn't see the ditch. Lyonell was in the wagon bed. The ditch was narrow enough for the mules to step across, but when the front wheels of the wagon dropped into the ditch, Andrew was thrown onto the rigging behind the mules. That startled the mules and they began to run. Andrew fell under a front wheel but held the lines as he was dragged along on his belly until he got the mules stopped, thus saving his little boy from a run-away. Lyonell said his father had a "whelp" across his back that stood out the size of a man's forearm.

Andrew didn't do much fishing because of all the farm work he had to do, so when he did go, he took all the family along to have a big outing. Lyonell recalled a fishing trip they took around 1925 when he was about 5 years old and his Grandfather Halbrook was about 85. They loaded all the gear they needed for cooking and camping into a wagon and traveled the three miles from Cleveland to a small creek that ran between the Liberty Cemetery and John Halbrook's home. Andrew's brother, Will, and several others had wagons there. Some of the men cut down a tree, hooked their horses to it, and dragged it through a "hole" upstream to muddy the water and make the fish come to the surface. They got so many fish, including a very large trout (or bass) that they decided to bring Grandpa down to join in the fish fry.

Andrew had also brought the T-Model that he used for carrying the mail. Andrew's brother, Allen, offered to drive it to get Grandpa and they agreed that Lyonell could ride along. When his Grandpa got into the single bench seat, Lyonell crawled over the back of the seat and rode in the homemade mailbox. He leaned over the seatback to be between the men so that he could listen in on their conversation.

Lyonell said that when they got to the camp and his Grandpa saw the many big fish, his grandpa's eyes just "danced" and "flashed." He said that Grandpa's eyes always did that when he was pleased and excited. Lyonell's Grandpa Halbrook died within a year or so of that time. I think Lyonell's eyes "danced" a little, too, at the memory of that long-ago event.

Arnold Walls was Lyonell's first brother-in-law. Arnold married Rose around 1925. Arnold must have been a strong young man and a willing worker. He was a good hand to help with the Halbrook's crops. Arnold had been plowing all day with "Big Jim," the mule that Andrew had bought from his brother, Jim. Big Jim was good for plowing, but not for riding. At the end of the day, Arnold was tired and wanted to ride to the house. He thought maybe Big Jim was tired out, too, and since the road was muddy, maybe Jim couldn't get away from him. After Arnold and Andrew got the harness loose and had Big Jim out in the muddy road, Arnold said, "I believe I can ride him to the house if you'll get a twist on his nose and hold him while I get on." Andrew put a loop of rope around Big Jim's nose and tightened it with a stick. Arnold started to get on Big Jim and Andrew said, "Hurry, Arnold, the twist is about to come off!" And when the twist came off, Arnold came off!

Andrew was building houses in the county seat 20 miles from home and sent word that he needed more lumber. It was in the afternoon and Arnold was out in the field plowing when the word came. He hooked up a team to the wagon and went to the sawmill just south of town to pick up the lumber. Rose had fixed him a sack supper and he headed on to the county seat before dark. He probably got to the county seat by midnight. Perhaps there was another wagon ready for his return trip or they may have quickly unloaded the wagon he drove in. Arnold was a good horse man and his team was in good shape, so after some feed and water they were ready for the return trip. The horses knew the way home, so Arnold was able to nap along the way. By morning he was back home and out in the field plowing.

Hettie's brother, George Rhoads, and his family lived in a community on the bank of the Arkansas River east of the foot of Petit Jean Mountain called Paw Paw Bend. One of the families had sold a piano to another family and George Rhoads was providing his wagon and team to haul it. Several men were there to load the piano and one of them suggested securing it some way to keep it from shifting. George said it wouldn't be a problem and hurried his team down a bank to the road. The piano fell over and crushed his head. George, Jim and Ed Rhoads were Hettie's brothers. Ed was also living in Paw Paw Bend when George was killed and he decided to move back to Cleveland. Some of their goods may have been moved by truck, but Ed also moved some by wagon. Ed and Hettie's son Clyde (about 24) were making a trip from Cleveland back to Paw-paw Bend to haul another load. Lyonell was about 8 years old and he got to go with them. It was about a 10-hour trip by wagon. They left at sundown and arrived about sunup. Lyonell rode on a quilt in the wagon bed but the ride was still pretty rough. He did sleep some and awoke during the night to see something large fly past the moon. *Submitted by Brenda Halbrook Tyler.*

HALE - John Middleton Hale was born Dec. 30, 1851, Panola County, MS, a son of Nicholas Jackson and Eveline G. Tipton Hale, who first came to Arkansas from Mississippi in a covered wagon in 1859. They settled at Scottsville in Pope County and in 1872, was caught up in the Pope County Militia War. John Middleton was a young man during those terrible times and his family suffered dearly, as his father was a Mason and Patriot Arc leader of the community. On July 13, 1872 his father and brother William T. were taken prisoners, and in an ambush attempting to murder the prisoners, William T. was shot and fell from his horse. He crawled out into the brush and made it to a neighbor who hid him, but he died soon after. Nicholas escaped without a scratch and made it to Dover to tell what happened. Both Nicholas and Eveline died in 1875 and are buried on their homestead at Scottsville. They had eight children: William T., Matthew Tolbert, George Washington, Thomas Jefferson, Albert Ross, Holly, Laura Ann Jackson F.

On March 3, 1874, John married Susan Elmina Noel Hale. They had seven sons and one daughter, several of which were Conway County residents. John and Elmina moved the family to Rover, Yell County about 1892. Elmina died May 11, 1897, leaving John with seven children still in the home and the baby not yet a year old. She is buried in Hunt's Chapel Cemetery at Rover. John remarried and moved his family to Mill Creek, Indian Territory. He was in the "Great Land Rush" when that area was opened for settlement.

John later moved back to Arkansas and lived at Morrilton for several years in the 1920s and 1930s. He lived near his son Sam, who lived on Ola Street. By the early 1930s he returned to Oklahoma and died there in 1940. John is buried in Drake-Nebo Cemetery in Murray County, OK.

Their children were:

1) William Noel (b. 1875) md. Ida Robinson and had five children. They lived in Yell County, then moved to Murray County, OK.

2) Samuel William (b. 1878) md. Dovie Arbuckle. They had three children and lived at Morrilton.

3) Luther Jackson (b. 188) md. Mary Luella Conn and lived in Morrilton.

4) Holly Buford (b. 1883, died in infancy).

5) Zachariah Nathan "Zack" (b. 1885) md. Martha Lovata Venable. They lived in Ada Valley and South Oppelo.

6) Reese Hogan (b. 1888) md. Lola Hill. They had three daughters and lived in Oklahoma.

7) John Herbert Arnold "Doc" (b. 1891) md. Jessie Hawkins and had one son. Jessie died and John married Josephine Elkins, had nine children and lived in Oklahoma.

8) Mary Altie Belle "Maybelle" (b. 1896) had nine children. They, also, settled in Oklahoma. *Submitted in memory of Hale families.*

HALE – Lola Mae Hale (b. May 6, 1923 in Willow Bend, Conway County, AR) was a daughter of Luther Jackson and Mary Luella Conn Hale. She graduated from Morrilton School, and on Dec. 25, 1946 in Morrilton, she married William Harold Sanders, a son of Hector and Ruth Turner Sanders. William was born June 20, 1925 in Bigelow, Perry County, AR. Lola worked at the Cotton Mill, Levi Manufacturers and was a Tupperware dealer for many years. Lola today works at T.C. Vaughan Senior Citizen Center. Lola attends the First Assembly of God Church of Morrilton. She loves to read and sew. Lola is the only surviving member of her parent's 10 children.

William and Lola Sanders and their three children: Tommy, Nancy and Marilyn.

William served in the US Navy (Seabees) and was a policeman at Morrilton. He drove a taxi and worked at a filling station. William died April 26, 1986 in Morrilton, and is buried in Elmwood Cemetery.

When Lola's father decided to sell his house in the 1950s, she and William bought his house, and Lola still lives there today. They had lived next door at 1204 West Rock Street. For a while, they moved to Los Angeles, CA but returned to Morrilton in 1971.

They had three children: Marilyn Ruth (b. June 16, 1948, in Morrilton) attended Morrilton School. In 1966 she married Billy Dean Jones of Perry. He was born March 26, 1947. They had two daughters, Tina Renee' and Tamela Lee'Ann. Marilyn retired from Levi Strauss and Billy was a truck driver. They have resided in North Little Rock, AR since 1967.

Tommy Harold (b. April 2, 1957, Los Angeles, CA) married in 1978 to Bernice Lee Gipson (b. Sept. 13, 1959). They have two children, Christopher Michael and April Renee.' Tommy was a long haul truck driver for many years. They reside in Sherwood, AR where he is employed at Mountaire Feed Inc. as a transportation supervisor.

Nancy Cheryleen (b. Aug. 4, 1959, Morrilton) graduated from Morrilton School. She married Jerry Palmer Bullington and they had one son, Jerry Palmer Jr. They divorced and she married William Harris. They have resided in Conway for several years. *Contributed by Marilyn Sanders Jones.*

HALE – Luther Jackson Hale (b. Oct. 23, 1880 at Scottsville, Pope County, AR), a son of John Middleton and Susan Elmina Noel Hale, had seven brothers and one sister. About 1892 the family moved to Rover and his mother died in 1897, leaving his father with several small children. John remarried and moved to Indian Territory.

As a young man, Luther was with his father in a place near Ft. Smith for "The Great Land Rush" when Southwest Oklahoma Indian Territory was opened for settlement. Luther and his cousin rode their bicycles the whole way through. "And

Luther Jackson Hale celebrating his 100th birthday

that wasn't the only time that bike made the trip." Luther returned to Arkansas and his eye caught the sight of Miss Mary Luella Conn (b. March 30, 1885 in Yell County), a daughter of John David Conn (Irish) and Tyme Darthula Carter (Dutch).

In 1904 they married. It was an elopement as her mother was against her leaving home. They lived in numerous places, as their 10 children were born, losing three in infancy. Finally they settled at Morrilton. They lived in numerous places in Conway County before buying property. Some were Willow Bend, Portland Bottoms, Cardon Bottoms, Paw Paw Bend, Ada Valley and Morrilton. About 1932 Luther built two houses at 1202 Rock Street and next door.

Mary died in 1953 and Luther sold his home to his daughter, Lola Sanders. He married Lula Payne and they moved to Dougherty, OK. Luther traveled back to Morrilton to visit many times, and when he did, there was always a big family gathering and potluck dinner. As he neared his late 90s, Lula had been confined permanently to the nursing home and Luther's health failed, so he was moved back to Morrilton to live with his daughter Essie Holsted. He lived to the ripe old age of 100 years and six months, although he never acted like he knew he was supposed to be old. He kept young by riding his bicycle well into his 90s. He died April 22, 1981.

Their children were Marvin Arthur (b. 1905) md. Ruby Tharp and had three children, and he was a Morrilton taxi driver for years; Sister Hale (b. 1906, died in infancy); Earnest David (b. 1906) served in US Army. He married Violet Hubbard, had seven children, and lived at Adona; Henry Melvin, (b. 1912) md. Glynis Treadaway, had two daughters and lived at Morrilton; Essie Bonetha (b. 1914) md. Marvin Holsted, had one son and lived at Lloyd's Community, Morrilton; Hazel Odelia (b. 1916) md. Allen Brimmage, had eight children and lived in Ada Valley; Luther Lawrence (b. 1919), married first, Loraine and second, Ludie Siegler, no children; Auston (b. 1922, died in infancy); Lola Mae (b. 1923) md. William Sanders, had three children and lived at Morrilton; Edwina (b. 1926, died in infancy).

Many of Luther and Mary's descendants still live in Conway County and surrounding area. *Contributed in memory of my mother, Hazel Hale Brimmage Ware.*

HALE - Samuel William "Sam" Hale (b. Dec. 3, 1878 in Scottsville, Pope County, AR) was a well known resident of Morrilton. He was the second oldest and a son of John Middleton and Susan Elmina Noel Hale. Sam had six brothers and one sister: William Noel, Luther Jackson, Holly Buford, Zachariah Nathan "Zack," Reese Hogan, John Herbert Arnold "Doc" and Mary Altie Belle "Maybelle."

Sam's family moved to Rover, Yell County about 1892, then moved to Mill Creek, Indian Territory. Sam and his father and siblings were part of the "Great Land Rush." Sam at first went with the family to Mill Creek, OK, but returned to Arkansas and in 1903, he married Dovie Nancy "Della" Arbuckle from Yell County, and they had three children.

Sam farmed the Dowdle Estate's farm for 46 years and retired. They lived on Ola Street in Morrilton. Their children attended Morrilton School. Sam died on Feb. 14, 1967 in Morrilton and Dovie died March 18, 1970. Both Sam and Dovie are buried in Elmwood Cemetery at Morrilton. Their children were:

Eliza L. "Mina" Hale (b. May 1, 1905) md. Olgar McDonald. Both were schoolteachers. Eliza taught for 42 years and retired in 1972 at Jenks, OK, then moved to Sherwood in Pulaski County. They had no children. Olgar preceded her in death and she died about 1991, at Little Rock. Both Eliza and Olgar are buried in Elmwood Cemetery at Morrilton.

Bertha L. May Hale (b. _, d. Feb. 10, 1982) md. Mr. Averyt. Both are buried at Elmwood Cemetery.

John William Hale (b. July 9, 1914) md. Mosa Dean Thompson and had a son named John Dean. John and Mosa Dean divorced and John William married

Eria Hale and had another son, Sammy. John lived in Morrilton. He is buried in Elmwood Cemetery.

The Hale families believed in gatherings when someone came for a visit, usually there were lots of relatives around as long as the out of towners were in the area. And at least one big potluck dinner happened, where everyone far and near attended. I remember those times very well. It was a time to get to see all my cousins at one time. *Contributed in memory of Eliza Hale McDonald.*

HALE – Zachriah Nathan "Zack" Hale (b. Aug. 24, 1885 in Pope County AR) was a son of John Middleton and Susan Elmina Noel Hale. He was a child when his family, to include brothers Luther and Sam (who later became Morrilton residents), made the "Great Land Rush" into Indian Territory, now Oklahoma. They settled at Mill Creek in Murray County, OK. What an experience that must have been! Zack returned to Arkansas by 1908 and met Miss Martha Lovata Venable (b. Nov. 13, 1891). She was from the Boston Mountain area of Pope County. They met while she and family were picking cotton and they married on Nov. 15, 1908. They lived in several locations in Conway County to include Willow Bend, Portland Bottoms, Ada Valley in mid-1940s, Lower Oppelo and Morrilton. Zack worked on the WPA at Morrilton and was a farmer. He worked with his brother Sam, on the Dowdle Estate Farm, for several years.

"Zack Hale" is remembered to have been a very kind, social and colorful man, not unlike his siblings. They rarely met a stranger who didn't become an immediate friend.

Ludie Sigler Hale tells of the first time she met Zack Hale. "Before she married Lawrence, Zack's nephew, she was on her way to visit a relative who lived at Oppelo. She had made a stop in Morrilton. It was commonly known that she made the same drive on a regular schedule.

It seems Zack was close by and was looking for a ride to Oppelo where he then lived. Someone pointed out Ludie's car and told Zack, "That car is going your way." Since the owner wasn't around, Zack decided to climb into the back seat and take a nap while he waited.

Ludie got into her car and was crossing the river bridge, when Zack rose up from the back seat and said "Hi, I'm Zack Hale" and started to explain. Well! You didn't need to have been there to imagine her fright. She tells that story so many years later, with such fondness of him.

Zack died 1970 and Martha died 1981, both are buried in Wolf Cemetery at Oppelo. Zack and Martha had six children;

1) Lee (b. 1910) md. Era Noland and had four children: Shirley Lee, Patsy, Billie Jean and Allen Loyd. Lee died in 1990 and is buried at Elmwood Cemetery.

2) Autie Mae (b. 1912) md. Jesse Lee McElroy and had three children: Betty Jewel, Vittie and Orval Lee. Autie lives in California.

3) Earnest (b. 1914) md. Ruby Tilly. He served in the US Army and died in WWII.

4) Aubrey "Short," served in the US Army.

5) Deva Lorene (b. 1920) md. Raymond William Windham and had two children, Jeanette Lovata and Gene Ruben. Deva lived in Missouri and is deceased.

6) Ople Edmond (b. 1923) md. Lois Dunn and had two daughters, Mary L. and Debbie L. Opal and Lois live at West Morrilton. *Contributed by Fay Miller.*

HAMMOND - Our grandfather, Milton V. Hammond (b. 1854 in Alabama) was a very young child when his family moved to Tennessee. When he was about 25 years old he decided that he wanted to see what was west of the Mississippi River. He rode a mule to head west and wandered around for a while, then settled down at Cleveland in Conway County.

In a short time he met our grandmother, Melinda Scoggins, who came to Cleveland with her brother and his family from Alabama. They fell in love and were married in 1881 or 1882. As Milton was a blacksmith and farmer (as his father was) they homesteaded 120 acres of land and put in a blacksmith shop. Milton and Melinda had six children: Manuel (b. 1883); Phena (b. 1885); twins-Henry and Ben Franklin (b. 1886), Ben Franklin died when he was a baby; John William (b. 1888); and Jenney (b. 1890). Can you imagine caring for six children all less than 7 years of age?

There are four grandchildren still living: Lucille Scroggins, Lila Little, Issac Hammond and Beal Hallbrook.

Our father, John Hammond, married Dove Williams Newton and they had four children: Huie Hammond (deceased), Lucille Scroggins, Dhew Hammond (killed in WWII in August 1942) and Lila Little.

There are nine descendants still living in Conway County and 56 others living in different parts of Arkansas and other states.

Since our grandfather had to work his farm during the day, he had to work at night in his blacksmith shop to keep all the farmers' equipment in good working condition, and their horses shod. I was told that the people that lived near the shop could hear that hammer ringing loud and clear on that anvil late at night, with him singing as he worked. He was a Methodist. However, he took his family to the Advent Christian Church in Cleveland. *Submitted by Lucille Scroggins and Lila Little.*

HANNA

HANNA – George William Hanna (b. Sept. 25, 1898, Cheeksville area of Conway County, AR, d. May 29, 1978, Tulsa, Tulsa County, OK) was the son of E.E. Hanna and Ruby Zachary Hanna. George's father died when he was very young, and his mother remarried Joe Chepas.

George William married Grace Pearl Rankin on July 19, 1918 in Conway County, AR. Grace (b. Aug. 3, 1903, Perry County, AR, d. Sept. 26, 1971, Tulsa, Tulsa County, OK) was

George William and Grace Pearl Rankin Hanna

the daughter of Henry Clay and Emma B. Mulkey "Mulkie" Rankin. George William and Grace Pearl Rankin Hanna are buried in Robertsville Cemetery, Conway County, AR.

George and Grace made their home in Granny's Hollow, Conway County, AR. They are parents of 10 children, all born in Granny's Hollow:

1) Lillie Olevia (b. July 19, 1919, d. Feb. 9, 1921, Granny's Hollow, buried Robertsville Cemetery, Conway County, AR).

2) Euell Henry (b. Nov. 3, 1922) md. Margie Ruth Harrison on July 14, 1943, Oakland, CA. Margie, daughter of Mr. and Mrs. Harrison, and Euell Henry were parents of Euell Henry Hanna Jr. and Dawna Lynn Hanna.

3) Mary Loreda (b. April 21, 1925) md. James

Calvin Edwards on Feb. 19, 1944 in Conway County, AR. Their children are James Adell "Dale" and Doyle Eugene Edwards. James Calvin, son of John Henry and Cary Delayce Bullock Edwards, died May 13, 1989, Canyon Hill, Caldwell, ID and is buried at Caldwell Cemetery.

4) Georgia Pearl (b. June 21, 1927) md. Arbon Floyd Langford on Dec. 17, 1944. They are parents of Barbara Janette Langford.

5) Mildred Jewel (b. May 22, 1931) md. Marion Thompson on Dec. 2, 1948 in Conway County, AR. Marion was born Nov. 17, 1930 in Arkansas. They are parents of Ronald Dale and Charles Burt Thompson.

6) Carrell William (b. July 9, 1933) md. Ruth Irene Coffman on Oct. 14, 1950 in Conway County, AR. Ruth Irene was born Feb. 6, 1935, Hector, Pope County, AR. They are parents of Carrell Williams Jr., Janice Elaine, Brenda Ruth and George Edwards. Carrell and Ruth now make their home in Hector, Pope County, AR.

7) Cecilia Joyce (b. Sept. 5, 1935) md. Frank Vale on Aug. 12, 1955. They are parents of Frank Jr., Shelia and Veronica Lynn.

8) Everett Louis (b. Aug. 28, 1937) md. Kay Frances McHenry on June 18, 1959. Kay was born Sept. 13, 1941, Claremore, Rogers County, OK. They are parents of Terri Kay, Leslie Gayle and Kindel Lynn.

9) James Henry (b. Sept. 5, 1944) md. Georgia Lea Spencer on Feb. 10, 1967, Sperry, OK. Georgia Lea was born July 14 in Susanville, CA. They are parents of Jamie Katherine and Blake Joseph.

10) Vivian Fay (b. Nov. 3, 1945) md. Gary Howard on Aug. 6, 1965. They are parents of Sherry Lynn, Lorie Ann and Beverly Dawn.

George and Grace owned their own land with a small house, living room, bedroom and a long room across the back which served as a kitchen/dining room. They planted a garden, fruit trees, berries and grapes. Much of Grace's time was spent canning vegetables, fruit, jams and jellies; washing in an iron pot with a washboard outside no matter the weather; cooking on a wood stove, biscuits, corn bread, pies, fruit cobblers and the best coconut cake.

They were hard workers and the children helped with the chores and younger children when they weren't in school. Children attended school in Granny's Hollow and Jerusalem. The family attended Church of Christ, where George was an Elder and song leader. Grace recited Bible verses by heart to the children.

As our family grew, George decided they needed a bigger house. Digging the foundation, mixing the sand and concrete, the children never seeing this before. There was some sand left for the children to play in.

What an exciting day when they moved in, six rooms, two porches, kitchen and dining room with shelves from the floor to the ceiling for Mom to keep her "canned goods."

George stopped farming in 1938/39 and started working as a carpenter. During the 1940s, he was working away from home and helping build the "Army Camps."

Grandma Emma Rankin lived with us until her death in 1943. She was crippled with arthritis, never complaining, sitting in her rocking chair on the front porch with her Bible.

George and Grace moved to Tulsa, OK in 1950, living in the "Brookside area" until their death. *Submitted by Mildred Thompson/Wanda Dilbeck.*

HARALSON

HARALSON - William Henderson W.H. "Jake" Haralson and Iva Fridell Haralson moved from the Union Grove Community near Atkins to the Wesley Chapel "Possum Trot" Community in 1928. He and Uncle Will Murdock bought a cotton gin and named it the Murdock and Haralson Cotton Gin, and dad bought a grocery store nearby.

The cotton gin burned down in 1937, but was built back and in continuous use until it had to be shut

down because not enough cotton was being grown - because all of the men had to leave their crops and go to WWII.

My daddy built a home on North Division Street and we moved to Morrilton in 1945. He passed away in 1948 and my mother in 1957. They had nine children that I have listed from oldest to youngest. Charles Clarence Haralson, Thelma Williams, Daisy Cooper, Raymond Haralson, Mary Crawford, Virgie Chapman, Lorene Rowell, Stanford Haralson and Bette Wilson Voss. *Written by Bette Voss.*

HARDIN

HARDIN - Ruth Geneva (Norwood) Hardin was the fourth child of six born to Jacob Sidney and Fannie (Wilson) Norwood. She attended the Bald Knob and Plumerville Schools before her family moved from Plumerville to Woodruff County in the 1920s. She graduated from Fitzhugh High School near Augusta in 1934. A year and a half later, on Christmas Day, she married Raymond Hardin, who had grown up in the vicinity. They lived in south Jackson County, where they farmed and raised two children.

Ruth Norwood Hardin

Sid Norwood grew up in Conway County to become a farmer, the occupation of his ancestors since coming to this country during colonial times. He would try to make a living for his family during hard times, years that would comprise a long-term agricultural depression in rural America, the economic situation no doubt contributing to his move to northeast Arkansas.

His wife, Fannie Wilson Norwood, grew up in Plumerville where her father, Charles M. Wilson, farmed cotton around Portland Bottoms. C.M. Wilson was born in Conway County to Elijah and Jane (Ballard) Wilson, who married in Conway County in 1860. Elijah Wilson was born in Alabama, and Jane Ballard in Tennessee. The Jesse Ballard family had moved to Perry County about 1850 with several of the children, including Jane, living in Conway County after the death of their parents. Fannie's mother, Geneva (Garrison) Wilson, was the daughter of Allen and Elizabeth (Durham) Garrison, both of whom had come with their families from northern Georgia in the late 1850s to populate the Georgia Settlement of the county.

Sid Norwood's father, Daniel B. Norwood, came to Conway County from western North Carolina in 1858. He married his first wife, Elizabeth Cone, in 1859. They had three surviving children before Elizabeth's death in 1872. The same year Daniel married Kindness Tiner, the daughter of James Elias and Sarah Tiner, who had settled in the county after Civil War's end. Elias Tiner was born in South Carolina and married his first wife, Sarah Moon, in Hall County, GA in 1834. They moved to Mississippi where they lived for many years before moving to Jefferson County, AR, where Sarah died in 1862. Elias married his second wife, Amanda Melvina Goodman, there in 1864 and moved the family to Conway County, where they lived in Springfield until Elias's death in

1881. He raised a family of 16 children and is buried in Kilgore Cemetery next to his daughter, Kindness (Tiner) Norwood, and granddaughter, Amy Norwood.

Daniel B. Norwood was born in 1834 in Franklin County, GA, where his family lived before moving to an area nestled in the Blue Ridge Mountains of western North Carolina. He was the oldest of four brothers who resettled in Conway County during the years before and after the Civil War. His brother, Enoch Norwood, traveled with him to Arkansas in 1858 and possibly died during the war. After the war his brothers, John Floyd Norwood and Elisha Norwood, settled in Conway County, where both remained and raised families. *Submitted by Diane H. Norton.*

HARMAN - Hezekiah Harman (b. Nov. 17, 1763, Orange County, NC) was the son of Zachariah Harman and Rebecca Petty. He married Keziah Petty Dillard, his cousin, about 1783. Hezekiah became an ordained minister of the Baptist church in 1800. He served as pastor of the New Hope Baptist Church, the May Chapel Baptist Church and the Bear Creek Church in Chatham County, NC during his life time.

Hezekiah and Keziah Harman had the following children: Alexander (b. Jan. 28, 1786) md. Sarah Poe; Hezekiah Jr. (b. ca. 1796); John (b. ca. 1798) md. Mary E. Marks; Joseph; Milbry (b. Jan. 8, 1785) md. Charles Riddle; Frances (b. 1787) md. Joseph Poe, died after 1850 in Pope County, AR; Nancy; Mary (b. 1796) md. Guilford Petty; Susan married Edward B. Jones; Elizabeth married Briton Gross; and Martha (b. 1793) md. Dempsey Harrington, died in Van Buren County, AR.

Keziah Harman died Oct. 9, 1820 in Chatham County, NC.

Hezekiah took sick while attending church at Bear Creek and died on March 29, 1832 in Chatham County, NC.

"The Sandy Creek Baptist Association" at its 100th annual session at Love's Creek Meeting House in Chatham County in 1858, gave a short history of Hezekiah and his style of preaching. His sermons were old fashioned and were termed as "spiritualizing." When some of his audience seemed to be asleep and others outside the house were heard talking, he has been known to say, "Those gentlemen out of doors, will you please not talk so loud, or you will wake up those who are in the house."

It was also stated that Hezekiah was a soldier in the Revolutionary War before he was of age and fought in the Battle of Cane Creek. Maga Poe Watkins is just one of the many great-great-grandchildren of Hezekiah living in Van Buren and Conway counties in Arkansas.

HARMAN - Zachariah Harman, one of the progenitors of the Harman line in Conway and Pope County, AR, was born on Aug. 15, 1741 in Virginia. His parents are unknown. Zachariah married Rebecca Petty, daughter of William and Elizabeth Petty, on Jan. 28, 1763 in Virginia. The couple eventually settled in Chatham County, NC, where Zachariah became a land holder. He was elected sheriff of Chatham County in 1785 and held that position until 1796. Zachariah provided aid and assistance to the Revolution by his civilian service. His DAR national number is 534028.

Zachariah and Rebecca had the following children: Hezekiah (b. Nov. 17, 1763), Frances (b. 1765), John (b. 1768), Catherine (b. 1787), Martha (b. 1774), Elizabeth (b. 1779), Merriman (b. 1784), Rebecca (b. 1786), Zachariah Jr. (b. March 12, 1789).

Zachariah died in 1808 and is buried in Chatham County. Rebecca died Aug. 5, 1830 in Monroe County, GA. Zachariah Harman is the great-great-great-grandfather of Maga Anne Poe Watkins of Conway, County, AR.

HARMON – James Louis Harmon (b. Nov. 21, 1856 in Indiana) was the son of Wilson Harmon and Elizabeth "Lucy" Endicott. About 1875-79 the Harmon family joined a wagon train and moved from Indiana to-

ward Indian Territory (Oklahoma). James Louis separated from his family during the journey and ended up at Cave City, in Independence County, AR. James Louis married Martha Jane Crow on Feb. 23, 1881 in Independence County. Martha Jane (b. June 16, 1858 at Cave City) was the daughter of John Henry Crow and Sarah Jane Rollins. James Louis was a farmer. He and Martha Jane settled at Cave City where four of their five children were born.

About 1890 James Louis moved his family to near Tilly, in Pope County, AR, where their fifth child was born. James Louis built a log house on the 160 acres of land he homesteaded in Pope County. The log house was small but adequate in size to hold the few primitive pieces of furniture the family possessed. A large fireplace was built at one end for heat and cooking. The house had a wooden floor. James Louis and Martha taught their children to work at an early age. James Louis taught his sons to plant, plow, clear land, build barns and split rail fences, raise livestock, hunt, trap and do all the other things involved in farming and providing for a family. Martha taught the girls to cook, clean, spin, weave, sew, make candles and soap, preserve food and make a home. A flax patch was planted and maintained for use in making linen cloth. Wool was shorn from sheep and then picked, carded and spun into yarn for weaving and knitting. Only the wealthy could afford to buy material or clothing from a store. Every house had a spinning wheel and weaving loom that were used to make all manner of clothing for everyone in the household. Even rugs for the floors were made on the loom. Also found in every household was at least one huge iron kettle that was used for everything from doing the laundry, to making soap and rendering lard.

Martha Jane died Oct. 26, 1915 and James Louis died April 4, 1917. They are buried in Archie Valley Cemetery east of Tilly. Their children were:

1) Sarah Almeda "Meda" Harmon (b. Nov. 21, 1881, d. March 23, 1931) md. Richard Christopher Omar Walker. Children: Iva, Pearl, Anna, Grover, Flossie, Charles, Leoah and Jewel Walker. This family settled in Conway County.

2) Charles Sherman Harmon (b. April 2, 1883, d. Dec. 19, 1963) md. Allie Cossey. Children: Roy, Aggie, Connie and Tempie Harmon. Sherman then married Effie Emerson. Children: Reba and Wavel Harmon.

3) Oliver Schuyler Harmon (b. April 1, 1885, d. May 17, 1959) md. Sarah Ann Bruce. Children: Lonnie, Ola, Effie, Arves, Loyd, Rhoda Belle, Azalee and David Harmon. Schuyler then married Mrs. Helen Chadwick.

4) Effie Ann Harmon (b. Jan. 23, 1887, d. Oct. 2, 1963) md. James William Monroe Horton. Children: Lunie, Belle, Opal, Orville, Meda, Maggie and Edna Horton. This family settled in Conway County.

5) William Listenbee Harmon (b. Sept. 28, 1897, d. Oct. 13, 1973) md. Minnie Hibberts. Children: Cleburn, Ida and Bulah Harmon.

HARMON - Wilson "Wilse" Harmon (b. 1828 in Indiana) probably had a brother, John Lewis Harmon. Wilson settled in Gibson County, IN prior to 1850 and married Elizabeth "Lucy" Endicott on April 20, 1851 in Posey County, IN. Elizabeth (b. 1834 in Indiana) was the daughter of Joseph Nation Endicott and Elizabeth Varner.

Wilson was a farmer, probably a sharecropper. He settled in Posey County to raise his family. He moved his family to Gallatin County, IL about 1868. Between 1875 and 1879, Wilson loaded his meager belongings into a wagon and his family joined a wagon train headed toward Indian Territory (Oklahoma). Wilson's family appears on the 1880 Boone County, AR census. Wilson settled for a time near the Indian Territory (now Oklahoma) line in either Sebastian County, AR or present day LeFlore County, OK. Elizabeth probably died 1890-1894. She is buried in the Old Hall Cemetery in the Old Kully Cho Ha Commu-

nity of the Choctaw Nation at Cameron, LeFlore County, OK. Soon after Elizabeth's death Wilson moved to McAlester, OK and lived with his daughter Amy Willis. Wilson died there about 1894. His son Andrew rode a mule from his home at Whitefield, OK to McAlester when his father died.

Wilson and Elizabeth had 16 children, but only seven lived to adulthood:

1) Joseph Harmon (b. June 16, 1852, d. March 20, 1922) md. Nevada Ann Hughes, daughter of Samuel Hughes and Selina Majors. Children: Dicie, Oliver, Arthur, Charles, Walter and Ira Harmon.

2) Joanna Harmon (b. Sept. 29, 1853) md. Ira Thomas Conger.

3) Emma Amy Harmon (b. Aug. 29, 1854, d. Sept. 7, 1945) md. James M. Willis, son of John Willis and Ollie King. Children: Anna, Mary, Maggie, Schuyler, Dolly, Roscoe and Gertrude Willis.

4) James Louis Harmon (b. Nov. 21, 1856, d. April 4, 1917) md. Martha Jane Crow, daughter of John Henry Crow and Sarah Jane Rollins. Children: Almeda, Sherman, Schuyler, Effie and Willie Harmon.

5) Martin V. Harmon (b&d. April 18, 1858).

6) Elizabeth Harmon (b. Oct. 10, 1859, d. Dec. 24, 1859).

7) Mary W. Harmon (b. Dec. 24, 1860, d. Oct. 15, 1861).

8) George W. Harmon (b. Sept. 13, 1862, d. Sept. 20, 1863).

9) Dicey Harmon (b. May 11, 1864, d. Oct. 11, 1865).

10) Andrew Jackson Harmon (b. Jan. 7, 1865, d. Feb. 21, 1955) md. Lula C. Booth, daughter of David Booth and Alpha Autry. Children: Maudie, Roscoe, Jess, Bettie, Flora Belle, Joseph, Dosha, Wilburn and Amy Harmon.

11) Arvis C. Harmon (b. Jan. 20, 1868, d. Aug. 25, 1874).

12) Flora Belle Harmon (b. Jan. 26, 1870, d. Aug. 16, 1938) md. James Monroe Dolan. Children: Ethel, Julia, Lillie Elizabeth, Alma, James, Benjamin, Carl, Lena, Gertrude, Luther and Jack Dolan.

13) Martha W. Harmon (b. February 1872, d. Feb. 2, 1957) md. ___ Tidwell. Sons: Ernest and John Tidwell. She then married William Thomas Looney, son of William Looney and Elizabeth Woolard. Children: Maggie, Thomas, James, Maudie, Gertrude, Jessie, Sadie, Frances Josephine and Mary Looney.

14) Ida May Harmon (b. Sept. 1, 1874, d. March 7, 1954) md. William Craig Mouser. Children: Esther, Dessie, Maggie, Delmer, Callie, Arval and Mary Mouser.

15) Charles Harmon (b&d. May 20, 1877).

16) Newton Harmon (died as infant).

HARRIS - The William Mathews Harris family came to Arkansas in the early 1870s, purchasing farms in Conway, Pope, and Franklin counties. He was also known as William Monroe Harris. William was enumerated in the 1880 Pope County census, Northfork Township, as postmaster. After purchase of 20 acres in Conway County from Pleasant Houston Spears in 1889, the Harrises moved to the site in Jerusalem, where they resided in a large two-story house, torn down in the 1930s. Harris was a prosperous farmer, and also engaged as manufacturing partner in Harris & Callahan in 1889. The 1893 Griffin Township tax list records Harris paying the third highest taxes in the township on sundry items: pleasure carriage, gold watch, cattle, mules, hogs, as well as manufactured goods. The year 1894 brought a family tragedy and reversal of fortune, forcing the sale of the Jerusalem property to George Burris; the property was later sold to M.A. Thompson then to Robert Stroud, whose descendants reside there today.

William Mathews Harris (b. Aug. 6, 1846, Hall County, GA) was the son of Clark M. Harris and Nancy Garner, who were married in 1838 in Gwinnett County, GA. Nancy, daughter of Thomas and Elizabeth Thompson Garner, died ca. 1848, leaving her husband with five children: Thomas, Mary, William, Jane, and Clark. With the advent of the Civil War, Clark married Mary Ann Beny and their son Benjamin Franklin Harris was born in 1863. Clark and son Thomas joined the 35th Georgia Infantry, while William also served the Confederate army as a private in Company I, 24th Georgia Infantry. He fought in battles of 2nd Manassa, Harper's Ferry, Seven Pines, and was captured at Spotsylvania Courthouse and taken to prison at Point Lookout, MD. After being exchanged, he removed with his father to Gordon County, GA where he married Nov. 24, 1866 to Clarinda Caladonia Cowan (b. Jan. 29, 1847, Gordon County, GA, d. Feb. 21, 1924, Tag. Pope County, AR). William died Nov. 22, 1926, Atlanta, GA. Clarinda was the daughter of William Wallace Cowan, who had immigrated with his parents, William and Elizabeth Cowan, from County Antrim, Ireland. Clarinda's mother was Lettie Hewitt, daughter of Rev. James Hewitt and his wife, Elizabeth Apsley Osheal, whose father, Jethro Osheal of Spartanburg District, SC, served as a lieutenant in the Revolutionary War.

William Matthew Harris and Clarinda Caledonia Cowan, ca. 1885.

The children of William and Clarinda who lived to adulthood and marriage were Caladonia (b. 1876, d. 1957) md. Scott Standrige; William Thomas (b. 1879, d. 1953) md. Nevada Weatherman, then Polly Humphrey; Abna May (b. 1882, d. 1962) md. William Thomas Casey; James Fletcher (b. 1886, d. 1958) md. Mattie Ella Roberts; Mary Lou Patricia (b. 1892, d. 1918) md. Benjamin Lawson; Rebecca Vada (b. 1893, d. 1923) md. John Peters.

The author's grandmother, Opal Lee Harris (b. 1913, d. 2000) was a daughter of Boss Harris, and wife of Clyde Calvin Bunton (b. 1914, d. 2001), all of Russellville. In 2004, Gary Harris, grandson of Boss' brother Will Harris, resides in Morrilton and owns a physical therapy clinic. The author, David Travillion Bunton, resides in Russellville, AR. *Written by David Travillion Bunton.*

HART - Frank Wilcox Hart (b. Nov. 25, 1900 in Oppello, AR) was the son of Louis Taylor Hart and Marnie Wilcox Hart. He married Essie Jane Ingram, daughter to Henry Taylor Ingram and Tabitha Ann Goodall Ingram. Essie was born on March 6, 1903. They were both raised in the United Methodist Church and were the parents of following children:

Frank and Essie Hart

1) Heneretta Hart (b. 1922, d. July 1924).
2) Frankie Dean (b. Dec. 19, 1924) md. Alton Atkinson and they were parents of three daughters: (a) Betty Dean Atkinson married Fred Fletcher of Handford, CA, two children, Allan Fletcher and Leann (Fletcher) Been. Allan married Jan Sandell, two children, Madison and Peyton. Leann married Brian Been and they have two children, Sidney and Cabel Been of Iowa. (b) Mary Jane Atkinson married Jerry Boren, one child Deana Lois Boren. (c) Alice Atkinson passed away in 1981.
3) E.J. Hart (b. June 26, 1928) md. Betty Brinkley

and they have three daughters: (a) Jackie Hart married Bryan Herner, Texas; (b) Barbara Hart married David Jones and they have two daughters, Amanda and Elizabeth Jones, Bentonville, AR. (c) Teresa Hart married Pete Peterson of West Memphis, AR.
4) Zeta Faye Hart (b. July 10, 1934) md. Gay Embry of Atkins, two sons: (a) Gaylord Embry married Peggy Beck, two children, William Ray "Will" Embry, Russellville and Morrilton, and Rebecka Embry of Morrilton. Gaylord was later married to Rita Martin of Oklahoma City, OK. (b) Jeffrey Phillip Embry of Atkins, married Darla Cahoone of Little Rock, AR. Two children, Benjamin Phillip Embry of Little Rock and Anna Lucille Embry of Conway, AR.
5) Lewis Taylor Hart (b. July 2, 1936, d. March 1990) md. Mary Alyce Tiner, parents of two children: (a) Shelia Hart married Randell Hettinga of Russellville, one son Zack Hettinga of Russellville, AR. (b) Lewis Randel "Randy" Hart married Dena Rainboe of Missouri, they have three children: Luke, Hannah and Kylee Hart, Missouri.
6) Othel Paul "Tuffy" Hart (b. Oct. 3, 1939) md. Pat Martin of Cedar Bluff, AL. They have four children: (a) Paula Hart married David Dahlke. Three sons: Paul David, Dain and Boe Dahlke, all of Alabama. (b) Steve Hart married Joan Pruitt, two children and one grandchild. Stephanie Hart, Houston Hart and Addison Hart, all of Conway. (c) Janelle Hart married Chris Vaught, one child Chole Vaught. Janelle and Chole live in Morrilton. (d) Pattie Hart married Brian Beijen of Mountain Home, two daughters, Breanna Beijen and Hart Beijen, all of Morrilton.
7) Charles "B.B." Hart (b. Dec. 31, 1942) md. Clara Jo "Jody" Pinson of Hot Springs, AR, parents of three children: (a) Meredith Gaye Hart married Gary Tharp, two children, Dalton Tharp and Grayson Tharp of Siloam Springs, AR. (b) Frank Hart married Kim Taylor, three children: Taylor, Bailey and William "Will" Hart of Little Rock, AR. (c) Charles Thomas Hart of Camden, AR.

Frank, Essie and Heneretta are buried at the Wolf Cemetery at Oppello. Alton, Frankie, Lewis and Alice are buried at the Elmwood Cemetery at Morrilton, AR. *Submitted by Zeta Hart McPherson.*

HARWOOD - Edith Catherine Brown became the bride of Garrett Lafayette Harwood on June 21, 1930. They made their home in Center Ridge on a farm down Oak Road for nearly 70 years. They were the parents of three children: Johnnie Sue (b. Oct. 9, 1931, d. Sept. 25, 1933); Mary Rebecca "Becky" (Eoff) (b. 1944) and Jeff Morris (b. 1947).

Edith was the daughter of Rebecca Lucinda Qualls Brown and Drew Morris Brown. She completed eighth grade at Formosa High School where she played basketball. Her siblings were Juanita, Ollie, Caldonia, twins-Don and Doris, Billie, Merlene, Marion and Onvie. Edith was the third child.

Garrett is the son of Mary Ella Cole Harwood and Thomas Jefferson Harwood. His siblings were Eva Lee H. Scroggins (b. 1897), Wilma Ethel H. Stobaugh (b. 1899), Lillian Beatrice (b. 1902, d. 1910), Freidie Hutto (b. 1907), Clara Pearl H. Powell (b. 1912), Mildred Opal H. O'Brien (b. 1914), Roberta H. Williams (b. 1917) and Loeta Fay H. Flowers (b. 1919). Garrett went to school through eighth grade in the Pleasant Hill Community.

Garrett and Edith were farmers. Edith went to the fields daily with Garrett. After baby Johnnie Sue died, Tressie Flowers Watters said of Edith, "She worked harder than any man ever did. She got so skinny that she could have blowed away in a strong wind. I remember when she finally was going to have another baby. She was sitting on a three legged milk stool milking one morning, big as a house with Mary Beck, and I told her, 'I don't think a woman in your condition ought to be sitting on a three legged stool.' We had a great laugh about that because I was carrying my child, too! We made a fine looking pair of women!"

In their later years, Garrett spent his free time

going to the store each day, after his son and daughter-in-law, Jeff and Brenda (McCoy) Harwood bought Center Ridge Grocery. "Pa" spent the better part of each day sitting on the bench visiting with whoever decided to come in. Edith gardened and canned lots of food; she was known for her crocheting also. Garrett and Edith sold their farm to daughter and son-in-law, Becky and Fred Eoff, but lived there until 1989 when Edith suffered a massive stroke that left her unable to walk and to talk. At that time, Jeff and Becky built them a house behind Center Ridge Grocery that would accommodate Granny's wheelchair. She was often seen being wheeled out to the store so she could say hi to all her old friends. Edith died in 2003 after being married for 73 years. In 2005 Garrett still lives, but he is in very poor health.

HARWOOD - Jeff and Brenda Harwood married in September 1967. They moved to Florida where Jeff enlisted in the Navy, and their first daughter, Diana Marie, was born there in 1970. They moved back to Dutton Mountain and in 1977 they opened E & H Dairy with Jeff's sister and her husband, Becky and Fred Eoff. In 1978 their second daughter, Cindy Jane, was born.

Brenda Gail is the daughter of Dan and Virginia (Bennett) McCoy. She was born in 1946 and graduated from Nemo Vista High School. Brenda's siblings are Jack McCoy and Dannie Sue McCoy Fort.

Jeff Morris (b. 1947) is the son of Edith (Brown) and Garrett Harwood. Jeff's siblings are Johnnie Sue Harwood (b. 1931, d. 1933) and Mary Rebecca "Becky" Harwood Eoff (b. 1944).

Jeff and Brenda bought Center Ridge Grocery as partners with Ronnie Stell. Later Stell got out of the store business, and Brenda sold the chicken houses to become a full-time store owner. Jeff and Brenda are known for their friendly, helpful personalities and their willingness to help a neighbor. Their sandwiches and pizzas are favorite meals for many in the community! Center Ridge Grocery is the central social point in the area; farmers and truck drivers make it their daily stop!

HASLER - Joseph A. Hasler (b. Jan. 12, 1843 in Switzerland) came to Conway County and settled in the Vinson Chapel Community north of Morrilton. Joseph married Mary Ann Hooker on Nov. 21, 1881 in Conway County, AR. Mary Ann was born in July 1854 in Marshall County, TN to William F. and Mary Jane (Smith) Hooker. Mary Ann's known brothers and sisters were Lucy Hooker, Frances Emily Hooker, George Hooker and Sarah Hooker.

William Henry Hasler and Mary Jane Hasler Zachary

On Aug. 30, 1888 in Fort Smith, AR, Joseph Hasler took his oath of allegiance and became a United States citizen. The famous hanging judge, Isaac C. Parker, gave the oath.

Joseph and Mary's children were William Henry Hasler (b. April 18, 1891 Conway County, AR, d. Dec. 15, 1965 Poplar Bluff, Butler County, MO); Mary Jane "Janie" Hasler Zachary (b. March 29, 1894 Vinson Chapel, Conway County, AR, d. May 3, 1983 Conway, Faulkner County, AR). Joseph and Mary Ann had a set of twins that were born and died sometime between 1882-90. It is unknown where the twins are buried. William Henry Hasler's first marriage was to Anna Parish Cobb. She had two children from a recent marriage, Leonard Cobb and Lola Cobb. William and Anna Hasler had three children: Elmer, Elbert and Carl Welton Hasler. Anna Parish Cobb Hasler died shortly after the birth of Carl and William married Mrs. Cora Williams Hays Musgrave. William and Cora had two children: William Jasper "Bill" Hasler and Lovina L. Hasler Chism Ivy. Cora had five girls by her first marriage: Myrtle, Ella, Ester, Sybil and Alta Hays. She had one son by her second marriage, Harry C. Musgrave.

Mary Jane "Janie" Hasler married George Washington Zachary Jr. in Vinson Chapel, Conway County, AR on Jan. 31, 1915. George (b. Feb. 22, 1884 in Dover, Pope County, AR) was the son of George Washington Zachary Sr. and Mary Frances Fellers Zachary. Mary Jane and George Zachary's children are Lois May Zachary Nicholson, William Virgil Zachary, Rose Mildred Zachary Chism, Mary Helen Zachary Nicholson Anderson, Eugene Luther Zachary, Leo Zachary, Cleo Zachary, John Quitman Zachary and Jimmy Doyle Zachary. George Zachary Jr. was married the first time to Nellie Treadaway and they had two children: William Carl Zachary and Terry Lou Zachary Nelson. George W. Zachary died Feb. 14, 1977 in Morrilton, Conway County, AR and is buried beside Janie in Elmwood Cemetery, Morrilton, Conway County, AR.

Joseph A. Hasler died June 14, 1922 in Vinson Chapel, Conway County, AR and Mary Ann died sometime between 1920-30. She is buried beside her husband in the Skinner Cemetery, Conway County, AR. They do not have a marker but are buried on the south end of the first row next to the highway. *Submitted by Rose Zachary Chism.*

HAWKINS - Estes Ray Hawkins (b. Jan. 29, 1921 in Center Ridge, Conway County, AR) was killed in an automobile accident on April 25, 1959. He was the son of John Carl Hawkins and Nettie Mae Dockins. Ray married Emma Louise Baskins (Aunt Snooks, as we know her) who was born July 23, 1920. She was the daughter of Jess and Ora Baskins. They had two children:

Ray and Snooks Hawkins

1) Monte Hawkins (b. July 17, 1940 in Conway County, AR, d. May 24, 2004 in North Augusta, SC) was a retired health physicist with Westinghouse at the Savannah River site in South Carolina. He married Mildred Teasley (Sam) on June 10, 1977. At the time of his death his children were Scott Raymond Hawkins (md. Shannea); Bradley William Hawkins; Robert B. Crawford; Rhonda C. (md. Frank Cogburn), children are Michelle Leigh Cogburn, Franklin L. Cogburn III, Paige Evelyn Cogburn, Kristine L. Cogburn.

2) Larry Hawkins (b. Sept. 4, 1943 Conway County, AR, d. Jan. 29, 2000 in Richmond, VA) was general manager of Reynolds Metals Global Bauxite and Aluminum Business Unit. He traveled the world doing business for Reynolds during his career. Larry married Coralie Ridling Feb. 4, 1967. She was the daughter of Paul P. Ridling and Juanita Adams.

Growing up and all through his life, Ray was an avid hunter and fisherman, going to wet his hook each and every opportunity he had. He was one of those guys who thought that a hook would rust if not always kept in the lake. Ray was a graduate of Nemo Vista High School. He was an Army Veteran of WWII. After coming home from the war, he attended what is now known as Arkansas Tech University in Russellville. He was also the owner operator of a dairy bar on North Moose Street. At the time of his death, he was an appraiser for the State Land Office. *By Beth Hawkins Miller.*

HAWKINS - George Washington Hawkins (b. February 1866 in Conway County, AR) was the son of John Washington and Susan Ann Watson Hawkins. He married Emily Orange Stell, daughter of Asbury Baxter and Rachel Hobbs Jones Stell, on Oct. 3, 1886. George and Emily's marriage record can be found in

Conway County Courthouse Marriage Records, Book E, p. 472.

Emily and George (holding Lela), children l-r: Lola, Myra, Winnie, Pearl, Myrtle, Ann, Rachel and Glendon, 1901.

George had nine children by Emily before deserting the family after 1904. He had a checkered reputation before and after the desertion. George died on Feb. 22, 1924 in Washington County, AR, according to the Arkansas Death Index. Their children were:

1) Myrtle Hawkins (b. August 1887) md. Walter Berry and had two daughters, Syble Wyoma (b. Jan. 18, 1910) and Aphra LaVelle (b. Dec. 25, 1912).

2) Ann B. Hawkins (b. November 1888) md. Walter Henry and had three children: Emma Dean Henry, Buddy Henry and Helen Henry.

3) Winnie Pearl Hawkins (b. Oct. 5, 1891, d. Jan. 17, 1988) md. David Gillard Jones and had 10 children: Druid Glaytus Jones, Hoyt Gillard Jones, Zenoma Aulene Jones, Vivian Marguerite Jones, Edith Christine Jones, Ruby Pearl Jones, Dorothy Estelle Jones, Beatrice Laverne Jones, Thaddeus Leon Jones and Martha Janet Jones. (See also this family's history in the first Conway County History book.)

4) Mary Rachel Hawkins (b. Jan. 17, 1893, d. May 17, 1959) md. John Vottaman Bowling and had five children: J.V. Bowling, Betty Jean Bowling, Stanley Hawkins Bowling, Laoma Jeanece Bowling and Johnnie Vivian Bowling. After John's death, Mary Rachel married a Mr. Howard.

5) Myra Vivian Hawkins (b. March 1895, d. 1904).

6) Iva Lola Hawkins (b. Dec. 22, 1896, d. Jan. 27, 1956) md. George Washington Miller and had seven children: Harold Gloyd Miller, Frances Mildred Miller, Howard Hawkins Miller, John Hargis Miller, Anna Lowena Miller, James Milton Miller, and Wyoma Rachel Miller.

7) Glendon H. Hawkins (b. July 1898, d. April 1979) md. Eunice Cardin and had one daughter, Betty Ann Hawkins.

8) Ruby Lela Hawkins (b. March 3, 1900, d. Nov. 15, 1982) md. Benny J. Bolton and had four children: Zonoma Bolton, Emma Dale Bolton, J.D. Bolton and Benny Hugh Bolton.

9) Gloyd Hawkins (b&d. 1904).

Emily Orange (b. Jan. 4, 1869, d. May 4, 1940) is buried in Wilder Cemetery in Conway County. *Submitted by Dorothy Estelle Jones Francis.*

HAWKINS - There is little known about Hugh H. Hawkins. He seems to elude the normal paper trail left by most. What we do know is his name, Hugh H. and he was born Feb. 19, 1867 in Conway County, AR and died April 6, 1899 in Aplin, Perry County, AR. Hugh was the son of John Washington and Susan Ann Watson Hawkins. Hugh married his first wife Mary Lodisky Brown on Dec. 30, 1888. She was the daughter of John H. and Levesta Lucindia Ledbetter Brown. Mary, also known as Dica, was born July 1873 in Arkansas and died between 1900 and 1903 in Conway County, AR. Hugh and Dica had one child, John Carl Hawkins (b. Jan. 29, 1891 in Center Ridge, Conway County, AR, d. July 9, 1931). He married Nettie Mae Dockins, the daughter of J.R. and Sarah Prince Dockins. She was born Dec. 24, 1894 in Cen-

ter Ridge, AR and died Aug. 27, 1982. Hugh and Dica divorced.

Hugh H. Hawkins and Mary Lodisky Brown, ca. 1890.

Hugh was married a second time to Ada Elizabeth Hardin on Aug. 4, 1896. She was the daughter of John Sanford and Cicely Hanna McKnight Hardin. Ada (b. June 14, 1874, d. Dec. 19, 1953) and Hugh had one daughter Norine (b. Dec. 22, 1897, d. October 1900 in Perry County, AR). Hugh and Norine are buried in Smyers Cemetery, near Aplin, Perry County, AR. Sometime after Hugh's death, Ada married a man who's last name was McGehee.

Dica married for a second time to Newman Wilkes on April 26, 1896. He was the son of Samuel Taylor and Ella Tullis Wilkes. He was born Feb. 24, 1876 and died May 20, 1944. They had two daughters: 1) Louella Lula Lucinda Wilkes (b. March 18, 1897, d. 1978) md. Alfred Lee Parish (b. 1896, d. 1990) on Nov. 22, 1917. Their children were Burce Lilbert, Dortha Lee, Dicia Vanteen, and Wanda Lou. 2) Ola Wilkes (b. Aug. 7, 1898, d. March 31, 1983) md. Joseph H. Fleming on Sept. 7, 1920. He was born Oct. 14, 1895 and died Sept. 4, 1979. Their children were Jerita, Mary Magdalene and Reba Jo. *Submitted by Mary Beth Hawkins.*

HAWKINS - J.C. Hawkins (b. Jan. 8, 1929 in Center Ridge, Conway County, AR, d. Sept. 23, 1982) was the son of John Carl and Nettie Mae Dockins Hawkins and the youngest of seven children. At the age of 2-1/2 years old, his father died and things were very difficult for his family. His mother went to work running a store and working in a cannery among other jobs. His oldest sister Clemmie and her husband Oda took care of him while she worked. He being the youngest child everyone spoiled him terribly. This of course made him a very mischievous young man. He was always picking at his sister Glenna, because they were closest in age, and getting her in trouble. One time their mother had made them kiss each other through the spokes of the back of a chair, boy did he hate that! This was after Glenna had told on him for popping the lids on the grape juice that had been canned for the winter (in his young foolish mind he thought it would ferment and make wine, just like that). He and his family moved from Center Ridge to Morrilton in 1939, where he attended school in Morrilton and played football his high school years for the Morrilton Devil Dogs (Number 65). While in high school he worked at the Corner Drug Store in the Soda Fountain Shoppe. J.C. graduated in

J.C. and Rose Hawkins, 1981.

1946, enlisted in the National Guard in 1947 and was honorably discharged as corporal in 1950.

J.C. was a nice looking young man and the girls seemed to follow him around a lot. Until, one night he needed a wake up call. He called the operator and asked if she would call him at a certain time the next morning. She told him it was against company policy to do so. But, you know ole sweet talking J.C.; well he got his wake up call, not only that one but for several days in a row. Several mornings of these calls and he decided he wanted to see just whom that nice little voice on the other end of the line belonged to so they arranged to meet in front of Warren's Café. Well, six weeks later on March 12, 1950 they became Mr. and Mrs. J.C. Hawkins and he got those wake up calls for the next 32 years. She was Rose Elladene Grimmett (b. Dec. 13, 1929 in Little Rock, Pulaski County, AR, d. Jan. 20, 2004), daughter of Ernest Wailon Grimmett and Nora White Grimmett Chandler. Rose lived with her mother and grandparents, Charles and Mary White in Ferndale, Pulaski County, AR, until moving to the Atkins, Russellville area with her mother and stepfather Roy Chandler. Rose was a 1947 graduate of Russellville High School.

J.C. went on to enlist in the US Air Force and was sent to California and from there to Washington State before returning to Arkansas. This was during the Korean conflict. (Rose went with him, July 1951-February 1953). He was honorably discharged as staff sergeant on Feb. 22, 1953. They moved to Little Rock where he was a taxi driver until he took a job with R.J. Reynolds Tobacco Company as a sales representative, during which time he took a Dale Carnegie Course on speaking.

In 1954 J.C. and Rose started their family; their first child was born in March of that year,

1) Joe Carl married Marilyn Rose Paladino and their children are (a) John Carl married Andrea Marie DeWinter; their children are Cameron Lewis, Savanna Rose and Paige Marie. (b) Joe Keith married Pamela Rose Gangluff; their children are Nathaniel Joe and Theresa Rose "Tess."

2) Gary Lee married Gloria Jean Bradley (divorced) and their child Clinton Lee married Amanda Greer.

3) Mary Elizabeth married Ralph W. Ruff Jr. (divorced) and their children are (a) Christopher Wayland married Cynthia Ann Wells; their children are Sydney Claire and Janna Elizabeth. (b) Kevin Lynn. In 1990, Mary Elizabeth "Beth" married Charles Edward Miller.

4) Melynda Rose married Benton Delane Thomas.

In about 1959-60 the family moved to Morrilton. J.C. worked as a deputy sheriff for a while. Their next adventure was a service station on the east end of town, known as the Skelly Station, where big trucks came in and were cleaned and washed as well as greased and oiled. Rose and J.C. fixed flats, pumped gas and even cooked bar-b-que sandwiches in the back. After this J.C. went to work for the state as an appraiser.

It is about this time we lived on North Oak St. There were shrubs in front of the house and one Halloween we got all dressed up to go out just as it was getting dark, and Daddy made us go out the back door for some reason which we couldn't figure out. Well, when we reached the front of the house there he was with a sheet thrown over his head, jumping up out of the bushes screeching booooooo at us, and all four of us ran screaming back into the house, afraid to go back outside. He laughed at us for years. What a Dad! Do you think this bothered any of us, not at all, when we returned home from our evening of fun, we sat on the floor where we divided our candy up and all the candy that no one would eat, we gave to dear ole Dad. Daddy had a great sense of humor, was a generous person, so much so that as they say "he would give you the shirt off his back if he thought you needed it." We, being children, thought that he might have been a little on the strict side, at least for our taste. He loved hunting and fishing.

In 1967 J.C. suffered three heart attacks thus changing all of our lives.

Rose not only worked as a telephone operator and side by side with J.C. at the station, she also worked at Morrilton Plastics. When Daddy had his heart attack she went to work at the Conway County Health Department. In 1970 they bought the James Lanni farm in Center Ridge and moved again (Daddy said home again). Funny thing happened to ole J.C. when the grandchildren were born, he started to change. That strict man we children had known didn't seem to be there anymore. Whatever those grandsons wanted, well, you know… Then in 1978-79 they built a poultry house and raised chickens.

After J.C.'s death Rose continued in the poultry business until 1989-90 when she retired. Rose was called on for many years to work at the election polls. She seemed to really enjoy doing this because it let her be out among so many people she hadn't seen for such a long time. All of that being said, I must add that not only did my mother work outside the home but there can never be given enough praise or honor to the woman we call Mother (knowing the endless worries, tireless, thankless jobs she had to do and the sleepless nights, changing of dirty diapers, cooking, cleaning, laundry and most of all the never-ending self-sacrifice and supply of love and understanding given without question).

In 1998, Rose learned of her leukemia and began a journey of numerous ups and downs with several spirals, twists and turns with various trying times and trials, through which she handled it all with such grace and poise. Rose and J.C. were members of the Church of Christ and it was through her faith and trust in God and the love for her family that kept her going strong. She really loved her grandchildren, always showing their pictures and making sure she kept her camera close at all times, just in case she could get that next great shot. Rose loved to go to ball games of any kind. She and a close friend, Gwen Kirtley, could be seen front and center at every game. She was a member of the Birdtown Home Extension Club. She loved to have flowers around the house indoors and out. She was particularly fond of roses.

J.C. and Rose worked very hard together to raise their four children and to have the family living on the farm in Center Ridge. They were always willing to help their friends and neighbors and were very community minded. Their daughter Mary and husband Charles Miller now live on the farm. *Submitted by the children of J.C. and Rose Hawkins.*

HAWKINS - John Carl (everyone knew him as Carl) and Nettie married on Jan. 20, 1910 in Center Ridge AR. Carl (b. Jan. 29, 1891, d. July 9, 1931) was the son of Hugh H. Hawkins and Mary Lodisky Brown Hawkins. Carl died after suffering a leg injury in a truck accident. His leg was crushed and amputated twice, after which infection caused his death. Nettie (b. Dec. 24, 1894, d. Aug. 27, 1982) was the daughter of Bob and Sarah Prince Dockins. They had seven children:

John Carl and Nettie Mae Dockins Hawkins.

1) Leona Inez (b. Aug. 27, 1910, d. Dec. 8, 1910).
2) Clemmie Helen (b. Sept. 18, 1911, d. Sept. 22, 1991) md. Oda Trece Stobaugh on Nov. 17, 1928. Oda (b. April 12, 1907, d. June 10, 1978) was the son of James J. and Mirah Jane Stobaugh.

3) Marlin Conover (b. April 22, 1913, d. Sept. 16, 1995) md. Katheryn Marvine Treadwell on April 11, 1948. Katheryn (b. Feb. 3, 1925) is the daughter of Monroe Treadwell and Kate Maxwell Frazier.
4) James Hugh "Jimmy" (b. Jan. 28, 1915, d. Aug. 13, 1992) md. Alma Irene Oliger on Dec. 21, 1940. She was born March 18, 1921 and is the daughter of Claude Oliger and Elizabeth Jordan Oliger.
5) Estes Ray (b. Jan. 29, 1921, d. April 25, 1959) was killed in an automobile accident. He married Emma Louise Baskins (b. July 23, 1920) on Oct. 8, 1938. She is the daughter of Jess and Ora Kissire Baskins.
6) Glenna Cathelene (b. Sept. 19, 1926) md. Herman Layne Long on June 30, 1946. Herman (b. Oct. 15, 1924, d. Nov. 22, 1998) was the son of Ira Long and Addie Lector Cupp Long.
7) J.C. (b. Jan. 8, 1929, d. Sept. 23, 1982) md. Rose Elladene Grimmett on March 12, 1950. Elladen (b. Dec. 13, 1929, d. Jan. 20, 2004) was the daughter of Wailon Grimmett and Nora White Grimmett Chandler.

Carl was a barber by trade. His shop was set up in a side room at the local grocery store. His cousin said, as a child he remembers seeing Carl walking to the barber shop on Saturday mornings. Carl would always be wearing a very neatly starched and pressed white shirt, this made a great impression on him at the time. Carl gave haircuts and shaves. We have the book where he kept his records; it shows not only the prices of haircuts and shaves, but also what people owed him for his services. Carl was a man with a huge sense of humor.

Carl and his family also sharecropped and farmed cotton, after the harvest he would take the bale of cotton into Morrilton to sell.

Carl and Nettie were somewhat musically inclined. Carl played the fiddle and Nettie played the guitar. Marlin learned to play the mandolin. Some of the time they would play for the public. When they would play for the public, Marlin would become very sleepy and the people would pitch nickels and dimes at him, so he would stay awake and play his mandolin.

After Carl's death, Nettie ran a store in Center Ridge and one in the Austin area. She also worked in a cannery. She and her family would later move to Morrilton, where she lived the rest of her life. She loved flowers and gardening of all kinds, always having a beautiful yard full of blooms. Closing my eyes, I can still see MaHawk, this is what some of the grandchildren called her, moving about the small kitchen in her house. The wonderful aroma coming from the kitchen was just out of this world. Fried chicken, stewed potatoes, okra, dumplings, peas, and of course don't forget the butter rolls in the oven. What a cook! Can't you just smell it?

She wore her silver hair curled up in a small bun on the back of her head. When she combed it out at night it came down to her waist. She always wore her apron and those black "Granny" shoes. Never were you called by your own name, she called you by whatever came to mind first.

This in no way covers all aspects of the life of this family or how hard the times were for them after Grandpa Carl died. It took more than MaHawk, as we called her, to raise the children. Their oldest son Marlin must be given recognition for all he sacrificed and did to help in their up bringing. *Submitted by Joe C. Hawkins.*

HAWKINS - John Washington Hawkins was born March 31, 1838 to Nathaniel and Mary Hawkins. Nathaniel was born in 1794 in Virginia. In 1794, Kentucky was a part of Virginia. Nathaniel and family were in the 1840 Census in Todd Count, KY. The other children of Nathaniel and Mary were Elizabeth (b. ca. 1831); Thomas David (b. Sept. 27, 1835); Margaret (b. ca. 1839); Nathaniel E. (b. ca. 1842); Mary (b. ca. 1843); Alberton (b. ca. February 1850); and Martha

Jane (b. 1853). The family moved from Kentucky to Arkansas in 1848. Nathaniel, Mary and all the children were listed in the 1850 Federal census in Conway County, AR.

John Washington and Susan Ann Hawkins seated holding unknown great-grandchildren. Standing L-R: granddaughter, and daughter - Mary "Molly" Hawkins Caperton.

John Washington was the first to move out of the family home, marrying Susan Watson Nov. 9, 1856. Susan Ann was the daughter of Harrison C. and Mary (Tatom) Watson. Harrison was born in North Carolina ca. 1810 and Mary was born ca. 1814 in Tennessee. The children of John Washington and Susan Ann were Henry E. (b. ca. 1858) md. Susanna J. Whitson; Mary L. (b. ca. 1859) md. Millard Filmore Caperton; George Washington (b. February 1866) md. Emily Orange Stell; Hugh H. (b. ca. 1868) md. first, Mary Lodisky Brown and second, Ada Hardin; John Egbert (b. April 15, 1870) md. Mary Elizabeth Thomas; Thomas Nathaniel (b. May 14, 1871) md. Mattie Harris; Robert Burt (b. ca. 1876) md. Bettie Lee first and Ester __ second; Claude Roston (b. March 14, 1881) md. Emma Etta Carlton.

John Washington served in the Civil War in the First Arkansas Mounted Rifles, Co. I, CSA, and was discharged in 1865 with rank of private. He was wounded in battle in 1862, taken prisoner and sent to Camp Chase, OH. He was later exchanged near Vicksburg, MS aboard the steamer *Metropolitan* on Dec. 2, 1862. On Oct. 13, 1864 he was shown as receiving clothing in the Fairground Hospital in Vineville, GA. He was later furloughed from the Way Hospital in Meridian, MS (March 5, 1865).

John was a Mason and a member of the Springfield Lodge. His funeral was conducted with Masonic honors. He was also a Baptist and was ordained a deacon in the Cedar Missionary Baptist Church in 1888. John died on Dec. 10, 1892 and was buried in Wilder Cemetery. His grave is marked with a fieldstone, with the letters JWH carved into it. Susan Ann lived until Aug. 17, 1924. It is believed that she was buried in Mt. Pleasant Cemetery, but the grave was unmarked.

HAYRE - Syble Hayre (b. 1902) was a daughter of Robert Smith Hayre and Minnie Frier Jones. She was sibling to five brothers and three sisters: Iva Virtius (b. 1904), Malvin J., Paul Leon (b. Jan. 27, 1913, d. May 6, 1995) md. Eloise Farmer, Evamae, Fleda Grace, Robert Smith Jr. and twins, Willard and Millard. Her paternal grandparents were William Nathan Hayre and Lucinda Kelley who hailed from Kentucky.

l-r: Clyde Nowlin and Syble (Hayre) Nowlin

Syble married Claude Nowlin Sept. 16, 1922 in Conway County, AR. Claude was the son of James Bryant Nowlin and Nellie Dodson Hays, who, for a time, lived in Morrilton, but later moved to Little Rock. The Nowlins had several years in the area and one result was the marriage of Claude and Syble. Not much is known at this writing about the couple, except they had moved to Fort Smith, AR for a time. Claude joined the armed forces during WWII, and one could assume that Syble may have come back to Morrilton during that time, like so many war brides. Trying to save and conserve commodities was a priority during that time, and often young wives helped their parents with rationing cards by combining households. This writer does not know for certain.

At some point, this couple either divorced or Claude died because Syble remarried. Edward L. Mikels became her second husband. It is to be left for further investigation to determine what became of this beautiful woman who for a time enjoyed being a member of the Nowlin family and to what fate her first husband, Claude Nowlin, was consigned. *Submitted by Maud Nowlin.*

HEISTAND - In 1955 Mary Ann Allen and Dale Dee Heistand were married. Mary Ann (b. Jan. 15, 1939) was the third child of eight born to James Andrew and Mary Louvenia Blankenship Allen of the Pleasant View Community two and a half miles south of Jerusalem, AR, on what is now Granny Hollow Road. Dale was born to Francis Bert and Jenny Maria (Benscoter) Heistand Oct. 9, 1933 in Little Sioux, IA. He was the youngest of five children. Dale was a handsome redheaded guy standing six foot one inch.

Dale and Mary Ann Heistand

When he and Mary met, he was in the Air Force at Lowry Air Base in Denver, CO. Mary was working in Denver. They met on a Sunday afternoon, where Mary was panning for gold with a cousin and her family in the mountains, and Dale and two buddies were camping. The one buddy said, "I'll bet you a dollar you won't talk to that girl, and I'll bet if you do you won't get a date with her." He took the challenge and came over. One of the guys had a camera and insisted on taking their picture. Dale moved closer to put his arms around Mary, and Mary later learned they were amused at her southern accent when she said "Listen here fellow." That day Dale asked for her phone number, and carved it in his billfold with his pocketknife. On Wednesday he called and arranged a date. They were quite taken with each other and when Mary had to come home to finish school, he promised her he'd come see her when he got his furlough, which he did and brought her an engagement ring. They were married that same year, the first couple to marry at Jacksonville Air Base in Jacksonville, AR. They lived in Altus, OK until Dale's discharge.

Their son Glen Dale was born June 24, 1956 at the base costing $5.00. They moved back to Conway County after Dale's discharge. Dale had surgery for a malignant brain tumor June 1960 at the V.A. Hospital in Little Rock, AR. He lived four years working as an auto mechanic. His tumor returned taking his life March 13, 1965, leaving a young widow and an 8-year-old son. Dale was a member of the Church of Christ. He is buried at Robertstown Cemetery near Jerusalem, AR. Glen attended grade school at Jerusalem, AR. The school consolidated with Wonderview School in the 1960s. Glen Dale was married to Kathy McGuire Dec. 17, 1976. They both were graduates of Wonderview High School. Glen took an auto-mechanics course at Vo-Tech in Morrilton, AR. He also became a certified Honda Mechanic, and was employed in Russellville, AR several years. Glen and Kathy made their home in Hattieville, AR, living in Russellville, AR for a short time. In 1999 he and Kathy were divorced. They had one child, Treva

Marie (b. Dec. 6, 1990) whom they adopted Jan. 17, 1991. In 2001 he married Janie Carter Shumate. They operate the Mower Zone in Morrilton, AR, where they make their home.

HENDERSON - Burton and Bettye Jean Montgomery Henderson (See Ottis Lawton Montgomery) were married in Hutchinson, KS on June 29, 1954. Burton was born in San Pedro, CA, the son of Fred Oren and Irene Estelle Henderson. Burton "Burt" attended the University of California at Berkley and graduated with highest honors from the US Navy Post Graduate School in Monterey, CA and Florida Atlantic University. Burton retired from the US Navy after serving 21 years as a naval aviator. He was also a mechanical engineer and became a college professor, retiring from the University of Arkansas at Little Rock in 1998. After Burton's retirement from the US Navy in 1968, they lived in Ft. Lauderdale, FL until they moved to Petit Jean Mt. in 1981.

Burton and Bettye Henderson family. Seated: Burton Henderson holding Madeline Rose Taylor and Bettye Henderson holding McKenna Grace Taylor. Standing l-r: Douglas Taylor, Caroline Taylor, Susan Henderson, Elizabeth "Beth" Powell and Richard Powell.

Bettye always thought of herself as a wife and mother. She graduated from Lindenwood University in St. Charles, MO. After moving to Arkansas, Bettye became a real estate broker and established Petit Jean Properties, Inc.

Burton and Bettye have three daughters: Elizabeth Ann "Beth" is married to Richard Wayne "Rick" Powell and they live in Little Rock. Beth is a lead micro services analyst and Rick is an account executive with a communications company. Susan Neal Henderson retired from Pier 1 Imports and became the owner and principal broker of Petit Jean Properties, Inc. Dr. Caroline Blythe is married to Douglas Wayne Taylor. They have two children, McKenna Grace Taylor and Madeline Rose Taylor. The Taylors live in Arkadelphia, AR where Caroline is a professor in the Music Department at Ouachita Baptist University. Douglas "Doug" is a SAN architect.

Burt and Bettye Henderson lived on Petit Jean Mt. from 1981-2002, when they bought a home and 30 acres on the Arkansas River in Morrilton in what was the original town of Lewisburg. They still own about 150 acres on Petit Jean Mt.

HESS - The Hess family originated in the state of Hesse or Hessen in that part of West Germany which was once Prussia. The name Hess means "the hooded people." The Hess family was of German descent. About 1811, Samuel Hess migrated to an area called Lawrence County of the Missouri Territory. In 1812 Lawrence County became part of the Arkansas Territory. About 1814, his brother Solomon Hess settled in that area. In 1819 that area of Lawrence County became Independence County in the Arkansas Territory. Samuel and Solomon Hess became very wealthy and prominent farmers and ginners in the area. They were said to make the best moonshine liquor in that part of the country. They lived near Marcella, in what later

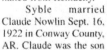

became Stone County, AR. The area where they lived was referred to as "Hess Town."

Solomon Hess (b. 1793, possibly in Illinois) md. Nancy (last name unknown) about 1812 in Kentucky. Nancy was born 1794 in Virginia. About 1814, Solomon moved his family to Lawrence (now Independence) County in the Arkansas Territory. Solomon settled near his brother Samuel Hess, who had moved there about 1811. Solomon was a farmer and a skilled stone mason, who is credited with building some very fine rock chimneys. Solomon signed his will on Oct. 21, 1839 in Independence County. He died about November 1840. Solomon's will was probated in Independence County Court on Dec. 17, 1840. On Feb. 17, 1841, the court gave authorization for "viewing and appraising the slaves and other personal property produced by Nancy Hess, executrix of the estate of Solomon Hess, deceased." On June 30, 1849, an agreement was filed in Independence County in which all of Solomon Hess' heirs were named.

Children of Solomon and Nancy Hess - the eldest born in Kentucky and the rest in Arkansas: (1) William Hess (b. 1813, d. 1861) md. Permelia Sutton, then Angeline Roberts; (2) Joseph W. Hess (b. 1815, d. 1879) md. Mary Louise Keizer, then Eliza ___; (3) unknown son Hess (b. 1819); (4) Martin Medford Hess (b. 1820, d. 1857) md. Elvira J. O'Neal; (5) Hiram Hess (b. 1822); (6) Thomas Wright Hess (b. 1825, d. 1851-59) md. Harriett Johnson, then Elizabeth Ann Johnson; (7) Mary Ann B. Hess (b. 1828) md. James T. Bone and (8) Evaline Jane Hess (b. 1829) md. Charles O'Neal.

Hiram Hess, son of Solomon and Nancy, was born 1822 in Independence County, AR. He married Sarah (last name unknown) in 1847. Sarah was born 1824 in Tennessee. Hiram was a farmer and a Methodist minister. In 1858 Hiram moved his family to Newton County, AR where he bought 10 acres of land in 1861. Hiram was in Stone County, AR in 1873 when one of his daughters married. Hiram died prior to Jan. 8, 1875 in Stone County.

Children of Hiram and Sarah Hess: (1) Christina Hess (b. 1847) md. __ Meadows, then C.P. Casey; (2) William Hess (b. 1848, d. before 1860); (3) Julia Ann Hess (b. 1853, d. 1876) md. Dockery Berry Giddens Jones; (4) Rola Virginia Hess (b. 1855) md. James P. Cartwright and (5) Sarah Martha Hess (b. 1858) md. W.F.M. Griffin.

HOELZEMAN

HOELZEMAN - Joseph N. Hoelzeman (b. March 26, 1908 in Morrilton) was the eldest son of Aloys Hoelzeman (b. 1882, d. 1959) and Margaret Koch Hoelzeman (b. 1886, d. 1958). He attended Sacred Heart School until reaching the eighth grade, when he had to drop out of school to help his father with carpentry work to support the family. Although he always spoke regretfully about not being  able to attend high school, he read all the books and magazines he had time for throughout his life and was indeed self-educated.

He was a master carpenter and prided himself on his exacting work. He was well-known for his artistry in cabinet-making.

Joe Hoelzeman met his future wife, Bernice Lienhart, through her friendship with his sister, Teresa. They married on July 10, 1940, and drove through the state of Texas on their honeymoon in a car they borrowed from Bernice's brother Bud.

Mr. Hoelzeman served his country in the US Army during WWII, having been drafted at the age of 36. He was to serve less than one year, however, and was discharged due to a problem with his back.

Joe and Bernice were devout Catholics and centered their lives around Sacred Heart parish and school.

They raised nine children, who also attended Sacred Heart School. After retirement, the couple spent countless hours each week doing volunteer work for the parish and the community of Morrilton.

Their eldest son, Joe Jr., died in 1969 at the age of 26. Their living children are Mary Crutcher of Memphis, Janie Hightower of Little Rock, Becky Hartman of Harrison, Katie Hodge of Little Rock, Agnes Bass of Little Rock, Judy Hoelzeman-Schneider of Little Rock and Bruno Hoelzeman and Michael Hoelzeman of Morrilton. Michael and Bruno each owns and operates a small business in the community.

Joe and Bernice Hoelzeman had 16 grandchildren, five of whom reside in Morrilton. As of this date, there are 16 great-grandchildren in their family. Mr. Hoelzeman died in 1990 after a brief illness and Mrs. Hoelzeman died in 2004.

Joseph Hoelzeman Sr.'s siblings were Bernard "Ben" Hoelzeman who married Dorothy Berkemeyer in 1934 and moved to Little Rock. Ben died in 1979 and his wife is also now deceased.

Margaret Hoelzeman married D.L. McArthur in 1945, and lived in Perry County. Margaret McArthur has lived in the old McArthur home in Perry County since her husband's death.

Teresa Hoelzeman Kaufman married Clem Kaufman and lived most of her married life in McGehee, where they owned a farm. Mrs. Kaufman now lives in Morrilton, having moved here after her husband died.

Louise Hoelzeman Carruthers married Dr. Earl C. Carruthers after working with him in his dental office for several years. She continued to be his dental assistant in his offices in the First State Bank Building, until their retirement. In the late 40s, the Carrutherses built a home high on a hill overlooking Morrilton, where they farmed and raised cattle, along with operating his dental office. That home remains a Morrilton landmark today and is where Mrs. Carruthers still lives. Their son Robert farms the acreage now.

Katherine Hoelzeman married Jack B. Mobley in 1947. He was in the construction business until his death in 1973. Later, Katherine married Bob DeSalvo and they presently live in Morrilton.

Aloys Hoelzeman Jr. married Terese Huber in 1958. They lived in the old Hoelzeman home on Highway 95, north of Morrilton, then built a new home off Highway 64 East, where Mrs. Hoelzeman lives now. Aloys (Junior) Hoelzeman died in 2004.

HOLDEN

HOLDEN - Archibald Holden (b. 1804 in South Carolina) moved to Tennessee before 1825 where he married Jemima (last name unknown). Jemima was born 1804 in Tennessee. Archibald was a farmer. He appears on the 1830 Wayne County, TN census. Tax records show he paid a poll tax in Wayne County in 1832, 1836 and 1838. About 1841 he moved his family to Mississippi, where two of his children were born. Between 1845-49, Archibald moved his family to Arkansas. He appears on the 1850 Jackson County, AR census, as does Isaac Holden (b. ca. 1799 in South Carolina). Archibald and Isaac may have been brothers. Between 1851-58, Archibald moved his family to Izard County, AR. Jemima died 1861-68. Archibald moved his family to Independence County 1865-69. He married Frances (last name unknown) between 1865-68. Frances was born 1842 in Alabama. Archibald died 1879 in Stone County, AR.

Archibald and Jemima had eight children: (1) Rebecca Jane Holden (b. 1826, d. 1900-1910) md. Henry Roberts; (2) Prudence Holden (b. 1833); (3) Richard James D. Holden (b. 1835); (4) Lucinda "Biddy" Holden (b. 1836); (5) Jonathan Holden (b. 1840); (6) Simeon Holden (b. 1842); (7) Jeremiah Jasper Holden (b. 1845) md. Sarah J. Gilson and (8) Mahala Elizabeth Holden (b. 1851) md. unknown George, unknown Williams, then George Roper.

Archibald and Frances had two children: (9) Harriet Tennessee Holden (b. 1868) md. J.R. Siler and (10) Aaron J. Holden (b. 1868, d. 1955) md. Augusta Pogue.

Richard James D. Holden (b. 1835 in Tennessee) was the eldest son of Archibald and Jemima. He married Martha Caroline George about 1858, probably in Izard County, AR. Martha George (b. 1838 in Tennessee) was the daughter of James Sevier George and Nancy (last name unknown). Richard was a farmer. Richard, Martha and their 1-year-old son Presley appear on the 1860 Izard County census. Richard paid taxes there in 1861. Richard joined the Confederate Army during the Civil War. He was mustered into Co. G, 8th Arkansas Infantry, on Sept. 1, 1861 at Pocahontas in Randolph County, AR. On Oct. 9, 1862 he was detailed as a nurse to Harrodsburg, Mercer County, KY. He left Kentucky in late January 1863 to return to Arkansas but wound up in a camp near Bell Buckle, in Bedford County, TN. He appears on a list of absentees dated May 7, 1863. It is unknown when he returned to Arkansas. Richard and Martha had a child born in Mississippi in 1865. They returned to Arkansas prior to 1870. Martha died in April 1874 in Stone County, AR. Their youngest child was a year and a half old when Martha died. Richard married Sary (or Mary) J. Moore on May 17, 1874, in Stone County. They appear on the 1880 Marion County, AR census. Richard probably died soon after 1880.

Richard Holden and Martha George had four children: (1) Presley Sanford Holden (b. 1859, d. before 1870); (2) Margaret Elizabeth "Betty" Holden (b. 1865, d. 1954) md. Jess H. Holt; (3) James W. Holden (b. 1870) md. Sarah Pierce and (4) Frances Adaline Catherine Holden (b. Oct. 14, 1872, d. Oct. 17, 1964) md. Thomas Jefferson Bridgman.

Richard and Sary had at least one child, Nancy Holden (b. 1878).

HOLLIMAN

HOLLIMAN - Columbus Ward and Lillie Pettit married in 1906 in Bee Branch, AR. They had one foster son, Woxie Crosby. In 1933 they moved to England where they cotton farmed.

Bill and Ann (Holliman) Welcher, just a few days after they were married, Nov. 11, 1956, and Virginia and Weldon Holliman.

Ann, Weldon and Lillian Holliman, 1955.

Lillie had a sister, Pearl Pettit, who married Arthur Holliman in 1918. They had eight children: Monroe, Marion, Windell, Howard, Lillian (b. 1927), Winfred, Ann (b. 1933) and Weldon (b. 1936).

Pearl died in 1937 in California, and Arthur could not take care of all the children so he brought Lillian, Ann and Weldon to Arkansas to stay with Columbus and Lillie on the cotton farm.

In 1952 Columbus retired and moved to

Morrilton on Roy Chaney's place. Weldon worked for Mr. Chaney until he got a job at the oil mill in 1954.

In 1956 Weldon married Virginia Lewis from Center Ridge. They moved to Fort Smith in 1957. They had three children: Karen (b. 1957), Michael (b. 1960) and Jeannie (b. 1968). Weldon worked for Whirlpool until his death in 1993.

Ann went to work for Oberman in 1953 and worked until 1963. While working there, she married William "Bill" Welcher in 1956, who was from Atkins. He was a truck driver for Atkins Pickles Company and then for B & B Trucking until his death in 1986. Bill and Ann had two children, Jimmy (b. 1957) and Sandra (b. 1959).

Jimmy graduated from Morrilton High School in 1976. He played football on the 1973 State Champion team. In 1977 he married Karen Briggler. They had three children: Bernadette (b. 1978), Christopher (b. 1982) and Matthew (b. 1986). Bernadette is employed by American Management and has one daughter, Ryley Jade (b. 2002). Christopher married Patricia Bronkema in 2003 and he is employed at Morrilton Packing. Matthew is a student at UCA in Conway. Jimmy passed away in 2003.

Sandra graduated in 1978 from Morrilton High School where she played in the band. In 1979 she married Joey Cannon. They had two children: Joshua (b. 1981) and Carrie (b. 1984). Joshua married Jacquie Kennedy in 2000. They have two children, Allyson (b. 2002) and Anna (b. 2003). Joshua is a deputy sheriff for Conway County. Carrie is employed in Conway.

In 1996 Sandra married David Holman. David has three children: Chastity, Bailey and Slade. Sandra works at Regions Bank.

In 1989 Ann married Bob Shumate. Bob's wife Grace died in 1988. They had three children: Elaine, Sarah and David.

Elaine married Dewey Hankins. They have three children: Sarah, Tracy and Patti. Sarah married Mark Ramsfield and they have four children: Brandon, Kayla, Savannah and Caleb. Tracy married Gary Neif. They have one son, Trey

Sarah Shumate married Ronnie Curtis. They have two children, Christy and Brad. Christy married Chris Garrett. They have two children Forrest and Braydon. Brad and Jennifer have a son Blake.

David lives in Little Rock.

Bob retired from Terminix in 1992. Ann worked for Morrilton Plastics for 29 years and retired from South Conway County School in 1998. Bob and Ann live on N. Division Street in Morrilton, where Bob has a small work shop and Ann has a Flea Market Booth up town. In 2005 they are park attendants at Old Post Road Park in Russellville.

Lillian married Hugh Rowell in 1965. He had the fix-it-shop on Center St. for many years. He died in 1986. Then in 1939 Lillian married Troy Bell from Hamsburg, AR. Troy played music at the Senior Adult Center. Troy died in 2001. Lillian still lives on Center Street in Morrilton. *Submitted by Ann Shumate.*

HOLSTED - Marvin Patric Holsted (b. July 29, 1912 at Marshal, AR), a son of Abner and Dicey Griffin Holsted. After Dicey's death, Marvin, his brother Jessie and their father Abner, moved to Conway County in 1942. Abner died in 1952.

On Feb. 2, 1946, Marvin married Essie Bonetha Hale, a daughter of Luther Jackson and Mary Luella Conn Hale of Morrilton. She was born Jan. 7, 1914 at Drake, Carter County, OK. They lived at Lord's School Community, five miles north of Morrilton on Highway 95. They had one son, Dewey Dale, born June 24,

The Holsteds: Marvin, Dewey and Essie, 1950.

1948, at Morrilton. He attended Lord's School until it was consolidated with Wonderview. Marvin worked at AP & L, then Morrilton Dairy for many years. He was also a carpenter and raised chickens and cattle. He worked at Crompton Arkansas Mills (The Cotton Mill). Essie attended school at Hannaford.

Her first job was at The Cotton Mill. After she married Marvin, she worked at Jamell's Clothing Store at Morrilton, then she was content to be a housewife. In later years she took into their home ladies for home health care - mostly family members. When her father's health failed him well into his 90s, he was moved from Oklahoma to her home for his health care. He celebrated his 100th birthday in her home.

Both Marvin and Essie are deceased and are buried in Elmwood Cemetery.

Dewey married first Betty Jean Williams of Plumerville. They had four children and they all attended school at Sacred Heart.

1) Michael Allen (b. June 4, 1967) md. Sonja Hill of Oppelo and they had two daughters, Chelsea and Payton. Michael died after battling cancer on Sept. 27, 1994, and is buried at Plumerville.

2) Shannon Renae (b. Sept. 30, 1970) md. first, Tim Jackson, and second, Greg Ingram. They have two sons, Carson and Keaton.

3) Ashley Deanne (b. Oct. 16, 1973) md. Erick Branson.

4) Chad Dustin (b. July 28, 1975) md. first, Christy Calva and they had one son, Chase Allen,. He then married Teri Berg.

Dewey married second, Linda Marie Malone. She was a daughter of Alfred Farrell and Pearlie Mae White Malone who lived for a time in Conway County. She was born Nov. 4, 1956, Dewey and Linda lived in his parents' home for several years, then built their new home on the property. Dewey worked at Levis Strauss Manufacturing, then at the Crompton Mills, then Green Bay Packing Arkansas Kraft Division in the paper making process. Linda worked at Levis and at Green Bay Packing Arkansas Craft Division. She was a forklift operator and Brown Plant operator. *Contributed by Dewey Holsted.*

HORTON - Isaac Horton (b. May 12, 1759 in London, England) immigrated to America in 1775, when he was 16 years old. Isaac enlisted to serve in the Revolutionary War on March 20, 1781 in Marshfield, MA. He served with the Massachusetts Continental Line in the 6th Massachusetts Regiment and later transferred to the 3rd Regiment. He served as a boatman, transporting officers, soldiers, and orders up the Hudson River from West Point to New Windsor and Newbury, NY. He was honorably discharged at West Point, NY in 1783. Isaac married Hannah Farris about 1784. Hannah (b. Dec. 9, 1759 in Salem, Westchester, NY) was the daughter of James Farris.

About 1800-04, Isaac moved his family to Montgomery County, VA. Around 1815 the family moved to Anderson County, TN. Isaac applied for a military pension in 1818. Isaac and his sons: Nathaniel, James and William, paid taxes in Campbell County, TN in 1823. Isaac moved his family to Lawrence County, TN prior to 1825. Isaac began receiving his pension in 1825. About 1828 Isaac settled his family in Wayne County, TN. In 1830 he bought 13 acres of land below the old mill on Indian Creek. Isaac built a log house there along the banks of Indian Creek. Hannah died between 1845-47 and was laid to rest on the hill above Isaac's log house. This was the beginning of what became known as the Isaac Horton Cemetery. Isaac married Mary "Polly" Weaver on May 18, 1848 in Wayne County. Mary was mute. Isaac was 89 and Mary was 38 when they married. Isaac outlived all four of his sons. Isaac died Feb. 28, 1854 in Wayne County, at the age of 95 years. He is buried beside Hannah in the Isaac Horton Cemetery.

Children of Isaac and Hannah: (1) Mary Ann Horton (b. 1785) md. Perrin Wright; (2) Hannah Parley Horton (b. 1787, d. 1861) md. Robert Stooksberry;

(3) Isaac Horton Jr. (b. 1788, d. 1853) md. Mary "Polly" Watts; (4) Nathaniel Horton (b. 1790, d. 1848); (5) James Horton (b. 1791, d. between 1793-1825) and (6) William Horton (b. 1795, d. 1835) md. America Cheek.

Nathaniel Horton (b. 1790 in New York) was the second son of Isaac and Hannah. He married Malinda Atkinson about 1818. Malinda (b. 1800 in North Carolina) was the daughter of William Nathaniel Atkinson and Celia Elizabeth Prince. Nathaniel paid taxes in Campbell County, TN in 1823 and moved his family to Wayne County, TN prior to 1830. Nathaniel was a farmer. He died August 1848 in Wayne County and Malinda died in 1880. They are buried in the Isaac Horton Cemetery.

Children of Nathaniel and Malinda: (1) Mary Horton (b. 1819, d. 1879) md. Josiah Youngblood; (2) William Melvin Horton (b. 1823, d. 1865) md. Rachel Thornton, then Arenna Jane Thornton; (3) Hannah Horton (b. 1828, d. 1899) md. Rial Brewer; (4) George S. Horton (b. 1829); (5) Nathaniel H. Horton (b. 1831, d. 1870) md. Mary Margaret "Peggy" Berry; (6) Peter Gales Horton (b. 1833, d. 1894) md. Sarah Margaret Ayers; (7) Malinda Caroline Horton (b. 1836, d. 1907) md. George Willis Horton; (8) Isaac James Horton (b. 1839) md. Louretta Ayers; (9) Nancy Catherine Horton (b. 1841); (10) Stephen Horton (b. 1843); (11) Sarah A. Horton (b. 1846) md. John Wesley Lay.

HORTON - John Ellison Horton (b. Aug. 7, 1858 in Wayne County, TN) was the fourth child of Nathaniel H. "Than" Horton and Mary Margaret "Peggy" Berry. Than married Sarah Jane Woody on Oct. 5, 1877 in Wayne County. Sarah Jane (b. Feb. 12, 1861 in Wayne County) was the daughter of John J. Woody and Nancy Jane Stanfield. John was a farmer. He appears on the 1880 Wayne County census with his wife and 1-year-old son, James. John moved his family to Searcy County, AR in 1881. An article published in the *Marshall Mountain Wave*, July 4, 1941 by Dan W. McInturff states, "There were 25 or 30 people in the group that trekked over hills, through valleys and canebrakes, through swamps, and over the famous Crowley's Ridge. Some had mule teams and others had oxen. They left Wayne County, TN, Sept. 23, 1881 and arrived at their destination Nov. 26, 1881." It is believed that John and his family were in that wagon train.

John ran the post office at Ella, in Searcy County, for a time. He moved his family to Douglas County, MO about 1908 and settled on Fox Creek, where he farmed. Later he exchanged his farm for a mercantile business at Pryor, MO. John owned and operated this dry goods store for many years. Sarah Jane died at Pryor on March 3, 1936. John died three months later on June 7, 1936. John and Sarah had six children:

1) James William Monroe Horton (b. Nov. 21, 1878, d. March 4, 1952) md. Mary A. Horton on Feb. 7, 1901. Mary (b. Jan. 10, 1878, d. 1902 in childbirth) was the dau. of William Winthrop Thomas Horton and Tennessee A. Parks. No children. Will then married Effie Ann Harmon on June 25, 1905. Effie (b. Jan. 23, 1887, d. Oct. 2, 1963) was the daughter of James Louis Harmon and Martha Jane Crow. Children: Lunie, Belle, Opal, Orville, Meda, Maggie and Edna Horton. Will's family settled in Conway County.

2) John Edmondson Garfield Horton (b. Jan. 22, 1882, d. Aug. 10, 1967) md. Irene Victoria Brewer on Jan. 7, 1903. Children: Walsie, Clifford, Claude, Coy, Verna, Clell, Eunice and Evea Horton. Ed's family settled in California.

3) Mary Magnolia Icephene "Nola" Horton (b. June 6, 1884, d. June 26, 1962) md. Francis Marion Aday on Sept. 8, 1904. Children: Ressie, Eulka, Dillard, Ruby, Dennard and Clifford Aday. Nola's family settled in Pope County, AR.

4) Gertrude P. Horton (b. Oct. 17, 1889, d. 1898).

5) Elmore McClure "Clura" Horton (b. Nov. 26, 1892, d. May 11, 1976) md. Thomas Harrison E.

Mathis on April 19, 1916. Children: Evelyn and Thomas Mathis.

6) Clyde Alexander Horton (b. May 13, 1895, d. Nov. 13, 1955) md. Pernie Coffman. Children, Leonard and Lyle Horton.

HORTON - Nathaniel H. "Than" Horton (b. Oct. 15, 1831 in Wayne County, TN) was the son of Nathaniel Horton and Malinda Atkinson. Than married Mary Margaret "Peggy" Berry in 1850. Peggy (b. 1828 in Tennessee) was the daughter of William Berry and Sarah Weatherford. Than was a farmer. He served as a private in Co. B, 2nd Tennessee Mounted Infantry in the Civil War. Than died in May 1870 and is buried in the Isaac Horton Cemetery in Wayne County. Peggy began drawing Than's Civil War pension July 25, 1890. She died Nov. 21, 1897 and is buried beside her husband. Than and Peggy had eight children:

1) Emiline Paralee "Emily" Horton (b. January 1851, d. March 19, 1928) md. William Morton Franks. Five children: (a) Thomas Marion Franks; (b) John William Franks married Mary Belle Sutterfield; (c) Jasper Edwin Franks married Mary Etta Sterling; (d) George Washington Franks married Ollie Fox. George and Ollie settled in Conway County. Their children: Jasper, Lonnie and Thomas Franks. George, Ollie and Jasper are buried in Cedar Creek Cemetery in Conway County; (e) Mary Lena Franks married Berry W. Green.

2) William J. Horton (b. 1854).

3) Joseph Griffin Horton (b. Feb. 15, 1856, d. April 4, 1930) md. Mary Catherine Woody, dau. of Joseph Josiah S. Woody and Mary Ann Margaret Ingram. Three children: Ella, Paralee and Annie Horton.

4) John Ellison Horton (b. Aug. 7, 1858, d. June 7, 1936) md. Sarah Jane Woody, dau. of John J. Woody and Nancy Jane Stanfield. Six children: James William Monroe Horton (settled in Conway County), John Edmondson Garfield Horton, Mary Magnolia Icephene Horton, Gertrude P. Horton, Elmore McClure Horton and Clyde Alexander Horton.

5) Margaret Martha Malinda "Lindy" Horton (b. Feb. 4, 1861, d. Jan. 1, 1936) md. Robert Wesley Baugus. The Baugus family lived in Conway County. Seven children: (a) Ora Baugus (md. George W. Joslin), children: Albert, Alvin, Lola, Mable (md. Walter Reynolds), Arlin, Fabell, Ruth and Mildred Joslin (md. Selby Anderson); (b) Clara Baugus (md. Oscar Johnson), children: Mary (md. Luther Pettingill), Jessie and Decie Johnson; (c) Ellen Baugus (md. Orville Johnson), children: Elmer, Jewel, Emery, Gladys, Loyce, Howard, Loyd, Ella and Della Johnson; (d) Ethel Baugus died at age 14; (e) Clifford Baugus (md. Dessie); (f) Wilford Baugus (md. Alma Ruby Stell), children: Daisy, Paul, Darryle, Opal, William, Bill, Betty, Gracie and Jimmie Baugus; (g) Oma Baugus.

6) David Wilson Horton (b. 1863, d. 1931) md. Callie Hailey. No children.

7) Peter A. "Pony" Horton (b. Jan. 15, 1866, d. Feb. 7, 1939) md. Sarah B. Horton. Children: Una, Vernie, Okla, Opal and Troy Horton.

8) Sarah L.E. "Sally" Horton (b. April 30, 1869, d. Oct. 20, 1901) md. Thomas W. Estes, children: Jesse, Earl, Margaret and Ruth Estes.

HORTON - James William Monroe "Will" Horton (b. Nov. 21, 1878 in Wayne County, TN) was the son of John Ellison Horton and Sarah Jane Woody. In 1881, Will's family moved to Searcy County, AR. Will married his cousin, Mary A. Horton, on Feb. 7, 1901 in Searcy County. Mary (b. July 1879 in Searcy County) was the daughter of William Winthrop Thomas Horton and Tennessee A. Parks. Mary died in childbirth in 1902. The baby died unborn. Mary is buried beside her parents in Canaan Cemetery in Searcy County.

Will married Effie Ann Harmon on June 25, 1905 at Ella, in Pope County, AR. Effie (b. Jan. 23, 1887 at Cave City in Independence County, AR) was the daughter of James Louis Harmon and Martha Jane Crow. Will and Effie settled in Pope County, near Tilly,

where four of their children were born. In 1913, the family moved to Una in Searcy County, where two more children were born. Will homesteaded farm land in Searcy County where he built a house for his family. He farmed, hunted and trapped. He also dug ginseng and golden seal roots and sold or traded them for needed supplies. In 1918, Will sold his farm and moved to Douglas County, MO where his parents were living. His youngest child was born in Douglas County.

Will moved his family to Conway County, AR in 1921 and settled in the Cedar Creek Community where he farmed. In 1925 the family moved to the Pleasant Hill Community in Conway County. For short periods of time during the 1930s the family also lived at Sunny Side, Portland bottoms near Plumerville and at Overcup. In 1939, Will moved his family from Overcup to Solgohachia. In 1951 they moved back to the Overcup Community. Will died March 4, 1952 at Overcup. Effie died at Morrilton on Oct. 2, 1963. They are buried in Friendship Cemetery near Solgohachia. Will and Effie's children:

1) Lunie Elsie Leoah Horton (b. July 18, 1906, d. July 31, 1980) md. Ausbie Haywood Nichols, son of Eugene Nichols and Annie Carroll. No children.

2) Bertha Martha Belle Horton (b. March 28, 1908, d. May 13, 1983) md. Roy Maddox Carruthers, son of Robert Crouthers and Emma Maddox. No children.

3) Sarah Opal Salina Horton (b. June 4, 1910, d. Feb. 1, 1997) md. Harry Hill, then William Edward Cupp. Children: Dorothy Hill (md. Wilmer Gene Holland) and Opaline Hill (md. Charles Harold Masters).

4) Orville Tolbert Horton (b. Aug. 24, 1912, d. Sept. 16, 1968) md. Elon Irene Groom, daughter of Robert Groom and Susan Reddeck. Children: Orla Horton (md. Robert Roberts); Jenwyl Horton (md. Michael John Miller Jr.); Betty Horton (md. Roger Winter); David Tolbert Horton and Darrell Horton (md. Karen Kerspert).

5) Meda McClure Horton (b. March 1, 1914, d. July 25, 1987) md. Joe Galen Henson. No children.

6) Maggie May Horton (b. May 25, 1915) md. Herbert Howard Bridgman (son of Thomas Jefferson H. Bridgman and Frances Adaline Catherine Holden). Children: Katherine Bridgman (md. Roy McClure) and Carol Bridgman (md. Albert Wren).

7) Edna Esther Horton (b. April 30, 1919, d. Jan. 12, 1984) md. Marion Houston Keith, son of John Lee Keith and Ellen Flowers. No children.

HOUSTON - John Hawkins "Hawk or James" Houston was born 1835 in Tennessee. His parents died of yellow fever after arriving in the US from Scotland in 1837 when he was about 2 years old. Rigdon Howard brought John, along with his brother and sister, to Arkansas. John was brought to Conway County, but his siblings were taken to Crawford County. Hawkins and Margaret Gregory, wealthy owners of 19 slaves, raised young John. John became an active Royal Arch Mason and a teacher at a Masonic School. He served as Justice of the Peace at Conway County for four years and served in the Civil War for the South from 1862-65 in Co. F, 36th Arkansas Infantry.

John married his first wife, Mary Arn of Tennessee, in 1856. They had Marcelius D. (who later became Conway County Treasurer from 1892-94), John Hawk, Sarah F., George L., Margaret Jane, Henry M., Mary A., Charles Roach, Luther and Mary.

John married his second wife, Joanna Elizabeth Guest, on May 1, 1884. John and Joanna had twins, Effie and Jeff, who died at ages 3 and 1. John and Joanna also had three other children.

John Hawk Houston, a son from the first of these two marriages, was a respected farmer. He married Pamela Cornelia Josephine Conley from Conway County on Nov. 6, 1881. They settled on a wooded section of land in Old Hickory that is still in the Houston family today. John was a member of the Masonic Lodge at Atkins and a charter member of the Woodmen of the World. He and his wife also helped start the

Mount Vernon Cumberland Presbyterian Church in the 1880s. John was also the Conway County Coroner from 1874-76. John and Pamela had John Hawk Jr., Elbert B., Eva Josephine, Maudie Grace and Eugenia Francis. The earliest marked graves in the Mount Vernon Cemetery are of infants, Henry and Sarah Houston, who died in 1867. These may be more children of John and Pamela.

John Hawk Houston Jr. was a carpenter and contractor. He was under contract to work on Ferguson Bridge on Highway 124 and Kelly Bridge between Old Hickory and Jerusalem. John was the Master Mason of Morrilton Masonic Lodge 105. He also worked under the WPA on the first rock building at Wonderview School.

John married his first wife, Ida Belle Massingill, and made a home at Old Hickory. They had Alberta "Berta," Williard Edna, James Mackey "Mack," Johnie Pauline and John Hawk "J.H." Houston III. Ida Belle died of complications after a miscarriage in their home in Old Hickory.

Next, John Jr. married Ida's niece, Bertha Mae Massingill. Together they had Billy Joe, Mary Joe and Franklin Delano Houston. Bertha Mae died of bullous pemphigoid, a blood disease, and was buried beside her first husband in the Old Hickory Cemetery. John Jr. also died and was buried in the Old Hickory Cemetery beside his first wife.

Franklin Delano Houston was born in Old Hickory but moved to Indiana after getting out of the military, to work on the railroad as a switchman. In Dyer, he met Shirley Eileene Burton. They were married on May 16, 1957. Their sons were Robert Dale and Ricky Dean. Frank and Shirley have since returned to live in Old Hickory, as well as their son Ricky Dean, on the land once owned by both John Hawk Sr. and Jr.

Ricky Dean married Patricia Ann Reynolds from Jerusalem in 1980. They had three daughters: Ashley Diane, and twins-Carly Kathleen and Kelly Eileene. On May 24, 2005, Ashley and her husband Michael Wright of Springfield had a son, Houston Michael. *Submitted by Kelly Houston.*

HUBBARD – On Oct. 19, 1921, Charlie McKinley Hubbard married Rosie Ellen Epperson. Charlie (b. Sept. 11, 1900 in Casa, AR) was the son of William Elisha Hubbard Jr. and Sara Ann McCabe Hubbard.

Rosie Ellen Epperson was the daughter of William Thomas Epperson and Venie Eveline Pope Epperson. She was born on Jan. 16, 1903 in Adona, AR. They lived most of their lives in Willow Bend bottoms in Conway County.

Charlie and Rosie Hubbard

Charlie was a farmer and Rosie was a housewife and worked by her husband's side. They raised six children: Daisy Eveline, Violet Pauline, Lily Adeline, William Charles, James Arnold and Barbara Ann.

Violet wrote the news for the Willow Bend section of the *Morrilton Democrat* until her death at 21. She died from heart problems in 1944. The other children all married and lived in Conway County for several years before moving to other areas. Daisy married Leland Crow in August 1938 and they made there home in Santa Marie, CA. Lily married Vernon McDonough in October 1943 and they made their home in Oklahoma, then later in Morrilton. William married Helen Mae Barker in July 1948, and they made their home in Overcup. Arnold married Amy Ellen Teal in October 1948 and they made their home in Oakhurst, OK. Barbara married Bobbie Lee Cooper in September 1959 and they made their home in Morrilton.

Rosie loved to have lots of flowers in her yard and she enjoyed gardening. Her favorite pass time was crocheting and quilting. She passed away in 1957 at the age of 53 with stomach cancer, leaving her husband and five children. All their children were married with the exception of Barbara who had just graduated high school in May before her mother passed away in September.

Charlie married Bessie Barnes in 1958. Bessie and her son, Wayne Barnes, from a previous marriage, moved out to the Willow Bend bottoms with Charlie and Barbara. In 1963 they bought a place on Hwy. 113 at what is now known as Hubbard Loop. It had a small house but lots of space for gardening and chickens. They tore down the house and built a bigger place. They lived on Hwy. 113 until their death. Bessie died first in May 1985 with heart complications. Charlie outlived her by three years. Charlie had a stroke and lived out his last year and a half in Morrilton Manor, he died in August 1988 at the age of 89.

Two children are still living in the Conway County area. Lily and Barbara both live in Morrilton. William's widow, Helen, still lives in Morrilton and Arnold's widow, Amy, still lives in Oklahoma. *Submitted by William C. Hubbard.*

HUBBARD - William Elisha "Lish" Hubbard Sr. (b. April 20, 1839 in Hall County, GA) is listed in the 1860 Perry County census as living in the Petit Jean Township, Rose Creek Community. He married Hannah Elizabeth Fitch, a daughter of James C. Fitch. To this union was born William Elisha Hubbard Jr. William Elisha Sr. was conscripted into Company K, 3rd Arkansas Cavalry of the Confederacy. He deserted near Chattanooga, TN on Oct. 2, 1863, was captured and taken to Louisville, KY. He pledged an oath to the United States and was released north of the Ohio River. There he stayed for the remainder of the Civil War.

Five generations starting from oldest to youngest: Jess Hubbard, Rayborn Hubbard, Billy D. Hubbard, Teena Marie Hubbard Jenkins and Crockett Jenkins

When he returned home to Rose Creek, he had been gone about five years. After his return, he and Hannah Elizabeth added to their family. Other children were James Thomas, Mary Jane, Robert Anderson, and George Riley. George Riley died at a young age. Hannah Elizabeth died (exact date not known) and William Elisha Sr. married her sister, Mary Jane Fitch Reed. Mary Jane's husband had died, leaving her with a daughter, Franklin Jane Reed. To the union of William Elisha Sr. and Mary Jane was born Sarah Missouri, Charlie Leroy, Francis Marion and Henry Clay. William Elisha Sr. died Feb. 17, 1912, and is buried at Aunt Dilly Cemetery, in the Rose Creek Community. Mary Jane died Oct. 12, 1913, and is also buried at Aunt Dilly Cemetery.

William Elisha "Billy" Hubbard Jr. (b. June 11, 1862) md. Sarah Ann McCabe (b. Jan. 26, 1864), a daughter of Marion McCabe. They had five sons and five daughters. James Thomas married Barbara Ellen Robertson and they had eight children. Mary Jane, the daughter, married Edward Parish Whitfield and had two children. Robert Anderson married Liz Teel and had eight children. Sarah Missouri married Garfield Brixey and had nine children. Francis Marion married Samantha Whitfield, a daughter of Edward Parish Whitfield and a stepdaughter to Mary Jane, and had five children. Charlie Leroy was married to Nora Schimmel and this ended in divorce. Henry Clay did not marry.

From the union of William Elisha "Billy" Hubbard Jr. and Sarah Ann McCabe, three of their sons: William Matthew, Robert Jessie and Charles McKinley came to reside in Conway County during the 1920s

and 30s. All three of the brothers eventually settled in a community southwest of Morrilton known as Willow Bend. This community is located on the north side of the Arkansas River directly across from the point of Petit Jean Mountain.

Robert Jessie "Jess" Hubbard (b. March 22, 1892), his wife Lily Mae Dempsey (b. April 8, 1895) and their two daughters, Retta Estell and Zettie Hubbard moved to Willow Bend in the fall of 1936. Jess rented the Rob Stallings farm and began sharecropping. Jess and Lily's son, Rayborn, along with his family, joined them on this farm in November 1939. From the fall of 1936 until Jess retired in 1959 and Rayborn retired in 1983, they farmed the Rob Stallings farm. Rayborn (b. Oct. 4, 1916) md. Sarah Laverne Wagner (b. June 13, 1921) on July 7, 1935. From this union there were two children, Sarah Joe Hubbard Brannon (b. March 8, 1936) and Billy Dale Hubbard (b. Sept. 10, 1939). Sarah Joe married Ernest Dean Brannon (b. Dec. 4, 1932) on July 20, 1955. From this union there is one son and three daughters: Howard Lynn (b. July 13, 1956), Janet Kay Brannon Fougerousse (b. Nov. 25, 1957), Susan Gail Brannon Freyaldenhoven (b. March 7, 1961) and Cynthia Jean Brannon Brekeen (b. Nov. 18, 1965). Billy Dale married Lois Jean Taylor (b. Aug. 23, 1941, in Perry County) on Dec. 18, 1959. From this union there were two children, Teena Marie Hubbard Jenkins (b. May 15, 1961) and Jeffrey Michael Hubbard (b. Nov. 19, 1966). Retta (b. Sept. 7, 1914) md. Jack Lentz (b. Dec. 5, 1912) on Oct. 17, 1936. From this union there were five children: Shelby Jean Lentz Bull (b. Aug. 29, 1937); Farrell D. (b. Dec. 28, 1939); Jessie Darrell (b. Oct. 7, 1943); Jimmy Wayne (b. Oct. 2, 1945); and Terry Don Lentz (b. Jan. 18, 1958).

William "Will" Matthew Marion Hubbard (b. Nov. 16, 1889) md. Nancy Adline Moore. Will and Adline had twins, Lester and Lessie, and three other sons: Matthew "Mack," Earl and George. Adline passed away Feb. 8, 1919 when George was 6 months old. George was reared by his paternal grandparents, William Elisha "Billy" Hubbard Jr. and Sarah Ann. Will married a second time to Elsie Jane Price. To this union were born three daughters: Vida, Opal, and Grace.

Will sharecropped in the Cardron Creek, Paw Paw Bend and Willow Bend areas. At the time of his death, on March 22, 1956, he had moved from the Willow Bend area into Morrilton. Elsie Jane died June 4, 1969.

George Hubbard, the youngest of the three sons, served on the Morrilton City Council as alderman for 32 years. He and his youngest sister, Grace Rainwater of Cabot are the only surviving children of Will.

Charles "Charlie" McKinley Hubbard (b. Sept. 11, 1900) md. Rosie Ellen Epperson (b. Jan. 16, 1903). From this union were born two sons, William Charles (b. Sept. 26, 1929, d. Dec. 11, 2003) and James Arnold (b. April 2, 1931, d. Aug. 25, 1985). There were four girls: Daisy Eveline Hubbard Crow (b. Jan. 30, 1923, d. Jan. 4, 2004); Violet Pauline (b. Feb. 9, 1924, d. June 6, 1944); Lily Adaline Hubbard McDonough (b. Nov. 19, 1927) and Barbara Ann Hubbard Cooper (b. Nov. 14, 1939). Upon the passing of Rosie Hubbard, Charlie married Bessie Myrtle Ruff Barnes on Aug. 5, 1958. Charlie moved into Morrilton in 1963 from Dr. Harl Carruthers farm in the Willow Bend Community.

HUBBARD - On July 4, 1948, William Charles Hubbard married Helen Mae Barker. William was the son of Charlie McKinley and Rosie Ellen Epperson Hubbard. He was born Sept. 26, 1929 in Morrilton. Helen was the daughter of Robert Don and Minnie Mae Mathis Barker. She was born June 19, 1934 in Morrilton, AR.

They met in the Assembly of God Church in Morrilton. William was dared to sit by Helen during church, by his Uncle Jess Epperson. William was a farmer in the Willow Bend Bottoms when they were first married. Helen was only 14, so being an adult

Helen and William Hubbard

was a new experience for her. They moved to Morrilton where William worked for the Cotton Mill. They had two sons, Charles Don and James Arvil. Charles lived only a few months and died. They buried him at Aunt Dilly Cemetery at Rose Creek. William and his brother, James Arnold, were so close that William decided to move to Tulsa to be near him and he went to work for Flint Ink Inc. in 1953. The couple had two more children, Linda Kay and Ricky. Ricky died shortly after birth. They returned to Arkansas to bury this child next to his brother.

Flint Ink transferred William to Dallas in 1959 so he moved with his job. It was quite a change for his small family in such a large town. While they lived here they had three more children: Karen Jo, Kimberly Ann and Melissa Rosemae. The two older children started school while Helen took in ironing and baby sat children to help William make ends meet. William was ordained into the ministry in June 1967. In 1967 they returned to Morrilton to raise their children in a small town. William went back to work at Crompton Mills, and with the children all in school, Helen went to work there also.

In 1968, the Hubbard's built a home on land they had received from Helen's parents. It was on Hwy. 9 at Overcup. In 1975, William went to work for Arrow Automotive as a parts handler until he retired in 1991. William was the pastor of Bald Knob church until his health got bad. He worked on small engines at a shop that he built at his home. Helen worked at Tate Container then Union Camp until 1992, when she suffered a heart attack and had to have a quadruple bypass.

The five Hubbard children all graduated from Morrilton High School, which pleased their parents, and one went to college. They all married and had children and have lived near the family for several years. The four daughters all live close to their mother. Three live in Conway County: Linda, Karen and Melissa. Kim lives in Perry County. James lives in North Carolina.

William passed away in December 2003 with many health problems. Helen remains in the family home in Overcup. There are many grandchildren and great-grandchildren that live near their grandmother. *Submitted by Helen Hubbard.*

HUGGINS - Abraham Lincoln Huggins (b. April 15, 1861 at Rose Creek, Perry County, AR) was the son of John Hazard Huggins and Anna Drucilla Hagerty. He married May 23, 1886 to Frances Olivia Rook (b. Dec. 27, 1871).

Children of this couple: (1) Cornelia (b. June 6, 1889 in Carden Bottoms, d. April 23, 1940) md. Dec. 22, 1904 to Byron Ashcraft, the son of William Columbus Ashcraft and his cousin, Nancy Jane Ashcraft. (2) Frank Harmon (b. May 23, 1883 in Fame, McIntosh County, Indian Territory, OK) md. Edna Marie Merideth Dec. 15, 1925. (3) Alta (b. Jan. 14, 1898, Rose Creek, Perry County, AR) md. Joe Loyd.

Abraham Lincoln "Abe" and Frances Olivia Rook, 50th Anniversary.

Family lore tells us that before 1883 A.L. and his family migrated to Eastern Oklahoma, then Indian Territory where they made friends with the Indians. The name of the Chief of the Cherokee was Frank Harmon. When the baby was born May 25, the Chief persuaded the Mother to name her child after him. The father, Abraham Lincoln Huggins, had share cropped for Chief Harmon and when he became ill, the Indians restored him to health. A.L. returned to Arkansas in the Fall of 1896.

Abraham Lincoln Huggins is a proved first cousin of my Grandfather Robert Mathew Huggins. Both men were one of a set of twins, their twin died at birth.

Around 1915-17 Alta Huggins was teaching school at Rose Creek at age 17. She got her Teaching Certificate from Teacher's College in Conway and took her test at the Perry County Courthouse. She also taught at Bigelow, where she met and married Joe Hughes Loyd on June 25, 1921, as written by Michele Coffman.

In August 1983 a member of the family received an answer to a query that had been put in the *Pettit Jean Headlight* on the family, and it was answered by Miss Aubra Brickey, a retired school teacher, living in Bigelow. Miss Brickey remembered the Huggins family, especially daughter Alta and a grown son Frank, who moved to Bigelow about 1920. Alta, being a school teacher, taught in the grades, two if not three years, with my sister Clara and they became close friends. Clara married in June 1921 and Alta and her boyfriend were brides maid and best man at Clara's wedding. Soon Alta and Hugh married. The brother Frank was a pharmacist here and later in Little Rock. The whole family moved to Little Rock early in the 1920s due to the closing of a large lumber mill. Clara went to live in Corpus Christie, TX and remained there the rest of her life. Clara Earline Brickey Thompson was born Dec. 24, 1894. *Submitted by Frank Huggins Jr.*

HUGGINS - Benjerman Carrol "Son" Huggins (b. Feb. 10, 1872 in Arkansas, d. May 20, 1940) is buried in Atkins City Cemetery. In 1927 he married Cleo Sweeden in Pope County. Cleo (b. Nov. 15, 1905, d. Jan. 7, 1988) is buried near Son in the Atkins City Cemetery. Son Huggins was a merchant dealing in general merchandise.

Benjerman Carrol "Uncle Son" Huggins

In a letter dated Oct. 22, 1978, his wife, Cleo, wrote an outline of Uncle Son's family from things he told her. Here is what she wrote:

"His father's name was Ben and his mother's name was Mary. His father was a farmer. One of Ben's brothers was a very good doctor. The doctor's son was Abe and his wife Ollie, they came and visited me and Son for a whole week. They lived in Little Rock. Abe had a son and a daughter, the son was a registered pharmacist in Little Rock. Abe's daughter married a Loyd. She and her husband and their two daughters spent the day one Sunday with Son and I."

"Aunt Matt's children came to see us. Albert Reed and daughter, Ruf Reed and family, Dorothy Alford and her husband. Her husband was a preacher. Aunt Matt would come to see us at the store once a year and Son would give her a new dress." This Reed family seems by name, etc. to be the Ruf Reed - Mattie Isom who lived in Pope County, Mattie, in correspondence with the Reeds, no relationship has been established at this time, although they think they are related."

"Son built his first store at the foot of Pettit Jean on Rose Creek. He made a share crop with Mr. Stubbs and saved $100, he caught the steamboat to Little Rock and bought lumber and stock of goods for the little store. He said it cost $1 or 1.50 roundtrip to go to Little Rock on the steamboat. He took me over to

see the little store building, it was on the bank of the little creek on Mr. Stubbs land. He didn't have to pay rent as Mr. Stubbs got the little building when he closed the store. He said his parents were buried in the Rose Creek Cemetery over there, but we did not go to the cemetery as it was across the creek."

"Son was so small when his mother died he did not remember her. He was about 10 years old when his father died."

"Buck's name was Robert and his wife was Mattie. The girl that Son called L was, I believe, Ellen on your record. She married a Pitts, had two little boys and lived in Ola. Mrs. Branson was Kate or Katharine. I didn't know Myrt's name, he was M.H., lived in Dover and married Nancy Cloud. One of his sons was Benjerman Carrol Huggins. I met all of Myrt's children and they visited us. One of the boys lived at Dover and he always comes by to see me when he is down this way. I met several of Buck's children, Rue Montgomery came to see Son several times when he was on his death bed. She was a very sweet person. In later years I visited in her home and in the Rest Home, she always seemed to enjoy my visits. I visited Buck's wife and Harley and his wife in Tulsa. I also met Mrs. Albert Deeter, Buck's daughter."

In 1911 the John Branson family moved to Atkins from their farm; about a year later, Son came to Atkins and put in a store and boarded with the Bransons." *Submitted by Mary Diaz.*

HUGGINS - Benjerman L.G. Huggins (b. ca. 1842 probably near Gadsden, AL, d. ca. 1895 in Conway County, AR) was the son of Robert Huggins (b. 1809 North Carolina) and his wife Nancy Hazard (b. 1812 in Missouri). The family came from Alabama to Arkansas ca. 1850 and settled in Galley Rock on Lot No. 3.

In the 1860 census of Anderson County, TX, he is living in the household of Dr. William J. Pride and his wife, Zero Huggins. The Priddys were married in Pope County in 1864 and she is presumed to be Ben's sister, daughter of Robert and Nancy Huggins. Ben and the Priddys must have come back to Arkansas by 1861, when it is believed that Ben married Mary Barmore, daughter of Ellen Barmore (b. 1823 W Canada), her father is unknown at this time, but may have been the John Sidney Barmore who had a land grant in early Pope County and was on a wagon train to California in 1849 from Yell County.

In the 1870 census of Perry County, AR, Ben and Mary are there in Rose Creek Township with four of the children, living in the same area as Robert and Nancy, Dr. Wm. Priddy and Zerah. John Hazard Huggins and many other relatives and friends. Grandpa Robert Mathew Huggins "Buck" (b. Jan. 21, 1862) is the oldest of Ben and Mary's children. All the children are listed in the 1870 census of Perry County, except Myrtle Hazard Huggins. The children named are Robert Mathew "Buck" (b. Jan. 21, 1862) md. Mattie Cumi Gasaway; Lennie/Linda Ellen (b. 1864) md. John Wesley Pitts (both died after 1900); Catharine (b. March 31, 1863) md. Jonathan Luke Branson; Benjerman Carroll "Sonny" (b. ca. 1868) md. Cleo Sweeden, and later Myrtle Hazard (b. Jan. 8, 1876) married Nancy Jane Cloud.

On Jan. 10, 1861 B.L.G. Huggins enlisted at Perryville, AR in Company H, 10th Arkansas Infantry Regiment, Confederate States of America, the same company that his two brothers-in-law, J.C. and N.M. Isom had joined. Ben Huggins was discharged May 12, 1862; because of such a short period of time, we believe he may have been injured and pensioned by the military.

On Dec. 19, 1874 Ben bought land from the Little Rock/Ft. Smith Railroad located in Section 30 Conway County, AR, laying, I believe, in Pettit Jean Township. Probably Myrtle Hazard Huggins was born

on this property, and Ben and Mary are possibly buried on this property.

Ben was elected the Justice of the Peace for Pettit Jean Township, Conway County on Sept. 4, 1878.

We believe that Ben died prior to February 1895, as his property was divided into five parts, meaning that each of his five children received a share. We have found where Robert and Ellen had signed their shares over to Myrtle Hazard Huggins. We have looked for many years for a burial spot for Ben and Mary, and none have ever been found, leading us to assume they were buried on the family estate in Pettit Jean Township, Conway County, AR. *Submitted by Katharine Turner.*

HUGGINS - Born ninth in a family of 10 children to Martha Cumi Gasaway and Robert Mathew Huggins "Buck," Harley Theodore Huggins was born Sept. 14, 1908 on beautiful Pettit Jean Mountain. About 1922 the family left the Arkansas Mountains and migrated to Dora, Seminole County, OK. Harley, then called Ted, was about 14 years old at that time.

Harley T. Huggins

In an old letter from his Aunt Cleo, she states that she and Uncle Son bought a radio in 1928 and that they heard a band from Tulsa, which included a Harley Huggins. When she inquired about him, she found that he was the son of Uncle Son's brother, Buck Huggins.

Aunt Lillie said *"Memories of You Dear"* was written by Harley and was on an album about four years ago (1984) and she says it made the charts. She felt Harley was not paid for any of the songs he wrote. Over the years some of the names of his songs have been lost, but he also wrote *"Together Forever"* and *"I'm Sorry We Said Goodbye."*

Harley started solo on the Shawnee, OK radio station, probably about 1926, and was on for 15 minutes a day at 11:45 a.m. Everything stopped for 15 minutes, as he mentioned family and always remembered our birthdays. Later he played and sang with the Alabama Boys in Tulsa, several years in competition with Bob Wills and his brothers, Johnnie Lee and Luke Wills. Late in the 1930s he went over to play with Johnnie Lee Wills.

Harley stayed with Johnnie Lee Wills, brother of Bob Wills, through the early 1940s. After Pearl Harbor on Dec. 7, 1941 the band began to disintegrate, with the boys joining the Services to help with the defense of the country. Bob Wills was also having a problem, having a band to play for different engagements, and drafted some of the players from his brother's bands. Harley was one of those in 1942, when Bob was called by Columbia Studios in Hollywood, to return to Hollywood with a small string band of musicians to play in several movies being planned with Russell Hayden. Harley played in four of these movies. Russell Hayden was the featured star with Wills and his small combo, which included himself on fiddle and vocal, Harley Huggins on rhythm guitar and vocals, Joe Holley on fiddle, Luke Wills on bass and jug, Leon McAuliffe on steel and vocals with Millard Kelso on tenor guitar, banjo and accordion. These films were made between 1942 and 43. These movies were *The Lone Prairie, A Tornado In The Saddle, Riders Of The Northwest Mounted* and *Silver City Raiders. Riders Of The Northwest Mounted* was made Feb. 15, 1943 at Columbia Pictures and Harley sang two solos, *Song Of The Rippling Stream* and *Bluebonnet Lane*. He also sang as a group on *When You're A Mountie* by Bob and Luke Wills, Leon McAuliffe and Harley Huggins.

After these movies were finished, most of the band returned to Tulsa, and shortly after Harley was drafted in to the US Army. He was trained in the Signal Corps as a radio operator and stationed in England, where he spent most of his 18 months in the service of his country.

Tired of life on the road, Harley quit Bob Wills shortly after recording his own composition, *I'm Feeling Bad*, in December 1945 and played with a few small local groups around Fresno before quitting the music business. He became a real estate broker and agent and worked at this up until his death on April 9, 1984. He is buried in Red Rock Cemetery in Fresno, CA. *Submitted by Jean Huggins.*

HUGGINS - John Hazard Huggins (b. ca. 1835, North Carolina) was the son of Robert and Nancy Huggins. John first married Annie Saulter and to them was born Frannie and Clemmie, who married a Fairchild.

John second married Anna Drucilla Hagerty, daughter of Joab and Penelope Gay Hagerty; children born to them:

1) Abraham Lincoln Huggins (b. April 15, 1861, Rose Creek, Perry County, AR) md. May 23, 1886 to Francis Olivia "Ollie" Rook. He is buried Martin Cemetery, Little Rock, died Oct. 20, 1941.

2) Robert Hazzard Huggins (b. Sept. 3, 1865, Arkansas) md. Nov. 5, 1887 to Ella Rook, sister of Ollie. He died Nov. 20, 1927 and is buried Brearley Cemetery, Dardnells, AR; one child, Blanche.

John married Elizabeth C. Rook, St. John; they were parents of a baby boy. The baby and Elizabeth both died soon afterward.

John Hazzard Huggins served during the Civil War from Pope County as a 1st lieutenant in 2nd Mounted Rifles from Wilson Creek.

On July 2, 1881 he was certified to practice medicine in Arkansas. *Submitted by Frank Harmon.*

HUGGINS - Katherine Huggins (b. March 31, 1866 in Carden's Bottom, AR, d. Jan. 24, 1948 at Atkins, AR) was the daughter of Benjamin L.G. Huggins and his wife, Mary Barmore/Barrymore. On Feb. 20, 1893 she married Johnathan Luke Branson in Carden Bottom, Yell County, AR. J.L. Branson (b. Aug. 26, 1869 in Indiana, d. Feb. 6, 1942 in Russellville, AR) was the son of William H. and Naomie Branson. J.L. and Katherine were one of the pioneer families of Atkins. They had six children: Elton Lee, Cora, Racy, Aurel, an infant son and Oddie.

Elton Lee (b. Jan. 21, 1894, d. June 2, 1963) md. Blanche Croom of Atkins. They had two children: (1) Sara Katherine Branson Harper (b. May 24, 1918) md. John Harper of Wynne and (2) Elton Lee Jr. (b. Nov. 22, 1923, d. Feb. 12, 1978) md. Betty Greer of Conway. In 1916 Elton was a cashier in the Bank of Atkins and later was employed in the state auditor's office. At the time of his death, he was the deputy prosecuting attorney of Drew County in Monticello

Cora (b. June 23, 1895, d. Jan. 20, 1990) md. Mackey Settles of Harrisburg. They had one daughter, Mary Elizabeth Settles Fortenberry (b. Oct. 16, 1918, d. April 15, 1990) md. Harold Newton Fortenberry of Marked Tree, AR.

Racy (b. Oct. 22, 1898, d. Jan. 16, 1994) md. Roland Montgomery of Atkins in 1924. She was widowed and later married John McCool of Sheridan in 1945. Racy owned "Racy's" (a general merchandise store) in Atkins from 1947-62.

Aurel (b. Sept. 3, 1900, d. June 17, 1992) md. Stanley Haney, an Atkins farmer, in 1922. They had one son, John Franklin Haney (b. Nov. 21, 1923, d. May 26, 1979) md. Virginia Winn of Russellville. Aurel was employed at the Merchants and Farmers Bank until 1947, when she became the bookkeeper for Racy's in Atkins.

Oddie (b. Sept. 12, 1909, d. March 25, 1995) md. Wade McConnell Turner, son of Wade Hampton and Maude McConnell of Atkins), they have one

daughter, Mary Katherine Turner Diaz, living in Atkins.

J.L. Branson continued to farm the land in Cardon Bottom until his death in 1942. He and Katherine moved the family to Atkins in 1910 and built the house, which is still standing on Town Hill in Atkins. After moving to Atkins, he opened a general merchandise store, which he operated until 1915. Later he managed the Ark-Mo Lumber Company. When the library in Atkins was built in 1933, J.L. Branson donated the transom windows for the new library. He also donated and helped lay the bricks for the first building of the Methodist Church in Atkins, which stood at the present corner of Church Street (Hwy. 105) and NE 3rd Street until 1977. J.L. was a member of the Woodsmen of the World, a lifetime member of the Methodist Church and an honorary member of its Board of Stewards. *Submitted by Mary Katherine Turner Diaz.*

HUGGINS - Linda Ellen Huggins was referred to Lennie or L. by her family. She was born before 1870, probably in Perry County, AR. Lennie was my grandfather's sister. She is with her parents, Ben and Mary Huggins, and her siblings in the census of 1870 of Rose Creek, Perry County, AR. Linda Ellen was surely named for her grandmother Ellen Barrimore.

Virgil Arthur Pitts, son of Lennie Huggings and John Wesley Pitts.

Lennie was married Jan. 10, 1892 to John Wesley Pitts. They are in the 1900 census of Yell County with two little boys, Virgil (b. 1893) and Ben (b. 1895). Shortly after the 1900 census Lennie and John Westley took sick and died. They had tried to help their sick family and friends and became sick too.

These two little boys, Virgil and Ben, were raised by J.W.'s brother, Robert Richard (Uncle Bob) Pitts, and his new wife, Hattie Mae Waller, along with nine children they had of their own.

Virgil Arthur Pitts (b. April 21, 1893 in Yell Count) md. _ Elkins and had one daughter, Juanita Pitts Kirtley. Virgil and Juanita went to eastern Oklahoma after the separation of Virgil and his wife, where he worked for Dickson-Goodman Lumber Company for 25 years in Coweta and Pawhuska. After retirement Virgil opened a store in Pawshuka and later he had one in Bartlesville, OK. Virgil died in 1957 of uremic poisoning.

Benjerman Franklin Pitts (b. 1895 Yell County, AR) served in WWI and was shell-shocked. He went to California ca. 1930 and was never heard from again.

John Wesley Pitts descends from Lewis Pitts and Jane Elizabeth Pitts. *Submitted by Mrs Jean Wingert.*

HUGGINS - Martha Huggins (b. 1849-50 in Alabama) was the daughter of Robert and Nancy Huggins. She and her sister Frances are with her parents in the 1860 census of Wilson District, Yell County, AR. She is also with her parents in the 1870 census of Rosecreek District, Perry County; she is evidently a widow, as her name is Martha Johnson, no male Johnson is mentioned and she has two small children, Lillian or Lilly (b. ca. 1868) and Alice M. or Allison.

Martha has probably died by 1880. In the 1880 census Lillian (b. 1868 AR), father born in Georgia and mother born in Alabama. Catharine M. Allen (b. ca. 1877 Arkansas), father born Tennessee and mother born Alabama. These children are in the household of Nathaniel Isom and his wife, Frances C. Huggins, sister of Martha Huggins Johnson Allen, Lillian 14 years old and Catharine is 3 years old in the 1880 census of Wilson District. Lillian is named in the Deed of Conveyance for Robert Huggins in 1889 in Conway County, where his heirs are named, she is listed as Lily

or Lillian Wood (Mrs. Joseph) along with her aunt Frances Huggins Isom.

Martha's second husband was Drury M. Allen and Martha Catharine Allen is his daughter (b. ca. 1877). Martha probably died in childbirth. Another possible child of Drury and Martha is McWillie Allen (female). Drury M. Allen died 1918 and is buried in Ada Valley. We have not found Martha's final resting place. *Submitted by Agnes Huggins.*

HUGGINS - Myrtle Hazzard Huggins was my grandfather, Robert Mathew Huggins's, youngest brother. We have not found Uncle Myrt in the census, but we know first hand he is part of the family. My family tells a story of the two men sharecropping in the early days, and there were visits between the two families as late as the 1940s.

Myrtle Hazzard Huggins and Nancy Jean Cloud, 50th anniversary.

Myrt was born Jan. 8, 1876, Petit Jean Township, Conway County, AR to Benjerman L.G. Huggins and Mary Barmore. It is said that Myrtle made his first crop at the age of 14, and it was probably on this land where he was born. At age 20 he married Nancy Jane Cloud from Scottsville, Pope County, AR. Probably their first year was spent at this location too, as family tell of her rowing him across the water to do his day's work (in Carden Bottoms) and picking him up again when the day was finished.

Feb. 15, 1904 the Dardnell Land Office approved the application of Myrtle Hazard Huggins, 27 years old. He then lived at Dover, Pope County, AR.

Those children were:

Wilmer (b. April 27, 1897, Scottsville, Pope County, AR, d. Sept. 26, 1986, Visalia, Tulare County, CA) md. Lena May Derryberry on March 16, 1918.

Zelma (b. Jan. 29, 1899, Scottsville, Pope County, AR, d. May 9, 1938, El Cajon, CA) md. first, Salem Jamell on Feb. 12, 1918 and second, Eugene Cole.

Velma (b. Feb. 3, 1903, Scottsville, Pope County, AR, d. Feb. 11, 1903, Pope County, AR).

Vernon (b. May 9, 1904, Dover, Pope County, AR, d. March 21, 1982, Hamblin, Jones County, TX) md. Jessie Mae Weaver on Dec. 24, 1926.

Olaf (b. May 8, 1909, Dover, Pope County, AR, d. June 19, 2000 Tulsa, OK) md. Bernice May on Dec. 7, 1932.

Opal Mildred (b. Dec. 10, 1910, Russellville, Pope County, AR, d. Sept. 2, 2000 Dover, Pope County, AR) md. William Cecil Jones on Oct. 16, 1929.

Alta Skee (b. July 6, 1912, Pope County, AR, d. Dec. 23, 1911, Porterville, CA) md. George "Mac" Wallace on July 27, 1932.

Benjamin McClunia (b. Oct. 19, 1915, Dover, Pope County, AR, d. May 7, 1990) md. Cleona M. Lang on Aug. 12, 1939.

Idelle (b. April 22, 1918, Dover, Pope County, AR, living) md. Lonnie Washington Wallace on Nov. 21, 1933.

On a visit to see Opal Mildred Huggins Jones in the 1970s, she told me that her father "Uncle Myrt," had been a small business man at one time in his life. He had a wagon outfitted with needles, buttons, broom, etc. that he traveled the county selling to those housewives who could not make a trip to town and needed these every day items to keep the family going. In memory of Uncle Myrt, I have a hand carved wall piece showing the old trading wagon with the tail gate down ready for business.

Uncle Myrt died in Dover, Pope County, AR on March 20, 1947; he is buried by his wife, Nancy Jane Cloud Huggins, in Pollard Cemetery, north of Dover, AR. *Submitted by Lucille Huggins.*

HUGGINS - The first mention that I found of Robert Huggins (b. 1809 North Carolina) in Arkansas was in the book, *Heart Within A Valley*, by John C. Stroud, this is a history of Atkins, formally known as Galley Rock. According to Mr. Stroud, Robert Huggins owned Lot No. 3 on Water Street in Galley Rock in 1850, though the name is misspelled Hoggins. It is spelled correctly on the map given in the book as Robert Huggins.

In 1854 Robert Huggins was the executor of the estate of John S. Paschal, who married Evelina Hawkins in Pope County in 1848.

During this period in Galley Rock in the 1850s, Robert Huggins, Justice of The Peace, performed seven marriages in Pope County.

Old Robert Huggins is on the 1851 Tax List for Pope County, but I have not found him until the 1860 census of Wilson District, Yell County.

On Nov. 6, 1860 Robert Huggins bought 40 acres of land for $100 in Perry County, and on Dec. 6, 1860 he bought 40 acres more for $100, all in Perry County, Rose Creek Township. Could this be the land that the family was all together on in the 1870 census? Robert is 61 years old and Nancy is 58.

In the 1860 census of Wilson District, Yell County, Robert and Nancy had two daughters living at home, Frances (b. 1845, Alabama) and Martha (b. 1849-50, Alabama). Frances Huggins married Nathaniel Isom; there were no children that I found, although they raised several nieces and nephews. Martha Huggins married __ Johnson who died or they divorced before 1870 census, as she is still living with Robert and Nancy and with children Lillie A. (b. 1868) and Allison (4 months old).

A Deed of Conveyance filed for record in Conway County Jan. 14, 1889 names the heirs of Robert Huggins, deceased, as John H. Huggins, Frances Isom and Lillian Wood (Mrs. Joseph Wood) all of Yell County, and Ben L. Huggins and Zerah York of Conway County. Lillian is the child of Martha Huggins Johnson and lived with her parents in the 1870 census. Martha later married Drury M. Allen and died in childbirth ca. 1880. Zerah first married William H. Priddy in Pope County ca. 1854; he died in 1874 and is buried at Perryville, AR. After 1874 Zerah married __ York. *Submitted by Bob Huggins.*

ROBERT MATTHEW HUGGINS history is in the student bios, page 47.

HUGGINS - On March 9, 1854, Zerah Huggins, daughter of Robert and Nancy Huggins, married William H. Priddy in Pope County, AR. In 1860 William Priddy owned Lot No. 8 and part of Lot No. 9 in Gally Rock. In the census of Anderson County, TX he is referred to as Dr. William H. Priddy (b. ca 1830 in Virginia). Zerah was born ca. 1836 in South Carolina. In the 1860 census of Anderson County, TX, two children are listed. They are Ida (b. 1857, Texas) and Thomasina (b. 1859 Texas), and also Zerah's brother Ben Huggins (b. 1846 in Alabama), a boarder in the home.

In the 1870 census of Rosecreek, Perry County, AR, Zerah and William are listed with their two daughters and a son, John W. Priddy (b. 1864 in Arkansas). Ben is living separately with his new wife Mary (Barmore) and their family. John H. Huggins and Robert and Nancy Huggins also live in the same neighborhood.

Ida W. Priddy married J.A. McBath; she seems to have had two sons who may have died young. She died Feb. 17, 1887 and is buried in Ragsdale Cemetery, in Perry County.

Thomasina Priddy married William Bethel Hogan, son of Mattison Clay Hogan and Susan Lee, daughter of William and Mary Lee. Their children were Hallie (b. May 12, 1882, Yell County); Jordan "Jerd" (b. Jan. 10, 1884, Yell County); and Cecil (b. Sept. 8, 1900, Brush Hill, McIntosh County, Indian Territory, OK).

John W. Priddy and Mandie Burns had one son, Layton Priddy.

Dr. William H. Priddy died Jan. 17, 1874 and is buried in Ragsdale Cemetery, Perry County, near his daughter, Ida Priddy McBath. His birth date is listed as Dec. 30, 1829. *Submitted by Mrs. Clarence Wingert.*

HULL - Elizabeth (Vann) Cummins-Burrows-Hull (b. Nov. 14, 1849, in what is now Perry County) was the only child of Cyrus Vann and Mary Ann James Vann. She married Andrew Jackson Cummins following his discharge from the Union Army on Sept. 10, 1865. He was from Indiana and they met while he was stationed in Lewisburg. They had one child, Mary Ann (b. Nov. 27, 1866). Following the death of Andrew from war related injuries, she married David Burrows on Feb. 20, 1870 and moved to Plumerville. She and David had a son, William Cyrus.

Maude Hull Taylor, Nodie Hull Bowdre and Mary Ann Cummins Patterson, 1906.

On the death of David, she married George Washington Hull on July 5, 1876. They had two daughters, Nodie and Maude. Following the death of her father, her mother married Andrew Jackson McCravin. Following her divorce from Andrew, she and Elizabeth, now the widow of George Washington Hull, opened up a boarding house in

Elizabeth Vann Cummins Burrows Hull, 1890.

Plumerville. The boarding house was famous for the murder of John M. Clayton, brother of Governor Powell Clayton. Clayton was in Plumerville to investigate the theft and burning of a ballot box from his recent bid for Congress. The murderer was never found.

Mary Ann and Elizabeth were founding members of the Methodist Church in Plumerville. Elizabeth died March 15, 1916, and is buried in the Plumerville Cemetery.

Her daughter Mary Ann Cummins (b. Nov. 22, 1866) md. Dan Patterson (b. Nov. 20, 1857 in LaCon, AL). He came to Arkansas in 1880 and they married May 15, 1883. Their children were Annie Elizabeth (md. Moses Terrell Kenimer); Mayme Hortense (md. Luther Malone, divorced); Neill (died young); Dan (md. Vernona Halbrook); Edward Hubert (md. Lula Fiske) and Maude Mildred (md. Eugene Melton Garrison).

Mary Ann died June 22, 1930 and Dan died March 31, 1945.

Daughter Nodie married Thomas Bowdre and daughter Maude married James J. Taylor. The family home in Plumerville was recently replaced with a carwash. A part of the boarding house is still standing and the magnolia tree planted by great-grandmother Elizabeth is still standing. *Submitted by Valda Jean Garrison Rose.*

HUMPHREY - The Humphrey family gradually made its way to Conway County, AR from John Humphrey (b. ca. 1739 in Pennsylvania) to his son John Jr. (b. 1765 in Berkes, PA) and his wife Susanna Bradford, to their son William Humphrey (b. Nov. 25, 1796 in Walton, GA) and his wife Nancy Stephens (b. Aug. 3, 1796 in Oglethorpe, Macon, GA), to their son William Samuel (b. June 19, 1826 in Walton County, GA) and his wife Susan Beavers (b. 1826 in Walton County, GA), to their son, Richard Allen Humphrey.

l-r: Richard Allen Humphrey and his father-in-law, Jesse Gray.

Richard Allen "Dock" (b. April 10, 1853 in Blount County, AL) was one of 11 children born to William and Susan. In 1880 Richard was living with H.T. and Jane Gordon in Washington, Conway, AR. Richard and Fannie Gray were married on Nov. 18, 1891 in a double ceremony with their friends, Alice Phelps (aunt to Bertha Phelps Humphrey) and Charlie Pate, at the home of Mr. and Mrs. G.H. Morrill in Morrilton, AR. In 1900 Richard was living in Morrilton City with his wife Fannie and their five children.

A trunk of Gray/Humphrey memorabilia survived a fire in Morrilton at the 204 South Ola home of Gene and Annie Waller (Richard's daughter). Included in the old trunk was a formal letter from Richard to Fannie, asking permission to take her for a Sunday drive before they were married. Newspaper records indicate Richard operated a saloon in a nearby town; however, after the wedding, the couple became farmers in the Carden Bottoms Paw Paw Bend section of Conway County. Richard enjoyed a close friendship with his father-in-law, Jesse Gray.

Richard died after a brief illness on July 3, 1911 in Morrilton. He is buried in the Lewisburg Cemetery without a marker. The family was quite poor and could not afford the cost of burial in the Elmwood Cemetery; burial in Lewisburg was free.

Widow Fannie and her seven children struggled in poverty on the farm. In 1916 her father bequeathed to her a house on West Church Street and it was a welcome relief, although the sons still had to look hard for any work they could find in those years. The 1930 Arkansas Census, Conway County, Welbourne Township, shows Fannie living at 610 West Church Street in Morrilton with three of her children: Hervey, Hallie and Frances Marie. Hervey is listed as a truck driver in the dray business. Following a work-related accident, Hervey later moved his wife, Bertha Phelps, and their six children to Oklahoma City, where he died in 1945 from the accident injuries. Bertha and the children then moved to California.

Three of Richard and Fannie's grandchildren still live in Conway County. *Submitted by F.H. Jensen.*

HUMPHRIES - Shadrack Humphries (b. Jan. 9, 1774 in Jackson County, GA) was the son of Joseph and Rebecca Humphries. He grew up in Jackson County, which was originally a part of Franklin County, GA. This land was inhabited by the Creek Indians. Shadrack's father was a veteran of the Revolutionary War, having served as a Captain in the 2nd Company of the Gum Log Company of the Georgia State Militia. Joseph Humphries was also a Justice of the Inferior Court of Jackson and Franklin counties.

Fort Yargo, now a state park in Georgia, has located upon its grounds a log block house built by Joseph Humphries and his sons. It was built for their protection from the Creek Indians. Shadrack married Sarah Camp, daughter of James and Mary Berry Camp, about 1804 in Jackson County, GA. Sarah's grandfather, John Camp, was also a veteran of the Revolutionary War. There is a family dispute as to which side he served on, he was accused of having accepted a captain's commission in the King's army in 1783, however, this charge was never proven. Family members state that John Camp served as a lieutenant in the Sullivan Independent Company of Volunteer Scouts of 96th District in South Carolina. John and his son Thomas fought in the battle of Kings Mountain where Thomas was wounded. John, along with his son James and other family members moved to Winder, GA around 1800.

Shadrack and Sarah had the following children: James (b. 1804) md. Margaret Black; Joseph (b. 1805); Alfred (b. 1807); Barry (b. April 1809) md. Anna Lucas and Amanda Carrington, died 1861 in Washington County, TX; Stephen (b. 1811); Shadrack Jr. (b. 1813) md. Mary Matthews; Marinda Humphries (b. June 12, 1815) md. John W. Williams, died 1900, Pope County, AR; Sexton (b. 1817); Jackson (b. 1820) md. Barbary Smith, died Howard County, AR; Starling (b. 1822) md. Lucinda Herlong, died 1864 in Ohio.

Shadrack died between 1822-27 and Sarah Camp Humphries died Feb. 6, 1832, both in Walton County, GA. They are the great-grandparents of Maga Poe Watkins.

HUNTER - Dr. Ulysses Hunter was born on Nov. 14, 1938 in Blackwell, AR to the late Harrison Hunter Jr. and Eddie Mae (Thompson) Hunter, and departed this life March 13, 2001. Dr. Hunter, an associate professor of mathematics at California State College at Hayward, CA since 1964, returned to Conway County last week to visit his grandparents at Blackwell who raised him.

Dr. Ulyssess Hunter

Hunter, 29, is the personification of a self-made man. Raised by his grandparents, William "Bud" Horton, 88 and Phillis, 78, after his mother died when he was age 2. Hunter picked cotton to keep himself in school and his perseverance paid off with a bachelor of science degree in mathematics from Arkansas AM&N College at Pine Bluff in 1959 and a masters degree and Ph.D. from Perdue University in 1961 and 1964 respectively. He received a yearly $50 scholarship at AM&N and at Perdue, he was aided by a teaching assistantship.

A 1955 graduate of L.W. Sullivan High School at Morrilton, several local teachers and others encouraged him to continue his education. The teachers he listed were Miss Margaret Sanders, Mrs. Emily Brown, and Mrs. Emma Thomas Bagby. He said he also received encouragement from Herman Garrett and Ike McDaniel.

Recalling his cotton picking days, he said he used to pick 400 lbs. per day. He said his older brother in service also aided him. At AM&N, he waited tables, served as a leader for a blind boy, and as a senior, taught remedial math for income. He married Joanne Hall of Maghee. They met at AM&N College and they have one son Michael, 8. *Submitted by V.M. Cunningham Steward.*

HUTCHCROFT - Theodore Hutchcroft (b. January 1931) was raised on a dairy and seed corn farm near Mediapolis, IA. He graduated from Mediapolis High School in 1948; earned a BS in agricultural journalism from Iowa State College (now University) in 1953, an MA in communication from The American University, and a PhD in education from Iowa State in 1978. He served in the US Army September 1953 to August 1955, including a year in the 513th MI Group, USAREUR, Frankfurt a. Main, Germany.)

He married Beverly Jane Walk of South English, IA, in June 1953. She was born in South English, IA, in July 1933, graduated from Kinross High School in

1950 and earned a BS in dietetics from Iowa State College in 1954.

Bev and Ted Hutchcroft with their daughters (l-r), Jill, Jayne and Julia, and son-in-law Barry Wanner, August 2003 on Petit Jean Mountain.

They lived in Des Moines from September 1955 to November 1956, where he was with the Iowa Farm Bureau. They moved to Fairfax County, VA in December 1956; when he joined the Office of Information, US Department of Agriculture. He became Information Director of the National 4-H Foundation in February 1959. The family lived in San José, Costa Rica from July 1968 to December 1975 where he was Director of the Inter-American Rural Youth Program. They returned to Ames, IA, in January 1976 where he was vice president, council for agricultural science and technology. In March 1983 he joined International Agricultural Development Service and they moved to Dhaka, Bangladesh for an assignment with the Bangladesh Agricultural Research Council. IADS was merged to become Winrock International in 1985 with headquarters on Petit Jean Mountain.

The Hutchcrofts moved to Petit Jean in May 1986 where he became a Senior Program Officer/Communication for Winrock International. They lived in Los Banos, Philippines from February 1992 to January 1994 when he was interim head, Information Center, International Rice Research Institute. H retired from Winrock International in October 1994.

They have three daughters: Jayne, a high school teacher of anthropology at Lincoln School, San José, Costa Rica; Jill, an assistant professor of biochemistry, Purdue University, West Lafayette, IN; and Julia, a medical secretary, Orthopedic Clinic, University of Minnesota Hospitals, Minneapolis.

In their high school days, both Beverly and Ted were active in their local Methodist Youth Fellowship and 4-H Clubs. He was an International Farm Youth Exchange delegate to the United Kingdom in 1949. They have been Girl Scout and 4-H leaders in various communities.

Hutchcrofts are members of the First United Methodist Church, Morrilton. She is a member of the Pathfinder Club, the Petit Jean Extension Homemakers Club and the Petit Jean Garden Club. They are founding members of the Petit Jean Mountain Community Association. He is president of the Friends of the Conway County Library, a board member of the Conway County Community Foundation, and a member of the Conway County Genealogical Association and of the Veterans of Foreign Wars. They are members of the Conway County Republican Committee. He edits newsletters for the PJMCA, the Friends group, amid the County Republican Party.

HUTSON - Richard Alexander Hutson, (b. 1944 in Georgia) md. Martha Jane Martin of Tennessee in 1870. They had one son John Henry Hutson (b. 1873 in Arkansas). John Henry Hutson married Sarah Alice Huddleston in Clinton, AR, Van Buren County. They had three sons: William J. "Bill" Hutson, Luther Hutson and John Hutson, and one daughter, Lena Hutson Summerhill.

John Henry Hutson and family moved to Conway County sometime around 1910-15. They settled for a period of time around the Cyprus Creek area.

William "Bill" Hutson married Wilma J. Brewer in early 1920s, and they had three sons and one daughter: Billie J. Hutson, Logan "BC" Hutson, Howard Eugene Hutson and Theresa A. Williams.

William Hutson had one son, Jimmy Hutson (Martin) by his first wife. Jimmy was killed in an automobile accident in 1985 at age 63.

William Hutson and family lived for a period of time across the river from Petit Jean Mountain, where he farmed with his mother-in-law, Sidney Kissire. Following the birth of three sons, the family moved to the Pleasant Hill area west of Center Ridge, Conway County, where they engaged in farming and the two older sons started to school at Pleasant Hill.

In the mid-1930s the family moved to Scott, AR, Pulaski County, where they farmed.

In 1938, the family moved back to the Center Ridge area where the two older sons attended Nemo Vista School. Then in early 1942, the family moved to England, AR, Lonoke County, where they lived until after WWII ended.

William Hutson died in July 1978 and Wilma Hutson died in September 1990; both are buried in Elmwood Cemetery, Morrilton.

Son Billie Hutson, after a tour of duty in the Air Force during the Korean War, settled in Fort Worth, TX and earned his chemical engineering degree from Texas Christian University. He is now a retired certified registered nurse anesthetist and advanced nurse practitioner. Logan "BC" Hutson lives in Cabot, AR and following a tour of duty in the Navy, 1945-48, and in the Army during the Korean War, attended the Baptist Seminary in Little Rock. He has been a Baptist minister for 48 years and is currently pastor of Cedar Creek Missionary Baptist Church, Springfield, AR. He is also a retired chief petty officer of the Naval Reserve.

Howard Eugene Hutson graduated from Morrilton High School in 1950. Following a tour of duty in the Air Force during the Korean War, he began a career with Continental Oil Well Supply of Forth Worth, TX. He was killed west of Morrilton on Highway 64, May 15, 1957 at age 24. He is buried in Elmwood Cemetery, Morrilton.

Theresa Hutson Williams lives in Everman, TX and is employed in a law firm in Forth Worth. *Submitted by Logan "BC" Hutson.*

INGRAM - James Robert Ingram (b. June 3, 1861 in Hamilton County, IL, d. Dec. 9, 1942 in Conway County, AR) was the son of Francis Alexander and Edith Anna (Gunter) Ingram. James Robert Ingram married Mary Eldora Burton on Oct. 19, 1889 in Hamilton County, IL. Mary Eldora Burton (b. Aug. 7, 1871 in Hamilton County, IL) was the daughter of Thomas and Mary (Goin) Burton.

Mary Eldora Burton Ingram

The Ingrams lived in McLeansboro, Hamilton County, IL until about 1897. They moved the family to Clay County, AR and lived in the Rector area. Mary Eldora died there on Dec. 4, 1902. James and Mary Eldora have four children: Thomas Francis "Frank" Ingram, Nancy Jane "Janie" Ingram, Bessie Belle Ingram and Melinda Eveline "Evie" Ingram.

1) Frank (b. March 9, 1891 in Hamilton County, IL) md. Elsie Virginia McKay, daughter of James B. and Ollie J. (Mobley) McKay, on June 25, 1910 in Clay County, AR. Frank and Elsie have one son, James Robert Ingram.

2) Janie Ingram (b. Feb. 12, 1893 in Hamilton County, IL, d. Dec. 4, 1976) md. Henry T. Hammonds on June 4, 1933 in Conway County, AR. Henry (b. Feb. 9, 1886, d. June 1968) was the son of Milton V.

and Melinda Hammonds. Janie and Henry are buried in Cleveland Cemetery, Conway County, AR. They had one son, Isaac Bill Hammonds.

3) Bessie Belle Ingram (b. March 4, 1895 in Hamilton County, IL., d. July 12, 1972 in Morrilton, Conway County, AR) md. Benjamin Campbell on Oct. 26, 1914 in Conway County, AR. Benjamin (b. April 14, 1894 in Okay, Pope County, AR, d. July 7, 1975 in Cleveland, Conway County, AR) was the son of William Frazier and Maizy Elizabeth (Wright) Campbell. Benjamin and Bessie are buried in Elmwood Cemetery, Morrilton, Conway County, AR. They had four children: Raymond Claud Campbell, William Francis "Frank" Campbell, Mary Eathel Campbell Freeman and Lela Marie Campbell Huffman.

4) Evie Ingram (b. Dec. 6, 1897 in Rector, Clay County, AR, d. April 28, 1988 in Stillwell, Adair County, OK) md. Samuel Lee Bookout on June 27, 1920 in Pope County, AR. Samuel (b. April 1, 1897, Round Mountain, near London, Pope County, AR, d. April 8, 1977 in Stillwell, Adair County, OK) was the son of William Logan and Rhoda Lilly (Myers) Bookout. Samuel and Evie are buried in Tyler Springs Cemetery in Stillwell. Their children are Cora Juanita Bookout Beaumont, Janetta Lee Bookout Henson Warnock, Paul Samuel Bookout, William Richard Bookout, Robert E. Lee Bookout, Gordon Logan Bookout, Garland Franklin Bookout and Greta Elnora Bookout.

After the death of Mary Eldora, James married Ada Hedgecock (b. Feb. 15, 1875, d. Sept. 16, 1956) on Nov. 12, 1907 in Clay County, AR. James and Ada Ingram are buried in the Reid Cemetery, Cleveland, Conway County, AR. They had one daughter, Mary Edith Ingram (b. Sept. 8, 1914 in Conway County, AR, d. Dec. 18, 1994 in Lane, Vaneta County, OR). She married Leonard M. Blake in December 1929 in Conway County, AR. Leonard (b. Nov. 23, 1903 in Van Buren County, AR, d. May 2, 1993 in Lane, Vaneta County, OR) was the son of Ripley D. and Amanda (Driver) Blake. They had four children: Leonard Lee Blake, R.D. Blake, Claudie Marie Blake and Norman Blake. *Submitted by Lela Campbell Huffman.*

ISENMAN – Johan "John" Isenman (b. Dec. 27, 1842 in Zell Baden, Germany) md. Anna Marie Wellman (b. Dec. 8, 1845 in Zell Baden, Germany) in about 1876. In order to provide support for the remaining family, John Isenman and his brother Fredrick emigrated to the United States in 1872 after the death of their mother.

Their sister, Pauline Isenman, remained in Germany with their father. Pauline (b. Jan. 21, 1850) md. Heinrick George Bayer on July 19, 1880 in Hofweier, Germany. Heinrick was born April 22, 1855 in Oberknich, Germany and died March 19, 1938.

Fredrick Isenman (b. Feb. 25, 1857 in Baden, Germany, d. Sept. 14, 1946 in Little Rock, Pulaski County, AR) md. Caroline "Lena" Grabherr about 1885. Lena was the daughter of Joseph Grabherr (b. 1833, d. 1899) and Theresia Kreideniss (b. 1840, d. 1918). Lena (b. May 16, 1862 in Baden, Germany, d. Sept. 11, 1898) was buried at Sacred Heart Cemetery, Morrilton, Conway County, AR.

Fredrick Isenman's second marriage was to Anna Basler Held about 1900. Anna (b. 1873, d. Oct. 9, 1938 in Little Rock, AR) and Fredrick are buried at Calvery Cemetery, Little Rock, Pulaski County, AR.

Shortly after arriving in America, John and Fredrick Isenman lived in the Chicago, IL area. John later moved to Decorah, IA. Fredrick arrived in Oppelo, Perry County, AR in the mid-1850s. John and Anna Marie Isenman arrived in Oppelo, AR in the late 1880s. John and Anna Marie had two daughters:

1) Emerelia "Emma" Isenman (b. Sept. 22, 1877 in Decorah, IA) md. John Albert Grabherr on Jan. 10, 1899 in Saint Elizabeth Catholic Church in Oppelo, AR. John Albert was born Nov. 8, 1868 in Baden, Germany and died July 25, 1933 in his home. Emma died May 24, 1951 at Saint Anthony Hospital,

Morrilton, AR; both are buried at Saint Elizabeth Cemetery, Oppelo, AR.

2) Mary Ann Isenman (b. Aug. 12, 1879 in Decorah, IA) md. Henry Boniface Nagel on Nov. 25, 1901 in St. Elizabeth Church, Oppelo, AR. Henry was born May 17, 1875 in Peru, IL. and died August 8, 1956 in Morrilton, AR. Mary Ann died April 6, 1966 in Little Rock, Pulaski County, AR; both are buried at Sacred Heart Cemetery, Morrilton, Conway County, AR.

John and Anna Marie Isenman bought 120 acres of land for 33 cents an acre in 1890. This parcel of land was originally owned by the Little Rock and Fort Smith Railroad. Their homesite, a log cabin, was located about a half mile west of what is now known as the Timberlake and Arena Road intersection. John farmed the land and Anna Marie kept the house. Both were members of Saint Elizabeth Catholic Church. John died Nov. 9, 1906 and Anna Marie died Oct. 20, 1893; both died in Oppelo and are buried in Saint Elizabeth Cemetery, Oppelo, AR. *Submitted by Ben Donaldson.*

ISOM - Charlie George Isom married Max Anne Trujillo in 1973. They lived in Little Rock, where he worked at Dixie Culvert Company, they moved to Clinton (where both their parents lived); he worked at ConAgra chicken plant and worked part time for True Value Hardware or part time caring for chicken houses. They moved to Conway where Charlie carpooled to Orbit Valve Company in Little Rock, making complicated valves for oil lines. In 1982, they came to Center Ridge in Conway County. They

Charlie and Max Anne Isom

lived at the Otho Guinn place for years. They bought land, then bought a house in Morrilton and had it moved onto their land in Center Ridge, where they live.

Michael, David, Tammy, Suzanne, Alvin, Dustin and John Isom.

Charlie and Max Anne had two daughters and five sons. Upon moving to Center Ridge, Tammy and Alvin finished fourth/second grade there at Nemo Vista School, and all seven children continued through twelfth grade there. As of this writing, Alvin, Dustin, and Suzanne have continued their education and learned a profession.

Charlie's family lived in Clinton, AR (Van Buren County) all their life. Charlie was one of 14 children. His father, Charlie Bryan Isom, took any work to support his large family — raising chickens, sawmill, driving a truck, delivering mail, accepting dumping fees at the city landfill. At the time of this writing, Gracie still lives in the house her husband built in Clinton. His parents were George Davis Isom and Elsie Pearl Isom. Gracie's parents were Jackson Bigelow and Joe Ann Bigelow.

Max Anne's family lived in Truth or Consequences, New Mexico (formerly Hot Springs until the name was changed for a TV show), where her father's family, Jose and Clara Trujillo, lived. She finished tenth

grade there, then they moved to Clinton, AR where her mother's parents, Leonard and Maude Cullum, lived. Max worked for the Chevrolet dealership; Pat worked at the hospital then the cord plant, until Max opened his own business. Max team roped in the rodeos with his son, and people who knew him came to love New Mexico because he did. Max and Pat worked at Max's Body Shop in Clinton until his death. Later Pat remarried to Odis Reed, who retired from the Navy, and they adopted three girls. Max Anne's great aunt, Gladys Cullum Denton, taught school in Conway County and Van Buren County after graduating from eighth grade. As laws changed and more education was required, she returned to school/college each time, then continued to teach, a total of 67 years.

Charlie George Isom was born in Clinton, AR in 1952. Max Anne Trujillo was born in Truth or Consequences, New Mexico in 1955. Wherever they lived, their place of worship was the Church of Christ. Charlie has been with Pilgrim's Pride (formerly ConAgra) chicken plant for 14 years. Max Anne is an artist and author (also part time speaker and art teacher). Of their children who have families of their own, Tammy and Dewayne Sykes settled in Clinton; Alvin and Janet (Johnson) Isom moved from Center Ridge to Vilonia; Dustin and Kristina (Scott) Isom in Center Ridge; Suzanne Hamilton in Center Ridge. They have blessed their parents with 10 grandchildren. Single as of this writing are John, who lived in Scotland and moved back to Center Ridge; Michael Isom of Center Ridge; and David Isom, a senior at Nemo Vista High School in Center Ridge. Charlie and Max Anne celebrated their 32nd wedding anniversary the year of this writing, 2005.

JACKSON - Cecil Everette Jackson (b. 1904 on Petit Jean Mountain, Conway County, AR) was the son of James William Jackson, who was reared in Nashville, TN and came to Arkansas as a young man, and Mary Aneta "Molly" McAlister of Pulaski County, AR. His parents were married in 1887. His father was born in 1864 and died in 1931. His mother was born in 1872 and died in 1933. They are buried on Petit Jean Mountain. His brothers and sisters were James Harrison Jackson, Florence America Jackson (Wright), Clarence Leonard Jackson, Carl Cleveland Jackson, William Coleman Jackson, Laura Etta Jackson (McVay), Howard Roosevelt Jackson, Augusta Jackson (Porter), Ward Johnson Jackson and George Edward Jackson, all deceased.

Cecil Jackson, Minnie Jackson and grandson Van Moore, 1968.

In 1926 he married Minnie Victoria Kimberlin of Atkins, Pope County, AR. She was born in 1907, the daughter of J.A. "Buck" Kimberlin and Clara Matthews Kimberlin.

He lived most of his life in Conway County, AR. In 1955 he had a massive heart attack and retired from the Conway County Sheriff's Department where he had worked as a deputy sheriff for several years. Minnie came to Conway County as a young bride. Before her marriage, she was a teacher at Bells Chapel in Pope County. She retired from the Conway County Library in the late 1980s. They had four daughters: Cecil Pauline Jackson (Cupp), Clara Jean Jackson (Moore) who died in 1997, Mary Sue Jackson (Pettus) and Shirley Anne Jackson (Bean).

They were of Baptist faith and members of the First Baptist Church in Morrilton, Conway County, AR. He died in 1974 and she died in 1991. Both are buried at Elmwood Cemetery in Morrilton, Conway County, AR. *Submitted by Shirley Bean.*

JACKSON - Charles Reid Jackson (b. Oct. 7, 1908 Center Ridge, AR, d. Aug. 30, 1956, buried at Whitter, CA) md. Beatrice Edna Buchanan on Aug. 9, 1941 at Las Vegas, NV. She was born June 7, 1918, Bakersville, NC.

Their daughter Barbara Ann Jackson (b. Oct. 15, 1943, Covina, CA) md. Carl Robert Campbell on Dec. 25, 1960 at Morganton, NC. He was born June 17, 1941, Valdese, NC. Their children are:

Charles Reid Jackson, Morrilton High School.

1) Robert Christopher "Chris" Campbell (b. Jan. 2, 1962, Valdese, NC, d. May 19, 1985, buried at Valdese, NC) md. Eulah Mae Green (b. Jan. 1, 1960 at Ellenboro) on June 1, 1984. Their child is Brandon Lee Campbell (b. April 5, 1985, Valdese, NC).

2) Patrick Durand "Pat" Campbell (b. Feb. 18, 1967, Valdese, NC) md. Karen Warren Aug. 4, 1986 at Schwalbach, Germany. She was born July 28, 1956 Wiesen fels, East, Germany. Their children are Jessica Catherine Campbell (b. Sept. 5, 1987, Schwalbach, Germany) and Jennifer Patricia Campbell (b. Oct. 7, 1989, Schwalbach, Germany).

3) Carl Dwayne "Hoody" Campbell (b. April 29, 1971 Valdese, NC) md. Kimberly Christine "Kim" Harris March 29, 1989 at Graffney, SC. She was born May 18, 1972, Lenoir, NC. Their daughter is Amanda Marie Campbell (b. Nov. 7, 1990 Morganton, NC).

JACKSON - Franklin Taylor "Frank" Jackson married Bessie Lee Finch Dec. 12, 1915. She was born March 22, 1891, and died Sept. 3, 1968. Both are buried at Center Ridge.

Franklin Taylor and Bessie Lee Jackson. Children l-r: James Lee, Elsie Jane and Harold Finch.

Their children are:

1) Elsie Jane Jackson (b. Dec. 10, 1916 at Center Ridge) md. Thomas Augustus Cathey Dec. 9, 1939 at Cleveland, AR. He was born March 15, 1907 at Scotland, AR. Their son Lowell Thomas Cathey was born Sept. 12, 1940 at Cleveland, AR.

2) James Lee Jackson (b. Sept. 15, 1918 at Center Ridge) md. Audrey Carolyn Russell in July 1945. She was born July 17, 1915 in Cleveland, AR and died May 4, 1978. Their children are (a) Robert Henry Lee "Bob" Jackson (b. March 24, 1946 at Center Ridge, AR) md. Barbara Hallett (first); their children are Rebecca Leeann, Stephanie Laverne and Hannah. (b) Carolyn June Jackson (b. June 1, 1947, d. June 4, 1977). (c) James Larry "Jim" Jackson (b. Sept. 30, 1948, Morrilton, AR) md. first, Joy, divorced, their child James Russell "Russ" Jackson (b. May 1, 1977, Morrilton, AR). James married second to Lanell "Nell" Jackson. (d) Mary Alice Jackson (b. April 9, 1950, Morrilton, AR). (e) Linda Joyce Jackson (b. March 2,

1952, Morrilton, AR) md. Tommy Dean Acton Aug. 13, 1971. Their children are Melissa Catherine Acton (b. May 21, 1972, Harrison, AR) md. July 7, 1990 to Sherman Ray Tiner Jr. (b. July 7, 1964); Michelle DeLynn Acton (b. Feb. 16, 1974, Neosho, MO); and Lisa Marie Acton (b. June 1, 1976 Conway, AR).

3) Harold Finch Jackson (b. Aug. 25, 1921 Center Ridge, AR) md. Arlene Frances Anderson on July 6, 1958 at Castle Rock, CO. Their child is Vincent Alan Jackson (b. May 10, 1959 Seattle, WA).

4) Lula Alice Jackson (b. Feb. 26, 1923, Center Ridge, AR) md. Marshall Monroe on Dec. 5, 1948. He was born Oct. 1, 1915, Center Ridge, AR. Their children are:

(a) Jerry Wayne Anderson (b. April 10, 1951) md. Connie Cash, divorced. Their children are Phillip Jeffrey Anderson (b. Sept. 22, 1971) and James Patrick Anderson (b. May 11, 1975).

(b) Carl Lynn Anderson (b. Nov. 25, 1953) md. Carolyn Betner on Dec. 5, 1974. Their child is Lesia Michelle (b. Feb. 15, 1977).

5) William Cornelius "Bill" Jackson (b. Dec. 22, 1924, Center Ridge, AR) md. Ada Ruth Permenter (b. May 31, 1924, Oppelo, AR) on June 7, 1950.

JACKSON - James Bayless Jackson (b. Aug. 16, 1902, Morrilton, AR, d. July 6, 1965 and buried at Little Rock, AR) md. Willamae Owens (b. Jan. 2, 1910) on Feb. 14, 1930

Their daughter Carolyn Mary Jackson (b. May 29, 1935, Little Rock, AR) md. John R. Stotts (b. Oct. 5, 1928, Searcy, AR) on April 11, 1957 in Little Rock, AR. They have three children:

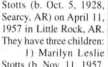

1) Marilyn Leslie Stotts (b. Nov. 11, 1957, Little Rock, AR) md. Richard Eugene "Rick" Layton on Sept. 15, 1990 at Little Rock, AR.

James Bayless Jackson

2) John Christopher "Chris" Stotts (b. April 23, 1960, Little Rock, AR) md. Sarah Angel Martin (b. June 6, 1960, Fort Smith, AR) on July 6, 1983.

3) Allyson Ann Stotts (b. Nov. 23, 1963, Little Rock, AR) md. David Harold Pickering (b. Jan. 20, 1961, Fort Smith, AR) on April 26, 1985. Their child is Melanie Diane Pickering (b. June 4, 1990, Little Rock, AR).

JACKSON - Dr. James Henry Jackson (b. March 23, 1860, d. May 13, 1933) md. Alice Annie Dean on March 2, 1890. She was born Sept. 15, 1870 and died July 17, 1925. Alice's mother was Mary Jane Cleveland (b. Aug. 5, 1847, d. June 18, 1926. Mary Jane's other children were Annie Dean Bruadaway, Homer Dean, Oscar Dean, Lula Dean Reveley, Will Dean, Hawk Dean and Nettie Dean.

Dr. James Henry Jackson and Alice Amie Dean Jackson.

James and Alice's children were Franklin Taylor Jackson (b. Sept. 20, 1891, d. Sept. 24, 1945); Andrew Norvin Jackson (b. Jan. 16, 1893); Iola Jane Jackson (b. May 1, 1894, d. March 18, 1924); Daughter Jackson (b. Sept. 8, 1895, d. Dec. 30, 1895); Wilford

Jackson (b. Sept. 8, 1895, d. February 1915); Nettie Jackson (b. Dec. 15, 1899, d. March 19, 1916); James Bayless Jackson (b. Aug. 16, 1902, d. July 6, 1965); Oscar Jackson (b. Feb. 14, 1905, d. 1961); Mary Susan Jackson (b. April 20, 1906, d. Jan. 9, 1969); Charles Reid Jackson (b. Oct. 7, 1908, d. Aug. 30, 1956); Lawrence Woodrow Jackson (b. Aug. 5, 1910, d. Sept. 12, 1993) and Thomas Morgan Jackson (b. April 21, 1915, d. April 26, 1918).

JACKSON - Lawrence Woodrow "Larry" Jackson (b. Aug. 5, 1910, Center Ridge, AR, d. Sept. 12, 1993) md. Vida Mae "Vi" Edwards Oct. 17, 1931. She was born Nov. 25, 1913 Center Ridge, AR and died Jan. 16, 2002. Their children are:

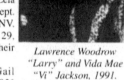

1) Billy Dean "Bill" Jackson (b. Dec. 30, 1932 Springfield, AR) md. Lela Judith "Judy" Shaw Sept. 3, 1955 at Las Vegas, NV. She was born Dec. 29, 1935 Poteau, OK. Their children are:

Lawrence Woodrow "Larry" and Vida Mae "Vi" Jackson, 1991.

a) Beverly Gail Jackson (b. Aug. 14, 1956 Santa Monica, CA) md. Gary Wayne Golden Aug. 11, 1979 at Rancho Palos Verdes, CA. He was born July 19, 1956. (Divorced) Their children are Jennifer Lynn Golden (b. March 31, 1982, Torrance, CA) and Robert Wayne Golden (b. June 21, 1985, Fort Smith, AR).

b) Susan Diane Jackson (b. May 23, 1958, Torrance, CA) md. Daniel William Boone Jr. June 28, 1980 at Rancho Palos Verdes, CA. He was born Dec. 2, 1955, Los Alamos, NM. Their children are Kimberly Anne Boone (b. Feb. 19, 1984, Los Angeles, CA) and Daniel William "Danny" Boone III (b. Sept. 27, 1987 Fort Smith, AR).

c) Steven Andrew "Steve" Jackson (b. March 9, 1962, Torrance, CA) md. Lisa Catherine Colley March 3, 1984 at Fort Smith, AR. She was born Sept. 12, 1963. Their children are Jillia Catherine "Jill" Jackson (b. Feb. 14, 1985, Fort Smith, AR) and Jeffrey Steven "Jeff" Jackson (b. Aug. 20, 1989, Fort Smith, AR).

d) William Lawrence "Billy" Jackson (b. Dec. 31, 1966, Redondo Beach, CA) md. Louann Troy June 1, 1987 at Las Vegas, NV. She was born April 8, 1968. (Divorced) Their child is Krystle Ann Jackson (b. Dec. 12, 1988, Ventura, CA). Second marriage to Sherri Venice Blagg May 25, 1991 at Eureka Springs, AR. She was born Feb. 15, 1967, Fort Smith, AR and died Feb. 24, 2000. Their child is Kayla Jackson (b. Aug. 28, 1993).

2) Betty Sue Jackson (b. April 8, 1940, Center Ridge, AR) md. Richard Lee "Dick" Van Valkenburg March 28, 1964. He was born May 17, 1935, Hardy, NE. Their children are (i) Richard Eric "Eric" Van Valkenburg (b. Jan. 21, 1967, Fresno, CA) md. Michelle Lynn Cox May 23, 1993 at Fresno, CA. She was born Dec. 29, 1967. Their child is Richard Jackson "Jack" Van Valkenburg (b. Sept. 6, 2001, Clovis, CA). (ii) Curtis Lee "Curt" Van Valkenburg (b. May 17, 1971, Fresno, CA).

JACKSON - Oscar Jackson (b. Feb. 13 or 14, 1905, d. 1961, buried in Little Rock, AR) md. Opal May Addington Jan. 19, 1929, Conway County, AR. She was born Aug. 7, 1911, died May 30, 1965 and buried in Little Rock, AR. Their children are:

1) Norvin Andrew "Andy" Jackson (b. June 11, 1930, Center Ridge, AR, d. Oct. 11, 1969, buried at Spring, TX) md. Estelle Ballentine in 1948. She was born October 23, ___. Their children are Beverly Ann Jackson (b. April 27, ___) and Kathy Jackson (b. Sept. 23, ___).

2) James Edward "Jim" Jackson (b. June 4, 1938, Adona, AR) md. Shirley Ann Finney May 6, 1960 at

Dallas, TX. She was born March 19, 1935, Dallas, TX. Their children are:

Oscar Jackson

a) adopted son Quade Jackson (b. Aug. 22, 1966, Killeen, TX) md. Holly Ann Kephart (b. Nov. 30, 1966 Phoenix, AZ). Their children are Amy Michelle Jackson (b. Jan. 16, 1986, Plano, TX) and Kevin James Jackson (b. April 2, 1988, San Antonio, TX).

b) Shawn Lee Jackson (b. May 27, 1970, Dallas, TX).

JACKSON – The Ward Jackson family lived at 107 Stephens St., Morrilton, AR. Ward Jackson hauled lumber, state to state, for M.H. Pierce and Gifford Lumber companies.

Back row: Ward Sr., Blanche, Ward Jr., Tommy; middle row: Annetta, Lonnie and in front is Martha.

In 1965 they moved to Blackwell, AR and went into farming and raising cattle. *Submitted by Ward Jackson Jr.*

JENKINS - Harry Jenkins II (b. Feb. 18, 1876, in Anderson County, SC), son of Lawrence Jenkins and Minerva Greenlee, and Ida (b. Oct. 4, 1884 in Abbeville, SC), daughter of Thomas Twine Baskin and Emma Elizabeth Swain, moved to Arkansas. There they are shown on the 1910 Federal Census, showing Harry married to Ida Baskin for the past seven years. This is Harry's second marriage. Harry and Ida lived on Maple Street in Morrilton. Conway

Ida Emma Asula Baskin 1884-1948

County, Howard Township, AR. The 1920 Census has Ida listed as 35 years old and Harry is listed as 45 years old. The family moved to Plumerville, Conway County, AR on Springfield Road. The land was called Diggs Addition or Cardon Bottoms.

Children of Harry and Ida were Helen Jenkins; Margie Jenkins (b. 1905, d. 1924) md. Samuel McDaniel; Lawrence Jenkins (b. 1906, d. 1985) md. Eva Fields; Harry Thomas Jenkins (b. 1907, d. 1988) md. Ruth Naomi McDaniel; Edith Jenkins-Calvin (b. 1908, d. 1930) md. Robert Calvin; Ila Maud Jenkins (b. 1914, d. 1934); Rose Bell Jenkins-Alexander (b. 1919, d. 1992) md. Wearlee Alexander; Herbert Ladell Jenkins (b. 1921, d. 1986) md. Theola, then Josephine.

JOHNSON - On Christmas Eve of 1859, Amos and Clarkie Johnson and their family arrived on Petit Jean Mountain. Their family consisted of their three children: Nancy, William and Columbus "Lump." Their daughter Nancy and her husband Theodore Montgomery had three children: William "Billy," Robert and Sally. (Sally was born in Maumelle en route to Petit Jean). William Johnson was married to Emily E.

Knowles. They brought six slaves with them. (See the biographies of Theodore and Nancy Montgomery, John Manly and Margaret Alice Montgomery, and Burton and Bettye Henderson.)

Clarkie Swanigan Barnett Johnson was born in County Donegal, Ireland. We do not know at what age and under what circumstances she came to the United States. She married a Mr. Barnett (We do not know his first name.) They lived in Baker County, GA, where they owned a plantation. After Mr. Barnett died, Amos Johnson, a neighbor, agreed to help her manage the plantation. Clarkie Barnett and Amos Johnson fell in love and were married in 1834.

After what the family referred to as "an unfriendly discussion over slavery," Amos and Clarkie and a brother of Amos decided to move to Texas. In the fall of 1859, they came to Greenville, MS, where they boarded a steamboat and traveled up the Mississippi River to the Arkansas River to Little Rock. They set up camp in Maumelle and stayed there until Nancy Montgomery delivered their third child, a daughter named Sally.

While they were in Maumelle, they met a Mr. Haggerty who was taking his cattle to market. Upon seeing Mr. Haggerty's cattle, Amos Johnson said, "wherever those cattle came from is where we are going!" When Nancy Montgomery was able to travel after the birth of Sally, Amos and Clarkie Johnson and their families went to Petit Jean Mt. Amos Johnson's brother continued to Texas.

Mr. Haggerty told them about the mountain near his farm and said that it was the most beautiful place he had ever seen. The ground was good for crops and cattle grazing. The Haggerty's farm was below the west side of Petit Jean Mt. The Johnson, Montgomery and Haggerty families remained friends until Mrs. Haggerty died. Mrs. Haggerty regularly rode her horse up the Mountain to visit the Johnsons. Her visits normally lasted two or three days. It was Mr. and Mrs. Haggerty who told the Johnsons and Montgomerys the story of Petit Jean.

Amos and Clarkie Johnson's first home on Petit Jean Mt. was near what is now Sound-Craft Systems, Inc. They had selected that site because of an excellent artesian well. The Johnsons and Montgomerys eventually acquired approximately 1,200 acres of land on Petit Jean Mt. Most of the land was from near the present Sound-Craft Systems, Inc. and along Montgomery Trace and Winrock Drive. Their descendants have continued to own some of the original property.

There were two other families living on Petit Jean when Amos and Clarkie settled there, the Owen West and Chester Morris families had moved to Petit Jean two or three years earlier.

In 1860, Amos Johnson was killed by a falling tree as he worked to clear the land. His grave was the third one in the Petit Jean Mt. Cemetery. (The first two were the Walker children.) Clarkie Johnson continued to raise her family on Petit Jean Mt. and lived there until she died in 1878. Clarkie was buried next to Amos in the Petit Jean Mt. Cemetery.

See the biographies of Theodore and Nancy Montgomery; John Manly and Margaret Alice Montgomery; Ottis and Ruby Montgomery and Burton and Bettye Henderson. *Submitted by Mrs. Burton Henderson.*

JOHNSON – Frank Main Johnson (b. June 27, 1885 at Oxley, Searcy County, d. April 6, 1952 near Lonoke, AR) was the son of William Main Johnson (b. March 26, 1859, Walker County) and Martha Kuykendall (b. Sept. 15, 1853 in Gwinnett County, GA). Martha was the daughter of Frank Francis Kuykendall and Mary Elizabeth Thompson, who walked from Georgia to Searcy County, AR ca. 1859 with all of the family possessions and small children in a two-wheeled oxcart. Many of the Kuykendalls owned slaves, but Frank Francis did not believe in this practice and took his family to Searcy County to avoid the future troubles he believed that would engulf Georgia in armed con-

Frank and Callie Johnson

flict. He "jumped from the frying pan right into the fire," because he was chained to other men and force-marched to Little Rock. There he was made to join the Confederate Army or be shot.

Frank M. Johnson's grandparents were: James Main Johnson (b. 1834 in Gwinnett County, GA). He was in Co. A, 3rd GA Confederate Cav., 4th GA Inf. and on July 24, 1864, he was killed and robbed by the bushwhacker Gatewood and his gang. His wife, Amanda Disharoon (b. March 1835) had recently given birth to twin sons - the above William and George (who later lived at Plumerville). Amanda Disharoon was the daughter of William and Elizabeth Downey Disharoon of Walker County, GA. All of her family came to Arkansas and into Texas.

Frank Johnson married Caldonia "Callie" Edith Fox at Flag, Stone County, AR in 1909. Callie (b. March 2, 1890, at Flag) was the daughter of Martha Ann Ramsey (b. June 6, 1866, d. Nov. 20, 1932) and William M. Fox (b. March 15, 1863, d. April 9, 1940). Martha was the daughter of Bradford Ramsey and very proud of her Ramsey family. Her father was an officer in the Union Army. Callie died of cancer at England, AR on Sept. 27, 1965 and was laid to rest beside Frank in the Mulberry Cemetery near England, AR. Frank was a teamster and worked in the woods until the forest were depleted in the Ozarks, then, he moved his family to Conway County with several other related families.

Frank and Callie Johnson had the following children:

1) Girtha Jewel (b. June 29, 1910 in Searcy County, killed Oct. 8, 1948 in Jefferson County). Her first marriage was at Hill Creek on Nov. 28, 1928 to John Wesley Maupin.

2) Lela Delphia (b. April 26, 1912, Searcy County, d. Dec. 9, 1965 in Lonoke County) md. Henry Houston McElroy on Oct. 26 1935 at Hill Creek, Conway County.

3) Veva Dorothy (b. April 26, 1912) was Lela's twin. She died on June 11, 1989. On Dec. 8, 1928 she married William Thurman Robinson and they lived most of their lives in Morrilton. Both are buried in the Scroggins Cemetery.

4) Bervie Lois (b. Feb. 7, 1915 in Searcy County) md. Ellis Martin of Robertstown, Conway County on Dec. 9, 1930. They eloped to his uncle's home at Keo in Lonoke County.

5) Francis Edith (b. June 26, 1919 at Hill Creek, Conway County) md. Andy McElroy on Dec. 3, 1934 at Morrilton.

6) William Troy Johnson (b. April 11, 1922 at Cedar Creek, Conway County) was the only son. On Aug. 6, 1925 at England, AR, he married Lena Lucille Tucker, the daughter of Rotton and Hattie Rhoads Tucker, also of Conway County.

7) Martha Lucille Johnson (b. Jan. 24, 1925 at Cedar Creek, Conway County, d. July 18, 1995, Cabot, AR) married first, Otis Theoda Reed of Humnoke, AR.

8) Louise Johnson was the last child of Frank and Callie. She died young and may be the child buried in the old Antioch Cemetery off Highway 95 in Conway County.

Frank was crippled by rheumatoid arthritis and by 1938 he was unable to work. He was in pain much of his life and unhappy that he had to be supported by his children. All of them loved him dearly. *Submitted by John Curtis Maupin.*

JOHNSON – George W. Johnson (b. May 1864 in Walker County, GA) was the twin of John Johnson and the son of James Main and Amanda Disheroon Johnson. His father was killed July 24, 1864 by bushwhackers while he was home on leave to see the new twin sons. He came to Searcy County, AR, with his mother and her family in 1870/71. When they first arrived, they lived with his older brother Joseph on Bear Creek. George married Dec. 11, 1884 to Mary Jane Kuykendall, the daughter of Francis and Elizabeth Thompson Kuykendall. She was born in October 1850 in Georgia. George and Mary Jane are buried at Mt. Pleasant Cemetery, near Plumerville, Conway County, AR. On the 1920 census for Conway County, they are living in the town of Plumerville as roomers in the home of G. Dodson.

George and Mary Jane had five children:

1) George Orvel Johnson (b. February 1886 in Searcy County) md. Dona Ellen Baugus (b. 1886/88) on July 9, 1905. Marriage certificate shows her age as 17 and George as 19. George Orvel and Dona moved to Pacific Beach, CA and are thought to have died there. Their known children are Elmer B. Johnson (b. 1907); Jewel M. Johnson (b. Jan. 12, 1909, d. Dec. 4, 1910, buried in the Kuykendall Cemetery by her great-grandparents); Emery Johnson – no information; Gladys Johnson – no information; Lois Johnson – no information; May Johnson – no information; Fay Johnson (twin).

2) Frank Oscar Johnson (b. March 1888) md. Clara A. Baugus/Baugis (b. ca. 1890), the sister of George Orvel's wife (?). They had several children, but not all names are known: Mary M. (b. 1908), Jessie C. and Dessie (b. 1920). Only Jessie is listed on census. They also moved to California and we have no more information.

3) George Volmie Johnson (b. May 1890 in Searcy County) at the age of 24 on May 2, 1915, at Plumerville, Conway County, he married Emmer Huie (b. 1898). They had several children, but only their son Huie is known. Volmie and Emmer lived at Bald Knob and at McCroy (1930). They are buried in Mt. Pleasant Cemetery near Plumerville, Conway County.

4) Seaborn A. Johnson (b. June 2, 1893, d. June 25, 1930) md. Azzie A. Price (b. Dec. 31, 1896, the daughter of William Russell Price (b. March 11, 1861, d. April 9, 1936) and Irene Bell Price (b. Oct. 12, 1871, d. Oct. 9, 1961). Azzie remarried, but when she died on Oct. 31, 1971, she was buried by Seaborn and share a large stone at Mt. Pleasant Cemetery. Seaborn and Azzie had following children:

a) Fred C. Johnson (b. ca. 1916, killed in action Oct. 8, 1944 in France during WWII) never married. He is buried in Mt. Pleasant Cemetery near his parents, Seaborn and Azzie.

b) Chester Clemon Johnson (b. July 16, 1917 in Conway County) md. Mary R. Whitaker on Jan. 6, 1945, at Springfield, AR. Mary listed her age as 16 and of Springfield. Chester died March 18, 1985 and was buried at Mt. Pleasant Cemetery. Mary lives at Plumerville. They had four daughters: Jane Johnson (b. Feb. 5, 1946) md. Joe Gillam; Patsy Johnson (b. March 25, 1948) md. Martin Richardson; Joyce Johnson (b. June 24, 1953) md. David Garrett; Pam Johnson (b. Sept. 5, 1956) md. Jerl Cato.

c) Pauline Opal Johnson (b. Oct. 16, 1918) was killed about June 19, 1920. Her parents were visiting at the home of Matt Harness of Cypress Creek, Springfield, AR when a rifle was accidentally discharged. Pauline was in her father's lap and the bullet first hit the father then killed his baby girl. There is a marker at Mt. Pleasant for her.

d) George Russell Johnson (b. ca. 1920) was married and living in Ontario, CA. No other information known.

e) Lorene Annalee Johnson (b. July 17, 1922, d. Aug. 28, 1993), while living at Springfield, AR, married on Oct. 11, 1941 to William "Bill" E. Holliman (b. Aug. 29, 1906), also of Springfield. They moved to Lake Village, AR and were the parents of 10 children, with five reaching maturity. Bill died June 26, 1988 and they are both buried at Mt. Pleasant Cemetery.

f) William "Bill" D. Johnson (b. April 22, 1924 in Springfield, Conway County, AR, d. Aug. 15, 1996)

was a veteran of WWII and a member of the Oak Grove Free Will Baptist Church at Lake Village, AR. Bill never married. He was buried at Mt. Pleasant with his other family.

g) Woodrow A. "Woody" Johnson (b. Sept. 12, 1926, d. Nov. 11, 1976) is buried at the foot of his mother's grave at Mt. Pleasant.

h) Mary Bell Johnson (b. Sept. 22 1928 at Springfield, Conway County, AR) md. Elmer Holiman, the son of her sister Lorene's husband. She died May 31, 1997(?) at her home in Lake Village, AR. She was a member of the First Free Will Baptist Church of Lake Village. She was buried at Mt. Pleasant Cemetery. Other than her husband, her survivors were Ronnie Holiman of West Warwick, RI; J.M. Holiman of Sheridan, AR; Glenn Holiman of Lake Village, AR; Anthony Holiman of Eudora, AR; and daughters: Anne Garrett, Wanda Aaron and Sandy Schuk, all of Lake Village, AR.

i) May Johnson (b. May 12, 1931) md. Buddy Ireland and had two daughters. She married second, Bill Brown with no issue. May lived at Lake Village and Harrisburg, AR.

After the death of Seaborn, Azzie married G.W. Hines on May 29, 1942. They were divorced and she married a Mr. Browning and had a son, James Browning of Morrilton.

5) Oma Johnson was the last child born to George W. and Mary Jane Kuykendall Johnson. It is believed that she also married a Baugus and went to California.

This concludes the known information of the George W. Johnson line. Family photographs show that he and his wife Mary Jane inherited the family affliction of rheumatoid arthritis, as their left arms and hands are shown drawn and crippled, the same as his older brother William and Martha Kuykendall (his wife) Johnson. Note: George and William Johnson married sisters. *Submitted by John Maupin.*

JONES - The Jones family originated in Wales. Jones was at one time the most common surname in Wales. The name Jones means "son of John." The Jones family immigrated to America prior to 1613. Dockery Berry Giddens Jones (b. March 27, 1849 in Georgia) may have been the son of Thomas F. and Martha Jones, both born in Alabama. (Berry named his first son Thomas.) Berry migrated to Arkansas prior to 1871 and settled near Mountain View, in Izard (now Stone) County. He married Julia Ann "Julie" Hess on July 6, 1871, probably near Mountain View. Julie (b. Nov. 7, 1853 in Independence County, AR) was the daughter of Hiram and Sarah Hess.

Berry and Julie settled near Mountain View where their two children were born. Berry was a farmer and sometimes called "Saddler" Jones, which probably meant he worked with leather, making and repairing saddles, harness and other items. Julie died at Mountain View on March 8, 1876, probably in childbirth. She was only 23 when she died. Berry was left to care for a daughter less than 2 years old and a son little more than 3.

On Oct. 25, 1876, a little more than six months after the death of his wife, Berry Jones married Sarah Jane Edwards at Mount Vernon in Faulkner County, AR. Sarah (b. Nov. 27, 1854 in Arkansas) was the daughter of Mrs. Mary A. Edwards. Several children were born to Berry and Sarah, but only five lived beyond a few days of age. Sarah died about 1886 and Berry soon married his third wife, Sarah's sister, Samantha Paralee Edwards (b. April 10, 1858 in Arkansas). Between 1893 and 1900 Berry moved his family to Formosa in Culpepper Township of Van Buren County, AR. Sometime after 1913, Berry and Paralee moved to near Bee Branch, in Van Buren County. Paralee died Feb. 29, 1936 and Berry died eight months later on Oct. 23, 1936. They are buried in the Bee Branch Cemetery.

Children of Berry Jones and Julie Hess:

1) James Thomas Edward Jones (b. Sept. 7, 1872, d. Aug. 8, 1938) md. Myra I. Langston. Children: Troy,

B.F., Lulia, Claude, Eula, Bulah, Bertha, Benjamin and Avalee Jones.

2) Eliza Julia Jones (b. June 20, 1874, d. Feb. 24, 1913) md. Dora Bannon McClure. Children: Julia (md. Major Jordon, then Ed Hall), Georgia (md. Jimmy Drake), Harmon, Charles William, Nellie, Luther and Susie (md. Elmer Smith).

Children of Berry Jones and Sarah Edwards:

3) George Giddens Jones (b. November 1877, d. Nov. 22, 1878).

4) Paralee S. Jones (b. 1878).

5) Mattie Izora Jones (b. 1880) md. Jasper Hardin. No children.

6) Nora Maria Jones (b. 1882) md. Joe Jones, then Ben Ray. Children: Malford, Josie and Bertha Jones.

7) Page Cleveland Jones (b. 1885, d. Aug. 18, 1886).

Children of Berry Jones and Paralee Edwards:

8) Rosa Virginia Jones (b. Aug. 30, 1888, d. March 27, 1962) md. Charlie Lay. Children: Ralph Jones and Irene Lay.

9) Charles Leonard Jones (b. Oct. 16, 1892, d. July 11, 1979) md. Lucille. Children: Clyde and Merle Jones.

JONES - Edwin A. and Norma Jean Burris Jones came to Morrilton in 1958 with their two young daughters, Carol Jean (b. 1951) and Eddie Ann (b. 1955). Edwin Jones was born at Ola, AR, to Nymph and Grace Marie Mason Jones in 1925. Jean Jones was born in Russellville to Lewis and Beulah Anderson Burris in 1929. Both Edwin and Jean Jones have roots in Conway County, going back to their grandparents and great-grandparents. Edwin's paternal grandmother, Adeline (Addie) Nelson Jones (b. 1881, d. 1972) remembered burying her infant daughter at a cemetery "north of Morrilton" in the early 1900s. That grave has been lost, as Addie remembered only that a "cedar plank" marked the grave.

Addie's husband John (b. 1875, d. 1916) and her father-in-law, David (b. 1844, d. 1916), were originally from Leslie and operated a jewelry business in Morrilton for a while (dates and name of the jewelry store are unknown) before opening a store and watch repair at Ola. Both David and John Jones, Edwin Jones' paternal grandfather and great-grandfather, died in a flu epidemic in January 1916 at Ola, two days apart, leaving Addie and Edwin's father, who was 16 at the time. Edwin's maternal grandparents were Delia Middleton Mason and John Mason who lived at Casa. It is believed that Delia's father, Dr. Middleton, practiced medicine in Conway County.

Jean Burris Jones' paternal grandparents were Ernest Burris and Ida McCauley Burris of Russellville, and they, too, had roots in Conway County. Ida McCauley Burris' Irish parents, Patrick McCauley (d. Oct. 26, 1896) and Mary "Mimi" Gillette McCauley were buried at the cemetery on Elmwood Highway 287. Mimi Gillette McCauley was laid to rest in the Mausoleum. Jean Jones' great-grandfather, George W. Burris and his wife, Mary Mathilda Whorton Burris, are buried at St. Joe, north of Atkins, on land they gave for the church building and cemetery there. Jean Jones' maternal grandparents were John Robert and Mary Epps Anderson of Russellville, who are buried at East Point Cemetery in Pope County.

Edwin has one brother, John Jones of North Little Rock. Jean has one half-sister, Mary Neal Noah, of Russellville. Jean's half-brother, Robert Andrew Neal, passed away in 1996.

The Jones family came to Morrilton to operate Tri County Gas, which was then located across from Burris Grocery on St. Joseph Street. Burris Grocery (now John's Grocery) was owned and operated by Jean's great uncle, Ott Burris, and his wife, Gertrude.

Carol Jean Jones Burt is married to Raymond Burt and resides at Morrilton. She has two daughters, Melanie Dawn Wirges Covey of Sarasota, FL, and April Marie Howell of Arkadelphia. Carol has two grandsons, Ian Patrick Covey and Ethan Edwin Howell, and two stepchildren, Alexandra and Nicholas Burt of Sarasota.

Eddie Ann Jones Dixon is married to Don Dixon, the son of Von and Ruby Lee Stell Dixon, and resides in Morrilton. Don and Eddie have three children: their daughter Whitney LaDon Dixon, and Don's children, Kimberly Jane Dixon and Doug Brandon Dixon.

Edwin and Jean Jones live on Lee Drive, where they raised their daughters and are members of Calvary Baptist Church, where they have been members since 1958. *Submitted by Carol Jones Burt.*

JONES - Katie Lou Vinson was born Sept. 16, 1874 at Aplin in Perry County, AR and died on Nov. 1, 1957

in Conway County, AR at her granddaughter's house at Oppelo. She married John Casual Jones Dec. 22, 1890 in Perry County, AR. John was born on Feb. 25, 1870 in Pontotoc County, MI and died on Feb. 21, 1941 in Ada Valley. John and Katie are both buried in the Ada Valley Cemetery in Conway County, AR. They had four children:

Charlie Caswell Jones

1) Nellie Jones (b. April 15, 1892, d. Sept. 2, 1898 Perry County, AR) is buried in the Harper Cemetery.

2) Lillie Belle Jones (b. Aug. 7, 1894 in Aplin, Perry County, AR, d. Dec. 8, 1945) md. Otto Allison Lawson June 23, 1914 in Perry County, AR. Otto (b. Feb. 18, 1893 in Edge Van Buren, AR, d. June 23, 1952) and Lillie both died in Drumright, OK and are buried in the Oak Hill Cemetery. They had five children.

3) William Thomas Jones (b. Dec. 21, 1896, Perry County, AR, d. July 10, 1973 in Little Rock, AR. He married Vida Wallace on Feb. 4, 1923 in Ada Valley, Conway County, AR. They had three children.

4) Charles Casual Jones (b. Nov. 6, 1900 in Perry County, AR) md. Alta Fudge on Oct. 30, 1945 in Conway County, Morrilton, AR. Charlie and Alta are both buried in the Ada Valley Cemetery. They had no children.

Katie and John were going to the Assembly of God Church in Perry County, Houston, AR between 1900 and 1914. They moved to Ada Valley later, where Charlie ran a grocery store. There was a big potbelly wood stove close to the back of the store. He had a checkerboard on top of a pickle barrel by the stove, and would challenge anyone that came into the store to play with him. He ran the store for many years before retiring. After retiring he moved to Morrilton, AR and later to Perryville, AR. The store was torn down some years later. *Submitted by Bobbie Anderson.*

JONES - Meredith Greenfield "Cotton" Jones was the son of M.H. and Nellie Jones of Helena, AR. "Cotton" married Pearl E. Newkirk on Petit Jean Mountain in 1947. Pearl was the daughter of De Forest and Gladys Newkirk. The Newkirks came to Morrilton in 1929, when the J.C. Penney Store opened. "Cotton" and Pearl taught school at Tillar (Desha County), AR. He as superintendent, she as the physical education teacher. They had two sons, Ralph Newkirk Jones (b. 1948) and Meredith C. Jones (b. 1951), born at St. Anthony's Hospital on Green Street. Cotton was a veteran of WWII and in the Army Reserves. He was recalled to Korea in 1951. He moved his family back to Morrilton to be near Pearl's parents, "the Newkirks"

Upon being honorably discharged with the rank of captain from Korea, Mr. Jones was principal of the Perryville High School. Later, he was the first paid business manager of the Morrilton Chamber of Commerce. He was employed at Mobley Construction as salesman for 17 years. Captain Jones was in the Morrilton National Guard for 22 years. He retired as

lieutenant colonel. Governor Faubus called out the National Guard Headquarters at Morrilton, Headquarters Company 2nd Battalion, 153rd Infantry Division, during the integration of Central High School in Little Rock in 1957. Soon, President Eisenhower sent in Federal Troops.

M.G. Jones family, 1980. Back row, l-r: Meredith Cole Jones Sr., DeForest Newkirk, Sgt. Ralph Jones, Meredith "Cotton" Jones and Cindy Jones. Front, l-r: Cathy (Simpson) Jones, Jared Jones, Cathy (Carroll) Jones, M. Cole Jones Jr., Mrs. Gladys (Burch) Newkirk, Pearl (Newkirk) Jones, Jennifer Jones.

In 1939, Meredith "Cotton" Jones received a scholarship to play football at the University of Arkansas at Fayetteville and was a Razorback letterman. He graduated in 1942, was in *Who's Who in American Colleges and Universities*, member of Kappa Sigma Fraternity, Scabbard and Blade, Blue Key and captain of the ROTC. He later returned to Fayetteville after WWII and received his masters in education in 1947.

Pearl Newkirk graduated from Morrilton High School in 1944. She attended the University of Arkansas and was a member of the Chi Omega Sorority.

The Jones' had a third child, Cynthia "Cindy" (b. 1962). She graduated from Morrilton High School, as did her brothers. She married Warren H. Stobaugh III and they have two children, Chase and Rebecca, attending Morrilton Middle School in 2005.

The M.G. Jones eldest son, Ralph Newkirk Jones, is a retired US Army sergeant. He is a veteran of Vietnam and Granada. He married Cathy Simpson and had two children, Jennifer and Jared, both MHS graduates. Jennifer married Scott Bratton of Pottsville. They had two children, Sidney and Gwendolyn Pearl.

Jared Forest Newkirk Jones married Kim Lum. Both graduated from the University of the Ozarks and are now living in Clarksville.

Meredith Cole Jones and wife, Cathy Carroll, had one son, Cole. Meredith and Cathy graduated from MHS, then Meredith graduated from Arkansas Tech University in Russellville. Cathy was a nurse for Dr. Thomas Buchanan. They moved to Plano, TX. Cole graduated from Plano High School and San Marcos University, TX. Meredith is employed with Hunt Oil in Dallas, TX.

Pearl was widowed in 1985. She has taught in the Morrilton school system. She was employed at the Conway County Hospital in 1974, retiring in 1986. She was a free lance artist and taught art classes. She lives in the oldest brick home in Morrilton. Four generations of the Jones family have lived there. She is a member of the G.F.W.C. Adelaide Club of Morrilton, Daughters of the American Revolution - General William Lewis Chapter, Petit Jean Garden Club, G.F.G.C., an original member of the Conway County Arts Council, Depot Museum Board, past president of the Senior Adult Center and was a Mid-South Water Colorist. She was a Girl Scout Leader, Cub Scout Den Mother and active in PTA. She has been a member of the First United Methodist Church of Morrilton for over 70 years. *Submitted by Mrs. M.G. (Pearl Newkirk) Jones.*

JORDAN – George Samuel Jordan "Sam" (b. Dec. 21, 1887 in Springfield, AR) was the third child and

first son of Jessie Price and Amanda Mallett Jordan. He was the grandson of Henrietta Casharago and George Washington Mallett, and Sarah Reed and Samuel H. Jordan.

Sam left Arkansas as a young man to help construct the Galveston Seawall after the 1900 storm that killed over 6,000 people. There he met and married Wilhelmina Marie Eddleman of Fort Worth,

Wilhelmina Marie Eddleman and George Samuel Jordan

TX on Feb. 26, 1913 in Texas City, TX. Sam died on Feb. 17, 1929 and Marie died Feb. 2, 1945; they are buried side by side in the Galveston Memorial Park Cemetery at Hitchcock, TX.

To this union four children were born: Mary Amanda Jordan Gace (b. Dec. 27, 1914, d. May 12, 1998); Anna Mae Christine Jordan Mattern (b. Dec. 23, 1916, d. Aug. 17, 1998); Sammie Maude Jordan Ivy DeCoito (b. June 23, 1918, d. Oct. 27, 1968); and George Samuel Jordan Jr. (b. April 12, 1926, d. May 11, 1999). Mary, Christine, and Sammie were all born in Texas City, TX, and George Jr. was born in Galveston, TX.

Mary Amanda married Gaza Gace (b. Aug. 6, 1906, d. Aug. 24, 1985) and to this union four children were born: Gaza Samuel (b. March 6, 1933); George David (b. Sept. 11, 1934); Mary Amanda Gace Lemire (b. Sept. 21, 1935) and Elizabeth Jane Gace Bliss (b. Dec. 26, 1942).

Anna Mae Christine married Buryl Benton Mattern (b. Aug. 10, 1908, d. Dec. 29, 1979) and to this union four children were born: Anna Mae Mattern (b. July 23, 1938); Buryl Benton Mattern Jr. (b. Sept. 21, 1935, d. Dec. 13, 1999); Patricia Ann Mattern (b. Dec. 15, 1947, d. Dec. 15, 1987); and Darrlyn Mattern (b. March 6, 1971).

Sammie Maude married first to James William Ivy (b. June 6, 1915, d. April 3, 1980) and to this union two children were born, Ethel Marie Ivy Fiesel (b. Dec. 8, 1937) and Betty Estella Ivy Donaldson (b. Oct. 7, 1941). Sammie married the second time to Joe DeCoito.

George Samuel Jr. married Virginia Ferrell Meador (b. Sept. 12, 1923) and to this union four children were born: Gloria Jean Jordan (b. Nov. 16, 1948); Barbara Ann (b. Sept. 15, 1950); George Samuel Jordan III (b. Aug. 17, 1952) and Linda Carol (b. March 13, 1956). *Submitted by Jane Bliss and Mary Lemire.*

KAUFMAN — Henry Kaufman (b. April 23, 1874) was the son of Henry Frank Kaufman (b. Dec. 6, 1838, d. March 17, 1904) and Maria Theis Kaufman (b. 1845, d. April 25, 1889) who came from Westphalia, Germany in 1880 to settle in St. Vincent. On April 30, 1900, he married Bertha Basler (b. Aug. 24, 1877) who had come to St. Vincent with her parents, Florian and Louise Ilgner Basler, from Schon Walde, Silesia, Germany, also in 1880.

F.H. "Henry" Kaufman and Bertha Basler Kaufman.

Together Henry and Bertha had 10 children who lived to adulthood: Fred, Ben, Carl, Clemens, Louis,

Herman, Florian, Elizabeth, Marie and Leo. Henry farmed and was a cattle buyer. Once the cattle were bought, they had to be driven overland on horseback to Morrilton to market. In 1927, he purchased the general store, which he owned and operated until 1968, and which is still a local landmark. Kaufman Lane in St. Vincent is named because of the family home place and store. The family was instrumental in bringing telephone service to St. Vincent by running the first phone line there from Morrilton. They were all very active in agriculture, and the younger children participated in 4-H. Bertha was very involved in programs through the Extension Service, including the raising of large numbers of capons for market. The family was also among the first to implement new government programs for diversified farming and conservation practices. During WWII, four sons (Ben, Herman, Florian and Leo) served in the armed forces at the same time, while three sons (Carl, Clemens and Louis) were deferred from service because of the need for farm products.

Fred (b. 1901, d. 1962) md. Rose Beck and they had two children. Fred was engaged in farming in St. Vincent.

Ben (b. 1904, d. 1980) was an International Harvester dealer in Morrilton until 1971. He lived in St. Vincent and raised cattle.

Carl (b. 1906, d. 1963) was engaged in farming at St. Vincent and later moved to McGehee, where he also farmed.

Clemens (b. 1909, d. 1983) md. Teresa Hoelzeman and they had four children. He was a farmer at McGehee before retiring to Springdale.

Louis (b. 1911, d. 1992) md. Louise Ehemann and they had five children. Louis was a farmer and rancher at the homestead in St. Vincent.

Herman (b. 1913, d. 1997) md. Margaret Rippengal and they had two sons. He lived in Hattieville and was engaged in ranching and real estate.

Florian (b. 1915, d. 1976) was a farmer in St. Vincent and later moved to Arizona where he was a chef at Mohave Resort.

Elizabeth (b. 1918) md. Henry Thines and together they owned and operated the Thines Food Market in Downtown Morrilton.

Marie (b. 1920) md. Robert Highter and they had six children. They lived in Vermont, where they owned a dairy farm and later a bed and breakfast.

Leo (b. 1923) md. Elizabeth Gottsponer and they had six children. Leo lived in Haley, where he farmed and was employed by the US Post Office. He is now retired and living in Russellville.

Henry died Feb. 22, 1969; Bertha preceded him in death on Jan. 31, 1951.

KAUFMAN — Louis Kaufman was born on Oct. 2, 1911 to Frank Henry Kaufman and Bertha Basler Kaufman in St. Vincent, AR. Both of his parents came from Germany at an early age. His father, Henry, ran the local "Kaufman Grocery Store" in St. Vincent with his brother Frank.

Louis married Louise Ehemann from Atkins, AR on April 28, 1952 in Atkins. Her parents were Mike Ehemann from Mansfield, OH, and Maggie Klar from Zell, Germany. Louis and Louise had five children: Dale, Gary, Mary Beth, Brenda and Sheila.

Dale (b. March 29, 1953) md. Sharon Hudson from Stamps and they had four children: Kendra, Amy, Kristen and Brandon. Dale and his wife, Jeana Spradley, are both veterinarians in Russellville, AR.

Gary (b. Sept. 11, 1955) farms the home place in St. Vincent, raising turkeys and beef cattle. He has four children: Jason, Brittany, Amber and Emily. They were chosen as the Conway County Farm Family of the Year in 1994.

Mary Beth (b. May 7, 1957) md. Raymond Gunther from New Dixie. They have two sons, Travis and Tyler. Mary Beth was a CPA in Little Rock and now volunteers at St. Joseph's School in Conway.

Brenda (b. Oct. 10, 1959) md. Jay Pinkston from Bryant and they have two sons, Drew and Matthew. Brenda is in management at Aimco Equipment Company in Little Rock.

Sheila (b. Nov. 5, 1960) md. Bill Kerst from DeQueen and they have four sons: Ryan, Adam, Jeffrey and Brad. Sheila taught first grade in Clarksville before moving to Hot Springs, and is now very active in Boy Scouts and works as a bookkeeper for 1st Community Trust Co.

Louis and Lou operated a turkey and cattle ranch and farmed rice and soybeans in St. Vincent and the Hattieville area. The farm kept everyone busy, not just their children but lots of teenagers in the area grew up working there. Louis and Lou won Conway County Farm Family of the Year in 1973 and Arkansas Turkey Producer of the Year in 1975. Louis died Oct. 30, 1992. Louise resides on the family farm in St. Vincent. *Submitted by Sherry Kaufman.*

KEARNEY - William Kearney, son of Patrick and Sophia Apjohn Kearney, was born in Ireland in 1847. He immigrated with his family to New York from Ireland, by way of Liverpool, arriving aboard the S.S. *Cornelia* on Oct. 11, 1849, at the age of 3. His family moved to Cincinnati, Hamilton County, OH, where he grew to adulthood prior to moving with his family to Waynesville, OH around 1866.

William Kearney

Sometime before October 1871 he moved to Morrilton, AR and on Oct. 10, 1871 was appointed by Conway County Clerk D.H. Thomas (placed in office following the removal of Clerk W.R. Hinkle by State Senate impeachment), as the legal and lawful deputy clerk (AHC Microfilm: Conway County Roll 21, Conway County Court Records, Book "G", page 430, 1868-1872). The following year Kearney was elected to the office of Conway County Clerk in which he served 1872-74.

He was said to be cheerful, genial, witty and an individual of many talents. Following his tenure in public office he was co-owner with Sam T. Watson, and served as editor and publisher of a weekly Lewisburg newspaper, *The Western Enterprise*, until May 1874 when Eugene B. Henry became editor and proprietor, but discontinued the publication a month later. He also worked as a bookkeeper. On Tuesday morning, Jan. 23, 1880 at 5 o'clock, Billy Kearney died from pneumonia at the Lewisburg home of his brother-in-law and sister, Mr. and Mrs. William Pitt Egan. He had taken ill on the previous Thursday and died after an illness of five days in duration. The attending physician was Dr. Adams.

William Kearney, who never married, is buried in an unmarked grave in the Lewisburg Cemetery. *Submitted by Dr. Buford Suffridge.*

KEMP - Albert Kemp was born in Alabama in January 1844. The 1880 Federal Census shows him as a 36-year-old farmer who could not read nor write. Both of his parents were listed as having been born in Virginia. He married Charlotte Logan/Wolf in Cold Water, MS. In 1880 they had seven children in the home. Six of these children were Albert and Charlotte's children. The seventh child was listed as Albert's stepson Mike. Charlotte was born in Cold Water, Tate County,

Parthenia Kemp McDaniel

MS on April 26, 1846. She could not read nor write. Charlotte's parents were listed as having been born in Virginia.

Children of Albert and Charlotte: Mike (b. 1867, Mississippi); Delia Kemp-Hail (b. 1870, Mississippi, d. 1954, Plumerville, AR); William Kemp (b. 1872, Mississippi); Ledger/Robert Walter (Major) Kemp (b. 1874, Mississippi); Washington Kemp (b. 1875, Mississippi); Annie Kemp (b. 1877, Mississippi, d. 1904, Plumerville, AR); John W. Kemp (b. 1880, Plumerville, AR); General Kemp; Dink Kemp (b. 1884, Plumerville); Parthenia (Mamagrand) Kemp-McDaniel (b. 1885, Plumerville, d. 1963, Plumerville).

After the 1880 Census, I have been unable to trace William, Ledger and Washington Kemp.

In the 1900 Census, Albert is 56 years old and has been married to Charlotte for 38 years. They are living in Welborn Township, Conway County, AR. Annie is still in the home of Albert and she is 21 years old. Dink, aged 16, is in the home, as well as Parthenia, age 15. Others in the home are two grandsons of Albert, believed to be the sons of Delia. They are Moses (b. January 1885) and John (b. 1889).

The 1910 Federal Census shows Albert as 69 years old and Charlotte as 64. They have been married for 48 years. Annie is now deceased. In the home are Albert's grandchildren, Jessie (age 8) and Marsetra (age 11). These are believed to be Annie's children. Robert Walter (Major) is 37 and married to Redy Ann. They have five children. General is living in Fort Smith, Sebastian County, AR. Dink is living in Little Rock, Pulaski County, AR.

KEMP - In 1891 Louis Kemp and Martha Knox Kemp came from Georgia to Morris Mountain. The name was later changed to Friendship Mountain. Louis was a white man whose family was named Camp. He was disowned by his father and his father's parents because he was born to a Cherokee Indian woman. He married a black woman (Martha Knox). His name was changed to Kemp and he and his wife came to Morris Mountain located 3-1/2 miles east of Center Ridge, AR. His family lived in Conway, Morrilton and Plumerville, AR and they owned stores in Plumerville and Conway for many, many years. Louis continued to stay in contact with his family and he would travel to Conway and Plumerville by wagon and they would give him goods from the stores that they owned. No other family contact was had between Louis and his family. His children never had any contact with their father's side of the family.

Louis and Martha Knox Kemp

Louis and Martha had three children: Wade, Elizabeth and Dewey.

Wade married Birdie and moved to Solmon Grove Community and they had five children: Louis, Mimie, Earl, Annabel and Elizabeth II.

Elizabeth married Will Dooley and they had seven children: Martha, Holcy, Georgia, Mary, Velva, Orlean and Effie Mae.

Dewey married Miley Dooley and they had two children, Ruth and Ray.

Louis and Martha were very industrious people, they helped in establishing the Friendship Baptist Church in 1891. The church was built out of logs and all the men of the community helped to build the church. They also helped each other to build their log huts to live in. He was a farmer and Martha was a homemaker and helped on the farm. They owned horses, cows, hogs and chickens. They worked hard to raise their family. They instilled in them Christian principles. Louis and Martha were very generous people. He would go to Conway, Morrilton and Plumerville and get large sacks of flour, meal, sugar and other grocery staples and share with others in the community that were in need. They raised all their vegetables, meats, sorghum, eggs and milk. Martha canned and preserved much food for the winter. *Submitted by Johnny Jones.*

KENDRICK – James M. Kendrick and Jane Gideon lived in Pope County and she is buried on Crow Mountain. James (b. 1832, d. May 17, 1863) died under curious circumstances. According to a granddaughter, Delphia Verlon Kendrick Bowden he was taken during the Civil War and never returned. She thought he might be buried in the Lewisburg Cemetery but cemetery records do not so reflect.

Their children were Melissa P. Kendrick Brance (Jackson), Pernica A., Margaret J. Kendrick McNulty, Susan M. Kendrick and grandfather to Mary K. Williams (spouse of the author), William Francis (Nancy Ann Harris).

William was born Oct. 24, 1842 and died July 30, 1925 in Ada Valley where he is buried. Nancy Ann (b. May 25, 1857, d. Sept. 2, 1934) is buried in the Bowden Cemetery, Crow Mountain, Pope County. William was the pastor of the Ada Valley church when it was part of the Methodist organization.

Their children include Richard W. (b. April 1, 1875, d. June 1, 1930) (Martha Ellen Morphis); Rosa Florence Kendrick Bowden Wiliker (b. April 16, 1879, d. March 24, 1948) (Herman); Lillie A. Kendrick Jobe (b. Dec. 5, 1883, d. May 4, 1924) (John K "Doc"); Victoria Kendrick Parrish Morgan (b. April 20, 1885, d. Dec. 28, 1951) (Monroe Parrish); George Henry (b. June 12, 1887, d. Aug. 19, 1953) (Carrie Young, Lee Warren, Helen, and, perhaps, others); Delphis Verlon Kendrick Bowden (b. Dec. 23, 1889, d. March 4, 1978) (Alonso Jackson Bowden); Claud Olen (b. Feb. 14, 1892, d. March 11, 1960) (Jestin Harris, Rosetta Warren Cowan, Minnie Bell Rinehart Grice Mash, Lily Pope Yarbrough and another Minnie); Ira V. (b. April 14, 1899, d. June 12, 1967) (Maud Artie Williams (sister-in-law of Mary Pearl) and Mary Pearl Kendrick Williams (b. Nov. 26, 1894, d. Dec. 23 1974) (Lamar). Many are buried in Ada Valley.

Lamar Williams, well known in Ada Valley, moved late in life to a house in Morrilton.

Children of Lamar and Pearl include Cleotha Elizabeth Williams Hallman (Dibbrell) of Rock Falls IL; Junior Irvin who died as a logger in Port Orford, OR and is buried in Ada Valley; Raymond E. Sr. (Rose Ciccarelli) lives in Seaford, DE as does Mary K. Williams (Archie Dalton); Evelyn Imajean Williams Himmelberg (Gilbert) lives in Vienna, VA near Cleva Glentaline (Robert Williams) in Arlington, VA. Other children died young. All were raised in Ada Valley and graduated from area schools.

KENDRICK - The Kendrick family of Ada Valley began with William Francis and Nancy Ann Harris. Nancy Ann was the daughter of David Harris and Charlotte Morphis. William was the son of Jane

Gideon and James M. Kendrick. James never returned from the War Between the States and is believed to be buried in the Lewisburg Cemetery.

William was born in Tennessee per birth certificate. William is buried in the Ada Valley cemetery and Nancy Ann is buried in the Bowden Cemetery on Crow Mountain, Pope County.

Their children were Richard W. (md. Martha Morphis); Rosa (md. first to William Bowden, then to Herman Wiliker); Lithe (md. John Jobe); Victoria (md. Monroe Parrish then Ranzel Morgan); George Henry (md. Lee Warren then Carrie Young then Helen); Delphia Verlon (md. Alonzo Bowden); Claude Olen (md. Justine Harris, Rosetta Warren, Minnie Bell Rinehart, Lillie Yarbrough, et al); Pearl (md. Lamar Williams); Ira Victor (md. Maude Artie Williams then Ora).

Old Bill moved from Pope County where he preached at Crow Mountain and at Gumlog (Double Springs) to become pastor at what was then the Methodist Church in Ada Valley. He was apparently a "Supply" pastor, not recognized in Methodist annals.

Many descendants of this pair are well known and several still reside in Ada Valley, at least one of whom (Alfretta) is still prominent in the now Ada Valley Community Church.

KENNAMER - John S. Kennamer (b. 1846, Madison County, AL) lived in Kennamer Cove until he moved his family to Springfield, Conway County, AR in 1871. His son Jacob Presley Kennamer (b. April 11, 1851 in Marshall County, AL) moved there with him at the age of 20.

Jacob Presley Kennamer with wife, Nicy Powell Kennamer, about 1920, Springfield, AR.

Jacob Presley Kennamer married Eunice "Nicy" Sarah Letha Mary Elizabeth Powell (b. June 8, 1855 in Mississippi) on Dec. 23, 1874. Nicy's father, William H. Powell and his wife Margaret moved to Conway County, AR about 1876. Oral family history has been that the Powells had a large plantation before the Civil War in Mississippi and were very wealthy. My great-grandmother had been to finishing school and passed what she learned along to her daughters. The Union soldiers burned their entire plantation to the ground and the Powells lost everything. Arkansas was a fresh start for several family members.

All the children born to the union of Jacob and Nicy were born in Springfield, Conway County, AR:

1) Nancy Ollie Kennamer (b. Oct. 14, 1875, d. Dec. 31, 1925) md. William Lewis Mallett. Their daughter Ethel Ollie married Charles Cathcart, their daughter Daucie married John Virgil White. Both couples moved to Carrizo Springs, TX with Maude and Ave White and Maude's brother Frank Kennamer and family.

2) Rachel Margaret (b. Jan. 30, 1877, d. Sept. 18, 1915) and her husband, George Jordan, lived in Ripley, Payne County, OK. Great Aunt Rachel came to Carrizo Springs, TX for their mother, my great-grandmother Kennamer, when my grandmother was stricken with tuberculosis. It was a very hard time - my grandmother and her mother had never been separated, and very sadly Great Grandmother Kennamer died during that time of separation on March 9, 1937. My great-grandfather had passed away in Springfield,

AR Dec. 23, 1920. She is buried in Ripley, Payne County, OK. Grandma White overcame TB and thankfully, experienced a good return to health.

3) Zachary "Zack" Taylor (b. Sept. 4, 1879, d. Sept. 1, 1962).

4) John William "Will" (b. Jan. 23, 1881, d. Jan. 18, 1961).

5) James Franklin "Frank" (b. Sept. 3, 1885, d. April 1932).

6) My grandmother Maude Alzonia (b. Sept. 22, 1890 in Springfield, Conway County, AR) md. William Avery "Ave" White, Sept. 10, 1916 in Springfield, Conway County, AR.

My grandfather was a farmer and a carpenter. They belonged to and were active members in good standing with the Baptist Church. My grandmother devoted her life to her family and her church. She was a Sunday school teacher, choir director, and played the piano or organ for Church services. Grandmother was also a professional music teacher and very skilled with sewing. She was able to duplicate clothes from pictures or a store display. She had the ability of a young woman taught the sewing skills of a refined young lady—such as embroidery, crocheting and tatting. She was able to make the finest lace. She died Oct. 13, 1966 after a long, full life in El Paso, El Paso County, TX, beloved by and surrounded by her family. She was survived by three of her children, 10 grandchildren and six great-grandchildren.

My maternal grandfather William Avery "Ave" White (b. Dec. 27, 1879 in Haysville, Clay County, NC) first appears in the 1900 Conway County, AR, Union Township census living with his uncle John F. Norwood. His mother, Nancy Melissa Norwood, had died sometime after the 1880 Clay County, NC, Hayesville Township census, where she is shown living with her husband James R. White and two sons, James A. (age 1) and William A. (age 6-1/2).

His children and grandchildren, very fondly called him "Papa." He loved people and never met a stranger. When we grandchildren were around, he would spend more time with us than he would the grown-ups. He taught us great and wonderful things, like how to catch crayfish, how to get rid of wasps, how to grow things, and how to make everyday things into something useful. He made each set of his granddaughter's child-sized tables, chairs, doll cradles, and beauty tables with mirrors. Papa also passed along wisdom he had learned about relationships, his beliefs in God and the Bible. He could sight read music and sing too! He also lived a long, full life and died in El Paso, El Paso County, TX, on Oct. 10, 1970, beloved by and surrounded by his family. Survived by three children, 10 grandchildren, and eight great-grandchildren. *Submitted by Kathryn Elizabeth McElhannon, granddaughter of Maude Kennamer and Ave White and great-granddaughter of Nicy Powell and Jacob Presley Kennamer.*

KING - Oather Ray King and Dorothy Lee Reynolds were married Aug. 26, 1957 in Morrilton. Dr. King (b. April 9, 1925, Ada Valley) graduated from Perry High School and immediately left for the US Navy from 1943-46 without getting a leave home. During high school he worked at Imboden's Corner Drug Store. After his discharge he enrolled in Hendrix College, graduating in 1949. That fall he taught history at Fort Smith High School, the following year assistant principal and dean of boys, then principal of Albert Pike and Rogers Elementary Schools. During this time he completed a MSE from UA Fayetteville.

In 1955 the family moved to Fayetteville so Ray could pursue a D.Ed. in elementary education which he received in 1958. He taught in the College of Education until 1964 when he became full professor and head of the Elementary Education Department at Sam Houston State Teachers College in Huntsville, TX. He retired from SHSU in December 1985.

Dorothy (b. June 20, 1928 at Jerusalem), daughter of Elvia Lester and Connie Webb Reynolds, was 8 when the family moved to Morrilton. She graduated from Morrilton High School, Abilene Christian College and University of Arkansas. She worked in insurance agencies in Morrilton and Fort Smith, and taught third grade in Huntsville, TX for 19 years.

Ray and Dot King, Petit Jean Mtn., August 1996.

Upon Oather's retirement they moved to Petit Jean Mountain where they still live. They have been active in the Downtown Church of Christ where he was an elder. He also served on the board of SCH and CRC and active in Kiwanis since 1965. He traveled to Central and South America on medical missions and both to many other countries in the Americas, Asia, Canada and Europe. Hobbies included fishing, hunting, gardening, and collecting barbed wire.

Dot taught Mission classes for children at the Downtown Church of Christ, was a member of Delta Kappa Gamma and River Valley Quilters and collected Coca Cola memorabilia.

Children and grandchildren are Karen and Dr. Sid Womack of Russellville and their children Karah Kristen Hosek and Sarah Ashlee Wilson; Robin Reynolds King and Carol and their children Emily Hallene King and Peter Montgomery King of Bethesda, MD.

KING - William Talmadge King and Hattie Mae Sisson were united in marriage Nov. 4, 1913 in Conway County. They lived in Ada Valley until 1932 when the family moved to Perry.

William Talmadge King (b. Aug. 1, 1892 in Ada Valley) was the son of Talmadge King and Mary Ellen Ellison King. He married Hattie Mae Sisson (b. June 3, 1896, Kentucky), daughter of John Ferdinand Sisson and Mary Lula Caroline Howard Sisson. W.T. and Hattie were the parents of two sets of twins: Connie Mae and Bonnie Rae (b. Sept. 13, 1918) and Odis Fay and Oather Ray (b. April 9, 1925).

Connie Mae married Chester Howard Williams (MO) and have one son, Chester Howard Williams Jr. Bonnie Rae died in December 1918. Odis Fay married Virginia Dare Cragar (Perry, AR) and they have two children, Charlotte Faye (Batchelor) and Kirk Warren King. Oather Ray married Dorothy Lee Reynolds (Morrilton) and they have two children, Karen Kay (Womack) and Robin Reynolds King.

William Talmadge "Willie" had a shoe repair shop in Perry for many years where he repaired saddles, belts, and any kind of leather as well as shoe repair. He later was a boiler operator on the Mississippi River for several years. Hattie was a people person and enjoyed quilting and clubs. After his death, she moved to Park Place Apartments in Morrilton and pieced quilts, played dominoes and enjoyed her neighbors. She was a member of the Downtown church of Christ.

W.T. died June 28, 1968 and Hattie died Jan. 3, 1990. Both are buried in the Ada Valley Cemetery.

KIRKLAND - William F. Kirkland (b. Sept. 3, 1857 in Marshall County, MS) was a merchant of Solgohachia. His parents, Mulkie S. (b. Nov. 3, 1834) and Marinda (Ragsdale) Kirkland, were natives of Alabama, and their children were William F., Calvin C., Lee A. and David O. Mr. Kirkland was a planter by occupation, and for a long time was a minister in the Missionary Baptist Church. He emigrated from Alabama to Mississippi and in 1888 he moved to Conway County. William F. died Aug. 28, 1900 in Plumerville. He was an active member of the Masonic fraternity, was a Royal Arch Mason and held all the principal offices in the lodge. William F. was reared and educated in Marshall County and at the age of 22 began

farming for himself on rented land. He married Geaudemala Shackelford, daughter of John James Thomas Shackelford.

Geaudemala Shackelford

Mala, as she was known, was born in Lamar County, AL. The Shackelford family moved to DeSoto County, MS where Mala met W.F. Kirkland and they married Nov. 29, 1888. In 1889 the family moved to Arkansas and W.F. began merchandising in Solgohachia. William Frankland and Geaudiemala had a son, William Dale, and a daughter, Aethal Glenn. W.F. went blind at about the age of 45. Mala continued to run the family's Five and Dime store many years after William Franklin died. She lived to be 104 years old.

William Franklin, Dale and Glenn were remarkable people because they all went blind very early in life and all were very successful in spite of their handicap.

Dale's failing sight forced him to quit his job as a rural mail carrier by the age of 23. Shortly after, he became totally and permanently blind. He turned to magazine sales to support himself and his wife, sister and mother. He became unusually successful as a salesman, working primarily for Curtis Publishing Co. He traveled by train and bus. His contact in each community would pick him up and take him around to his customers. It is reported in a Morrilton, AR newspaper article that he sold more than two hundred thousand subscriptions and was probably the top salesman in the nation at the time. Even though blind, he became a highly skilled cabinetmaker, raised ponies, and bought and sold land. He specialized in building fine, wooden cases for grandfather clocks, miscellaneous furniture, and many other wood crafted items. He made coffee tables for all of his cousins. Dale left a very large sum of money to the church with the understanding that the interest on the money would be distributed to all of his living relatives until their death.

Glenn graduated from Conway College, taught speech, drama, and music at Fulton High School and at Arkansas State Teacher's College, she also taught an adult Sunday School class at the Plumerville Baptist church for nearly 55 years. She was blind for a substantial portion of that time. *Information provided by William Smith, Terrell Stepp, Ruth Shackelford and Maurice Shackelford. Source: Articles—The Arkansas Baptist Biographical and Historical Memoirs of Arkansas.*

KISSIRE- Ellanda Jane Kissire, daughter of John Kissire and Mary Ann Williams, was born in January 1859 in Center Ridge, Conway County. On Nov. 7, 1875 she married Andrew Jackson "Jack" Williams, son of Aaron Leroy P. Williams and Martha Ann Hill.

Children of Ellanda Jane and Jack Williams were Mary Lugenia (md. Allen Ambers Hill), Martha Ann "Mattie" (md. John E. Kirkland), Margaret Delphinia "Dell" (md. Lark Howard and Needham Ance Flowers), Ollie Pearl (md. Charlie Hill), John Jackson (md. Charity Howard) and Arthur Lee (md. Duffy Hazel Scott).

After the death of Andrew Jackson Williams, Ellanda Jane married Lark Howard on Sept. 28, 1895. Their children were Cassie Emmeline (md. David William "Will" Bostian), Charles McKinley (md. Bessie Brewer) and Gertie (md. Grover Garfield Polk).

Ellanda Jane Kissire Williams is buried in Grandview Cemetery and the death date on her headstone is 1902, but her daughter Gertie was born in 1904 so we don't know the real date of death. *Submitted by Phyllis Maulding Campbell.*

KNIGHTEN - James Edgar Knighten (b. 1885, d. 1919) was the son of Willis Franklin and Mary E. Young. He married Nellie Bradford (b. 1889, d. 1921) in 1906 at Cleveland, AR. Both died and are buried in the Cleveland Cemetery. His brother M.C. married her sister Edith. They were daughters of Nancy Sarah Ann Massey and James Monroe Bradford of Cleveland

Nellie and Ed's first child was Virginia "Virgie" (b. 1907, d. 1986) md. Garland Shepherd and had two daughters. They lived in North Little Rock, AR where both died and are buried. One daughter, Mary V. (md. Ken Brooks), still resides there.

Other children were Anna Mae (md. Ben Francis) born 1909, Emily (md. Zeb Redding), Evelyn (md. Ralph Ring), Ollie Ruth (b. 1914, d. 1915) and James Edgar (b. 1916, d. 1918). The deceased are buried out of state except, Ollie Ruth and James Edgar who are buried in Cleveland Cemetery.

KNIGHTEN - Joseph Franklin Knighten (b. ca. 1810 in South Carolina) md. Ludince Kilpatrick (b. ca. 1820, in Tennessee). Both families emigrated from Ireland. The original spelling of the family name may have been "Knight." Their children were Willis Franklin, Jessie Presley and Thomas. The only information found about Thomas was a birth date of about 1856. Since eight of W.F.'s children were born in Alabama, it is assumed that he moved there with his parents. There is a corner of Alabama that is still referred to as "the Knighten territory." Joseph also married two other wives, Ann in 1860 and Lutensia in 1870.

Jessie P. Knighten was born about 1853 in South Carolina. He died in 1911 and is buried in Morgan County, AL. He married Mary Ann Alvis (b. 1855 in Alabama) on Dec. 24, 1874 in Morgan County, AL.

Willis Franklin Knighten married Mary Elvira Young. He was born July 23, 1848 in Jefferson, AL. Mary was born in Alabama on May 27, 1848, city unknown. Very likely her name was spelled Younger, according to stories passed down within the family. It is unknown when they moved to Cleveland, AR. He died Feb. 12, 1918 and she July 19, 1918 in Cleveland, AR where they are buried.

Eight of their children are listed as being born in Alabama. No place of birth is listed for the others. The oldest of their 12 children was Martha Ann "Babe" born about 1867 in Alabama. She married William Johnson who was born in the 1880s in Evansville, IN. Their children were Arthur John, Lillie Frances, Lucy, Steven, William, Emma, Clara June, Grady, Marion and George Henry. Babe and W.M. both died in the 1930s.

The second child was Sarah (b. about 1870 in Alabama). She married a Hale and they had two children, John and Laura.

John W. was born about 1872 in Alabama. At age 23, he married Emma Griffin, age 16, on May 28, 1895. Ellen was born about 1874 in Alabama. She married a Grandy (sp) Graham.

Willis Wright (b. June 8, 1876 in Morgan County, AL, d. July 16, 1960) md. Daisy Mae Willcut (b. Nov. 2, 1880 in Cullman, AL, d. May 13, 1955 in Longview, TX). Her mother was a Shamblee. There were 13 children in this family. A separate history follows for them because of their Arkansas connections.

Lillian or Lydia was born about 1876 or 77 in Alabama. All that is known is that she married a Griggins.

Emma J. (b. ca. Oct. 25, 1879 in Morgan County, AL) md. James McDonald Graham in 1898.

Nancy Jeanettie "Nettie's" birth date is listed as about 1881. She married F.M. "Mack" Ledbetter March 19, 1897 in Conway County. Nettie and F.M. had 12 children, some of whom married, reared families, died and were buried in Conway County. Their names were John Franklin (b. Oct. 26, 1898), Arbie Annis (md. Samuel Phillips and died in childbirth), Arty Francis, Ellen Izora married David Hill and at this writing her son D.B. resides in Springfield, AR, Lillian Dale (md. Harold Taylor); Joseph Cullen, James Madison "J.M. or Jake" (md. Rosemary Mitchell), McKinley "Mack," Zella (died in early 2005) and her twin Della, and Cartha Dean "Tommie". The Ledbetter family lived in Solgohachia, AR until they moved to Alma, CO in 1934. Irene's son, D.B. Hill, resides in Springfield, AR at the time of this writing. McKinley, after marrying and living in California for years, returned to Morrilton, AR where he married Ruby Miller Ruff, widow of Lloyd Ruff. He is buried in Friendship Cemetery at Solgohachia, AR.

Robert Franklin (b. Jan. 25, 1883 in Winston, AL, d. March 21, 1969 in Holbrook, AZ, where he is buried) md. Sadie Mae Carpenter in 1903. She is listed as being born in Arkansas. She died in 1919 and is buried in Pawhuska, OK. She was the daughter of Susan Tommy Barnes and Will Carpenter. They had three children: Frank Wesley (b. Sept. 10, 1906, d. Sept. 10, 1927); Ralph Fredrick (b. July 20, 1910, d. August 1967) md. Emma Lloyd Townsend; and Geraldine Mae Knighten (b. July 12, 1914, d. March 16, 1991). She was born in Lanty, AR, married D.F. Tadlock in 1933 and a J.H. Casey July 20, 1946 in Phoenix, AZ. Ralph is buried in Superior, AZ.

Robert Franklin was married again June 30, 1920 in Pawhuska, OK to Cora Esther Miller. Eight children were born to this union. A separate history of this couple follows because of their Arkansas connections.

A separate history follows of the next two children, James Edgar and Millard Columbus, as they married and reared their families in Cleveland, AR. The last born, Noah Knighten (b. March 3, 1890, d. March 13, 1911), is buried at Scroggin Cemetery near Lanty, AR.

KNIGHTEN - Millard Columbus Knighten (b. Sept. 8, 1887, d. March 4, 1950) was the son of Willis Franklin and Mary Young. His brothers were John W., Willis Wright, Robert Franklin, James Edgar and Noah. His sisters were Martha Ann "Babe," Sarah E., Ellen, Lydia "Lillian," Emma and Nancy Jeanettie "Nellie." He was born in Alabama and moved with his family to Cleveland, AR when a young boy.

Millard married Edith Bradford (b. May 10, 1891, d. Dec. 26, 1977), daughter of James Monroe and Nancy Sarah Ann Massey Bradford, on May 24, 1908 in Cleveland, AR. His brother Edgar married Edith's sister Nellie. Both couples are buried in Cleveland Cemetery.

Their children were born in Cleveland, Conway County, AR. The family moved to Arizona in 1935. Millard and Edith returned to Morrilton, AR in 1945. They moved to Petit Jean Mountain, where M.C. died. Edith moved back to Morrilton after his death, where she remained until her death.

Gaston Monroe (b. April 15, 1909, d. Oct. 19, 1945) died in a motorcycle accident and is buried in California. He married Esther Jemison Nov. 25, 1929 in California. They had no children. Esther later remarried and had two daughters. She and the children always remained in touch with the Knighten family, visiting several times.

Lillie Knighten (b. April 4, 1912, d. Sept. 2, 1926 of a ruptured appendix) is buried in Cleveland Cemetery.

Agnes Knighten (b. April 25, 1915, d. Oct. 31, 1970) md. Lloyd Bradley on April 26, 1930. Their children were Joe Carroll, Rodrick Berwyn and Lynnie. She later married Gene Tollison on Feb. 9, 1939. Their children were Norma Jean, Marion and Roger. She then married Johnny Grande in 1946. Born to them was Edith Juanita. Agnes died in a car accident and is buried in Blythe, CA.

Lorene Knighten (b. Nov. 15, 1917) md. Oscar Brents on April 26, 1930. The infant born to them is

buried in Cleveland Cemetery. She was briefly married to Lee Mason. On May 15, 1946 she married Warren Stone, whose father was a member of the founding family of Phoenix, AZ. To them was born one child, Helen. She and Carl Huntstiger had one daughter, Christine. They divorced and Helen later married George Reed. Lorene passed away in 1999 in Washington state, where her family had moved. She was laid to rest with Warren in Phoenix, AZ.

Norma Knighten (b. July 11, 1920, d. July 2, 1922) is buried in Cleveland Cemetery.

Millard Berwyn "Slick" (b. Jan. 1, 1923) md. Sharon H. Knighten, daughter of Jewell and Hervey Harwood, June 27, 1953. They lived in Morrilton, AR where Slick was a postal carrier and cattle farmer at Cleveland, AR. Sharon taught at Morrilton High School and was a program advisor in the State Department of Education, Vocational – Technical Division. They had one daughter, Karen Kimberly, who married James Oelke from Charleston, AR, and they had two sons, Matthew James (b. July 22, 1982) and Wesley Berwyn (b. May 12, 1991 on Mothers Day). Both were born in Little Rock, AR. After M.B. "Bill" passed away Jan. 7, 2003, Sharon moved to Harrison, AR, where Kim and her family lived. M.B. is buried in Cleveland Cemetery.

Robbie Fred "Bob" Knighten (b. July 19, 1925, d. March 8, 2003) md. Theo Edith Christ Frazier (b. Jan. 19, 1916, d. June 30, 2003) in Morrilton, AR on Nov. 2, 1945. He was an electrical engineer and WWII veteran. He and Theo lived in several foreign countries, where Bob worked with oil companies. They did not have children. Edward and Carlyon Frazier and their children of Louisville, KY, completed their immediate family. Both are buried in the Cleveland Cemetery.

In the early 1960s Edith Knighten married E.O. Stewart of Sweetwater, TX. He was a minister of the Church of God of the Abrahamic Faith. She and E.O. had known each other for many, many years as he held meetings in Cleveland prior to the time she and Millard moved to Arizona. Her father was a minister of this same faith, and in fact, established the congregation and built the chuch in Cleveland, AR soon after he moved there.

They lived in Sweetwater, TX after marrying and he is buried there. Edith returned to Morrilton, AR and lived with M.B. and Sharon until her death Dec. 26, 1979. She is buried in the Cleveland Cemetery next to M.C.

KNIGHTEN - Robert Franklin Knighten was born in Winston, AL and died in Holbrook, AZ. His first wife was Sadie Mae Carpenter, born in Condon, AR (this is an error - it is probably Conway or Camden, AR). They were married in 1903. She died in 1919 and is buried in Pawhuska, OK. Their children were:

1) Frank Wesley (b. Sept. 10, 1906, d. Sept. 10, 1927).

2) Ralph Fredrick (b. July 20, 1910, d. August 1967 in Superior, AZ) was married to Emma Lloyd Townsend (b. June 17, 1913 in Chicota, TX, d. April 26, 1996 in Van Buren, AR). Their son Edwin (b. March 8, 1938) is in Van Buren, AR at this time. Other children were Glenna Arnell and Margot Elaine.

3) Geraldine Mae Knighten (b. July 12, 1914 in Lanty, AR, d. March 16, 1991) md. Davis Franklin Tadlock on May 5, 1933 and on July 20, 1946 she married James Henry Casey in Phoenix, AZ.

Robert Franklin married Cora Esther Miller Jan. 30, 1920 in Pawhuska, OK, with her father officiating. Robert died March 21, 1969 and is buried in Holbrook, AZ; Esther died May 3, 1994 and is also buried in Holbrook, AZ. The following information addresses only those family members who lived in Arkansas or are presently living there. Children born to them were Dorothy, Cora Lee, Robert Franklin Jr., Jess Willard, Mary Ellen, Anna Mae, Ethel Jean and Nancy Pamela Jane. The first five were born in Pawhuska, OK. Anna Mae was born in Kaw City,

OK; Ethel Jean in Glendale, AZ and Nancy in Superior, AZ.

In the 1940s the family moved from Arizona to Clinton, AR. Robert was a deputy sheriff, had a grocery store and café there. He also farmed on Crowell Mt. Anna Mae married William Henry Avery in 1947 in Clinton, AR. At this writing, she lives in Brownwood, TX. Mary Ellen married Kenneth Earl Lea in 1948 in Russellville, AR. She presently lives in Miami, OK with her husband, Bill Reichstadt.

Ethel Jean "Jeanne" returned from Arizona to Little Rock, AR, where she and a cousin completed nursing training at St. Vincent School of Nursing. While there, she met and married Joseph Earl Cross, who was in medical school. They moved to DeWitt, AR where he was in medical practice until his death Jan. 17, 1983. He and David are buried in West Memphis, AR. They had four sons: Joseph Miller (b. Feb. 9, 1957) is a Baptist minister and lives in Branson, MO; Michael Justin (b. June 23, 1958) practices medicine in Fayetteville, AR; David Earl (b. Jan. 25, 1961, d. Jan. 28, 1961 in Little Rock, AR); Jason Wayne (b. Sept. 2, 1966) also lives in Arkansas. Jeanne still resides in DeWitt, AR.

The deceased children as of this writing are Dorothy Jane K. Evans (d. June 27, 1970) is buried in Lyman, WA; Jess Willard (d. May 7, 1973 in Vancouver, WA) is buried in Willamette National Cemetery in Portland, OR; Nancy K. Archer (d. August 2001) is buried in Flagstaff, AZ.

KNIGHTEN - Willis W. "Will" Knighten (b. Jan. 8, 1876 in Morgan County, AL) was the son of Willis F. and Mary F. Young Knighten. He married Daisy Mae Willcut and they had 13 children. She was born in Cullman, AL on Nov. 2, 1880, died May 13, 1955 and was buried in Longview, TX. Their children were:

Dewey Franklin (b. July 23, 1899 in Cullman, AL, d. June 27, 1967 in Longview, TX) md. Mae Gage.

Willie Robert (b. Aug. 8, 1901 in Isley, AL, d. Aug. 10, 1968 in El Dorado, AR and is buried there).

Jessie Paul (b. March 10, 1905 in Arkansas, d. April 29, 1929 in El Dorado, AR, buried in Bauxite, AR).

Lydia Eula Knighten Watts (b. Aug. 20, 1906 in Cleveland, AR, d. Sept. 25, 1983 in New Orleans, LA, buried in Marrero, LA).

Mary Imogene Knighten (b. Aug. 5, 1908, Quinlan, TX) married, but had no children.

W.D. Knighten (b. April 9, 1910, d. 1989 in Kilgore, TX, buried in Longview, TX).

Stella Knighten (b. Feb. 15, 1912 in Cleveland, AR, d. Dec. 29, 1983 in Pittsburgh, TX) md. Robert William Green and they had two daughters.

Clinty Dell Knighten married a Parrish in Longview, TX on June 1, 1932. Children were Paul, Patrick and John.

The next two Knightens are not identified in the genealogy source. Reason given was that they are still living.

Pearl Knighten (b. Oct. 4, 1918 in Cleveland, AR, d. June 12, 1925, buried in Bauxite, AR).

Another Knighten is not identified for same reason as given above.

Thelma Jo Knighten (b. Jan. 12, 1923 in Bauxite, AR, d. May 12, 1992 in Pittsburgh, TX and is buried there).

LAFAYETTE - William "Will/Bub" Lafayette was born in February 1894 in Conway County, AR to Andrew and Polly Davis Lafayette. Polly's parents were Solomon and Mary Young Davis of Lexington County, SC. Polly was born Nov. 20, 1859. Solomon and Mary were also the parents of Wade, Walter, William S., John Edward, Henry P., Reed, Mary A., Scott, Eliza, and Henry Davis.

David Andrew Lafayette (b. January 1843 in Lexington County, SC) md. Polly in 1878. The family moved to Conway County, AR in the 1880s. David Andrew was buried in Morrilton's Oddfellows Cemetery Dec. 26, 1915. Polly was buried May 15, 1939, also in Oddfellows. They were the parents of 12 children: Jessie Lafayette Manuel, Edward, James, Harold, Nancy, Walter Reed, Eliza, Lula Essie Marshall, Margaret, Laska L., Mae Lafayette Brown and William "Will/Bub" Lafayette.

William Lafayette

Will Lafayette married and divorced Lola Cyrus, daughter of Mattie Perry Cyrus Brown and Logan Cyrus. Will and Lola were the parents of four children: Lloyd Allen Lafayette, Charles Reed Lafayette, Willie Floyd Lafayette, and Mattie M. Lafayette. He married Annie Bryson who died in 1972. Will was a hard worker. He owned his home on Kissire Hill where he and Lola raised their children to adulthood. He owned and operated a hog slaughtering business and owned rental properties. In addition, Will was a carpenter and brick mason. He was the contractor and builder of his beloved Trinity C.M.E. church when it was rebuilt in May 1972. The church is located at 402 North Chestnut Street in Morrilton. Will was a long time trustee of the church.

William became ill in 1982. His daughter returned to Arkansas to care for him during his illness and demise. Will died in August 1982 in Morrilton, Conway County, AR and is buried in Oddfellows Cemetery. *Submitted by Thomas A. Lafayette.*

LANNI - James Vincent Lanni was born of Natale and Antonia Piedmonte Lanni in the Catholic Point Community of Center Ridge, AR, on April 12, 1918. He had three brothers and three sisters. He also had one half-brother and two half-sisters from his father's first marriage to Marie Carmine DeSalvo, who died in 1910. During the Depression, he moved with several in his family to Ohio for work, staying there until he was called to service in the US Army in WWII. Most of his time in the service was spent in the South Pacific, the last years in the Philippine Islands.

1985–the James and Germaine Veys Lanni Family. Front row seated l-r: Jimmie Lanni, James Lanni and Germaine Veys Lanni. Second row, standing l-r: Adam Jones, Karen Lain, Amy Jones and Mark Diehl. Third row, standing l-r: Terry Diehl, Lori Jones, Betty Diehl, Susan Jones, Wayne Jones, Donald Lain, Jackie Lain holding Chris Lain, Richard Lanni and Teri Lanni. Not pictured: Edwin Diehl and Katelyn and Kristen Lanni.

Germaine Marie Veys was born of Jules and Josephine Muyle Veys of Pittem, Belgium, on Aug. 16, 1910. She had six brothers and five sisters. In approximately 1935 she accompanied her brother, a Catholic priest, to the Philippines to help him at his mission in the Northern provinces.

This is where James met Germaine. He was a mechanic and fixed her bicycle. At the end of the war she came to the United States and stayed in Ohio with his sister until he returned. They then moved back to Center Ridge to get married, but they had to wait until a law was passed that foreign war brides would become citizens if they married a GI. They were wed Feb. 9, 1946.

They had six children: Lorraine Mary (b. 1946 and died soon after birth), Susan Diana (b. 1948), Beatrice Josephine "Betty" (b. 1949), Jacqueline Marie "Jackie" (b. 1951), James Vincent Jr. "Jimmie" (b. 1953) and Richard John "Dickie" (b. 1957).

James hauled milk from the local farmers to Morrilton to the Cheese Factory and worked part-time for the Conway County Agriculture ASCS office, until he began traveling the state as a compliance supervisor for the state ASCS office. Germaine was a homemaker. They lived in Center Ridge until 1969 when they moved to Pine Bluff, where he was employed by Jefferson County ASCS office.

James died June 3, 1992, in Pine Bluff at 74 years of age and Germaine died Feb. 19, 2003, in Pine Bluff at 92 years of age.

Susan married Chester Wayne Jones in 1967, lives in Center Ridge and they have three children: Lori, Amy and Adam Jones. Betty married Edwin Diehl in 1971, lives in Conway, and they have two children, Terry and Mark Diehl. Jackie married Donald Lain in 1977, lives in Pine Bluff and they have two children, Karen (md. Jeff Morrison) and Christopher Lain. Jimmie lives at the Conway Human Development Center in Conway. Dickie married Terri Lucas in 1983, they live in Pine Bluff and have two children, Katelyn and Kristen Lanni. *Submitted by Susan Lanni Jones.*

LANNI - Louis J. Lanni, known as Luigi to some and as Louie to most, was born Oct. 5, 1924, to Italian immigrants, Natale and Antonia Piedmonte Lanni, who made their home on a small farm off Highway 9, south of Center Ridge.

America was deeply involved in WWII when 18-year-old Lanni entered the United States Army in late summer of 1943. His basic training consisted of a 4-month tenure with Troop R of the 2nd Regiment at Fort Riley, KS, before being

PFC Louis Lannie – 1943. He was KIA, WWII, May 29, 1944.

sent to Fort George G. Meade, MD, with Company C, 10th Battalion of the 3rd Replacement Regiment, where he underwent six weeks of intensive training.

By the end of February 1944, Lanni had been assigned to join the Allied Forces with the 34th Infantry Division at Anzio, a small port on the southwest coast of Italy. Military historians report that the battles at Anzio were some of the most savage fighting of WWII with continuous bombing, shelling, and fighting, resulting in utter mental and physical exhaustion of the troops. Replacements were needed to offset the heavy loss of Allied troops. Lanni was one of the soldiers of Rifle Company F in the 168th Infantry Regiment that went ashore on the beachhead to relieve the war-weary troops.

During the major offensive to break out of the beachhead and liberate Rome, the 168th was stopped by enemy troops at Villa Crocetta on May 29. Allied troops became pinned down and were being picked off one by one by the German defenders. Lanni and his platoon sergeant moved forward in a bold attempt to reach an outpost that had become entrapped. They were under direct fire from an enemy tank when Lanni was hit in the head. Because of the ferocity of the battle, it was impossible to evacuate his body at that time without endangering the lives of others.

On March 27, 1945, Lanni's remains, properly identified by his identification tags, were interred in the United States Military Cemetery at Nettuno, Italy. As if destined by fate, Louis Lanni was killed on his parents' native soil, not too many miles from the homes near Campobasso.

After the war his remains were returned to the states for burial in St. Joseph's Cemetery, Catholic Point Community at Center Ridge, with military honors by the Morrilton Veterans of Foreign Wars post. Private First Class Lanni was awarded the Purple Heart Medal posthumously. His other commendations were a Bronze Star, the European-African-Middle East Campaign, and the Good Conduct Medal. His unit, F Company, was awarded the Presidential Unit Citation for their actions in the Anzio battles.

Private First Class Louis Lanni's military history is short, but his daring feat to risk his life to help his fellow soldiers is none-the-less gallant. He personifies the valor of the fallen soldiers of Conway County and all US troops who made the supreme sacrifice - a sacrifice so great that it erased their opportunity to return and live the freedom for which they fought. *Submitted by Loretta Paladino-Jackson.*

LANNI – Mateo (Matthew) Lanni (b. April 22, 1878 in Ripabottoni, Campobasso, Italy) was the son of Nicola Lanni (b. Dec. 6, 1847, d. Aug. 16, 1917) and Maria Crescentia Santelio Lanni (b. October 1856, d. Jan. 25, 1942). His grandparents were Pietro Cristanziono Lanni (b. May 13, 1828) and Cleonice Leonarda Maria Lepore Lanni (b. March 8, 1825). His great-grandparents were Domenico Lanni and Rosalia Silvaggio Lanni. Matthew was the brother of Pete, Natale, Frank, Tom and Mary Lanni Andrews. Matthew's family arrived in New York in 1884. His family worked there until 1897 when they moved to Center Ridge, AR where they farmed, grew cotton and raised cattle.

Maria Rosario Paladino

Matthew and Elizabeth Fabrizio Lanni

Matthew Lanni married Maria Rosario "Molly" Paladino on Feb. 2, 1899. Maria Rosario "Molly" was born in 1882 in St. Louis, MO. She was the daughter of Francesco "Frank" Paladino (b. April 2, 1842) and Elena "Lena" Iannuzzi (b. Dec. 18, 1848 in Valle Dell'Angelo, Salerno, Campania, Italy). Frank and his family arrived in New York City in 1879 and settled in St. Louis, MO for several years before arriving in Center Ridge, AR. Maria was the sister of Tony, Rocky, Angelo, Pete and Robert "Robbie" Paladino. Matthew and Maria had one daughter, Antonia Marie (b. Oct. 12, 1899). Maria Rosario Paladino Lanni died in May 1900 and is buried at St. Joseph Cemetery, Center Ridge, AR.

Matthew Lanni married Elisabetta (Elizabeth) Fabrizio, daughter of Guiseppe and Lucia Zarlenga, on Jan. 14, 1903 at St. Joseph Church, Catholic Point, in Center Ridge, AR. Elizabetta (b. Feb. 26, 1882 - church records in Italy indicate Feb. 23, 1883 - in Castleverrino, Isernia, Italy) came to Center Ridge, AR in October 1902 to marry Matthew. Matthew and Elizabeth had 10 children: Lucy (b. May 14, 1906); Nick (b. Dec. 18, 1907); Joseph (b. Feb. 8, 1909); Mary Christina "Babe" (b. Sept. 24, 1910); Annie (b. April

3, 1912); Leonard (b. Feb. 28, 1914); Marie (b. July 7, 1917); Daniel (b. Dec. 9, 1919); Margaret (b. Sept. 2, 1921) and Rosalia, who died as an infant.

Matthew Lanni died Oct. 24, 1950. Elizabeth Fabrizio Lanni died July 6, 1964. They were buried at St. Joseph Cemetery, Catholic Point, Center Ridge, AR. *Submitted by Sandra Lanni and S.L. Paladino.*

Annie Lanni, daughter of Matthew and Elizabeth Fabrizio Lanni, was born April 15, 1912 and died Jan. 20, 1929 at the age of 16. *Submitted by Marie Lanni Freyaldenhoven.*

Antonia Marie Lanni, daughter of Matthew Lanni and Maria Roserio "Molly" Paladino Lanni, was born Oct. 12, 1899. Antonia Marie Lanni married Luigi "Louie" DiPasqua of Chicago, IL on Feb. 24, 1927 at St. Joseph Church, in Center Ridge, AR. Luigi (b. Nov. 17, 1897 in Pietrabondante, Compobasso, Italy) was the son of Pasqualino DiPasqua and Leonica Nerone DiPasqua. Luigi traveled to Arkansas from Chicago with his brother, Jim DiPasqua (Pasck) to visit and go hunting. During his visit, he met Antonia. Jim DiPasqua was married to Virginia DeSalvo, daughter of Joseph and Johannina Lombardo DeSalvo. After Antonia and Luigi were married in 1927, they moved to Chicago, IL. They had four children born in Chicago: Pasqualino "Pat," Matthew, Anthony and Lorraine Elizabeth. Antonia died Jan. 9, 1971 and Luigi died Sept. 3, 1987. They are entombed at Queen of Heaven Mausoleum, Hillside, IL.

Pasqualino "Pat" DePasqua (original spelling DiPasqua) (b. July 5, 1928) md. Shirley Mae Fromel in Chicago on Sept. 15, 1952. Shirley Mae (b. April 28, 1933) was the daughter of John Andrew and Frances WB Clegg Fromel of Chicago. Pat and Shirley DePasqua had two children: Keith Allen (b. April 30, 1957) and Paula Rene' (b. May 25, 1961). Paula married Larry Allen Sharmota (b. Sept. 28, 1961) on Nov. 26, 1986.

Matthew DePasqua (b. June 26, 1929) md. Mary Verona (b. May 27, 1936 in Ottawa, IL) on June 30, 1956 in Rockford, IL. They had three children: Matthew, Jeanine Marie and Louis.

Matthew DePasqua Jr. (b. June 9, 1957 in Chicago, IL) md. Kathleen Sturm (b. Aug. 18, 1963) on May 26, 1984. They had two children born in Downers Grove, IL: Amanda Ann (b. Sept. 9, 1986) and Tammy Marie (b. July 22, 1989, d. July 6, 1999). Matthew Jr. and Kathleen divorced in 1993.

Jeanine Marie DePasqua (b. Oct. 13, 1959, in Oak Park, IL) md. Michael J. Colella (b. Oct. 16, 1957 in Triggiano, Ban, Italy) on Aug. 29, 1981. They had two children: Dominic (b. Sept. 17, 1986 in Elk Grove Village, IL) and Rosa Marie (b. Aug. 2, 1960 in Maywood, IL).

Louis DePasqua (b. Aug. 7, 1962 in Oak Park, IL) md. Deborah Jean Jurczykowski on July 2, 1983. They had two children born in Elk Grove Village, IL: Louis Richard (b. Nov. 27, 1985) and Lea Jean (b. April 28, 1988). Deborah died Jan. 13, 1990.

Anthony DePasqua (b. Oct. 20, 1930) md. Frances Addotta (b. July 16, 1935) on June 18, 1955 in Rockford, IL. Frances is the daughter of Peter and Elenore Saladino Addotta. Anthony and Frances have two children, Mark and Denise.

Mark DePasqua (b. April 7, 1957) md. Michele Ann Swanson on July 4, 1982. They had two children born in Rockford, IL, Jessica Marie (b. July 21, 1988) and Natalie Rene (b. Feb. 25, 2002).

Denise DePasqua (b. July 18, 1961) md. Kenneth Douglas Fell (b. April 15, 1954) on July 15, 1984. They had two children born in Rockford, IL: Samantha Pandora (b. July 26, 1985) and Kade Diane (b. April 24, 1989).

Lorraine Elizabeth DePasqua, daughter of Antonia and Luigi DePasqua, was born Dec. 29, 1939 in Chicago, IL. Lorraine married Richard A. Miller on Aug. 1, 1964, at St. Frances of Rome Church in Cicero, IL. Richard (b. July 9, 1937 in Chicago, IL) is the son of Harry and Cecile Miller. *Submitted by the children of Antonia M. Lanni DePasqua.*

Leonard Lanni, son of Matthew and Elizabeth Fabrizio Lanni, was born in Center Ridge, AR on Feb. 28, 1914. Leonard moved to Chicago, IL in 1937. He married Carmella on Nov. 30, 1940 at Our Lady of Pompeii Church, in Chicago, IL. Leonard and Carmella had three children: Leonard Jr. and Ronald (twin boys born in 1942) and one daughter Sandra Lee (b. 1947). In 1978, after retirement, Leonard and Carmella moved to Conway, AR. They lived in Conway for seven years. In 1986 they moved back to Illinois. Leonard Sr. died Oct. 5, 1999, and is entombed at Queen of Heaven Cemetery in Hillside, IL.

Leonard Lanni Jr. married Irene Sulski in 1972. Leonard and Irene have two children: Christopher Leonard (b. 1975) and Monica Lynette (b. 1977).

Ronald Lanni married Donna Pas in 1979. Ronald and Donna have two children: Alicia Ann (b. 1983) and Melanie Kristina (b. 1985).

Sandra Lanni married Vincent Mula in 1971. Vincent and Sandra have two children: Renee Marie (b. 1975) and Lori Anne (b. 1977). *Submitted by the children of Leonard Lanni.*

Lucy Lanni, daughter of Matthew and Elizabeth Fabrizio Lanni, was born on May 14, 1906. Lucy married James "Jim" Zarlingo (b. Oct. 18, 1894) on Jan. 22, 1922. James was the son of Alexander and Michelina D'Alusio Zarlingo and brother of Maria Paladino, wife of Angelo Paladino, Annunciata "Linzy" wife of Lewis DeSalvo and Tony Zarlingo.

Lucy and Jim Zarlingo

James was a lay teacher until 1926, when the Benedictine Sisters began teaching the children of the community. Lucy and Jim had one daughter, Mary Elizabeth (b. Oct. 30, 1922 in Center Ridge, AR).

Mary Elizabeth married John Louis Paladino, son of Anthony "Tony" and Erminia "Minnie" Rossi Paladino on Jan. 27, 1947. They had one daughter, Sharon Louise (b. Sept. 24, 1947, at St. Vincent's Infirmary, Little Rock, AR). John operated Paladino's Café with his brother Frank J. Paladino at 3rd and Main Street in North Little Rock, AR. Mary and John were divorced in February 1950. That same year Mary Elizabeth and her daughter moved to Chicago, IL.

Mary Elizabeth on June 27, 1959 married James "Jim" Frank Horak (b. Jan. 6, 1919), the son of James Joseph and Antonie Horak of Cicero, IL. James and Mary Elizabeth lived in Cicero, IL until October 1968, when they moved to Center Ridge, AR. Jim Horak died April 28, 1978 and is buried at St. Joseph Cemetery, Center Ridge, AR. James Zarlingo died April 3, 1960 and is buried at St. Joseph Cemetery, Center Ridge, AR. *Submitted by Mary E. Horak and Sharon L. Paladino.*

Margaret Lanni, daughter of Matthew and Elizabeth Fabrizio Lanni, was born Sept. 2, 1923. Margaret married Maurice Henry Courtney in November 1939. Margaret died Feb. 10, 1940 and was buried at St. Joseph Cemetery, Conway, AR. *Submitted by Sharon L. Paladino and Sandra L. Lanni Mula.*

Marie Lanni, daughter of Matthew and Elizabeth Fabrizio Lanni, was born July 27, 1917. She married Joseph Freyaldenhoven (b. Dec. 12, 1913) on Jan. 12, 1937 at St. Joseph's Church, Center Ridge, AR. Joseph was the son of Paul and Josephine Rolf Freyaldenhoven of Conway, AR. Marie and Joseph had three children: Joe Allen, Paul Lynn and Donald Eugene. Donald Eugene was born Nov. 29, 1948 and died from an automobile accident Aug. 15, 1982. Joseph Freyaldenhoven died July 31, 1997. They were buried at St. Joseph Cemetery, Conway, AR.

Joe Allen Freyaldenhoven (b. March 4, 1939), son of Marie and Joseph Freyaldenhoven, married

Rosie Margaret Moix (b. Oct. 19, 1940). She was the daughter of Maurice Moix Sr. and Eleanor Moix of Conway, AR. Joe and Rosie were married at St. Joseph Church, Conway, AR. They had three daughters and two sons: Dee Ann, Todd Allen, Stephen, Beth and Lauran (b. Oct. 14, 1971).

Dee Ann Freyaldenhoven (b. Aug. 21, 1962) md. Michael Townsend (b. March 15, 1960). They were married on May 10, 1984, in Conway, AR. Dee Ann and Michael had five children: Tabitha (b. Feb. 16, 1985), Michael Jacob "Jake" (b. July 11, 1986), Mitchell (b. Jan. 25, 1988) and twin girls, Haley and Whitney (b. Oct. 7, 1993).

Todd Allen Freyaldenhoven (b. Oct. 14, 1963) md. Susann Gunther (b. May 4, 1964). They were married on Oct. 23, 1987 in Bigalow, AR. They had three sons: Matthew (b. March 29, 1989), Brandon (b. Nov. 23, 1992) and Spencer (b. Aug. 7, 1995).

Stephen Freyaldenhoven (b. April 8, 1966) md. Misha Shah (b. May 23, 1967). They were married on Sept. 10, 1994 in San Antonio, TX. They had three children: Kaesha (b. Nov. 27, 1996), Kannan (b. Feb. 13, 1999) and Kavi (b. Feb. 10, 2001).

Beth Freyaldenhoven (b. May 4, 1968) was married on June 30, 2000 to Jeff Crowder (b. Feb. 9, 1964). They were married in Conway, AR.

Paul Lynn Freyaldenhoven (b. May 7, 1944), son of Marie and Joseph Freyaldenhoven, was married on April 4, 1964 to Linda Schrekenhofer (b. June 30, 1944). Linda Schrekenhofer is the daughter of George and Elviria Schrekenhofer. Paul and Linda were married at St. Joseph Church, Conway, AR. They had three children: Michelle, Shawn and Jason. Jason was born on Nov. 5, 1972.

Michelle Freyaldenhoven (b. Nov. 11, 1965) was married on Nov. 4, 1988 to David Romine (b. Dec. 3, 1966),the son of Ray and Willa Romine of Conway, AR. Michelle and David were married at St. Joseph Church, Conway, AR. They had three children: Nick (b. Dec. 14, 1990) and twin girls: Madison and Morgan (b. Nov. 29, 1998).

Shawn Freyaldenhoven (b. Nov. 4, 1966) was married on May 3, 2003 to Tara Cook (b. Aug. 26, 1972) at St. Andrews Cathedral, Little Rock, AR. Tara Cook Freyaldenhoven is the daughter of David Cook, Cookeville, TN and Donna Reaves of Little Rock, AR. *Submitted by the children of Marie Lanni Freyaldenhoven.*

Mary Christina "Babe" Lanni, daughter of Matthew and Elizabeth Fabrizio Lanni was born Sept. 24, 1910. Mary Christina moved to Chicago, IL in the early 1930s. She married William "Bill" Oulehla of Oak Park, IL on July 3, 1948. William (b. July 25, 1917) was the son of Frank and Mary Oulehla of Berwyn, IL. Mary and William lived in Cicero, IL until 1978, when they moved to Conway, AR. William died May 16, 1984. After his death, Mary returned to Illinois in 1984, and lived with her niece, Lorraine DePasqua Miller. Mary died on March 20, 1977. Mary and William were buried at Woodlawn Cemetery, Forest Park, IL. *Submitted by Lorraine DePasqua Miller*

Nick Lanni, son of Matthew and Elizabeth Fabrizio Lanni, was born Dec. 18, 1907. Nick married Margaret Moll on June 11, 1940. They had one daughter, Mary Ann. Nick died on Feb. 21, 1996 and was entombed at Rest Hill Memorial Park, No. Little Rock, AR.

Mary Ann Lanni (b. March 9, 1943, in Morrilton, AR) md. William Anthony Rand. They had five sons: Wayne Anthony, Jeffrey Scott, Gregory Keith, Mark Albert, William Nicholas and one daughter, Antoinette.

Wayne Anthony Rand (b. Jan. 7, 1962) md. May 6, 1989 to Dorothy Dennise Bentley (b. Aug. 12, 1969). They had two daughters, Lanni Nicole (b. Oct. 21, 1993) and Leslie Victoria (b. Aug. 15, 1995) and one son Landon Bentley Rand (b. April 1, 2002).

Jeffery Scott Rand (b. July 6, 1963) md. Karen Ann Camp (b. Aug. 1, 1965) on March 18, 1989. They had two sons, Nicholas Scott (b. June 4, 1993) and Allen Jeffery (b. Sept. 10, 1996).

Gregory Keith Rand (b. July 17, 1964) md Lisa Ann Evans (b. Jan. 14, 1966) on March 13, 1993. They have one son Gregory Evans (b. Nov. 12, 2001).

Mark Albert Rand (b. Nov. 19, 1965) md. Jennifer Elaine Morris (b. April 4, 1967) on Dec. 18, 1999.

William Nicholas Rand (b. Dec. 20, 1969) md. Ann Louise Pruitt (b. April 10, 1968) on March 7, 1998. They have two sons, Colson William (b. July 12, 1999) and Garrett Alexander (b. May 2, 2001).

Antoinette Rand (b. June 19, 1971). *Submitted by Mary Ann Lanni Rand.*

Daniel Lannie, son of Matthew Lanni and Elizabeth Fabrizio Lanni, of Center Ridge, AR was born Dec. 9, 1918, brother of Lucy Zarlingo, Nick, Joseph, Mary Christina Oulehla, Annie, Leonard, Marie Freyaldenhoven and Margaret Courtney.

Sergeant Lannie, age 23, was a member of the 405th Technical School Squadron at Sheppard Field, TX. He reported to Camp Robinson June 11, 1941 and was later sent to Jefferson Barracks, St. Louis, where he was assigned to the US Army Air Corps.

Young Lannie was sent to Technical School at Sheppard Field, TX, when he graduated Oct. 16, 1941. He was promoted to corporal Nov. 1, 1941 and to sergeant a month later. He was advanced to staff sergeant Aug. 4, 1942.

Staff Sergeant Lannie attended school at Catholic Point and graduated from the Nemo-Vista High School at Center Ridge in 1937. He was associated with the Little Rock branch of Swift & Company for eight or nine months prior to entering the service of the US Armed Forces.

Before returning to civilian life in 1945, he received the Air Medal and the Distinguished Flying Cross.

The following was submitted by the children of Daniel Lannie:

Daniel Lannie, son of Matthew Lanni and Elizabeth Fabrizio Lanni, was born in Center Ridge, AR on Dec. 9, 1918.

Daniel moved to Chicago, IL and married Livia DiCarlo on Nov. 30, 1946, and they had two children, Daniel "Danny Boy" (b. 1948) and Linda Lee (b. 1956).

Linda Lannie married Edward Kazmierczak on March 31, 1979. They had two children, Lisa Lynn (b. 1984) and Lauren Marie (b. 1988).

Daniel Sr. died April 9, 1984 and was entombed at Queen of Heaven Cemetery in Hillside, IL.

Joseph Lannie, son of Matthew and Elizabeth Fabrizio Lanni, was born on Feb. 8, 1909. He married Mary Rose Paladino on June 22, 1932. Mary Rose (b. Dec. 25, 1912) was the daughter of Rocci and Ann DeSalvo Paladino. Joseph and Mary Rose had three children: Anita, Mildred "Millie" and Matthew "Sonny." Joseph died Feb. 17, 1975 and Mary Rose died Jan. 15, 1998. They are buried at St. Joseph Cemetery, Center Ridge, AR.

Anita Lannie (b. Nov. 4, 1932) md. Ernest John Miller (b. Feb. 26, 1930) on Feb. 23, 1957. Ernest is the son of Simon and Elizabeth Miller. Anita and Ernest had six children: Regina Ann, Barbara Elaine, Yvonne Louise, Ernest John II, Mariam Theresa and Paul Joseph.

Regina Ann Miller (b. Nov. 25, 1957) had one son Eric Jason (b. Oct. 8, 1976). Eric Jason married on Aug. 28, 1999 to Sandy Hunter (b. Jan. 21, 1977).

Barbara Elaine Miller (b. Jan. 26, 1959) md. Vernon James Illich (b. Nov. 22, 1951) on Aug. 7, 1993. Barbara had two stepdaughters, Candice and Bobbi Illich. Candice (b. June 25, 1974) was married on June 24, 1997 to Mr. Buck. They had one son Dalton (b. June 6, 1999). Bobbi Illich (b. July 10, 1987) was married on April 20, 2001 to Mr. Barela. They had one son Reyes Barela (b. Nov. 18, 1999).

Yvonne Louise Miller (b. July 7, 1960) was married on June 6, 1981 to William Flppen (b. Feb. 27,

1965). They had two children: Elizabeth (b. Oct. 2, 1982) and William (b. Aug. 5, 1986). Elizabeth has one son Trey Williams (b. March 16, 2003).

Ernest John Miller II (b. Sept. 3, 1961) was married on Oct. 7, 1995 to Denyse Michele Garey (b. Sept. 22, 1962). Ernest II had two stepdaughters: Natalie Garey (b. Jan. 29, 1982) and Emma Garey (b. March 18, 1983). Ernest and Denyse had one daughter Meredith Lannie Miller (b. May 4, 1996).

Mariam Theresa Miller (b. Jan. 17, 1962) was married on Aug. 1, 1987 to George Hopkins (b. Jan. 7, 1958). They had two children: Clayton (b. March 20, 1993) and Jacob (b. May 22, 1996).

Paul Joseph Miller (b. Jan. 17, 1964) was married on Oct. 2, 1992 to Karan Ann Robinson (b. June 29, 1963). They had three children: Chelsea Alexis (b. May 14, 1988); Brooke (b. July 21, 1993); and Kristen Danielle (b. Nov. 16, 1997).

Mildred "Millie" Lannie (b. June 27, 1935) was married on May 4, 1957 to Paul F. "Bob" McManus (b. Dec. 8, 1935). They had two children, Michael P. and Vickie.

Michael P. McManus (b. Jan. 15, 1960) was married on March 26, 1982 to Thersa Roush (b. May 6, 1961). They had two children: Chelsie N. McManus (b. Dec. 13, 1984) and Chase B. McManus (b. Dec. 27, 1988). Michael and Thersa were divorced in December 2004. Michael married Gail Ernst (b. Oct. 26, 1961) on Nov. 26, 2004. Michael's stepson, Tommy Gullahorn, was born Feb. 17, 1995.

Vickie McManus (b. Oct. 18, 1963) was married on July 9, 1994 to Walter Anger (b. Oct. 10, 1961). They have two children: Kristen Laney (b. June 26, 1996) and Austin (b. Oct. 25, 1999).

Matthew "Sonny" J. Lannie (b. Feb. 28, 1939) was married on Dec. 14, 1962 to Wanda Hays (b. Dec. 4, 1932). They had one daughter Tonya (b. March 18, 1968). Tonya Lannie was married on Aug. 26, 1988 to Scott Booher (b. Feb. 20, 1962). Matthew died Sept. 13, 2003 and Wanda died Nov. 1, 1981. Matthew is buried at St. Joseph Cemetery, Center Ridge, AR. Wanda is buried at Magness Cemetery, Wilburn, AR. *Submitted by the children of Joseph Lannie.*

LASATER - Three Lasater brothers and their families, moved to Solgohachia, AR from Malden, MO in 1900. These brothers were Stanford (b. 1868), William (b. 1875) and David Benjamin Cardwell (DBC) (b. 1857). They were the sons of Johnathan C. (b. 1838) and Olive Wooster Lasater and were originally from Weakley County, TN. Johnathan was the son of Dr. Jacob B. Lasater (b. 1819), a physician. The Tennessee Lasaters came from North Carolina, where the name was originally spelled Lassiter. The name spelling was changed in the 1790s. The Lasater brothers were farmers and they established farms in the vicinity of Overcup and Solgohachia. Many of their descendants have remained in Conway County.

Stella Lasater

Stanford first married Mal Riddick and they had five children. They were: Oxley; George; Bright; David and Lawrence. Stanford next married Kate Grooms and they had 10 children. These were: May, Lila, Brooxie, Joe, Lessie, Jemmy, Majorie, Fanny, Vernon and Lucille. He then married Alice Bostian. It is interesting that Stanford's son Oxley married Josephine Bostian and later Stanford married Josephine's first cousin, Alice Bostian.

William's wife was named Bara and they had four children: Daisy Pearl, Deloris, Maxine and William. Daisy Pearl married Porter Bostian and they had Deloris, Maxine and William.

DBC had married Betty Stewart (b. 1869) while he was in Missouri and they had nine children - four of which died at a young age. The survivors were Sallye, Stella, Iva, Lucy and Bill.

Sallye (b. 1891) md. Homer Bearden and had Homer M. and Hillman. Homer M. "Brownie" md. Opal Lee McDaniel (b. 1912) and had Laura (b. 1930), Nancy (b. 1933), Marian (b. 1941) and twins, Annette and Janette (b. 1944). Hillman was out of the area during most of his life. All the members of this family are buried in the Sologohachia Friendship Cemetery.

Stella (b. 1897) md. Clifford Atkinson (b. 1893) and had Millicent (b. 1920), Randal (b. 1922), Drexel (b. 1926), James (b. 1929) and Robert (b. 1930). Stella, Clifford and their children left the area and moved to Little Rock in 1935. Randal and Robert had careers in the US Navy. Drexel retired from the US Border Patrol and James retired from the General Electric Co. Stella, Clifford and Millicent are buried in the Sologachia Friendship Cemetery.

Iva (b. ca. 1900) md. Herbert Dickson and had two daughters, Betty (b. 1922) and Lou (b. 1922). Betty married Dee Halbrook and settled in Conway, AR where Dee was a very successful dentist. Lou married Bill Gibson and moved to Texas.

Luey (b. ca. 1905) md. Hazel Adams (b. 1907) and had Louie Edwin (b. ca. 1926), Billy Jean (b. 1927), Carol Dean (b. 1931), Shirley (b. 1940), Linda (b. 1945) and Larry (b. ca. 1947). Luey left Conway County during WWII to pursue defense work and settled in Kansas City after the war.

Bill married Electra Brewer and they had a daughter Jo Ann. Jo Ann married Glenn Powell and they had Glenda (b. 1951), Janis (b. 1958) and Steve (b. 1960).

LEACH - On Jan. 24, 1940 Henry Scott Leach and Lois Ann Ashley were married. Henry (b. March 28, 1916) was the son of Jessie Louis Leach and Sarah Francis Leach married in 1906. Jessie (b. 1881) moved to Arkansas from the Oklahoma Territory. Jessie and Sarah Leach lived on the E.E. Mitchell Farm in Oppelo, AR during 1923 when you had to pay a toll of 10 cents per footman and 50 cents per horse and wagon to cross the Arkansas River Bridge from Oppelo to Morrilton. Jessie and Sarah had 10 children: Hez (b. 1910, d. 1996); Janie (b. 1914); Henry (b. 1916); Wesley (b. 1918, d. 2003); Fred (b. 1920); Mayme (b. 1922); Ruben (b. 1926); Bob (b. 1928); Jewel (b. 1930, d. 1932) and Violet (b. 1933).

In 1929 during the depression, Henry and Wesley worked for $0.75/day combined for Loftus, clearing land in what was known as Old Dixie near Bigelow, AR. Jessie and Hez worked with them for $0.75/day each. From 1935-38 Henry worked for the Civilian Conservation Corps created in 1932 for the fight against soil erosion and declining timber resources, utilizing the unemployed of large urban areas.

After Henry and Lois were married, they lived on the E.E. Mitchell Farm in Oppelo before moving to Water Plant Road in Oppelo. Henry then worked for South Conway County School District, driving a school bus.

During 1940 through 1960 Henry and Lois had three girls: Shirley Jean (b. Oct. 3, 1940); Ida Mae (b. Dec. 18, 1944) and Patricia Ella (b. July 28, 1949) and two boys, John Henry (b. Feb. 9, 1948) and Finas Anthony Ray (b. Aug. 10, 1960, d. April 2000).

In 1944 during WWII, Henry and Hez were declined for draft. Henry was declined because he was considered a class F. Hez was declined because he worked at the shipyard and was needed there. Two of his brothers, Fred and Wesley, were drafted for the war. In 1959 Henry's father Jessie died and in 1979 his mother Sarah died. In 1966 Henry worked for Arkansas Craft in Oppelo and worked there until he retired in 1981. In 1987 Henry's oldest son John had a tractor-trailer accident and is now a paraplegic. In

2000 Henry's youngest son Ray died of a four-wheeler accident. Henry and Lois still live in Oppelo on Water Plant Road, and have 17 grandchildren, 25 great-grandchildren and two great-great-grandchildren.

LEDBETTER - James Baty Ledbetter (b. Nov. 1, 1829 in Bedford County, TN) was the son of Martin Stanley and Eliza McKinley Ledbetter. In 1847 he married Cynthia Bane, the daughter of Andrew and Margaret Bane. In 1836 the part of Bedford County where the Ledbetter family lived, became Marshall County. Three of their children were born there: William W. (b&d. 1848), Margaret (b. April 10, 1850) and Edna Jane (b. 1853).

James Baty and Carolina Ledbetter

J.B. moved his small family to Lawrence County, MO between 1853 and 1851 His wife Cynthia died in 1855 at the time their son Curtis was born. He returned to Marshall County, TN with his small children and his mother-in-law kept the baby until her death.

In 1859 he married Caroline Barrett Thompson, daughter of William and Lavina Thompson, and returned to Missouri with his new wife and two small daughters. While there, their first daughter Mary Elizabeth was born on June 26, 1860.

J.B. then moved his family to Pope County, AR. The family remained at this location while James served in the Confederate Army during the Civil War. Information taken from Caroline's widow's application states that he served in a regiment of Stirman's Battalion from about 1861 until the end of the war.

In a 1885 biography published by Goodspeed, J.B. states that he moved to Conway County, AR in 1865. He homesteaded land about five miles southwest of Springfield. This area was later known as Hill Creek.

The remainder of J.B. and Caroline's children were born at Hill Creek: Eliza Izora (b. March 23, 1867); James Baty Jr. (b. Dec. 6, 1869); Charlie Stanley (b. July 20, 1872); and Farrier McKinley (b. Nov. 3, 1877).

J.B. was a farmer, and he and Caroline remained on the farm in Hill Creek until his death on Sept. 4, 1909. Caroline then lived with her son Charles Stanley in Springfield until her death on Sept. 20, 1916. They are both buried in the Scroggins Cemetery near Springfield. Their farm is now part of the Conway Reservoir and lays partially under water.

Further information on the J.B. Ledbetter family: Margaret married George Farior Scroggins on Jan. 13, 1869, the son of John and Sarah Blackfox Scroggins. Their children were James Mattison, Ida, Sarah Callie, Elbert Eleaney, John Andrew, George Ashur, Hugh, Edna Jane, and Lawn. She died on Oct. 18, 1924 in Solgohachia, Conway County, AR.

Edna Jane married Joseph Bell ca. 1871. Their children were Frances J., Hugh M., Sallie May., Maggie, Joseph, Samuel, Zella and Edward. She died about 1895 in Hill Creek, Conway County, AR.

Mary Elizabeth married William Horace Brown on May 17, 1877. William was the son of Allen and Eveline Stell Brown. Their children were Junia Arieon, Lillian M., James Horace, Laura E., Dora Wilma, Ruth Elizabeth, and Emmett Clairon. She died on Aug. 23, 1926 in Shirley, Van Buren County, AR.

Eliza Izora married Thomas Green Love on July 8, 1883, the son of Wiley and Martha Tidwell Love. Their children were Rommie Mack, Lonnie F., Myrtle R., Izora A., Daulphus and Thomas G. Jr. She died on Nov. 23, 1952 in Scotland, Van Buren County, AR.

James Baty married first, Rosa Belinge on Feb. 23, 1897, the daughter of John and Salina Marthell Belinge. Their children were Martin Lilburn, Clarence Ruel, Emmett Naplean, James Baty III and Celena Mae. He married second, Susie Mar Florence Anderson on Nov. 30, 1930, the daughter of Albert S. and Lula C. Haigwood Anderson. Their children were Verlie Caroline, Emma Evalee, Opal Marie, Bonnie Sue, Mack Albert and Charles Stanley. He died on Nov. 26, 1954 in Botkinburg, Van Buren County, AR.

Charlie Stanley married first, Nora Coleman in 1891 and had Jesse M. In 1893 he married second, Mary Jane Stell. They had children: Louise Mae, William Miles, Eliza Izora, Elizabeth B., Lou Cindy, Claude Stanley, Charles Sanford, Robert Bayles, Mary Frances, Bonnie, Paul and Pauline. He died on April 25, 1925 in Solgohachia, Conway County, AR.

Farrier McKinley married Nancy Janettie Knighten on March 29, 1897. Their children were Johnny Franklin, Arbie A., Ellen I., Artie E., S. Irene, Lillian D., J. Cullen, James Madison, McKinley, Zella, Della and Cartha Dean. He died on Dec. 28, 1961 in Salida, Chaffee County, CO. *Submitted by Mrs. Mack L. Ledbetter.*

LEE - John U. Lee was born on July 25, 1870 at Annapolis, MO to William F. Lee and Lucinda Steel. William married Lucinda on Jan. 14, 1866. Lucinda was born in 1848 and William in 1846. William and Lucinda had four children: John U., Willie, Samuel and Elizabeth. William F. died of wounds sustained in the Civil War and died Feb. 26, 1872.

John U. Lee family in 1914. Row 1, l-r: Bessie, Wrennie, John D., Robert and Lillie; 2nd row: Arthur, Isabel, John U., Sarah holding Madeline, Ollie and Oscar. Bonnie and Beulah are not pictured.

Lucinda remarried after William died. She married William Marlow on Aug. 19, 1873. Their children were Evelyn, Lillie, Rose and Frances. Lucinda died of pneumonia Feb. 18, 1909 and is buried at Witts Springs, AR.

John U. married Sarah Jane Colyott on Feb. 21, 1894. Sarah (b. Feb. 5, 1874 in Reynolds County, MO) was the daughter of Alexander and Mary Keathley Colyott. The children of John U. and Sarah Jane were Arthur (b. March 14, 1897, d. March 23, 1976); Ollie Sarrat (b. Sept. 8, 1895, d. May 20, 1987); Lucy Williams (b. Nov. 24, 1899, d. Dec. 3, 1986); Samuel Oscar (b. Jan. 15, 1901, d. April 1, 1965); Bessie Baker (b. March 11, 1903, d. Aug. 28, 1991); Lillie Mullins (b. Feb. 20, 1904, d. Feb. 28, 1985); Wrennie Israel (b. Jan. 17, 1906, d. Feb. 16, 1997); Robert Earl (b. Feb. 13, 1909, d. Nov. 15, 1996); John D. (b. June 14, 1911); Madeline Diamond (b. Oct. 24, 1913, d. Feb. 4, 1997); Bonnie Ratliff (b. April 30, 1916, d. July 7, 2003); and Beulah Costephens (b. Sept. 23, 1918).

John U. died in Ellington, MO on June 8, 1947. Sarah Jane Lee died in Haskell, OK on June 23, 1933 and is buried at Bixby, OK Cemetery. Many descendants of John U. Lee and Sarah Jane Lee still reside in Conway County.

LEE - Mark Edward Lee was born Aug. 14, 1961 in Dinuba, CA to Tommy E. Lee and Monterey Stroud Lee. Mark graduated from Hector High School, Arkansas Tech and UCA. He taught school at Mansfield, AR and Wonderview. He was a coach, teacher, counselor, and high school principal. Mark married Victoria Gunderman (b. July 19, 1967), daughter of Ray and Delores Gangluff Gunderman, on Oct. 14, 1989.

Their children are Orry Michael (b. Aug. 5, 1990); Alexandria Marie (b. Feb. 22, 1993); Maggie Rose (b. July 7, 1995); and Quinton Edward (b. Sept. 20, 2001). They continue living at Wonderview.

(Left) Mark Lee family: Mark and Victoria with children: Orry, Quinton, Maggie Lee and Alexandria. (Right) Brent Lee family: Brent and Ashley with children: Parker, Karson and Cassie.

Brent Allen Lee (b. Dec. 25, 1963 in Dinuba, CA) graduated from Hector High School and attended Arkansas Tech. Brent has been in farming, raising cattle and continues to be involved in raising swine. Brent married Ashley Fountain, daughter of Charles and Peggy Tackett Fountain on March 28, 1987. Ashley was born June 6, 1968. Their children are: Karson Charles (b. March 29, 1996) and twins, Parker Thomas and Cassie Paige (b. Nov. 23, 1999 at Russellville, AR). They continue living on their farm near Jerusalem.

LEE - Robert Earl Lee was born at Witts Springs, AR on Feb. 13, 1909 to John U. Lee and Sarah Colyott Lee. On Nov. 11, 1933 he married Ima Wilson, daughter of B.E. Wilson and Maggie Stobaugh Wilson. Ima was born at Jerusalem, AR on July 18, 1915. Their children: Jackie Charles (b. Jan. 19, 1935, d. Feb. 17, 1977); Tommy Edward (b. Feb. 25, 1936); Frances Evelyn (b. Feb. 27, 1938); and Shirley Alene (b. Jan. 30, 1944).

Robert Earl Lee Family: Ima Wilson Lee, Tommy, Frances, Jackie, Robert and Shirley.

Their grandchildren are Mark E. Lee and Brent A. Lee, sons of Tom and Monterey Lee. Janene Ward Richert, Kelli Lee Eimers and Kimberly Ward Potter, daughters of Frances and Gary Ward. Christopher Kyle Russell, Veronica Russell, Matthew Stephen Russell and Brian Lee Russell, children of Shirley and Donald Ray Russell.

Their great-grandchildren are Orry Michael Lee, Alexandria Marie, Maggie Rose and Quinn Edward, children of Mark and Victoria Lee; Karson Charles Lee, Parker Thomas and Cassie Paige Lee, children of Brent and Ashley Lee; Amber Hayes, James Hayes and Kaitlyn Raska, children of Kim Potter; Mason, Ashlyn and Morgun-Ray Russell, children of Matthew and Virginia Russell.

They lived in California for 30 years and moved to Jerusalem, AR in 1976. Ima died Sept. 13, 1982 and Robert died Nov. 15, 1997. They are both buried at Cedar Creek Cemetery at Jerusalem, AR.

LEE - Tommy E. Lee was born in Checotah, OK, on Feb. 25, 1936, to Robert Earl Lee and Ima Wilson Lee. The family moved to California in 1940. Tom graduated from Mt. Whitney High School in Visalia, CA, in 1955. He was in the US Air Force for four years. He married Monterey Stroud on July 18, 1958. They met in California. Monterey (b. June 2, 1939), daughter of Fayburn Stroud and Effie Ramsey Stroud, gradu-

Tommy E. and Monterey Stroud Lee

ated form Dinuba High School and from Fresno State College.

Tom and Monterey had two sons, Mark Edward (b. Aug. 14, 1961) and Brent Allen (b. Dec. 25, 1963), both born in Dinuba, CA.

They moved to Jerusalem, AR, in April 1969. Monterey taught school at Jerusalem and Hector, AR. Tom farmed, raising broilers, cattle and swine. Tom and Monterey are both retired and still live in Jerusalem.

LIENHART - Bruno J. Lienhart with his wife Katie Byrne Lienhart and a family of three boys and three girls, moved to Morrilton from Conway, AR, in June 1930. He had been a farmer and the owner of a general store in Faulkner County, but the economy of the time led him to Conway County to begin a new business venture.

The Bruno Lienhart family.

Mr. Lienhart was familiar with the Morrilton territory, having traveled it for several years helping to educate landowners in diversified farming. He was active in dairy and livestock development, and in association with Faulkner Dairy Company of Conway, he operated a wholesale and retail distribution plant for their products on North Moose Street in Morrilton, buying milk products from local farmers. When the dairy filed for bankruptcy in 1935, Lienhart became the Ward Ice Cream distributor for the area. After alcohol prohibition was lifted in 1933, Ward's became, in addition, the distributor for Falstaff, Budweiser and other beers.

The company remains in the family at this time, operated by Bruno Lienhart's grandson, Otto Lienhart II, as Lienhart Distributors and is located at Highway 9 and 980 in Morrilton.

Both Bruno Lienhart and his wife Katie were children of immigrants; his ancestors from Germany and hers from Ireland and Germany. His parents were pioneer settlers of Faulkner County, where he was born in 1887. Katie Byrne was also born in Conway in 1889. Bruno and Katie Lienhart were the parents of:

Theresa Gertrude (Tead) (b. 1914, d. 1993) md. George Riedmueller (b. 1910, d. 1981) of Morrilton. George operated Riedmueller Grocery on Main Street in Morrilton during the 1940s and 1950s, and later was in the insurance business. Theresa and George had six

children: Barbara Jean Nabholz of Conway, George Riedmueller IV "Buddy" of Perry County, Elaine Lynch of Fort Smith, Jim Riedmueller of Morrilton, Charles Riedmueller of Rogers, AR, and Lon Beck of St. Vincent, AR.

Bernice Julia "Sis" Hoelzeman (b. 1915, d. 2004) md. Joseph N. Hoelzeman Sr. (b. 1908, d. 1990). She worked as an assistant to agricultural agent Jim Moose in the courthouse offices before her marriage. Mr. Hoelzeman was a carpenter. He and Bernice raised nine children: Mary Crutcher of Memphis; Joseph Hoelzeman Jr. who died of cancer in 1969 at the age of 26; Janie Hightower of Little Rock; Becky Hartman of Harrison; Katie Hodge, Agnes Bass and Judy Hoelzeman-Schneider, all of Little Rock; and Bruno and Michael Hoelzeman, both of whom reside in Morrilton.

Bernard Thomas "Bud" Lienhart (b. 1918, d. 1996) md. Melba Linebarger (b. 1922, d. 1989). He was an insurance adjuster in Morrilton until his retirement. Bud and Melba had three children: Tom Lienhart of Vilonia, Debbie Lienhart of California and Patti Franklin of Morrilton.

Ethel Marie (b. 1919, d. 1999) md. J. Fred Hart (b. 1918, d. 2002) of Little Rock. Ethel and Fred lived in Little Rock and raised six children: Fred Jr., Mary Katherine, Anne, Paul, Theresa and Margaret.

Otto Louis (b. 1921, d. 2004) md. Jeanette Sponer (b. 1926, d. 1973). He took over the Budweiser distributorship after his father Bruno died. They had one son Otto II. Jeanette died in 1973. Otto Sr. married Betty "Ish" King in 1978.

Julius Bruno (b. 1922, d. 1951) was a University of Arkansas graduate who taught for a short time after college, and was an insurance agent at the time of his death from leukemia at the age of 29.

The six Lienhart children graduated from Sacred Heart High School, and those who remained in Morrilton were faithful and dedicated members of Sacred Heart Catholic Church.

All three Lienhart sons saw active duty in the US Navy during WWII.

Both Bud and Otto were very active in the Morrilton business community, as their father had been, volunteering their efforts toward the betterment of life in Morrilton at every opportunity.

Bruno Lienhart died in 1953 and Katie Byrne Lienhart died in 1972.

LIERLY - Athalene Lierly Crook, Lonnie and Margaret Lierly's second daughter, was born Nov. 25, 1928. She graduated from Nemo Vista High School in Center Ridge after a girlhood spent living and working on the farm. She moved to Little Rock, where she eventually went to work for Westinghouse. A co-worker insisted that Athalene meet her brother, Floyd Crook. Floyd made quite an impression the first time he met Athalene's parents. A private pilot, not content with a typical entrance, Floyd landed a Taylorcraft airplane in a field near their house. The mule broke the fence and the chickens didn't lay eggs for a week afterward. In spite of that beginning, Athalene married Floyd in 1952 and they lived in California for several years before settling in North Little Rock.

Floyd, a Navy veteran of WWII, worked as a dispatcher and dock foreman in the freight business. Athalene worked in retail for many years and eventually retired from the Arkansas State Revenue Department, but her primary calling was as mother to Melissa, Mona and Lonnie. Athalene had many interests and talents. An avid gardener, she could always be found tending to her flower beds and vegetables. She also crocheted, sewed and painted in oils. Her paintings are proudly displayed in the homes of her family.

Melissa is a graduate of Harding University. She has a master's degree the University of South Florida and a juris doctorate from the University of Arkansas at Little Rock, School of Law. She is a law librarian who inherited her mother's love of gardening. Her husband, Douglas Serfass of Yardley, PA, a graduate

of Moravian College, is a website developer. They live in Little Rock.

Mona attended Arkansas State University in Beebe. After a career in restaurant management in Russellville and Hot Springs, she moved to Little Rock, where she works for the Arkansas State Revenue Department. Mona inherited her mother's talent for oil painting and enjoyed working on projects with her.

After graduating from the University of Arkansas at Little Rock, Lonnie served in the US Army. He is married to Kimberly Goheen of North Little Rock. Lonnie is a special agent with the Drug Enforcement Administration. Kim is a graduate of the University of Central Arkansas and received a master of business administration from the University of Arkansas at Little Rock. She is a certified public accountant and auditor. They live in Houston, TX with their son, Zachary Colton Crook. Lonnie, like his namesake grandfather, is a talented woodworker.

Athelene passed away on May 15, 2001. She left behind a legacy of love. *Submitted by Melissa Serfass and Mona Crook.*

LIERLY - Fayedean Lierly Anders (b. Nov. 24, 1923) was the oldest daughter of Lonnie and Margaret Lierly. She grew up in the Middleton Community of Center Ridge, AR, graduating from Nemo Vista High School. She moved to Little Rock, where she attended Draughon's School of Business. She worked for many years as a bookkeeper for auto dealerships in central Arkansas. Fayedean married Otis Anders of Jersey, AR, also a bookkeeper. They lived most of their married life in Little Rock. During WWII they moved to Richmond, CA, where they both worked as bookkeepers in the shipyards.

Their son David spent much of his childhood with his grandparents, Lonnie and Margaret Lierly, because he did not like life in the city. David married Betty Bryant, daughter of Hershel and Lorrine Bryant of Center Ridge. David and Betty both graduated from Nemo Vista High School. David, a truck driver for Wal Mart and Master Bladesmith, and Betty, a homemaker, have two children, Jerome and Lucretia.

Jerome met wife Kathy while living in Colorado. They now live in Center Ridge. Jerome is also a Master Bladesmith. David and Jerome are the only father and son Master Bladesmiths certified by the American Bladesmith Society.

Lucretia and husband Jim Williams live in Perryville, AR. Lucretia, a graduate of the University of Central Arkansas, is a county extension agent in Perry County. Jim works for the Pepsi Cola company. Their beautiful daughter is named Avery Elizabeth.

David and Betty make their home in Center Ridge, near the home place where Lonnie and Margaret lived. David still prefers life in the country. Otis Anders died in May of 1965. Faydean lived to see her two grandchildren, but passed away Nov. 20, 1975 after a long battle with heart failure. *Submitted by David Anders.*

LIERLY - John Lierly and his wife moved to Arkansas from Illinois in the 1800s. They had two sons, John and Tazzie Lierly. Tazzie moved to Oklahoma. John settled in Center Ridge, AR, where he married Ida Bennett. John and Ida had three sons: Lonnie, Grover and Willard, and three daughters. None of their daughters survived to adulthood. Beulah died at the age of 18, Addie at age 3 and another baby girl passed away shortly after birth.

Lonnie and Margaret Lierly

Lonnie Earl Lierly (b. Feb. 12, 1897) as a young man met a pretty young lady named Margaret Louise

Starkey. Lonnie would ride his old mule Goldie for miles just to court Margaret. Margaret (b. July 6, 1900) was the oldest of six children of Richard and Delana Starkey. Her brothers and sisters were John, Jess, Ruby, Jim and Minnie.

Lonnie and Margaret were married March 12, 1922. They made their home in the Middleton Community of Center Ridge, where they were the much-loved parents of three daughters: Fayedean, Athalene and Lillian. All three daughters graduated from Nemo Vista High School in Center Ridge, and eventually moved to Little Rock, AR where they reared their families.

Lonnie, an Army veteran of WWI, made his living as a farmer and carpenter. He grew cotton to sell, and corn for the family and the livestock. He could build anything. The farmhouse he built for Margaret in Middleton still stands today (granddaughter Denise lives there). During the early 1940s and WWII, he moved twice, along with his family, to work in war industries. In North Little Rock, AR, he worked at Camp Robinson building ammunition boxes. He later worked in the shipyards in Richmond, CA. During the war years, Margaret had to make ends meet by managing the family's ration books to purchase staple foods such as sugar and items such as gasoline, tires and shoes.

After WWII Lonnie and Margaret mostly lived on their farm. Margaret was a homemaker. She always kept a big beautiful garden, keeping the entire family supplied with its bounty. If she couldn't feed you at her table, she would send you home with a ready-made meal. Lonnie and Margaret's six grandchildren loved nothing more than to spend a time on the farm with their Pa and Granny. Granny could even make shelling peas seem like fun. And there was nothing more exciting to the grandchildren than riding out through the fields on the tailgate of Pa's old pickup truck.

Margaret succumbed to leukemia, passing away on Jan. 20, 1974. Lonnie, never the same without his Margaret, died of a heart condition Oct. 25, 1976. Family and friends still gather at the homeplace and remember the good old days, when Lonnie and Margaret brightened their lives. *Submitted by Lillian Heath.*

LIERLY - Lillian Lierly Heath (b. March 14, 1933) is the youngest daughter of Margaret and Lonnie Lierly. After graduation from Nemo Vista High School she also moved to Little Rock. She married Charles H. Heath, who grew up in Benton and Ferndale. They live in North Little Rock, where they raised their two children, Denise and Jimmy. Charles and Lillian each had two careers. Charles, a WWII veteran of the Army Air Corps, was a diesel mechanic and driver for several freight companies. His second career was as a school bus driver for Pulaski County. The children loved to ride Mr. Heath's bus, always bringing him gifts on Christmas, Valentine's Day and other holidays. Lillian was first an insurance secretary and underwriter. She retired from her second career with the Arkansas State Revenue Department. However, mother and grandmother are her preferred job titles. Lillian works in ceramics and porcelain, creating beautiful dolls and decorative pieces.

Denise graduated from Oak Grove High School. She married Jim Webb and they have a daughter, Leigh Ann. Denise, formerly a bookkeeper, lives on the family home place in the Middletown Community of Center Ridge where she keeps and cares for her horses. Leigh Ann is her grandmother Lillian's pride and joy. An honor student, Leigh Ann received an associate's degree from Pulaski Technical College and a bachelor's degree from the University of Arkansas for Medical Sciences School of Nursing. Leigh Ann married Navy Lieutenant Clayton Shane, a helicopter pilot flight instructor and graduate of the US Naval Academy. Upon completion of his training, they will live in San Diego, CA.

Jim obtained a general equivalency diploma so that he could leave high school early to join the Navy.

Back row: Charles and Jimmy Heath, Randy Barnhouse; middle: Lillian (Lierly) Heath and Denise Barnhouse; front is Leigh Ann Webb Shane.

After his Navy career, Jim lived and worked in California before moving back to Arkansas. Jim lived his too-short life to the fullest. He passed away on Dec. 22, 1993. *Submitted by Leigh Ann Shane.*

LILLEY - Rufus Wayne Lilley Jr., better known to friends and family as "Corkey," was born in Conway County, Morrilton, AR in 1937 to parents, Rufus Wayne Lilley Sr. and Lillian Leon Charton. Wayne Jr.'s mother was the daughter of Walter Henry and Donna Cruchfield Charton. Walter H. Charton's grandfather was born in France and entered the United States of America in 1842. Wayne Jr.'s dad was the son of Rufus Issac and Mamie Kennedy Lilley. Rufus Issac Lilley's mother was a native Cherokee woman in Oklahoma and he was born on a Cherokee reservation. Mamie Kennedy came from Atlanta, TX.

Madge and Wayne Jr. Lilley - December 1958.

Walter Henry Charton (grandfather of Wayne Lilley Jr.) delivering ice in Morrilton, dated mid-20s or early Depression years.

Wayne Jr. "Corkey" graduated high school from Sacred Heart Catholic School of Morrilton in 1955. After attending two years at Arkansas State Teachers College, now known as University of Central Arkansas in Conway, Corkey spent six months in the US Army at Fort Jackson, SC and finished his military service with the National Guard Unit in Morrilton.

Wayne "Corkey" married Edna Madge King in June 1958. Madge was born in 1939 to parents Lewis Wallace King and Edna Monteen Moore in Faulkner County, Conway, AR. She had one brother Lewis Dale King who died in January 2000.

Madge graduated from Morrilton High School in 1957. Corkey has three brothers: Allen Leon Lilley now deceased, and twin brothers Larry Kay and Garry Ray Lilley.

Wayne "Corkey" and Madge have three children,

all born at the old St. Anthony's Hospital in Morrilton: Rufus Wayne Lilley III (b. January 1961); Angela Kay Lilley (b. December 1962) md. James Bently Pew of Conway, AR; and William Thomas Lilley (b. March 1965) md. Deborah Lynn Johnson of Morrilton. Among their three children, Corkey and Madge have seven grandchildren to be proud of: Amber Nicole Lilley, Trevor Wayne Lilley, Samantha Kay Pew, James Austin Pew, Andrew Harrison Pew, Jennifer Brooke Lilley and Joshua Taylor Lilley.

Wayne Jr. "Corkey" took over Lilley Paint Co. from his father in 1960, building a successful business and continues to work in the business after turning it over to his son Wayne. Through the years Corkey was involved in several community activities. He worked in the Morrilton Junior Chamber of Commerce for many years serving as president for one year. He was a member of Ducks Unlimited for many years, serving as their president 1984-85; and served on the Planning and Zoning Commission for the city of Morrilton.

Through the years Corkey has enjoyed playing the guitar, rodeoing, hunting and fishing with friends and family. Corkey and Madge still reside in Morrilton.

LITTLE - Elmer Claud Little (b. April 15, 1903, d. Nov. 6, 1977) was the son of Alexander Davis Little and Elnora Josephine Brigham Little. A.D. Little (b. Aug. 1, 1861, d. Jan. 28, 1923) and Elnora (b. April 8, 1860 in Arkansas, d. July 8, 1938) are both buried at Elmwood Cemetery in Morrilton, AR. They were married Nov. 14, 1878 by D.H. Upchurch, minister of the ME Church. They were living in Moreland Community in Pope County

Claud and May Little

when they married. They lived for a time in Scott County, but primarily spent their life in Conway County. They had 12 children, with Claud being the youngest.

Claud's paternal grandparents were Holland Little and Elizabeth Alice Andrews Little. His maternal grandparents were Melvin "Marquis" Lafayette and Mary Ann Brigham. Holland was born about 1838/1840 in Georgia and Alice was born in North Carolina in 1829. Melvin "Fate" and Mary Ann Brigham were both born in Tennessee about 1830.

On July 31, 1926 Claud married Lela May Huett in Conway County. May (b. April 13, 1905 at Solgohachia, d. Jan. 26, 1980 in Morrilton) was the daughter of David Richard Huett and Beulah Virginia Greer Huett. D.R. Huett (b. Oct. 5, 1881, d. Sept. 30, 1910/18) and Beulah (b. Feb. 8, 1882, d. Sept. 2, 1967) are buried at Kilgore Cemetery. They were married Dec. 6, 1903 in Conway County.

May's paternal grandparents were James Madison Huett and Harriet Caroline James. J.M (b. April 3, 1857 in Arkansas, d. Aug. 11, 1944) and Caroline (b. April 6, 1858/59 in Mississippi, d. Oct 18, 1909) are buried at Kilgore Cemetery.

May's maternal grandparents were William L. Greer and Leretta R. Bird. W.L. (b. July 5, 1855/59 in Arkansas, d. Jan. 13, 1909) and Lee (b. Oct. 31, 1863 in Mississippi, d. June 29, 1915) md. Oct. 23, 1881 and had six children, with Beulah being the oldest. Both are buried at Friendship Cemetery in Solgohachia, AR.

Claud and May spent their married life in Conway County and had five children. They were Ruby Marvell, Hulon Emmett, Vivian Marie, David Marshall and Jerry Layne. Ruby (b. Dec. 16, 1926, d. Sept. 23, 1994) md. William Curtis Dixon on Aug. 1, 1942. They had six sons: John C., James Donald, Curtis Jr., Steve Owen, Billy Joe and Lloyd Clay.

Hulon married Ann Atkinson and they had one son and one daughter, Michael Lynn and Debbie.

Vivian married Leon Hill and they had one daughter and one son, Sharon Kay and Carl Allen. David married Mary Scroggins and they had two daughters and a son: Marchelle Lee, Melanie Renee and Derrick Marshall. Jerry married Carol Cornell and they had one son and one daughter: Jeffery Layne and Jennifer Lynn. He later married Norma McCoy.

Claud spent his working years and retired from the city of Morrilton. May was a "housewife." Both were rather quiet, soft spoken people. They both loved their children and grandchildren. Claud loved to fish and they both enjoyed gardening. *Submitted by Brenda J. Dixon.*

LOFTIS - Ellen Castleberry Loftis (b. May 4, 1881 at Center Ridge, Conway County, AR) was the daughter of Robert W. Castleberry (b. ca. 1862, Bradley County, AR, died before 1900 census) and Charity Emaline Spence (b. August 1858, died after 1920 census).

Clinton LaFayette Loftis, known as Fate, was born Feb. 3, 1882 at Bee Branch in Van Buren County, AR, and was the oldest son of Laborn Barton and Martha Ann Elizabeth Quattlebaum Loftis. He married Ellen Castleberry on Sept. 21, 1902 in Conway County, AR.

Fate and Ellen Loftis with children, Levi and Elvy.

Her grandparents were Elizatu Rose (b. December 1828 in Alabama) and Richard D. Spence (b. ca. 1818 in North Carolina). Her father's parents were Martha Jane White (b. 1840 in Mississippi) and John S. Castleberry (b. August 1837). Martha White Castleberry married Joseph Etheridge after the Civil War in Bradley County. Then they moved to Conway County. The young couple, Charity and Robert Castleberry, appears on the census with Mary and Joseph Etheridge after their marriage on April 22, 1880. This was Charity's second marriage. She first married Anderson Williams. So Ellen had a stepsister.

Charity and Robert had six other children: Tom (b. April 19, 1882, d. April 8, 1949) md. first, Levicy Loftis and second, Pearl Litton; Herbert (b. September 1882, d. 1971) md. first, Ada Hardin and second Ovalee Loftis; Mary Katherine (b. June 3, 1887, d. April 20, 1961) md. Merrick Barlett; Aruther (b. March 1888 married Cyretha; John J. (b. April 2, 1890, d. April 13, 1983) married Lavanda Cross; Robert (b. Dec. 4, 1891, d. June 25, 1966).

Ellen and Fate moved to Conway County before June 2, 1918, because my father Luther was born at Center Ridge and they are on the Conway County Census in 1920. They moved to Lonoke County when Floyd was a child. Ellen was shelling corn for the chickens when a hard dry kernel hit in the eye. Although a doctor treated her, she lost her eye and she had a prosthesis, or glass eye, which she usually didn't wear.

Fate and Ellen had 10 children, who included three sets of twins, yet only five lived to adulthood. Surviving children were:

Levi Boleth (b. 1904, d. June 8, 1973) md. Eura Leo Webb, daughter of Martha Webb, on Feb. 15, 1923. Levi married three other times.

Delcie (b. September 1910, d. Dec. 8, 1910) is buried in Quattlebaum Cemetery.

Minnie Esther (b. May 23, 1915, d. Oct. 10, 1991) md. first, Roland Manning in 1931 and second, Johnny McCullar on July 28, 1945.

Thomas Lester (b. 1915) md. Faye Cullum, daughter of Elbert "Dick" Andrew and Martha Lavinia Roberts Cullum, on July 11, 1938 in Van Buren County. Esther and Lester were the only set of twins to live to adulthood.

Margaret (b. Oct. 19, 1917, d. Jan. 2, 1925 at Center Ridge) died of the measles and pneumonia at 7 years, 2 months and 18 days old.

Luther Clinton (b. June 2, 1918, d. Oct. 9, 1993) md. Ola Carlene McKin, daughter of John Calvin and Willie L. Gray Mckin, on Jan. 3, 1938 in England, AR.

Ruby Floyd (b. June 4, 1923, d. May 19, 1995) had a twin, Lloyd who did not survive.

Clinton LaFayette (d. April 11, 1954) and Ellen (d. Sept. 30, 1956) are buried in Quattlebaum Cemetery along with Luther, Esther and Levi. Lester is buried at Union Valley in Lonoke County. Elmer, Elvy and Lloyd may be buried at Center Ridge. *Submitted by Martha Loftis Kehoe, granddaughter.*

LONG - Herman Layne Long (b. Oct. 15, 1924 in Springfield, Conway County, AR, d. Nov. 22, 1998) was the oldest child of Ira and Lector Cupp Long. Herman was always into everything, playing jokes and pulling pranks on everyone. On Feb. 6, 1943 he entered the US Navy but served with the Marines; this was during WWII. He was discharged as a pharmacist's mate 2nd class on March 2, 1946.

Herman was such a good-looking man and quite a catch, some would say. When Herman returned home he began

Glenna Cathelene (Hawkins) Long and Herman Layne Long, June 30, 1946.

dating Miss Glenna Cathelene Hawkins, daughter of John Carl and Nettie Mae Dockins Hawkins. Glenna (b. Sept. 19, 1926 in Center Ridge, Conway County, AR) was the sixth of seven children. While dating they frequented Warren's Café to hang out, as well as at the Corner Drug Store for milkshakes and ice cream at the soda fountain. There were steak suppers at Armour's Café. Sometimes they went hiking and canoeing on Petit Jean Mountain. After this fun filled courtship they were married on June 30, 1946.

Herman and Glenna both graduated from Morrilton High School (he in 1942 and she in 1943). Herman went on to State Teachers in Conway for a short time. He then ran the Long's Phillip 66 Service Station on the corner of Highway 64 West and Will Street. In January 1949 he returned to school at Arkansas Tech in Russellville. From there it was off to Oklahoma State University, where he received his master's degree. He then taught at Paris High School for one year and taught school at Newport for a year, followed by a job with R.J. Reynolds Tobacco Company of Little Rock. In the 1955-56 school year Herman began his teaching career at Arkansas Tech University in Russellville. Then, moving the family to Indiana (1963-65) where he obtained his EdD in business education at Indiana University. He was a member of Phi Delta Kappa and a distinguished member of Delta Pi Epsilon, both educational fraternities. He returned to Arkansas Tech University then retired in 1990.

After high school Glenna worked in the Circuit Clerk's Office; from there she worked for J.E. Brazil, an Attorney - Abstract Office. Upon moving back to Russellville, she worked in the Academic Dean's Office. She also worked within the banking institution in the Trust Department. She retired in 1988. Herman always loved to hunt and fish but one of his most favorite places was the pawnshop, that's where he always found his little treasures. Glenna was the gardener and loves flowers. She is always in the kitchen

cooking up something for someone. She is one of the best cooks around! They have always been ready to help whenever they were asked, no matter what the task. After retiring, Herman and Glenna also spent time traveling, working with their church and spending time with their family.

They have two children: 1) Stephen Layne who has two children, April Kristen and Evan Layne. April has one child, Mackenzie Kristen Watson. 2) Linda C. has one child, Zachary Wayne Reddell who has one child, Logan Paige Reddell.

Herman and Glenna shared 52 years of marriage. They have always been a very special couple to all who have known them.

LONG - The earliest record of John D. Long in Union Township, Springfield, Conway County, AR is Sept. 7, 1859, when he purchased 275 acres from a family named Murray, according to Conway County records. John D. would have been about 19 years old at that time. The farm property was located northeast of Springfield, toward Cedar Creek.

After buying the farm, John D. returned home to Bradley County, TN not coming back to Conway County permanently for about 14 years. The Civil War was one reason for the extended delay, because military records provide evidence that he served as a private in the 43rd Tennessee Infantry CSA Company D Quartermaster Department, along with his older brother, Thomas A. Long. who was a sergeant in the same company.

John D. Long (b. 1840 at Bradley County, TN) is most likely the second of six children of Louis and Mary A. born in Tennessee. John D. married Cornelia E. Bolton of Hamilton County, TN on Feb. 25, 1869. Cornelia was the oldest of possibly 11 children born to Allison Lance "Yell" Bolton and Jane Steele, born in Virginia, living in Tennessee. For geographical reference, Chattanooga is located in Hamilton County and Bradley County is the next county to the east.

In about 1873 John D. and Cornelia moved from Tennessee to the Conway County property, bringing daughter Marcy A. and son John Louis with them. Additional children, born in Arkansas were John H., William Ike, Delia and Eugene. Eugene was one of twins, the other of which did not survive. It appears that at least two of Cornelia's brothers (Bolton) also came to Arkansas and were Springfield merchants in following years.

John D. apparently died sometime between 1890 and 1900, most likely of tuberculosis. Cornelia died sometime before 1910 because she is not listed on the 1910 census. John D. and Cornelia may be buried near Cedar Creek or Springfield, though no records or grave markers have been found. The original farm was apparently sold by Eugene after his mother Cornelia's death.

Eugene, the youngest child, was born in 1881. Eugene told his daughter that he made a "hand" on the family farm by the age of seven. He later worked as a carpenter in Plumerville, after fire destroyed part of that town. He returned to the farm to help his mother after his father died.

Eugene married Mary Elizabeth Ford of Van Buren County. Her parents were William Cellers Ford, son of Thomas Cellars Ford and Martha Ellender McKee, and Alpha Etta Barnes, daughter of David D. Barnes and Mary Elizabeth Hill. William Cellers Ford died a relatively young man and Alpha Etta later married Thomas Alfred Sloan.

Eugene and Mary Elizabeth moved to England, Lonoke County, AR for the work that was available in that area at the time. They had three children: Ruby Lee, Ralph and Roy. Mary died in childbirth with Roy on Friday night, Oct. 13. 1922. Eugene and Mary Elizabeth are buried together at Mulberry Cemetery near England.

John Louis Long, the second child and oldest son, and his wife Josie Parker are buried at Cedar Creek Cemetery, northeast of Springfield. The lower picture on page 182 of the book, *Conway County - Our Land, Our Home, Our People*, shows several of John Louis and Josie's children.

Hopefully, other Conway County residents know the history of the other children of John D. and Cornelia E. Long and will share that information. *Submitted by Ruby Lee (Long) Tarver, daughter of Eugene and Forrest Michael Long, son of Roy Long.*

LORD - James Lord and his brother, George, sons of Joseph and Sarah Lord, emigrated from Rochdale, England in 1844. They are the descendants of Thomas and Dorthy (Bird) Lord who emigrated to the colonies on the ship, *Elizabeth*, in 1635. Henry the III of England married Sarah Lord, one of our ancestors. Our ancestors go back many generations to Captain Stanley Lord, who was Master of the ship, *The Californian*, which was not far from the *Titanic* when it sank. Also, Walter Lord who wrote the book "A Night to Remember."

George settled in the Lords Schoolhouse Community, and is my great-great uncle. He built the first schoolhouse in this community, therefore, it is named after him. He and his family are buried in Gordon's Chapel and Campground Cemeteries. His daughter, Hattie, married Dixon Malachi James.

James Lord married Hannah Lord, his cousin. They settled in Rushville, IL. They had four children: Joseph (b. 1826); Sarah (b. 1811) md. Richard Lester; Mary (b. 1814) md. Alexander Mosley of Scotland; Margaret (b. 1822) md. Michael Sweeney of England.

Joseph S. (b. 1826) md. Judidia Boyd (b. 1848 in Indiana). Joseph went overland to the California Gold Rush, where he made his fortune. They had 12 children: James Madison (b. 1849) md. Parthene Parnell; Mary (b. 1854) md. Thomas Kent; William (b. 1853) md. Ellen Cain; Anna (b. 1855) md. William Davis; Robert (b. 1857) md. Susan Zygette of Sweden; Sarah (b. 1859) md. Jacob Clark; Joseph (b. 1861) md. Cora Linn; Josephine (b. 1861) md. Dillard Harris; Amanda (b. 1863) md. Herb Moore; and Charles (b. 1870) md. Nellie Malone.

James Madison, my grandfather (b. 1849 in Rushville, IL, d. 1898) was a Mason, a trapper and a US Marshal. He traveled down the Ohio River to Arkansas, where he met Parthene Parnell. They were married in Nelson, OK, Indian Territory on July 28, 1885. On Aug. 20, 1889, he went to McCurtain County, OK, during the Gold Rush Fever, and purchased land on March 12, 1899, but never reclaimed this land. They later settled in Locksburg, Sevier County, AR. He was killed in 1898 while returning from taking a prisoner to Fort Smith, AR, eight miles from Provo, Howard County. About one mile from his home he was shot off of his horse. They had four children: James Damon, Mary Louise, Edmond and Parthene Florance.

Parthene Florance (b. 1898, d. 1985) md. John Allen Nicholson Feb. 2, 1919. They had three children: Clarenda Corrine (b. 1920, d. 1969); John Allen "Johnny" Jr. (b. 1930, d. 1980) and Janie Bell (b. 1935-).

Clarenda Corrine married Robert Swope Dec. 19, 1939. Their children are Allen Royce (b. 1940), Phyllis (b. 1941), Robert Blayne (b. 1943), Carolyn Sue (b. 1945), Rocky Lane (b. 1949) and Judy Estelita (b. 1953).

Johnny Allen married (1) Joyce Hale, (2) Cleo Marie Issacs and (3) Lavern Flannery. He has two children, Benita Irene (b. 1953) and Venita Marie (b. 1957).

Janie Bell (b. 1935) md. Howard Upchurch and John Reedy. Her children are Connie Ann (b. 1953), Sharon Rose (b. 1955), Howard Thomas Jr. (b. 1955), Alan Howard (b. 1957), Mark Anthony (b. 1958) and Rhonda Renee (b. 1962).

Parthene had five great-grandchildren: Gregory (b. 1973), Susie (b. 1975), Angela (b. 1978), Raymond (b. 1980), Shaun (b. 1992) and Jacob (b. 1991). She had one great-great-grandchild, Ashylnn Nichole (b. 2002).

Most of these descendants live at Lords School-house Community. *Submitted by Janie Nicholson Reedy and Rhonda Reedy Tanner.*

LOWDER - The family of Jeremiah Lowder was one of several families who came to Conway County with a wagon train from North Carolina. Deed records find Jeremiah M. Lowder and family in Conway County on Dec. 1, 1859. Jeremiah purchased land on that day from Johnson and Mary Bennett. However, Joshua Moses, county clerk, did not record the deed until April 2, 1860. The land Jeremiah bought was purchased for $400 and is recorded in the Deed record as the NW corner of the NE quarter of Section 28, Twp 9N, of Range 16W containing 51 acres.

George D. Lowder and wife, Lizzie Bowman Lowder, approximately 1939.

Jeremiah's family on the 1860 Census consisted of the following individuals: (See 1860 Census, Conway County, Lick Mtn. Twp. page 109, Household 815): Jeremiah M. Lowder, Head of Household, age 37, Farmer, Place of birth North Carolina; Persilla M., wife, age 28, Cook, Place of birth North Carolina; Robert F., son, age 10, Place of birth, North Carolina; Mary F., daughter, age 6, Place of birth North Carolina; Catherine E., daughter, age 4, Place of birth North Carolina; Frances M., daughter, age 1, Place of birth North Carolina; Cloubon Rose, laborer, age 61, Place of birth Tennessee.

By 1861, the Civil War began and Jeremiah enlisted on Oct. 7, 1861 at Lewisburg, AR for an initial 12-month period. He enlisted as a private in Company A, 17th Regiment Arkansas Infantry and was later transferred to Company D, 21st Regiment Arkansas Infantry (Civil War Service Record Card #798). Jeremiah never returned to Conway County as he was killed in battle at Tupelo approximately 1862. Before leaving for the war, George and Persilla had their last child, George David Lowder, born Dec. 7, 1860. It is through George Lowder that I am descended.

George D. Lowder grew up in Conway County around Lick Mountain. He left the area some time in the 1890s and moved to Van Buren County, where he raised his family. George married Elizabeth Frances Bowman of Isbell Creek, Pope County on Aug. 4, 1902. George's family is listed on the Arkansas, 1910 Census in White Oak Twp., Van Buren County, Household No. 181 as George D. Lowder; Lizzie, wife; Roxa E.; Bettie; Rubie, Henry and Grady Lowder. They later had two more sons, Lester and Andrew Lowder. His daughter, Rubie Lowder, was my grandmother.

George D. Lowder sold his land in Conway County Nov. 30, 1920 to officers of the then known Lowder Cemetery in Cleveland, AR. George owned two farms in Van Buren County that were separated when he and his wife Lizzie divorced on Sept. 26, 1929. He lived with family members after the divorce until his death. George Lowder's death was published in the *Morrilton Democrat*, Conway County, AR on March 20, 1941, and listed under the Cleveland Section. He died of pneumonia in the home of his daughter, Mary Raberson, on March 14, 1941. He was buried in Lowder Cemetery, Cleveland, AR beside his mother, Persilla M. Lowder. *Submitted by Paul Adcox.*

MAIDEN - William Maiden (b. 1808 in Virginia) md. Margaret (last name unknown) prior to 1831 in Virginia. Margaret was born 1808-13 in Virginia. At least three children were born to William and Margaret in Virginia. About 1836 William moved his family to Ohio, where at least four children were born. About 1846 the family moved to Illinois where two more children were born. The family moved to Indiana about 1850, where the last child was born. Prior to 1860, the family moved to Iowa and settled in Henry County.

William was a farmer and had a good deal of money when he settled in Henry County. He soon bought a great deal of farmland. In 1860 William's real property was valued at $9,000 and his personal property at $2,000. The 1870 Henry County census showed the family living in Scott Township. Living in the same area was their daughter and son-in-law, Rebeca and William Adamson, and their family. Also living in that area was their son Henry and his wife. Three sons: William, John and James were still living at home. John was teaching school and William and James were farming with their father. Margaret died after 1870.

William married Cordelia (last name unknown) after Margaret's death. Cordelia was born in 1838. William died 1897 and is buried in Winfield-Scott Cemetery near Winfield, IA. Cordelia died 1937 and is buried beside William. Children of William and Margaret included:

1) Simeon B. Maiden (b. 1830) md. Sarah. Children: Charles, Simeon Jr., William and Margaret Maiden. Simeon married second to Caroline. Children: Annie, Mary and Joseph Maiden.

2) Caroline Maiden (b. 1833).

3) Elizabeth Maiden (b. 1834, d. 1922) md. William D. Shultz.

4) Rebeca A. Maiden (b. May 29, 1836, d. June 16, 1922) md. William Sheppard Adamson. Children: Anne (md. Louis Edwin Bush), Grant and John Adamson.

5) Henry Maiden (b. 1839) md. Margaret.

6) William F. Maiden (b. 1843) md. Katie. Children included William J. Maiden.

7) John Maiden (b. 1845).

8) Jacob B. Maiden (b. 1847) md. Emma. Children: Minnie and Willis Maiden. Jacob then married Mary. Children: Hazel and Olive Maiden.

9) Jack Taylor Maiden (b. 1849) md. Margaret. Children included: Daisy, Bertha and Jennie Maiden.

10) James M. Maiden (b. 1851, d. 1896) md. Mary. Children: Milton, Willie and Alva Maiden.

Several descendants of the Maiden family moved to Conway County in the early to mid-1900s. A number of these descendants remain in the area today.

MAHAN - Jimmie Mahan III (b. 1822 in Kentucky) md. Emily White (b. 1827 in Kentucky). Jimmie and Emily moved to Conway County in 1863. Emily died during the journey and was buried on the trail. Jimmie settled in the Hogan Creek area (five miles east of Center Ridge near Van Buren County). In 1865 Jimmie married Tine Poteet. Jimmie died circa 1903 and is buried in Center Ridge Cemetery. Jimmie and Emily White Mahan's children:

1) Nancy (b. 1847) md. Joseph Atkinson. Children: Margaret (md. James Fulkerson), Mary C. Jane (md. James H. Mason, Sophronia (md. John Mason), Jesse (md. Tennessee Newberry), Samuel, Cora (md. Charles Cullum.

2) Dempsey (b. 1848) md. Nancy Jane Shewmake Adams. Children: Johnny (md. Lucy Johnson and Hattie Allen) and Jimmy, a bachelor.

3) Lucy (b. 1850) md. Thomas Yow and had Neely who married a Foster; Lucy married George Crabtree. Children: Lue, Berlie, Jim, Bill and Charlie.

4) John Melton (b. 1851) md. Sophronie Steely (no children).

5) Jesse W. (b. 1853) md. Harriet Stripling. Children: Nanny (md. Joe Geary), Jodie (md. Charlie Willis), Lue (md. Joe Halbrook), Iola (md. Frank Bowman), Taylor (md. Hattie French), Dovie (md.

Jim Eaton, Ethel (md. Allen Polk). Jesse married second to Genie Stripling Rhoades and he married third to Frances Nicholson.

6) James Irving (b. 1853, a twin to Jesse) md. Mary Starkey. Children: Irvie (md. Triphena Paxton, Addie (md. Lona Doughty), Harvey (md. Lantie Latimer), Frank (md. Minnie Byrd), Lowell (md. Loretta Dockins), Della (md. Albert Nichols), Webb (md. Lottie Byrd), Vincent (md. Katie Kelley).

7) Will (b. 1855) md. Mary Ann Lockhart. Children: Jane (md. Bob Jones), Zora (md. Fred Huffman, Thomas French, Truman Crownover), George (md. Dora Carpenter), John (md. Orie Brown), Princie (md. Jim Brown), Deanie (md. __ Norwood), Darby (md. Alma Latimer), Jack (md. Fronie Brown), Harrison (md. India Tackett), Floyd, Floy (md. Otto Tindall).

8) Mary (b. 1857) md. George Stripling. Children: Bill (md. Flora McMahan), Jess (md. Della Stobaugh), Ella (md. Ray Cooper), Claud (md. Ina French), Maud (md. __ Settles), Mandy.

9) Eliza Jane (b. 1859) md. William W. Reed. Children: John (md. Rose Halbrook), Lula (md. Tom Crigg), Betty, Henry (md. Ruth Glover).

10) Nicholas (b. 1861) md. Martha Starkey. Children: Wesley (md. Alice Doughty), Martin (md. Lottie Byrd), Larkin (md. Effie Tackett), Jess (md. Lela French), Arthur (md. Evie Geary), Belle (md. Pink Knopp).

Jimmie and Tine Poteet Mahan's children: Larkin (b. 1868) md. Alice Gilbert and Jane Morrow Rainwater; Martha (b. 1870) md. Bill Geary; Henry (b. 1872) md. Marie Cooper and Annie Hurst; Lelia (b. 1874) md. Will Harris; Dorothie (b. 1876) md. Drew Bryant; Miles Melvin (b. 1879) md. Nora Marlow and Rosie Harris. *Submitted by Richard Mahan.*

MALLETT - Jesse L. Mallett (b. Dec. 2, 1861 in Mallettown, Conway County, AR) was the son of John and Sabra Elizabeth (Cargile) Mallett. He was a direct descendent of Stephen (Etienne) and Marie Mallet; Huguenots who came to America in 1699 and settled in Manakin, Henrico County, VA.

Front row: Vernon and Orpha Johnston; children are Alton and Willie Mae, early 1930s.

Jesse Mallett and Mary Cordelia "Delia" Miller were married Oct. 12, 1884, in Conway County, AR. Mary (b. April 3, 1871, in Greenbrier, AR) was a daughter of Warren "Jack" and Rebecca (Honeycutt Hensley) Miller. Warren "Jack" (b. 1845, in Gilmer County, GA) was the son of Daniel B. and Barbara (Pettit) Miller. Mary Miller's siblings were Lockey Victoria (md. Isaac William Allinder) and Andrew J. (md. Lydia Bell Mallett). Children born to Jesse L. and Mary Cordelia "Delia" Mallett were Drucie (md. Walter Norwood), Irvin L. (md. Ethel Mount), Marvin E. (md. Blanche Lyons), Edna (md. Edd Howell), Orpha (b. May 6, 1898), Ruby (md. Virgil Price), Ray, Wilma L. (md. Clarence Hart).

My grandparents were Vernon Clarence and Orpha (Mallett) Johnston. They were married Nov. 19, 1916, in Faulkner County, AR. Vernon (b. Aug. 9, 1895) was a son of John C. and Rosie (Bramlett) Johnston, in El Paso, White County, AR. Children of John C. and Rosie Johnston were Leona, (md. __ Black), Agnes, Vernon, Horest (twin) (md. Flonnye Cleo Dallas), Forest (twin) (md. Sammie Clouette) and John C. Jr.

John C. (b. Jan. 12, 1863) was the son of James and Amanda Jane (Ward) Johnston. Sometime after his wife Rosie died, John moved to Republican, AR. He is listed as one of the earliest settlers of this Union Township Community, located about four miles northwest of Greenbrier.

Vernon and Orpha Johnston lived in Conway County, then moved to Republican, where they owned a general store. Their children were Alton Theodore (md. Ellen M. Donals) and Willie Mae (md. William R. Hinkle). In the early 30s, the store caught fire; Vernon and Orpha and their two children escaped with only the clothes on their back. A friend of the family, Judge Clark, owned a farm located close to Hope, and offered to let the Johnstons live on it until they got back on their feet. Vernon took his family and Joe Tolby, a friend who lived with them, and moved to the Green Lasater Community, where they farmed.

My father, Alton, would bring the produce to Hope, and sell it from a wagon. Later the family would move to Hope, where Vernon went to work for South Arkansas Implement Company. Vernon was the bookkeeper, and Alton worked there as a salesman. Alton married Ellen Donals on Dec. 24, 1940. Alton served in WWII in the European Theatre, with the 82nd Airborne as a paratrooper. When he returned from the war, he and his wife Ellen and their two children, Priscilla and Larry, made their home in Hope, AR.

Vernon, Orpha, Alton and Ellen, are all buried in Memory Garden Cemetery, just outside of Hope. Their daughter Willie Mae is still living at this writing. *Submitted by Priscilla Johnston Davis.*

MALLETT - Joseph Columbus Mallett (b. Feb. 10, 1882) was the son of George Washington Mallett and Henrietta (Casharago) Mallett. George's ancestors, of French descent, came to this country as early as 1699. Joe's grandfather, Jessee II, and grandmother, Matilda Tabitha (Sterling) Mallett, were numbered in the 1890 History of Conway County as some of the earliest settlers. They moved here in 1841 from Monroe County, GA, and settled in what is now called Mallettown, where Joseph Columbus, more commonly called Joe, was born.

Papa, Mama, Carl, Lorene, 1908

Joe's mother, Henrietta "Hetty" (Casharago) Mallett was a native of Genoa, Italy. She came to Arkansas (at the age of 7) in 1850 with her parents. They settled in Prairie County near Des Arc, later moved to Faulkner County and finally settled in Mallettown.

Joe was a farmer and very active in the Methodist Church at Mallettown. He regularly taught Sunday school until shortly before his death at age 98. His father George donated the land for the Mallettown Cemetery. Joe married Lula "Abbie" Duncan on Aug. 17, 1902. Abbie's parents were John Q. and Tabitha Duncan. To this union two children were born, "Carl" Columbus and Henrietta Vaughn. Abbie died Oct. 26, 1905.

Joseph Columbus's second wife was "Lona" Elizabeth Salter, daughter of John Milton Salter and Mary Henrietta (Pearson) Salter. Joe and "Lonie" were married Dec. 22, 1907. To this marriage 10 children were born: Alta Lorene, Carrie Ophelia, Norma

Cleo, Opie Dalton, Thurman Othelian, Willie Marie, J.C., Milton Leon, Gwynnith Louise and Grace La Verne. Lonie died Aug. 10, 1928.

After the death of his wife, being both mother and father to a family of 10 children must have been a very difficult task for Joe. The older girls helped with household chores, the sons tended to the fields with Papa and everyone became attentive parents to the younger children. Joe's mother, Hetty, also helped when the family needed her. Joe grew so close to his family that it is no wonder that he is, to this day, affectionately called "Papa" by all his children, grandchildren and great-grandchildren.

Joseph Columbus "Papa" Mallett died April 21, 1980, and is buried in the Mallettown Cemetery between both of his beloved wives.

Carl Columbus married Clemmie Browning (both deceased). Their children are Abby Elizabeth "Happy," Henrietta Louise "Lou," and Carl "Dean" Mallett.

Alta "Lorene" married Joe Castleberry (both deceased). Their children are James "Travis" and Della "Jocile."

"Carrie" Ophelia married Harold Martin (both deceased). Their children are Harold "Harry" Mallett, "Ruth" Carolyn and Joseph "Wayne." They live in California.

"Norma" Cleo married Eli Clouette (both deceased). Their children are "Peggy" Lou (deceased) and Forest Eugene "Gene" Clouette. Norma's second marriage was to Bill Hoth (deceased).

"Opie" Dalton married Audrey Mae Johnson (both deceased). Their children are Ronald "Ronnie" Dalton, "Gary" Glen, and twins Lonie "Jean" and Ollie "Jane." Opie's oldest son by a previous marriage is Opie "Dale" Mallett.

"Thurman" Othelian married Ruby Jones. They live in Conway, AR, and are the parents of "Joe David" Mallett.

Willie "Marie" married F.E. Scroggins (both deceased). They have three children: "Kay" Marie, "Marilyn" Jo and "Bruce" Eugene.

J.C. married Alice Elma White. They live in Oklahoma City. Their daughters are "Barbara" Lynn Mallett and Janet "Jan" Gayle (Mallett) Lake.

Milton "Leon" (deceased) has a daughter, Lona Ruth "Sue."

"Gwynnith" Louise married Lester Ledbetter (deceased). They share three children: "Lynnette," Sanford Leslie "Les" and "Kevin" Gwynne.

Grace "LaVerne" married Robert Bane (both deceased). Their children: Robert "Keith" (deceased), John "Warren," "Nancy" LaVerne (deceased), and "Karen" Elizabeth (Bane) King.

Papa's homeplace is currently being restored by Karen (Bane) King and her husband David. It has been kept in the family, where loved ones often return "home to remember." The house holds many memories of "Papa" and family. *Submitted by Jan Lake.*

MARTIN - John V. Martin (b. 1817 in Virginia), son of Joel and Fanny Martin, had a brother George W. (b. 1818 in Tennessee). There may have had other siblings who have not yet been located. Joel and Fanny were born in Virginia in 1787. The three families were living near each other in Hardin County, TN in 1850. They were farmers.

John V., with his wife and children, moved into Union Township, Conway County, AR before 1860. Joel and Fanny have not been located after 1850. George with his family moved from Tennessee to Ouachita County, AR. John V. moved to Van Buren County before 1880. His wife Sarah died before 1880; Sarah may have been his third wife. His children were William Joel (b. 1841, d. 1927) md. Mary Ann Ables, he served in the Civil War; Frances W. (b. 1845); Mary Ann (b. 1847); Sarah Berthena (b. 1849, d. 1931) md. Jack Summers and later married William A. Webber; John Ruben (b. 1854, d. 1930) md. Delila Goodman (b. 1850, d. 1905); John Anderson (b. 1856, d. 1929) md. Sarah Ann Kerley; Alveta (b. 1863); and Louisa b. 1865). John V. died between 1880 and 1900.

John Ruben Martin family. Seated: John Ruben Martin, Delila (Goodman) Martin. Standing l-r: Daniel H. Martin, Robert Houston Martin and Eli Mansfield Martin - 1904.

John Ruben, son of John V. and Sarah Martin, married Delila A. Goodman in 1871. Delila was daughter of William E. and Martha Caroline (Merriman) Goodman. Delila died in 1905 and is buried in Harness Cemetery, Stone County, AR. In early 1910 John Ruben moved from Leslie, Searcy County, AR to the Hill Creek Community in Conway County. He died in 1930 and is buried in Mt. Pleasant Cemetery, Hill Creek.

John and Delila had 12 children, but only nine lived to adulthood. They were:

1) Georgia A. (b. 1872, d. 1938) md. John W. Passmore. Children: William (md. Dorothy Wilson), Jefferson (died age 13), Wesley (never married), Susan (md. Adam Richardson), Viona (md. Claud Branscum), Millas (md. Arthie Jollie), Miller (md. Jessie Clemons), John (md. Maud Bassinger), Mark (md. Mammie Laster), Bertha (died age 12), Bitha (md. Dan Barnett), Amos (md. Myrtle Sterlin), and Olus (md. Mattie Delk).

2) Joel Jefferson (b. 1876, d. 1964), merchant and farmer, married Sarah Jane Wilson. Children: Julia (md. Russell Hudspeth), Lillie (md. Charles Turner), and Irvin (md. Aulene Jones).

3) Riley A. (b. 1878, d. 1953) md. Aretty King. Children: Mary Bell (md. Charlie Williams), Lona (md. Noah Tiner), Emline (md. Ed Johnson), Ollie (md. Guy Spires), Floyd died at young age, Bertha (md. Marion Bond), Hestlee (md. Charles Bond) and Vestle (md. Joe Hartline).

4) John Wesley (b. 1880, d. 1939) md. Mary E. Mitchell. Children: Arminta (md. Arden Faulk), Loyd (md. Ollie Fryer) and Gertha (md. Ersle Standridge).

5) Martha A. (b. 1882, d. 1958) md. William Thomas Passmore, no issue.

6) Eli Mansfield (b. 1883, d. 1978) md. Nellie Mae Watts. Children: Dicy (md. Walter Baker), Uless (md. Mary Helen Cobb), and Leta (md. John Cobb Jr.)

7) Robert Houston (b. 1885, d. 1967) md. Hannah Mary Sutterfield. He was a merchant and farmer. Children: Roy (md. Mayona Bridgman), Elsie (md. Truman Childress), Nelsie (md. Hiram Prince), Lora (md. William Lampley), and Gladys (md. Irvin Carter).

8) Mary Lenora (b. 1866, d. 1927) md. Johnnie Noah Cooper. Children: Noah (md. Lea Mallett), Vurla (md. Clarence George), Vurda (md. Marvin Stover), Girlie (md. Homer Stracener) and Gurtha (md. Fred Ussery).

9) Daniel H. (b. 1890, d. 1972) md. Melvina M. Chadwick. Child: Merdie (md. Wilma Rhoades).

Before 1930 Riley and his family moved to California; Mansfield and family moved to Oklahoma. The other seven remained in Arkansas, most of them in Conway County. Several of the John Ruben Martin descendants still live in Conway County. *Submitted by Jemolee (Martin) Cole.*

MASON - Ada Mason Bryant Stroud (b. Jan. 1, 1905 at Center Ridge), daughter of James H. and Mary J. Atkinson Mason. She married C.A. Bryant and they were the parents of six daughters:

Standing, l-r: Stuart and Stephanie Spencer, Thetus McCoy; seated: Ada Mason Stroud, Lynda Spencer.

1) Maxine (deceased) md. Melvin Polk and had one son, Darryl Ray. He married Mary-lynn Adams. He has PhD in engineering and they reside in Austin, TX. They have one daughter, Amy Rebecca.

2) Thetus married Herman Stell and had a daughter Lynda Kay. Thetus served in the Women's Marine Corps in WWII. She is the widow of Mack McCoy and resides in Little Rock. Lynda Kay Stell Spencer is media specialist in Little Rock school system. Her son Stuart Spencer is an attorney. Daughter Stephanie is a resident in UAMS.

3) Nadine married Howard Ridgely in Washington DC. Two daughters: Karen married Ronnie Matthews and they have daughter Christy and two grandsons. Leanne married Barry Bland and both are teachers in Conway schools. Leanne and Barry have Samantha and Annabelle.

4) Charlene married Bill Looney, lives in Little Rock, has a daughter Rebecca Diane (deceased) and son Randy. Randy and his wife Rita Sutterfield Looney are both attorneys in Little Rock. Their children are Kyle and Bekah.

5) Jimmie Lee married Norman "Stormy" Smith. Children are Larry Joe (md. Sonya Breeding). Larry is principal of middle school in Conway. Their daughters are Sara Kathryn and Natalie. David Brian (md. Mary Curran), works for ARKLA. Their children are Clint and Lindsay. Debbie (md. Thomas E. Lambert) is a teacher in Conway. Their children are Laurie and Michael. All live in Conway.

6) Mary Jo married Robert Cline and they live in Maumelle, AR. Robert is owner of a computer company. Their sons are Thomas Scott and Robert Allen. Allen's son is Robert Peyton. Scott married Rhonda Waymore and they live in Tennessee.

J.H. Mason, "Pa," used to sing to Ada and her sisters; his verse for Ada was "Prettiest little girl in Arkansas. Pretty as she can be, cheeks as red as roses, eyes as blue as the sea, and her name is Ada Lee" - those were happy times.

Ada quit school young to marry, but was determined her children and grandchildren would get as much education as possible. All of Ada's grandchildren graduated from college. Ada later married Roy Stroud and they lived in Oregon for awhile, then moved back to Conway, Faulkner County, AR. Ada was a member of the Church of Christ. She was a very talented seamstress, quilter and cook. She was employed in the cafeteria at UCA for many years. She died March 15, 1999, and was buried at Center Ridge Cemetery.

MASON - Frances V. Mason (4A) was the fourth child of J.H. and Rebecca Damaras Harriet Hill Mason, who survived childhood. She was born Dec. 12, 1881 and died in 1949. She was about 11 years old when J.H. Mason married Mary Centelia Jane Atkinson. She was 10 when her mother died. Frances married J. Galloway Howard (b. Sept. 8, 1887, d. Nov. 12, 1963). They had one son Thelbert Othello (b. April 23, 1909, d. Sept. 13, 1952). Thelbert married Dorothy Bryant and they had one son Kenneth (b. Dec.

19, 1931, d. November 1992). Kenneth married Jettie Harrelson Oct. 3, 1974.

Galloway, Frances and Thelbert Howard, ca. 1918.

Frances was very close to Emma who was born in 1894 when Frances was 13. Frances helped her stepmother rear Emma, Fred and Dewey. She and Galloway lived for some time in the Catholic area southeast of Center Ridge; later they owned and operated a general store in Center Ridge. Galloway and all the Howards were enthusiastic sportsmen, especially baseball and basketball. One time Galloway told Kenneth that every member of the baseball team that was playing at Center Ridge had the last name of "Howard," or was related to the Howards. Galloway had a great sense of humor and was always telling jokes and pulling pranks on the younger generation. Frances enjoyed him and his jokes, having a good sense of humor herself.

Kenneth said that one of the big thrills for him while growing up in the Center Ridge area, was the annual 4th of July picnic. He enjoyed the baseball games between the local teams and remembered the hamburger stand and baseball throw doll rack. He remembered the ice cream sold at the hamburger stand, which was two scoops for a nickel. The one in charge would chant "Stack 'em high, stack 'em high, 365 days till another 4th of July."

Frances and Galloway, Thelbert and Dorothy, Kenneth and Jettie were all active workers in the Church of Christ. *Submitted by M. Bostian.*

MASON - Fred Orville (b. June 7, 1895) was the second child and first son born to James Harrison Mason and Mary Jane "Sis" Atkinson Mason. Fred attended the one-room school as all the children did in Center Ridge. He loved to play basketball on the dirt "court" even in the dead of winter. Some of his teammates were Olen Fullerton, Edmond Stobaugh, the Etheridge boys, Polks and Gordons. This love for sports endured all his life, even af-

Belle and Fred O. Mason - 1971.

ter all his sports had to be "spectator" sports. The St. Louis Cardinals were his team!

After finishing the eighth grade or 8 terms, he took the teachers exam, passed it and taught several terms at nearby schools, Austin, Greasy Valley, Grandview, to name a few. Then WWI broke out and he enlisted in the US Navy and was assigned to the medical branch. He made two trips to France aboard the USS *Mercury*, transporting home the wounded and sick servicemen.

He returned home and after taking some courses at Arkansas Tech College, began teaching again in one or two room school houses. About this time a young lady, Mary Isabelle Miller from Culpepper Mtn. in Van Buren County, came to Center Ridge to teach all eight grades in a one room school. She had taught several terms in the Van Buren County rural schools. Teachers in the early 1900s were not only expected to do a good job of instructing students, but also to build wood fires, sweep floors, draw drinking water, etc. Fred and

"Miss Belle" met in the school room, "courted" several months, then married in Morrilton on March 15, 1921. Belle did not teach any more until WWII, when there was a real shortage of teachers and she taught seventh grade at Nemo Vista.

Around 1925 Fred passed the Civil Service exam and was appointed one of the two mail carriers at Center Ridge. The other one was Jake Richardson. Their routes were each about 50 miles long and they took the mail to all their patrons, six days a week, rain or shine, snow or sleet. It was not unusual for them in the days long before air conditioners or heaters, to get their Model T's or Model A's stuck in the dirt road, or slide off in a ditch, and to have to walk miles to find some kind soul to come help push them out. Fred wasn't much of a complainer and "took it as it came."

They were members of the Church of Christ and Fred was member of Masonic Lodge for over 50 years, member of Arkansas Realtors and was delegate to the Nat'l Republican Convention in San Francisco in 1964. Belle died in 1986 and Fred died in 1989. They are buried at Center Ridge.

Their children: Kenneth Orvid (b. Feb. 5, 1922) graduated from Harding College with degree in history and political science and served in US Coast Guard. He married his college sweetheart, Mildred Knowles. Kenneth died in April 1953 and is buried at Center Ridge.

Ferrel Orville (b. March 23, 1924) also attended Harding college, served in US Air Force and US Maritime Service. He went to New Orleans, worked as contractor, realtor and hotel owner. He married Georgia Nassie and they have three children: Marylynn, Susan and David L., and six grandchildren.

Mary Carolyn, shortened to Mary Lynn, was born Dec. 28, 1927. She attended Harding College and U of A and taught home economics. She married D.V. Bostian and has four sons: Bruce, Stephen, Charles and Keith, and nine grandchildren. *Submitted by Mary L. Mason Bostian.*

MASON - Isaac Dewey Mason, the fourth child born to James H. and Mary C. Jane Mason, was born Sept. 9, 1898 in Center Ridge. He died July 15, 1976 in Fort Smith, AR and was buried in the Center Ridge Cemetery. He married Minnie Evelyn Fullerton (b. April 9, 1891, d. Jan. 6, 1974) and to them three children were born: Sammie Sue Mason (Watts), James Henry Mason, and a son who died shortly after birth. Dewey and Minnie moved to Morrilton to put their children in the Arkansas Christian College Academy, which later became Harding University after moving to Searcy. Dewey was a lay-minister of the Church of Christ and a postman. He and Minnie celebrated their 50th wedding anniversary several years before their deaths.

Dewey and Minnie Mason 50th Wedding Anniversary

Sammie Sue Mason (Watts) (b. April 15, 1919, d. March 1992) was a graduate of Harding University and obtained her master's degree from the University of Arkansas. She taught in the Fort Smith schools for many years, and worked as a high school counselor the last years before her retirement. She loved to travel, was a dedicated worker in her church, and in all things pertaining to education. She loved her "kin folks" and helped to start Mason reunions. She married Clyde Watts (b. Sept. 13, 1913 in Bexar, AR, d. Jan. 11, 1985) and to that union was born one daughter, Evelyn Sue Watts (Walker). Evelyn Sue's husband is Charles Neal Walker of Akron, OH. She is a college graduate and teaches school.

James Henry Mason (b. Aug. 14, 1924) graduated from Harding University and from Washington University, St. Louis, MO with a degree in dentistry. He practiced dentistry until his retirement in Fort Smith, AR. He married Ella Margaret "Margie" Pryor of Morrilton (b. Jan. 23, 1923) and to that union two sons were born: Rodney and Bob.

Rodney married Lottie and works for the government in an executive position with Social Security. He has a serious back problem, but has not let the crippling effects deter him in any way. He placed fifth in the Tulsa, OK 15k Wheelchair Race in 1992, and is also an ardent fisherman, evidenced by pictures of his big catches.

Bob married Vicky. He followed in his father's footsteps and is a practicing dentist in Ft. Smith. The fourth generation of the Dewey Mason family to date is represented by Amy and Lucas, children of Bob and Vickie, grandchildren of James Henry and Margie. *Submitted by J. Mason.*

MASON - James Harrison Mason married his second wife, Mary Centelia Jane Atkinson, Jan. 8, 1893. To this union nine children were born:

Mary Jane "Sis" Atkinson and James H. Mason on wedding day, Jan. 8, 1893.

1) Emma Viola Mason (b. Jan. 23, 1894, d. July, 1975) md. John Calloway Bradley. Their children were Eva Lee Bradley (Cralle) and Thelma Bradley (Bradley).

2) Fred Orville Mason (b. June 7, 1895, d. January 1989) md. Belle Miller and had three children: Kenneth Mason, Ferrell O. Mason, and Mary Lynn Mason (Bostian).

3) Samuel Lafayette Mason (b. Dec. 27, 1896, d. Oct. 5, 1897).

4) Isaac Dewey Mason (b. Sept. 9, 1898, d. July 15, 1976) md. Minnie Fullerton and had three children: Sammy Sue Mason (Watts), James Henry Mason and one died in infancy.

5) Joseph Theodore Mason (b. Sept. 9, 1900, d. Sept. 9, 1901).

6) Mary Damaras Mason (b. Oct. 10, 1902, d. Feb. 19, 1911). Double services were held for her and her younger brother, Laurice H. Mason.

7) Ada Lee Mason (b. Jan. 1, 1903) md. Britt Bryant. Their children are Maxine Bryant (Polk), Thetus Bryant (Stell, McCoy), Charlene Bryant (Looney), Jimmie Lee Bryant (Smith), Nadene Bryant (Ridgely), Mary Jo Bryant (Cline). Ada divorced Britt and married Roy Stroud.

8) Nancy Leota Mae Mason married Hulon Epperson. Their children are Betty Jo Epperson (Mourot) and Donald Mason Epperson. *Submitted by F. Mason.*

MASON - John Calvin Mason (b. Nov. 25, 1873, d. May 17, 1952) was the son of James Harrison Mason (b. Oct. 4, 1850, d. July 16, 1927) and Rebecca Damaras Harriet Hill (b. Dec. 25, 1849, d. April 1891).

James Harrison and Rebecca had 10 children, with John Calvin being the oldest. Only six of these children survived. His siblings were S.E. (b. 1878, died as a youth); Roxie A. (b. 1880, d. 1903); Frances V. (b. 1881, d. 1949); Chester A. (b. 1883, d. 1972); James Blaine (b. 1886, d. 1975).

John Calvin's mother Rebecca passed away when he was about 18 years of age, and about two years later his father married Mary Centelia Jane Atkinson

and to this union nine children were born: Emma Viola (b. 1894, d. 1975); Fred Orville (b. 1895, d. 1989); Samuel Lafayette (b. 1896, d. 1897); Issac Dewey (b. 1898, d. 1976); Joseph Theodore (b. 1900, d. 1901); Mary Damaras (b. 1902, d. 1911); Ada Lee (b. 1903); Nancy Leota Laurice; Laurice Harrison (b. 1901, d. 1911).

John Calvin and Saphronia Mason

John Calvin married Sephronia Elizabeth Atkinson (b. Oct. 11, 1873, d. April 30, 1945) who was a sister to Mary Centalia Atkinson. To this union was born: E.L. (b. Oct. 5, 1896, d. Aug. 21, 1922); Flora Maye (b. Dec. 18, 1897, d. Jan. 29, 1902); Baby, unnamed (b&d. Dec. 30, 1899); Joseph Elmer (b. March 27, 1901, d. May 14, 1971) md. Lora Prince, daughter Gladys; William Chester (b. Dec. 28, _, d. May 19, 1912); Samuel (b. Dec. 23, 1904, d. Jan 30, 1905); James Aaron (b. Jan. 1, 1906, d. 1978) md. Ida McMahan, children are Wanda Faye, Orville Lee and Ronald Odell; Lonnie Venson (b. April 1, 1908, d. May 9, 1971) md. Celia Davis, children: Daniel Othello, Bernice Allene, Mary Evelyn, Wilma Lee, Alice O'Dean, Johnnie Venson, Lonnie Wayne, Lena Mae, Bennie Ray, Ferrell Lynn, Marvin Leon, Quinton Earl, Sidney Harold, Katherine Marie; Lee Hamilton (b. Dec. 22, 1911, d. Dec. 23, 1975) md. Thelma, son Marvin Raye married Flonell, married Pat; John Wilburn (b. March 5, 1914) md. Edna Masterson, children: Elizabeth Ann, Johnnie Louise, Verdia Mae, Mary Lee and Janice Ruth.

For many years Pa and Ma Mason (as their grandchildren called them) lived on the Fullerton place just above Center Ridge, not far from Pa's parents, who were the original "Ma and Pa Mason." Pa was a farmer, raising cotton and corn. They had a small orchard and garden where he and Ma enjoyed growing unusual varieties of vegetables. They liked spinach and always had it in their garden. Each year Ma planted a Jack-a-bean vine at the end of the porch to provide shade.

Ma was under 5' tall, but spunky. She was capable of throwing a tantrum by flinging herself to the ground and well…just having a fit. She was an excellent seamstress, making her own wardrobe of long dresses from beautiful brocades and organdy fabrics. Pa always wore his suit coat everywhere he went.

Ma and Pa were members of the Church of Christ and are buried in the Center Ridge Cemetery.

Following Ma Mason's death, Pa married Miss Alice from Nebraska. She wore lots of makeup and nice clothes. She passed away before Pa did.

MASON - John Samuel Roberts, aka Samuel Mason, was a highly decorated soldier who fought with General Forrest's Cavalry, was wounded and lost his leg while fighting during the Civil War.

After the war when John returned home to Alabama, he was involved in a conflict with a local interloper concerning a conflict with his wife. This led to a shooting and John Roberts left Alabama and changed his name to Samuel Mason. Samuel settled in Tennessee and went to work for a successful horse breeder. He married the man's daughter, Cosie, and they went to Memphis, where Samuel attended and completed medical school.

After medical school, Dr. Samuel Mason and wife went to Arkansas where he had relatives located in Conway and Pope counties. Dr. Mason and wife finally settled in Hattieville, AR. Dr. Mason had an extremely successful practice there and raised his children, Walter, Sula, Maggie, Sidney, Joe, Drew and Essie.

Dr. Walter Lee Mason

Essie and Maggie both married Hattieville men and became prominent citizens of north Conway County. Essie married Joe Golden and they had six children: Mason, Sybil, Bill, Emmett, Mary and Jimmy. Maggie married Oscar Beason, a local merchant and they had two children, Walsie and Zelby.

Ardella Massingill Mason

Walter Mason went to Memphis and attended medical school and returned to Conway County. He married Ardella Massingill, daughter of Marion and Mahalia Massingill. They had one child, Barbara Mason. Ardella died when Barbara was 2 years old; therefore, she spent much of her young life with her aunts, Bertha and Mattie Massingill.

(Left) Barbara Mason Rowell with Blanch Calon.

A few years later, Dr. Walter Mason married Bertha Alewine and they had two children, Walter A. and J.L.

Barbara married George Rowell of Hattieville and had two children, Della Jane and Bobby. Barbara spent most of her adult life in Hattieville until moving to California in 1952. J.L. moved to California as a young man and worked as an electrician and mechanic. He had three children: Carolyn, Ellen and Lewis. Walter "Little Doc" moved to California after graduation from Atkins High School. He was a highly decorated soldier during WWII. After serving his country, he worked for the US Treasury Department as a customs and narcotic agent. He had one child, Barbara "Babs."

Dr. Samuel Mason was a prominent physician in Conway County; however, his life took a tragic turn at the end. Although his son, Dr. Walter Mason did everything in his power to care for him, Dr. Samuel Mason lost touch with reality in the end. The article appeared in the *Arkansas Gazette* on Nov. 10, 1908.

Dr. Walter Mason dedicated his life to serving the people of Conway and Pope counties. However, he also experienced a great tragedy in his life. The article appeared in the *Arkansas Gazette* on Dec. 26, 1906 and the *Atkins Chronicle* on Jan. 8, 1907. *Submitted by Bobby George Rowell with thanks to Sue Roberts.*

MASON - Lawson Anderson Mason was born Jan. 15, 1860 to Samuel S. and Elizabeth Shoemake Mason, Conway County, AR. On May 8, 1881 in Conway County, Lawson married Ellen D. McGinty, the daughter of James W. McGinty and Emily C. Scroggins, both of Conway County. Ellen was raised by her grandparents, James Madison and Samantha Stell Scroggins of Conway County. Ellen was born Aug. 18, 1862 in Arkansas.

Lawson Mason family: Back l-r: James Madison Mason, Lizzie Mason, Della Mason. Front l-r: Lawson A. Mason, Donna Mason, Ellen McGinty Mason, Maggie Mason.

Lawson and Ellen moved to Indian Territory, OK in 1892. According to Lawson, they came with a small group of pioneers, some six or eight wagons. They stopped over in LeFlore County, OK. It has been believed for years that Elizabeth Mason was buried beside Samuel in the Gaylor Cemetery in Conway County. However, in a recently found interview at the Oklahoma Historical Society, Lawson states his mother was buried at "old Shake Rag in the Choctaw Nation." Research has shown that to be what is now Bokoshe, LeFlore County, OK. She died in 1896, so apparently she remained in LeFlore County while Lawson and Ellen went on to what became Pontotoc County, OK. Some of Ellen's Scroggins family either moved with them or were already settled there. A number of Scroggins descendants still live in the Ada, OK area.

Lawson is thought to have participated in the land run of 1898, which opened up land south of the Canadian River. They settled near Washington, McClain County, OK. Lawson was chairman of the Anti-Horse Thief Association. Oklahoma, not being a state at the time, was home to a large number of outlaws, and stolen horses were a common occurrence. Later, he became good friends with the governor of Oklahoma, Alfalfa Bill Murray. Lawson ran a whiskey still and when he would get caught he would make a phone call and get off the hook. Presumably he was calling his friend, Governor Murray.

My father, Lawson's great-grandson, born in 1935, could remember going with Lawson to the stills when he was a child.

Lawson and Ellen had six children. The oldest being 1) James Madison Mason (b. Jan. 25, 1882, d. Feb. 7, 1940 in Conway County) md. Madlin Sumpter and had 16 children - 12 of whom lived to be adults.
2) Della Frances Mason (b. 1885, d. 1918) md. David Thomas McMahan, also of Conway County. They had five children.
3) Donna Delaney Mason (b. 1899, d. 1955) md. Jay Elwin Claunch and had a large family.
4) Lizzie Mason (b. 1890, d. 1910) md. _ Walker.
5) Mary Magdalene Mason (b. 1892, d. 1987) md. William Harve Lenderman and had four children.
6) Munro Mason (b. Dec. 9, 1900, d. Dec. 30, 1902) was their youngest child.

Ellen came down with tuberculosis and the family moved to New Mexico for the drier air. It didn't help so they came back to Oklahoma. Ellen died in 1908 and is buried at the cemetery in Washington, OK.

Lawson remarried in 1911 to Elizabeth Muse Lenderman (b. 1864, d. 1934), widow of Caleway Linderman. Lawson remained in Washington until 1949 when he passed away. He is buried next to Ellen in the Washington Cemetery. *Submitted by Vicci Mason Flatt.*

MASON - Lena Mae Mason (b. Jan. 2, 1941 in Center Ridge, AR), daughter of Lonnie Venson and Celia Davis Mason. Her brother Lonnie in trying to say, "little sister," inadvertently gave her the name, "Tootie," which was to be her nickname till she grew up and left home. Her siblings are Daniel Othella, Bernice Allene, Mary Evelyn, Wilma Lee, Alice O'Dean, Johnnie V., Lonnie Wayne, (Lena), Bennie Ray, Ferrell Lynn, Marvin Leon, Quinton Earl, Sidney Harold and Katherine Marie.

Lena attended Nemo Vista elementary school till fifth grade, then moved with her parents and siblings to Southeast, MO. Following her graduation from Gideon High School in May 1959 she moved to St. Louis, MO where she lived until November 1961 when she married Duane Lawrence Tolbertson of Hayward, CA (formerly of Storden, MN).

Duane was a career Marine, which took them all over the United States, both the East and West Coast, and a 3-year-tour of duty in Hawaii. She loved living in Hawaii so much she wanted her mother to see it too, so she flew Celia to the Islands for a 6 week visit. She loved the military life with the exception of the unaccompanied tours of duty overseas during the Vietnam era. Duane retired as a master gunnery sergeant E-9, USMC in 1977.

Upon his retirement, the family settled in Oceanside, CA. Her home state of Arkansas is still dear to her heart and she returns frequently to visit her family and take lots of pictures. Children born to this union are:

David Duane (b. Jan. 20, 1963 in Vallejo, CA) md. Jasmine Lee Chin. Children: Tyson (Jasmine's son), Ariel Lee (b. May 3, 1986), Ashley Marie (b. Dec. 31, 1987). Divorced, married Pamela Bland.

Daniel Wayne (b. Jan. 22, 1965 in Vallejo, CA) md. Sabrina Lynn Moody. Children: Justin Daniel (b. Nov. 28, 1993), Matthew Lawrence (b. Dec. 14, 1996) and Maverick Timothy (b. Oct. 23, 2001).

Rebecca Joann (b. March 18, 1970 in Manassas, VA) md. Martin Rodrigues. Divorced. Note: Daughter, Rebecca was adopted as an infant in Manassas, VA.

Lena attended Cosmetology School in Honolulu, HI and became a licensed cosmetologist in 1975 in Oceanside, CA. She is a talented hairdresser, seamstress, cook, artist, computer geek and digital camera buff. Her motto is, "never stop learning." She is a perpetual student of computer classes. A doting grandmother, whose grandchildren call her "Honey," instead of Grandma.

Duane and Lena are both active members of the Church of Christ in Vista, CA. Duane is an elder, teacher, bible scholar and webmaster for the church's website. Lena is the official photographer in charge of photos for the website, pictorial directory or where there is a need for photographs. Lena taught Cradle Roll Classes for many, many years but now assists Duane in developing classes for Bible studies held in their home. *Submitted by D.L. Tolbertson.*

MASON - Lonnie Venson Mason (b. April 1, 1908, in Center Ridge, AR) was son of John Calvin and Sophronia Atkinson Mason. His siblings were E.L., Flora Maye, baby who died in infancy, Joseph Elmer, William Chester, Samuel, James Aaron (Lonnie V.),

Lonnie and Celia Mason

Lee Hamilton and John Wilburn. He attended school through eighth grade at Nemo Vista, after which he went to work on the farm.

On Aug. 31, 1925 he married Celia Catherine Davis (b. March 21, 1911), daughter of Daniel Webster Davis and Hulda Ward of Bee Branch (or Damascus). Lonnie and Celia lived on a farm in the Center Ridge area and raised cotton, corn, cows, and sold milk to the dairy. He was a carpenter, bricklayer, cabinet maker, farmer, barber and loved to play checkers. His checkerboard said Lonnie on one end and Loser on the other. He butchered hogs, cured meats in the smoke house, made great sausage, broke horses to pull a wagon and to plow. In 1950, he moved his family to Southeast, MO.

In the early 1960s he quit farming and took the job as chief of police in Risco, MO. In 1963 Lonnie and Celia moved to Solgohachia, AR, and lived there till Lonnie passed away May 9, 1971 from heart problems. Celia lived there until Sept. 22, 1988. She succumbed to strokes and kidney failure. Both are buried in the Mason Family plot in the cemetery beside the Church of Christ in Center Ridge, AR. They were members of the Church of Christ.

Children born to this union:

Daniel Othella (b. June 27, 1929, d. Feb. 21, 2003) md. Katherine Guinn. Children: Shirley, Sheila and Sondra.

Bernice Allene (b. Jan. 5, 1927, d. 1937).

Mary Evelyn (b. Sept. 28, 1929) md. Kenneth E. Anderson. Children: Melissa Elaine, Kenneth Clay, Barbara Leanna and Melanie Andre.

Wilma Lee (b. April 30, 1931) md. William C. Gambill. Children: James Mason and Nancy Lynn.

Alice O'Dean (b. Jan. 25, 1933, d. June 4, 1992) md. Thomas B. Hairston. Children: Thomas Victor, Linda Susan and Timothy Mark.

Johnnie Venson (b. March 20, 1935, d. Jan 26, 1987) md. Irene Plough. Children: Johnnie Venson Jr., Larry Wayne, Janice Kay. Divorced, married Dora; children, Marvin Wayne and Vincent Leon.

Lonnie Wayne (b. Dec. 23, 1939) md. Mary Leta Flowers. Children: Charles, Carolyn and David Allen.

Lena Mae (b. Jan. 2, 1941) md. Duane L. Tolbertson. Children: David Duane, Daniel Wayne and Rebecca Joann (adopted).

Bennie Ray (b. June 27, 1943) md. Ella Berry, no children, divorced; he married Chris of Germany. Children: Nicole (Chris's daughter), Danny and Jessica (deceased).

Ferrell Lynn (b. Dec. 20, 1944) md. Beverly Harris. Children: Tammie Regina, Ramona Lynn, Delana Renea. Divorced, married Barbara Eades.

Quinton Earl (b. Dec. 28, 1947, d. April 20, 1993) married Linda Lee Gwin. Children: Christina Lee and Michael Earl.

Marvin Leon (b. Aug. 8, 1946) md. Linda Gail Davis. Children: Kevin Leon, Marlana Gail, Keith Erick (deceased) and Amanda Kaye.

Sidney Harold (b. July 5, 1949, d. Oct. 26, 1986) md. Jill Brandt. Children: Shane, Carrie, Erika. Divorced.

Katherine Marie (b. July 28, 1951) md. Thomas Joe Williams. Children: Thomas Joseph II "Jody," Andrew Venson and Maria Einett.

Baby girl to be named Margaret Ann Mason. Stillborn Oct. 3, 1953.

MASON - Samuel Selathiel Mason (b. 1828, probably in Lincoln County, NC) came to Conway County, AR before 1849 from Gaston County, NC with his older brother William Alexander Mason. A story that a 94-year-old cousin in Gaston County remembers her mother relating is: Selathiel, being a young man, was supposed to go with the wagon train headed for Arkansas only as far as the first day's journey and then return home. Someone insisted he go all the way to Arkansas with them. He replied "I will if you give me your Bowie knife," which they did, and he kept going West with them until they reached the state called Ar-

kansas. His parents never saw him and his brother again.

James Harrison Mason family - 1921.

Wm. Alexander purchased land in Conway County Dec. 25, 1849. He settled in Pope County and we have no record of him ever living in Conway County. However, the issue is made cloudy by the fact that Pope and Conway boundary lines were disputed for some 17 years. Anyway, we wonder if the property in Conway County may have been given to his young brother and his bride, for Selathiel and Elizabeth C. Shumake were married on that same date, Dec. 25, 1849.

Elizabeth C. (b. 1830 in Tennessee) was the daughter of James and Nancy Baird Shumake, who came to Conway County before 1840.

Elizabeth and Selathiel lived several years in Union Twp., Post Office Springfield, which was the county seat for awhile. All of their children: James Harrison, Marcus Layfayette, John Stark, Mary F., Lawson A., Elizabeth Ann, Nancy Emma and Wm. Harrison, were born while they lived in Union Twp. Because Mary F. does not appear with the other children in later censuses, it is believed she died young.

Selathiel enlisted in the Union Army at age 34, and served six months. It has been said that our ancestors who served with the Union Army were not "Yankee lovers," but simply believed that the owning of slaves was wrong. He was a private in Company "B," Arkansas Infantry Battalion (Union) organized at Batesville, AR, June 10, 1862, by amalgamation of two companies of volunteers from Conway County, brought into (occupied by Fed. Forces under General Samuel R. Curtis) by Thomas J. Williams and George M. Galloway. In the organization of Co. "B," Williams was chosen captain, Galloway first lieutenant and Nathan Williams second lieutenant. Selathiel also served at Helena, AR and his name appears on the Muster Out Roll at Benton Barracks, MO.

Selathiel served as justice of the peace for many years. Because that name is very unusual, and his first name was Samuel, many times on legal papers he signed them simply "S. Mason." It is interesting that he performed the marriage of our other great-grandparents, Nancy Mahan and Joseph Banks Atkinson on July 25, 1868.

Selathiel died Oct. 23, 1873, at age 45. He was buried in Gaylor Cemetery, now abandoned, which is about two miles east of Center Ridge. His and one other Civil War veteran are the only graves with markers. They have only their names and "Co. B" inscribed on them. We had thought for many years Elizabeth was probably buried there also, but their son Lawson A., who moved to Oklahoma Territory, stated that Elizabeth was buried in LaFlore County, OK.

After Selathiel's death, Elizabeth applied for and received a widow's pension of $12 per month for her and the children, which she drew until her death, Feb. 4, 1896. Selathiel and Elizabeth had acquired quite a lot of personal property and real estate before his death. Elizabeth seemed to be a very resourceful person, having a knowledge of business affairs. She made several legal transactions after becoming a widow, being assisted by her cousin, Wilson C. Shewmake.

These pioneer ancestors must have had tremendous strength and courage! We give tribute to these ancestors who gave us our heritage. In researching their

lives, we feel as if we knew them, and only wish we could have known them better. *Submitted by Mary Mason Bostian.*

MAUPIN – Bobby Lee Maupin (b. Aug. 26, 1934 on Rock Street, Morrilton, Conway County, AR) is the third son of John Wesley and Girtha Jewel Johnson Maupin. His paternal grandparents were John Wesley Maupin (b. November 1876, d. Dec. 23, 1902) and Hariet Ella McClure (b. Aug. 6, 1877, d. May 4, 1939). His maternal grandparents were Frank M. Johnson (b. June 27, 1885, d. April 6, 1952) and Caldonia "Callie" Edith Fox Johnson (b. March 2, 1890, d. Sept. 27, 1965).

Bobby Lee Maupin, age 18

Bobby Lee first attended school at the old Hannaford School near the Cotton Mill, where both of his parents worked. In 1942, the family moved to Tucker, between Prison Camp 1 and 2. His mother refused to move to California, so his father abandoned his family and went to California. Bobby's mother promptly filed for a divorce which was granted.

Bobby lived with his mother until her death on the night of Oct. 8, 1948 when she was murdered by his step-father, Harvey Rorie. Bobby Lee was 14 and went to live with his father and attended school at Sylvan Corners Grammer School in Citrus Heights, CA. He did not feel welcome in his father's home so he lived with his older brother, Johnny, who had a good job at a grocery store in Roseville, CA. Although he liked school in Roseville, it was difficult to adjust to a new environment without his mother. He returned to Morrilton to live with his Uncle W.T. and Aunt Veva Robinson, and again attended school at Morrilton.

When the Korean conflict started, he was again living with his brothers, Johnny and Edward, in Roseville. Johnny got his draft notice for the Army and could not get a deferment, so Bobby enlisted in the Army so they could serve together. Johnny had gone to Arkansas on a final visit and joined the Air Force. At 17, Bobby was sitting in the muddy dug-outs on a hillside in Korea. At one time he had been a driver for the Allied Commander, General Van Fleet and was now a medic. Bobby took his R and R leave to Nagoya, Japan to see his brother John, who was at the Air Force headquarters. John did not like the stories he heard, and when Bobby returned to Korea, he was soon notified that he was being sent home.

Senator Sparkman of Alabama invoked the Sullivan Act and let the Army know he was shocked that they were so desperate for men that they would put an orphan 17 year old in such of a hell hole as Korea, and that his brother was in the same theater of operations. John was safely in Japan, but subject to duty in Korea. Bobby Lee was soon a happy young civilian in Roseville, CA.

Bobby Lee returned to Morrilton to drive a truck for his uncle W.T. He loved his uncle so much, it's surprising that he did not pay Uncle W.T. to let him drive! He was at last a happy young man. He got to haul a load of marble from Georgia, made a few trips to Missouri for feed, plus the locals. Late one night he was on his way home from Missouri when the rig got away from him up in the Ozarks. Suddenly Bobby found himself in a cold creek bed with water quickly rushing into the cab and steam hissing from the hot engine. He was trapped and feared being burned alive, but suddenly, there was help. His neck was broken in three places and his left arm in four places. After a stint in the VA hospital at Little Rock, he returned to California with a full collar neck brace, but spirits high.

I wish there was more space to describe his additional accidents; a steel beam fell and hit his hard

Arkansa Head, breaking his neck in several places, plus his back. Full body cast for over a year and too many operations to remember. Bobby Lee was always smiling even if he might be gritting his teeth in pain.

He married Nancy Nell Leffingwell, a native of Sacramento, CA. on July 14, 1956, in Nevada. They have three children:

1) Robin Lynn born at Stockton, CA. She was a 3-year graduate of Casa Roble High School in Orangevale. Her first husband died of cancer. She and their son, Shane Gilbeau, live at Cleveland next to her parents.

2) Bobby Lee Maupin (b. Aug. 29, 1958 in California) is also a graduate of Casa Roble High School. He is a manager of a Wal-Mart Store near Roseville, CA. He married Shirley Kapusihinsky of Sacramento. They have children: Christina, Jennifer Ann and Bobby Lee Maupin III.

3) Michael Wayne (b. March 28, 1961) came to Conway County with his parents and helped build their new home. He is an excellent carpenter like his father. He married Deborah Jean Couch of Kennesaw, GA. They have two daughters and one son and now live in Georgia. *Submitted by John O. Maupin.*

MAUPIN – Edward Francis Maupin (b. Sept. 29, 1932 at 308 Rock Street, Morrilton, AR) was the second son born to John Wesley and Girtha Jewel Johnson Maupin. His great-grand-

parents were John Wesley Maupin (b. 1836 in Wayne County, TN) and Lida Louisa Cooper (b. 1847), who came to Searcy County about 1859, and William Fox (b. 1836) and Martha Ann Ramsey Fox. Martha was the daughter of Bradford Ramsey of Stone County, AR.

John Wesley Maupin on bottom.

Edward first attended school in 1938 at the old Perryville School, then went to school in Morrilton until his parents moved into a house that was just west of the western city limits sign of Morrilton. Because the family was no longer residents of Morrilton, the children were transferred to the old 2-room school of Hannaford. Edward's parents both worked at the Cotton Mill when WWII was declared.

Ed Maupin on bottom.

In May of 1942, before the end of the school year, the family relocated with other family members to Jefferson County, AR. They lived on the gravel road that came from Tucker and passed Tucker Prison Camp 1 and 2. Their house faced Camp 2. At that time, prisoners were hired out to the local farmers to work in the fields or farm the prison land, so each day long lines of men would march by the house on the dirt road that went straight between the camps. Several times Edward, his brothers and cousins stood outside the prison fence and saw the men given their evening punishment for not picking their assigned quota of cotton or for breaking some rule. Punishment was with a leather strap about six inches wide and three feet long with a brass "ring" on one end. The prisoner was placed face down over a table and the trustee that administered the blows, held the strap with both hands and let it hang down his back. With a swift swing, he would bring the wide belt down on the mens' back. Many looked shocked and cried out as if they had not expected much pain.

Edward's parents divorced and his father went

to California to find work. He failed to send money to feed his children. Edward and his younger brother, Bobby, would work as a team and chop the same row of cotton together to "make-a-hand" to help support the family. His older brother was able to chop a row alone to qualify as "a hand," but the pay was so low that they feared starvation. The boys were always grateful for a loving mother that never scolded or gave them the strap for not meeting a quota. She gave her children love and treated them as individuals who deserved respect.

In 1946, Girtha remarried to Harvey Rorie and the family was happy for a few years, but in 1948, she left her husband and took her children to live on a farm leased by her brother at Plum Bayou. She worried about Harvey's small children and wanted to take them, but he would not let them go. Girtha refused to return to him, so on Oct. 8, 1948, after midnight, he came to the house, murdered her and burned the house to hide his horrible crime. He denied killing Joyce and Frankie, but knew they were there by their mother when he threw the match.

After this tragic loss, Edward went with his brothers to live with their father in California, but it was difficult to recover since he was so close to his mother and little sister. He lived with his brother Johnny instead of his father. When his brother Johnny got drafted and Bobby enlisted in the Army, Edward tried to enlist several times, but was told he was "possible diabetic."

In 1952, he married Thressa Messick at Reno, NV. Of course, he was then drafted into the Army! Thressa was born on Nov. 14, 1935 near Ft. Worth, TX. Their first child, Debra Ann, was born at Ft. Bolvour, VA on Sept. 29, 1953. Terry Lynn was born June 5, 1960 at Roseville, CA, and their son, John Lee Maupins, was born on March 19, 1962 at Roseville. When Edward was in the second grade, his father started using an "S" on his name, so Edward has continued to use this ending to the family name.

While he was in the Army, he became a telephone lineman and continued in this career after his discharge. He loved working outdoors and with a crew of men, but eventually he was "kicked upstairs" until he was the district representative of his company in Alaska, when he retired and moved to Cleveland, Conway County. He loved his huge ponds stocked with channel cat fish and soon had the waters covered with mallards and Canadian geese. He had always loved horses and now he could raise his own. Edward passed away at the age of 64, on a Tuesday, Sept. 9, 1997 and is buried in the Liberty Cemetery at Cleveland. Tess is still at home in Cleveland. *Submitted by John Curtis Maupin.*

MAUPIN - John Curtis Maupin was born on Sept. 20, 1930 at Geridge, Lonoke County (settlement was near Humnoke, AR). He was the first son born to John Wesley and Girtha Jewel Johnson Maupin. Shortly after his birth, his parents returned to Morrilton. The "Great Depression" was in full swing and they were forced to share a house with Frank and Callie Johnson and their children. John Wesley swept the streets of Morrilton at night with a push-broom, and found other work during the day to help the families survive. He went to the "bottoms" of Point Remove

John Curtis Maupin, taken 1963 in Germany.

and filled gunny sacks with "poke salet greens," which he hauled to Morrilton. Despite the laughter and teasing of the family, Wes sold all of the greens and made many more trips to fill orders.

When John Curtis was 9 months old, his two front

teeth fell into his mother's hands as he was nursing. A huge carbuncle on his neck was almost destroying his throat. The local doctor refused to treat the ill child, and told the parents that they had waited too long to seek treatment. The condition was fatal since the growth had reached the "wind pipe." No one in the household could sleep except when the father held the child to his shoulder while sleeping in a rocking chair, then the crying would stop.

Late one night while the family members were at last getting some rest, Wes placed a blanket and clean sheet on the kitchen table, lit another oil lamp and placed the baby on the table. Wes sterilized a razor and tweezers. He had cotton and bandages ready. The first touch of the razor gave him a shock because the carbuncle split open with such force it shot the putrid pus almost into his face. The baby did not make a sound as each of the 19 heads (some say 22) of the growth was carefully dug out to their roots. The gapping hole was sterilized and packed with cotton, then a bandage was wrapped around the infant's neck. It was now almost daylight, and due to the silence in the house, the family started to awake. The grandfather, Frank Johnson, was in a rage and threatened John Wesley with prison for "deliberately killing that boy." Instead of killing his first born, John Wesley performed a miracle and gave him life a second time.

I never knew of this operation until I was a grown man and my aunts related the event. Only one of my central teeth grew back, the gap was eventually closed, and this odd defect always got a lot of attention at the dentist office. Perhaps it never grew back so that I would always be reminded of my father's love. John Curtis (then J.C.) was stunted in growth, had a left "crossed-eye," and was in such poor health that he did not start school until he was 8 years old. He and his 6-year-old brother, Edward, could pass as twins and started first grade together at the old Perryville School. John Curtis started to read when he was about 5 and was able to read a newspaper at 8, so he was quickly placed in the second grade. The boys next attended school in Morrilton, which they hated because of the teachers. They loved Mrs. McDonald at the old Hannaford School. John Curtis loved learning and continued his education by taking college courses while he was in the Air Force.

During the Korean Conflict (War), he was stationed at Nagoya, Japan. He was stationed at the Strategic Air Command (SAC) when he was sent to Saigon, Vietnam. When he returned home to California, he found the woman he had been searching for, Sharon Lee Bergren Cline. They were married at Citrus Heights, CA on July 26, 1969. Sharon's daughter by a previous marriage, Roberta Lynn, was adopted by John. On Sept. 12, 1972, John and Sharon were blessed with the birth of a son, Chad Evert Bissel Maupin. John Curtis retired from the Air Force in 1974 after 22 years of service.

In 1985 he retired from his civil service position, Sharon retired from her position at the bank, they sold their home and relocated to beautiful Cleveland, Conway County. Chad graduated from the Wonderview High School in 1990. He worked at the Kroger store while in school, but is now the graphic artist at BSW Advertising, Inc., in Plumerville. On Feb. 14, 1994 Chad married Rhonda Suzane Tester Thompson. Their daughter Kelsey Ann Maupin was born Jan. 21, 1997 at the St. Mary's Regional Hospital in Russelville. Rhonda is the daughter of Thomas "Woody" and Donna Tester of Hill Creek and she is employed as a bookkeeper with Allison Ford. *Submitted by Curtis Maupin.*

MAUPIN - John Wesley Maupin (b. 1903) was the only child of John Wesley Maupin (b. November 1876) and his wife Harriet Ella McClure Maupin. His mother was born at Des Arc, AR on Aug. 6, 1877, the daughter of William Holliway McClure (b. Feb. 29, 1832) and Nancy E. Cargile (b. Nov. 29, 1836). John Wesley was born at Ledwedge, Perry County, AR on Feb. 22,

1903. His father was shot and killed by a cousin, Robert T. Dicus, on Dec. 23, 1902, near Bigelow, Perry County, so he never knew his father. His parents were married at Morrilton Conway County, on Dec. 25, 1900. Harriet Maupin married Oliver Curtis Powell on Sept. 16, 1903 in Perry County, so this was the

John Wesley Maupin

only father he knew. The family lived in both Perry and Conway counties until John Wesley was a young man.

He enlisted in the US Army. After a tour of duty at the Presidio in San Francisco, and at Fort Lewis in Washington, he gladly returned to Conway County. While he was visiting his uncle Dode McClure at Hill Creek, he met Girtha Jewel Johnson, the daughter of Frank and Callie Johnson. Girtha Jewel (b. June 29, 1910 in Searcy County, d. Oct. 8, 1948 in Jefferson County, AR) and John Wesley were married on Nov. 28, 1928 at Hill Creek by Joe Robinson, Justice of Peace.

Girtha was the mother of nine children by the time she was 27 years old. They were Virgil Fay (b. Feb. 12, 1924) md. Jesse Hicks; Donnie Ray (b. 1928, d. 1932); John Curtis (b. Sept. 20, 1930) md. Sharon Lee Bergren; Edward Francis (b. Sept. 29, 1932, d. Sept. 9, 1997) md. Thressa Messick; Bobby Lee (b. Aug. 26, 1934, Morrilton) md. Nancy N. Leffingwell; twin-Louis Franklin (b. April 6, 1936 at Charter Oak, MO) and twin-Frankie Louis (b. April 6, 1936, d. Oct. 8, 1948); twins (b. Aug. 12, 1938), Troy Gene (died September 1938) and Joyce Dean died Oct 8, 1948).

John Wesley and Girtha lived in Morrilton and Conway County most of their married life. At one time the family rented the old brick home of Dr. Jones in Plumerville, and Wes peddled his bike to the cotton mill plant in Morrilton. Girtha and Wes were both working at the Cotton Mill and lived near the Morrilton city limits sign where the Lewis Livestock Sale Barn is now located. Johnny "J.C.," Edward and Bobby were in the same room at the old Hannaford School, when WWII started. Mrs. McDonald was their wonderful teacher. John Wesley and Girtha Maupin relocated to Tucker, Jefferson County, with most of her family members, to farm with Sam Ferguson, who was also from Conway County. Instead of farming, Wes went to work at the Pine Bluff Arsenal. Girtha refused to relocate to California where workers were desperately needed due to the war, so Wes left her and his children. Girtha promptly filed for divorce.

John Wesley Maupin married Norma Jean Krammer, a native of Sacramento, CA. Norma was a licensed vocational nurse and worked at the old Sutter Hospital. This marriage was not successful and they were divorced after a couple of years. John Wesley married Margie Cox Hunt, the widow of Boss Hunt who had recently moved from Arkansas. Margie and John both worked at the McClellan Air Force Base.

Girtha Jewel Maupin Rorie and her two children, Frankie Louis and Joyce Dean, were murdered by her estranged husband, Harvey Rorie, on the night of Oct. 8, 1948. He burned the home in an effort to cover his crime, but was tried and executed at Tucker. The remaining sons, Johnny, Edward and Bobby Lee, went to live with their father in California. All three of these Maupin retired and came back to beautiful *Conway County. Submitted by J. Maupin.*

JOHN WESLEY MAUPIN JR. (b. November 1876 in Faulkner County) was the son of John Wesley Maupin Sr. (b. 1836 in Wayne County, TN) and Lida Luisa Ann Wilks Mar Cooper Maupin (b. 1842 in Wayne County, TN). Louisa (b. 1817, died in Izard County AR during the Civil War) was the daughter of Archibald "Archie" Cooper. He was a deaf mute. His

wife was Charity Charlotte Cooper (b. 1821 in Tennessee). They came to Searcy County before 1860 and owned the land behind the courthouse in the present town of Marshall.

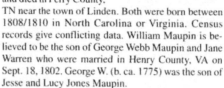

John Wesley Maupin Jr's grandparents were William and Elizabeth Maupin who lived and died in Perry County, TN near the town of Linden. Both were born between 1808/1810 in North Carolina or Virginia. Census records give conflicting data. William Maupin is believed to be the son of George Webb Maupin and Jane Warren who were married in Henry County, VA on Sept. 18, 1802. George W. (b. ca. 1775) was the son of Jesse and Lucy Jones Maupin.

Jesse was born about 1736 in Hanover County, VA which is now Louisa County. His exact date of birth and death are unknown, but it is believed he died about 1798 in Henry County, VA. Jesse was the 8th child and youngest son born to Daniel Maupin (b. March 25, 1700, d. Sept. 20, 1788) and Margaret Via Maupin (b. Aug. 3, 1701, d. April 1789). Daniel Maupin was the eldest living son of the immigrant Gabriel Maupin (b. ca. 1661 at Jargeau, France and died ca. 1719 at Williamsburg, VA). His mother was Marie Hersent Maupin (b. ca. 1661 in Normandy, France, d. July 26, 1748 at Williamsburg).

The Maupins were French Huguenots who had their lands confiscated and had to flee for their lives to Amsterdam to escape death at the hands of the Catholics after the revocation of The Edict of Nantes which had given them freedom of worship. Gabriel and Marie were married in the Wallonne Church that had been given to the French refugees for worship on Sept. 2, 1691. It is believed that Daniel was born at Southampton, England as the parents awaited passage to the colonies. There were four ships sent to the colonies with Frenchmen. Several family names on the lists of passengers probably have descendents in present day Conway County. For example, Martin, Robinson, Mallet, Guerin, Maus and several others.

The Maupin family arrived in Virginia aboard the ship "*Nasseau of Pool*" in March 1701 (or 1700 as the calendar had changed that year) The passengers were supposed to be sent to the French settlement of Mannikintown in the interior of Virginia, but most of them left the ship at Yorktown and scattered in the rural area around Williamsburg, then known as the "Middle Plantation." The second son, Gabriel Maupin, was born there in 1705, the first Maupin to be born in Virginia. The first son Daniel was granted 1,188 acres of land in western Albemarle County. He moved there in 1748 and purchased 300 acres that adjoined his grant.

On the 1900 Federal Census of Conway County, Welborn TS, Morrilton, West of Point Remove Creek, dated June 2, 1900, John Wesley Maupin Jr. is listed as a servant in the home of Moses and Mollie Davidson and their three sons. His future wife Harriet Mc Clure is listed as "adopted daughter" and her age is shown to be August 1880, 19 years old. (On the 1880 census she is 3 years old). Her relationship to the Davidson's has not been researched by this writer. John Wesley and Harriet were married at Morrilton on Dec. 25, 1900. He was shot six times with a Winchester rifle near Bigelow, Perry County, on Dec. 23, 1902, by his cousin, Robert T. Dicus. One family story relates that John won Robert's farm while gambling and demanded payment or the farm.

John Wesley and Harriet's only child was born the following February 22nd and named John Wesley Maupin after his father and grandfather. Harriet was the daughter of William Holloway Mc Clure and Nancy E. Cargile Mc Clure and was born at Des Arc, Prairie County, and died at Perryville on May 4, 1939. She is

buried in the Ada Valley Cemetery at the foot of Petit Jean Mountain. John Wesley's grave has not been located yet. *Submitted by John Curtis Maupin.*

MAXEY - The Maxey family probably originated in France. It is reported they fled from France to England, where they settled for an indeterminate length of time. Edward Maxey was born in either France or England. He married Elizabeth Ann Wyatt. They immigrated to America about 1700 and settled in Henrico County, VA. Edward probably died in Goochland County, VA, which was formed from Henrico County in 1728.

Edward Maxey II was born 1674 in France or England, the son of Edward and Elizabeth Maxey. Edward married Susannah Gates. He signed his will on April 18, 1737 in Goochland County, in which he named his wife and children. Edward died prior to 1740. Edward and Susannah had at least eight children.

Walter Justinian Maxey (b. 1719 in Henrico County, VA) was the youngest son of Edward and Susannah. He married Mary Netherland (or Bedford), who was born 1719. Walter eventually moved to Franklin County, VA, where he died in 1791. Mary died in 1798. Walter had at least 10 children.

Jeremiah Maxey (b. 1751) was the son of Walter and Mary. He married Mourning Hail in 1769 in Virginia. Mourning Hail was born 1751 in Virginia. About 1800, Jeremiah moved his family to Oglethorpe County, GA. Mourning died there prior to 1808. Jeremiah married Mary "Polly" Allen in 1808 in Oglethorpe County. Jeremiah died in 1810. Jeremiah and Mourning had 12 children. Jeremiah and Mary had two children.

Hail Maxey (b. 1770 in Bedford County, VA) was the eldest child of Jeremiah Maxey and Mourning Hail. He married Dicey Craighead in 1789 in Bedford County. Dicey (b. 1766 in Virginia) was the daughter of John Craighead and Jane Dicia Maxey. Dicey and Hail were first cousins. (Hail's father, Jeremiah Maxey, and Dicey's mother, Jane Dicia Maxey, were brother and sister.)

Hail and Dicey moved their family to Oglethorpe County, GA around 1800. Hail owned several hundred acres of rich farmland in Oglethorpe County. He also owned a grist mill. Hail had two successful draws in the 1832 Cherokee Land Lottery, obtaining tracts in Gilmer County and Walker County, GA. Dicey died between 1840-45 and Hail died in 1849. Hail and Dicey had nine children.

Bennett Hail Maxey (b. ca. 1808 in Oglethorpe County, GA) was the son of Hail Maxey and Dicey Craighead. He married Frances Eason in 1836 in Oglethorpe County. Frances Eason was born 1810 in Georgia. Bennett Hail and Frances raised their children in Georgia. The family moved to Izard (now Stone) County, AR prior to 1858. Bennett Hail was a farmer. Frances died prior to 1875, in Stone (formerly Izard) County. Bennett Hail signed his will on June 26, 1875 in Stone County, in which he named his son John H. Maxey, daughter Dicey Jane Bridgman and grandson John B. Bridgman. Bennett Hail died in Stone County in late 1875.

Bennett Hail and Frances had five children: Delilah Maxey (b. 1839, died before June 26, 1875); John H. Maxey (b. January 1840, d. June 30, 1926) md. Sarah Angeline M. Gilcrest; Dicey Jane Maxey (b. 1843, d. July 5, 1885) md. William T. Bridgman; James T. Maxey (b. 1844, d. June 20, 1862, in the Civil War); Martha Ann Maxey (b. 1846, d. 1870) md. William T. Bridgman.

MAXWELL - Luther Maxwell was a popular teacher who taught in many of the community schools in Conway County during the first few decades of the 20th century. He was the son of Alvus M. Maxwell and Mary Ann Harrington. When Luther was born on Aug. 22, 1892, the family lived in a little log cabin in Lanty, AR. Mary Ann went to the home of her mother,

Belfame Harrington, for the birth. Alvus and Mary Ann already had a 1-year-old son, Marvin. The Maxwells eventually moved about two miles west of Lanty to a location a mile or two north of Bull Mountain near what is now State Highway 95. They lived near the old McElroy school house, which was about a half mile from the highway.

Alvus M. Maxwell and Mary Ann Harrington. Children: Luther beside his father, Noah between father and mother, Marvin beside his mother, and Dove in mother's lap - 1898.

Luther Alonzo Maxwell and Eugenia Frances Houston, 1918.

Luther Alonzo Maxwell and Eugenia Frances Houston, ca. 1940.

Luther's brother Noah was born in 1894 probably at that location. Then Lucinda Bell was born in 1896, but died the following year. Luther was only 3-1/2 years old when Lucinda Bell was born and 5 when she died, but remembered her well and referred to her occasionally in later life.

During those years, Alvus had a small general store near the McElroy School. Luther would sometimes watch the store and remembered an evening during which he sold only one 2-cent spool of thread. Luther also went with his father on his peddling route. In the early days, the goods were hauled in a horse-drawn wagon or cart that had been customized to store and display products for the home. Later, Alvus bought a Model-T for his peddling route.

Alvus had to make a 12-mile trip to town to re-supply his stock. It was difficult to make the trip and return in one day. Horses or mules could pull a wagon at two to three miles per hour, so the round-trip was eight hours minimum. The men often spent the night at a wagon yard. The yard provided a secure place for the animals, and travelers could sleep in their wagons in the yard. By traveling to town in the afternoon and spending the night, travelers would have more time to conduct business and see some of the sights the next morning before returning home. After cars and trucks became available, it was easy to make the trip to town and return in a day.

Sometimes on these trips to town, Alvus would take the boys and give them his leftover poor quality skins for them to sell for spending money. Luther said that the man at the wagon yard was also a fur trader, but usually didn't want to buy skins from the boys. He would send the boys on to someone who would handle poor quality skins.

Luther probably started school in the fall of 1898. I think that he had been eager to start school, because he once said that the start of school was delayed at the request of the parents until the crops could be brought in. That sounds like something someone, who was eager to get started to school, would have remembered.

Luther's future bride, Eugenia Francis Houston, was born May 21, 1899, to John Hawk Houston Sr. (b. June 22, 1859, d. June 2, 1936) and Josie (b. Oct. 23, 1861, d. June 3, 1933). Luther was almost 7. On June 1st, 11 days after Eugenia was born to the Houstons, Luther's little brother Virgil was born to Alvus and Mary Ann.

Luther turned 8 years old during the last year of the century. The family had probably moved to the old home place by 1900. During that year, Alvus turned 30, Mary Ann was 31, Marvin 9, Luther 8, Noah 6, Dove 2, and Virgil 1. Luther's grandmother, Belfame Harrington, was a 60-year old widow living in Lanty with a son about Luther's age. His Maxwell grandparents, Jack and Lucinda, were 58 and 54 respectively and lived in Carroll County in north Arkansas.

Sister Kate was born Feb. 24, 1901, the first year of the new century. She was the final child of Alvus and Mary Ann. Luther would have started the third grade that fall. Schools had only eight grades a hundred years ago, so Luther would have completed school in 1906 or 1907 at about 15. He attended two years at the State Normal School in Conway, now the University of Central Arkansas. The Normal School prepared students for teaching, but they still had to pass a test prepared by the director of the school district in which they taught. Counties licensed teachers who passed the required tests. Apparently Luther completed his training and was licensed to teach by the time he was 18.

Luther's pen and ink record, in an old school record book, lists his school terms from 1911-21. He taught a winter term at Lone Grove School beginning Nov. 27, 1911, and finishing on Feb. 23, 1912. He was only 19 years old. His younger brothers and sisters were students during the terms at Lone Grove. Noah was 17 and in the sixth grade. Doyle was 13 and in the fourth grade. Virgil was 12 and also in the fourth grade. Katie was 10 and she was in the fourth grade, too.

Luther taught a 20-day summer term in July 1912 at Lone Grove and another in September. He was 20 years old by then. He then went to the Lord's School House for the 1912 fall term and the 1913 winter term. He taught a 2-month summer term at Vinson Chapel, where he had lived when he was a child.

Luther had a 5-month school term at Sand Town in the winter of 1913-14. He was back in Lone Grove for a 2-1/2 month summer term. He returned to Sand Town for the 1914-15 five-month term. He taught the 1915-16 term of school in Solgohachia.

Eugenia Houston was 17 in 1916, and she and Luther must have been acquainted with each other by the time she was 18. When Luther took her on a date the first time, her father told her brother John Hawk Jr. to "go check out that young fellow." Her brother said, "Don't worry about him, he's a really good fellow."

Luther was at Solgohachia again for the 1916-17 school term and then back at Lone Grove nearer home for the summer term of 1917.

On April 6, 1917 the US declared war on Germany. By the time Luther was 25 in August 1917, a selective service system had been established and all men between 21 and 30 were required to register for the draft. Luther had just completed the summer term at Lone Grove. He either enlisted or was drafted and

on Sept. 4, 1917, he was in the Army. He eventually qualified for Officer Candidate School and went to Camp Beauregard in Louisiana for training.

In April 1918, he went home on furlough to marry Eugenia Francis Houston on April 21, 1918 at Atkins, AR, not far from Old Hickory. Gene's brother, John Hawk Jr. was best man. Gene was just a month short of her 19th birthday and Luther was almost 26.

Luther completed Officers Training School at Camp Beauregard with the rank of 2nd lieutenant. It was the 4th Officers Training School, and he was in the Second Infantry Company. He was proud of his officer's rank, and had it inscribed on his tombstone 65 years later.

Luther and Eugenia settled into married life after his military service. He was 26 and she was 19. They lived with her parents, Hawk and Josie Houston, at Old Hickory. By July 1919, they had contracts to teach at Sunnyside School for the 1919-20 school term, but when they learned that she was pregnant, they had to get out of the contract. Pregnant women could not teach back then. When the Sunnyside job didn't work out, Luther got a contract to teach at Old Hickory, where his brother-in-law was on the school board. The pay of $3.00 a day was very good pay for the time.

TEACHER'S CONTRACT (State of Arkansas, County of Conway)

This agreement, between Cleve Massingill and John H. Houston Jr. as Directors of the School District No. 36 in the County of Conway State of Arkansas, and Luther A. Maxwell a teacher who holds a license of the first grade, and who agrees to teach a common school in said district, is as follows:

The said Directors agree, upon their part, in consideration of the covenants of said teacher, hereinafter contained, to employ the said Luther A. Maxwell to teach a common school in said District the term of four months, commencing on the 24th day of November A.D. 1919 to pay out of the funds the sum of $90.00/xx each school month. Luther filled out the form in his distinctive penmanship. It was signed by John H. Houston and G.C. Massingill.

Luther and Gene's first child, Eva Louise Maxwell, was born Feb. 17, 1920. They were probably still living with Gene's parents. Luther was 27 and Gene was 20. His parents, Alvus and Mary Ann, were 49 and 51 and Gene's parents were 60 and 58.

Luther taught the 1920 summer term at Round Mountain. He was back at Old Hickory for the 1920-21 school term. He probably taught the 1921-22 and the 1922-23 terms at Hattieville where Paul Turner, grandson of Dave and Kate Skipper, was one of his pupils.

Luther bought property east of his parents' farm on the top of Bull Mountain and built the family home at its present location around 1922. He was 30 years old.

Luther taught the 1923-24 school term at Lanty. The schoolhouse was not far from the location of the little log cabin the family had lived in when Luther was born 31 years earlier. Luther and his Lanty basketball team played Howard Bradford and his Cleveland team one time. Luther didn't like the way Howard and his team played, so he wrote a letter to Howard with his complaint. Howard wrote a scathing reply, which Luther kept for many years.

Luther and Gene had another daughter on May 9, 1924. They named her Katherine Grace, but she died at or soon after birth.

Around 1925 the family was living in Cleveland where Luther was teaching. He probably had the 1925-26 term. Louise and Lyonell Halbrook, her future husband, were 5 years old. Lyonell remembers that he would watch that pretty little red-headed girl, Louise, from the barn loft as she walked between his house and the gin to meet her father after school. Luther had a 1925 Model "T" at that time. It was the only gasoline-powered machine that he ever owned as far as I can tell.

Luther was losing his hearing by the time he was

155

30. He eventually stopped teaching because he felt that he could not maintain discipline if he couldn't hear the students. This was probably after the 1925 term at Cleveland. He was 33 in August 1925.

Luther's father Alvus died as he drove back from a trip to Morrilton on May 8, 1929. He had asked Luther to go with him, but Luther didn't want to. Of course, Luther regretted that decision after his father died. Soon after his father's death, Luther, Gene, and Louise went to New Mexico to visit Luther's brother, Virgil. They traveled in the Model-T and visited the Royal Gorge and Pike's Peak. After they returned home, Luther parked the Model-T in the barn and eventually sold it.

The family settled down in the house on the farm. Luther lived on his farm for another 30 years and was a respected member of the community. He had a reputation for wisdom and honesty. Many in the community came to him for advice about their business and legal affairs. He was secretary of the Lanty Masonic lodge and treasurer of the Lanty Methodist Church for many years. He was a Notary Public from the mid-30s to the late 40s.

Soon after his beloved wife died on Aug. 7, 1963, at the age of 64, Luther moved to Cleveland to live with his daughter's family. A large room had been added to their home to provide a place for him. He lived there until his death on April 22, 1973, at the age of 80 years, 8 months.

Grandchildren of Luther and Eugenia are James Skipper, Jeanne Skipper Rentfro, Brenda Halbrook Tyler, Marinelle Halbrook Paladino, Sherrye Halbrook Futterer and John Halbrook. *Submitted by James Maxwell Skipper.*

MAXWELL - William Virgil Maxwell, son of John Wesley Maxwell and JoAnna Josephine Robinson, was born in Arkansas Jan. 15, 1904 in the Bird Town Community. He met Evelyn McCasland, daughter of James H. McCasland and Alice Freaman, on a blind date about 1923. They were married Dec. 10, 1926 and lived in the Springfield area, where three of their children were born: James Francis (b. Nov. 12, 1927), Everett Leroy (b. Dec. 1, 1931) and Alice "JoAnn" (b. July 13, 1934).

Virgil and Evelyn Maxwell, 45th wedding anniversary; l-r: JoAnn, Jim, Wayne and Alice.

In 1937, during the Dust Bowl and also a depression, work was hard to find, so Virgil and Evelyn decided to go to California. They took six quilts, their small suitcase and their Bible. They packed it in a Model A Ford, along with Evelyn's brother Jack and his family, Virgil with his old felt hat, Evelyn with her velvet pill-box hat, and off they went.

Along the way, they stopped at a motel to eat and rest. The men and boys all went to the men's restroom and in a few minutes Jack (Evelyn's brother) came running out to find Evelyn saying, "Virgil has just lost it! He's in the restroom taking all the paper off the rolls and throwing it all over the floor." When Evelyn asked Jack why he was doing that, Jack said, "Virgil says he's looking for the cobs."

After five nights and six days, they finally arrived in Cutler, CA in Tulare County where some of Evelyn's family already resided. Virgil jumped out, waving his old felt hat at the family. Evelyn's hat was stomped in the floorboard, flat as a flitter and JoAnn

(age 3) had sat on Evelyn's lap until her big toe died. To this day, at 91 years of age, Evelyn's big toe is still numb.

It was late November and they all needed to work, so they rested a day or two, and someone heard there was cotton to pick in a small town by the name of Firebaugh in Fresno County. There were two or three families that went and picked cotton for about a month, when they were flooded out and came back to Cutler.

They lived in the Cutler area when their fourth child, Alice Faye was born April 3, 1940. They bought their first home there.

In 1946 Everett Leroy was killed when a car hit him and a friend on a bicycle. Both boys were killed. They were 14 years old. It was a sad time for this young couple.

In 1947 they bought five acres in a town called Orosi, about five miles out in the country from Cutler, where they farmed for several years. There, their youngest child (Robert Wayne) was born on July 4, 1947.

Virgil and Evelyn worked in farming most of their lives. This area is rich in agriculture of every kind. There are oranges, lemons, all kinds of tree fruit, row crops, berries, vegetables, cotton, table and wine grapes, and sugar beets. Evelyn also worked in a nursing home for 13 years. In 1961 she took a geriatric class at Fresno City College.

Virgil and Evelyn were married 52 very happy years. Lots of grandchildren, great-grandchildren and great-great-grandchildren! They both retired. Virgil passed away in 1978 and James Francis in 1984.

Evelyn, age 91, lives alone in Orosi where she is still active in quilting and gardening (vegetables and flowers). Alice "JoAnn" lives nearby in Cutler and Robert Wayne in Visalia, 15 miles from Orosi. Alice Faye lives in Bandon, OR. *Submitted by Cyrus Maxwell for JoAnn McGee Butler.*

McCAIGE - The McCaige family came from Ireland and were farmers. Samuel McCaig (b. ca. 1785 in Ireland, d. June 26, 1850 in Conway County) md. Elizabeth Leslie on March 21, 1812 in Humphrey County, TN. She was born about 1795 in York County, SC and died Nov. 25, 1875 in Searcy County, AR. They had six children.

Their son John Wesley McCaig (b. 1822 in Tennessee, died in California) md. Sarah Sutter, the niece of Capt. Sutter of early California history fame, before 1840 in Tennessee. She was born about 1822 in Tennessee and died Sept. 3, 1908 in California. John and Sarah had six children - four born in Tennessee, two in Arkansas. They came to Conway County around 1848. They left Conway County in April or May 1870 and went to California, settling first in San Francisco, then Wilmington, Downey, and finally settling in Puente in 1891.

Their fourth child was Susan C. (b. Jan. 8, 1818 in Tennessee). She married my great-great-grandfather, William A. Evans (see Evans family) on March 24, 1870. The couple helped the family move to California as part of their honeymoon. They then came back to Conway County to live. They are buried in the Evans Family Cemetery in Conway County. *Submitted by Jimmy Horton.*

McCLURE - Charles William "Charlie" McClure (b. Dec. 23, 1902 in White or Cleburne County, AR) was the son of Dora Bannon "Dode" McClure and Eliza Julia Jones. Charlie's mother died when he was 11 and his father soon re-married. In a short time Charlie and his siblings began leaving home to live with other family members. Charlie began working at a very early age.

Charlie married Velma Mae Branham on April 11, 1928 in Van Buren County, AR. Velma (b. March 20, 1914 at Formosa in Van Buren County) was the daughter of James William Branham and Gertie Mae Adaline Gloden. Velma had just turned 14 years old when she married the 26-year-old Charlie. Velma's

father wrote a note giving his permission for his daughter to marry.

The depression in the 1930s made life extremely hard for Charlie and his family. Charlie farmed around Formosa for a time. He also worked a couple of years on the Works Progress Administration program (WPA). The WPA built roads and many of the stone structures are still in use today. Charlie also worked for a time at a sawmill. Charlie and Velma taught their children to work from a very early age and the children grew up working in the cotton fields beside their parents. In later years Velma worked at St. Anthony's Hospital at Morrilton.

The older McClure children began their formal education in the Formosa School. In 1948 Charlie moved his family to Conway County. They settled in the Hannaford Community west of Morrilton, where the family farmed for several years. The children attended school at the Hannaford School. The family later moved into Morrilton and the children attended the Morrilton schools.

Charlie died March 7, 1976 at Morrilton and Velma died March 12, 1987. They are buried in McGhee Cemetery, near Adona in Perry County. Charlie and Velma had nine children:

1) Gracie Lillian McClure (b. Feb. 16, 1929, d. Feb. 28, 1929 at Formosa, AR) is buried Culpepper Cemetery in Van Buren County.

2) Willie Virgil McClure (b. Jan. 6, 1930, d. June 23, 1974) md. Billie Willis and had a daughter, Virginia McClure. He then moved to Kansas and married Constance "Connie" Henderson and had two sons, Virgil Ray "Butch" and Steve McClure.

3) Dorothy Lea McClure (b. 1933) md. Kermot Moore. They moved to Adona, AR. They had five children: Larry, Kenneth, Keith, Roger and Susan Moore.

4) Charlene McClure (b. 1936) md. Edmond Dugan. They had three children: Edna, Brenda and Judy Dugan.

5) Darrell Benjamin Franklin McClure (b. 1939) md. Janell Brown. They settled in Ada Valley and had two children, Benny and Nellia McClure.

6) Bobbie Dean McClure (b. July 18, 1941, d. March 28, 2002) md. Leroy Cole, then she married John Helton. The family moved to Kansas. They had one child, Rhonda Helton.

7) Jo Ann McClure (b. April 8, 1944, d. March 29, 1995) md. Cecil Hill. The family moved to Oklahoma. Their children are Dana and Diana (twins) and Lynn Hill.

8) D J McClure (b. 1946) md. Shirley Lackey and had daughter Pamela McClure. He then moved to Kansas and married Nelda Henderson. Their children are Todd, Charida and Tommy McClure.

9) Roy Leonard McClure (b. 1948) md. Katherine Ann Bridgman, daughter of Herbert Bridgman and Maggie Horton. Their children are Scott and Clint McClure.

McCLURE - Dora Bannon "Dode" McClure (b. March 12, 1871/72 in White County, AR) was the son of William Holliway McClure and Nancy Elizabeth Cargile. Dode was 9 years old on the 1880 White County Census. In 1891 he paid personal property taxes in White County. Dode married Eliza Julia Jones on Aug. 14, 1893 in White County.

Eliza (b. June 20, 1874 at Mountain View in Izard (now Stone) County, AR) was the daughter of Dockery Berry Jones and Julia Ann Hess. Dode was a farmer. Between 1901 and 1908, he moved his family to the town of Edgemont, in Cleburne County, AR. There Dode worked for a time at a sawmill. The 1910 census shows the family in the town of Edgemont. Dode moved his family to Culpepper Township near Formosa, Van Buren County, AR about 1911. Eliza died Feb. 24, 1913 near Formosa and is buried in Culpepper Cemetery.

Dode married Mary Margaret "Meg" Brewer on Dec. 23, 1915, in Van Buren County. Meg Brewer (b. May 1, 1895) had a 4-month-old son when they married. He used the McClure surname. Soon after Dode re-married, his children began leaving home to stay with other family members. Dode eventually moved to Morrilton in Conway County. He was interested in horticulture and planted redbud trees along Main Street in Morrilton. The trees grew and bloomed beautifully for many years until age and disease killed them. Dode died at Morrilton on Sept. 12, 1955 and was buried in Culpepper Cemetery. Meg later married Frank L. Hem. She died March 27, 1980. Meg and Frank are buried in Kilgore Cemetery in Conway County.

Children of Dode McClure and Eliza Julia Jones:
1) Julia Ancybell "Julie" McClure (b. Aug. 12, 1896, d. June 26, 1984) md. Major Harrison Jordon, then Ed Hall. Children: Bernice, Verna and Alma Jordon.

2) Baby McClure (b&d. 1898).

3) Georgia Ettamae "Georgie" McClure (b. Feb. 28, 1900, d. Jan. 20, 1981) md. James E. "Jimmy" Drake. Children: David, Luther Willie and Jewel Drake.

4) Harmon McClure (b&d. ca. 1901).

5) Charles William McClure (b. Dec. 23, 1902, d. March 7, 1976) md. Velma Mae Branham. Children: Gracie, Virgil, Dorothy, Charlene, Darrell, Bobbie, Jo Ann, DJ and Roy McClure.

6) Nellie McClure (b&d. about 1905).

7) Luther Conway McClure (b. June 4, 1906, d. Sept. 30, 1958) md. Thelma Pearl Shipley. Children: Carl, L.J., Orvin, Bill, Gene, Virgil Weldon, Lucille, Ruby, Owdia, Shirley, Patricia and Margaret McClure.

8) Susie Izora McClure (b. Aug. 11, 1908, d. Aug. 31, 1994) md. Elmer Smith. Children: Eliza, Penzol "Penny," Oral and Sherman Smith.

Children of Dode McClure and Meg Brewer:
9) Ernest M. McClure (Meg's son b. Aug. 12, 1915) md. Cassie Dancer.

10) William S. "Bill" McClure (b. March 15, 1916, d. Sept. 6, 1989) md. Rosey May Killion. Children: Bill Jr. and Frances McClure.

11) Stephen Scott "SK" McClure (b. Aug. 30, 1919, d. Sept. 23, 1970) md. Mary H. Doubleday. They had no children.

12) Daisy Lee McClure (b. Sept. 19, 1923, d. Jan. 20, 1996) md. Arnold G. Epperson. Daughter: Jan Epperson.

13) Peggy May McClure (b. 1927, d. Sept. 20, 1970) never married.

McCLURE - The McClure family originated in Scotland and was of Scottish or Scots-Irish descent. The McClure surname was taken from the name of the landlord or clan. It did not necessarily denote kinship. The word mac (mc) meant son of. Olaf the Black died around 1237 and his younger son Leod inherited the Islands of Lewis and Harris. The Clan MacLeod consisted of two main branches, the MacLeods of Lewis and the MacLeods of Harris. The Clan MacClure (McClure) was a Sept of the Clan MacLeod of Harris and entitled to clan rights including the use of the clan tartan.

Stephen McClure (b. 1798 in Kentucky) migrated to Illinois prior to 1825. He married Sarah Smith on April 6, 1825 in Clinton County, IL. Sarah (b. 1800 in Kentucky) was possibly the daughter of John Smith. Stephen appears on the 1825 and 1830 Clinton County Census. In 1837, he moved his family to Arkansas. He was in Searcy County prior to 1839 and in Conway County in early 1840. In 1849 he purchased 160 acres of land in Benton Township of Conway County. Stephen paid taxes on 320 acres of land in 1855. Sarah died in 1855 or early 1856. Stephen married Mary Allen on Sept. 4, 1856 in Conway County. Mary probably died in childbirth in 1857.

Stephen married Mrs. Louisa "Eliza" Goff about 1858. Louisa (b. 1818 in Kentucky) was the daughter of Zachariah Chandler and Elizabeth Kelly. Louisa was the widow of Jesse Goff. On Oct. 14, 1859, Stephen applied for guardianship of Louisa's five youngest children: Jesse, Wilson, Nancy, Elizabeth and Emily

Goff. Guardianship was granted by the court. (In 1873 Conway County was divided and Benton Township where Stephen lived became part of the newly formed Faulkner County.)

Stephen died about June 1873. Stephen and Sarah had 11 children:

1) John M. McClure (b. 1826, d. April 20, 1863 in the Civil War in Tennessee) married and may have had children, D.W. and Sauna. John then married Larrinora Russell on Oct. 13, 1859 in Conway County.

2) Robert S. McClure (b. 1828).

3) Rachael McClure (b. 1830, d. April 8, 1864, in childbirth) md. Israel Moore on July 2, 1863, in Conway County. Their child Rachael Moore married Frank Ramsey.

4) William Holliway S. McClure (b. Feb. 29, 1832) md. Nancy Elizabeth Cargile on Jan 14, 1855, in Conway County. Their children were Nenion, Robert Conway, Sarah, Dora Bannon, Harriet and Millard McClure.

5) Unknown daughter McClure (b. 1834, d. between 1841-49).

6) Valentine McClure (b. 1837, d. Aug. 28, 1862 in the Civil War) md. Mary Elen Scarlett. Children were Sarah Elizabeth and Lodusky Catherine McClure.

7) Melissa McClure (b. 1837).

8) Matilda McClure (b. 1839) md. John N. Bennett on Dec. 20, 1860, in Conway County. Children: Nancy, James, Samuel, Newton, Edward and Carroll Bennett.

9) Sarah McClure (b. 1841) md. Christopher C. Shipley on Sept. 18, 1858, in Conway County. Children: Rachael, Mary Ann, Jesse and Eugenia Shipley.

10) Stephen McClure Jr. (b. October 1842) md. Telitha Stanley.

11) James Orsen B. McClure (b. 1844, d. Feb. 2, 1899) md. Alzira Ann Scarlett. Children: Sarah Elizabeth, Mary Dallas, Nancy, Commie, Nora and Maude.

Stephen and Louisa had one child:
12) Alma McClure (b. 1858) md. George W. Goff.

McCLURE - William Holliway S. McClure (b. Feb. 29, 1832 in Clinton County, IL) was the son of Stephen McClure and Sarah Smith. William's family moved to Arkansas in 1837 and settled in Conway County in early 1840, when William was about 8 years old. He began farming with his father at an early age. In 1854, William purchased 80 acres of land in Conway County.

On Jan. 14, 1855, William married Nancy Elizabeth Cargile in Conway County. Nancy (b. May 29, 1836 in Kentucky) was the daughter of Nenion Elijah Cargile and Sarah Johnson. About 1859, William and Nancy moved to Madison County, AR, where they appear on the 1860 Madison County Census. William probably enlisted in the Confederate 34th Arkansas Infantry, Co. F, on Aug. 9, 1862 at Bentonville, Benton County, AR, for a term of three years or until the end of the war. He re-enlisted on Feb. 19, 1864.

On July 15, 1867, William and Nancy bought land in White County, AR. They raised corn and cotton as a money crop on their farm. The family appears on the 1870 and 1880 White County Census. Tax records show William was in Royal Township of White County in 1887. William and Nancy both died prior to 1900. Nancy, who died first, was buried in White County and William was buried in Faulkner County. Their children were:

1) Nenion Elijah McClure (b. 1855, Conway County, d. Dec. 6, 1856, Conway County).

2) Robert Ramsey Conway McClure (b. July 31, 1861, d. Sept. 1, 1887).

3) Sarah Ann Priscilla "Ciller" McClure (b. Aug. 22, 1868, d. Oct. 9, 1955, Conway County) md. John Alvy Laycook (Lacook) on Aug. 16, 1887 in White County, AR. They settled in Ada Valley in Conway County about 1910. Both are buried in Ada Valley Cemetery. They had six children, but only five lived to adulthood. Children: Maude (md. Met Ross then Dave Birdwell), Loy Lenzy (md. Velma Gertrude

Wallace), William Clyde, Irvy Gay Josey, Robert Lee and Baby Lacook (died in infancy).

4) Dora Bannon "Dode" McClure (b. March 12, 1871/72, d. Sept. 12, 1955, Conway County) md. Eliza Julia Jones. They had eight children, but only five lived to adulthood. Children: Julie (md. Major Jordon, then Ed Hall); Stillborn Infant; Georgie (md. Jimmy Drake); Harmon (died in infancy); Charles William (md. Velma Branham); Nellie (died in infancy); Luther (md. Pearl Shipley); and Susie McClure (md. Elmer Smith).

5) Harriet McClure (b. Aug. 6, 1877, d. May 4, 1939, Conway County) md. John Wesley Maupin on Dec. 25, 1900. John Maupin (b. Nov. 1877, d. Dec. 22, 1902 two months before the birth of his son). Harriet then married Curtis Powell. Harriet is buried in Ada Valley Cemetery. Children: John Wesley Maupin Jr. and Robert and Bulah Powell.

6) William Millard McClure (b. Nov. 24, 1879, d. July 17, 1969) md. Beatrice Maude Sutton on May 7, 1910. Maude, daughter of Cicero Lumpkin Sutton and Martha Jane Sublett, died May 10, 1976. They are buried at Texarkana, TX. Children: David, Willie Maude, James Barney, William Edwin and Martha Christine McClure.

McCOY - Dan McCoy was born in the Middleton Community of Center Ridge, AR. In 1945 he married Virginia Bennett, who was also born in Middleton. They were married at Morrilton, AR. Virginia is the daughter of Dick Bennett and Lula Harris. She had three brothers: Len "Shorty," Gene and Irvine (all are now deceased). Virginia worked at Compton Mills in Morrilton before becoming a full time homemaker.

l-r: Cora Jordan McCoy, Juanita, Jack and Dan McCoy.

Dan is the son of Jack McCoy and Cora Jordan. Dan has one sister, Juanita Moll, who is a member of the Birdtown Community. Dan is a Veteran of WWII and was a member of the US Navy. Dan spent the majority of his service years in the South Pacific. He worked for many years in the weaving room at Compton Mills.

Dan and Virginia had two daughters, Dannie Fort and Brenda Harwood, and one son Jack McCoy (deceased). They are the proud grandparents of six grandchildren. Brenda has two daughters, Diana Curry and Cindy Harwood. Jack has two daughters, Jackie Ellis and Brandi Hill, and two sons, Billy McCoy and Luke McCoy.

Dan still lives in the Middleton Community in the home he and Virginia built in the late 1950s. *Submitted by Dan McCoy.*

McCULLOUGH - James McCullough (b. ca. 1760 in Ireland) came to America around 1800 with his brothers. They first landed in South Carolina, then James and one brother moved to Knox County, TN. James married Elizabeth Brandon Oct. 11, 1801 in Knox County, TN. She was born 1784 in Albemarle County, VA and died before 1870 in Cherokee County, AL.

James and Elizabeth had eight children. Their first born was John (b. Sept. 29, 1803 in Knox County, TN, d. Nov. 3, 1887 in Blount County, TN) md. Hannah Boring Jan. 24, 1828 in Blount County, TN. She was born Sept. 27, 1805 in Virginia and died Dec. 26, 1884

Blount County TN. They are both buried in Middlesettlement United Methodist Church Cemetery, near Maryville, TN. They had eight children. Their fifth child was Joshua James (b. Nov. 2, 1837 in Tennessee) who was known as just "J.J." J.J. and his brother Cyrus came to Conway County around 1872. It is believed that Cyrus shot a man in Tennessee and that is why they came to Conway County. J.J. married twice; first to Mary C. Jones, Oct. 31, 1861 in Tennessee, second time to Tabitha Taylor Mason Osburn, Sept. 19, 1886 in Conway County. It is said they had a rocky marriage and were not married long. J.J. and Mary Jones had eight children. Their sixth child was Tennessee Lee McCullough, born Nov. 1, 1870 in Tennessee. She married Lonnie Lee Evans Sept. 24, 1895 in Conway County. (See Evans family.)

The McCulloughs were farmers. Some related families from Conway County are Russell, Miller, McInturf, Poteete, Jones, Gray, Evans, Harrison, Riggs, Griswood, Roberts and Farish.

McDANIEL - James McDaniel was born 1827 in the state of Kentucky. The 1880 Census shows that his father was born in Virginia and his mother was born in Maryland. The 1870 census shows James listed as James McDonald. James, his wife Ellen and their six children are living in Harrison, Hamilton County, TN. They also have a 12-year-old domestic servant living with them, by the name of Martha Spriggs. James is 42 years old and his wife Ellen is 31 years old and listed as a Mulatto, having been born

James McDaniel

in Virginia. The census shows Ellen Perkett (Puckett) as born in Charlottesville, VA on April 23, 1836. This census shows that James could possibly read but could not write. Ellen could possibly read and write.

After the birth of their son Martin Van Buren in 1870, the family left Tennessee and moved to Plumerville, AR. The twins, Isaac and Virginia, were born in Plumerville in 1874 and in 1878 Franklin was born.

The 1880 Federal Census listed the family as James McDaniel. The oldest son, William, is 26 years old and no longer in the home. Also Andrew G. is 15 and no longer in the home. The domestic servant Martha Spriggs is not in the home and Franklin is now 3 years old.

The 1880 Federal Census shows James as a 53-year-old farmer living in Plumerville, Conway County, AR. Between July 30, 1870 and June 26, 1880, the family changed. Four more children were born.

The children of James McDaniel and Ellen Perkett were William (b. 1854), Napoleon (b. 1859), John H. (b. 1861), Daniel A.L. (b. 1863), Andrew G. (b. 1865), Samuel H. (b. 1868), Martin Van Buren (Uncle Mart) (b. 1870), Virginia (Aunt Ginny) (b. 1874), Isaac (b. 1874) Franklin (Poppagrand) (b. 1877). Franklin married Parthenia Kemp in Plumerville, AR.

The 1900 Federal Census has this family listed as "Mcdannals." Napoleon is listed as a 42-year-old butcher by trade and he owns his home free and clear.

Martin Van Buren is a 29-year-old "railroad laborer." Franklin (Poppagrand) is listed as a 22-year-old "mill laborer." Issac is a 27-year-old carpenter and house builder.

The 1910 census shows Ellen McDaniel in the home of Franklin and Parthenia McDaniel. Ellen is now 72 years old.

On April 14, 1900 at the age of 74, James McDaniel was laid to rest in Plumerville, AR.

McELROY - Narvin Ray McElroy (b. April 14, 1936 in Conway County, AR) was the son of Tommy Lee McElroy and Eva Frances Chambers.

Narvin married Patsy Jean Walters of Atkins, AR. Children born to their union were Michael Ray (b. Nov. 1, 1966) and Marsha Gay (b. Feb. 10, 1970). Narvin died July 13, 1993 and is buried in the Bells Chapel Cemetery near Atkins, AR.

Narvin Ray McElroy and wife Patsy Walters McElroy.

McGLOFLIN - Fleeing the Potato Famine in Ireland, James Brown McLaughlin arrived in Philadelphia, PA in 1857 at the age of 11. He made the journey with an older cousin. He became an overseer for a plantation in South Carolina. When the Civil War began, he enlisted in the Confederate Army. After the war, he migrated across the southern states. Along the way, he met and married Amelia Howard. They had 11 children, but only seven survived. They were Elijah, James L., Nathan Abel, Susan Lou Critter Sarah, Samuel, Jeffrey and Marcus. James and Amelia were illiterate and when they crossed the Mississippi River to settle in Phillips County, the spelling of their name changed to McGloflin.

Nathan Abel met and married Lela Cox in Saline County, AR. Nathan worked for the railroad and also farmed on land owned by others (share cropping). He was a fine carpenter. Children of that family were Norman (died in infancy), Harold Raymond, Sam, Imogene, and Lela Sue. The family settled in Cabot where Harold was the captain of Cabot High School's first football team. Sam, also, played on that team.

Harold finished high school and taught school for a year. He moved to Little Rock to work at the Arkansas State Hospital. He met Margaret L. Williams at the tennis courts near the hospital. They married in 1930. Margaret's father was a captain in the Little Rock Fire Department. He encouraged Harold to work at the Fire Department, which led to a life-long interest in fire fighting. He was a volunteer fireman in Morrilton for many years. Harold and Margaret moved to Morrilton during the war, because Margaret was promoted to chief operator of Southwestern Bell's Morrilton Office. Harold was a fireman at Marche and visited on weekends. Their children are Gayle (Mrs. John Eden) and Sally Jo (Mrs. Max J. Mobley).

After the war ended, Harold bought and operated the telephone company in Perry for a while. He also was employed by the Morrilton Police Department, the cotton oil company, and Compton Mills before he bought and managed the Broadway Café.

When Margaret retired, she and Harold moved back to Little Rock so that he could work again for the State Hospital. He became a psychiatric technician and worked there for about 10 years, completing his requirements for retirement. Margaret took on the busiest PBX in the state at Arkansas Foundry while they lived in Little Rock.

Upon Harold's retirement, they moved to Petit Jean. They enjoyed their years on the mountain and made many new friends. Harold and Margaret were members of the United Methodist Church and charter members of the Young Couples Sunday School Class. Harold was a 32nd degree Mason and they were members of the Eastern Star for over 50 years. Harold and Margaret are buried on their beloved Petit Jean Mountain. *Submitted by M. Mobley.*

McINTURFF - William McInturff was born in Perry County in 1903. He, along with his sister Hazel McInturff Norwood were brought to Conway County as infants. Their mother and father passed away soon after they were born.

l-r: Ray Cook, Lula Oliver, William McInturff, Annie Roberts and Mary McInturff at the McInturff home 1947 or 1948.

Their Grandmother Oliver and two aunts, Mattie and Lula, and two uncles, Tommie and Sam Oliver, raised them. William grew up on a farm on what is now Road 287 in the Bald Knob Community. William's Uncle Tommie owned a farm about one-half mile from the old home place. At Tommie's death, William inherited the farm.

In about 1924, he met and married Mary Huie. They built a home on the place. To this union there was born three children: Corinne McInturff-Faulkner, W.T. McInturff and Christine McInturff, who passed away at the age of 5.

William farmed in the Bald Knob Community for many years. Corinne and W.T. grew up there and both graduated from Plumerville High School, Corinne in 1945 and W.T. in 1949.

Corinne married Elmo Faulkner in the late 1940s and they moved to California. In 1951 William, with his family, went to California for a visit to see Corinne and her family. They stayed for about six months and then returned home. They made several trips and eventually made California their home in 1959. Corinne lives near San Diego with her mother, Mary Huie McInturff, age 98.

In 1958 W.T. had married Alice Schmuland. In 1969 W.T. and Alice moved to Tacoma, WA. They had two children, Kevin and Lynette. W.T. still lives in Tacoma, near to both his children and their families. Alice passed away on Oct. 4, 2004.

McMILLAN (RHOADS) - Don Louis "Cowboy" (Rhoads) McMillan was born in Panama City, FL, Nov. 21, 1948, the son of USAF Capt. George Louis McMillan Jr. and Bonnie LaVelle Littig McMillan. He attended the University of Central Arkansas in Conway and was a professional rodeo cowboy. In 1967 he began a 20-year career in electrical distribution and construction as a journeyman lineman with Arkansas Power and Light Company, now Entergy, in Little Rock and Russellville.

Don, Blake, Marsha (Rhoads) McMillan family, Dec. 23, 2000 Christmas.

On Dec. 1, 1973 Don married Marsha Jewell Elkins in Little Rock, where they were both living, as both their parents had retired from the military and settled to be near the Little Rock Air Force Base. Marsha was born June 7, 1950, at Cherry Point, NC, daughter of USMC CWO-3 James Lewis Elkins and Ruby Mae Thompson Elkins. Her father served in three wars and was an aeronautical engineer. He was a championship marksman distinguished with the rifle and pistol, coached the National Marine Corps rifle and pistol team, and was selected to compete in the Olympic Competitions in Russia. Her mother graduated from the University of Cosmetology in Savannah, GA and managed the family properties and investments.

Don and Marsha (Rhoads) McMillan's wedding day with Marsha's parents, James and Ruby Elkins

Marsha's Conway County roots go back several generations. Her maternal grandparents were Johnnie Everett Thompson and Missouri Jewell Blankenship, and paternal grandparents, Charles Ross Elkins Sr. and Verna Verna Harvell (Gregory). Johnnie E. Thompson's parents were Thomas Harvey Thompson and Matilda Isabel Poteete. Missouri Jewell Blankenship's parents were Josepheus C. Blankenship and Ruby Dillard Zackery. Verna V. Harvell's parents were William Harvell and Rebecca Wiley. Charles Ross Elkins Sr.'s parents were James Riley Elkins and Francis Mooney. They all lived in the Jerusalem, Pleasant View area at some time in their lives.

In 1973 Marsha graduated from The University of Arkansas at Little Rock with a degree in music and sociology and started a career in social work and teaching piano, voice, and music theory, in Little Rock and Russellville. Marsha's parents had owned property in the county since 1946, even though they were pursuing a career in the military, having purchased the farm in Granny Hollow, known as Pleasant View, from her mother's parents when they decided to move to the Overcup area. In 1975, Marsha's parents moved to their farm after retiring from the military and the J.C. Penney Company.

Don and Marsha purchased adjoining property in 1976, when they decided to establish their home in Granny Hollow, to be near her parents. They began developing their cattle farm, while he worked for AP and L and she was employed by the State of Arkansas Social Services, then later as the social worker/counselor for Southern Christian Home in Morrilton. The Pleasant View School was once located on this property, which later became the home for the Pleasant View Church of Christ. Marsha's great uncle, Walter Elam, was once schoolmaster. Marsha's grandparents and other family members helped establish and attended the church. When Don and Marsha bought the property, this historic building had been neglected for many years. The roof was caving in and the floor was rotting out, which made the building unsafe and it could not be restored. They built broiler houses in 1980. In 1988 a swine farrow-to-finish facility was added and Don retired from AP and L to engage in full-time farming. Later they bought a second farrow-to-finish farm at Center Ridge.

Their only child, a son Blake Halston McMillan, was born Oct. 20, 1983. He attended Wonderview School, was home schooled for four years, then went to high school at Harding Academy in Searcy. He attended Oklahoma Christian University, ITT, and The University of Central Arkansas, before joining the US Air Force in June 2004.

Don and Marsha were active for many years in church, community service, and state and local politics. They developed several businesses during the course of their life together: Rocky Roads Farms, which later became DonMar Farms, Rhoads Construction, Rocky Roads Farms Dozer Service, D & R Forestry Services, DonMar Properties, and Beach Haven Senior Care. Don's biological father, Capt. George Louis McMillan Jr., a highly decorated Air Force fighter test pilot, was killed in a plane crash in 1949 (26 years old), after having completed 30 combat missions. Don's mother was left with two small sons, Ricky and Don.

A few years later the boys were adopted by Air Force pilot, Major Marvin Paty, who died an early death, leaving the young mother again with fatherless sons. When Don was 9 years old she married Air Force pilot, Lt. Col. John Ross Rhoads, who also adopted the boys. Don carried the name Rhoads for some 40 years. After the death of his mother and step-father, Don, Marsha and Blake petitioned the court to reinstate Don's birth name, McMillan to the family. In August 2002, the Don Rhoads family became the McMillan's.

On Sept. 13, 2003, Don, 54, was tragically killed by an employee of his company in Garland County near Hot Springs, leaving Marsha alone after 30 years, and Blake fatherless. After his father's death, Blake joined the Air Force. In March 2005, he graduated from US Air Force Technical School in navigational and meteorological systems. Marsha currently resides on their farm on Rhoads Drive and her Hot Springs home, and has started a new business, JonMar Trucking.

McQUAIN - Alex McQuain came to America in 1756 from Scotland. He began his new life in Pendleton County, VA where he married Mary Bodkin. Alex and Mary had 11 children - one was Hugh Alexander McQuain. Hugh married Catherine Cain in 1805 and had nine children - one was Joseph Winn McQuain.

Joseph Winn married Susan Priscilla Morgan in 1861. They had 12 children (four girls and eight boys). Joseph and Susan relocated to St. Louis, MO by 1868 and by 1873 they had moved on to Butler, KS. This is where their son Herbert Alexander was born in 1881. Herbert Alex eventually moved to Payne County, OK, met Ida Mae Hartzell and moved to Van Buren County, AR. Herb Alex and Ida Mae lived in the Choctaw-Clinton area. They raised 10 children, eight of them boys, the youngest being Herbert Finis McQuain.

In 1954 Herb Finis was working in Independence, MO, and he met Winnie Joe Russell. Winnie was from Scotland, AR, but she was living with family in Missouri so she could work there. Winnie actually met Herb Alex first, and later his son Herb Finis. Herb and Winnie married in 1954. The first of their eight sons was born in 1954. Herbert Michael led the team and was followed by Terry, Ronnie, Mark, Jerry, Scotty, Joe and Steve. All of the boys were born in Independence, MO except Steve. He was born in Morrilton.

Herb, Winnie and the boys made the long trip (on the then un-improved highways) at least every summer, sometimes more often, back to Arkansas to visit the families. They re-located to Arkansas about 1965 after losing their home to a fire. They lived in Scotland for a brief time before moving to the Birdtown area. After a short stay there, they moved to Overcup and eventually to Morrilton, where most of the family has remained.

The family has remained close over the years. We lost Michael in 1994 at age 39. In 2002 Jerry had

his only child and named him Michael in honor of his brother. We think of him often.

This is the last of the "BIG" McQuain families in Arkansas. Our boys have kept it small. Mike never married or had children; Terry has two girls, Charlotte and Kerry; Ronnie has a son Ronnie Jr. and daughter Marsha; Mark has a son Joshua and daughter Sarah. Mark lost his second child at birth, a girl named Jessica; Jerry has one natural son, Michael, and four stepchildren; Scotty has one son Brandon and a daughter Brittany; Neither Joe nor Steve has any children.

Of this generation, Ronnie has the only grandchild. Ronnie Jr. has a son, Alex Blake McQuain. As young men, Ronnie and Mark joined the US Army together and at this writing, their sons, Ronnie Jr. and Joshua, are serving in Iraq in the US Army National Guard, 206th Unit of 39th Infantry Brigade. We are very proud of them. *Submitted by Kim McQuain.*

MERRYMAN - In 1836, John and Sally Merryman were married in Decatur County, IN. John and Sally had three children: William M., Mary Ann and Mahala Jane. William M. married Nancy Ann Winn in Decatur County in 1860, they had nine children: Sarah Elizabeth, John H., Minnie Alice, Samelda Jane, William A., Nancy Ellen, Ardonia, James Riley and Eva Mae. The children were all born in Indiana.

William and Merica Merryman family.

The family was living in Van Buren County at the time of Minnie Alice's death in 1886. A homestead for 160 acres of land was granted to William in 1894. William was a barn builder by trade. At least one of his barns is still in use today. It was put together with wooden pegs. William himself was the first postmaster of Culpepper Mountain in Van Buren County.

Sarah Elizabeth, William's daughter, succeeded him as postmistress until 1914. Elizabeth was married to Marion Smith. They operated a general store and a gristmill until the early 1940s on Culpepper Mountain. They are said to have donated the first acre of land for the Culpepper Cemetery. They had nine children.

John Henry married Nancy A. Hockersmith and they had eight children.

Nancy Ellen married George Cleaver and they had seven children.

Ardonia Merryman never married.

Eva Mae married James Alfred Nicholson and they had five children.

James R. Merryman left Culpepper about 1899-1900 under dire circumstances and returned to Indiana. He rode a horse that he had borrowed from a neighbor and rode to the Mississippi River and turned it loose; strange as it seems, the horse returned home some months later. James Merryman's sister, Eva, married James Alfred Nicholson, who was murdered by Pete Barnes in 1899 (Gazette files, P.1, Vol. 2 1899). The writer had been told that Pete Barnes hid behind a tree and stabbed James A. Nicholson in the back as he and James Merryman were walking down the road near Scotland. He was killed. James Merryman told Barnes to get off of him (Nicholson), that he was dead. Barnes refused and Merryman picked up the gun that Nicholson was carrying and shot Barnes off of him. This resulted in his leaving Culpepper Mountain. It is assumed that he became a Baptist Minister. Eva married second, Lynn Shipley and third, Fender Prince.

Samelda Jane married first, George Dickinson, second, Joseph Nicholson and third, Thomas Story.

Minnie Alice married first, Mr. Helley and second, Emmett Bradley.

William Merryman married Merica L. Barnes. They had 11 children: John Cliff, Erby, Eston, Marvin, Sherman, Minnie Pearl, Eileen, Clara Mae, William Harv, James Elmer, and Orville. John Cliff married Ida B. Miller. They had two children, Opal and Othel. Marvin married Dora Lee Skinner. Minnie Pearl married John Wilson. Carla Mae married John Bradley. William Harv married Bertha Banks. James Elmer married Mamie Harris. They had five children: J.E., Lula Mae, Faye, Dewayne and Ruby. James Elmer owned a country store in the late 1920s, north of Wonderview in Conway County. Orville married Bell Pruitt.

Each fourth Sunday in May, families and friend meet at Culpepper Cemetery, paying homage to our loved ones buried here. It was they, who years ago, set aside this particular time for decoration, and it has been observed ever since. Then, as now, the day is filled with song, prayer, and dinner on the ground, and tales of the long journey in a wagon from Indiana to Arkansas, or from some other far away place.

MILLER - Matthias and Margaret Miller married in 1888. He is the brother of Nichalous Miller and she is a sister to Louisia Weber, both daughters of Peter and Anna Mary Wein Weber. Three of their oldest children were born in Pittsburgh, PA: Michael, Nichalous and Anna. The other of their six children were born in St. Vincent, AR - Catherine, Josephine, Martin, Clemons Joseph, Simon and Elizabeth.

Matthias and Margaret Miller

Michael married Thelma Marie Ridling, daughter of Andrew and Frances Bradley Ridling, and they had nine children: Rose Marie (md. Henry Miller of Little Rock); Mike (Jenwye Horton of Morrilton); Margaret Lantolo (deceased); Theresa (md. Alfred Thomas of Russellville); Mathilda Jo, (md. 1st, Carl Paladino (deceased) and 2nd, Andy Rossi, both of Center Ridge); Matthias (deceased); Carl (md. Beatrice DeSalvo of Center Ridge); Imelda (md. Allen Roberts of Little Rock); and Jim (md. Becky Fougerousse of St. Vincent).

Nichalous married Annie Volpert of Bigelow and they had four children: Joseph Edward (Earlene) of Broussard, LA; Anna Louise of Benton; Mary Margaret (Paul) Lee of Little Rock and Thomas (Sherry) of Youngsville, LA.

Anna Lachowsky married John Lachowsky of Morrilton and they had four children: Albert (deceased); James (deceased); John Jr., Hot Springs Village, AR; and Imelda Lachowsky of Los Angeles, CA.

Catherine married Carl Kordsmeier of Morrilton. They had 12 children: Carl William (deceased); Nick (Dolores Ilgner) (both deceased); Cyril (Eleanor Kock of Morrilton); Msgr. Charles (deceased); Herbert (Lorene Dussex of Morrilton); William (deceased) (md. Lorine Fredrick of Morrilton); Emil (Helen Moix of Conway); Gerald (deceased) (md. Elsie Nahen of Conway); Martin (Bernadine Massery of Conway); Margaret (Herman Baechie of Houston TX); Martha (William Lemonde of Springfield, OR); Lucille of Morrilton.

Josephine married Edgar Worthington of St. Louis, one son Edgar Jr., all deceased. They owned the Weather Bird Shoe Store in Little Rock, Capitol Ave, for many years.

Martin married Marie Ermann of Barlin. They

have six children: Martin (Rosemary Zakrzenski of Marche); Louise (Walter Bulter of Eureka Springs); Raymond (Dorothy Piechocki); John (Betty Nosal); Romana (Roy Dwight Jones) and Charles (Mary Szymanski) all of Marche.

Simon married Elizabeth Pfeifer of St. Vincent. They had four children: Ernest (Onita Lannie of Little Rock), Margaret (Bill Curtin of Boston, MA), Sister Stephanie of New Orleans, LA, and James (deceased) (md. Elizabeth Ann Beck of St. Vincent). After their divorce he married Eva Neely of Ft. Smith. Simon founded the Respiratory Therapy Dept. at St. Vincent Infirmary and is honored each year in April during RT week.

Elizabeth married Joseph Montana of Buffalo, NY and they had one son Joseph Jr., he and his wife Ann live in Dallas, TX. The Montana's owned the Montana Italian Restaurant on Broadway in Morrilton for several years before retiring. *Submitted by Rose Marie Miller.*

MOBLEY - The Mobley family originated in Mobberley, England. Among the first inhabitants of New England was John Mobberly, who settled in Prince Georges County, MD. Later, Mobleys were pioneers in Ohio and Iowa. Richard Oliver Mobley married Lydia Jane James in 1883. Richard tried his hand at several ventures. He prospected for gold, farmed, worked for a railroad company and eventually formed a construction company with his sons. Richard and Lydia were in the Great Land Rush in Oklahoma. They claimed a farm, but had to move because a black substance in the water made the children sick.

While Richard worked for the railroad, he developed a sliding door for boxcars that is still in use today. In Argenta (North Little Rock), AR, Richard and sons formed the Argenta Construction Company, and were among the first to pave streets in Little Rock. They traveled around Arkansas during the early years of the company, often living in tents near the sites.

Around 1920, Richard and Lydia with their children, John Bryce, Fay, and Max James and their families, moved to Morrilton, where Mobley Construction Company was formed. Richard noticed that the hot and cold made the concrete highway slabs deteriorate as they expanded and contracted. It was his idea to leave a small space between slabs to prevent that deterioration.

Bryce and Dee Mobley had three children: Jimmy, Fay and William. They moved to California for a while, but when the marriage failed, Bryce, Jimmy and Fay returned to Arkansas. Bryce managed the Dardanelle branch of Mobley Construction, where he met "Nootsy" Jackson and married her. Their children are Mary Lynn (Mrs. Ronnie Roberson) and Bryce.

Max married Mary Ellen Cholvin. Their sons were Richard (died in infancy); Max James Jr. "Mick," John Bryce "Bud" and Robert Joseph "Bob." When Max died in 1942, Mary sold their interest in Mobley Construction Company to raise and educate her sons. "Mick" and "Bud" flipped a coin to see which one would go to college first. "Mick" went first.

Upon finishing medical school Dr. Max Mobley married Mary Fletcher Strait. Max had already enlisted, but had to complete his residency in New Orleans before he was sent to Europe. In 1943, Mary died six weeks after Max James III was born. After the war ended, Dr. Max returned to Arkansas and married Hazel Virdelle Hill. Dr. Max practiced medicine in Russellville for many years.

Max III "Mickey" spent his early years with his maternal grandfather, Judge Audrey Strait, and his paternal grandmother, Mary Ellen Mobley Strait, who had married shortly before his birth. When Dr. Max remarried, "Mickey" went to live with him. Max III married his childhood sweetheart, Sally Jo McGloflin, and together they joined the Peace Corps for a 2-year project to Liberia, West Africa. That experience had a major impact in their lives, leading them to seek careers to help others. Max became a Ph.D. psycholo-

gist, then became deputy director for Treatment Services for the Arkansas Department of Correction. Sally became a special education teacher. They have two sons, Harold Blaise Mobley and Max James "Mickey" Mobley IV. A description of their families may be found in the article on the Strait Family.

John Bryce Mobley joined the Army, where h served in the Aleutians. He returned to Arkansas and finished college at Arkansas Tech where he played football. "Bud" married Katherine Holtzman. They raised five children: Ann (Mrs. Ken Smith), Susan (Mrs. Jim Yeager), John, Ellen and Karen.

"Bob" served on a mine sweeper in the Navy. He returned to marry Cicely Glendenning and became a pharmacist. Cicely and "Bob" raised eight children: Jane, Robert Joseph "Joe," Martha (Mrs. Andrew James), Marjorie (Mrs. Hablitz), Lydia, Richard, Mary Grace (Copping) and Audrey (Mrs. Mardis Jones).

Information for this article came from Ancestry.com genealogical files, the Mobley Family web-site, interviews with Mary Ellen Mobley Strait, Judge Richard Mobley and Robert J. Mobley. *Submitted by Max Mobley.*

MONTGOMERY - Bradley Hayward Montgomery, called Hayward, was born on Petit Jean Mountain Feb. 5, 1911, the youngest son of James Byron "Bud" Montgomery (See the biography of Theodore Montgomery). Hayward lived and farmed on Petit Jean until 1929, when he left the mountain and moved to North Little Rock to enter the sawmill business. In April 1937 he married Ruby Lucille McGlasson, the eldest daughter of Bascomb and Agnes McGlasson, who had

Bradley Hayward Montgomery with wife Ruby - 1937.

moved to North Little Rock from Saltillo, AR. To this union four children were born: Hayward Carl (md. Carolyn Burson); Gaye Delores (md. William Avants); Larry Don (md. Kay Rowland) and Debra Renee (md. Don Blakey).

Finances were slim during the depression years and when the sawmill business slowed, Hayward gave it up to become a produce broker, buying fresh produce and selling it to local groceries. Through thick and thin, Hayward saw that his family always had a good living and lived to see his children become computer programmers, aviation engineers, nurses and professionals.

Although Hayward left the mountain at age 18, he never forgot his roots and made sure his children knew and appreciated their heritage. Each year on Memorial Day, the entire family returned to the mountain for a family reunion at the community cemetery by the Lutheran Church. All his brothers and sisters and their children would meet at the cemetery to visit and clean the grave sites, have a potluck picnic, and get reacquainted.

Hayward had many stories about life on the mountain to tell his children, and one that always amused them was "Traveling to Morrilton." He had a Model T Ford that had little or no brakes and a gravity feed fuel system. Hayward said that when he and his brothers left the mountain to drive into Morrilton, they would stop at the mountain top, cut down a small sapling, chain it to the rear bumper of the Model T and use it as a drag brake to go down the slope. On the way home he would have to back the car up the mountain to keep the engine from stalling, since the gas tank was under the front seat and the gas was gravity fed to the engine.

Hayward died in 1996 and is buried at North Little Rock. He is survived by four children, eight grandchildren and nine great-grandchildren. The oldest son, Hayward Carl, retired in 2004, returned to his roots in Conway County and settled at Morrilton; Gaye Delores retired to Dallas, TX; Larry Don and Debra Renee both still live in North Little Rock.

MONTGOMERY - Hayward Carl Montgomery (called Hayward) (b. March 20, 1938 in Little Rock, AR) is the son of Bradley Hayward Montgomery, grandson of James Byron Montgomery, and great-grandson of Theodore Montgomery. Theodore Montgomery moved his family from Georgia to Arkansas in 1859 and settled on Petit Jean Mountain. The family lived and farmed on Petit Jean through the years until 1930 when Bradley Hayward left the mountain and moved to North Little Rock. There he met and married Ruby Lucille McGlasson. Hayward Carl was the first child of that union.

Front row: Michael Toczek, Matthew Toczek, Carolyn Montgomery, Kelly Montgomery. Back row: Hayward Montgomery, David Toczek, Carla Toczek, Pamela Montgomery, Michael Montgomery.

Hayward grew up in North Little Rock and in 1958 married Carolyn Joyce Burson, the youngest daughter of John Sanford Burson and Edna Lee Garrett. To this union two children were born, Carla Beth Montgomery (b. 1966) and Michael Wayne Montgomery (b. 1969).

Carla Beth graduated from the University of Arkansas at Little Rock with degrees in English and international studies, which included study abroad in Caen, France. In 1989 Carla married David Matthew Toczek of Hillsdale, MI, a graduate of the US Military Academy at West Point, NY. To this union two children were born, Michael David Toczek (b. 1991) and Matthew Aaron Toczek (b. 1994). As a military family, David and Carla move frequently, but currently they live in Heidelberg, Germany where David is a lieutenant colonel working on the staff of the Commanding General of NATO.

Michael Wayne graduated from the University of Arkansas at Little Rock with a degree in business administration. In 1993 he married Pamela Denise Crowder of Camden, AR, a graduate of the University of Arkansas. To this union was born one child Kelly Shea Montgomery (b. 1994). Michael currently lives in Landenberg, PA and is first vice president of MBNA, Wilmington, DE.

In 1963 Hayward joined the North Little Rock Police Department where he served for 12 years, first as a patrolman, then later as a detective working in the highest crime areas of the city. While working on the police department, Hayward studied and trained in electronics and computer science.

In 1975 Hayward left the police department and went into business designing and selling video recording and surveillance systems to the industrial market in Arkansas. He designed, sold, and installed the largest CCTV system in the state at that time to Timex Corporation in Little Rock, along with many other systems including a complete video production studio at Southwestern Bell. After 28 years in the commercial electronic business Hayward retired in 2003. He then contracted with Alltel Communications in Little Rock as a computer system administrator to program and maintain one of their nationwide computer systems.

In 2004 Hayward returned to Conway County

and moved to Morrilton, AR where he and Carolyn currently live.

MONTGOMERY - John Manly Montgomery (See biography of Amos and Clarkie Johnson and Theodore and Nancy Montgomery) married Margaret Alice Ferguson on Petit Jean Mt. Margaret Alice Ferguson was born near Spring Hill, TN to George Ferguson and Vesta Mueller Ferguson. Margaret Alice became an orphan when she was 6 years old and was adopted by Jim and Elvira Mundy, who brought her to Petit Jean Mt. shortly thereafter.

John Manly Montgomery family. John Manly and Margaret Alice Montgomery - 1905. Standing: Ottis Lawton, Bonnie Lovie, Gladys Easter. Center: Oma Gray (Betty) and Gerthel Lucille (Eugenia) (baby).

John Manly and Margaret Alice had nine children: Effie and Eva Crescent both died as infants. The surviving children were Gladys Easter, Bonnie Love, Ottis Lawton, Hazel Garnet, Betty Gay (Oma), Eugenia (Gerthel Lucille) and Jo Ann (Johnnie). Gladys Easter married Patrick Henry Hamilton. Bonnie Love married Walter Delile Bratcher. Ottis Lawton married Ruby Edith Gilley (See Ottis Lawton and Ruby Edith Montgomery biography.) Hazel Garnet died of pneumonia when she was 20 years old. Betty Gay married William Homer Gray of Bradford, AR. Eugenia married Frederick Lacefield. Jo Ann married Kenneth Cocks.

John Manly Montgomery was a farmer and a merchant. He owned and operated a general store just east of what is now the Lutheran Camp. Because of his reluctance to collect from his debtors, he was considered a better farmer than merchant. John Manly died in 1911 at the age of 46 years. He was buried in the Petit Jean Mt. Cemetery. The hearth stone from Theodore and Nancy's log home was used as his headstone. His widow, Margaret Alice, was advised by friends and family to sell the store because it was felt that a lady could not manage such affairs.

Shortly after John Manly died, Margaret Alice rented the farm and moved her children to Morrilton. Eventually, Margaret divided the property among her children. Her children and grandchildren still own a portion of the land, which had been homesteaded by their ancestors almost 150 years ago. Margaret subsequently married Colonel Gibson. *Submitted by Bettye Henderson.*

MONTGOMERY - Ottis Lawton was born on Petit Jean Mt. on Jan. 19, 1899 to John Manly and Margaret Alice Montgomery. (See biographies of Amos and Clarkie Johnson, Theodore Montgomery and John Manly Montgomery.) He grew up on Petit Jean Mt. and went to the Rebstock School. Ottis was a farmer and a builder. He built several of the homes that still exist on Petit Jean Mt.

In 1923, Ottis married Ruby Edith Gilley. Ruby lived at Cardon's Bottom, where her father was a planter and also a constable. In the summer, Ruby's family came to a house that her family owned, near what is now known as West Road.

Ottis and Ruby had four children: Glenna Belle (named for her maternal grandmother, Belle Wallace); Alice Dean (named for her paternal grandmother); Bettye Jean and Carroll LeeRoy "Monty" (named for

his maternal uncle). Dr. T.W. Hardison delivered all four children. Dr. Hardison and Ottis Montgomery shared a love of Petit Jean and when Bettye was born, they wanted to name her Petit Jean. Ruby refused to name her daughter Petit Jean but the rhyming name was acceptable to her.

Seated: Ottis and Ruby Montgomery. Standing, l-r: Bettye Jean, Carroll LeeRoy (Monte), Glenna Bell.

Ottis and Ruby lived in a 2-story white frame house on what is now Winrock Drive, but moved to Morrilton because of a desire for better schools for their children. They kept the property on Petit Jean Mt. and spent most of the summers on the Mountain.

Glenna Montgomery married Graham Addison Suggs of Pensacola, FL. They had six children: Graham Montgomery Suggs, Gregory Steven Suggs, George Michael Suggs, Patricia Galene Suggs, Bradley Lawton Suggs and Mary Christine Suggs. Graham Montgomery Suggs married Audry Anne Spears and they had one daughter, Jennifer Rebecca. Jennifer married Timothy Hammonds and they have three children: Graham Timothy, Olivia Madeline and Lauren MaKenzie. The Suggs and Hammonds live in Arlington, TX. Gregory Suggs married Denise Larson. Gregory was a gifted musician. He was killed in an automobile accident in 1972 while in Denver, CO performing. He is buried in the Petit Jean Mt. Cemetery. George Suggs married Karen Postier and they have three children: Melissa Renee, Brandy Michelle and Jeremiah Zachariah. Brandy is married to Johnny Childress and they have one son, Calvin. Bradley Suggs married Stephanie Rae Pace. They have one son, Tyler.

Alice Dean Montgomery was a sweet and beautiful little girl with strawberry blonde hair. She died when she was only 12 years old from complications from appendicitis. She is buried in the Petit Jean Mt. Cemetery.

Bettye Montgomery married Burton Henderson. See the Burton Henderson biography.

Carroll "Monty" Montgomery married Mary Belle Laird. They had two children, Mitchell and Megan Blythe. "Monty" died in 2001 and is buried in the Petit Jean Mt. Cemetery.

MONTGOMERY - Theodore and Nancy Montgomery came to Petit Jean Mt. on Christmas Eve, 1859. Theodore was born in North Carolina and moved to Baker County, GA in about 1830 where his father John had developed a plantation. It was there that he met and married Nancy Johnson, whose family owned a plantation nearby. The plantations were on along the banks of the Ichawaynochaway Creek.

When Theodore and Nancy Montgomery left Georgia, along with Nancy's parents and siblings (see the Amos and Clarkie Johnson biography), they had two children, William "Billy" and Robert. Their daughter Sally was born at Maumelle as they were traveling en route to Petit Jean Mt. After settling on Petit Jean Mt., four more children were born to them: James Byron "Bud," Columbus "Lump," John Manly and Josephine.

Theodore and Nancy's sons, except for William who died at a young age, acquired land on Petit Jean Mt. and became farmers there.

Robert was married at least twice and had one son Bill. Robert (d. ca. 1940) is buried in the Petit Jean Mt. Cemetery.

Sally married Tom Pynson, a farmer, and they lived on Petit Jean Mt. Both are buried in the Petit Jean Mt. Cemetery.

James Byron "Bud" (b. 1864) md. Lorenda "Rendy" Monday. They had nine children: Lee (Mrs. John Weaver); Elbert, whose first wife died, and whose second wife's name was Ruby; Ernest (md. Rosie Coble); Lawrence (md. Lucy Kelly); Feral; Odas (md. Maudie Boyd); Lisy (md. Elbert Ashcraft); Layton (md. Violet Stanhigh); and Havard (pronounced Hayward) (md. Ruby McGleeson). James Byron and Lorenda Montgomery and Lawrence and Lucy Montgomery are buried in the Petit Jean Mt. Cemetery.

Columbus married Fay Allen and they had three children: Vey (Mrs. Ernest Clayton), Effie (Mrs. Chester Carter) and Clarence. They are all buried in the Petit Jean Mt. Cemetery.

John Manly married Margaret Alice Ferguson, and they had nine children. Effie and Eva Crescent died as infants. The surviving children were Gladys Easter, Bonnie Love, Ottis Lawton, Hazel Garnet, Betty Gay, Eugenia and Jo Ann. Josephine married William Coble and they continued to live on Petit Jean Mt. Hazel Garnet died of pneumonia when she was 20 years old. *Submitted by Mrs. Bettye Henderson.*

MOORE - James Marion Moore was born about 1823 in Tennessee and died about 1864. Tradition is that he was killed by bushwhackers during the Civil War. The Oppelo area was hard hit by bushwhackers and Federals in the closing months of the war. On Dec. 1, 1864 a skirmish was fought along Cypress Creek between forces of the Confederacy and the Union stationed at Lewisburg; this creek runs along the south end of Lower Oppelo and the stream "Old Bap" feeds into it near Hwy. 9 and the county road.

Residents of Oppelo had been very helpful to the Southern Cause, and after the Federals destroyed Witt's Regiment (a quasi-official guerrilla group) in a battle just above what is now Morrilton during February 1865, the civilians of Oppelo suffered horrible and deadly raids. Sick old men were dragged from their beds and shot, and even several women were murdered. Many of the families who lived through the trouble just up and left in the months after - abandoning homesteads or selling out for pennies on the dollar. Land was cheap, and still a lot of it free for homesteading after the war.

James married June 27, 1844 in Roane County, TN to Elizabeth A. Taylor. It is believed she was the daughter of William Taylor, a resident of Roane County, TN. James and Elizabeth arrived in Perry County in time for the 1850 census where he is shown with wife and two children and, what we believe to be three brothers: Lewis J. age 21, Henry W. age 11 and Andrew J. age 9. There was also William M. Moore who married Nancy J. Taylor in Roane County, TN, and it is believed that brothers married sisters. Two other brothers came with James and Elizabeth - Daniel and Thomas. These records would indicate that the parents had died - the 1840 Roane County, TN census shows that were seven male children and two females.

The children of James and Elizabeth Moore were: Sarah J. married P.L. Sharp. I know nothing more on this family.

Columbus F. died at age 15.

Mary Ann married Wilburn C. Wood, their children were James W., John, Maggie, Robert "Bob," Bennett F.

Daniel W. married Lizzie Norman. Allie is the only child known.

John Henry died before 2 months old.

Thomas Hugh married Angeline Green; their known children were Maude and James T.

James Bennett married Lucy E. Todd; their children were Biddie F., Dora A., Claude A., Esther M., Stella and Nora Callie.

William A. died before his first birthday.

Martha E. married William J. Nix, see the Nix family. *Compiled by J.A. (Wear) Jenkins.*

MOOSE - Charles Reid Moose (b. Feb. 15, 1905 in Morrilton) was the son of Judge William Lewis and Linnie B. Moose. He graduated from Morrilton High School in 1924, attended Hendrix College one year, and graduated from Sweeney Mechanical School, Kansas City, MO, in 1927. He then went to Lambeth Air Field, St. Louis, MO, learned to fly and got his private pilot license.

On April 12, 1930, he and May Hope McClurkin (b. Nov. 20, 1908) of Conway married in Prescott. They lived in Little Rock and Mr. Moose worked in the Little Rock Airplane Factory where the

Lt. Commander Charles Reid Moose, May Hope Moose, Charles Jr., Robert Lewis, John Irving, William Cozart, David Nelson, Kathryne E.

"Little Rocket" was built. This plane came in first and won the race across the United States for light planes in 1932.

Mr. and Mrs. Moose moved to Morrilton in 1932 and lived in the family home place, 500 Green Street. Mr. Moose was a foreman in the Soil Conservation Service, CCC Camp at Solgohachia. He was transferred to the CCC Camp at Charlotte, AR, in 1937. The family moved to Little Rock in 1939 where Mr. Moose taught aviation for Central Flying Service at Adams Field and Ground School at Central High School.

After Pearl Harbor, Dec. 7, 1941, Mr. Moose moved his wife and five small sons to Morrilton where a new house had been built on the Moose home site. Then he joined the Navy Air Force and flew planes from the factories to the West Coast for the war against Japan. After the war he was stationed on Midway Island for a year as liaison officer. He retired from the Navy with the rank of lieutenant commander and returned to Morrilton.

Mr. Moose sold Ward Ice Cream products to grocery stores in Conway County and four surrounding counties. He did refrigeration repairs on Ward boxes in the stores. Then he went into business for himself, repairing commercial refrigeration motors as Moose Refrigeration Service. He owned a 2-place Taylorcraft, high-wing monoplane and took passengers for flights and for picture-taking over Conway County and surrounding areas. He and Stewart Nelson did commercial photography of homes and farms in Conway County. Mr. Moose had over 10,000 hours of flying time, Navy and personal. He died Feb. 25, 1984, in the Veterans' Hospital, Fort Roots, North Little Rock, of a malignant tumor on the brain. He is buried in Elmwood Cemetery.

Mrs. Moose graduated from Hendrix College in 1928 and earned a master of science in education from Arkansas State College for Teachers, Conway in 1960. She taught English and Latin in Almyra High School (1928-30), in Morrilton High School (1956-66), and Freshman English in the University of Central Arkansas (1966-73), when she retired. She was elected Teacher of the Year in 1963. Mrs. Moose has been active in church, school, and civic affairs. The Mooses belong to the Methodist Church where she taught Sunday School classes in the Adult Department for 60 years. She has been active in PTA units (a Life Member), AARP, the DAR, Delta Kappa Gamma, United Methodist Women (a Life Member), Conway County Retired Teachers, and the Petit Jean Garden Club.

Mr. and Mrs. Moose had six children, all graduated from Morrilton High School.

1) Charles Reid Jr. (b. 1932) attended Hendrix College for two years, was in the Navy Air Force for four years, graduated from the University of Florida Gainesville, FL, and earned a master's degree in electrical engineering at Drexal University, Philadelphia PA. He worked for the Bunker-Ramo Company in Canoga Park, CA. He lives in Baltimore, MD.

2) Robert Lewis (b. 1934) attended Hendrix College one year, was in the Navy four years stationed on the battleship *Iowa*, and graduated from the University of Arkansas, Fayetteville, with a degree in electrical engineering. He was employed in the McDonnell Aircraft Company, working on the first Gemini spacecraft when he was killed in a car wreck in St. Louis at age 28. He is buried in Elmwood Cemetery.

3) John Irving (b. 1937) graduated from Hendrix College and Arkansas Medical School in Little Rock. He served two years in the Navy Air Force Hospital in Orlando, FL. He is a medical doctor in Siloam Springs.

4) William Cazort (b. 1939) graduated from Hendrix College, earned a master's degree in electrical engineering on a scholarship to Columbia University, New York, and an EdD degree in natural sciences from Texas University in Houston, TX. He is head of the Physics Dept. in San Jacinto College in Pasadena, TX. He lives in Deer Park, TX.

5) David Nelson (b. 1941) graduated from Hendrix College and St. Paul's School of Theology, Kansas City, MO. He is pastor of the Rosewood United Methodist Church in West Memphis, AR.

6) Kathryn Elizabeth (b. 1948) md. Vic Kordsmeier Jr. and lives in Morrilton and works for the Kraft Paper Mill at Opello.

The Moose family now consists of 16 grandchildren, 45 to 30 years, and 22 great-grandchildren, 18 years to 6 months.

In 1880 James Miles Moose (for whom Moose Street was named) sold to the Methodist Church for $125, Lots 1 and 2, Block 10, Moose Addition, on the corner of Church and East (now Chestnut) Streets. The present United Methodist Church is the third building on that site. James Miles Moose was the grandfather of Charles Reid Moose.

MOOSE - The Moose family in Conway County came from Germany where the name was spelled Mussgenung, meaning "moss gatherer." Moss was collected for the stuffing of furniture.

David Moose came to Philadelphia in 1751. His son George was the first to change the spelling of the name. After the Revolutionary War the "genung" was dropped. The "Muss" part was spelled like the animal "moose."

May Hope Moose (b. Nov. 20, 1908).

George's third son was John (b. 1771), the progenitor of the Moose family in Conway County. The third of John's 10 children was John Lewis (b. 1803, d. 1888). After living in North Carolina and Tennessee, he went to California for the gold rush. Then he settled in Arkansas where Lewisburg is located.

The oldest son of John Lewis was James Miles Moose (b. 1827), the father of Mary Emily, Edwin C., William Lewis (b. 1857), Annie Laura, Alice Urilda, Eugenia (born in Texas for the Union Army was in Conway County where his home was burned), John Menifee, Annie, Sophia and James Sayle (b. 1874). In 1889 Annie married J.O. Blakeney, editor of *The Headlight*. James Miles built a new home at 711 Green Street. It is on the National Register of Historic Homes. His great-great-grandson, Edward Beamon Howell Jr., lives there.

By 1890 James Miles owned 800 acres of good farming and east of Division Street, so the first street east is Moose Street. On the west side, E.J. Morrill owned about the same amount of farming land, so the first street west of Division is Morrill Street.

There are several stories about the naming of the city of Morrilton. It is the only one in Arkansas, the United States, or the world, according to the Atlas. One story had the flipping of a coin which decided the name would be for Mr. Morrill. But one "l" was left off of the railroad sign, so the town has always been spelled Morrilton.

William Lewis came to Morrilton in 1880 where he and Mr. Charles C. Reid formed a law partnership. Later Judge Moose was Attorney General of Arkansas until his death in 1915. The Mooses had nine children, all born in Morrilton and graduated from Morrilton High School: William Lewis Jr., James Clifton, Mary Ellen, Elizabeth, Emily, John Fletcher, Virginia Darden, Susan Fuller and Charles Reid.

Clifton had two daughters, Margaret (Spires) and Mary (Howell). Mary Ellen (Mrs. Madison Hauk Dean) had two sons: M.H. Jr. and William Moose. Emily and Rev. W.F. Rogers had three sons: W.F. Jr., James and Dr. Henry Nelson II. Miss Darden Moose was the first woman lawyer in Little Rock. Charles Reid and wife (May Hope) had five sons and a daughter: Charles Reid Jr., Robert Lewis, Dr. John Irving, Dr. William Cazort, Rev. David Nelson and Kathryn E. (Moose) Kordsmeier.

Eugenia married C.C. Burrow; they had a son and seven daughters. When the Burrows moved from Moose Hill to a home on Green Street, the Burrow home became the first St. Anthony's Hospital. Mary Fletcher married Audrey Strait, a lawyer.

James Sayle Moose served several terms as mayor of Morrilton. His son James Jr. spoke seven languages and was US Ambassador to Damascas, Iran, Saudi Arabia, Paris (France) and the Orient. They had two children, James III and Duncan. They lived in the Moose home on Green Street when they were in Morrilton.

Over the years there have been many Moose names in the telephone directory. At the present time, there is only one - Moose, M.H., 500 Green Street, phone 354-4453, the only reversible number in Conway County. The owner is 96 years old, so soon there will be no Moose names in the directory.

Since James Lewis and Sarah Moose came to this area in 1835, many of their descendants in Conway County have been actively associated in business, cultural, social and educational affairs around the world. *Submitted by May Hope Moose.*

MORRILL - Lavinia Bedinger, daughter of Solomon Singleton and Mildred Berry (Washington) Bedinger, married Edward Henry Morrill on Feb. 22, 1882. Edward Henry Morrill was the son of Edward James and Harriet Morrill. E.J. Morrill, a native of Massachusetts, and his wife Harriet had lived in Perry County, MO before coming to Conway County in 1841. They settled in Lewisburg, south of the present-day Morrilton.

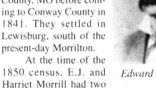
Edward Henry Morrill

At the time of the 1850 census, E.J. and Harriet Morrill had two sons, Edward Henry and George Hall, and a daughter Josephine. When E.J. Morrill's will was probated May 7, 1885, Josephine was not mentioned and was presumably deceased. E.J. Morrill made a bequest in his will, probated, to his granddaughter Lucy O. Griffin, possibly the daughter of Josephine.

Netta Washington (Morrill) Griffith, daughter of Edward H. and Lavinia (Bedinger) Morrill relates in a letter written in 1960, that when her grandfather, E.J. Morrill "...moved down the Arkansas River by flatboat to Lewisburg with his family. Lewisburg on the bank of the river was a thriving little town ... had 10 or 12 stores, two hotels. Their only transportation was stagecoach or steamboat which brought their merchandise from New Orleans. Grandfather was a merchant and druggist. In those early days, there were few railroads. In 1871 or 1872, a company was formed in Little Rock and began building a road to Fort Smith. The first survey was through Sardis Gap through Lewisburg. They asked Lewisburg to donate $1,000 to help build the railroad. They thought little of the 'Old train thing' as they called it ... felt they could get it anyway and wouldn't donate ... the company moved one (mile) north to where it is now. (The) Morrill and Moose (families) donated from their land which they owned, where the town of Morrilton was established. The first depot was a box car... The first residents of Morrilton, according to historic accounts, were Mr. and Mrs. George Morrill,.... They were the parents of the first child born at Morrilton, Julia..." The city of Morrilton began to develop, to the demise of Lewisburg. The city was incorporated by an act of the county court Jan. 16, 1880 as Morrillton. The spelling was later changed to Morrilton.

Edward Henry Morrill died at an early age, apparently as a result of a prank. While on a deer hunt and staying in a cave, a bucket filled with water was set up to topple on the unsuspecting person who walked under. The douse in the cold weather was blamed for Edward catching pneumonia, causing his death in 1888 at the age of 43. He left his widow, Lavinia (Bedinger) Morrill, with four young children, ages 7 months to 5 years: Edward Henry, Netta Washington, Edna and Mildred Antoinette. Lavinia (Bedinger) Morrill and her children lived in the Morrilton area for 12 or more years after the death of E.J. Morrill. The 1900 Conway County Census records Lavinia's sister, Henrietta "Netta" G. Bedinger, living with her and her four children. In the early 1900s Lavinia Morrill and her children moved to Terrell, Kaufman County, TX to be near close relatives.

At the historic depot in Morrilton, now a museum, there is now a plaque donated by the Morrill family which states: "In memory of Edward Henry Morril, 1845-1888, for whom the city of Morrilton is named, for his foresight in recognizing the importance of bringing the railroad to this community and his generosity in donating land for that purpose, this plaque is dedicated. Given in loving memory by his grandchildren on this 10th day of April 1999." *Contributed by Marion Singleton (Doug) Bedinger.*

MORROW - John Dale Morrow (b. July 29, 1920 in Birdtown), son of Thomas Bowden and Lavada Mayall Morrow, had three brothers (deceased) and five sisters: Ira, Floyd, Jim, Glena, Ruby, Cumi, Ila Faye and Arbra). John's father Tom moved the family to England in 1935 to farm. John Dale joined the Army in 1942 during WWII and served in New Guinea and South Pacific.

John Dale and Margaret Ann Morrow.

He married Margaret Ann Henson in 1948. Margaret Ann has two sisters, Mary Frances Noggle (deceased) and Katherine Norman of Florida. John Dale and Margaret Ann raised two daughters and twin sons. Marie Ann "Sissy" Hackett and Martha Dale Langhammer reside in Perryville, Jimmy Melton Morrow resides in North Little Rock and Thomas Felton Morrow resides on Tucker Mtn., Conway County. John Dale and Margaret Ann (as of this writing) have seven grandchildren and six great-grandchildren.

When their children were young, John Dale would take them for Sunday drives to Birdtown and surrounding communities. When driving Hwy. 9 around Birdtown and John Dale sees the pastures and hay grounds he tells stories about his "Papa" (he always called his father "Papa") surveying his neighbors land into terraces to prevent erosion. Those terraces are still obvious today.

John Dale retired in 1986 having worked for Arkansas Uniform and Linen for 32 years and Margaret Ann, LPN, retired in 1996 from the VA Hospital in Little Rock. After that, John Dale and Margaret Ann moved to Conway County for good to their cabin atop Tucker Mountain. They now live on Hwy. 9N at Cypress Creek. John spends his time on top of Tucker Mountain with his cattle and in the summertime he grows watermelons and works in the hayfields. Margaret Ann takes care of the house and gardens. If anyone wants to stop in for a visit - you could not be more welcome. Oh! Yes! You may even get a Tucker Mountain Watermelon.

MOUROT - Augustus or Gus(s) Mourot (b. June 6, 1883, d. March 31, 1968) and a brother were born in France and traveled to Canada with their parents. No one seems to know his parents names for sure, but maybe they were Joseph and Cecilia Mourot. His mother died at sea. Gus(s) was approximately 6 years old when they arrived. His father migrated down the Mississippi River looking for work and a place to settle. He began working for the railroad in St. Louis and worked down to Little Rock building tracks. Other relatives had already settled in the

Gus and Josie Mourot

Overcup Community. Joseph left little Joe and Gus(s) with them and continued with the railroad company, building tracks to the west. He was last heard from when he was in Fort Smith.

At the age of 35, Gus(s) married Josephine Pearl Bostian Lasater (b. Sept. 4, 1896, d. June 23, 1984), daughter of Charlie Alexander Bostian and Frances Elizabeth (Crowder), and they set up housekeeping in the Overcup Community, later moving to the Sardis Community. Gus(s) and Josie farmed their land in cotton, sweet potatoes, strawberries and watermelons. They also raised cattle.

Josie had been married to Oxley Lasater, who died of influenza. She had two children from that marriage and she and Gus(s) had 10 children They raised the 12 children in a two-story home built of log covered with clapboard on Highway 64 east of Morrilton. Most of the children attended school at the Sardis schoolhouse, which is the present day Sardis Community Building, and later the Morrilton Public Schools.

1) Oldest child, Pauline M. Lasater (b. Nov. 26, 1916, d. Oct. 23, 1996), Josie's child by her first marriage, was married to Robert Bowie. They had two children, a baby girl who died at birth and Jerry Bob who married Marinelle Halbrook.

2) Josie's second child, Beatrice Frances Lasater (b. Oct. 14, 1918) md. Leon Thompson. Their children are Gloria Jeanne Rankin (md. Jim Rankin) and Louis Thompson (md. Debbie Thomas). Gloria and Jim's children are Tammy (md. John Harrelson) and Jim Jr. (md. Joanna Ott). Jim and Joanna are raising her son, Adam. Louis and Debbie have a daughter Jennifer (md. Stephen Adams).

3) Claude Knight (b. Feb. 29, 1921, d. Feb. 21, 1968) md. Marie Meeler. They had five boys: (a) Jimmy married Donna McGee and they had one daughter Jamie who married Danny Kelley and they have son Steele. (b) Wayne married Adena Jones and has four children: Deanie married Greg Ragland and has children, Thomas and Maggie; Robert married Traci

O'Neal and has children: Morgan, Parker and Abigail; Rachel married Dustin Creech; Charlie married Melanie Duvall. (c) Gary married Pat Beck and has three children: Amy married Jon Williams; Rhonda married Heath Thomas and has Jarrett Austin; Matt married Stephanie Boyer and they have Madison. (d) Charles Edward "Eddie" was badly burned in a gas pipeline explosion in Nebraska and died on Dec. 5, 1968. (e) Ricky died April 11, 1985. Knight later married Kathryn Mayall and they had one son Todd.

4) (Twin) Ernest (b. March 27, 1924, d. June 20, 1973) md. Johnnie Ogden and had children: Paula Sue who married Tony Foiles and has children, Tessie and Brandon. Keith has son Collier Geiger.

5) Twin-Ernestine (b. March 27, 1924) md. Joe Taylor and has two sons: Larry married Blair McElroy and has daughter Melissa, who married Kevin Crosby, and a son Jeff. Joe and Ernestine's second son Randy died as an infant.

6) Joe (b. Nov. 17, 1926, d. Jan. 14, 1978) md. Grace Hunter.

7) Vera Josephine (b. Oct. 15, 1929, d. April 4, 1936) died of appendicitis.

8) Philip Charles (b. Feb. 29, 1932, d. Aug. 18, 1933) died of diphtheria.

9) Ralph Augusta (b. Aug. 14, 1934, d. May 9, 1937) died of diphtheria.

10) Bobbie Ann (b. April 18, 1937) md. John Zachary. They had six children: (a) Debra was married to Paul Longinotti and they had Kevin and Anthony, who married Janie and they have a son named Tony. Debra also married Gary Slepicka and had Justin and Aaron. Allen married Tammy Matheny and they had Holly. Sharon married Bobby "Sonny" Hill II and they had Bobby III. James married Heather. Roger married Michelle Carter. Cody, Danielle and Brandi. Mark is not married. Mary Jo married Thomas Watson and their children are Tiffany and Ashley. Tim is not married

11) Danny Augusta (b. Dec. 23, 1939) md. Kathryn Baldus and they had two daughters. Lee is married to Mark Roberson and they have Heather, Emily and Katy. Kathleen is married to David Oliver and they have Daniel Thomas and Rylee Elizabeth. Danny is now married to Nicki Beeson.

12) Ronny David (b. Aug. 22, 1942) md. Sue Freeman and they have four children. Scott was married to Tina Poole and they had two children, Kortney and Korey. Scott is now married to Leanne Folk. Greg was married to Tonya Froggatt and they had Amanda, Gregory and Samantha. Greg also has a child named Christopher. Michelle is married to Wayne Dixon and they have Alyssia Ruel. Sara Jo is married to Louis Carroll Jr. and they have Lacey Danae.

NAGEL – Henry Boniface Nagel (b. May 17, 1875 in Peru, IL) was the son of Joseph Nagel (b. 1840, d. 1906) and Elizabeth Merz (b. 1845, d. 1925). When arriving in Arkansas, the Nagel family lived in the New Dixie Community. Henry Boniface married Mary Ann Isenman on Nov. 25, 1901 at St. Elizabeth Church near Oppelo, AR. Mary Ann Isenman (b. Aug. 12, 1879 in Decorah, IA) was the

Henry and Mary Nagel, 50th wedding anniversary, 1952.

daughter of Johan "John" Isenman (b. 1842, d. 1906) and Anna Marie Willman (b. 1845, d. 1893). Henry and Mary were the parents of five children:

1) John Henry Nagel (b. July 31, 1903 at New Dixie, Perry County, AR, d. July 12, 1954 at Keaner, NE) md. Faye Iona Cobb on Dec. 21, 1940 at the St. Boniface rectory, New Dixie, AR.

2) Carl Albert Nagel (b. April 19, 1907 in Perry, AR, d. Dec. 7, 1997 in Jacksonville, FL) md. Eleanor Coughten May 25, 1940 in Our Lady of Lourds Church, New Orleans, LA.

3) Fred Gebhart Nagel (b. July 21, 1909 in Perry, AR, d. Feb. 25, 1990 in Little Rock, Pulaski County, AR. Fred's second marriage was to Theresa Lillian Pustka Sept. 16, 1948 in St. Joseph Cathedral, San Diego, CA.

4) Marie Ann Nagel (b. Oct. 16, 1912 in Perry, AR, d. March 14, 2000 in Little Rock, Pulaski County, AR).

5) Henrietta Elizabeth Nagel (b. June 27, 1919 in Perry, Perry County, AR, d. May 30, 1999 in Little Rock, AR). All the Nagel children are buried at Sacred Heart Cemetery, Morrilton, AR, except Carl Albert who is buried at Oaklawn Cemetery in Jacksonville, FL.

In the 1920s Henry Boniface Nagel bought the Perry Mercantile store previously owned by T.E. Homes and his two partners, which opened in 1917. Henry Boniface operated the mercantile store until 1938. During this period he was assisted by his son John Henry. The name of the store was known as H.B. Nagel & Son. O.O. Oates bought the Mercantile store in 1938 and it remained open until 1975. (The above information on mercantile store was obtained from Oran Oates.) The following ad was found in 1934 paper: H.B. Nagel & Son Leading Merchants in Hats and Caps-Fancy Dress Goods, Guaranteed BROWN BUILT Shoes, Fresh Groceries at Right Prices Phone 34 Perry, AR.

The Nagel Family moved to Morrilton, Conway County, AR shortly after selling the mercantile store, where Henry Boiniface was agent in charge of Perry and Conway counties for the Farm and Loan Association of the Federal Bank of St. Louis, MO. He was assisted by his daughter, Henrietta, until his retirement 30 years later. Their home was on the corner of Church and St. Joseph Street. Henry Boniface Nagel died Aug. 8, 1956 in Morrilton, AR. Mary Ann Isenman Nagel died April 6, 1966 in Little Rock, Pulaski County, AR. Both are buried at Sacred Heart Cemetery, Morrilton, Conway County, AR. *Submitted by Fran Donaldson.*

NEAL - Vestal Elder Newton Neal, known to friends and relatives as just Vess, Vestal or VN Neal, was born in Conway County, AR near Morrilton on Nov. 1, 1899. His father was John H. Neal. His mother was Mary Hall Black. Bertha Lela Williams also was born in Conway County near Morrilton on April 20, 1901. Her father was Henry Jasper "Buddy" Williams. Her mother was Cynthia Ella Wood.

Vestal and Bertha were married in Conway County on May 17, 1921. Their first son, James Loyd, was born in Conway County on April 12, 1923. In 1924 the Neals moved to Hartshorne, OK where Vestal worked in several coal mines in the vicinity of Hartshorne and Bertha owned and operated a cafe in Hartshorne. Their second son, Ancal, was born at Hartshorne in 1925. Sons Loyd and Ancal attended first grade school at Hartshorne.

The Neal family moved back to Arkansas in 1932 and lived near Lavaca. There they farmed and raised dairy cattle and beef cattle. Sons Loyd and Ancal attended Lavaca School, 1932-34.

In 1935 the Neals moved back to the Lords School Community, where Vestal and Bertha were married in 1921. There they operated a grocery store with living quarters in the back. A few months later, in 1936, the store building and all of its contents, together with their furniture and clothing were lost in a fire.

After the fire destroyed their store and home, the family moved to a 640-acre farm in the Lords School Community known as the Hannaford Farm. There they raised dairy and beef cattle. In addition to farming, Vestal started a cattle trading business and became well known in Conway County and surrounding counties as a livestock trader. Loyd and Ancal attended grade school at Lords School and transferred to Morrilton High School in the ninth grade. The family moved to Morrilton in 1942.

In 1950 the Neals built a building at 106 East Elm Street in Morrilton, and operated a grocery store there. Later Bertha Neal and Billie Neal operated a variety and store at the same location. It was called The Thrift Shop.

Loyd married Myrtle Lee "Sue" Boone in 1941. They had one daughter, Lena Carrol, born in 1942 in Morrilton. Loyd worked at the Morrilton Cotton Mill and managed a string band in his spare time, playing western and country music. Loyd died in 1949 and is buried in the Old Salem Cemetery in the Lords School Community. Lena Carrol attended grade school and high school in Morrilton and Harding College in Searcy. She and Wayne Thomas Jones were married in 1963. They live in Little Rock. Wayne works for Sears and Lena Carrol operates a grocery store.

After graduating from Morrilton High School, Ancal served three years in the US Navy during WWII. He later earned a civil engineering degree from the University of Oklahoma. He and Billie Dean House were married in Little Rock in 1952. Ancal and Billie live in Tulsa, OK, where Ancal is retired from Citgo Petroleum Corporation. They have two sons, Lloyd Alan and Bryan Douglas. Lloyd Alan married Janice Daniel in 1979. They have four children: Adam Scott, Julia Diane, David Alan and Benjamin Daniel. They live near Atlanta, GA. Lloyd is a CPA with the IRS. Bryan Douglas married Darla Jean Thomas in 1983. They live in Okmulgee, OK where Bryan is city attorney.

Bertha Lela Neal died Nov. 28, 1985 in Tulsa, OK. She is buried in the Old Salem Cemetery in the Lords School Community. Vestal Neal died in Morrilton on May 11, 1988. He is buried with Bertha and son Loyd in the Old Salem Cemetery. *Submitted by Ancal Neal.*

NELSON - The rickety-rackety old flatbed truck with homemade sideboards rolled north on Hwy. 95 on the last leg of the last 500-mile trek from Galveston County, TX, to Cleveland, AR - we were home! It was August 1966 and it had taken a year of long week-end and holiday trips to get everything relocated, but we were all there at last: Mama (Johanna Holzworth Nelson), Daddy (Charles Stephen Nelson), my sister Jo Ann, my brothers Steve and Tom, and me, Sherry. There was also Soccer, Cowboy and Pitty, the cows that belonged to us kids, along with our hogs and our dog, Uncle Sam.

Daddy had traveled all over the world in the navy during WWII, but he swore to his dying day that Arkansas was the most beautiful place he'd ever seen, and the place where he wanted to raise his kids. Mama and Daddy had both been raised in and around Galveston, but the area was growing too fast for what Daddy wanted. He found what he wanted in Cleveland - 160 acres with a spring running through it where we could hunt and fish and hike, and a community where everyone knew everyone and was always willing to help each other.

Today, I marvel that my parents would pack us all up and move where they didn't know a soul for 40 miles and didn't have a job waiting. We had left family, friends and security to live a dream. What none of us dreamed was that we would find so much more than we had left behind. It wasn't long before neighbors started showing up, and it wasn't long before those neighbors became our family and friends. Once school started and we met other kids in the community, their aunts and uncles and cousins and granny's and papa's became ours. We became part of the crowd that huddled around the potbelly stove at the garage on frosty mornings to wait for the bus. We became part of the family gatherings after church. We became part of watching chairs being recaned at the post office. Sometimes we climbed the hill and let "Aunt" Carrie's muscadine cookies become part of us. And finally that magical day when we each had our own horse and could ride the dirt roads with the other kids.

The first snow was an absolute wonder, but I

think Mama, the avid photographer, enjoyed it most of all. Daddy cut firewood and used that old truck to haul hay in the summer and pulpwood the rest of the year. We raised and sold cattle and hogs. Daddy and Jo Ann both worked at the cotton mill. Mama made sure we were well fed, well dressed and well mannered, and the rest of us went to school and did chores. Some time later we built two chicken houses and added that to our list of experiences. We grew and picked and canned and butchered and sewed and milked and made do and did without. Through it all we had each other, and we had our new family.

Many years have come and gone, but those childhood memories are as vivid as the days we lived them. We have all grown up and had our own children to make memories for - I hope we've done as good a job as our parents at that. When Daddy died, we buried him under an oak tree in one of the Cleveland cemeteries. Most people have to die to experience heaven, but Daddy felt that way every time he walked out the back door and saw eagles soaring in the sky, every time he walked the woods, every time he sat on the pond bank with a pole in his hand, every time he thought about my mama and his kids and grandkids and great-grandkids. No, my daddy didn't have to die to go to heaven - he just had to move to Cleveland.

NEWKIRK

NEWKIRK - De Forest Newkirk (b. Nov. 29, 1899, d. March 28, 1985) was born in Shelbyville, IL, the son of Rev. G.R. and Elizabeth (Hall) Newkirk. Gladys Newkirk (b. Nov. 1, 1898, d. Aug. 5, 1980) was born in Bellwood, NE, the daughter of Daniel P. and Minnie (Mabey) Birch. They married Dec. 27, 1921 in Bellwood, NE and came to Morrilton in 1929.

Dr. Forest Newkirk

Forest was a longtime civic and business leader in Morrilton and Conway County. He was a graduate of Nebraska Wesleyan University at Lincoln, NE. In his early years, he taught in a one-room school house in Nebraska and worked in a coal mine in Colorado. He was manager of the J.C. Penney Store in Morrilton from its beginning in 1929 until his retirement in 1960. He was a member of the Morrilton School Board (1961-64), president of the Morrilton Chamber of Commerce (1961), a past president of the Conway County Fair Board on which he served for over 45 years, a past president of the Morrilton Rotary Club of which he was a member for 35 years, recipient of the 1975-76 Rotarian of the Year Award, recipient of the Rotary Paul Harris Award, recipient of the Silver Beaver Award for his work for over 50 years with the Boy Scouts, charter member of the Community Service Board of Directors, and served on the Board (1961-64), a former chairman of Conway County Red Cross Chapter, a former member of the Advisory Committee on the Petit Jean Vocational-Technical School, and was instrumental in the development of the Morrilton City Park. He was a 32nd degree Mason and a member of the First United Methodist Church (his father was a Methodist minister). He served on the Board of Trustees and Board of Stewards of the Church.

Gladys was also a valued civic leader in Morrilton. She was a member of the Methodist Church, past president of the Women's Society of Christian Service, a member of the Daughters of the American Revolution, past president of the Literary Coterie, the first chairman of the Red Cross blood bank, held office in the PTA and was president of the PTA Council, taught Sunday School, was a Gray Lady at St. Anthony's Hospital, and for 25 years, was a leader in Girl Scout activities in Conway County. She and other Methodist ladies fed the Rotary Club the noon meal,

in the basement of the Library, making money to buy tables for the Methodist Church dining hall. During the Great Depression, she worked in the soup kitchen run by local businessmen for needy citizens. Her rescue of a youngster, in the 1950s, who had fallen into a water-filled well on Northwest Street, brought letters from all over the United States.

Some of the civic work done by Forest and Gladys was as a "team." At the request of V.L. Boren, Superintendent of Schools in the 1930-40s, they ran a boarding house for single teachers: Miss Rosa Moore, Principal of Central Ward School; Miss Ruth Pruitt, Central Ward; Harold Chastain, Principal at Morrilton High School; Bartus Gray, MHS; Coach McGivens, MHS; Coach Auburn Smith, MHS; and others. They took into their home for two years, Bill Patterson, later Morrilton Junior High School Principal, and Doyle Kirtley, who later moved to Texarkana, so the boys could play football in high school. Many youth activities, church and scouts, were held in the home.

D.F. and Gladys had two children: Ralph Robert Newkirk (b. Jan. 13, 1923; d. Dec. 15, 1944) and Pearl Elizabeth Newkirk (b. June 16, 1926). Ralph Robert Newkirk was educated at the University of Arkansas and was a member of Kappa Sigma Fraternity. He married Bobbye Scarlett, daughter of the Health Doctor, Dr. Will and Vivian Scarlett. Sgt. Ralph Robert Newkirk was a medic in WWII. Ralph was killed in the Battle of the Bulge in France while he was tending the wounded on the field. He was a member of the 347th Infantry, 87th Division, and is buried in the US Cemetery in Lorraine near St. Avold, France. On Petit Jean Mountain, in 1945, the Ralph Newkirk Beach was dedicated by Gov. Ben Laney, with Dr. T.W. Hardison giving the biographical sketch.

Pearl Elizabeth attended the University of Arkansas in Fayetteville where she was a member of Chi Omega Sorority. She also attended the John Robert Powers Modeling School in New York. She taught school in Tillar, AR and at Morrilton High School, was life guard and taught Red Cross swimming at the Morrilton City Pool, was a free lance artist, taught art in Russellville and physical education at Morrilton High School, was a member of "Our Town Singers," President of the Senior Adult Center (2002), a member of the GFWC Adelaide Club, the DAR, the Historical (Depot Museum) Society, the Petit Jean Garden Club, and worked at the Conway County Hospital for 13 years. She married Meredith "Cotton" Jones in 1947. He was born in 1923 and died in 1985. Cotton was the son of M.H. and Nellie (Greenfield) Jones of Helena. He received his master's degree at the University of Arkansas, where he was a varsity football letterman. He was Superintendent of the Schools at Tillar, AR, and was a lieutenant colonel in the National Guard. His group was called to Little Rock Central High School during the integration crisis. He was the first paid manager of the Morrilton Chamber of Commerce and was later employed by Mobley Construction Company. Mr. and Mrs. Newkirk and "Cotton" are buried in the Elmwood Cemetery in Morrilton.

Pearl and "Cotton" had three children: Ralph Newkirk Jones (b. April 6, 1948), Meredith Cole Jones (b. Nov. 17, 1951) and Cynthia Lynn Newkirk Jones (b. July 14, 1962).

Ralph married Cathy Jo Simpson and they had two children: Jennifer Jones (b. Aug. 28, 1974) and Jared Forest Newkirk Jones (b. Nov. 17, 1978). Sgt. Ralph Newkirk Jones fought in the Vietnam War and served in Granada; he received the Bronze Star, Gallantry Cross and the Army Air Medal. 1st Sgt. Jones was stationed at Schofield Bks., Wianie, HI. Ralph Newkirk Jones has made his home on Petit Jean Mountain, updating the cabin with running water and indoor plumbing, adding bedroom, bathroom and a garage in 2005. He has two grandchildren, Sidney Bratton and Gwendolyn Pearl Bratton, by his daughter, Jennifer (Jones) Bratton. They live in Pottsville, AR. His son Jared graduated from the University of the Ozarks in Clarksville and married Kim Lum in 2002. They

reside in Clarksville where both work in the Clarksville Schools.

Meredith "Bimbo" married Cathy Darleen Carroll; they had a son, Meredith Cole Jones II (b. June 3, 1975) who graduated from the University of San Marcos in Texas. Meredith was with the Arkansas State Parks System and was a cartoonist with the local newspaper, the *Headlight*. He moved to Texas where he was employed by Arko Oil Company, then Hunt Oil, in Plano, TX. His wife operated Cathy's Professional Cleaners.

Cynthia "Cindy" went to school at Morrilton High School, Arkansas Tech and Petit Jean Vo-Tech. She majored in Parks and Tourism and was with the Arkansas State Parks System. She also worked at DeGray State Park. She married Warren H. Stobaugh III and had two children, Chase and Rebecca.

The Newkirk-Jones home is at 309 West Church Street, the first brick house built in Morrilton. Built in 1880, it has 10 rooms and five fireplaces, square nails were used. There was no indoor plumbing, no gas and no electricity. Built by Morlock, it was known as the Dr. Bradley house. The Newkirks bought it in 1933 for $2,000 and did extensive remodeling. It was located on the old Highway 64, now Highway 113. Pearl N. Jones lives there now. The Newkirks also had a cabin on Petit Jean Mountain which they willed to Ralph Newkirk Jones where he now lives. The Morrilton home and the mountain "cabin" have always had an "open door" policy and a warm welcome awaits each individual and every group that comes to visit. *Submitted by Pearl (Newkirk) Jones.*

NICHOLS

NICHOLS - Edwin F. Nichols (b. 1802 in New York) probably had a brother Henry Nichols (b. 1800 in New York) and a brother William Nichols (b. 1805 in New York). Edwin married Hester (possibly Hyde) prior to 1827 in New York. Hester was born 1801, in New York. At least two children were born in New York.

Prior to 1835 Edwin moved his family to Illinois. Henry Nichols moved his family to Illinois prior to 1838 and William Nichols moved his family there prior to 1840. All three families appear on the 1840 Fulton County, IL census. William and Edwin are shown living next door to each other and Henry is living nearby. In 1850 Edwin's family lived in the town of Center in Fulton County. Edwin was a farmer. In 1850 Edwin's son, William, was working as a blacksmith. Edwin's daughter and son-in-law, Arlina and George R. Snyder were living near-by. Edwin Nichols died between 1850 and 1860, probably in Fulton County.

The 1860 Fulton County census shows Hester as head of the household. Two sons were still living at home. Living on one side of Hester was her daughter and son-in-law, Arlina and George Snyder, and family. Living on the other side was her daughter and son-in-law, Anna and Elbridge (Eldridge) Bush, and family. Prior to 1870, Hester moved into the house with her daughter and son-in-law, Arlina and George Snyder, and family. Hester is shown on the census to be 69 years old. Living next door to them is the family of Elbridge and Ann Bush. Hester may have died between 1870 and 1880.

Children of Edwin and Hester Nichols were:

1) Arlina M. Nichols (b. May 29, 1828) md. George R. Snyder. Children: Wilmer, Edgar, Charles, Flora (md. John Wesley Burham) and Arthur Snyder.

2) William W. Nichols (b. May 6, 1831).

3) Hannah M. Nichols (b. April 21, 1833, d. before 1840).

4) Anna E. Nichols (b. Aug. 20, 1835, d. Feb. 14, 1916) md. Elbridge G. Bush. Children: Carl, Louis Edwin (md. Anne H. Margaret Adamson), Walles, Frank, Artimus, Edward and Eugene Bush.

5) Daniel E. Nichols (b. May 30, 1838, d. Sept. 25, 1896) md. Mary Sanford. Children: Fannie, Albert, Esther, Rosa, Anna and Florence Nichols.

6) Hiram S. Nichols (b. 1840, d. before 1850).

7) George Franklin Nichols (b. Dec. 22, 1844, d.

April 13, 1902) md. Caroline Louk. Children: Wesley "Sel." Mettie (md. Jack Crowley), William Edgar, Maudie (md. Charles Scoville) and Donnie Franklin Nichols.

Several descendants of the Nichols family moved to Conway County in the early to mid-1900s. A number of descendants remain in the county today.

NICHOLS - Samuel Alexander Nichols (b. June 22, 1859 in Alabama) migrated to Conway County between 1880 and 1885 and settled in the Center Ridge area. Samuel married Mahala Jane Maxey on Feb. 22, 1885 in Conway County. Mahala (b. Feb. 22, 1867 in Coles County, IL) was the daughter of Samuel Madison Maxey and Mary Ann Humphries.

Samuel Maxey had moved his family from Illinois to Conway County between 1880 and 1885. Samuel Maxey was a descendant of Edward Maxey (b. mid-1600s in France or England) and Elizabeth Ann Wyatt. Samuel Nichols was a farmer in the Lick Mountain, Grandview and Center Ridge areas. Samuel, not yet 40 years old, died Jan. 19, 1899 at Center Ridge. Mahala died Aug. 10, 1930 at Center Ridge and is buried in the Pleasant Hill Cemetery near Center Ridge.

Children included Quinnie H. Nichols (b. Jan 30, 1886, d. Jan 27, 1924) md. Caleb Presley on Aug. 30, 1903, Conway County; Taylor Eugene Nichols (b. Feb. 4, 1888); Mary Alice Nichols (b. Nov. 20, 1889, d. May 28, 1961) md. Oliver Prince and Oscar Carroll, son of John J. and Frances Carroll; Elmer Albert Nichols (b. July 14, 1892, d. Dec. 24, 1945) md. Della Mahan on Nov. 22, 1914; Lester Earl Nichols (b. Feb. 3, 1894, d. Sept. 6, 1968) md. Hazel Crowell on Sept. 27, 1931; Willie Raymond Nichols (b. March 5, 1896, d. April 2, 1896); Samuel Pearl Nichols (b. April 13, 1897, d. June 29, 1960) md. May Brown on Nov. 12, 1921.

Taylor Eugene Nichols (b. Feb. 4, 1888 in Conway County) was the son of Samuel Alexander Nichols and Mahala Jane Maxey. Eugene married Annie Belle Carroll on Oct. 13, 1907 in Conway County. Annie (b. March 16, 1891 in Arkansas) was the daughter of John J. and Frances E. Carroll. Eugene was a farmer and lived his whole life in the Center Ridge area of Conway County. Eugene died Feb. 21, 1941 in Conway County and Annie died Sept. 3, 1961 at Morrilton. They are buried in Pleasant Hill Cemetery near Center Ridge. Children were Ausbie, Andrew, Ruby, R. Ray (md. Pauline Montgomery), Elmo (md. Dorothy Montgomery) and Elmira.

Ausbie Haywood Nichols (b. Aug. 26, 1908 at Center Ridge) was the son of Eugene and Annie (Carroll) Nichols. Ausbie married Lunie Elsie Leoah Horton on Aug. 21, 1930 in Conway County. Lunie (b. July 18, 1906, in Pope County, AR) was the eldest child of Will Horton and Effie Harmon. Ausbie and Lunie farmed in Conway County until the mid to late 1940s. At that time they bought property near Little Rock, where they lived for many years. Ausbie was a farmer, an auto mechanic and a fine carpenter. Lunie loved to tend her vegetable garden and always had beautiful flower gardens in both her yard and her garden. In 1973 they bought a house at Morrilton where they remained. Lunie died July 31, 1980 and Ausbie died Nov. 15, 1980. They are buried in Friendship Cemetery near Solgohachia in Conway County. They had no children.

NICHOLSON - The Nicholsons emigrated from Wales and Scotland in the early 1600s. In 1884 John Nicholson and Angeline (Bars) were married. John is the son of Ira and Jane (Maples) Nicholson. Angeline was the daughter of Joe and Leah (Gaye) Bars from North Carolina. Her ancestry is Irish Indian. John was born in Marietta, GA in 1843 and was a native of Georgia. Angeline (b. 1843) was a native of Georgia.

The Nicholson family moved from Georgia to Meridian, MS, then in 1875 to Arkansas. John died en route and is buried in Johnson County, AR. Angeline continued on to Conway and Van Buren County. They

had five children. Joseph, their oldest son, married Semelda Jane Merryman, daughter of Will Merryman of Rochester, IN, in 1890. Joseph had four brothers. John Henry (1885/91, died at age 19); Monroe (1873/27) md. Lorna Newman; Alfred (1876/99) md. Eva Merryman. NOTE: Andrew (1882/1900) married (1st) Mattie Harris (1887/1923), (2nd) Martha Chambers (1892/1970); (3rd) Josephine Cherry (1909/1985).

Joseph Adam (my grandfather) and Smeleda had six children. Joseph was a farmer, carpenter, masonry. Culpepper Cemetery holds many tombstones he made for friends and relatives. Dovie (b. 1892, d. 1978) md. Fred Bowing; Birdia (b. 1894, d. 1989) md. Eugene Story; Joseph died at birth; Clarenda died at age 9; John A. (b. 1896, d. 1982) md. Florance Lord; William (b&d. 1898).

John Allen (my father) married Florance Lord (b. 1898, d. 1985) on Feb. 2, 1919. She was the daughter of James and Parthene (Parnell) Lord, born in the Indian Territory, which is now Locksburg, AR. John served in WWI and took his training at Camp Pike, AR. They lived in England, AR and Oklahoma before buying their home in the Lords School Community near Morrilton in 1939. John was a farmer, carpenter and an ordained minister. He built many homes and businesses in Morrilton.

They had three children:

Clarenda Corrine (b. 1920, d. 1969) md. Robert Swope, six children: Robert Blayne (b. 1942, d. 1995) md. first, Barbara Bird, second Juanita Byrum. Children, Theresa and Michael. Royce died at birth in 1940. Phyllis died at age 6 months in 1941. Carolyn Sue (b. 1945) md. Robert Vasquez of Texas. Children: Deborah (b. 1966) md. Walter Stanley of Virginia. Children: Corrine (b. 1990), Adam (b. 1992), Robbie (b. 1973) md. Karey of New Hampshire. Children: Emily (b. 1990) and Megan (b. 1992). Rocky Lane (b. 1949) md. first, Kathy Fabry and second, Kim Osbourne. He has four children: Bryan (b. 1973) who has Hayden; Katie (b. 1975) md. a Collins, three children: Keala (b. 1995), Kelsea (b. 1993), Conner (b. 1999) and Corrine "Corey" (b. 1988). Judy Estelita (b. 1953) md. Dean Robnett of Oklahoma.

Johnny Jr. (b. 1930, d. 1980) married three times: Joyce Hale, Cleo Marie Issacs, Lavern Flanner. Two children: Benita Irene (b. 1953) md. Howard Clifton. Venita Marie (b&d. 1957).

Janie Bell (b. 1935) married twice: Howard Upchurch (b. 1930, d. 1989). John Reedy (b. 1924, d. 1999), seven children. Cocanaugher, two children: Gregory (b. 1973, d. 1990). Angela (b. 1978), one child Ashlynn Nicole (b. 2002). Sharon Rose (b. 1955) married 1. Daniel Morton 2. Bill Grantham. One child Johnnie Sue married Tim Hale. Alan (b. 1957) married 1. Carlotta Jones, 2. Cindy Reynolds. Two children, Raymond (b. 1980) and stepson Jacob (b. 1991). Howard Jr. died at birth in 1955. Mark Anthony died at birth in 1958. Rhonda Renee (b. 1962) md. Gregory Tanner, one child, Shaun Greggory (b. 1992).

The latter generation lives in Conway, Pope and Perry counties. *Submitted by Janie Nicholson Reedy.*

NIX - William Jennings Nix (b. Jan. 14, 1856, Alabama) was the son of Thomas M. Nix and Elizabeth Gasaway. He died Jan. 3, 1918 Bentley Twp., Conway County, AR. Wm. J. Arrived in Conway County before the 1880 census and on Feb. 18, 1884 he married Martha Elizabeth Moore. Martha (b. Sept. 5, 1863 in Oppelo) was the daughter of James M. Moore and Elizabeth Agnes Taylor, both natives of Tennessee.

The ancestry of Wm. Jennings is not yet proven, but it is believed his father Thomas A. Nix, born in South Carolina, married a second time after the death of his mother and there were two half brothers, John T. and James T. It is believed the parents of Thomas Alexander Nix were Jennings Nix and Lucinda "Letty" Alexander.

The 1860 Blount County, AL census shows Thomas Nix with wife Melley and sons, James T. and John

T., and next door is William W. Gasaway with family and one son shown as William, age 4. On the 1870 census Wm. Gasaway has moved to St. Francis County, AR and William J. is still with him.

The photo for this family was taken about 1902. Sitting is William Jennings and Martha Elizabeth (Moore) Nix with child Grace Missouri. Standing l-r: is Lilburn W., Cecil Mattie, Dora Letty, Josie Myrtle and Ora Lee.

The children of Wm. J. and Martha were (1) Willie Agnes (died at age 4); (2) James Marion (died at birth); (3) Josie Myrtle married Oscar Allen Wear, children: Ora Hazel, J. Darrell, Hugh B., Woodrow W., D. Marie, O. Leon., E. Louise, Ina D. and Charles B.; (4) Ora Lee married John Samuel Davis and their children were Garland, Ora B. and James Marion; (5) Lilburn W. died at age 17; (6) Dora Letty married Henry Berger and their child was William J.; (7) Cecil Mattie married Charles R. Carroll, they had no children; (8) Mary Velma died at age 1; (9) Grace Missouri married Marion Francis and their children were Mildred E., Betty Lou, Marian, Paul J., Joyce June, Bobby Joe and Barbara Ann.

Wm. J. had an 80-acre homestead in Conway County Sec. 12, Twp. 5N, Rng 17 W. When the Nix home was torn down in the 1990s, the original log cabin was found under the clapboard cover. *Submitted by Mrs. JoAnn (Wear) Jenkins.*

NOLAND - Nolar, Sydney, Josephine and Willie Noland were the daughters of William Franklin Noland and Sarah Matilda Beatty. William (b. 1860) was the son of Thomas and Mealy Noland. Sarah was born in 1862.

William Franklin Noland and Sarah Matilda Beatty, circa 1890.

William Noland's father, Thomas Johnson "T.J." Noland, was born Dec. 10, 1826 in Tennessee. His mother, Parmelia "Mealy" Margaret Riddling, was born in Georgia in 1827. They came to Arkansas from Mississippi in 1858 and settled in Lone Grove.

William and Sarah were married on Oct. 12, 1879 in Conway County, AR. In the 1880 census, William Noland was listed as 20 years old and Sarah as 18. In October 1880, their first child, Ivy Nolar Noland was born. Their second daughter, Sidney Noland, was born Dec. 24, 1883.

William's father, T.J. Noland, died in 1887 at the age of 60 and was buried at Lone Grove. Mealy was 59 and William was 27. T.J. and Mealy's oldest son, Alfred, was about 40 years old. T.J.'s will indicates that there had been a rift between him and his three oldest children. This may have split the family. Mealy apparently went to live with Alfred.

William and Sarah's third daughter, Mayola Josephine Noland, was born on July 22, 1890.

William died about January 1894 at the age of 34. He left Sarah, a 32-year-old widow, pregnant with their fourth child and with three daughters, ages 4, 11 and 13. Their fourth daughter, William Franklin Noland, was born April 5, 1894. Sarah named little Willie in honor of her late beloved husband. It is possible that Sarah and her four daughters may have been in dire circumstances. Sarah may have been estranged from her husband's older, more prosperous relatives because of the rift over the will.

Nolar married Linus Clarence Roe three years later on April 3, 1897, at the age of 16-1/2. So Linus took a new wife, her three sisters and their mother. That must have been a big load for a young husband of 23.

However, that same year Sidney, almost 14, married James W. Brewer, son of Wesley Brewer and Matilda, on Sept. 7, 1897. This must have provided some relief for Nolar, Linus and the rest of the family.

In March 1898, the first grandchild of William and Sarah Noland, Georgia O. Roe, was born to Nolar and Linus Roe. Sarah died between 1897 and 1900, so it is possible that she did not see this grandchild. She was in her late 30s when she died.

In 1900, Mealy Noland, age 68, the grandmother of the Noland sisters, was a widow living with her son Alfred in McLaren Township. Nolar, age 19, the oldest Noland sister, was married to Linus Roe and they had a daughter Georgia who was 2. Nolar's sisters, Josephine and Willie, were living with them. Sidney, the second Noland daughter, was also married. Josephine and Willie were 9 and 6.

Another grandchild of William and Sarah, Fred Roe, was born to Nolar and Linus after the 1900 Census.

Sidney's first child, daughter Bessie Dean Brewer, was born Jan. 26, 1903. Sidney was 19 years old. She had been married for five years. About that time Nolar and Linus produced another granddaughter of William and Sarah Noland, Nona Roe.

Grandma Mealy Noland died and was buried at Lone Grove in 1904.

Around 1905, Nolar and Linus had a son named Clyde who was the father of Rusty Roe. The Roe household consisted of Linus, 31; Nolar, 25; daughter Georgia, 7; son, Fred, 4; son, Clyde, baby; and Nolar's sisters: Jo, 14 and Willie, 11. Jo and Willie had to do the boys work on the farm and that may be one reason Jo got married at such a young age. As Georgia got older, she and Willie took up the farm chores. Willie would often tell her girls how she worked on the farm, even splitting rails for fences.

Sidney's second child, daughter Wilma James Brewer, was born Dec. 27, 1907. This was also the year that Sidney's younger sister, Mayola Josephine Noland, married James Arthur Skipper.

More grandchildren of William and Sarah Noland were born to the Noland sisters: Thelma Skipper, Noland Roe, Albert Edward Brewer, and W. Irving Skipper.

William Franklin "Willie" Noland, age 18, married David Lindsey Krisell on July 3, 1912. This was about the year Sidney's first husband, James Brewer, died. Sidney was about 29 years old with three young children when she was widowed.

By early 1914, Sidney had married John Isaac Kissire, son of Thomas Kissire and Martha Bowling. More children came along: John Paul Kissire, David Wilbourn Krisell, William Jefferson Kissire, Florence Matilda Krisell, Pauline Skipper, Margarette Lavern Krisell and James A. Skipper Jr.

John Isaac Kissire, Sidney's second husband, died March 26, 1922. Sidney had been widowed twice by the time she was 39.

Willie's fourth child, Sybil Maxine Krisell, was born Nov. 8, 1923. She was grandchild number 18. Willie's fifth child, Edith Eileen, was born Aug. 6, 1926. Willie's sixth child, William Walton Krisell, was

born Aug. 4, 1929. He was the 20th Noland grandchild.

Joe Noland Skipper, son of Jim and Jo, was born in 1931. He was grandchild 21.

Willie's seventh child, Betty Jo Krisell, was born April 19, 1932. The year this twenty-second grandchild of William Franklin Noland and Sarah Matilda Beaty was born, Nolar Noland Roe was 52, Sidney Noland Kissire was a widow at age 49, Josephine Noland Skipper was 42, and Willie Noland Krisell was 38.

Mayola Josephine Noland Skipper died March 29, 1939, at the age of 48.

Ivy Nolar Noland Roe died Dec. 27, 1941, at the age of 61.

Sidney Noland Brewer Kissire died June 14, 1964, at the age of 80.

William Franklin "Willie" Noland Krisell died Aug. 22, 1979, at the age of 85. *Submitted by J.M. Skipper.*

NORWOOD - George Claud Norwood (b. Nov. 4, 1890 in Center Ridge, Conway County, AR) was the son of Daniel B. and Kindness (Tiner) Norwood. He married Hazel Ophelia McInturff on Aug. 29, 1921 in Plumerville, Conway County, AR. Hazel, daughter of Neal and Cora (Oliver) McInturff, was born Feb. 11, 1902 in Adona, Perry County, AR.

Claud and Hazel are the parents of eight children: George Cornelius "Neal," Gladys Amelia, Martha Louise, Mary, Donald Wayne, Wendell Lane, Edwin Harrison and Elmer Baxter.

Claud and Hazel Norwood

George Cornelius "Neal" Norwood (b. Oct. 24, 1922 in Springfield, Conway County, AR, d. Nov. 22, 1991 in Poplar Bluff, Butler County, MO) is buried in the Chapel of Memories Mausoleum in Poplar Bluff. Neal married Elizabeth Beatrice "Bea" Duncan on Nov. 14, 1942 in Knobel, Clay County, AR. Bea is the daughter of George and Stella (Hollaman) Duncan. Neal and Bea are the parents of one daughter, Brenda Louise Norwood Morgan.

Gladys Amelia Norwood married Edgar Joseph Worsham Jr. on Feb. 21, 1946 in Longview, Gregg County, TX. He is the son of Edgar Joseph and Sally (Dooley) Worsham Sr. Gladys and Edgar are the parents of two children, Joseph Edgar Worsham and Gloria Ann Worsham Bailey.

Martha Louise Norwood married Herman Eugene Garton on Aug. 25, 1946 in Reno, Washoe County, NV. Herman, son of Herman and Vada (Bailey) Garton, was born on Oct. 20, 1921 in Revels, Woodruff County, AR. He died Oct. 15, 1994 in LeGrand, Merced County, CA. Martha and Herman are the parents of four children: Virginia Ruth Garton Harrison, George Eugene Garton, Barbara Louise Garton Beltz and Nancy Ann Garton.

Mary Norwood, a stillbirth and twin to Martha, was born and died in Springfield, Conway County, AR.

Donald Wayne Norwood married Mabel Irene Roberts on May 21, 1953 in McDougal, Clay County, AR. Mabel is the daughter of Silas Benjamin and Lela Mae (Garis) Roberts. Wayne and Mabel are the parents of seven children, Kirby Wayne, Kenneth Eugene, Kippy Dale, Karl Alan, Kelly O'Neal, Rachel Kathleen and Kevin Ray. Wayne and Mabel divorced and he currently resides in Poplar Bluff.

Wendell Lane Norwood married Prilla Dean Fisher on June 19, 1956 in Ann Arbor, Washtenaw County, MI. Prilla is the daughter of Lester and Alsie (Powers) Fisher. Wendell and Prilla are the parents of one son, Stuart Lane Norwood.

Edwin Harrison Norwood married Frankie Lavon

Keelin on Dec. 3, 1961 in Datto, Clay County, AR. Frankie is the daughter of Frank and Freda (Black) Keelin. Edwin and Frankie are the parents of three daughters: Julia Ann Norwood Brand, Mary Ellen Norwood O'Brien and Cecilia Ilene "Ceci" Norwood. Edwin and Frankie are divorced and he currently resides in Corning, Clay County, AR.

Elmer Baxter Norwood (b. Aug. 29, 1941 in Fitzhugh, Woodruff County, AR, d. Aug. 22, 1975 in Poplar Bluff) is buried in the Memorial Gardens Cemetery in Poplar Bluff. He married Kathleen Linda Browning on June 9, 1962 in Poplar Bluff. Linda is the daughter of Doc and Maude (Graham) Browning. Elmer and Linda are the parents of two sons, Phillip Browning Norwood and David Lance Norwood.

George Claud Norwood died on March 25, 1961 in Poplar Bluff. Hazel Ophelia died on Oct. 23, 2004 at the age of 102 in Poplar Bluff. They are buried in the Cochran Cemetery in Poplar Bluff. *Submitted by Donald Wayne Norwood.*

NORWOOD - Donald Wayne Norwood, son of George Claud and Hazel Ophelia (McInturff) Norwood, was born in Springfield, Conway County, AR. He married Mabel Irene Roberts on May 21, 1953 in McDougal, Clay County, AR. Mabel, daughter of Silas Benjamin and Lela Mae (Garis) Roberts, was born in Pollard, Clay County, AR.

Donald Wayne and Mabel are the parents of seven children: Kirby Wayne Norwood, Kenneth Eugene Norwood, Kippy Dale Norwood, Karl Alan Norwood, Kelly O'Neal Norwood, Rachel Kathleen Norwood and Kevin Ray Norwood.

Donald Wayne Norwood

Kirby Wayne was born in Ft. Hood, TX. He married Ann Dilliard on June 26, 1988 in Little Rock, Pulaski County, AR. Ann is the daughter of Edward and Lois (Wilson) Dilliard. Kirby and Ann have one daughter, Katherine Anne Norwood, and they currently reside in Little Rock, AR.

Kenneth Eugene was born in Jonesboro, Craighead County, AR. He married Zoe Ann Melick on Feb. 14, 1976 in Tacoma, Pierce County, WA. Zoe is the daughter of Richard "Dick" and Sarah (Taylor) Melick. Ken and Zoe have two sons, Adam Wayne Norwood and Benjamin James Norwood. Ken and Zoe currently reside in Peach Orchard, WA.

Kippy Dale was born in Corning, Clay County, AR. He married Rosemary Chism on March 4, 1983 in Morrilton, Conway County, AR. Rosemary is the daughter of Kenneth Edward and Mary Joyce (Freeman) Chism. Kip and Rosemary have three children: Nicholas O'Neal Norwood, Mary Whitney Norwood and Nathan Edward Norwood. They all currently reside in Morrilton.

Karl Alan Norwood was born in Corning, Clay County, AR. He is unmarried and currently resides in Jackson, TN where he is involved in the construction and remodeling business.

Kelly O'Neal was born in Corning, Clay County, AR. He married Brigitte Theresa Blevins on June 23, 1978 at Soap Lake, Grant County, WA. Brigitte is the daughter of Travis Blevins and Maxine Ellis Blevins. Kelly and Brigitte are the parents of two daughters, Amanda Beth Norwood and Jennifer Ashley Norwood. Kelly and family currently reside in Spokane, WA.

Rachel Kathleen was born in Morrilton, Conway County, AR. She is unmarried and currently lives in Greenville, SC where she is involved in several business endeavors.

Kevin Ray was born in Morrilton, Conway County, AR. He married Angela Anna Corkill on Aug. 18, 1996 in Ocho Rios, Jamaica. She is the daughter of Paul and Sarah (Maldonado) Corkill. Kevin and Angela have one child, Ashley Nicole Norwood. Kevin and family currently reside in Austin, TX.

Mabel and Wayne divorced in 1973. Mabel lives in Morrilton beside her son Kip and family. She is retired and enjoys traveling, family research, reading and growing a vegetable and herb garden. Donald Wayne lives in Poplar Bluff, Butler County, MO. Until recently after suffering a light mini stroke, he enjoyed participating in Senior Olympics, working in the garden, bowling and going to watch high school football games. *Submitted by Kirby Norwood.*

NORWOOD - George Cornelius "Neal" Norwood (b. Oct. 24, 1922 in Springfield, Conway County, AR) was named for his father and his grandfather, Cornelius "Neal" McInturff. He was the oldest son of George Claud and Hazel Ophelia McInturff Norwood. He died Nov. 22, 1991 in Poplar Bluff, MO and is buried in the Chapel of Memories Mausoleum in Poplar Bluff, Butler County, MO.

George Cornelius Norwood and wife Beatrice Duncan married Nov. 24, 1942.

He married Elizabeth Beatrice Duncan Nov. 24, 1942 in Knobel, Clay County, AR, daughter of George and Stella Hollaman. Beatrice was born in Hickory Ridge, Cross County, AR. Their daughter, Brenda Louise Norwood, was born in Knobel, Clay County, AR. She married Lynn Hershell Morgan Aug. 6, 1961 in Poplar Bluff, Butler County, MO. He was born in Ironton, Reynolds County, MO. Their children are Bryan Lynn and Misty Michelle, both born in Poplar Bluff, Butler County, MO. Misty married Rodney Keith Ray, Oct. 9, 1989 in Poplar Bluff, MO. Rodney was born in St. Louis, MO. Their son, Logan Hunter Ray, was born in Poplar Bluff, MO. *Submitted by Brenda Louise Morgan.*

NORWOOD – Gladys Amelia Norwood was born in Springfield, Conway County, AR. Her parents were Claud and Hazel O. McInturff Norwood. She married Edgar J. Worsham Jr., son of Edgar J. and Sally Dooley Worsham. He was born in Dallas, Dallas County, TX. They are the parents of Joseph Edgar and Gloria Ann Worsham.

Joseph "Joe" was born in Longview, Gregg County, TX. He married Christina Jeanne Doney June 13, 1970 in Electric City, Lincoln County, WA.

Gladys Norwood and Ed Worsham, married Feb. 21, 1946.

She was born in Great Falls, Cascade County, MT. They are the parents of Scott Edgar, Jason John and Jolee Christina Worsham. Scott, born in Omak, Okanogan County, WA, married Devin Michelle Bost April 4, 1998 in Brewster, Douglas County, WA. Their daughter, Josie Olivia, was born in Omak, Okanogan County WA.

Jason was born in The Dalles, Wasco County, OR, married Amy Angelina Jaime in Orlando, Orange County, FL. She was born in Yakima, Yakima County, WA.

Jolee was born in Omak, Okanogan County, WA. She teaches fourth grade in Houston, TX. Scott teaches H.S. math classes in Creswell, OR. Jason teaches business education classes in Orlando, FL. Their father, Joseph "Joe," is high school principal in Neah Bay, WA, and their mother, Jeanne, teaches kindergarten in Neah Bay, WA. Their grandmother, Hazel Ophelia McInturff Norwood, taught school in a one-room school, all grades, during the years 1919 through 1921 in the Jacklett School near Morrilton, AR.

Gloria was born in Richland, Benton County, WA and married John Daniel Bailey June 20, 1970 in The Dalles, OR, son of Russel and Christine Fisher Bailey. Daniel "Dan" was born in Kelso, Cowlitz County, WA. Their children are Patrick Andrew, Jeffery Todd and John Joseph Bailey. Pat was born in Wenatchee, Chelan County, WA. Jeff was born in Longview, Cowlitz County, WA. John was born in Longview, Cowlitz County, WA. Gloria teaches fourth grade in the Longview, WA school district. *Submitted by Gloria Ann Worsham Bailey.*

NORWOOD - Kippy Dale "Kip" Norwood was born in Corning, Clay County, AR, the son of Donald Wayne Norwood and Mabel Irene (Roberts) Norwood. Kip has one sister, Rachel Kathleen Norwood and five brothers: Kirby Wayne Norwood, Kenneth Eugene "Ken" Norwood, Karl Alan Norwood, Kelly O'Neal Norwood and Kevin Ray Norwood.

Kip Norwood family.

Kip married Rosemary Chism on March 4, 1983 at Lewisburg Missionary Baptist Church in Morrilton, Conway County, AR. Rosemary, daughter of Kenneth Edward Chism Sr. and Mary Joyce (Freeman) Chism, was born in Morrilton, Conway County, AR. Rosemary has one sister, Tammie Joyce Chism Shipp, and two brothers, Kenneth Edward "Kenny" Chism Jr. and William Alan Chism.

Kip and Rosemary are the parents of three children: Nicholas O'Neal "Nick" Norwood, Mary Whitney Norwood and Nathan Edward Norwood. All three children were born in Morrilton, Conway County, AR. Nick graduated from Morrilton High School in May 2002 and attends University of Arkansas Community College at Morrilton. Whitney graduated from Morrilton High School in May 2004 and attends the University of Central Arkansas in Conway. Nathan currently attends high school in Morrilton.

Kip graduated from the University of Central Arkansas in May 1981 with a bachelor's degree in business administration. He works at Arkansas Kraft-Green Bay Packaging in Morrilton, where he just completed his 25th year. Rosemary graduated from Wonderview High School in May 1981. She is a stay-at-home mom and in her spare time enjoys researching the family history and quilting. They enjoy camping, fishing, hunting and spending time at the cabin they built. Kip and Rosemary are charter members of the Conway County Genealogical Association, which formed in 1997. The family currently makes their home in Morrilton. *Submitted by Kip Norwood.*

NORWOOD – Martha Louise Norwood was born in Springfield, Conway County, AR. Her parents were

Claud and Hazel McInturff Norwood. She married Herman Eugene Garton Jr. Aug. 25, 1946 in Reno, Washoe County, NV. He was the son of Herman E. and Vada Bailey Garton of Augusta, AR. Herman was born Oct. 20, 1921 in Revels, Woodruff County, AR and died Oct. 15, 1994 in Le Grand, CA. Their children are Virginia Ruth, Barbara Louise, George Eugene and Nancy Ann.

Martha L. Norwood, husband Herman Garton and daughter Nancy Garton

Virginia was born in Merced, Merced County, CA. She married Jimmie Lee Harrison May 1, 1973 in Planda, CA. Jim was born in Cottage Grove, Lane County, OR, son of James and Barbara Lee Harrison. Their children are Michelle Lynn and Heather Noel Harrison.

George was born in Merced, Merced County, CA and married Christine Duvall Valasquez June 28, 1981 in Seattle, King County, WA, daughter of Carroll and Ilene Duvall. They divorced in 1989. George married Karren Louise Bradshaw July 12, 1991 in Pasco, Franklin County, WA, daughter of Robert Bradshaw and Mary Haley. Karren was born in Kennewick, Benton County, WA. Their children are Jarrod Robert and Molli Le Ellen Garton, born in Richland, Franklin County, WA.

Barbara Louise Garton was born in Merced, Merced County, CA. She married David Gordon Beltz June 22, 1974 in Merced, Merced County, CA, son of Francis and Ruby Beltz. David was born in Merced, Merced County, CA.

Barbara and Dave's children are Matthew David, Rachel Louise and Nathan Joseph. Matthew was born in San Diego, San Diego County, CA. Nathan was born in Merced, Merced County, CA. Rachel was born in San Diego, San Diego County, CA. She married Jovian Miller Aug. 10, 1998 in Mariposa, Mariposa County, CA, son of Bruce Welcher and Yuvonne Miller Dixon. Their son, Jedediah Nathan Miller, was born in Merced, Merced County, CA. They divorced in 2003. Rachel married David Cabezut Jan. 29, 2004 and their son, Nicholas Shawn Cabezut was born in Merced, Merced County, CA.

Barbara and David Beltz are both school teachers in California schools.

Nancy Ann was born in Merced, Merced County, CA. Nancy is unmarried and lives at home with her mother. *Submitted by Barbara Louise Garton Beltz.*

NORWOOD – Wendell Lane Norwood was born in Springfield, Conway County, AR. His parents were Claud and Hazel Norwood. On June 19, 1956 Wendell and Prilla Dean Fisher married in Ann Arbor, Washtenaw County, MI. Prilla, daughter of Lester and Alsie Powers Fisher, was born in Scotts Hill, Henderson County, TN.

Their son Stuart Lane, born in Memphis, Shelby County, TN, married Julian Elaine Hoyt, who was born in Seattle,

Wendell Norwood, wife Prilla and son Stuart Norwood.

King County, WA, a daughter of George Clark and Jacqueline Nadine Carlson Hoyt.

Stuart and Jill are the parents of a son Timothy James Norwood, born in Seattle, King County, WA. *Submitted by Stuart Lane Norwood.*

NOWLIN - Born as Glenna Carroll Nowlin, she was the only child of Glenn Silas Nowlin and Willie Mae Skinner Nowlin. She later officially changed the spelling of her name to Glynna Carole Nowlin. Glynna (b. July 14, 1925 in Morrilton, AR) was delivered by her paternal grandmother, Nellie Dodson Hays Nowlin, who was an herbalist and midwife. The Nowlin family lived in Conway County until the Depression, moving out to California where Glenn found work at his brother's service station. They enjoyed the sojourn in California, especially Glynna, who developed a life-long love of the state even when the family moved back to Arkansas. They settled this time in Little Rock, where they had many family and friends. Glynna attended Little Rock Central High School, later to be called Central High School.

Glynna Carole Nowlin and her husband, Paul Earle Gordon

On Oct. 30, 1942, she married Paul Earle Gordon, who had recently joined the US Navy. They began their marriage in Chicago at the naval training base. Paul was born Nov. 13, 1923 in Almyra, Arkansas County, AR, the son of Alfred M. Gordon and Lutie Brown Gordon. He shipped out after basic training and was away at sea for most of WWII, serving as a medic, while Glynna moved into the house with her parents and sisters, whose husbands also were serving their country. The house was just around the corner from her parent's home. Their first child, Jerry Lynn, was born Oct. 18, 1943.

Upon his return from the service, the family moved to North Little Rock. They were living here when their second child, Paula Carole, was born on May 25, 1948. Her older brother was very protective of his baby sister. They had barely begun to make a normal life, when the Korean conflict called into service again those who had remained in the Naval Reserve. Paul was among that number and was ordered to report for duty. He served for two years and was discharged around 1952.

This little family then moved to Ft. Worth, TX, where they began to realize that little Jerry was having trouble standing and walking. At the time, not any information was forthcoming about his condition. During this time, they had moved to Atlanta, GA. A trip to New York for some therapy for Jerry, doctors made the diagnosis of Muscular Dystrophy, a fact which would change the nature of this family forever.

Glynna worked for many years as a secretary for a large grocery store chain and Paul became a chiropractor; they lived in Little Rock during this time. Jerry lived with his disease until Nov. 24, 1960 when he developed pneumonia and passed away at the age of 17. He is buried at Pinecrest Cemetery in Saline County, AR. Paula married Danny Stobaugh, a native of Morrilton and they had two sons, David Allan and Scot Sherman.

Glynna and Paul were divorced in 1966. Paul never remarried and he died April 16, 1994. Glynna married Chet Hodges and they were divorced. She then married Clyde L. Price of Little Rock in 1968 and they moved to California, where Glynna again enjoyed living. Glynna became a widow in 1994 and moved back to Arkansas. She died Jan. 20, 2002 in Hot Springs, AR. She is buried in the Houston National Cemetery, in Houston, TX next to her third husband.

OLIVER - Annie Corine "Cora" Oliver, daughter of William Thomas and Mary Catherine (Bradford) Oliver, was born Dec. 17, 1876 in Eupora, Webster County, MS. She married Cornelius "Neal" McInturff on Feb. 10, 1901 in Conway County, AR. Neal, son of Thomas William and Dicey Elizabeth (Eoff) McInturff, was born in May 1875 in Arkansas.

Neal and Cora (Oliver) McInturff

Cornelius McInturff's brothers and sisters were John Wesley McInturff, James L. McInturff and Deborah Jane McInturff Youngblood. Cora's brothers and sisters were George William Oliver, John James Oliver, Thomas Lorenza Oliver, Lula Charity Oliver, Mattie Eudora Oliver and Samuel Clarence Oliver.

The McInturffs moved to Perry County, AR and settled in the small town of Adona. It was there that their children were born: Hazel Ophelia McInturff (b. Feb. 11, 1902) and William Wesley McInturff (b. Oct. 8, 1903).

Neal got a job with a lumberyard/sawmill in the town of Perry to support the family. Neal purchased a set of books from the Little Rock School of Medicine and was studying to be a doctor. He traveled by train one day a week and took tests at the school. The train would let him off at the sawmill and he would walk home. It was at this sawmill that he drank from a bucket of stagnant water and contracted the dreaded swamp fever. He died on Oct. 20, 1904 and is buried in the McGhee Cemetery in Perry County. Cora took their two small children and went to live with her mother, Mary C. Oliver, in Bald Knob Community in Conway County. Cora became ill with the fever as well and died on Nov. 8, 1904. She is buried in the Oak Grove Cemetery north of Morrilton, Conway County, AR.

Grandma Oliver, with the help of two maiden daughters and two bachelor sons, took the two small children in and raised them. At the age of 17, Hazel took her teacher's exam and took her first job at the Jacklett School, three miles from her home. Later that year, she graduated from Plumerville High School. She also attended Hendrix College in Conway, Faulkner County, AR.

Hazel married George Claud Norwood on Aug. 29, 1921 in Plumerville, Conway County, AR. Claud, son of Daniel B. and Kindness (Tiner) Norwood, was born Nov. 4, 1890 in Center Ridge, Conway County, AR.

Hazel and Claud are the parents of eight children: George Cornelius "Neal" Norwood, Gladys Amelia Norwood Worsham, Martha Louise Norwood Garton, Mary Norwood, Donald Wayne Norwood, Wendell Lane Norwood, Edwin Harrison Norwood and Elmer Baxter Norwood.

George Claud Norwood passed away on March 25, 1961 in Poplar Bluff, Butler County, MO. Hazel lived the reminder of her life in Poplar Bluff and passed away at the age of 102 on Oct. 23, 2004. They are buried in the Cochran Cemetery in Poplar Bluff.

William Wesley McInturff married Mary Magdalene "Maggie" Huie on Aug. 9, 1925 in Plumerville, Conway County, AR. Maggie, daughter of George and Mary Lou (Izsa) Huie, was born on Sept. 2, 1904 in Arkansas. William and Maggie are the parents of three children: Annie Corine McInturff Faulkner, William Thomas McInturff and Mary Christine McInturff.

William Wesley McInturff passed away on May 9, 1977 in Orosi, Tulare County, CA. He is buried in the Smith Mountain Cemetery in Orosi. Maggie Huie McInturff currently resides in California. *Submitted by Gladys Norwood Worsham.*

OLIVER - Mary Catherine "Katie" Bradford, daughter of Rev. George S. and Mary Jane (Kent) Bradford was born Sept. 25, 1840 in Tennessee and died Feb. 9, 1920 in Morrilton, Conway County, AR. Katie married William Thomas Oliver in March 1861 in Calhoun County, MS. William (b. May 31, 1838 in Georgia, d. Sept. 3, 1903 in Morrilton, Conway County, AR) was the son of Samuel and Charity (Cain) Oliver. Katie and William are buried in the Oak Grove Cemetery, Morrilton, Conway County, AR.

W.T. and Katie Oliver family

Katie and William's children are George William Oliver, John James Oliver, Thomas Lorenzo Oliver, Lula Charity Oliver, Mattie Eudora Oliver, Annie Corinne Oliver and Samuel Clarence Oliver.

1) George William (b. Oct. 3, 1862 in Mississippi, d. July 25, 1898 in Conway County, AR) md. Frances Lou Dora Marmon (b. May 22, 1866, d. July 1957). Their children are Edgar Layefette Oliver and Maybell Oliver.

2) John James Oliver (b. Nov. 11, 1865 in Jackson, MS, d. Sept. 11, 1934 in Fort Smith, Sebastain County, AR) married first to Charlotte Annie Scoggins on Jan. 9, 1892 in Conway County, AR. Charlotte (b. 1876, d. Nov. 27, 1892) was the daughter of Squire Henry and Mary Francis (Cook) Scoggins. She is buried in Elmwood Cemetery, Morrilton, Conway County, AR. They had one daughter, Annie Charlotte Oliver Williams. After Charlotte's death, John married Elizabeth Minnie Scoggins on May 8, 1897 in Conway County, AR. John James and Elizabeth Minnie are buried in Forest Park Cemetery in Fort Smith. Elizabeth, daughter of Squire Henry and Mary Francis (Cook) Scoggins, was born Jan. 8, 1881 in Conway County, AR and died March 21, 1937 in Fort Smith, Sebastain County, AR. Their children are Pearl Loraine Oliver Wilson Carruthers, Mary Opal Oliver Vernon and Eleanor Ruth Oliver Ashmore Moody Little.

3) Thomas Lorenzo Oliver (b. July 12, 1868 in Mississippi, d. Dec. 18, 1928 in Bald Knob, Conway County, AR) never married and is buried in the Oak Grove Cemetery, Morrilton, Conway County, AR.

4) Lula Charity Oliver (b. Feb. 26, 1871 in Mississippi, d. Sept. 4, 1961 in Morrilton, Conway County, AR) never married and is buried in the Oak Grove Cemetery.

5) Mattie Eudora Oliver (b. Oct. 30, 1873 in Mississippi, d. Oct. 5, 1940 in Bald Knob, Conway County, AR) never married and is buried in the Oak Grove Cemetery.

6) Annie Corinne "Cora" Oliver (b. Dec. 17, 1876 in Eupora, Webster County, MS, d. Nov. 8, 1904 in Bald Knob, Conway County, AR) is buried in Oak Grove Cemetery. Cora married Cornelius "Neal" McInturff on Feb. 10, 1901 in Conway County, AR. Neal (b. May 1875 in Arkansas, d. Oct. 20, 1904 in Perry, Perry County, AR) was the son of Thomas William and Dicey Elizabeth (Eoff) McInturff. He is buried in the McGhee Cemetery, Adona, Perry County, AR. Their children are Hazel Ophelia McInturff Norwood and William Wesley McInturff.

7) Samuel Clarence Oliver (b. Oct. 20, 1880 in Solgohachia, Conway County, AR, d. Feb. 27, 1939 in Little Rock, Pulaski County, AR) never married and is buried in Oak Grove Cemetery. *Submitted by Martha Louise Norwood Garton.*

ORR - John Riley Orr (b. Aug. 21, 1889 in Stone County, AR) was the son of James T. Orr (b. March 2, 1867) and Mary Frances Seats Orr (b. 1865), a Cherokee Indian Princess and daughter of George Washington Seats). He married Ivor R. Bell Mitchell on Jan. 9, 1910 and settled in the Grandview Community. They had three children: Ruby Lee Orr (b. Feb. 17, 1911), Ernest Orr (b. Nov. 3, 1912) and Otis Orr (b. Feb. 14, 1918).

John and Ivor Orr

1) Ruby Lee Orr married James Roscoe Chism on Aug. 23, 1929 and settled in Grandview at the old Orr homestead. They had three children: Nellie Chism (b. April 23, 1935), Betty Marie Chism (b. Jan. 17, 1942) and James Riley Chism (b. Oct. 5 1949). All three children were born in Conway County, AR.

A) Nellie Chism married Clell Laudis Stobaugh on May 6, 1954. They had two children, David Glenn Stobaugh (b. April 30, 1955) who married Ann Addison on April 21, 1979 in Lipan, TX. They had one son Justin David (b. March 9, 1987). Cynthia Louise "Cindy" Stobaugh (b. Oct. 17, 1959) md. Donald Karman O'neal May 25, 1978 in Conway County, AR. They had two children, Felicia Dawn O'neal (b. Jan. 2, 1979). Felicia married Steven Davenport, they had one daughter, Brook Nichole Davenport (b. Dec. 18, 2001). Karmon and Cindy had a son Wesley Shawn (b. Nov. 19, 1980). Wesley married Corrina Moore on March 15, 2005.

B) Betty Marie Chism married Jimmy Harold "Jim" Dixon on April 28, 1961 in Conway County. They had three children: Betty Gail Dixon (b. Oct. 9, 1962) and Leslie Dixon, they had one son Mitchell Keith Dixon (b. Sept. 9, 1985). Divorced, Betty Gail married Donald Eller on Oct. 17, 1987. They are the parents of Luke Ashdon Eller (b. Feb. 10, 1989) and Andrew Randall Eller (b. June 25, 1993). Betty Gail died Sept. 13, 1997 in an auto accident and is buried at Grandview Cemetery in Conway County, AR. Deronda Lee Dixon (b. April 23, 1966) md. Tony Freeman and had one daughter Ashley Nichole Freeman (b&d. Aug. 2, 1985, buried in Grandview Cemetery Conway County). Divorced, Deronda married Fred Givens Jr. Oct. 17, 1987. They are the parents of two daughters, Heather Lee Givens (b. March 3, 1989) and Jenna Marie Givens (b. Aug. 19, 1994). Randall Harold Dixon (b. March 7, 1970) md. Lynice Lee Anne Sharp on May 5, 1989. They are the parents of Krysten Lynice Dixon (b. Nov. 15, 1989) and Stefanie Janelle Dixon (b. July 1, 1991).

C) James Riley "Jimmy" (b. Oct. 5, 1949) md. Mary Evelyn Guinn on Oct. 4, 1968. Jimmy and Evelyn are the parents of two children, Dena Lynn Chism (b. June 23, 1972) and James Gregory "Greg" (b. July 26, 1978). Dena married Boyce Smith Sept. 4, 1999. They are the parents of Morgan Nicole Smith (b. July 4, 2001) and Carson Lane Smith (b. Dec. 27, 2004).

2) Ernest Orr married Ruth Everett on Feb. 24, 1934. They had two children. James Everett Orr (b. Oct. 22, 1943) md. Judith Ann Sole (b. March 31, 1945). James and Judith had two children, Lori Orr (b. Oct. 22, 1967) and Angie Orr (b. March 6, 1974). Angie married Brian Eaton and they had two children, Mason Eaton (b. Dec. 4, 2001) and Kennedy Eaton (b. Dec. 20, 2004). Ernestine Orr (b. Dec. 24, 1936) md. Charles Howard Elms on Oct. 21, 1955. They had three children: Debra Ruth Elms (b. Sept. 29, 1958), Tina Marie Elms (b. Aug. 30, 1957) and Charles Howard Elms Jr. (b. July 20, 1956).

Debra Elms married Mitchell Dean Hanley on Sept. 9, 1977. They had one son, Joshua M. Hanley (b. March 5, 1978). Joshua married Denise Walthall on July 15, 2000. They had one son Cade Daniel Hanley (b. July 15, 2003). Debra divorced Mitchell Hanley and married Daniel Goettel. After Daniel's death, Debra married Juan Gomez July 3, 2004.

Tina Marie Baedke (b. Aug. 30, 1957) had two children, Micheal Potter (b. Aug. 9, 1977) and Melissa Potter (b. Jan. 4, 1980). Tina married Roger Baedke on Nov. 11, 2000. Roger had two children, Anthony Baedke (b. March 14, 1977) and Amy Baedke (b. Oct. 20, 1979). Anthony Baedke married Heather Bruns and they had six children: Slaone Morrow (b. Jan. 8, 1994); Autumn Baedke (b. Oct. 14, 1997); Leif Bruns (b. Oct. 17, 2001); Ava Baedke (b. April 17, 2002); Forrest Bruns (b. April 7, 2002) and Kade Baedke (b. Dec. 1, 2004). Melissa married Kenneth Wayne Chennell Jr. Sept. 1, 2000. They had two children, Allie Marrie Channell (b. April 22, 2001) and Dawson Lee Channell (b. March 28, 2002).

Charles Elms Jr. (b. July 20, 1956) md. Joan Brislen in 1984 and had one child, James John Elms (b. Feb. 20, 1985). Charles Elms Jr. divorced and married Mary Hylen on May 19, 1994. Mary had two daughters, Kristina (b. Aug. 11, 1974) and Cindy (b. Oct. 5, 1972). Kristina married Mike Pauaous in 1994. They had two children, Kayla (b. Sept. 14, 1994) and Cheyenne (b. Sept. 14, 1994). She was widowed in 1994 and remarried Larry Larimore. They had two children, Serenity Hope (b. March 4, 1998) and Samual Robert (b. May 30, 1999). Cindy married Brian Mandziara in 1997. They had two children, Ashley (b. July 10, 2000) and Brianne (b. Oct. 17, 2003).

3) Otis Orr (b. Feb. 14, 1918) lived a short life; he died at only three months old on May 13, 1918.

Deaths and places of rest pertaining to this family are listed below:

Otis Orr, buried in the Grandview Cemetery, Arkansas May 13, 1918.

Alitha A. Jane Orr buried in the Grandview Cemetery, Arkansas.

Kerby A.B. Orr buried in the Grandview Cemetery, Arkansas.

John Riley Orr buried in the Grandview Cemetery, Arkansas Feb. 25, 1948.

George W. Orr buried in Helena, AR.

Margaret A. Orr buried in Grandview, TX.

Ada V. Orr buried in Odessa, TX.

Chester L. Orr buried in Tucson, AR.

Artle Orr buried in Luling, TX.

George Seats buried in Grandview Cemetery, Dec. 28, 1923.

Sarah Seats buried in Grandview Cemetery, Arkansas.

James T. Orr burial spot unknown, Arkansas.

Mary Frances Seats Orr buried in Old Odessa Cemetery, Texas, March 9, 1943.

Ivor Mitchell Orr buried in Grandview Cemetery, Arkansas Sept. 18, 1979.

Ruby Orr Chism buried in Grandview Cemetery, Arkansas April 17, 1982.

James Roscoe Chism buried in Grandview Cemetery, Arkansas May 1, 1990.

Ruth Orr buried in Mount Washington Cemetery, Independence, MO, March 17, 1998.

Ernest Orr buried in Mount Washington Cemetery, Independence, MO, March 17, 1998.

Randall Dixon buried in Grandview Cemetery, Arkansas Jan. 10, 1994.

Gail Dixon Eller buried in Grandview Cemetery, Arkansas Sept. 13, 1997.

OWENS - Charles Belt Owens was born in Batesville, AR, Feb. 11, 1919 to Louis Bernard and Mytle Ozias Owens. His family moved to Texarkana, where he was reared and graduated from high school. He dropped out of the University of Arkansas during WWII to enlist in the US Naval Air Corps and served in VRF-1 as a ferry pilot, test pilot and liaison officer. In 1942 he married Jean Winburne, daughter of John Newton and Dica E. Scroggin Winburne. In 1946 after the war, Charlie and Jean moved to Morrilton where she had been born and reared.

Charlie tried farming, selling groceries, and being part owner of an automobile agency before joining Johnston Insurance Agency in 1953. He bought the agency a few years later and went into a partnership with A.J. Meadors. After A.J.'s death, he bought the family's interest and became sole owner of Central Insurance and Real Estate Agency. Charlie was active in civic affairs and was the second president of the Morrilton Lions Club. He was on Morrilton's first planning and zoning commission and was chairman of the Conway County Industrial Board. He also served as president of the Morrilton Chamber of Commerce and the Rotary Club. He was active in the First United Methodist Church and served as chairman of the Board of Trustees, the Finance Committee, and the Building Committee.

His wife Jean and their children, Charles B. and Melinda Jean Carnahan, of Springdale, graduated from the University of Arkansas as did five of their nine grandchildren, the others from UCA, Mississippi State U., Bob Jones U. and Texas A&M. Before going to Washington, DC, as a secretary to the Undersecretary of Labor, in Morrilton she was a member of the Book Review Club, Adelaide Club, Redbud Garden Club and various fund raising committees, and on the board of the River Valley District Human Relations Board. She was an accountant in her husband's office. They both retired in 1985 and are still living in Morrilton.

PACELEY - Benjamin F. Paceley (b. 1821 in Ohio) md. Elzira Parmer (b. 1829 in Ohio) in 1847 in Ohio. Benjamin, Elzira and their 2-year-old son James appear on the 1850 Hamilton County, OH census. Living with the family was Elzira's 16-year-old brother, Andrew J. Parmer. Benjamin was working as an inn keeper at the time. By 1860 Benjamin had turned to farming in Hamilton County. Benjamin's six older children were born in Hamilton County. In 1865 Benjamin moved his family to Indiana. The family lived in Spencer County, IN for a time in the 1870s.

At least seven children were born to Benjamin and Elzira: James Paceley (b. 1848); William James Paceley (b. Feb. 26, 1851, d. 1888) md. Amelia Cline, daughter of Peter Cline and Dorcas Brown; Harriet Ellen Paceley (b. Oct 1, 1857, d. Dec. 27, 1939) md. Melvin Ice; Mary Ann Paceley (b. Dec. 27, 1858) md. Abraham Herron; Lewis F. Paceley (b. Feb. 27, 1861); Horace Edward Paceley (b. 1864) and Sallie E. Paceley (b. Jan 8, 1866) md. Samuel E. Beeler.

Horace Edward Paceley (b. Jan. 20, 1864 in Hamilton County, OH), son of Benjamin and Elzira. Horace married Elizabeth Jane Cline on March 23, 1891. Elizabeth (b. 1864 in Monroe County, OH) was the daughter of Peter Cline and Dorcas Brown. Horace settled his family at Muscatine, IA. Horace was a farmer. He died April 18, 1906 at Muscatine. Buried next to him is his infant son.

Elizabeth and her four daughters appeared on the 1910 city of Muscatine census. The two older daughters were working at a button factory at Muscatine. Stella, age 17, was a driller at the factory and Ida, age 15, was a carder at the factory. Stella married between 1910 and 1918. Ida married in 1919. In 1920, Elizabeth's daughters, Mary and Clara, were working as sorters at a button factory in Muscatine. Daughter Stella, who married a few years prior to 1920, was widowed and living with her mother and sisters in 1920. She was working as a finisher at a button factory. For many years one of the major industries at Muscatine was the manufacture of muscle shell buttons. Since Muscatine was located on the Mississippi River there was a ready supply of shells. There were several button factories in Muscatine at that time. The Pearl Button Company was one of the major button producing factories.

At least five children were born to Horace and Elizabeth:

1) Infant Son Paceley (b. 1891, died as infant).

2) Stella M. Paceley (b. July 18, 1893, d. Dec. 5, 1952) md. John Theo Machu (b. Jan 10, 1891, d. April 20, 1918). no children.

3) Ida Florence Paceley (b. April 4, 1895, d. April 20, 1972) md. John Cleveland Wren. Children: Pearl married Howard Montgomery; Robert married Elizabeth Annie Bush; and Kenneth Wren.

4) Mary E. Paceley (b. Dec. 27, 1898, d. December 1973) never married.

5) Clara H. Paceley (b. 1901, d. before 1972) never married.

A number of Paceley descendants settled in Conway County in the early to mid-1900s. Several descendants still reside in the area.

PALADINO -
Military bio of Andrew "Andy" R. Paladino (b. Sept. 9, 1921), son of Anthony "Tony" and Minnie Paladino of Center Ridge, AR, was the brother of Mary Rossi, Frances DeSalvo, Frank J., Father Christopher, Amelia Whitten, Sister Lucille, Paul, John, Joseph, Henrietta Rowland, Henry, Lawrence and Florence Andreas.

Andrew Paladino

Andy took his basic training with the Army Air Corps at St. Petersburg and Clearwater, FL in July 1942. He studied airplane mechanics at Keesler Field, MS, for six months and advanced mechanical training on B-24s at a mechanics school in San Diego, CA. Andrew trained at a gunnery school in Laredo, TX for six weeks. In April 1943, he was assigned to a plane crew at Pocatello, ID, with the 536th Bomb Squad, where he received overseas training. After Pocatello he was sent to the 3rd SSU Squad, Langley, VA. TSgt. Paladino left for the South Pacific from Hamilton Field, California in December 1943, with the 13th Air Force, where he flew 42 combat missions as an engineer gunner on a B-24 bomber in New Guinea and the Solomon Islands. He returned to Fort McDowell, CA, Jan. 10, 1945.

Andrew was awarded the Sharpshooter Badge with Carbine Bar, WWII Victory Medal, Good Conduct Medal, American Campaign Medal, Asiatic-Pacific Theater Medal w/Silver Star, Air Medal w/Silver OLC and Aviation Tech Badge. Sgt. Paladino received an honorable discharge under the Army point system on July 13, 1945 from Camp Chaffee, AR.

Andrew Paladino, his wife Melba Humphrey, and their eight children: Philip, David, Beverly, Daniel, Carolyn, Ralph, Jan and Terry, tragically perished in a home fire Jan. 15, 1962. *Submitted by the Paladino family.*

PALADINO -
Anthony "Tony" Paladino (b. May 21, 1877, d. March 10, 1961) and wife Ermenia "Minnie" Rossi (b. May 9, 1887, d. Nov. 2, 1961) were descendants of some of the original settlers of the community of Center Ridge, AR. Their heritage is derived from two branches of immigrants from the Northern and Central Regions of Italy.

June 1932

Francesco and wife Lena Iannuzzi arrived in New York City in 1879 from the village of Valle Dell' Angelo, Province of Salerno, in the Region of Campania, Italy, and eventually settled in St. Louis.

MO, in 1880. They were the parents of six children: Anthony "Tony," Rocky, Robert, Angelo, Peter and Maria Rosaria "Molly."

November 1961

Joseph Rossi and wife, Mary Pedrazolli, established their residence in Center Ridge from Termenago, Italy (near the Austrian border), in ca. 1886. Mary was a schoolteacher in southern Austria before migrating to America. Joseph and Mary were the parents of nine children: Paul, Joseph "Bep," Mary Lucille, Emma, Josephine, Frances, Ermenia "Minnie," Christine and Lucia. Joseph died Feb. 22, 1896, and at that time, Mary turned her efforts to horse breeding.

She later married Albert Agnello on Nov. 22, 1899, an employee of the railway system in Arkansas, and this union produced eight children: Anthony, Peter, Adolph, Andrew, Catherine, Della, Augustine and Abraham.

Primary agriculture pursuits at that time centered on staples and poultry for family consumption. However, the sale of cotton, horses and corn were pursued for monetary benefits.

On Nov. 3, 1900, Tony Paladino and Minnie Rossi married in Catholic Point (Center Ridge). They were to enjoy over 60 years together. They produced 17 children: Frank, Angelo, Paul, John, Andrew, Joseph, Henry "Hank," Larry, Mary, Frances, Amelia, Anna, Henrietta "Etta," Florence "Babe," three boys, all named Joseph, who perished in infancy. The original 40 acres of Paladino Farms in Center Ridge was purchased for $75 from Dr. Holloway in 1902. Tony concentrated his efforts on poultry and vegetable crops and soon thereafter expanded in the raising of cotton, corn, dairy farming and the production of beef cattle (Black Angus).

Tony's endeavors in the agriculture economy of Arkansas culminated in being named Progressive Farmer of the Year and Master Farmer of Arkansas in 1941. He was recognized locally as a leader in establishing the community electrification program and applied its purpose economically in being one of the original purchasers in Conway County of the electric milking machine for his dairy herd. He also was active in the local school board, which established a fully recognized school for the children of the community.

As of 2005, the 14 children who survived infancy, eight are deceased.

Angelo joined the Benedictine Order at Subiaco and was ordained a Catholic priest, Father Christopher, on June 6, 1939. During his tenure he served as teacher, Head Prefect, founder and director of Camp Subiaco, Subprior, financial manager, and Pastor of St. Joseph Parish, Paris. He died Jan. 21, 1972.

Anna joined the Benedictine Order at St. Scholastica's in Fort Smith and took her final vows in June 1932 as Sister Lucille. She was a teacher at St. Scholastica, Shoal Creek until her death May 9, 1933.

Mary married Frank Rossi Jan. 6, 1921. Their marriage produced seven children. She died during childbirth Aug. 16, 1941. (See Rossi history.)

Andrew, after serving our country in WWII, settled in Center Ridge with his wife Melba, managing the family farmland, primarily producing Black Angus cattle and hay. He and Melba and their eight children perished in a tragic fire, including the original family homestead, Jan. 15, 1962. (See military bio.)

John (Colonel, USAF, retired) produced four children (one deceased). He served our country in WWII as an Air Force pilot. His being awarded the Distinguished Flying Cross with notable commentaries in national, state, and local newspaper magazines recognized his aeronautical achievements during the Korean War. He died Jan. 16, 1988. (See military bio.)

Frank J. and wife Jackie produced one child. After serving our country in WWII, he owned and operated Paladino's Café, North Little Rock over 40 years. His business establishment was well known as a central meeting place for political and civic leaders in the community. He died June 2, 1988. (See military bio)

Amelia married Bill Whitten May 2, 1939 producing one child. She died Dec. 6, 2000.

Frances married Tony Luke DeSalvo Sept. 12, 1934 and produced 10 children. She died April 20, 2001. (See DeSalvo history)

Paul Peter married Autie Faye Simmons May 19, 1944 producing one child. Paul served our country in the US Marine Corps. He later owned and operated The Old South Restaurant in Russellville, AR. He died June 13, 2005. (See Paladino history.)

Henry "Hank" A. married Betty Jo Barnes Oct. 21, 1951 producing four children. After serving our country in an extensive military career he settled with his family in Clarksville, AR. At this time he purchased a hardwood pallet mill in Knoxville, AR, which became his family owned and operated business. Hank died June 19, 2005. (See Paladino military history.)

The original 40 acres farmed by Tony and Minnie has since grown to over 900 acres and is primarily responsible for beef cattle and cultivation of pine tree forests. The farm today is owned by their descendants and known as The Paladino Farms, Inc. *Compiled by Patsy Paladino.*

PALADINO -
Barbato Paladino was born June 21, 1860 in Italy and died March 17, 1939. He married Donata Chavlerila. She was born March 23, 1867 in Italy and died June 1, 1942. Both are buried in St. Joseph Cemetery, Conway County, AR.

Barbato and Donata Paladino about 1932

Their children were:

1) Rosie married Joseph "Bep" Rossi on Nov. 10, 1904 at St. Joseph Catholic Church. Bep (b. Aug. 19, 1893) was the son of Joseph and Maria "Mary" Pedrazolli Rossi.

2) Carmalla (b. Feb. 25, 1889, d. Feb. 3, 1925) md. Camillo "Kill" DeSalvo, son of Luca and Beatrice DeSalvo. He was born April 10, 1885 and died Jan. 1, 1968.

3) Josie M. (b. Jan. 28, 1889, d. Jan. 2, 1974) md. Carmie DeSalvo, son of Joseph and Johannia Lombardo DeSalvo. He was born Nov. 25, 1891 and died Dec. 29, 1965.

4) Mary Rose (b. Sept. 19, 1894, d. May 20, 1977) md. Pete Lanni on Jan. 29, 1920. He was the son of Nicola and Maria Crescentia Santelio Lanni. Pete was born Aug. 2, 1880 and died April 23, 1970.

5) Madaline (b. Sept. 14, 1897, died in 1907).

6) Mary Angeline (b. 1900, d. 1987) md. Frank DeSalvo on Feb. 1, 1921. Frank (b. 1894, d. 1981) was the son of Joseph and Johannia Lombardo DeSalvo.

7) Pauline (b. 1902) md. Jim Christopher on Jan. 9, 1922. He was born about 1899.

8) Angelo Anthony "Doc" (b. Feb. 27, 1905, d. Nov. 15, 1962) md. Amelia Beatrice DeSalvo on Nov. 20, 1929. She was the daughter of Joe Luke and Mary Louise Rossi DeSalvo. Amelia was born Nov. 2, 1911.

9) Donna (b. Nov. 23, 1909, d. Jan. 5, 1992) md. Clemens Hamlings (b. Aug. 1, 1914, d. July 11, 1966).

10) Mary Frances (b. Jan. 16, 1912, d. May 26, 1989).

When first arriving in America, Barbato and Donata came through St. Louis, MO. Somewhere between 1880 and 1884 they came to Conway County, AR and settled in the community of Catholic Point. Barbato had a brother here as well; his name was Frank. Barbato and Donata never mastered the English language and could only speak a little broken English. They were well known and loved throughout the community. Everyone knew Barbato as "Uncle B." Like all the early settlers, they were farmers, with crops of corn and some cotton. Growing all that they ate, canning and drying to preserve for the winter. They also grew animals for their use, such as the milk, meat to cure, and making sausage. Donata was like all the other wives of the community, sewing and quilting to keep her family in clothes and warm in the winter.

Barbato and Donata were very active in their community and in the church. Their faith was the center of their lives and what carried them through the lean years and what always kept them happy and at peace in their lives.

PALADINO - Frank J. Paladino (b. Oct. 18, 1906) was the son of Tony and Erminia "Minnie" Paladino of Center Ridge, AR. He was the brother of Mary Rossi, Frances DeSalvo, Father Christopher, Amelia Whitten, Sister Lucille, Paul, John, Andrew, Joseph, Henry, Henrietta Rowland, Lawrence and Florence Andreas.

Paladino a T-5 was inducted into the army in September 1943, received his basic training at Camp Berkeley, TX and trained for overseas near

Frank J. Paladino, ca. 1950

Maryville CA. He went overseas from San Francisco, April 1, 1944. He was sent over with a replacement outfit, unassigned to any branch of the service but after landing in the Southwest Pacific, he was assigned to an anti-aircraft artillery unit as cook. He was stationed in New Guinea, on Goodenough Island and Trobriand Islands, then back to New Guinea the latter part of 1944. He was stationed at Finschhafen, New Guinea. In May 1945 he was sent to the Philippines.

Frank married Tula "Jackie" Spradling Nov. 27, 1939, had one child. He died June 2, 1988 and was interred at St. Joseph's Catholic Cemetery, Center Ridge, AR. *Submitted by the Frank Paladino family.*

PALADINO - Henry "Hank" A. Paladino (b. April 15, 1927), son of Anthony "Tony" and Erminia "Minnie" Paladino of Center Ridge, AR, was brother of Mary Rossi, Frances DeSalvo, Frank J., Father Christopher, Amelia Whitten, Sister Lucille, Paul, John, Andrew, Joseph, Henrietta Rowland, Lawrence and Florence Andreas.

Paladino entered the Air Corps out of Subiaco Academy in 1945, when he volunteered to serve in what is known as the US Air Force. He was sent to Europe at the end of

Henry A. Paladino

WWII and was stationed in Italy, Libya, North Africa and Athens, Greece, as a control tower and approved controller operator for our aircraft, and instructor for foreign students.

He was a technical sergeant and reservist when he returned to civilian life in 1950. He attended the University of the Ozarks in Clarksville, AR before being recalled to active duty in his second year when the war broke out in Korea. He attended officer's training school in Kansas and graduated in 1951, quickly earned a promotion to lieutenant. For the next three years, he returned to Europe in Western Germany as a communication officer in the Army Headquarters to oppose the threat of Russians.

After his tour in Europe, he was stationed for aviation training as a fixed wing and helicopter pilot upon returning to the U.S. in 1955. Followed by a one-year tour where he served on the 18th Parallel separating North Korea from South Korea, as a tactical pilot and communications officer where he was promoted to the rank of captain.

Returning to the United States, Paladino was sent to Alabama as a test pilot in research and development programs for avionics. He was then assigned to Command and General Staff College in Kansas where he was promoted to major. Following graduation, Paladino was assigned to a classified board where he developed aircraft systems and organization of Air Assault operations for war where he would carry our units into combat with helicopters.

Paladino was assigned to the Air Mobile Division as an Assistant Division G-4 for a one-year combat tour in Vietnam in 1965, where he was awarded three Commendation Medals, Bronze Star, five Air Medals and Legion of Merit. He was with the first unit that was sent to war using this technology, the First Air Assault Cavalry Division. He flew over 50 combat missions against North Vietnam forces in both helicopter and fixed wing. He flew both gunships equipped with machine guns and rockets, as well as, transporting soldiers into combat. He also transported equipment, supplies and was responsible for evacuating wounded soldiers to field hospitals.

In 1967 he returned to the US. Paladino was promoted to lieutenant colonel and served his last military assignment at the Department of Army Headquarters in Washington, DC, at the (Pentagon) as assistant program manager of the Army's No. 1 priority development program, the "Armed Helicopter Program." The US Congress later canceled this program as the Vietnam War came to a close and was replaced with the Apache Armed Helicopter Program in 1971. The Apache Armed Helicopter is being used today in Iraq. He retired with the rank of lieutenant colonel from the Army in Washington, DC, in 1972.

Henry married Betty Jo Barnes on Oct. 21, 1951. He passed away June 19, 2005 and is survived by four children: Kevin J. Paladino of Lamar, Steve H. and his wife Sheryl Paladino of Clarksville, Kimberly Paladino of Woodbridge, VA, and Michelle and her husband Dr. David Tanner of Russellville; five grandchildren: Jason Paladino, Jessica Paladino, Justin Brown, Julie Paladino and Wayne and his wife Kasey Brown; a two step-grandchildren, Richie Tanner and Maegan and her husband Billy Hampton; great-grandchild, Madison Brown, and four stepgreat-grandchildren: Cecelia, Gabriel, Sophia Hampton and Paizley Bratton. *Submitted by the children of Henry A. Paladino.*

PALADINO - John Louis Paladino (b. Sept. 23, 1919, in Center Ridge, AR, d. Jan. 16, 1988) was entombed at Rest Hills Cemetery, North Little Rock, AR. He was the son of Anthony "Tony" and Erminia "Minnie" Paladino of Center Ridge and brother of Mary Rossi, Frances DeSalvo, Frank J., Father Christopher, Amelia Whitten, Sister Lucille, Paul, Andrew, Joseph, Henrietta Rowland, Henry, Lawrence and Florence Andreas.

John married Mary Elizabeth Zarlingo on Jan.

27, 1947 at St. Joseph in Center Ridge, AR. Mary Elizabeth was the daughter of James "Jim" and Lucy Lanni Zarlingo. They had one daughter, Sharon Louise Paladino (b. Sept. 24, 1947). John and Mary were divorced in February 1950. John operated Paladino's Café with his brother Frank J. Paladino in North Little Rock, AR, before being recalled to the military on Oct. 10, 1950.

John L. Paladino.

John married Lucretia Ida Eagle (b. Oct. 20, 1924 in Lonoke, AR) on Sept. 2, 1950 in Benton, AR. Lucretia "Lou" was the daughter of Oscar and Ida Plummer Eagle. John and Lou had three children:

Deborah Ann "Debi" Paladino (b. Oct. 28, 1952 in Wareham, MA) md. Thomas Jacob "Tom" Knight, May 5, 1985 in Setauket, Long Island, NY. Tom (b. Sept. 10, 1955 in Oceanside, NY), son of Richard and Lois Knight of St. James, NY, had three children: Ashley Elizabeth Knight (b. Sept. 5, 1986); Emily Alexandra Knight (b. Dec. 21, 1987) and Dylan Maxwell "Max" Knight (b. Dec. 12, 1990). All three children were born in New Brunswick, NJ.

Donald Anthony "Don" Paladino (b. Oct. 29, 1954 in Newport News, VA) md. Ronda Melia Elliott Aug. 2, 1975 in Malvern, AR. Ronda (b. June 12, 1955), daughter of Lesil and Mary (Riggan) Elliott of Malvern, had two sons, Nick Elliott Paladino (b. March 31, 1979) and Andrew John Paladino (b. Aug. 13, 1981). Nick and Andy were born in Little Rock, AR. Nick married Jennifer Lynne Spence on July 31, 2004 in Magnolia, AR. Jennifer is the daughter of Kenny and Jada Spence of Magnolia.

Anthony Michael "Tony" Paladino (b. March 9, 1961 in Colorado Springs, CO) md. Carla Sue Roberson March 5, 1983 in Vanndale, AR. Carla (b. Sept. 18, 1961), daughter of Mr. and Mrs. Leroy Roberson of Vanndale, had one daughter, Lauren Nicole Paladino (b. Oct. 9, 1985 in Jonesboro, AR). Tony died March 28, 1992 and is entombed at Rest Hills Cemetery, North Little Rock, AR.

John was inducted into the Army Air Corps at Camp Robinson in July 1941, took his basic training at Jefferson Barracks, MO and aviation mechanic training at Chanute Field, IL for six months. He was stationed as an airplane mechanic at Moody Field, Valdosta, GA for approximately a year. He was promoted to rank of corporal and one month later to sergeant. From Moody Field he was sent to Stuttgart AAB for four months of flight training. He took his cadet training at Cleveland, OH; preflight at San Antonio, TX; primary at Chickasha, OK; and advanced training at Frederick AAF, OK. While there he received his wings and commission as 2nd lieutenant Dec. 23, 1944. From there, he was stationed at San Marcus, TX as a flying instructor. He was a reservist when he returned to civilian life in 1945.

John was recalled to active duty Oct. 10, 1950 as 1LT with the 154th Ftr. Sqdn., Arkansas Air National Guard (at that time a part of the 136th Ftr. BW in Korea). In April 1951 while stationed at Langley Field AFB, VA, 1LT Paladino was flying a two plane formation on a routine training mission over Prince George County when 1LT Wm. Butcher saw flames near the tail of Paladino's F-84. Butcher told him by radio and Paladino used the ejector seat and was thrown clear of his plane deep in the woods near Spring Grove. Paladino landed in the trees a few feet above the ground. He unfastened his parachute harness and stepped out uninjured. He built a fire with waterproof matches given to him by his wife, for warmth and to keep animals away. He was found many hours later by a 70-man search party from Langley Field. He was transferred to Korea in May 1951 to participate in the Korean War.

Capt. Paladino was one of six Arkansas men with the 136th Fighter-Bomber Wing who received the Air Medal for meritorious achievement while participating in aerial flights over enemy-held territory in Korea from May 27-July 29, 1951. On Oct. 24, 1951 Capt. Paladino was awarded the Distinguished Flying Cross for striking and destroying three active locomotives during inclement weather and heavy ground fire.

On Nov. 15, 1951 in Korea, Capt. Paladino was racing back to base at 600 mph at 32,000 feet in his Republic F-84 Thunderjet, when his oxygen apparatus failed and without warning he passed out. In one of the most spectacular examples of teamwork and unorthodox rescue in aviation history, his combat teammates and good friends, Lt. Jack Miller and Lt. S. Woody McArthur, maneuvered their wingtips under Paladino's wings and for some 15 tense minutes succeeded in maintaining directional control and guided his plane on a thin cushion of air streaming between the wing tips of the three planes, down to 13,5000 feet when Paladino regained consciousness, as well as control of his plane and made a successful landing. Approximately 10 years later Major Paladino looked back on the rescue as a rare and fortunate incident that turned out because of the right people at the right moment.

"Pal" as he was known, completed 100 missions in Korea. Upon return to the States, he was stationed at Otis AFB, MA; Langley AFB, VA; Seymour-Johnson AFB, NC; Ent AFB, CO; Little Rock AFB, AR; Grissom AFB, IN and Barksdale AFB, LA. He continued an illustrious career in the USAF, receiving his Command Pilot Wings at Thule AFB Greenland in 1960. He spent three tours of duty in Southeast Asia during the Vietnam War, where he flew another 100 missions and was the deputy commander of maintenance at Da Nang AFB. He retired from the US Air Force Sept. 1, 1972 with the rank of full colonel from Offutt AFB, NE after having a distinguished military career. *Submitted by the children of John L. Paladino.*

PALADINO - Joseph Anthony Paladino (b. June 12, 1923, in Center Ridge, AR) is the son of Anthony "Tony" and Erminia "Minnie" Paladino of Center Ridge. He is brother of Mary Rossi, Frances DeSalvo, Frank J., Father Christopher, Amelia Whitten, Sister Lucille, Paul, John, Andrew, Henrietta Rowland, Henry, Lawrence and Florence Andreas. Joe married Geneva Nelda Gilliam on Jan. 5, 1946 at St. Joseph in Center Ridge, AR. Geneva was born Feb. 25, 1925 in Jacksonville, AR to Guy and Frannie Youngue Gilliam.

Etta, Geneva, Joe and Johnny - 1946

He attended college at the University of Arkansas in 1944, where he played for the Arkansas Razorbacks as right guard. He worked at his brother Frank's restaurant, Paladino's Café, in North Little Rock from 1944-46, where he met his wife Geneva.

He worked for ABC (Alcohol Beverage Control) for 4 years. Due to his investigating experience he then worked for ATF (Alcohol, Tobacco, and Firearms) for 21 years, in Little Rock, Hot Springs, Hugo, OK, and

Muskogee, OK where he retired on Feb. 26, 1977. He moved back home and built a house near Center Ridge. He and Geneva had four children:

1) William Joseph "Bill" Paladino (b. July 4, 1946 in Little Rock) had one son by his first marriage named William Joseph Jr. "Joe Bill" (b. Nov. 5, 1967 in Camp Lejeune, NC) who married Vickie Renee Burks in May 1980. She was born March 10, 1957 to Thad and Patricia Burks. They had three children: Aaron Jacob Paladino (b. Aug. 19, 1981, d. Nov. 15, 1989); David Andrew Paladino (b. Aug. 15, 1984) and Daniel Phillip Paladino (b. July 5, 1988).

2) Steven Anthony Paladino (b. Dec. 15, 1954 in Little Rock) md. Cheryl Lyn Smith on June 3, 1978 in Muskogee, OK. She was born May 31, 1957 in Pawnee, OK to Rayburn and Darlene Smith. They have three children: Jason Aaron Paladino (b. May 7, 1979 in Little Rock, AR); April Dawn Paladino (b. Oct. 5, 1981 in Muskogee, OK) and Tony Ryan Paladino (b. Sept. 18, 1982 at home in Springfield, AR).

3) Terry Andrew Paladino (b. April 26, 1963 in Little Rock) has one daughter by his first marriage, Ashley Ann Paladino (b. July 18, 1986). He married Stephanie Jo Wingo on Oct. 23, 2004. Stephanie was born Aug. 20, 1964 in Morrilton, AR to Virgil and Sue Wingo.

4) Lori Irene Paladino (b. Nov. 7, 1964 in Little Rock) md. Robert Milan Ross on July 1, 1989 at St. Joseph in Center Ridge. Robert (b. Fe. 29, 1964) is the son of Frank and Geraldine Ross. They have three children: Taylor Maria Ross (b. March 10, 1993 in Conway, AR); Rachel Nicole Ross (b. April 21, 1995 in Little Rock, AR) and Natalie Milan Ross (b. June 21, 2001 in Conway, AR). *Submitted by the children of Joseph A. Paladino.*

PALADINO - Lawrence "Larry" Paladino (b. Aug. 15, 1929 in Center Ridge, AR), son of Anthony "Tony" and Erminia "Minnie" Paladino and brother of Mary Rossi, Frances DeSalvo, Frank J., Father Christopher, Amelia Whitten, Sister Lucille, Paul, Andrew, Joseph, Henrietta Rowland, Henry and Florence Andreas.

Larry R. Paladino

He was a graduate of Subiaco Academy in 1948 and while attending Subiaco, he played quarterback on the football team and pitcher on the baseball team. In 1947, an outstanding Subiaco Football Team played for the State Championship against Little Rock Central in the War Memorial Stadium. Also, at Subiaco in 1948, Larry pitched a no-hitter against Booneville High School.

He attended and graduated from UCA in Conway, AR, and played quarterback on the football team and pitcher on the baseball team. He was selected on the All Conference Teams in 1950 and 1951. He pitched two no-hitters in semi-pro baseball during the summer of 1949.

Larry signed a professional contract with the New York Giants Baseball Team (presently known as the San Francisco Giants) at the end of his junior year in 1951 and played in the Giants organization until 1956. Larry's best year was 17 wins and 8 loses. He also coached football, basketball and taught at George Washington High School in Danville, VA in the off-season.

Paladino served and became an officer in the Arkansas and Virginia National Guards from 1951-59. In 1958, Westinghouse, ALD hired Larry as a public relations and sales manager, establishing coin operated laundry stores in all the Central States of our nation. In 1963, Speed Queen division of McGraw Edison hired Larry to develop their commercial appliance market. Raytheon then bought out McGraw Edison and assigned him to Washington, DC, East

Coast market, for a four-year period and then to New York, as a regional manager, until his retirement. Larry also owned two concession companies in New York City.

He loves to visit the farms at Center Ridge, where he served as president of Paladino Farms, Inc. for 12 years. Larry has been an avid sportsman, and has a great love for golf, holding a +1 handicap. He won the Senior Tour (today it is the Champions Tour) Pro-Am Tournament in 1983 and 1984. Larry has won 20 golf club championships in New York, New Jersey and Florida and his 11th at the famous Island Country Club in Marco Island, FL in March 2005.

Larry has been selected by the CMAA (Club Managers Association of America) to play for the National Club Championship in a tournament to be held at Pinehurst, NC in November 2005, sponsored by the Golf Channel, Nike and Toshiba.

Larry has a son, Lawrence "Chris" Paladino. Chris married Elizabeth Jennings McRoberts in 1997. Chris is vice president and financial advisor for Milkie Ferguson Investments, Inc. in Dallas, TX. *Submitted by the family of Larry R. Paladino.*

PALADINO - Paul P. Paladino (b. Dec. 2, 1917, Center Ridge, Conway County, AR), was one of the 17 children of Tony and Minnie (Rossi) Paladino. His siblings are Mary Lena (b. 1902); Frances (b. 1903); Frank Joseph (b. 1906); three sons, all named Joseph, died in infancy; Angelo Donnato (b. 1909); Amelia (b. 1910); Anna Josie (b. 1913); Paul, John Louis (b. 1919); Andrew Rosario (b. 1921); Joseph Anthony "Joe" (b. 1923); Henrietta "Etta" (b. 1925); Henry Albert "Hank" in 1928; Laurence Raymond (b. 1929); and Florence "Babe" (b. 1932).

Paul P. Paladino

Angelo became a priest named Father Christopher and Anna Josie became Sister Lucille. Anthony died in March 1961 and Minnie died in November 1961. Both are buried in St. Joseph's Catholic Church Cemetery along with many of the pioneer fami-

Autie Faye Simmons and Paul Peter Paladino on their wedding day in 1944.

lies who had settled this area and helped develop it.

Paul attended Catholic High School in Little Rock, AR, while living with his older brother, Frank and his family. It was quite an experience for a young man from a small community to be educated away and he took every advantage of it. He played football for the school and graduated with a fine ability to conduct his life. He then attended Loyola University in New Orleans before going to the University of Arkansas at Fayetteville, where he was a member of the Varsity Football Eleven. While there, he saw a very pretty young woman and remarked to his friends "there's the girl I'm going to marry." They scoffed at him, but on May 19, 1944, Paul married Autie Faye Simmons at the chapel on the US Marine Base at Quantico, VA.

Paul enlisted in the US Marine Corps Reserve at age 27 and was called to active duty in 1943. He was stationed at Arkansas A&M College, Monticello in the V-12 Naval Unit for six months, then took his boot training at Paris Island, SC. He graduated from the Marine Corps School at Quantico, VA, in July 1944 with a rank of second lieutenant, then was sent to Camp Pendleton, Oceanside, CA for further training. He went overseas in December 1944 and took part in the Okinawa campaign. He attained the rank of captain. After the war he returned to the University of Arkansas, graduating in 1949 with a degree in agriculture.

After college, Paul was the first to be hired by AP&L as poultry specialist in 1950. He later joined Arkansas Valley Industries as director of hatcheries. He and Faye built up a business, The Old South restaurant in Russellville, which is still a gathering spot in the town. They lived for awhile in Little Rock, but settled and made their home place in Russellville, Pope County, AR.

Faye Paladino (b. July 27, 1924, La Grande, OR), daughter of Arthur Simmons and Mary Sallee and had one brother Christopher Jacy Simmons (b. Feb. 5, 1913) and one sister Claudia Wilma (b. Jan. 1, 1917). Faye Paladino was a tall, beautiful woman whose joy of living surrounded everything she did. She and Paul were members of St. John's Catholic Church and they developed many deep friendships around the city. She and Paul fell in love and stayed that was for nearly 60 years.

Faye Paladino, sadly, passed away Aug. 1, 2003 after an exhaustive battle with many illnesses. She is missed greatly, but will be remembered by many as kind, loving and generous. Simple words cannot describe this fine woman. Paul continued to live in their homeplace, replete with many happy memories of their life together until his death on June 13, 2005. Both he and Faye are buried at St. Joseph's Catholic Church in Center Ridge, AR.

Paul and Faye had one son, Paul Arthur "P.A." (b. July 22, 1956 in Little Rock, Pulaski County, AR). P.A. lives in Russellville also. *Submitted by the family of Paul Paladino.*

PAXSON - Joseph Taylor Paxson, son of Benjamin F. Paxson and Sarah E Carter, was born Jan. 15, 1849 in Walton County, GA and died Aug. 3, 1908 in Grandview, Conway County, AR. He married Matilda Agnes Kelley, daughter of Edward Sylvester Kelley and Mary Ann Gipson, about 1877 near Springfield, Greene County, MO. She was born Jan. 16, 1857 in Virginia and died Nov. 26, 1938, England, Lonoke County, AR. Joseph and Matilda are both buried in Grandview Cemetery.

Back row: Anna, Barty, Phena. Front row: Irpeel, Joseph T., Fred, Matilda A., Chloe, Phosa.

Joseph Taylor Paxson's third great-grandparents, William and Abigail (Pownall) Paxson, were Quakers who emigrated from Buckinghamshire Parish, Great Britain to Bucks County, PA in 1682 with William Penn.

Joseph T. Paxson attended the Lexington College of Bible at the University of Kentucky at Lexington in 1869. In 1872 he and Thomas M. Foster established New Hope Christian Church, Gwinnett County, GA.

Family stories say that immediately after their marriage, Joseph and Matilda traveled by mule to Arkansas. Joseph T. Paxson preached several places on the way to Arkansas. They stayed about two years in Baxter County, AR before heading down to Conway County. His credentials as a minister of the Church of Christ were filed in Conway County, AR on Jan. 3,

1881. He helped to build the church and school at Grandview. Joseph preached at Grandview, Hogan School, and possibly at other locations. Joseph T. Paxson homesteaded in Grandview and received his Homestead Certificate May 4, 1885.

Joseph and Matilda had 14 children, with six of them dying at an early age. The names of these children are engraved on the side of their parents' tombstone at Grandview Cemetery. The children who died young were Willie, Amos, Lemuel, Lydia, Ruth and Theophilus.

All of the Paxson children were given Bible names:

1) Anna Lou (b. September 1878, died 1953, Conway County, AR) married John F. Anderson Oct. 23, 1898. Their children are Nettie, Alonzo, Vernon, Lily, Claudie and Kenneth Edsel. Kenneth still lives in Grandview and now owns the Paxson land.

2) Tryphena Olive (b. March 9, 1880 in Conway County, d. Jan. 8, 1967 in Tucson, AZ) md. John Irving Mahan Aug. 3, 1900. Their children are Roy Edward, Odessa Elizabeth, Edna Jeanette, Matilda Ruth, John Irving, Chloe Pearle, Paul Edison, Rachel Beatrice, John Rayburn and Hazel Lorraine.

3) Bartholomew Milligan (b. Feb. 15, 1882 in Conway County, d. June 14, 1941, Little Rock, AR) md. Emma Jane Woods on Feb. 15, 1906, High Hill, Montgomery County, MO. Their children are Eugene Woods, Irl Bartholmew, Olive Frances, Lois Jane, Harold Dean and Joseph Milton.

4) Tryphosa Jane (b. October 1886, Conway County, d. 1961, Kenosha, WI) md. John A. Scoville. They had no children to survive infancy.

5) Chloe Belle (b. March 8, 1889, Grandview, AR, d. Sept. 4, 1967 in Little Rock, AR) md. Joseph Lucian Gordon Feb. 13, 1910, Center Ridge, AR.

6) Irpeel Joshua (b. November 1890 Center Ridge, AR, d. 1972 in Tucson, AZ) md. Eola Parry in 1932 in Indiana. They had one daughter, Janet Nadine.

7) Sylvanus Frederick (b. Dec. 11, 1894 Conway County, d. Feb. 8, 1983, Botkinburg, Van Buren County, AR) md. Susan L. Meaders Dec. 24, 1916, Center Ridge, AR. Their children are Mildred Maxine, Norman Emmett, Sylvan Frederic, Wilma Faye and Freda Sue.

8) Eunice (b. Sept. 9, 1898, Grandview, AR, d. April 25, 1987, Little Rock, AR) md. James Beavers Dec. 12, 1917. Their children are Mildred Leilah, Lowell W. and J. Othel. *Submitted by Mrs. Peggy Gordon.*

PAYNE - As passed down through the years and partially recorded in an old tattered and worn Bible, the story of the Payne's begins. Mary Smith, during the mid-1700s, in South Carolina raised four children: Rebecca, James, Annie, and Joe.

1930s, l-r: Charlie, Tessie, Robert, Tecumpia, Mary, Margie, Henry, Artelia, Tommy, Cozetta, Ira "Big Boy," Cleo, Leo and Ive Payne.

Years later, Rebecca met and married Hampton Payne. To this union 13 children were born: James Eddie, Lee Andrew "Buster," Thomas, Webster, Ezekiel "Zeke," Ruben, Luther, Willie, Mary Elisabeth, Wadie, Sudie, Amy and Sissy. The family lived in Shelby County, Memphis, TN for a while.

As they matured (mid to late 1800s) the family moved to Arkansas and settled in the Mt. Olive Com-

munity, Conway County. James Eddie and Lee Andrew "Buster" later went onto Oklahoma to settle. Each family member seemed to raise 10 to 15 kids.

Thomas met and later married Elizabeth "Lizzy" Bell on Jan. 27, 1892. They raised 15 kids together: Charlie Andrew "Sonny" (b. Aug. 6, 1892, d. March 26, 1985); James Robert "Buddie" (b. May 6, 1894, d. June 27, 1963); Henry Dewitt Payne (b. July 28, 1900, d. Feb. 2, 1976); Thomas "Tommie;" Ive "Buck" (b. Oct. 6, 1921, d. Dec. 15, 1966; Ira "Big Boy;" Leo "Boomie" (b. July 1, 1930- ?); Cora; Mary Elizabeth; Tessie "Tee" (b. May 28, 1905, d. April 19, 1989); Cozetta "Watt" (died July 6, 1957); Artelia "Ris" (b. 1909, d. 1993); Margie "Bysie" (b. April 15, 1918, d. Feb. 1, 1989); Tecumpia "T;" and Cleo "Shoomie" (b. July 1, 1930, d. July 2003).

The children were raised to share and care for each other. As a whole for generations, the family grew crops not only to feed themselves but sold, traded, and gave to others throughout their community. From the late 1800s to the late 1970s, Hampton, Tom, Sonny and Buddy Payne's families were known for their hard work to produce sweet corn, peas, peanuts, greens, cabbage, okra and some of the sweetest and largest watermelons as well as eggs, sausage, molasses, pears, plums, apples and peaches in Conway County. The girls all did sewing and were some of the best cooks around.

Charlie Andrew "Sonny" Payne met and married Dovie Samantha Johnson. Sonny had one other child, Berniece "Pinkey" Lambert (b. May 1916, d. September 1978). To this union, 10 children were born. James Althimer (b. Jan. 28, 1918, d. May 23, 1996); Emmett Jerry (b. June 6, 1919, d. April 1984); Charlie Dewitt "Doc" (b. 1921, d. June 23, 1996); Doyle McCleve (b. Sept. 19, d. September 1975; Edgar Doris "Ed" (b. March 24, 1924, d. August 1997); Robert Thomas "Braus" (b. June 13, 1933 to November 2003; Charlie Algertha Renell (b. October 1916, d. Nov. 28, 1980; Glodie Evanglene; Thelma Lee and Gladys Omeria (b. May 1932, d. December 2002).

James Althimer Payne met and later married Jerlean Hart on June 3, 1945. He served his country in WWII until September 1946 when he was honorably discharged after receiving multiple injuries during his tour. They resided in Kansas City, MO until 1954, then returned to the Mt. Olive Community in Plumerville, AR and settled down. They had four children: James E. (b. Dec. 7, 1955); Gloria Y. (b. Sept. 28, 1962); Phyllis A. (b. Aug. 3, 1965) and Anthony Wayne (b. July 17, 1967, d. July 20, 1967). This is only a look into our large family.

PAYNE - I traced Samuel Payne from Stone County to Dover in Pope County. I found that he was born in Alabama on Aug. 11, 1837 and that his parents were from Pennsylvania. Samuel married first to M.E. Lancaster on Dec. 31, 1874 and second to Cynthia Barnett on Nov. 7, 1887.

Samuel Payne and Cynthia Burnett Payne

When Samuel's son William "Bill" Payne (b. Jan. 11, 1883 in Stone County, AR) moved to Pope County, AR, he married on March 23, 1900 to Miss Elizabeth "Betty" Branch (b. Dec. 4, 1880). William and Betty moved to Riverview, Conway County, AR and raised seven children: William Houston (b. Feb. 3, 1900); Mary "Lizzie" (b. Jan. 7, 1902); John Oscar (b. March 15, 1906); Mary May (b. July 13, 1908); Bessie Ann (b. Oct. 15, 1910); Georgie Lee (b. Jan. 31, 1913) and Eddie Elmer (b. June 7, 1921).

William Houston Payne met and married Miss Essie (Ezzie) Ethel Parham in Pope County, AR.

Essie's parents were John Wesley Parham and Mary Francis Mooney, and they had two other daughters, Vernie and Louvina. William and Essie had five children that were raised in Arkansas and Missouri.

Imo Ethel Payne (b. Feb. 3, 1926) md. William Henry Anderson and had four children.

1) David Earl (b. Jan. 14, 1942) md. Roberta Bingham on Jan. 24, 1961. They had three children: Lex, Sonya and Jon Paul.

2) Gene (b. July 17, 1943) md. Barbara Mosley and had two children, Victor and Victoria. He also married Carol Cody and he adopted her two girls, Jamie and Shannon.

3) Patricia (b. Aug. 18, 1945) md. (1st) Jackie Boyd; (2nd) Eugene Potts and had two children: Michael and Kimberly; (3rd) Johnny Strassle and they had one child Melissa.

4) Barbara (b. July 9, 1951) md. Delbert Vales Sept. 21, 1967 and they had two children, Mark and Candy.

Imo then married Edward Mitchell and had one daughter, Sheila Jean.

Jack Loyd Payne (b. Dec. 25, 1927) md. Maggie Russell and they had two children, Brenda and Nelson. He then married Lois Moody Kennedy and they had two boys, Timmy and Michael.

Annie Lou (b. Sept. 19, 1933) md. Aug. 18, 1950 to Jessie Raymond Lecroy (b. Jan. 1, 1926) and they had five children: Martha, Linda, Debra, Darlene, Melissa.

Ruby Jewel (b. June 25, 1936) md. Charles Cluck and had two children, Scotty and Kathy. Ruby married second, Ronnie Dockins (b. Aug. 2, 1944). Ronnie had two children by a previous marriage, Leigh and Carol.

Willie "Buddy" (b. Aug. 5, 1939) md. Mary Helen Davis on April 2, 1958. She was born March 6, 1943 and they had two children, Tony and Allen.

Murial was born between 1937 and 1938 and died between 1939 and 1940. *Submitted by William Anderson.*

PEITZ - Peter A. Peitz (b. Dec. 2, 1868) moved to Morrilton from Pittsburgh, PA in 1885 at age 17. He had followed his brother (Ammon Peitz), a religious brother of the Holy Ghost Fathers, who was assigned to their mission at "Marienstadt" on Monastery Ridge, north of Morrilton.

Parents of Peter (John and Margaret Peitz) had immigrated from Germany around 1850. Peter married Teresa Riedmueller (b. July 10, 1872). He purchased property on Monastery Ridge and was engaged primarily in farming. Their children were Margaret Mueller, Carl Peitz, Wilbert Peitz, Alphonse Peitz, Marie Ross, Josephine Zaloudek, Frances Zaloudek, Zita Denny, Agatha Loveless, James Peitz, John Peitz and Elizabeth Anderson, all of whom are deceased.

Peter died Jan. 4, 1943 and Teresa died Jan. 4, 1933; both are buried in Sacred Heart Cemetery.

Carl F. Peitz, son of Peter A. Peitz (b. Aug. 7, 1893) was a lifelong resident of Morrilton. He purchased property on Monastery Ridge and was engaged in farming and carpentry. He was a veteran of WWI. He married Teresa Bellinghausen (b. Oct. 15, 1893) who had taught at the "Ridge" school prior to their marriage. Their children are: Angela Pfeifer (b. Sept. 16, 1920, d. March 8, 2003); Ruth Hettman (b. Aug. 23, 1922, d. March 12, 2005); Mildred Peitz (b. March 11, 1924 of Conway, AR); Charles Peitz (b. Feb. 19, 1926, d. 1928); Edward Peitz (b. June 5, 1928 of Hot Springs Village); Alfred Peitz (b. April 20, 1930, d. Jan. 26, 1990); Bernice Smith (b. April 18, 1932 of Fort Smith, AR); and Mary Lachowsky (b. March 1, 1934) of Conway, AR).

Carl married second, Eleanor Koscielny in 1950, who died July 12, 1972. Carl died March 27, 1982 (age 89) and Teresa died Nov. 25, 1942 (age 49), both are buried in Sacred Heart Cemetery. *Submitted by Mildred Peitz.*

PERRY - George (Rabun) Perry (b. Aug. 31, 1835 in Atlanta, GA) was the son of Emmaline Rabun. His siblings were Minerva, Charles, Creed, Baker, Fannie, Tabitha Rabun and Lucy Perry, who married Jim Webb and resided in Brinkley, AR. George and Martha Ferguson-White Gates were married Nov. 17, 1860 at Peach Creek, Panola County, MS by Thomas Fitzgerald. Martha (b. 1840 in Richmond, VA) was the daughter of Africans Thomas and Hannah Ferguson White. Her siblings were Mary Elizabeth Ferguson White Humphrey, who lived in Claredon, AR, and Thomas Ferguson White Cryer Gates, who moved to Perry and Conway County. Hannah was sold to the White plantation in Mississippi, where Samuel White became her husband, hence the change of names.

Children of George and Martha Perry: Back l-r: W.W., Charles and John H. Perry; front: Ellen, Sarah and Emmaline.

George joined the Union Army Nov. 23, 1863 and was honorably discharged Sept. 23, 1865 at Helena, AR. Afterwards, he moved his family to Memphis, TN where they lived until 1877 when they moved to Perry County, AR. They moved to Conway County in 1887. George was a deacon at Pleasant Hill Baptist Church in Perry County. He died January 1894 at the age of 57 and was buried in the church graveyard. His tombstone is on Martha's grave in Oddfellows Cemetery in Morrilton.

Martha Ann died May 10, 1926 in Morrilton, AR. She received a Widow's Pension from the government until her death. She is buried in Oddfellows Cemetery in Morrilton, AR under George's headstone.

George and Martha's children were Rev. William Wesley Perry (b. 1861) and Hannah Perry (b. 1863), born near Sardis, Mississippi County, TN; Ellen Perry Anderson (b. 1867); Sarah Elizabeth Perry Clark (b. 1869); Charles Baker Perry (b. 1875); Emmaline Perry Bennett Little (b. 1873); Mattie Perry Cyrus Brown (b. 1877 in Tennessee); John Henry who was born in Redemption, Perry County, AR; and George, who died in infancy, is buried in Shelby County.

Rev. William Wesley Perry married Georgia Ann Ward from Tennessee. Their oldest daughter, Willie Perry Bell Holloway, was born in Arkansas. The family moved to St. Louis, MO where second daughter, Edna Pearl, was born. Rev. Perry ran a grocery store and print shop in St. Louis in addition to pastoring the Compton Hill Baptist Church. Georgia Ward Perry taught Sunday School for 50 years. She worked in her neighborhood in sewing circles and for a young women's Christian organization.

Rev. William Wesley Perry died Aug. 4, 1943 in St. Louis, MO. Their daughter Willie married Henry Bell and William Holloway. She was a member of Compton Hill Baptist Church. She died June 1968 and was buried at Jefferson Barracks, MO. She had one son, William Bell.

Daughter Edna Perry married Marshall Powell, an electrician and plumber. Edna died in May 1962 in St. Louis. Marshall preceded her in death in December 1961 They were parents of eight children: George, Ruth, David Marshall, Ursula, William, Charles, John, and Georgia Powell Bailey. *Submitted by Georgia Powell Bailey.*

PETTINGILL - William Luther Pettingill (b. Feb. 4, 1901 in Lincoln, NE) was the third child of George and Annie (Venable) Pettingill. The Pettingill family moved to Plumerville, AR around 1905. In 1924 Luther married Mary Lola, daughter of Oscar and Claire (Baugus) Johnson. William Luther and Mary Lola had eight children together.

The Luther Pettingill Family: George, C.C., Luther, Kenneth, Bill, Betty, Kay, Mary, Emma Jean, Clara.

1) Emma Jean married Albert Newland at Wichita, KS. They had one child, Mark Allen.

2) William Frank "Bill" served over two years in the US Army. He returned home to continue farming and married Bennie Jean Lear, daughter of Ben and Nossie Lear of Plumerville. They had one son, Ricky. Bill later married Nadine Smith.

3) Betty Lou married Fred Guinn, son of Orville and Mary Guinn of Morrilton. They had three children: Debra, Steve and Paul.

4) George Oscar, a farmer, married Lois Cook, daughter of Johnny and Laura Cook. They had three children: Laura Ann, George Michael and Mary Elizabeth. He later married Toni Peolis at Cabot, AR.

5) Calvin Curtis "C.C." served 23 years in the US Air Force. He married May Ruth Cook, daughter of Johnny and Laura Cook, and they had two children, Linda and Nita.

6) Kenneth Joe served 21 years in the US Air Force. He married Mary Elizabeth Creach, daughter of John and Artie Creach at Plumerville. They had two sons, Kenneth Joe Jr. and Timothy Scott.

7) Clara Ann married Jethro L. "Pete" Sharp (who served 28 years in the US Air Force). He is the son of Luther and Rosa Sharp. They have two sons, Brian Keith and Carey.

8) Doris Kay married Gary McArthur, son of Shirley and Ester Belle McArthur. They had two daughters together, Michelle and Mandy.

The Pettingill Family lived in the Portland Bottoms where they farmed with a sizable community and the first seven of their children were born there. The flooding seemed a frequent occurrence, but in 1938 they moved out and stayed in Plumerville, where their last child was born. Luther Pettingill, as he was called by those who knew him best, was a very successful farmer. His income was like most during the depression years, required supplementing by hunting and fishing to survive.

Luther Pettingill loved farming. He continued improving his trade all his life. At one time the family farm had 1,200 acres in cultivation. All this was made possible by his lifelong beloved wife and partner, Mary Lola. She was a wonderful homemaker, working endless hours to provide the needs of such a large family. Family work, church and friends was what they loved. For a long number of years Annie Pettingill, Luther's Mother, lived with the family. Both Luther and Mary are buried at the Plumerville Cemetery.

PINTER - The Jacob Pinter family came to America in 1880 and bought a farm north of Morrilton in the Overcup Community. The family engaged in general farming activities. The children moved to different places and activities as they grew up. A son, Peter, remained on the farm. Peter and his wife, Anna

(Hoelzeman), had a family of three girls and seven boys. During WWII, five of their sons were in active military duty, a sixth son worked in an aircraft factory and the seventh son was conscripted for military service just as the war was at an end.

Pinter home built in 1893. People in the vehicle are Peter and Anna Pinter and one of their children. Time period is between 1910 and 1920 approximately. The mail box says "P. Pinter." The house was replaced in 1965.

The principal activities on the farm during that period of time (1900-40) consisted of very diversified activities. The family primarily lived off the farm and its products. Cotton was the mainstay cash crop and during this period for several years, sweet potatoes, Irish potatoes and strawberries played a prominent source of cash income. The farm raised and butchered quite a few hogs each winter and the meat was cured and had a ready market. There were always plenty of chickens to supply the egg and poultry needs of the family. The family always had several milk cows and fresh butter went to market. The farm always had quite an acreage of corn that went to feed the horses, mules, hogs and chickens on the place. With time, the milk cows number grew and in later years milk was sold to the local cheese plant.

Peter Pinter's youngest son, Ben, stayed on the farm and he and his wife Catherine (Siebenmorgen) spent 40 years operating a grade A dairy operation which produced milk for the local market for many years, and eventually went into the overall market for the state of Arkansas. The farm currently functions as a cow/calf beef operation.

Ben and Catherine are the parents of 16 children, one dying at birth. At the present time, children Jane (Ussery), Paul and Gerry live in the area and work in Morrilton. Mary Beth (Hard) lives in Iowa; Steve, Tim, Ed, and Ann (Basco) live in Little Rock; Dr. Mike lives in Nashville, TN; Nita (Moix) Rogers, AR; Teresa (Mallett) and Christina (Flake) in Conway and Patrick lives in Fort Smith, AR; Frank and Ben live in Fayetteville.

The family enjoys their frequent gatherings and still call Morrilton HOME! *Submitted by Ben Pinter.*

PLUMMER - David Edward Plummer (b. March 3, 1950, in Jacksonville, FL) the son of Russell Plummer and Oma Montene Hopkins, the grandson of Elbert Oriel Plummer, the great-grandson of Thomas Plummer and the gg-grandson of Samuel Plummer.

David married Peggy Sue Christiansen in February 1966. They had daughters Michelle Rene (b. July 5, 1966), Aundrea Sue (b. Dec. 8, 1968), and Jodi Lynn (b. Oct. 23, 1972). David married Cynthia Frances Spiering on Dec. 28, 1974. They had daughters Angela Suzanne (b. Jan. 28, 1977) and Audra Beth (b. Sept. 17, 1979).

David Edward Plummer and wife Cynthia Spiering Plummer

Angela S. Plummer, ggg-granddaughter of Samuel Plummer and daughter of David Plummer.

Audra B. Plummer, ggg-granddaughter of Samuel Plummer and daughter of David Plummer.

David has had an interest in genealogy and researching the Plummer line beginning in 1965. *Submitted by David Plummer.*

PLUMMER – Elbert Oriel Plummer (b. April 28, 1890, in Plumerville, AR) was the last child of Thomas Plummer and Julia Ann Miller, and the grandson of Samuel Plummer. Elbert's siblings were Josie E., Minnie Ann, John Samuel, Thomas Lewis, Lillie Retter, Benjamin Wallace, and his twin, Albert Carl, who died before reaching the age of 1.

Elbert's parents died when Elbert was 10 years old. Who raised Elbert? More than likely it was an older brother or

Elbert Oriel Plummer

sister. The loss of parents at an early age was an unfortunate occurrence that has happened in every generation of this line for 200 years. Samuel lost his parents at age 7. Samuel's son, Thomas, lost his mother at the age of 2. Thomas' son, Elbert, lost both of his parents at the age of 10. Elbert's son, Russell, lost his father at age 16, and Russell's son, David, lost his mother at age 13 and his father at age 17.

Elbert was referred to as "Uncle Gib." Elbert worked for the Missouri Pacific Railroad and died at 5:30 p.m. on March 26, 1928, when he fell off a bridge in Hermann, MO.

Elbert married Mary Alice Mosley, daughter of William H. Mosley, on May 21, 1911, in Conway County, AR. Mary Alice was born on Feb. 23, 1895, near Conway in Faulkner County, AR and died Oct. 4, 1973, in Farmington, NM. They had four children, all of whom were born in Plumerville, AR: Russell Plummer (b. May 10, 1912, d. Aug. 22, 1967, in Sioux City, IA); Royce Plummer (b. Dec. 24, 1913, d. Oct. 22, 1914, in Plumerville, AR); William Oriel (b. Aug. 20, 1916, d. Dec. 4, 1988 in Scott, LA); Nadine Plummer (b. July 19, 1919, d. April 8, 1921 in Dermott, AR).

Elbert's tombstone spells his middle name Orrell, while letters from his wife spells his middle name as Oriel, and his grandson spells his middle name Orriel. *Submitted by David Plummer.*

PLUMMER - Russell Plummer (b. May 10, 1912, in Plumerville, AR) was the son of Albert Oriel Plummer and Mary Alice Mosley, the grandson of Thomas Plummer and Julia Miller, and the great-grandson of Samuel Plummer and Henrietta Ells.

Russell married Oma Montene Hopkins of Mayflower, AR, on Jan. 14, 1939. Russell and Oma had three sons: Russell Oriel (b. Jan. 17, 1940 in Monroe, LA); Robert Allan (b. Jan. 16, 1949, d. Jan. 18, 1949) and David Edward (b. March 3, 1950).

Oma Hopkins Plummer died April 30, 1963, in Jacksonville, FL, and Russell Plummer died on Aug. 22, 1967, in Sioux City, IA, Both are buried at Oaklawn Cemetery in Jackson, FL.

Oma Hopkins Plummer and Russell Plummer

Sons of Elbert O. Plummer: (left) William O. Plummer; (right) Russell Plummer.

Russell served in WWII as an instructor in food preparation at Fort Hood, TX. He was in restaurant management for the majority of his working career. *Submitted by D. Plummer.*

PLUMMER - Russell Oriel Plummer (b. Jan. 17, 1940, in Monroe, LA) was the son of Russell Plummer and Oma Montene Hopkins, the grandson of Elbert Oriel Plummer, the great-grandson of Thomas Plummer and the great-great-grandson of Samuel Plummer.

(l-r) Russell Oriel Plummer, Sandra (Reda) Plummer, Caroline Frances Plummer, Jeffrey Michael Plummer, Lisa Marie (Duncan) Plummer, Jessica Ann Plummer, Jennifer Marie (Plummer) McDade, Scott McDade.

Russell married Sandra Reda on Sept. 1, 1961, in Lake City, FL, where they reside to this day. Russell and Sandra had two children, Jeffrey Michael Plummer (b. Oct. 21, 1964) and Jennifer Marie (b. Nov. 26, 1970).

Russell earned a degree as a pharmacist and practices his profession in Florida. Sandra was a registered nurse and practiced in this vocation for many years.

Jeffrey Plummer is a lieutenant commander in the US Navy and is currently stationed at the Pentagon in Washington, DC. Jeffrey married Lisa Marie Duncan on July 6, 1991. They have twin daughters, Caroline Frances and Jessica Ann, who were born on March 26, 1998.

Jennifer Marie Plummer married Scott McDade on Feb. 26, 2000. Jennifer and Scott make their home in Paducah, KY. *Submitted by D.E. Plummer.*

POE - Frances "Fanny" Harman Poe (b. ca. 1787 in Chatham County, NC) was the daughter of Hezekiah and Keziah Petty Dillard Harman. Frances grew up in Chatham County, NC. Her father, Hezekiah was a land holder and a Baptist preacher. Her grandfather, Zachariah Harman, was a well known citizen of Chatham County and held the position of sheriff of the county for a period of 11 years. Frances married Joseph Poe, son of David and Elizabeth Morton Poe, about 1807 and went to live on her grandfather's plantation where her husband, Joseph, was an overseer of the tobacco farms.

Frances and her family left Chatham County around 1814 and moved to Kentucky, possibly Todd County, where her brother Alexander and his family were living.

Frances and Joseph left Kentucky and moved to Tennessee, living first in Robertson County and later in Henry County. In 1839 Frances and Joseph moved to Pope County, AR. Shortly after their arrival in Pope County, Joseph died. Frances lived with her son, Josephas "Joe" Poe, until her death sometime after the 1850 census of Pope County was taken.

The following children were born to Joseph and Frances Harman Poe: Lydia (b. 1808, d. 1849 in Pope County) md. John Caudle; Mary (b. 1809) md. James Caudle; William D. (b. 1811, d. ca. 1865 in Pope County) md. Tabitha Ridgeway; John Morton (b. May 4, 1813, d. 1877 Pope County) md. Edna Turner; David Poe (b. 1815, d. June 24, 1895 in Linn County, KS); Keziah (b. 1818, died in Kansas) md. Kirney C. Kirby; Alexander H. (b. 1820, d. 1862 in Pope County); Josephas Francis Poe (b. Dec. 20, 1822, d. Jan. 15, 1897 in Pope County) md. Isabelle Jane Rankin; Sarah Francis (b. 1825) md. William E. Rowland. Josephas and Frances Harman Poe were the great grandparents of Maga Poe Watkins.

POE - George Marion Poe (b. Dec. 30, 1847 in Appleton, AR) was the son of Josephas Poe and Isabelle Rankin Poe. George's grandparents were Joseph and Frances Harman Poe of Henry County, TN and Robert and Isabelle Rankin of Gibson County, TN. They were early settlers of Pope County, AR. George's earliest known ancestor was an Englishman named Samuel Poe who settled in Essex County, VA in the early 1700s.

George M. Poe

George married Melissa Miranda Williams in Conway County on Oct. 3, 1872. Melissa was the daughter of John W. Williams and Miranda Humphries Williams. John and Miranda moved to Pope County after the Civil War from Walker County, GA. John served as Post Master of the Glass Village Post Office from 1872 until his death in 1878. John had the honor of having two Williams grandfathers serve in the Revolution and be present at the surrender of General Cornwallis to George Washington's army at Yorktown.

George and Melissa had the following children: Arminda Minnesota Poe (b. Aug. 8, 1873, d. May 15, 1946 in Clarksdale, MS) md. first, John Craig and second, A.G. Hartgrove; William Luther Poe (b. Nov. 18, 1874) md. Molly Roach; Rhoda Alice Poe (b. June 13, 1877, d. Aug. 17, 1953 in LeFlore County, OK) md. first, William Ramsey and second, Thomas Satterfield; Elijah Jackson Poe (b. June 17, 1879, d. Feb. 3, 1922 in Hulbert, OK); John Masterson Poe (b. Sept. 24, 1881, d. Aug. 23, 1967, Poteau, OK) md. Ida Couch; Maga Anne Poe (b. Jan. 13, 1885, d. March 19, 1958 in Morrilton, AR, buried Lost Corner Cemetery) md. Samuel Garfield Watkins.

Melissa Miranda Poe died March 26, 1889 and was buried in the Rock Springs Cemetery near Jerusalem, AR. George left Arkansas after the death of Melissa and moved to Oklahoma, and remained there until his death on March 4, 1935. He was buried in the New Hope Cemetery near Spiro, OK. *Submitted by Ginny Campbell.*

POE - Josephas Francis Poe, or "Joe Poe" as he was known by the family and in the community, was born in Robertson County, TN on Dec. 20, 1822. He was the son of Joseph and Frances Harman Poe. His family moved to Pope County, AR in 1839. His father, Joseph Poe, died shortly after their arrival. His mother, Frances, lived with him until her death.

Josephas Poe's family were originally from Virginia and Chatham County, NC. His grandfather, David Poe, was a soldier in the Revolutionary War, a member of the Third Regiment of the North Carolina Line. David's father, Simon Poe Jr., was a farmer in Chatham County. His grandfather, Simon Senior, was an early settler of Chatham County arriving there from Caroline County, VA in 1759.

Josephas married Isabelle Jane Rankin, daughter of Robert and Isabelle Rankin, on Nov. 8, 1842, in a double wedding with Isabelle's sister, Selena, and her fiancé, William Johnson. Josephas built a cabin in 1843 on 120 acres of land he later obtained title to by homestead grant in 1860, and began his marriage. Josephas and Isabelle were members of the Cumberland Presbyterian Church in Appleton. Josephas was the church secretary for a period of 40 years.

Josephas was a farmer, wagon maker and carpenter. He and Isabelle had the following children: Christopher C. Poe (b. 1845, d. April 4, 1887) md. Lucinda Gray and Lucinda Stewart; George Marion Poe (b. Dec. 30, 1847, d. March 4, 1935 in LeFlore County, OK) md. Melissa Miranda Williams; Theron Monroe (b. Oct. 12, 1849, d. Dec. 12, 1934); Mary Anne (b. April 22, 1853, d. Dec. 15, 1927) md. William Bachus; Martha Jane (b. Aug. 15, 1856, d. March 23, 1871); W.S. Poe (b. October 1857, d. 1858); Sophronia C. (b. July 31, 1861, d. Oct. 31, 1924) md. Stephen Powers, Marsh Harris; Sarah Ellen (b. 1864, d. March 21, 1899) md. Lee Jack Fisher; Dorietta (b. 1865) md. James Conley; Isabelle Frances (b. 1859, d. July 18, 1896) md. Cyrus Bartlett.

Josephas F. Poe died Jan. 15, 1897 and was buried in the Appleton Cemetery in Appleton, AR. Isabelle Jane Rankin Poe died Feb. 14, 1899 and was buried beside her husband in the Appleton Cemetery.

They were the great-grandparents of Arlie L. Watkins of Conway County, AR.

POLK - Jasper Allen Polk (b. Nov. 29, 1888) was a son of William Thomas Polk. Allen married Linner Ethel Mahan on Oct. 16, 1908. She was born April 13, 1893 and was the daughter of Jesse and Harriet (Stripling) Mahan. Jasper Allen Polk died April 5, 1928 and is buried at Center Ridge, AR.

Jesse Mahan was born in Hardin County, TN in 1855, died in 1909 and was buried at Old Whipple Cemetery near Center Ridge. Harriet Stripling was born in 1856, died in 1898 and buried at Center Ridge. Jesse and Harriet were parents of six girls and one boy.

Allen and Ethel Polk were active in church, community and social activities. Allen was a leader of the church choir and taught singing. He participated in sports and played in the first basketball game held at Center Ridge on Thanksgiving Day, 1906. Allen was a farmer, blacksmith and carpenter. They were parents of five sons listed below.

1) Laudis Thelbert Polk (b. July 14, 1909, d. Feb. 11, 1972, buried at Center Ridge) md. Dewel Mable Hartwick on Oct. 8, 1927. Dewel Mable (b. Jan. 26, 1909, d. Dec. 2, 1998) was a Van Buren County native. They were parents of two daughters: Bennie Yvonne "Snooks" (b. Aug. 4, 1935) and Rebecca Jane "Becky" (b. July 21, 1945).

2) William Jesse "Bill" Polk (b. June 6, 1910, d. Jan. 8, 1983) is buried at Yellville, (Marion County) AR. On Dec. 9, 1939, he married Mary Ardell Cowdrey (b. July 10, 1919). Mary now resides in Harrison, AR. Bill and Mary are parents of one daughter, Mary Elizabeth "Beth" (b. Aug. 26, 1944) and one son William Allen "Bill" (b. April 17, 1946).

3) Glyn Wood Polk (b. April 29, 1915, d. April 17, 1988) is buried at Center Ridge. On Sept. 16, 1946, he married Conway County native, Norma Montine Sledge (b. Nov. 18, 1918). Montine now resides in Morrilton. Glyn and Montine are parents of one daughter and two sons. Linda Lou (b. March 3, 1948), Glyn Allen "Bud" (b. Jan. 13, 1951) and John Gregory "Johnny" (b. Jan. 21, 1963).

4) Ardith Taylor "Puppy" Polk (b. Nov. 12, 1918). First marriage in 1935 to Bertie Stanton Bryant (b. Aug. 27, 1919), a Conway County native. They are parents of one son, Artel Lee Polk (b. Jan. 17, 1936). Second marriage on June 13, 1942 to Rosebelle Muliwai "Tura" DeMello (b. Feb. 24, 1923), a native of Hono-

lulu Territory of Hawaii. Tura died Dec. 2, 2002. They are parents of one son James Allen Polk (b. March 22, 1956). Ardith now resides in Center Ridge, AR.

5) Doris Bratton "Doc" Polk (b. Jan. 19, 1920, d. Dec. 26, 1959 in Mead, OK) is buried at Center Ridge, AR. On Sept. 3, 1949 he married Gertrude Roller, a native of Mead, OK. No children.

Ardith Taylor Polk, CWD US Army Retired. Pearl Harbor Survivor, WW II, Korea, 23 yrs. active military service.

After the death of the Polk boys' parents, the younger brother Glyn 13, Ardith 10 and Doris 8, lived with the eldest brother, Laudis and wife Dewel, both age 19, who had been married approximately one year. Bill, who was 18 at the time, was now living on his own.

The Polk brothers were sports enthusiasts, participating in baseball, football and basketball. After leaving the farm to pursue their careers, the boys were re-united in 1951 after 18 years.

For a more in depth look into the Polk family history see the *Conway County, Our Land Our Home, Our People.* See Robert Bruce Pollock (Polk) Family, William Carroll "Gosh" Polk Family, and The Jasper Allen Polk Family. *Submitted by Ardith Taylor Polk.*

PONDS - John Bascom "Backey" Ponds (b. April 1, 1868 in South Carolina) was the son of Michael and Francis Pond. Backey's siblings included Alice, George, Estella, Mary, Lizzie, Thomas, and Cromwell. Alice, George and Backey settled in Morrilton, while Thomas moved to Richmond, CA, and Cromwell lived in Salt Lake City, UT and finally in Oakland, CA. Alice married Richard Boozer and was the mother of Moses Davis (md. Elizabeth Washington), Anna

John Bascom Ponds

(md. Felix Mason), Otto, Richard Jr. and Naomi (md. Will Hensley). George married Ida Swagger. Alice and George also settled in Morrilton.

Backey married Ida Armstead from Tennessee on Dec. 31, 1891 in Conway County, AR. They were the parents of two children: Estelle Ponds (named for his sister) and Tollie Ponds. Ida died in childbirth in 1897 when Tollie was born. About 1903, Backey married Ella Mason from Tennessee. Ella's widowed mother, Mariah Mason, and her daughter Arabella Parks, also a widow, lived with Backey and Ella. Estelle died before she was 20 years old and Tollie died at age 22.

Backey's daughter, Estelle Ponds, married Arthur Nash. She and Arthur were the parents of one child, a daughter, Larlean Nash Oliver, who married Samuel Oliver, the son of Ferry R. and Margaret Oliver.

Backey's son, Tollie Ponds, and Ms. Bowles were the parents of a son, Zetora "George" Ponds who lived and died in Dallas, TX. He and his wife Julia Ann were the parents of a son Tollie Ponds II. Tollie Ponds and Mary Thornton Haywood were the parents of a son, Frank John Ponds. Frank married Mae Esther Brown and they were the parents of one child, a daughter.

Backey was a member of the St. Matthew Baptist Church west of Morrilton on what is called St. Matthew Hill. He worked as a sharecropper on or near what was known as Germantown and is now Kenwood, as did many of Morrilton Black American citizens. He eventually owned a house on West Broadway, in Morrilton, where he lived out the rest of his life. All four houses and lots on that block were owned by family members. Backey's granddaughter, Larlean Nash Oliver and her husband, Samuel Oliver, and their family lived with him and cared for him until he died. Backey died Oct. 20, 1945 in Morrilton, AR and is buried in Oddfellows Cemetery. *Submitted by Blanche O. Banks.*

PONDS - John E. "Jack" Ponds (b. June 5, 1891 in Morrilton, AR) was the son of George and Ida Swaggert Ponds, natives of Lexington County, SC. Ida was the daughter of Hannibal Swaggert. George and Ida were married March 23, 1888 in Morrilton. George died Feb. 4, 1916 and was buried in Bethany Hill Cemetery. Jack's brother Thomas Pervis Ponds (b. 1894) md. Delores Temple from Jamaica and settled in Everett, WA, where he worked as a landscape gardener. There were no children.

John "Jack" and Addie Ponds.

Jack married Addie Oliver in 1909. Addie (b. Oct. 23, 1888 in Morrilton) was the daughter of Reuben and Margaret Holland Oliver. Reuben and Margaret were the parents of Addie, Ferry Oliver, Charlie Oliver, and Julia Oliver Wells. Reuben was the father of three other children in a previous marriage. They were Mary F. Oliver (b. ca. 1869), James "Jim" Oliver (b. 1872) and Sarah J. Oliver (b. ca. 1874).

Jack Ponds was a soft spoken, proud man, who often walked in the shadow of keeping a thriving family of 10 children clothed, fed and sheltered. Jack was a sharecropper, an oil mill worker, and lastly a custodian for the Morrilton Public Schools at Sullivan High School. He worked dependably, consistently and faithfully until his retirement. Claude Ponds said that his mother was an organizer who budgeted, managed the money and paid the bills. Jack and Addie were faithful members of St. Paul A.M.E. Church.

John Ernest "Jack" died May 14, 1967 and is buried at Oddfellows Cemetery in Morrilton, AR. Addie died May 10, 1961 in Morrilton, AR and is also buried in Oddfellows Cemetery. "Jack" and Addie were parents of 10 children: James E., Marcus, Hattie Ponds Hart, Faye Ponds Jefferson, Pauline Ponds Wells, Charles, Hazel Ponds Waters Nelson, Mamie Ponds, Erby, Claude Ponds and Magdalene Ponds Hervey.

James married Lucille Manuel, daughter of William and Jessie Lafayette Manuel, and settled in Morrilton. The other children who settled in Morrilton were Marcus (md. Mary Smith); Hattie (md. Churt Hart); Faye (md. Rueben Jefferson); Pauline (md. Wood Olan Wells); Charles (md. Ruth James) settled in Everett, WA; Hazel (md. Fred Waters) lived in Little Rock, then moved to North Little Rock when she married W.D. Nelson; Mamie (md. Thomas Erby and raised her family in Kansas City, MO; Claude (md. Etta Wallace) and his family live in St. Paul, MN. Magdalene (md. Cardell Hervey) settled in Rockford, IL.

They imbued their children with a desire to succeed that was passed on to their descendants. Their descendants include a lawyer, a doctor, US Armed Forces officers, morticians, educators, carpenters, government workers, and other professions. Most importantly, these descendants are instilled with a work ethic, a sense of community service, and a strong spiritual connection evidenced by their active participation in the religious communities of their choice. *Submitted by Lillian Trimble.*

POTEETE - Jeff A. Poteete was born in Solgohachia, AR, on June 11, 1900. He was the second of five children born to Rufus C. Poteete and Roxie Ann Bearden Poteete. He had an older sister named Laura Ann and

younger siblings: Dora Lee, who lived less than two years, and brother Virgil Paul who died at age 4. His brother William was 9 years younger than Jeff. Jeff's paternal grandfather was William H. Poteete who came from Mississippi with Jeff's great-grandparents, Elvis S. Poteete and Mary Singleton Poteete.

Jeff Poteete and Maggie (Parker) Poteete - 1922.

They homesteaded in Conway County in 1862 with other family members. Jeff's paternal grandmother, Martha Ross Poteete, died before he was born. Jeff's maternal grandparents were Gus F. Bearden and Nancy Jane Autry Bearden, who also died before he was born. Jeff attended school from ages 5 to 18 at the Poteete School, which was located on land donated by his grandfather W.H. At age 9, Jeff started working as a field hand.

Jeff, his cousins and friends spent many hours at the Overcup creek where he was bitten in the foot by a copperhead snake in 1910. He had no ill effects. Jeff was a member of a baseball team named the Hickory Nut Knockers and a literary society.

In the winter of 1918-19, many people in Conway County had the influenza. Jeff and his mother, Roxie, went from house-to-house tending the sick. They both caught light cases of the flu. Jeff inherited his curly hair and his love of singing from his mother Roxie. His father taught him carpentry.

Margrete C. "Maggie" Parker was born on June 15, 1906, in Batesville, AR. Her parents were M.T. "Theo" Parker and Alice Spears Parker. She had one brother, John R. Parker, who was born in 1909. Maggie's paternal grandparents were Jake Parker and Mary Catherine Roseman Parker. Maggie attended school at Solgohachia and Overcup.

Jeff and Maggie met as children. They started dating in 1922 and were married on Feb. 25, 1923, at Overcup. They had three daughters: Lavene (b. March 6, 1927, in Morrilton); Nadene (b. Dec. 18, 1934 at Overcup); Gloria (b. May 28, 1947 at Lonoke). The family lived in the Morrilton area where Jeff worked as a farmer and carpenter. They raised a garden, had a milk cow, chickens and hogs. In 1940 Maggie and Jeff joined the Church of Christ.

Jeff, Maggie, and Gloria moved from Arkansas to the Oklahoma Panhandle in 1951, where Jeff and Maggie's oldest daughter, Lavene Smith and her husband Ray lived. Nadene followed when school was out.

In January 1953, Jeff began working for Panhandle State University in Goodwell, OK. Maggie died in June 1960, following a lengthy bout with cancer. Jeff lived at the college farm until June 1971, when he retired and moved to Guymon.

Jeff lived to celebrate his 100th birthday. He died on Aug. 25, 2000. *Submitted by Gloria Poteete Grice.*

POWELL - Hardin Powell and Angelica (Battles) Powell, who were both born in North Carolina in 1791, came to Arkansas from Tennessee in about 1845 with their six children. The eldest child, William (b. May 20, 1820), brought along his wife Susan (b. 1820), who was half Cherokee, and their two young daughters Mary Ann (b. 1842) and Rachael (b. 1844). The family settled in the Washington township area near Solgohachia. It is likely that some of Hardin's 11 brothers and sisters were already in the area.

William and Susan were farmers and would have seven more children to help run the family farm. Thomas (b. Aug. 21, 1848); twins Nancy and Charity (b. 1850); Sarah (b. 1854), John (b. 1856), and another set of twin daughters, Margaret and Susan (b. 1860). Susan, only in her early 40s, died sometime in the early 1860s, leaving William a widower with eight children still at home and the Civil War ravaging the country-

side. These must have been hard times for the family and William soon married a war widow Phoebe Caroline (Roberts) Gorento on Dec. 9, 1865. Phoebe (b. July 12, 1834) and her two children quickly settled in with the Powell family and soon another child was added, Josephine (b. 1866) and finally Isom (b. 1873). William died on May 29, 1881 and is buried at Old Antioch Cemetery just off Hwy. 95, about six miles north of Morrilton. Phoebe died Dec. 31, 1900 and is buried in Francis, OK.

The children all married and raised families except Charity and Susan, who we can find no record of after 1870. Thomas, William and Susan's eldest son, married Margaret Cooper on Sept. 14, 1871. They had one son, Richard. Margaret died soon after Richard's birth and Thomas then married Laura Ann Hall (b. Oct. 13, 1853), an orphan from Tennessee. Her parents, George and Anna Carolyn (Jackson) Hall ran a freight hauling business in Nashville and apparently both died during the Civil War. Laura and her two brothers, Thomas Payton "T.P." and James "Jim" came to the Jerusalem area with their maternal uncles, George and Jim Jackson. Jim raised Laura and James, and T.P. was raised by George.

Thomas and Laura had 10 children: Marion Daniel (b. Oct. 13, 1877); James Anderson (b. Dec. 12, 1878); Sarah Emma (b. June 29, 1881); twins, John Able and Morgan Lee (b. May 8, 1885); Benjamin Franklin (b. Sept. 4, 1888); Florence Mable (b. Nov. 15, 1890); Della Magnolia (b. Feb. 8, 1893), Josie Ellen (b. Nov. 27, 1895); Edward Washington (b. Feb. 6, 1899). Thomas died Dec. 5, 1922 and Laura on March 19, 1946, both are buried at Campground Cemetery on Lake Overcup.

Marion Daniel "Mamie," Tom and Laura's oldest child, married Inez Rosie "Rosa" Bostian (b. Jan. 13, 1883). She was the daughter of Charlie Alexander and Francis Elizabeth (Crowder) Bostian. Mamie and Rosa had nine children: Cora Estella (b. Sept. 6, 1899); Ella Elizabeth (b. June 28, 1901); Homer Alexander (b. March 15, 1903); Ernest Jackson (b. Oct. 1, 1906); Ethel Magnolia (b. Jan. 24, 1910); Inez Ola (b. July 25, 1916); Irene Lucille (b. July 25, 1919); Athula and James died in infancy.

Ernest Jackson "E.J." married Lela Marie Mullican (b. Sept. 29, 1909) on Oct. 25, 1925 at Old Hickory. Their marriage of over 66 years produced six children. The first son died at birth on Feb. 13, 1927; Glenn Jackson (b. Jan. 29, 1928) md. Joann Lasiter and had three children: Glenda, Janice and Steve; Gerald Ray (b. Feb. 3, 1930) md. Dorothy Green and had three children: Mike, Cathy and Mark; Alvin Daniel (b. Nov. 16, 1932) md. Johnnie Sue Williams on July 29, 1953 in Morrilton and had two children, Patricia Ann and Allen Troy; Thomas Faye (b. Feb. 4, 1937) md. Betty Green and had three children: Debbie, Gary and Neil; Thelma Jean (b. Nov. 30, 1938) md. Ernest McComb and had two children, David and Nancy.

Alvin Daniel and Johnnie (Sue) spent the first years of their marriage in Augusta, GA where Alvin was stationed with the US Army. Patricia Ann was born at Fort Gordon Army Hospital on Nov. 3, 1954. After a short visit to Arkansas following Alvin's discharge, they then moved to Wellington, KS, where Sue's mother, Zola May (Williams) Dusher, and Sue's stepfather, Bernard Dusher, had moved in 1951. Alvin and Sue went to work at the National Furniture Company, where Zola was also employed. Alvin drove a truck delivering furniture across the upper Midwest, where Alvin once said he had been to every town in North and South Dakota with a stop sign.

Allen Troy was born at St. Lukes Hospital in Wellington on Feb. 15, 1962. The family then moved to Wichita, where Alvin worked at Boeing Aircraft, then finally back to his chosen career, a truck driver for Winters Truck Line, where he drove until 1979, when a back injury ended his career. Pat married James Colby Harmon and had one daughter, Angela Ann. Pat resides in the Wichita area, where she owns a cleaning business. Allen married Mary Jo Orth and had two children, Allen Troy II and Andrew Aaron Travis. Allen then married Myra Jean German and had two children, Trevor Daniel and Blake Alexander Jean. Allen then married Jan Rene McCoy. Allen and Jan had no children and reside in the St. Louis area, where they own and operate an insurance agency with offices in St. Louis and Springfield, MO.

Sadly Ernest "Papa" passed away on Feb. 24, 1992 followed by Alvin on Sept. 16, 2002 and Glenn on Sept. 12, 2004. All are buried at Campground Cemetery. The family matriarch Lela Marie "Granny" is 95 and at this writing is still in reasonably good health with a sharp wit and a perfect memory, and is able to tell many stories from the "Olden Days." *Submitted by Allen Powell.*

POWELL - William Marion Hampton Powell, son of William Powell and wife Sarah, was born ca. 1810 in Georgia. His family, originally from Edgefield, SC, migrated through Georgia and Alabama, eventually settling near Aberdeen, Monroe County, MS, where William Powell died March 25, 1827. Sarah Powell was born ca. 1780 in South Carolina and died Aug. 16, 1852 in Lafayette County, MS.

William's siblings were Elizabeth Powell (b. ca. 1803 in Edgefield, SC); Bird Hampton Powell (b. Feb. 19, 1805 in Edgefield, SC); Sarah Powell (b. ca. 1811-1815 probably in Georgia); Charles Powell (b. April 22, 1816 in Georgia); Martha Powell (b. ca. 1817-1820 in Georgia or Alabama); Moses P. Powell (b. Oct. 19, 1821 in Marion County, AL) and Mary Ann Powell (b. ca. 1825 in Monroe County, MS).

William moved to Choctaw County, MS ca. 1835, where he met and married Margaret Faulkner in July 1837. Margaret (b. ca. 1815 in Edgefield, SC) was the daughter of Nathan Faulkner. Their first son Jesse Spear Powell (b. July 27, 1838 in Choctaw County, MS) was soon followed by son Charles Powell (b. ca. 1839). By 1840 William and family were in Chickasaw County, MS, where daughter Bramilla "Bramly" Charlotte Powell (b. ca. 1842) and son Salathiel M. Powell (b. ca. 1844) joined the family. Shortly after Salathiel's birth, William moved his family near Water Valley, Yalobusha County, MS, where sons, Nathaniel Hampton Powell and Isaac M. Powell, were born - Nathaniel on Feb. 2, 1846 and Isaac on March 30, 1848. William returned to Chickasaw County, MS, where son Moses Allen Powell was born July 1850 and daughter Margaret Samantha Powell was born ca. 1852. Last child was Eunice "Nicy" Sarah Letha Mary Elizabeth Powell (b. June 8, 1855, in Chickasaw or Lafayette County, MS).

William and Margaret resided in Dallas, Lafayette County, MS until 1870, migrating to Conway County in early 1872. With them came their sons, Isaac and Moses Powell; daughters, Margaret Samantha and Eunice "Nicy" Powell and grandson Andrew J. Smith. Son Salathiel Powell had died in Dallas, MS in 1862 and daughter Bramilla (Powell) Smith had died before 1870. Son Charles J. Powell with wife Mary, and daughters Sarah "Nicy" Powell and Bramilla R. Powell, also moved to Conway County. On May 3, 1874, son Isaac M. Powell married his cousin Mary Jane "Maude" Powell, daughter of Elizabeth and Levi Powell, and on the 23rd of December of that same year, daughters Margaret Samantha and Eunice "Nicy" Powell celebrated a double wedding. Margaret married John Stark Mason and "Nicy" married Jacob Presley Kennamer. In 1876 son Moses Allen Powell married his cousin Elvira Elizabeth Carpenter, daughter of Robert and Mary Ann (Powell) Carpenter.

William and Margaret's sons, Jesse and Nathaniel, stayed in Mississippi, marrying sisters Eliza C.J. Hood and Cynthia Elizabeth Malvina Hood, daughters of Reuben Harrison and Margaret (Hennegan) Hood. Jesse married Eliza April 17, 1861 and Nathaniel married Cynthia Feb. 12, 1874. By 1876 Jesse and Nathaniel had joined the rest of the family in Conway County.

In 1886 William and Margaret secured 76 acres near Center Ridge, AR. Their exact dates of death are unknown. Goodspeed published *Western Arkansas Biographies and Historical Memoirs: Conway County, Arkansas* in 1891, which included a biographical sketch on their son, Jesse Spear Powell. If Margaret was alive when the publication was printed, it does not state but William was "hale and hearty and in his 81st year." Both are believed to be buried in unmarked graves at Cedar Creek Cemetery, where grandson Jesse A. Powell is also buried. *Submitted by Jan Lawson.*

PRICE - Romie (b. 1911) and Florence Pruitt Price (b. 1914) of Dabney, AR, moved to the Morrilton area in the late 1940s, after spending several years in Malvern, AR, and Stockton, CA, during WWII.

1st row seated: Griff, Ethan, Donna Price, Luva Griffin. 2nd row standing: Willis and LaVada Price

They had their only son, Romie Willis Price (b. 1934) who attended school in Morrilton. During the late 1940s and 1950s, they operated a grocery store, used car lot, and eventually operated a Willys Auto Agency on Railroad Avenue.

Their son Willis married his high school sweetheart, LaVada Griffin, daughter of Barney and Luva Ferguson Griffin, in 1951 and lived in San Antonio, TX, until 1957 while he served in the Air Force. Upon returning to the Morrilton area he operated Price Motor Co. on West Broadway until 1966 when he joined Allison Ford Co. as sales manager. His wife, LaVada, joined the US Forest Service in Perryville, AR in 1961 where she served until 1994.

Their only son Romie Griffin Price (b. 1967) attended school in Morrilton. During the 1970s Willis remained as sales manager at the Ford Dealership until purchasing the Chevrolet Dealership in Morrilton in 1979.

During the 1980s, Romie and Florence passed away and in 1989 Willis sold Price Chevrolet, Inc. During the early 1990s Willis ran Price Motor Co. in Russellville, and eventually moved the company back to Morrilton. Their son Griff married Donna Windsor, daughter of Mike and Phyllis Windsor of Morrilton, in 1991 and later attended Petit Jean Vocational School. In 1998 he graduated from the University of Arkansas in Fayetteville with a bachelor's degree in architecture and went on to establish himself as an architect in the area. His wife Donna graduated from the University of Central Arkansas in 1991 and later became a teacher in the Perryville School District.

Griff and Donna's only child, Romie Ethan Price (b. 1999), attended school at Perryville, AR. Around the turn of the century, Griff and Donna returned to the Morrilton area, where Griff started his own business, taking on many architecture projects. Willis and LaVada spent their retirement years operating their car lot and traveling around the country. *Submitted by R.W. Price.*

PRINCE - Jeremiah Miles Prince, son of William Jasper and Martha Elizabeth Owens Prince, was born in Center Ridge, AR April 4, 1871 and died July 28, 1934. He married Sarah Caroline McMahan (b. July 3, 1875, d. Aug. 26, 1945) on Nov. 9, 1890. Their surviving children were:

The Miles Prince family.

1) Charolotta Elizabeth "Lizzie" (b. Aug. 28, 1891, d. Nov. 27, 1968).
2) Isaac Newton (b. Oct. 20, 1895, d. June 18, 1978) md. Della Jane Stobaugh.
3) Charity Jane (b. Nov. 7, 1897, d. May 21, 1991) md. Johnny W. Stobaugh.
4) Ethel Leona (b. Jan. 25, 1900, d. March 4, 1988) md. John Edmond Stobaugh.
5) John Orville (b. April 10, 1902, d. June 28, 1964).

John Orville married Reba Mae Dickson (b. Jan. 27, 1906, d. Sept. 24, 1979) on Aug. 5, 1921. (See Dickson history in *Our Land, Our Home, Our People*). They had two children:

1) Corba Earl (b. July 16, 1924 in Morrilton) md. Wynona Kirl Swanzy. Their children are Carolyn Swanzy and Holly Lynn Prince, who married David Shaw. Their children are Zackary and Clayton.
2) Gwendolyn "Gwen" (b. March 20, 1926 in Morrilton) md. Freddie Alfred Kirtley (b. Sept. 21, 1921 in Center Ridge, d. Dec. 13, 1985) on May 15, 1944. They had one son Freddie Earl (b. April 27, 1945 in Oklahoma City, OK). He married Linda Carol Fuller Poole on May 30, 1981. Their children are:
i) Jason Eric Poole (b. Oct. 27, 1971) md. Kristian Willis (b. Oct. 12, 1970) on June 12, 1993. Their children are Emily Brooke (b. Aug. 7, 1997), Andrew (b. Feb. 2, 2000) and Jack Thomas (b. Jan. 21, 2005).
ii) Veronica Rhae "Roni" (b. Feb. 25, 1983).
iii) Jaila Renee "Bugs" "Jr." (b. Dec. 28, 1984).
John Orville and Reba divorced and John married Gertrude Merrick (b. Jan. 14, 1908, d. Sept. 21, 1979). Their children were:
i) Mary Sue (b. July 22, 1929) md. Truman Thornton. Their children are Susan and Michael.
ii) Betty Lou (b. July 22, 1929) md. Charles Schonert. Their children are David, Terry and Carol.
iii) John Merrick (b. 1936) md. Peggy Murphy. Their child was Tia. *Submitted by Gwen Prince Kirtley.*

PRINCE – Miles, son of Isaac Prince and unknown wife Prince was born in 1815 in South Carolina and died after 1880 in Arkansas. He married Charity S. Halbrook about 1840; she was the daughter of William and Judith McGee/Magee Halbrook. She was born in 1815 in Tennessee and died after 1880 in Arkansas. Miles and Charity lived first in Perry County, TN near the Buffalo River and Cypress Creek.

In 1847 Miles helped to build the first house in Linden, 10 miles east of Perryville, Perry County, TN Deed Book Nov. 8, 1845 State of TN to Miles Prince, Page 507, a certain tract or parcel of land, containing twenty and one fourth acres by survey bearing date the tenth day of November 1845 lying in said county on Range Nine & Section Five on Buffalo River. This was a portion of the will of his father-in-law William Halbrook. Before the 1850 census Miles and Charity moved to Conway County, Lick Mountain Township, AR. Their children were:

1) Elizabeth "Lizzie" (b. Sept. 6, 1840, d. July 25, 1905) md. Alexander Gordon. Children: Joseph P., Roxie Ann, William Miles "Willie." She married

second, Isaac L. Bradley and their children were John, Charity, S. Buford, Maria, Isaac, A. Jasper.

2) Catherine (b. 1843 in Tennessee).

3) Sarah Jane (b. October 1845 in Tennessee) md. Joseph Watson. Children: William J., Charity C., Mary E., James H., Joseph M., Caroline, Manerva and John H.

4) William Jasper (b. June 2, 1846 in Arkansas, d. Aug. 4, 1897 in Arkansas) md. Martha Elizabeth Owens, the daughter of Ben Owens. Children: Isaac Newton, Sarah Elizabeth, Jeremiah Miles, Charity Stanten, William Fender, Joseph "Joe," Martha Ellen, Frances Jane, George, Rosie Maybell, Stanley, Ben, Judy Ann, Sophrona Cathryn "Cassie," Oliver B., James and Henry S.

5) Martha S. Ellen (b. 1851 in Arkansas) md. John Roland Polk Aug. 29, 1879. Children: Charity Ellen, Thomas Jefferson, Daniel Webster, Charles Alexander, William and Joe Taylor.

6) Johnathan F. "John" (b. 1853-55 in Arkansas) md. Sarah W. Foster in 1873. Children: Staton, Charity and Isaac J.

PRINCE - Roy Gene Prince Sr., son of Roy Junior and Willard Francis (Bryant), and Patricia Ann (Kuettle), daughter of Clemons and Esta Mae (Kissire), were married in 1965. Together they had four wonderful children: Cynthia, Roy Gene Jr., Esta Mae, and Alicia Francis. Roy Sr. works at United Motor Co. in Morrilton and Patricia is a homemaker.

Cynthia married Terry Lynn Epperson, son of Dole and Inez Epperson, in 1987. They had two wonderful children: Jessicia Marie and Trey Clemons.

Esta Mae married Robert Allen Gunderman, son of Charles Anthony and Ruth Ann (Swope), in 1986. Robert and Esta Mae had one child, Stacie Marie.

Roy Jr. married Theresa (Mays), daughter of Glen and Essie May Mays. Roy and Theresa had one child, Haley.

Alicia married Justin Lusk, son of Jim Lusk and Paula Lowe, in 2004.

Jessicia attends Morrilton High School, she is in the Beta Club, is on the Drill Team, and she plays the clarinet in the Morrilton Band. Trey attends Reynolds Elementary. Stacie attends Morrilton Middle School, she is in Beta Club, Science Club, Math Club, and is the treasurer of the CO Club. She also plays the clarinet in the Morrilton Band. Haley attends Bigelow Elementary.

PRINCE - William Jasper Prince (b. June 2, 1846 in Tennessee, d. Aug. 4, 1897), son of Miles and Charity Halbrook, is buried in Halbrook Cemetery. He married Martha Elizabeth Owens, daughter of Ben Owens. She was born April 1, 1849 and died July 1, 1933.

The Prince family, about 1916. Standing l-r: Martha Owens Prince Majors, Bill Majors, Sarah, Charity, Ellan, Judy, Cassie. Seated: Isaac Newton, Miles, Opal Mahan, William Fender, Joe, Oliver, Henry.

Their 17 children were Isaac Newton (b. Nov. 3, 1868, d. Feb. 8, 1940) md. Ellen "El" J. Polk; Sarah Elizabeth (b. Jan. 23, 1870, d. Dec. 30, 1960) md. first, William Thomas Polk on Jan. 1, 1887, and after his death she married second to James Robert "J.R." Dockins on Jan. 20, 1889; Jeremiah Miles (b. April 1871, d. July 28, 1934) md. Sarah Caroline McMahan

on Nov. 9, 1890; Charity Stanten (b. 1875, d. 1924) md. John H. Howard on Jan. 20, 1889; William Fender (b. Dec. 13, 1874, d. June 3, 1962) md. Rosa Hammond on Aug. 26, 1895; Joseph "Joe" (b. 1876) md. first, Maggie Brown on Jan. 25, 1895; his second wife was Lee Brown; Martha Ellen (b. 1877, d. 1933) md. Thomas J. Howard "Uncle Buddy" on July 14, 1893; Frances "Frannie" Jane (b. 1879); George; Rosie Maybell; Stanley; Ben (b. Oct. 19, 1882, d. April 3, 1904); Judy Ann (b. Oct. 19, 1882, d. Nov. 30, 1977) md. Benjamin Parker; Sophrona Cathryn "Cassie" (b. May 7, 1886, d. Oct. 22, 1953) md. John W. "Uncle Johnny" McNew; Oliver B. (b. April 1888) md. Ida Marlow in 1907; James (b. April 26, 1892); Henry S. (b. April 26, 1892, d. June 21, 1968) md. Lew Effie Stobaugh on Nov. 27, 1913.

William Jasper and Martha at one time owned a grocery store in Center Ridge. It was located in front of where the McNew House is now. Land Patent Records show on May 20, 1862, (original homestead entry) Document #4041 issue date May 20, 1885 from Little Rock Land Office, 120 acres. The description was NENE 34/ 10-N 15-W Van Buren County and W1/ 2 NW 35/ 10/N 15-W Van Buren County.

This land was at the time located in Van Buren County, but as boundaries changed, it became Conway County. After Jasper's death, Martha Elizabeth married William Merryman of Van Buren County. After his death, she married William "Bill" Majors. *Submitted by Melynda Thomas.*

PRUETT - Jefferson Monroe Pruett of Altus and Nancy Ann Zachary of Dover, married in 1902. Early in their marriage, they purchased a 110-acre farm at Old Hickory from his father, Tifford Milton Pruett. Jefferson Monroe and Nancy Ann began their family in Conway County. The family consisted of six sons and three daughters. These nine children married and produced 31 grandchildren. Many cousins of the Pruetts remain in Conway County and the surrounding area, such names as Allen, Blankenship, Hanna, Magar and Zachary.

Nancy Ann Pruett and her nine children, on her birthday, Oct. 29, 1938; front: Alva Pruett, Bonnie (Pruett) Lemingo, O'Della (Pruett) Venable, Edith (Pruett) Tackett, Nancy Pruett, Monroe Pruett; back: Elmer Pruett, Bill Pruett, Milton Pruett, George Pruett.

In 1945 Charles G. Venable and his wife, O'Della Maye Pruett Venable, purchased the 110-acre farm belonging to the heirs of Jefferson Monroe and Nancy Pruett. Previously, in 1942, the Venables had purchased Alf Cunningham's 60 acres from Mayne Hawkins. Later in 1966, they purchased 33-1/2 acres of the Taylor Bennett place. This combined acreage made a total of 203-1/2 acres bordering the corner of Mount Vernon and Granny Hollow Roads. Although Charles and O'Della lived in Morrilton, they ran cattle on the farm acreage. The land belonged to the Venables until their deaths and presently is owned by their two daughters and their spouses.

Thus, for over 100 years, the property has remained in the hands of Pruett descendants—a century of memories for the family. Memories continue in abundance for the grandchildren and great-grandchildren of the Venables. Present day memories include sleep-overs, hiking, fishing, 4-wheeling, ballgames and

picnics. *Submitted by Pat (Venable) Kissire and Shirley (Venable) Schnakenberg.*

PRUETT - Jefferson Monroe Pruett (b. Jan. 17, 1882, d. Feb. 12, 1936) and Nancy Ann (Zachary) Pruett (b. Feb. 12, 1882, d. Feb. 7, 1945) were married on April 27, 1902 at Altus, AR. Children were Elmer Lee, Mary Edith, Burl William, Alva Jefferson, Bonnie Dillard, O'Della Maye, Jesse Milton, Monroe Elisha and George Caleb. They were members of the Church of Christ in Granny Hollow. They are buried in the Old Hickory Cemetery.

Jefferson Monroe Pruett and Nancy Ann (Zachary) Pruett.

Mr. Pruett, as a young man, was a resident of Altus, AR, and worked for a short time in the coal mines around Altus and Denning. Ms. Pruett, and her family lived at Dover, north of Russellville. Mr. Pruett's father, Tifford Milton, and his second wife, Martha M. Horner-Adcock, lived on a 110 acre farm near the foot of Wildcat mountain on the Granny Hollow road. They had previously bought the property from Mr. Kibbie.

Behind their farm ran the West Point Remove creek. And down the creek a ways were several large bluffs, extending out over the water, where the young people loved to go swimming. This was called the Kibbie hole, named after Mr. Kibbie. Further down the creek, a quarter mile, upstream from the bridge, was Bluff Hole, a more suitable place to swim in. Tifford and his wife didn't live there long. She got homesick for her former home, and they moved back to Altus.

While living there on the farm, a child was born, and later died. They buried the child in the Mount Vernon Cemetery, located near the foot of Wildcat Mountain between the Cheeksville road and the Granny Hollow road. When they got ready to move back to Altus, they exhumed the body of the child and took it with them. The infant is buried in the Liberty Cemetery, at Altus.

About four years prior to Tifford and Martha's move back to Altus, J. Monroe and Nancy, who had gotten married at Alms in April 1902, traveled to Old Hickory in a covered wagon, which was about a three or four days journey, and purchased a small farm from Mr. Fellers. This land was about one mile east of the Hawkins store. While they lived there, three children were born: Elmer, Edith and Burl. When Tifford and Martha moved back to Altus, Monroe and Nancy sold the Fellers property and purchased his father's place. His father's property had a two story log house on it as their residence. They lived in the log house until 1919. Nancy's brother, Jess Zachary, built for them a large bungalow house near the log house.

While living in the log house, four children were born, Alva, Bonnie, O'Della and Milton. After moving into the new house, two more children were born, Monroe and George. Nancy and Monroe lived on the farm the rest of their natural life. After Nancy's death in 1945 the property was sold to a daughter, O'Della, and her husband, Charles Venable. After their death, their two daughters, Shirley Ann and Patsy Ruth inherited the farm. It's their desire to keep the property in the family. *Submitted by George Pruett.*

PRUETT - George Caleb Pruett lived on the farm with his mother. They planted a crop in 1944, and tilled the land during his last year in high school. On Aug. 2, 1944 he married Jackie Cody of Morrilton, and on August 7 he was drafted into the army.

George Caleb Pruett

With his departure, it left his mother to be alone on the farm, and his wife to live with her parents. George took his basic training at Camp Blanding, FL near Stark. Jackie went to Stark to be near him while he was in training.

In February 1945, after basic was over, his mother had emergency surgery. He got an emergency furlough to come home. He also brought home his wife, who was six months pregnant. A few days after arriving home, his mother passed away, and within three hours time Jackie gave birth to premature twin sons at her mother's home. They lived three hours. After burial of his mother and children, he was shipped overseas to Italy.

After the war they lived at Morrilton a while, then moved to Little Rock to go to college. They have lived in Pine Bluff since 1951. He worked 35 years with the government. They have two children, Pamela Jean and Kimberly Ann. *Submitted by Pamela Pruett Love.*

PRUETT – George was the last child born to Jefferson Monroe and Nancy Ann (Zachary) Pruett. He was born Nov. 21, 1924 at Old Hickory. He and his mother made a crop the year he graduated from high school at Wonderview in 1944. He married Jackie Cody, of Morrilton, Aug. 2, 1944.

He served two years in the Army during WWII. Five months was overseas duty in Italy. After the war he went to college under the GI Bill. After college he worked one year for the state as an auditor. He worked 35

George and Jackie (Cody) Pruett

years with the US Government. He and his wife have lived in Pine Bluff since 1951. Four children were born to this union, twin sons, who died at birth, two daughters, Pamela Jean and Kimberly Ann.

George, as a broker, and Jackie, as sales agent, managed a real estate business for several years in Pine Bluff. Since retirement, he loves gardening and maintaining their property. Jackie loves flowers and working in her yard. They are also very active in church work. George has written two books. One is entitled *A Son's Return to The Old Home Place*, a story about his home life on the farm with his family, Mother and Father and nine siblings. This book is on file in the Morrilton Public library. His other book is about his WWII experiences. *Submitted by Jackie Cody Zachary.*

PRUETT - Jessie Milton Pruett's father passed away in February 1936, leaving him and his two younger brothers to manage the farm with their mother. He quit high school to help run the farm. Milton remained on the farm for about three more years, then joined the CCC (Civilian Conservation Corps) and served in Ely, MN.

In the 1941-42 time frame, he left the CCC and worked as a carpen-

Jessie Milton Pruett

ter constructing barracks for the Army at Fort Leonard Wood and Neosho, MO. While in Missouri working, he married Pearl Hilderbrand.

In 1943 he was drafted into the Army. He trained at Fort Leonard Wood, after which he was shipped to the Pacific Theater of Operations. He saw action on Okinawa and was on Saipan when his mother died in February 1945. The Army refused him leave to come home for the funeral.

After the war he and his family lived in Oklahoma, operating a chicken farm and a restaurant. They later moved to California. He passed away Aug. 5, 2001. They had four children. *Submitted by Donna Pruett Cole.*

PRUETT - Monroe Elisha Pruett Monroe lived on the farm after his father died until 1941 when he married Mary Ruth Rainey of Morrilton.

In 1942 he was drafted into the Army. His basic training was in Freeport, TX. After basic he was assigned to Pamona, CA. He served in the Military Police.

After the war, he and his wife lived in Morrilton until the fall of 1946. They then moved to San Diego, CA with their

Monroe Elisha Pruett

three children. Monroe had a construction business, and Ruth operated a real estate office.

Their son Richard served in Vietnam and was seriously wounded. Monroe passed away in December 1986. *Submitted by Janice Pruett Evans.*

RAGSDALE - Thomas D. Ragsdale (b. 1803, d. 1878) and Mary Anne Kilgore (b. 1804, d. 1879) were married in 1823, probably in Robertson County, TN. They lived briefly in Humphreys County, TN, before moving to Conway County, AR, in 1833 or 1834.

Their first home was in Griffin Township, but by 1847, the family had moved to Union Township. Thomas D. established a farm, gristmill and cotton gin on Cypress Creek near where Highway 9 crosses the creek. The site was known as Ragsdale's Ford. On the map today, the area is termed Cypress Valley.

Thomas and Mary Anne had five children who survived to adulthood. Mary (b. 1830) md. Isaac H. Adams. They had a farm adjoining her parents' land. Sarah Jane (b. 1835) md. Dr. John Alexander Westerfield. Sarah Jane and John had a farm about two miles away. Louiza (b. 1838) md. John W. McCarley. They lived in Griffin Township. Louis (b. 1840) md. Isabel Boggess (b. 1849). Louis managed the family land after the Civil War. Margaret (b. 1842) md. Madison Elliott Moore and moved to his home in Greenbriar.

The Ragsdales and related families were prosperous. Thomas D. was a slaveholder. By 1860 he held six people whose work contributed to the family's success. Lewis was sent to college in Washington County, probably Arkansas College, until the outbreak of the Civil War.

When the war came, Lewis joined the 10th Arkansas Infantry at Springfield, AR, as first lieutenant of Co. K. He was in skirmishes in Kentucky, wounded at Shiloh, and captured after the fall of Port Hudson, LA. He was imprisoned at Johnson's Island on Lake Erie until the end of the war.

Although impoverished by the war and threatened by the civil disorders of the Reconstruction period, the Ragsdales and related families kept their land and were able to rebuild to a certain extent. Lewis operated the cotton gin and mill. Thomas D. died in 1878 and Mary Anne followed in 1879.

With the coming of the railroad, the related families took stock of their circumstances. Lewis, his father-in-law Charles Boggess, and brothers-in-law, John McCarley and John Westerfield, decided to leave farm-

ing and move their families to the railroad towns, now the centers of commerce, and enter business or the professions. They moved first to Atkins, then to Pottsville. The Moores and Adams elected to stay in Conway County.

Lewis returned to college at the Medical Department of the Arkansas Industrial University, forerunner of the present University of Arkansas Medical School, and graduated in 1886 at age 46. He held a medical license until 1914.

Lewis and Isabel had nine children: Albert Sidney Johnston (b. 1867), Charles (b. 1869), Excelsior Hannah (b. 1871), Mary Bell (b. 1974), Nettie (b. 1876), John Lewis (b. 1878), Robert Arthur (b. 1884), Nola Allien (b. 1889) and Wade (b. 1892). Five of the children: Sidney, E. Hannah, John, Robert and Wade, married and raised their children in Pottsville and Rusellville. Louis died in 1918. Isabel lived to be 97, dying in 1946.

RAINWATER - Edmund E. Rainwater was born in Spartanburg, SC, Nov. 28, 1850. His parents were Diana Bearden and Elias Rainwater. Berryman Hicks Bearden, father of John Will Bearden (Solgohachia area) was brother of Diana. The Rainwaters and Beardens came to Arkansas in 1852. Edmund is the grandfather of Jarrell Rainwater.

Seated: Edmond E. and Sarah Virginia Rainwater. Back l-r: Josie R., S.J. Bud, Charles E., William M. (relative of Sarah V.). Children in front l-r: Monroe, Arkie and Edmund E.

Edmund had five brothers and five sisters:
1) Nancy Christina (b. Feb. 22, 1842) md. S.V. Poteete, veteran of the Shiloh battle in the Civil War.
2) Rhoda Jane (b. Aug. 23, 1843) md. Joseph Daniel Poteete (S.V.'s brother).
3) Gustanna "Ann" (b. Jan. 25, 1845) md. Joseph Aldridge.
4) Jackson Daniel (b. Oct. 29, 1846), a Civil War Veteran, married Mary Roberts and after her death, he married Nancy Rowell.
5) John B. (b. 1848, d. young of "consumption" tuberculosis.
6) Robert (b. Jan. 30, 1852) md. Malissa Martin and second, Martha Ann Callahan.
7) Elias (b. December 1854), no other information.
8) Miles Benjamin (b. March 28, 1857) md. Pleasant Grinstead in 1879 and Deneatha Roberts in 1881 (Deneatha was a sister of Mary who was married to Jackson Daniel).
9) Mary A. (b. April 18, 1860) md. William Dunn.
10) Susan "Tice" (b. Dec. 5, 1863) md. J.C. Holmes.

Great-grandfather Elias died around 1863-64. In 1867, his widow Diana married Elvis Simeon Poteete, who was the father-in-law to her two daughters, Nancy Christina and Rhoda Jane.

Edmund married Sarah Virginia Poteete (b. Feb. 15, 1854), his little stepsister). My great-grandfather Poteete was married to both of my great-grandmothers on my Rainwater-Poteete side of my family. Edmund and Sarah had 10 children:
1-2) Saneter (b. 1875) and Rosette Ann (b. 1877), both died in 1878.
3) Charles F. (b. 1879) md. Sarah Callie Henderson; they had four children, all deceased.

4) William M. (my dad) (b. 1881) was married four times. First three wives died young; second wife had two sons, Virgil and Orrell, both deceased. My mother was Mollie Richardson of Center Ridge. Dad died in 1952 and Mom died in 1958.

5) Simeon J. "Bud" (b. 1884) md. Nancy Overton and Lavada Little.

6) Josie (b. 1887) md. John Gray, then Daniel Wright; she had five children. All are now deceased.

7) Edmon E. (b. 1889) md. Maude Hanserd, had one child, Faye Rainwater Sims of Morrilton.

8) Arkie D. (b. 1893) md. Henry Tiner, a first cousin of my mother; Henry was wounded in WWI and died young as did their two children. Bud has eight children. The only survivors are Louise Johnson of Overcup and Stella Lee Bearden of Kansas.

9) Monroe (b. 1894) md. Mary Pijot; they had three children, all still living: Miles Rainwater and Virginia Dillon, both of California, and Doris Jean Scroggin of Vilonia.

10) Burr (b. 1899) never married and drowned in the 1927 flood.

Grandchildren and great-grandchildren are too numerous to list in this account. Edmund E. died May 22, 1927 and his love since the Civil War, Sarah Virginia, died Nov. 23, 1916. She came to Conway County with the Poteete family from Tippah County, MS. *Submitted by Jarrell Rainwater.*

RAMER - John W. Ramer (b. 1798, d. 1874) was born in Kentucky to German immigrant parents. Around 1820 John married Elizabeth Lambert?? (b. 1800, d. 1835) and moved to Tennessee. Their Tennessee homestead became the town of Ramer, McNairy County. Their sons James, John and Andrew moved on to Arkansas, as did John's brother, thus establishing the Ramer name there.

Francis Marion Ramer with his grandson William Ramer Smith, summer 1944 in Plumerville, AR.

John's son Andrew B. Ramer (b. 1830, d. 1875) was ancestor of the Conway County clan. Around 1849 Andrew married Amanda Campbell (b. 1828, d. 1893) and they homesteaded thereabouts before 1860. Legend has it that Amanda was part Cherokee. Four of their children later lived in or near Plumerville: Mary Ann (b. 1861, d. 1923); John (b. 1864, d. 1945); Thomas Ruark (b. 1866, d. 1940); and Robert Daniel Ramer (b. 1868, d. 1919).

Mary Ann Ramer married John Vaughn. They had Willie (b. 1884, d. 1886); Ellen (b&d. 1886); Emma (b. 1887, d. 1969) md. Mark Jumper; Millie (b. 1890, d. 1986) md. Loma Faulkner; Elbert (b. 1892, d. 1929) md. Lonie Little; David (b. 1896, d. 1942) md. Dovey Williams; Ivey (b. 1899, d. 1900) and Julia (b. 1902, d. 1996) md. J.O. Scoggin.

John Ramer married Nellie Hugg. They had Cordy (b. 1896, d. 1963) md. Ella Fryer, who had Abby. Cordy married second, Susan Tiner, and they had Cordy Jr. (md. Maude McGarity) and Bobbie Jean (md. Bradley Thomas).

Ruark Ramer married Edith Griffin. They had James (b. 1887, d. 1966) md. Rachel Allen; Joseph (b. 1890-?) md. Josie Lindsey; Carrie (b. 1892, d. 1970) md. Homer Hall; Roy (b. 1894, d. 1972) md. Rachel; Eula (b. 1894, d. 1985) md. Will Martin; John (b. 1896, d. 1968) md. Clyde Groom; Myrtle (b. 1898, d. ?) md. Tom Atkinson; Pearl (b. 1900, d. ?) md. Duff Atkinson; Bertha (b. 1903, d. ?); Clara (b. 1904, d. ?), m. Gilmore; Earl (b. 1907, d. ?); Paul (no info.). Ruark married second, widow May Talley and they had Clarence.

Robert Ramer settled near Solgahachia. There in 1888 he married widow Mary Ann Catherine Hansard Birchfield (b. 1856, d. 1929), daughter of William J.S. "Buck" Hansard (b. ca. 1817, d. 1894) and wife Martha Loftis (b. 1828, d. 1906). Robert and Mary had Martha (b&d. 1889); Francis Marion (b. 1891, d. 1957); Noah "Barney" (b. 1894, d. 1918); Belle (b. 1898, d. 1977) and Lucy Ramer (b. 1901, d. 1976).

Barney Ramer married Ruby Reeves (b. 1900, d. 1918). They had Frances Elizabeth (b. 1918, d. 1919). All three died of influenza during the 1918-19 pandemic.

Belle Ramer married Roy Hogan (b. 1897, d. 1979), son of Joseph Hogan. Belle and Roy had Mildred (b. 1919, d. 2000) md. Roy Reynolds; Bonnie married Herbert Adams; Roy (b. 1924, d. 1925) and Joseph (b. 1925, d. 1966) md. Mary Griswood.

Lucy Ramer married Clyde Ramer's brother, Bryan Groom (b. 1899, d. 1993), son of Hewaska and Rachel Reddick Groom. Lucy and Bryan had Edwin (b. 1923, d. 1925); Ralph (b. 1926, d. 1975) md. Sybil Staggs and second to Bonnie New; Wanda married William Pryor.

Marion Ramer married in 1913 Amanda Licena "Sena" Roach (b. 1894, d. 1982). Her parents were Joseph D.M. Roach (b. 1856, d. 1935) and wife Amanda Ellen Stell (b. 1856, d. 1909). Marion and Sena had Raymond Loyd (b. 1916, d. 1980) and daughter Frances Marian. Loyd married Ruby Jackson, daughter of Adam Jackson of Morrilton. Frances married Jesse Dewey Smith (b. 1914, d. 2004) of Moro, AR.

Starting out, Marion Ramer taught school and worked as a bookkeeper. In 1923 he acquired a Plumerville mercantile store that he operated until his death. In the 1930s he supervised construction of a portion of the Arkansas River levee. He was elected mayor and served on the school board at Plumerville. Twice he was elected Conway County Clerk. *Submitted by William Ramer Smith.*

RANKIN - Barton "Bart" Edwin, son of Henry Clay and Emma B. Mulkey Rankin was born Dec. 23, 1892 in Perry County, AR. He died Jan. 14, 1930, at age 38 of typhoid fever and pneumonia at Robertstown, Conway County, AR. He married Mattie Lenora Barrett on March 12, 1911, in Conway County. Mattie (b. Sept. 19, 1894, in Cleveland, Conway County, d. Aug. 28, 1982, at age 88) was the daughter of Bill and Annie Andrews Barrett. Mattie's mother died when she was little and her grandmother, Granny Andrews, raised her. Bart and Mattie are buried at Robertstown Cemetery.

Barton "Bart" Edwin Rankin and Mattie Lenora Barrett Rankin.

Bart and Mattie were parents of J.C., Alvin Barton, Loweda, Annie Oleta, Nona Ruth and James Edwin. All were born in Robertstown.

J.C. (b. July 1, 1913) md. Syble Mae Massingill on March 15, 1941, in Conway County. Syble (b. May 25, 1921, in Old Hickory in Conway County) was the daughter of E.M. "Mad" and Jessie Ford Massingill. Syble died in July 2004 in Morrilton and was buried in Old Hickory Cemetery. They were the parents of Brenda Mae (b&d. Feb. 7, 1943) and Rebecca Ann (b&d. Dec. 12, 1944). Both are buried in Old Hickory Cemetery.

Alvin Barton (b. May 6, 1915, d. Dec. 25, 1996, in Conway County) was buried in the Robertstown Cemetery. He married Minnie Mae Franklin on Jan. 18, 1936 in Conway County. She was born Feb. 16, 1916, at Wetumka, Hughes County, OK. They were the parents of Donald Barton (b. Jan. 14, 1940 at Robertstown); James Doyle (b. Nov. 23, 1943 at Richmond, Contra Costa County, CA); Bobby Dean (b. January 1937, d. Jan. 8, 1937, buried at Robertstown Cemetery).

Loweda (b. Sept. 19, 1917, d. March 10, 1991 in Texas) md. Arthur Raymond Harrelson in Conway County. He was born Dec. 5, 1911, and died June 19, 1982 in Texas. They are both buried in the Robertstown Cemetery. They were the parents of James Barton, Arthur Ray Jr., Mary Anna, Mattie Sue, Rankin Dee, William Jay and Debra Jane.

Annie Oleta (b. Oct. 11, 1921, d. 1999/2000) md. Troy L. LeFler on Aug. 3, 1940, in Conway County. He was born March 10, 1917, in Scotland, Van Buren County, AR and died Nov. 24, 1954, in Conway County. Both are buried at Robertstown Cemetery. They were the parents of Oleta Ruth and Troy Lee Jr.

Nona Ruth (b. May 19, 1924) md. James Bernard Porter on April 24, 1939, in Conway County. He was born Sept. 11, 1919, in Conway County and died Oct. 9, 1976, in Morrilton. They were the parents of Lenora, James David and James Bernard Jr.

James Edwin (b. Sept. 16, 1928) md. Juanita J. Stracner on Sept. 30, 1950 in Morrilton. She was born Oct. 9, 1931 in Conway County. They were the parents of Barton Edwin and Kimberly.

Bart and Mattie made their home in Robertstown. They farmed their own land, planting crops, and Mattie worked in her garden. Bart owned and operated a sawmill.

The children attended school in Jerusalem, which was a three-mile walk to and from home. All of them had chores to do on the farm.

In 1930 Bart died, leaving Mattie a widow at age 36, with six children. These were hard times, but they were survivors. It took the family working together and each one doing their part in the hot, dry summers and cold winters. *Submitted by W. Dilbeck.*

RANKIN – Henry Clay Rankin and Emma B. Mulkey married in Perry County, AR. They made their home in Rankin Township and began their life together. All their children were born there. They were parents of Fred, Barton Edwin, Lalie Abigail, Lillie Mae, Charles Henry, Lois Augusta and Grace Pearl.

Henry Clay Rankin and Emma B. Mulkey Rankin.

1) Fred (b. March 1887, d. 1907/08 of pneumonia, buried Antioch Cemetery, Perryville, Perry County, AR) md. Essie Cantrell (b. September 1903, Perry County).

2) Barton Edwin (b. Dec. 23, 1892, d. Jan. 14, 1930) died of typhoid/pneumonia at age 38, Robertstown, Conway County, AR. He married Mattie Lenora Barrett on March 12, 1911, Conway County, AR. Mattie was born Sept. 19, 1894, Cleveland, Conway County, AR and died Aug. 28, 1982, Conway County, AR. Barton and Mattie are buried at Robertsville Cemetery, Conway County, AR. They were parents of J.C., Alvin Barton, Loweda, Annie Oleta, Nona Ruth and James Edwin.

3) Lalie Abigail (b. Aug. 11, 1893, d. Sept. 1, 1981, Shawnee, Pottawotomie County, OK at nursing home/hospital) md. Sept. 23, 1910, Conway County,

AR to Ples Lee Watson (b. May 10, 1891, Conway County, AR, d. June 30, 1972, at hospital, Oklahoma City, Oklahoma County, OK). Ples and Lalie are buried Wetumka, Hughes County, OK. Ples and Lalie, parents of Floy Mae, Grover Lee, Mavis Jewel, R.D., Ova Etheline, Zelma Rea, Lois Fay "Sonny" and Billy Wayne.

4) Lillie Mae (b. April 1894) md. Floyd Fisher about 1912, Conway County. She was pregnant with twins, got the measles and died at age 21 in 1915, Conway County. She is buried in Conway County. Floyd is buried Wetmuka, Hughes County, OK. He joined US Army and served in WWI. Floyd and Lillie were parents of a daughter Dona Mae (b. Aug. 21, 1913, Conway County, d. Dec. 11, 2000, Wetumka, OK, buried Wetumka Cemetery).

5) Charles Henry (b. May 1899, d. 1912) died at age 13, appendicitis, Conway County, buried at Robertsville Cemetery.

6) Lois August (b. Sept. 15, 1902, d. April 21, 1991, Tillamook, Tillamook County, OR) is buried Bay City IOOF Cemetery, Oregon. Married Sept. 27, 1921, Conway County, to Velma V. Cleek (b. March 6, 1906, Graysborg, Cape Girardeau, MO, d. June 3, 1977, Portland, Multonomah, OR, buried England, Lonoke County, AR). Lois and Velma were parents of David Thaddeus Augustus, Phillip Henry, Lois "Lela" Mae, Bobbie Jean, William Charles, Betty Jo, Herman Lee, Juanita and Janice Earl. Second marriage was to Vesta Whitten of Oregon; they were parents of Patsy Ann Rankin.

7) Grace Pearl (b. Aug. 3, 1903, d. Sept. 26, 1971, Tulsa, Tulsa County, OK) md. July 19, 1918, Conway County to George William Hanna (b. Sept. 25, 1898, Old Hickory or Cheeksville, Conway County, AR, d. May 29, 1978, Tulsa, OK). George and Grace are buried Robertsville Cemetery. They were parents of Lillie Olevia, Euell Henry, Mary Loreda, Georgia Pearl, Mildred Jewel, Carrell William, Cecilia Joyce, Everett Louis, James Henry and Vivian Faye.

Henry, age 18, and Emma, age 19, began their life together. Henry's life ended at the age of 36, due to pneumonia. Emma B., a strong willed, hard working, Christian, had the strength to endure the years to come as a young widow to raise her children. Emma lived to be 77. *Submitted by W.M. Dilbeck and mother.*

RANKIN – Henry Clay (b. September 1867, Perry County, AR, d. April 1903, Rankin Township, Perry County, AR), son of Edmond Hogan Rankin and Nancy Jane Spears Rankin, is said to be buried Antioch Cemetery, Perry County. Mary Loreda Hanna remembers visiting the cemetery with her mother, Grace Pearl Rankin Hanna.

Henry Clay married Emma B. Mulkey, Aug. 16, 1885, Perry County, AR. Emma B. (b. Jan. 13, 1866, Illinois, d. March 8, 1943, Granny's Hollow, Conway County) is buried Robertsville Cemetery, Conway County. Emma B., daughter of __ Mulkey, born in Illinois, and Delila Dell Safford Mulkey, born in Louisiana.

Delila Dell married Hugh Close in Illinois. Hugh, born in Texas, was a construction worker. They were parents of son Edgar Close (b. July 13, 1871, Illinois).

Delila Dell married Joseph Benton Turner in Illinois. They were parents of Herbert, "Hoot," and Isaac "Ike," and others. Herbert and Isaac were best known to children of Henry and Emma.

Henry and Emma made their home in Rankin Township, Perry County. Emma, a housewife, and Henry who worked as a lumberman in the sawmill, were parents of Fred, Barton E., Lalie A., Lilie M., Charles H., Lois A. and Gracie P., all born in Perry County.

Henry and Emma endured pain, hardship, and poverty but together they had the strength to overcome.

Henry took pneumonia and died, age 36. Emma, age 37, was left with seven children to raise. She and the children moved to Robertstown to be close to her half brother, Edgar Close, and other family members.

Emma and the children lived on a farm. They farmed the land and the boys worked at the local sawmill. When Barton Edwin was older, he owned his own sawmill.

Grandma Emma, as she was known, developed severe rheumatoid arthritis. She would not take any medicine. She was a devout Christian, reading her Bible daily.

Doc. Close wanted to send Emma to Hot Springs, AR for treatments, but she refused. Emma's health grew worse so she went to live with Lalie A., her daughter, in Wetumka, OK. She missed her friends and family in Granny's Hollow and went back to live her final days with her youngest daughter, Grace Pearl Rankin Hanna and family. *Submitted by Mrs. Robert C. Dilbeck.*

RANKIN – J.C. Rankin (b. July 1, 1913, Robertstown Community, three miles south of Jerusalem in Conway County, AR) was the oldest child of Barton Edwin Rankin and Mattie Lenor Barrett Rankin. He attended school at Jerusalem.

He married Syble Mae Massingill, March 15, 1941, Conway County, AR, daughter of E.M. "Mart" and Jessie Ford Massingill of Old Hickory, Conway County, AR. Syble attended school at Wonderview

J.C. Rankin and Syble Mae Massingill Rankin

while growing up. Syble (b. May 25, 1921, Old Hickory, d. July 2004, Morrilton, Conway County, AR) is buried Old Hickory Cemetery.

They were parents of two daughters, Brenda Mae (b. Feb. 7, 1943, d. Feb. 7, 1943) and Rebecca Ann (b. Dec. 12, 1944, d. Dec. 12, 1944), both are buried Old Hickory Cemetery.

J.C. and Syble made their home in Morrilton, Conway County, AR. J.C., a lifetime "lumber man" from his teenage years until his retirement from the Pinecrest Lumber Company, just outside of Morrilton. J.C. was a city alderman for 16 years in Morrilton, serving the community.

Syble retired from Ben Franklin Variety Store in Morrilton after many years of service as a sales clerk.

Both were members of the Calvary Baptist Church in Morrilton.

J.C., at the age of 88, still enjoys playing his fiddle with family and friends, and at Community Center and nursing home. He learned to play when he was in school and they put together a string band.

Our thanks to J.C. and Syble for a great visit in 1996, sharing their family history.

J.C., now 91 years old, is a patient at a nursing home in Morrilton. *Compiled by Wanda Mae Dilbeck (Rankin family cousin).*

RANKIN - One of the great-grandfathers of Arlie L. Watkins was Robert Rankin. He married his cousin, Isabelle Rankin, the daughter of Robert and Mary Cusick Rankin. Isabelle was the descendant of a Robert and Rebecca Rankin of Letterkenny, County Donegal, Ireland. They arrived in the colonies in 1750, settling in Lancaster County, PA. They moved to Guilford County, NC in 1753. Many of their descendants settled in Rowan County, NC, and McNairy and Gibson counties in Tennessee. Robert and Isabelle migrated to Pope County, AR in 1838.

Robert, Isabelle's husband, was born in 1787. His parents are unknown. Children born to Robert and Isabelle were Margaret D. Rankin; George W. Rankin (b. 1821, d. 1843 in Pope County, AR); Salenda (b. 1823) md. William Johnson; Isabelle Jane (b. Sept. 14, 1826, d. Feb. 14, 1899, Pope County, AR) md. Josephas Poe; Robert M. (b. Nov. 9, 1827, d. Sept. 17, 1894) md. Nancy Burns; Anthony L. (b. Jan. 3, 1830, d. Jan. 4, 1892) md. Patience Jones; William (b. 1832, d. 1862) md. Arabelle Hallock; Ruben (b. May 4, 1834, d. Aug. 17, 1909) md. Nancy Nash.

Robert was a farmer. He died in 1845, leaving Josephas Poe as the administrator of his estate. It was probated in Conway County. Robert was buried in the family cemetery located on his farm in Appleton, AR. Isabelle (b. 1791 in North Carolina, d. 1861 in Pope County) lived the rest of her life in Appleton, AR. She was buried in the family cemetery beside Robert and her son George, who was accidentally killed in 1843.

RASMUSSEN - Todd Stephen Rasmussen was born in Glendale, CA, in 1945 to Axel Peter Rasmussen and Barbara Jane (Van Amburgh) Rasmussen. Todd was reared by his mother and stepfather, Adolph Carpenter, who was a career soldier; thus, Todd became an "army brat" and lived in several states and Germany. When his stepfather decided to retire to Mountain Home, AR, Todd decided to attend Arkansas Tech in Russellville. While he was a student at Tech, Todd met and married (in 1966) Mary Clyde Davis who was from Hot Springs. Mary Clyde, the daughter of Helen Katherine (Isely) Davis and Jesse Jennings Davis Jr., was born in Hot Springs in 1946.

Todd Rasmussen family, shown at 2004 wedding of Jamie Rasmussen and Joe Bratton; l-r: Todd Rasmussen, Katie Rasmussen Jackson, Jamie Rasmussen Bratton, Victoria Jackson, Jeff Rasmussen holding Brooklyn Jackson. Second row: Mary Clyde Rasmussen, Joe Bratton, Jeff Jackson.

Both Todd and Mary Clyde graduated from Arkansas Tech in 1967 with degrees in English. That summer they moved to Morrilton with their son Jeffery Stephen Rasmussen (b. May 1967). Todd and Mary Clyde are both teachers—Todd is certified to teach secondary math, English, computers, and serve as a secondary principal. Mary Clyde is certified to teach English and elementary grades. They both taught for 30 or more years in various schools in Morrilton and Perry County until they retired. Upon retiring from public school teaching, Todd began working for Petit Jean College, which later became UACCM. Jeff Rasmussen is a graduate of UACCM and is a self-employed draftsman.

A daughter, Katherine Leigh, was born to the couple in 1971. She married Jeffrey Reese Jackson in 1994. They are the parents of two daughters, Victoria Katherine (b. 1996) and Brooklyn Reese (b. 2000). Katie, a graduate of UCA and St. Vincent's School of Radiology, is employed at St. Anthony's Hospital. Jeff Jackson is employed at Arkansas Kraft and attends school part time at UACCM.

Another daughter, Jamie Frances, was born to Todd and Mary Clyde in 1983. Jamie is currently a senior at UCA and plans to teach high school English upon graduation. Jamie married Joseph Allen Bratton in 2004. Joe is an electrician and employed by Little Rock Electrical Contractors. Jamie is the stepmother of Joe's daughter, Paizley, who was born in 2002. *Submitted by Mary Clyde Rasmussen.*

REDDIG - Susie Doss Reddig was sixth generation of Scotch-Irish immigrants who settled in Virginia in 1661. Her great-great-grandfather John Doss Sr. of Pittsylvania County, VA, served in The Virginia Continental Line commanded by General George Washington during the Revolutionary War. John Doss Sr. and John Doss Jr. both served in the East Tennessee Militia during the War of 1812. Her grandparents, John and Rebecca Walis Doss, moved to Arkansas and settled in Sharp County, AR. Samuel Newton Doss, her father, traveled to southern Missouri after the

Susie Doss Reddig

Civil War and stayed in Ozark County, MO, where he met and married Martha Jane Daves.

Susie Doss was born in Ozark County, MO on June 23, 1890 to Samuel Newton and Martha Jane Daves Doss. Her father Samuel was killed three months before her birth. Martha Jane and her four small children moved from Missouri to Pope County after Susie was born. Times were very hard for a widow with four children and under pressure of day to day of struggling. Martha had to give Susie and her brother Eldy to neighbors to raise. It was during that time and unknown circumstances that Martha and the other two children, Virgil and Ada, seemed to vanish. My grandmother lost contact with her mother.

Time passed and Susie was taken in by the Lehman Lemley family and worked as a servant at the age of 9. After she became a young woman she worked at the Potts Inn at Pottsville, AR. Jobs were scarce for women at the turn of the century and she cooked and cleaned to earn her keep. Shortly after working as a cleaning maid she began to care for the sick and elderly in the area. She was a kind and loving caregiver and was often sought for her loving care by many in the community.

It was in Pope County that she met William Grant Reddig. They lived on a houseboat on the Arkansas River, traveling up and down the Mississippi River. My grandfather painted smokestacks for a living. He at one time was first mate on a steamboat and navigated the Mississippi from Galveston, TX all the way up north beyond Missouri. They eventually went back down south and settled in Conway County.

Mr. W.G. "Shorty" Reddig established two cotton gins in Conway County and along with several partners owned and operated the "Copperhead Mercantile Store" in Plumerville. Cotton was "King" and the city of Plumerville was thriving at that time. The family was starting to grow and times were good.

Susie found her mother, brother Virgil and sister Ada living in Conway County. Mr. "Shorty" hired the Pinkerton Detectives and her brother Eldy's body was brought from the Oklahoma Territory. Martha Jane Doss who was blind and in failing health lived and was cared for by Susie until her death in 1929.

Today the old home still sits above Town Creek in Plumerville on Reddig Hill. The old homeplace was built before the Civil War. Amanda "Aunt Mandy" Matthews, who helped with the large Reddig brood, told my grandparents her parents were slaves to the original owners of the old place. It was she who helped establish the age of the original dwelling. After she retired she was killed when her clothes caught on fire.

Shorty and Susie raised their 12 children and brought them up in a Christian home. They attended the First Baptist Church. My Grandfather's name can be found on the cornerstone to this very day. Mr. W.G. passed away while on a business trip to Hot Springs in 1932. Susie had a long hard road ahead of her but with her "grit and determination," she conquered every obstacle placed before her. Susie held the family together through some very hard times. Hard work was no stranger to my grandmother. She operated the government sponsored Canning Kitchen and taught local women how to can and preserve food and she once again cared for the people of the community, when she worked as a nurse at St. Anthony's Hospi-

tal in Morrilton. The family didn't have many luxuries, but love and happiness were abundant and plenty for all.

In 1980 Susie Doss Reddig was called to her place in Heaven. A reward for a life well lived and a job well done. The old house still sits atop "Reddig Hill" and if you listen closely you can hear the music and laughter of generations of Reddig and Doss descendants. It remains in the Reddig family and is owned by James Kurtz, grandson of W.G. and Susie. The once big family of 12 is now only four: Dave Reddig, Louise Reddig McArthur, Rose Reddig Kurtz and Jean Reddig Lear. I live across the street and can look fondly at the "old place" whenever I want. This gives me great joy and peace for I was raised there and memories of my grandmother are strong.

"Mrs. Susie" never knew her father, who was half Cherokee, or from whom she descended. In 1999 I began searching with a tin-type photograph and Samuel Newton's name. After an incredible journey through countless volumes, numerous courthouses, I have been able to piece together the missing history of her family and heritage.

To my grandmother, family was precious because she knew very little about hers. How proud she would be of her heritage. Strong brave ancestors who came to the new land and helped settle this great nation. A grandmother who was of Cherokee birth. Great-grandfather who fought for freedom. Hardy pioneers who went west and cleared the wilderness. My grandparents were brave to venture out on the "Mighty Mississippi River" to raise several of their children on a houseboat. Anchoring at the "bottoms" south of Plumerville, putting down roots and helping build a community.

I lovingly dedicate this to her memory. Sandra Kurtz Samoyedny, granddaughter, Doss descendant, ninth generation.

REED - James Reed (b. Nov. 12, 1821 Tennessee, d. April 3, 1887 Conway County, AR, buried at Pleasant Hill Cemetery) moved his family to Van Buren County, AR prior to 1860, then to Lick Mountain Township in Conway County prior to 1875 where he remained the rest of his life. He lived in Alabama, Georgia and Bradley County, TN before settling in Arkansas. He was a farmer and Baptist Minister and a member of the Pleasant Hill Baptist Church in Conway County. During the Civil War he served in the CSA with General Price on his raid into Missouri.

James married three times. His first marriage was to Sarah Elizabeth Smith who died before 1858 in Tennessee. Their children are Joseph, James M., William W., Archibald, Nancy Elizabeth and Melvina. There is no information on Joseph or James. The 1860 Van Buren census record indicates that Archibald and William were born the same year and probably were twins. Archibald was not found in the 1870 census and may have died young.

William's first wife was Rebecca Lacy, second wife Sutha M. Halbrook and third wife was Louisa Jane Mahan. Nancy Elizabeth married Robert Bolen Gordon and Melvina married Alexander Gordon. Robert and Alexander Gordon were sons of Robert Boaz Gordon and Milly Pitts who migrated to Conway County in the mid-1840s.

James Reed's second marriage was to Anna Fuller. They married about 1856 in Arkansas and their children are Rosa Ann and Martha. Rosa Ann married Thomas W. Scroggin, a son of John Scroggin and Mary M. Inglebright.

James Reed married a third time to Mary Moody (a widow) on July 15, 1875 in Springfield, Conway County AR. Their children are Mary M. "Maggie," Robert A. and Charles Elmo. Charles married Emma May Stobaugh, daughter of Elisha Stobaugh and Mary Williams.

James Reed is my great-great-grandfather and information in this article is based on data received prior to February 2001. Additional information on the

Reed family can be found at http://www.angelfire.com/ar2/reed. *Submitted by Sharon Smith.*

REEDY - Charles Reedy (b. 1770, d. 1859), son of Clement and Mary (Hill) Reedy, emigrated to Tennessee to the town of Readyville in 1797. He was a historical lecturer and trailblazer. The Reedys are of French and English origin. Their shield is French. The oldest line of my family emigrated from France to Lincolnholt, Hampshire England in 1430. They emigrated from England to Glouchester County, VA in the early 1600s. From there to Tennessee, where my family came from.

I am a descendant of Col. Augutus and Mildred (Reedy) Warner, who married Lawerence Washington, grandfather of General George Washington, also the daughter of Mary Lee (Reedy) Fitzhugh, Mary Lee Randolph married General Robert E. Lee.

My great-grandfather was John Henry Reedy (b. 1865, d. 1910), a descendant of Charles Reedy, who settled in Readyville, TN. He married first Martha Mathis (b. 1868, d. 1895) and second, Clara Grisson (b. 1873, d. 1947). Children were Bertha (b. 1888, d. 1970); Verna (b. 1890); Joseph (b. 1891); Sarah (b. 1893, d. 1984); Eliza (b. 1895); Clarence (b. 1906) and Viva (b. 1901). The Reedys come from a long line of musicians and politicians - a cousin, Tom Reedy, was mayor of Faulkner County, AR.

Joseph "Jodie" (b. 1891) md. Pearl Barker. Children: Auby (b. 1916, d. 1978) md. Orel Smith. Children: Sammy (b. 1944), Ruth (b. 1944), John (b. 1944), Patty (b. 1954) md. Hubert Stoneger, Leona (b. 1946) md. Paul Pritchard.

Eliza (b. 1895) md. Burl Holland. Children: Zenobia (b. 1915) md. Loyd Thompson; Carmel (b. 1928) md. first, Noel Heavington and second, Al Brown.

Sarah "Sallie" (b. 1895) md. first, William Mabry and second, Baxter Setzier.

Bertha (b. 1888, d. 1970) md. first, Buddy Gibbs and second, Tom Wheatley. Children: Inez, Ruby, Eldon, Audrey, Howard.

Viva (b. 1901) md. first, Carroll Atkinson and second, Tommy Kimberlin.

Clarence (b. 1905, d. 1962), my grandfather, married Eunice Bush (b. 1907, d. 1979). Children: Richard (b. 1953) md. first, Pamela Page and second, Patricia Machen. Children: Richard Jr. (b. 1971) md. Alicia Simmons (child) Richard Thomas (b. 2003), Kelsey (b. 1990). Randall (b. 1955) md. Renee Keith, one child, Cheyenee (b. 1991). Robin (b. 1957).

Vancel Paul (b. 1941, d. 1989) was a disc jockey and nightclub owner. He married first, Judy Kirby; second Janice Hutchins; third, Gigi Gookin; fourth, Cherylinn Padechwits. Children: Paul (b. 1964), a musician. Three children: Clinton (b. 1987), Kelsey (b. 1992), Leleb (b. 1994). Jackie (b. 1963) md. Slyvia Willis. Child: Taylor, Tangela (b. 1970) md. Paul Cullum. Children: Brianica (b. 1988), Bretzen (b. 1994), Britzen (b. 1995).

Naomi (b. 1976), child: Alexis (b. 1995).

Vanessa (b&d. 1983).

Vanna (b. 1985).

Carolyn Ailene (b. 1944) md. Joe McHenry. Children: Dee Ann (b. 1963) md. Johnny Poteete. Child: Joseph Dalton (b. 1992).

Mark Todd (b. 1965) md. Traci Hitchcock. Children: Relee and Ryan (b. 1998).

Reva Jo (b. 1950) md. first, James Brailey and second, Bill Hayes. Children: Aisha Credit (b. 1976). Natasha (b. 1972) md. Authur Williams. Children: Authur Brandon (b. 1999), Maxwell Keaton (b. 2001), Elijah (b. 2002).

John Horace (b. 1924, d. 1999) was a concrete block maker, musician and songwriter. He sang on the radio in his early years. Married first to Mary Owens and second to my mother, Janie Bell Nicholson Dec. 23, 1960. Children: Shelia (b. 1957) md. first, Joe West and second, David White. Children: Dayton West (b. 1974), child: Kane (b. 1997). Reanna White (b. 1979), child: Haley (b. 1997).

Rhonda Renee (b. 1962) is a musician and singer. She was in the Olde Tyme Kuntry Band, A Little Bit of Ark (Play) on Petit Jean with the Our Town Players and the Our Town Singers. She still performs around the county. She married first, Gregory Tanner (b. 1974), child: Shaun Greggory (b. 1992).

I am the only Reedy in Conway County, the rest of my family lives in Faulkner County and Texas. *Submitted by Rhonda (Reedy) Tanner.*

REID - Alexander Reid, our first immigrant ancestor, was a Scots Highlander, born in Ulster, Ireland about 1698. He married Margaret McKay in Ireland about 1725. He died in Rowan County, NC, Jan. 11, 1775. According to his will, proved in 1777, he was old and very infirm. George Reid I (Esquire), fifth son of Alexander, the progenitor of the Arkansas Reid family, may have been born in Ireland. He married Margaret Katherine Chambers in June 1767 in Rowan County, GA. George and his sons made numerous claims from 1802 to 1835 for compensation for losses incurred during the Indian Wars. George Reid I and heirs were compensated for a total of eight horses "stolen" by Creek Indians. George Reid II (b. Nov. 27, 1774, in Rowan County, NC) md. Jane Gaston in 1798 in Greene County, GA. George was given permission to pass through Cherokee land on June 14, 1803. He served two terms in the Georgia State Legislature, fought in the War of 1812, and was commissioned captain in February 1813. He was also Justice of the Inferior Court 1819-21. His second son, Asa, is our Arkansas forefather.

About 1818 Asa (b. Feb. 14, 1799 in Gwinnett County, GA) md. Winney Castleberry (b. Feb. 19, 1800 in Georgia, d. Jan. 4, 1880 in Arkansas). Asa paid taxes in Conway County for the year 1846 in Lick Mountain Township. Later on they moved to Smyrna, on the banks of Point Remove Creek near its junction with Brock Creek. Asa and Winney are thought to be buried in the first Smyrna Cemetery or possibly in the McKay Cemetery. Winney's family had migrated to Arkansas in 1840. Henry Reid, sixth child of Asa and Winney, was my great-grandfather and 15 years old in the 1850 Census, Lick Mountain Township, Conway County. The siblings of Asa who continued on to Oklahoma refused to file for their Indian (Cherokee) Head Rights, and could not own land there. It is ironic that Point Remove is named for the gathering place where the Indians were held for shipment to Oklahoma via the Arkansas River. One long-time resident told me that his father was hired by the sheriff to guard large groups of prisoners there. This should be near the site of Cherokee Park at Morrilton.

Henry Reid married first Ruth Ann Prince (b. April 22, 1837, d. April 18, 1873, buried in the Smyrna Cemetery); he then married Eliza Ann Meeler. Eliza deeded the land for the Reid Cemetery. Eliza's sister and her brother Hosea Meeler are listed on the Cherokee rolls in Oklahoma. Henry served in the Union Army, and was a member of the GAR (The Grand Army of the Republic), founded in 1866. He listed himself as 6 feet 1/2 inches tall, light complexion, dark eyes. He died March 3, 1905 of a lung ailment contracted during the war. Henry and Eliza were the first Reids to occupy the log home known as the Reid House, which he helped build. Many generations of Reids, including myself, were born in the house. After the WWII, Grandpa Jim Reid sold the place to his nephew, Bill Reid of Morrilton, who promptly sold it to Arden Freeman and wife. The house was taken down and some of the logs were used to construct a corncrib, still standing across the road from the Reid Cemetery.

James Henry Reid "Jim" (b. March 12, 1877, d. Aug. 26, 1964 in Dos Palos, CA) md. Emma Senora Byers (b. Dec. 17, 1879, d. July 14, 1964, in Dos Palos, CA). Both are buried in Reid Cemetery, Allred, and Pope County, AR. The Henry and Jim Reid families spent part of the time in Oklahoma and part of the time in Arkansas. Eliza died in Oklahoma and was transported back to Arkansas for burial in the Reid Cemetery as she wished.

My father, Chester "Chek," was the fourth child of Jim and Emma. He married Nina Webb of Jerusalem and they had six children:

1) William Jackson, Lilbourn, MO, married Alfreda Vines (child Robin married Tanya Beasley, child Lindsey).

2) Lonnie Lee has children: Elizabeth (children, Jennifer and Alexander) and David (children, Blake and Zachary).

3) Ilda.

4) Barbara married Robert Wilson, child Rebecca (children Myka Dorshea and Jasper Ann Wilson).

5) Don L. was killed at 20 in an auto accident in California and is buried on Petit Jean Mountain.

6) James Ray who died in infancy and is buried at Matthews, MO. *Submitted by Ilda Reid.*

REID - Ilda Mae Reid (b. Oct. 1, 1935 in the Reid family log home at Smyrna, I am proud of that. The logs were squared, and I was grown up before I realized it was logs and not boards; there were rifle slits in the walls for protection and very few windows. At one time 120 guests and family members spent the night after a musical evening. There were only two main rooms, with a dog trot breezeway, a half back porch and full length front porch; kitchen with wood stove, very long plank table, and shelves across one end of the kitchen to hold all the fruit and vegetables Grandma canned to feed the crowds. The attic was huge, and it was there that Grandma kept her spinning wheel. The stairs were narrow and made a square turn.

It was a very happy place to grow up, with horses, cows, dogs and cats, there were children everywhere. We all lived within a half-mile, and there were no restrictions on where we could go or what we could do. Mud pies with real eggs (depression time with large families pooling income and eating most meals together). Grandpa Jim Reid did all the shopping. He took credit for creating the fashion of shorter and leaner dresses for women. Grandma always asked for 10 yards of material for a new dress. He watched it measured and cut, then decided that was too much material for such a tiny person. He then instructed her to use the 10 yards for TWO dresses!

There was lots of family, swimming, picking huckleberries, blackberries, wild plums, apples, etc. with Grandma Reid and all available cousins. Mealtimes had 15 to 30 people as a rule. The men ate, then the women and children. All the cooking was done on a wood cook stove. Fresh bread was baked for every meal, usually two kinds. There was always singing, story telling, and games. Grandma was well known for her ability to heal with herbs gathered with the assistance of whatever grandchildren were available. She may have been my inspiration to become an RN.

I married Elwood L. Calvert, born in September in Morgantown, WV. We met on a blind date and married eight days later in St. Louis, MO. Cal spent over 20 years in the US Army. While stationed in Taiwan, we traveled to Japan, Hawaii, Hong Kong, Kowloon, Guam, the Philippines, and Okinawa. While assigned to the Netherlands, we traveled to W Berlin, Belgium, Luxemburg, France, Spain, Switzerland, Portugal and to West Germany frequently. We also visited every state, plus Canada and Mexico and lived in many of them. Our children are:

1) Terri Ann Calvert Haines, RN, San Antonio, TX, was born March 9, 1953, Dos Palos, CA. Children are William Ramon Guzman, married to Melissa Smith, Memphis, TN. Children: Dalton, Chandler, Marshall and Wyatt. They are serving as Presbyterian Missionaries in Honduras at this time. Robert Eric Guzman, Las Cruces, NM. Bobby is raising his adopted brother, Dylon King. Angelique Michelle Richards, Sissy's children are Adrian, Tristan and Jimmy (who died at birth and is buried in the Reid Cemetery). Terri is divorced from both fathers.

2) Carla Raye Calvert Yeates, respiratory program assistant, San Antonio, TX, was born June 29, 1954, Herlong, CA. She married John Vernon Yeates in El Paso, TX. John retired after 20 years in the Army and died from Vietnam related illness in Memphis, TN. He is buried in Reid Cemetery. Children are James Elwood Stanley Yeates who married Eileen Collins in Las Vegas, NV, one child, Colin. Jesy is an engineer with John Deere now serving in Iraq as a captain in the National Guard. Johnette Vivian Yeates, elementary schoolteacher, married Wayne McWhorter near Hondo, TX. Their children are Bridgett, Bryana and Ashley Gail.

3) Chester Rink Calvert, OTR Truck Driver in Iraq. Children: Sonya Lynn Calvert who married Richard Sparks and their children are Caitlin and Chelsea. They live in San Angelo, TX. Gary Calvert, Russellville, AR. Another son, Brian Calvert, died in infancy and is buried at Walnut Grove in Pope County. Rink is divorced from their mother.

4) Ellen Lorraine Calvert, artist and art dealer, Clought, France and Memphis, TN, was born Jan. 25, 1960 in Morrilton, AR. Children are Jesse Dale Condley, Hot Springs, AR and Cameron Victor Calvert, Carnathan, France. Lori is divorced from both fathers.

5) Kris John Leon Calvert, 18 year Navy Veteran, building sub-contractor, Hattieville, was born May 13, 1961 in Morrilton, AR. He married Norma Jean Keene, trainer for ICT, in Morrilton, AR by Judge Jimmy Hart, followed by a covenant marriage in Maine. Children are Brandi Lee Calvert, Nashua, NH; Casey Jay and Justin David Calvert, Hattieville. Kris is divorced from their mother.

I was truly blessed to be able to spend so much time with my grandparents, cousins and other relatives while growing up, and I tried to pass that onto my children and grandchildren by keeping all of them for the summer months so that they could be together. Cal and I live at Jerusalem in a partially finished and partially converted garage. We would like to spend more time sailing, and are active in volunteer work. We also spend a lot of time with our children and grandchildren, traveling to visit and baby-sit. We have had a very interesting and varied life, believing in God and family and America, and we always return to Conway County. *Submitted by Ilda Reid Calvert.*

REYNOLDS FAMILY ROOTS - Our record starts when Christopher Reynolds was born in Kent County, England in 1530. He married and had all boys: George, Christopher, John, Thomas, Cornelius, Richard and Robert.

George Reynolds, son of Christopher Reynolds (b. 1555 in Kent County, England, d. 1634 in London, England) md. Thomasyn Church on Jan. 20, 1585. They had four sons and daughter: Thomas, John, Robert, Ann and Christopher.

Thomas Reynolds (b. 1590 in England), son of George Reynolds, married a woman named Mary. Together they had Rachel, Mary, John, William, Thomas, Cornelius, Edward and Richard.

John Reynolds (b. 1650), son of Thomas Reynolds, was in the United States when he married Sarah Grimes on Aug. 5, 1647. They had four children: twins, Jeffery and John, and Robert and Ann.

Robert "Bob" Reynolds (b. Jan. 6, 1677), son of John Reynolds, married a woman named Frances. They had Dominick, George, Robert, Rebecca, Ann and William.

William Reynolds (b. Feb. 10, 1725 in Nansemonc County, VA), son of Robert Reynolds, married Henrietta Hamilton. They had James, Jacob, William, Richard, Thomas and Hamilton. (The Reynolds family believes that the brothers, John and William Reynolds, are the same John and William Reynolds who appear in Alex Haley's novel *Roots*. The brothers lived in the right place at the right time, and lived on plantations with slaves. As in the novel, John was older than William).

Hamilton Reynolds (b. Oct. 3, 1761 in Anson County, NC), son of William Reynolds, married a Jewish girl named Rachel Clemet (b. Oct. 10, 1775 in Cob County, GA). They had 11 children: Huriah, Elizabeth, David, Nancy, Isaac, Clements, Polly, Millye, Henry, Hamilton, and Thomas. Rachel Clemet died in 1833. Hamilton, who lived to be 100 years old, died in 1861 in McNairy County, TN.

Huriah Reynolds (b. Nov. 5, 1791 near Ashland, NC), son of Hamilton Reynolds, married Elizabeth Hamm (b. Aug. 13, 1800, d. 1882). They had 14 children: Thomas Hamilton, William Carrall, Nancy Emily, James Marion, John Wiggin, Pheobe Jane, Huriah, Wesley Blasengame, George Riley, Joseph Pleasant, Anderson Pinkny, Winston Pettus, Elizabeth Darinda and Richard Randolph. Huriah and Elizabeth then settled in northern Alabama in Pruitton. Anderson Pinkny Reynolds had a daughter named Vetura Octavia (b. Feb. 14, 1873).

Wesley Reynolds (b. March 10, 1833, d. July 23 1901), son of Huriah Reynolds, married Sara Angeline Brewer on Nov. 9, 1854. Sara (b. Aug. 22, 1838, d. Feb. 5, 1936) was half Native American. Wesley married at age 21 and Sara was only 16. The family lived on a plantation and owned slaves. They owned about 100 slaves when the Civil War ended. Wesley and Sara told how the "colored people cried because they had nowhere else to go." After the war, the family had nothing left. They moved to Arkansas with one old "Nanny goat." The couple had 11 children: George Raymond, James Alexander, Thomas Hamilton, Elizabeth Forrest, William Hickman, Emily J., Hugh Randolph, John W., Anna Gertrude, Minnie Dorinda and Sherril K. Emily J. died at the age of 6.

George Reynolds (b. Aug. 8, 1856), son of Wesley Reynolds, married Sarah Ann Plunkett. They had twelve children, including James Randolph Reynolds.

James Randolph Reynolds (b. 1890 in Conway, AR, d. 1956 in Cave Junction, OR), son of George Reynolds, married Ruth Lueva Tackett (b. 1891 near Jerusalem, AR, d. Nov. 7, 1971 in Grante Pass, OR). They had Wilma Lee, Eldon Dee, Clifton B., Bernie Rhea, and two others who died as infants. Clifton B. died June 8, 1974.

Eldon Dee Reynolds (b. Aug. 14, 1924), son of James Randolph Reynolds, married Minnie Kathleen Huneycutt on Dec. 23, 1949. They had Keith Owen and Patricia Ann. Eldon Dee died Jan. 21, 1985 and Minnie Kathleen died Nov. 6, 1998.

Patricia Ann Reynolds (b. Feb. 25, 1961), daughter of Eldon Dee Reynolds, married Ricky D. Houston from Highland, IN. They had Ashley Diane, Kelly Eileene and Carly Kathleen. *Submitted by Carly Houston.*

RIDLING - The ancestors of Andrew J. Ridling came from Rotterdom, Holland. Jacob Von Reidlinger and family came on the ship *Queen of Denmark* in 1751 and settled in Lancaster County, PA. The name was changed at the Port of Entry.

Records show that the family owned property and sold it before moving to Coweta County, GA in 1836. Some of the family remained in Pennsylvania.

l-r: Roxie Dutton, Clara Brown, Fannie Ridling, Evelyn Sroczynski, Luther Ridling, Andrew Ridling, George Ridling and Thelma Marie Miller.

Moses Franklin Ridling moved his family to Conway County, AR about 1885.

Andrew Jackson, son of Moses Franklin Jr. and Laura Jenkins Ridling, was born Oct. 16, 1884 in Coweta County, GA and moved with his family as an infant. He died Sept. 30, 1962 in Morrilton and is buried in Middleton Cemetery on Dutton Mountain. In 1901 he married Frances "Fannie" Bradley, daughter of George and Laura Russell Bradley. She was born in Chicago, IL on May 10, 1882 and died March 25, 1957; she is buried at Middleton Cemetery. Her parents were from County Cork, Ireland. Her father died shortly before she was born and her mother when she was about seven months old, leaving her an orphan. Jessie Jacob and Lavica Evelyn Dutton Hall brought her to Morrilton and raised her at 306 N. St. Joseph St.

Their children: Thelma Marie was born Nov. 22, 1904 at Middleton, AR, died Aug. 14, 1963 at Lone Grove (St. Vincent) and is buried in Calvary Cemetery in Little Rock, AR. She married Michael J. Miller of St. Vincent on July 15, 1927 and had nine children: Rose Marie, Mike Jr., Margaret, Theresa, Mathilda Jo, Matthais, Carl, Imelda and Jim.

Roxie Ridling (b. Nov. 30, 1907 at Middleton, d. Jan. 29, 1992 in Oklahoma City, OK) md. Dewey Dutton of Dutton Mt. on April 4, 1930. Their children: John Lee, Vernon, baby girl buried in Middleton Cemetery, Euna, Athelene Guenter, Burvil Dean, Patsy, Barbara and Mary. They all lived in Oklahoma City.

Homer Ridling was born in 1910 and died in an accident Dec. 25, 1927 in Little Rock and is buried in Calvary Cemetery.

George Ervin Ridling (b. Nov. 11, 1911, d. May 4, 1973) md. Mary Caldonia Collins (b. May 25, 1925, d. July 12, 1993). Both are buried in Middleton Cemetery, Conway County, AR. Their children: Georgia, Willie, Catherine Brown and Lidea Mealler.

Christina Ridling died at about 8 years old and is buried in Lone Grove Cemetery.

Clara (b. 1914, d. April 18, 1994) md. Murrel Brown (b. 1900 in Ardmore, OK, d. 1970), both are buried in Oklahoma City, OK.

Twin Boys, unnamed about 1912, are buried in Lone Grove Cemetery.

Luther Monroe Ridling (b. April 17, 1916, d. July 21, 1992) md. Imalee Collins (b. Sept. 12, 1920, d. Aug. 1, 1987), both are buried in Middleton Cemetery. Their children: Ruby Jackson, Mary Jackson, Linda Norwood, Janice Rowe, Dwight and Luther Jr.

Evelyn Ridling (b. Nov. 17, 1919, d. Oct. 1, 2003) md. Harold Sroczynski of Detroit, MI on Oct. 28, 1944. Harold (b. Aug. 2, 1917, d. June 1, 1996) and Evelyn are buried in Middleton Cemetery. Their children: Frances (Glen) Summers, Jim (Sue) Lewis, Wayne (Sue Ann) and Donnie Sroczynski.

John Henry and his wife, Kansas Tiner Ridling, on Jan. 13, 1903 gave Lone Grove Baptist Church a deed to property to be used for a church and cemetery with an added note that any relative would be buried there without cost. J.H. Kaufman and Fred Hutto signed the deed.

School was also held in the church building for several years. My dad, uncle and aunts attended: Mike, Nick, Annie, Kate and Josephine. The education they received was excellent and prepared them for their futures. *Submitted by Mrs. Henry Miller*

ROACH - Samuel George Roach Sr. (b. Oct. 28, 1892 in Lyles, TN), was the son of John Wesley Roach and Margaret Elizabeth Green Roach. He had three brothers: Stanley, Wesley and Hollis, as well as three sisters: Jennie Roach Sensabaugh, Docia Roach Gooch and Mozell Roach Merrick; three half brothers: Lonnie, Weldon, General, and one half sister, Mary. Sam was married in Conway County to Olevia McGehee (b. June

Samuel George Roach Sr.

27, 1895) by Reverend Jim Alford. They were the parents of Inez, Bernice and Samuel George II, known as S.G. Olevia died Feb. 1, 1932 and is buried in Old Hickory Cemetery. Sam died March 6, 1958 in Hope, AR, and is buried there in Memory Gardens.

Inez (b. Oct. 18, 1915 in Solgohachia) md. Olen Newberry on Sept. 16, 1933 in Conway County by the Reverend Jim Alford. Their son Larry Olen (b. March 4, 1947 in Little Rock) md. Diane Meadors. Their children are Jana and Misti. Following Olen's tragic death in an automobile accident in 1951, Inez married Howard Bradley, who died August 2002. Her death was July 26, 2003.

Bernice (b. March 4, 1918) md. Jake McKuin Oct. 23, 1936 in Conway County by Reverend George Rowell. Their two sons are Bobby George (b. Aug. 3, 1941), Morrilton, and Barry Lynn (b. Dec. 23, 1944), San Diego, CA. Jake died May 20, 1965 and is buried in Elmwood Cemetery. Bobby married Mary Ann Williams Aug. 26, 1962 in Morrilton. Their children are Andrew (b. Oct. 29, 1964) in Kansas City, MO, and Joel (b. May 13, 1968) in Dallas, TX. Barry married Phyllis Scroggin Aug. 19, 1967 in Morrilton. Their children are John Daren (b. March 2, 1970); Laura Lindley (b. Aug. 2, 1971); and Timothy Dean (b. July 26, 1980) in Little Rock. Bernice's second husband was Marion Lindley, (md. June 9, 1967) in Morrilton by Reverend Morris Smith. Marion came to Morrilton from Washington as assistant production superintendent of Arkansas Kraft Paper Mill, died Feb. 28, 1979 in Morrilton, and is buried in Elmwood Cemetery.

S.G. Roach (b. Oct. 28, 1925) in Conway County, married Ruth Hewitt Feb. 20, 1949 in Washington, DC. Their children are Kathleen (b. April 4, 1954); Keith (b. June 27, 1956); Karen (b. April 4, 1959) in Detroit, MI, and Craig (b. Dec. 29, 1962) in Memphis, TN.

Sam's second marriage was to Jewell Shelton Canfield on Dec. 31, 1932 in Conway County. They had one son Athel (Dean) Roach (b. Jan. 28, 1934) in Conway County. Jewell died March 1937 and is buried in Smyers Cemetery in Perry County. Dean married Patricia Betts May 21, 1955 in Hope. Their children are Lisa (b. April 6, 1956), Dena (b. April 6, 1957) at Otis AFB, Falmouth, MA; Beth (b. May 13, 1961) at Shaw AFB, Sumpter, SC; and Susan (b. Jan. 27, 1966) at Seward AFB, Smyrna, TN. Sam's third marriage was to Alice Taylor Evans in 1938. She had one child, Jo Rene Evans, by a previous marriage, who lives in Wilmington, NC. One child, Elizabeth Ann, was born Dec. 3, 1942 to Sam and Alice in Morrilton. She lives with her husband, Loy Young, in Tulsa, OK.

For many years Sam Roach was a very diversified farmer. Not only was he one of the first Conway County farmers to terrace his land to prevent soil erosion, but he also was among the first to use the sugar cure method in preserving home cured meat. He later entered the insurance business, moving to Hope, AR in 1943, where he was owner of Roach Insurance Agency until his death. He was a member of Woodmen of the World, a 32nd Degree Mason, and an Elder in the Hope First Presbyterian Church. The Roach family, having migrated to Arkansas from Tennessee, was among the first settlers in the Wesley Chapel Community, located a few miles north of Morrilton. Today, three of Sam's children: Bernice, Dean and S.G., still call Morrilton "home." *Submitted by Bernice Lindley.*

ROBERTS - In 1850, Jessee Roberts, 53, and Jane Lay Roberts, 45, were living in Knox County TN. The children were Eli 16, Andrew J. 14, William B. 8, and Jessee L. 7. Only Phoebe Caroline Roberts (b. June 12, 1833) and Eli M. Roberts (b. July 1834) came to Conway County, AR.

Eli M. Roberts (b. July 1834) md. Louisa Wood in Conway County where she died. Eli married Angelica Powell (b. November 1847 in Tennessee). Her father was William Powell. Her mother was Susan and Susan's father name is unknown. Their children were Sarah Roberts (b. January 1870), Joseph Edward Roberts (b. Jan. 1, 1876, d. July 16, 1924 in Hot Springs, AR), buried with no grave marker in a cemetery near Hot Springs, AR. He married Ida Bell (Tennessee) Harris, born Feb. 1, 1878, in Tennessee, died February 1918, buried at Old Shiloh Cemetery near Paris, TX. Ida Bell (Tennessee) Harris' father and mother's names are Milton Harris and Imogene (Reedy).

Children of Ida Bell (Tennessee) Harris and Joseph Edward Roberts. Adar Harris; Mattie Harris, her spouse's name was John Ladd; brother Zack Harris (b. July 22, 1884); John Henry Harris (b. Dec. 12, 1886, d. Feb. 26, 1956), spouse's name was Sadie Hood; Robert G. Harris (b. Jan. 20, 1892, d. April 27, 1922) was buried at Lost Corner Cemetery, Conway County, AR, and later Lue Crabtree.

John W. Roberts (b. March 1, 1882, d. June 5, 1902); Thomas W. Roberts (b. Dec. 28, 1912, d. June 15, 1912); James Franklin Roberts (b. Dec. 18, 1886 in Solgohachia, d. March 21, 1959 in McGehee, AR), spouse Nannie Pat Garrett.

Gertrude (Gertie) Ann Roberts (b. Jan. 8, 1904 in Conway County, AR) md. May 13, 1921 in Morrilton, Conway County, AR. Spouse name is Autie (Aughtie) L. Lewis and they had three children. (1) Mozell married first, Alfred Croy; second, Orvil Hall; and third, Tom Howard. She lives at Pocola, OK. (2) Mildred married first, Oatha Juttet and second, James Smith. They live in Pocola, OK. (3) Joyce married Herman Edwards and they live in Benton, LA.

James Gresham Roberts (b. Oct. 23, 1906, Morrilton, AR, d. Jan. 11, 1997, buried at Lone Grove Cemetery in Conway County, AR) md. May 5, 1939 to Treddy Eunice (Hall) Roberts (b. June 21, 1916, d. Feb. 14, 1996, buried at Lone Grove Cemetery in Conway County, AR). Children of James Gresham Roberts and Eunice (Hall) Roberts:

1) Roy Lloyd Roberts (b. May 12, 1940) md. Rosa Lee (Ellis) Roberts (b. Dec. 1, 1946) on Sept. 5, 1970. Child: Michael Eugene Roberts (b. March 17, 1978).

2) Ruby Ann (Roberts) Herring (b. Dec. 24, 1943) md. Samuel Herring. Children: Belinda Ann Burnett (b. Feb. 14, 19__, died June 1978), Angela Kay Burnett, Samantha Lynn Herring.

3) Mary Elizabeth (Roberts) Edwards, married Milton Edwards. He is buried at Friendship Cemetery in Conway County, AR. Children of Mary Elizabeth and Milton Edwards are Betty Sue (Edwards) Hoffman, Robert Edwards, Anita (Edwards) Fraga, Monty Gale Edwards.

4) Jimmy Darrel Roberts buried at Forest Hills Cemetery, Alexander, AR. Married Shirley (Fenton) Roberts. Children of Jimmy D. Roberts and Shirley Roberts: Shela Denice (Roberts), Jenifer Roberts, Leo Danny Roberts married Martha (Mesinger) Roberts.

Mettie Marie (Roberts) was adopted by the (Bass), born 1914, married William Isacc Lowrance. Children of Mettie Marie (Roberts) and William Isacc Lowrance: Dorothy Lowrance, James Lowrance, Roy Edward Lowrance, Lettie Marie (Lowrance) Lowrance.

Roy Homer Roberts (b. Jan. 6, 1916 in Conway County, AR, d. April 12, 1962 at Little Rock, AR, buried at Long Grove Cemetery in Conway County, AR).

Ruby Jewel (Roberts) Polk, died Jan. 9, 1982 and is buried at Encinitas Cemetery in California. She was married to Raymond Polk.

Joseph Edward and Ida Bell (Tennessee) Harris children of Edward Roberts died 5 years old.

ROBERTS - Mary Mahalia Roberts was born on June 17, 1856. Family history and census records state she was born in Tennessee where she married John Autry while only a young girl. John Autry was born about 1839 in Tennessee. Mary and John were the parents of four children: William Ervin Autry, Sarah Jane "Sallie" Autry, Robert Autry and Georgie Autry. Little is known about John Autry. He died sometime between 1880-85 and is buried in the Johnston Cemetery in Sardis, Conway County, AR.

Mary Mahalia Roberts Autry Wills

Sarah Jane Autry, according to the 1880 Conway County Census Records, was born about 1872. It stated that she was 8 years old and born in Missouri. She married James Bridges on May 17, 1885 in Conway County. Her marriage record stated she was 17 years of age and had the permission of her mother to marry because her father was dead. This puts her born in about 1868. Sarah and James had two children: Matthew Hawkins Bridges (b. Dec. 28, 1888, d. Jan. 5, 1965) and Stella Bridges Pope (b. March 6, 1890, d. Oct. 5, 1970). Sarah died at a young age and is buried in the Johnston Cemetery beside her brother and father. Sarah's children lived on Wills Mountain in Van Buren County, AR with their grandmother for awhile until their father sent for them.

William Ervin "Uncle Bud" Autry (b. Oct. 22, 1872 in Tennessee, d. Jan. 20, 1904 in Morrilton) is buried beside his father in the Johnston Cemetery. William married Mary Mariellen Mitchell on Dec. 25, 1895 in Conway County. Mary, daughter of John Wesley and Margaret (Griggs) Mitchell, was born Jan. 14, 1883 in Morrilton, Conway County, AR. She died Feb. 12, 1966 in Morrilton and is buried in El Reno Cemetery, El Reno, Canadian County, OK. Mary was married three more times: Frank Whorp, Will Foster and Elmer Neely. Mary dropped the "E" in Autrey when she moved the family to Oklahoma.

William and Mary had four children: Roberta Jane Autry Riemar (b. Nov. 7, 1896, d. May 30, 1988); Georgia Mahalia Autry Mednikow (b. July 22, 1898, d. Dec. 12, 1971); Minnie May Autry Marquardt (b. Sept. 12, 1900, d. Aug. 22, 1992) and Wilma Grace Autry Miller (b. July 21, 1902, d. Sept. 10, 1957).

On the 1880 Conway County Census Record, Georgie Autry was born about 1873. It stated she was 7 years old and born in Missouri. Robert Autry was born about 1879. It said he was 1 year old and born in Arkansas. We do not know what happened to these two children after 1880.

On Jan. 28, 1888, Mary Mahalia married Lewis Joseph Wills in Conway County. Lewis was born May 27, 1865 in Pennsylvania and died Jan. 4, 1961 on Wills Mountain. They had one daughter, Annie Mary Wills Freeman (b. Feb. 2, 1889, d. March 26, 1978). Mary Mahalia Wills died April 11, 1931 on Wills Mountain. Matthew Bridges, Mary Mahalia, Lewis and Annie Mary are buried in the Liberty Springs Cemetery, Van Buren County, AR. *Submitted by Aleda Mills Bateman.*

ROHLMAN - Henry Bernard Rohlman Jr. was born in Morrilton Dec. 31, 1928 to Agnes Gunderman Rohlman and Henry B. Rohlman Sr. His sister, Mary Katherine Rohlman Henning, was born Feb. 7, 1926. Henry graduated from Sacred Heart High School in 1946. In 1950 while working at Greer's Store, he was drafted into the US Army, served a year in Korea and was discharged in November 1952. He married Elinor Ann Nabholz, daughter of Mary Strack Nabholz and Emil A. Nabholz in Conway, May 26, 1952. Their daughter Mary Virginia "Ginny" was born March 4, 1953. After his Army discharge, Henry returned to work for Greer's and in 1964 Mr. R.A. Greer sold Greer's to Henry, who operated the quality men and

Henry Rohlman and Elinor Rohlman

women's clothing store and jeans shop until he retired in 1994.

In 1971 Ginny graduated from Sacred Heart High School and in 1975 graduated from the University of Central Arkansas with a degree in nursing. In 1977 Ginny married William Jackson Bell, son of Bill and Florine Bell of Conway. They live in Conway where Ginny works at the Conway Regional Hospital and Jack works for the Conway School System as a school psychologist and counselor. Jack is an alderman on the Conway City Council. They have three children: Jeremy, Jessica and Lauren Bell.

Henry has been a member of the Morrilton Lions Club for 50 years and received the Melvin Jones Fellow Award in 1994. Elinor has been a member of the GFWC Adelaide Club for 45 years and was named "Citizen of the Year 1994" by the Morrilton Area Chamber of Commerce and also received the Arkansas Community Development Award in 1994. Henry and Elinor are retired but very active in church and civic activities.

ROSSI - Edward V. Rossi (b. Jan. 1, 1922 in Center Ridge, AR), son of Frank and Mary Paladino Rossi, enlisted in the US Air Force in 1942 at Camp Joseph T. Robinson, North Little Rock, AR. He was assigned to Keesler Air Force Base, Biloxi, MS and graduated from Airplane Mechanics School in 1943. A graduate of Aviation Cadet School, Rochester Business Institute, Rochester, NY, 1943 and received aerial gunner training at

Edward V. Rossi

Tyndall Field, Panama City, FL. He was assigned to begin pre-combat training at Davis-Monthan Field, Tucson, AZ, in B-24J bombers with the 494th Bomb Group.

Edward received advanced overseas combat training at Hickam Field, Honolulu, HI. In October 1944 he was assigned to the 7th Air Force in B-24J bombers, and flew to the South Pacific Theatre to the Island of Anguar (Palau Island Group). The 494th Bomb Group Mission was to retake the Philippines Island from the Japanese for General Douglas McArthur's return. (He was born in Little Rock, AR).

On Jan. 4, 1945, his 15th mission as a nose gunner, their target was Clark Field on the island of Luzon in the Philippines Islands. They were escorted to the target by P-38 fighters. The flak was very intense and their plane was hit just above the nose turret. After dropping the bombs they were attacked by a number of Japanese fighters. Ed got his first shot at a Zero at one o'clock high. Staff Sgt. Rossi fired several bursts which hit the Zero just aft of the pilot's seat. Rossi saw an explosion at this point and the Zero continued through their formation and clipped the wing of one of their planes. He then went into a dive and burst into flames and crashed in the sea.

Rossi flew 40 combat missions and he was awarded the Distinguished Flying Cross (DFC), Air Medal with one silver, five stars, one Bronze Air Medal and Philippine Liberation Ribbon.

Rossi returned to the States after flying his 40 missions. He was stationed at Santa Ana Air Base in Santa Ana, CA for rest leave. A directive came from the President in Washington DC that if you had 103 points you could be immediately discharged. Rossi had the required points so he was discharged from Camp Chaffee in Arkansas, July 26, 1945.

He enrolled at Western Michigan University, in Kalamazoo, MI and graduated with a BS degree in January 1950. He then signed a pro baseball contract with the Boston Braves baseball team. For 40 years he operated a successful State Farm Insurance Agency in Kalamazoo, MI and retired in 1995.

Ed and his wife Jean celebrated 55 years of marriage Sept. 3, 1949. They have five children, three daughters and two sons. They have nine grandchildren and one great-grandson.

ROSSI - Frank M. Rossi was born Feb. 24, 1899, in Center Ridge, AR, to Romedio and Adelaide Rossi, one of the first settlers of the Italian settlement of Catholic Point near Center Ridge, AR. Frank attended Center Ridge School, which is now known as Nemo Vista, where he was an outstanding basketball player. In 1917 he left home to seek employment in Chicago, IL. After one year there, he became homesick and went back to Center Ridge to help on the farm. On Jan. 5, 1921 he married Mary Lena Paladino, eldest daughter of Tony and Minnie Paladino at St. Joseph Catholic Church, Center Ridge, AR.

Frank was a successful cotton farmer, raising a record 42 bales of cotton in one year in the 1930s. When raising cotton was no longer profitable, he started a dairy herd and sold milk to a cheese factory in Morrilton. The dairy business gave way to the raising of beef cattle, later he purchased bulls from Winrock Farms (Santa Gertrudis breed) which is still carried on by his youngest son, Marion, at the same farm. Frank had a great interest in soil conservation and built several ponds and stocked them with fish. He also experimented with many soil building grasses to conserve the soil and to provide valuable feed for his cattle.

Frank and Mary had seven children:

1) Edward (b. Jan. 1, 1922) pitched for the Center Ridge baseball team, the Morrilton American Legion and the Morrilton Red Sox teams. He married Jean McCarty and lives in Kalamazoo, MI. They have five children: Mary, married Bruce Livingston and has two children, Heather and Jay; Thomas married Conni Bracken, no children; Nancy married Wendell Trantham and has three children: RaNae, Ross, and Rylee; David married Gitte Christopherson and has two boys, Peter and Thomas; Susan married Greg McGrail and has two children, Tyler and Amanda.

2) Louise (b. Feb. 2, 1923) md. Milton Crews and lived in Memphis, TN. Louise died Aug. 17, 1998 and Milton died July 13, 1990. They had two daughters, Diane married Glenn Campbell and had daughter Michelle; Anita married Mark VanderHorck and they had two daughters, Jessica and Amelia. Anita died in 2003.

3) Lucille (b. Oct. 6, 1925) md. James A. Conway (deceased Dec. 15, 2001). She lives in Kalamazoo, MI. Her two children are Mary Ellen (md. Joseph Stuart, no children) and James Patrick Conway.

4) Gloria (b. Sept. 24, 1927) md. Henry DeSalvo (deceased Feb. 24, 1976). Henry was the son of Tony Luke and Josephine DeSalvo of Center Ridge. Gloria lives in Hot Springs, AR. Their three children are Barbara, who married Douglas Peterson and they had three children: Brett, Todd and Kara. Stephen married Keely Ardmann. Mark married Dorsey Catlett Bond and had son Nicholas Andrew.

5) Reverend Raymond (b. April 30, 1933) was ordained a Catholic priest, May 15, 1958. He taught Latin at Little Rock Catholic High School for 20 years. He then served in various parishes in the diocese of Little Rock for 24 years. He now lives in retirement in Hot Springs, AR.

6) Charles (b. Feb. 16, 1937) md. Dorothy Erickson and lives in Houston, TX. They have four children: Rhonda Samperi who has three children: Blake, Logan and Jacqueline. Leigh married Britt Wiegand and has two sons, Carter and Blaine. Sharen married David Groppel and has two sons, Garrett and Gregory. Son, Alan Charles Rossi.

7) Marion (b. Aug 16, 1941) md. Betty Sponer of St. Vincent, AR. They have five children: Yvonne married Wayne Zackery, has a son Daniel. Johnny married Sundee Standly and has two children, Scarlett and Jeff Edward. Kenneth married Faryl Roberts, their two children are Francesca and Faith. Jennifer and

Cheryl Rossi. Marion and Betty raised registered beef cattle and live at the family homestead.

Mary Lena Paladino Rossi was born on Jan. 25, 1902 and died Aug. 16, 1941 from complications following the birth of their youngest son.

Frank M. Rossi was 70 years old when he took up the game of golf He built a unique nine hole golf course on his farm and named it "The Green Ranch Golf Course" which was written up in the *Arkansas Democrat*. Frank never remarried and lived with his son Marion and his family until his death on July 29, 1987 at age 88.

Frank and Mary are both buried in St. Joseph Cemetery at Catholic Point near Center Ridge, AR. *Submitted by Edward V. Rossi.*

ROSSI - Louise Rossi Crews (b. Feb. 2, 1923 in Center Ridge, AR) was the second child of Frank Rossi and Mary Paladino Rossi.

She enlisted in the WAVES (Women Accepted for Volunteer Emergency Service) of the US Navy in February 1944. Her training was conducted at Hunter's College, New York where she graduated with high honors. She was assigned to the US Naval Hospital, Oceanside, CA as pharmacist mate third class, *Louise Rossi Crews* where she served until her discharge in January 1946. She married Milton R. Crews in 1949 and has two daughters.

ROWELL - The most memorable recollection I have of my grandfather, Benjamin Franklin Rowell, the patriarch of the Rowell family, was when he was dying. Of course, I didn't realize he was dying. He had suffered a stroke and came to live his last days with us. And what made this even more exciting for a young boy of 7, was my other grandfather, Dr. Walter Lee Mason, was his physician. That year with two grandfathers was an impressionable experience for a young boy.

The Ben Rowell family: Mary, Anne, George and Jim.

Benjamin Rowell was born in or around Kosciusko, MS. He had a brother Oscar and a sister Mary. Mary married a Muirhead and had a rather large family. Benjamin left Mississippi when he was 18 years old. The reason he came to Arkansas is unclear; however, he apparently liked what he saw and decided to stay.

Ben met and married Eliza King, the daughter of James and Melinda King. Through hard work and thrifty living they purchased 160 acres next to the King place just south of Old Hickory.

Ben and Eliza had four children: Mary, Annie, Jim and George. They all lived and farmed the land until they married and started their own lives.

Annie Rowell married Sim Newberry of Old Hickory. They had four children: Jewel, Mary Vera, Rachel and Olin. Annie died at a young age.

George married Barbara Mason, daughter of Dr. Walter Mason and Ardella Massingill Mason. They had two children, Della Jane, who died at age 12, and Bobby, who was only 1 year old, when Della died.

George was a mail carrier in Hattieville for 29 years and was pastor of several churches in Pope and Conway counties. The George Rowells moved to California in 1952 where George spent 25 years as pastor of the First Baptist Church of Gardena. *Submitted by Bobby Rowell.*

ROWELL – Ben John Rowell was born May 12, 1931 in Possum Trot, AR, son of James McKinley Rowell and Sula McKinley Rowell. Ben was a Baptist preacher for 57 years and now lives in Rogers, AR.

Ben married Billie June Matlock on April 9, 1949. They have one daughter, Karen Jo, who married Lowell David Maloney. They have one son, John David Maloney. They live in Rogers, AR. *Submitted by Ben J. Rowell.*

ROWELL – Erby Earl Rowell Sr. was a son of Jim and Sula Rowell. Erby Sr. married Eula Mae Hogue. To this union one son was born, Erby Earl Rowell Jr. "Sonny."

Erby Rowell Jr. married Judy Waller. They have one son, Everett Rowell and one daughter, Marla Rowell.

Marla Rowell married Roger Stratton. They have three children: Sara, Joshua and Matthew Stratton.

ROWELL – Helen Rowell was born to Jim and Sula Rowell on June 28, 1916 in Conway County, AR. Helen married William Virgil "Bill" Hendricks (b. Sept. 18, 1906) on Sept. 4, 1937. To this union were born two daughters. Willie Faye (b. July 6, 1938) and Deloris Ann (b. Sept. 5, 1939). After graduation from high school, the daughters moved to Little Rock where they were both employed.

Deloris Ann married Dan Morgan in Little Rock, AR on June 25, 1961. One son, Brooks Sherwood Morgan, was born to Dan and Deloris on Aug. 20, 1963.

Bill Hendricks died Feb. 21, 1964 in Morrilton. Helen moved to North Little Rock in 1965 to be with her daughters. Helen remained in North Little Rock and shared a home with Willie Faye until her death on April 9, 2002.

Brooks Morgan married Melissa Dwyer on Jan. 17, 1987, in North Little Rock, AR. To this union were born two daughters: Taylor Elizabeth Morgan (b. Dec. 16, 1988) and Bailey Brooke Morgan (b. March 4, 1991).

ROWELL – James "Jim" Rowell married Sula Childress. To this union were born seven children: Tony, Helen, Erby, Pauline, Jimmy, Sarah Jane and Ben

Tony married Lorene Haralson in February 1933. They were farmers and mail carriers, where both retired with Tony having 52 years of service. Lorene also retired from Crompton Mills. They had one daughter Virginia Ruth and one son Tony Jr.

Virginia married Boyd Norwood and they have a daughter Trudy Brents. She has two children, Katie and Strap Brents.

Boyd worked construction and they were poultry and cattle farmers. Boyd retired from Conway County Road Forman in 1997.

Tony Jr. married Bettye McCoy and they have one son Monty Rowell and one daughter Sheree Rowell.

Monty married Nancy Latham. They have two children, Angela and Brandon Rowell.

Tony Jr. worked at Crompton Mills and raised cattle. He was elected Conway County Tax Assessor in 1986 and served 14 years (1987-2000) until he retired in December 2000. *Submitted by Tony Rowell Jr.*

ROWELL – James "Jimmy" M. Rowell, fifth child of Sula and Jim Rowell, married Eulene Bradley in

1940. In 1944 they moved to California to help in WWII by working in the aircraft industry, of which Jimmy still operates his own company.

To this union two daughters were born. Deborah, who married Fred Heldoorn. They have four children: Kellee, Michael, Nicole and Christopher. The second daughter, Sandra, married Stephen Connors. All of the families reside in California.

ROWELL - Mary Rowell married Buddy Wade. They had no children and spent their entire life in Conway County.

ROWELL – Pauline Rowell was the child of Jim and Sula Rowell. She married O.D. Fellers. They had one daughter, Carol Ann, who married Antoin Kuettle. To this union, three children were born: Toni, Mark and Tami.

Pauline married Frank Hubbard and they were married for more than 50 years before his death. They spent their entire married life in California, where she still lives.

ROWELL - Sarah Jane Rowell (b. Aug. 25, 1928), daughter of James McKinley Rowell and Sula McKinley Rowell, married Robert Hamlett. They had one son, Gary Hamlett, who lives in Valencia, CA. Sarah is deceased. *Submitted by Ben J. Rowell.*

SCARLETT - Jacob E. Scarlett (b. 1817 in North Carolina) may have been the son of John Scarlett (b. April 9, 1791). Jacob probably was a brother to James Madison Scarlett. Jacob moved to Indiana prior to 1834. He married Nancy (last name unknown) about 1835. Nancy was born 1810 in Kentucky. Five children were born to Jacob in Indiana. About 1846, Jacob moved his family to Arkansas. Jacob and James Scarlett probably traveled from Indiana to Arkansas together. Jacob settled in Van Buren County, AR, prior to 1850 and was a farmer. Jacob died between 1852 and 1860. Children included: Lewis J. Scarlett (b. 1836); Elizabeth Scarlett (b. 1838); Pamelia A. Scarlett (b. 1840); Austin E. Scarlett (b. 1842, d. 1864 in the Civil War); Alzira Ann Scarlett (b. 1844); James D. Scarlett (b. 1849); Nancy A. Scarlett (b. 1852).

Alzira Ann Scarlett (b. April 1844 in Indiana) was the daughter of Jacob and Nancy Scarlett. She married James Orsen B. "Orin" McClure on Nov. 7, 1867, in Van Buren County, AR. Orin McClure (b. 1844 in Conway County) was the son of Stephen McClure and Sarah Smith. Orin enlisted in the 8th Arkansas Confederate Cavalry, Co. E, on Jan. 5, 1863, in Conway County. He was later assigned to the 10th Arkansas Cavalry, Co. E, and taken prisoner of War by the Union Army. He was paroled at Jacksonport, in Jackson County, AR, on June 5, 1865. Orin and Alzira settled in Van Buren County for a time. Orin was a farmer. Prior to 1880, they moved to White County, AR. Besides their own children, they raised Orin's niece, Rachael A. Moore, who was orphaned when she was very young. Orin moved his family to Independence County, AR in the mid-1880s. Orin died Feb. 2, 1899 in Independence County. Alzira received Orin's Civil War Pension in 1901. She died March 3, 1919, in Independence County. Children included:

1) Sarah Elizabeth McClure (b. Jan. 25, 1869, d. Oct 18, 1959) md. J.G. Burns on July 19, 1885. Sarah then married Major James Harris on Oct. 21, 1897. Children included: Major Orsen Harris, Beulah Harris, Obert Harris, Thelma Harris and Carl Vernon Harris.

2) Mary Dallas "Allie" McClure (b. Nov. 12, 1871, d. Oct. 21, 1932) md. William Allen Davidson on Jan. 3, 1900. Children: Arthur Andrew Davidson and Oscar Obid "Ought" Davidson.

3) Nancy V. "Dollie" McClure (b. July 1873, d. Jan. 2, 1913 in a pneumonia outbreak) md. James C. Speed on Dec. 2, 1893 (James died Jan. 11, 1913). Children: Effie, Boyer, Zora, Bryan, Jeanne, Hazel, Annvel and Herman.

4) Commie A. McClure (b. November 1874-died before 1908) md. Arthur Riley Harris (later married her sister Maude). Child: Clarence Harris.

5) Nora Florence McClure (b. Aug. 22, 1879) md. Andrew Jackson "Jack" Harris.

6) Maude Magalene McClure (b. Nov. 8, 1886) md. Arthur Riley Harris (after the death of her sister, Commie). Children: Dora, Pearl Alzira, Thurman James, Deward Orson, Earl Arthur and A.L.

SCARLETT - James Madison Scarlett (b. July 15, 1813, in North Carolina) may have been the son of John Scarlett (b. April 9, 1791). James was probably a brother to Jacob E. Scarlett. James moved to Indiana prior to 1834. He married Abigail Chance about 1835. Abigail was the daughter of Jonathan Chance, who practiced medicine in Van Buren County, AR, in the mid-1800s. Four children were born to James in Indiana. About 1846, James moved his family to Arkansas. Abigail died prior to 1849. James married Melinda N. McClure about 1849. Melinda McClure was born April 1, 1824, in Illinois. James settled in Conway County prior to 1850. He was a farmer and a Methodist Protestant minister who performed many marriages in Conway and Van Buren Counties in the mid-to late 1800s. He started the Scarlett Masonic Lodge No. 283 that was chartered at Shiloh in 1873 and merged with Sugar Loaf Lodge at Heber Springs, AR in 1937. James died Oct. 22, 1875, in Cleburne County, AR. Melinda died June 10, 1896.

Children of James Scarlett and Abigail Chance:
1) Mary Elen Scarlett (b. 1837).
2) Nathan Calvin Scarlett (b. 1840, d. 1864 in the Civil War) md. Zilla Holland.
3) Lucinda Scarlett (b. 1842).
4) Minor Scarlett (b. May 10, 1844).
5) Anna M. Scarlett (b. Oct 24, 1848).
Children of James Scarlett and Melinda McClure:
6) Sarah Scarlett (b. 1852) md. Ezekiel W. Ward, son of Clarborn Ward and Martha P. Cargile, daughter of John Cargill Jr. and Nancy Elizabeth Lewis.
7) William L. Scarlett (b. 1854) md. Sarah E. New.
8) Emeline Scarlett (b. 1856) md. John Ballard.
9) Naomi Scarlett (b. 1857) md. Milton Williams.
10) James Scarlett (b. 1858, died young).
11) Melinda Scarlett (b. 1860).
12) Leonia Alice Scarlett (b. April 10, 1863, d. Jan. 22, 1959) md. Stephen Wison Bates. Children: Olen, Virgil, Minnie, Paul, Audra and Le Roy.

Mary Elen Scarlett (b. Feb. 16, 1837 in Indiana) was the daughter of James Scarlett and Abigail Chance. She married Valentine McClure on June 12, 1856. Valentine (b. 1837 in Arkansas) was the son of Stephen McClure and Sarah Smith. Valentine purchased 160 acres of land in 1857 in Van Buren County. He was a farmer. They had two children. On March 3, 1862, Valentine enlisted in the 31st Arkansas Confederate Infantry, Co. F, in Van Buren County. The 31st Infantry was sent to Tennessee. Valentine died in service on Aug. 28, 1862. On Feb. 6, 1864, Mary married James H. Shipley, who was born March 1818, in Tennessee. The family moved to Texas prior to 1880. Mary died April 20, 1920, in Bell County, TX. She and James Shipley had four children.

Children of Valentine McClure and Mary Scarlett:
1) Sarah Elizabeth McClure (b. Nov. 1, 1859, d. March 12, 1943) md. George Washington Crone. Children: Nancy Elen, Ida, Talular, Walter, Lee Edger, Stella, George, William and Louis.
2) Lodusky Catherine McClure (b. Dec. 8, 1861).
Children of James Shipley and Mary (Scarlett) McClure: Minor Scarlett Shipley (b. 1865); Nancy P. Shipley (b. 1867); Amanda Eva Shipley (b. 1870); Etta Shipley (b. 1872) md. J.C. Allison.

SCROGGIN - The Scroggin's history extends beyond the 1600s when our ancestors immigrated to the United States from the countries of England and Scot-

land. Some of the research goes back to George Scroggin (b. 1660). He died between 1696 and 1700 in the state of Maryland. His wife Susanna was also born in England about the same time.

Skipping several generations to Dennis Quilla (sometimes spelled Quiller) Scroggin, the first child of Roberta Humphrey Scroggin and Sarah Barnes, was born Sept. 9, 1883 at Springfield, AR. He died April 21, 1958, Morrilton, AR. He married Oct. 30, 1899 to Matilda Jane Starkey, daughter of Richard Isiah Starkey and Margaret Spence. Matilda was born Oct. 9, 1879, Springfield, AR and died Nov. 24, 1962, Springfield, AR. They had 12 children, one of whom was Junia Jewell Scroggin, Kacie's great-grandmother. She is 91 years old and the only child living as of March 2005. She was born 1914 near Center Ridge, AR and married Willie Everett "Shine" Stover Sept. 28, 1935. He was born Dec. 3, 1912, at Center Ridge and died Aug. 2, 1987, Conway, AR. They have one daughter, Willie Gay (b. 1939 at Center Ridge). She married Lewis Earl Miller at Morrilton in 1959. He was born 1937 in the Hill Creek Community, near Plumerville, AR. They have two daughters, Tawnia Gay (b. 1965) and Crystal Ann (b. 1968) at Morrilton.

Tawnia married Kenneth Michael Hoelzeman Oct. 3, 1986 at Mt. Pleasant Baptist Church near Plumerville. He was born 1958 at Morrilton. They have three children: Kacie Lynn (b. 1990); Haley Renee (b. 1994) and Bret Andrew (b. 1997). All were born in Little Rock, AR. They attend schools in Morrilton and church at Mt. Pleasant. Tawnia teaches second grade at Reynolds Elementary School in Morrilton. Kenny is a self employed chicken grower for Pilgrim's Pride and raises beef cattle north of Plumerville. Crystal married Kevin Emil Rehm Dec. 17, 1988 at the First Baptist Church, Morrilton. He was born 1966 at Morrilton. They have two daughters, Stephanie Leigh (b. 1991) and Hannah Maria (b. 1994) at Little Rock. Both attend St. Joseph School in Conway, AR. Crystal is a librarian at Theodore Jones Elementary School and Kevin owns Central Arkansas Electronics in Conway.

Other children born to D.Q. and Matilda were James Madison "Matt" (b. March 23, 1901, d. Feb. 23, 1982) md. Irene Hawkins; Jesse Baxter "Jess" (b. Dec. 18, 1903, d. July 8, 1982) md. first Vivian Lacefield and second, Hazel Williams; Christopher Columbus "Lum" (b. Oct. 2, 1905, d. Sept. 3, 1998) md. Beatrice Blanch Mallett; Chloia Easter (b April 19, 1908, d. April 26, 1997) md. William Edgar Dowdy; Genevia Icillene "Icie" (b. Jan. 10, 1912, d. Aug. 2, 1999) md. Johnnie "Chick" Matthews; Fairy Eugene (b. March 3, 1916, d. Oct. 29, 1981) md. Marie Mallett; Leoda (b. Feb. 1, 1920, d. March 23, 1929). Four other children died in infancy. *Written by great-great-granddaughter Kacie Lynn Hoelzeman.*

SCROGGIN - Harold Franklin Scroggin was born Nov. 21, 1937 on the old Scroggin home place which was homesteaded by his great-grandfather James Madison Scroggin. He is the son of Mitt Lindsey and Mary Ellen McKuin Scroggin. Harold's mother died in 1937 when Harold was about 6 weeks old. He was raised by his grandparents, Bert and Sallie Starkey Scroggin.

Harold graduated from Catholic Point Grade School. He graduated from Nemo Vista High School in 1956. He excelled in basketball while in high school and had the honor of being on the number one team in the district. They went to state three times and Harold won two scholarships. He attended college at UCA at Conway and received 40 hours of in service training.

Tammy Welch, the granddaughter we raised.

He married Joy Garrett in 1958. They had two children, Barbara and Wesley. Barbara married Bobby Hensley and they had one child, Lindsey Hensley. Barbara's second marriage was to Mark Flowers. They have one child, Julia Flowers. Wesley married Oralynn Henry and had one child, Kerry Scroggin. Wesley's second marriage was to Joy Crawford and they had a son, Austin Ridge Scroggin.

Harold worked at Nemo Vista School for a period of about 10 years and later retired in the year 2000 from C.W.I. in Conway, AR. Harold married Pat Tilley Welch on Nov. 28, 1974 in Conway County. Pat is the daughter of Paul David and Ola Mae Watkins Tilley. She had two children from her previous marriage, James Ray Welch and Rose Welch. James Welch married Debbie Trotter and they have one son, James Eric Welch. Rose married Wesley Hart and had one daughter, Melanie Hart. Melanie married Jodi Box and they have two children, Katilyn and Kyleigh Box.

Harold and Pat raised a granddaughter, Tammy Welch. She married Chris Mahoney and they have one daughter, Bailey Mahoney.

Harold and Pat, at the present time, are living in Center Ridge and enjoying their retirement by gardening, hunting and fishing.

SCROGGINS - Dennis Scroggins was the son of Robert Henson Scroggins and Isabelle Williams. Robert's father, Henson Scroggins and his wife Malinda Carpenter originally settled near Cleveland and in fact, the Lost Corner Cemetery was known at first as Scroggin Cemetery, Henson having donated the land that was used. Isabelle's father, Leroy "Dick" Williams was one of the sons of Thomas Jefferson Williams, a former combatant in the Civil War who was shot down in his own front door by Confederate sympathizers. Both families have rich histories, but this subject, Dennis Scroggins, has no less a story to tell.

Dennis Scroggins and Mary Elizabeth "Lizzie" Stobaugh Scroggins.

He was born July 11, 1892 in Conway County. Other siblings were Caroline or "Callie" who later married Wiley Harrison Scroggins; Garfield (b. 1895, d. 1967) md. Bertha Watkins; John S. md. Cora Watkins; Herbert (b. 1901, d. 1971) md. Nellie Polk; William Kerry (b. 1906, d. 1988) md. Laura Bell Hill and Columbus md. Bonnie Bell.

Dennis was married to Mary Elizabeth "Lizzie" Stobaugh sometime around 1916. Lizzie was the daughter of George Washington Stobaugh and Margaret Ann Brinkley. She was born Dec. 16, 1884 and was a sweet natured lady who was loved by everyone she came to know. They had but one child, a small little baby girl who died very soon after her birth. The little babe is buried at Lost Corner. Dennis and Lizzie lived next door to Lizzie's brother, Orville and his wife, Etta Stobaugh, and their thriving household of 11 children. All of the kids and eventually, grandchildren, enjoyed the close relationship of these households. Soon, one of Orville's children, George, became so attached to Dennis and Lizzie, he was like their own child. So much so, that in fact, when the Scroggins moved to Morrilton, little George went to live with them. Eventually, this couple would officially adopt George, though not changing his name.

Later, Orville and Etta, too, moved to Morrilton

and lived near them. Dennis and Lizzie opened a restaurant in Morrilton called "The Streetcar Cafe, housed in an old dining car. It was frequented by many people from Morrilton and the business prospered. In later years, they sold the cafe and Dennis began to buy land and other interests around town. They owned land on Harding Street in Morrilton. One family member said he was a fine carpenter and built many houses in town. When Lizzie died on Sept. 19, 1966, Dennis buried his wife next to their infant daughter at Lost Corner. After some time, he married Mae Scroggin Flowers (b. 1904, d. 1971). She, too, is buried at Lost Corner Cemetery. Dennis later passed away June 4, 1974 and was buried near Lizzie at the Lost Corner Cemetery where so many of their relatives are interred as well.

SCROGGINS - Hayes Scroggins was a son of Leroy Scroggins and his third wife, Mary A. Harvey, married Sept. 26, 1897, Conway County. His parents are buried in Lost Corner Cemetery near Cleveland. Hayes had one sister, Laura Ann. He was orphaned at the age of 6 and lived with cousins until the age of 18.

Hayes and Bertie Scroggins, Cleveland, AR

Laura Ann married Ollie Gaines. They had three children: Elmer, Irene and Wilburn. Ollie moved to Oklahoma after Laura's death in 1922. Both boys later joined the military service during WWII. They settled in Vancouver, WA. Irene lives in California. Laura Ann is buried in Mallettown Cemetery near Birdtown, AR.

Hayes (b. April 1, 1902, d. Oct. 15, 1976) md. Bertie Alvertie Russell (b. Feb. 21, 1902, d. June 4, 1975), the daughter of George Washington and Vesta Brents Russell. They lived on the homestead he inherited from Leroy and expanded the acreage to 400, lying in both Conway and Van Buren counties. He raised cattle, corn, cotton, etc. and in the 1960s joined the broiler craze. He and Bertie had six children: Euin L.G., Weldon D., Mildred Marie, Eathel Fern, Doyle J. and Claudia Jean.

Euin (b. March 6, 1924) md. Eloise Brunson (b. Aug. 10, 1927, d. May 13, 2001). Both graduated from University of Arkansas. Both taught in the Judsonia and Searcy schools. Euin later worked for the State Dept. Eloise was an advanced math teacher with two masters and taught in White County for more than 50 years. They have one child, John Lee.

Weldon (b. Sept. 1, 1925) md. Euleta McCall (b. July 19, 1930, d. April 15, 1991). They lived on a farm near Cleveland and raised broilers and turkeys. They later moved to Morrilton where Weldon worked for Arkansas Kraft and Arrow. Three children were born to them: Marie (deceased), Devon and Betty Sue.

Mildred (b. July 21, 1928, d. Jan. 20, 2003) md. James K. Mahan (b. Feb. 13, 1915, d. June 12, 2001). Mildred graduated from UCA and was a schoolteacher for 30 years. Most of it was in the Damascus and Southside-Bee Branch schools. James was a farmer and Church of Christ minister. Three children were born to them: Loretta, Roger Wayne and Harold James.

Fern (b. Jan. 20, 1930) md. Walter Robert Hornbuckle (b. June 6, 1930) of Dallas, TX, and taught commercial subjects in Southside-Bee Branch and Wabbaseka, AR schools and Draughon's Business College, Dallas, TX. She left the education field and worked as a legal secretary in the Field Research Dept., Mobil Oil Co., Dallas. There she met Robert, who had an EE degree from Southern Methodist University. His

work took them to White Sands Missile Range, Kwajalein, Marshall Islands, New Jersey, Illinois and back to Texas. They moved to Conway County in 1992. They have two sons, Greg Allen and Bruce Abbott.

Doyle (b. April 22, 1932) md. Mary Jones (b. March 6, 1933). Doyle attended UCA before joining the Navy. After his discharge, he opened a barbershop in North Little Rock and ran a Registered Hereford Cattle Ranch at Scotland on the side. He is active in the annual National Chuckwagon Races at Clinton and is a trail boss for the Arkansas Trailriders Association. Mary worked for Addressgraph-Multigraph Corp. in Little Rock and Farm Bureau Ins. Co. at Clinton. They have one child, Sherry Doylene.

Claudia Jean (b. March 15, 1938) md. her high school sweetheart, Dewey Crow (b. Sept. 3, 1938, died Jan. 12, 1990). Jean loved her vegetable garden and helping take care of the cattle on their farm near Cleveland. Dewey worked on the side in the Woodlands Dept. of Arkansas Kraft. Jean moved to Morrilton a few years after Dewey's death. They had two sons, Steve and Randall. *Submitted by Fern Scroggins Hornbuckle.*

SEATS - Once upon a time there was a beautiful Indian Princess. She was about five feet tall and had beautiful black hair. Her daddy was Chief of their Cherokee Tribe. His name was George Washington Seats. Her name was Mary Frances Seats. The year was 1865. Her tribe lived in Tennessee and Kentucky. She lived in a permanent village and at Thanksgiving time their ceremony was called Busk. They were thankful

Mary Frances Seats Orr

for fruits and corn on the cob, beans, peanuts, pumpkins, and squash represented the harvest. These were among 86 plants before the white man came.

They played games and had athletic contests, dances, storytelling and playing ball. They hit the ball with sticks that resembled tennis rackets. They had foot and horse races. On long winter nights their musical instruments included drums, flutes and rattles of every kind. They had songs for every occasion: lullaby, work, love, games, medicine, war, and religious ceremonies. Women of the tribe usually did most of the work while the men hunted and fished. The bow and arrow, hatchet, or tomahawks were their weapons. Dogs were used while hunting. They speared fish from canoes dug out of large trees. Metal work included the use of copper for spear points and knives. Most tribes were expert workers with flint and stone tools and weapons. Even in our day the tribes have high skills in setting precious stones in silver work. The ladies wore dresses made of buckskins. Sometimes they painted them.

In the 1800's the Federal Government began sending large indian populations to Oklahoma to land know as the Indian Territory. Some Indians who started in winter snows had to cross many mountains and rivers to get there. These harsh conditions took many lives. The ones who lived finally made it to Oklahoma. The Little Indian Princess and her family couldn't find a home there as the area was so crowded. Their tribe settled in northern Arkansas.

The Little Princes met and married James Orr on Sept. 14, 1888. His dad was a German immigrant. They had four boys and four girls: John Riley (b. Aug. 21, 1889); George W. (b. Oct. 21, 1891); Kerby (b. May 9, 1903); Artle Ivon (b. Oct. 17, 1905); Alitha Jane (b. Jan. 9, 1894); Margret Allenea (b. Sept. 12, 1896); Ada Viola (b. May 17, 1899); and Chester Laverne (b. May 2, 1901).

John Riley Orr was my great-grandfather. They were true to indian culture. In the 1900's the family made a move to Conway County in the Grandview Community. They lived at the foot of Lost Mountain. James T. Orr with his two sons, William George and John Riley, helped dig the hand dug well at the Grandview Community school and church building. This family became a large part of the Grandview Community. In the 1920s Mary Frances Orr and her younger children left behind John and William, making a move from Arkansas to Texas. Texas became their home but they still made many trips to visit their family in Arkansas. *Submitted by Deronda Givens*

SHADDOX - Sarah Louise Shaddox was born on Jan. 12, 1863 in Walker County, GA, to Ezekiel and Nancy Shaddox. Her father Ezekiel was born in Stokes County, NC on July 23, 1837, one of six known sons of Ezekiel Shaddox Sr. and his wife Tilletha Ivey, natives of North Carolina. Her mother Nancy was a child of Shadrach and Mary (Turner) Carson.

Ezekiel and Nancy were married in 1857, and by 1860 they had two daughters: Tilletha Frances, 3, and Mary, 6 months old. Lula was born in 1863 and her father went off to war when she was 10 months old.

Ezekiel died in 1864. His military records say he deserted at Turner's Point, GA on July 21, 1864, but actually he died of measles, rampant in many military camps during that war. After Ezekiel's death, his widow and children migrated to Arkansas. In 1870 they lived in Woodruff County, with Lula's step-father, William H. Ward.

In August 1880, Lula married James Jonas Ward (no relation to her late step-father) in Woodruff County. No children were born to them, because "Jimmy" died soon after their marriage. Lula moved to Conway County about 1881 with her thrice-widowed mother, Nancy (Smith), and a half-sister and half-brother, Dora and Robert Ward.

Lula married Fletcher Alexander Griffin on Sept. 29, 1886 in Conway County. They had four children before he died of lung disease on April 13, 1894.

1) Mary Ella Griffin (b. July 9, 1887, d. Nov. 15, 1926) md. about 1903 to Arthur Norwood, son of Lucinda (Autry) and William E. Norwood. Arthur and Ella's children were Clister, Edna Ruth, Inez, Ollie J. and Wayne Norwood.

2) Myrtle Griffin married Samuel B. Sledge on Jan. 27, 1904. Sam and Myrtle shared the same birth date, Dec. 17, 1888. Sam died March 19, 1973, and Myrtle died April 11, 1981. Both were buried at Cedar Creek Cemetery. Their children were Carlos, Arnold, Olvie, Romie, Audrey, Loyd and Glen Sledge.

3) John Franklin Griffin (b. Sept. 23, 1891, d. March 28, 1893).

4) Fletcher Ada Griffin (b. April 1, 1894, d. April 16, 1973) md. Chester Owens (b. 1889, d. 1968). Ada and Chester Owens were buried at Friendship Cemetery at Solgohachia. Their children were Dessity Mae, Herbert, Florence, Lillian, Inez, Carles, Christine, Kenneth, and Norma.

Lula married a third time. On Nov. 12, 1904 she married John Watson Sledge. They moved from Springfield to Morrilton about 1926. John died in June 1932 and was buried beside his first wife (Minerva Jane Purcell) at Damascus. Lula died June 17, 1944 and was buried in the Springfield Cemetery, near her mother's unmarked grave.

Lula owned the book *Rotteck's History of the World*, published in 1857 by Leary and Getz, Chicago, IL, where she recorded birth, marriage, and death dates of Shaddox and Griffin family members on various pages.

We are fortunate the book was preserved by Lula's descendants, because most of the information she recorded is not available through other sources. Our sincere thanks to Glenda Sledge Fuller for sharing Lula's records with us. *Submitted by Nada Guthier.*

SHEWMAKE - The name Shewmake has been spelled many ways down through the years -

Shumacher, Shoemaker, Shoemake, Shumake. In the 1800s there were many people here by the name of Shumake/Shewmake. James and Jesse were among the early settlers, moving here from Tennessee. They were both shown on Conway County 1840 census, only four years after Arkansas became a state.

Jesse Shewmake (b. 1816, Tennessee) md. Viva Tracey who was born in Tennessee. She died 1843. They had three children: Pleasant G., Wilson C. (b. Dec. 13, 1840) and a child who died in infancy. Jesse married Martha. He died after 1890. This is from *Goodspeed's Reminiscences and Memoirs of Conway Co, 1890.* Also from same source: Company B, 1st AR Inf. Battalion (Union), organized at Batesville June 10, 1862 by amalgamation of two companies of volunteers from Conway County brought into Batesville recently occupied by federal forces under Samuel R. Curtis, by Thomas J. Williams and Geo. M. Galloway; in the organization of Co. B, Williams was chosen Captain, Geo. M. Galloway first lieutenant and Nathan Williams 2nd lieutenant.

Shewmake (Shoemake) Wilson C., 21, received disability discharge Nov. 24, 1862. He was born in Conway County and was a farmer. It is not known for sure, but is believed that Jesse was nephew of James Shumake, born ca. 1795 in Tennessee. James married Nancy Baird (b. ca. 1799, Davidson County, TN) was the daughter of Isham (pronounced Isom) H. Baird born in Ireland. Isham Baird and Clarissa Bushnell were married in Sumner County, TN in 1825. Clarissa was born ca. 1795 in York County, SC and died in Arkansas. It is not known where Isham died.

James and Nancy Shumake's daughter Elizabeth C. married Samuel Selathiel Mason in Conway County Dec. 25, 1849. They lived in Springfield for a time when it was the county seat. *Submitted by Mary Mason Bostian.*

SHIPP - Weighing in at 10-1/2 pounds and 21 inches long, I entered this world March 20, 1971. I am the "proud daughter" of Eddie and Sue Shipp. A few days after the beginning of my life, I arrived at my white house half bricked up, in Center Ridge of Conway County. I was beginning to wonder if I would ever get to see my new home. My dad, Eddie Shipp, could not seem to get over the fact that I wasn't the little boy he had

Edi Cathlene Shipp

hoped for. Finally, my mom Sue Shipp convinced my dad that other children would make fun of me if my name was Eddie Scott. He agreed and they decided on Edi Cathlene Shipp. We arrived at my new home March 23, 1971. Once again, another individual disappointed in my arrival. My sissy Sherry did not want a baby sister, she wanted a baby puppy.

As years began to go by, I enjoyed growing up in Conway County. I loved playing in our yard until dark, eating fresh vegetables out of the garden, raising my pets and working in my daddy's shop.

My playground equipment consisted of one swing. This swing would definitely be recalled this day and time. It was a board on a rusting chain, looped over a log, which was nailed to two posts, not cemented. Did I have fun? I had a blast.

Wow, what gardens we would plant each summer. You would think we were in charge of feeding everyone in Conway County. Even though it was lots of work for the whole family, I sure enjoyed making dolls out of the oversized, yellow cucumbers. Was I creative or what?

Those poor animals that had to be my pets. The most beneficial lesson I learned from being a young pet owner is to not carry my sisters' baby duck by the

neck. Come to find out, my sister did get a puppy that day I came home from the hospital, but she did not let me touch it.

Eddie Shipp's Garage, those were the days. I could change the oil in vehicles, help my dad tear down motors, help inspect the buses and assist in knocking out kingpin bushings. I'm sure I did a lot more tearing down than putting together. I may not have been Eddie Scott Shipp, but I was daddy's little grease monkey.

I'm very thankful for being raised in Conway County. I am now 33 years old and a GT-Specialist for the Russellville School District. Through my gifted students, I still play, create, own a class pet and fix items they break. I now answer to Mrs. Cathlene Price. *Submitted by Cathlene (Shipp) Price.*

SHIPP - On May 28, 1965 Eddie Arnold Shipp and Sue Crisel were married in the living room of her parents. Sue was born and raised in Monroe County, AR, near Holly Grove. Her parents were Olin Elmo Crisel and Lorene Beatrice Smith Crisel. Both are deceased now. She has four sisters: Barber Ann (deceased), Paulette (deceased), Patricia Ann and Maybell. Sue and her sisters grew up in the cotton patches of

Shipp Family, 1976.

the Arkansas delta along with numerous cousins. She graduated from Holly Grove High School as valedictorian in May 1965, four days before she was married.

Eddie is the son of Oma Mae McCoy and Noah Kaleb Shipp. They are both deceased. He has three brothers and one sister: Leonard Shipp, Dewey Shipp, Alvin Shipp and Judy Shipp Baldwin. They all grew up in Sheepskin Valley where they all still live, except for Eddie who only lives about seven miles away in the Pleasant Hill Community.

After they married, Eddie and Sue made their home in Conway County where Eddie was born and raised. They had their first child in 1966. When Sherry Sue was 3, the family moved into the home they have lived in now for 35 years. In 1971, a second daughter, Edi Cathlene was added to the family. Sherry teaches at Wonderview High School, and Cathlene teaches G/T classes at Dwight Elementary in Russellville. Sherry is married to James Earl Latimer, and they have two sons, Justin Scott Shipp who is a senior at UCA and Marshall Wyatt Latimer who is in the first grade at Nemo Vista. Cathlene is married to Kevin Shawn Price and they have one son, Shawn Wayne Price.

Eddie worked for the county a while before he went to work for Allison Ford Company. In 1979, Eddie began working for Nemo Vista School District as a bus driver and mechanic. He plans to retire in July 2006 and devote his time to enjoying his grandchildren and working on the farm.

Sue worked at a couple of local factories, that have since closed, before going to Nemo Vista as a custodian, study hall teacher, and finally high school secretary. She completed her degree in education at ATU in 1998 and has been teaching at South Side Bee Branch High School since then. She plans to retired in 2009 and join Eddie and the grandchildren on the farm.

Eddie and Sue worship at the Center Ridge Church of Christ and have many wonderful friends in Conway County. Life is good!! *Submitted by Sue Shipp.*

SIMMONS - Coma Delana Simmons was born Jan. 13, 1880 in Pope County. In later years, she moved to Morrilton, AR. She was a member of the Morrilton

First United Methodist Church for many years.

She became employed by O'Neal's Department Store and worked there for 50 years.

Miss Coma, as she was affectionately called by most of those who knew her, lived to the age of 86 years and 5 months. Miss Coma passed away June 13, 1966 and is bur-

Miss Coma Delana Simmons

ied in the Atkins City Cemetery in Pope County. *Submitted by Pauline Merryman.*

SISSON - Nettie Sisson was my great-grandmother. I have relied on census records, marriage records, deed records, land grants, and death records copied from the original books whenever possible in constructing her family history. I was also fortunate to have discovered Lemuel Sisson's family Bible among Nettie's papers. A very active Sisson genealogy community has traced the Sisson family in the United States back to two main lines, the "Rhode Island" branch and the "Southern" branch. Thanks to help from David Arne Sisson of the Rhode Island line and Southern specialists Chuck Ward, Libby Clay, Beverly Brown and Katherine Hardiman; Nettie's lineage can be followed back along a Southern branch to South Carolina. Information on both Sisson lines can be obtained from Carol Sisson Regehr, family archivist and manager of *SISSON-L@rootsweb.com.*

Nettie Sisson, Hattie Laurence and James D. Sisson.

Nettie Sisson (b. Sept. 5, 1882 in Morrilton, Conway, AR) was the last of 12 children of Lemuel D. and Mary Adeline Cox Sisson. Lemuel (b. Dec. 20, 1838, Alabama) md. Mary Adeline Cox Jan. 22, 1859 in St. Clair County, AL. She was born Feb. 18, 1839 in Alabama, the daughter of Emmanuel Cox and Sarah McNeil. Lemuel died testate in Morrilton, Conway County, AR March 16, 1912. Mary Adeline died testate March 30, 1930 at Nettie's home at 403 S. Morrill in Morrilton. Both are buried in Elmwood Cemetery, Morrilton.

Lemuel was the fifth of 11 known children of Dannison and Lucinda Stockman Sisson. Dannison (b. Jan. 15, 1810 in Georgia) md. Lucinda Stockman May 25, 1830 in Georgia. She was born Jan. 15, 1815 in South Carolina. Their first three children were born in Georgia: James Marion (b. April 5, 1831); William M. (b. Feb. 8, 1833) and Emilee (b. April 24, 1835). The family moved to Alabama about 1836, and the rest of the children were born there: Catherine (b. Dec. 28, 1837); Lemuel (b. Dec. 20, 1838); Daniel S. (b. Feb. 25, 1841); Braxton (b. March 18, 1843); Benson S. (b. March 15, 1846); Zachery Taylor (b. Dec. 22, 1848); Mary Ann (b. Nov. 11, 1851) and David W. (b. ca. 1858). Dannison died Jan. 4, 1885 in Talladega County, AL and Lucinda died May 17, 1886 also in Talladaga County. They are buried in the Sisson Cemetery in that county.

Dannison was the son of William Sisson (b. ca. 1777 in South Carolina, died before 1860 in Alabama) and Susannah (born after 1780 in South Carolina, died

before 1850 in Alabama). This William Sisson was also the progenitor of the Van Buren County, AR Sissons through his son William B. Sisson and William B.'s son, William R. Sisson, who married Melva Blackwell Quattlebaum. Many researchers believe that William Sisson (b. ca. 1777) was a descendant of William Sisson (b. 1739 in Brunswick County, VA) and Frances Shearin. This early William Sisson died Jan. 21, 1796 in Spartanburg, Union County, SC.

Judging by the census records and the birth dates and places of the children, the Lemuel D. Sisson family migrated to Arkansas from Alabama about 1869. They are found in the 1870 Conway County, AR Census in Howard Township, Post Office Lewisburg, p. 8. According to the Lemuel Sisson family Bible, Lemuel and Mary Adeline Sisson had 12 children.

1) Sarah C. Sisson (b. Oct. 10, 1859 in Talladega County, AL) first married Rufus M. Rodgers on Dec. 31, 1882. They had one child Verna Addie (b. Dec. 3, 1883) who married Albert Zerrel O'Daniel July 15, 1900 in Morrilton, Conway, AR. Albert died May 15, 1940 in Phoenix, AZ, and Verna died April 2, 1973 in Phoenix. Sarah C. married second, Wilburn M. Batson on Feb. 23, 1888 in Morrilton. They had three children: Charles (b. June 1890, d. May 9, 1912 in Germantown, Conway County); Mamie (b. August 1894) md. Elbert Owens; Lee Roy (b. June 1, 1896) md. Ruth Ellen Williams on Aug. 13, 1916, and died Jan. 9, 1943. Sarah C. Sisson Batson died April 2, 1901, and is buried in Elmwood Cemetery, Morrilton, Conway, AR.

2) Francis E. "Fanny" Sisson (b. Oct. 20, 1861 in Alabama, d. Sept. 11, 1883).

3) John W. Sisson (b. Oct. 22, 1862 in Alabama). (Note: that birth date is the one on his tombstone - the family Bible says Nov. 7, 1862). According to the Family Bible, he first married Kitty Adams, date unknown. He then married Clyde Pool May 1, 1919 in Garland County, AR. Clyde was born ca 1879. John W. died Nov. 16, 1925 in Mena, Polk County, AR, and was buried in Elmwood Cemetery, Morrilton, Conway, AR. He was a gambler and wore a ring with two one-carat diamonds.

4) George Washington Sisson (b. Jan 18, 1865 in Alabama, died before 1912).

5) William F. Sisson (b. Sept. 20, 1866 in Alabama, died before 1912).

6) Sidney C. Sisson (b. Feb. 18, 1868 in Alabama, d. Dec. 16, 1904) is buried in Elmwood Cemetery, Morrilton, Conway County, AR.

7) Dector "Dock" Sisson (b. Feb. 18, 1869 in Alabama, died before 1912).

8) Robert Daniel Sisson (b. Aug. 20, 1870 in Arkansas) md. on Aug. 26, 1894 to Margaret Ophelia Riley, daughter of Robert Riley and Angeline Weaver in Conway County, AR. Margaret (b. Feb. 1, 1873 in Independence, Randolph County, AR, d. Aug. 14, 1959) and Robert are buried in Elmwood Cemetery, Morrilton, AR. They had six children:

a) Minnie Allene (b. March 31, 1904) md. Lee Pack on March 19, 1922.

b) Robert Lemuel Jr. (b. Jan. 9, 1896, d. Aug. 16, 1942 in Maryland) is buried in Elmwood Cemetery in Morrilton. He was a US Navy veteran.

c) Franklin L. (b. Sept. 12, 1897) md. Amy Garner on Oct. 14, 1918. He died April 2, 1968 and buried in Elmwood Cemetery, Morrilton.

d) Jack Westley (b. Feb. 12, 1899) md. Theresa Borhosalin on Feb. 22, 1925. He died Dec. 1, 1972 in New Hampshire.

e) Evelyn Margaret (b. Oct. 15, 1915 in Morrilton, Conway, AR) first married Robert Lloyd Heigle on Aug. 31, 1933 in Morrilton and had three children: Robert L., Mary K., and Margaret. Robert Lloyd was born ca. 1914. She married second, Robert Bradley Skipper (b. May 1914, d. April 8, 1952) on Dec. 22, 1945. She married third, Robert Lee Leland on Jan. 6, 1956 in Morrilton. They had one child John R. (b. Dec. 28, 1956).

f) Lillie Angeline (b. March 4, 1908) md. Leonard

Thomas Riggs on Dec. 24, 1927. She died Oct. 7, 1974 and was buried in Riggs Cemetery, Conway County, AR.

9) Ella Sisson (b. Feb. 22, 1876 in Arkansas, d. Aug. 20, 1884).

10) James Danason Sisson (b. Feb. 6, 1879 in Arkansas) md. Lillie Bess Kershaw and had one daughter Bess. Bess (b. Oct. 13, 1906, died in a fire Feb. 26, 1956 in Newport, Jackson County, AR). She owned a children's clothing store and was a veteran of WWII. James died after 1948. (Note: the spelling of James' middle name is according to the family Bible. However, it is likely that the correct spelling is "Dannison," the given name of his grandfather.)

11) Hattie Virginia Sisson (b. July 18, 1881 in Arkansas) md. Henry Laurence and had two children: John Robin (b. Dec. 22, 1903 in Terrell, Kaufman, TX, d. April 1958) and Mary Sidney (b. July 30, 1905 in Terrell, TX, d. February 1982 in Austin, TX) married a Becker. Hattie died in a car accident in Ft. Stockton, Pecos County, TX where she had lived much of her life. She came there in 1912, moved to Sanderson, TX in 1923 and returned to Fort Stockton in 1933. She is buried in East Hill Cemetery, Pecos County, TX.

12) Nettie Sisson (b. Sept. 5, 1882) married on June 3, 1900 to Phillip Frank Drilling (see related article) in Faulkner County, AR. They had three children:

a) The oldest was my grandfather Allen Leonard Drilling (b. June 29, 1901 in Morrilton) who was baptized July 28, 1901 at Sacred Heart Parish in Morrilton. He married Carmon Belle Miller (see related article) June 26, 1923 in Plumerville, Conway, AR. They had one child, my mother Betty Jane, who is still living. Allen Leonard died Sept. 3, 1986 in Heber Springs, Cleburne, AR and Carmon Belle died May 30, 2000 in Heber Springs. Both are buried in Corning Cemetery, Clay, AR.

b) The second child, Hattie Virginia Drilling (b. April 27, 1903 in Morrilton) first married Clarence Naff March 1, 1918 in Conway County, AR. They were divorced Sept. 18, 1922 in Conway County. She married second, Mark Eyre Switzer April 18, 1923 in Eureka, KS. They had one child, Donald Eyre (b. Jan. 7, 1927 in Pawhuska, Osage County, OK, d. July 13, 1986 in St. Petersburg, FL). Donald Eyre is buried in Corning Cemetery, Clay County, AR. Mark Switzer was a sheriff, and was killed in the line of duty Jan. 12, 1927 in Pawhuska, OK at the age of 29. He was buried in the City Cemetery in Pawhuska. She married third, Arthur McDaniel Nov. 11, 1929 in Conway County. He was born Sept. 11, 1904 and died March 8, 1935. Hattie was proprietor of a ladies dress shop in Monticello, AR. She died Nov. 5, 1943 in Little Rock, Pulaski, AR, and was buried in Elmwood Cemetery in Morrilton.

c) The third child, Arthur Bernard Drilling (b. Jan. 17, 1905 in Morrilton, d. June 5, 1961 in New York City) was buried in Memorial Gardens Park, Hot Springs, Garland, AR. He married Florida Francis "Floy" Harris ca. 1924. She was born Jan. 11, 1906 and died Jan. 5, 1986. He was a bridge builder, and a superintendent with US Steel, American Bridge Division, and was in charge of building the Mackinac Bridge. They had four children: Arthur B. Jr. (b. Nov. 10, 1925, d. Nov. 12, 1979) was buried in Memorial Gardens Park; Carolyn (b. June 24, 1927 in Morrilton, d. January 1987 in Florida) was buried in Memorial Gardens. The other children, Marinette and John Allen, are still living.

The marriage of Nettie Sisson and Philip Drilling ended in divorce Oct. 29, 1906 and on Aug. 14, 1907 Phillip Frank Drilling married Maggie M. Thompson. Nettie subsequently married J. Walter Roberts on June 29, 1912 in Conway County. He died in 1916. She married last, O.J. Alexander on April 2, 1920 in McAlester, Pittsburg County, OK. Nettie died Nov. 6, 1968 at St. Anthony's Hospital in Morrilton and is buried at Elmwood Cemetery in Morrilton. *By Janet Claire Porterfield.*

SKINNER - James Calvin Skinner (b. April 16, 1875, Clarendon, Monroe County, AR) was the second of 11 children born to John Washington Skinner and Susan Clarentine McCray. John Washington was also born in Monroe County, AR in 1852, whose family had come from Alabama and Mississippi. John and Susan had eight children. After the death of Susan Clarentine in 1881, John Washington married her sister, Louise McCray; and together, they had three daughters. All of the children of Susan and John called this stepmother, their own mother's sister, "Aunt Lou."

James Calvin Skinner and Cecil Alice Carroll Skinner

James Calvin Skinner was a tall, thin man who earned his living for a time as a "barkeep." He also raised race horses, according to family members. At some point in his life, the family had made its way to Caruthersville, MO and became "renters," working various lands there.

James married Cecil Alice Carroll in Caruthersville, Pemiscot County, MO on March 14, 1897. Cecil was the daughter of John Rueben Carroll and Mary Jane "Molly" Wallingsford. She was born March 1, 1879, probably in Tennessee. It is believed that all of the nine children of James and Cecil were born in Caruthersville, but none of them stayed there. The family moved to Perry County, AR, back to Caruthersville, then back to Perry County, and then to Conway County. The children were Johnnie Elvis "Brother" (b. 1897, d. 1931); Susan Zeola "Zeke" married to William Collier (b. 1899-); Calvin Leroy; Jessie Belle (Jess) married to Royce Morrow (b. 1902, d. 1971); Willie Mae "Bill" married to Glenn Silas Nowlin (b. 1904, d. 1989); James Edward; Ralph Buchanan "Peck" (b. 1908, d. 1967); Mary Clarentine "Ruth" married to Olen Windham (b. 1910-); and Georgia B. "Mug" married to Argus Edmondson (b. 1912, d. 2005).

The Skinners moved to Oppelo, Conway County, AR at some point. James Calvin and Cecil became members of the Riverview Baptist Church where J.C., as he was known, became a deacon. Ralph Buchanan Skinner lived near them most of his life after serving in WWI. The husband of Mary Clarentine "Ruth," Olen Windham, still had family ties to Conway County and her sister Georgia B., who married Argus Edmondson, lived near St. Elizabeth's Church in one of the two homes James Calvin Skinner built. (He and Cecil lived in the other.) The houses are still in use.

Willie Mae and her husband Glenn Nowlin lived in Morrilton when their daughter Glenna Carroll Nowlin (see sketch of Glenna Nowlin) was born in 1924. Their son Johnnie Elvis was a lineman for the power company at Perry when he accidentally touched a live wire and was electrocuted. Susan Zeola was a really good shot with rifle or handgun, dubbed, "The Annie Oakley of Missouri" in a newspaper article about her. Willie Mae joined the WACS during WWII when her husband was told he could not join the Army because he was blind in one eye. James died in 1952 and Cecil in 1966; both are buried in Wolf Cemetery, Oppelo, AR.

SKINNER - Ralph Buchanan Skinner, better known to his family as "Peck," was born the seventh child of James Calvin Skinner and Cecil Alice Carroll (see sketch of James and Cecil). He was born Feb. 22, 1908, probably in Caruthersville, Pemiscot County, MO. He was, as a young boy, quite a "card," always playing practical jokes on his brothers and sisters. In one family photo for example, Peck is dressed as a girl and his sister, Willie Mae, is dressed like a boy. Both of them are smiling like the imps they were.

There was another story of Peck when he was small, this time perpetuated against him. The kids were playing in the old barn on their property and they all thought it would be fun to ride the tricycle in the loft. They had a rope up there, tied to the brace and pulley, and had all jumped out to swing out onto the hay that was piled below. So,

Ralph Buchanan "Peck" Skinner

they took the tricycle and all took turns riding it around. When it was Peck's turn, no one thought to tell him to watch out for the open loft door, and he rode it straight out and down he went. Fortunately, there was enough hay to break his fall. But, when their father found out what had happened, he spanked all of "us kids" as my grandmother used to say.

Ralph grew to manhood and served during WWI in the US Army, though if he was drafted or enlisted, no one knows. On Aug. 10, 1929, he married Dora Calloway of Oppelo, AR. Now, this is a sort of mystery, as there are no family members left who remember much about Ralph. One member told that his wife's name was Buena. The family research is not complete, so one will have to wait for the sequel to find out for certain. Ralph did have at least one child, Millie Dale. She grew to adulthood and married a man named Cisco.

Ralph attended Riverview Baptist Church with his parents, who were also members. He was said to have been a deacon at one point. He died Feb. 7, 1967, and is buried at Wolf Cemetery, at Oppelo, AR.

SKINNER - Willie Mae Skinner (b. Nov. 2, 1904) was the fifth child of James Calvin Skinner and Cecil Alice Carroll Skinner in Caruthersville, Pemiscot County, MO. Growing up poor, she and her brothers and sisters worked in every conceivable occupation - picking cotton, farming, digging ditches, domestic help; whatever they could do to help the family. They learned to can home grown vegetables and to "make do." They moved from Missouri, coming to Perry

Willie Mae Skinner Nowlin

County first, then they moved back to Missouri, and then, mysteriously, back to Arkansas, this time, Conway County to live near Oppelo.

Willie Mae met Glenn Silas Nowlin (b. April 25, 1901) and they were married Oct. 29, 1922 in Perry County. Glenn was born in Natural Steps, Pulaski County, AR and perhaps his parents, James Bryant Nowlin and Nellie Dodson Hays Nowlin had moved into Conway County by that time. No one knows how they met, but the result was a daughter, Glenna Carroll Nowlin (b. July 14, 1924). Willie Mae's mother-in-law, Nellie Nowlin, served as mid-wife for the birth, done at home, with no help for the pain of it except the herbs Nellie concocted from local roots and leaves. Nellie was known as a healer to the locals. The experience was so traumatic for Willie Mae, she swore she would not have another and she did not. She and Glenn moved to California during the Depression. He worked for his brother, Claude Nowlin, who owned a gas station; she worked as a domestic, cleaning a local apartment building. Glenna began school there and developed a life-long affection for California. When the family later moved back to Little Rock, AR, she was terribly disappointed.

Glenn always referred to Willie Mae as "Bill," as did the whole family. When still a child, Glenn was rendered blind in one eye by an encounter with a rooster. When WWII broke out and he tried to enlist, he was rejected due to his blindness. Willie Mae promptly joined the Women's Army Corps (WAC) and began her training at Ft. Oglethorpe, GA.

Willie Mae's ancestral roots were Irish. Her great-grandmother, Mary Jane Wallingsford Carroll, had taught her many old Irish ballads which Willie Mae sang when she cooked or cleaned. She had a great laugh and loved to tell ghost stories to her grandchildren, Jerry and Paula. She loved *"The Carol Burnett Show"* and worked the crossword puzzle every day, though she never finished the eighth grade. She never learned to drive and lived for many years in the home she and Glenn restored in Little Rock. Her last years were spent in Boulder City, CO, near her only child, Glenna. She died there April 7, 1989.

SKIPPER - James Arthur "Jim" Skipper Sr. was an early postmaster at Solgohachia. He was born June 19, 1882 to David James and Mary Katherine Skipper at their family farm near Lanty in Conway County, AR. His Grandfather Skipper had settled in Conway County in 1856 and had several hundred acres of land near Round Mountain. When James was born, his mother and father were 33. He had four older sisters: Mary, 12; Harriet, 10; Lou, 8; and Betty, 3 and an older brother, John Quincy, 5. The Skippers had lived in the area for 26 years.

James Arthur Skipper and Mayola Josephine Noland, with daughter Thelma, 1908.

Another brother David was born in 1885. He lived only a few months. Born between 1885 and 1894 another sister Rosie Elmer, a brother Carl Toby and a final sister Ethel Pauline were born.

Mayola Josephine Noland, Jim's future bride, was born July 22, 1890 to William F. Noland, age 30, and Sarah M. Beaty, age 28. They lived in Lanty. William was from Alabama and Sarah was from Georgia. Jo's father died when she was 4 and her mother died when she was 10.

Jim turned 18 in 1900. There is no record of his education, but based on his later employment as a postmaster, he must have had a good education for the time. Somewhere in the area his future bride, Jo Noland, turned 10. Jim and Jo exchanged the following notes in 1905 and saved them for the rest of their lives:

Arthur, Ark.
Oct. 3d 1905.
Miss Jocie Noland
Lanty, Ark.
Kind friend
    You may be surprised to receive a letter from me but I thought I would write you a few lines and see if you would correspond with me and if it be agreeable with you, I would like to have your company for the 3d Sunday in this month. If you have not got any objections to me coming write and let me know. Hoping to hear from you.

Her reply was:
Lanty, Ark.
Oct 9th - 1905
Mr. James Skipper
Arthur, Ark.
Kind friend
    Your letter was veary much suprising indeed. I

never thought of hearing from you but your company for the 3d Sunday will be exceptable with me if so you can write and tell me what time you will be heare and if you can not all right.

From a kind friend

Josie Noland

When the golden sun is setting and your mind from home is free

When of others you are thanking will you sometimes thank of me.

Josie

Jo was 15 and Jim was 23 when they exchanged these notes and there were some spelling errors as you can see. They were married a year later on Jan. 6, 1907. He was 24 and she was 16-1/4. Although it was not uncommon for women her age to be married, perhaps the fact that she had been an orphan since the age of 10 might have been a factor.

Jim was appointed postmaster of Solgohachia in 1908. Republican Teddy Roosevelt was president at the time. The appointment lasted until 1913 when Democrat Woodrow Wilson became president. The appointment certificate was signed by George V.L. Meyer, Postmaster General.

Jim's father, Dave, died on Dec. 24, 1909 at the age of 60 and was buried in the McLaren Cemetery in Lanty. A nice monument still marks his grave. The monument has the initials of the International Order of Odd Fellows on it. Jim was 27 and Jo was 19. Mary Katherine, Dave's wife, was 60. Jim was also a member of the Odd Fellows.

Jim and Jo's second child, David William, was born on Nov. 23, 1911. Grandma Louisa Skipper was 62. At the time David was born, a man named Irving lived in the community and had a monkey. A visiting friend looked at baby David and said, "Why he's as ugly as Irving's monkey." "Irving" became his nickname and stayed with him. If Joseph W. Skipper's middle name was William, then Irving was probably named David for his grandfather and William for his great-grandfather. He eventually had his name changed to Irving.

Jim's mother Mary died Feb. 9, 1912, at the age of 65. Her casket was purchased from R.E. Echols, Dealer In Furniture, Carpets, Wall Paper, Shades, Etc. - Undertaking a Specialty. It cost $30. The order was made on the 9th for Mrs. D.J. Skipper. She was buried beside Dave in the McLaren Cemetery at Lanty. Jim was almost 32 and Jo almost 24 when his mother died. Thelma was 6 and Irving was 2. Jim and Jo had been married for seven years.

With both his parents dead, the family land in dispute and worn out from over 50 years of farming, and no chance for a postmaster job with a Democrat president in office, Jim probably decided to make a new start elsewhere. The swamp land around England, AR, had been drained and cleared and had very rich soil for farming and Jim may have been told or may have realized that there would be an opportunity to get an appointment to the job of postmaster at England if a Republican president was elected.

Jim and his family and perhaps Carl Toby and his family moved to England early in 1917. It could have taken up to a week to reach England from Round Mountain. They traveled in wagons and camped along the way. Even if they had had cars and trucks, the journey would have been difficult because of the poor roads. Average speed by auto was about 20 mph. Thelma remembered that it was cold. She was almost 9 years old and Irving was 5.

Jim and Jo's third child, Mildred Pauline, was born Jan. 25, 1919, in England, AR. Pauline may have been named for her Aunt Ethel Pauline, Jim's youngest sister.

Jim and Jo's fourth child, James Jr., was born Nov. 7, 1921. Jim was 39 and Jo was 31. Thelma was 13, Irving was 10, and Pauline was almost 2.

In 1922, at the age of 40, Jim received an appointment as postmaster of England, AR. The certifi-

cate is dated July 1st and signed by Warren G. Harding, who had taken office in March of 1921. A farmer, C.F. Skipper, saw the appointment notice in the *Gazette* and wrote to compare family histories. C.F.'s father, William F. Skipper, had come from Alabama in 1855.

Jim and Jo's baby boy, Joe Noland Skipper, was born on Feb. 19, 1931. Jim was 48 and Jo was 40.

Jim's 50th birthday was June 19, 1932. Jo was almost 42, Thelma was 24, Irving was almost 21, Pauline was 13, James Jr. was almost 11, and Joe Noland was 1. Thelma had been married for three years, Irving for two years. Democrat Franklin D. Roosevelt soundly defeated President Hoover with the promise to end prohibition and with the theme song *"Happy Days Are Here Again."* Of course the days were not so happy for Jim, since the election of a Democrat meant the loss of his job as postmaster.

Jim and Jo celebrated their 30th wedding anniversary on Jan. 6, 1937. Thelma had written a letter to them and Jo wrote the following letter in return:

"England, Ark., Jan. 6,1937: Dear Daughter, I never thought I would be writing my eldest child a letter on my 30th (wedding) anniversary, but here I be. Through all the joy and sorrows and weary at 30 years still happy and Dad is still the dearest man of my heart. We have fought the battles of life side by side true to each other and love each other as much as we did when we took one another for better or worse 30 years ago this afternoon. June 6, 1907 don't seem so long ago...

Jo died Wednesday, March 29, 1939 She had had an almost constant loss of blood. She had consulted doctors for some time about cures and was a little hesitant about surgery. The letters to Thelma and to the doctor about this situation are sad to read. As Thelma's calendar tells, Jo had surgery, but soon began to get worse. Thelma's daughter, Virginia, said that a blood clot resulting from the surgery was actually what killed her.

James Arthur Skipper died Feb. 9, 1940, at the age of 57. Jim suffered from headaches and nosebleed, probably from high blood pressure. He and Joe Noland often slept together since they were the only ones left at home. Jim came home not feeling well and in the night had a massive stroke that left him mostly paralyzed and unconscious. Joe was pinned to the bed by Jim's arm. They got Jim to the hospital and he died there. *Submitted by James Maxwell Skipper*

SKIPPER - James Maxwell Skipper was a 1959 graduate of Wonderview High School. Known to friends and family as Jimmie, he was the oldest child of Louise Maxwell of Lanty and James Arthur Skipper Jr. of England, AR. James Arthur Skipper was the son of James Arthur Skipper Sr. "Big Jim" and Josephine Noland, both of whom were born and raised near Solgohachia in Conway County. Big Jim was postmaster of Solgohachia from about 1908-12 before moving his family to England where James Jr. was born and raised. Louise was the only child of Luther Maxwell of Lanty and Eugenia Houston of Old Hickory. She was born in Old Hickory and raised on the family farm in Lanty, but attended Morrilton High School.

James Maxwell Skinner and Ann Louise Jones on their wedding day, June 27, 1962.

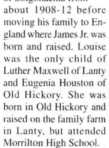

James Maxwell Skipper at University of Arkansas - 1962.

James and Louise met at UCA (then ASTC)

and started married life in Little Rock, where Jimmie was born on Feb. 11, 1941. The following year, twin sisters, Jeanne and Josephine, were born. Josephine died of a congenital heart defect at the age of 13 months. James worked with an oil company in support of the war effort and was transferred to Lake Charles, LA. He was drafted in 1944 and moved the family back to live with Louise's parents in Lanty. They were still there when news of James' death came in 1945.

Louise married Lyonell Halbrook, a life-long resident of Cleveland, and the family moved there in 1947. Lyonell and Louise built a beautiful rock house and raised six children there: Jimmie and Jeanne and Brenda, Marinelle, Sherrye and John Halbrook.

Jimmie attended six years of elementary school at Cleveland, then six years at Wonderview High School where he participated in sports and was active in the Future Farmers of America. He qualified as an Arkansas State Farmer and won a Rockwin Scholarship. He attended the University of Arkansas and received a bachelor's degree in electrical engineering in 1963.

Jimmie married Ann Louise Jones while attending the University and their first child, James Maxwell Skipper Jr., was born there in 1963. Ann is the oldest child of Jesse and Maurice Jones of west Texas. Over the years Ann and her parents have lived in Texas, Colorado, South Dakota, Missouri, Illinois and Iowa in addition to a period of time in northwest Arkansas before settling in Springdale, AR. Ann has a younger sister Frances and younger brothers, Chester and Grady.

After graduation from the U of A, Jimmie was hired by the NASA Manned Spacecraft Center (now Lyndon B. Johnson Space Center) in Houston, TX. He, Ann and little Jimmy moved to Houston, then moved to Pearland, just south of Houston, where they had a new house built. Three more children were born there: Louis Lee, Rebecca Louise and John Luther. All the children attended and graduated from the Pearland Independent School District public schools and went on to obtain other degrees.

Jimmie (now known as Skip to friends and associates) began work for NASA on June 10, 1963 just after the final Mercury Program space flight. He was involved with the Gemini program and was a volunteer test subject in the Gemini space suit to certify it for operation in the minus 300° cold of space for the first US extra-vehicular activity (space walk). He worked with space suit development testing and astronaut training for all the manned space projects from Gemini through Apollo, Skylab, Apollo-Soyuz, Shuttle, and the International Space Station. He retired in 1998 after 35 years with NASA.

Skip and Ann still live in the house they built in 1964. They are active members of the Shadycrest Baptist Church in Pearland where they have been members since it was formed in 1971. Skip has been a photographer since early childhood and has collected many old family photos, space program photos, and travel photos and has put them on the Internet as stories in the Skipper Family Magazine at the URL: www.jamesmskipper.us. In addition to raising the family and keeping the home, Ann has been involved with church and PTA activities. She has worked in various arts and crafts over the years, selling some at Christmas craft shows and hosting craft parties for women of the community. *Submitted by James M. Skipper.*

SLEDGE - Henry and Betsy Sledge's family came to Conway County nearly 175 years ago when Arkansas was still a territory. Family historians of the 19th century claimed Henry had several daughters plus seven or eight sons, with at least two of those sons serving under the Confederate Flag during the Civil War. Actually, one son served on the Confederate side, was captured, exchanged and paroled. He and a brother then enlisted in the 3rd Regiment of the Arkansas Mounted Volunteers, Union Troops.

The Sledge surname originated in English mills where goods were hauled about on sledges. The first Sledge immigrants left Pensford, Somerset, England to escape the Bloody Assizes which took place in 1685. Our ancestor, Charles Sledge, arrived in Virginia in 1686.

Henry Sledge (b. 1794, Virginia) was a sixth generation descendant of Charles and wife Mary (Clarke). Henry married Betsy Pate, Aug. 29, 1814, in Williamson County, TN. According to land records, their family was in Giles County, TN in 1830.

Their final move was about 1832, when they settled on Cadron Creek, near present day Springfield. Henry died about 1848 and Betsy died in 1857. Their resting place is unknown but they probably were buried on their own land, as was the custom among early pioneers. Their known children and grand-children were:

Thomas P. Sledge (b. 1816). First wife unknown, son James Franklin. Second wife, Louisa (Hawkins ?). Children: Thomas C., John Watson and Martha. Third wife, Martha (Garrison) Blaylock. Children, Susan Jenkins and Mary Savannah. Fourth wife, Mrs. Mary A. Goats. (Thomas died not long after they married in 1880.)

Austin J. (b. 1819). First wife, Arena (unknown). Children: William and Elizabeth J. Second wife, Mary Mitchell. Except for the son William, the family disappeared from all records before 1870. William, unmarried, died in 1886 in Faulkner County.

Cynthia (b. 1820). Husband, Thomas MacMillan. Children: Sarah, William, Elizabeth Mary, Emeline, John M., Daniel G., Hardy (Harris/Harrison), Isabella and Susan MacMillan.

John H. (b. 1826). First wife, Margaret (Unknown). Children: Mary and John. Second wife, Sarah Carter. Child: Lucinda. (After John H. died in 1857, John and Lucinda went to live with the Thomas Sledge family.)

Susan (b. 1829). Husband, John Holt. Children: Sarah, William and Andrew Holt. (Susan was widowed by 1870.)

Hardy/Harry (b. 1830). Wife unknown, Child. Peter. (Hardy/Harry died before 1870, so Peter lived with Henry and Martha Sledge.)

Rosetta (b. 1832). Husband, John Pryor Hogue. Children: Sarah Malinda, Henry Gibson, Archibald Y., Elizabeth A., John, Mary and Rebecca Hogue.

Henry (b. 1834). Wife, Sara Stewart who died in 1859. Second wife, Martha Wood. Child: Nancy Elizabeth (Lizzie).

Elizabeth M. (b. 1839). First husband (Unknown) Rodgers. No children. Second husband, Asa Allen. Children, Henry and Calhoun Allen.

Benjamin Sledge (b. 1841, d. before 1857).

Jackson Sledge may have been a son of Henry and Betsy Sledge, also. His name appeared only once on Conway County's tax list (1847). Since there is no further record, it is presumed he died before 1850. *Submitted by N.C. Guthier.*

SMITH - Andrew Jackson Smith was born in Corinth, MS on Oct. 10, 1866. By the time he was 6 years old, death had taken both of his parents. As a result, he came to Arkansas in approximately 1872 to live with his maternal grandparents (his mother's name was Nicie Powell Smith) named William and Margaret Powell. The 1880 census lists the Powells and their grandson as living in Union Township.

On Dec. 13, 1885, Andrew married Susan Florence Williams who was the daughter of Anderson (known as Doc) and Melinda Beck Williams. The 1900 census lists the Smith household as: Andrew, Susan, three boys, and Susan's mother, Melinda Williams. The boys were: William T. (Truman), Freed F., and Otto Orville (O.O.) Smith. A daughter Lola was born in 1902. Susan Florence died on Sept. 11, 1905. Following her death, her mother took over the household duties and helped raise the four children.

Andrew lived in Atkins, AR from 1902-17 where he was a farmer. In 1917, he moved to Morrilton, AR and established a grocery store with gasoline pumps on highway 64 East, next to the Pierce-Young Planer Mill. The Mill was located near the site of what is now (2004) Sonic Drive-In. In 1933, he moved Smith Grocery Store to 701 East Broadway and operated it from this location until he retired. He died on Jan. 28, 1960. In all, Andrew Jackson Smith lived in Conway County for 72 years. He was a member of the Cedar Creek Baptist Church and of the Springfield Masonic Lodge. He was a Masonic Lodge member for 64 years.

Andrew Jackson Smith and Family, ca. 1940. From left: Lola Smith Autry, O.O., Freed, W.T. and Andrew Jackson Smith.

Andrew Jackson and Susan Florence Smith descendants' histories are as follows:

William T. (Truman) Smith (b. April 19, 1887, d. March 23 1975) was preceded in death by his wife Alma Long Smith (d. 1966). They had no children. He was the owner of a shoe store that later became Jumper's Shoe Store. After selling the shoe store, he established a general store on North Moose Street in Morrilton, AR that he operated until he retired.

Freed E. Smith (b. July 11, 1895, d. Dec. 22, 1955) served overseas in the Co. F, 153rd Infantry during WWI. Freed was a member of the American Expeditionary Force and saw action in the Verdun sector and the Meuse-Argonne offensive. He returned to Morrilton, AR after being discharged. Once home, he married Gracie Alfred Brickey (b. Oct. 26, 1900, d. Jan. 1, 1978) in 1921. Freed was elected as a city alderman several times and served Morrilton well on the city council. Smith was also a member of Morrilton Masonic Lodge 105 F&AM. He was the owner/operator of Smith Grocery (which he ran after his father retired) until his death in 1955. Freed and Gracie had two children, Mary Frances Smith and Lewis Earl Smith.

Mary Frances Smith married Herman Hesson in 1941. Herman, a native of Fort Smith, AR, was an employee of the *Morrilton Headlight*, a weekly newspaper. He later purchased the half-interest of the paper that was owned by Christina Van Marion and became co-publisher with Earl Haynes. The Hessons moved to Conway, AR in 1958. They have one son Gary who was born on Oct. 27, 1954. Gary Herman Hesson married Patsy Ann Troutman in 1973. They are the parents of one son. Their son Kristopher Gary Hesson has two daughters, Alia Hesson-Blaylock and Wynter Aiel Hesson.

Lewis Earl "Red" Smith (b. Jan. 4, 1925, d. March 10, 1985) md. Laura Lou Bearden. To this union, three boys and one girl were born. The boys (from eldest to youngest) are Danny Smith, Jerry Smith and Timmy Smith. Their sister (the youngest sibling) is Dawn Smith. They lived in Morrilton, AR for several years while Lewis was self-employed in a heating, air-conditioning, and appliance repair service. During this same time, Lewis was also a member of the Morrilton Fire Department for 20 years. The Smith family then moved to Little Rock, AR where Lewis was employed by a large heating and air-conditioning company.

O.O. Smith was born in 1898 and died on Dec. 27, 1996 at the age of 98. He moved to Pittsburg, TX and went into the grocery business there. He married a local girl named Frances Vanilla Warrick. They had one child, Ethel Smith. When Freed Smith, his brother, died in 1955, O.O. and his family returned to Morrilton, AR. He purchased the family store and operated it until he sold it to Rupert Lynch. Following this sale, O.O. bought a grocery store just east of the Rialto Theater. He purchased the store from Dutch Morgan. This store, originally Steve Laux sold the store to Charlie Wofford who operated it for several years before selling it to Morgan. After operating this store and living in Morrilton for a number of years, the family returned to Texas, which is where O.O. died.

Lola Smith (b. July 10, 1902, d. June 1987) md. Walter Autry and moved to Oklahoma. She owned a restaurant in Shawnee, OK and was later a dietician for Oklahoma Baptist University until she retired. The Autrys had five children: Burman, W.F., Dorothy, Juanita and Joyce Beth. *Information researched and submitted by Gary H. Hesson.*

SMITH - Nancy Lucinda Carson (b. Aug. 18, 1835 in Haywood County, NC) claimed her cousin was noted Indian Scout, "Kit" Carson, and that is a distinct possibility, but we have not been able to prove nor disprove that claim, due to myriads of Carsons named Samuel, James, John, William, Joseph, Robert and so on.

However, we do know Nancy's grandfather was Robert Carson, who lived in Tennessee since he was a small child. His son, William Shadrach Carson, was born in Tennessee about 1804. Robert Carson died when Shadrach was about 18, and Shadrach went to live with his Carson relatives in Haywood County. He married Mary "Polly" Turner on March 2, 1826. She was a daughter of Robert and Nancy Turner of Haywood County.

Nancy Lucinda Carson was their fourth child. Her brothers and sisters were Robert B., Samuel, John Shadrach, Sarah Angeline, Adaline, James, Jane, Joseph, Margaret, Harriet (Adelaid?), William and Martha.

On her 22nd birthday (1857) Nancy married Ezekiel Shaddox, son of Ezekiel and Tilletha (Ivey) Shaddox in Walker County, GA, where both the Carson and Shaddox families lived at the time. By 1860, Nancy and Ezekiel's family included two daughters, (Tilletha) Frances, 3, and Mary, 6 months old. A third daughter (Sarah Louise) was born in January 1863.

The War Between the States erupted in 1861. In November 1863, Ezekiel enlisted in Company D, 22nd Battalion, Georgia Heavy Artillery. He died at Turner's Point, GA, two days before his 27th birthday, on July 21, 1864, not from battlefield injuries, but from dreaded measles. After the war, Nancy and the children migrated to Arkansas.

About 1865, Nancy married William H. Ward, a widower with four minor children. They lived at Augusta, Woodruff County, AR, where Nancy bore him two more children: Eudora (Dora) Ward (1866) and Robert W. Ward (1868). William Ward died in November 1870, and Nancy was widowed again, with small children to raise.

She married David Smith on Aug. 8, 1871. Family legend claims she had a child by Mr. Smith, and that he took the child and disappeared. Their marriage is documented in Woodruff County, but there is no further trace of David Smith, his age, in the Federal Census records.

Nancy and her surviving children (Sarah Louise Shaddox, Dora and Robert Ward) moved to the Springfield area about 1881. Family lore says Nancy traded some cows and/or pigs to J.F. Keller for 40 acres in Union Township. On Feb. 2, 1883, her daughter Dora married Mr. Keller, after his first wife died, leaving him with four young children. Dora (Ward) gave him three more children before she died. Her children were Marcus W. (b. 1884), Joseph A. (b. 1885) and Ora (b. 1888) Keller.

Nancy Lucinda "Cinda" Smith resided with her grandson, Joseph Keller and his family in 1910. The

Federal Census of Union Township shows she was a widow, had her own income and had borne five children, with two still living (Sarah Louise Sledge and Robert Ward). She died before 1920 and was buried in the Springfield Cemetery in an unmarked grave. *Submitted by Mrs. Thomas Guthrie.*

SPIER – "Where Did They Put Him?" The search for the gravesite of Pleasant Calloway Spier (b. 1844, d. 1888). Genealogy is like opening a mystery book, you never know what will be found until the last page is read; sometimes the ending is disappointing, sometimes very pleasing.

Gravestone of Pleasant C. Spier.

In the search for my first great-grandfather's grave, I solved not one, but two mysteries. One of course was his burial place, two was the dates of birth and death. I had looked at several records for clues, military records, marriage and death records and found nothing. I even went to all the cemeteries in and around the Morrilton area that I could locate; I also visited with a cousin whom I had met in 1996, she had nothing to offer as to the location. I have worked on my mother's paternal line for the better part of 20 years and had not been able to locate the burial place for Pleasant Calloway Spier.

In October 2002, my wife and I took a vacation to the Morrilton area. She wanted to fish for catfish in the Arkansas River. I wanted to solve the mystery "Where Did They Put Him?" I had found the application for his homestead on the BLM-GLO website, so I knew the location of the property. I found several deeds of the property. On the fourth one dated Aug. 18, 1904, Number 14-621, there was an exception for "ten square feet for the burial site for P.C. Spier." I was overwhelmed in realizing I had found the gravesite.

I went to the campground where my wife was fishing and related to her what I had discovered. We went and took pictures of the house and layout of the land, and didn't even see the white spot at the base of a big oak tree. When we left the place, we went to visit my cousins who live on the quarter section that joins Great-Grandpa's homestead on the north. I asked my cousin if there was a way we could go in to the property on which the grave was located. She asked why and I told her my great-grandfather was buried there someplace. She excitedly examined, "I know where there is a grave." Anxiously we got into her Gator and made our way to a big oak tree. She showed us the spot, I pulled the bottom half of the stone away and there lying in the leaves and dirt was the top half of the stone. She pulled it out and we cleaned it off, stood the bottom up and placed the top on, and there was "Pleasant C. Spier" with birth and death dates. *Submitted by Alton E. Bailey*

STACKS – The Stacks family living in Conway County are descendants of William Stacks (b. 1764 in North Carolina). Family legend says William was full blooded Irish, and was a blacksmith who lived to be at least 101 years of age. One of William's sons, Benjamin, was born in 1797. Benjamin later moved to Newberry, SC, where he married Martha Valentine. Their son Benjamin Jefferson Stacks was born in Newberry County, SC, March 22, 1818. In the mid-1820s, William Stacks and several of his sons and daughters migrated from South Carolina to Campbell and Fayette counties near Atlanta, GA, then later to Walker, Pickens, Greene, and Tallapoosa counties in Alabama. One son, Thomas Stacks, later moved to Tippah County, MS. Another son, John James Stacks, remained in Campbell County, GA, where his descendants still reside.

l-r: Benjamin Rufus, Pleasant Tidwell and William Benjamin, photo taken in early 1900s.

Benjamin Jefferson Stacks and Ursula Jane West were married Jan. 19, 1843. In Fayette County, GA. Ten children were born to Benjamin J. and Ursula: Jackaline Louisa (b. 1847), Eula Lucinda (b. 1848), Joseph (b. 1849), Johanna (b. 1850), Benjamin Rufus (b. 1852) Arsula Jane (b. 1855), William Benjamin (b. 1860), Marinda Melvina (b. 1861), Pleasant Tidwell (b. 1863) and Mary Elizabeth "Dolly" (b. 1865).

Like his brother, several uncles, and cousins, Benjamin Jefferson Stacks fought for the South during the Civil War. According to his widow's pension application, he served in Company B, 10th Alabama Cavalry, CSA. Following the end of the Civil War, with Atlanta burned to the ground by General Sherman and the economy of Georgia devastated, Benjamin Jefferson and Ursula decided to move their extended family west to start a new life in Texas. Traveling in nine covered wagons drawn by oxen, some were riding horses and mules, while some were walking and driving livestock. On their way west, the family stopped for extended periods, apparently making crops in Walker County, AL, and later in Tippah County, MS, where other Stacks kin had settled. As fate would have it, the Stacks never made it to Texas. As they crossed Cadron Creek into Conway County, AR, they met an old friend from Georgia, who told them of readily available land and grass nearby. They arrived in Plumerville, Jan. 1, 1870 and camped at Mrs. Reddig's place (then the Jim Lucas place), later settling in the "Georgia Community," now known as Caney Valley, northeast of Plumerville.

The children of Benjamin Jefferson Stacks and Ursula West Stacks married as follows: Jackaline Stacks md. John Rice; Johanna Stacks md. Francis Marion Thomas; Benjamin Rufus Stacks was married four times: (1) Evaline Harris, (2) Mary Rachel E. Tate (died in childbirth), (3) Lockie Elizabeth McDaniel (died in childbirth) (4) Mary Alice Faulkner Ledford; Arsula Jane Stacks md. Franklin Melton Garrison; William Benjamin Stacks md. Maggie E. Mackey; Pleasant Tidwell Stacks md. Merilla Russell; and Mary Elizabeth "Dolly" Stacks md. William Jasper Fields.

Benjamin Jefferson Stacks died in 1881 and Ursula West Stacks died in 1902. They and many of their descendants are buried at Mt. Pleasant Cemetery in the Hill Creek Community north of Plumerville and at Plumerville Cemetery. Many of their descendants still live in Conway County, including Madolyn Stacks Rogers, the youngest daughter of Benjamin Rufus Stacks and Mary Alice Faulkner Stacks, who lives in Morrilton. R.B. Stacks, son of Benjamin Rufus Stacks Jr., lives in Van Buren County near Bee Branch. Farrell Ray Stacks and Billy Stacks, grandsons of William Benjamin Stacks; Dalton Stacks and William R. "Bill" Stacks, grandsons of Benjamin Rufus Stacks, all live in Conway County. *Submitted by William R. "Bill" Stacks.*

STACKS – William R. "Bill" Stacks, is a grandson of Benjamin Rufus Stacks. Bill was born in 1935 near Plumerville, AR, the son of Hollie and Margaret Grace Gifford Stacks, and is a 1953 graduate of Morrilton High School. Bill retired as Southern Region Director for AP and L (Entergy Arkansas) in 1994, following a 40 year career with the power company. He also served as chief labor negotiator for the company.

Mr. and Mrs. William R. "Bill" Stacks

Enlisting as a private in the Army National Guard in 1953, Bill graduated from the Guard's Arkansas Military Academy and rose to the rank of captain before retiring after 20 years service. He holds an honorary doctor's degree in public service from the University of Arkansas at Pine Bluff, and is former president of Arkansas Literacy Councils, Inc., the Morrilton Chamber of Commerce, and Conway County Industrial Development Corporation. Bill founded football and basketball programs for elementary-aged boys in Benton, and was a co-founder of the Saline County Boys Club. He served as campaign chairman of the Jefferson County United Way and was co-chairman of the UAPB College/Industry Cluster.

Bill and his wife, the former Mary Jane Poteete, returned home to Morrilton upon his retirement in 1994, where he continued to devote his life to the betterment of his community. He served as president of Vision 2020 Conway County and is a member of the Stewardship Committee of First Baptist Church in Morrilton. Bill also serves as president of the South Conway County Public School Foundation, an organization he co-founded in 1995.

He served two years as chairman of the Beautification Committee of the Morrilton Area Chamber of Commerce, and continues to serve as volunteer coordinator for Conway County's clean up and beautification efforts. Bill is a member of the board of the Rialto Community Arts Center, and various other organizations. He is a member of Plumerville Masonic Lodge 253, and is a 32 degree Mason. In August 2002, he was honored by the Arkansas Economic Developers as "Volunteer of the Year" for the Second Congressional District. In 2003, Mr. Stacks was selected as Morrilton's "Citizen of the Year" for his volunteer work in the community. The Stacks' have three children: Pete, Toni and Brian, and six grandchildren. *Submitted by Bill Stacks.*

STANFIELD – The Stanfield family immigrated from England to America in the late 1600s. Robert Stanfield (b. 1702 in Bristo Parish, Prince George, VA) md. Frances Merryweather before 1724 and produced at least four children.

William Stanfield (b. 1730 in Prince George County, VA) was the son of Robert and Frances. He married Sarah (last name unknown). William and Sarah were in Randolph County, NC in 1756 and in Halifax County, VA in 1777. William died in Abbeville District, SC prior to August 1806 and Sarah died 1812 in Abbeville District. They had at least four children.

John (b. 1756 in Randolph County, NC) was the son of William and Sarah Stanfield. John married Sarah Roberts in 1777 in Halifax County, VA. Sarah (b. 1757 in Virginia) was the daughter of William Roberts. John entered the Revolutionary War as a private from Guilford County, NC. He was later promoted to a lieutenant and then a captain. John and his family lived in Randolph County for many years. In 1787, John represented Randolph County as an elected member of the House of Commons of the General Assembly of North Carolina. Prior to April 1794, John moved to Abbeville District (now Laurens County), SC. He died there in 1805. In 1848, Sarah began drawing a pension on John's Revolutionary War service. Sarah died 1854 in Marshall County, AL. They had at least 13 children.

William "Billy" Stanfield (b. 1787 in Randolph County, NC) was the son of John and Sarah. He married Mary (last name unknown) in 1810. William eventually settled in Wayne County, TN. William was a Baptist preacher and owned a tavern at one time.

Wayne County records show he also traded in slaves. Mary died 1851 in Wayne County and William died here in early 1860. They had six children: (1) Lucinda A. Stanfield (b. 1811, d. 1889) md. Robertson Talley; (2) James William Stanfield (b. 1813, d. 1851); (3) Elizabeth Ann Stanfield (b. 1817) md. Lewis B. Pierce; (4) Peyton Smith Stanfield (b. 1824, d.1888); (5) Pricy Jane Stanfield (b. 1826) md. Thomas H. "Ken" Dickerson and (6) Nancy Elitha Stanfield (b. 1828, d. 902) md. John Westley Shull.

James William Stanfield (b. Feb. 13, 1813 in Georgia) was the son of "Billy" and Mary Stanfield. He married Elizabeth Helton in 1834. James was a plantation owner and a farmer. Elizabeth died July 1851 in Wayne County, TN and James died two months later in September 1851. Their children:

1) Nancy Jane Stanfield (b. Nov. 23, 1835, d. Dec. 3, 1886) md. John J. Woody. Children: Jim, Joseph, Malinda, Charity, Polly Ann, Sarah Jane (md. John Ellison Horton), John, Arena, Elijah, Thomas and Cornelius Woody.

2) Elizabeth M. Stanfield (b. 1836) md. Beasley Ingram. Children, Mary and Jane Ingram.

3) Thomas Peyton Stanfield (b. 1838, d. Jan. 3, 1865, in the Civil War) md. Comfort Annis Woody. Children: Robert, James, Mary Jane, Joseph, Elizabeth and Annis Stanfield.

4) Elijah Martin Stanfield (b. 1841) md. Sarah Jeffries Turnbull. Children: Mary, Courtney, Lucinda, Robert, John, Elijah and Cord Turnbull.

5) John A. Stanfield (b. Aug. 4, 1843, d. Jan. 16, 1893) md. Elizabeth Jane Copeland. Children: Malinda, James, Eletha, Sarah, Nancy, Mary, Flora, Elijah, Jesse, Emma and John Stanfield.

6) Lucinda M. Stanfield (b. 1849).

STELL - Asbury Baxter Stell (b. 1826 in Gwinnett County, GA) was the son of Robert and Winnie (Gentry) Stell. Robert Stell (b. March 2, 1792 in Newberry County, SC), was the son of Dennis and Sarah (King) Stell. Winnie (Winifred) Gentry was the daughter of Johnathan and Elizabeth (Moody) Gentry and was born about 1791 in Hamilton District, SC. Dennis Stell was the son of John Stell and Susannah (Malone) Stell and was born in 1765 in Pendleton District, SC. John Stell was a soldier in the American Revolution. He was born in Keighley, Yorkshire, England on Feb. 18, 1743.

Rear (l-r): Belle and Asbury Baxter Stell, Jr., Emily Orange Stell Hawkins, J.D.M. Roach. Middle: Hoyt Jones (boy). Front: David Gillard Jones.

Robert Stell was one of the earliest settlers in Conway County. He and Winnie moved to Conway County in 1835. Their children who came with them to Arkansas were Eveline (b. 1813), John King (b. Feb. 9, 1814), Robert Bayless (b. 1815), Samantha Lucy (b. 1823), Asbury Baxter (b. 1826), Catherine (b. 1829) and Miles Lancelot (b. April 29, 1831). Also moving to Arkansas in 1835 was Robert's brother, Dennis Quimby Stell. Dennis served as an Arkansas Representative from 1840-42 and an Arkansas Senator from 1844-46. Robert Stell served as Conway County Judge from 1854-56.

Asbury Baxter was married twice in Conway County. His first wife was Isena (Licena) Willbanks, daughter of Hiram and Sarah (Stell) Willbanks. (Sarah was Asbury's grand aunt). The Willbanks moved in 1835 from Gwinnett County to help form the Georgia Community in Conway County. Asbury and Isena's children were Sarah J. (b. 1846), Mary (b. 1848), Josephine (b. 1851), Georgia Ann (b. Dec. 9, 1853) md. John Caperton Griswood; and Amanda Ellen (b. Jan. 18, 1856) md. Joseph David M. Roach. In the 1850 Conway County Census, Lucinda Willbanks was shown living with Asbury and Isena. Lucinda was the sister of Isena and later married Asbury's brother, Miles Lancelot Stell. Isena Stell died before the 1870 census.

Asbury's second wife was Rachel Elizabeth Hobbs Jones. Rachel was the daughter of John and Martha (Marthena Ann Haskins) Hobbs and was born Oct. 8, 1831 in Tennessee. Rachel first married Martin J. Jones in 1856 in Tennessee. Martin's parents (Allen and Elizabeth Hicks Jones) and Rachel's parents moved to Conway County before 1850, since both families are in the 1850 census in Conway County. There is no death date for Martin but Rachel married Asbury about 1865 or early 1866. The children born to Asbury and Rachel were Licera (b. 1866); Emily Orange (b. Jan. 4, 1868) md. George Washington Hawkins; Asbury Baxter Jr. (b. October 1871) md. Belle Roberts; Winnie (b. 1873) md. Jermie Fields; and Martha (no dates).

Asbury served in the Civil War. Rachel applied for and received a pension for Asbury's service in Company 1 10th Arkansas Cavalry, CSA. His service dates are listed as about 1862-65. The amount was $50 and was approved on Aug. 15, 1901. Asbury's occupation in the censuses was listed as a farmer. He was evidently a kind-hearted person, since several censuses show other family and neighbor's children living in his home.

Asbury died on Oct. 6, 1884 and Rachel Elizabeth died July 11, 1903. Asbury and Rachel are buried in Wilder Cemetery in Conway County. Also buried at Wilder are his daughter Emily Orange Hawkins, his son Asbury Jr. and his wife, Belle, as well as Asbury's parents, Robert and Winnie Stell. *Submitted by Emery L. Francis.*

STEWART - I realized my grandmother's mother had a name when I was 5 years old. Thirty-five years later, I discovered the name of my great-grandmother's grandmother. My grandmother, Lillie Dorothy Stewart Toombs, planted the seed of knowledge when she taught me her mother's name was Neta Roland Stewart. That seed was nurtured and fed through the years. After Mama Lillie died in 1997, I journeyed to the past. The setting was Morrilton, AR. The city Mama Lillie took her first breath, in 1917. Effie Stewart Johnson, her sister lived there from birth to her death in 2004.

Children of Nita Roland Stewart, l-r: Lillie Stewart Toombs, Johnnie Cunningham, Effie Stewart Johnson, Ruth Cunningham and Ora Stewart Hodges.

It was here that Mama Lillie learned the lessons of life she would share with me. Neta was mother to Ruth, Johnny, Lillie, Little Charlie, Effie and Ora. Other children were born but did not survive to adulthood. Neta married Charlie Stewart in February 1914.

She made and sold "hot tamales" to help support her family. I imagine Neta passed the knowledge of life to her children as she'd learned from Mariah Holyfield Roland.

Aunt Ruth spoke often of Mariah's love for horses. She also remembered her grandmother riding a beautiful white horse. As the eldest child of Neta, she lived in the home of Mariah and John Roland with her mother. She remembers her grandfather performing a variety of duties. He was an herbalist. His gardens were often among the best in the city. He assisted with the rituals of death in their community. He was a janitor, cleaning the city he loved. Mariah and John married in August 1880.

Mariah's mother is Mary Holyfield. Her siblings are Rena and Nancy Holyfield. Mariah was born in Arkansas around 1854 and her mother was born in Georgia.

One hundred and fifty years after the birth of Mariah, the death of Effie Stewart Johnson marked the end of one branch of the family tree rooted in the soil of the city of Morrilton, county of Conway, and state of Arkansas.

The seeds from this branch have spread over the United States with a cluster in Little Rock, AR. The history of this branch was passed generation to generation in the oral tradition. As the first great-great-great-granddaughter of Mary Holyfield, mother of Mariah Holyfield Roland, mother of Neta Roland Stewart, mother of Lillie Dorothy Stewart Toombs, mother of Louise Stewart Shields, mother of Rhonda Stewart, it is with pride of my ancestors that I tell their story. The knowledge of their lives fertilizes the dreams in my life. This knowledge smoothes the turbulence of unseen forces while elevating the confidence in my potential for positive influence in this land called America. This knowledge allows me to determine the strength of my "link" in this chain of life.

STOBAUGH – Billie Jean Stobaugh was the oldest daughter of Orville and Etta Sheridan Stobaugh, born in Center Ridge, AR on April 25, 1928. She attended Nemo Vista School and after graduation went to Arkansas State Teachers College in Conway. After one year of school, she married E.L. Wilson, son of Elijah and Venia Mae (Newman) Wilson. She worked for a time at Armors Café in Morrilton. She and E.L. had four children: Barbara Ann, Eddie Lewis, Michael Stobaugh and Alice Renee.

Billie Jean Stobaugh

E.L. Wilson served in the US Army in the famous unit of WWII, the Big Red One. After the war, he went to work as a plumber with the R.J. O'Bryant Plumbing Co. Billie was very supportive of the local VFW club, raising money, etc. Later, Billie opened Wilson's Dairy Bar. It was here that many of the memories of her children and brothers and sisters were created. She sold 5 cent ice cream and you could get five hamburgers for $1 through a drive-up window. Billie created one of the most favored dishes of her regulars, made up of chili and then beef stew. A customer would simply ask for the "Mix." It could also be bought in a quart size fruit jar to carry home.

Edith Deeter and Pansy Russell worked there also, as well as her brother Danny and me, her daughter Barbara. I remember selling cookies to raise money for the VFW on the sidewalk in front of the business. Many of the Morrilton police force and businessmen and women in the city were regulars. Later, E.L. opened a liquor store in the adjoining building and they cut a pass-through window so one could buy a meal as well. Both businesses were closed in the mid-1960s, after their divorce. E.L. Wilson died March 10, 1966 and is buried at Friendship Cemetery.

Billie then got a job with the Children's Colony at Conway as a teacher of life skills for the retarded children housed there. Billie loved her job and the children, often bringing one of them home with her on holidays or special dinners with her family. Her home was located at 405 West Valley, a home originally built as a parsonage in 1890, for the Presbyterian Church on Church Street.

Billie married William Hershel "Bill" Martin, a brick mason from Possom Trot, the son of William "Will" and Eula Martin. Bill and Billie later opened and ran the liquor store. He was a very kind and gentle man and they had a very strong, happy marriage. Billie's youngest child, Alice, so loved Bill that he officially adopted her, when she was yet in grade school. He and Billie had another daughter, Amy Kay Martin born in the 1970s.

Billie became ill and Bill was diagnosed with cancer. Billie died on May 30, 1995 and Bill just three months later on Aug. 28, 1995. They are buried together in Elmwood Cemetery in Morrilton. *Submitted by Barbara Evans.*

STOBAUGH – Burvil Dean Stobaugh was the second son of Orville and Dollie Etta (Sheridan) Stobaugh.

Dean Stobaugh and Mary Geneva Fryer Stobaugh

He was born Nov. 30 1925, in Center Ridge, AR. The young Stobaugh family at that time consisted of Orville and Etta and the oldest child, Odie Sherman Stobaugh, who was also born in Center Ridge in September 1923. The couple with their two sons had many family members in the surrounding countryside and they worked hard to provide for the children.

Then, in October 1927, little Odie became very sick. He had developed an abscess of his tonsils and shortly thereafter, passed away at barely the age of 4 years. They buried him at the Lost Corner Cemetery next to his grandparents, George Washington Stobaugh and Margaret Brinkley Stobaugh. This tragedy, so soon encountered by the Stobaughs perhaps explains their deep attachment for Dean which developed through the years. Though, another year would usher in a daughter, Billie Jean, followed by the others - Patsy Ruth, Bettie Lou, Donald Jay, Varnold Ray, George Lynn, Ronald Wayne, James David and Danny Carl.

Dean, like the other children, learned to work hard for farm life in those Depression days was difficult and trying. It imbued Dean with a sense of wanting to improve his lot in life. He opened a service station and garage when he was of age and began to raise cattle on his land, just east of Morrilton on Highway 64.

He married Mary Geneva Fryer, daughter of Jerry and Safronia V. (Martin) Fryer, who was born Aug. 9, 1920. Throughout their marriage, they remained childless. Several of his brothers worked his cattle with him, learning to ride and handle the herd.

Dean was a successful rancher, ultimately raising cows that were bought by Winthrop Rockefeller, among others. He died of a heart attack on Jan. 20, 1973, at the very young age of 48. He is buried at Elmwood Cemetery next to his parents. Mary Geneva Fryer Stobaugh died June 9, 1997 and is buried next to her mother, Fronia Fryer at Elmwood Cemetery.

STOBAUGH - Danny Carl Stobaugh was the youngest son of Orville Stobaugh and Etta Sheridan Stobaugh. (See sketch on Orville Stobaugh.) He was born Nov. 12, 1948 in Morrilton's St. Anthony's Hospital. When he was just a teenager, his mother was accidentally killed in an auto accident and his father died of a heart attack. He attended schools in Morrilton, graduating in 1966 from the new Morrilton High School. After high school,

he moved to Little Rock to live with his sister, Patsy Stobaugh Dunn and her family.

Danny Stobaugh, wife Paula and sons Scot (on left) and David.

He began his working career in the mail room of Worthen Bank and Trust Company. Quickly, he was promoted to the Transit Department where it was his job (at such a young age as 19) to balance the bank's deposits. He was promoted time and again until reaching the title of assistant vice president. He had worked in the Correspondence Department, meeting and working with all the banks around the state which did business with Worthen.

On March 31, 1967, he married Paula Carole Gordon (b. May 25, 1948) of Little Rock, also an employee of Worthen Bank. They bought a small house and began their family, first with David Allan and then Scot Sherman.

When Danny left Worthen Bank, he took his career in another direction - that of investment brokerage, working first with Brittenum & Associates; then Swink and Company, and eventually, Stephen's, Inc. Each different position gave him more insight into the business and his contacts around the state had grown in addition. A new trend of installing investment brokers within banks began and Worthen Bank was no exception; Danny returned for a time, then went to One Bank's investment department. When that bank closed its department, Danny was hired by Llama Company in Fayetteville, moving there in 1989. Afterwards, Danny moved to A.G. Edwards and Sons and continues at this firm, serving as both broker and branch manager of the Russellville, AR office.

David Allan married Elissa Jensen in 1991 in Ft. Smith. They had one daughter, Catherine Elise in 1992, and soon after were divorced. David then married Dena L. Turner of Ozark, AR and they have three girls: Scottie, Anna and Sarah.

Scot was 22 when he was robbed and murdered while washing his clothing at a laundry in Little Rock, AR. He died March 16, 1993 and is buried at Elmwood Cemetery in Morrilton. He had not ever married nor had children.

Danny and Paula continue a quiet life in Russellville, living on a 40 acre farm they have owned since 1985, raise a few cattle and enjoy their four grand-daughters.

STOBAUGH - Edmond "Shep" Stobaugh was born around 1817 in Tennessee, probably Franklin County. His father was also named Edmond Shepherd and the only name we have for his mother is Sarah or Sary as she was later known. Edmond married Jane McDaniels and they began their very large family. John W. (b. 1841); William (b. 1843); Isaiah or Isaac (b. 1845); James A. "Jim" (b. April 1846) md. Sidney Williams in 1865; Thomas (b. 1846); Parmelia (b. 1850); Elisha Jefferson "Jeff" (b. April 7, 1851) md. Mary Jane Williams; Nancy Jane (b. 1853) md. Charles W. "Phela" Beavers; Sarah J. (b. 1856) md. Needham Flowers; Martha A. (b. 1858), Annanias Frances "Frank" (b. 1862) md. Susan Keith.

Shep served during the Civil War as a private in Co. B, AR 1st Inf. Reg. (Union) and later in the 3rd AR Cavalry, Co. B, (Union). He was awarded bounty land in Conway County as a result of his service and

returned to the profession of farming and blacksmithing.

In 1888 his wife Jane McDaniels passed away. He remarried at the age of 60 on Nov. 19, 1888 to Mrs. Martha J. Brents Hammond, widow of James H. Hammond, who was then 35 years of age. Review of the Widow's Pension she filed, finds this physical description of Shep. He was 45 upon joining the service. Five feet, seven inches tall, with fair completion, blue eyes and light brown hair and was a blacksmith. The $25 pension was paid to Mrs. Stobaugh until her death in April 1919.

This man who had himself 11 children to raise, must have been a very compassionate fellow. He took in his niece and nephew, George Washington and Martha Ann Stobaugh, after his brother Samuel Adams Stobaugh died. Samuel and his wife Elizabeth had four children, but nowhere is found mention of either Elizabeth or the two older girls, Lucinda and Elizabeth A., after the 1860 census recording. So, Uncle "Shep," as he was known to George and Martha, helped them come to adulthood. George later married Margaret Brinkley and had 11 children of his own, nine of whom grew to adulthood, and Martha Ann married Willis Freeman and they, too, had a large family.

Today, descendants of both Edmond and Samuel continue to live in the same area and revere the memory of these two brothers.

STOBAUGH - Elisha Jefferson "Jeff" Stobaugh (b. April 7, 1851 in Scott County, AR) was a son of Edmond Shepherd Stobaugh and Jane McDaniel Stobaugh, who had moved at an earlier time from Tennessee into Van Buren County, then over to Scott County for a time, then back into Van Buren County. Elisha was raised on various farms and his education was like that of other boys whose families existed on farmland. Then in 1868, he married Mary Jane Williams, the daughter of Leroy P. Williams and Martha Ann Hill Williams, who were natives of Franklin County, TN.

Elisha Jefferson Stobaugh and Mary Jane Williams Stobaugh

The Williams family are descendants of a Cherokee maiden, Rebecca Jackson, who had married Nathan Williams of North Carolina. To this union were born 11 children: James J. "Jim" (b. 1869) md. Miriah Jane Bradley; Sarah Elizabeth (b. 1872) md. George W. Ring; Laura A. (b. 1875) never married; Rebecca J. (b. 1877); twins born in 1880: John F. married Mary E. Beckham and Clarisy married Alex J. Bradley; Emma May (b. 1886) md. Charlie E. Reed; William Harrison "Will" (b. 1888) md. Bess Howard; George Washington (b. 1890) md. Ethel Harwood; Nora (b. 1892) md. Floyd Allen Hill, and Effie Lew (b. 1895) md. Henry S. Prince.

Jeff Stobaugh improved his farmland, beginning with only 15 acres, progressing to 280 acres, making one of the best farms in the township. His success was a result of hard work and good management. Mr. Stobaugh was a Republican by politics and a member of the Sons of Veterans (Mason Camp). He and his family were members of the Christian Church.

Mrs. Stobaugh passed away in 1911 and is buried at Pleasant Hill Cemetery. On Nov. 18, 1924, he married Mrs. Mary Elizabeth "Lizzie" Grayson Owens, the widow of George Owens. Mrs. Owens was the daughter of Robert Grayson and Bettie Wilson Grayson, who was born about 1886 in Conway County, AR.

Jeff Stobaugh died Aug. 8, 1935 and is buried in Pleasant Hill Cemetery. His grandson, Audy Ray Stobaugh has inherited the family's knack for good land management. He and his family were named the "Arkansas Farm Family of the Year" in 2004, a fact which Elisha Jefferson, no doubt, would be extremely proud.

STOBAUGH - The Reverend Franklin Owen Stobaugh is said to have been the first inhabitant of Center Ridge, AR. He moved into the county in 1872 from Van Buren County, where most of his family had been. He bought land, built a home and raised 11 children. The house was across the street from the old post office and he began farming, doing blacksmithing work and wagon building, as well. Uncle Frank, as he was commonly known, became very prosperous over the years, improving his land and talents. He became the pastor of the Christian Church at Center Ridge and was a member of the Napier Post, GAR No. 72 and served as its quartermaster.

F.O. is the son of John J. Stobaugh and Sarah Rogers Stobaugh, who were both from Tennessee. They moved to Mississippi and in about 1825, came to Arkansas. F.O. (b. Sept. 17, 1845) was the fifth of 11 children of Rev. John J. (a Confederate veteran, fatally wounded at the Battle of Corinth, MS). His oldest brother was Edmond Shepherd (b. 1835); then came Matilda Ann (b. 1838) who married George Huie; Malinda Jane (b. 1838) md. Robert O. Fullerton; James Allen (b. 1842) md. Jane Huie and Mary E. Williams; William Hiram (b. 1849) md. Nancy P. Dowdy and Winifred "Winnie" Arminta Traywick; Robert David (b. 1848) md. Martha E. Lovell; an unknown child (b. 1851); Mary Elizabeth (b. 1854) md. Francis Marion Jones; Amanda E.C. (b. 1857) md. Steven Scott Williams; and Samuel L. (b. 1861) md. Mary Melinda Bell Bailey. This Samuel later changed the spelling of the surname to Stobuck, for what reason, no one knows.

F.O. enlisted in the 3rd AR Cav. in Capt. Thomas J. Williams' Co. in the spring of 1863, where he served until 1865. Upon his return home in 1866, he married Martha Jane Maddox, daughter of James and Elvina Maddox. They bore 11 children: Ida Ann (b. 1870) md. Bumpass Brinkley and Truman Bethbel Robbins; Martin T. (b. 1873) md. Nancy Jemima "Nannie" Jones; Ruth J. (b. 1876), who we believe married Dell Copeland; Ada Catherine (b. 1879) md. Jon Wellington Halbrook; Mary (b. 1887); Benjamin Franklin (b. 1888) md. Ruth May Ayers; Mary Lizra (b. 1867); Rebecca Ann (b. 1876); Frank O. (b. 1876); Susan Adella (b. 1881) and Stella (b. 1883).

F.O. established the Stobaugh Hotel in Center Ridge and continued to improve his farm land. He passed away Oct. 17, 1925 and is buried at Pleasant Hill Cemetery in Conway County. It is unknown if his wife Martha is buried near him or not. His will was probated on Oct. 20, 1925, and finalized Feb. 21, 1933 (File No. 2052) in the Conway County Courthouse.

STOBAUGH - George Washington Stobaugh (b. Dec. 20, 1857) was the fourth child of Samuel Adams Stobaugh and Samantha Elizabeth Amanda Eubanks Stobaugh. It is believed that he was born in Van Buren County, AR. His father, Samuel must have died before the 1860 Census of that county, because only his wife Elizabeth and the four children: Lucinda, Elizabeth A., Martha Ann and George Washington, are listed on that record. Later in 1870, Martha Ann and George W. were living with their father's brother, Edmond Shepherd "Uncle Shep"

George Washington Stobaugh

Stobaugh in Liberty Township of Van Buren County; apparently having lost both parents. This is confirmed by family tradition, which tells of George being raised by his Uncle Shep, who with his wife Jane McDaniels had a very large family of their own.

Another tradition has it that the mother and the two older girls died in a terrible fire, but that cannot be confirmed by any other means. In a previous volume of this county's history, it was mistakenly printed that Samuel's son was a different George Washington Stobaugh (who married Nancy Bartlett). This George (b. Jan. 20, 1856), however, was the son of Annanias and Nancy (Riley) Stobaugh. Annanias and Samuel were brothers, so these two boys with the same name were in fact, first cousins.

On July 5, 1878, George married Margaret Ann Brinkley, daughter of Bumpass B. Brinkley and Martha Ann Hill Williams Brinkley (b. Feb. 11, 1861). Martha Ann Hill had previously been married to Leroy P. Williams who had perished during the Civil War. Martha and Leroy had seven children, which presumably were brought into her second marriage. Martha Ann and Bumpass had eight more children, one of whom was Margaret Ann Brinkley.

Together, George and Margaret had 11 children, two of whom died very young. Of the others the oldest was Laura (b. March, 28, 1879, d. Nov. 8, 1952) who married John T. Williams on Jan. 12, 1898; Martha Elizabeth "Lizzie" (b. Dec. 16, 1884, d. Sept. 19, 1966) md. Dennis Scroggins; James Monroe (b. Dec. 22, 1888, d. Dec. 21, 1954) md. Lucinda "Cindy" Scroggins about 1908; W. Henry (b. Nov. 18, 1890, d. Jan. 28, 1968) md. Callie S.; Effie Mae (b. Oct. 21, 1892, d. March 17, 1973) md. William Motton Guinn on Aug. 2, 1908; Johnnie W. (b. Sept. 11, 1894, d. July 21, 1975) md. Charity J. Prince; Della J. (b. December 1895, d. 1961) md. Newton Prince; Hettie (b. Nov. 1, 1898, d. Oct. 12, 1983) married William Scroggins; and Orville (b. Aug. 9, 1901, d. Dec. 25, 1964) md. Etta Sheridan on Dec. 20, 1921.

George and Margaret lived a simple life as farmers in Cleveland, Springfield and Center Ridge communities in Conway County. They are listed as early as 1880 on the census at Lick Mountain Township. Both of them had extensive family within this area as well as Van Buren County, just over the border. The family tradition has said they lived in "The Gulf" which is the name locals call the area. No one can say just why it is called thus, but there is a Gulf Mountain nearby. To have raised such a large family, the Stobaughs must have been successful farmers and caretakers of the land. The two lived to see their remaining nine children grown to maturity and married with children. They left a legacy of rich family tales and legends.

George passed away June 5, 1931, Martha on Dec. 28, 1936. Both are buried in Lost Corner Cemetery near Cleveland, AR. *Submitted by Patsy Ruth Stobaugh Dunn.*

STOBAUGH - James A. "Jim" Stobaugh, who was a son of Edmond Shepherd Stobaugh and Jane McDaniel Stobaugh, was a progressive farmer living in the Lick Mountain Township of Conway County. At the time of the writing in *Goodspeed's Biographical Sketches*, James was one of five children of Edmond and Jane still living. The Stobaugh children born to Edmond and Jane were: John W., William, James Allen (the subject of this piece), Isaac, Thomas, Parmelia, Elisha Jefferson, Nancy Jane, Sarah Jane, Martha A. and Annanias Francis (called Frank); 11 children in all.

James was most probably born in Scott County, AR in April 1846. He grew to manhood farming with his family. There was little in the way of education for the children of Edmond and Jane. Then, war came to our country and James enlisted in the 1st Arkansas Infantry, Company B of the Union Army. The date was June 1861, just at the outbreak of the conflict. After a period of six months, he was discharged and rejoined

the service under the 3rd Arkansas Cavalry, Company B which operated in Central Arkansas until the close of the war. He received a gunshot wound in his left shoulder at Lewisburg, AR. He was married the year the war ended to Miss Martha Sidney Williams, a daughter of Leroy P. and Martha Ann (Hill) Williams. Mrs. Stobaugh was born in Conway County and she gave birth to five children: Jane (b. 1871), Amanda (b. 1873), Henry (b. 1878), Minnie A. (b. March 1884) md. Samuel T. Wilkes in 1905. The identity of the fifth child has not been uncovered.

Mr. Stobaugh improved a good farm first in Van Buren County where they lived until about 1876, when he settled around the community of Center Ridge. The farm totaled about 120 acres, 65 of which was under a good cultivation; all reportedly acquired through the sweat of his brow. Politically, he was a Republican and was a member of the Napier Post of the GAR. He and his wife were devout members of the Christian Church. At this writing, we do not know his date of death nor where he is buried.

STOBAUGH - James Allen Stobaugh was one of the sons of Edmond Shepherd Stobaugh and Jane McDaniels Stobaugh. He was probably born during their time in Scott County, AR in April 1846. He grew to manhood on his father's farm with little advantage for education. In June 1861, he, like so many others in the state, enlisted in the Union Army, Co. B, 1st AR Inf. for a six month term. Upon his release at Helena, AR, he returned home to re-enlist in Co. B. 3rd AR Cav., operating in central Arkansas until the close of the War. He had received a gunshot to his right shoulder during a skirmish at Lewisburg.

On Jan. 19, 1865, he married Martha Sidney Williams, daughter of Leroy P. Williams and Martha Ann Hill Williams. She was born in Conway County and gave birth to five children: Jane (b. 1871), Amanda (b. 1873), Henry (b. 1878) Minnie A. (b. 1884) who married Samuel T. Wilkes in 1905; and another child whose name is not known.

The family came over from Van Buren County in the year 1876 to settle in the woods near Center Ridge where a fine farm of about 120 acres was established. It is unknown just when James and Sidney died (they are last seen on Census records in 1880) or where they are buried, but one must suspect they are among the number of unmarked graves of that era, known only to their Maker. Politically, he was a Republican and was a member of the Napier Post GAR. Both he and Mrs. Stobaugh were solid members of the Christian Church.

STOBAUGH - James J. or "Jim" as he was known, was one of the sons of Elisha Jefferson Stobaugh and Mary Jane Williams Stobaugh, born about 1869. The family lived as farmers and Jim soon became an adult, along with his 11 brothers and sisters. (See sketch of Elisha Jefferson Stobaugh). On Oct. 19, 1890, he married Miriah Jane Bradley, who was the daughter of Isaac T. "Ike" Bradley and Elizabeth "Lizzie" Prince.

Together, they had five children who grew into adults: Della (b. Sept. 30, 1891, d. Aug. 27, 1958) md. Jess H. Stripling; John Edmond (b. March 31, 1897, d. Sept. 28, 1953) md. Ethel Prince; Lona "Lonnie" Jefferson (b. July 15, 1895, d. Dec. 25, 1979) md. Rosa A. Marlowe; Clyde V. (b. Sept. 12, 1905, d. May 21, 1990) md. Frances "Frankie" Gilmore; and Oda Trece (b. April 12, 1907, d. June 10, 1978) md. Clemmie Helen Hawkins.

Jim Stobaugh (d. 1933) and Miriah Jane (d. 1964) are both laid to rest at Center Ridge Cemetery, Center Ridge, AR in Conway County, where they lived and raised their family.

STOBAUGH - James Treba "Jimmy" Stobaugh (b. March 24, 1921 in Morrilton) was one of the children of James Monroe Stobaugh and LouCinda "Cindy" Scroggins Stobaugh. LouCinda's parents were James Monroe Scroggins and Sarah Catherine McCoy, they being from a long line of early settlers of the area. James Monroe Stobaugh was one of the sons of George Washington Stobaugh and Margaret Ann Brinkley Stobaugh, also from families who settled in this state at an early date.

Jimmy Stobaugh was educated in Conway County schools and joined the Coast Guard during WWII, serving on

James Treba "Jimmy" Stobaugh

one of the LST boats, which carried troops from one port to another. His LST participated in the invasion of Normandy, hauling the troops onshore. After that service, his LST was employed taking the troops from England over the Channel onto to French soil; his being distinguished by having carried the most troops.

Jimmy then joined the Arkansas State Police having graduated second in his class of thirteen. This was probably a crucial time in the history of the State Police as most of the county sheriffs really resented any other group "coming into their town" to do their job. But, Jimmy was of such a good nature, he quickly made friends with the local sheriff and they had a good working relationship.

On Sept. 6, 1946, he and Mary Frances Ruffiner were married at the Catholic Rectory in Morrilton, AR. Mary was born Jan. 30, 1928 in Morrilton also. She and Jimmy were a team. They had a healthy respect and love for each other and their life together. On Dec. 27, 1955, they had a daughter, Rebecca Sue "Becky" Stobaugh. She was born while the family lived in Little Rock, AR. Becky married Terry Lee Waldo on Feb. 14, 1984 in Denver, CO. Their daughter is Jennifer Marie Berry (b. Dec. 12, 1975 in Fayetteville, Washington County, AR). Jennifer later married Matthew Craig Fleming on Dec. 12, 1998 in Russellville, Pope County, AR. Jennifer and Matthew have two daughters to date: Megan Marie and Kristen Leigh.

Jimmy Stobaugh retired from the Arkansas State Police after 37 years of faithful service. He was well respected by all who had the opportunity to work with him. Jimmy passed away Dec. 9, 2002 in Russellville after a short-lived illness. Mary Stobaugh continues to live in Russellville, near their daughter Becky.

STOBAUGH

STOBAUGH – Orville Stobaugh (b. Aug. 9, 1901 in Center Ridge, AR) was the son of George Washington Stobaugh and Margaret Ann Brinkley. His father was a farmer, living in Van Buren and Conway counties, so his early life involved the usual labor of that lifestyle. During his early manhood, he was hired as a school bus driver for the Nemo Vista School district.

Then, on Dec. 12, 1921, he married his soul mate, Etta Sheridan, who

Orville Stobaugh and Etta Sheridan Stobaugh

was the 14-year-old daughter of Dr. Odie Jacob Sheridan and Elizabeth "Betty" Williams. Etta was born Sept. 30, 1907 in Scotland, Van Buren County. Her father "Jake" was a traveling veterinarian; her mother Betty was the daughter of Jackson Griffith Williams and Martha Ann Hatley, both children of early settlers of Van Buren County and Pope County.

Orville had many different occupations through the years; once a farmer (and through the Great Depression, many of the children worked the farm with him). Upon moving to Morrilton, he worked for a time at the Morrilton Cheese Factory. He later be-

came a carrier for the *Morrilton Democrat* newspaper, and at one point, he opened a fish market in Morrilton.

Etta and Orville had a total of 11 children: Odie, Dean, Billie, Patsy, Bettie, Don, Varnold, George, Ronald, Jimmy and Danny. They raised them in the Church of Christ religion.

1) Odie Jacob (b. Sept. 16, 1923, on the farm at Center Ridge). A tragedy befell this young family when at the age of 4, "little" Odie died Oct. 9, 1927 of an abscess of his tonsils after an infection had set in. He is laid to rest at Lost Corner Cemetery.

2) Burvil Dean (b. Nov. 20, 1926) md. Mary Geneva Fryer. He died of a heart attack on Jan. 28, 1973 and is buried at Elmwood Cemetery.

3) Billie Jean (b. April 25, 1928) md. E.L. Wilson and they had four children: Barbara Ann, Edward Lewis, Michael Stobaugh and Alice Renee Wilson. E.L. died March 10, 1966 and is buried at Friendship Cemetery. Billie then married William Hershel Martin and of this marriage was born daughter Amy Kay. Because she loved him so, Bill Martin legally adopted Billie's youngest daughter Alice who changed her name to Alice Martin. Billie Jean died May 30, 1995 and Bill Martin died Aug. 28, 1995, both are buried at Elmwood Cemetery.

4) Patsy Ruth married William Harvey Dunn, II. They had two sons, William Harvey III and Gary Lynn. "Little" Harvey passed away at the age of 24 and is buried in Hot Springs, where his parents and brother live.

5) Bettie Lou Stobaugh was born next and married the cousin of Harvey Dunn, Allen Dunn. They had two daughters, Phyllis Kay and Patricia Ann.

6) Donald Jay married Mary Ann Matthews, daughter of Lloyd and Lorraine (Merritt) Matthews, on June 13, 1959. They had three children: Sharon Lorraine "Lori," Donald Jay Jr. and Elizabeth Ann, all born in Little Rock.

7) Varnold Ray was born next and married Carolyn Stacks, daughter of William Edgar "Ed" and Vesta Mae (Littleton) Stacks. They had three children: Steven Ray, Mark Allen and Stephanie Kay.

8) George Lynn was born in Center Ridge and married Bobbie Sisson. They had Terry Lynn. On Nov. 25, 1971, he married Jeanette Kordsmeier, a daughter of Otto Kordsmeier and Mary Lena (Paladino) Kordsmeier, and they had Tracey Lynn and Jimmey Dean Stobaugh.

9) Ronald Wayne was the next son born to Orville and Etta. On Aug. 18, 1965 he married Victoria Irene Cupp, daughter of Floyd and Pauline Cupp, and they had Matthew Wayne. Later, Ronald married Donna Fay Jones, daughter of Hillary and Margaret (Swallow) Jones.

10) James David Stobaugh (b. Aug. 17, 1946) md. Becky Lilley, daughter of Raymond and Roberta Lilley, and produced a daughter, Etta Shantelle. Jimmy was killed in an automobile accident in Athens, TX on March 16, 1975 and is buried at Elmwood Cemetery.

11) Danny Carl, the youngest child, married the former Paula Carole Gordon, daughter of Paul Earle Gordon and Glenna (Nowlin) Gordon of Little Rock, on March 31, 1967. They produced two sons, David Allan and Scot Sherman. Scot was murdered by a man who robbed him on March 16, 1993 and is buried at Elmwood Cemetery.

Etta Sheridan Stobaugh was killed in a head-on automobile accident on July 29, 1963 on Highway 10 near Lake Maumelle. She left a legacy of love and respect, not only among her children, but the entire community of people who knew her. Orville Stobaugh died of a heart attack on Dec. 25, 1964. They are both buried at Elmwood Cemetery next to their sons, Dean and Jimmy. Though this writer never met them, their influence among family members is still felt and remembered with great affection, a testimony of the care with which they lived their lives. *Submitted by Paula Stobaugh*

STORY

STORY - James Story (b. May 29, 1846 in Hector, Pope County, AR) was the son of Henry Haws Story (b. 1799 North Carolina, d. 1858) and was listed on the Cherokee Indian roll under Henry Haws Story. The mother of James was Nancy Elizabeth Taylor (b. 1810 in South Carolina and died in Pope County, AR).

James Henry Story and wife Mahalia Elizabeth Jones Story, great-grandparents of Jim Huett.

James siblings were Elizabeth (b. 1838, TN) md. Melvin Reed; John Story (b. 1842 Pope County, AR); and James Story who married March 9, 1871 in Pope County to Mahala E. Jones (b. Aug 11, 1847 in Pope County, d. Feb. 9, 1930).

The children of James Story and Mahala F. Jones are Mahalia Josephine Story (b. Nov. 11, 1869, d. Feb. 16, 1960) md. Leonard Ashcraft (their children are named under John Leonard Ashcraft in this book); Nancy Elizabeth (b. January 1873 Gumlog County, AR); Louise S. (b. Sept. 17, 1874); Rhoda (b. Dec. 28, 1876, d. Aug. 2, 1968); Georgeanna (b. Feb. 13, 1878); Stephen W. (b. ca. 1879, died as a baby); Mary Jane (b. Dec. 18, 1881); James Albert (b. March 4, 1889).

Mahalia Josephine Story and John Leonard Ashcraft's old home still stands in Conway County where all their children were born. The family lived for many years in Conway County. *Submitted by Lee Huett*

STOVER

STOVER - It is said that these families came by flatboat to Arkansas in 1850 from Davidson County, TN. They put into the Duck River near Waverly, TN, and stopped at Lewisburg and settled in the surrounding areas. Most of them settled at or near Bentley Township (Riverview) then Perry County, but later with the changing of the county lines that part of the county fell into Conway County.

It is believed that John D. Stover, may have died in late 1850 in Tennessee, after the census was taken, but before the trip began, as it is documented that Catherine (Kitty Garland) Stover, a widow with minor children, acquired land, took possession by October 1850 and lived in Conway County, as did most of their 10 children. No record found of her death or what became of her minor children. Many of John and Kitty's descendants still live in the area today.

1) Elisha Garland (b. 1819) md. Mary Elizabeth Greer, had two sons, moved to Arkansas, had another son and died in now Conway County.

2) John Barnes (b. 1821) md. Minerva Fowler, had six children, moved to Bentley Township, bought and cleared land at Riverview. Minerva died and John married second, Mary Jane, an American Indian, and had four more children. Both wives and John died and are buried in Bentley Township.

3) Elizabeth (b. 1823) md. Elisha (Elihu?) Wilson, moved to Conway County and lived near Plumerville.

4) Lucinda (b. 1825) moved to Bentley Township, married John Christopher Geyer, a J.P., and lived in Conway County, on the river near Sandtown Road, then moved to Perry County, died and is buried in Edlin Cemetery, Stoney Point, Perry County.

5) Orville Henderson (b. 1826) md. Nancy Smith and is documented to have been in Cypress Mill in Perry County. He had land holdings in Conway County and sold their land to his brother John Barnes. They

moved to Obion County, TN and had six children. After Nancy died, Orville married to a Mrs. Fullerton

6) Martha Jane (b. 1827) md. David C. Pinkerton and moved to Cypress Mill, AR. David died in 1858 and Martha married his widowed brother, Joseph Pinkerton, and moved to Crawford County.

7) Sarah G. (b. 1830) moved to Arkansas, married first Robert P. Edlin, had four children and moved to Stoney Point. Robert died and Sarah married second, George W. Holmes, had a son. She married third, Mr. Womack. Both John and Sarah are buried in Edlin Cemetery at Stoney Point.

8) Jacob (b. 1832) moved to Arkansas and married Drusilla Traweek. He served in Union Army, moved to Crawford County and had nine children. Jacob and Drusilla died and are buried in Blanco County, TX.

9) Delila (b. 1835) came with her mother to Arkansas.

10) James (b. 1836) both minor children came with their mother Catherine to Arkansas, but no records found of what became of them. *Contributed in memory of Stover families.*

STOVER – James Alfice "Jimmy" Stover (b. Nov. 7, 1886 in Lawrence County, Danville, AR, d. April 24, 1975, Morrilton) was the son of Loranza Dow Stover Jr. and Cordelia Cornelius. His parents moved to a farm near Center Ridge in February 1887. Jimmy's father (b. Jan. 11, 1860, d. Aug. 19, 1946) and his mother (b. Jan. 10, 1866, d. Aug. 9, 1945) are both buried at Mt. Pleasant Cemetery, near Plumerville. Jimmy's grandfather Loranza Dow Stover Sr. came from Virginia, settled in Decatur, AL., and married Manda Blankenship, birth and death date unknown. He operated a gristmill and farmed. Loranza Sr. (b. March 12, 1829, d. May 18, 1921) is buried at Danville, AL.

Mandie Flowers Stover and Jimmy Stover at 50th wedding anniversary. Willie Everett "Shine" Stover, Jewell Scroggin Stover, Myrtle Shipp Stover, Lorenzo Stover, Leola O'Brien Williams (niece of J.A. Stover), T.J. Williams, William Cecil Stover and Lottie Johnson Stover.

On Nov. 8, 1905 Jimmy married Manda "Mandie" Isabel Flowers (b. May 19, 1889, Center Ridge, d. Jan. 12, 1978 at Morrilton), daughter of Benjamin Franklin and Angeline Hill Flowers. Manda's father (b. 1851, d. 1897) and her mother (b. 1863, d. Jan. 23, 1938) are all buried at Pleasant Hill Cemetery near Center Ridge.

Jimmy and Manda's three sons were born at Center Ridge. They raised the boys on a farm where cotton and corn was the main money crop. After the boys married, Jimmy and Mandie continued growing cotton and corn and started a small dairy heard in the Birdtown Community. The milk was transported in 5 and 10 gallon metal cans to Morrilton and sold to the cheese plant.

The oldest son, William Cecil (b. Oct. 31, 1907, d. March 13, 1972) md. Lottie Johnson (b. May 21, 1907, d. Sept. 10, 1997) on Oct. 22, 1925. Cecil, Lottie and his brothers are buried at Kilgore Cemetery. They had three children: J.C., Laverne and Alfretta. J.C. (b. Dec. 7, 1929, d. Sept. 27, 1990) md. Louise Manning on Jan. 7, 1953. They had four children: Bruce, Amber, Brenda and Brian. Laverne (b. 1932) md. Ardith

Kellar on Dec. 29, 1950. They have twin sons, Steven and Stanley, and a daughter Linda. Alfretta (b. 1941) md. Joseph Mitchell Oct. 3, 1959. They have one son Joseph Kimball and a daughter Kelli.

James Loranza (b. May 9, 1911, d. July 1, 1963) was the middle son and a WWII veteran. He was married to Roberta Harwood and Myrtle Shipp Kirtley. No children were born to these unions.

Willie Everett "Shine" (b. Dec. 3, 1912, d. Aug. 2, 1987) was the youngest son. "Shine" married Jewell Scroggin on Sept. 28, 1935. Jewell was born in 1914. They have one daughter Willie Gay (b. 1939). She married Lewis Miller on March 29, 1959 and has two daughters, Tawnia Gay and Crystal Ann. Tawnia married Kenny Hoelzeman in 1986. They have three children: Kacie, Haley and Bret. Crystal married Kevin Rehm in 1988. They have two daughters, Stephanie and Hannah.

Jimmy and his brothers were Baptist deacons. Brothers were Edgar (b. March 11, 1892, d. March 2, 1978) md. Annie Cleaulan; Oscar (b. Sept. 10, 1893, d. Feb. 24, 1966) md. Joan Garrisow; Arvil (b. Jan. 25, 1899, d. Dec. 19, 1987) md. Roxie Mallett; Thomas (b. March 1, 1896, d. Oct. 29, 1973) md. Vida Mallett; Marvin (b. April 25, 1906, d. June 10, 1979) md. Vurda Cooper; three sisters: half sister Hattie (b. Nov. 23, 1881, d. Nov. 11, 1969) md. Martin O'Brien; Alma (b. Nov. 13, 1901, d. Nov. 13, 1961) md. Milford Roach; and May (b. Feb. 18, 1889, d. Jan. 20, 1965) md. Thomas C. Scroggins. *Submitted by Gay Stover Miller.*

STOVER – The Stover family, as a family unit, in 1850 embarked on a most dangerous journey to Arkansas by flatboat along the Duck River in Tennessee to the Mississippi and to the Arkansas River. It is believed that the men probably traveled first to Arkansas and obtained land and returned to Tennessee for their families as some of the children show on census as being born in Tennessee after October 1850. John Barnes Stover (b. 1821, Davidson County, TN), a son of John D. and Catherine

John Barnes Stover

"Kitty" Garland Stover, married in 1841 to Minerva Fowler (b. ca. 1824 in Waverly, TN). John cleared the bottomlands and farmed a large acreage at the foot of the ridge at Riverview in Bentley Township. He owned several hundred acres combined. About 1824 in Waverly, TN, he built his home on the ridge at Riverview, overlooking his lands and the Arkansas River.

John and Minerva had six children:
1) John Barnes Jr. (b. 1842, died before 1860).
2) Sarah Elizabeth (b. ca. 1846) md. John S. Brown in 1870 and lived at Riverview next door to her father. They had three children, but only one survived infancy. They moved to California.
3) Lucinda Caroline (b. 1848) md. William H.H. VanWinkle and lived at Riverview. William served in the Confederate Army. William and Lucinda took guardianship of her father's estate and her two minor sisters (twins) when her father died in 1874. Five of Lucinda's children are buried at Stover Cemetery on the homestead.
4) Jacob Nancy Ellen (b. 1851) md. William C. King and is probably buried in Stover Cemetery.
5) Thomas Jefferson (b. 1852 at Riverview) md. Sarah Susan McGhee and raised his family at Casa in Perry County. It has been difficult to convince those families of today of their ancestry.
6) James S. (b. ca. 1855, d. by 1860).

Minerva died after November 1855 at Riverview. John then married second, Mary Jane (a Native American Indian) before 1860. She was born 1835 in Tennessee. They had four children:

7) Rachel B. (b. 1859) md. John R. Snap and lived at Riverview.
8) Mary Jane (b. 1862).
9) Martina Bitanna "Marthena" (b. Nov. 4, 1886, a twin, at Riverview) md. Henry Haydon Pryor, and mothered three children. She died in childbirth and both she and infant are buried in Stover Cemetery.
10) Artemisia Celestie "Bettie" (b. Nov. 4, 1866, a twin, at Riverview) md. William Thomas Thompson and mothered 10 children. They lived at Riverview. Many of their descendants still live in the area. Both William and Artie are buried in Wolf Cemetery.

Mary Jane died after 1870. John Barnes died by 1875. Minerva, John, Mary Jane and several of their children and kin are buried in Stover Family Cemetery on their homestead at Riverview. *Contributed in memory of Artemisia Celestie Stover.*

STRAIT - Henry Straight left England and arrived in America before 1685. He was a wheelwright who settled in Greenwich, RI. His son Henry Jr. and grandson John became blacksmiths there. John's son John Jr. moved his family to Hartford, NY. Next, the family migrated to Kentucky, settling in Allen County, then Bowling Green. James Wright Strait met and married Mariah Ross, a Cherokee maiden. They moved to Clark County, AR in 1849. The family moved to Yell County in 1861.

In 1862, Wright was killed by bushwhackers near Gravelly, in Jefferson County. That same year his son Powhatten N. "Bud" Strait enlisted in the Federal Army, Co. 1, 1st Arkansas Infantry with Captain Samuel M. Bard and was in the Battle of Fayetteville, Poison Springs, and a number of other skirmishes. Upon his discharge in 1864, he returned to Magazine Township, where he resumed farming and in connection operating a general merchandising store. He became postmaster of Magazine Township. He married Olive Whatley. They had 10 children: Olive J., William Powhatten, Charles W., Jerusha, Booker, James R., Emma A., Viola, Mathulda, and Leona.

Judge William Powhatten "W.P." and Lillie Dorthea Warren Strait moved to Conway County by 1896. "W.P" was a pioneer lawyer and state representative from Conway County. They had three children: Audrey Lee, Ruby Lois and Freedie. Ruby and Freedie died in the great flu epidemic.

"W.P." built the house located at 304 W. Church St. for his family; selecting each piece of wood that went into it. Audrey spent much of his early life in that home. He attended Morrilton High School and Henderson State College. He became a respected lawyer and a well respected circuit judge. His concept of an organization of community services to provide services to troubled youth led to the organization of Community Services, Inc. which serves six counties from offices in Morrilton and Russellville. Audrey married Mary Fletcher Burrow. Their children were Audrey Lee Jr. "Sonny" Strait and Mary Fletcher Strait.

Sonny Strait married Gracie Jewel Davis. Their children are: Mary Lou Strait (Mrs. Ron Comstock) and William "Bill" Strait.

Mary Fletcher Strait married Dr. Max James Mobley II. Their child is Dr. Max James Mobley III.

Max III married Sally Jo McGloflin. Their honeymoon was spent in training for a two year Peace Corps project to Liberia, West Africa. Upon their return, they both finished college degrees, which would enable Max to become a psychologist, then Deputy Director for Treatment Services for the Arkansas Department of Correction; and Sally to become a special education teacher. Max and Sally raised two sons: Harold Blaise Mobley and Max James "Mickey" Mobley.

H. Blaise Mobley married Felicity Maret Fleming and they had Thea Meghann Mobley. When their marriage dissolved, Maret moved back to Australia with Meghann. Blaise then married Merredith Nicole Bates, who had a son, Nathan Anthony McVey (Mobley), from a previous marriage. Their other children are Jeremiah Blaise Mobley and Benjamine Max Mobley. Blaise is a registered nurse. Blaise and "Nikki" moved to Morrilton in 2002.

"Mickey" Mobley married Eva Leeann Calhoun. Their children are Evan James Mobley and William Thomas "Will" Mobley. Mickey is a registered nurse. Leeann teaches English and Spanish. They will reside in Morrilton soon.

Information for this article comes from newspaper articles from *The Morrilton Headlight* and *The Arkansas Gazette*, interviews with Mrs. Mary E. Cholvan Mobley Strait, and a great deal of research in the Arkansas Historical Commission, the Tennessee State Archives, the public libraries of Morrilton, AR; Greenwich, RI; and Bolling Green, KY. *Submitted by Mr. and Mrs. Max Mobley*

STRIPLING - William Wiley and Mariah Mince Stripling were the parents of the Stripling family that came to Conway County in 1867. William Wiley was born in 1824 and died 1863 in Bradley County, AR. Mariah then married Woody K. Davis and moved to Conway County in 1867. Mariah and William Wiley Stripling's children:

1) Margaret Eugenia "Genie" (b. 1852, d. 1908) md. William D. Rhoades first and Jesse W. Mahan second.

2) John J. (b. 1854, d. 1890) md. Nancy Scroggins, daughter of Leroy and Julia Williams Scroggins. Children: Henry md. Exie Barker, Belva md. William Barker, Franklin md. Mattie Elders, Julia md. Robert Barker, Sallie md. George Ford, Jennie B. md. a Craig.

3) Harriet (b. 1855, d. 1896) md. Jesse W. Mahan. Children:

(a) Nanny (b. 1877, d. 1962) md. Joe Geary. Children: Arval, Marvin, Lonnie, Evie, Adam, Wayne, Dovie and Edith.

(b) Jodie (b. 1879, d. 1947) md. Charlie Willis. Children: Syrus, Cleavie and May.

(c) Leu (b. 1883, d. 1947) md. Joe Halbrook. Children: Aril md. Jewel Williams, Faye md. a Childress and a Sigler, Glennie md. a Guiling, Quinton md. Opal Bradley.

(d) Iola (b. 1885, d. 1968) md. Frank Bowman. Children: Ivan and Elsie.

(e) Taylor (b. 1888, d. 1970) md. Hattie French. Children: Oneta md. Ray Privett, Tressie md. Homer Smith, Jim md. Mildred Scroggins, Helen md. Robert Black, Dick md. Dorothy Garriott, Bill md. Rose Morris, Jerry md. Modean Kirtley.

(f) Dovie (b. 1890, d. 1928) md. Jim Eaton.

(g) Ethel (b. 1893, d. 1928) md. Allen Polk. Children: Laudis md. Dewell Hartwick, Bill md. Mary Cowdrey, Glen md. Montine Sledge, Ardith md. Bertie Bryant and Tura DeMello, Dorse md. Gertrude Roller.

4) George (b. 1857, d. 1955) md. Mary Mahan. Children: Bill md. Flora McMahan, Ella md. Ray Cooper, Jess md. Della Stobaugh, Claud md. Ina French, Maud md. a Settles, Mandy.

Mariah died ca. 1889 and is buried in Quattlebaum Cemetery on Bee Branch Mountain.

Mariah and Woody K. Davis had one daughter Susie Catherine (b. 1868, d. 1952, buried at Augusta, AR) md. Manley Willis. Children: Guy, Ara, Cecil, Vera, Horace, Hubert, Ruth.

Descendants of Harriet Stripling Mahan and Jesse Mahan living in Conway County are Quinton Halbrook, Dick, Eddie, Jimmie, Janet, Michael Mahan, Karen Hamilton, Tressie Smith, Ruth, Allen Johnson, Bennie Latimer, Becky Zimmerman, Linda Roberts, Bud, Johnny, Ardith Polk, Danita Buckholtz, Paula Trafford and Jamie Honeycutt.

Descendants of George and Mary Mahan Stripling living in Conway, County are Sharon Knighten and Karen Williams Koch. *Submitted by R.L. Mahan.*

STROUD - Amos Price Stroud, son of Sally Halbrook Stroud and Roy Louis Stroud, married Glynda June Boyle on June 20, 1957. June was the

daughter of Myrtice Wade Boyle and Lee Boyle, in Old Hickery. Price and June had three children: Roy Lewis Stroud (b. April 12, 1958); Cynthia Renee Stroud (b. June 24, 1959); and Cheri Lynn Stroud (b. Oct. 29, 1961).

Price Stroud with great-grandson Hank Jordan Pruitt and daughter Cheri - 2003.

June Stroud died May 10, 2004 of lung cancer. Their son Roy Lewis Stroud was killed in an accident in Russellville, AR on July 18, 2004.

Cindy married Bruce Bradford in December 1985. They have three children: John Price Bradford, 18; Cody David Bradford, 16, and Miranda Bradford, 13.

Cheri married Lyndon Ray Pruitt on June 26, 1980. Lyndon owns Pruitt Motor Company on Hwy 9B. They have three children: Brandon Kyle Pruitt (b. April 24, 1981); Jordan Drew Pruitt (b. Sept. 28, 1983) and Dustin Thomas Pruitt (b. July 19, 1988). Both sisters and their families all live in Conway County.

SUFFRIDGE - Buford Joseph Suffridge Jr., son of Buford Joseph Suffridge and Catherine Helen Totten, was born at St. Anthony Hospital, Morrilton, AR. Nov. 21, 1940. His parents moved from the Totten home on Green Street to Perryville in March 1942. A 1958 graduate of Perryville High School, he attended the University of Arkansas at Fayetteville graduating with a bachelor of science in bacteriology. The summers of 1962, 1963 and 1965 he was a seasonal park ranger for the National Park Service at Carlsbad Caverns National Park, NM.

Dr. Buford Joseph Suffridge and his wife Lynda on their 40th anniversary.

He enrolled in the University Of Tennessee College of Dentistry, graduating Sept. 22, 1968. He was employed by the North Carolina Department of Public Health in Hickory, NC until March 10, 1969 when he reported for active duty at Pensacola Naval Air Station, Pensacola, FL. The next two years he served at Naval Air Station, Whiting Field, Milton, FL.

On March 9, 1971 he was released from active duty and moved to Morrilton where he practiced dentistry until June 1972, when he entered the orthodontic residency program at Saint Louis University Medical Center and graduated in June 1974 with a master of science degree with specialty in orthodontics. He moved to Little Rock, AR and associated in the practice with Drs. Alstadt, Bost, Golden, Suffridge and Parker from July 1974 until March 1975, when he opened his practice of orthodontics in North Little Rock, AR, retiring Sept. 13, 2000. From June 2001 until June 2003, he taught part time in the Orthodontic Graduate Program at The University of Tennessee College of Dentistry, Memphis, TN with the rank of assistant professor.

Following his two years of active duty with the US Navy he continued his naval career in the reserves, retiring with the rank of captain July 1, 1995. He is a 1997 graduate of the Missouri School of Auctioneering

and a licensed auctioneer in the state of Arkansas and a graduate of the Dale Carnegie Course. He is a member of Perryville Masonic Lodge No. 238, F&AM, Arkansas Scottish Rite and Scimitar Shrine Temple Little Rock, AR and has been a member of the West Little Rock Lions Club since 1974, having served twice as president and edits the monthly club bulletin, *The Lions Mouth.* As a correspondent of the *Perry County Edition of the Petit Jean Country Headlight*, he writes "Glimpses From The Past." He is a member of the Perry County Historical and Genealogical Society and is serving as president. He is a lifetime member of the Methodist Church.

He married Lynda Sue Childers, the daughter of Pinckney Robert and Jim Searcy Childers of Little Rock, AR at Westover Hills Presbyterian Church on July 31, 1964. They have three sons: Dr. Calvin Buford Suffridge (b. April 29, 1970), an endodontist; Dr. Phillip John Suffridge (b. Oct. 27, 1971) an ophthalmologist; and Dr. Joseph Bradley Suffridge (b. July 16, 1974), an endodontist, and five grandchildren. *Submitted by Bufford J. Suffridge Jr.*

SUFFRIDGE - Buford Joseph Suffridge Sr. (b. Dec. 20, 1905, d. May 27, 1983) was owner and operator of the B.J. Suffridge Lumber Co. He moved from Oklahoma City to Perryville in 1937 and to Morrilton in 1938 following his marriage to Catherine Helen Totten. He moved back to Perryville in March 1942 and served a term as mayor of Perryville, was a Mason, member of the Scottish Rite and the Scimitar Shrine. He owned the Perry County Phone Co. in partnership with Paul Van Dalsem

Buford Joseph Suffridge Sr. about 1955.

and owned and operated a caged layer egg business in the mid-1950s. He built and operated Coffee Creek Landing boat dock on Harris Break Lake. He was a contractor, building many of the homes and commercial buildings in Perryville, including two homes he built for his family and the old Perry County Bank building. In partnership with several others, he was a charter owner of the Perry County Bank. He served on the Arkansas Prison and Parole Board during the McMath Administration.

His father, Calvin Britton Suffridge (b. Sept. 4, 1883 in Claiborne County, TN, d. May 14, 1943 in Oklahoma City), buried in Rose Hill Memorial Park in Tulsa, OK, was the son of Bannister Suffridge and Mahala Odell. Bannister Suffridge (b. 1845, d. 1888) was the son of Thomas Suffridge and Sarah Dobbins. Mahala Odell (b. 1840, d. 1926) was the daughter of William Odell and Rebecca Margaret Beeler. Rebecca Margaret Beeler was the daughter of Joseph Beeler, a Revolutionary War veteran. Calvin Britton Suffridge moved from Claiborne County to Knox County, TN with his mother and siblings after the death of his father in 1888.

As a young man, he moved to Texas where he met and married Myrtle Mae McAnulty in Angelina County, TX, the sixth child of Joseph Abraham McAnulty and Narcissus Beasley. Calvin and Myrtle Mae had six children: Buford Joseph Suffridge (b. Dec. 20, 1905, Frost, Navarro County, TX, d. May 27, 1983, Perryville, Perry County, AR, buried in Elmwood Cemetery, Morrilton, AR). Eva Elsada Marie Suffridge (b. Oct. 5, 1907, Kirbyville, Jasper County, TX); Thomas Hal Horton Suffridge (b. Oct. 4, 1909, Camden, Polk County, TX, d. Nov. 10, 1995 in Tulsa, OK); Leora Suffridge (b. Oct. 28, 1911, Blueridge, Limestone County, TX, d. Nov. 5, 1998 in Tulsa, OK); Pearl Almarine Suffridge (b. Aug. 26, 1913 in Kosse, Limestone County, TX, d. April 25, 1948, Stoutland, Monroe County, MO); and Doris May Suffridge (b. Jan.

17, 1916, Kosse, Limestone County, TX, d. June 14, 2003, Deridder, LA).

Buford Joseph Suffridge married first, Gladys Rhea Herndon in Wewoka, Seminole County, OK on July 5, 1930, but they divorced July 8, 1936 in Seminole County, OK. He married second, Catherine Helen Totten of Morrilton, AR, at 12:15 a.m. on Dec. 25, 1938. They had two children, Buford Joseph Suffridge Jr. (See article) and Catherine Gladys Suffridge. Catherine Gladys "Katy" Suffridge, a dental hygienist and associate professor at the UAMS School of Dental Hygiene, married first, Dr. Nathan Leland Dodd, a physician, on June 3, 1967 at Perryville, AR. They had one child, Catherine Elizabeth "Kate" Dodd. Catherine Gladys Suffridge and Nathan Leland Dodd divorced. Catherine Gladys Suffridge married second, Dr. Lonnie Charles Warren of Little Rock.

Catherine Elizabeth Dodd married Travis Paul Tokar of Fayetteville, AR, and they have one child, Catherine Olivia Tokar. *Submitted by Dr. Buford J. Suffridge Jr.*

SUFFRIDGE - Catherine Helen Totten Suffridge was born at home on Oct. 10, 1910 in Morrilton, Conway County, AR, the oldest daughter of Percy Norman Totten and Gladys Mary Egan. Percy Norman Totten (b. April 6, 1866, in Paris, Brant County, Ontario, Canada, d. March 7, 1924 at Morrilton, Conway County, AR) married first, Olive Egan. They divorced and he married second, Gladys Mary Egan on Feb. 1, 1904 at Morrilton, AR. She was the sister of his first wife and was born July 7, 1882 at Morrilton and died Feb. 3, 1953 at Perryville, AR. P.N. and Gladys Totten are buried in Elmwood Cemetery in Morrilton.

Catherine Helen Totten Suffridge

P.N. Totten was the son of Norman Totten, who was engaged in the railroad business in Canada and his wife Catherine Christie, daughter of Thomas Christie, who had immigrated to Bowmanville, Canada from Dundee, Scotland, in 1835. Norman Totten was the son of Daniel Totten and his wife Christina Jamison. Daniel Totten owned and operated a woolen mill in Paris, Canada. Norman Totten immigrated to the United States moving from Paris, Canada to Buffalo, NY, then to Chicago, IL.

Gladys Mary Egan, the mother of our subject, was the child of Irish immigrants. Her father, William Pitt Egan, came from County Roscommon, Ireland and settled in Cincinnati, OH. Her maternal grandparents, Patrick Keamey and Sophia Apjohn came from Pallas Green, County Limerick, Ireland arriving in New York City on the *Cornelius* in October 1849 moving almost immediately to Cincinnati, OH.

Catherine graduated from Morrilton High School in 1928 and attended Arkansas State Teachers College for two and a half years with a major in education and a minor in biology. She finished her degree at Harding College with a major in history and a minor in English. She attended the University of Illinois in Chicago for a summer term where she studied art and education. She was offered an opportunity to study in Paris, but was not able to accept the offer because of family obligations. Her first position as a teacher was in Burdette, AR, where she taught for two terms and a summer. Later she spent many years teaching elementary school in Morrilton and Perryville. She met Buford Joseph Suffridge, who owned and operated the Morse-Suffridge Lumber Company in Perryville.

Catherine and Buford married at 12:15 a.m. on Dec. 25, 1938 at the home of her mother on Green Street in Morrilton. Leaving teaching she worked as a clerk typist at the Perry County Health Department for 30 years before her retirement. An active member of the Perryville United Methodist Church, she served for many years as the treasurer. Buford and Catherine Suffridge had two children, Dr. Buford Joseph Suffridge Jr. and Catherine Gladys Suffridge, both born at St. Anthony's Hospital in Morrilton. *Submitted by Buford J. Suffridge Jr.*

SWEEDEN - Conway County Sweeden Families in the Civil War. Sadly, they were split just as the nation and the great state of Arkansas was - uncle against nephew, brother against brother, father against son. These soldiers are believed to be the sons of Thomas and Emmaline Sweeden.

1) Private Lewis Sweeden served with the Confederate Cavalry, Company F, 10th Regiment, Texas Cavalry (Locke's) and the 14th Regiment, Texas Cavalry, CSA (Johnson's Mounted Volunteers). Formed in Panola County, TX, these units spent lots of time in Arkansas protecting Little Rock from the Union Army. They belonged to Parson's Brigade. Lewis is in Conway County by 1870 with children. He is "murdered" in 1881 per Bible Records.

2) Private John Sweeden enrolled in the 31st Regiment Arkansas Infantry, CSA, Company C in January 1862, born Arkansas, 36, black eyes, dark hair, fair complexion 5'8" tall, found on the 1860 Conway County Census. Records indicate he may have survived the war based on the birth date of his last-born child, but his wife is remarried by 1870. Their son James Jr. is a Union soldier.

3) Henry Sweeden enlisted on Feb. 1, 1862, Company E, 5th Sergeant. Age 18 born in Arkansas, farmer, light eyes, hair, complexion, 5'8" tall. Received an Oklahoma pension in 1915. Henry is on the 1870-80 Conway County Census.

4) Private Patrick Sweeden, age 24, born Arkansas, farmer, light eyes, hair and complexion, 6'0" tall.

5) Private Parrium Sweeden, enrolled Nov. 21, 1863 in the 3rd AR Union Cavalry, Co. I. Age 18, farmer, height 5'10", eyes black, hair dark, complexion dark. Born Clark County, AR. He survives the war but dies Nov. 20, 1865 around age 20.

6) Private Robert Sweeden, age 26, height 5'9-1/2" tall, eyes dark, hair black, complexion dark, farmer. Born Lawrence County, AR. Died of smallpox June 26, 1864 at Lewisburg, Conway County. Robert is in the 1860 Census of Conway County, age 24 with his young wife Sarah Marshall (Patterson) and his nephew James Patrick, son of his brother Lewis, CSA.

7) Private James Sweeden Sr. enlisted Feb. 1, 1864, height 6' 10-1/2," eyes black, hair black, complexion dark, farmer, age 23, born Lawrence County, AL. He may have survived the war, but was later killed (before 1870) while rocking his baby on the front porch, by an unknown assailant. He was possibly called James Mack.

Grandson of Thomas Sweeden and Emmaline Sweeden, son of John. Enlisted in the 3rd AR Union Cavalry, Private James Sweeden Jr., height 5'8", eyes dark, hair dark, complexion dark, farmer, age 18. Born in Clark County, AR. Died Jan. 19, 1864, Little Rock. His father was a CSA soldier.

I haven't found family connections to these men yet; Company B, 2nd Regiment Arkansas Mounted Rifles, and CSA: Carroll Sweeden and Private John L. Sweeden, both enlisted July 15, 1861, from Point Remove, both killed within weeks on Aug. 10, 1861 in the Battle of Oak Hill or Wilson's Creek, MO. *Submitted "In Their Memory" by Carolyn F. Tucker*

SWEEDEN - Sarah Marshall (Patterson) Sweeden (b. Oct. 4, 1840 in Conway or Pope County), widow of Union Soldier Robert Sweeden, son of Thomas and Emmaline Sweeden. Robert died during the Civil War at Lewisburg, Conway County, of smallpox. They married in Conway County, she 20, while both resided in Conway County, Jan. 8, 1860. They had no children of their own and she never remarried.

Her parents were Tennessee born. Robert Patterson and Cynthia Flowers, daughter of Henry and Elizabeth (Marshall) Flowers. Elizabeth is in the 1840 Point Remove Township of Conway County, which was indian land. Sarah and Robert Sweeden are in the July 1860 Griffin Township, Conway County census with whom I believe is his nephew, son of his brother Lewis, James Patrick, age 7.

Her Uncle Henry Flowers, her mom's brother, is a constant in her life. She is with him in 1850 Pope County, age 10. Then widowed she is with him in 1870 and 1880 Liberty Township, Van Buren County.

In November 1887, Sarah paying $14, applies for land via the Homestead Act, application no. 16043, Section 18, Township 10N of Range 17W, 160 acres at Rondo, Van Buren County. She lived there since 1881, unable to read or write, records requiring her signature have "her mark," an X. She stated "my improvements consist of two dwelling houses, lot, stable, crib, about 20 acres cleared land, valued at $200." Nov. 14, 1892 R.E. Patterson, publisher of *The Bommerang*, a newspaper published at Bee Branch in Van Buren County, swore the following was in his newspaper for six months, Sarah named these witnesses to her "continuous residence as proof in support of her land claim: Ed Cowan, P.B. Hearne, Geo. G. Eddy, and Willis Freeman, all of Sang, AR. Nov. 14, 1892, she testified she "was 52 years old, Post office: Sang, AR, born in Arkansas, built her home in December 1881, established residence January 1882: house 16 x 18, smoke house, 3 cribs, 2 stables, orchards, 30 acres in cultivation, value $300. Family is two nieces, lived here continuously and myself am unmarried, never absent from my home, cultivated 30 acres for 5 seasons. It is timbered ordinary agricultural land mass, valuable for agriculture, never sold or mortgaged." Another witness was her cousin, Joseph Ed Flowers, age 36 and again cousin Willis Freeman, age 29, both of Sang, Van Buren County. On November 1892, she paid $4 receiving her Final Certificate July 6, 1893, recorded Vol. 12, page 385.

Sarah's sister Catherine (b. ca. 1832) md. Preston Hearne. Their daughter Cynthia Hearne (b. ca. 1856) md. Benjamin Wilson, having a daughter named Catherine Luvicia Wilson, who marries W.H. "Henry" Weatherman. This niece Luvicia Wilson is with Sarah in the 1900 Van Buren County, White Oak Township census.

Sarah dies June 2, 1926 of "old age" in North Fork Township, Pope County, a widow, age 86, buried at Dry Creek Cemetery in Pope County by her neighbors. Informant on her death certificate was W.H. "Henry" Weatherman, of Sang, AR, husband of niece Luvicia. *Submitted by C.F. Tucker.*

TANNER - My ancestors coat of arms was established in Ireland in the year 1613. We came to Ireland from Cornwall, England then to Virginia where Henry Tanner (b. 1775, d. 1865) was in the War of 1812 in Johnstons 3rd Reg. of East Tennessee Militia, in 1814. He died in Alabama. Children: John (b. 1812), Catherine (b. 1815) md. Peter Flinn, Charles (b. 1820), Rachael (b. 1825), Jacob (b. 1827) md. Elizabeth, Evaline (b. 1830) and Lucy (b. 1832).

John (b. 1812, d. 1876 in Tennessee), son of Henry Tanner, married Laura Jane Williams (b. 1821, d. 1884). They moved from Jackson County?, AL to Perry County, AR. He was of Dutch descent. Children: Charles (b. 1897), Rachael (b. 1840), Luta (b. 1841), John (b. 1846), Elizabeth (b. 1848), Juith (b. 1851), George (b. 1855) and Jacob (b. 1861).

Charles (b. 1837, d. 1907), son of John and Laura Jane (Williams) Tanner, married Mary Bryant. He was in Co. C. 49th Alabama Regiment, fought in the Battle of Shiloh Baton Rouge and Cornith, MS. Children: Clayburn (b. 1866), John Henry (b. 1867), Mary Jane (b. 1870), Martha (b. 1870), George (b. 1873), Murtie (b. 1876), Charles (b. 1878) and Elisey (b. 1880).

George William (b. 1873, d. 1932), son of Charles and Mary Bryant Tanner, was my great-grandfather.

He married Molly Henry (b. 1822, d. 1926). Children: Jessie (b. 1901), Willie (b. 1902), Lillie (b. 1905), Rosa (b. 1906), Annie (b. 1909), George W. (b. 1912), C.B. (b. 1918), Charlie, Johnnie, Mollie.

George Washington (b. 1912, d. 1991) was my grandfather and he married Rosa Bell Smith. He was a farmer, cattleman and military engineer. Children as follows:

Georgia (b. 1931) md. James Manning; children: Virginia, James II and Michael.

Helen (b. 1933) md. first, William Brents (b. 1930, d. 1983) and second, Johnny Wood. Children: Marita Brents (b. 1952) md. James Roach. Children: James Jr. (b. 1972) and Shane (b. 1975). Romona Brents (b. 1954/57), Willie Brents (b. 1955) md. Jesse Sledge. Child: Jessie (b. 1985). William Brents (b. 1958) md. Jimmie Sykora, child, Jennifer (b. 1977). Stepson Charles Wood (b. 1948) md. Janet Drost.

Jimma Dean (b&d. 1936).

Rose Marie (b. 1937) md. Russell Allen. Children: Rhonda (b. 1959) md. Ronald Atkinson. Children: Jacob (b. 1983), Kaitlin (b. 1989), Kelsey (b. 1990), Rusty (b. 1962).

Margie (b. 1941) md. Darrell Abshere. Children: Darrell II (b. 1962) md. Pamela Herring, children: Darrell III (b. 1984), Trey. Mona (b. 1963) md. Robert Bratcher. George (b. 1964) md. Charlotte King.

George II (b. 1944) md. (1) Phyllis Pebbles, (2) Teri Faith, (3) Cathy Fannon. Children: Sheila (b. 1964) md. William Wiles, child William. Deborah (b. 1966) md. (1) Dayton May (2) Tim Cowgur, children: Kendall May (b. 1983) and Christopher Cowgur. Christina (b. 1969) md. Billy Bufford. Yvonne (b. 1972) md. Tony May, children: George (b. 1987) and Terri (b. 1990).

Sherry (b. 1947) md. Ronnie Foster, children: Karne (b. 1967) md. Dawayne Milsap, children: Joshua and Hannah. Kelly (b. 1969) md. Gary Cummings, children: Channing (b. 1992) and Kilmney (b. 1995). Kristy (b. 1973) md. Jeffery Windham, children: Abigiail (b. 1996), Grace (b. 1999) and Andrew (b. 2001).

David (b. 1948) md. (1) Elizabeth DeSalvo, (2) Michele Paladino, child Megan (b. 1970) md. (1) Stavy George (2) Billy Hampton. Children: Cecilia George (b. 1993), Gabe and Sophia Hampton. Richard (b. 1973).

Rocky Layne (b. 1955) md. Marilyn Martin, daughter of William (W.O. and Anna Bartlett) Martin, child, Gregory Layne (b. 1974) md. Rhonda Reedy. *Submitted by Gregory Layne Tanner and Grandmother Rosa (Smith) Tanner.*

THOMPSON

THOMPSON – Aaron Carl Thompson (b. 1894, d. 1956) was born at Riverview in Conway County the fourth child born to William Thomas and Artemisia Celeste Stover Thompson. Aaron Carl served in the US Army and was stationed in France, Hawaii and the Philippines. He later lived in Little Rock and worked for the Rock Island Railroad where he met and married Minnie Bess Adams, originally of Three Creeks, Union County, AR.

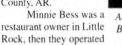

Minnie Bess was a restaurant owner in Little Rock, then they operated it together. They had a daughter and then the Depression hit. By 1933 they moved to Perry County to live on the land given to him by his dad. This land has been in his family since 1912, which was given to his son Charles and he still holds ownership today. Their family grew to four children adding Aaron Carl Jr., Vernon Byrd and Charles Albert.

Aaron Carl and Minnie Bess Adams Thompson

Aaron Carl Sr. was raised a farmer. He loved to hunt. He raised cattle and registered Poland China hogs, which Aaron and his boys showed at the county and state fairs with pride. He also milked cows and sold cream. Aaron died in 1956 and Minnie died in 1967. Both are buried in Wolf Cemetery at Opello.

1) Artie Ideli (b. 1932 in Little Rock, Pulaski County, AR) graduated Perry School in 1949. Artie graduated Arkansas State Teachers College at Conway in 1953. She married Ted Howell of Piggott, AR. Artie retired from School at Piedmont, MO, and lives in Missouri. Artie and Ted have three children: Marjorie Elizabeth "Beth," Ted Houston Jr. and September Dawn.

2) Aaron Carl Jr. (b. 1933 in Perry County) graduated at Perryville School in 1951. He delayed his graduation a year so he could graduate with his childhood sweetheart, Mary Louise Wurz of Bigelow, whom he married. He served in the US Air Force. Aaron Jr. and Louise have one child, Nila Sue. Aaron was a painting and finishing contractor. He specialized in walls and ceilings. After 1967 he became a Southern Baptist Minister. His church was at Redfield, AR near Little Rock.

3) Vernon Byrd Thompson "Buckshot" (b. 1935 in Perry County) graduated at Perryville School in 1952. He served in the US Army in 1954-56. He then went to Quincy, IL, where he met and married Donna Marie Robertson. Vernon and Donna have one son, Vernon Byrd Thompson Jr. "Lil' Buck," who lives on East Thompson Rd., Perry, AR.

4) Charles Albert Thompson "Charlie" (b. 1941 in Perry County) attended Perryville school but graduated at Clarkton, MO in 1959, where his sister Artie lived. He married first, Evelyn Louise Biswell and had one son Charles Albert Thompson Jr. "Lil' Charlie." Charles Sr. divorced and married second, Betty Hastings. Both Charles Sr. and Charlie Jr. live on East Thompson Rd., Perry, AR. Charlie Sr. is a self contractor, his trade of choice is carpentry. He has worked in pre-fab built home factory. He has lived over 60 years in the same house he was born in. *Contributed by Charles Thompson.*

THOMPSON

THOMPSON - Little is known about William Thomas Thompson before he came to Oppelo. The story goes that William Thomas Thompson was born Oct. 6, 1859 in Cadron Township of then Conway County. His parents are unknown at this time. Some said "He was raised by his Aunt Becky Bradford." In 1880 William suddenly appeared in the Oppelo area as a horse trader looking for work. He was employed by William VanWinkle for work at the Stover Farms Estates at Riverview, where he met and married Artemisia Celeste "Bettie" Stover.

Artemisia Celeste was born a twin on Nov. 4, 1866, in Bentley township, daughter of John Barnes and Mary Jane (Jayne) Stover. Their marriage took place on Oct. 8, 1882. William was 23 and Artemisia was 16 years old. William farmed and they lived at Riverview and raised their family there. William didn't talk much, he was a businessman and when he had something to say, it usually concerned business."

William died in 1916 but Artemisia lived on for many more years at Riverview. She died in 1947. Both William and Artemisia are buried at Wolf Cemetery at Oppelo. William's only known relative was his Aunt Beckey Fisher Bradford, who would ride the train from Cadron to Morrilton to visit him and William would meet her at the station with the buggy. William and Artemisia had nine children, losing four in infancy.

1) M.J. (b. 1887, d. 1888).

2) John William (b. 1890, d. 1941) md. Willi... Allen. They had three children: Helen, John Ha... and Willene.

3) Mose Barnes (b. 1891, d. 1976) md. Cecil... Hart. They had six children: Leon, Mosa Dean, Vain, M.B., Billie Hargis, Betty Jeanette.

4) Aaron Carl (b. 1894, d. 1956) md. Minnie E... Adams. They had four children: Artie Ideli, Aaron Ca... Jr., Vernon Byrd and Charles Albert.

5) Earnest Thomas Asbury Thompson (b. 1896, d. 1977). Earnest married Ada Evelyn Permenter. They had three children: Earnestine, Guy Nathaniel and Patsy Nell.

6) Grace Mae Thompson (b. 1899, d. 1976) was the only girl. Grace married Joseph Adam Brown. They had eight children: William Adam, Odis Odell, Betty Alice, Ida Mae, Joseph Bradley, Lela June, Aaron Claude and Nila Grace.

7) Infant son-1 Thompson (b&d. on same day in 1901).

8) Infant son-2 Thompson (b&d. on same day in 1901).

9) Buster Thompson (b. 1905, d. 1906) lived four months. *Contributed by Charlie H. Thompson.*

THORNTON

THORNTON - Caroline Thornton (b. January 1838 in South Carolina) was the mother of Samuel and James Melvin Airhart before her marriage to James Thornton. I don't know what happened to Samuel, but James Melvin Airhart settled in Morrilton, along with several of the Thornton children.

Rev. James Melvin Airhart (b. December 1857 in South Carolina, d. Dec. 25, 1944 in Morrilton) was ordained as a minister by Bishop L.H. Holsey, one of the original Bishops of the C.M.E. Church. He married Elizabeth Hyler (b. June 10, 1862) also of South Carolina. Elizabeth died Oct. 18, 1923 in Morrilton. They were parents of Lonnie Benjamin Clayborn Airhart, Edward, Zeddie, James T., Pearl Airhart Booth, Mamie Airhart Evans, Josephine Airhart Edwards and Carrie Airhart Carter. Lonnie Airhart was the proprietor of a movie theatre and restaurant in Morrilton before he moved to Hayti, MO. He also was a barber and operated a barber shop in Missouri before returning to Morrilton where he died. Zeddie married Ella Steward and they became the parents of four children. Ella was the mother of three children from a previous marriage.

Caroline married James Thornton in 1870 in South Carolina. He also was a South Carolinian, born in 1830. Caroline moved to Morrilton where she and her daughter, Lizzie Thornton Brown, and granddaughter Cora lived with her son Frank. Her Thornton children were: Burrell, Ella, Pearson, Julia, Green, Henry, John, Columbus Frank and Lizzie. Green, Henry and Columbus settled in Morrilton.

Henry Thornton married Lemuel Boozer (b. Sept. 23, 1872) on Dec. 24, 1888. Lemuel (b. Sept. 23, 1872) was buried March 17, 1913 in Oddfellows Cemetery

Green William Thornton (b. June 10, 1865 in Lexington County, SC) md. Hattie Boozer, also from South Carolina. They owned farmland and ran a grocery store. They lived on Highway 64 West. She may have been Lemuel's sister. They are buried in the same cemetery section. They had no children but served as surrogate parents for many children from South Carolina, as many families did following the war. Green and Hattie both died in California where they moved as they began to age.

Columbus Frank Thornton, known only as Frank, was born Dec. 4, 1872 in South Carolina. Frank married Margaret Smith, daughter of Jim and Lucinda Smith, on July 9, 1894. Margaret

Columbus Frank Thornton

...ith (b. July 1873) was the daughter of James and ...anda Smith. Frank and Margaret were the parents ... Julia Thornton Bowles, Carlene Thornton ...kland, Christine Thornton and Mary Rebecca ...nton Haywood. After Margaret's death, Frank ...ed Mabel Brame, the daughter of Rev. and Mrs. ...or Brame. They became the parents of five chil...en, all of whom are still living. Frank Thornton died ...n April 13, 1947 in Morrilton, Conway County, AR ...d is buried in Oddfellows Cemetery in Morrilton. ...ibmitted by Columbus Frank's great-granddaughter ...argarette Banks.*

...HORNTON - James Thornton (b. 1830, South ...arolina, death unknown) and Caroline Thornton (b. ...anuary 1838, South Carolina, d. in Morrilton, Conway ...ounty, Arkansas) were listed in the 1870 census of ...ollow Creek Township, Lexington County, SC. Green ...hornton was enumerated in the 1870 census of Lex...ngton County, SC in the home of I.W.T. Hayes, a Eu...opean-American school teacher, and his wife Naomi. ...he assumption has been that Caroline was born a ...layes, but there really is no concrete evidence that I ...ould find to verify this information. (*The source of ...he information shared by Carl Stricklin was from ...ountry Publishers, P.O. Box 277, Ripley, Oklahoma)* ...une 10, 1870, A.D.J. Hayes, Assistant Marshal, Enu...nerator, page 351B #14, household number 105, fam...ly number 105, enumerated the Thornton family as ...ollows. James was listed as age 31 and Caroline, age ...4, both of them born in South Carolina. Their chil...ren in this census were:

Samuel, age 17.

Melvin, age 13 (was this James Melvin Airhart/ ...arhart born Dec. 1, 1857 who lived and died in Morrilton and was said to be the son of Caroline Thornton. (*This information came from Leo Frank Thornton[In a letter written in 1997] and confirmed by James Thornton, sons of Columbus Frank Thornton and by Carl E. Strickland/Stricklin, Carlean Thornton Stricklin's son, in telephone conversations.*)

Pearl Airhart Booth, his daughter told me of the Airhart/Thornton relationship. She, Lonnie, Mamie, and Zeddie said I was their cousin but never explained how. James Airhart's date of birth matches Caroline's second child, Melvin who was 13 years old at the 1870 census.)

Burr (Burrell), age 12; Pearson, age 7; Ellen, age 6; Julia, age 5; Henry, age 2; James Snelgrove, age 12 (Unidentified relationship); Green Thornton, age 4.

Information supplied to the census enumerator in 1900 states that Caroline Thornton, Columbus Frank's mother, was a widow who was married to her husband for 30 years, which would place the marriage date about 1870. Only three children were born after this date. They were Columbus Frank, John, and Lizzie. The other eight children were born prior to that date. The eight children born before 1870 may have been her oldest children that she possibly brought to the marriage.

There is no explanation in the census regarding James Snelgrove and he does not appear in the household again. I have no evidence that either Melvin Thornton or James Snelgrove is the James M. Airhart mentioned above. Melvin was 13 years old at the 1870 census which would have made his birthdate about 1857 the same date as James Airhart. There is a J.M. Airhart listed in Schedule 2, Slave Inhabitants in the vicinity of Lexington County, SC, State of South Carolina, enumerated on June 4, 1860. He lists one 17 year old black female slave - whatever that means. and we'll probably never know what that meant. I have not found a Thornton slaveholder in the Lexington County slave schedule of 1860. Perhaps James was in another county. Caroline may have been in Lexington County but I have no way of finding out.

Caroline Thornton (Frank's mother), age 62, born January 1838 in South Carolina was a widow who in 1900 said she had been married for 30 years before she was widowed, placing the marriage about

1870. If this is correct, Caroline's older children were born before she married James Thornton and their children together would have been John, Columbus Frank, and Lizzie Thornton. I can find no other information about Caroline. I don't know when she died or where she is buried neither have I found nothing to indicate that her husband, James Thornton, was ever in Conway County. Considering the times and the events of this period of time, it's very possible that he was not alive at this time. However, since Caroline was living with Frank in Conway County, I assume that she also is buried in Conway County.

The Thorntons neighbors in 1870 South Carolina were Jacob and Pamelia Monts, Green Monts, J.B. Mills, A.M. Long, A.E. and Eliza Drafts, T.I. and A.M. Warner, Lepe and Nancy Hayes, Hannah Seay, A. and Louisa Hairston. Elizabeth Sease and N. Hipp are shown in the household of Jacob Monts. (*These may or may not be sources of information regarding them. According to Lonnie Davis, another researcher with Conway County ties (Lafayette and Davis families) A.E. Drafts had labor contracts with some African Americans whose families migrated to Conway County following the War of Rebellion, so there's another of the endless possibilities.*)

In the 1880 census of Lexington County, SC enumerated June 11, 1880, the family of James and Caroline Thornton appear in Saluda Township. (*Page 487B #10 of Supervisor's District 2, Enumeration District 13.*) James is a farmer and Caroline's occupation is keeping house. Ella, Julia, Green, and Henry are shown as working on the farm. Their neighbors are Anne Lebrow, John and Elise Thomas, William Curry, and Christine Rawl. Samuel Thornton does not appear in any of the censuses of Conway County.

Melvin Thornton also does not appear unless he is James M. Airhart with the "M" being Melvin. Based on the information I have received I am including the Airhart information I have in this space:

Rev. James M. Airhart was born December 1857 and died December 25, 1944. This is consistent with the Melvin Thornton birthdate. He could have been an older child of Caroline Hayes, and may or may not have taken C. Frank Thornton's name after the marriage to Caroline. He may not have been reared in this family at all. Considering the propensity to using middle names, it's highly possible that this is accurate. (Columbus, used his middle name, Frank). Rev. James M. Airhart (name was spelled Earhart in 1910) was married to Elizabeth Hyler also from South Carolina. (The Hyler name appears several times in Conway County census records.) Their children were Lonnie (b. December 1880); Edward (b. June 1882); Pearl (b. Dec. 16, 1890); Josephine (b. October 1891); Zeddie (b. March 12, 1895); Carrie Bev (b. 1901); Mamie (b. 1903); and James T. (b. 1906).

Pearl Airhart was married to Henry Booth (b. Aug. 6, 1873). They were parents of a son William H. Carter Booth (b. Nov. 29, 1928, d. June 17, 1930). Henry Boothe died Dec. 26, 1941 and Pearl died June 23, 1974 in Morrilton.

Zeddie Airhart married Ella Sanders (b. Jan. 1, 1892) and they were parents of Lillian, L.T. and Joseph Airhart.

Carrie Bev married a Carter. They were the parents of Airhart (Boots) and Aaron Carter.

Pearl Airhart Booth, Mamie Airhart Evans, "Old Man" Airhart (Was this James? I don't remember his name - or was it Will?), Zeddie Airhart, and Lonnie Airhart, all told me I was their cousin.

In the household next to the Airharts lived the family of Mamie Hyler who had several children. However, Mamie does not appear in any more censuses. However, her son Adam appears in the household with Hattie Boozer Thornton in the census of 1910. A Mamie Hyler who lives in Lexington County, Saluda Township, SC (December 2000). This Mamie Hyler was married to a James Pope Black and they were parents of two daughters, Annie Mae and Myrtle Black. Most likely this is a coincidence. There was a

Mamie Hyler in Conway County, AR, a widow, who lived in household #248 in 1900. (The Airharts were in #246.) Mamie's children included Adam Hyler (b. 1892) who lived with Hattie Boozer in 1910. The other children were M_____(b. 1885), Evan (b. 1888), Lucinda (b. 1890), Ellen (b. 1891), Elijah (b. 1895) and Willie (b. 1899). I have not found any of the others after 1900. Inf. from 1900 census of Conway County, AR. There was a Mamie Hyler who married T.H. Holland in Morrilton on Oct. 16, 1900 and a Lena Hyler who also married a H.H. Holland Sept. 13, 1900. I don't know if there's a relation to these Hylers.

Burrell (Burr) Thornton was born in 1858 in South Carolina. In the 1870 census of Lexington County, SC, Burrell is listed as Burr, 12-year-old son of James and Caroline Thornton. He appears in the 1880 census of Lexington County, SC, Hollow Creek Township, married to Linah. They are the parents of a daughter, Cora E. Thornton (b. March 1880). (No maiden name for Linah). Cora lived with Frank and Margaret Thornton's family in 1900 when she was 20 years old. (The age and year match the 1880 Lexington County Census where she is shown as the daughter of Burrell and Linah).

In the 1910 Census of Conway County, AR, Welburn Township, Burrell appears with his wife Belle as a 42-year-old Black male. Belle is 33 years old. She and Burrell have been married five (5) years. This is shown as his second marriage and her first marriage. Belle is the mother of two children, both living. They are Herbert Denton, 18 years old and Huless Magauss, age 14. They are enumerated in the census as household 6, family 6. (Burr's brother Frank Thornton appears in the next numbered household with his wife, Margaret and four children.) Huless is buried in Oddfellows Cemetery. His tombstone bears the inscription: "Son of Belle Thornton." (He is buried as a Thornton, not a Magauss)

Pierson (Pierce) Thornton was born in 1870 in South Carolina. According to the census of Lexington County, Hollow Creek Township in 1870, Pearson Thornton is seven (7) years old and living in the household with his parents James and Caroline Thornton along with his other brothers and sisters. Pearson is not shown in the Thornton household in 1880. They were living in Saluda Township at that time and only seven children were in the household: Ellen, Julia, Green, Henry, John, Columbus, and Lizzie.

In 1900, a Pierce Thornton is shown living in Hollow Creek Township in Lexington County, SC on June 8, 1900. (Enumerator's District 41, Sheet B, Line 65, Household number 99, Family number 99. He is 40 years old and shows a birth date of December 1859. He has been married 21 years which would make his marriage date around 1879 when he would have been 20 years old. His wife is shown as Elizabeth with two children: Eddie (b. September 1879), age 20 and Franklin (b. March 1882), age 18 both living in the household. Pierce, Eddie and Franklin are shown as farm laborers renting the property. Farm schedule is shown as #92.

In the 1910 census of Lexington County, a Pierce Thornton is shown in the May 6, 1910 census, living in Hollow Creek Township, Lexington County, SC in Enumeration District 38, page 270, line 31. He is shown with wife Lizzie (Elizabeth?), age 48 and he is age 50. It shows they have been married 30 years and that Lizzie is the mother of two living children. They have a daughter named Eddie C. age 15 who is listed as adopted by Pierce. (In 1900, they had a son named Eddie who was 20 and who would be 30 at this census. Perhaps this is his daughter.) They rent farm land and the farm schedule is #330. They are family #318 in dwelling #304. (*I don't have a 1920 census from Lexington County. Perhaps part of this family still lives in Lexington County.*) I have found no further information about Ellen, Julia, and Henry Thornton except that in the censuses of 1870 and 1880. I don't know whether or not they moved to Arkansas.

Green William Thornton (b. June 10, 1865 in

Lexington County, SC) md. Hattie Boozer, also from Lexington County. He appears in the 1870 and 1880 censuses of Lexington County, SC as a four year old and as a 14 year old. In the 1900 census of Conway County, AR, enumerated on June 2, 1900 Green and Hattie appear in Supervisor's District 4, Enumerator's District 14, Sheet 2, Line 34, dwelling number 23 and household number 24. Green is 34 years old and Hattie is 31 years old. Hattie is shown as the mother of one living child and they have been married 12 years, placing their marriage date about 1888.

The following people lived in the household with Green and Hattie in 1900: Atha Reed (Green's niece), age 6, born February 1894 in Arkansas. Her father is from Mississippi and her mother is from South Carolina. Adam Hyler (listed as a boarder), age 8, born 1892 in Arkansas. Both his parents are from South Carolina; Audrey Thornton (Green's nephew), age 3, born May 1897, born in Arkansas. His father is from Arkansas and his mother is from South Carolina; Lula Thornton (listed as a boarder), age 10, born December 12, 1889 born in Arkansas. Her father is from Arkansas and her mother is from North Carolina; Jamie Graham (listed as a boarder), age 12, born April 1888 in Arkansas. Both parents are from Arkansas; Thomas Griggsby (listed as a boarder), age 28, born March 1872 in Tennessee. Both parents are from Tennessee.

In the 1910 Census of Welborn Township, Conway County, AR, Green W. Thornton appears in household #15, family 15 on line 8 on Germantown Road. His is listed as a 44-year-old black male head of the household. Hattie is listed as a 39-year-old mulatto with one child born in Arkansas. The inhabitants of the household in 1900 do not appear on this census. Household inhabitants in 1910 in addition to Green and Hattie are: Odra Thornton (Green's nephew), male mulatto, age 12, born in Arkansas. His father is from Arkansas and his mother was born in South Carolina. We don't know who the parents were. Otto Boozer (Hattie's nephew), male mulatto, age 18 born in Arkansas. Both parents from South Carolina. (Otto is the son of Richard Boozer and Alice Ponds Boozer. (Richard Boozer, Sr. was Hattie's brother.)

In the Conway County, Welburn Township census of 1920 Green and Hattie appear in District 19, Sheet 112, Line 22, dwelling 360, household #378. Green is listed as a 54-year-old Black Male and Hattie. None of the 1900 occupants of the household appear in the census. The 1920 household occupants in addition to Greene and Hattie are: Otto Boozer (Hattie's nephew), 28-year-old Black male; Richard Boozer (Hattie's nephew), 18-year-old Black male. (Son of Alice Ponds Boozer & Richard Boozer, Sr.); Aaron Davenport (listed as a lodger), 16-year-old Black male.

Green William Thornton died Dec. 19, 1954 in Los Angeles, California. (California Death Records, 1940-97 Data Base Searched Dec. 12, 2000)

Columbus Frank Thornton was born Dec. 4, 1872 in Edgefield County, SC. (All the information I have shows Lexington County, not Edgefield County so I may be missing some pieces.) He appears in the household of James and Caroline Thornton in Hollow Creek Township in 1870 and Saluda Township, Lexington County, SC in 1880. Frank married Margaret Smith, daughter of Jim Smith and Lucinda ? July 9, 1894 in Conway County, AR. They were both 21 years old.

Columbus Frank Thornton and Margaret Smith July 9, 1894 were married in Conway County, Arkansas. (Marriage book 1, page 53, Conway County records. They were both listed as age 21.)

MARGARET SMITH THORNTON'S FAMILY - Margaret Smith was born July 1873 in Conway County, Arkansas to Jim Smith and Lucinda Brooks (Smith???). I am not sure if her name was Lucinda - the name came from what I was told by Emily Thomas Brown, who said that these were her relatives and that Lucinda was her aunt. I have found no evidence of who Harry Brooks was or what Emily Brooks maiden name was, nor have I seen them in any other

place. He was 82 years old in 1880 and she was 70, so they may not have survived until there was another census. So there is that mystery. Margaret's father, James Smith, was born in Maryland, as were his parents. His birth date appears to have been 1856, according to his age in 1920 which is shown as 64.

Mary Smith was born about 1876 to James Smith and Lucinda (Brooks?). She was four years old in June 1880. Mary married William Lee Mitchell on Dec. 22, 1890 in Conway County, Arkansas. Mary Smith and Lee Mitchell were the parents of two children, Margaret and William "Bill" Mitchell. (Mary Mitchell died when Margaret was about five years old and William was a baby. Their father and his second wife, Tempie Owens Mitchell, raised both children to adulthood).

Margaret Mitchell Hinton (b. March 8, 1907) md. Frank Hinton from Houston, TX shortly after the beginning of World War II. He preceded her in death. Margaret died in Morrilton, AR Nov. 25, 1998.

William Mitchell (nicknamed "Stick") (b. 1902 in Morrilton, AR) md. Arvie Templeton from the Happy Bend community. (This information came from Bobbie Lee Mitchell in May 2001 in a telephone call). William died about 1983 in Morrilton.

Henrietta Brooks or Smith - I could find no information about Henrietta.

James Smith was shown as married to Priscilla Cole in 1880 with children Thomas Cole, daughter, Josephine Bradley, sons, Benjamin and Terry Bradley. It's not clear if all of these were their children separately or of their union.

James Smith married Tennessee Dickens from Dardanelle, Yell County, AR on June 15, 1890 in Conway County, AR. Tennessee Dickens was born in 1868. James and Tennessee were parents of six children: Corrie Smith Jackson, who married Jim Jackson; Viola Smith Mills; Louise Smith; Percy Smith; Leslie Smith; Butler Smith, and Elizabeth Smith.

June 4, 1900, Margaret Smith is shown with husband Frank Thornton in Supervisor's District 4, Enumerators District 14, Sheet #2, line 780, Welbourne Township, Conway County, Frank Thornton is listed as a 26-year-old Black male born in South Carolina, both parents born in South Carolina. Margaret, his wife, is listed as a 26-year-old Black female. They have been married seven years. Margaret is the mother of seven (7) children, four of whom are living in 1900.

They were: Julia Thornton, age 5, born June 1895 in Arkansas; Christina Thornton, age 3, born January 1897 in Arkansas; Carlina Thornton, age 3, born January 1897 in Arkansas and Mary (Rebecca) Thornton, age 2, born January 1898 in Arkansas. Other residents of the home in 1900 are as were: Lizzie Brown (Frank's sister), age 23, a widow who had been married three (3) years., (1897) who was born in South Carolina, both parents from South Carolina; Cora Thornton (Frank's niece), age 20, born March 1880 in South Carolina. Both parents from South Carolina; Caroline Thornton (Frank's mother), age 62, born January 1838 in South Carolina, a widow who was married for 30 years, placing the marriage date about 1870. I can find no other information about Caroline.

The 1910 Census. Margaret shows as wife of Frank Thornton. She is 36 years old. They had been married 14 years. She was the mother of 8 children, 4 of whom were living. Margaret Smith died sometimes between 1910 and 1922. Only Frank, his wife, and four children are in the household. Children and ages: Julia, age 15; Christina, age 13; Carlina, age 13 and Rebecca, age 11 (This is Mary Rebecca). Frank Thornton married Mable Brame in 1922 and they became parents of five children, all of whom are living (2002). Frank Thornton died April 13, 1947 in Morrilton, Conway County, Arkansas and is buried in Oddfellows Cemetery in Morrilton in the Thornton Section of the cemetery.

Children of Columbus Frank Thornton and Margaret Smith Thornton:

Julia Thornton Bowles was born in Morrilton,

AR, Jan. 21, 1895. She was the daughter of Columbus Frank Thornton and Margaret Smith Thornton. Julia was a member of the St. Matthew Baptist Church. She married David Bowles in 1914 (David Bowles was born June 9, 1895 in Arkansas and died in 1947 in England, Arkansas.) After David's death, Julia moved to Coffeyville, KS where she lived for many years. Julia died July 13, 1966 in Columbus, OH. They were parents of two daughters: Mable Orlean Bowles Brown and Ruby V. Bowles Austin.

Ruby V. Bowls Austin was born in Morrilton, AR on March 31, 1915. She was married and divorced from E.L. Austin of Morrilton and Waterloo, IA. Ruby is deceased.

Mable Orlean Bowles Brown (b. May 10, 1917 in Morrilton, AR) was a professional cook. She retired from Capital University in Columbus, OH May 10, 1979, after working for many years as their head cook. She and Clarence Brown were married February 2, 1957. Orlean was a member of the Gospel Tabernacle United Holiness Church of American where she served as vice president of the Senior Usher Board and was in charge of the kitchen. Orlean died in 1989 in Columbus, OH.

Christina Thornton (b. Feb. 8, 1897) was twin to Carlina Thornton. Christina was the mother of a son named Manoy, who was nicknamed "Boney."

Carlina Thornton Stricklen was born Feb. 8, 1897 in Morrilton, AR to C. Frank Thornton and Margaret Smith Thornton. She married Samuel Stricklin (formerly Strickland) Sept. 12, 1914. Carlina and Samuel Stricklin (Strickland) were the parents of 10 children. They were: three living descendants who live in Arkansas and in Kansas, and the following other children (deceased): Sammie Henry Stricklen, Garland Stricklen, Julia Vanella Stricklin (called Vanella), Thelma Stricklin, James Henry Stricklin; Eddie Green Stricklin and Mary Rebecca Stricklin

Mary Rebecca Thornton Haywood (b. Feb. 28, 1888 in Morrilton, AR) was the daughter of Frank Thornton and Margaret Smith Thornton (Margaret was the daughter of Jim Smith and Lucinda Smith. Mary was the mother of one child, Frank John Henry Ponds, born July 16, 1917. Information about Frank is in the Ponds family history. Mary married Burt Haywood. The family lived in Morrilton's west end until Frank helped Mary purchase a house in downtown Morrilton on North Division Street. Mary was a member of Trinity C.M.E. Church most of her life until she became a Jehovah Witness shortly preceding her death in May 1953.

TICE - Robert Lee Tice (b. May 19, 1875 in Tennessee), son of "Unknown" and Jane Tice. Robert married Rebecca Ann Mills in 1893. Rebecca was the daughter of John Mills and Henryetta Andrews Mills. She was born July 17, 1863 in Georgia. According to the census, Robert's father was born in Georgia and his mother was born in North Carolina.

In 1900, Robert was in Conway County in Washington Township.

Robert and Rebecca Tice

The 1900 census said that Rebecca had three children, two of which were living. Her parents were born in Georgia. Also listed with them were a son, John H., age 3, and Rutha J., age 1. Both of these children were born in Arkansas. Also, living with them was Robert's mother, Jane. Jane was 67 years, born in North Carolina, had nine children, eight of whom were still living. Robert was a farmer. Rebecca (d. Dec. 19, 1942) and Robert (d. Aug. 17, 1958), both are buried in Friendship Cemetery in Solgohachia. The couple had three children: John Henry, Ruth Jane and Hazel Beatrice.

Robert Lee was a preacher and also wrote Overcup Community news for the local newspaper.

John Henry (b. Nov. 20, 1896, d. April 11, 1918) is buried in Friendship Cemetery in Solgohachia.

Ruth Jane Tice (b. Sept. 28, 1898 in Lonoke, AR) md. Huie Robert Williams. She died April 27, 1985 in Little Rock, AR. Huie died Oct. 18, 1952. They are buried in Old Salem Cemetery. Their children include Herman, Euna Pearl, Dorothy Dalton, R.H., Robert Lee, Fatha Faye, Leroy, Mary Lee, Dewitt, Billy Earl and Helen Ruth.

Hazel Beatrice (b. July 22, 1902) md. William Miles Ledbetter on July 10, 1923. She died Feb. 28, 1987 in Missouri and William Miles died Jan. 13, 1980. They are buried in Friendship Cemetery. Their children include Henrietta, Eddy Lee, Virginia Dale and Charles Edward. *Submitted by Fay Beavers.*

TILLEY - On Aug. 26, 1933, Avis Rhoades and Hector Tilley were married at Cleveland, AR. Avis (b. Dec. 9, 1915) was the daughter of Coma Wolverton and Sam Rhoades, who were married in 1910. Sam Rhoades died in 1917, and Coma married George Walls. Avis had two sisters, Hester Walls and Imo Jean Walls, and two brothers, Troy Walls and Arlie Walls.

Coma Wolverton was the daughter of Ann Wolverton and W.F. Wolverton. The Wolverton family moved from McNairy County,

Hector Tilley and Avis Rhodes Tilley

TN, to Wolverton Mountain in Conway County, in the mid-1800s.

Sam Rhoades was the son of Jim Rhoades of Cleveland. Sam had two sisters, Mattie Rhoades and Ettie Rhoades, and four brothers: Jim, George, Ed and El Rhodes.

Hector Tilley (b. May 30, 1915, d. July 15, 2002) was the son of Lou Ella Guinn and Wayne Tilley. He had one brother Rufe, who died as a young man.

Avis was a home maker and worked in Detroit, MI during WWII, and worked at Levi Strauss in Morrilton from 1948-72. They lived In Morrilton most of that time, but later moved back to Cleveland. Hector was employed some time with the Morrilton Police Department. *Submitted by Hector Tilley.*

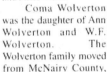

TILLEY - Ola Mae Watkins (b. July 10, 1920 in Conway County, AR) was the daughter of Samuel Garfield and Maga Anne Poe Watkins. Ola grew up in Conway County and married first, Richard Boyer, in 1938. Unfortunately, Richard died shortly after their marriage of typhoid fever.

Ola married second, Paul David Tilley on Feb. 23, 1939 in Conway County. Their union produced two children: David Lee Tilley (b. Nov. 27, 1939) and Mable Marie "Patsy" Tilley (b.

Ola Mae Tilley

Nov. 27, 1940). Paul David Tilley was tragically killed in a train accident in Pope County on July 28, 1942. He was buried in the Lost Corner Cemetery near Cleveland, AR.

Ola married twice more and had five other children: Joe, Bill, Margaret and Christine Cravens; and Linda Sue Lowe. Ola also died tragically in an accident. She was living in Kermit, TX when she was killed in a car accident while on her way to work on Sept. 16, 1969. Ola was returned home and buried beside her second husband Paul in the Lost Corner Cemetery

near Cleveland, AR. *Submitted by Mable Marie "Patsy" Tilley Scroggin.*

TILLEY - Paul David Tilley (b. May 2, 1921 in Arkansas) was the son of Charles and Isabelle Mitchell Tilley. Paul grew up in Conway County with his four brothers, A.H., M.W., Dewey and J.A. Tilley. When he was 16 years old he joined the Civilian Conservation Corp and went to Pierce, ID. He spent six months in Idaho before returning home to Conway County.

Paul and Ola Tilley

Paul married Ola Mae Watkins, daughter of Samuel and Maga Poe Watkins, on Feb. 23, 1939. Their union produced the following children:

David Lee Tilley (b. Nov. 27, 1939) and Mable Marie "Patsy" Tilley (b. Nov. 27, 1940). David Lee Tilley married Lois Waites. Children born to them are Paula (b. July 7, 1964) and Stacey (b. April 17, 1967).

Mable married first, James Welch. Children born to them are James Ray Welch (b. Aug. 8, 1958) and Rose Marie Welch (b. Nov. 10, 1960). Mable married second, Harold Scroggin of Center Ridge, AR.

Paul was killed in a train accident on July 28, 1942 in Russellville, AR. He was brought home to Conway County and buried in the Lost Corner Cemetery near Cleveland, AR. *Submitted by Ray Welch.*

TOOMBS - The US Census for 1930 lists several family members living in Conway County, AR. Preston Toombs lives in Birdtown Township. McClaren Township lists Toombs residents for Thadeus, Pauline, Arthur, Lowell, Ruby, Raleigh, Horatio, Eleanor and Phyllis. Welborn Township has Richard Toombs as a resident. He is not the Richard Toombs in the 1880 US Census. He is a grandchild. The father and grandfather of the people listed above is Richard Toombs.

Richard Toombs, age 30, married to Mollie, age 23 was living in Washington Township in Conway County. Thadeus, Edward, Willis, Ula and Arthur are the children living at the time. At least one more son, Clarence, would be born in Conway County. Richard migrated to Conway County from Shelby County, TN. Records indicate he was born in Virginia.

There are hundreds of Richards' offspring still living in Arkansas, while others have scattered across the nation. *Submitted by Rhonda C. Stewart.*

TOTTEN - Percival Norman Totten (b. April 6, 1866, Paris, Brant County, Ontario) was the son of Norman Totten and Catherine Christie. Norman Totten (b. Nov. 13, 1840 at Paris, Brant County, Ontario, d. Feb. 23,

Percival Norman Totten

Gladys Mary Egan Totten, wife of Percy Totten

1899 at Chicago, Cook County, IL) was the son of Daniel Totten (b. Dec. 25, 1807 in New York, d. April 3, 1877 in Brant County, Ontario), who had moved to Brant County around 1830 and built a woolen factory at Paris, Ontario.

His mother Catherine Christie (b. June 19, 1844 at Melbourne, Ontario, d. June 1, 1920 in New York City) was the daughter of Thomas Christie (b. Dec. 29, 1815 in Perth, Scotland, d. Dec. 30, 1879 at Bowmanville, Durham County, Ontario) and Catherine Morton (b. May 22, 1820, Montreal, Quebec, d. Dec. 28, 1881 at Bowmanville, Durham County, Ontario). Catherine Morton was the daughter of a contractor, Robert Morton (b. 1796, Coupar Angus, Scotland, d. March 28, 1873, buried in Brant County, Ontario) and Helen Young. Robert Morton retired and moved from Montreal to Brantford, Ontario and built a house that he later sold to Alexander Graham Bell's father. It was there that Mr. Bell invented the telephone. The house stands today, a museum administered and owned by Canadian Bell Telephone.

The Totten family immigrated to the United States in 1871 to Buffalo, Erie County, NY. Norman Totten became a naturalized citizen on Oct. 21, 1879. In 1893 he worked at the World's Columbian Exposition in Chicago, and there he met Olive (Ween) Egan of Waynesville, OH.

Olive was born in Lewisburg, AR, the first child of W.P. and Kate Kearney Egan, but had been sent to Waynesville, OH to live with her Grandmother Kearney due to being born with a cleft palate which could be treated by doctors in Ohio but not Arkansas. P.N. and Olive married Aug. 20, 1894 at Waynesville. They later divorced and PN. married Olive's sister, Gladys Mary Egan in Conway County, AR on Feb. 1, 1903.

P.N. held various positions in Morrilton. He owned a confectionery, was general manager of the Federal Compress and was an engineer for highway construction and the bridge over the Arkansas River at Morrilton. He was also with the Davies Construction Company. He served as Mayor of Morrilton in 1908. He was a 32 degree Mason, Consistory of Little Rock and a member of Morrilton Lodge No. 105.

The children of P.N. and Gladys Totten were Frank Norman Totten (b. July 21, 1906, d. Oct. 21, 1987); Catherine Helen Totten (b. Oct. 10, 1910); Patricia Norma Totten (b. March 20, 1914, d. May 22, 1995); and Gladys Egan Totten (b. Oct. 17, 1916).

P.N. Totten died March 7, 1924 at Morrilton of cancer. Gladys died at Perryville Feb. 3, 1953 of pernicious anemia. Both are buried in Elmwood Cemetery at Morrilton. *Submitted by Lynda Suffridge.*

VARNER - The Varner family originated in Germany. The spelling "Varner" is said to be a French version of the German patronymic name "Werner." Early Varner immigrants arrived in America around 1632. Adam Varner married Christina R. (last name unknown), probably in Germany. Adam and Christina were probably both born in Germany. Adam and Christina immigrated to America and settled in Virginia where several, if not all, of their children were born. Records of Shenandoah County, VA show the birth of their son John in 1772. Adam is named in a list of tithables in Augusta County, VA in 1782 and 1785. Adam settled in Pendleton County, VA about 1785. He was granted a land patent on 300 acres of land in Pendleton County in 1799. Adam probably died between 1810-20. Christina died 1824-30. They had at least 12 children: Adam, Henry, Conrad, Abraham, Peter, Jacob, John, George, Catherine, Margaret, Regina and Joseph.

Jacob Varner was born 1768-71 in Virginia, the son of Adam and Christina Varner. Jacob appears on the 1787 Rockingham County, VA tithables list. He was under the age of 21. Jacob married Sarah Ficklin about 1791. Jacob and Sarah appear on the 1800 Bourbon County, KY census, as do Jacob's brothers, Adam and Conrad Varner. The family was in Harrison County, KY in May 1810 when Jacob gave consent for their daughter Jane to marry. The family moved to Indiana between 1810-20. They were in Posey County, IN in 1820 and 1830. Sarah died 1830-36 in Posey County. On Dec. 29, 1836 Jacob married Mrs. Mary Stum, a widow from White County, IL. Jacob died prior to 1840. Jacob and Sarah had at least eight children:

1) John Varner (b. 1792, d. Feb. 2, 1870) md. Rebecca McCarty. Children: Elizabeth, Samuel, William, James, Mary, Sarah, Robert, Angeline and Maria.

2) Jane Varner (b. 1795, d. March 24, 1876) md. Andrew Fitzwater. Children: Charity, Jacob, John, George, Andrew, James, Sarah and Mary Ann Fitzwater.

3) Elizabeth Varner (b. 1797, d. 1870) md. Joseph Nation Endicott. Children: John, James, George, William, Joseph, Arvis, Sarah, Emily, Charles, Samuel, Elizabeth (md. Wilson Harmon), Welmet, America and Martin Endicott.

4) Polly A. Varner (b. 1798) md. William Wilson. Children: James, Robert, Humble, Nancy, Andrew, Henry and William Wilson.

5) James B. Varner (b. Oct. 31, 1800, d. June 20, 1886) md. Emily Denby. Children: Frances, Joseph, James, Mary, William, Emily and Martha Varner.

6) Sarah Varner (b. 1805) md. Joseph Stoker.

7) Emily Varner (b. 1808) md. Gillis "Billy" Driskill.

8) Thomas Varner (b. 1809) md. Elizabeth Centers. Children: Francis, Sarah, Nancy, Mary, Thomas and George Varner.

VENABLE – Thomas William Venable (b. 1798 in Virginia) migrated to Georgia while young. He married Sarah Martha Stell, daughter of John Wesley and Elizabeth (King) Stell, in Hall County, GA, on April 20, 1820. Four children were born to them in DeKalb County, GA before they migrated to Conway County in 1839. Another son was born in 1845.

Martha died about 1867 and Thomas died intestate about 1870. Both were buried in Springfield Cemetery. Thomas owned about 235 acres, which was divided among his "only heirs," according to documents found in Chancery Court Records. Those named were James, Z.A.P. and George Fenable: Thomas, King, Alex, Martha and Emily Griffin; John L., Martha A.E., Thomas J., Elenor C. and William D. Steele.

Caroline C. Venable (b. 1823) md. William Stell/ Steele, a merchant, about 1846. They lived in Dallas County in 1850 and 1860. Other than their children listed above, there was a son James, who died before 1860. Caroline was deceased by 1871.

James P. Venable (b. 1826) joined the gold rush to California in 1849/50 but returned home in 1853, and became a merchant. In 1856 he married Harriet Elizabeth Francis Hardin, daughter of Jonathan and Elizabeth Hardin, who was the first child born (1837) at Enola, then in Conway County. Her father, Jonathan Hardin, was said to be one of the wealthiest men in the area, owning 3,000 acres of land.

James and Elizabeth lived in Pulaski County when he was State Legislator (1860). He also was a justice of the peace and a county judge in Conway County.

In July 1861, he enlisted in Company B, 10th Arkansas Regiment Infantry, C.S.A. He was appointed captain, but resigned because of illness. Later he enlisted in Company I, 10th (Witts) Arkansas Cavalry Regiment.

His children were Jonathan W., Katie, May and Bessie.

Margaret Eliza Venable (b. 1829) md. John W. Griffin before 1850. Their children were Thomas William, John King, Fletcher Alexander, Martha F., Emily and James. John and Eliza Griffin died before 1870, and most of their children were raised by Venable family members. James, their youngest child, died before October 1871.

Zebulin "Z.AP" (b. November 1836) md. Susan Hobbs, daughter of John and Martha Hobbs, in July 1860. Lula E., Zebulin's daughter, was born in

1874. She married Alex H. Stephens, a physician, in 1898. Zebulin helped organize Company I, 10th Arkansas Regiment, C.S.A. in July 1861. He was appointed captain, fought at Shiloh, captured at Port Hudson, LA, and imprisoned at Johnson Island, OH until the War ended. He resumed farming afterwards and was elected State Representative in 1888. He died in 1902 and his wife died in 1908.

George Washington Venable (b. 1845) enlisted in Company B of the 10th (Witts) Arkansas Cavalry Regiment, C.S.A. during the Civil War. George and his brother James were both paroled June 5, 1865 at Jacksonport, AR.

George married Jane Raybone (Rayburn) in 1867. Their daughter Jennie was born about 1869. After Jane died. George married Tennessee Agnes Wilson in 1875. His children by "Tennie" were James Arthur, Ethel Mae, Ruth, and perhaps others. George died in 1889 in Elm Springs, Washington County.

VENABLE – Thomas W. Venable was born in Virginia about 1798, but migrated to Georgia at an early age. In Hall County, GA, on April 20, 1820, he married Sarah Martha Stell. Her parents were John Wesley Stell and Elizabeth (King). Thomas and Martha Venable had at least two sons, James and Zebulin, and two daughters, Eliza and (unknown), born in Georgia. The family migrated to Conway County about 1839, where their son George was born about 1845.

Martha Venable died about 1867 and Thomas died about 1870. They were buried in the Springfield Cemetery.

James P. Venable was born October 1826 in DeKalb County, GA. About 1850 he went to California seeking gold, but returned home in 1853 and became a merchant. In 1856, he married (Harriet) Elizabeth (Francis) Hardin, daughter of Jonathan and Elizabeth Hardin. She was said to be the first child born in Enola about 1837. Her father owned 3,000 acres of land and was the one of the wealthiest men in the area.

James and Elizabeth Venable lived in Pulaski County in 1860 while he served as a State Legislator. Later on, he was a justice of the peace and also the county judge in Conway County.

In July 1861, he enlisted in Company B, 10th Arkansas Regiment Infantry, C.S.A. He was a captain, but resigned due to illness. Later, he enlisted in Company I, 10th (Wilts) Arkansas Cavalry Regiment serving until the end of the war.

James' children were Jonathan W., Katie, May and Bessie L. Venable.

Zebulin (Z.A.P.) Venable (b. Nov. 16, 1836 in DeKalb County, GA) md. Susan Hobbs in Conway County in July 1860. Susan was a daughter of John and Martha Hobbs, Zebulin helped organize Company I, 10th Arkansas Regiment, C.S.A., in July 1861. He was appointed captain and fought at Shiloh, was captured at Port Hudson, LA, and imprisoned at Johnson Island, OH for 23 months until the war ended. He resumed farming after the war, and was elected state representative in 1888 by a majority of about 800 votes. Zebulin died in 1902 and Susan died in 1908. They rest at Springfield Cemetery.

Zebulin and Susan had only one child, Lula F. Venable, born about 1874. She married Alex H. Stephens, a physician, in 1898, in Conway County. Their only child did not survive.

George Washington Venable (b. July 5, 1845, d. April 5, 1889 in Elm Springs, Washington County) enlisted during the Civil War in Company B of the 10th (Witts) Arkansas Cavalry Regiment, C.S.A. He and his brother James were both paroled June 5, 1865 at Jacksonport, AR.

George married Jane Raybone (Rayburn) Dec. 19, 1867. A daughter Jennie was born about 1869. On Oct. 11, 1875, George married Tennessee Agnes Wilson of Lewisburg. The 1880 Census lists his children as Jennie, James Arthur and Ethel Mae. A daughter Ruth, and possibly others, were born after 1880.

Margaret Eliza Venable (b. 1829) md. John W.

Griffin before 1850 in Conway County. They became parents of four sons: Thomas, King, Alex and James, and one daughter Martha Emily. Eliza and her husband died before 1870, and their children were raised by Venable family members. *Submitted by Nada C. Guthier.*

WADE - Edmond Wade was born ca. Jan. 11, 1808 in Lauderdale County, TN, which was Chickasaw land at the time. His mother Elizabeth, possible Green, and unknown Wade, possible Hampton, had left Virgini' where his sister Sarah (b. ca. 1805) and brother Joh (b. ca. 1806) and had Edmond in Tennessee. Sister Elizabeth was also born in Tennessee ca. 1813. The family moved to Illinois, where they had Richard Calvin (b. ca. 1815) and Joseph (b. ca. 1819).

The family is believed to have moved to Missouri, where they had Frances Jane (b. ca. 1822) and Thomas Hampton (b. ca. 1823). We believe the father died there and Elizabeth then moved her family to Lawrence County, AR, which was an Indian Reservation then. It is believed that she married a half Cherokee named Green, from possible Mississippi, who was father to William Green (b. ca. May 10, 1818, Mississippi), who with his brother Jim James Green (b. ca. Jan. 20, 1823, Arkansas) migrated between 1831-46 to Bastrop, TX by covered wagon and settled on Gen. Edward Burleson Plantation in Texas.

William Green married Hannah King (b. ca. 1824, Kentucky, d. Oct. 6, 1901 Texas) who was daughter of Nathaniel King, who was half Cherokee from North Carolina. James Green was married to Sarah Kitchell, daughter of Celia Williams, niece of Aaron Williams. They had sisters: Elizabeth (b. ca. Jan. 20, 1823, Arkansas, d. Feb. 29, 1908, Texas) who married Aaron Williams (b. Oct. 13, 1815, Tennessee, d. 1900, Texas) who migrated to Texas in 1845 and sister Mary Ann Green (b. ca. 1825, Arkansas, d. 1897, Texas) who married first, Benjamin King, son of Nathaniel King in Arkansas. He died and she married David Pinson (d. 1872). She was living next door in Arkansas to Nathaniel King, who was her father-in-law. She moved to Texas beside her brother James in Texas. It is believed that she is daughter of Elizabeth Wade and Green.

Edmond Wade married Sallie Williams in Arkansas and had Sarah Jane (b. April 17, 1840, d. 1864) who married Matthew Marion McCabe (b. Aug. 8, 1835, Arkansas, d. July 23, 1924, Adona, AR) and had John Hampton Wade (b. 1842, Arkansas, d. 1881 Texas) who married Sara Conway (b. ca. 1835, d. 1864, Arkansas) who had Sarah Lou (b. ca. 1862, Arkansas) and Martha (b. ca. 1864, Arkansas). He migrated to Texas after that to Col. Burleson Plantation and married Julia Ann Neely on April 4, 1867, who was born May 31, 1850, Kentucky, d. Jan. 11, 1933, Texas, and had six children with her, including William Green Wade, and then Elizabeth (b. ca. 1844, Arkansas, d. March 23, 1923, Arkansas, Yell County) who married Edmond Alexander Smith in 1872.

After Sallie died, Edmond married Sarah Ann McCabe Holbein, ca. 1829 in Arkansas, daughter of James McCabe, and had Nancy (b. March 26, 1850); William (b. ca. 1852, d. 1860); Margaret (b. March 6, 1854); Edmon (b. Jan. 28, 1856); Catherine (b. Jan. 13, 1861); Julia (b. March 13, 1863); Louise (b. Dec. 23, 1859).

Edmond signed up to serve in the Union Army and died six months later of pneumonia and smallpox, leaving a wife and small children. His son John also was in the Union Army, and after he got out in 1864, he migrated to Texas with his two small children. In 1850, Elizabeth McCabe (b. 1829) was living in Edmond's house. She was a sister to Sarah. Many of the Greens lived at Georgetown, on Green's Farm.

These are the ancestors of Billy and Bo White of Morrilton and Plummerville, AR. Early Arkansas settlers during the 1800s. Parents of Billy and Bo are Mary Wade and Allen White, who are from Texas and Louisiana, who now live in Conway County, AR, who are also in this book. Billy is married to Amy Harris and has two children, Christian and Billy. Bo has children Chelsey Rose, Mary Danielle and Caitlin Cheyenne.

WALKER – John Caldwell Calhoun Walker came to Conway County, AR between 1881-84. He was born April 4, 1857 in Tippah County, MS. His great-grandfather, John Walker (supposed son of Alexander Walker and Esther Gray), had been born in 1732 and lived with his family in Chester County, SC, in the Rocky Creek Community. John married Jane (last name unknown) and had John Jr., Samuel, William, Martha, Charles and Alexander.

Charles Walker, born between 1770-80 in South Carolina, married Elizabeth (last name unknown) in South Carolina. They had at least eight children: Charles Jr., Hugh, Lucinda, Alexander, Thomas, Mary, Amanda, and Jane. From Chester County, the family moved to Dallas County, AL for a brief period of time in the 1820s, then on to Tippah County, MS in the 1830s.

Hugh Walker (b. 1814 in South Carolina) md. Mary Caroline Maxcy (daughter of Edward Maxcy and Mary Polly Nelson). They had two children, Amanda Jane (b. 1851, Mississippi) and John Caldwell Calhoun (b. 1857, Mississippi). In 1858, Hugh died. Mary C. Walker remarried Oswald Owens on Aug. 10, 1858 in Tippah County, MS. John married Melvina Ann Love in Union County, MS on Jan. 6, 1879. They had five children: William Calvin, Margie Caroline, Martha Antha, Hugh E. and Johnnie Oliver.

The family moved to the Hill Creek Community just prior to 1884, where John built a log house. Wilder and Wilbanks owned the cotton gin and a house at Hill Creek, which they traded both for John's log house and the 80 acres it stood on. The land where the old log house stood is now covered under Lake Brewer. The white house where they lived has also been torn down. John contracted pneumonia and died Feb. 4, 1893.

William Calvin Walker (b. Jan. 3, 1881 in Mississippi) md. Emily Elvia Griswood (b. Aug. 5, 1880 in Clinton, AR) on Sept. 15, 1900 in Conway County, AR. Together, they had nine children including: Mildred (md. Roy Bradford), Mamie Alice (md. Orville Langrell), Forrest (died at a year old), Aubrey (md. Golda Thomas), Hazel (md. Luther Poteete), William Orville (md. Loeta Reynolds), J.C. (md. Thelma Holland), Jack Arlie (md. LaVelle Deaver) and Myrtle Irene (md. Dalton Stacks).

William Calvin Walker was instrumental in the moving of Portland Baptist Church from the bottoms of Portland to Plumerville. He donated the land and helped reconstruct the building where Portland Baptist Church now sits. He also owned a general store in Portland Bottoms around 1911. The family moved to England, AR for a time before moving back to Plumerville years later.

Jack Arlie "Red" Walker married Mildred LaVelle Deaver. He was born June 14, 1915 in Plumerville, AR. They married on Dec. 4, 1937 in Conway County, AR. They had eight children: Naomi, Harold, CB, Lucretia, Anthony, Gwyned, Arlianne and Kevin. Red died on June 13, 1984 in Little Rock, AR. LaVelle died March 12, 2003 in Morrilton, AR. *Submitted by Anthony Walker.*

WALLACE – Myrt and Nancy Jane Cloud (Osborn) were married in Pope County, AR on July 5, 1896. They had nine children. Eight they raised to be grown. Idell was youngest of these nine children.

Idelle Huggins Wallace is the only living child of Myrt and Nancy Jane Huggins. At this time, April 6, 2005, she is a resident of Miner Nursing Center, Sikeston, MO. She has six living children, 15 grandchildren, 26 great-grandchildren and five great-great-grandchildren.

Idelle Huggins and Lonnie Wallace married on Nov. 21, 1933 in Dover, Pope County, AR and lived there off and on until Feb. 22, 1946. They had lived in California and Arkansas until that time. They moved to Mississippi County, MO on February 22nd. Lonnie was farmer most of the rest of his life.

While Lonnie was in WWII, she took care of six of us children and did what she had to do to give us a good life and show us we were loved and cared for. We lived in Pope County, AR at that time, near her mother and father, Nancy and Myrt Huggins.

Idelle Huggins Wallace, last living child of Myrtle Hazard Huggins and Nancy Jane Cloud.

Idelle was the typical farmer's wife. She kept house, sewed, gardened and canned the vegetables and meat that they raised. She was an excellent seamstress. She made all our clothes until we were grown and married, and then some. She enjoyed crafts. She worked in the fields with Lonnie and hauled the grain raised to the elevator at harvest time. They enjoyed traveling and visiting family and friends, so did a lot of that in the off season for farming.

When Lonnie decided to retire about 1971, they purchased a home in Charleston, MO. He never really retired. He worked for an electric parts factory for a while and then went back to farming, which he continued until his death, June 10, 1978. Idelle was active in community works. She was active until 2001 when she had to have her left leg amputated below the knee due to an infection of the bone that would not heal. She was always active in her church, Wyatt Baptist Church, Wyatt, MO.

She loved having her family around her and especially those grandchildren and greats. They were great parents for their children and we grew up with discipline and lots of love, and we knew it. *Submitted by Loretta Wallace McGee.*

WALLACE - Levi W. Wallace was born between 1820-1828 in Marion County, AL. The names of his parents are unknown. It is known that he had a brother named Joseph Wallace, who was born in March of 1839 in Alabama. Levi is shown on the 1860 census of Wise County, TX living in the household of Nicholas B. Haney, working as a well driller.

Levi married Sena Anne Wells, daughter of Jesse and Martha Overlin Wells, on April 2, 1861 in Denton County, TX. Jesse

Sena Anne Wells Wallace and grandson Henry Luther Carr - 1901.

and Martha who were married in Orange County, IN on Sept. 27, 1832, had moved to Washington County, MO by 1850, and to Texas by 1860. Sena had two sisters, Sarah E. (b. 1846) and Elizabeth Jane (b. 1849). Her brother William J. Wells was born in Indiana in 1837.

Levi enlisted in the Union Army on Sept. 4, 1864 at Fort Smith, AR. He served in Company C of the 14th Kansas Cavalry. Levi was listed as "missing in action in the field as a scout near Fort Smith, AR" on Sept. 26, 1864. He had been captured by Confederate forces and later was released on parole at Red River Lodge, LA on Feb. 26, 1865. Levi rejoined his unit at Pine Bluff and was later honorably discharged at Fort Gibson, Indiana Territory on June 25, 1865.

Levi's physical description on his army payroll records was stated as 43 years old, 5 foot 6 inches, with dark complexion, dark eyes and black hair, occupation, farmer.

Levi and Sena, along with her parents, Jesse and Martha Wells, moved to Conway County, AR, in 1867. They settled near Hattieville, AR where Levi filed for a 160 acre homestead grant on Section 12, Township 8, Range 17 West. He received title to this land in 1877.

Levi and Sena and their first child, Letha Wallace, are listed on the 1870 census of Conway County, AR. Also listed as living in Levi's household was a Levi H. Wallace, age 20, born in Alabama. The relationship of Levi W. Wallace to Levi H. Wallace is unknown. Levi H. Wallace later married Sarah Reid, daughter of Henry and Ruth Prince Reid and moved to Oklahoma.

Joseph Wallace, Levi's brother, and a veteran of the Confederate States Army, joined Levi in Conway County after 1870. He had been living in Pontotoc County, MS with his first wife, Martha A. McCurley, and his son Robert Sylvester Wallace. Joseph married Nancy Warren in 1883 and had three more sons: John Franklin, James Marion and Virgil Wallace. Joseph was living in the household of Robert and Mintie Wells in 1920. His date of death is unknown.

Levi and Sena farmed their homestead at Hattieville. Their union produced the following children: Letha Frances Wallace (b. March 2, 1869, d. 1940) md. Newton Floyd Andrews on Feb. 27, 1884. Letha was buried on Levi's Wallace homestead in the Wallace Wells Cemetery. Alice Wallace (b. July 12, 1872, d. 1953 Oakhurst, OK) md. first, James Watkins and second, Chester Ward. Sena Idora Wallace (b. Oct. 15, 1875, d. 1947 in Wagoner, OK) md. first, Charles Andrews and second, W.F. Fritts. Mary Elizabeth "Molly" Wallace (b. March 2, 1881, d. 1964, Oklahoma City, OK) md. first, Thomas Carr and second, Walter Grimes. Louraney Arella Wallace "Lou" (b. June 26, 1885, d. Jan. 4, 1959 in Oklahoma City, OK) md. first, Chester Mathis and second, Ben Guyn.

Levi W. Wallace died June 18, 1887 of tuberculosis he contracted while in a prisoner of war camp. He was buried on his homestead in the Wallace Wells Cemetery. Sena Wells Wallace married again in 1888 to Thomas Dunham. She died in 1916 and was buried beside Levi Wallace in the Wallace Wells Cemetery located on their homestead land. *Submitted by Billie Campbell.*

WAMPLER - The Wampler family originated in Switzerland. The family spoke German and attended German Lutheran and Reformed Churches. Family naming patterns in some German areas resulted in all of the sons and daughters of a family having the same first name, but different second or middle names. Johann (or Hans) for the sons and Anna for the daughters were the primary first names used. The children were usually called by their second or middle name.

Heinrich Wampfler married Verna Herren. They had at least one son, Hans Wampfler, born Nov. 20, 1616, at Diemtigtal, Switzerland. Hans married Magdalene Knutt on Oct. 15, 1647 at Diemtigtal. Magdalene Knutt was born Jan. 9, 1620 at Diemtigen, Switzerland. They had at least one son, Christian Wampfler, born Dec. 3, 1654 in Diemtigtal. (Note: The surname was spelled Wampfler in early documents but later spelled Wampler.) Christian married and produced at least five children: Johann Christian Wampfler (b. 1685); Anna Magdalena Wampfler (b. 1692, d. 1725) md. Samuel Mettauer; Johannes Wampfler (b. 1696, d. 1776); Johann Peter Wampfler (b. 1701) and Johann Michael Wampfler (b. 1702, d. 1760). Christian Wampfler died Jan. 28, 1715 at Sparsbach, Alsace, Germany.

Johann (Hans) Peter Wampfler (b. 1701 in Sparsbach, Germany) was the son of Christian Wampfler. He married Anna Veronica Lung in 1719 at Zollingen, Germany. Veronica was born in Zollingen, the daughter of Jacob Lung and Elizabeth Wildermuth. Peter Wampfler immigrated to America with his family on the ship *Lydia*, landing at Philadelphia on Sept. 29, 1741. He settled his family on 200 acres of land he purchased in the Swiss and German community in Lancaster County, PA. Peter died in early 1749 in Lancaster County.

On April 24, 1749, Veronica made application to be administratrix of his estate. Her sons, Michael and Peter, signed her application bond. Peter and Veronica had at least nine children, all born in Germany: Anna Magdalene Wampler (b. 1720) md. Mathias Boger; Hans Peter Wampler Jr. (b. 1722, d. 1792); Hans Michael Wampler (b. 1724); Anna Veronica Wampler (b. 1726) md. John Jacob Brennelsen; Anna Barbara Wampler (b. 1729); Anna Elizabeth Wampler (b&d. 1732); Anna Catherine Wampler (b. 1734, d. 1735); Hans Georg Wampler (b. 1736, d. 1815) and Hans Adam Wampler.

Hans "John" Michael Wampler (b. Nov. 19, 1724, at Hinsingen, Germany) was the son of Johann (Hans) Peter and Anna Veronica Wampfler. He married Anna Elizabeth (last name unknown), in 1750, in Lancaster County, PA. Anna Elizabeth was born in 1727. John Michael became a naturalized citizen on Aug. 17, 1765. He moved his family to Fincastle County, VA where he appears on the 1771 tithables list. In 1774, a 270 acre tract of land was surveyed for him in Fincastle County. John Michael died after April 18, 1789, probably in Wythe County, VA. Anna Elizabeth died in 1807.

Children of John Michael Wampler and Anna Elizabeth (birth order and dates unknown) included: Elizabeth Wampler (b. Aug. 12, 1752) md. Ludwig Heinrich Abel; Lovice Wampler (b. 1755); George Wampler (b. 1756, d. 1835); Catherine W. Wampler married George Kinser and (Unknown) Hardin; Esther Wampler married Jacob Kinser; Christopher Wampler (b. 1763); Michael Wampler Jr. (b. 1764) and Peter Wampler (b. 1766).

WATKINS - Arlie Lee Watkins (b. April 2, 1916 in Conway County, AR) was the son of Samuel Garfield and Maga Anne Poe Watkins. Arlie grew up in Conway County, attending school at the Shot Gun Ridge School near Cleveland, AR. He joined the Civilian Conservation Corps in 1937 and worked for a while in Pierce, ID.

After his return home, he married Eva Chambers on Dec. 29, 1937. Arlie was a farmer.

Arlie L. Watkins, 1943.

He left his farm in 1942 when he volunteered to join the US Army. He was assigned to General Patton's Third Army, Company B of the 312th Combat Engineers, 87th Division. Arlie arrived in Germany just in time to fight in the Battle of the Bulge in the Ardennes. Arlie returned home in July 1945 on leave and was discharged in October 1945.

Arlie sold his farm at Cleveland after the war, and moved to Colorado and California to work cutting timber. Later, Arlie returned to Arkansas and worked as a grader operator for Conway County. He died April 12, 1991 and was buried in the Lost Corner Cemetery near Cleveland.

He and Eva had the following children: Narvin Ray McElroy (Eva's child by a first marriage), Virginia Lee Watkins, Buddy Watkins and Arlie Lynn Watkins.

Eva Frances Chambers, the daughter of Henry (Horace) and Martha Ellen Andrews Chambers, died May 12, 1996 and was buried in the Lost Corner Cemetery beside her husband. *Submitted by Arlie Lynn Watkins.*

WATKINS - Arlie Ray Watkins (b. March 21, 1947) was the son of Arlie Lee and Eva F. Chambers Watkins. Arlie Ray was known by family and friends as "Buddy." He attended schools in several different states and eventually graduated from Morrilton High School at Morrilton, AR.

Buddy married first, Sarah Juanita Jones on Aug.

11, 1967. Their union produced three children: Kyle Lynn Watkins (b. June 29, 1968), Kimberly Gail Watkins (b. March 18, 1973) and Kevin Ray Watkins (b. Sept. 7, 1970, d. Feb. 3, 1971). Buddy and his third wife, Deborah Parker Watkins, had one child, Jeremy Ray Watkins (b. July 18, 1980).

Buddy Watkins and family. Front: Jeremy Ray Watkins; back, l-r: Anita Boyette Watkins, Valarie Boyette, Arlie Ray "Buddy" Watkins and Kyle Lynn Watkins - 1988, Conway, AR.

Buddy worked for Amtram Corporation in Conway, AR. He died July 4, 1989 of colon cancer. He is buried near his parents and his small son Kevin in the Lost Corner Cemetery near Cleveland, AR. *Submitted by Kimberly Watkins.*

WATKINS - Roland Watkins was born in 1825 in South Carolina. His parents are unknown. Census records show that his father was born in Virginia and his mother was born in South Carolina.

Roland is shown living in Fayette County, AL on the 1860 census. He was residing on a farm he had purchased in 1858, which was located on the border of Tuscaloosa and Fayette counties in Alabama. Roland married Melinda Roberts, daughter of Josiah and Mary Linsey Roberts. Roland and several other families who lived in Fayette County, AL decided to move to Conway County, AR in 1867. The names of some of the families who moved during this time were Roland and Matilda Maddox Andrews, William and Louisa Simmons Andrews, Amos and Matilda Andrews Roberts, Daniel, Ezekiel and Sarah Andrews, and Nancy Andrews Howell, Thomas and Charles and Phoebe Andrews Maddox, Sarah Maddox, George and William Martin Hopson, David and Margaret Cranford, William and Jane Poe, Andrew Morris and his son, W.D. Morris. Several of these families settled in Conway County, others settled in Logan and Washington counties.

Roland purchased 80 acres of land located on Lick Mountain. Later he also received title to an 80 acre homestead grant. Roland and Melinda Roberts Watkins had the following children: Sarah Watkins (b. 1849, Alabama) md. a Henderson; John Roland Watkins (b. 1851, Alabama) md. Hannah McGinty, died after 1880; Iba Jane Watkins (b. 1853, Alabama) md. William Martin Hopson, buried Crossroads Cemetery in Pope County, AR; Evaline Watkins (b. 1854 in Alabama); William Watkins (b. 1855 in Alabama) md. Matilda Adeline Andrews, died after 1897, buried in Lost Corner Cemetery near Cleveland, AR; Daniel Andrew Watkins (b. 1857 in Alabama) md. Adeline Scroggins and Ida Martin, died 1903-04, buried Lost Corner Cemetery near Cleveland, AR;

Mary Watkins (b. 1861, Alabama, died between 1895-1900) md. Robert McNew; Nancy Watkins (b. 1863 in Fayette County, AL); Ezechial Watkins (b. 1864 in Fayette County, AL) md. Mandy Keith, Margaret Montgomery and Martha J. Phillips in Franklin County, AR in 1892; Howell Watkins (b. 1864 in Fayette County, AL); James B. Watkins (b. 1865 in Fayette County, AL) md. Alice Wallace and Cora B. (maiden name unknown) in Sebastian County, AR; Rhoda Watkins (b. 1868 in Conway County, AR).

Roland and Melinda Roberts Watkins sold their farm on Lick Mountain in 1899 and moved from

Conway County. Their place of death and burial i unknown. *Submitted by Kyle Watkins.*

WATKINS - Samuel Garfield Watkins (b. April 2 1883 in Conway County, AR) was the son of William and Matilda Adeline Andrews Watkins. He lived or his grandfather Roland's farm located at Lick Mountain, AR. The death of both his parents at the age of 1[?] years forced Samuel to leave Lick Mountain and go to live with an uncle, Jim Andrews, of Jerusalem, AR.

Samuel G. Watkins and Maga Anne Poe Watkins.

Samuel married Maga Anne Poe, the daughter of George Marion and Melissa Miranda Williams Poe, on Nov. 3, 1901. Samuel was a farmer. He and Maga had the following children: Ester Watkins (b. June 12, 1902) md. Harrison Scroggins, died Nov. 23, 1989; Orville Watkins (b. 1903, d. 1906 of diphtheria); Amy Alice Watkins (b. June 1907) md. Jim Bryant, died 1993 in Indiana; Ira Luther Watkins (b. June 1907) md. Bessie Bryant, died 1976 in Missouri; Nona Mae Watkins (b. Dec. 3, 1909) md. Frank Farrish, died in 1993; Dovie Ruth Watkins (b. Oct. 24, 1914) md. Lonzo Henderson, died in 1985; Arlie Lee Watkins (b. April 2, 1916) md. Eva Chambers, died April 12, 1991; Ola Mae Watkins (b. July 10, 1920) md. Paul Tilley, died Sept. 16, 1969; Nola Mae Watkins (b. July 10, 1920, d. July 10, 1920; Clara Marie Watkins (b. Oct. 17, 1922) md. William L. Maxwell, died Dec. 29, 2001.

Samuel died on Oct. 9, 1976 and Maga Anne Poe Watkins died March 19, 1958. They are buried in the Lost Corner Cemetery near Cleveland, AR. *Submitted by David Lee Tilley.*

WATKINS - William Watkins (b. 1855 in Fayette County, AL) was the son of Roland and Melinda Roberts Watkins. He traveled to Conway County, AR in 1867 with his parents and grew up on his father's farm located on Lick Mountain.

William married Matilda Adeline Andrews, daughter of William and Louisa Simmons Andrews, in 1877. "Bill" and "Till" as they were called by the family, had the following children: John Roland Watkins (b. 1878, died in a coal mine accident in

Arlie and Eva Chambers Watkins - 1942. Grandson of William and Matilda Andrews Watkins.

Coffeyville, KS while still a young man); Thomas Watkins (b. 1881) md. Della Watkins, died in 1954, buried at Lost Corner Cemetery; Samuel G. Watkins (b. April 2, 1883) md. Maga Anne Poe, daughter of George Marion Poe and Melissa Miranda Williams Poe, died 1976, buried at Lost Corner Cemetery; James William Watkins (b. 1887) md. Rozilah D. Fox, died 1950 in Lubbock, TX; Galloway Watkins (b. 1888) md. Bessie Lily, died 1968 in Fouke, AR; Harrison Watkins (b. 1889) md. Ester Williams, Mae Wilson and Theresa Kirtley, died in Missouri; Nora Watkins (b. 1895-96) married unknown, buried in the Buttermilk Cemetery in Pope County, AR.

William Watkins died of typhoid fever about 1897 and was buried in the Lost Corner Cemetery near Cleveland, AR. Matilda Andrews Watkins died in 1899 of a stroke and was buried in the Bolton Wells Cemetery near Jerusalem, AR. *Submitted by Jeremy Ray Watkins.*

WATSON – Ples Lee, son of Andrew Watson and Samatha K. Roberts Watson, was born May 1891 Conway County, AR and died June 30, 1972, Oklahoma City, OK "hospital, broken hip, blood clot." Ples Lee married on Sept. 3, 1910, Conway County, MO to Lalie Abigial Rankin, daughter of Henry Clay and Emma B. Mulkey Rankin, died September 1981, Shawnee, Pottawotomie, OK. Nursing Home. Ples Lee and Lalie Abigail are buried at Wetumka, Hughes County, OK.

Family of Ples Lee and Lalie Abigail Rankin Watson. Front, l-r: Ova, Ples, Floymae, Lalie and Zelma Rae; back: Billy, Grover, Mavis, R.D. and Lois Fay.

Ples Lee and Lalie Abigail made their home in Robertstown, Conway County, AR. They were parents of eight children, all living to be grown: Floy Mae, Grover Lee, Mavis Jewel, R.D., Ova Etheline, Zelma Rea, Lois Fay "Sonny" (born in Conway County, AR), Billy Wayne (born Wetumka, Hughes County, OK).

Floy Mae (b. June 30, 1912, Conway County, AR, d. Nov. 8, 1994, Eufaula, McIntosh County, OK) md. Clarence Edgar Robinson (b. Aug. 14, 1912, Soper, Choctaw County, OK, d. Sept. 11, 1992, McAlester, Pittsburg County, OK) on Dec. 23, 1931, Wetumka, Hughes County, OK. Both are buried Oak Hill Cemetery, McAlester, Pittsburg County, OK. Parents of Wanda Mae Robinson.

Grover Lee (b. Dec. 6, 1913, Conway County, AR, d. Feb. 24, 1999, Wetumka, Hughes County, OK) md. Ida Helen Phipps (b. June 12, 1914, Whiterock, TX, d. Aug. 1, 2003, Holdenville, Hughes County, OK) on Nov. 2, 1935, Wetumka, Hughes County, OK. Both buried Wetumka, Hughes County, OK. No children of this union.

Mavis Jewel (b. Dec. 9, 1916, Conway County, AR, d. Sept. 24, 2002, Wetumka, Hughes County, OK) md. Louis M. Sanders (b. April 23, 1915, Wetumka, Hughes County, OK, d. Feb. 17, 1992 Wetumka, Hughes County, OK) on July 24, 1940, Wetumka, Hughes County, OK. Louis M. served in US Army February 1943 to December 1945, WWII. Both buried at Wetumka, Hughes County, OK. Parents of Jewel Dean and Norma Jean Sanders.

R.D. (b. Oct. 13, 1919, Conway County, AR, living at this time) md. Alma L. Mauldin (b. Oct. 29, 1923, Cement, Caddo County, OK, living at this time) on June 9, 1940, Harlingen, Cameron County, TX. R.D. served in US Army, WWII. Parents of Gloria Jean, Olivia Lee, Linda Lorene and Elaine Watson.

Ova Etheline (b. Dec. 13, 1923, Conway County, AR, living at this time) md. Pete Amerson in about 1942. He was born Wetumka, Hughes County, OK, deceased, Wetumka, Hughes County, OK. Parents of Carol Faye Amerson.

Zelma Rea (b. April 13, 1925, Conway County, AR, living at this time) md. William H. Jackson (b. Aug. 1, 1921, Salt Lake City, UT, d. April 12, 1999, Eufaula, McIntosh County OK) on Oct. 16, 1943, Norman, Cleveland County, OK. Buried McAlester, Pittsburg County, OK, Memory Gardens Cemetery. William "Bill" served in US Navy, WWII in the Pacific. Parents of Shelia Rea Jackson.

Lois Fay "Sonny" (b. July 30, 1928, Conway County, AR, d. March 1977, VA Hospital, Oklahoma City, Oklahoma County, OK, buried Wetumka, Hughes County, OK). Served in US Army 1948-50. Married Nov. 18, 1948, Muskogee, Muskogee County, OK to Betty Jean Butler (b. Aug. 27, 1930, Wetumka, Hughes County, OK, living at this time). Parents of Dwight Anthony and Debra Lynn Watson.

Billy Wayne Watson (b. Jan. 21, 1932, Wetumka, Hughes County, OK) served in US Army. He married June 9, 1951, Artesia, NM, to Shirley Rae Dilbeck (b. May 3, 1934, Gladewater, Upshur County, TX), both living at this time. Parents of Theresa Jean Watson.

Ples and Lalie, hard working farmers, went through some hard times. Depending on their crops, raising a garden, canning food for winter, hay for horses and milk cows. Then came the tornado in 1926. They were eating supper at that time and the schoolteacher was staying with them. They got into the cellar just in time, when the cellar door blew off. In a matter of minutes, the house and everything was gone. Neighbors, family and friends came, bringing food, clothing and helped clean up and rebuild. Then came the drought and depression. This is when they decided to move to Wetumka, Hughes County, OK to begin a new life. Ples's sister's family had already moved there. *Submitted by Wanda M. Dilbeck.*

WEAR – Dr. Hamilton Bradford Wear arrived in Arkansas in 1858 - he and his family are shown on the 1860 Conway County census. He married in 1857 to Nancy Ann Townsend, daughter of Robert B. and Rispha (Hiett) Townsend, natives of South Carolina. Wear children were Caswell Bolen md. Perneacy Ellen Adams, Mary Ann Ellen md. Joseph Solomon Williams, James Wiley died young, Francis Elizabeth md. Joseph L. Harris, Martha Annis Tennessee md. Joseph Alphonzo Lovelace, Robert King md. Bell Henderson, Sarah Matilda md. William Virgil Timmons, William Hamilton Taylor md. Kate McArthur, and Oscar Allen md. Josie Myrtle Nix.

Hamilton Bradford studied medicine in Cherokee County, AL, then in 1856 to the Medical College at Nashville, TN and after that at Atlanta, GA, where he graduated. He first practiced medicine in Cherokee County, AL, then emigrated to Arkansas. In 1861 he enlisted as surgeon captain in the Confederate Army, Company I, Arkansas Infantry.

Years later, Dr. Wear moved across the Arkansas River to Perry County, where, with George Lovelace and others, he helped establish the town of Houston and became the first Postmaster (1881).

Hamilton B. Wear (b. April 29, 1829 Blount County, TN) was the son of William Weir/Wear and Mary Ann Tipton. His grandparents were James Weir, born Virginia, and Margaret Sharp, born Virginia.

James was a Revolutionary War veteran and his name appears on a monument in Maryville, Blount County, TN. Great-grandfather was Hugh Weir and his wife's name is unknown.

Most of the children of Dr. Wear lived their entire lives either in Conway or surrounding counties.

Caswell Bolen died Seminole, OK, and his children were William Ernest, Claude Otis, Hamilton Stanley, Martha Ann, James Garrett.

Mary Ann Ellen Williams died Jamestown, CA, and her children were John H., Nancy Ann, Hardy L., Dewitt B., Ethel, Jodia N., Willie O., Virginia A.

Francis Elizabeth Harris died in Arkansas approximately one year after her marriage, presumably in child birth.

Martha Annis T. Lovelace died in Perry County, and her children were Verta, Odar M., Joseph D., Ruby N., Sybil N., Robert Z., Pink E., Nellie L., Mark H., and Fred J.

Robert King is buried Conway County; he and Bell had only one child, Laura. Robert K. married second to Violet Jones and their children were Roberta, Gordon K. and Reva D.

Sarah Matilda Timmons died Conway County and her children were Mattie Ruth, Deward D., Mary L., Oscar V. and Grace T.

William Hamilton died Conway County, and his children were Jewell, Ruby K., William D.

Oscar Allen died Conway County, and his children were Ora Hazel, J. Darrell, Hugh B., Woodrow W., D. Marie, O. Leon, E. Louise, Ina D. and Charles B.

J. Darrell was the father of the compiler of this family history – he died 1983, as did my mother, Hazel F. Smith. I had only one sibling, my sister Marilyn Y., and she died 2002.

I am very proud of my ancestry and hope to continue locating more of our history. *Compiled by JoAnn Wear Jenkins. email jj1j2jenkins@cox.net*

WEATHERFORD - The Weatherford family was of English descent. The name was originally spelled Whitheford. After immigrating to America, the Whitheford/Weatherford line mixed with Indian blood, some say Cherokee and others say Creek.

Thomas Whitheford (b. 1585 in Warwickshire, England) md. Margaret Waring in 1609 in Tamsworth, England. They had at least five children: William, Elizabeth, John, Maria and Thomas.

John Whitheford (b. 1615 in Warwickshire, was the son of Thomas and Margaret. John immigrated to America prior to 1642 and settled in Virginia. John married, probably in Virginia, and produced at least one son. John died April 1706 in James City County, VA.

William Whitheford (b. 1645 in York County, VA) was the son of John Whitheford. William married

None of the children in front are known to me. Second row, l-r: _, Mary Ann Ellen (Wear) Williams, _, _, Joseph Alphonzo Lovelace, Martha Annis Tennessee (Wear) Lovelace, Josie Myrtle (Nix) Wear, Oscar Allen Wear, Robert King Wear, _, Kate (McArthur) Wear, William Hamilton Wear. Standing l-r: _, Martha E. Nix, Ora Lee Nix, _, _, _, _, Caswell Bolen Wear, _, _, _, _. Note: If anyone can identify the unnamed people I would appreciate hearing.

and produced at least seven children: Thomas, William, Richard (William "Red Eagle" Weatherford, a Creek Chief descended from this line), John, James, Charles and Ann. The spelling of the name Whitheford changed during this time and William's children spelled their name Weatherford.

William Weatherford (b. 1678 in Virginia) was the son of William Whitheford. He married Susanna Waller in 1699 in Virginia. Susanna (b. 1680 in New Kent County, VA) was the daughter of Thomas Waller and Anne Keate. William Weatherford and his brother Richard moved their families to Lunenburg County, VA in the 1740s. William and Susanna had at least five children: John, William Jr., Lucy, Richard and Major Weatherford. William died 1756 in Lunenburg County. Susanna died there in 1758.

William Weatherford Jr. (b. 1703 in New Kent County, VA) was the son of William and Susanna. William married Susannah (probably Wilkerson) and they had at least one child. William died 1760 in Lunenburg County, VA.

Wilkerson Weatherford (b. 1726 in Virginia) was the son of William Jr. and Susanna. Wilkerson migrated to North Carolina. He married Susanna (last name unknown). Wilkerson and Susanna had at least six children: Hilkiah, Agnes, Ursula, William, Mary and John S. Weatherford.

William Weatherford (b. 1759 in Mechlenburg County, NC) was the son of Wilkerson and Susanna. William married Margaret Ann Polk in Mechlenburg County. Margaret Polk (b. 1760) was the daughter of William Polk Jr. and Sarah Weatherford. Some say that Margaret was a relative of President James K. Polk. Prior to 1815, William and Margaret moved their family to Tennessee. They were pioneer settlers of Pinhook, now called Lutts, in Wayne County, TN. Weatherford Creek in Wayne County was named for William. At one time there was a Weatherford Post Office located at the head of Weatherford Creek. William was a farmer.

William and Margaret both died between 1840-50, in Wayne County. Their children were Josh Weatherford, William Weatherford, Hill K. Weatherford, Vicey Weatherford md. Stephen Daniel, Joel Wilson Weatherford md. Nancy Beckham, Ursala Weatherford, md. Green D. Robbins, then Thomas McDonel, Margaret Weatherford md. _ Davis, John Weatherford, Sarah Weatherford md. William Berry (Children: Mary Margaret "Peggy," William, Rebecca, John, George, Sarah Ann, James and Nancy Berry), Joseph Weatherford and Rebecca Weatherford md. Green Berry Beckham Jr.

WEBER – Elizabeth, daughter of Peter and Anna Mary Weber, married Ben Berkemeyer of Atkins. They moved to San Luis Obisco, CA and had five children: Joseph, Marie, Charlie, Francis and Ben Jr. They owned the Union and Pacific Markets. Ben, a butcher, and his brother Henry was a baker. Henry was also born and raised in Atkins, AR.

Louisia "Lucy," daughter of Peter and Anna Mary Weber, also was born in Germany and came to America with her parents to Pittsburgh, PA in 1881. Louisia married Nichalous Miller, Matthias's brother, in St. Mary's Church in St. Vincent, AR.

The couple moved back to Pittsburgh, PA where they raised eight children: Matthias, Nichalous Jr., Charles, William, Joseph, Sue and Margaret. The family, all double cousins of Matthias and Margaret's children, worked in coal mines, owned Miller Brothers Feed and Seed Store in Hays, PA and were musical, having their own band called the Barn Yard Frolics Band. It was much in demand. They also have relatives in Conway County today. *Submitted by R.M. Miller.*

WEBER - In 1887 Peter and Anna Mary Weber moved to St. Vincent, Conway County, AR and bought a farm with an old log house, small barn and good well in the Lone Grove Community. They moved to

---

Arkansas after a coal mine fire which damaged Mr. Weber's lungs and doctors ordered him to move to a warmer climate from Pittsburgh, PA. They had three daughters: Elizabeth, Louisia and Margaret.

Elizabeth Weber Berkemeyer, Margaret Weber Miller and Lucy Weber Miller.

Elizabeth, daughter of Peter and Anna Mary Weber, married Ben Berkemeyer of Atkins. They moved to San Luis Obisco, CA and had five children: Joseph, Marie, Charlie, Francis and Ben Jr. They owned the Union and Pacific Markets. Ben was a butcher and his brother Henry was a baker. Henry was also born and raised in Atkins, AR.

Louisia "Lucy," daughter of Peter and Anna Mary Weber, was born in Germany and came to America with her parents to Pittsburgh, PA in 1881. Louisia married Nichalous Miller, Matthias's brother, in St. Mary's Church in St. Vincent, AR. The couple moved back to Pittsburgh, PA, where they raised eight children: Matthias, Nichalous Jr., Charles, William, Joseph, Sue and Margaret. The family, all double cousins of Matthias and Margaret's children, worked in coal mines, owned Miller Brothers Feed and Seed Store in Hays, PA and were musical, having their own band called the Barn Yard Frolics Band. It was much in demand. They also have relatives in Conway County today.

Margaret married Carl Kisel of Pittsburgh and they had two sons, Carl Jr. and Peter. After the death of Carl and Carl Jr., Margaret moved to Arkansas with her son Peter. In 1888 she married Matthias Miller, the brother of her sister Louisia's husband, Nichalous. The couple, along with Peter, returned to Latrobe, PA. They had three children: Michael, Nichalous and Anna. With her father's failing health, they returned to Arkansas to help care for him. Mr. Weber died in 1899. After his death Mrs. Weber became the parish housekeeper at St. Mary's Church. She died in 1907 and is buried in the family plot at St. Vincent beside her husband. The couple had six more children, all born at St. Vincent: Catherine, Josephine, Martin, Clemons Joseph, Simon and Elizabeth.

Peter Kisel md. Caroline Gottsponer of St. Vincent and they had nine children: Joseph Frank, Margaret (she was a midwife who delivered many of the area babies), Rose Ann, Carl, Aloys, Marie, Carolina, Chris and Joseph. Joseph Frank died at 7 years. Margaret md. Joseph Miller of St. Vincent, they had three children. Rose Ann md. Matt Davis. After Matt's death, Rose md. Ivo Cochron of Lonsdale, AR, they had three children. Carl md. Eva Wagner, they had six children. Aloys md. Mary Ann Zokysek, they had three children. Eva and Mary Ann were both from Lakin, KS. Carolina md. Cicel Hughs of Billings, MT, they had five children. Marie md. Joseph Fakey of Pueblo, CO, they had one child. Chris md. Virginia Carthell of Benton, AR, they had two children. Joseph md. Gertrude Maier of Germany and lives in Colorado Springs, CO, they have three children. All Kisel children were born at St. Vincent. They moved to Lakin, KS in 1937, but still have many relatives in Conway County. Only Marie and Joseph and survive. *Submitted by Rose Miller.*

WELCH - Essie (b. Dec. 20, 1905 in Hattieville), daughter of Robert and Rosie Fellers, attended school

---

in Macedonia, Conway County, AR. She married Thomas William McKinley Welch on May 20, 1923.

Essie Frances Fellers Welch 100th birthday, with nine of her 11 children: Standing, l-r: Edgar Welch, Lottie Sue Denton, Raymond Welch, Don Welch, Betty Liemke, Frances Rhea Welch, Jim Welch. Sitting: Hattie Faye Faught, Essie Fellers Welch, Dwayne Welch. Bill Welch (not in picture), Jay Welch (deceased).

Essie and Thomas are the parents of 11 children: Hattie Faye Welch, Hershel Dwayne Welch, Edgar Noel Welch, Lottie Sue Welch Denton, Raymond Lee Welch, Jerry Don Welch, Betty Rose Welch Liemke, Frances Rhea Welch, Jimmie Carol Welch, Billy Ray Welch and Jay Thomas Welch.

Her children provided her with 28 grandchildren, 37 great-grandchildren and 20 great-great-grandchildren.

Essie has lived in this area most of her life, spending the last few years enjoying her favorite past time, fishing. *Submitted by Brenda Liemke.*

WELCHER-WILCHER-WILSHER - The first of the family to settle in Conway County was Samuel Houston Wilsher, who came to St. Vincent in the mid-1890s and married Mrs. Virginia Frances Clifton Young on Feb. 15, 1896 (Book I, page 477). Both had been previously married. Virginia, known as Jennie, was born in 1862 and died March 7, 1934, Fort Worth, TX. She first married James Young in 1878 in Conway County with issue: Sarah Frances (md. William Monroe Guffey), James "Bud," Lee Vick, John and Jesse. After Young's death, Jennie married briefly to Frank Tinney. After the death of Samuel Wilsher, she married George Dicus on Oct. 5, 1899 in Conway County by whom she had Rosie Dicus, who married Charles Harvell, then Heron Bryant.

By his first wife, Josephine Dillard, Samuel Wilsher had issue born in Marion County, AR: Lawrence (b. 1874), Alonzo (b. 1881, died Sacramento, CA); George (b. 1883, d. 1949 North Little Rock); Josephine (b. 1887, d. 1957, Arkansas) md. Tom Davis; Arizona (b. 1890, d. 1963 Fayetteville, AR) md. Thomas Redding James.

Samuel Wilsher and Jennie Clifton had two children: Essie Frances Welcher (b. Dec. 6, 1896) and Samuel Houston Welcher Jr., who later changed his name to Samuel Earl Welcher (b. March 20, 1898). Family tradition states that Samuel Sr. was on the way to the mill with corn to be ground, when someone shot and killed him and took his horse. He is buried near Morrilton. Essie married first to John Wesley Mounce (b. 1865, d. 1942) with issue: Carl Earl Houston Mounce (b. 1917, d. 1985) who married Alice Ophelia Forgy and had two sons, John Wesley and Gaston Earl. Essie was the widow of Frank Snideman at her death on Feb. 27, 1979, Morrilton.

Samuel Earl Welcher married Gladys Leona Townsend (b. 1906, d. 1982) with issue: Ida Virginia (md. Douglas Sloan), Mildred Marie (md. Raymond Stateham), Geraldine Lula (md. Ronald Hightower), Samuel Earl, Bobby Joe, Betty Jean (Hansel Williamson) and Albert Lee. Samuel died April 9, 1969 followed by Gladys in 1982, both at Fort Worth, TX.

The Wilsher family removed from Cannon County, TN to Marion County, AR, ca. 1868-69. Ancient family records provided by the Welcher family istorian, David Travillion Bunton, Russellville, AR, eveal the ancestor Joseph Wilcher marrying Hannah Preston, daughter of William Preston, in Lincoln County, KY, with issue William H. Wilcher (b. 1817) nd Charles Madison Wilcher (b. 1818). After Joseph's eath in Lincoln County, TN, Hannah removed to Cannon County, where she married Vach Crabtree.

By first wife Nancy Close, William H. had issue: Thomas (b. 1841) and James (b. 1843). William hen married Emeline "Emily" Gilley (b. 1826 Warren County, TN), daughter of Edward Gilley and Mary Collins of Lee County, VA. Issue of William and Emily: John (b. Oct. 13, 1847, Cannon County, TN, d. Nov. 20, 1917, Freck, AR) md. Elizabeth Canzada Carter, then Martha Jane Kyles; William (b. 1851) md. Hannah Hudspeth; Martha (b. 1853) md. Taylor Bogle; Samuel Houston (b. 1856) md. Josephine Dillard, then Jennie Clifton; George (b. 1859). John and Elizabeth's daughter Canzada Wilsher (b. 1879, d. 1922) md. John Lonzo Bunton. *They are the grandparents of the submitter, Clyde J. Bunton.*

WEST - Owen West was born in 1819 in North Carolina. His family had moved to Gibson County, TN by 1840. On Oct. 12, 1841 he married Jane McClure (McClur) in Gibson County, TN. Owen and Jane had four children in Gibson County, TN before moving to Petit Jean Mountain in 1854 - James McDaniel, John, Etna and Samuel. Owen purchased a cabin and some land from John Walker. The cabin still stands west of the Petit Jean State Park. Owen and Jane had four more children after moving to Arkansas: William Wiley, Elijah and Elisha (twins), and Ephraim Miles.

Seven sons of Owen and Jane West. Top l-r: Ephriam, Elisha, Elijah, William; bottom: Samuel, John and James McDaniel.

The large family needing more room, moved just south of the cabin close to the Conway-Perry County line. Owen was a logger and saw miller. They owned much of the land on top of Petit Jean and Rose Creek. Most of their children stayed in the area and built homes and businesses. Being unable to pay the taxes on all of the property on Petit Jean Mountain, the state took it. It is now the State Park.

In 1880 Census the family still were in Conway County. Owen was listed as age 60 and Jane, 57.

The picture above are the seven sons of Owen and Jane. They lost the only daughter they had between 1860-1870. All of Owen and Jane's children and grandchildren were buried along with them in the Petit Jean Cemetery, Conway County, AR.

Owen West (b. 1819, North Carolina, d. 1893 Conway County, AR) md. on Oct. 12, 1841 to Jane McClure/McClur (b. 1821, Kentucky, d. 1899 Conway County, AR). Children:

1) James McDaniel "Mack" (b. December 1843, Gibson County, TN, d. 1900-1910) md. first Tabatha "Tilly" Morris and second, Mary Matthews.

2) John H. "Jack" (b. Dec. 4, 1845 Gibson County, TN, d. March 18, 1899, Yell County, AR) md. Dec. 6, 1866, Yell County, AR to Laura Ellison.

3) Etna (b. 1848, Gibson County, TN, d. 1860-70, Arkansas).

4) Samuel G. "Sam" (b. March 1852, Gibson County, TN, d. July 18, 1943, buried Petit Jean Mountain Cemetery, Conway County, AR) md. Harriet Morris.

5) William Wiley "Wile" (b. Jan. 4, 1854, Arkansas, d. July 31, 1953, buried Petit Jean Mountain Cemetery, Conway County, AR) md. Feb. 22, 1872, Yell County, AR to Rhoda A. Carlock.

6) Elijah "Lige" (b. July 5, 1858, Arkansas, d. July 2, 1931, buried Petit Jean Mountain Cemetery, Conway County, AR) md. first, Arkie Laws on Feb. 8, 1877; second, Laura Brown on Oct. 28, 1880 and third, Laura Alice Rankin Huffstuttler on Oct. 29, 1919.

7) Elisha, "Lish" (b. July 5, 1858, Arkansas, d. Aug. 14, 1940, buried Petit Jean Mountain Cemetery, Conway County, AR) md. Eugena Laws.

8) Ephraim Miles "Eph" (b. Aug. 28, 1860, Arkansas, d. Oct. 8, 1949, buried Petit Jean Mountain Cemetery, Conway County, AR) md. Tempia Ann Morgan on April 9, 1879 Conway County, AR.

Elisha "Lish" West (b. July 5, 1858, Arkansas, d. Aug. 14, 1940, buried Petit Jean Mountain Cemetery, Conway County, AR) was a Baptist minister. Eugena Laws (b. March 1858, d. Feb. 20, 1930, buried Petit Jean Mountain Cemetery). Parents, Stephen and Nancy Laws.

Children:
1) Dan (b. 1878).
2) Son (b. May 1880).
3) Daisy md. Jim McCabe. Children: Mary Jemina, Lester and Vester.
4) Isofene md. Jape McCabe. Children: Dan, Archie, Matthew "Mack."
5) Ollin L. (b. May 8, 1885, d. May 14, 1963, buried Old Liberty Cemetery, Perry County, AR) md. first, Cassie Isom on Dec. 14, 1901, Perry County, AR; second, Nola Ashcraft on July 29, 1903, Perry County, AR; third, Maizie Thomas (b. July 19, 1880, d. March 7, 1969, Perry County, AR).
6) Alvin (b. Aug. 8, 1886, d. Aug. 22, 1953, age 67), buried Aunt Dilly Cemetery, Perry County, AR. He married first, Jessie Kirtley on June 11, 1909, Perry County, AR and second, Girthel Story on Aug. 12, 1927, Perry County, AR.
7) Elsie (b. Aug. 7, 1890, d. May 7, 1967) md. Thomas S. "Sid" Robertson (b. March 27, 1890, d. April 12, 1959), both are buried at Aunt Dilly Cemetery, Perry County, AR. Child: Verdie.
8) Ervin (b. April 1894, d. Nov. 14, 1985) md. Florida Brixey on Jan. 17, 1916 Perry County, AR. Children: Rayburn (b. November 1916); Vallen (b. May 1918); Garland (b. April 1921); Iletha (b. June 1923); Gladys (b. October 1926); Melma (b. July 1929); Frank (b. May 1932); Daniel (b. November 1936).
9) Nance (b. 1896).
10) Nova Lee (b. April 2, 1898, d. Dec. 8, 1977, buried McGhee Cemetery, Perry County, AR) md. first, Charlie Pearson and second, Rube McDaniel.
(11) Emma Jean (b. Aug. 1, 1900, d. Oct. 28, 1973, buried McGhee Cemetery, Perry County, AR) md. Audrey Barnes on Dec. 23, 1917, Perry County, AR.

Owen and Jane's lives centered around church and church activities. Their children, grandchildren and great-grandchildren were musically inclined and they could all sing beautifully.

James McDaniel, the oldest of Owen and Jane's children, volunteered for the Civil War. He sent word to the Northern Armed Forces that he would like to join them and that he would be hiding in a bear cave on Petit Jean Mountain. His wife Tabatha would take him something to eat and drink in the night, and let it down into the cave with a rope. Fearing the Southern Army, she would take different routes each night. When the Northern Army reached Dardenelle they sent a messenger for him. He lived to tell many hair raising tales of his time in the services. Vida Mae West McGhee and Oma West Turner were his grandchildren.

Elisha (one of the twins) was a Missionary Baptist preacher and preached all over the country in different churches. Elisha's son Olin also was a Missionary Baptist preacher and was known to have preached from Plumerville to Centerville, riding an old mule

and sometimes swimming the Arkansas River in order to get to his appointment at some church. He helped organize many Missionary Baptist Churches. It was known that he baptized as many as 25 at one given Revival meeting. He also preached in different states and organized churches there. Olin's son, Olen, also was a Missionary Baptist preacher and preached in several states and pastored churches in Louisiana, and here in Arkansas. Olen's daughter, Sheila West Edwards, got this history together. After all these many years, Sheila and her family still center their lives around the Missionary Baptist Church.

Olen and Mary Magdaline "Maggie" Minnie married on Feb. 29, 1940 and had nine children: Walter Louie (b. June 29, 1941); Stanley Phillip (b. Aug. 16 1942); Portia West Drye Robinson (b. Sept. 11 1944); Murphy Don "Butch" West (b. Jan. 22, 1948); Vickie West Anderson (b. April 27, 1950); Sheila West Edwards (b. July 22, 1951); Steve Eugene West (b. Oct. 11, 1954); Eulita West Fitch (b. Sept. 9, 1958); Jeffery Wayne West (b. April 30, 1960).

Sheila married Robert Allen Edwards on Dec. 27, 1968. They had two daughters, Rhonda Annette (b. Oct. 11 1969) and Robin Arlene (b. Nov. 28, 1971). Robin married James Michael Bird on July 28, 1989. They have a son Terrell Allen Bird (b. Aug. 7, 1995). Rhonda married Thomas Scott Polk on Aug. 16, 1991. They have one daughter Shawnee Montana Hope and one son Brant Cooper Polk. Olen West (b. Dec. 29, 1923, d. Jan. 23, 1996). Mary Magdaline Minnie West (b. Jan. 31, 1924, d. July 29, 1997).

One hundred fifty years have passed since the young couple, Owen and Jane, settled on Petit Jean Mountain. Their lives have left its mark on this county and this country. *Submitted by Shelia Edwards.*

WHITE - George Cleveland White was born Oct. 16, 1886 in Haysville, Clay County, NC to James Ransom White and Nancy Melissa Norwood. Oral family history is that the family moved to Conway County, AR area in 1890. As an adult, George moved to Knoxville, Johnson County, AR in 1910 when he married Bessie Mae Anderson, daughter of Andrew Anderson and Bettie Bowman. Born to their union: Opal Lee, Velma Mae, Cleve Edward (nicknamed Bob), Leona Belle, Agnes Louise, James Murray and Georgia Ruth.

George Cleveland White with wife, Bessie Anderson White and daughter, Opal, about 1912 – Arkansas.

George White was a barber in Clarksville for many years. My dad was a barber in Clarksville when I was small. It may have been the only shop in town, I don't remember another one. During the war, we moved to a farm at Knoxville. Dad and Mom planted cotton, peanuts, and other crops. My brother Bob was in the service, and my dad felt that farming would be one way to show our patriotism. We also had a great garden, raised and milked cows and sold the milk to a dairy. My parents raised hogs to kill for food and stored the meat in a smoke house. I went to school in Knoxville through 8th grade, then rode the bus to Lamar to attend high school. When I was in the 10th grade, we moved back to Clarksville, where Dad, Mom and I lived until their death.

Opal Lee (b. April 1, 1911) md. Zearl Henderson in June 1928. They lived in Clarksville, then moved to Alvarado, TX. Opal passed away Dec. 23, 1990 and Zearl died June 24, 1994. To their union was born Aliene (md. Pete Burns on June 4, 1954); Billy (md. Belia Sarmeinto Sept. 12, 1952); Jimmy Wayne (md. Loretta) died in 1986; Carmalita (md. Bill Carter Feb. 8, 1963); Alice Fay; and Charlene who is deceased.

Cleve Edward "Bob" (b. Aug. 9, 1915) md. Irene

Stewart in 1944 and died Jan. 17, 1972. To their union was born Dorinda Irene. They lived in Fayetteville, AR.

Agnas Louise (b. July 1921, died in infancy on unknown date).

James Murray (b. April 19, 1927, died at about age 3 on unknown date).

Velma Mae (md. Baxter Lee Bridges March 26, 1934). Mr. Bridges passed away Feb. 3, 2000. To their union was born Barbara Ellen, Patsy Jane, Tommie Lee, Virginia Lee (md. David DuPont), and Glenda Fay (md. Larry Spangler). She lives in Sikeston, MO with her daughter, Pat.

Leona Belle (md. Louis Fowler on Dec. 31, 1938). Louis died Nov. 8, 1997 in Hartman, AR. To their union was born Amos Darrell (md. Betty Ann Turner), Joe Don (md. Frankie Jo Moore), Peggy Louise (md. Bobby Joe Johnson), Billy Ray (md. Judith Lynn Gean) and Anna Ruth (md. Douglas Ray Underwood).

Leona Belle (md. Rannel Cargile about 1979). Mr. Cargile passed away Dec. 1, 2002 in Van Buren, AR. Leona lives with her daughter, Anna in Barling, AR.

Georgie Ruth (md. O.G. Johnston June 20, 1953) and they make their home in Gladewater, TX. To their union was born Carol Ann (currently a PhD Professor of English, Dickinson College, Carlisle, PA), and Donna Lynn (md. Joe Lawrence Niehus). *Submitted by Georgia Ruth White Johnson, daughter of George Cleveland White and granddaughter of Nancy Norwood and James Ransom White.*

WHITE - James "Jim" Abram White (b. Aug. 23, 1878 in Haysville, Clay County, NC), son of James Ransom White and Nancy Melissa Norwood. Oral family history is that the family moved to Conway County, AR area in 1890. He married Elizabeth "Lizzie" Herring Dec. 2, 1902. They settled in Dublin, AR and began raising a family.

From an obituary article: "Mr. White, as a young man farmed in Oklahoma for several years before moving to Tulare County, CA to continue farming. During WWII, Mr. White worked

James "Jim" Abram White, about 1950, Atwater, CA.

for the Kaiser Shipyards in Richmond, CA. He retired in 1946 and moved to Atwater, Merced County, CA." This is where Jim and Lizzie lived out the remainder of their lives. Jim died in April 1979; Lizzie preceded him in death in 1969.

Born to their union is Arnold, Clyde; Lena; Leo Luther (d. Nov. 21, 2004) md. Pauline Dailey; Pearl (md. Ben White); Ralph; Clister Evelyn (b. Dec. 10, 1906, d. June 2, 1976) md. Henry Lee Hinsley); Harold "Bud" and Helen (b. 1914, d. 1935).

Jim White's obituary article also states that he and Lizzie "had 21 grandchildren, 33 great-grandchildren, and one great-great-grandchild." *Submitted by Roy White, cousin to James Abram White and grandson of James Ransom White.*

WHITE - James Ransom White was born to William D. "Wadd" White and Tempie Slatton in October 1848 in Haysville Township, Clay County, SC. James Ransom married Nancy Melissa Norwood Feb. 22, 1872 in Haysville, Clay County, NC, daughter of William Norwood and Elvirah.

To their union was born James Abram, William Avery, George Cleveland and John Virgil. Oral family history states there were also three daughters born to the couple, who tragically died in a diphtheria epidemic. There are no records of their daughters names, dates of their deaths, nor location of their burials. Tra-

ditional oral family history speculation is that Nancy Melissa died in the same diphtheria epidemic. She last appears in the 1880 North Carolina US Census. Oral family history states that James Ransom White moved his family to Conway County, AR area in 1890.

Eliza Ann Mackey White (widow of James Ransom White) with four of their grown children, l-r: Zonia, Susan, Dolly and Ollie (twins), 1950, Little Rock, AR.

James "Jim" Abram White (b. Aug. 23, 1878 in Haysville, Clay County, NC) md. Elizabeth "Lizzie" Herring on Dec. 2, 1902 in Dublin, AR. To their union was born Arnold, Clyde, Lena, Leo Luther (d. Nov. 21, 2004), Pearl, Ralph, Clister Evelyn (b. Dec. 10, 1906, d. June 2, 1976), Harold and Helen (b. 1914, d. 1935). Jim and Lizzie made their home in Atwater, CA. Lizzie died Sept. 1, 1969 in Winton, CA and he died in April 1976 in Atwater, Merced County, CA.

William Avery "Aye" White (b. Dec. 27, 1879 in Haysville, Clay County, NC) md. Maude Alzonia Kennamer Sept. 10, 1916 in Springfield, Conway County, AR. To their union was born: Hubert Edwin (b. Aug. 28, 1917, Springfield, Conway County, AR, d. Nov. 9, 1998); Erma Leala (b. Oct. 27, 1918, Springfield, Conway County, AR, d. Oct. 20, 1932); Leatha Deryl (b. Aug. 26, 1922, d. May 15, 1999); and Ava Louise (b. April 18, 1927, d. Feb. 9, 1989). They made their home in Springfield, AR until 1922 when they moved to Carrizo Springs, TX. Maude died Oct. 13, 1966 and Ave died Oct. 10, 1970 in El Paso, El Paso County, TX.

George Cleveland White (b. Oct. 16, 1886 in Haysville Township, Clay County, NC) md. Bessie Mae Anderson (b. March 3, 1891) before 1910. To their union was born Opal Lee (b. April 1, 1911, d. Dec. 23, 1990); Velma Mae; Cleve Edward (b. Aug. 9, 1915, d. Jan. 17, 1972); Leona Belle; Georgia Ruth; Agnes Louise (b. July 1921, died in infancy); and James Murray (b. April 19, 1927, died about age 3 at unknown date); George Cleveland White died January 1962 in Knoxville, Johnson County, AR and Bessie died April 15, 1983, Ozark, Franklin County, AR.

John Virgil "Virg" White (b. Oct. 16, 1886 in Haysville, Clay County, NC) md. Alma Daucie Mallett about 1916. They made their home in Union Township, Conway County, AR. To their union was born Irpell C. (b. January 1917, died between 1940-44, during WWII); Elizabeth (b. 1920); Jimmie Ruth (b. Nov. 23, 1923, d. April 17, 2002); and Wanda (b. 1926, d. January 2005). All their children were born in Springfield, Conway County, AR.

James Ransom White was widower of Nancy Melissa Norwood for perhaps eight or nine years, when he married Elizabeth Rhoades (b. Jan. 23, 1870, d. Jan. 28, 1898). They made their home in Clinton, AR. To their union Robert Harlan was born on July 10, 1896 and died April 3, 1979).

James Ransom White met and married Eliza Ann Mackey (b. 1871, d. 1964) on Oct. 17, 1899. To their union was born Rufus Lee (b. 1901); Clarcie May (b. July 23, 1902); Zonia (b. Feb. 13, 1904); Charles Ransom (b. Dec. 23, 1906); Ollie and Dollie (twins b. Feb. 21, 1908 in Springfield, Conway County, AR) Ollie died Nov. 11, 1979 and Dollie died June 16, 2004). Eliza Mackey brought Susie Ann Barnes (b. 1889) from her first marriage into the family, just as James Ransom White brought all his sons

that were still at home. *Submitted by Roy Joe White, son of Ollie White and grandson of James Ransom White*

WHITE - John Virgil White was born Oct. 16, 1886 in Haysville, Clay County, NC to James Ransom White and Nancy Melissa Norwood. Oral family history is that the family moved to Conway County, AR area in 1890. Nicknamed "Virg," he married Alma Daucie Mallett about 1916. They made their home in Union Township, Conway County, AR.

John Virgil White with wife, Daucie Mallet White and son Irpell about 1918, Springfield, AR.

To their union was born Irpell, Joe Bill, Elizabeth, Jimmie Ruth, and Wanda. John Virgil White earned a living for his family by farming. When Daucie's uncle, Frank Kennamer, told of the opportunity to buy lush farmland in Texas, they moved there with other family members. One of Virg's brothers, Ave White, and one of Daucie's sisters, Ethel, and their families joined together for the move to Carrizo Springs, Dimmit County, near San Antonio, TX.

Unfortunately, no one anticipated a severe drought in just a few years. John Virgil moved his family back to Arkansas, but the tragedy had taken a severe toll. Daucie and Virg divorced about 1930. She remarried John Porphir, who lived near Kensett, AR and they moved to Michigan after a few years. Virg stayed for a while with his brother George on his farm in Knoxville, AR, but eventually bought his own home in Knoxville. John Virgil White is enumerated on the United States 1930 census in Union Township, Conway County, AR as a farmer. He passed away in Knoxville in 1958.

Irpell White (b. Jan. 24, 1919 in Springfield, Conway County, AR) was killed on Oct. 20, 1942, while serving his country in the Philippines in the US Army during WWII. The family brought his body back home, and he is buried in the Springfield Cemetery, Springfield, Conway County, AR.

Elizabeth White (b. 1920 in Springfield, Conway County, AR) md. Preston Carter and they made their home at Coloma, MI. She is now living in a nursing home in South Haven, MI.

Jimmie Ruth White (b. Nov. 23, 1923 in Springfield, Conway County, AR) md. Walter Dawson in 1940. Mr. Dawson died in 1942. Jimmie Ruth married Elmer F. Johnson in 1944. They made their home in Watervaliet, MI. She passed away April 17, 2002.

Wanda White (b. 1926 in Springfield, Conway County, AR) md. Charles Martin in 1946. They made their home in Watervaliet, MI. Wanda passed away in January 2005. *Submitted by Val Soulard, daughter of Jimmie Ruth White Johnson and granddaughter of John Virgil White.*

WHITE - Robert Harlan was born on July 10, 1896. His father, James Ransom White, was widower of Nancy Melissa Norwood for perhaps eight or nine years when he married Elizabeth Rhoades (b. Jan. 23, 1870, d. Jan. 28, 1888) Sadly, Robert Harlan wasn't even 2 years old when his mother died and the only child from their union.

He went by his middle name, Harlan. He married Dorotha Garrison

Robert Harlan White with wife, Dorotha Garrison White about 1922, Springfield.

(b. 1903, Arkansas) in 1920. They are found in Conway County Marriages Book X, p. 155 as Harlin White, 24, and Dortha Garrison, 19, on Feb. 19, 1922. It is unknown when they moved, but they made their home in Oklahoma where Harlan was a realtor and had a real estate office in Oklahoma City. He died in 1977 in Oklahoma City, Cleveland County, OK, and is interred in Resthaven Gardens Cemetery there.

Garrison H. White was born to their union in December 1923. One of Harlan's cousins, Pearl White, remembers a daughter was also born to Harlan, and thinks her name was Donna Sue.

Pearl White states that Harlan was a popular, wonderful singer and he performed in many places. She also states that he taught in singing schools.

Harlan's son Garrison is also a realtor in Oklahoma City, OK and still lives there. Garrison married Dorothy. To their union was born Gary Don in 1953 and Penny Kay in born in 1950. *Submitted by Kathryn McElhannon, great-granddaughter of James Ransom White and grand niece of Robert Harlan White.*

WHITE - William Avery White was born Dec. 27, 1879 in Haysville, Clay County, NC to James Ransom White and Nancy Melissa Norwood. Oral family history is that the family moved to Conway County, AR area in 1890. Called "Ave" he married Maude Alzonia Kennamer (b. Sept. 22, 1890), daughter of Jacob Kennamer and Nicy Powell, on Sept. 10, 1916. Mr. and Mrs. Ave White lived in Springfield, Conway County, AR until they moved to Carrizo Springs, TX in August 1922. Born to their union: Hubert Edwin, Erma Leala, Letha Deryl, and Ava Louise (my mother).

William Avery "Ave" White and wife Maude Kennamer White with children Hubert and Erma, about 1920, Springfield, AR.

At this time, my mother is deceased as well as all her siblings. Hubert (b. Aug. 28, 1917 in Springfield, Conway County, AR, d. Nov. 9, 1998 in Chandler, TX); Erma Lela (b. Oct. 27, 1918 in Springfield, Conway County, AR, died following complications from an appendectomy on Oct. 20, 1932 in Carrizo Springs, TX); Deryl (b. Aug. 26, 1922 in Cushing, OK while the family was moving to Carrizo Springs, TX, d.

William Avery "Ave" White and wife, Maude Kennamer White about 1950, El Paso, TX

May 15, 1999 in El Paso, TX); Ava Louise (b. April 18, 1927 in Carrizo Springs, Dimmitt County, TX, d. Feb. 9, 1989 in El Paso, El Paso County, TX, following a lengthy battle with cancer).

There was no reason to anticipate the lush Carrizo Springs, TX farmland would undergo a drought in just a few years and although very happy there, life became very hard. This unfortunately happened during the Depression and everyone pulled together to provide for their families. Papa was able to gain employment for a period of time with the railroad, riding "shotgun" for the armored money cars between Sierra Blanca, TX and Tucson, AZ. My grandparents subsequently moved to Sierra Blanca.

My mother, called Louise, married Frank Stoehner of Honey Grove, TX during WWII. He had joined the Army and was assigned with a detachment guarding a prisoner of war camp in the desert near where my grandparents lived in Sierra Blanca. My grandparents later moved to Clint, TX when Papa became employed on a large farm. My parents had set up housekeeping in El Paso, TX, near Ft. Bliss Army Base there. Daddy was with Headquarters' Troop, 7th Cavalry. His lower leg and ankle were shattered when a jeep he was driving had brake failure. He was transferred to the 8th Corps Medical Detachment at William Beaumont Army Hospital and trained as a physical therapist, where he served the remainder of the war. His troop shipped out overseas without him, assigned to combat, landing to fight with other groups at Iwo Jima. Almost none of Daddy's troop lived to come home.

I was the first of their four children, born at William Beaumont Army Hospital just before the end of WWII. Daddy stayed in the El Paso area after his tour of duty ended, gaining employment with another large farm in Clint, TX. In a few years, Daddy had an opportunity for employment at a large dairy farm in Arrey, NM, near today's Truth or Consequences. By this time my siblings began arriving.

Daddy attended special training at an agricultural college in Denver, CO, Graham Scientific Breeding School, graduating as a Certified American Breeders Service technician. He was transferred to the home dairy in El Paso, TX, Price's Dairy, which is a subsidiary of Borden's today. He matched and cross-matched bloodlines in order to artificially breed the large dairy head, improving the cattle many times over as far as milk production, offspring, and show herds.

Daddy, Frank Frederick Stoehner, was born Dec. 21, 1919 in Honey Grove, Fannin County, TX. He and Mother, Louise White, married Jan. 21, 1943 in Las Cruces, Dona Ana County, NM. Daddy passed away from diabetic complications on July 29, 1989, just five months after mother died Feb. 9, 1989. They both died beloved by and surrounded by their family. They are buried side by side at Restlawn Cemetery in El Paso, El Paso County, TX, and are survived by four children and 10 grandchildren. Both were active members in good standing with the Lutheran Church, Missouri Synod. *Submitted by Kathryn Stoehner McElhannon, daughter of Louise White and Frank Stoehner and granddaughter of Maude and Ave White.*

WHITE - In 1996 Allen and Mary Wade White came to live in Perry County, AR. They were married in Gilmer, TX in 1966. Mary's ancestors came from Virginia, North Carolina, Tennessee, Illinois, Missouri, Arkansas and Texas.

Elizabeth Wade came in 1828 to Lawrence County, AR with her children: Edmund, John, Richard Calvin, and possible other children: Sarah, Elizabeth, Frances Jane, Thomas Hampton and Joseph, after husband Hampton, 1753 Virginia, had died in Missouri. (Unproven.) Edmond and brothers went to Conway County.

Mary L. Wade and Allen White

Edmund's first wife is said to be Sallie Williams. Edmond died of smallpox and pneumonia in May 1864 while serving in Union Army. He and Sallie had John (b. 1842 Arkansas, d. 1881 Texas) who also served in the Union Army and whose first wife, said to be Sarah Conway, died in childbirth, leaving him with Sarah Lou (b. 1862 Arkansas) and Martha (b. 1864), and his sister Sarah Jane (b. 1839, d. 1864) Fouche La Fave River, who married Matthew Marion McCabe (first white child born in Perry County on Aug. 8, 1835 Arkansas, d. July 23, 1924, Adona, AR), died at the end of the Civil War as did his father and many uncles and cousins. She was only 25 and had young children.

There are several McCabes at this time married to Wades and related families. His sister Elizabeth (b.

1844 Arkansas, d. 1923 Arkansas) md. Edmund Alexander Smith in 1872. She looks Native American in her picture and her family claims she and Sarah were Choctaw.

After the deaths of all these family members, John moved to Texas to Col. Burleson's Plantation where he married Julia Ann Neely (b. May 31, 1850 Kentucky, d. Jan. 11, 1933 Texas) on April 4, 1867 in Texas. Julia was living with sister Sophrania Neely Borrer, wife of Issac Borrer (have ties with Aaron Williams and Charity Nation), and sister Susan Ann Neely Lackey, wife of Elijah Lackey.

John and Julia had son John S. who married Zella Mae and had children, Ginny (b. 1896) and Zella (b. 1898) who were all lost in the 1900 Galveston Hurricane. Rumor is that Ginny survived. Also, James C. ? and Jesse Hampton (who married Maggie Alice Ferrill) and William Green (b. Nov. 16, 1874, Texas, d. Nov. 19, 1938 Texas (who md. Jessie O. Kirk (b. Nov. 24, 1891, d. Feb. 7, 1959 Texas) (Mary's line) and Margaret Angeline married Charles Sumner True and George W. married Bessie Mae Hodge.

Julia married John Williams, had one son Elijah Thomas Williams who married Miram Kirk. John died young and left behind a young wife and children; records and photos were lost and family only in recent years found out who his family was. We still do not know all of family. Julia had married third time to George White.

John's father, Edmond (b. ca. 1808 Lauderdale, TN) married second March 23, 1853 to Sarah Jane McCabe Holbein (b. 1831, d. 1880-1900), daughter of Thomas Lovell McCabe. Their children were William (b. 1850), Margaret (b. 1854), Edmond (b. 1856), Louise (b. 1859), Catherine (b. 1861), Julia (b. 1863) and Sarah had two girls, Nancy (b. ca. 1849) and Mary Ann Holbein (b. 1848). His sister, Elizabeth (b. 1839), daughter of James McCabe was living with them in 1850.

Edmond's brothers, John (b. Dec. 26, 1806 Virginia) md. Clarissa Gardner and Richard Calvin (b. 1815) md. Ailsa Gardner, were early settlers of Perry County, AR. Their mother Elizabeth married second, Green (unproven) who was half Cherokee from Mississippi. His son William (b. May 10, 1818) md. Hannah King (b. 1824 Kentucky) and later moved to Texas with brother, James (b. Jan. 20, 1823) who married Sarah Kitchell, daughter of Celia Williams (Aaron Williams and Charity Nation).

Sister Elizabeth Green (b. Jan. 20, 1823 Arkansas, d. Feb. 29, 1908 Texas) md. Aaron Williams Jr. (b. Oct. 13, 1815 Tennessee, d. 1900). Sister Mary Ann Green (b. 1825 Arkansas, d. 1897 Texas) md. Benjamin King, son of Nathanial King and she married David Pinson (b. 1847 Arkansas, d. 1872). They are rumored to be children or stepchildren of Elizabeth Wade (unproven). In Perry on Wade's Crossing there is Wade's Cemetery, where many family of John and Clarissa are. Also, Liberty in Casa and Adona in Yell County, family are buried.

There is a link from Richard Calvin's daughter Sarah Wade who married John Pryor, that goes back to Edward of England (Edward, Edward, Andrew, Andrew, Robert, Sarah, Elizabeth Stokes, John Pryor, John Pryor and Sarah C. Wade).

Allen White was the son of George W. White (b. June 1, 1915, Louisiana, d. Dec. 22, 1989, Louisiana) and Mary Cellalee Aaron (b. April 9, 1920, Louisiana, d. July 14, 1970, Louisiana), daughter of Bob Aaron and Susannah. George is the son of James David White of Arkansas, who died in Louisiana, who married Maggie Lillie Elizabeth Jones (Frisby) March 3, 1800, who was the daughter of Susan Jones, Oct. 6, 1861, Camden, AR–May 5, 1942 Louisiana, and Jessie Lee Frisby Jr., April 6, 1891 Arkansas. Susan was daughter of David Jones, ca. 1820 Ireland-1870 Arkansas and Frances Susan Le Beouff ca. 1837 Arkansas-ca. 1874 Arkansas, who was daughter of Susan Clover Sept. 1, 1823 and Andreas La Beouff II ca. 1805, Ouachita Territory, LA. Andreas was the son of

Andreas La Beouff and Genevieve Fogul, who were early settlers of Ouachita Territory.

We are kin to the McCasland-Wade's of Mt. View, Jonesboro, and Batesville also. William H. Wade line is Edward, Edward, Andrew, Andrew, William or Robert married Mary Callicut, Samuel's daughter Rhoda Wade married Wade Barrick McCasland, son of Jane McCasland Nov. 20, 1817 Tennessee, married William Marriott Wade 1841 Tennessee, Jan. 16, 1821 Tennessee, whose son William Alexander Wade April 9, 1935 Arkansas married Martha White, daughter of Rhoda's sister, Mary Ann Wade and John W. White. William Marriott Wade, son of Noah Jasper Wade 1780 and Twynn Rebecca Satterfield 1753 South Carolina and Noah is son of David Bingley Wade ca. 1755 South Carolina. We are still a work in progress, both past and present. *Submitted by Mary Wade White.*

WILLIAMS - Arlie Andrew Williams (b. 1925, d. 1994) was born in Center Ridge, AR, those were the last words we would hear his sweet voice say. He was one of the kindest souls to ever live, a gentle giant, a quiet soft spoken "bear" of a man, second father to me and my children. Born to Henry and Laura (Keith) Williams, raised by a farm family to be a farmer. Disliking school and needed at home to work, he wasn't forced to attend. Therefore, he couldn't read well or write much more than his name. Reading road signs to him greatly improved my reading. He had them memorized. He was being sure I was learning to read.

l-r: Ron Flowers Jr., Arlie Williams, Alex Bowen and Shane Burris.

His family left Conway County for Jackson County, AR, as my grandparents did, they wound up farming at Amagon. Arlie married my sister, Martha Ann, daughter of Edmond and Mildred (Ray) Flowers. Their baby, Esther Pauline, lived only a few days shortly before I was born in 1957. Mama was very sick, so I went home without her. They helped take care of me. Folks in town thought I was their baby.

My limited farm knowledge is from visits to the Williams farm. Milking cows, feeding chickens, gathering eggs, churning butter, pumping water outside, and carrying it inside. Sleeping on homemade feather mattresses under homemade quilts. Bathing in a washtub after the sun warmed the water, using coal oil lanterns for light and an outhouse bathroom. Women labored over a hot stove preparing delicious meals, then eating leftovers. Men from the fields ate first.

Arlie farmed his entire life, sometimes seven days a week, often-long days. He loved driving combines and tractors. He and Martha helped raise my boys. They loved him very much and will miss him forever. He loved watching cartoons, wrestling and "shoot 'em ups," fixing small appliances, and arm wrestling with the kids.

He retired from Wilman's Farms in Jackson County when his health failed. When Arlie's neighbor was complaining about his parking in the empty lot between them, Daddy bought it for him.

Mother's Day 1994 is my happiest; Arlie survived his first ventilator battle to come home that day! Happily I felt as though we'd cheated death, I knew our time together was limited. The very thing he loved to do, farm, caused his lung condition. He never smoked, although over and over he was asked. De-

cades of inadvertently inhaling farm pesticides and plant dust caused it. Permission was requested and given to publish his case in medical journals.

On Nov. 5, 1994, Arlie went to heaven. His nephews were pallbearers. His beautiful monument reflects an entire farm scene with a tractor. Because he was here, I know there are angels among us.

Remembering Arlie, I think of the Bible scripture: "I thank God upon every remembrance of You." He lives forever in our hearts. *Submitted "In his precious memory" by his niece, Mrs. Carolyn Tucker.*

WILLIAMS - Eddie Williams was the second child born to Robert and Syvellia Williams. His father Robert Williams was born in South Carolina in 1877. His mother, Syvellia Templeton Williams was also born in South Carolina in 1879. His grandfather, Syrus Williams, was born into slavery in 1854 in Darlington County, SC. The Underground Railroad was still in operation at that time. The Underground Railroad was in operation from 1830-65.

Eddie Williams

Eddie Williams married Rena Swinton on March 4, 1934. He farmed and read meters for the water department of Morrilton, AR until his death. This was a special job for African-Americans in the 1950s. He lived in the Happy Bend Community, which was located near Pope and Conway counties line. He walked the Tally Lane everyday to catch the Greyhound bus to Morrilton, AR to work.

Eddie Williams and Rena Williams had a unique family of 10 girls and one boy. Eddie loved to take his family to church. They attended Diggs Chapel A.M.E. Zion Church of Blackwell, AR.

Eddie Williams died in Morrilton Hospital on May 2, 1957. He was buried in Rose of Sharon Cemetery in Blackwell, AR. *Submitted by Gertrude Williams McCoy, his daughter.*

WILLIAMS - Descendants of Frederick S. Williams. Generation No. 1: Frederick S. Williams was born after September 1838 in Maury County, TN, and died Oct. 3, 1886 in Washington, Conway, AR. He married first Priscilla Witt, Oct. 13, 1859 in Washington Township, Conway, AR. She was born about 1838 in Conway, AR. He married second, Mary Ann Stringer Sept. 7, 1875 in Conway, AR, daughter of Reuben Stringer and Sarah Edge. She was born 1850 in Lumpkin, GA and died 1906 (unproven where or exactly when).

Frederick was shown on the 1850 census in Marshall County, MS, in the 1860, 1870 and 1880 census in Washington Township, Conway, AR. Mary Ann Stringer was shown on the 1850 census, age 2, in Lumpkin, GA. The 1870 census shows her in the Welborn Twp., Conway County, AR. The 1880 census shows her in Washington Twp., Conway County, AR. She is shown to be age 24 on Sept. 9, 1875. At the time of their marriage Frederick was age 35 and Mary Ann was age 24.

The children of Frederick and Priscilla were: Sidney Oscar Williams (b. July 18, 1863 in Conway County, AR, d. Sept. 26, 1944 in Yell County, AR); James Anderson Williams (b. April 25, 1866 in Conway County, AR, d. Dec. 23, 1939 in Conway County, AR); Columbus Lafayette Williams (b. August 1869 in Arkansas, d. November 1906 in Springfield, Conway County, AR); Charlie M. Williams (b. ca. 1870); Thomas Henry Williams (b. July 1, 1872, d. Aug. 15, 1953).

The children of Frederick and Mary Ann were S.T. Williams (male) (b. 1880); Victoria Williams (b. Oct. 27, 1883 in Morrilton, Conway County, AR, d. June 1, 1976 in Fresno, Fresno County, CA).

Generation No. 2.

Sidney Oscar Williams married Sallie Gordon June 12, 1887 in Conway County, AR. She was the daughter of James Gordon and Elizabeth Crow. She was born Aug. 16, 1870 in Conway County, AR and died Oct. 16, 1941 in Yell County, AR. Children of Sidney and Sallie:

1) Orville Bradley Williams (b. Dec. 20, 1889 in Conway County, AR, d. Dec. 20, 1971, Hanford, Kings, CA) md. Madoline James on Aug. 9, 1914 in Conway County, AR. She was born Sept. 30, 1896 and died Sept. 9, 1979.

2) Ben Franklin Williams (b. Sept. 17, 1895, d. Feb. 26, 1959) md. Wilma on Oct. 6, 1922 in Conway County, AR.

3) Walter Williams (b&d. ca. 1901, Morrilton, Conway County, AR).

4) Nettie Williams born about 1903.

5) Dudley Carl Williams (b. March 23, 1908 in Morrilton, Conway County, AR, d. Jan. 25, 1952 in Morrilton, Conway County, AR) md. Lera L. Ramsey, Nov. 15, 1925.

James Anderson Williams married Frances Robinson Jan. 2, 1895 in Conway County, AR. She was born Feb. 3, 1872 in Conway County, AR died Aug. 3, 1951 in Conway County, AR. Their children were:

1) James Eardy Williams (b. March 20, 1897 Conway County, AR, d. June 28, 1976) md. Mabel Gordon June 27, 1920.

2) Jennie Williams (b. Feb. 23, 1901).

3) Oral Williams (b. Feb. 7, 1903).

4) Laura Williams (b. Dec. 18, 1904).

5) Eugene Williams (b. July 24, 1909 in Morrilton, Conway County, AR, d. Dec. 30, 1969).

6) Verline Williams (b. June 1, 1912).

Columbus Lafayette Williams married Ida Belle Dancer Sept. 5, 1895 in Conway County, AR. She was born November 1874 in Tennessee. Their child was James I. Williams (b. August 1895 in Conway County, AR).

Charlie M. Williams married Malissa Perry Sept. 24, 1891. She was born about 1872. Their child was Walter Williams (b. ca. 1896).

Victoria Williams married Walter Andrew Kuykendall Dec. 27, 1901 in Conway County, AR. He was the son of John Kuykendall and Kisira Hopkins, born May 26, 1881 in Fort Payne, Dekalb County, AL, died May 6, 1955 in Yuba City, Butte County, CA. Their children were:

1) Mildred May Kuykendall (b. June 19, 1903 in Morrilton, Conway County, AR, d. 1929, in Gore, OK) md. Sam Chompton in 1926.

2) Charles Andrew Kuykendall (b. June 28, 1905 in Springfield, Conway County, AR, d. Sept. 23, 1974 in Roseville, Placer County, CA) md. Hazel Hendrickson in 1929. She was born about 1910.

3) Mary Edna Kuykendall (b. April 28, 1907 in Bono, Faulkner County, AR, d. June 5, 1988 in Solano, CA) married first, Cecil Clarence German, Sept. 1, 1923 in Muskogee, Muskogee Co. OK. He was born Oct. 10, 1904, Indian Territory, Nowata, OK, d. Oct. 15, 1971, Sonoma, Sonoma, CA; married second, George Michael Neary after 1951. He was born June 15, 1908 in Iowa and died Jan. 25, 1994 in Solano, CA.

4) Virdie Kuykendall (b. Dec. 14, 1908 in Aday, Perry County, AR, d. 1911 in Conway or Yell County, AR).

5) Willie Ethel Kuykendall (b. Jan. 23, 1909 in Centerville, Yell County, AR) md. Charles Vincent Hughes Sept. 14, 1922.

6) Claudia Faye Kuykendall (b. Oct. 22, 1914 in Morrilton, Conway County, AR, d. Oct. 1, 1916, Welborne Twp., Conway Co. AR).

7) Blanche Mildred Kuykendall (b. Aug. 9, 1916 in Morrilton, Conway County, AR, d. July 12, 1938 in Porter, Muskogee County, OK) md. Bert McCoy.

8) Jessie Wilma Kuykendall (b. Aug. 19, 1918 in Morrilton, Conway County, AR) md. Roland Raymond McDaniel March 2, 1934. He was born about 1915.

9) Joe Bill Kuykendall (b. Nov. 17, 1920 in Lee, Pope County, AR, d. July 7, 1926 Gore, Muskogee County, OK). *Submitted by Dianna German Anderson.*

WILLIAMS - Henry Jasper Williams was born Dec. 2, 1859 in Conway County, AR to William Haywood Williams and Esther Gordon Williams. Henry Jasper was known as "Buddy." He married Cynthia Ella Wood, daughter of John Hamilton "Hamp" Wood and Mary Frances Burns Wood, Aug. 14, 1888 in Conway County. Henry Jasper and Cynthia Ella had the following children: Walter Lee (b. July 30, 1889); Arthur Bennett (b. July 26, 1892); Ada (b. March 6, 1894); Huie Robert (b. Nov. 16, 1896); Rutha Ellen (b. Feb. 10, 1899); Bertha Lela (b. April 20, 1901); Delia Etta (b. Sept. 2, 1903); and Cora Edna (b. July 5, 1891).

Henry Jasper and Cynthia Ella Williams and granddaughters.

Walter Lee Williams married Maudie Delilah Gordon, daughter of Samuel and Callie Williams Gordon, Jan. 9, 1910. He died Feb. 13, 1940 in Harlengen, TX.

Arthur Bennett Williams married Hettie Albertie Dickson Aug. 9, 1914 in Conway County, AR. Arthur was a carpenter and died Oct. 16, 1973 in Morrilton. Hettie Albertie "Bertie" was born Jan. 10, 1898 and died Sept. 7, 1984 in Morrilton. Arthur and Bertie are buried in Old Salem Cemetery in the Lord's School House Community. They had six children: Afton Buryl, Vernon D., Lorene, Helen Irene, Nora Inez and Charles Edward. Lorene was only about eight months old when she fell into a fire. She died as a result of the burns.

Ada Williams married Bob Batson, son of Oscar Batson and Clara Willis Batson. She died Jan. 13, 1916 from complications in childbirth. She is buried in Old Salem Cemetery. Ada and Bob had the following children: Clara and Ada Syble. Clara (b. Feb. 4, 1914, d. Oct. 15, 2000) md. Harmon G. Greer. Clara and Harmon are buried in Old Salem Cemetery. Ada Syble died Sept. 21, 1984 in Houston, TX.

Huie Robert Williams married Ruth Jane Tice Aug. 14, 1916 in Morrilton, AR. He died Oct. 18, 1952 in Morrilton and she died April 27, 1985 in Little Rock. They are buried in Old Salem Cemetery.

Rutha Ellen Williams married Lee Roy Batson Aug. 13, 1916 in Morrilton. Lee Roy was born June 1, 1896 in Germantown, AR to Wilburn Batson and Sarah Sisson Rodgers Batson. Rutha died Feb. 19, 1971 in Houston, TX and is buried in Old Salem Cemetery. Rutha and Lee Roy had two children, Verna (b. Oct. 19, 1918 in Melbourne, AR) and a baby boy (b. June 13, 1922, d. Sept. 4, 1922). The baby boy is buried in Old Salem Cemetery.

Bertha Lela Williams married Vestal Elder Newton Neal May 17, 1921 in Morrilton. She died Nov. 28, 1985 in Tulsa, OK. Vestal was born Nov. 1, 1899 to John Neal and Mary Black Neal. He died May 11, 1988 in Morrilton. They are buried in Old Salem Cemetery. Their children are James Loyd and Ancal.

Delia Etta Williams married Bob Batson April 20, 1919. They had two children, Ellas Howard and Rheba Aleece. Delia died Jan. 22, 1999 in Little Rock, AR and Bob died Nov. 14, 1956. Both are buried in Old Salem Cemetery.

Cora Edna Williams married William Haywood Williams III. Cora died Oct. 18, 1943 and is buried in Old Salem Cemetery. They had two children, Elva and Bessie M. Bessie married Lester Wood. *Submitted by Mrs. Euna Beavers.*

WILLIAMS - Jackson Griffith Williams, son of John Littleton Williams and Mary Garner. John Littleton had previously been married to Mary Sidney Hill. Mary died around 1847 and John remarried in December 1848. He and Mary Garner had seven children: Thomas Jefferson (b. 1849); Nancy (b. 1851, d. 1928); William Day "Bill Day" (b. 1852); Nathan H. (b. 1854, d. 1919); Henry B. (b. 1857); Jackson Griffith (b. Dec. 21, 1859) and Sarah Jane (b. 1862).

Martha Ann Hatley Williams and Jackson Griffith Williams

Jackson G. was born in Arkansas, probably Van Buren County. John Littleton enlisted in the 31st AR Infantry, Co. C and was sent with his brothers to Helena, Phillips County, AR for duty. While there, John L. developed bilious fever and died Aug. 12, 1862. John L. had fought in the Indian Wars, the War with Mexico and followed his patriotism into the Union Army, prepared to fight again.

Jackson Griffith married Martha Ann Hatley, the daughter of John Hatley and Elizabeth Perry. They were married in Van Buren County, AR on Dec. 25, 1879. These two were the parents of 15 children, most of whom settled and lived in Conway County. The children were Cora (b. 1880, d. 1881); Mary Alice (b. 1882, d. 1968); Elizabeth "Betty" (b. 1884, d. 1963) md. Odie Jacob "Jake" Sheridan; John Littleton (b. 1886, d. 1929) md. Bertha Magnolia Tester; Julia (b. 1888, d. 1913); Ida M. (b. 1890, d. 1970) md. Tom Whitfield, unknown Scott and Bob McIntyre; William "Bill" (b. 1892) md. Belle Emerson and Maudie Eubanks; Lillie B. (b. 1894, d. 1986) md. Bill Burnett; Rosa or Rosia, died as a child; Dollie M. (b. 1897, d. 1987) md. Clifford Lindsey; Lucie Ann (b. 1899, d. 1993) md. Maston Lonza Tester; James Thomas (b. 1901, d. 1973) md. Rose Ellen Brents; Pearle (b. 1903) md. Scott Sloan and Gene Strieff; Annie (b&d. 1905); Martha (b. 1907, d. 1991) md. William Spencer Tester.

Martha Ann Hatley Williams was born Sept. 26, 1863 in North Carolina. Her father and mother are buried in Pope County, AR, where presumably she had also lived when a child. Martha had six brothers and sisters: Sarah (b. 1853), Adam W. (b. 1856), Mary (b. 1861) md. Sam Kilpatrick in 1888, Littleton Perry (b. 1866) md. Eva Barton, Taletha, and William (b. 1870). Its believed they were all born in North Carolina.

Story has it that one day, Jackson Griffith was working outside in the heat of the day when he went over to the water trough to fetch a drink of water. When he had drunk, he straightened up, wiping off his face. Suddenly, he realized he could no longer see anything. The family believes it was from a heat stroke that he suffered, but nothing is sure about that. At any rate, he lived the rest of his life without his eye sight. He died April 15, 1916 and Martha Ann died on Aug. 29, 1941, and they are buried at Foster Cemetery, near Scotland, AR. One of their grandchildren, James Lowell, son of James Thomas and Rose Williams, is also resting with them.

WILLIAMS - The history of the Williams family and its different branches, had its beginning in America with John Williams of Welsh descent who settled in York County, VA before 1645. His wife's name is unknown. Their children were John Williams Jr., Edward, Obediah, Richard and William.

John Williams Sr. married Mary Keeling who, after his death settled along the Panuky River. One of her sons, Lewis, established Williams Ferry where George Washington crossed to visit the Chamberlains and met Martha Custis, whom he later married.

Another son Daniel (b. 1669 in York County, VA) md. Ursula Henderson. They had seven children: Mary, John, Jane, Joseph, Henry, Mary Mitchell and Daniel. According to the terms of his will, he bequeathed to each of his children considerable land, livestock, a feather bed and Negro servants.

Andrew Jackson Williams and wife, Ellanda J.

Children of Andrew Jackson Williams and Ellanda J. Williams and Lark Howard: in front, from right: J.J. Williams, Arthur Lee Williams, Charles Howard; back: Delphinia Williams, Martha Ann Williams, Mary Williams, Ollie Pearl Williams, Cassie Howard, Gertie Howard.

Colonial John Williams distinguished himself at the Battle of King Mountain in the Revolutionary War in 1780 by killing the commander of the British forces. Henry Williams was born in North Carolina where he was a landowner and attorney. His wife's name was Elizabeth. Their children were Daniel, Joseph, Nathan, Nancy Elizabeth, Susan, Sally and Jane.

Grandmother Charity Elizabeth Howard Williams Walker

Nathan Williams (b. 1770-1780 in Caswell County, NC) md. Rebecca Jackson, daughter of John Jackson, a Cherokee Indian. Nathan was also a large landowner. He later moved to Crowcreek Valley in Franklin County, TN. They had eight children: Thomas Jefferson (b. 1811), Mary (b. 1810), William (b. 1814), Leroy P. (b. 1822), John Littleton (b. 1823), Wriley (b. 1825), Julia Ann (b. 1827) and Susan C. (b. 1831). All of their children moved to Conway and Van Buren counties before 1850s.

Leroy P. Williams married Martha Ann Hill, daughter of Jonas and Mary Hill. Their children were Nathan, John, Sidney, Rebecca, Mary J., Andrew J. and Elizabeth.

Andrew Jackson Williams (b. 1854, d. 1894) md. Ellanda J. Kissire (b. 1859, d. 1902). Their children were John J. Williams, Arthur Lee, Delphinia, Ollie Pearl, Martha Ann and Mary. After the death of Andrew J., Ellanda Jane married Lark Howard. Their children were Cassie, Charles and Gertie. When Ellanda died, Lark married Delphinia, his stepdaughter who was the oldest, to help raise the children. They had two children, Maudie and Helen. After Lark's death, Delphinia married Ance Flowers. They had one son Carl.

J.J. Williams married Charity Elizabeth Howard. Charity was a sister to Lark Howard. They had three children: Zola Mae, Conniver Lee and Gladis Muriel.

Zola Mae married Marvin Williams. They had

one child, Johnnie Sue. Conniver Lee married Dora Wilson; they had one child, Larry Joe. Gladis Muriel married Ira McCoy. They had one child, Carolyn Sue.

J.J. was an elder in the Pleasant Hill Church of Christ. He rang the bell on Sunday morning to announce worship services. The preacher would have Sunday dinner with John and Charity. She was a devout Christian and was always ready to help any neighbor who needed it. Charity always baked the communion bread for the Lord's Supper. Her granddaughter Sue West of Wichita, KS says she remembers her grandmother wringing a chicken's neck in preparation for Sunday dinner.

It was rumored that J.J. had money buried around their house. In fact his granddaughter says she has seen him bury money beside the garage. Sometimes during evening services lights could be seen through the church windows. They thought it was someone looking for the money.

The Williams descendants, along with their cousins the Hills, Howards and others, can be proud of their pioneering ancestors through whom they can claim "kin" to governors, judges, congressmen, and such notable individuals as General Robert E. Lee, the 11th President of the United States James Polk and even the Chamberlain to William the Conqueror. *Submitted by Sue West.*

WILLIAMS – John B. Williams, born in Texas County, MO, came to Arkansas with his elder sister, Mary Margaret Bates, and her family. They eventually settled in Yell County. Two other brothers came with her, Wilson Furd and James Carroll. Nothing can be found about James Carroll. Furd settled in Ada Valley, where he was a blacksmith prior to moving to Morrilton. They were the children of James William Carroll and Caroline, grandchildren of William and Mary Webb. The parents and grandparents died in Texas County, MO.

John B. married Joe "Josie" Anna Barker, daughter of the Ada Valley druggist and Cumberland Presbyterian minister, John Ewing Barker and Missouia Allen. The Barkers are buried in Hominy, OK. John B. is buried in French Prairie Cemetery, Ione, Logan County. Josie later moved back to Ada Valley and married Claude Knowles. Joe Anna is buried in the Ada Valley Cemetery. None of the Williams family now reside in Ada Valley. Mary K. Williams, daughter of Lamar and Pearl, married Archie Dalton and still owns the family farm. It has one campsite and lots of pine and honeysuckles.

Their children were Lemoin (Lamar Ewing) married Mary Pearl Kendrick, both buried Ada Valley; Maud Artie (md. Ira V. Kendrick); Glovie never married and is buried Ada Valley; John B., Jo Anna "Josie"; Missouri Sue (md. David Cramer, then Jack Carter), buried Roland, AR; Carroll Moody (md. Mary Elizabeth Greathouse), buried Ada Valley Cemetery; Myrtle Sylvia (md. Hugh Strait), buried in Connecticut.

W. Furd married Martha Reeves. Their children were: Beulah (md. Mack Chambers), buried in Ada Valley; Claude (md. Margaret), both buried in Elmwood Cemetery; Etta Irene (md. James Alexander Deaton), both buried Elmwood Cemetery (one cemetery book has name spelled as Ella; Carroll (md. Gertrude), buried in Elmwood.

Three of Furd's grandchildren still live in Morrilton: Syretha Chambers Loyd, Mary Etta Deaton and Billie Deaton, longtime city councilman.

WILLIAMS - John W. Williams was the grandfather of Maga Poe Watkins of Conway County, AR. He was born in South Carolina in 1809. He was the son of Louis and Winifred Williams. He married Marinda Humphries, daughter of Shadrack and Sarah Camp Humphries on Dec. 23, 1830 in Walton County, GA. John and Marinda moved to Walker County, GA in 1835 and began farming a short distance from his father. They had the following children:

James Lewis (b. April 20, 1832, d. 1870) md. Mary White; Jane Vashtie (b. Oct. 25, 1836) md. Frances Hopkins; Mary Caroline (b. June 2, 1839, d. Jan. 3, 1892) md. John Self; Martha Victory (b. March 19, 1842, d. Sept. 21, 1876) md. William Hopkins; Sarah Winifred, born March 31, 1847, d. Aug. 26, 1898) md. James Boland; Melissa Marinda (b. Aug. 11, 1854, d. March 26, 1889) md. George Marion Poe; Jackson Jeremiah (b. Dec. 29, 1857, d. May 2, 1915) md. Elloit Rosie Bruton; Elizabeth Mary (b. Aug. 10, 1858, d. Jan. 22, 1890) md. Ruben A. Rankin.

John and Marinda moved from Walker County, GA to Pope County, AR after the Civil War. John became Post Master of the Glass Village Post Office in 1872 and retained that position until his death on Sept. 30, 1878. Marinda Humphries Williams lived with her daughter, Jane Hopkins until her death on Dec. 18, 1900. John and Marinda are buried in the Appleton Cemetery in Appleton, AR.

WILLIAMS - Lamar Ewing Williams and Mary Pearl Kendrick Williams moved in the early 30s from Pope County to Ada Valley, Conway County. They first lived on the Kendrick place, formerly occupied by the Reverend William Francis Kendrick. Reverend Kendrick was a pastor of the Methodist Church prior to his death in 1925. The church is now the Ada Valley Community Church. See church history elsewhere.

Two other places of worship existed in the valley. They were "brush arbors" functioning in the warm months and consisting primarily of "revival type gatherings." One was located near the Ada Valley Cemetery (Blue Point Road) and the other near the school (near the junction of Ada Valley Road and Ault Road). At one such meeting, Bill Ellison, JE Warren and Dean Rinehart pulled a trick on two families. They substituted the babies of Mrs. Williams and Mrs. Warren. They switched blankets. Being a boy and a girl, the trick was discovered at diaper changing time.

The school taught through the eighth grade although, per Mrs. Williams, it formerly taught the high school grades. Children had to choose either Oppelo or Adona or Morrilton for additional education. Most selected Adona to go to both junior and senior high at the same place.

Lamar's grandfather, John Ewing Barker, was the druggist in the valley earlier in the century. He was also a Cumberland Presbyterian minister and a Mason. The Masons and the Woodmen of the World met over the school house. (See separate article.) There was one grocery store in the valley when Lamar and Pearl moved there, operated by Marvin Brimmage. Later stores were operated by Dezzie and Columbus

Abston and Charlie Jones. Sadly, now there are none.

The valley supported itself prior to WWII primarily by agriculture. In the late 30s, the WPA was a big source of income. At least two sawmills operated, one of which was extant in 2004. There was a cannery established at the Scott place. That property is still in the Scott family although the cannery is long gone. One of the farmers (and blacksmith) was an uncle of Lamar. W. Furd Williams. Furd was the grandfather of Bill Deaton, longtime Morrilton councilman.

Homecoming, always well attended with people from California, Delaware and points between, continues each year on the first Sunday in June. (Ed. note: Come at 10 AM for the best congregational gospel singing anywhere, sans sermon.). Far fewer families reside in the valley now although many still own the old farms and are well represented at homecoming. Several of the current residents have lived there all their lives. *Submitted by Mary Williams.*

WILLIAMS - Louis Williams, the great-grandfather of Maga Anne Poe Watkins, of Conway County, AR, was born on Nov. 29, 1785 in Virginia. He was the son of John Williams, an Englishman and a soldier in the Revolution. Louis married Winifred Williams, who was born in 1786 in South Carolina. "Winnie," as she was called, was the daughter of another John Williams, a Welshman, and also a soldier of the Revolution. The two John Williams were at the surrender of General Cornwallis to George Washington's army at Yorktown.

Louis and Winnie lived in Walker County, GA on a plantation they had built in 1840 located near Chestnut Flats. Their union produced 10 children. Their oldest son, John W. Williams, was Maga's grandfather.

Winnie Frances Williams died on Oct. 8, 1850 of typhoid fever. Louis married a second time to Sarah Moon in 1855. Louis died on June 4, 1863 during the Civil War. Shortly before his death, one of his sons, Jeremiah Jackson Williams, was killed at the battle of Resaca, which took place near the Williams plantation. Jeremiah was brought home and both he and Louis are buried on the plantation grounds.

Louis Williams was an active member of the Baptist Church and a local leader in the Democratic Party. He is listed as a member of the Coosa Baptist Association. He is shown attending their conventions in Walker County, GA between 1853 and 1857.

WILLIAMS - Ollie Pearl Polk (b. July 4, 1896, d. Sept. 8, 1997) md. Charley Etheridge on Dec. 18, 1913. He was born April 20, 1897. Ollie and Charley had

Front row of boys 3rd from left is Franklin Miller. 2nd row: _, Glenna Williams, Harold Rankin, Donald Cunningham, Odell Wallace, A.J. Yarbrough. 3rd row: Jewell Price, Faye Abston, Jessie Thomas, Eulene Fudge, Emogene Yarbrough, Imajean Williams, Hazel Brown, Irene Yarbrough, Nell Wallace, Thelma Yarbrough, Monteen Anderson, Deloin Miller; 4th row: Mildred Cunningham, Ione Fudge, Mary Katherine Williams, Juanita Rankin, Cliva Yarbrough, Nina Abston, Frances Yarbrough, Jewell Edwards and Teacher Audrey Oliger.

two children: Martha Elizabeth Etheridge (b. Jan. 31, 1919) and William Andrew Etheridge (b. Oct. 31, 1924, d. Feb. 18, 1926).

After the death of Charley Etheridge, Ollie married on Dec. 29, 1931 for a second time to Enoch Williams (b. April 4, 1904, d. July 7, 1987). Ollie and Enoch had one child, Wanda Lou Will-

Enoch and Ollie Williams

iams (b. Jan. 22, 1935) who married Luther Gleen Bryant June 28, 1954. He was born April 8, 1934. They had two children:

1) Glenn Russell Bryant (b. July 6, 1956) md. Sandra Dell Woods Sept. 12, 1975. They had three children: (A) Jason Glenn Bryant (b. April 13, 1977) md. Elizabeth Lee Vargas Dec. 28, 1997. She was born Aug. 3, 1974. They have one child, Nathaniel Glenn (b. Nov. 20, 1998). (B) Justin Russell Bryant (b. Jan. 29, 1980). (C) Jessica Dell Bryant (b. Feb. 24, 1984). Glenn Russell and Sandra Dell Bryant divorced in 1991. Glenn Russell Bryant married second, Karen Webb on June 20, 1992. They have one child, Ashley Michelle Bryant (b. May 29, 1994).

2) Mark Anthony Bryant (b. May 25, 1970) md. Jodi Ann Thompson Aug. 16, 1997. She was born Feb. 15, 1973. They have two children: Shelby Ann (b. Feb. 13, 1998) and Ethan Taylor (b. March 6, 2000).

Martha Elizabeth Etheridge married William Avery Stobaugh on Jan. 4, 1936. Martha and Avery had five children:

1) Rebecca Sue Stobaugh (b. March 27, 1938) md. Bill Baldwin June 26, 1954. They had three children: (A) Tammy Kay Baldwin (b. Oct. 27, 1957) md. Henry Sissions Oct. 7, 1987. No children. (B) Billy Baldwin Jr. (b. Jan. 23, 1964) md. Melinda Hazelip Feb. 9, 1991; they have one child, Megan Rebecca Baldwin. (C) Chris Andrew Baldwin (b. Sept. 16, 1972) md. Dana Hicks Aug. 1, 1992, they have two children: Haley Danielle (b. Oct. 3, 1999) and Clayton Andrew (b. Jan. 2, 2003).

2) Glenda Ruth Stobaugh (b. June 25, 1944) md. Landon Carr July 4, 1961. He died Feb. 24, 1965. They had one son, Wesley Bryan Carr (b. July 4, 1963) md. Ronda Harris Feb. 14, 1982. They had one child, Christopher Landon Carr (b. April 14, 1983). Wesley and Ronda Carr divorced in 1987 or 1988. Wesley Bryan Carr then married Thresha Banks on Feb. 14, 1989. Glenda Ruth married a second time to Jerry Barber on Aug. 12, 1967 they had two children: (A) Angela Lynn Barber (b. Oct. 1, 1969) md. Michael Wilburn in September 1988. They have two children, Jera Mica Wilburn (b. March 23, 1989) and Jamie Lynn Wilburn (b. Oct. 8, 1991). (B) Alan Randall Barber (b. March 30, 1976).

3) Margaret Ann Stobaugh (b. March 31, 1947) md. Walton Weaver Aug. 12, 1966. They had four children: (A) Martha Michelle Weaver (b. June 16, 1967). (B) Melissa Dawn Weaver (b. June 27, 1969) md. Steve Pecot March 18, 1990. They have two children, Lyndon Wayne Pecot (b. Oct. 10, 1991) and Madison Elaine Pecot (b. Oct. 20, 1995). (C) Marcus Walton Weaver (twin) (b. May 28, 1975) md. Valarie Ann Brogdon May 22, 2004. D) Michael Ray Weaver (twin) (b. May 28, 1975).

4) Kathy Rhea Stobaugh (b. July 11, 1953) md. Larry Jones March 25, 1972. They have three children: (A) Lora Elizabeth Jones (b. June 21, 1979) md. Giuseppe Galoti (b. May 10, 1978). (B) Sara LeAnn Jones (b. July 1, 1981) md. Brian Lee Leija Oct. 9, 2004; he was born July 2, 1980. They have one child, Keaten Avery Leija (b. Feb. 27, 2005). (C) Larry Kyle Jones (b. Dec. 7, 1988).

5) William Charles Stobaugh (b. April 4, 1957, d. Dec. 31, 1957).

WILLIAMS – My father was born William Edward Wyatt to Abner and Virginia (Langley) Wyatt on Feb. 16, 1909 at Shirley, AR. I don't have all the facts, but I do know that his parents were divorced. When he was 3 years of age, he and his 5-year-old sister Beatrice were adopted by Rollins and Noma (Rhodes) Williams. They lived in the New Liberty Community located north of Cleveland in Conway County, just south of the Van Buren County line.

Edward and Verda Williams - 1985.

He attended the Shot Gun Ridge School and helped work on the farm. During his late teen years, he drove a truck hauling timber to Morrilton.

My mother was born Verda Lou Elam to James Richard and Martha Ellen (Turner) Elam on May 30, 1904 in the Mt. Zion Community just north of Jerusalem, AR. She was the sixth child and was 8 years old when her father died. He left his wife with a 40-acre farm and 10 children, ranging in age from 17 years to 4 months old.

She struggled to provide for her children. She and the children worked the farm and some of the boys hired out to the neighbors. The baby died when he was less than a year old of unknown causes. One of the older boys died when he was 19 during the flu epidemic.

My mother attended the Mt. Zion School, a one-room school with classes for first to eighth grades. She said that she loved school and attended after she had completed the eighth grade, but finally stopped after her brother got the teacher's job. She didn't like going to school to her brother.

In 1925 my grandmother married Daniel Scott. In 1926 they rented out her farm and moved to the New Liberty Community. Three of her children, including my mother, were still living at home.

My parents were married April 21, 1929. They lived with his parents and farmed with them the first year of marriage. They managed to buy the essentials for housekeeping and the next year made a deal with a lady in the neighborhood to sharecrop her farm. She gave two rooms of her four-room home to them to live in. They worked hard and lived frugally, moving often during the early years of marriage.

They were parents of four children: Gordon Lee (b. Oct. 21, 1930) who died four months later from pneumonia. This was the biggest tragedy of their lives. He is buried in the Old Liberty Cemetery in Van Buren County.

Treva Pearline was born Dec. 21, 1931 at Jerusalem, AR. They were farming Grandma Scott's farm that year. Treva was delivered by Grandma's brother, Dr. Edgar Close.

I, Elva Rea, was born July 3, 1933. They had moved back to the New Liberty Community. This was during the heart of the depression and money was hard to come by. A mid-wife, "Aunt" Sleety Shipp, delivered me and my younger sister. Daddy owned a sweater that "Aunt" Sleety's son liked, so they gave it to her as payment for delivering me.

Wanda Fay was born Aug. 28, 1934 at the Lost Corner Community. They paid "Aunt" Sleety with a new quilt that Mama had made for delivering her.

In 1936 we moved back to the New Liberty Community and in a few years were able to buy the 80 acre farm that we were renting. Daddy grew corn, cotton and hay. We milked several cows, raised a few hogs

and chickens. We grew a large garden and had an apple and peach orchard.

During the summer months, Mama stayed busy canning and drying fruits and vegetables. She always found jobs for us girls. Her motto, "idle hands are the devil's workshop." We chopped cotton, milked cows, picked blackberries and helped Mama with the canning. We went to church twice every Sunday. Not much time for the devil's workshop, but I do have to admit that we did get into mischief with our next-door neighbors, Bertha and Irene, and our cousins when they visited.

We girls loved animals and always had several cats and a dog. We even loved the cows and Daddy was very sly. He was trying to build up his dairy herd, and every time that he bought another cow, he would let one of us claim and name her. Of course, if she was our cow, we could also milk her. After about three cows apiece, we wised up.

Two of the biggest highlights of my childhood were when Daddy bought a "brand-new" wagon. I was 8 years old and when I was 13, came the biggest one. He bought a used car! We girls really enjoyed that car.

We moved to Matthews, MO in 1948. Arnold Walls hauled our furniture, one cow and our dog in his truck. I sneaked my favorite cat, with Daddy's help, into the back of the car. We sold our cows, but left our cats and team of mares with Grandpa and Grandma Williams. We didn't milk cows in Missouri, but we did chop and pick lots of cotton.

Daddy rented a farm and moved our team, Murt and Maud, up here. He finally sold them and bought a tractor. We were sad to see the mares go, but Daddy did enjoy farming with his tractor and didn't retire until his health failed.

After high school all three of us girls worked as telephone operators for Southwestern Bell in the Sikeston, MO office. Wanda made a career with them and transferred to St. Louis. There she held several different positions before retirement. Her two daughters followed in her footsteps and are still employed by Southwestern Bell. The company has transferred them to Texas.

Daddy and Mama celebrated their 60th wedding anniversary on April 21, 1989. He died May 14, 1989 and she died Oct., 2, 1993. They are buried in the Garden Of Memories Cemetery in Sikeston, MO.

Their descendants are: Treva married Clyde "Peck" Wisdom. They live in Sikeston, MO and own "Peck's Enterprises," a franchise of the *St. Louis Post Dispatch*. They have five children: Gale Wisdom of Jackson, MO; Linda Manes of Salcedo, MO; Clyde Wisdom, Gregory Wisdom and Nancy Driskill of Sikeston, MO. They have 14 grandchildren (two are deceased) and three great-grandchildren.

I, Elva, married Lee Kenedy. We live near East Prairie, MO and we farm. We have three sons: Gary lives at Matthews, MO; David lives at East Prairie, MO and Roger lives at New Madrid, MO. We have seven grandchildren and three great-grandchildren.

Wanda married Dallas Sawyer and he is deceased. She is retired and lives in Universal City, TX. She has three children: Sharon Sadlon of Schertz, TX; Jennifer Ousley of Grandview, TX and Michael Sawyer of Elsberry, MO. She has 10 grandchildren and one great-granddaughter.

Daddy and Mama enjoyed their large family and lived a good Christian life, setting a good example for all of us. Daddy was a great story teller and all the grandchildren loved to listen to him tell about the "good-old- days." We all thought that Mama was the best cook in the whole world and everyone seemed to make it to their house every Sunday for dinner. The grandchildren's favorites were her chicken and dumplings and homemade rolls. *Submitted by Elva Kenedy.*

WILLIAMS - William Haywood Williams was born Nov. 8, 1822 in North Carolina to John D. Williams and Susanna Hobbs Williams. He married Esther S. Gordon Nov. 20, 1844 in Fayette County, TN. Esther was born about 1823 in Maury County, TN to Josiah Gordon and Susannah Gambrell Gordon.

The 1850 census of Marshall County, MS shows William H., Esther S., son John and son Anthony H. According to family stories, Esther and Bill traveled by covered wagon westward from Tennessee to Arkansas, arriving about 1850 in Conway County. They settled in Lewisburg Township, which is now Washington Township in the area presently known as Lord's School House Community.

William Haywood Williams

By the 1860 census they were in Conway County. William Haywood "Bill" was listed in the census as being an overseer of property. Listed with him and Esther are Franklin, Haywood, Edmond J. and a 6 month old baby.

Before the Civil War, Bill was the overseer for landowners, N.S. Howe and Henry Paine of Massachusetts. In 1874 he purchased 160 acres from them. This land was located one half mile west of what is now State Highway 95 in Conway County. By the 1880 census, Marian Williams, a nephew age 28, Dora Gordon, a niece age 14, and Charlie, a nephew age 13, were living with him and Esther. Bill also ran a cotton gin north of Morrilton in the Lord's School House Community. In 1893 he had an accident at the cotton gin which resulted in amputation of his left arm. His son, Henry Jasper "Buddy," then took over the gin. It is said that he would not eat with the family, but had a round table in the living room where he ate his meals alone. Bill lived with Sam and Callie Gordon after Esther's death, and then later lived with Henry Jasper and Cynthia Williams. Bill gave the land and the cotton gin to Emma Jane Wood and Henry Jasper Williams for them to take care of him for the remainder of his life. Bill died about 1911 in Conway County and Esther died April 24, 1899 in Conway County. Both are buried in Old Salem Cemetery in Lord's School House Community.

The children of Bill and Esther are as follows: John Franklin (b. 1847 in Tennessee); William Haywood II (b. 1849 in Tennessee); Emma Jane (b. Nov. 8, 1856 in Arkansas) and Henry Jasper (b. Dec. 2, 1859 in Arkansas).

John Franklin married Janie Upchurch Sept. 13, 1888.

William Haywood II married California Batson Nov. 26, 1882 in Tennessee. William Haywood died in January 1887. Their children are Walter, Florence, William Haywood III and Elbert Williams.

Emma Jane married John Hamilton "Hamp" Wood in 1882. She died July 15, 1939.

Henry Jasper "Buddy" married Cynthia Ella Wood Aug. 14, 1888 in Conway County. He died Dec. 9, 1939. They are both buried in Old Salem Cemetery. *Submitted by Mrs. Burnie Beavers.*

WILLIAMS - Wilson "Furd" Williams and brother John B. Williams, along with their sister, Mary Margaret Williams Bates, migrated from Texas County, MO after 1876. Mary Margaret and her family migrated to Yell County. She and her family are buried in the Harkey Valley Cemetery of Arkansas 7 south of Dardanelle. Their parents were James William Carroll and Caroline Williams, who came with his parents, William and Mary Webb Williams from Warren County TN.

John B. Williams and Furd were living in 1880 in the household of their sister's family in Texas County, with another brother who cannot be traced. John B. lived most of his adult life in Logan County

and is buried in French Prairie Cemetery near Ione. He married Joe Anna "Josie" Barker.

The elder Barker (John Ewing) was at one time, the druggist in Ada Valley. Apparently, after the death of John about 1912, she moved to Ada Valley, possibly with her father. She died in Roland, AR, in 1964 and is buried in Ada Valley Cemetery.

John and Joe Anna had several children, most of whom are buried next to her in Ada Valley. Their children were Maud Artie Williams Kendrick (Ira V.); Lemoine "Lamar" (Mary Pearl Kendrick); Glovie L.; Myrtle "Sylvia" Williams Strait (Hugh); Carroll Moody (Mary Elizabeth Greathouse); Missouri Sue Williams Cramer Carter (Jack).

Lamar Williams, well known in Ada Valley, moved late in life to a house in Morrilton. Children of Lamar and Pearl include Cleotha Elizabeth Williams Hallman (Dibbrell) of Rock Falls IL; Junior Irvin who died as a logger in Port Orford, OR and is buried in Ada Valley; Raymond E. Sr. (Rose Ciccarelli) lives in Seaford, DE as does Mary K. Williams (Archie Dalton); Evelyn Imajean Williams Himmelberg (Gilbert) lives in Vienna, VA near Cleva Glentaline (Robert Williams) in Arlington, VA. Other children died young. All were raised in Ada Valley and graduated from area schools.

Wilson "Furd" married Martha Reeves and lived both in Ada Valley and Morrilton. Both are buried in Ada Valley. Their children include Beulah Williams Chambers (Mack) who lived in Morrilton and are buried in Ada Valley. Beulah's children include Syrthea Chambers Loyd (Jimmy) presently living in Morrilton. Other children include Claude (Margaret); Carroll (Gertrude); Etta Irene Williams Deaton (James Alex). All except Gertrude are buried in Elmwood Cemetery.

Etta's children include: Marietta Deaton Driggers Russell (Ray); Jimmie Dean (recently deceased) (Ruth Coffman Trafford) and Billie Eugene (Helen Louise Long). Billie, in 2002, announced his imminent retirement after 37 years as Morrilton city councilman and vice-mayor.

WILLS - Annie Mary Wills, daughter of Lewis Joseph and Mary Mahalia (Roberts) Autry Wills, was born on Feb. 2, 1889 in Lanty, Conway County, AR. She married Homer Freeman on Dec. 8, 1908 on Wills Mountain, Van Buren County, AR. Homer, son of Willis and Martha Ann (Stobaugh) Freeman, was born Sept. 5, 1886 in Sang, Van Buren County, AR and died June 21, 1958 in Benton, Saline County, AR. He is buried in Cedar Creek Cemetery, Jerusalem, Conway County, AR. Annie died

Annie Wills Freeman with son, Arden Freeman.

on March 26, 1978 in Jerusalem, Conway County, AR. She is buried beside her parents in Liberty Springs Cemetery, Van Buren County, AR.

Annie and Homer are the parents of five children: Artie Mahalia, Alta, Arden William, Alene Bretty and Ardee Lewis.

Artie (b. Oct. 31, 1909 in Gridley, Van Buren County, AR) md. John Calvin Creach on Nov. 19, 1927 in Jerusalem, Conway County, AR. John, son of Benjamin and Elizabeth (Rony) Creach, was born on Jan. 22, 1903 in Cross Timbers, Hickory County, MO. Artie and John are the parents of four children: Zelma Dewell Creach, John Dempsey Creach, Cletus Carroll Creach and Mary Elizabeth Creach Pettingill. John Calvin died on April 23, 1985 in Morrilton, Conway County, AR. Artie died on Dec. 30, 1999 in Perryville, Perry County, AR. They are buried in the Liberty Springs Cemetery, Van Buren County, AR.

Alta (b. Oct. 29, 1912 in Gridley) md. Weldon Taft Mills on Sept. 26, 1938 in Cleveland, Conway

County, AR. Weldon, son of Thomas Roland and Lela Virginia (Brown) Mills, was born on Oct. 4, 1908 in Gridley. Weldon died Dec. 26, 1972 and is buried in Cedar Creek Cemetery. Alta and Weldon are the parents of six children: Evern Edwin Lawless, Mack Sheldon Mills, Virginia Aleda Mills Bateman, Lena Joy Mills Poe Cossey, Barney Alton Mills and Alta Cordell Mills New.

Arden (b. Jan. 17, 1915 in Gridley) md. Mary Eathel Campbell on Dec. 23, 1939 in Conway, Faulkner County, AR. Mary Eathel, daughter of Benjamin and Bessie Belle (Ingram) Campbell, was born on Dec. 13, 1920 in Okay, Pope County, AR. Arden and Eathel are the parents of four children: Mary Joyce Freeman Chism, Janice Arden Freeman Roberts, Gerald Don Freeman and Darrell Dean Freeman. Arden died on Sept. 17, 1992 in Morrilton, Conway County, AR and is buried in the Liberty Springs Cemetery.

Alene (b. April 29, 1919 in Gridley) md. James Thomas Campbell on July 30, 1934 in Cleveland, Conway County, AR. James Thomas, son of Jessie Thomas and Phoebe Catherine (Collie) Campbell, was born on Sept. 15, 1911 in Cleveland, Conway County, AR. Alene and Thomas are the parents of three children: Vesta Marie Campbell Burnette, Marjorie Louise Campbell Ralston and James Thomas Campbell Jr. Thomas died on Nov. 4, 2002 in Ft. Cobb, Caddo County, OK. Alene died on Feb. 20, 2003 in Oklahoma City, Oklahoma County, OK. Alene and Thomas are buried in the Oak Grove Cemetery in Ft. Cobb.

Ardee Lewis (b. April 12, 1923 in Gridley) lived with his mother and never married. Lewis was a young man when he developed muscular dystrophy. He led a courageous battle with his illness his entire life. He died on March 25, 1985 in Morrilton and is buried in Liberty Springs Cemetery. *Submitted by Rosemary Chism Norwood.*

WILLS - Lewis Joseph Wills was born on May 27, 1865 in Scranton, Lackawanna County, PA. His parents, John Robert and Josephine (Martin) Wills immigrated to the United States from Switzerland. Lewis started working when he was only 9 years of age. Pamphlets were circulated in Scranton telling of the advantages of living in Arkansas. At the age of about 21, he came to Little Rock, Pulaski County, AR seeking employment. He was told of a glass factory in Morrilton, so he came up the river on a steamboat. He lived and worked in the Morrilton area for a while.

Sitting: Lewis Joseph Wills. Standing (l-r): Alta Freeman Mills, Alene Freeman Campbell, Artie Freeman Creach. Back row: Arden Freeman and Lewis Freeman.

He was living in the small community of Arthur, when he met a widow, Mary Mahalia Roberts Autry. She and her first husband, John Autry, had four children: William Ervin Autry, Sarah Jane Autry Bridges, Georgie Autry and Robert Autry. Lewis and Mary Mahalia married on Jan. 27, 1888 in Conway County, AR. After they married, they moved to Lanty, Conway County, AR where their daughter, Annie Mary Wills, was born on Feb. 2, 1889. The Wills family left Lanty and moved to a farm northwest of Cleveland, Conway County, AR. Then they moved to the McKay Place and lived in a house that was supposedly haunted. Lewis Wills took the family and homesteaded 80 acres on what is now known as Wills Mountain in Van Buren County, AR.

Annie Mary Wills married Homer Freeman on Dec. 8, 1908 on Wills Mountain. Homer (b. Sept. 5, 1886 Pope County, AR) was the son of Willis and Martha Ann (Stobaugh) Freeman. He died on June 21, 1958 in Benton, Saline County, AR and is buried in the Cedar Creek Cemetery, Jerusalem, Conway County, AR.

Annie and Homer were the parents of five children: Artie Mahalia Freeman Creach (b. Oct. 31, 1909, d. Dec. 30, 1999); Alta Freeman Mills (living); Arden William Freeman (b. Jan. 17, 1915, d. Sept. 17, 1992); Alene Bretty Freeman Campbell (b. April 29, 1919, d. Feb. 20, 2003) and Ardee Lewis Freeman (b. April 12, 1921, d. March 25, 1985). Annie Mary died on March 26, 1978 in Jerusalem, Conway County, AR.

Mary Mahalia Roberts Autry Wills died on April 11, 1931 on Wills Mountain and Lewis died on Jan. 4, 1961 on Wills Mountain. Annie, Mary Mahalia and Lewis are all buried in Liberty Springs Cemetery, Van Buren County, AR. *Submitted by Alta Freeman Mills.*

WILSON - James Robert Wilson (b. 1966) md. Sharon Leigh Eoff (b. 1967) on June 21, 1986. Both were from the Center Ridge Community having been transplanted by their families in upper elementary. The Wilsons, Lonnie and Mary, had retired to Center Ridge in 1976 from their military life, and the Eoffs, Fred and Becky, had moved to Center Ridge to begin a dairy partnership with Jeff and Brenda (McCoy) Harwood.

James and Sharon were both graduates of Nemo Vista High School where they participated in many activities. James, a member of the class of 1984, was involved in the Future Farmers of America, serving in various officer capacities, baseball, and was a member of the Center Ridge Fire Department. Sharon was on the basketball team, an officer in the Future Homemakers of America, and was president of the National Beta Club.

Jacquelynn, Juleighanna, Sharon, James and Geoffrey Wilson

After their marriage in 1986, James continued to work at Arrow Automotive while Sharon finished a degree in English and biology at the University of Central Arkansas (BSE in 1989, MSE in 1997). When Sharon began teaching at Wonderview High School, James went on to UCA to pursue his college degree in technology education (BSE in 1997). Sharon later taught at Perryville Jr-Sr High School and has been employed with the South Conway County Schools first as an English teacher and in 2005 as Reynolds Elementary Principal. James first taught at Oak Grove High School in North Little Rock and is currently with Greenbrier Schools as the EAST facilitator and EITE teacher at Greenbrier Jr. High.

Their family has been made complete by the addition of children Geoffrey Brian (b. 1994) and twin daughters, Juleighanna Paige and Jacquelynn Hope (b. 2001). Geoff is an active member of the Plumerville Bulldogs summer baseball program where he was on the AABA 1st Runner-up State Tournament team in 2003. They also won the district championship and the Morrilton Youth Association Tournament that year!

In 2005 Geoff coordinated a "Change Angel" fundraiser at Northside Elementary for Arkansas Children's Hospital and was proclaimed "Head Angel" by radio station B 98.5 and the hospital! He won a ski trip to Aspen for his efforts. Juleigh and Jacque are ever supportive of big brother Geoffrey. They serve as cheerleaders for his ball teams. They stay with their Nan and Pop, Becky and Fred Eoff, while everyone is

at school. They are also frequent visitors of Uncle Lynn, Uncle Joe, and Mrs. Jettie.

The family is active in Plumerville First Baptist Church. James serves as assistant song leader, grounds committee member, and both he and Sharon are Sunday School teachers. The kids are active in the Children on Mission and Mission Friends classes on Wednesday nights. James also serves on the Plumerville Fire Department and the Plumerville Planning and Zoning Committee. He is a board member on the Plumerville Youth Association. Sharon serves on the Plumerville Park and Recreation Commission and has helped to get a city playground built in downtown Plumerville.

WILSON - Mary Louise Tarble became the bride of Lonnie Fay Wilson on July 9, 1956. Lonnie was a member of the Army and they spent the next 20 years with him serving his country and Mary moving around to accommodate the military life with their five children. Lonnie served in both Korea and in Vietnam, making two tours in Vietnam.

Mary was the daughter of Minnie Lucille Kelly Tarble Taylor (b. Feb. 25, 1911, d. Feb. 8, 2000) and Calvin Tarble Sr. and Harry Platt Taylor (b. 1898, d. 1967). Her siblings are Dolores and Calvin Jr. and Robert Taylor. Grandma Taylor lived with Mary and Lonnie in Center Ridge until her death in 2000.

Lonnie was the son of Ilda "Ike" Bell Flowers Wilson and William Thomas "Tommy" Wilson. He has one brother, Frankie Gerald, who retired in Center Ridge. Lonnie retired from the military and later from Arrow Automotive in Morrilton.

Lonnie and Mary's five children have provided 18 grandchildren. The children are Geneva Josephine, Lonnie Fay Jr., OraLea, James Robert and Charles Thomas.

Geneva has four children: Michele Pawlik Robinson, John Pawlik Jr., Noah Shipp and Samuel Wilson. Michele and her husband Jason Robinson have one son, Dillon. John and his wife, Brandi have one daughter, Reanna, and are expecting another child in 2005.

Lonnie Fay Jr. and his wife Margie live in Wisconsin. They have three children: Jamie, Amanda and Debbie.

OraLea has three children. They are Jessica, David and Thomas Bostian.

James and his wife Sharon have three children: Geoffrey, Juleighanna and Jacquelynn.

Charles and his wife Darlena have four children: Kaila, Rachel, Claudia and Nathan.

Mary and Lonnie have enjoyed their retirement years. Mary is an avid bowler, and Lonnie enjoys gardening. They help out with family members and grandkids in their spare time.

WIRGES - Gene and Betty Wirges moved to Morrilton in Conway County, AR, when they purchased the *Morrillton Democrat* and *Perry County News* newspapers in 1957. Gene was editor and Betty served as business manager. The newspapers were sold to other interests in 1977.

Both from Little Rock, Gene was born Dec. 5, 1927 to Joe and Elizabeth (Wollhower) Wirges and Betty was born Dec. 3, 1926 to Rufus and Mary (Creighton) Carter. Gene's grandparents (Wirges and Wollhower families) settled north of Morrilton after immigrating from Germany in the 1800s.

Joe Wirges was a noted newspaper police reporter, winning one of the first "Big Story" awards for solving and reporting a murder mystery for the *Arkansas Gazette.*

Gene Wirges was at the center of a political struggle and authored the book *Conflict of Interests.*

Gene and Betty Wirges had five children: Ronald Wirges of Hollister, MO; Mrs. Victoria Wirges-Stanton of Little Rock; Gregory Wirges of Little Rock; Mrs. Karen "Shelly" Culbertson of North Little Rock; and George Wirges of Little Rock.

There are 11 grandchildren: Melanie Wirges Covey of Sarasota, FL; Veronica Wirges of North Little Rock; Mindy Wirges of Little Rock; Nigel and Tracey Wirges of Little Rock; Courtney Ugolini Webber of North Little Rock; Eric Ugolini of Olympia, WA; Kaitlyn Culbertson of North Little Rock; and Alex, Kayleigh and Shelby Wirges of Little Rock.

There are two great-grandchildren, Ian Covey of Sarasota, FL, and Tristan Webber of North Little Rock.

Betty Wirges died Oct. 22, 1977. Gene Wirges is retired and currently resides in Little Rock. *Submitted by Shelly Culbertson.*

WOFFORD - The earliest records show that the Wofford family in America originated in what is now Staffordshire, England. The name was originally spelled Walford and can be traced back to William Wofford, born around 1510. His great-grandson, named William as well, moved to Maryland in the 1630s. The family then migrated southward to South Carolina and later Mississippi. It is from there that Jesse Joseph Wofford, youngest son of Nathaniel Wofford and Comfort Snow, married Clarissa Wilson. They had eight children, and some of these children, along with Jesse Joseph and his wife, came to Conway County, AR in the early 1860s.

Their children were Eleanor, Nancy, Levi, Sarah, Mary, Green, Emily and Madeline. In the early 1870s Conway County was divided and part of it became Faulkner County, many of these children remained in Faulkner County, but never far from their siblings. Eleanor married a John Luster in Conway County and eventually moved to Faulkner County. Levi married Mary McGinty on Aug. 10, 1865, and his descendants relocated to the area around Independence, MO. Mary married George Belcher and then moved on to other parts of Arkansas.

Green married Mary Elizabeth Belcher in 1874 and some of their descendants remained in what is now Conway County. Green and Mary had five children: James Hamilton, William Jesse, John, Susie and Thomas Madison. Both Green and Mary died before Thomas was two months old. Their children were divided amongst family and friends. Current research can provide no information on James, John or Susie. William Jesse (or Tobe) moved away from Conway County but his son Charlie eventually returned and it is believed that his descendants remained in Conway County.

Thomas Madison (youngest son of Green, and often called Matt) married Maude Maybelle Moore. They lived around Springfield and moved later to the Jerusalem area. They had four daughters: Linnie May, Maggie Evalena (or Lena), Dovie Jo, and Edna Faye. They married Lonnie J. McCoy, Tarlton Ward, Lawrance Reid (known as Doodger), and Heavner Reid respectively. These members of the Conway County Community are connected to, and are ancestors of, many other families now residing in Conway County such as James, Garrett, Shipp, Nicholson, Zachary, Ward, Church, Vandeveer, Mitchell, Thompson and others. *Submitted by Lana Dale (McCoy) and Jeff James.*

WOLLEY - William "Bill" Theron Wolley (b. Nov. 15, 1900 in Plumerville, Conway County, AR) was the eldest son of Theron Burke Wolley and Quintella "Quincey" Lee Snyder. Born in Peoria, IL in August 1858, Theron was the son of Luther M. Wolley born about 1825 in Indiana and Martha P. Robeson, born in Kentucky about 1827 as daughter of the famous Illinois evangelist James Robeson and Jane A. Earle. James had been born in South Carolina May 21, 1797 and married Jane Oct. 23, 1822 in Hopkins County, KY. Jane, daughter of Virginians Baylis Earle Jr. and widow Anna Hewlett (Moseley), was born March 2, 1806 in Christian County, KY. Baylis' parents were Mary Prince and Baylis Earle Sr. who was one of the first county judges and first county commissioners in Spartanburg County, SC.

Quincey was born in Springfield, Conway County, AR, Sept. 12, 1867 to William J. Snyder and Martha Ann Roberts. William was born in Greenville, TN, April 17, 1847 to Margaret and William Snyder, and had come to Conway County, AR, about 25 years before his death in Springfield, AR, Nov. 21, 1893. He engaged in the saddlery and mercantile business

William T. Wolley - January 1919

in his shop on the southwest corner of the courthouse square. Martha, born May 1844 in North Carolina to John L. Roberts and Sarah Proby, married William Aug. 6, 1866. She died May 20, 1921 and is buried in Scott Cemetery, Saline County, AR. Her parents were both born about 1813 in North Carolina, immigrating to Conway County, AR about 1849 when they purchased a large farm that now is north of Plumerville about five miles. John was buried Nov. 14, 1863 at Little Rock National Cemetery, dying from injuries sustained while serving as a private in Company B, Third Arkansas Cavalry, Union forces.

When he was still very young, Bill's parents moved to a farm at Salem Township just northwest of Benton in Saline County, AR. Their children were raised on about 210 acres that are today lovely hilly wooded upscale subdivisions. In 1917, Bill enlisted in the US Navy as an aviation apprentice. Nine years later, he was in Pensacola, FL, earning his Navy Pilot's wings. The following year he married Nellie Mae Mudge, daughter of Idahlia Gertrude Lang and Wareham A.G. Mudge of Muscogee, a logging community just north of Pensacola, FL. Their marriage was the first of three generations of his family in which the newlyweds had met because of the husband's military assignment to the Florida Panhandle.

Their three daughters: Bette Marie, Virginia Lee, and Patricia Ann, all married Navy or Marine Corps men. Bette married LT Walter Decker in August 1951, and Ginny and Pat had eloped to Pascagoula, MS on July 4, 1951 to marry their flight school student sweethearts, Bill Garman and Theodore Zieckas.

Virginia's daughter, Constance Lee Garman, met Navy Supply Corps Commander Bruce Wayne Rova at a Gulf Breeze United Methodist Church gathering in May 1992, and two years later they too were joined in marriage, carrying on the tradition of her grandfather.

When William T. Wolley died at age 91 at the Gulf Breeze, FL hospital, the *Pensacola News Journal* wrote, "His 30-year Navy career was the stuff movies are made of." He was one of the first enlisted pilots and flew off the earliest carriers - USS *Langley* (CV-1), USS *Saratoga* (CV-3), USS *Enterprise*, and the original USS *Lexington* (CV-2). He was part of the first group of aviators to prove carrier-based planes were possible by landing and taking off the USS *Langley* (CV-1). He was part of a search party that looked for lost aviator, Amelia Earhart, and while stationed in Hawaii in the mid-1930s, he bombed the volcano Mauna Loa to divert lava flow away from the city Hilo. Bill retired as a lieutenant commander, having served in both WWI and WWII. Nell died in 1984. They both are buried at Rose Lawn Cemetery east of Gulf Breeze. *Submitted by Bruce Rova.*

WOMACK - Dr. Sid Womack and Karen Kay King were married May 19, 1972. Sid T. Womack was born in Abilene, TX to Don and Thelma Caffey Womack on May 9, 1950. The family lived at Truby, TX in Jones County on a farm. After attending Anson High School, Sid attended Abilene Christian University were he met Karen Kay King. After marrying, Sid attained a M.Ed. from Sam Houston State University and a Ph.D. from Texas A&M.

Karen Kay King was born in Fort Smith, AR on Aug. 10, 1953 to Ray and Dorothy King. The family moved to Fayetteville, AR and then to Huntsville, TX where Karen attended Huntsville High. Karen graduated from SHSU with a BAT in elementary education and an M.Ed. in elementary education and has taught school for 28 years. Karen earned a M.Ed. in instructional technology from ATU in 1995 and is librarian at London Elementary School. Dr. Womack teaches secondary education at Arkansas Tech University and serves on the board of Southern Christian Home. Dr. Womack also preaches part-time for the Mill Creek Church of Christ at London, AR and has served the West Side Church of Christ as deacon. They have lived in Russellville for 18 years. They have two children: Karah Kristen Womack Hosek is married to Matthew Philip Hosek and they have a son, Mark of Wylie, TX, and Sarah Ashlee Womack Wilson is married to Douglas Alan Wilson of Russellville, AR.

WOOD – Don Wood was born Feb. 16, 1918 in Oppelo, AR to Bennett Floyd Wood and Ulah Bell Baker Wood. He was one of three children born to them. On Oct. 6, 1950, he married Euna Pearl Williams. Euna was born May 16, 1919 to Huie Robert Williams and Ruth Jane Tice. Don and Euna lived at Oppelo in the home with his parents for several years. When Floyd and Eula decided to leave the farm and move to Morrilton, Don and Euna

Don and Euna Wood

bought it from them. Don raised vegetables for the family as well as to sell. He also had greenhouses and raised plants to sell.

Don followed construction work and was gone many hours a week. Euna helped with the gardens and fruit trees and also the greenhouses. She sold milk, butter and eggs. They lived on the family farm until 1975, when they also moved to Morrilton. Don and Euna had five children: James Don, Euna Fay, Reba Dianne, Nancy Louise and Mary Ann. Don had a heart attack in November 1985 and only lived about two weeks. He died Nov. 29, 1985. Euna had cancer and died May 7, 1988. They are both buried in Wolf Cemetery in Oppelo, AR.

James Don Wood is a truck driver and resides in Roland, OK. He married Rhonda Warnick. He has six children: Dawn Raynelle, Tina Marie, James Andrew, James Don Jr., Samantha Belle and Jared Daniel. Dawn is married to Anthony Joseph Powell and has three children: Michael Brennan, Katileigh and Summer Cheyenne. Tina has one son, Joseph Wesley.

Euna Fay Wood married Burnice "Burnie" Lee Beavers March 8, 1973 in Morrilton, AR. Euna owns and operates a daycare and until recently owned and operated Rocky Point Craft Shop. Burnie was a carpenter. They have three children: Steven Lee, Bobby Allen and Timothy David. Steven is married to Rachel Deanne Langle and has two children, Alanna Jordan and Evan Lee.

Reba Dianne Wood married Danny Charles Charton March 11, 1974 in Morrilton, AR. Dianne is a housewife and cares for her grandchildren. Danny owns a cattle farm and chicken houses. They have three children: Jeffrey Charles, Daniel Scott and Matthew Don. Jeffrey married Teisha Poe and has two children, Payton Jewell and Gabriella Reece. Scottie has one son, Alexander Scott. Matthew married Marie Tollefson.

Nancy Louise Wood married Dennis Ferrall McCoy June 28, 1975 in Morrilton, AR. Louise is a daycare worker and Dennis works for Arkansas Kraft. They have two sons, Jamie Allen and Jason Keith. Jamie married Martie Hamlin and has three children, Talyn Angelique, Jayden Clara and Drayke Hunter.

Jason married Tabitha Burlie and has one child, Emily Marie.

Mary Ann Wood married Robert Louis Jennings Nov. 27, 1981 in Morrilton, AR. Mary works for a Christian bookstore in Russellville and Rob works for a bread delivery company. They have three children: Joshua Louis, Rebecca Ann and Jennifer Alaine. Jennifer Alaine died April 16, 1988 and is buried in Wolf Cemetery in Oppelo. *Submitted by Steve Beavers.*

WOOD - John Hamilton "Hamp" Wood was born August 1852 or according to other records, Sept. 7, 1851 in Arkansas. He first married Mary Frances Burns in 1870. She died about 1879. Hamp then married Emma Jane Williams in 1882. Emma Jane was the daughter of William Haywood Williams and Esther Gordon Williams. She was born Nov. 8, 1856 in Arkansas.

Hamp and Mary Frances had the following children: Cynthia Ella (b. Dec. 12, 1870); twins, Lillie Bell and William H. (b. July 29, 1875). Cynthia Ella Wood married Henry Jasper Williams and died April 14, 1945. Lillie Bell married Henry Franklin Gordon Oct. 28, 1895 and died Feb. 16, 1941. Lillie Bell is buried in Old Salem Cemetery in the Lord School Community in Conway County. William H. married Vernona Poteete Roberts. They had three children: Tina (md. Wilson C. Burns), Retha (md. a Kyle) and Murvin Wood.

Hamp and Emma Jane had the following children: Robert Luther (b. November 1883); Esther (b. July 1885); Nettie Irene (b. October 1887); Charles Benjamin (b. Feb. 15, 1890); Oliver Herbert (b. March 1892); Emma Florence (b. Dec. 31, 1893); and Laura Ninnie (b. October 1896).

Robert Luther married Laura Ann Collums. Robert Luther and Laura both taught school in Morrilton, then moved to Conway. Esther married Don Dickson. Nettie Irene married R. Louis Cargile. They had no children. Charles Benjamin married Fatha Lela Hairston. They owned and operated "Wood's Variety" in Morrilton for many years. They had one son, Charles B. Williams Jr. (b. Dec. 1, 1919). Charles Sr. died Aug. 28, 1964 in Morrilton. Charles Jr. died May 28, 1978 in Morrilton and Fatha died Oct. 21, 1982. They are all three buried in Elmwood Cemetery in Morrilton. Oliver Herbert married Josie Gist and had one son, Lester Wood. Emma Florence died Nov. 6, 1901 and is buried in Old Salem Cemetery. Laura Ninnie Wood married Porter Fryer and had one daughter, Maurine.

According to the 1880 census for Conway County, Hamp and Cynthia Ella were living in Welborn Township in Lewisburg. He was a farmer. With them were William H. and Lillie, 4 years old and James Wood, age 23, who was a brother to Hamp. According to this census, Hamp's parents were born in Mississippi. According to family stories, Hamp was blind for the last 14 years of his life. Hamp died Oct. 29, 1934 and Emma Jane died July 15, 1939 in Conway County. They are buried in Old Salem Cemetery in Lord's School House Community. *Submitted by E.F. Beavers.*

WOODS - Gloria June (Allen) Woods was born in Morrilton, AR, to James Andrew "Andy" and Mary Luevenia (Blankinship) Allen on April 1, 1960. The family resided in Granny's Hollow, south of Jerusalem. Gloria was the youngest of eight children. Her siblings include: Paul David Allen, Rita Jo Gipson, Judy Lane Freeman (deceased), Evelyn Faye Stroud Baxley, Mary Ann Heistand Gullett Fowler, James Benton Allen, and Lola Ruth Stone Ulry. Gloria attended Jerusalem Grade School, grades 1-8, then went on to attend Wonderview High School, grades 9-12, in which she graduated as valedictorian of her class in 1978.

Gloria went on to attend Harding University, Searcy, AR, where she was blessed to meet, date, and marry Jeffrey Lynn Woods, of St. Louis, MO on Aug. 8, 1981. The two went on to graduate from Harding in

1982, Gloria with a BS in vocational home economics, and Jeff with a BA in Bible.

Jeff and Gloria Woods Family. Gloria and Jeff, Jessica (Emma), Jonathan, Hannah and David Woods, 2001.

After graduation, both Gloria and Jeff went on a mission trip to Kenya, Africa, in which their lives would be forever changed. They viewed the world differently and their parents' faith had now become their own. They immediately began work at Southern Christian Children's Home, Morrilton, in which they were house-parents for disadvantaged children and Jeff was activities director. They later served as relief house-parents, when their first child, Jessica Lynn, was born in 1984. Jeff remained on staff for another year in public relations, after which his position was terminated.

Gloria then went to work at First National Bank of Conway County, and Jeff found work at the Conway County Water Distribution District. The couple made the Downtown Church of Christ, Morrilton, their church home in which Jeff served as Downtown Church's first part-time youth minister. Within a year, the Lord answered prayers and Jeff accepted a full time youth minister's position in Tullahoma, TN, in which they spent six productive years. One week after they moved there, Gloria's Daddy died. Two months later on Sept. 30, 1986 Jonathan Andrew was born, and he was named after his Grandpa "Andy." Within 21 months Hannah Elizabeth joined the family.

Jeff and Gloria, along with their three children, moved to Paducah, KY where Jeff served as youth and family minister. A second son, David Jeffrey, was born there on April 8, 1994.

Within three years they moved to St. Louis, MO, to be near Jeff's parents, Haskell and Elizabeth Woods, as his dad's health was failing. God was gracious, as Haskell's health continued to improve and the young family spent seven years nearby. Jeff ministered at McKnight Road, Maryland Heights, and Bonne Terre. Gloria taught in Parkway, Rockwood, and North County Schools. One regret is that while the family lived in St. Louis, MO, Gloria's mother, Mary Lue, of Jerusalem, AR, died.

The couple returned to Searcy, AR where Jeff received his marriage and family therapy master's degree and is currently minister of involvement at the Cloverdale Church. Gloria works at Harding University as academic coordinator for the Upward Bound Program.

WOODY - Richard Woody I was born 1590 in England. He married Ann (last name unknown). Richard and Ann immigrated to America in 1642 and settled in Boston, MA. Ann died there 1656-58. Richard died there in 1658. They had at least four children including Isaac Woody (b. 1631 in England). Isaac married Dorcas Harper in 1656 at Boston. Dorcas Harper was the daughter of Joseph Harper. Isaac and Dorcas had at least nine children, including John Woody I, (b. 1659 in Boston).

John married Mary (last name unknown). John died 1692-95. John and Mary had at least one son, John Woody II (b. 1687 in Boston). John II married Mary (last name unknown). They had at least one son, John Woody III (b. 1715 in Boston). John III married Mary Lindley in 1738 in Harford County, MD. John and Mary (Lindley) had five children. In 1742, John

married Mary Gowan. John and Mary (Gowan) had at least five children. John died 1762 in Orange County, NC.

Joseph (b. 1748 in Baltimore County, MD) was the son of John Woody III and Mary Gowan. Joseph married Sarah Thompson in 1769. Sarah Thompson was born 1750 and died 1822 in Orange County, NC. Joseph died there 1815-18. Joseph and Sarah had at least nine children including Robert Woody (b. 1781 in Orange County). Robert married Rachel Rickets in 1802 in Orange County. Robert and Rachel had at least three children including Joseph Woody (b. 1805 in Orange County). Joseph settled in Wayne County, TN prior to 1826. He married Mary "Polly" Cypert in 1827 in Wayne County. Mary (b. 1804 in Wayne County) was the daughter of Frances Cypert II and Abigail Johnson. Joseph was a farmer. He died 1865 in Wayne County. Mary died there in August 1884. Children of Joseph and Mary: John J. Woody (b. 1828); Elizabeth Woody (b. 1830) md. William Stanfield; Rachel Emeline Woody (b. 1832, d. 1895) md. John Cromwell; Joshua Anderson Woody (b. 1834) md. Angeline Stanfield; Comfort Annis Woody (b. 1835, d. 1908) md. Thomas Peyton Stanfield; Infant Woody (b&d. 1837); Mary A. Woody (b. 1838) md. William Ingram; Joseph Josiah S. Woody (b. 1840, d. 1916) md. Mary Ann "Margaret" Ingram and Ivy Woody (b. 1848).

John J. Woody (b. 1828 in Wayne County, TN) was the son of Joseph and Mary. John married Nancy Jane Stanfield in 1851 in Wayne County. Nancy Jane (b. 1835 in Wayne County) was the daughter of James William Stanfield and Elizabeth Helton. John was a farmer. Nancy died 1886 in Wayne County and is buried in Mt. Hebron Cemetery. John died after 1900 while visiting his daughter, Sarah Jane Horton in Van Buren County, AR. He is buried in Zion Hill Cemetery in Van Buren County.

Children of John and Nancy: James Franklin Woody (b. 1852, d. 1929) md. Malissa S. "Rose" Reid, then Mary Minerva Balentine; Joseph W. Woody (b. 1854) md. M.J. Stanfield; Elizabeth Malinda Woody (b. 1856) md. R.M. Reid; Charity M. Woody (b. 1857, d. 1886); Mary "Polly" Ann J. Woody (b. 1859, d. 1894) md. Andrew Nelson Johnson; Sarah Jane Woody (b. 1861, d. 1936) md. John Ellison Horton; John P. Woody (b. 1863, d. 1885); Arena Rachel Woody (b. 1865); Elijah A. Woody (b. 1867, d. 1955) md. Mary White; Thomas J. Woody (b. 1870); Charles Cornelius P. "Neal" Woody (b. 1873, d. 1948) md. Bru Nettie Phillips.

WREN - Robert Laverne Wren was born June 28, 1924 at Muscatine, IA, the son of John Cleveland Wren and Ida Florence Paceley. Robert served in the US Navy, Air Force and Army and served in WWII. He married Elizabeth Annie "Betty" Bush in 1946, at Muscatine, IA. Betty was born Jan. 5, 1927 at Wayland, Henry County, IA, the daughter of Earl Louis Bush and Mary Myrtle Abel.

Robert and Betty divorced about 1954. Betty's parents, Louis and Mary Bush, had moved to Conway County, AR so Betty and the children moved there after her divorce. They lived in Conway County for a few years, then moved to Johnson County. Betty married Willie Ervin Felkins on June 2, 1956. He was a state trooper and was injured in an automobile accident in Missouri not many years after they married. Betty moved her family back to Conway County, AR after the accident, to be near her parents. Betty worked as a nurse for many years. Willie Felkins died Sept. 19, 1963 at Morrilton.

Robert married Mrs. Hazel Logel in 1962 in Missouri. They lived in Muscatine, IA after their marriage. Robert was employed for a number of years at the Alcoa plant at Muscatine, IA. Robert died June 5, 1984 at Muscatine. Hazel died in 1985. Betty (Bush) Wren Felkins died Jan. 10, 2001 in Conway County, AR and is buried in Friendship Cemetery at Solgohachia, AR.

Children of Robert Wren and Elizabeth "Betty"

Bush: Carol Ann Wren (b. 1947, Muscatine, d. 1951, Muscatine, IA); Richard Anthony Wren (b. 1948, Muscatine, IA) never married; Diana Louise Wren (b. 1949, Muscatine, IA) md. Oscar Collins, Bill Hanna and Bobby Flowers. Children: Diana Kay and William Billy" Hanna; Albert L. Wren (b. 1950, Muscatine, IA); Nancy Kay Wren (b. 1951 Henry County, IA) never married; Donald Eugene Wren (b. 1953, Johnson County, IA, d. 1953, Mt. Pleasant, IA)

Albert (b. 1950 in Muscatine, IA), son of Robert and Betty Wren, grew up in Conway County, AR. He enlisted in the US Army in 1967, and after being honorably discharged in 1970, he returned to Morrilton where his mother lived. Albert married Carol Susan Bridgman in 1971 in Conway County, AR. Carol (b. 1951 at Solgohachia) was the daughter of Herbert Bridgman and Maggie Horton.

Albert joined the National Guard in 1973 and re-enlisted in the Army in 1974, making a 20-year-career of the military. He and his family were stationed in Oklahoma (twice), Germany (twice), Maryland and Kentucky. He also served a tour of duty in Korea. Albert retired at Ft. Knox, KY in January 1992 and returned to Conway County, AR. He and Carol bought a home at Plumerville, AR. Albert is currently employed as a truck driver. Carol did clerical work in the military and worked in the South Conway County School District for some years. They have two children:

1) Anthony Wayne Wren (b. 1972) md. Leigh Huie and has a son, Devon. Wayne then married Tammi (Butterball) Gay and has three step-children: Kenneth, Kevin and Kendall Gay.

2) Tonya Marie Wren (b. 1984 in Wegberg, Germany).

WREN - William Thomas Wren (b. 1822) md. Mary Montgomery in 1844. Mary was born 1824 in North Carolina. William and Mary settled in Kentucky, where a child was born in 1845. Mary died before 1849, possibly in childbirth. William and Mary had one child: James Alfred Wren (b. 1845). William moved to Spencer County, IN. 1846-49. He married Allena (Overall) Hamilton on Aug. 9, 1849 in Spencer County. Allena Overall (b. 1822) was the widow of Joseph Hamilton. Joseph and Allena had a daughter, Amanda. William was a farmer. He and Allena had four children: Frances Wren (b. 1850) md. Harvey Pruett; Mary Wren (b. 1854) md. William Burgess; William Thomas Wren Jr. (b. 1856) md. Eliza Householder and Luther Wren (b. 1859).

James Alfred Wren (b. Sept. 27, 1845 in Kentucky) was the son of William Wren and Mary Montgomery. James married Mary Jane Martin on Aug. 21, 1867 in Spencer County. Mary Jane (b. Dec. 24, 1848) was the daughter of John and Elizabeth Martin. Mary Jane's mother married a second time to John Hagens and had three children: Francis, John and Jefferson Hagens. John Hagens had a son, William Hagens, from a previous marriage. Mary Jane had a brother, Thomas Martin. James farmed in Spencer County until about 1885, when the family moved to New Madrid County, MO.

Prior to 1907, they moved to Muscatine, IA. James worked as a cutter in a button factory in Muscatine. He died there June 26, 1919. Mary Jane died there Aug. 4, 1926. Children of James and Mary Jane were: David Wren (b. 1874, d. before 1890); Mary Elizabeth Wren (b. Aug 18, 1877, d. Jan 31, 1944) md. Ulysses Grant Cooley; Samuel Wren (b. 1880, died young); John Cleveland Wren (b. 1885); Sarah Ann Wren (b. March 1, 1888, d. Sept. 12, 1980) md. Edward W. Wagler; Joseph Christopher Wren (b. Feb. 26, 1891, d. May 13, 1946) md. Amy Townsend and James Wren (died as infant).

John Cleveland Wren (b. Feb. 8, 1885 at New Madrid, MO) was the son of James and Mary Jane. John married Emma Rapp on March 27, 1907. Emma (b. April 5, 1888 in Kansas) was the daughter of Paul Rapp and Katrina Kempf. John and Emma lived in

Muscatine where John worked for the Pearl Button Factory as a button cutter. John and Emma had four children. Emma died Nov. 1, 1916 at Muscatine.

John married Ida Florence Paceley on May 22, 1919. Ida (b. April 4, 1895 in Iowa) was the daughter of Horace Edward Paceley and Elizabeth Jane Cline. John and Ida had three children. John died March 8, 1969, at Muscatine. Ida died there on April 20, 1972.

Children of John and Emma: Beulah Jane Wren (b. Jan. 3, 1909, d. March 27, 1909); William Thomas Wren (b. 1910) md. Ruth Maria Newlen; John Louis Wren (b. Aug. 8, 1912, d. July 10, 1930) died after being bitten by a rabid fox) and Ellen Pauline Wren (b. Aug 8, 1915, d. Feb. 15, 1917).

Children of John and Ida:) Pearl Ida Wren (b. 1922, d. April 4, 1962) md. Howard Montgomery; Robert Laverne Wren (b. June 28, 1924, d. June 5, 1984) md. first, Elizabeth Annie "Betty" Bush, daughter of Earl Louis Bush and Mary Myrtle Abel, then second, Hazel Logel; Kenneth Gene Wren.

YARBROUGH – Sarah Carroll was born in 1839 in Georgia, according to the 1880 census. She married Thomas Yarbrough in Alabama in 1856. He was the son of Franklin and Elizabeth Foster Yarbrough. Sarah and Thomas had four sons: William Franklin (b. 1858); James Sidney (b. 1860); John B. (b. 1862) and Thomas Lee (b. 1864).

In 1860, Thomas and Sarah were living in Chambers County, AL with two sons, William and Sidney. They were living next door to Thomas' parents and his 12 siblings. Also living in this household was John Carroll.

Thomas died Jan. 30, 1864 during the Civil War. He was a private in the Confederate Army, Company K, 60th Regiment, Alabama Volunteers.

Sarah moved to Arkansas with her boys and was living at Tulip in Dallas County, AR in 1870. Also living with them was Evaline Carroll, age 53.

Sarah married her second husband, D.M. Allen, on Dec. 27, 1877 in Ada Valley, Conway County, AR. In the 1880 census in Higgins Township, Conway County, AR, Sarah was listed as being in bad health. Their children were Willie, age 7, and Martha (b. May 1880).

Sarah and Drury Allen had two more children; Charles Carroll (b. Aug. 6, 1881) and Walter C. (b. June 9, 1883). Sarah Carroll Yarbrough Allen was a member of the Baptist Church. She died in 1886 in Conway County, AR and is buried in Barnes Cemetery, Ada Valley, AR. Her youngest Yarbrough son, Thomas Lee Yarbrough, lived in Ada Valley until his death in 1945.

Thomas Lee married Francis Sharp (b. 1866, d. 1933). To this union was born John (b. February 1885); Carroll (b. November 1887); Alta, (b. August 1889); Ethel (b. May 1892); Herman (b. December 1893); Bill (b. November 1896); Charlie (b. November 1900); Garland (b. 1909). They also raised their grandson, Clay Yarbrough. Most of the Yarbroughs in Conway County are descendants of Thomas Lee Yarbrough and his children.

This information is from research files of Thelma Yarbrough Fletcher and Walter Allen family. Written by Irene Yarbrough Young

YOUNG – Augustus Layton "Gus" Young was born March 18, 1883 in Old Powell, near Pyatt, Marion County, AR. He was the son of George Washington Young (b. 1847, Arkansas, d. 1921, Arkansas) and Nancy Caroline Lancaster (b. 1854, Tennessee, d. 1955, Arkansas). He married Alma McDowell Dodd (b. 1890, Arkansas, d. 1941, Arkansas) on Feb. 26, 1907 in Bellefonte, Boone County, AR, the daughter of David Henry Neal Dodd and Hattie LaRue McDowell. They had one son, George Henry "G.H." who was born June 3, 1908 in Dodd City, Marion County, AR. In 195?, Mr. Young married second, Mrs. Lola (Hogan) Matthews (b. 1894, d. 1983) of Morrilton.

Mr. Young had an insurance business, was in-

volved in mining and farming in Yellville, Marion County, AR, before moving to Morrilton in 1925, when he and M.H. Pierce organized the Pierce-Young Lumber Company, which continued until 1945. They bought land and timber rights in many parts of Central Arkansas for the timber to be used at the Lumber Company. Mr. Young was also a farmer in Conway County in the Point Remove Bottoms area, as well as in Marion County. He raised cattle, maintained forest land and was involved in the Young Store located at Pyatt.

In 1937 Gus and Alma built their home on South East Street just down from the Methodist Church. Mr. Young personally picked all the wood that was used in the home.

In 1939, they took a trip west, taking their grandson, David Layton Young, which included Pikes Peak, CO; Salt Lake City, UT; Boise, ID, where they visited with Dodd relatives; Vancouver, British Columbia; San Francisco, CA; Los Angeles, CA; Hoover Dam outside Las Vegas, NV; The Petrified Forest in Arizona; Albuquerque, NM, and back to Morrilton.

Alma and Gus were members of the First Methodist Church in Morrilton and Alma was very active in the Women's Society and enjoyed playing bridge. Gus enjoyed the outdoors, including fishing and hunting. He was a Mason. Alma died in Yellville, of a heart attack while visiting relatives on April 9, 1941. Mr. Young died Dec. 12, 1958, also from a heart attack, which he suffered at his home. They are both buried in Elmwood Cemetery. *Submitted by C.Y. Moulton.*

YOUNG - G.H. (George Henry) Young was born June 3, 1908 at Dodd City, Marion County, AR, the son of Gus (Augustus Layton) Young (b. 1883, d. 1958) and Alma McDowell (Dodd) Young (b. 1890, d. 1941). He married Margaret Catharine Lay (b. Aug. 1, 1911, d. July 5, 1961) on Nov. 4, 1930 in Cleburne County, AR. Margaret was the daughter of Horace B. Lay (b. 1879, Arkansas, d. 1919, Arkansas) and Lula Maud Claunch (b. 1878, Arkansas, d. 1963, Arkansas). She was attending Gallaway College when they married. They had two children, David Layton Young (b. Oct. 28, 1932, d. Dec. 8, 1963) and Margaret "Catherine" Young Hale Manasco Moulton, the submitter of this sketch. G.H. married a second time in 1962 to Mrs. Lena Nowlin. No issue from the second marriage.

G.H. Young attended College of the Ozarks in Clarksville and Draughan's School of Business in Little Rock. He was involved with heavy equipment for several years, building levees in eastern Arkansas, as well as water and sewer work in Forrest City and Stuttgart. In 1952, he moved from Morrilton to Boydell, Ashley County, AR to run a plantation he bought from his father-in-law, Mr. A.J. Nesbitt, after Mr. Nesbitt had a stroke. G.H. began by preparing the acreage for the planting of rice rather than cotton, which had been the staple of the area. This consisted of building ditches, putting in pulps and constructing ponds or water holding areas.

After establishing the rice production, G.H. moved back to Morrilton and started a wholesale distributing company by the name of Warehouse Distributing Company. He was a "middle" man for grocery items, vending machines, canned goods, candy and cigarettes. During this time he also had farm land in the Blackwell area, plus the acreage he had inherited from his father, Gus Young in northern Arkansas.

G.H. retired in 1963 to the Hot Springs area where he lived on Lake Hamilton. In 1966 he built a home in the Dodd City, Marion County, AR, where he cleared inherited land for cattle (from his father and grandfather) and moved back to his roots, Marion County, AR. He raised Black Angus cattle and pasture lands.

He was a 32 degree Mason, enjoyed fishing, hunting of all kinds, good food, and old friends. He was a Methodist and was instrumental in the construction of the organ of the First Methodist Church in Morrilton in memory of his wife, Margaret Catharine (Lay) and his mother, Alma McDowell (Dodd) Young.

G.H. died in his home in Marion County, AR on Aug. 1, 1976 of a heart attack. He is buried in Elmwood Cemetery, beside his first wife, Margaret (Lay) Young. *Submitted by Catherine Y. Moulton*

YOUNG - My great-great-great-grandfather, Isaac R. Young, was born in South Carolina in 1808. Sometime between 1808-34, Isaac had moved to Tennessee. His wife, Emiline(?) was born in Tennessee in 1813. Isaac and Emiline were married around 1834 in Tennessee and had two children, Abram and Isaac Jr. (my great-great-great-grandfather).

Isaac, Emiline and the two boys moved to Tishomingo County, MS, around 1840. Five more children were added to the family after moving there - Ellen, Mary, George, James and Susan, making a total of seven children.

Isaac R. Young Jr., his wife Caroline, youngest daughter Liddia and grandson Eddie Young, Winchester's only son in about 1902.

My great-great-grandfather, Isaac R. Young Jr., was born in Tennessee in 1837. On April 21, 1859, Isaac Jr. married Caroline Hutchins. Caroline was born in Georgia in 1840. It is said she came from a well-to-do plantation-type family. While living in Mississippi, Isaac Jr. served in Co. B 26th Mississippi Regiment during the Civil War.

Isaac and Caroline were blessed with six children, all born while living in Mississippi: Silvester, Winchester, Hester, Mary Hattie, and Liddia.

Sometime in 1878, Isaac came alone to Conway County. It has been told to me he homesteaded land there and built a one-room log cabin with no floor, as part of the agreement for homestead.

In late 1878 or early 1879, he returned to Mississippi, loaded his family and belongings in a wagon and moved them to Ada Valley. Upon arriving at the cabin, it is said Caroline refused to live in that one-room cabin with the dirt floor. She also refused to budge from the wagon. After promising her he would add a room and a floor, she reluctantly gave in.

Silvester Young, his wife Sarah, and children: from left, Elbert (my grandfather), Nan, Mary, Sennie, Ike, in Sarah's lap is Jeff and in Silvester's lap is adopted child Connie - about 1906.

My great-grandfather, Silvester Young, was born Nov. 27, 1864, in Tishomingo County, MS. Silvester moved to Ada Valley in Conway County some time in late 1878 or early 1879, along with his father, mother, and four sisters. He was 13 years old at the time.

In 1888 or 1889, Silvester married Sarah Higgins. Sarah was born March 24, 1867, in (?) Arkansas. I put a question mark because the only document I have seen shows her being born in Arkansas, but does not say where in Arkansas. However, the Higgins were a prominent family in early Ada Valley history having the township named after them. Also there is a Higgins Cemetery located in Ada.

Tom and Ann Higgins, Sarah "Higgins" Young (my great-grandmother) is sitting in her father's lap. Her twin brothers, Mike and Tommy are to the left and right. I don't know her two sisters' names - about 1873.

Silvester and Sarah were blessed with six children: Sennie, Nan, Ike, Mary, Elbert and Jeff. They also raised an adopted child, Connie.

For a brief two-year period, I was told, they moved to Texas. However, Silvester and Sarah lived almost their entire married life in Ada Valley. Silvester died in 1937 at the age of 72. Sarah died in 1953 at the age of 86. I was 7 years old at the time and can remember her well.

Elbert Silvester Young, my grandfather, was born in Ada Valley, Conway County, on Aug. 19, 1897. Elbert married Jewell Vim Roberts, who was born in Oklahoma on April 9, 1903. Elbert and Vim bought land from his dad and mom, Silvester and Sarah, and built a house there. Cleo Young's house now sits in the exact spot as the old house.

Elbert and Vim had five children: Vertie Elmo, Pauline, Othell, Fred Vernon and Cleo. They lived at the old home place from 1918-41. They built a new house on property about 200 yards west of the old home place. That is where they finished raising their children and lived out their lives. Elbert passed away May 24, 1973, at the age of 75. Vim passed March 30, 1997, just 10 days short of her 94th birthday.

Elbert Silvester and Jewell Vim Young in front of their homeplace around 1946.

Young family from left: Othell, Pauline, Elmo (my dad), Vernon, Jewell Vim, Cleo, Elbert Silvester, in front of the old house place - January 1972.

Vertie Elmo Young, my father, was born July 10, 1920, in Ada Valley. On Nov. 22, 1941, he married Lola Marie Rankin. Marie, my mother, was born Nov. 13, 1924, in Antlers, OK. I don't know what year the Rankin family moved back to the valley, but at the time my father and mother were dating, they lived on the Will Warren property, the place was just north over the hill from where Tommy Warren now lives.

Elmo Young, Roger Young and Marie Young holding Bobby Young about August 1944.

My brother, Bobby Young, was born in Ada Valley on Sept. 7, 1942. My parents and my brother moved to Morrilton while my father was serving in the military during WWII. I was born March 7, 1944, while my parents were living on Childress Street in Morrilton. Fortunately, my father was granted a furlough so he could be with his family during my birth. Sometime in late 1944, Dad was sent to the Philippines to serve in the war against Japan.

In 1946, we moved into the house my dad, his brothers and other friends and relatives helped to build. In 1960, we moved to Oppelo. The house my dad built in Ada Valley is still standing and is owned by Augie Warren and his family.

My son Ronnie Young and his family live in the house at Oppelo that my dad, brother and I built.

On Jan. 23, 1965, I married Shirlene Scroggin, a twin, of Cleveland. We built a house next to Lakeview Landing on Lake Overcup. We moved into the house in January 1970. After 33 years we still live there. We have two children, Ronnie and Sheila, and three grandchildren: Lance, Grant and Garrett. I am very happy to say my children and their families all live in Conway County.

There are many, many more Youngs I have not mentioned. For instance, Isaac, my great-great-grandfather, had a brother, George W. Young, who moved here from Mississippi. He lived on the Conway-Perry County line. His offspring live in the Oppelo and Adona areas.

My grandfather, Elbert Young, had two brothers, Ike and Jeff, who married and raised their families in Ada Valley. Aunt Pauline, Uncle Othell and Uncle Cleo all raised their families in Ada Valley. But since I am writing the story, I get to run my line.

I may no longer live in Ada Valley, but I go there often. I haven't lived there in 43 years but a very large chunk of my heart says Ada Valley is still my home and always will be. *Submitted by Roger Young.*

ZACHARY - George Washington Zachary Jr. was born Feb. 22, 1884 in Dover, Pope County, AR. His first marriage was to Nettie Treadaway on July 8, 1906 in Conway County, AR. George and Nettie were the parents of two children, William Carl Zachary and Terry Elizabeth Zachary Howard Hampton. Nettie was born on Feb. 18, 1889 and died on Aug. 23, 1912 from complications during pregnancy. She is buried in Old Hickory Cemetery, Conway County, AR.

George and Janie (Hasler) Zachary

William Carl Zachary married Marie Crowder and they had no children. They divorced and he married Lillian Dye Pope. William Carl and Lillian had no children.

Lillian had one son from a previous marriage. Terry Elizabeth Zachary married first to a Howard, they divorced and she married Nelson Hampton. Their children are Kenny Hampton and Steve Hampton.

George Washington Zachary's second marriage was to Mary Jane Hasler in Vinson Chapel, Conway County, AR on Jan. 31, 1915. Mary Jane, daughter of Joseph A. and Mary Ann (Hooker) Hasler, was born on March 29, 1894 in Vinson Chapel, Conway County, AR. Mary Jane and George Zachary's children are Lois May, William Virgil, Rose Mildred, Mary Helen, Eugene Luther, Leo, Cleo, John Quitman and Jimmy Doyle Sr.

George Washington Zachary Jr. died Feb. 14, 1977 in Morrilton, Conway County, AR. Mary Jane Hasler Zachary died May 3, 1984 in Conway, Faulkner County, AR. George and Janie are buried in Elmwood Cemetery, Morrilton, Conway County, AR.

Lois married Johnny Edward Nicholson and their children are Vonnie Sue Nicholson Shipp, Charles H. Nicholson, Emily Dean Nicholson Smith, Terry Maxine Nicholson Lowder, Ruby Marcelle Nicholson Shier, Larry Edward Nicholson, Wendell Harold Nicholson, Dwight Andrew Nicholson, Anthony Lynn Nicholson and one infant who died at birth.

William Virgil Zachary married Bobbie Lou Wright and their children are Terry Lou Zachary DeLong Smith and Richard Wayne Zachary.

Rose Mildred Zachary married William Archie Chism and their children are Betty Ruth Chism, Howard Lee Chism, Kenneth Edward Chism Sr., Billy George Chism and Carl Eugene Chism.

Mary Helen Zachary married Chris Nicholson and they had one child: Shirley Nicholson Atkinson Powers. Mary Helen and Chris divorced and she married Oliver Anderson. Their children are Karen Anderson Graham, Gary Anderson, Pam Anderson Lawson, Sandra Anderson Wooten and Michelle Anderson Johnson.

Eugene Luther Zachary married Mildred Landry and their children are Roscoe Zachary and Jeanetta Susan Zachary Vaivin.

Leo Zachary married Kathleen Carr and their children are Robert Lee Zachary, Linda Joyce Zachary Jones and Steven Brian Zachary.

Cleo Zachary married first to Norma Jean Hester and their children are Wilma Jean Zachary Winn, Cleo Eugene Zachary and Robert George Zachary. Cleo and Jean divorced and he married Carolyn Sue Ward. Cleo and Carolyn's children are Lynn Zachary, Melanie Zachary Jones, Greg Zachary, Mike Zachary and Ca'Lyn Zachary.

John Quitman Zachary married Bobbie Ann Mourot and their children are: Debbie Zachary Longinotti Slepicka, John Alan Zachary, Sharon Zachary Hill, Mark Anthony Hill, Mary Jo Zachary and Timmy Clark Zachary.

Jimmy Doyle Zachary married Maxine Hubbard and their children are Jimmy Doyle Zachary Jr. and Scott Zachary. *Submitted by Rosemary Chism Norwood.*

ZACHARY - Rose Mildred Zachary was born in Vinson Chapel, Conway County, AR, the daughter of George Washington Zachary Jr. and Mary Jane Hasler Zachary. Rose married William Archie Chism on Feb. 2, 1937 in Conway County, AR. William, son of John Pleasant "Doc" and Maggie Lou (Conley) Chism, was born Dec. 31, 1910 in Lanty, Conway County, AR. He died Oct. 5, 1974 in Morrilton, Conway County, AR and is buried in Vinson Chapel Cemetery. Rose and William are the parents of five children.

William and Rose Chism

Their first child, Betty Ruth Chism was born in Vinson Chapel, Conway County, AR. Betty lives with her mother in Vinson Chapel and never married.

Howard Lee Chism was born in Vinson Chapel, Conway County, AR. He served as corporal in the US Marine Corps in Thailand and the Philippines until he was honorably discharged in 1962. He married Cheryl Ann Helton on Feb. 14, 1964 in Morrilton Conway County, AR. Cheryl is the daughter of Joe and Gertie (Underhill) Helton. Howard and Cheryl are the parents of two girls: Valerie Diane Chism and Michelle Lee Chism.

Kenneth Edward Chism Sr. was born in Vinson Chapel, Conway County, AR. He married Mary Joyce Freeman on May 27, 1961 in Morrilton, Conway County, AR. Mary Joyce is the daughter of Arden William and Mary Eathel (Campbell) Freeman. Kenneth and Mary are the parents of four children: Tammie Joyce Chism Shipp, Rosemary Chism Norwood, Kenneth Edward "Kenny" Chism Jr. and William Alan Chism.

Kenneth Edward Chism Sr. was killed in a truck accident on his way home from work on March 31, 1985 in St. Vincent, Conway County, AR. He is buried in Liberty Springs Cemetery in Van Buren County, AR.

Billy George Chism was born in Morrilton Conway County, AR. He served in the US Army in Korea and was honorably discharged in 1969. Upon his return home, he married Margaret Ann Norwood on Nov. 27, 1969 in Morrilton, Conway County, AR. Ann is the daughter of Virgil and Opal (Mansfield) Norwood. Bill and Ann are the parents of three children: Michael Clint Chism, Crystal Jane Chism Gullett and Billy Lance Chism.

The last child to be born to Rose and William is Carl Eugene Chism. He was born in Morrilton, Conway Count, AR. Carl served in the US Marine Corps during the Vietnamese War and was honorably discharged in 1972. He married Deborah "Debbie" Eugenia Caudell on Jan. 26, 1973 in Morrilton, Conway County. Debbie is the daughter of Elmer Caudell and Sherry (Rainbolt) Caudell. Carl and Debbie are the parents of three children: Robert William "Bobby" Caudell, Deborah Chism and Zachary Todd Chism. *Submitted by Nicholas O'Neal Norwood.*

ZARLINGO - Alexander (Alessandro) "Sandy" Zarlingo (original spelling Zarlenga) was born Nov. 1, 1858, (circa) in Italy. Alexander was the brother of Maria Zarlingo. Maria married Domenic "Tom" Lanni, brother of Nicholas Lanni, on Sept. 29, 1892. Alexander Zarlingo married Michelina D'Alusio, born in Italy on March 20, 1858. They had five children: Maria (b. Sept. 20, 1889), Anthony (b. June 1, 1891), Bibiana (b. Feb. 16, 1893), James (b. ca. Oct. 18, 1894) and Annuciata "Lenzy" (b. Feb. 14, 1897). Michelina D'Alusio Zarlingo died on Feb. 24, 1900 and buried at St. Joseph Cemetery, Center Ridge, AR.

Maria Zarlingo married Angelo Paladino (b. Feb. 4, 1909), the son of Frank and Lena Paladino.

Anthony Zarlingo (d. Feb. 8, 1892) and Bibiana Zarlingo;s date is presently unknown.

The Alexander Zarlingo family.

James "Jim" Zarlingo married Lucy Lanni (b. May 14, 1906), the daughter of Matt Lanni and Elizabeth Fabrizio Lanni. They had one daughter, Mary Elizabeth (b. Oct. 30, 1922).

Annuciata "Lenzy" married Lewis DeSalvo (b. Feb. 14, 1897), the son of Luke and Beatrice DeSalvo.

After the death of Alexander's first wife Michelina, Alexander Zarlingo married Jessiminia (Gelsomina) "Minnie" Fabrizio on Dec. 9, 1900. Minnie Fabrizio, first cousin of Elizabeth Fabrizio Lanni, was born in Italy on Nov. 18, 1869 (circa). Alexander and Minnie Zarlingo had one son, Liberantonio "Tony" Zarlingo (b. Sept. 20, 1901). Tony died Jan. 1, 1942 and is buried at St. Joseph Cemetery, Center Ridge, AR.

Records indicate that Alexander Zarlingo purchased land in Center Ridge, AR around the 1880s. In 1924, Alexander donated land to build a new church that was needed in Center Ridge, Catholic Point, because of the growing population. The new red brick church was named in honor of St. Joseph.

Alexander Zarlingo died Sept. 17, 1928 and Jessimina Zarlingo died Oct. 15, 1941. They were buried at St. Joseph Cemetery, Center Ridge, AR. *Submitted by Sharon L. Paladino.*

ZIMMEREBNER - The unity in marriage of three early Conway County families developed a large legacy of descendants and countless future generations. Louise Stoll of Germany boarded the ship *Atalanta* with her parents, Anton and Euphrosina Hund Stoll, in 1865. Euphrosina, age 21, died during the voyage to America and was buried at sea. Louise married Frank Mundus (who had emigrated from Pekelsheim, Germany in 1875) at St. Vincent in 1880. Frank and Louise had 11 children: Mary Louise, Antonio, John, Joseph (md. Bertha Jokish), Martin, Henry, William (md. Frieda Zeiter), Leo (md. Anna Burkalhen, then Francis Grossnickle), Ben (md. Rose Burnett), Michael and Emma.

Michael Marcus Zimmerebner was born May 25, 1872 in Grossarl, Austria to Martin and Maria Rohrmoser Zimmerebner. His older siblings were also born in Austria, but the younger were born in America after the family immigrated in 1883. They settled in the St. Vincent Community, where Martin farmed the land. Mike's brothers and sisters were Elizabeth, Martin (md. Angeline Gotsponer), Robert, Margaret (md. William Rachaner), Mary Magdalen (md. Simon Zeiter), Annie Otilia (md. Joseph Beck), Rose, and Emma (md. Frank Beck).

Michael and Mary Mundus Zimmerebner.

Mike Zimmerebner married Mary Louise Mundus, the eldest child of Frank and Louise, on Jan. 8, 1900. Mike remained at St. Vincent, where he farmed in the area now known as Ranger Road and also was a member of the early community band. Mike and Mary Zimmerebner had the following children: Elizabeth, Paul (md. Josephine Schneider), Cecilia (md. William Hegeman), Benard (md. Hildagard Beck), Ida (md. William Boehmer), Josephine (md. Pete Mergenschroer), Margaret (md. Pete's brother Joe Mergenschroer), Gus (md. Ella Elliot), Emma (md. Ed Lenggenhager), Martin, Mike (md. Nell Canton) and Frank (md. Nell Carlton after his brother Mike's death. Mike, Mary Louise, his parents, her father and grandfather, and many of their family are buried at St. Vincent Cemetery.

Most of the Mike Zimmerebner family moved to Little Rock where summer reunions and Christmas parties were held annually at the home of Ed and Emma Lenggenhager. Mike's eldest daughter Cecilia moved to Conway after marrying William Hegeman of nearby Atkins. They operated a grocery business at several downtown Conway locations for many years.

Their eldest daughter is Lucille, who married Clarence Schierlang, with three sons: David, Fred and John, and two daughters who died in infancy, Patricia and Mary. John and his wife Lorie have three children: Tiffany, Patrick, Chris, and two grandsons. Other children of Will and Cecilia Hegeman are Margaret, who married Glenn Davis, with four children and seven grandchildren; Theresa, who married Herb Nahlen, with three children, and two grandchildren; Bill, who married Martha Imboden, with two children, and three grandchildren; and Louis, who married Elizabeth Barton, with two children and one grandson.

A family reunion in 2003 brought together 100 members of this family that formed its roots, whether through fate or mere chance, in St. Vincent. *Submitted by John Schierlang.*

157; Vonnie, 93; Walter Garland, 61; William, 61; William E., 94; William G., 62; William T., 61; William Vardman, 93
Benscoter, Jenny Maria, 122
Benson, Brenda Dixon, 95; Franklin, 95
Bentley, Dorothy Dennise, 141; Eli, 62; Mae, 89; Mae/May, 62; Mary Jane, 62; Oliver Tolls, 62
Beny, Mary Ann, 119
Berg, Teri, 124
Berger, Dora Letty Nix, 166; Henry, 166; Sarah, 110, 111; Sarah E., 110; William J., 166
Bergis, Cynthia Bradshaw, 66; John B., 66
Bergren, Sharon Lee, 154
Berkemeyer, Ben, 212; Ben, Jr., 212; Charlie, 212; Dorothy, 123; Elizabeth Weber, 212; Francis, 212; Henry, 212; Joseph, 212; Marie, 212
Bernhard, William A., 19
Bernstine, Doris, 50
Berry, Aphra LaVelle, 120; Cally, 62; Charles, 87; Deanna Conley, 87; Edmund, 62; Edmund G., 62; Elizabeth Janice, 87; Ella, 152; Elmira Jane Cypert, 62; Frances, 62; Frances Wayne Hensley, 62; George, 212; H.H., 8; James, 212; James Ellison, 62; John, 212; John D., 62; John Wyatt, 62; Johnnie Keith, 62; Joseph George, 62; Lucinda King, 62; Luke, 15; Mary, 129; Mary Margaret, 62, 124, 125, 212; Mary Martin, 62; Mary Sawyer, 61; Mildred, 60; Myrtle Hawkins, 120; Nancy, 212; Nancy Emaline, 62; Nancy Margaret Newman, 62; Orville Benjamin, 62; Patsy, 62; Polly, 62; Rebecca, 62, 212; Sarah Ann, 212; Sarah Ann Elizabeth, 62; Sarah Matilda, 167; Sarah Weatherford, 62, 125, 212; Susannah, 62; Susannah Taylor, 62; Susie Mae Chote, 62; Syble Wyoma, 120; Taft, 64; Taliaferro, 62; Taliaferro L., 62; Walter, 120; William, 62, 125, 212; William Alderson, 62
Beschorner, Agnes, 62; Andrew, 62; August, 62; Eleanor, 62, 86; Elizabeth, 62, 63, 86; Magdalena Comes, 62, 86; Margaret, 62, 63, 86; Mary Thome, 62; Paul, 62, 86; William, 62, 86
Best, T.R., 27
Beth, Sonny Elliott, 45
Betner, Carolyn, 132
Bettis, Charles, 37
Betts, Patricia, 186
Bevart, 60
Beverage, Ada, 104
Bevers, 60
Bevert, 60
Bice, Martha Bradshaw, 66
Bigelow, Gracie, 131; Jackson, 131; Joe Ann, 131
Biggers, Bessie, 105
Biggs, Hugh M., 37
Bill, J.R., 8
Billings, Addie, 103
Bingham, Alexander, 63; Bonnie Lee, 63; Brittiany Marie, 63; Edith Hopkins, 63; Edith Loretta, 63; Edwin Leon, 63; Gertrue, 110; Guy Lawson, 63; Laura Ann, 63; Margie Luellen Lawson, 63; Margie Lynn Stone, 63; Megan Renee, 63; Patty Relli, 63; Robert Dominic, 63; Robert Lee, 63; Roberta, 53, 175; Roberta Luellen, 63; Tami Ferguson Miller, 63
Birch, Daniel P., 165; Gladys, 165; Minnie Mabey, 165; Robert, 15
Birchfield, Mary Ann Catherine Hansard, 182
Bird, Amelia, 64, 105; Amelia Dunn, 63, 64; Anita Robin, 60; Arthur Othonel, 64; Barbara, 166; Daniel G., 64; Dewey Gordon, 107; Dorthy, 147; Edther, 107; Elbert Samuel, 107; Elizabeth, 63; Elizabeth E., 64; Emma, 63; Fay M., 107; Huett Franklin, 107; Imogene Gladys, 107; Jacob H., 64; Jacob, Jr., 63, 64; Jacob, Sr., 63, 64; James Jacob, 64; James Madison, 64; James Martin, 64; James Michael, 213; James W., 63, 107; Jane, 64; Jerry Wayne, 60; John, 47, 63, 64, 105; John A., 64; Josie, 64; Juanita Faye Beavers, 60; Kevin Robert, 60; Lena, 109; Leretta R., 145; Luretta, 63; Luther H., 63; Mary, 64, 105; Mary C., 63, 64; Matin, 64; Mattie, 63; Melissa Renee, 60; Nancy Brickey, 63, 64; Nettie, 64; Ralph Dale, 107; Richard Othnice, 64; Robert L., 107; Robert Thelton, 60; Robin Arlene Edwards, 213; Rosa Narsis Gordon, 107; Roy Lane, 107; Ruth, 107; Samuel Porter, 107; Susan, 64; Susan Alice, 63, 107, 108; Susan F., 63, 107; Talitha, 64; Terrell Allen, 213; Terry Alan, 60; William, 63; William Buford, 64
Birdwell, Dave, 157; Maude Laycook Ross, 157
Bishop, Addie, 64; Allen Dalton, 64; Artymace Helena Vanhook, 64; Bertha Huie, 64; Bertha P. Huie, 64; Betty Eoff, 64; Carmie, 64; Catherine Mae, 64; Cyril Clyde, 64; Emmer Eveline, 64; Farrie, 64; Florabel Douglas, 64; Frank, 64; Gladys, 64; Hazel Goldie Flora New, 64; Iris, 64; James Elmer, 64; John, 64; Johnathan, 64; Juanita Chism, 81; Kittie Bell, 64; Lawrence Wilburn, 64; Lela May Andrus, 64; Lena, 64; Lena P., 113; Leta Faye Fitzgerald, 64; Lillian Stobaugh, 64; Lois, 64; Lola, 64; Mary Elizabeth Carolina, 59; Mary Iola Harmon, 64; Mary Susan Carolina Allen, 64; Nobie Lee, 64; Norene, 64; Opal, 64; Robert Earl, 64; Rubye Ernest McCasland, 64; Sarah Price, 64; Sarah Quinn, 64; Sybil, 64; Thomas, 64; Thomas L., 64; Tolbert Francis, 64; Tolbert Francis, Jr., 64; Violet, 64; William Daniel, 64; William Perry, 64; Wilma Inez, 64; Winnie, 64
Bissett, Maxine, 21
Bissop, Mary Susan Carolina Allen, 64
Biswell, Evelyn Louise, 204
Bizell, Edith, 20
Bizzell, Mary Alice, 80, 83
Black, Annie Mae, 205; Catherine, 39; David, 42; Freda, 167; Harold, 9; Helen Mahan, 202; James Pope, 205; Leona Johnston, 148; Lizzie Baskin, 58; Mamie Hyler, 205; Margaret, 130; Marshall, 71; Mary Evaline, 112; Mary Hall, 164; Mrs. D.T., 39; Myrtle, 205; Robert, 202; William, 9
Blackfox, Sarah, 143
Blackmon, Alice Jackson, 65; Amelia, 64; Annie, 64; Arbie, 64; Ben, 64; Benjamin, 64; Benjamin, II, 64; Bertha Jefferson, 64; Beulah, 64; Booker C., 64; Daniel, 64; David, 64; Dessie, 64; Edgar, 64; Edward Stokes, 64; Ella, 64; Elliott, 64; Emma Brown, 64; Ethel, 64; George, 64; George Washington, 64; George Washington, Jr., 64; Georgia Ann, 64; Girtha, 64; Hattie, 64, 65; Huey, 64; Jane, 64; Jeremiah, 64; Jessie Lee, 64; John, 64; John Henry, 65; Lamond, 64; Liza, 64; Lula Mae, 64; Matilda, 65; Matilda Mitchem, 64, 65; Mattie, 64; Maxine Elizabeth, 64; Melie Pauline, 64; Mildred Vera Catherine Webb, 64; Minnie, 64; Obadiah, 64; Paul Lawrence, 64; Rena, 64; Robert, 64; Ruby, 64; Virgie, 64; Wayne Apollis, 64; Willie, 64
Blackshear, Horace, 107; Susan Gordon, 107
Blackstock, Christy, 66; Kathryn Lee Bradley, 66
Blackwell, Arbie Blackmon, 64
Blagg, Sherri Venice, 132
Blair, Margaret R., 55; Mary Reynolds, 55; Samuel, 55
Blake, Amanda Driver, 131; Claudie Marie, 131; Eunice Wilma Mills, 103; Leonard Lee, 131; Leonard M., 131; Mary Edith Ingram, 131; Norman, 131; R.D., 131; Ripley D., 131; Zela Mills, 103
Blakeney, Annie Laura Moose, 162; J.O., 162
Blakey, Debra Renee Montgomery, 160; Don, 160
Blanch, Beatrice, 49
Bland, Annabelle, 149; Barry, 149; Betty, 46; Leanne Ridgely, 149; Pamela, 151; Samantha, 149; Wilmer, 9
Blankenship, Annie, 57; Artency, 57; Elizabeth Keeton, 57; Flarra Bell, 57; Jimmy, 57; Joe Cephas, 57; Josepheus C., 159; Kizzie Chism, 57; Manda, 201; Mary Louvenia, 103, 122; Missouri Jewell, 159; Ruby Dillard Zackery, 159; Ruby Zachary Hanna, 57; William, 8, 57
Blankinship, Mary Luevenia, 222
Blansett, Cheryl Ann Deaton, 91; Jonathan Andrew, 91; Joshua Deaton, 91; Luke Allan, 91; Ralph Andrew, 91
Blaylock, Alia Hesson, 195; Martha Garrison, 195
Blevins, Brigitte Theresa, 167; Maxine Ellis, 167; Travis, 167
Bliss, Elizabeth Jane Gace, 135; Jane, 77, 135
Blount, Nancy Jane, 87; R.J., 8
Blue, Joe H., 30
Blunt, Reuben, 8
Bodkin, Mary, 159
Boehmer, Ida Zimmerebner, 226; William, 226
Bogan, Jorene, 108
Boger, Anna Magdalene Wampler, 210; Mathias, 210
Boggess, Charles, 181; Isabel, 181
Boggs, June Chism, 81
Bogle, Martha Wilcher, 213; Taylor, 213
Bohannon, Seavia Ellen, 95
Boland, James, 218; Sarah Winifred Williams, 218
Bolton, Allison Lance, 146; Benny Hugh, 120; Benny J., 120; Cornelia E., 146, 147; Emma Dale, 120; J.D., 120; Jane Steele, 146; Ruby Lela Hawkins, 120; Zonoma, 120
Bonagofski, Vicki, 60
Bond, Bertha Martin, 149; Charles, 149; Dorsey Catlett, 188; Hestlee Martin, 149; Marion, 149
Bonds, Mrs. Travis, 42
Bone, James T., 123; Mary Ann B. Hess, 123
Booher, Scott, 142; Tonya Lannie, 142
Booker, James W., 78; Mary Eliza Chambers, 78
Bookout, Cora Juanita, 131; Garland Franklin, 131; Gordon Logan, 131; Greta Elnora, 131; Janetta Lee, 131; Melinda Eveline Ingram, 130, 131; Paul Samuel, 131; Rhoda Lilly Myers, 131; Robert E. Lee, 131; Samuel Lee, 131; William Logan, 131; William Richard, 131
Boone, Christine Alison, 96; Daniel William, III, 132; Daniel William, Jr., 132; Kimberly Anne, 132; Myrtle Lee, 164; Susan Diane Jackson, 132; Sylvon, 84
Booth, Alpha Autry, 118; David, 118; Henry, 205; Lula C., 118; Pearl Airhart, 204, 205; William H. Carter, 205
Boozer, Addie, 65; Alice Ponds, 65, 177, 206; Anna, 177; Annie, 65; Annie Jerlean, 65; Aretha Davis, 65; Bernice, 65; Caroline Brockington, 65; Elizabeth Washington, 65, 177; Evalina, 65; Hattie, 65, 204, 205, 206; Hazel, 65; James C., 65; John Hampton, 65; Lemuel, 65, 204; Lovell Davis, 65; Lovie Tresvant, 65; Mary, 65; Moses, 65; Moses Davis, 65, 177; Naomi, 65, 177; Oliver Davis, 65; Otto, 65, 177, 206; Pauline, 65; Rachel, 65; Richard, 65, 177, 206; Richard, III, 65; Richard, Jr., 65, 177; Salena Davis, 65; Tollie H., 65
Boren, Deana Lois, 119; Jerry, 119; Mary Jane Atkinson, 119; Victor, 40
Borhosalin, Theresa, 192
Boring, Hannah, 157
Borrer, Issac, 215; Sophrania Neely, 215
Boson, Eva, 52; Eva Regina, 52; Jacob, 52
Bost, Devin Michelle, 168; Emily, 38
Bostian, Abbie, 84; Alice, 142; Anna, 99; Athalene, 12; Audrey, 12; Bessie Evaline Groom, 113; Betty, 83; Beverly West, 113; Bonnie Lee, 112; Bruce, 150; C.W., 79; Carlena, 99; Cassie Emmeline Howard, 138; Charles, 150; Charles W., 79; Charles Waymon, 112; Charlie Alexander, 163, 178; D.V., 150; Daisy Pearl Lasater, 142; David, 221; David Henry, 12; David William, 138; Deloris, 142; Edith Mae, 112; Ellie Kathryn, 113; Emmet E., 112; Eugene Orville, 113; Frances Elizabeth Crowder, 163; Francis Elizabeth Crowder, 178; Gene, 12; George T., 112; Geraldine, 12; Inez Rosie, 178; Irple, 12; James E., 112; Jessica, 221; Josephine, 142; Josephine Pearl, 163; Katherine, 12; Keith, 150; Lorraine, 12; M., 149; Mark, 113; Mary Carolyn Mason, 150; Mary Lynn Mason, 150; Mary Mason, 152, 191; Maxine, 142; Orville Wayne, 112; Philip, 113; Robert Wesley, 113; Ruby, 79; Ruby Katherine, 79; Stephen, 150; Thomas, 221; Thomas Houston, 112; Velma L. Groom, 112; Virgil David, 112; William, 142; Willie Mae Watkins, 79; Wilma Dale, 113
Bostic, Martha, 39
Bourq, 73
Bowden, Alonso Jackson, 137; Alonzo, 137; Charlie, 90; Delphia Verlon Kendrick, 137; Rosa Florence Kendrick, 137; Rosa Kendrick, 137; William, 137
Bowdre, Nodie Hull, 129; Thomas, 129
Bowerman, Edith, 47
Bowers, Crettie May, 86
Bowie, Jerry Bob, 163; Marinelle Halbrook, 163; Pauline M. Lasater, 163; Robert, 163
Bowing, Dovie Nicholson, 166; Fred, 166
Bowles, David, 206; Julia Thornton, 205, 206; Mable Orlean, 206
Bowling, Betty Jean, 120; Hi, 7; J.V., 120; John Vottaman, 120; Johnnie Vivian, 120; Josephine, 105; Laoma Jeanece, 120; Martha, 167; Mary Rachel Hawkins, 120; Stanley Hawkins, 120
Bowls, Ruby V., 206
Bowman, Bettie, 213; Eddie, 29; Elizabeth Frances, 147; Elsie, 202; Frank, 202; Iola Mahan, 147, 202; Ivan, 202
Box, Jodi, 190; Katilyn, 190; Kyleigh, 190; Melanie Hart, 190; Rachel, 105
Boyd, Jackie, 53, 175; Judidia, 147; Mary Lena Maxwell, 80; Maudie, 162; Morris Scott, 80; Patricia, 175; Patricia Jeanette Anderson, 53; Thomas Dean, II, 80; Thomas Dean, III, 80
Boyer, Elizabeth Carol, 97; Ola Mae Watkins, 207; Richard, 207; Stephanie, 164
Boyette, Valarie, 210
Boyle, Glynda June, 202; June, 35; Lee, 202; Myrtice Wade, 202
Bracken, Conni, 188
Bradford, Beckey Fisher, 204; Bruce, 28, 29, 44, 202; Cindy, 44; Cody, 44; Cody David, 202; Cynthia Renee Stroud, 202; Edith, 138, 139; Erwin, 73; Eulene, 44, Gary, 44; George S., 169; James Monroe, 138, 139; John A., 44; John Price, 44, 202; Johnny, 44; Lee, 73; Lela Frances Burke, 73; Mary Catherine, 169; Mary Jane Kent, 169; Mildred Walker, 209; Miranda, 44, 202; Nancy Sarah Ann Massey, 138, 139; Nellie, 138; Roy, 209; Susanna, 129
Bradley, A. Jasper, 180; Agnes Knighten, 139; Alex J., 198; Alex Joseph, 65, 66; Alicia Nicole, 65; Alta Mae, 66; Alta May, 65; Ardith Lynn, 65, 66; Benjamin, 206; Benny Leon, 66; Bluford, 65; Borda Jean, 65; Borden, 65; Carla Mae Merryman, 160; Charity, 65, 180; Charity Jane, 65; Clarisy Williams, 198; Cyretha Parker, 66; Delmas V., 95; Delmas Vincent, 65, 66; Eddie, 65; Edna Mae, 66; Elene, 66; Elisabeth Prince Gordon, 65; Elizabeth Prince, 199; Elizabeth Prince Gordon, 179; Emma V. Mason, 65; Emma Viola Atkinson, 56; Emma Viola Mason, 150; Emmett, 160; Erma, 66; Esther Edwards, 66; Eulene, 66, 188; Eva L., 65, 66; Eva Lee, 65, 150; Frances, 160, 186; George, 186; Gloria Jean, 121; Howard, 186; Inez Roach Newberry, 186; Isaac, 180; Isaac L., 180; Isaac Newton, 65; Isaac T., 199; Isaac Taylor, 65; Jasper, 65; Jerry Norman, 65; Jerry Norman, Jr., 65; Joe Carroll, 139; John, 160, 180; John Calloway, 56, 65, 150; John Thomas, 65; Josephine, 206; Joy Faye, 66; Joyce Lynn, 66; Judy Catherine, 65, 66; Kathryn Lee, 66; Leona Stripling, 108; Lloyd, 139; Loretta, 66, 95; Lynnie, 139; Margaret Ann Ridling, 65; Maria, 180; Mariah Jane, 65; Marvelle Bryant, 66; Mary Kissire, 66; Minnie Alice Merryman Helley, 160; Miriah Jane, 198, 199; Mr., 28; Nancy Emaline Pierce, 65; Nella Lou, 65, 66; Opal, 202; Opal Mahan, 66, 95; Patrick C., 65, 66; Riley J., 65, 66; Robert, 21; Rodrick Berwyn, 139; S. Buford, 180; Samuel, 65; Sarah Bryant, 66; Spencer Lee, 65; Terry, 206; Thelma, 65, 150; Wilbern, 66; William, 65
Bradshaw, Catherine, 9; Cynthia, 66; Ed, 66; Eliza, 70; Ellen Ruth, 66; Henry, 66; Henry, Jr., 66; Iris, 66; James, 77; Julia Gabrielle Mourot, 66; Karren Louise, 168; Mable, 66; Malinda Caroline Wilks Wallace, 66; Martha, 66; Mary Ann Sutterfield, 66; Mary Atkinson, 57; Mary Bell Freeman, 66; Mary Elizabeth, 66; Mary Haley, 168; Mary Jane Casharago, 77; Nathaniel, 66; Robert, 168; Ruby, 66; Sarah, 77; Sybil, 21, 66; William Jasper D., 66; William Jasper, Jr., 66; William P., 57
Bradshear, W.W., 9
Brady, Elizabeth Jane Chambers, 78; John, 78
Braggs, B.T., 72
Brailey, James, 184; Reva Jo Reedy, 184
Brame, Mabel, 205; Mable, 206; Major, 205
Bramlett, Rosie, 148
Branahm, Lorene Griggs, 67
Brance, Jackson, 137; Melissa P. Kendrick, 137
Branch, Elizabeth, 174
Brand, Julia Ann Norwood, 167; Thomas, 19
Brandley, Alex, 97; Esther Lavester Edwards, 97
Brandon, Elizabeth, 157
Brandt, Al, 53; Betty Allen, 53; Jill, 152; Michael, 53
Branham, Arenna, 106; Arenna May, 66; Arenna R., 66; Barbara Jo, 67; Clyde, 66; Clyde William, 67; Debra, 67; Della, 66, 67; Effie, 66; Effie Mae, 67; Eliza Jane Osborn, 66, 106; Frances, 66; Frances W., 66; Gail, 67; Gary, 67; Gertie Mae Adaline Gloden, 66, 106, 156; Hannah Jane, 66; Inez Griggs, 67; James, 66; James Lacey, 66, 106; James W., 66; James William, 66, 106, 156; Jane H., 66; Jeremiah, 66; Jewel, 66; Jewel Dean, 67; John, 66, 67; Joyce, 67; Larry, 67; Leroy, 66, 67; Lewis L., 66; Loretta, 67; Lucinda Adaline, 66, 106; Lucretia King, 66; Mae Speaks, 67; Mandy Jane, 66, 106; Margaret McCochran, 66; Mary Frances, 67; Mary Lucille Anderson, 67; Odious, 66; Odious Lee, 67; Pearlie, 66; Pearlie Ann, 67;

Rolen E., 66; Samantha Elizabeth, 66; Sarah Ann Arenna, 66; Susanna E., 66; Susie Belle Whitehead, 67; Tennessee Paralee, 66; Theodoshia Davis, 66; Uriah, 66; Velma, 66, 157; Velma Mae, 67, 69, 156, 157; Viona, 66; William, 66, 106
Brannon, Cynthia Jean, 126, Ernest Dean, 126; Howard Lynn, 126; Janet Kay, 126; Minnie, 114; Sarah Joe Hubbard, 126; Susan Gail, 126
Branom, America Isabel Garrett, 66; Annie Moland, 66; Belle Wright, 66; Essie Greenhill, 66; Harvey Terrell, 66; John S., 66; Lucy R., 66; Maggie, 66; Marshall S., 66; Maudenia, 66; Pearl White, 66; William Wesley, 66
Branscum, Claud, 149; Viona Passmore, 149
Branson, Ashley Deanne Holsted, 124; Aurel, 128; Betty Greer, 128; Blanche Croom, 128; Catharine Huggins, 127; Cora, 128; Elton Lee, 128; Elton Lee, Jr., 128; John, 127; Johnathan Luke, 128; Jonathan Luke, 127; Katherine Huggins, 128; Naomie, 128; Oddie, 128; Racy, 128; Sara Katherine, 128; William H., 128
Brant, Frances E., 73; Lenora, 73; Mary Elizabeth, 73; Maxine, 97; Sarah J., 73
Brashier, Betty Crye, 90
Brasier, Barbara Ellen Maxwell, 80; Deborah Kay, 80; Ernest Ray, 80; Leo, 80; Melvin Keith, 80
Bratcher, Bonnie Love Montomery, 161; Mona Abshere, 204; Robert, 204; Walter Delile, 161
Bratton, Doris Polk, 177; Gwendolyn Pearl, 135, 165; Jamie Frances Rasmussen, 183; Jennifer Jones, 135, 165; Joseph Allen, 183; Paizley, 172, 183; Scott, 135; Sidney, 135, 165
Braud, Alton Lewis, 67; Betty Aldredge, 67; Colette Marie Lovelady, 67; Gilbert Gay, 67; Gilbert Gay, Jr., 67; Jacob Pierre, 67; Jeremy Kyle, 67; Joshua Ryan, 67; Karen Gay, 67; Pamela Marie, 67; Phyllis Ann Nauman, 67; Rachael, 67; Rachael Anne McKinney Wills, 67; Serena Joyce, 67; Shirley Bowdle, 67; Steven David, 67; Susan Sutherland, 67; Terri Lynn, 67; Yve Pierre, 67
Braudway, Bessie, 70
Braxton, Leta, 90
Brazil, J.E., 37, 146; Mrs. Bernard, 42
Brazzell, Melissa, 54
Breeden, L.O., 62; P.O., 62
Breeding, Sonya, 149
Breezley, Michael, 83; Ruth Elaine Morphis Martin, 83
Brekeen, Cynthia Jean Brannon, 126
Brennelsen, Anna Veronica Wampler, 210; John Jacob, 210
Brent, Louisa, 74
Brents, Alverda, 68; Alvin Garfield, 67; Benjamin Harrison, 68; Berma, 67; Carl, 30; Charles Linberg, 67; Charles Wesley, 68; Charlie, 30; Della Irene Crye, 90; Eunice, 68; Helen Tanner, 204; James Wesley, 68; Jennifer, 204; Jimmie Sykora, 204; John Mansfield, 68; Joshua, 68; Katie, 188; Landy McKinley, 67; Leland, 37; Leon, 13; Lloyd, 90; Logan Blain, 68; Lorene Knighten, 139; Louis, 67; Loyd, 29, 30; Lucy, 67; Mae, 67; Margaret Isabelle Williams, 67; Marita, 204; Martha J., 198; Marvin Luther, 68; Mary, 5; Mary Ann, 67; Mary Elizabeth Lynch, 67; Millie Ann Frazier, 68; Minnie Mae, 68; Minor Hamilton, 68; Noah Sherman, 67, 68; Oscar, 139; Patsy, 90; Pleasant Mitchell, 68; Priscilla D. Upchurch, 68; Priscilla Jane, 68; Priscilla Upchurch, 68; Rafel, 67; Rea, 67; Robert Washington, 68; Romona, 204; Rose, 67; Rose Ellen, 217; Ruth, 67; Safronia Adeline, 107; Sarah Alverda, 68; Simon, 30; Simon Alexander, 68; Strap, 188; Suraney, 68; Thomas Bellflower Phillips, 67; Thomas Landy, 67; Thomas McKinley, 67, 68; Trudy Norwood, 188; Una Scoggins, 67; Vesta, 68; Wesley Columbus, 67, 68; William, 204; Willie, 204; Wilma, 68
Brewer, Albert Edward, 167; Arrie Anna, 61; Bertie, 61; Bessie, 138; Bessie Dean, 167; Buleah, 61; David, 15; Electra, 142; Hannah Horton, 124; Hazel Lavern, 61; Irene Victoria, 124; James W., 167; Mary Esther, 61; Mary Margaret, 156, 157; Matilda, 167; Melvin Green, 61; Oragon Elizabeth Bennett, 61; Rial, 124; Sara Angeline, 186; Sidney Noland, 167; Stella, 61; Wesley, 167; Wilma J., 130; Wilma James, 167
Breyel, Theresa Louise, 110
Brice, Betty, 50; Emily Butler, 68; Gertrude, 68; Sarah Alverda Brents, 68; William Thomas, 68; William Thomas, II, 68
Brickey, Aubra, 127; Clara Earline, 127; Eleanor Dobkins, 63, 64; Gracie Alfred, 195; John, 63, 64; Mary Elizabeth Garner, 63, 64; Mary Garner, 63, 64; Nancy, 63, 64; Peter, 63, 64; William, 63, 64; Winifred Lucas, 63, 64
Bridewell, Charles, 20
Bridgeman, Christine, 70; Etta Ruth Chism, 83; Harold, 70; Jacob Aaron, 83; Jimmy, 70; John B., 70; Katie Elizabeth, 83; Leonard Archie, 70; Lillie May Cargile, 70; Marcus Allan, 83; Rosa, 70; Sandee Dae Trafford, 83; Stephanie Nichole, 83; Sturl, 70; Sturl D., 83; Terry Gene, 83; Timothy Wayne, 83; Tonya, 83; Travis D., 83; Vickie Gayle Price, 83
Bridges, Alexandria Delores, 44; Allyson Denise, 44; Barbara Ellen, 214; Baxter Lee, 214; Billy Ray, 68; Carl Deon, 80; Carolyn, 68; Carrie, 69; Charles, 68; Floyd, 68; Glenda Fay, 214; Glenda Grace, 83; J.W., 68; James, 187; James L., 68, 69; John Robert, 69; Josephine, 68; Joyce Fay, 68; Judy, 68; Katie Moore, 80; Lela Mae Lowry, 68; Linda, 44; Malinda Lawson, 69; Marilyn, 68; Mary, 44; Mary Jane, 69; Matthew Hawkins, 68, 187; Nellie, 74; Ollie, 69; Patsy Jane, 214; Richard, 68; Robert, 44, 68; Ronald, 44; Sarah Jane Autry, 68, 69, 187, 220; Stella, 187; Stella Adeline, 68, 69; Stephanie, 44; Tarra, 44; Tommie Lee, 214; Velma Mae White, 214; Virginia Lee, 214; Wes, 80; Wilma, 68
Bridgman, Ada, 70; Adelia Proctor, 69; Aggie, 70; Aggie Josephine, 70; Alfred, 69; Alma Hazel Moore, 68; Andrew Jackson, 69; Ann, 69; Ann E., 69; Ann Eliza L., 69; Anna, 70; Annie, 69; Benjamin, 69; Benjamin Elliott, 69; Benjamin Franklin, 69; Betty, 70; Betty Lou Barker, 58; Bill, 69; Calvin, 69; Carol, 70, 125; Carol Susan, 69, 223; Charles, 69; Charlotte S., 69; Clarence, 15, 58, 70; Claudius, 69; Cleo, 70; Cora, 69; Creed, 69; Cynthia Barron, 69; David, 69; Dessie Fryer, 70; Dicey Jane Maxey, 70, 154; Dora, 69; Dorothy York Moss, 70; Edgar, 70; Eliza, 69; Eliza Bradshaw, 70; Elizabeth, 69; Elizabeth Stanfield, 70; Ellen, 70; Emily, 69; Emily J., 69; Emily Susan H., 70; Emmett, 69; Ettie Jane, 70; Eva, 69; Frances Adaline Catherine Holden, 69, 70, 105, 123, 125; Frank, 69, 70; Franklin, 69; Franklin David, 69; Gertha Mayona, 70; Grady, 69; Harmon, 70; Hazine J., 70; Hellen, 70; Herbert, 156, 223; Herbert Howard, 69, 70, 125; Herman, 70; Howard, 69; Ina Fryer, 70; Isaac, 69, 70, 74; James, 69; James Everett, 69; James Franklin, 69, 70; James Isaac, 70; Jane Butler, 69, 70, 74; Jewell, 69; John, 69; John B., 154; John Butler, 70; John F., 69; John W., 69; John Washington, 69; John Washington, Jr., 69; Josephine, 69; Katherine, 70, 125; Katherine Ann, 69, 156; Leo, 70; Lillian Myrtle, 70; Linda, 70; Lonnie, 70; Lucinda, 69; Lucinda Gibson, 69; Lucinda Jane, 69; Maggie Horton, 156, 223; Maggie May Horton, 69, 70, 125; Margaret, 69; Margaret Ann Hall, 69; Mariam, 69; Mariam Brown, 69; Marion, 69; Marion Franklin, 69; Martha, 69; Martha Ann Maxey, 70, 154; Martha D., 69; Mary, 69, 70; Mary Brown, 69; Mary Catherine, 69; Mary Jane, 70; Mary Queener, 69; Matilda J. Prock, 69; Maude, 69; Mayona, 149; Mildred, 70; Miller Creed, 69; Missouri Belle, 69; Nancy, 69; Nancy Teague, 70; Nora, 70; Oliver P., 69; Oliver P., Jr., 69; Orville, 69; Perry, 70; Rebecca Kidwell, 69; Robert E. Lee, 69; Rufus Calvin, 70; Ruth Davis, 69; Ruth E. Lamb, 69; Sampson D., 69; Sampson David, 69; Sandra, 70; Sarah Bunker, 70; Sarah Jane Hinkle, 69; Sarah Jane Owens, 69; Sherman, 70; Susan, 69; Susan Barron, 69; Thomas, 69; Thomas Jefferson, 123; Thomas Jefferson H., 69, 70, 105, 125; Thomas W., 69; Thurman, 70; Thursa Jane, 69; Vandver, 69; Verna, 70; William, 69; William Berry, 70; William Calvin, 69; William Henry, 70; William T., 69, 70, 154; Willis, 70; Willis Andrew, 70; Zacharia, 69
Briggler, Karen, 124; Linda Fuller, 104; Raymond, 104
Brigham, Elnora Josephine, 145; Mary Ann, 145; Melvin Lafayette, 145
Brightwell, Frances Berry, 62; Samuel, 62
Brimmage, Allen, 116; Alta Mae Yarbrough, 70, 71; Angela Louise, 70; Autum Hazel, 70; Betty, 70; Beverly Ann, 70; Dorothy Mae, 70, 71; Emma Jean, 70; Fay, 70; George Allen, 70, 71; George Eugene, 70, 71; George Franklin, 70; Georgie Fay, 70, 71; Hazel Odelia Hale, 70, 71, 116; Heidi Murriell, 70; Henry Evrett Allen, 70, 71; Henry Holland, 71; Jeannie Turner, 70; Katherine Louise, 70, 71; Lizzy Piney, 70; Luther Marvin, 70, 71; Luther Thomas, 70, 71; M.E., 70; Mamie Ellison, 71; Marvin, 218; Mary Elizabeth, 71; Mary Frances, 70; Mary Luella, 70; Nila Sue, 70; Opal Turner, 70; Roxie Arant, 70; Ruby Marie, 70, 71; Sandy Jane Whitney, 70; Shirley Jean, 70; William Henry, 70
Brinkley, Agnes Bumpass Cazort, 71; Alexander, 52, 71; Alexandria, 71; Alma Smith, 71; Berlin, 71; Betty, 71, 119; Bumpass, 71, 199; Bumpass B., 71, 199; Bunk, 71; Elizabeth Jinkins, 71; Ethel, 71; Georgia Ann, 52, 53; Hattie Bruce, 71; Ida Ann Stobaugh, 199; Ida Ann Stobaugh Robbins, 71; Jessie Lee, 71; Joel Alexander, 71; John, 71; John Alexander, 71; John Harrien, 52; John S., 71; Joseph, 71; Joseph B., 71; Julia A. Scroggins, 71; Kerry, 71; Laura Lee Wagley, 71; Lola May, 71; Margaret, 198; Margaret Ann, 71, 190, 199, 200; Margaret Maxwell, 71; Marietta, 71; Martha Ann, 71; Martha Ann Hill Williams, 71, 199; Martha J., 71; Martha J. Jones, 71; Martha Jane, 71; Mary L. Winters, 71; Maryetta D., 71; Nancy Jones, 52; Peggy Dove, 71; Reba Hazel, 95; Simeon, 71; Thelma, 71; William, 71; William B., 71; William H., 71; William U., 71
Brisbane, Henry, 67
Brislen, Joan, 170
Brison, Richard, 58
Brixey, Florida, 213; Garfield, 126; Sarah Missouri Hubbard, 126
Broadnex, Katie, 72
Brockington, Addie, 85; Caroline, 65; Charlie, 85; Gertrude, 85; Hellin, 85; Julia McDaniel, 85; Martha, 85, 86; Peggy, 85; Phillip, 85; Sam C., 85
Brockman, Cassie La'Shae, 44; Kevin, 44; Khadejah, 45
Brockway, Earl, 81; Joyce, 81; Joyce Faye Delong Moody Sensabaugh, 80, 81; Velma Brown McCoy, 81
Brogdon, Valarie Ann, 219
Bronkema, Patricia, 124
Brookings, Laurance, 20
Brooks, Emily, 206; Harry, 206; Henrietta, 206; Ken, 135; Lucinda, 206; Mary V., 138; Roger, 20
Brown, Aaron Claude, 204; Al, 184; Allen, 143; Arlene Marie, 71, 72, 97; Audrey, 72; Austin Jacob, 59; Betty Alice, 204; Beverly, 192; Bill, 134; Billie, 119; Caldonia, 119; Carmel Holland Heavington, 184; Catherine Ridling, 186; Celestine, 72; Christie Newsom, 68; Clara Marie, 96; Clara Ridling, 186; Clarence, 206; Deborah Anne Bean, 59; Don, 119; Dora Wilma, 143; Dorcas, 86, 170; Doris, 119; Doyle, 97; Drew Morris, 119; Edith, 119; Edith Catherine, 119; Elizabeth Carol Boyer, 97; Ellen Faye, 80, 81; Ellen McClaren, 80; Emily, 130; Emily Thomas, 206; Emily Virginia Thomas, 72; Emmett Clairon, 143; Ethel, 97; Eveline Stell, 143; Famie Jewell Chism, 80; Fronie, 148; Grace Mae Thompson, 204; Hazel, 218; Henry Wallace, 80; Ida Mae, 204; Irene, 21; Isaac, 69; James Doyne, 80; James Horace, 143; Janell, 156; Jim, 148; Jimmy, 15; John, 55; John H., 120; John S., 201; Joseph Adam, 204; Joseph Bradley, 204; Juanita, 119; Junia Arieon, 143; Justin, 172; Karissa, 104; Kasey, 172; Kendra, 104; Kimberly, 72; Laura, 213; Laura E., 143; Lee, 180; Lela June, 93, 204; Lela Virginia, 75, 103, 220; Levesta Lucindia Ledbetter, 120; Lillian M., 143; Lizzie, 206; Lizzie Thornton, 204; Lutie, 169; M., 8, 78; Mable Orlean Bowles, 206; Madison, 172; Mae Esther, 72, 177; Mae Lafayette, 140; Maggie, 180; Margaret Ann, 80; Mariam, 69; Marie Sledge, 80; Marion, 119; Martha Crow, 89; Martha Perry Cyrus, 72; Mary, 55, 86; Mary Allen, 52; Mary Ann Eddy, 96; Mary Annette Mills, 103; Mary Elizabeth Ledbetter, 143; Mary Jane, 80, 81; Mary Lodisky, 120, 121, 122; Mattie, 20; Mattie Perry Cyrus, 72, 140, 175; May, 166; May Johnson Ireland, 134; Merlene, 119; Monroe, 89; Murrel, 186; Nila Grace, 204; Odis Odell, 204; Ollie, 119; Ollie Charton, 96; Ollie Elizabeth Gordon, 98, 109; Onvie, 119; Orie, 148; Peggy Janell, 106; Perry W., 85; Princie Manan, 148; Rebecca Lucinda Qualls, 119; Rita Ann, 83; Robert E., 97; Robert Warren, 71, 89, 97; Ruth Elizabeth, 143; Sarah Elizabeth Stover, 201; Shirley Ann, 80; Shirley Marie Edwards, 71, 89, 97; Taylor Ashley, 59; Terry Lee, 97; Thelma, 80, 81; Therlo, 109; Tollie L., 80; Tollie Lucien, 80; Ulysses, 72; Velma, 80, 81; Wallace, 80; Wanda, 26; Wayne, 172; Wiley, 96; William, 26; William Adam, 204; William Bruce, 59; William Henry, 72; William Horace, 143; William Perry, 72
Browning, Azzie A. Price Johnson Hines, 134; Clemmie, 148; Doc, 167; James, 134; Kathleen Linda, 167; Maude Graham, 167
Bruadaway, Annie Dean, 132
Bruce, Ann E. Bridgman, 69; Charles, 80; Daniel, 69; Danny, 80; Hattie, 71; Mariam, 69; Mary Lena Maxwell Boyd Hearn, 80; Nancy Bridgman, 69; Sarah Ann, 118; William, 69; Willis, 69
Brumwell, Sarah, 61
Bruns, Forrest, 170; Heather, 170; Leif, 170
Brunson, Eloise, 190
Bruton, Elloit Rosie, 218
Bryant, Ada Lee Mason, 150; Ada Mason, 149; Alexander, 79; Alexander John, 52; Amanda, 73; Amy Alice Watkins, 210; Arthur, 64; Ashley Michelle, 219; Benjamin, 79; Bertie, 202; Bertie Stanton, 177; Bessie, 210; Betty, 144; Beverly Jean, 73; Billy Gene, 72; Bobby, 15, 16; Brian, 28; Britt, 150; C.A., 149; Caroline M., 73; Cerrena, 107; Charlene, 149, 150; Charles Decatur, 73; Chris, 16; Delores, 72; Dorothie Mahan, 148; Dorothy, 149; Drayton, 73; Drew, 148; Elizabeth, 73; Elizabeth Andrews, 55; Elizabeth Lee Vargas, 219; Elsie Holmes, 101; Ethan Taylor, 219; Eurie Frank, 79; Evelyn Pearl, 72; Frances Beatrice, 72; Frank, 72, 73, 86; Franklin, 72; Gertrude Baker, 66; Glenn Russell, 219; Harriet, 66; Hazel Leota, 72; Helen, 95; Heron, 212; Herschel, 66; Hershel, 144; Howell, 73; Ina May Jones, 72; James Monroe, 107; Jamie Atkinson, 57; Jane Blackmon, 64; Jason Glenn, 219; Jessica Dell, 219; Jim, 65, 210; Jimmie Lee, 149, 150; Jodi Ann Thompson, 219; John, 73; John Barry, 79; John Thomas, 107; Judy Catherine Bradley, 66; Justin Russell, 219; Karen Webb, 219; Landon, 66; Leathal, 66; Lenora, 73; Levi, 73; Lorrine, 144; Lou Ella, 107; Lucy, 73; Luther Gleen, 219; Lynn, 16; Mae, 73, 86; Mark Anthony, 219; Martha, 73; Marvelle, 66; Mary, 203; Mary Jo, 149, 150; Mattie Mae, 72; Maxine, 72, 149, 150; Minerva, 73; Minerva Ann Ragsdale, 73; Myrtle J., 107; Nadene, 150; Nadine, 149; Nadine Lucille, 72; Nancy A., 73; Nancy Zellar, 107; Nathaniel Glenn, 219; Norma, 15, 16; Orville, 66; Peggy, 16; Rick, 15; Robert H., 79, 80; Robert Henry, 79; Rosie Dicus Harvell, 212; Roxie Ann Gordon Halbrook, 107; Roxie Gordon, 65; Samuel, 66; Sandra Dell Woods, 219; Sarah, 66; Sarah George, 73; Shelby Ann, 219; Susan Phillips, 79; Susannah, 52; T. Wesley, 73; Theo, 66; Thetus, 149, 150; Thomas W., 73; Walter, 79; Wanda Lou Williams, 219; William, 79; William J., 55; Williard Francis, 180; Zoy Charton, 79, 80
Bryles, Allen, 9; Forest, 9; Forrest, 90
Bryson, Annie, 140
Buchanan, Beatrice Edna, 132; Thomas, 135; Vickie, 39
Buck, Candice Illich, 142; Dalton, 142; Joseph, 86; Susanah, 86
Buckholtz, Danita, 202
Bufford, Billy, 204; Christina Tanner, 204
Buford, Jane, 78
Bugh, F.H., 42
Buie, Edgar Jackson, 80; Jarvis Lee, 80; Jean, 80; Pauline Euna Maxwell, 80; Una Faye, 80
Bull, Bernice, 80; Billye Ruth, 80; Shelby Jean Lentz, 126
Bullard, Arthur William, 95; John Aaron, 95; Raymond Lee, 95; Rebecca Dixon, 95; Travis Wesley, 95
Bullington, Jerry Palmer, 116; Jerry Palmer, Jr., 116; Nancy Cheryleen Sanders, 116; Tennie Edith, 84
Bullock, Cary Delayce, 117
Bulter, Louise Miller, 160; Walter, 160
Bumpass, Winifred, 71
Bunker, Sarah, 70
Bunton, Canzada Wilsher, 213; Clyde Calvin, 119; Clyde J., 213; David Travillion, 119, 213; John Lonzo, 213; Opal Lee Harris, 119
Burgess, Fannie, 91; Gene, 26; Mary Wren, 223; William, 223
Burham, Flora Snyder, 165; John Wesley, 165
Burk, Josephine, 93
Burkalhen, Anna, 226
Burke, Afton Allen, 73; Albert, 73; Carol, 95; Edith Robinson, 73; Francois, 73; Fronia, 73; Irene Muriel, 73; Lee Bradford, 73; Lela Frances, 73; Leo, 73; Lillie, 73; Lou Noline, 73; Louis Arthur, 73; Lucille Stobaugh, 73; Mack

231

234

Marnie, 71; Mary Ellen, 138; Mary Jane, 71
Ells, Henrietta, 176
Elms, Charles Howard, 170; Charles Howard, Jr., 170; Charles, Jr., 170; Debra Ruth, 170; Ernestine Orr, 170; James John, 170; Mary Hylen, 170; Tina Marie, 170
Embrey, Ann, 74; William, 74
Embry, Anna Lucille, 119; Anne, 74; Benjamin Phillip, 119; Bill, 9; Darla Cahoone, 119; Gay, 119; Gaylord, 119; Jeffrey Phillip, 119; Nancy, 74; Peggy Beck, 119; Rebecka, 119; Rita Martin, 119; Robert, 74; William Ray, 119; Zeta Faye Hart, 119
Emerson, Belle, 217; Effie, 118; John L., 18; Rick, 17
Endecott, Anna Gouer, 98; Anne Gillam, 98; Elizabeth Cogan Gibson, 98; Elizabeth Winthrop Newman, 98; Hannah Gosling, 98; John, 98; Joseph, 98; Joseph, Jr., 98; Mary Smith, 98; Zerubbabel, 98
Enderlin, Amos, 31; Joseph J., 31
Endicott, America, 98, 208; Arvis, 98, 208; Charles, 98, 208; Elizabeth, 98, 118, 208; Elizabeth Varner, 98, 118, 208; Emily, 98, 208; George, 98, 208; James, 98, 208; John, 98, 208; Joseph, 98, 208; Joseph, III, 98; Joseph, IV, 98; Joseph Nation, 98, 118, 208; Martin, 98, 208; Samuel, 98, 208; Sarah, 98, 208; Welmet, 98, 208; Welmet Nation, 98; William, 98, 208
Engelhoven, Virgil, 37
Engle, Edith, 93
Ennis, Vicki, 38; Vickie, 39
Eoff, Artie Elizabeth Campbell, 75, 76, 98; Becky, 221; Betty, 64; Betty Jo Bishop, 99; Carolyn Elizabeth, 99; Daniel Grady, 75; Dicey Elizabeth, 169; Edna Pearl, 99; Erma Lorene, 98; Ernest, 98; Fred, 221; Freddie Earl, 98, 99; Garland, 98; Garrett Daniel, 98; Grady, 98, 109; Grady Daniel, 98, 99; Grady Lynn, 99; Gyva, 98; Hettie, 98; Hettie Melvina Gordon, 98, 99, 109; Irvin, 98; Irving J., 75, 76; James Gordon, 99; Katie Burns, 98; Leonard, 98; Mary Rebecca Harwood, 98, 119; Michael Wayne, 99; Ora, 75, 98; Patton Arnold, 99; Sallie, 107; Sharon Leigh, 98, 221; Soloman, 98; William Hoover, 98
Epperson, Ada Lee Atkinson, 56; Arnold G., 157; Betty Jo, 150; Cynthia Prince, 180; Daisy Lee McClure, 157; Dole, 180; Donald Mason, 150; Earnie, 101; Eunice, 101; Frankie, 101; Hulan, 56; Hulon, 150; Inez, 180; Jan, 157; Jess, 126; Jessicia Marie, 180; Nancy Leota Mae Mason, 150; Rosie Ellen, 125, 126; Terry Lynn, 180; Trey Clemons, 180; Venie Eveline Pope, 125; William Thomas, 125
Erby, Annie Blackmon, 64; Mamie Ponds, 178; Thomas, 178
Erickson, Dorothy, 188
Ermann, Marie, 160
Ernst, Gail, 142
Erwin, S.H., 42; S.N., 42
Estelle Ponds, 177
Estes, Earl, 125; Jesse, 125; John, 74; Joseph Nathaniel, 68; Josie Morningstar, 68; Margaret, 125; Ruth, 125; Sarah Hannah, 68; Sarah L.E. Horton, 125; Susan Butler, 74; Thomas W., 125
Etheridge, 149; Amber Caroline, 45; Charley, 218, 219; Joseph, 146; Martha Elizabeth, 219; Martha White Castleberry, 146; Ollie Pearl Polk, 218, 219; Walter Jr., 45; William Andrew, 219
Ethridge, Jack, 28
Eubanks, Jerry, 15; Maudie, 217; Samantha Elizabeth Amanda, 199
Evans, Alice Taylor, 186; Almyra J., 99; Almyra Jane, 99; Alvis, 99; Anna Bostian, 99; Anna Skipper, 99; Anthony, 86; Arbie, 99; Augustus, 99; Azora George, 99; Barbara, 198; Benjamin, 99; Bro., 29; Carl Edward, 99; Carlena Bostian, 99; Charley, 99; Clara, 99; Claud, 99; Cory, 99; Dorothy Jane K., 139; Dotch Leroy, 99; Edith, 99; Elisha, 99; Elizabeth Campbell, 99; Elmo, 99; Etta Guess, 99; Eulus E., 99; Eva, 99; Eva Nell Minton, 99; Floyd A., 99; Gary, 100; Genara Jobe, 99; Georgia Mayhue, 99; Harriet, 99; Jane, 99; Janice Pruett, 181; Jennie N., 99; Jo Rene, 186; Julie Deaton, 99; Lee Gettus, 99, Leroy, 99; Leroy Pope, 99; Lisa Ann, 142; Lish, 99; Lonnie Lee, 99, 158; Louisa, 99; Mamie Airhart, 204, 205; Margaret Henry, 99; Martha A., 99; Mary Ann Faulkner, 100; Mary Savannah Fielder, 99; May, 99; Maye, 99; Minus, 99; Orvel, 99; P.P., 90; Peter H., 99; Raymond, 37; Reddick, 99; Susan C. McCaig, 156; Susan C. McCaige, 99; Susan Lorean, 99; Susanah Buck Cline, 86; Tennessee Lee McCullough, 99, 158; Thomas, 99; Thomas Pope, 99; Viny Rhodes, 99; William A., 99, 156; William Clarence, 99; William W., 99; Willie, 99; Wilma Sanders, 99
Evatt, Rachel, 83; Rachel P., 87
Everett, Ruth, 170

F

Fabrizio, Elisabetta, 140, 141, 142; Guiseppe, 140; Jessiminia Gelsomina, 226; Lucia Zarlenga, 140
Fabry, Kathy, 166
Fain, Ruby Fay, 55
Fairbanks, Ann, 100
Faith, Teri, 204
Fakey, Joseph, 212; Marie Kisel, 212
Fannon, Cathy, 204
Fargo, Mary Augustine, 31
Farino, Roccena, 92
Farish, Carolyn, 20; Claude M., 33; Harold, 21; Ruby, 21
Farley, Jane H. Branham, 66; William H., 66
Farmer, Elizabeth, 91; Eloise, 122
Farris, Hannah, 124; James, 124
Farrish, Frank, 210; Nona Mae Watkins, 210
Faubus, Orval, 32
Faulk, Arden, 149; Arminta Martin, 149; Bernie Viola Stell, 112; George Washington, 112; Viola Stell, 112
Faulkner, Ann Fairbanks, 100; Anna Corene McInturff, 100; Annie Corine McInturff, 169; Barbara Ann, 100; Barbara Smoljan, 100; Bonnie Ledbetter, 100; Corinne McInturff, 158; Donald, 100; Elmo, 158; Ethel Lee Groom, 100, 113; Helen Ayers, 100; Herman Floyd, 100; Jeanne Corene, 100; Jennifer Megan, 100; Jessica Ruth, 100; Jessie Fay Davison, 100; John, 99; Karen, 100; Kimberly Diane, 100; Larry Lee, 100; Leanna Garner, 99; Linda Nichols, 100; Loma, 182; Loma Ishmel, 99, 100, 113; Margaret, 179; Mary Ann, 100; Megan Ann, 100; Michael, 100; Millie Ann Vaughn, 99, 113; Millie Vaughn, 182; Nathan, 179; Roy Franklin, 100, 113; Ruth Muriel, 100, 113; Ruthie Muriel, 12; William Elmo, 100; William Floyd, 100; William Larry, 100; William Nathan, 100
Feldkamp, Joseph, 31
Felkins, Aaron, 100; Allen, 100; Andrew, 100; Angeline Standridge, 100; Anna, 100; Anne, 100; Annie, 100; Artemesia, 100; Bathsheba, 100; Beatrice, 100; Bersheba Cundiff, 100; Bessie, 100; Billie, 100; Edna, 100; Eliza, 100; Elizabeth, 100; Elizabeth Annie Bush Wren, 74, 100, 223; Elizabeth Bush, 69; Elizabeth Bush Wren, 52; Elizabeth Ross, 100; Elizabeth Standridge, 100; Emma, 100; Esther Doss, 100; Eva, 100; Flora, 100; George, 100; Harriet Jane, 100; Harrison, 100; Henley J., 100; Henry, 100; Hetta, 100; Jack, 100; James, 100; James Ervin, 100; James W., 100; Jane Williams, 100; Jimmy, 100; Joel, 100; John, 100; John, Jr., 100; Josephine Dillon, 100; Juanita, 100; Keziah, 100; Keziah Bell Prewitt, 100; Keziah Prewitt, 100; Lee, 100; Lucinda, 100; Lucinda Ann, 100; Malinda Shepard, 100; Margaret, 100; Marinda, 100; Martin, 100; Mary, 100; Mary Frances, 100; Mary Nordin, 100; Mary Susan, 100; Mary Young, 100; Missouri Tennessee Dillon, 100; Nancy, 100; Nancy Eastep, 100; Rachel, 100; Reuben, 100; Richard, 100; Sally, 100; Sarah, 100; Tennessee, 100; Thomas, 100; William, 100; William, Jr., 100; William Martin, 100; William Thomas, 100; Willie, 52, 74, 100; Willie Ervin, 100, 223; Willy, 100; Wilson Clemence, 100
Fell, Denise DePasqua, 141; Kade Diane, 141; Kenneth Douglas, 141; Samantha Pandora, 141
Fellers, Carol Ann, 189; Essie, 212; Mary Frances, 120; O.D., 189; Pauline Rowell, 189; Rhea Moore, 80; Robert, 212; Rosie, 212; William E., 80
Felts, Osellia Arnold Mosely, 75
Fenton, Shirley, 187
Ferguson, Birtha, 80; Carolyn Chism, 80, 84; George, 161; Henry N., 80, 84; Henryetta, 80; Luva, 111; Margaret Alice, 161, 162; Marvin, 26; Vesta Mueller, 161
Ferrel, Clifton, 54; Fannie Bell Anderson, 54; Oscar, 54
Ferrill, Maggie Alice, 215
Ferrin, M.E. Griffin, 112; S.D., 112; Stephen Decatur, 112
Feyen, Margaret, 86
Ficklin, Sarah, 98, 207, 208
Fielder, Ann, 99; Mary Savannah, 99; Nick, 99
Fields, Colleen, 26; Effie, 104; Eva, 133; Jack, 9; Jermie, 197; Mary Elizabeth Stacks, 196; William Jasper, 196; Winnie Stell, 197
Fiesel, Ethel Marie Ivy, 135
Finch, Bessie Lee, 132
Finkbeiner, John, 46
Finley, Earnest, 29
Finnery, Cynthia, 83
Finney, Shirley Ann, 132
Fiser, Helen, 21; Herbert, 37
Fisher, Alsie Powers, 167, 168; Clem, 31; Dona Mae, 183; Floyd, 183; Lee Jack, 177; Lester, 167, 168; Lillie Mae Rankin, 182, 183; Prilla Dean, 167, 168; Sarah Ellen Poe, 177
Fiske, Lula, 129
Fitch, Dain S., 70; Dorothy Mae Brimmage, 70; Eulita West, 213; Grover Allen, 70; Hannah Elizabeth, 126; James C., 126; Mary Jane, 126; Paul Marion, 70; Terry Dale, 70; Tressa Gail, 70; True, 70; Wanda Sue, 70
Fitzgerald, Cheryl, 50; Leta Faye, 64; Thomas, 175
Fitzhugh, Mary Lee Reedy, 184
Fitzwater, Andrew, 208; Charity, 208; George, 208; Jacob, 208; James, 208; Jane Varner, 208; John, 208; Mary Ann, 208; Sarah, 208
Fivecoat, Susan Matilda, 72
Flaherty, John, 31
Flake, Christina Pinter, 176
Flanner, Lavern, 166
Flannery, Lavern, 147
Flatt, Vicci Mason, 151
Fleeman, Alice, 33
Fleming, Felicity Maret, 201; Jennifer Marie Berry Waldo, 200; Jerita, 120; Joseph H., 120; Kristen Leigh, 200; Mary Magdalene, 120; Matthew Craig, 200; Megan Marie, 200; Ola Wilkes, 120; Reba Jo, 120
Flemming, Irene, 75
Fletcher, Allan, 119; Betty Dean Atkinson, 119; Cullin, 90; Fred, 119; George, 8; Jan Sandell, 119; Leann, 119; Madison, 119; Peyton, 119; Thelma Yarbrough, 224
Flinn, Catherine Tanner, 203; Peter, 203
Florence, Andreas, 173
Florian, Anna, 96
Flournoy, Evalina Boozer, 65
Flower, Marietta Brinkley, 71
Flowers, Addie, 102; Alice, 102; Allen, 102; Alma, 102; Alta, 102; Ance, 71, 217; Angeline Hill, 201; Areminta Sides, 101, 102; Ashlyn, 101; Barbara Scroggin Hensley, 190; Benjamin Franklin, 201; Bessie Polk, 101; Bobby, 223; Bud, 15; Bytha, 53, 102; Bytha Tennessee, 101; Carl, 217; Carolyn, 101, 102; Christine Ward, 101; Clara Anderson, 102; Claudia Josephine Wagley, 102; Columbus Henderson, 53, 100, 101, 102; Cynthia, 203; Debra Hanley, 101; Delphinia Williams Howard, 217; Diana Louise Wren Collins Hanna, 223; Dollie Bell, 109; Donald, 101; Donald, Jr., 101; Donald Ray, 101; Drew, 101; Drucilla Claretta Anderson, 53, 100, 101; Dustin, 101; Edmond, 21, 54, 102, 216; Edmond Columbus, 54, 101; Edward, 104; Edwin, 101, 102; Eliza Jane Gilliam Duron, 101; Elizabeth, 103; Elizabeth A., 102; Elizabeth Jane Gilliam Duron, 102; Elizabeth Jane Sweeden, 100; Elizabeth Jane Sweeden Carr, 102; Elizabeth Janie Sweeden, 54; Elizabeth Marshall, 60, 101, 102, 203; Ella Mae Wagley, 102; Ellen, 125; Ellen Arizona, 102; Elmer Sevier, 101, 102; Elzonia, 102; Esther Pauline, 216; Eunice Epperson, 101; Genia Hillis, 102; Greg, 37; Henry, 60, 101, 102, 203; Henry Edmond, 100, 102; Ida Polk, 102; Ilda Bell, 221; Jacob, 101, 102; Jacob Marion, 102; James Monroe, 102; James P., 102; James Raymond, 101; Jeanette Stewart, 101; Jewel McNabb, 102; John Henry, 102; John T., 102; Joseph, 102; Joseph Alonzo, 101; Joseph E., 102; Joseph Ed, 203; Julia, 190; Lavicia Elizabeth Gilliam, 101, 102; Linda Lynette, 101; Lisa, 102; Loeta Fay Harwood, 119; Louis Jefferson, 102; Louisiana J., 101; Manda Isabel, 201; Margaret Delphinia Williams Howard, 138; Mark, 9, 190; Martha, 101; Martha Ann, 216; Mary, 102; Mary Ann Josephine Elizabeth, 101; Mary Leta, 152; Mildred, 54; Mildred Pauline Ray, 101; Mildred Ray, 216; Millard, 102; Mima, 60; Nancy, 101; Nancy A., 104; Nancy Arilla, 101; Nancy Miranda, 102; Nancy Polk, 102; Needham, 198; Needham Ance, 138; Oda, 53, 102; Oda McArthur, 101; Rachel Clark, 102; Raymond, 101; Robert Ance, 102; Ronald, 101; Sarah Fannie Griffin, 102; Sarah J. Stobaugh, 198; Sarah Vella Polk, 102; Sula Nova, 102; Susan A., 102; Walter, 102; Zack, 101
Floyd, Newton Andrews, 54
Fogul, Genevieve, 216
Foiles, Brandon, 164; Paula Sue Mourot, 164; Tessie, 164; Tony, 164
Folk, Leanne, 164
Ford, Alpha Etta Barnes, 146; G.W., 26; George, 202; Martha Ellender McKee, 146; Mary, 100; Mary Elizabeth, 146; Sallie Stripling, 202; Thomas Cellars, 146; William Cellers, 146
Forgy, Alice Ophelia, 212
Fornash, Bobby, 46; Bradley, 46; Doris, 46; Kelly, 46; Lindsay Nicole, 46; Meagan Elizabeth, 46; Melanie Tipton, 46; Robert, 46
Forrest, S., 9
Fort, Ann Cherry McGill, 102; Dannie McCoy, 157; Dannie S. McCoy, 102, 103; Dannie Sue McCoy, 119; Edward, 102; Geraldine, 102; Wallace R., 102, 103
Fortenberry, Harold Newton, 128; Mary Elizabeth Settles, 128
Fortner, J.B., 75
Foshee, Allen Lynn, 80; Angela Gail, 80; Frances, 80; Ida Mae Maxwell, 80; Irvin, 80; James Andy, 80; Lisa Ann, 80; Pamela Jean, 80; Rentha Mae, 80; Sharon Jacqueline, 80; Stanley Irvin, 80
Foster, Bernice Boozer, 65; Elizabeth, 224; Karne, 204; Kelly, 204; Kristy, 204; Mary Mariellen Mitchell Autry Whorp, 187; Neely Yow, 147; Ronnie, 204; Sarah W., 180; Sherry Tanner, 204; Thomas M., 174; Will, 187
Fougerousse, Becky, 160; Janet Kay Brannon, 126
Fountain, Ashley, 143; Charles, 143; Peggy Tackett, 143
Foust, Katherine, 39, 41
Fowler, Addie Billings Sosbee, 103; Amos Darrell, 214; Andrea, 53; Andy, 53; Anna Ruth, 214; Armour, 103; Betty Ann Turner, 214; Bill, 113; Billy Dale, 103; Billy Ray, 214; Frankie Jo Moore, 214; Glen Marion, 103; James Robert Lee, 103; Joan Camille, 103; Joe Don, 214; Judith Lynn Gean, 214; Leona Belle White, 214; Leta Loftus, 103; Marjorie, 103; Mark Billings, 103; Marquis Lyndon, 103; Mary Ann Allen Heistand Gullett, 113; Mary Ann Heistand Gullett, 222; Mary Bell Ghrell, 103; Mary Volage Allen Cody, 53; Mildred Louise, 103; Minerva, 200, 201; Peggy Louise, 214; Stephen Lee, 103; William James, 103; Wilma Jean, 103
Fox, Andrew Freeman, 96; Arel, 26; Caldonia Edith, 133, 152; Jeffrey Lee, 96; Johnathon Jerry, 96; Martha Ann Ramsey, 133, 153; Ollie, 125; Rozilah D., 210; Stephanie, 110; Stephanie Lynne Donaldson, 96; William, 153; William M., 133
Fraga, Anita Edwards, 187
France, Jessie, 103; Mrs. Frank, 39
Francis, Anna Mae Knighten, 138; Barbara Ann, 166; Ben, 138; Betty Lou, 166; Bobby Joe, 166; C.E., 8; Dorothy Estelle Jones, 120; Emery L., 197; Grace Missouri Nix, 166; Joyce June, 166; Linda Redditt, 66; Marion, 166; Mildred E., 166; Paul J., 166; Rev., 31
Frank, 226
Franklin, Andrea, 46; Ann, 38; Araya, 46; Elizabeth, 65; Frances Andrews, 54; Jessica, 46; Lloyd, 46; Matthew, 54; Minnie Mae, 182; Mrs. Lucinder, 9; Patti Lienhart, 144; Rayford, Sr., 46; Rayford, Jr., 46; Sarah Lee Lavern Horton, 110; Shawna, 46
Franks, Emiline Paralee Horton, 125; George Washington, 125; Jasper, 125; Jasper Edwin, 125; John William, 125; Lonnie, 125; Mary Belle Sutterfield, 125; Mary Etta Sterling, 125; Mary Lena, 125; Ollie Fox, 125; Thomas, 125; Thomas Marion, 125; William Morton, 125
Frantz, Barbara Ann Kymes, 81
Fraser, Lou Ellen, 75
Frasier, Daniel R., 75; Elizabeth, 75; Lou Ellen, 75
Frazier, Carlyon, 139; Edward, 139; Kate Maxwell, 121; Millie Ann, 68; Theo Edith Christ, 139
Freaman, Alice, 156
Fredrick, Lorine, 160
Freeman, Abe, 103; Alene Bretty, 103, 220, 221; Alta, 103, 220, 221; Anita, 104; Annie M. Wills, 88; Annie Mary Wills, 103, 187, 220, 221; Annie Wills, 69; Ardee Lewis, 220, 221; Arden, 82, 185; Arden William, 74, 82, 103, 220, 221, 226; Arlie, 103; Artie Mahalia, 88, 103, 220, 221; Ashley Nichole, 81, 170; Ashley Nicole, 94; Beverly, 104; Clovie, 104; Darrell Dean, 76, 103, 220; Deborah, 104; Deronda Lee Dixon, 81, 94, 170; Dyke, 103; Eathel Campbell, 69, 82; Edward, 104; Elizabeth Flowers, 103; Ethel Ashcraft, 56; Gerald, 30; Gerald Don,

238

Eveline, 125, 126; Earl, 126; Elsie Jane Price, 126; Francis Marion, 126; Frank, 189; George, 126; George Riley, 126; Grace, 126; Hannah Elizabeth Fitch, 126; Helen Mae Barker, 58, 125, 126; Henry Clay, 126; James Arnold, 125, 126; James Arvil, 126; James Thomas, 126; Jeffrey Michael, 126; Karen Jo, 126; Kimberly Ann, 126; Lessie, 126; Lester, 126; Lily Adeline, 125, 126; Lily Mae Dempsey, 126; Linda Kay, 58, 126; Liz Teel, 126; Lois Jean Taylor, 126; Mary Jane, 126; Mary Jane Fitch Reed, 126; Matthew, 126; Maxine, 225; Melissa Rosemae, 126; Nancy Adline Moore, 126; Nora Schimmel, 126; Opal, 126; Pauline Rowell Fellers, 189; Rayborn, 126; Retta Estell, 126; Ricky, 126; Robert Anderson, 126; Robert Jessie, 126; Rosie Ellen Epperson, 125, 126; Ruby Cody, 86; Samantha Whitfield, 126; Sara Ann McCabe, 125; Sarah Ann McCabe, 126; Sarah Joe, 126; Sarah Laverne Wagner, 126; Sarah Missouri, 126; Teena Marie, 126; Vida, 126; Violet, 116; Violet Pauline, 125, 126; William C., 126; William Charles, 58, 125, 126; William Elisha, Jr., 125, 126; William Elisha, Sr., 126; William Matthew, 126; William Matthew Marion, 126; Zettie Hubbard, 126

Huber, Terese, 123

Huddleston, J.D., 15; Sarah Alice, 130

Hudlow, Josephine, 9

Hudson, Cordell, 42; Mary Ann, 57; Sharon, 136

Hudspeth, A.A., 37; Hannah, 213; Julia Martin, 149; Russell, 149

Huett, Annie Lucille Ashcraft, 56; Beebe, 39; Beulah Virginia Greer, 145; Carlotta Williams, 107; David, 107; David Richard, 145; David Wesley, 64; Emma Jeanette Gordon, 107; Freddie, 107; Harriet Caroline James, 145; Iris Bishop, 64; Jacob Calvin, 107; James Madison, 145; Janet Dold, 96; Jim, 56; Jimmie, 56; John Amos, 107; Lee, 200; Lela May, 145, 146; Leo, 56; Lue Ella Allgood, 107; Mable, 107; Mitzi, 56; Sreathie Ethel Gordon, 107

Huff, Leona, 104

Huffman, Annie Lee, 65; Bobbie McCoy, 88; Doyle, 88; Fred, 148; Jim, 88; Judy Ann, 88; Laudis Ray, 74; Lela Marie Campbell, 74, 131; Nancy Adline House, 65; William Henry, 65; Zora Mahan, 148

Huffstuttler, Laura Alice Rankin, 213

Hugg, Alvis, 8; Nellie, 182

Huggins, A.L., 56; Abraham Lincoln, 55, 126, 127, 128; Agnes, 128; Alta, 126, 127; Alta Skee, 128; Anna Drucilla Hagerty, 126, 128; Annie Saulter, 128; Ben, 128, 129; Ben L., 129; Benjamin L.G., 128; Benjamin McClunia, 128; Benjerman Carroll, 127; Benjerman L.G., 127, 128; Bernice May, 128; Blanche, 128; Bob, 129; Burton, 47; Catharine, 127; Clara Yates, 47; Clarence, 47; Clemmie, 128; Cleo Sweeden, 127; Cleona M. Lang, 128; Clifford, 47; Cordelia, 56; Cornelia, 55, 126; Edith, 47; Edna Marie Merideth, 126; Elizabeth C. Rook, 128; Ella Rook, 128; Elmer, 47; F.H., 55; Frances, 129; Frances C., 128; Frances Olivia Rook, 55; Francis Olivia Rook, 128; Frank Harmon, 126, 127; Frank, Jr., 127; Frannie, 128; Gerthel Jean, 47; Harley, 47; Harley Theodore, 127, 128; Idelle, 128, 209; Jean, 128; Jessie Mae Weaver, 128; John H., 129; John Hazard, 126, 127, 128; Katherine, 128; Lena May Derryberry, 128; Lennie/Linda Ellen, 127; Lilly Shirley, 47; Linda Ellen, 128; Lucille, 128; Martha, 128, 129; Martha C., 52; Mary, 127, 128; Mary Barmore, 127, 128, 129; Mattie Cumi Gasaway, 64, 105, 127; Mavis, 47; Myrtle Hazard, 127; Myrtle Hazzard, 128; Nancy, 52, 128, 129; Nancy Hazard, 127; Nancy Jane Cloud, 127, 128; Olaf, 128; Opal Mildred, 128; Robert, 52, 105, 127, 128, 129; Robert Hazzard, 128; Robert M., 47; Robert Mathew, 127, 128; Syble, 47; Velma, 128; Vernon, 128; Viola, 47; Wilmer, 128; Zelma, 128; Zerah, 129; Zero, 127

Hughes, Charles Vincent, 216; Nevada Ann, 118; Samuel, 118; Selina Majors, 118; Willie Ethel Kuykendall, 216

Huie, Bertha, 64; Bertha P., 64; Emmer, 134; George, 169, 199; Jane, 199; Joseph M., 109; Leigh, 69, 223; Mary, 158; Mary Lou Izsa, 169; Mary Magdalene, 169; Matilda Ann Stobaugh, 199; Ora Jane Gordon, 109; Sarah, 107

Hull, David, 17; Elizabeth Vann Cummins Burrows, 129; George Washington, 129; Maude, 129; Nodie, 129; Vicki, 17

Humphery, Mary Elizabeth, 175; Bertha Phelps, 129; Fannie Gray, 111, 129; Frances Marie, 129; Hallie, 129; Hervey, 129; John, 129; John, Jr., 129; Melba, 171; Nancy Stephens, 129; Polly, 119; Richard Allen, 129; Susan, 111, 112; Susan Beavers, 129; Susanna Bradford, 129; William, 129; William Samuel, 129

Humphreys, Carl E., 18

Humphries, Alfred, 130; Amanda Carrington, 130; Anna Lucas, 130; Barbary Smith, 130; Barry, 130; Jackson, 130; James, 130; Jennifer E., 76; Joseph, 129, 130; Lucinda Herlong, 130; Margaret Black, 130; Marinda, 130, 218; Mary Ann, 166; Mary Matthews, 130; Rebecca, 129; Sarah Camp, 129, 130, 218; Sexton, 130; Shadrack, 129, 130, 218; Shadrack, Jr., 130; Starling, 130; Stephen, 130

Hund, Euphrosina, 226

Hundertmark, William H., 18

Huneycutt, Minnie Kathleen, 186

Hunt, Boss, 154; Margie Cox, 154; Morris G., 18, 19

Hunter, Brandon, 15; Doug, 15; Eddie Mae Thompson, 130; Grace, 164; Harrison, Jr., 130; Joanne Hall, 130; Michael, 130; Sandy, 142; Ulysses, 130

Huntstiger, Carl, 139; Christine, 139; Lorene Knighten Brents Mason Stone, 139

Hurley, B.L., 15; Curtis B., 62

Hurst, Annie, 148

Hutchcroft, Bev, 38; Beverly Jane Walk, 130; Jayne, 130; Jill, 130; Julia, 130; Ted, 5; Theodore, 130

Hutchins, Caroline, 224; Janice, 184

Hutchison, Jeannie, 39; Will, 70

Hutson, Billie J., 130; Celia, 59; Howard Eugene, 130; Jimmy, 130; John, 130; John Henry, 130; Lena, 130; Logan, 130; Luther, 130; Martha Jane Martin, 130; Richard Alexander, 130; Sarah Alice Huddleston, 130; Theresa A., 130; William J., 130; Wilma J. Brewer, 130

Hutto, Fred, 186

Hylen, Cindy, 170; Kristina, 170; Mary, 170

Hyler, Adam, 205, 206; Elizabeth, 204, 205; Lena, 205

Hylton, Deana, 29; Wesley, 29

I

Iannuzzi, Elena, 140; Lena, 171

Ice, Harriet Ellen Paceley, 170; Melvin, 170

Ike, Bob, 16

Ilgner, Dolores, 160; Louise, 135

Illich, Barbara Elaine Miller, 142; Bobbi, 142; Candice, 142; Vernon James, 142

Imboden, C.A., 37; Martha, 226

Inglebright, Mary M., 184

Ingram, Ada Hedgecock, 74, 131; Bessie Belle, 74, 103, 130, 131, 220; Carson, 124; Edith Anna Gunter, 130; Edward Dale, 49; Elizabeth M. Stanfield, 197; Elsie Virginia McKay, 130; Essie Jane, 119; Francis Alexander, 130; Greg, 124; Henry Taylor, 119; James, 105; James Robert, 74, 130, 131; Jane, 197; Keaton, 124; Mary, 49, 197; Mary A. Woody, 223; Mary Ann, 223; Mary Ann Margaret, 125; Mary Edith, 131; Mary Eldora Burton, 74, 130, 131; Melinda Eveline, 130, 131; Nancy Jane, 130, 131; Robert, 49; Sarah Delila Cole, 105; Shannon Renae Holsted Jackson, 124; Tabitha Ann Goodall, 119; Thomas Francis, 130; William, 223

Ireland, Buddy, 134; May Johnson, 134

Irick, Allie, 42; Emma, 42

Isely, Helen Katherine, 183

Isenman, Anna Basler Held, 131; Anna Marie Wellman, 131; Anna Marie Willman, 109, 164; Caroline Grabherr, 110, 131; Emerelia, 109, 110, 131; Fred, 110; Fredrick, 131; Johan, 109, 131, 164; Mary Ann, 131, 164; Pauline, 131

Isley, Helen, 21

Isom, Alvin, 131; Cassie, 213; Charlie Bryan, 131; Charlie George, 131; David, 131; Dustin, 131; Elsie Pearl, 131; Frances C. Huggins, 128; Frances Huggins, 129; Francis A., 58; George Davis, 131; Gracie Bigelow, 131; Janet Johnson, 131; John, 131; John C., 58; Kristina Scott, 131; Mattie, 127; Max Anne Trujillo, 131; Michael, 131; Nathaniel, 128, 129; Suzanne, 131; Tammy, 131; Victoria Barrimore, 58

Israel, Carlys, 60

Issacs, Cleo Marie, 147, 166

Ivey, Tilletha, 191, 195

Ivy, Betty Estella, 135; Ethel Marie, 135; James William, 135; Lovina L. Hasler Chism, 119; Sammie Maude Jordan, 135

Izsa, Mary Lou, 169

J

Jackson, Ada Ruth Permenter, 132; Adam, 182; Alice, 65; Alice Annie Dean, 132; Amy Michelle, 133; Andrew, 62; Andrew Norvin, 132; Annetta, 133; Arlene Frances Anderson, 132; Audrey Carolyn Russell, 132; Augusta, 131; Barbara Ann, 132; Barbara Hallett, 132; Beatrice Edna Buchanan, 132; Bessie Lee Finch, 132; Betty Sue, 97, 132; Beverly Ann, 132; Beverly Gail, 97, 132; Billy Dean, 97, 132; Blanche, 133; Brooklyn Reese, 183; Carl Cleveland, 131; Carolyn June, 132; Carolyn Mary, 132; Cecil Everette, 59, 131; Cecil Pauline, 131; Charles, 27; Charles Reid, 132; Clara Jean, 131; Clarence Leonard, 131; Corrie Smith, 206; Elmo, 46; Elsie Jane, 132; Estelle Ballentine, 132; Euna Faye Dixon, 94; Florence America, 131; Franklin Taylor, 132; Garland, 94; Gary, 94; George, 178; George Edward, 131; Hannah, 132; Harold Finch, 132; Herman W., 18; Holly Ann Kephart, 133; Howard Roosevelt, 131; Iola Jane, 132; James Bayless, 132; James Edward, 132; James Harrison, 131; James Henry, 132; James Larry, 132; James Lee, 132; James Russell, 132; James William, 131; Jeffrey Reese, 183; Jeffrey Steven, 132; Jillia Catherine, 132; Jim, 178, 206; John, 217; Joy, 132; Judy, 97; Katherine Leigh Rasmussen, 183; Kathy, 132; Kayla, 132; Kevin James, 133; Krystle Ann, 132; Lanell, 132; Larry, 94; Laura Etta, 131; Lawrance, 97; Lawrence Woodrow, 132; Lela Judith Shaw, 132; Linda Joyce, 132; Lisa Catherine Colley, 132; Lisa Dawn Chism, 84; Lonnie, 133; Loretta Paladino, 140; Louann Troy, 132; Lula Alice, 132; Lyndon, 37; Lyndon M., 27; Martha, 133; Mary Alice, 132; Mary Aneta McAlister, 131; Mary Ridling, 186; Mary Sue, 131; Mary Susan, 132; Minnie Kimberlin, 59; Minnie Victoria Kimberlin, 131; Nettie, 132; Norvin Andrew, 132; Opal May Addington, 132; Opha, 46; Oscar, 132; Peggy, 20; Quade, 133; Rebecca, 71, 198, 217; Rebecca Leeann, 132; Robert Henry Lee, 132; Ruby, 182; Ruby Ridling, 186; Shannon Renae Holsted, 124; Shawn Lee, 133; Shelia Rea, 211; Sherri Venice Blagg, 132; Shirley Ann Finney, 132; Shirley Anne, 59, 131, 132; Stephanie Laverne, 132; Steven Andrew, 97, 132; Susan Diane, 97, 132; Thomas Morgan, 132; Tim, 124; Tommy, 133; Valery, 27; Victoria Katherine, 183; Vida Edwards, 97; Vida Mae Edwards, 132; Vincent Alan, 132; Ward Johnson, 131; Ward, Jr., 133; Ward, Sr., 133; Wilford, 132; Willamae Owens, 132; William Coleman, 131; William Cornelius, 132; William H., 211; William Lawrence, 132; Zelma Rea Watson, 211

Jacob, 102; John Porter, 52

Jacobi, Kathryn Leigh, 81

Jaime, Amy Angelina, 168

Jamell, Salem, 128; Zelma Huggins, 128

Jamerson, James, 64; Violet Bishop, 64

James, Adaline, 89; Amos, 89; Andrew, 160; Archibald, 89; Arizona Wilsher, 212; Dale, 5; Dixon Malachi, 147; Ellie Kathryn Bostian, 113; Gary, 28; Harriet Caroline, 145; Hattie Lord, 147; Janet Lynn, 113; Jeff, 221; Jettre, 89; Leroy, 89; Lydia Jane, 160; Madoline, 216; Margie, 89; Martha Mobley, 160; Mary Ann, 74, 129; Maude, 89; Nettie Crow, 89; Norma, 20; Paralee, 89; Petris, 89; Rachel Margaret Lucretia Crow, 89; Retha, 89; Ruth, 178; Sarah, 89; Susan Ann, 113; Talmage, 89; Thomas Redding, 212; William, 113

Jamison, Christina, 203

Janesko, Angela, 31

Jarett, Michelle Lynette, 72

Jefferson, Bertha, 64; Faye Ponds, 178

Jefferson Monroe Pruett, 180; Rueben, 178

Jemison, Esther, 139

Jenkins, Edith, 133; Eva Fields, 133; Harry, II, 133; Harry Thomas, 133; Helen, 133; Herbert Ladell, 133; Ida Emma Asula Baskin, 58, 133; Ila Maud, 133; J.A. Wear, 162; JoAnn Wear, 166, 211; Josephine, 133; Lawrence, 133; Margie, 133; Minerva Greenlee, 133; Rose Bell, 133; Ruth Naomi McDaniel, 133; Teena Marie Hubbard, 126; Theola, 133

Jennings, Earl, 62; Janna, 50; Jennifer Alaine, 222; Joshua Louis, 222; Mary Ann Wood, 222; Nelly Marie Taylor, 62; Rebecca Ann, 222; Robert Louis, 222; Z.B., 9

Jensen, Elissa, 198; F.H., 129; Frances, 111

Jerschied, Charles M., 18, 19

Jessie, W.M., 9

Jett, John Wyatt, 105; Susan M. Webb, 105

Jinkins, Elizabeth, 71

Jobe, Cynthia, 99; Dovie, 99; Genara, 99; Gerlina, 99; Grettie, 99; John, 137; John K., 137; Lillie A. Kendrick, 137; Lithe Kendrick, 137; Lona, 99; Lovie, 99; Ona, 99

Johannes, Emily Breanne, 47; Thomas Dee, 47; Thomas Dee, II, 47

John, 8

Johns, Mary Gladys Egan Hanna, 97

Johnson, Abigail, 90, 223; Alice M., 128; Allen, 45, 202; Allice, 52; Allison, 129; Amanda Disharoon, 133; Amos, 133, 161; Amos M., 52; Andrew Nelson, 223; Arthur John, 138; Audrey Mae, 148; Azzie A. Price, 134; Bellefame, 84; Bellefane, 80; Bervie Lois, 133; Bobby Joe, 214; Britney, 45; Caldonia Edith Fox, 133, 152; Callie, 153, 154; Carroll Gene, 70; Chester Clemon, 134; Claire Baugus, 175; Clara A. Baugus, 134; Clara Baugus, 125; Clara June, 138; Clarkie, 161; Clarkie Swanigan Barnett, 133; Columbus, 133; David, 45; Deborah Lynn, 145; Decie, 125; Della, 125; Dessie, 134; Dona Ellen Baugus, 134; Dovie Samantha, 174; Dustin, 45; Ed, 149; Edna M., 90; Effie Stewart, 197; Elizabeth, 77; Elizabeth Ann, 123; Elizabeth Nicole, 46; Ella, 125; Ellen Baugus, 125; Elmer, 125; Elmer B., 134; Emery, 125, 134; Emily E. Knowles, 133; Emline Martin, 149; Emma, 138; Emmer Huie, 134; Emoline McGehee, 78; Fay, 134; Francis Edith, 133; Frank, 153, 154; Frank M., 152; Frank Main, 133; Frank Oscar, 134; Fred C., 134; George, 133; George Henry, 138; George Orvel, 134; George Russell, 134; George Volmie, 134; George W., 133, 134; Georgie Fay Brimmage, 70; Girtha Jewel, 133, 152, 153, 154; Gladys, 125, 134; Grady, 138; Harriett, 123; Howard, 125; Huie, 134; James Main, 133; Jane, 134; Janet, 131; Jesse, 90; Jessie, 125; Jessie C., 134; Jewel, 125; Jewel M., 134; Jimmie, 70; Jimmie Carroll, Jr., 70; Jimmie Ruth White, 214; John B., 58; Joseph C., 58; Joyce, 134; Lela Delphia, 133; Lena Lucille Tucker, 133; Lillian, 128; Lillie A., 129; Lillie Frances, 138; Lilly, 52; Lois, 134; Lorene Annalee, 134; Lottie, 201; Louise, 133, 182; Loyce, 125; Loyd, 125; Lucy, 138, 147; Marcia, 46; Marion, 138; Marquita Renae New Sanchez, 103; Martha Ann Knighten, 138; Martha C. Huggins, 52; Martha Huggins, 128, 129; Martha Kuykendall, 133; Martha Lucille, 133; Martin Van Buren, 78; Mary, 125; Mary Ann J. Woody, 223; Mary Bell, 134; Mary Jane Kuykendall, 134; Mary Lola, 175; Mary M., 134; Mary R. Whitaker, 134; May, 134; Merle, 26; Michelle Anderson, 225; Minnie Bennett Smith, 62; Nancy, 133, 161; Nancy Emoline, 78; Natalie, 46; Oma, 134; Orville, 125; Oscar, 125, 175; Pam, 134; Patsy, 134; Pauline Opal, 134; Peggy Louise Fowler, 214; R.H., 28; Salenda Rankin, 183; Sally, 113; Sarah, 77, 157; Seaborn A., 134; Selena Rankin, 177; Steven, 138; Vasco, 62; Veva Dorothy, 133; William, 133, 138, 177, 183; William D., 134; William Main, 133; William Troy, 133; Woodrow A., 134

Johnston, Agnes, 148; Alton Theodore, 148; Amanda Jane Ward, 148; Anne, 27; Carol Ann, 214; Carroll W., 37; Donna Lynn, 214; Ellen M. Donals, 148; Flonnye Cleo Dallas, 148; Forest, 148; Georgie Ruth White, 214; Horest, 148; J.W., 37; James, 148; Jim, 27; John C., 148; John C., Jr., 148; Larry, 148; Leona, 148; Martha, 91; O.G., 214; Orpha Mallett, 148; Priscilla, 148; R.H., 29; Rosie Bramlett, 148; Sammie Clouette, 148; Vernon, 148; Vernon Clarence, 148; Willie Mae, 148

Jokish, Bertha, 226

Jollie, Arthie, 149

Jolly, Al, 29; Rosie, 111

Jones, A.B., 77; Aaron, 48; Adam Jones, 140; Adeline Nelson, 134; Adena, 163; Alicesten, 96; Allen, 197; Alta Fudge, 135; Amanda, 119; Amy, 140; Ann Louise, 194; Annie, 96; Annie Jewel, 113; Audrey Mobley, 160; Augusta, 96; Aulene, 149; Avalee, 134; B.F., 134; Barbara Hart, 119; Beatrice Laverne, 120; Benjamin,

Loftis, Clinton LaFayette, 146; Delcie, 146; Ellen Castleberry, 146; Eura Leo Webb, 146; Faye Cullum, 146; Laborn Barton, 146; Levi Boleth, 146; Levicy, 146; Lloyd, 146; Luther Clinton, 146; Margaret, 146; Martha, 182; Martha Ann Elizabeth Quattlebaum, 146; Minnie Esther, 146; Ola Carlene McKin, 146; Ovalee, 146; Ruby Floyd, 146; Thomas Lester, 146
Loftus, Leta, 103
Logan, B.C., 93
Logan/Wolf, Charlotte, 136
Logel, Hazel, 223, 224
Loggins, J.B., 26
Loh, Barbara, 39
Lombardo, Johannia, 92, 171; Johannina, 141
Long, A.M., 205; Addie Lector Cupp, 121; Alma, 195; Anna Dortha, 93; April Kristen, 146; Cornelia E. Bolton, 146, 147; Delia, 146; Elmo, 91; Elmo Floyd, 93; Evan Layne, 146; Forrest Michael, 147; Glenna Cathelene Hawkins, 121, 146; Helen Louise, 91, 93, 220; Herman Layne, 121, 146; Ira, 121, 146; John D., 146, 147; John H., 146; John Louis, 146, 147; Josie Parker, 146, 147; Lector Cupp, 146; Linda C., 146; Louis, 146; Marcy A., 146; Marmary Dicus, 91; Marmary Truman Dicus, 93; Mary A., 146; Mary Elizabeth Ford, 146; Mattie, 83; Ralph, 146; Roy, 146, 147; Ruby Lee, 146, 147; Stephen Layne, 146; Thomas A., 146; Wanda Dean, 87; William Ike, 146
Longinotti, Anthony, 164; Debbie Zachary, 225; Debra Zachary, 164; Janie, 164; Kevin, 164; Paul, 164; Tony, 164
Loomis, Maridell Cunningham, 55
Looney, Bekah, 149; Bill, 149; Charlene Bryant, 149, 150; Elizabeth Woolard, 118; Frances Josephine, 118; Gertrude, 118; James, 118; Kyle, 149; Maggie, 118; Martha W. Harmon Tidwell, 118; Mary, 118; Maudie, 118; Randy, 149; Rebecca Diane, 149; Rita Sutterfield, 149; Thomas, 118; William, 118; William Thomas, 118
Loong, Eugene, 146
Loonie, Jessie, 118; Sadie, 118
Lopes, Rebecca, 83
Lord, Amanda, 147; Anna, 147; Charles, 147; Cora Linn, 147; Dorthy Bird, 147; Edmond, 147; Ellen Cain, 147; Florance, 166; George, 147; Hannah, 147; Hattie, 147; James, 147, 166; James Damon, 147; James Madison, 147; Joseph, 147; Joseph S., 147; Josephine, 147; Judidia Boyd, 147; Margaret, 147; Mary, 147; Mary Louise, 147; Nellie Malone, 147; Parthene Florance, 147; Parthene Parnell, 147, 166; Robert, 147; Sarah, 147; Stanley, 147; Susan Zygette, 147; Thomas, 147; Walter, 147; William, 147
Lore, Mary, 38
Louis, Earl Bush, 52
Louk, Caroline, 166
Love, Bertha Balch, 58; Charles Allen, 58; Daulphus, 143; Edgar Earle, 58; Eliza Izora Ledbetter, 143; Izora A., 143; Jim, 29; Leon, 86; Lonnie F., 143; Marion Ryland, 58; Martha Tidwell, 143; Melvina Ann, 209; Myrtle R., 143; Pamela Pruett, 181; Rommie Mack, 143; Sarah Clemmons, 86; Thomas G., Jr., 143; Thomas Green, 143; Wiley, 143; William Earl, 58
Lovelace, Charles, 37; Fred J., 211; George, 211; Joseph Alphonzo, 211; Joseph D., 211; Mark H., 211; Martha Annis Tennessee Wear, 211; Nellie L., 211; Odar M., 211; Pink E., 211; Robert Z., 211; Ruby N., 211; Sybil N., 211; Verta, 211
Lovelady, Colette Marie, 67; Tammie, 69
Loveless, Agatha, 175; Royce, 37
Lovell, Martha E., 199
Lovett, Charlie Allen, 52; Dallas Wesley, 52; Ernest Elmer, 52; McWillie Allen, 52; Walter Murphy, 52; William Bryan, 52
Lowder, Andrew, 147; Bettie, 147; Catherine E., 147; Elizabeth Frances Bowman, 147; Frances M., 147; George David, 147; Grady, 147; Henry, 147; Jeremiah, 147; Jeremiah M., 147; Lester, 147; Mary F., 147; Mary Francis, 75; Persilla M., 147; Robert F., 147; Roxa E., 147; Rubie, 147; Terry Maxine Nicholson, 225
Lowe, Linda Sue, 207; Ola Mae Watkins Boyer Tilley Cravens, 207; Paula, 180
Lowrance, Dorothy, 187; James, 187; Lettie Marie, 187; Mettie Marie Roberts, 187; Roy Edward, 187; William Isacc, 187
Lowry, Lela Mae, 68
Loyd, Alta Huggins, 126, 127; Comfort Annis Cypert, 90; Jimmy, 220; Joe, 126; Joe Hughes, 127; John, 90; Lena Ann, 87; Lois M., 20; Martha, 99; Michael, 87; Michael Jason, 87; Millie Jane Conley, 87; Syretha Chambers, 218; Syrthea Chambers, 220; William, 99
Lucas, Anna, 130; Hazel, 112; James L., 37; Jim, 196; Steve, 95; Tammy Dixon, 95; Terri, 140; Winifred, 63, 64
Ludwig, Maria Sophie, 105
Luebker, Charles Edward, 45
Lum, Kim, 135, 165
Lung, Anna Veronica, 209, 210; Elizabeth Wildermuth, 209; Jacob, 209
Lusas, Estella, 53
Lusk, Alicia Francis Prince, 180; Jim, 180; Justin, 180; Paula Lowe, 180
Luster, Eleanor Wofford, 221; John, 221
Lute, Martha Elizabeth Campbell, 75; Rudolph, 75
Lweis, Berma Brents, 68
Lyell, Winnifred, 54
Lyles, Cleon, 37
Lynch, Elaine Riedmueller, 144; Mary Elizabeth, 67; Rupert, 35, 195
Lynn, Dawna Hanna, 117; Jeffrey Woods, 223
Lyon, J., 8
Lyonell, Halbrook, 7, 11
Lyons, Barbara Barrett, 88; Blanche, 148; Gary, 88
Lytle, Heather Dawn Watson, 97; McKinzy Michelle, 97; Shanan Dale, 97; Sky Ashley, 97

M

Mabey, Minnie, 165
Mabry, Sarah Reedy, 184; William, 184
MacDonald, Virginia Lea, 57, 58
Machen, Patricia, 184
Machovec, Rudolph A., 19
Machu, John Theo, 170; Stella M. Paceley, 170
Mackey, Eliza Ann, 214; Maggie E., 196
MacMillan, Cynthia Sledge, 195; Daniel G., 195; Elizabeth Mary, 195; Emeline, 195; Hardy, 195; Isabelia, 195; John M., 195; Sarah, 195; Susan, 195; Thomas, 195; William, 195
Macy, Mitchell, 55; Sarah Jane Andrews, 55
Madden, Mary Dalorosa, 31
Maddox, Charles, 210; Elvina, 199; Emma, 125; Emma H., 88; Fanny, 109; James, 199; Martha Jane, 71, 199; Matilda, 54, 55; Phoebe Andrews, 210; Sarah, 210; Thomas, 210; William, 54
Magaha, Joseph B., 18
Magee, Judith, 88
Mahan, Addie, 148; Alice Doughty, 148; Alice Gilbert, 148; Alma Latimer, 148; Annie Hurst, 148; Arthur, 148; Belle, 148; Bill, 202; Chloe Pearle, 174; Darby, 148; Deanie, 148; Della, 148, 166; Dempsey, 147; Dewey Wesley, 91; Dick, 202; Dora Carpenter, 148; Dorothie, 148; Dorothy Garriott, 202; Dovie, 147, 202; Edna Jeanette, 174; Effie Tackett, 148; Eliza Jane, 148; Emily White, 56, 147; Ethel, 148, 202; Evie Geary, 148; Floy, 148; Floyd, 148; Frances Nicholson, 148; Frank, 148; Fronie Brown, 148; Genie Stripling Rhoades, 148; George, 148; Harold James, 190; Harriet Stripling, 147, 177, 202; Harrison, 148; Harvey, 148; Hattie Allen, 147; Hattie French, 147, 202; Hazel Lorraine, 174; Helen, 202; Henry, 148; India Tackett, 148; Iola, 147, 202; Irvie, 148; Jack, 148; James Irving, 148; James K., 190; James M., 56; Jane, 148; Jane Morrow Rainwater, 148; Jennifer Lynn Deaton, 91; Jerry, 202; Jess, 148; Jesse, 177; Jesse W., 147, 202; Jim, 202; Jimmie, III, 147, 148; Jimmy, 147; Jodie, 147, 202; John, 148; John Irving, 174; John Melton, 147; John Rayburn, 174; Johnny, 147; Katie Kelley, 148; Lantie Latimer, 148; Larkin, 148; Lela French, 148; Lelia, 148; Leu, 202; Linner Ethel, 95, 177; Lona Doughty, 148; Loretta, 190; Loretta Dockins, 95, 148; Lottie Byrd, 148; Louisa Jane, 184; Lowell, 95, 148; Lucy, 147; Lucy Johnson, 147; Lue, 147; Margaret Eugenia Stripling Rhoades, 202; Marie Cooper, 148; Martha, 148; Martha Starkey, 148; Martin, 148; Mary, 148, 202; Mary Ann Lockhart, 148; Mary Starkey, 148; Matilda Ruth, 174; Michael, 202; Mildred Scroggins, 190, 202; Miles Melvin, 148; Minnie Byrd, 148; Modean Kirtley, 202; Nancy, 56, 147, 152; Nancy Jane Shewmake Adams, 147; Nanny, 147, 202; Nicholas, 148; Nora Marlow, 148; Odessa Elizabeth, 174; Oneta, 202; Opal, 66, 95, 180; Orie Brown, 148; Paul Edison, 174; R.L., 202; Rachel Beatrice, 174; Richard, 148; Roger Wayne, 190; Rose Morris, 202; Rosie Harris, 148; Roy Edward, 174; Sophronie Steely, 147; Taylor, 147, 202; Tine Poteet, 147, 148; Tressie, 202; Triphena Paxton, 148; Tryphena Olive, 174; Vincent, 148; Webb, 148; Wesley, 148; Will, 148; Zora, 148
Mahan-Yow, Lucy, 87
Mahoney, Bailey, 190; Chris, 190; Tammy Welch, 190
Maiden, Alva Maiden, 147; Annie, 147; Bertha, 147; Caroline, 147; Charles, 147; Cordelia, 147; Daisy, 147; Elizabeth, 147; Emma, 147; Henry, 52, 147; Jack Taylor, 147; Jacob B., 147; James M., 147; Jennie, 147; John, 147; Joseph, 147; Katie, 147; Margaret, 52, 147; Mary, 147; Milton, 147; Minnie, 147; Rebeca A., 74, 147; Rebecca A., 52; Sarah, 147; Simeon B., 147; Simeon B., Jr., 147; William, 52, 147; William F., 147; William J., 147; Willie, 147; Willis, 147
Maier, Gertrude, 212
Majors, Martha Elizabeth Owens Prince Merryman, 180; Selina, 118; William, 180
Maldonado, Sarah, 168
Malik, Angela Ann DeSalvo, 92; Hamid, 83; James Joseph, 92; Jo Ann Morphis, 83; Shawn, 83
Mallet, Marie, 148; Salley, 77
Mallett, Abby Elizabeth, 148; Alice Elma White, 148; Alma Daucie, 214; Alma Henritta, 77; Alta Lorene, 148; Amanda, 77, 135; Anderson Gordon, 77; Audrey Mae Johnson, 148; Barbara Lynn, 148; Barbara Lynn Halbrook, 115; Beatrice, 49; Beatrice Blanch, 189; Blanche Lyons, 148; Carl Dean, 148; Carrie Ophelia, 148; Clemmie Browning, 148; Columbus, 148; Daniel Harrison, 77; Daucie, 137; Drucie, 148; Edna, 148; Edwin Monroe, 77; Elizabeth Salter, 148; Ethel, 214; Ethel Mount, 148; Ethel Ollie, 137; F.M., 56; Fannie, 90; Gary Glen, 148; George Washington, 77, 135, 148; Grace La Verne, 148; Gwynnith Louise, 148; Heneritta Annett Casharago, 77; Henrietta Casharago, 135, 148; Henrietta Louise, 148; Henrietta Vaughn, 148; Irvin L., 148; J.C., 148; James A., 90; James O., 90; Janet Gayle, 148; Janet Gayle Halbrook, 115; Jesse L., 148; Jessee, II, 148; Joe, 77; Joe David, 148; John, 148; Joseph Columbus, 77, 148; Kelly, 77; Lea, 149; Lena Elizabeth, 77; Lizzie, 61; Lois Mae Crye, 90; Lona Ruth, 148; Lonie Jean, 148; Lula Abbie Duncan, 77; Lula Duncan, 148; Lydia Bell, 77, 148; Lynn, 95; Mae, 90; Marie, 49, 189; Marvin E., 148; Mary Ann Stacia Atkins, 56; Mary Cordelia Miller, 148; Mary Elizabeth Smith, 77; Matilda Tabitha Sterling, 148; Milton Leon, 148; Minnie Casharago, 77; Minnie Casharago Wharton, 77; Molly Perry, 77; Nancy Ollie Kennamer, 77, 137; Norma Cleo, 148; Ollie Jane, 148; Opie Dale, 148; Opie Dalton, 148; Orpha, 148; Ray, 148; Regina Dixon, 95; Ronald Dalton, 148; Roxie, 201; Ruby, 148; Ruby Jones, 148; Sabra Elizabeth Cargile, 148; Sarah Catherine, 77; Stephen, 148; Teresa Pinter, 176; Thurman Othelian, 148; Vida, 201; Virgil, 77; William Lewis, 77, 137; William Louis, 77; Willie Marie, 148; Wilma L., 148
Malone, Alfred Farrell, 124; Linda Marie, 124; Luther, 129; Mayme Hortense Patterson, 129; Nellie, 147; Pearlie Mae White, 124; Susannah, 197
Maloney, John David, 188; Karen Jo Rowell, 188; Lowell David, 188
Manan, Princie, 148
Manasco, Margaret Young Hale, 224
Mandziara, Ashley, 170; Brian, 170; Brianne, 170; Cindy, 170
Manes, Linda Wisdom, 219
Mann, Bridgette, 45
Manning, Emma, 48; Emma Eileen, 48; Georgia Tanner, 204; James, 204; James, II, 204; Louise, 201; Marshall Stuart, 48; Michael, 204; Minnie Esther Loftis, 146; Virginia, 204
Mansfield, Opal, 82, 226
Mantus, Caudine Ridling, 57
Manuel, Jessie Lafayette, 140, 178; Lucille, 178; William, 178
Maples, Jane, 166
Maratta, J., 8
Markham, R.T., 8
Marks, Mary E., 118
Marlar, Dolphia Ann Taylor, 62; John Allen, 62
Marler, Barbara, 5
Marley, Edward G., 31
Marlow, Evelyn, 143; Frances, 143; Ida, 180; Lillie, 143; Lizzie, 56; Lucinda Steel Lee, 143; Nora, 148; Rose, 143; William, 143
Marlowe, Rosa A., 199
Marmon, Frances Lou Dora, 169
Marney, Francis, 19
Marquardt, Minnie May Autry, 187
Marr, Eliza Jane, 61
Marshall, Ann, 98; Elizabeth, 60, 101, 102, 203; Jacob, 90; Margaret Scypert, 90
Marshaw, Edward L., 20
Martin, Alveta, 149; Amy Kay, 198, 200; Anna, 49; Anna Bartlett, 204; Aretty King, 149; Arminta, 149; Aulene Jones, 149; Bertha, 149; Bervie Lois Johnson, 133; Betty, 50; Bill, 83; Billie Jean Stobaugh Wilson, 197, 198, 200; Billy, 70; Carmie Bishop, 64; Carol Ann, 49; Carrie Ophelia Mallett, 148; Claud, 64; Cynthia, 77; D. Hugh, 105; Dale, 94; Daniel H., 149; Delila A. Goodman, 148, 149; Dicy, 149; Dillon, 94; Dustin, 94; Eli Mansfield, 149; Elizabeth, 223; Ellis, 133; Elsie, 149; Emline, 149; Eula, 198; Eula Ramer, 182; Fanny, 148; Floyd, 149; Frances, 70; Frances W., 148; George W., 148; Georgia A., 149; Georgia Lee, 93; Gertha, 149; Gertha Mayona Bridgman, 70; Gladys, 49, 149; Hannah Sutterfield, 70; Harold, 148; Harold Mallett, 148; Hestlee, 149; Irvin, 149; James, 70, 105; James L., 76; Jemolee, 70; Jeweldean Grabher, 110; Joel, 148; Joel Jefferson, 149; John, 42, 223; John Anderson, 148; John Lewis Reddick, 112; John Ruben, 148; John V., 148; John Wesley, 149; Jordan, 94; Joseph Wayne, 148; Josephine, 220; Julia, 149; Krysten Lynice Dixon, 94; Leta, 149; Lillie, 149; Lona, 149; Lora, 149; Loretta Lynn, 49; Louisa, 149; Loulee, 64; Loyd, 149; Lynice Sharp Dixon, 94; Malissa, 181; Marilyn, 204; Martha A., 149; Martha Jane, 130; Mary, 62; Mary Ann, 148; Mary Ann Ables, 148; Mary Bell, 149; Mary E. Mitchell, 149; Mary Helen Cobb, 149; Mary Jane, 223; Mary Lenora, 149; Maryland Rose, 49; Mayona Bridgman, 149; Melvina M. Chadwick, 149; Merdie, 50, 149; Molly, 105; Nellie Mae Watts, 149; Nelsie, 149; Ollie, 149; Ollie Fryer, 149; Opal Bishop, 64; Pat, 119; Rachel Adaline George Dark, 105; Ricky Lynn, 83; Riley A., 149; Rita, 119; Rita Gail, 83; Rob, 70; Robert, 105; Robert Houston, 149; Roy, 149; Roy Jefferson, 70; Ruth Carolyn, 148; Ruth Elaine Morphis, 83; Safronia V., 198; Samuel J., 27; Sarah, 148, 149; Sarah Angel, 132; Sarah Ann Kerley, 149; Sarah Berthena, 148; Sarah Frances Grabher, 110; Sarah Jane Wilson, 149; Thomas, 223; Uless, 149; Vestle, 149; Virginia, 20; W.O., 49; W.S., 49; Wanda White, 214; Will, 182; William, 198, 204; William Hershel, 198, 200; William Joel, 148; Wilma, 50; Wilma Rhoades, 149
Mash, Minnie Bell Rinehart Grice, 137
Mason, Aaron, 56; Ada, 149; Ada Lee, 150; Alice, 150; Alice O'Dean, 150, 151, 152; Amanda Kaye, 152; Amy, 150; Anna Boozer, 177; Annie Boozer, 65; Ardella Massingill, 151, 188; Barbara, 151, 188; Barbara Eades, 152; Belle Miller, 150; Bennie Ray, 150, 151, 152; Bernice Allene, 150, 151, 152; Bertha Alewine, 151; Beverly Harris, 152; Bob, 150; Bobby, 188; Carolyn, 151, 152; Carrie, 152; Celia Catherine Davis, 151, 152; Celia Davis, 56, 150, 151; Charles, 152; Chester A., 150; Chris, 152; Christina Lee, 152; Cosie, 150; D.D., 8; Daniel Othella, 151, 152; Daniel Othello, 150; Danny, 152; David Allen, 152; David L., 150; Delana Renea, 152; Delia Middleton, 134; Della Frances, 151; Della Jane, 188; Dewey, 149; Donna Delaney, 151; Dora, 152; Drew, 151; E.L., 150, 151; Edna Masterson, 56, 150; Elizabeth Ann, 150, 152; Elizabeth C. Shumake, 152, 191; Elizabeth Muse Lenderman, 151; Elizabeth Shoemake, 151; Ella, 177; Ella Berry, 152; Ella Margaret Pryor, 150; Ellen, 151; Ellen D. McGinty, 151; Elmer, 56; Emma, 149; Emma V., 65; Emma Viola, 150; Erika, 152; Essie, 151; F.M., 65; Felix, 177; Ferrel Orville, 150; Ferrell Lynn, 150, 151, 152; Ferrell O., 150; Fionell, 150; Flora Maye, 150, 151; Frances V., 149, 150; Fred, 149; Fred Orville, 149, 150; Georgia Nassie, 150; Gladys, 150; Grace Marie, 134; Ida McMahan, 56, 150; Irene Plough, 152; Isaac Dewey, 150; J.H., 149; J.L., 151; James Aaron, 150, 151; James Blaine, 150; James H., 147, 149, 150; James Harrison, 56, 149, 150, 152; James Henry, 150; James Madison, 151; Janice Kay, 152; Janice Ruth, 150; Jessica, 152; Jill Brandt, 152; Joe, 151; John, 134, 147; John C., 56; John Calvin, 150, 151; John Samuel Roberts, 150; John Stark, 152, 179; John Wilburn, 150, 152; Johnnie Louise, 150; Johnnie V., 151; Johnnie Venson, 150, 152; Johnnie Venson,

Jr., 152; Joseph Elmer, 150, 151; Joseph Theodore, 150; Katherine Guinn, 152; Katherine Marie, 150, 151, 152; Keith Erick, 152; Kenneth, 150; Kenneth Orvid, 150; Kevin Leon, 152; Larry Wayne, 152; Laurice H., 150; Laurice Harrison, 150; Lawson A., 152; Lawson Anderson, 151; Lee, 56, 139; Lee Hamilton, 150, 152; Lena Mae, 150, 151, 152; Lewis, 151; Linda, 26; Linda Gail Davis, 152; Linda Lee Gwin, 152; Lizzie, 151; Lonnie, 56; Lonnie Venson, 150, 151, 152; Lonnie Wayne, 150, 151, 152; Lora Prince, 56, 150; Lorene Knighten Brents, 139; Lottie, 150; Lucas, 150; Madlin Sumpter, 151; Maggie, 151; Marcus Layfayette, 152; Margaret Ann, 152; Margaret Samantha Powwell, 179; Mariah, 177; Marlana Gail, 152; Marvin Leon, 150, 151, 152; Marvin Raye, 150; Marvin Wayne, 152; Mary C. Jane, 150; Mary C. Jane Atkinson, 147; Mary Carolyn, 150; Mary Centelia Jane Atkinson, 56, 149, 150; Mary Damaras, 150; Mary Evelyn, 150, 151, 152; Mary F., 152; Mary Isabelle Miller, 149; Mary J. Atkinson, 149; Mary Jane Atkinson, 149; Mary Lee, 150; Mary Leta Flowers, 152; Mary Lynn, 150; Mary Magdalene, 151; Marylynn, 150; Michael Earl, 152; Mildred Knowles, 150; Minnie Evelyn Fullerton, 150; Minnie Fullerton, 150; Munro, 151; Nancy Emma, 152; Nancy Leota Laurice, 150; Nancy Leota Mae, 150; Orville Lee, 150; Pat, 150; Quinton Earl, 150, 151, 152; Ramona Lynn, 152; Rebecca Damaras Harriet Hill, 149, 150; Rodney, 150; Ronald Odell, 150; Roxie A., 150; S.E., 150; Sammie Sue, 150; Sammy Sue, 150; Samuel, 150, 151; Samuel Lafayette, 150; Samuel S., 151; Samuel Selathiel, 152, 191; Sephronia Elizabeth Atkinson, 150; Shane, 152; Sheila, 152; Shirley, 152; Sidney, 151; Sidney Harold, 150, 151, 152; Sondra, 152; Sophronia Atkinson, 147, 151; Sophronia E. Atkinson, 56; Sula, 151; Susan, 150; Tammie Regina, 152; Thelma, 150; Verdia Mae, 150; Vicky, 150; Vincent Leon, 152; Walter A., 151; Walter Lee, 151, 188; Wanda Faye, 150; Wilburn, 56; William Alexander, 152; William Chester, 150, 151; William Harrison, 152; Wilma Lee, 150, 151, 152
Massery, Bernadine, 160
Massey, Joe, 37; Nancy Sarah Ann, 138, 139; Willie Ellen, 81
Massingill, Ardella, 151; Bertha, 151; Bertha Mae, 125; E.M., 182, 183; G.C., 155; Ida Belle, 125; Jessie Ford, 182, 183; Laverne, 37; Mahalia, 151; Marion, 151; Mattie, 151; Syble Mae, 182, 183
Masters, Charles Harold, 125; Harold, 91; Maxine Deaver, 91; Opaline Hill, 125
Masterson, Edna, 56, 150; Elizah, 66; Lucy R. Branom, 66
Matheny, Tammy, 164
Mathers, Thomas, 8
Mathes, Minnie Mae, 58
Mathis, Chester, 209; Elmore McClure Horton, 124; Evelyn, 125; Louraney Arella Wallace, 209; Martha, 184; Minnie Mae, 126; Thomas, 125; Thomas Harrison E., 124
Matlock, Billie June, 188; Danny Jay, 76; Della Campbell, 74; Della Jean Campbell, 76; J.V., 76; Maracella Anne, 76
Matson, Mary Rose, 88
Mattern, Anna Mae, 135; Anna Mae Christine Jordan, 135; Buryl Benton, 135; Buryl Benton, Jr., 135; Darrlyn, 135; Patricia Ann, 135
Matthews, Amanda, 184; Christy, 149; Clara, 131; Claude, 37; Genevia Icillene Scroggin, 189; J.M., 37; Johnnie, 189; Karen Ridgely, 149; Lloyd, 200; Lola Hogan, 224; Lorraine Merritt, 200; Mary, 130, 213; Mary Ann, 200; Ronnie, 149
Mauk, Charles F., 76; Cheryle Lee, 76; David Fredrick, 76; Dennis Charles, 76; Lisa Gail, 76; Richard Dale, 76; Ruby Anne Campbell, 76
Mauldin, Alma L., 211
Maupin, Bobby, 153; Bobby Lee, 152, 153, 154; Bobby Lee, III, 153; Chad Evert Bissel, 153; Christina, 153; Daniel, 154; Deborah Jean Couch, 153; Debra Ann, 153; Donnie Ray, 154; Edward Francis, 153, 154; Elizabeth, 154; Frankie Louis, 154; Gabriel, 154; George Webb, 154; Girtha Jewel, 154; Girtha Jewel Johnson, 133, 152, 153, 154; Hariet Ella McClure, 152; Harriet Ella McClure, 153; Harriet McClure, 77, 154, 157; Jane Warren, 154; Jennifer Ann, 153; Jesse, 154; John Curtis, 133, 153, 154; John O., 153; John Wesley, 77, 133, 152, 153, 154, 157; John Wesley, Jr., 154, 157; John Wesley, Sr., 154; Joyce Dean, 154; Kelsey Ann, 153; Lida Louisa Cooper, 153; Lida Luisa Ann Wilks Mar Cooper, 154; Louis Franklin, 154; Lucy Jones, 154; Margaret Via, 154; Margie Cox Hunt, 154; Marie Hersent, 154; Michael Wayne, 153; Nancy N. Leffingwell, 154; Nancy Nell Leffingwell, 153; Norma Jean Krammer, 154; Rhonda Suzane Tester Thompson, 153; Roberta Lynn, 153; Robin Lynn, 153; Sharon Lee Bergren, 154; Sharon Lee Bergren Cline, 153; Shirley Kapusihinsky, 153; Terry Lynn, 153; Thressa Messick, 153, 154; Troy Gene, 154; Virgil Fay, 154; William, 154
Maupins, John Lee, 153
Maus, Annalee, 51; Hamilton, 51; J.B., 51; John, 50; Lawrence, 31; Lawrence P., 31; Stephen, 51
Maxcy, Edward, 209; Mary Caroline, 209; Mary Polly Nelson, 209
Maxey, Bennett Hail, 70, 154; Bobby John, 95; Delilah, 154; Dicey Craighead, 154; Dicey Jane, 70, 154; Edward, 154, 166; Edward, II, 154; Elizabeth Ann Wyatt, 154, 166; Frances Eason, 70, 154; Hail, 154; James T., 154; Jane Dicia, 154; Jerald, 95; Jeremiah, 154; John H., 154; Lillard Catherine Dockins, 95; Lorene, 95; Mahala Jane, 166; Marie, 95; Martha Ann, 70, 154; Mary Allen, 154; Mary Ann Humphries, 166; Mary Netherland, 154; Mourning Hail, 154; Olen F., 95; Samuel Madison, 166; Sarah Angeline M. Gilcrest, 154; Susannah Gates, 154; Walter Justinian, 154
Maxwell, Alice Faye, 156; Alice JoAnn, 156; Alvus M., 154, 155, 156; Barbara Ellen, 80; Barry Wade, 80; Bernice Bull, 80; Billye Ruth Bull, 80; Clara Marie Watkins, 210; Cyrus, 156; D., 8; Dana Lynn, 80; Dennis, 16; Dove, 155; Doyle, 155; Edith Melvinia, 80; Elna Louise, 80; Eugenia, 115; Eugenia Francis Houston, 155, 156; Eugenia Houston, 194; Eva Ethel Chism, 80; Eva Louise, 155; Evelyn McCasland, 156; Everett Leroy, 156; Frances Foshee, 80; Gary David, 80; Geneva Mae, 109; Gordon Lee, 80; Gregory Lance, 80; Ida Mae, 80; Jack, 155; James Francis, 156; James Milburn, 80; James V., 80; James Victor, 80; Janet Denise, 80; JoAnna Josephine Robinson, 156; John Wesley, 156; John Westerfield, 80; Josephine Robinson, 80; Kate, 155; Katherine Grace, 155; Kenny Allen, 80; Linda Diana, 80; Louise, 115, 194; Lucinda, 155; Lucinda Bell, 155; Luther, 11, 115, 154, 155, 194; Luther A., 11; Luther Alonzo, 155, 156; Margaret, 71; Marilyn Lance, 80; Martha, 103; Marvin, 155; Mary Ann Harrington, 154, 155; Mary Evelyn 80; Mary Lena, 80; Melvin Hayes, 80; Noah, 155; Pauline Euna, 80; Randy Howard, 80; Robert Wayne, 156; Stephen Erman 80; Vicki Annette, 80; Virgil, 155, 156; Virginia Cain, 80; Vivian Jewell, 80; Wesley Obadiah, 80; William L., 210; William Virgil, 156
May, Bernice, 128; Dayton, 204; Debbie Weems Watson, 83; Deborah Tanner, 204; George, 204; John, 58; Kendall, 204; Phil, 83; Terri, 204; Tony, 204; Yvonne Tanner, 204
Mayall, Betty Irene Dicus Hester, 93; Elmer, 95; Gloria Jean, 82; Kathryn, 164; Leona, 95; Margaret J. Dockins, 95; Sherrill, 93; Thomas, 95
Mayberry, Loreatha Gunnels, 64, 65
Maye, O'Della Pruett, 180
Mayfield, Betty Jones, 87; Elizabeth Sue Jones, 63; Kimberly Ann, 63; Lisa Marie, 63; Ross Richard, 63; Terry Lynn, 63
Mayhew, Douglas Bradley, 87; Glenn Max, 87; Millie Jane Conley Loyd, 87
Mayhue, Aubrey, 99; Frank, 99; Georgia, 99; Jasper, 99; Nona, 99; Reba, 99
Mays, Essie May, 180; Glen, 180; Theresa, 180
McAlister, George, 61; Ira, 61; Leila Mae, 61; Mary Aneta, 131; Orville, 61; Sallie Mae Bell, 61; Willie Bell, 61
McAnulty, Joseph Abraham, 202; Myrtle Mae, 202; Narcissus Beasley, 202
McArthur, D.L., 21, 123; Doris Kay Pettingill, 175; Ester Belle, 175; Gary, 175; Kate, 211; Louise Reddig, 184; Mandy, 175; Margaret Hoelzeman, 123; Michelle, 175; S. Woody, 173; Shirley, 175
McAuliffe, Leon, 127
McBath, Ida W. Priddy, 129; J.A., 129
McCabe, Archie, 213; Daisy Laws, 213; Dan, 213; Elizabeth, 208; Isofene Laws, 213; James, 208, 215; Jape, 213; Jim, 213; Lester, 213; Marion, 126; Mary Jemina, 213; Matthew, 213; Matthew Marion, 208, 215; Sara Ann, 125; Sarah Ann, 126; Sarah Jane, 215; Sarah Jane Wade, 208, 215; Thomas Lovell, 215; Vester, 213
McCaig, Elizabeth Leslie, 156; John Wesley, 156; Samuel, 156; Sarah Sutter, 156; Susan C., 156
McCaige, 156; John, 99; Susan C., 99
McCall, Euleta, 190; Robert, 8
McCallie, Sam, 15
McCarley, John W., 181; Louiza Ragsdale, 181
McCarrol, Dorothy, 20
McCarty, Jean, 188; Rebecca, 208
McCarver, Ollie, 109
McCasland, Alice Freaman, 156; Evelyn, 156; James H., 156; Jane, 216; Rhoda Wade, 216; Rubye Ernest, 64; Wade Barrick, 216
McCauley, Ida, 134; Mary Gillette, 134; Mimi Gillette, 134; Patrick, 134
McClain, Agnes Lorene Gordon, 108; 108
McClanahan, Diana, 88
McClaren, Ellen, 80; L.E., 38; Myrtle, 114
McClean, Frances Elizabeth Burrow, 73; Tom, 73
McClure, Alma, 157; Alzira Ann Scarlett, 157, 189; Beatrice Maude Sutton, 157; Benny, 156; Benny Lloyd, 106; Bill, 157; Bill, Jr., 157; Billie Willis, 156; Bobbie, 67, 157; Bobbie Dean, 156; Carl, 157; Cassie Dancer, 157; Charida, 156; Charlene, 67, 156, 157; Charles Blaine Thomas, 106; Charles William, 67, 69, 134, 156, 157; Clint, 69, 156; Commie, 157; Commie A., 189; Constance Henderson, 156; D.J., 67, 156, 157; D.W., 157; Daisy Lee, 157; Darrell, 67, 157; Darrell Benjamin, 106; Darrell Benjamin Franklin, 156; David, 157; Derrick Shane Jack, 106; Dode, 154; Dora Bannon, 77, 134, 156, 157; Dorothy, 67, 157; Dorothy Lea, 156; Eliza Julia Jones, 134, 156, 157; Ernest M., 157; Frances, 157; Gene, 157; Georgia, 134; Georgia Ettamae, 157; Georgie, 157; Gracie, 67, 157; Gracie Lillian, 156; Hariet Ella, 152; Harmon, 134, 157; Harriet, 77, 154, 157; Harriet Ella, 153; James Barney, 157; James Orsen B., 157, 189; Jane, 213; Janell Brown, 156; Jo Ann, 67, 156, 157; John M., 157; Jonathan, 69; Julia, 134; Julia Ancybell, 157; Julie, 157; Katherine Ann Bridgman, 69, 156; Katherine Bridgman, 125; L.J., 157; L.M., 13; Larrinora Russell, 157; Lauren Lea Brooke, 106; Lodusky Catherine, 157, 189; Louisa Goff, 157; Lucille, 157; Luther, 134, 157; Luther Conway, 157; Margaret, 157; Martha Christine, 157; Mary Allen, 157; Mary Dallas, 157, 189; Mary Elen Scarlett, 157, 189; Mary H. Doubleday, 157; Mary Margaret Brewer, 156, 157; Matilda, 157; Maude, 157; Maude Magalene, 189; Melinda N., 189; Melissa, 157; Millard, 77, 157; Nancy, 157; Nancy E. Cargile, 153, 154; Nancy Elizabeth Cargile, 77, 156, 157; Nancy V., 189; Nelda Henderson, 156; Nellia, 156; Nellie, 134, 157; Nenion, 77, 157; Nenion Elijah, 157; Nora, 157; Nora Florence, 189; Orvin, 157; Owdia, 157; Pamela, 156; Patricia, 157; Pearl Shipley, 157; Peggy Janell Brown, 106; Peggy May, 157; Rachael, 157; Robert Conway, 77, 157; Robert Ramsey Conway, 157; Robert S., 157; Rosey May Killion, 157; Roy, 67, 69, 125, 157; Roy Leonard, 156; Ruby, 157; Sarah, 157; Sarah Ann Priscilla, 77, 157; Sarah Elizabeth, 157, 189; Sarah Smith, 157, 189; Sauna, 157; Scott, 69, 156; Shannon Hancock, 69; Shirley, 157; Shirley Lackey, 156; Stephen, 157, 189; Stephen, Jr., 157; Stephen Scott, 157; Steve, 156; Susie, 134, 157; Susie Izora, 157; Tammie Lovelady, 69; Tara Lea Givens, 106; Telitha Stanley, 157; Thelma Pearl Shipley, 157; Todd, 156; Tommy, 156; Valentine, 157, 189; Velma Branham, 157; Velma Mae Branham, 67, 69, 156, 157; Virgil, 67, 157; Virgil Ray, 156; Virgil Weldon, 157; Virginia, 156; William Edwin, 157; William Holliway, 153, 156; William Holliway S., 77, 157; William Holloway, 154; William Millard, 157; William S., 157; Willie Maude, 157; Willie Virgil, 156
McClurkin, May Hope, 162
McCochran, Margaret, 66
McComb, David, 178; Ernest, 178; Nancy, 178; Thelma Jean Powell, 178
McConnell, Athalene, 27; Maude, 128
McCool, John, 128; Racy Branson Montgomery, 128
McCoole, Jackson, 78
McCowan, Bill, 53; Cloteen, 53; Danny, 53; James, 53; Jerry, 53; Larry, 53; Melvin, 53; Paul, 53; Robert, 53; Ruby Allen, 53; Sylvia, 53
McCoy, Aimee, 85; Aldon, 80; Bert, 216; Betty Jewell, 80; Bettye, 188; Billy, 157; Blanche Mildred Kuykendall, 216; Bobbie, 88; Brenda, 98, 102, 119, 157, 221; Brenda Gail, 119; Carolyn Sue, 218; Cora Jordan, 157; Cynthia Ann Reid, 85; Dan, 102, 119, 157; Dannie, 157; Dannie S., 102, 103; Dannie Sue, 119; Dennis, 15; Dennis Ferrall, 222; Drayke Hunter, 222; Elmore Art, 80; Emily Marie, 222; Gertrude Williams, 216; Gladis Muriel Williams, 218; Harold, 15; Herbert Hoover, 81; Jack, 102, 119, 157; Jamie Allen, 222; Jan Rene, 179; Jason, 15; Jason Keith, 222; Jayden Clara, 222; Jeremy, 85; Jerry, 34; John, 67; Jonathan, 85; Lana Dale, 221; Larry, 34; Larry Winston, 80; Leslie, 34; Linnie May Wofford, 221; Lonnie J., 221; Luke, 157; Mack, 149; Martie Hamlin, 222; Mike, 85; Nancy Louise Wood, 222; Norma, 146; Oma Mae, 191; Rickey Lynn, 81; Sarah Catherine, 199; Shirley Louise, 81; Tabitha Burlie, 222; Talyn Angelique, 222; Thetus Bryant Stell, 150; Velma Brown, 81; Virginia Bennett, 102, 119, 157; Vivian Jewell Maxwell, 80; William Victor, 80
McCraige, Sarah Sutter, 99
McCravin, Andrew Jackson, 129; Julia, 105; Martha Melinda, 105; Mary Ann James Vann, 129; Thomas Monroe, 105; William, 105
McCraw, C.P., 26
McCray, Louise, 193; Susan Clarentine, 193
McCroy, 109
McCullar, Johnny, 146; Minnie Esther Loftis Manning, 146
McCullough, Cyrus, 158; Elizabeth Brandon, 157; Hannah Boring, 157; James, 157; John, 157; Joshua James, 158; Mary C. Jones, 158; Tabitha Taylor Mason Osburn, 158; Tennessee Lee, 99, 158
McCurley, Martha A., 209
McDade, Jennifer, 176; Jennifer Marie Plummer, 176; Scott, 176
McDaniel, Andrew G., 158; Arthur, 192; Daniel A.L., 158; Ellen Perkett, 158; Franklin, 158; Hattie Virginia Drilling Naff Switzer, 192; Ike, 130; Isaac, 158; James, 158; Jane, 199; Jessie Wilma Kuykendall, 216; John H., 158; Julia, 85; Lockie Elizabeth, 196; Margie Jenkins, 133; Martin Van Buren, 158; Napoleon, 158; Nova Lee Laws Pearson, 213; Opal Lee, 142; Parthenia Kemp, 136, 158; Roland Raymond, 216; Rube, 213; Ruth Naomi, 133; Samuel, 133; Samuel H., 158; Virginia, 158; William, 158
McDaniels, Jane, 198, 199
McDonald, Caroline, 82; Doyle Newton, 82; Eliza L. Hale, 116; Emma E. Anderson, 82; Jennafer Janell, 82; John S., 82; Kristy Kay, 82; Lindsey Gail, 82; Martha, 87; Newton A., 82; Olgar, 116; Richard, 82; Tammy Medlock, 82
McDonel, Thomas, 212; Ursala Weatherford Robbins, 212
McDonough, Lily Adeline Hubbard, 125, 126; Vernon, 125
McDowell, Hattie LaRue, 224
McElhannon, Kathryn, 215; Kathryn Elizabeth, 137; Kathryn Stoehner, 215
McElroy, Andy, 133; Autie Mae Hale, 116; Betty Jewel, 116; Blair, 164; Eva Frances Chambers, 158; Francis Edith Johnson, 133; Henry Houston, 133; Jesse Lee, 116; Lela Delphia Johnson, 133; Marsha Gay, 158; Michael Ray, 158; Narvin Ray, 158, 210; Orval Lee, 116; Patsy Jean Walters, 158; Tommy Lee, 158; Vittie, 116
McFearson, Henry, 8
McGarity, Maude, 182
McGee, Claude, 18; Donna, 163; Floy Goodall, 106; Loretta Wallace, 209
McGehee, Ada Elizabeth Hardin Hawkins, 120; Emoline, 78; Olevia, 186
McGhee, Sarah Susan, 201
McGill, Ann Cherry, 102; Hattie Boozer, 65
McGinty, Ellen D., 151; Emily C. Scroggins, 151; James W., 151; Mary, 221
McGlasson, Agnes, 160; Bascomb, 160; Ruby Lucille, 160, 161
McGleeson, Ruby, 162
McGloflin, Amelia Howard, 158; Elijah, 158; Harold Raymond, 158; Imogene, 158; James Brown, 158; James L., 158; Jeffrey, 158; Lela Cox, 158; Lela Sue, 158; Marcus, 158; Margaret L. Williams, 158; Nathan Abel, 158; Norman, 158; Sally Jo, 160, 201; Sam, 158; Samuel, 158; Susan Lou Critter Sarah, 158
McGoflin, Gayle, 158; Sally Jo, 158
McGrail, Amanda, 188; Greg, 188; Susan Rossi, 188; Tyler, 188
McGraw, C.P., 26

Stacy Maybelle Sikes Cotton, 65; Thomas J., 65
Pierson, Elzada, 54; Rosa, 54
Pijot, Mary, 182
Pike, Mary E., 61; Peggy Evelyn, 108
Pimpleton, Ollie, 22
Pinckney, C., 106
Piney, Lizzy, 70
Pinkerton, David C., 201; Joseph, 201; Martha Jane Stover, 201
Pinkham, J.B., 37
Pinkston, Brenda Kaufman, 136; Drew, 136; Jay, 136; Matthew, 136
Pinson, Clara Jo, 119; David, 208, 215; Mary Ann Green King, 208
Pinter, Ann, 176; Anna, 176; Anna Hoelzeman, 175; Ben, 176; Catherine Siebenmorgen, 176; Cetherine, 38; Christina, 176; Ed, 176; Frank, 176; Gerry, 176; Jacob, 175; Jane, 176; Mary Beth, 176; Mike, 176; Nita, 176; Patrick, 176; Paul, 176; Peter, 175, 176; Steve, 176; Teresa, 176; Tim, 176
Pitts, Benjerman Franklin, 128; Hattie Mae Waller, 128; Jane Elizabeth, 128; John Wesley, 127, 128; Joseph, 108; Juanita, 128; Lennie/Linda Ellen Huggins, 127; Lewis, 128; Linda Ellen Huggins, 128; Martha Barbee, 108; Millie, 106; Milly, 107, 108, 184; Robert Richard, 128; Virgil Arthur, 128
Plant, Elizabeth, 77; Margaret, 77; Mary, 77
Plough, Irene, 152
Plummer, Albert Carl, 176; Albert Oriel, 176; Angela Suzanne, 176; Audra Beth, 176; Aundrea Sue, 176; Benjamin Wallace, 176; Caroline Frances, 176; Cynthia Frances Spiering, 176; D.E., 176; David Edward, 176; Elbert Oriel, 176; Henrietta Ells, 176; Jeffrey Michael, 176; Jennifer Marie, 176; Jessica Ann, 176; Jodi Lynn, 176; John N., 19; John Samuel, 176; Joseph, 176; Josie E., 176; Julia Ann Miller, 176; Lillie Retter, 176; Lisa Marie Duncan, 176; Mary Alice Mosley, 176; Michelle Rene, 176; Minnie Ann, 176; Nadine, 176; Oma Montene Hopkins, 176; Peggy Sue Christiansen, 176; Robert Allan, 176; Royce, 176; Russell, 176; Russell Oriel, 176; Samuel, 13, 176; Sandra Reda, 176; Thomas, 176; Thomas Lewis, 176; William C., 13; William Oriel, 176
Plunkett, Sarah Ann, 186
Poe, Alexander H., 177; Arminda Minnesota, 177; Carla Michelle, 103; Christopher C., 177; David, 176, 177; Dorietta, 177; Eddie, 103; Edna Turner, 177; Elijah Jackson, 177; Elizabeth Morton, 176; Frances Harman, 118, 176, 177; George Marion, 177, 210, 218; Ida Couch, 177; Isabelle Frances, 177; Isabelle Jane Rankin, 177, 183; Jane, 210; John Masterson, 177; John Morton, 177; Joseph, 118, 177; Josephas, 177, 183; Josephas Francis, 177; Keziah, 177; Lena Joy Mills, 103, 220; Lucinda Gray, 177; Lucinda Stewart, 177; Lydia, 177; Maga Anne, 118, 177, 210; Marsh Harris, 177; Martha Jane, 177; Mary, 177; Mary Anne, 177; Melissa, 177; Melissa Marinda Williams, 177, 210, 218; Merle Ball, 103; Molly Roach, 177; Rhoda Alice, 177; Samuel, 177; Sarah, 118; Sarah Ellen, 177; Sarah Francis, 177; Simon, Jr., 177; Simon, Sr., 177; Sophronia C., 177; Tabitha Ridgeway, 177; Tazel, 103; Teisha, 222; Theron Monroe, 177; W.S., 177; William, 210; William D., 177; William Luther, 177
Pogue, Augusta, 123
Poindexter, Mickey, 27; Paul, 104
Polk, Allen, 148, 202; Alvin, 101; Amy Rebecca, 149; Andrea, 15; Ardith, 202; Ardith Taylor, 95, 177; Arnold, 28; Artel Lee, 177; Bennie Yvonne, 177; Bertie Bryant, 202; Bertie Stanton Bryant, 177; Bessie, 101; Bill, 202; Brant Cooper, 213; Charity Ellen, 180; Charles Alexander, 180; Daniel Webster, 180; Darryl Ray, 149; Dewel Mable Hartwick, 177; Doris Bratton, 95; Dorse, 202; Ellen J., 180; Ethel Mahan, 148, 202; Gertie Howard, 138; Gertrude Roller, 177, 202; Glen, 202; Glyn Allen, 177; Glyn Wood, 95, 177; Grover Garfield, 138; Hannah Jane, 109; Ida, 102; James, 15, 218; James K., 212; Jamianne, 45; Jasper Allen, 177; Joe Taylor, 180; John Gregory, 177; John Roland, 180; Laudis, 202; Laudis Thelbert, 95, 177; Linda Lou, 177; Linner Ethel Mahan, 177; Margaret Ann, 62, 212; Marie, 81; Martha Marie, 94; Martha S. Ellen Prince, 180; Mary Ardell Cowdrey, 177; Mary Cowdrey, 202; Mary Elizabeth, 177; Mary-lynn Adams, 149; Maxine Bryant, 149, 150; May Olliger, 101; Melvin, 149; Montine Sledge, 202; Nancy, 102; Nellie, 190; Norma Montine Sledge, 177; Ollie Pearl, 218, 219; Raymond, 187; Rebecca Jane, 177; Rhonda Annette Edwards, 213; Rosebelle Muliwai DeMello, 177; Ruby Jewel Roberts, 187; Sarah Elizabeth Prince, 95, 180; Sarah Vella, 102; Sarah Weatherford, 212; Shawnee Montana Hope, 213; Thomas Jefferson, 180; Thomas Scott, 213; Tura DeMello, 202; William, 102, 180; William Allen, 177; William Carroll, 177; William Jesse, 95, 177; William, Jr., 212; William Thomas, 95, 102, 177, 180
Pollock, Robert Bruce, 177
Ponds, Addie Oliver, 178; Alice, 65, 177, 206; Charles, 178; Claude, 178; Cromwell, 177; Delores Temple, 178; Ella Mason, 177; Estella, 177; Etta Wallace, 178; Faye, 178; Francis, 177; Frank John, 177; Frank John Henry, 206; George, 177, 178; Hattie, 178; Hazel, 178; Ida Armstead, 177; Ida Swaggert, 177, 178; James E., 178; John Bascom, 178; John E., 178; Julia Ann, 177; Lizzie, 177; Lucille Manuel, 178; Mae Esther Brown, 72, 177; Magdalene, 178; Mamie, 178; Mary, 177; Mary Smith, 178; Mary Thornton Haywood, 177; Michael, 177; Pauline, 178; Ruth James, 178; Thomas, 177; Thomas Pervis, 178; Tollie, 177; Tollie, II, 177; Zetora, 177
Pool, Clyde, 192
Poole, Andrew, 179; Emily Brooke, 179; Gertrude Merrick, 179; Jack Thomas, 179; Jason Eric, 179; Kristian Willis, 179; Tina, 164
Pope, Elizabeth Sharp, 69; Esrom Isom, 69; Frank, 69; Fredrick, 69; Ida Belle, 69; Lillian Dye, 225; Stella Adeline Bridges, 68, 69; Stella Bridges, 187; Tillman, 29; Venie Eveline, 125; William Izak, 69
Porphir, John, 214
Porter, Augusta Jackson, 131; J.B., 111; James Bernard, 182; James Bernard, Jr., 182; James David, 182; Lenora, 182; M., 8; Mattie, 52; Nona Ruth Rankin, 182; William H., 40
Porterfield, Janet Claire, 192
Postier, Karen, 161
Poteet, Tine, 147, 148
Poteete, Albert, 21, 22; Annie Thomas, 22; Arthur, 21; Arthur D., 22; Bernice, 51; Bob, 21; Dee Ann McHenry, 184; Diana Bearden Rainwater, 181; Dora, 21, 22; Dora Lee, 178; Elvis S., 178; Elvis Simeon, 181; Emma, 21, 22; "Fate", 21; Gloria, 178; Hazel Walker, 209; Ida, 21, 22; Jacqueline, 22; Jeff A., 178; John Miles, 22; Johnny, 184; Joseph Dalton, 184; Joseph Daniel, 22, 181; Lafayette, 22; Laura Ann, 178; Lavene, 12, 178; Luther, 21, 209; Luther Eugene, 22; Margrete C. Parker, 178; Martha, 22; Martha Ross, 178; Mary, 21, 22; Mary Elizabeth, 22; Mary Jane, 196; Mary Singleton, 178; Matilda Isabel, 159; May, 21, 22; Miles, 21; Nadene, 178; Nancy Christina, 22; Nancy Christina Rainwater, 181; Napoleon, 22; "Poley", 21; Rhoda Jane, 22; Rhoda Jane Rainwater, 181; Robert Lafayette, 22; Roxie Ann Bearden, 178; Rufus, 21, 22; Rufus C., 178; S.V., 181; Sarah Virginia, 22, 181; Sim, 26; Simeon Vinson, 22; Tollie, 21, 22; Vernonia, 21, 22; Virgil Paul, 178; William, 178; William H., 178; William Humphrey, 22
Potter, Kim, 143; Kimberly Ward, 143; Melissa, 170; Micheal, 170
Potts, Eugene, 175; Gene, 53; Kim, 53; Kimberly, 175; Michael, 53, 175; Patricia, 175; Patricia Jeanette Anderson Boyd, 53
Povall, Rachel, 60
Powell, Allen, 15, 109, 179; Allen Troy, 178, 179; Allen Troy, II, 179; Alvin Daniel, 178, 179; Andrew Aaron Travis, 179; Angelica, 186; Angelica Battles, 178; Anthony Joseph, 222; Arlie, 97; Athula, 178; Benjamin Franklin, 178; Betty Green, 178; Bird Hampton, 179; Blake Alexander Jean, 179; Bramilla Charlotte, 179; Bulah, 157; Cathy, 178; Charity, 178; Charles, 175, 179; Clara Pearl Harwood, 119; Cora Estella, 178; Curtis, 77, 157; Cynthia Elizabeth Malvina Hood, 179; David Marshall, 175; Dawn Raynelle Wood, 222; Debbie, 178; Della Magnolia, 178; Dorothy Green, 178; Edna Perry, 175; Edward Washington, 178; Eliza C.J. Hood, 179; Elizabeth, 179; Elizabeth Ann Henderson, 122; Elizabeth Gordon, 109; Ella Elizabeth, 178; Elvira Elizabeth Carpenter, 179; Emily Isabelle Gilbert, 97; Ernest Jackson, 178, 179; Ethel Magnolia, 178; Eunice, 179; Eunice Sarah Letha Mary Elizabeth, 137, 179; Florence Mable, 178; Gary, 178; George, 175; Georgia, 175; Gerald Ray, 178; Glenda, 142, 178; Glenn, 142; Glenn Jackson, 178; Hardin, 178; Harriet Ella McClure Maupin, 153; Harriet McClure Maupin, 77, 157; Homer Alexander, 178; Inez Ola, 178; Inez Rosie Bostian, 178; Irene Lucille, 178; Isaac M., 179; Isom, 178; James, 178; James Anderson, 178; Jan Rene McCoy, 179; Janice, 178; Janis, 142; Jesse A., 179; Jesse Spear, 179; Jo Ann Lasater, 142; Joann Lasiter, 178; John, 175, 178; John Able, 178; Johnnie Sue Williams, 178; Josephine, 178; Josie Ellen, 178; Laura Ann Hall, 178; Lela Marie Mullican, 178, 179; Levi, 179; Margaret, 137, 178, 195; Margaret Cooper, 178; Margaret Faulkner, 179; Margaret Samantha, 179; Marion Daniel, 178; Mark, 178; Marshall, 175; Martha, 179; Mary, 179; Mary Ann, 178, 179; Mary Jane, 179; Mary Jo Orth, 179; Meriden, 97; Michael Brennan, 222; Mike, 178; Morgan Lee, 178; Moses Allen, 109, 179; Moses P., 179; Myra Jean German, 179; Nancy, 178; Nathaniel Hampton, 179; Neil, 178; Nicy, 215; Oliver Curtis, 154; Patricia Ann, 178; Phoebe Caroline Roberts Gorento, 178; Rachael, 178; Ray, 97; Richard, 178; Richard Wayne, 122; Robert, 157; Rosa Elizabeth Gordon, 109; Ruth, 175; Sally, 97; Sarah, 178, 179; Sarah Emma, 178; Salathiel M., 179; Steve, 142, 178; Susan, 178; Thelma Jean, 178; Thoma, 178; Thomas Faye, 178; Trevor Daniel, 179; Ursula, 175; William, 175, 178, 179, 186, 195; William H., 137; William Marion Hampton, 179
Powers, Alsie, 167, 168; Grace, 88; Shirley Nicholson Atkinson, 225; Sophronia C. Poe, 177; Stephen, 177
Prather, Henry, 28
Pratt, Jean Ann, 63
Prendergest, Francis X., 31
Presley, Caleb, 166; Flossie, 58; Quinnie H. Nichols, 166
Preston, Hannah, 213; William, 213
Prewitt, John, 100; Keziah, 100; Keziah Bell, 100; Mary Ford, 100
Priba, Cleo, 91
Price, Ada, 78; Amos, 44; Arlene Marie Brown, 71, 72, 97; Azzie A., 134; Barbara Chism, 81; Bobby Wayne, 71, 72, 97; Bud, 78; Cathlene Shipp, 191; Clyde L., 169; Darwin, 78; Donna Windsor, 111, 179; Edi Cathlene Shipp, 191; Edna, 78; Edward, 78; Elsie Jane, 126; Florence Pruitt, 179; Glynna Carole Nowlin Gordon Hodges, 169; Ina Grace, 78; Irene Bell, 134; Jeannie, 5, 39; Jeffrey Austin, 72; Jeffrey Lynn, 71, 72; Jennifer Marie, 71, 72; Jewell, 218; Karen, 26; Kevin Shawn, 191; LaVada Griffin, 179; LaVada Marie Griffin, 111; Mary, 57; Mary Claudia Chambers, 78; Michelle Lynette Jarett, 72; Polly, 56; R.W., 179; Romie, 179; Romie Ethan, 111, 179; Romie Griffin, 111, 179; Romie Willis, 111, 179; Roy, 78; Ruby Mallett, 148; Sarah, 64; Shawn Wayne, 191; Vickie Gayle, 83; Virgil, 148; William Russell, 134; Willis, 179
Priddy, Ida W., 129; John W., 129; Layton, 129; Mandie Burns, 129; Thomasina, 129; William H., 129; Zerah Huggins, 129
Pride, William J., 127; Zero Huggins, 127
Priest, Elizabeth Butler, 74; William, 74
Prince, Alicia Francis, 180; Alosia E., 54; Ben, 180; Betty Lou, 179; Beulah Smith, 109; Carolyn Swanzy, 179; Cary, 109; Cassie, 56; Catherine, 180; Celia Elizabeth, 124; Charity, 180; Charity Halbrook, 65, 106, 180; Charity J., 199; Charity Jane, 179; Charity S. Halbrook, 179; Charity Stanten, 180; Charolotta Elizabeth, 179; Corba Earl, 179; Cynthia, 180; Cyretha Ann Dockins, 95; Della J. Stobaugh, 199; Della Jane Stobaugh, 179; Effie Lew Williams, 198; Eisora Gordon, 109; Elisabeth, 65; Elizabeth, 106, 107, 179, 199; Ellen J. Polk, 180; Esta Mae, 46, 180; Ethel, 199; Ethel Leona, 179; Eva Mae Merryman Nicholson Shipley, 159, 160; Fender, 160; Frances Jane, 180; Fred, 95; George, 180; Gwendolyn, 179; Haley, 180; Henry S., 180, 198; Hiram, 149; Holly Lynn, 179; Ida Marlow, 180; Isaac, 179; Isaac J., 180; Isaac Newton, 179, 180; James, 180; Jeremiah Miles, 179, 180; John Merrick, 179; John Orville, 179; Johnathan F., 180; Joseph, 180; Judy Ann, 180; Julia B., 54; Lee Brown, 180; Lew Effie Stobaugh, 180; Lora, 56, 150; Maggie Brown, 180; Martha Elizabeth Owens, 95, 179, 180; Martha Ellen, 180; Martha S. Ellen, 180; Mary, 82; Mary Alice Nichols, 166; Mary Sue, 179; Miles, 65, 106, 179, 180; Nelsie Martin, 149; Newton, 199; Oliver, 166; Oliver B., 180; Patricia, 180; Patricia Ann Kuettle, 46, 180; Peggy Murphy, 179; Reba Mae Dickson, 179; Robert Hervey, 95; Rosa Hammond, 180; Rosie Hammonds, 95; Rosie Maybell, 180; Roy Gene, 46; Roy Gene, Jr., 180; Roy Gene, Sr., 180; Ruth Ann, 185; Sarah, 120, 121; Sarah Caroline McMahan, 179, 180; Sarah Elizabeth, 180; Sarah Elizabeth, 95, 180; Sarah Jane, 180; Sarah W. Foster, 180; Sophrona Cathryn, 180; Stacie Marie, 46; Stanley, 180; Staton, 180; Theresa Mays, 180; Tia, 179; Wayde, 9; Willard Francis Bryant, 180; William, 95; William Erastus, 109; William Fender, 180; William Jasper, 95, 179, 180; Wynona Kirl Swanzy, 179
Pritchard, Leona Smith, 184; Paul, 184
Privett, Oneta Mahan, 202; Ray, 202
Proby, Sarah, 222
Prock, Matilda J., 69
Proctor, Adelia, 69
Pruett, Alva, 180; Alva Jefferson, 180; Bill, 180; Bonnie, 180; Bonnie Dillard, 180; Burl, 180; Burl William, 180; Edith, 180; Elmer, 180; Elmer Lee, 180; Frances Wren, 223; George, 180; George Caleb, 180, 181; Harvey, 223; Jackie Cody, 181; Jefferson Monroe, 180, 181; Jesse Milton, 180; Jessie Milton, 181; Kimberly Ann, 181; Mary Edith, 180; Mary Ruth Rainey, 181; Milton, 180; Monroe, 180; Monroe Elisha, 180, 181; Nancy Ann Zachary, 180, 181; O'Della, 180; O'Della Maye, 180; Pamela Jean, 181; Pearl Hilderbrand, 181; Tifford Milton, 181
Pruitt, Ann Louise, 142; Bell, 160; Brandon Kyle, 202; Buddy, 44; Cheri, 35; Cheri Lynn Stroud, 202; Cheri Stroud, 44; Dustin Thomas, 202; Hank Jordan, 202; Joan, 119; Jordan Drew, 202; Kyle, 35; Lyndon Ray, 202; Ruth, 165
Pryor, Ella Margaret, 150; Henry Haydon, 201; John, 215; Kelley, 20; Martina Bitanna Stover, 201; Sarah Wade, 215; Wanda Groom, 182; William, 182
Purcell, Minerva Jane, 191
Purks, Mary C., 74
Purvis, Elizabeth, 93
Pustka, Theresa Lillian, 164
Putnam, Sarah, 112
Putterbaugh, Ben, 29
Pynson, Sally Montgomery, 162; Tom, 162

Q

Qualls, Leslie, 45; Rebecca Lucinda, 119; Will, 45
Quattlebaum, Martha Ann Elizabeth, 146; Melva Blackwell, 192
Queener, Mary, 69
Quindley, J., 9; John, 8
Quinn, Sarah, 64
Quisenberry, Herald, 26

R

Raberson, Mary, 147
Rabun, Emmaline, 175; Tabitha, 175
Rabun-Perry, George W., 85
Rachaner, Margaret Zimmerebner, 226; William, 226
Rachel Reddick, 182
Ragland, Deanie Mourot, 163; Greg, 163; Maggie, 163; Thomas, 163
Ragsdale, Albert Sidney Johnston, 181; Charles, 181; Excelsior Hannah, 181; Isabel Boggess, 181; John Lewis, 181; Louis, 181; Louiza, 181; Margaret, 181; Marinda, 138; Mary, 181; Mary Anne Kilgore, 181; Mary Bell, 181; Minerva Ann, 73; Nancy, 106, 107, 108, 109; Nettie, 181; Nola Allien, 181; Robert Arthur, 181; Sarah, 106, 107, 108; Sarah Jane, 181; Thomas D., 181; Wade, 181; William, 106, 107, 108
Rahiller, Rosa Anna, 52
Rainboe, Dena, 119
Rainbolt, Sherry, 82, 226
Rainey, Albert, 56; Beulah Fulkerson, 56; John H., 95; L.E. Dockins, 95; Mary Ruth, 181
Rainwater, Arkie D., 21, 22, 182; Burr, 182; Charles, 21, 22; Charles F., 181; Cloud Knight, 73; Delores, 91; Deneatha Roberts, 181; Diana Bearden, 181; Edmon E., 182; Edmund, 21; Edmund E., 22, 181, 182; Elias, 181; Ellis, 21; Faye, 182; Grace Hubbard, 126; Gustanna, 181; Jackson Daniel, 181; Jane Morrow, 148; Jarrell, 9, 12, 181, 182; John B., 181; Josie, 182; Lavada Little, 182; Lula Doyle Burrow, 73; Malissa Martin, 181; Martha Ann Callahan, 181; Mary A., 181; Mary Pijot, 182; Mary Roberts, 181; Maude Hanserd, 182; Mayne, 21; Miles, 182; Miles

249

253

254

Printed in the USA
CPSIA information can be obtained
at www.ICGtesting.com
JSHW060050150824
68134JS00032B/2707